For more resources, visit the Web site for

The Making of the West

bedfordstmartins.com/hunt

FREE Online Study Guide

GET INSTANT FEEDBACK ON YOUR PROGRESS WITH

- Chapter self-tests
- Key terms review
- Map quizzes
- Timeline activities
- Note-taking outlines

FREE History research and writing help

REFINE YOUR RESEARCH SKILLS AND FIND PLENTY OF GOOD SOURCES WITH

- A database of useful images, maps, documents, and more at *Make History*
- A guide to online sources for history
- Help with writing history papers
- A tool for building a bibliography
- Tips on avoiding plagiarism

FOURTH EDITION

The Making of the West

PEOPLES AND CULTURES

Volume A: To 1500

Lynn Hunt
University of California, Los Angeles

Thomas R. Martin
College of the Holy Cross

Barbara H. Rosenwein
Loyola University Chicago

Bonnie G. Smith
Rutgers University

BEDFORD/ST. MARTIN'S
Boston ♦ New York

For Bedford/St. Martin's

Publisher for History: Mary Dougherty
Director of Development for History: Jane Knetzger
Developmental Editor: Danielle Slevens
Senior Production Editor: Karen S. Baart
Production Editor: Marcy Ross
Senior Production Supervisor: Jennifer L. Peterson
Senior Executive Marketing Manager: Jenna Bookin Barry
Associate Editor: Robin Soule
Production Assistants: Elise Keller and Victoria Royal
Copyeditor: Janet Renard
Indexer: Leoni Z. McVey, McVey & Associates, Inc.
Cartography: Mapping Specialists Limited
Photo Researcher: Bruce Carson
Permissions Manager: Kalina K. Ingham
Senior Art Director: Anna Palchik
Text Designer: Lisa Buckley
Page Layout: Boynton Hue Studio
Cover Designer: Billy Boardman
Cover Art: Estate of farm master, mosaic, 4th century A.D. Roman, from Tabarka, Tunisia, North Africa. The Art Archive/Bardo Museum Tunis/Gianni Dagli Orti.
Composition: Jouve
Printing and Binding: RR Donnelley and Sons

President: Joan E. Feinberg
Editorial Director: Denise B. Wydra
Director of Marketing: Karen R. Soeltz
Director of Production: Susan W. Brown
Associate Director, Editorial Production: Elise S. Kaiser
Managing Editor: Elizabeth M. Schaaf

Library of Congress Control Number: 2011939727

Manufactured in the United States of America.

1 2 3 4 5 6 15 14 13 12 11

For information, write: Bedford/St. Martin's, 75 Arlington Street, Boston, MA 02116 (617-399-4000)

ISBN: 978-0-312-67268-3 (Combined Edition)
ISBN: 978-0-312-57571-7 (Loose-Leaf Edition)
ISBN: 978-0-312-58343-9 (High School Edition)
ISBN: 978-0-312-67269-0 (Volume I)
ISBN: 978-0-312-57569-4 (Loose-Leaf Edition, Volume I)
ISBN: 978-0-312-67271-3 (Volume II)
ISBN: 978-0-312-57570-0 (Loose-Leaf Edition, Volume II)
ISBN: 978-0-312-58340-8 (Volume A)
ISBN: 978-0-312-58341-5 (Volume B)
ISBN: 978-0-312-58342-2 (Volume C)

Acknowledgments: *Acknowledgments and copyrights are printed at the back of the book on page C-1, which constitutes an extension of the copyright page. It is a violation of the law to reproduce these selections by any means whatsoever without the written permission of the copyright holder. At the time of publication all Internet URLs published in this text were found to accurately link to their intended Web site. If you do find a broken link, please forward the information to* history@bedfordstmartins.com *so that it can be corrected for the next printing.*

Preface

History requires constant rethinking and rewriting, because current events make us see the past in a new light. The fall of the Berlin Wall in 1989; the attacks of September 11, 2001; and the world economic crisis that began in 2008 are dramatic examples of how events shift our perspective. As a result of these events, communism, Islam, and globalization all took on different meanings — not just for the present, but also in ways that compel us to reconsider the past. To take just one example, Islam has been part of the history of the West since its founding as a religion in the seventh century, and yet until the last two decades most textbooks of the history of the West gave it relatively little attention. No one would think of limiting its coverage now.

As this book goes into its fourth edition, we authors feel confident that our fundamental approach is well suited to incorporating changes in perspective. We have always linked the history of the West to wider developments in the world. A new edition gives us the opportunity to make those links even stronger and more global, and thereby help students better understand the world in which they live. Instructors who have read and used our book also confirm that the synthesis of approaches we offer — from military to gender history — enables them to bring the most up-to-date conceptualizations of the West into their classroom. We aim to integrate different approaches rather than privileging any one of them.

Our primary goal has been to create a text that demonstrates that the history of the West is the story of an ongoing process, not a finished result with one fixed meaning. We wanted also to make clear that there is no one Western people or culture that has existed from the beginning until now. Instead, the history of the West includes many different peoples and cultures. To convey these ideas, we have written a sustained story of the West's development in a broad, global context that reveals the cross-cultural interactions fundamental to the shaping of Western politics, societies, cultures, and economies. Indeed, the first chapter opens with a section on the origins and contested meaning of the term *Western civilization*.

Equally valuable to instructors has been the way our book is organized in a chronological framework to help students understand how political, social, cultural, and economic histories have influenced one another over time. We know from our own teaching that introductory students need a solid chronological framework, one with enough familiar benchmarks to make the material easy to grasp. Each chapter treats the main events, people, and themes of a period in which the West significantly changed; thus, students learn about political and military events and social and cultural developments as they unfolded. This chronological integration also accords with our belief that it is important, above all else, for students to see the interconnections among varieties of historical experience — between politics and cultures, between public events and private experiences, between wars and diplomacy and everyday life. Our chronological synthesis provides a unique benefit to students: it makes these relationships clear while highlighting the major changes of each age. For teachers, our chronological approach ensures a balanced account and provides the opportunity to present themes within their greater context. But perhaps best of all, this approach provides a text that reveals history as a process that is constantly alive, subject to pressures, and able to surprise us.

Cultural borrowing between the peoples of Europe and their neighbors has characterized Western civilization from the beginning. Thus, we have insisted on an expanded vision of the West that includes the United States and fully incorporates Scandinavia, eastern Europe, and the Ottoman Empire. Latin America, Africa, China, Japan, and India also come into the story. We have been able to offer sustained treatment of crucial topics such as Islam and provide a more thorough examination of globalization than any competing text. Study of Western history provides essential background to today's events, from debates over immigration to conflicts in the Middle East. Instructors have found this synthesis essential for helping students understand the West amid today's globalization.

In this edition, we have enhanced our coverage of Western interactions with other parts of the world and the cross-cultural exchanges that influenced the making of the West. Chapter 2, for example, demonstrates that despite the Dark Age, Greek civilization stayed in contact with civilization in the Near East as it reinvented itself — and that this cultural interaction produced a reemergence with profound differences from the social and political traditions that had existed in Greece before. Chapter 14 shows how the gold and silver discovered in the New World combined with growing confrontations over religion within Europe to reshape the long-standing rivalries among princes, treating these topics together to illustrate how earlier forms of globalization influenced daily life, religious beliefs, and the ways wars were fought. Chapter 27 features a revised, updated discussion of decolonization and the end of empire in Asia, Africa, and the Middle East, including a new document on torture in Algeria. Chapter 29 includes current coverage of recent events in the Middle East, the global economic crisis, the rise of economies in the Pacific and the Southern Hemisphere, and globalized culture and communications.

As always, we have also incorporated the latest scholarly findings throughout the book so that students and instructors alike have a text on which they can confidently rely. In the fourth edition, we have included new and updated discussions of topics such as fresh archaeological evidence for the possible role of religion in stimulating the major changes of the Neolithic Revolution; the dating of the Great Sphinx in Egypt, the scholarly debate that could radically change our ideas of the earliest Egyptian history; the newest thinking on the origins of Islam; the crucial issues in the Investiture Conflict between pope and emperor; the impact of the Great Famine of the fourteenth century; the slave trade, and especially its continuation into the nineteenth century; and, in a brand-new epilogue, the ways in which scholars are considering recent events within the context of the new digital world.

Aided by a fresh and welcoming design, new pedagogical aids, and new multimedia offerings that give students and instructors interactive tools for study and teaching (see "Versions and Supplements" on page ix), the new edition is, we believe, even better suited to today's Western civilization courses. In writing *The Making of the West: Peoples and Cultures*, we have aimed to communicate the vitality and excitement as well as the fundamental importance of history. Students should be enthusiastic about history; we hope we have conveyed some of our own enthusiasm and love for the study of history in these pages.

Pedagogy and Features

We know from our own teaching that students need all the help they can get in absorbing and making sense of information, thinking analytically, and understanding that history itself is often debated and constantly revised. With these goals in mind, we retained the class-tested learning and teaching aids that worked well in the previous editions, but we have also done more to help students distill the central story of each age and give them more opportunities to develop their own historical skills.

Compared with previous editions, the fourth edition incorporates more aids to help students sort out what is most important to learn while they read. Completely redesigned Chapter Review sections feature new, dynamic activities asking students to identify and discuss the chapter's key terms, encouraging students to go beyond rote memorization and consider each term's importance in context. We have also added questions in three different places: to the documents (which are described more fully below), to the end-of-chapter timelines, and to the Making Connections sections. Posed at the end of the documents, questions help focus students' attention on the main themes and concepts expressed in them. The questions at the end of the timelines encourage students to think about possible links between political, economic, social, and cultural events. We have added more questions to the Making Connections feature because instructors find these questions to be useful in prompting students to think across the sections of any given chapter. To further help students as they read, we have worked hard to ensure that chapter and section overviews outline the central points of each section in the clearest manner possible, and we have condensed some material to better illuminate key ideas.

The study tools introduced in the previous editions continue to help students check their understanding of the chapters and the periods they cover. Boldface key terms and names have been updated to concentrate on likely test items. Those terms and people are defined in a running glossary at the bottom of pages and collected in a comprehensive glossary at the end of the book. Review questions, strategically placed at the end of each major section, help students recall and assimilate core points in digestible increments. Vivid chapter-opening anecdotes, timelines, and conclusions further reinforce the central developments covered in the reading.

To reflect the richness of the themes in the text and offer further opportunities for historical investigation, we include a rich assortment of single-source documents (two to three per chapter), 30 percent of them new to this edition. Nothing can give students a more direct experience of the past than original voices, and we have endeavored to let those voices speak, whether it is Frederick

Barbarossa replying to the Romans when they offer him the emperor's crown, Marie de Sévigné's description of the French court, or an ordinary person's account of the outbreak of the Russian Revolution.

Accompanying these primary-source documents are our five unique skill-building features. Reviewed with users and revised for the fourth edition, these features extend the narrative by revealing the process of interpretation, providing a solid introduction to historical argument and critical thinking, and capturing the excitement of historical investigation.

- ***Seeing History*** features guide students through the process of reading images as historical evidence. Each of the ten features provides a pair of images for comparison and contrast, with background information and questions that encourage visual analysis. Examples include comparisons of pagan and Christian sarcophagi, Persian and Arabic coins, Romanesque and Gothic naves, pre- and post–French Revolution attire, and portrayals of soldiers in World War I.
- ***Contrasting Views*** features provide three or four often conflicting primary-source accounts of a central event, person, or development—such as Julius Caesar, Charlemagne, Magna Carta, Martin Luther, the English Civil War, and late-nineteenth-century migration—enabling students to understand history from a variety of contemporaneous perspectives.
- ***New Sources, New Perspectives*** features show students how historians continue to develop fresh insights using new kinds of evidence about the past, from tree rings to Holocaust museums.
- ***Terms of History*** features explain the meanings of some of the most important and contested terms in the history of the West—*civilization*, *nationalism*, and *progress*, for example—and show how those meanings have developed and changed over time.
- ***Taking Measure*** features introduce students to the intriguing stories revealed by quantitative analysis. Each feature highlights a chart, table, graph, or map of historical statistics that illuminates an important political, social, or cultural development.

The book's map program has been widely praised as one of the most comprehensive and inviting of any survey text. In each chapter, we offer three types of maps, each with a distinct role in conveying information to students. Four to five full-size maps show major developments, two to four "spot" maps—small maps positioned within the discussion right where students need them—serve as immediate locators, and "Mapping the West" summary maps at the end of each chapter provide a snapshot of the West at the close of a transformative period and help students visualize the West's changing contours over time. For this edition, we have added new maps and carefully considered each of the existing maps, simplifying where possible to better highlight essential information, and clarifying and updating borders and labels where needed.

We have striven to integrate art as fully as possible into the narrative and to show its value for teaching and learning. Over 430 illustrations—30 percent of which are new—were carefully chosen to reflect this edition's broad topical coverage and geographic inclusion, reinforce the text, and show the varieties of visual sources from which historians build their narratives and interpretations. All artifacts, illustrations, paintings, and photographs are contemporaneous with the chapter; there are no anachronistic illustrations. Substantive captions for the maps and art help students learn how to read visuals, and we have frequently included specific questions or suggestions for comparisons that might be developed. Specially designed visual exercises in the Online Study Guide supplement this approach. A new page design for the fourth edition supports our goal of intertwining the art and the narrative, and makes the new study tools readily accessible.

Acknowledgments

In the vital process of revision, the authors have benefited from repeated critical readings by many talented scholars and teachers. Our sincere thanks go to the following instructors, whose comments often challenged us to rethink or justify our interpretations and who always provided a check on accuracy down to the smallest detail.

Robert Beachy, *Goucher College*
William E. Burns, *George Washington University*
Kevin W. Caldwell, *Blue Ridge Community College*
Patricia G. Clark, *Westminster College*
Oliver Griffin, *St. John Fisher College*
Rebecca K. Hayes, *Northern Virginia Community College–Manassas*
Anne Huebel, *Franklin Pierce University*
Steven Kale, *Washington State University*
Jeff Kleiman, *University of Wisconsin–Marshfield*
John Leazer, *Carthage College*

Charles Levine, *Mesa Community College*
Mauro Magarelli, *William Paterson University*
Kelly Obernuefemann, *Lewis & Clark Community College*
Ann Ostendorf, *Gonzaga University*
Maryanne Rhett, *Monmouth University*
Sarah Shurts, *Montclair State University*
Mark Stephens, *Chabot College*
Frank Van Nuys, *South Dakota School of Mines and Technology*

Many colleagues, friends, and family members have made contributions to this work. They know how grateful we are. We also wish to acknowledge and thank the publishing team at Bedford/St. Martin's who did so much to bring this revised edition to completion: president Joan Feinberg, editorial director Denise Wydra, publisher for history Mary Dougherty, director of development for history Jane Knetzger, developmental editor Danielle Slevens, freelance editors Jim Strandberg and Debra Michals, associate editor Robin Soule, senior executive marketing manager Jenna Bookin Barry, senior production editor Karen Baart, freelance production editor Marcy Ross, managing editor Elizabeth Schaaf, art researcher Bruce Carson, text designer Lisa Buckley, page makeup artist Cia Boynton, cover designer Billy Boardman, and copyeditor Janet Renard.

Our students' questions and concerns have shaped much of this work, and we welcome all our readers' suggestions, queries, and criticisms. Please contact us at our respective institutions or via **history@bedfordstmartins.com**.

Versions and Supplements

Adopters of *The Making of the West* and their students have access to abundant extra resources, including documents, presentation and testing materials, the acclaimed Bedford Series in History and Culture volumes, and much much more. See below for more information, visit the book's catalog site at **bedfordstmartins.com/hunt/catalog**, or contact your local Bedford/St. Martin's sales representative.

Get the Right Version for Your Class

To accommodate different course lengths and course budgets, *The Making of the West* is available in several different formats, including three-hole punched loose-leaf Budget Books versions and e-books, which are available at a substantial discount.

- Combined edition (Chapters 1–29)—available in hardcover, loose-leaf, and e-book formats
- Volume 1: To 1750 (Chapters 1–17)—available in paperback, loose-leaf, and e-book formats
- Volume 2: Since 1500 (Chapters 14–29)—available in paperback, loose-leaf, and e-book formats
- Volume A: To 1500 (Chapters 1–13)—available in paperback format
- Volume B: 1340–1830 (Chapters 13–20)—available in paperback format
- Volume C: Since 1750 (Chapters 18–29)—available in paperback format

The online, interactive **Bedford e-Book** can be examined at **bedfordstmartins.com/hunt** or purchased at a discount there. Your students can also purchase *The Making of the West* in other popular e-book formats for computers, tablets, and e-readers.

Online Extras for Students

The book's companion site at **bedfordstmartins.com/hunt** gives students a way to read, write, and study, and to find and access quizzes and activities, study aids, and history research and writing help.

FREE **Online Study Guide.** Available at the companion site, this popular resource provides students with quizzes and activities for each chapter, including multiple-choice self-tests that focus on important concepts; flashcards that test students' knowledge of key terms; timeline activities that emphasize causal relationships; and map quizzes intended to strengthen students' geography skills. Instructors can monitor students' progress through an online Quiz Gradebook or receive email updates.

FREE **Research, Writing, and Anti-plagiarism Advice.** Available at the companion site, Bedford's **History Research and Writing Help** includes **History Research and Reference Sources**, with links to history-related databases, indexes, and journals; **More Sources and How to Format a History Paper**, with clear advice on how to integrate primary and secondary sources into research papers and how to cite and format sources correctly; **Build a Bibliography**, a simple Web-based tool known as The Bedford Bibliographer that generates bibliographies in four commonly used documentation styles; and **Tips on Avoiding Plagiarism**, an online tutorial that reviews the consequences of plagiarism and features exercises to help students practice integrating sources and recognize acceptable summaries.

Resources for Instructors

Bedford/St. Martin's has developed a wide range of teaching resources for this book and for this course. They range from lecture and presentation materials and assessment tools to course management options. Most can be downloaded or ordered at **bedfordstmartins.com/hunt/catalog**.

HistoryClass for The Making of the West. HistoryClass, a Bedford/St. Martin's Online Course Space, puts the online resources available with this textbook in one convenient and completely customizable course space. There, you and your students can access an interactive e-book and primary sources reader; maps, images, documents, and links; chapter review quizzes; interactive multimedia exercises; and research and writing help. In HistoryClass you can get all of our premium content and tools and assign, rearrange, and mix them with your own resources. For more information, visit **yourhistoryclass.com**.

Bedford Coursepack for Blackboard, WebCT, Desire2Learn, Angel, Sakai, or Moodle. We have free content to help you integrate our rich content into your course management system. Registered instructors can download coursepacks with no hassle and no strings attached. Content includes our most popular free resources and book-specific content for *The Making of the West.* Visit **bedfordstmartins.com/coursepacks** to see a demo, find your version, or download your coursepack.

Instructor's Resource Manual. The instructor's manual offers both experienced and first-time instructors tools for preparing for lecture and running discussions. It includes chapter review material, teaching strategies, and a guide to chapter-specific supplements available for the text.

Guide to Changing Editions. Designed to facilitate an instructor's transition from the previous edition of *The Making of the West* to the current edition, this guide presents an overview of major changes as well as changes in each chapter.

Computerized Test Bank. The test bank includes a mix of fresh, carefully crafted multiple-choice, matching, fill-in-the-blank, short-answer, and essay questions for each chapter. It also contains the Chapter Focus, Review, Important Events, and Making Connections questions from the textbook and model answers for each. The questions appear in Microsoft Word format and in easy-to-use test bank software that allows instructors to easily add, edit, re-sequence, and print questions and answers. Instructors can also export questions into a variety of formats, including WebCT and Blackboard.

PowerPoint Maps, Images, Lecture Outlines, and i>clicker Content. Look good and save time with *The Bedford Lecture Kit.* These presentation materials are downloadable individually from the Instructor Resources tab at **bedfordstmartins.com/hunt/catalog** and are available on *The Bedford Lecture Kit* Instructor's Resource CD-ROM. They include ready-made and fully customizable PowerPoint multimedia presentations built around lecture outlines with embedded maps, figures, and selected images from the textbook and detailed instructor notes on key points. Also available are maps and selected images in JPEG and PowerPoint formats; content for i>clicker, a classroom response system, in Microsoft Word and PowerPoint formats; the Instructor's Resource Manual in Microsoft Word format; and outline maps in PDF format for quizzing or handing out. All files are suitable for copying onto transparency acetates.

***Make History*—Free Documents, Maps, Images, and Web Sites.** *Make History* combines the best Web resources with hundreds of maps and images, to make it simple to find the source material you need. Browse the collection of thousands of resources by course or by topic, date, and type. Each item has been carefully chosen and helpfully annotated to make it easy to find exactly what you need. Available at **bedfordstmartins.com/makehistory**.

Videos and Multimedia. A wide assortment of videos and multimedia CD-ROMs on various topics in Western civilization is available to qualified adopters through your Bedford/St. Martin's sales representative.

Package and Save Your Students Money

For information on free packages and discounts up to 50%, visit **bedfordstmartins.com/hunt/catalog**, or contact your local Bedford/St. Martin's sales representative.

Bedford e-Book. The e-book for this title, described above, can be packaged with the print text at a discount.

***Sources of The Making of the West*, Fourth Edition.** This companion sourcebook provides written and visual sources to accompany each chapter of *The Making of the West.* Political, social, and cultural documents offer a variety of perspectives that complement the textbook and encourage students to make connections between narrative history and primary sources. Over thirty new documents and visual sources highlight the diversity of historical voices that shaped each period. To aid students in approaching and interpreting documents, each chapter contains an introduction, document headnotes, and questions for discussion. Available free when packaged with the print text.

***Sources of The Making of the West* e-Book.** The reader is also available as an e-book. When packaged with the print or electronic version of the textbook, it is available for free.

The Bedford Series in History and Culture. More than one hundred titles in this highly praised series combine first-rate scholarship, historical narrative, and important primary documents for undergraduate courses. Each book is brief, inexpensive, and focused on a specific topic or period. For a complete list of titles, visit **bedfordstmartins.com/history/series**. Package discounts are available.

Rand McNally Atlas of Western Civilization. This collection of over fifty full-color maps highlights social, political, and cross-cultural change and interaction from classical Greece and Rome to the postindustrial Western world. Each map is thoroughly indexed for fast reference. Available for $3.00 when packaged with the print text.

The Bedford Glossary for European History. This handy supplement for the survey course gives students historically contextualized definitions for hundreds of terms—from *Abbasids* to *Zionism*—that they will encounter in lectures, reading, and exams. Available free when packaged with the print text.

Trade Books. Titles published by sister companies Hill and Wang; Farrar, Straus and Giroux; Henry Holt and Company; St. Martin's Press; Picador; and Palgrave Macmillan are available at a 50% discount when packaged with Bedford/St. Martin's textbooks. For more information, visit **bedfordstmartins.com/tradeup**.

A Pocket Guide to Writing in History. This portable and affordable reference tool by Mary Lynn Rampolla provides reading, writing, and research advice useful to students in all history courses. Concise yet comprehensive advice on approaching typical history assignments, developing critical reading skills, writing effective history papers, conducting research, using and documenting sources, and avoiding plagiarism—enhanced with practical tips and examples throughout—have made this slim reference a best seller. Package discounts are available.

A Student's Guide to History. This complete guide to success in any history course provides the practical help students need to be effective. In addition to introducing students to the nature of the discipline, author Jules Benjamin teaches a wide range of skills, from preparing for exams to approaching common writing assignments, and explains the research and documentation process with plentiful examples. Package discounts are available.

The Social Dimension of Western Civilization. Combining current scholarship with classic pieces, this reader's forty-eight secondary sources, compiled by Richard M. Golden, hook students with the fascinating and often surprising details of how everyday Western people worked, ate, played, celebrated, worshipped, married, procreated, fought, persecuted, and died. Package discounts are available.

The West in the Wider World: Sources and Perspectives. Edited by Richard Lim and David Kammerling Smith, this first college reader to focus on the central historical question "How did the West become the West?" offers a wealth of written and visual source materials to reveal the influence of non-European regions on the origins and development of Western civilization. Package discounts are available.

Brief Contents

Contents

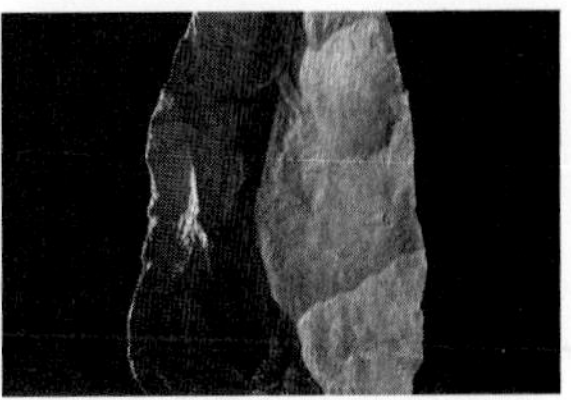

CHAPTER 3

The Greek Golden Age

CHAPTER 4

From the Classical to the Hellenistic World

CHAPTER 7

The Transformation of the Roman Empire

284–600 C.E. 205

CHAPTER 8

The Heirs of Rome: Islam, Byzantium, and Europe

600–750 243

CHAPTER 9 From Centralization to Fragmentation

CHAPTER 10 Commercial Quickening and Religious Reform

CHAPTER 11

The Flowering of the Middle Ages

1150–1215 345

CHAPTER 12

The Medieval Synthesis—and Its Cracks

1215–1340 381

Maps and Figures

Maps

Prologue

Chapter 1

Chapter 2

Chapter 3

Chapter 4

Chapter 5

Chapter 6

Chapter 7

Chapter 8

Chapter 9

Chapter 10

Chapter 11

Chapter 12

Chapter 13

Figures

Special Features

Documents

Contrasting Views

New Sources, New Perspectives

Terms of History

Seeing History

Taking Measure

To the Student

This guide to *The Making of the West* introduces the tools and features designed to help you study and do well in your Western Civilization course.

In-text tools help you focus on what's important as you read.

Read the **chapter outlines** to preview the topics and themes to come.

Read the **Chapter Focus** questions at the start of each chapter to think about the main ideas you should look for as you read.

Consult the **running glossary** for definitions of the bolded **Key Terms and People**.

Use the **Review Questions** at the end of each major section to check your understanding of key concepts.

Preview chapter events and keep track of time with **chapter timelines**.

CHAPTER 1

Early Western Civilization

4000–1000 B.C.E.

Kings in ancient Egypt believed that after they died the gods would judge them as rulers to decide their fate in the afterlife. In *Instructions for Merikare*, for example, written sometime around 2100–2000 B.C.E., an Egyptian king gives his son Merikare the following advice: "Make secure your place in the cemetery by being upright, by doing justice, upon which people's hearts rely. . . . When a man is buried and mourned, his deeds are piled up next to him as treasure." Being judged pure of heart led to an eternal reward; if the dead king reached the judges "without doing evil," he would be transformed so that he would "abide [in the afterlife] like a god, roaming [free] like the lords of time." A vital part of the justice demanded of an Egyptian king was to keep the country unified under a strong central authority to combat disorder.

Ordinary Egyptians, too, believed that they would win eternal rewards by living justly, which for them meant worshipping the gods and obeying the king and his officials. An illustrated guidebook containing instructions for mummies on how to travel safely in the underworld, com-

ancient Italy's many peoples, but Greek literature, art, and philosophy influenced Rome's culture most of all. This cross-cultural contact that so deeply influenced Rome was a kind of competition in innovation between equals, not "inferior" Romans imitating "superior" Greek culture. Like other ancient peoples, Romans often learned from their neighbors, but they adapted foreign traditions to their own purposes and forged their own cultural identity.

The kidnapping legend belongs to Rome's earliest history, when kings ruled (753–509 B.C.E.). Rome's most important history comes afterward, divided into two major periods of about five hundred years each—the republic and the empire. Under the republic (founded 509 B.C.E.), male voters elected their officials and passed laws (although an oligarchy of the social elite controlled politics). Under the empire, monarchs once again ruled. Rome's greatest expansion came during the republic. Romans' belief in a divine destiny fueled this tremendous growth. They believed that the gods wanted them to rule the world by military might and law and improve it through social and moral values. Their faith in a divine destiny is illustrated by the legend of the Sabine women, in which the earliest Romans used a religious festival as a cover for kidnapping. Their conviction that values should drive politics showed in their determination to persuade the Sabine women that loyalty and love would outweigh the crime of kidnapping that turned them into Romans.

Roman values emphasized family loyalty, selfless political and military service to the community, individual honor and public status, the importance

sonal ambition before the good of the state, they destroyed the republic.

CHAPTER FOCUS How did traditional Roman values affect both the rise and the downfall of the Roman republic?

Roman Social and Religious Traditions

Roman social and religious traditions shaped the history of the Roman republic. Rome's citizens believed that eternal moral values connected them to one another and required them to honor the gods in return for divine support. Hierarchy affected all of life: people at all social levels were obligated to patrons or clients; in families, fathers dominated; in religion, people at all levels of society owed sacrifices, rituals, and prayers to the gods who protected the family and the state.

Roman Moral Values

Roman values defined relationships with other people and with the gods. Romans guided their lives by the ***mos maiorum*** ("the way of the elders"), or values handed down from their ancestors. The Romans

mos maiorum: Literally, "the way of the elders"; the set of Roman values handed down from the ancestors.

753 B.C.E. Traditional date of Rome's founding as monarchy

509 B.C.E. Roman republic established

396 B.C.E. Defeat of Etruscan city of Veii; first great expansion of Roman territory

700 B.C.E. | 600 B.C.E. | 500 B.C.E. | 400 B.C.E.

509–287 B.C.E. Struggle of the orders

451–449 B.C.E. Creation of Twelve Tables, Rome's first written law code

387 B.C.E. Gauls sack Rome

operate, the Greeks opened the way for the rise of a new power—the kingdom of Macedonia—that would end their independence in international politics. The Macedonian kings did not literally enslave the Greeks, as the Spartans did the helots, or usually even change their local governments. They did, however, abolish the city-states' freedom to control their foreign policy.

REVIEW QUESTION How did daily life, philosophy, and the political situation change in Greece during the period 400–350 B.C.E.?

The Rise of Macedonia, 359–323 B.C.E.

The kingdom of Macedonia's rise to superpower status counts as one of the greatest surprises in an-

Special features introduce the way historians work and sharpen your critical-thinking skills.

Numerous **individual primary-source documents** offer direct experiences of the past and the opportunity to consider sources historians use.

DOCUMENT

The Rape and Suicide of Lucretia

This story explaining why the Roman elite expelled the monarchy in 509 B.C.E., thus opening the way to the republic, centers on female virtue and courage, as do other stories about significant political changes in early Roman history. The values attributed to Lucretia obviously reflect men's wishes for women's behavior, but it would be a mistake to assume that women could not

Tarquinius said he loved her, begging and threatening her in turn, trying everything to wear her down. When she wouldn't give in, even in the face of threats of murder, he added another intimidation. "After I've murdered you, I am going to put the naked corpse of a slave next to your body, and everybody will say that you were killed during a disgraceful adultery." This

came to have his fun, to my despair, but it will also be his sorrow—if you are real men." They pledged that they would catch him, and they tried to ease her sadness, saying that the soul did wrong, not the body, and where there were no bad intentions there could be no blame. "It is your responsibility to ensure that he gets what he deserves," she said; "I am blameless, but I will not free myself from punishment. No dishonorable woman shall

Contrasting Views provides three or four often conflicting eyewitness accounts of a central event, person, or development to foster critical-thinking skills.

CONTRASTING VIEWS

The Nature of Women and Marriage

Greeks believed that women had different natures from men and that both genders were capable of excellence, but in their own ways (Documents 1 and 2). Marriage was supposed to bring these natures together in a partnership of complementary strengths and obligations to each other (Document 3). Marriage contracts (Document 4), similar to modern prenuptial agreements, became common to define the partnership's terms.

praise of your excellence or blaming your faults.

Source: Thucydides, *History of the Peloponnesian War*, Book 2.45. Translation by Thomas R. Martin.

2. Melanippe Explains Why Men's Criticism of Women Is Baseless (late fifth century B.C.E.)

The Athenian playwright Euripides often por-

women make them flourish in every way. In this way women's role in religion is right and proper.

Therefore, should anyone put down women? Won't those men stop their empty fault-finding, the ones who strongly believe that all women should be blamed if a single one is found to be bad? I will make a distinction with the following argument: nothing is worse than a bad woman, but nothing is more surpassingly superior than a worthy one.

New Sources, New Perspectives shows how new evidence leads historians to fresh insights—and sometimes new interpretations.

NEW SOURCES, NEW PERSPECTIVES

Papyrus Discoveries and Menander's Comedies

Fourth-century B.C.E. Greek playwrights invented a kind of comedy, called New Comedy, that is today's most popular entertainment—the situation comedy (sitcom). They wrote comedies that concentrated on … sonality types … rocky course … most plots. A… medians creat… bubble-heade… cally servants, … vealed by the…

These comic plays inspired many imitations, especially Roman comedies, which inspired William Shakespeare (1564–1616) in England and Molière (1622–1673) in France. Their comedies, in turn, led to to-

day we can read most of *The Girl from Samos* and parts of other plays. In this way, Menander's characters, stories, and jokes have come back from the dead.

Recovering plays from papyrus is difficult. The handwriting is often difficult to make out, there are no gaps between

Seeing History pairs two visuals with background information and probing questions to encourage analysis of images as historical evidence.

SEEING HISTORY

The Shift in Sculptural Style from Egypt to Greece

As Greek civilization revived during the Archaic Age (750–500 B.C.E.), artists took inspiration from the older civilizations of Egypt and the Near East, with sculpture in particular emerging as an important mode of cultural expression. Greek sculptors carved freestanding *kouros* ("young male") statues whose poses recalled the Egyptian style that remained unchanged for two thousand years: an erect posture, a striding leg, and a calm facial expression staring straight ahead. And yet important differences, both religious and stylistic, exist between Egyptian statuary and the Greek sculpture influenced by it.

ralism and idealization of the human body that would characterize the later Greek classical style (see the illustration on page 93). What evidence do you see of that in the differences between the two sculptures?

Question to Consider

- **What cultural factors do you think could account for Egyptian statues keeping the same style over time, while the style of Greek statues changed?**

Terms of History identifies a term central to history writing and reveals how it is hotly debated.

TERMS OF HISTORY

Civilization

Our word *civilization* comes from the ancient Roman word *civilis*, which meant "suitable for a private citizen" and "behaving like an ordinary, down-to-earth person." Historians connect civilization especially with urbanization and the ways of life that characterize city existence. Also, the word *civilization* often expresses the judgment that being civilized means

and intellectual refinement. **6.** cities or populated areas in general, as opposed to unpopulated or wilderness areas. **7.** modern comforts and conveniences, as made possible by science and technology.

All these definitions imply that *civilization* means an "advanced" or "refined" way of life compared to a "savage" or

lization has become so accepted that it can even be used in nonhuman contexts, such as in the following startling comparison: "some communities of ants are more advanced in civilization than others."[1]

Sometimes *civilization* is used without much definitional content at all, as in the Random House dictionary's third definition. Can the word have any deep meaning if it can be used to mean "any type of culture, society, etc. of a specific place,

Taking Measure data reveals how individual facts add up to broad trends and introduces quantitative analysis skills.

TAKING MEASURE

European Emigration, 1870–1890

Country of Origin

Sweden, Norway, Finland, Denmark 7%; Italy 10%; France, Belgium, Netherlands, Switzerland 2%; British Isles 47%; Germany 18%; Austria 2%; Spain 5%; Portugal 2%; Russia 7%

Destinations

Asiatic Russia 6%; New Zealand 2%; Australia 5%; British West Indies 1%; United States 63%; Uruguay 2%; Brazil 6%; Argentina 10%; Canada 5%

The suffering caused by economic change and by political persecution motivated people from almost every European country to leave their homes for greater secu-

and the United States. Both countries were known for following the rule of law and for providing economic opportunity in urban as well as rural areas.

Question for Consideration

- **Where did the majority of these migrants originate? What historical factors prompted them to leave their**

Art and maps help you to analyze images and think about events in their geographical context.

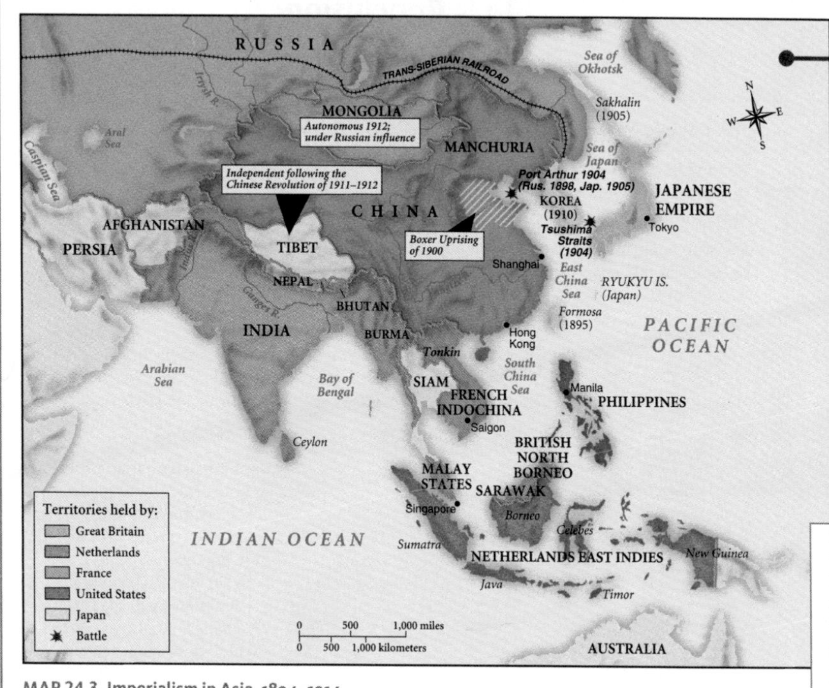

MAP 24.3 Imperialism in Asia, 1894–1914
The established imperialists came to blows in East Asia as they struggled for influence in China and as they met a formidable new rival—Japan. Simultaneously, liberation groups like the Boxers were taking shape, committed to throwing off restraints imposed by foreign powers and eliminating these interlopers altogether. In 1911, revolutionary Sun Yat-sen overthrew the Qing dynasty, which had left China unprepared to resist foreign takeover, and started the country on a different course.

Full-size maps show major historical developments and carry informative captions.

"Spot" maps offer geographic details right where you need them.

B.C.E., the Romans spent the next hundred years warring with the nearby Etruscan town of Veii. Their 396 B.C.E. victory doubled the Romans' territory. By the fourth century B.C.E., the Roman infantry legion of five thousand men had surpassed the Greek and Macedonian phalanx as an effective fighting force because its soldiers were trained to throw javelins from behind their long shields and then rush in to finish off the enemy with swords. A devastating sack of Rome in 387 B.C.E. by marauding Gauls (Celts) from beyond the Alps proved only a temporary setback, though it made Romans forever fearful of foreign invasion. By around 220 B.C.E., Rome controlled all of Italy south of the Po River, at the northern end of the

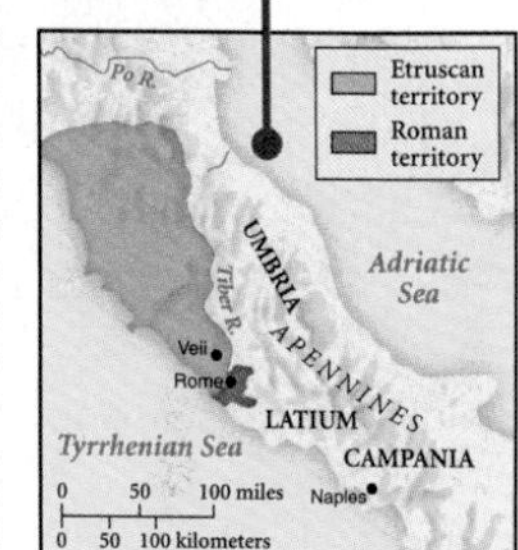

Rome and Central Italy, Fifth Century B.C.E.

Mapping the West summary maps provide a snapshot of the West at the close of each chapter.

MAPPING THE WEST

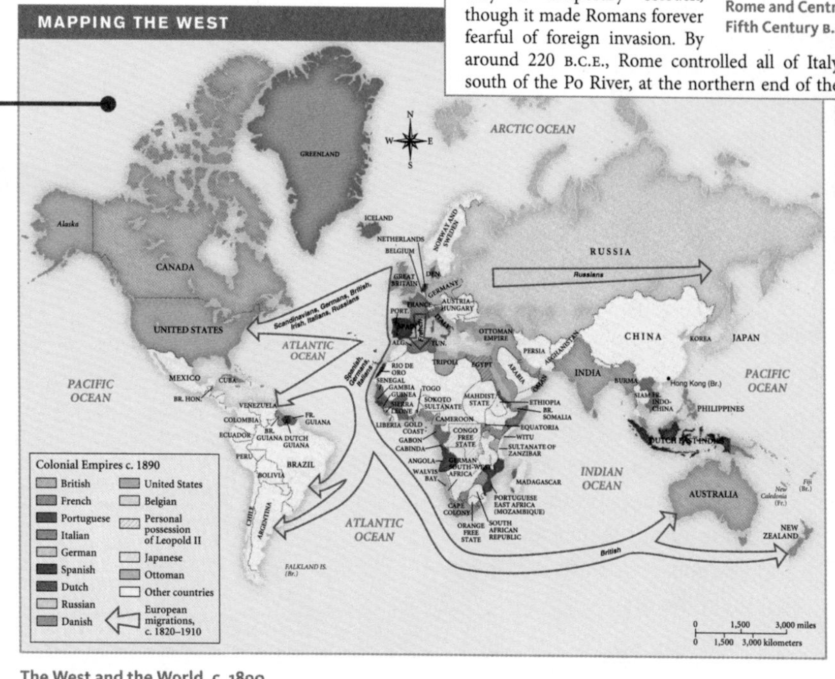

The West and the World, c. 1890
In the late nineteenth century, European trade and political reach spanned the globe. Needing markets for the vast quantities of goods that poured from European factories and access to raw materials to produce the goods, governments asserted that the Western way of life should be spread to the rest of the world and that resources would

End-of-chapter materials enable you to synthesize what you've learned and provide ideas for further research.

Read the **chapter conclusions** to review how the chapters' most important themes and topics fit together and learn how they connect to the next chapter.

Conclusion

The third-century civil wars brought the Roman Empire to a crisis that Diocletian's creation of the
…nd reorganization of government tem-
…eved, but Diocletian's reforms only de-
…vision of the empire. In the late fourth
…grations of non-Roman peoples fleeing
…ought intense pressures on the central
… Emperor Theodosius I divided the em-
…stern and eastern halves in 395 to try to
…administration and defense. When Ro-
…ities bungled the task of integrating bar-
…s into Roman society, the newcomers created kingdoms that eventually replaced imperial government in the west. Roman history increasingly divided into two regional streams, even though
…ian in the sixth century
…niting the empire and re-
…ration of barbarian tribes
…ransformed not only the
…society, and economy but
…, as they developed their
…le organizing themselves
…n territory. The economic
… weakness that accompa-
… changes destroyed the
…elite, which had been one
…erial stability, as wealthy
…ficient country estates and

Consult the **For Further Exploration** boxes at the end of each chapter, which guide you to additional primary-source materials and related Web resources.

FOR FURTHER EXPLORATION

- **For additional primary-source material from this period**, see *Sources of the Making of the West*, Fourth Edition.
- **For Web sites, images, and documents related to topics in this chapter**, visit *Make History* at bedfordstmartins.com/hunt.

Visit the **free online study guide**, which provides quizzes and activities to help you master the chapter material.

Chapter 11 Review

Online Study Guide bedfordstmartins.com/hunt

Key Terms and People

In the grid below, identify the term or person and explain its historical significance. (To do this exercise online, go to bedfordstmartins.com/hunt.)

Test your knowledge of the important concepts and historical figures in the **Key Terms and People** grids by identifying each term and explaining its significance.

Term	Who or What & When	Why It Matters
Romanesque (p. 350)		
Gothic architecture (p. 351)		
Henry II (p. 354)		
common law (p. 357)		
Philip II (Philip Augustus) (p. 358)		
Magna Carta (p. 359)		
Frederick I (Barbarossa) (p. 362)		
troubadours (p. 366)		
chansons de geste (p. 368)		
chivalry (p. 369)		
Franciscans (p. 369)		
Fourth Crusade (p. 372)		

Answer the **Review Questions**, which repeat the chapter's end-of-section comprehension prompts.

Review Questions

1. What was new about education and architecture in the twelfth and early thirteenth centuries?
2. What new sources and institutions of power became available to rulers in the second half of the twelfth century?
3. What do the works of the troubadours and vernacular poets reveal about the nature of entertainment—its themes, its audience, its performers—in the twelfth century?
4. How did the idea of crusade change from the time of the original expedition to the Holy Land?

Answer the analytical **Making Connections** questions, which will help you link ideas within or across chapters.

Making Connections

1. What were the chief differences that se… period 1150–1215 from those of the peri…
2. How was the gift economy associated … economy with the Gothic style?
3. How do political developments—the gr… ment of strong monarchies, the growth … and popularity of vernacular literature … centuries?

Review the **Important Events** chronologies and answer the chronology question to make sure you understand the sequence of and relationships between major events in the chapter.

Important Events

Date	Event	Date	Event
1139–1153	Civil War in England	1202–1204	The Fourth Crusade
1152–1190	Reign of Frederick Barbarossa	1204	Fall of Constantinople to crusaders
1154–1189	Reign of King Henry II	1204	Philip takes Normandy, Anjou, Maine, Touraine, and Poitou from John
1176	Battle of Legnano	1209–1229	Albigensian Crusade
1180–1223	Reign of Philip II Augustus	1212	Battle of Las Navas de Tolosa; triumph of the *reconquista*
1182–1226	Francis of Assisi	1214	Battle of Bouvines
1189–1192	The Third Crusade	1215	Magna Carta

- Consider three events: **The Third Crusade (1189–1192), The Fourth Crusade (1202–1204),** and **the Albigensian Crusade (1209–1229).** What were their various causes and results? How were they differently waged and led?

Consult the **Suggested References** to find additional Web and print sources for further research.

SUGGESTED REFERENCES

For the new schools, Abelard is a key primary source, while Clanchy provides perceptive background. Cultural and artistic developments are discussed in both Burl and Coldstream. Bartlett and Bradbury are essential for politics.

*Abelard's *The Story of My Misfortunes*: http://www.fordham.edu/halsall/source/abelard-sel.html

Aurell, Martin. *The Plantagenet Empire, 1154–1224*. Trans. David Crouch. 2007.

Bartlett, Robert. *England under the Norman and Angevin Kings, 1075–1225*. 2000.

Bouchard, Constance Brittain. *"Every Valley Shall Be Exalted": The Discourse of Opposites in Twelfth-Century Thought*. 2003.

Bradbury, Jim. *Philip Augustus: King of France*. 1998.

Burl, Aubrey. *Courts of Love, Castles of Hate: Troubadours and Trobairitz in Southern France, 1071–1321*. 2008.

Cheyette, Fredric L. *Ermengard of Narbonne and the World of the*

Coldstream, Nicola. *Medieval Architecture*. 2002.

**Crusade of Frederick Barbarossa: The History of the Expedition of the Emperor Frederick and Related Texts*. Trans. G. A. Loud. 2010.

Gaunt, Simon, and Sarah Kay. *The Troubadours: An Introduction*. 1999.

*Goldin, Frederick. *Lyrics of the Troubadors and Trouvères: Original Texts, with Translations*. 1973.

Gothic architecture: http://www.bc.edu/bc_org/avp/cas/fnart/arch/gothic_arch.html

Hudson, John. *The Formation of the English Common Law: Law and Society in England from the Norman Conquest to Magna Carta*. 1996.

Moore, R. I. *The Formation of a Persecuting Society: Power and Deviance in Western Europe, 950–1250*. 2nd ed. 2007.

Pegg, Mark Gregory. *A Most Holy War: The Albigensian Crusade and the Battle for Christendom*. 2008.

Robson, Michael. *The Franciscans in the Middle Ages*. 2006.

Stephensen, David. *Heavenly Vaults: From Romanesque to Gothic in Euro-*

Primary documents help you to understand history through the voices of those who lived it.

In each chapter of this textbook you will find many primary sources to broaden your understanding of the development of the West. Primary sources refer to firsthand, contemporary accounts or direct evidence about a particular topic. For example, speeches, letters, diaries, song lyrics, and newspaper articles are all primary sources that historians use to construct accounts of the past. Nonwritten materials such as maps, paintings, artifacts, and even architecture and music can also be primary sources. Both types of historical documents in this textbook — written and visual — provide a glimpse into the lives of the men and women who influenced or were influenced by the course of Western history.

To guide your interpretation of any source, you should begin by asking several basic questions, listed below, as starting points for observing, analyzing, and interpreting the past. Your answers should prompt further questions of your own.

1. **Who is the author?** Who wrote or created the material? What was his or her authority? (Personal? institutional?) Did the author have specialized knowledge or experience? If you are reading a written document, how would you describe the author's tone of voice? (Formal, personal, angry?)

2. **Who is the audience?** Who were the intended readers, listeners, or viewers? How does the intended audience affect the ways that the author presents ideas?

3. **What are the main ideas?** What are the main points that the author is trying to convey? Can you detect any underlying assumptions of values or attitudes? How does the form or medium affect the meaning of this document?

4. **In what context was the document created?** From when and where does the document originate? What was the interval between the initial problem or event and this document, which responded to it? Through what form or medium was the document communicated? (For example, a newspaper, a government record, an illustration.) What contemporary events or conditions might have affected the creation of the document?

5. **What's missing?** What's missing or cannot be learned from this source, and what might this omission reveal? Are there other sources that might fill in the gaps?

Now consider these questions as you read "Columbus Describes His First Voyage (1493)," the document on the next page. Compare your answers to the sample observations provided.

DOCUMENT

Columbus Describes His First Voyage (1493)

In this famous letter to Raphael Sanchez, treasurer to his patrons, Ferdinand and Isabella, Columbus recounts his initial journey to the Bahamas, Cuba, and Hispaniola (today Haiti and the Dominican Republic), and tells of his achievements. This passage reflects the first contact between native Americans and Europeans; already the themes of trade, subjugation, gold, and conversion emerge in Columbus's own words.

Indians would give whatever the seller required; . . . Thus they bartered, like idiots, cotton and gold for fragments of bows, glasses, bottles, and jars; which I forbad as being unjust, and myself gave them many beautiful and acceptable articles which I had brought with me, taking nothing from them in return; I did this in order that I might the more easily conciliate them, that they might be led to become Christians, and be inclined to entertain a regard for the King and Queen, our Princes and all Spaniards, and that I might induce them to take an interest in seeking out, and collecting, and delivering to us such things as they possessed in abundance, but which we greatly needed. They practise no kind of idolatry, but have a firm belief that all strength and power, and indeed all good things, are in heaven, and that I had descended from thence with these ships and sailors, and under this impression was I received after they had thrown aside their fears. Nor are they slow or stupid, but of very clear understanding; and those men who have crossed to the neighbouring islands give an admirable description of everything they observed; but they never saw any people clothed, nor any ships like ours. On my arrival at that sea, I had taken some Indians by force from the first island that I came to, in order that they might learn our language, and communicate to us what they know respecting the country; which plan succeeded excellently, and was a great advantage to us, for in a short time, either by gestures and signs, or by words, we were enabled to understand each other. These men are still travelling with me, and although they have been with us now a long time, they continue to entertain the idea that I have descended from heaven.

Source: Christopher Columbus, *Four Voyages to the New World*, trans. R. H. Major (New York: Corinth Books, 1961), 8–9.

Question to Consider

- **In what ways were Columbus's early impressions of native Americans both respectful and condescending?**

1. **Who is the author?** The title and headnote that precede each document contain information about the authorship and date of its creation. In this case, the Italian explorer Christopher Columbus is the author. His letter describes events in which he was both an eyewitness and a participant.
2. **Who is the audience?** Columbus sent the letter to Raphael Sanchez, treasurer to Ferdinand and Isabella — someone who Columbus knew would be keenly interested in the fate of his patrons' investment. Because the letter was also a public document written to a crown official, Columbus would have expected a wider audience beyond Sanchez. How might his letter have differed had it been written to a friend?
3. **What are the main ideas?** In this segment, Columbus describes his encounter with the native people. He speaks of his desire to establish good relations by treating them fairly, and he offers his impressions of their intelligence and naiveté — characteristics he implies will prove useful to Europeans. He also expresses an interest in converting them to Christianity and making them loyal subjects of the crown.
4. **In what context was the document created?** Columbus wrote the letter in 1493, within six months of his first voyage. He would have been eager to announce the success of his endeavor.
5. **What's missing?** Columbus's letter provides just one view of the encounter. We do not have a corresponding account from the native Americans' perspective nor from anyone else traveling with Columbus. With no corroborating evidence, how reliable is this description?

Note: You can use these same questions to analyze visual images. Start by determining who created the image — whether it's a painting, photograph, sculpture, map, or artifact — and when it was made. Then consider the audience for whom the artist might have intended the work and how viewers might have reacted. Consult the text for information about the time period, and look for visual cues such as color, artistic style, and use of space to determine the central idea of the work. As you read, consult the captions in this book to help you evaluate the images and to ask more questions of your own.

Authors' Note

The B.C.E./C.E. Dating System

"When were you born?" "What year is it?" We customarily answer questions like these with a number, such as "1987" or "2012." Our replies are usually automatic, taking for granted the numerous assumptions Westerners make about how dates indicate chronology. But to what do numbers such as 1987 and 2012 actually refer? In this book the numbers used to specify dates follow a recent revision of the system most common in the Western secular world. This system reckons the dates of solar years by counting backward and forward from the traditional date of the birth of Jesus Christ, over two thousand years ago.

Using this method, numbers followed by the abbreviation B.C.E., standing for "before the common era" (or, as some would say, "before the Christian era"), indicate the number of years counting backward from the assumed date of the birth of Jesus Christ. B.C.E. therefore indicates the same chronology marked by the traditional abbreviation B.C. ("before Christ"). The larger the number following B.C.E. (or B.C.), the earlier in history is the year to which it refers. The date 431 B.C.E., for example, refers to a year 431 years before the birth of Jesus and therefore comes earlier in time than the dates 430 B.C.E., 429 B.C.E., and so on. The same calculation applies to numbering other time intervals calculated on the decimal system: those of ten years (a decade), of one hundred years (a century), and of one thousand years (a millennium). For example, the decade of the 440s B.C.E. (449 B.C.E. to 440 B.C.E.) is earlier than the decade of the 430s B.C.E. (439 B.C.E. to 430 B.C.E.). "Fifth century B.C.E." refers to the fifth period of 100 years reckoning backward from the birth of Jesus and covers the years 500 B.C.E. to 401 B.C.E. It is earlier in history than the fourth century B.C.E. (400 B.C.E. to 301 B.C.E.), which followed the fifth century B.C.E. Because this system has no year "zero," the first century B.C.E. covers the years 100 B.C.E. to 1 B.C.E. Dating millennia works similarly: the second millennium B.C.E. refers to the years 2000 B.C.E. to 1001 B.C.E., the third millennium to the years 3000 B.C.E. to 2001 B.C.E., and so on.

To indicate years counted forward from the traditional date of Jesus's birth, numbers are followed by the abbreviation C.E., standing for "of the common era" (or "of the Christian era"). C.E. therefore indicates the same chronology marked by the traditional abbreviation A.D., which stands for the Latin phrase *anno Domini* ("in the year of the Lord"). A.D. properly comes before the date being marked. The date A.D. 1492, for example, translates as "in the year of the Lord 1492," meaning 1492 years after the birth of Jesus. Under the B.C.E./C.E. system, this date would be written as 1492 C.E. For dating centuries, the term "first century C.E." refers to the period from 1 C.E. to 100 C.E. (which is the same period as A.D. 1 to A.D. 100). For dates C.E., the smaller the number, the earlier the date in history. The fourth century C.E. (301 C.E. to 400 C.E.) comes before the fifth century C.E. (401 C.E. to 500 C.E.). The year 312 C.E. is a date in the early fourth century C.E., while 395 C.E. is a date late in the same century. When numbers are given without either B.C.E. or C.E., they are presumed to be dates C.E. For example, the term *eighteenth century* with no abbreviation accompanying it refers to the years 1701 C.E. to 1800 C.E.

No standard system of numbering years, such as B.C.E./C.E., existed in antiquity. Different people in different places identified years with varying names and numbers. Consequently, it was difficult to match up the years in any particular local system with those in a different system. Each city of ancient Greece, for example, had its own method for keeping track of the years. The ancient Greek historian Thucydides, therefore, faced a problem in presenting a chronology for the famous Peloponnesian War between Athens and Sparta, which began (by our reckoning) in 431 B.C.E. To try to explain to as many of his readers as possible the date the war had begun, he described its first year by three different local systems: "the year when Chrysis was in the forty-eighth year of her priesthood at Argos, and Aenesias was overseer at Sparta, and Pythodorus was magistrate at Athens."

A Catholic monk named Dionysius, who lived in Rome in the sixth century C.E., invented the system of reckoning dates forward from the birth of Jesus. Calling himself *Exiguus* (Latin for "the little" or "the small") as a mark of humility, he placed

Jesus's birth 754 years after the foundation of ancient Rome. Others then and now believe his date for Jesus's birth was in fact several years too late. Many scholars today calculate that Jesus was born in what would be 4 B.C.E. according to Dionysius's system, although a date a year or so earlier also seems possible.

Counting backward from the supposed date of Jesus's birth to indicate dates earlier than that event represented a natural complement to reckoning forward for dates after it. The English historian and theologian Bede in the early eighth century was the first to use both forward and backward reckoning from the birth of Jesus in a historical work, and this system gradually gained wider acceptance because it provided a basis for standardizing the many local calendars used in the Western Christian world. Nevertheless, B.C. and A.D. were not used together as a system until the end of the eighteenth century. B.C.E. and C.E. became common in the late twentieth century.

The system of numbering years from the birth of Jesus is far from the only one in use today. The Jewish calendar of years, for example, counts forward from the date given to the creation of the world, which would be calculated as 3761 B.C.E. under the B.C.E./C.E. system. Under this system, years are designated A.M., an abbreviation of the Latin *anno mundi*, "in the year of the world." The Islamic calendar counts forward from the date of the prophet Muhammad's flight from Mecca, called the Hijra, in what is the year 622 C.E. The abbreviation A.H. (standing for the Latin phrase *anno Hegirae*, "in the year of the Hijra") indicates dates calculated by this system. Anthropology commonly reckons distant dates as "before the present" (abbreviated B.P.).

History is often defined as the study of change over time; hence the importance of dates for the historian. But just as historians argue over which dates are most significant, they disagree over which dating system to follow. Their debate reveals perhaps the most enduring fact about history—its vitality.

FOURTH EDITION

The Making of the West

PEOPLES AND CULTURES

Prologue

The Beginnings of Human Society

To c. 4000 B.C.E.

In 1997, archaeologists working in the East African nation of Ethiopia discovered fossilized skulls that dated from at least 160,000 years ago. These bones are the oldest remains ever found from the species *Homo sapiens* ("wise human being")—people whose brains and appearances were similar though not identical to ours. This discovery excited scientists because it supported the "out of Africa" theory about human origins, which claims that *Homo sapiens* first appeared in Africa perhaps as early as two hundred thousand years ago and then spread from that continent all over the world. In contrast, recent discoveries of human remains in Asia have reignited debate over the "out of Africa" theory, bringing back the once-discarded idea that human beings arose independently in different parts of the earth.

The innovations that early human beings made in technology, trade, religion, and social organization formed the basis of our modern way of life. They also led to the emergence of war. As the discoveries of the skulls in Ethiopia and the human remains in Asia show, researchers continue to find evidence that adds to our knowledge about the past and therefore our thinking about how the past relates to the present. This process of discovery always involves questioning and debate. When we study history, therefore, we have to expect uncertainty and disagreements, especially about how to interpret past events, what those events meant then, and what they mean today.

Stone Age Handaxe
Archaeologists regard stone cutting tools like this one, called a handaxe, as the first great invention. Stone Age peoples made handaxes for hundreds of thousands of years, probably using hammers made from bone or wood to chip off flakes from the stone to create knifelike edges for cutting and scraping. This sharp tool would have been especially useful for butchering animals, such as the hippopotamuses that African hunter-gatherers killed for meat. Shown here at its full size (about seven and three-quarter inches top to bottom), this handaxe was, like all others, shaped to fit the human palm; users probably wrapped the tool in a piece of hide to protect their hands from cuts. (*© The Trustees of The British Museum/Art Resource, NY.*)

Scientists studying fossilized bones and those studying human mitochondrial DNA (the type inherited from the mother) have shown that it took millions of years for the earliest human species to emerge. According to the "out of Africa" theory, human beings exactly like us first developed in sub-Saharan Africa more than fifty thousand years ago. Starting about forty-five thousand years ago, those human beings began moving out of Africa, first into the Near East[1] and then into Europe and Asia.

This migration took place in the period commonly called the Stone Age, during which human beings made their most durable tools from stones, before they learned to work metals. Human society began in the Stone Age, which archaeologists divide into two parts to mark the greatest turning point in human history: the invention of agriculture and the domestication of animals and the enormous changes in human society that these innovations brought. The first part, the **Paleolithic** ("Old Stone") **Age**, dates from about 200,000 B.C.E. to about 10,000 B.C.E. The second part, the **Neolithic** ("New Stone") **Age**, dates from about 10,000 B.C.E. to about 4000 B.C.E.

Archaeology—the study of physical evidence from the past—is our only source of information about the Stone Age; there are no documents to inform us about the lives of early human beings because people did not invent writing until about 4000–3000 B.C.E. Historians sometimes label the time before the invention of writing *prehistory*, because *history* traditionally means having written sources about the past. Historians also usually do not apply the word *civilization* to human society in the Stone Age because people then had not yet begun to live in cities or form **political states** (people living in a defined territory and organized under a central authority). The first cities and political states emerged about the same time as writing, as we will see in Chapter 1.

It was in the Neolithic Age that, instead of only hunting and gathering food in the wild, people learned how to produce their own food by raising crops and domesticating animals. The technological innovations of agriculture and animal husbandry produced lasting changes in human society, especially in strengthening social hierarchies, supporting gender inequality, and encouraging war for conquest. Historians continue to debate what was positive and what was negative in the consequences, intentional and unintentional, that this turning point produced for human society.

CHAPTER FOCUS What were the positive and the negative consequences for human life when people learned how to produce their food by farming instead of only hunting and gathering food in the wild?

The Paleolithic Age, 200,000–10,000 B.C.E.

Human society began during the Paleolithic Age and was organized to suit a mobile way of life because human beings in this early period roamed around in small groups to hunt and gather food in the wild. The most notable feature of early Paleo-

[1]The term *Near East*, like *Middle East*, has undergone several changes in meaning over time. Both terms reflect the geographical point of view of Europeans. Today, the term *Middle East*, more commonly employed in politics and journalism than in history, usually refers to the area encompassing the Arabic-speaking countries of the eastern Mediterranean region as well as Israel, Iran, Turkey, Cyprus, and much of North Africa. Historians, by contrast, generally use the term *ancient Near East* to designate Anatolia (often called Asia Minor, today occupied by the Asian portion of Turkey), Cyprus, the lands around the eastern end of the Mediterranean, the Arabian peninsula, Mesopotamia (the lands north of the Persian Gulf, today Iraq and Iran), and Egypt. In this book we will observe the common usage of the term *Near East* to mean Egypt and southwestern Asia.

Paleolithic Age: The "Old Stone" Age, dating from around 200,000 to 10,000 B.C.E.

Neolithic Age: The "New Stone" Age, dating from around 10,000 to 4000 B.C.E.

political states: People living in a defined territory with boundaries and organized under a system of government with powerful officials, leaders, and judges.

200,000–160,000 B.C.E. Beginning of Paleolithic ("Old Stone") Age

50,000–45,000 B.C.E. *Homo sapiens sapiens* migrate from Africa into southwest Asia and Europe

10,000–8000 B.C.E. Neolithic ("New Stone") Revolution in the Fertile Crescent and the Sahara

8000 B.C.E. Walled settlement at Jericho (in modern Israel)

7000–5500 B.C.E. Farming community thrives at Çatalhöyük (in modern Turkey)

200,000 B.C.E. | 50,000 B.C.E. | 10,000 B.C.E. | 0

lithic society was that the group probably made important decisions in common, with all adult men and women having a more or less equal say. Over time, however, Paleolithic peoples created a more complex social organization as they developed trade to acquire goods from long distances, technology such as fire for heat and cooking, religious beliefs to express their understanding of the divine and of the mystery of death, and social hierarchies to denote differences in status.

The Life of Hunter-Gatherers

The characteristics of human society in the Paleolithic period originally reflected the conditions of life for **hunter-gatherers**, the term historians use for people who roamed all their lives, hunting wild animals and foraging edible plants. They never settled permanently in one place. Although they knew a great deal about how to survive in the natural environment, they had not yet learned to produce their own food by growing crops and raising animals. Instead, they hunted game for meat; fished in lakes and rivers; collected shellfish along the shore; and gathered edible plants, fruits, and nuts.

Archaeology reveals that a change in weather patterns apparently motivated hunter-gatherers of the modern type of human being, ***Homo sapiens sapiens***, to begin wandering out of Africa around 50,000–45,000 B.C.E. (*Homo sapiens sapiens* means "wise, wise human being"; the repeated *wise* is meant to distinguish this later type from the earlier and slightly different type, called simply *Homo sapiens*.) Long periods without rain drove game animals into southwestern Asia and then Europe to find water, and at least some of the mobile human populations who hunted them in African lands followed this moving food into new continents. There is no evidence to explain why some hunter-gatherers left Africa in the Paleolithic period while others stayed behind.

When *Homo sapiens sapiens* hunter-gatherers reached Europe and Asia, they met earlier types of human beings who had already migrated out of Africa, such as the heavy-browed, squat-bodied Neanderthal type (named after the Neander valley in Germany, where their fossil remains were first found; their body type is often used to represent "cavemen" in popular art). Eventually, after walking across then-existent land bridges to reach the Americas and Australia, *Homo sapiens sapiens* replaced all earlier types of people around the globe.

Archaeological excavations of hunter-gatherers' campsites tell us about their lives on the move, showing that over time they invented new forms of tools, weapons, and jewelry and began burying their dead with special care. Anthropologists have also reconstructed the lives of ancient hunter-gatherers from comparative study of the few groups who lived on as hunter-gatherers into modern times, such as the !Kung San of southern Africa's Kalahari Desert, the Aborigines in Australia, and the Coahuiltecans in the American Southwest. These two categories of evidence suggest that Paleolithic hunter-gatherers banded together in groups numbering around twenty or thirty to hunt and gather food that they shared among themselves. Their life expectancy was about twenty-five to thirty years for both men and women. Since they had not learned to domesticate animals or to make wheels for carts, they walked everywhere. Because women of childbearing age had to carry and nurse their babies, it was difficult for them to roam long distances. They and the younger children therefore gathered plants, fruits, and nuts close to camp and caught small animals such as frogs and rabbits. The plant food that they gathered provided the majority of the group's diet. Men did most of the hunting of large animals, which frequently took them far from camp to kill prey at close range with rocks and spears; butchered hippopotamus bones found near the skulls in Ethiopia show that early humans hunted these dangerous animals. Women probably participated in hunts when the group used nets to catch wild animals.

Each band of Paleolithic hunter-gatherers moved around searching for food, usually ranging over an area that averaged roughly sixty miles across in any one direction. They tended not to intrude on other bands' areas, but there were no set boundaries or central settlements to identify a band's territory. To judge from battles observed between surviving tribes of hunter-gatherers, conflicts between Paleolithic bands were more skirmishes than total battles, and there was as much display as serious fighting; for ancient hunter-gatherers, there was nothing to take from another group that one's own group did not already possess, except other people. Hunter-gatherers' constant walking, bending, and lifting kept them in fine physical shape, but they counted on their knowledge as much as their strength for both hunting and the occasional battle. Most important, they planned ahead for cooperative hunts at favorite spots, such as river crossings or lakes with shallow banks, where experience taught they were

---

hunter-gatherers: Human beings who roam to hunt and gather food in the wild and do not live in permanent, settled communities.

***Homo sapiens sapiens*:** The scientific name (in Latin) of the type of early human being identical to people today; it means "wise, wise human being."

Building with Bones
This reconstruction shows how Paleolithic people built shelters using bones from mammoths they hunted. Dating from about fifteen thousand years ago and found in Ukraine in east-central Europe, this closely fitted structure reveals how hunter-gatherers made the maximum use of the bodies of dead animals. *(C. M. Dixon / Ancient Art & Architecture Collection, Ltd.)*

likely to find herds of large animals fording the stream and drinking water.

Paleolithic hunter-gatherers also used their knowledge to establish camps year after year in particularly good spots for gathering plants. They took shelter from the weather in caves or temporary dwellings made from branches and animal skins. On occasion, they built sturdier shelters, such as the dome-like hut found in Ukraine that was constructed from the bones of mammoths. They never built permanent homes, however; they had to roam to survive.

Hunter-gatherers probably lived originally in egalitarian societies, meaning that all adults enjoyed a general equality in making decisions for the group. This cooperation reflected the fact that men and women both worked hard to provide food for the group, even if they tended to divide this labor by gender, with men doing more hunting and women more gathering. At some point, however, differences in social status began to emerge. Most likely, age was the first basis of social status: older people of both genders won prestige and probably positions of leadership because of the wisdom gained from long experience of life in an era when most people died of illness or accidents before they were thirty years old. Women past childbearing age who helped out in multiple ways and strong, clever men who hunted dangerous animals also likely held high status.

Innovations in Paleolithic Life

Paleolithic people made changes in their lives that turned out to be important for the later development of civilization. In technology, learning how to create ever sharper edges and points in stone, bone, and wood led to better weapons for hunting and tools for digging out roots and making clothes from animal skins, thereby increasing the chances for survival. The discovery of how to make fire was especially important because Paleolithic people had to endure the cold of extended ice ages, when the northern European glaciers moved much farther south than usual. The coldest part of the most recent

Bison Painting in the Cave at Lascaux
Stone Age people painted these bison (European bison) on the rock walls of a large cave at Lascaux in central France around 15,000 B.C.E., to judge from radiocarbon dating of charcoal found on the floor. Using black, red, yellow, and white pigments, the artists made the deep cave into an art gallery by filling it with pictures not only of these bison but also of horses, deer, bears, and wooly rhinoceroses. Some scholars have suggested that the scenes symbolized the importance of hunting to the people who painted them, but this guess seems wrong because the bones from butchered animals found in the cave are 90 percent reindeer, while no reindeer pictures exist in the cave. *(Caves of Lascaux, Dordogne, France / The Bridgeman Art Library International.)*

ice age started about twenty thousand years ago and created a harsh climate in much of Europe for nearly ten thousand years. Hunter-gatherers' knowledge of how to control fire led to the invention of cooking. This was a crucial innovation because it turned indigestible plants, such as grains, into edible and nutritious food.

Long-distance trade also began in the Stone Age. When hunter-gatherers encountered other bands, they exchanged things they had made, such as blades and jewelry, as well as natural objects such as flint or seashells. Trade could move valuable objects great distances: for example, ocean shells worn as jewelry made their way far inland through repeated swaps.

Archaeological discoveries suggest that Paleolithic hunter-gatherers developed religious beliefs, a crucial factor in the evolution of human society, and reveal that ancient peoples saw religion as necessary for living a successful and just life. Some late Paleolithic cave paintings found in Spain and France hint at hunter-gatherers' religious ideas as well as display their artistic ability. Using strong, dark lines and earthy colors, Paleolithic artists painted on the walls of caves that were set aside as special places, not used as day-to-day shelters. The paintings, which primarily depict large animals, suggest that these powerful beasts played a significant role in the religion of Paleolithic hunter-gatherers. Still, there remains a great deal we do not yet understand about their beliefs, such as the meaning of the dots, rectangles, and hands that they often drew beside their paintings of animals.

Important evidence for early religious beliefs also comes from the discovery of specially shaped female figurines at late Paleolithic sites all over Europe. Modern archaeologists call these statuettes of women with extra-large breasts, abdomens, buttocks, and thighs Venus figurines, after the Roman goddess of sexual love (see the illustration on the right). The oversized features of these sculptures suggest that the people who made them had a special set of beliefs and rituals regarding fertility and birth.

Anthropologists study Paleolithic burial sites to find clues to what these early peoples believed about the mystery of death and the possibility of an afterlife. The early skulls found in Ethiopia have missing jaws and marks in the bone, hints that the living cut away the flesh from the heads of the dead to prepare their remains for a new future after burial (and not for cannibalism, as some have said). More evidence for Paleolithic ideas on fundamental questions about life and death come from the care with which corpses were decorated with red paint, flowers, and seashells. Some researchers conclude that these careful preparations for burial mean that early human beings already had complex religious ideas about what happened to them after they died.

Prehistoric Venus Figurine
This limestone statuette, four and a half inches high, was found at Willendorf, in Austria. Carved in the later Paleolithic period and originally colored red, it probably was meant to have symbolic power expressing the importance of women's fertility. The emphasis on the woman's breasts, hips, and pubic area have led scholars to call such statuettes Venus figurines, after the Roman goddess of love and sex; archaeologists have uncovered many of them all across Europe. Since no written records exist to explain the significance of such figurines' hairstyle, obesity, and prominent sexual characteristics, we can only speculate about the complex meanings that early peoples attributed to them. How would you explain this figurine's appearance? *(Museum of Natural History, Vienna, Austria, photo SuperStock.)*

Burials reveal more than religious beliefs; they also show that, by late Paleolithic times, hunter-gatherer society had begun to mark significant differences in status among people. Those who were buried with valuable items such as weapons, tools, animal figurines, ivory beads, and bracelets likely had special social standing. These object-rich burials reveal that late Paleolithic groups had begun organizing their society according to a **hierarchy**, a ranking system identifying certain people as having more status and authority than others. This is the earliest evidence for social differentiation, the marking of certain people as more respected, richer, or more powerful than others in their society.

Despite their varied status, knowledge, and technological skill, prehistoric hunter-gatherers lived precarious lives dominated by the relentless search for something to eat. Survival was a risky business. The groups that survived were those that cooperated in finding food and shelter; profited from innovations such as fire, tools, and trade; and taught their children the knowledge, beliefs, and social traditions that had helped them endure in a harsh world.

REVIEW QUESTION **What were the most important activities, skills, and beliefs that helped Paleolithic hunter-gatherers survive?**

---

hierarchy: The system of ranking people in society according to their status and authority.

The Neolithic Age, 10,000–4000 B.C.E.

By around 10,000–8000 B.C.E., people in the Near East had opened the way to a different kind of society by learning to grow their own food and build permanent farming settlements that housed larger populations than the twenty- to thirty-member bands of hunter-gatherers. In this new society, dominance by men replaced the general equality in status and decision making between men and women that likely existed in earlier times. In addition, war became a prominent part of human life.

The inventions of agriculture and permanent settlements in the Neolithic Age occurred over a long time, but once established they changed forever the way human beings lived; eventually, these changes would make civilization possible. Daily life as we know it still depends on farming and the domestication of animals, developments that began at the beginning of the Neolithic Age. These radical innovations in food acquisition caused such fundamental changes in human life that they are called the **Neolithic Revolution**.

Neolithic Revolution: The invention of agriculture, the domestication of animals, and the consequent changes in human society that occurred about 10,000–8,000 B.C.E. in the Near East.

The Neolithic Revolution and the Production of Food

Revolutionary change took place in human history in the Neolithic Age when hunter-gatherers learned to sow and harvest crops and to raise animals for food. Exactly how they gained this knowledge remains mysterious. Recent archaeological research, however, indicates that it took thousands of years for people to develop agriculture. The process began in the part of the Near East that we call the Fertile Crescent, whose hilly regions happened to have the right combination of soil, water, climate, and wild mammals for the invention of farming and the domestication of animals. The Fertile Crescent stretches in an arc, or crescent, along the foothills and lowlands that run northward from modern Israel across southeastern Turkey and Syria and then turn in a southeasterly direction down to the plain of the lower stretches of the Tigris and Euphrates Rivers in what is now southern Iraq (Map 1).

The slow trial-and-error process through which former hunter-gatherers developed agriculture had complex origins. Recent archaeological excavations at Göbekli Tepe, a site in southeastern Turkey whose name means "stomach-shaped little hill," have revealed stone-lined rooms in the earth decorated with stone pillars eight or more feet tall that are carved to depict boars, bears, birds, snakes, and other animals. Freestanding sculptures of animals seem to have been placed atop the rooms' walls. Radiocarbon dating suggests these rooms were built around 9300 B.C.E., which would make them contemporary

Stone Structures in the Neolithic Revolution
These ruins of stone-built structures from around 9300 B.C.E., many decorated with incised drawings of animals, were found at Göbekli Tepe in Turkey. Since their construction would have required many workers for a long time, archaeologists speculate that people's desire to build these large structures led to them developing agriculture so they could stay in one place long enough to accomplish their goal. *(Marcia Chambers/© dbimages/Alamy.)*

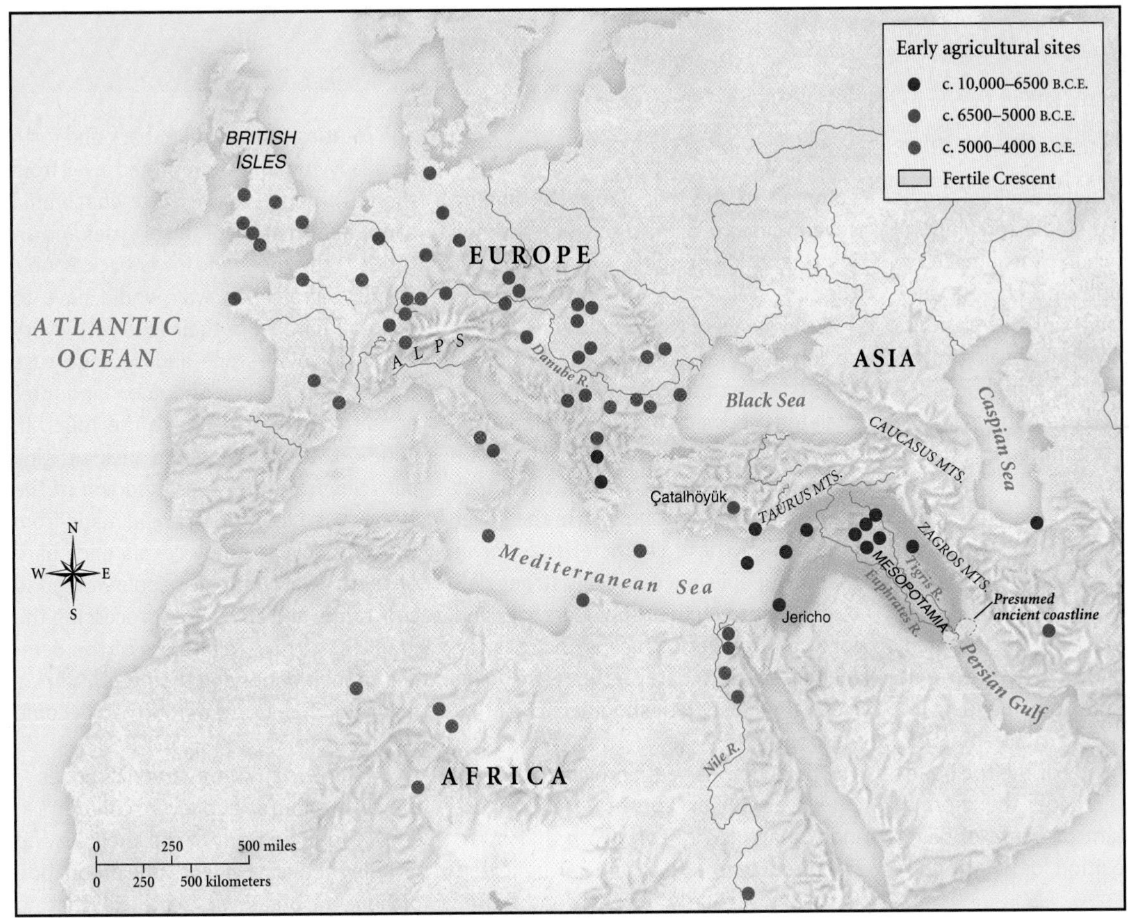

MAP 1 The Development of Agriculture
From around 10,000 to 8000 B.C.E., people learned to plant seeds to grow nourishing plants and to domesticate animals in the Fertile Crescent, the foothills of the semicircle of mountains that curved up and around from the eastern end of the Mediterranean down to Mesopotamia, where reliable rainfall and moderate temperatures prevailed. At about the same time, domestication of animals took place in the grasslands then flourishing in the Sahara region of Africa. The invention of irrigation in the Fertile Crescent allowed farmers to grow lush crops in the region's arid plains, providing resources that eventually spurred the emergence of the first large cities by about 4000 B.C.E.

with the first attested agriculture or perhaps even earlier. Some scholars speculate that hunter-gatherers built these monuments to express their religious beliefs. According to this theory, since a large group had to remain in one place for a long time to complete such elaborate structures and art, they had to develop agriculture to feed themselves. In this way, farming was a consequence of this new, concrete expression of religious ideas.

Only further archaeological research can reveal whether Stone Age religious activity was a cause of the Neolithic Revolution or vice versa. What seems certain is that climate change contributed significantly to the Neolithic Revolution. About ten to twelve thousand years ago, the long-term weather pattern in the Fertile Crescent became milder and rainier than it had been during the ice age that had just ended. This change promoted the growth of abundant fields of wild cereal grains. Similarly, recent archaeological research reveals that increased rain in the Sahara Desert, in central Africa, created there lush grasslands called savannahs that attracted hunter-gatherer nomads from the southern part of the continent; in a slow process of change, these people built settlements, domesticated cattle instead of only hunting wild animals, and created intricate pottery suited to their new way of life.

The hunter-gatherers living in the Fertile Crescent began to gather more and more of their food from the now easily available wild grains. This regular supply of food in turn promoted human fertility, which led to a growth in population, a process that might have already begun as a result of the milder climate. The more children that were born, the greater the need to exploit the food supply efficiently. Over centuries, people learned to plant part of the seeds from one crop of grain to produce another crop. Since Neolithic women did most of the gather-

NEW SOURCES, NEW PERSPECTIVES

Daily Bread, Damaged Bones, and Cracked Teeth

The invention of agriculture helped people produce a more predictable and plentiful supply of food, which in turn allowed the population to expand. This change came at a price. Recent scientific research in biological anthropology and osteological archaeology (the study of ancient bones and teeth) has uncovered dramatic evidence of the physical stress endured by some of the individuals working in early agriculture. Excavators at Tell Abu Hureyra in Syria have found bones and teeth from people living around 6000 B.C.E. that reveal the pain that the new technology could cause. The big toes of these ancient people especially show proof of extreme and prolonged dorsiflexion—bending the front of the foot up toward the shin. Dorsiflexion made the ends of the toe bones become flatter and broader than normal through the constant pressure of being bent in the same position for long periods of time.

What activity could the people have been pursuing so doggedly that it deformed their bones? The only posture that creates such severe bending of the foot is kneeling for extended periods. Osteologists confirmed that kneeling was common in this population by finding several cases of arthritic changes in knee joints and lower spines in skeletons at the site.

But why were the people kneeling for so long? Other bone evidence offered the first clue to solving this mystery. The skeletons showed strongly developed attachment points for the deltoid muscle on the humerus (the bone in the upper arm) and prominent growth in the lower arm bones. These characteristics mean that the people had especially strong deltoids for pushing their shoulders back and forth and powerful biceps for rotating their forearms. Whatever they were doing made them use their shoulders and arms vigorously.

The skeletons' teeth provided the next clue. Everyone except the very youngest individuals had deeply worn and often fractured teeth. This damage indicated that they regularly chewed food full of rock dust, which probably resulted from grain being ground in rock bowls.

The final clue came from art. Later paintings and sculptures from the region show people, usually women, kneeling down to grind grain into flour by pushing and rotating a stone roller back and forth on heavy grinding stones tilted away from them. This posture is exactly what would cause deformation of the big toes and arthritis in the knees and lower back. People grinding grain this way would have to push off hard from their toes with every stroke down the stone, and vigorously use the muscles of their shoulders and forearms to apply pressure to the roller. In addition, the flour would pick up tiny particles from the wearing down of the stones used to grind it; bread made from it would have a sandy consistency hard on teeth. That Neolithic people worked so constantly and so hard at processing the grain they grew, regardless of the damage to their bones and their teeth, shows how vital this supply of food had become to them.

At this Syrian site, everyone's bones—men's, women's, and even children's—show the same signs of the kneeling and grinding activity. Evidently the production of flour for bread was so crucial that no gender division of this labor was possible or desirable, as it seems to have become in later times. Regardless of who used it, this new technology that provided essential food for the community took its toll in individual pain and hardship.

ing of plant food, they had the greatest knowledge of plant life and therefore probably played the major role in the invention of agriculture and the fashioning of tools needed to turn grains into food, such as grinding stones for making flour. At this early stage in the development of agriculture, women and children did most of the agricultural labor, using hand tools to grow and harvest crops, while men continued to hunt to obtain meat.

During the early Neolithic Age, people also learned to breed and herd animals that they could eat, a development that helped replace the meat previously acquired by hunting large mammals, many of which had by now been hunted to extinction. Fortunately for the people in the Fertile Crescent, their region was home to surviving large mammals that could be domesticated. Unlike the zebra or the hippopotamus found in Africa, the wild sheep, goats, and cattle of the Fertile Crescent could, over the span of generations, be turned into animals accustomed to live closely and interdependently with human beings. The sheep was the first animal to be domesticated as a source of meat, beginning about 8500 B.C.E. (The dog had been domesticated much earlier but was not usually eaten.) By about 7000 B.C.E., domesticated animals had become common throughout the Near East. In this early period of domestication, some people lived as pastoralists, meaning they obtained their food mainly from the herds of animals they kept, frequently moving around to find fresh grazing land. They also cultivated small temporary plots from time to time when they found a suitable area. Other people, relying more and more on growing crops for their livelihood, kept small herds close to their settlements. Men, women, and children alike could therefore

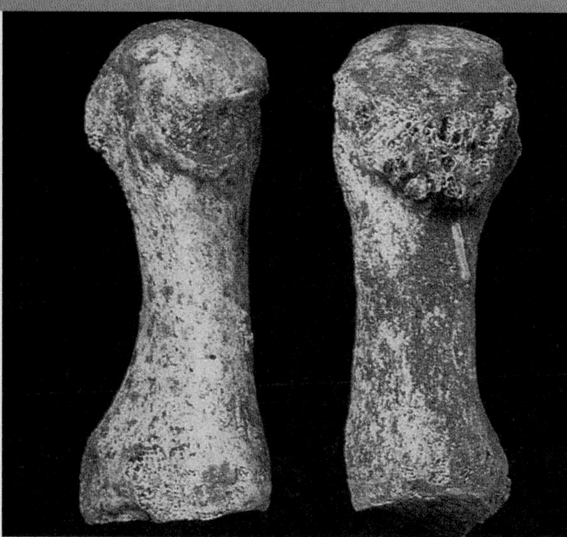

Bones from Tell Abu Hureyra, Syria
These big toes from a middle-aged man reveal severe arthritic changes to the joint. Osteologists interpret this damage as evidence of extreme and prolonged dorsiflexion, or bending of the foot. *(© Natural History Museum, London.)*

Sculpture from Giza, Egypt
In this statuette, a woman grinds grain into flour. The sculptor shows her rubbing her severely flexed left foot with the toes of her right foot, probably trying to ease the throbbing resulting from hours of kneeling. *(Courtesy of the Oriental Institute of the University of Chicago.)*

Questions to Consider

1. What other new technologies that have increased productivity and bettered human life have also involved new pains and stresses?
2. How do you decide what price—financial, physical, emotional—is worth paying for new technology? Who will make those decisions?

Further Reading

Abu Hureyra: http://www.mnsu.edu/emuseum/archaeology/sites/middle_east/abuhureyra.html

Hillman, G. "Traditional Husbandry and Processing of Archaic Cereals in Recent Times: The Operations, Products, and Equipment Which Might Feature in Sumerian Texts." *Bulletin on Sumerian Agriculture* 1 (1984): 114–52.

Molleson, Theya. "Seed Preparation in the Mesolithic: The Osteological Evidence." *Antiquity* 63 (1989): 358.

Moore, A. M. T. "The Excavation of Tell Abu Hureyra in Syria: A Preliminary Report." *Proceedings of the Prehistoric Society* 41 (1975): 50–71.

tend the animals. These earliest domesticated herds seem to have been used only as a source of meat, not for products such as milk or wool. Hunting never completely disappeared, but it evolved into an activity mainly for establishing men's masculinity and prestige—something that would be increasingly important as humans moved toward civilization.

The Neolithic Origins of Civilization

The Neolithic Revolution laid the foundation for civilization and our modern way of life. The remarkable new knowledge of how to produce food and the consequent division and specialization of labor emerged through innovative human responses to the link between environmental change and population growth (see "New Sources, New Perspectives," above). Furthermore, the Neolithic Revolution reveals the importance of **demography**—the study of the size, growth, density, distribution, and vital statistics of the human population—to the study of history.

Two central features of Neolithic farming villages helped create conditions that eventually led to urban-based civilization: they were permanent, and they supported larger populations than were characteristic of hunter-gatherer society. First, to be able to raise crops, people had to stop roaming and settle in one place with adequate land and water. Farming communities thus sprang up in the Fertile

---

demography: The study of the size, growth, density, distribution, and vital statistics of the human population.

Tower in the Stone Wall of Neolithic Jericho
The circular mass in the center of this photograph is the base of a tower in the stone wall that the people of Jericho (today in Israel) built to protect their community around 8000–7000 B.C.E. This is one of the earliest defensive walls ever discovered; most of the people in this era still lived in unwalled collections of mud huts, but the inhabitants of Jericho had reached a more complex level of social organization that allowed them to collaborate on major building projects. The agricultural fields that lay outside the walls supplied the overwhelming majority of Jericho's economy, while the wall surrounding their settlement provided security for the residents' homes and storehouses and thus protected their improving standard of living. *(Photo © Zev Radovan/The Bridgeman Art Library International.)*

Crescent starting around 10,000 B.C.E., sharing the region with pastoralists. Second, parents began to have more children because agriculture required a great deal of labor and because the fields and herds supplied readily available food. At the same time, living in close quarters with domesticated animals, which might well be penned right next to or even inside the house, exposed people to new epidemic diseases transmitted from animals to humans. Hunter-gatherers had largely escaped this danger because they had no groups of animals around them every day, although they could sometimes become infected by eating diseased wild animals. Since many viruses that afflict people today — for example, the avian influenza (bird flu) virus — originated in domesticated animals, we are still living with this unintended consequence of the Neolithic Revolution.

Much bigger and more densely packed than the temporary settlements of the Paleolithic Age, early farming communities built sturdy houses of mud brick and used containers made of pottery (whose broken remains provide evidence for chronology and cultural development). The first homes were apparently circular huts, like those known in Jericho (in what is today Israel). Around two thousand people had settled in Jericho by 8000 B.C.E., their huts sprawling over about twelve acres.

Jericho's remains also reveal that war became a prominent part of life during the Neolithic Revolution. The most remarkable part of the village was the massive fortification wall surrounding the community. Ten feet thick, the wall was crowned with a thirty-foot-diameter stone tower enclosing a flight of stairs; this massive structure shows that the inhabitants of Jericho feared attacks by their neighbors (see the illustration above). The presence of the tower suggests that growing prosperity brought by the Neolithic Revolution had also spurred war for conquest and acquisition. Religion remained central to the lives of the Neolithic inhabitants of Jericho, as evidenced by the human skulls that they covered with plaster and paint, perhaps to honor their ancestors.

Neolithic people from the Fertile Crescent opened the way for civilization to develop in other regions by gradually spreading their knowledge of agriculture abroad. Farmers looking for more land migrated westward from the Near East and brought the new technology of farming into areas where it was not previously known. Although recent scholarship argues that human beings in other areas, especially Asia, independently developed agriculture and the domestication of animals, migrants from the Near East were the ones who spread this knowledge across Europe by 4000 B.C.E.

Daily Life in the Neolithic Village of Çatalhöyük

An archaeological site northwest of the Fertile Crescent, in present-day Turkey, provides vital evidence for the vast changes in human life brought on by the spread of knowledge during the Neolithic Age, especially how agriculture's efficiency in providing food led to the division and specialization of labor.

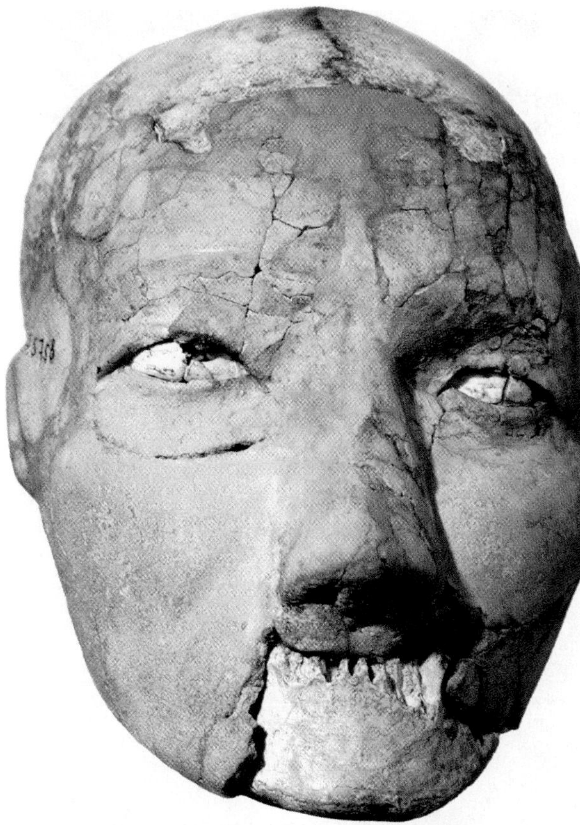

Decorated Human Skull

The inhabitants of Jericho buried human skulls under the floors of buildings in their Neolithic town. They made the skulls look more lifelike by applying plaster and shells. It seems possible that these carefully decorated remains expressed respect and religious awe for ancestors. *(Archeological Museum, Amman, Jordan/Giraudon/The Bridgeman Art Library International.)*

At this site a large mound rises from a plain near a river. Known to us only by its modern Turkish name, Çatalhöyük (meaning "Fork Mound"), the site reveals what daily life was like in a Neolithic farming community. By 7000 to 6500 B.C.E., the farmers of Çatalhöyük had erected a settlement of mud-brick houses sharing common walls. They constructed their dwellings in the rectangular shape still used for most homes today, with one striking difference: they had no doors in their outer walls. Instead, they entered their homes by climbing down a ladder through a hole in the flat roof. Since this hole also served as a vent for smoke from the family fire, getting into a house at Çatalhöyük could be a grimy experience. But the absence of exterior doors also meant that the walls of the community's outermost houses served as the village's fortification wall to defend it against attacks.

The people of Çatalhöyük fed themselves by growing wheat, barley, and vegetables such as field peas; they diverted water from the nearby river to irrigate their fields to increase their harvests. They also kept domesticated cattle to provide their main supply of meat and, by this time, hides and milk. They continued to hunt, too, as we can tell from the hunting scenes they drew on the walls of some of their buildings, recalling the cave paintings of much earlier times. Unlike hunter-gatherers, however, these villagers no longer had to depend on the hit-or-miss luck of the hunt or risk being killed by wild animals to acquire meat and leather. The village's population reached perhaps six thousand at its height, and its inhabitants practiced a wide array of occupations.

The diversity of occupations at Çatalhöyük reveals a significant change from earlier times, anticipating the division of labor characteristic of the later cities of the first fully developed civilizations. Since the community could produce enough food to support itself without everyone having to work in the fields or herd cattle, some people could develop crafts full-time. Just as others in the community produced food for them, craft specialists produced goods for those who provided the food. Craft specialists continued to fashion tools, containers, and ornaments in the traditional way—from wood, bone, hide, and stone—but they now also worked with the material of the future: metal. So far, archaeologists are certain only that metalworkers at Çatalhöyük knew how to fashion lead into pendants and to hammer naturally occurring lumps of copper into beads and tubes for jewelry. But traces of slag, the scum that floats on molten metal, have been found on the site, suggesting that the workers may have begun to develop the technique of smelting metal from ore. This tricky process—the basis of true metallurgy and an essential technology of civilization—required temperatures of 700 degrees centigrade and took centuries for metalworkers to perfect. Other workers at Çatalhöyük specialized in weaving textiles, and the scraps of cloth discovered there are the oldest examples of this craft ever found. Like other early technological innovations, metallurgy and the production of cloth apparently also developed independently in other places.

Trade—another central aspect of human existence that became increasingly prominent in the Neolithic Age—also figured in the economy of this early farming community. The trading contacts the Neolithic villagers made with other settlements increased the level of economic interconnection among far-flung communities that had begun in the Paleolithic Age. Trade allowed the people of Çatalhöyük to acquire goods from far away, such as shells from the Mediterranean Sea to wear as ornaments and a special flint from far to the east to shape into ceremonial daggers. The villagers acquired these prized materials by offering obsidian in exchange, a local volcanic glass whose glossy luster and capacity to hold a sharp edge made it valuable.

Model of a House at Çatalhöyük
Archaeologists built this model of a house to show how Neolithic villagers lived in Çatalhöyük (today in central Turkey) from around 6500 to 5500 B.C.E. The wall paintings and bull-head sculpture had religious meaning, perhaps linked to the graves that the residents dug under the floor for their dead. The main entrance to the house was through the ceiling, as the houses were built right next to one another without streets in between, only some space for dumping refuse; the roofs served as walkways. Why do you think the villagers chose this arrangement for their settlement? *(Çatalhöyük Research Project.)*

Just as members of the community saw trade as vital to their economic prosperity, they saw religion as essential for their spiritual needs. The shrines and burial sites uncovered by archaeologists offer us hints about these beliefs and practices. The villagers outfitted their shrines with paintings and sculptures of bulls' heads and female breasts, perhaps as symbols of male and female elements in their religion. Like the hunter-gatherers before them, they sculpted figurines depicting large-breasted, large-hipped women who perhaps represented goddesses of birth, although some figurines recently found with skeletal designs suggest they were also related to ideas about death. The villagers' deep interest in the mystery of death is demonstrated by the skulls displayed in their shrines and by wall paintings of vultures devouring headless corpses. They buried their dead, some holding skulls decorated with painted plaster, under the floors of their houses. Perhaps they, too, believed their dead ancestors had power and therefore wanted to keep them close by. A remarkable wall painting also suggests that the people of Çatalhöyük regarded the volcano looming over their settlement as an angry god whom they needed to please. As it turned out, a volcanic eruption overwhelmed Çatalhöyük about fourteen hundred years after its foundation, and the settlement never recovered.

Along with religion, hierarchy was also important to the people of Çatalhöyük. They had a clear social hierarchy, another example of the lasting changes that occurred in the Neolithic Age and influenced the development of civilization. The villagers developed a hierarchical society because they needed leaders to plan and regulate irrigation, trade, the exchange of food and goods between farmers and crafts producers, and the defense of the community against enemies. These leaders held more authority than had been required to maintain peace and order in Paleolithic hunter-gatherer bands because their responsibilities were more complicated. Furthermore, households that were successful in farming, herding, crafts production, and trade generated surpluses in wealth that set them apart from those whose efforts proved less fortunate.

The Emergence of Gender Inequality in the Neolithic Age

As hierarchy became increasingly important, the social equality between men and women that had existed in hunter-gatherer bands dwindled during the Neolithic Age. By about 4000 B.C.E., when the first political states had begun to emerge in the Near East, **patriarchy** was the rule. (Patriarchal political states also emerged at various other distant places around the world, including India, China, and the Americas—whether through independent development or some process of mutual influence we cannot yet say.) The reasons for the appearance of patriarchy remain uncertain, but they perhaps involved gradual changes in agriculture and herding over many centuries. After about 4000 B.C.E., farmers used plows pulled by large animals to cultivate land that was difficult to sow. Men apparently operated this new technology of plowing, probably because it required much more physical strength than digging with sticks and hoes, as women had done with hand tools in the earliest period of agriculture. Men also looked after the larger herds that had become more common in settled communities; people were now keeping cattle as sources of milk and raising sheep for wool. The herding of a community's large groups of animals tended to take place at a distance from the home settlement because the animals continually needed new grazing land. Free from having to nurse children, men took on this task, as they had with hunting in hunter-gatherer populations.

As agriculture became more intensive and therefore required more and more labor than had food gathering or the earliest forms of farming, the increasing pressure to bear and raise children probably tied women to the central settlement. Women also took responsibility for the new labor-intensive tasks needed to process the secondary products of larger herds. For example, they now turned milk into cheese and yogurt and made cloth by spinning and weaving wool. Men's predominant role in agriculture and herding in the late Neolithic period, combined with women's lessened mobility and increasingly home-based tasks, apparently led to women's loss of equality with men in these early times of human society.

patriarchy: Dominance by men in society and politics.

REVIEW QUESTION What benefits and what drawbacks did the Neolithic Revolution bring to human life?

Conclusion

Permanent homes, fairly reliable food supplies from agriculture and domesticated animals, specialized occupations, hierarchical patriarchies, and war characterized Western history from the Neolithic period forward. For this reason, the broad outlines of the life of Neolithic villagers might seem unremarkable to us today. But the Neolithic way of life in built environments surrounded by cultivated fields and herds would have seemed astounding, we can guess, to Paleolithic hunter-gatherers such as the roaming hippopotamus hunters of Africa who now rank as the earliest known *Homo sapiens*. The Neolithic Revolution was the most important change in the early history of human beings; it overturned the ways in which people interacted with the natural environment and with one another. Now that farmers and herders could produce a surplus of food to support other people, specialists in art, architecture, crafts, religion, and politics could emerge. Hand in hand with these developments came a new division of labor by gender that saw men begin to take over agriculture and herding while women took up new tasks at home, leading to a loss of gender equality. At the same time, war between newly prosperous communities became common. These changes altered the course of human history and spurred the development of Western civilization as we know it today.

FOR FURTHER EXPLORATION

- **For additional primary-source material from this period**, see *Sources of the Making of the West*, Fourth Edition.
- **For Web sites, images, and documents related to topics in this chapter**, visit *Make History* at bedfordstmartins.com/hunt.

Prologue Review

Online Study Guide bedfordstmartins.com/hunt

Key Terms and People

In the grid below, identify the term or person and explain its historical significance. (To do this exercise online, go to bedfordstmartins.com/hunt.)

Term	Who or What & When	Why It Matters
Paleolithic Age (p. P-2)		
Neolithic Age (p. P-2)		
political states (p. P-2)		
hunter-gatherers (p. P-3)		
Homo sapiens sapiens (p. P-3)		
hierarchy (p. P-5)		
Neolithic Revolution (p. P-6)		
demography (p. P-9)		
patriarchy (p. P-13)		

Review Questions

1. What were the most important activities, skills, and beliefs that helped Paleolithic hunter-gatherers survive?
2. What benefits and what drawbacks did the Neolithic Revolution bring to human life?

Making Connections

1. Explain whether you think human life was more stressful in the Paleolithic period or the Neolithic period.
2. What do you think are the most important differences and similarities between Stone Age life and modern life? Why?
3. How might historians draw conclusions about religious beliefs of Stone Age people, given that there are no written records?

Important Events

Date	Event
200,000–160,000 B.C.E.	Beginning of Paleolithic ("Old Stone") Age
50,000–45,000 B.C.E.	*Homo sapiens sapiens* migrate from Africa into southwest Asia and Europe
10,000–8000 B.C.E.	Neolithic ("New Stone") Revolution in the Fertile Crescent and the Sahara
8000 B.C.E.	Walled settlement at Jericho (in modern Israel)
7000–5500 B.C.E.	Farming community thrives at Çatalhöyük (in modern Turkey)

■ How might the changes characterizing the **Neolithic Revolution (10,000–8000 B.C.E.)** relate to the creation of the **walled settlement at Jericho (8000 B.C.E.)**?

SUGGESTED REFERENCES

Çatalhöyük: Excavations of a Neolithic Anatolian Höyük: http:// www.catalhoyuk.com/

Clark, J. Desmond, et al. "Stratigraphic, Chronological and Behavioural Contexts of Pleistocene *Homo Sapiens* from Middle Awash, Ethiopia." *Nature* 423 (June 12, 2003): 747–52.

Diamond, Jared M. *Guns, Germs, and Steel: The Fates of Human Societies.* 2005.

Ehrenberg, Margaret. *Women in Prehistory*. 1989.

Fagan, Brian M. *People of the Earth: An Introduction to World Prehistory.* 13th ed. 2009.

Hodder, Ian. *The Leopard's Tale. Revealing the Mysteries of Çatalhöyük.* 2006.

Klein, Richard G. *The Human Career. Human Biological and Cultural Origins.* 3rd ed. 2009.

Lewis-Williams, David, and David Pearce. *Inside the Neolithic Mind: Consciousness, Cosmos and the Realm of the Gods.* 2005.

Mithen, Steven. *After the Ice: A Global Human History 20,000–5000 BC.* 2004.

Moore, A. M. T. *Village on the Euphrates: From Foraging to Farming at Abu Hureyra.* 2000.

Renfrew, Colin. *Prehistory: The Making of the Human Mind.* 2009.

Scarre, Chris. *The Human Past: World Prehistory and the Development of Human Societies.* 2009.

Wenke, Robert J. *Patterns in Prehistory: Humankind's First Three Million Years.* 5th ed. 2006.

White, Tim D., et al. "Pleistocene *Homo Sapiens* from Middle Awash, Ethiopia." *Nature* 423 (June 12, 2003): 742–47.

CHAPTER 1

Early Western Civilization

4000–1000 B.C.E.

Kings in ancient Egypt believed that after they died the gods would judge them as rulers to decide their fate in the afterlife. In *Instructions for Merikare*, for example, written sometime around 2100–2000 B.C.E., an Egyptian king gives his son Merikare the following advice: "Make secure your place in the cemetery by being upright, by doing justice, upon which people's hearts rely. . . . When a man is buried and mourned, his deeds are piled up next to him as treasure." Being judged pure of heart led to an eternal reward; if the dead king reached the judges "without doing evil," he would be transformed so that he would "abide [in the afterlife] like a god, roaming [free] like the lords of time." A vital part of the justice demanded of an Egyptian king was to keep the country unified under a strong central authority to combat disorder.

Ordinary Egyptians, too, believed that they would win eternal rewards by living justly, which for them meant worshipping the gods and obeying the king and his officials. An illustrated guidebook containing instructions for mummies on how to travel safely in the underworld, commonly called the *Book of the Dead*, explained that on the day of judgment the jackal-headed god Anubis would weigh the dead person's heart on a scale against the goddess Maat and her feather of Truth, with the bird-headed god Thoth carefully writing down the result. Pictures in the *Book of the Dead* also show the Swallower of the Damned—a hybrid monster with a crocodile's head, a lion's body, and a hippopotamus's hind end—who crouched behind Thoth ready to eat the heart of anyone who failed the test of purity. Egyptian mythology thus taught that living a just life was the most important human goal because it was the key to winning the gods' help for a blessed existence after death.

The Afterlife in Egyptian Religion
This illustration comes from the ancient Egyptian *Book of the Dead*, a collection of illustrated instructions and magic spells buried with dead people to help them in the afterlife. It shows the deceased standing in front of offerings made to Osiris, the god of the underworld. He is seated on a throne with his sister and wife, the goddess Isis, and her sister standing behind him. The myth of Osiris, who died and was cut up into pieces but then reassembled and resurrected by Isis, expressed Egyptians' belief in an eternal life after death. *(The Art Archive/Egyptian Museum, Cairo/Alfredo Dagli Orti.)*

The earliest examples of Western civilization arose in Mesopotamia, Egypt, Anatolia (today Turkey), Crete and other Aegean islands, and Greece. Each of these societies believed in the need for a centralized authority, but the forms of that authority differed. In Egypt, a single central authority united the country; in the others, smaller independent states competed with one another. All believed that religion and justice were basic building blocks for organizing human life. They believed that many gods existed, but their particular religious beliefs and practices differed. In contrast to the Egyptians, for example, the Greeks believed that most people could expect only a gloomy, shadowlike existence following their deaths.

Trade and war brought these societies, with their sometimes differing religious beliefs and practices, into frequent contact. They exchanged not only goods and technologies but also ideas. Thus cultural diversity has always characterized Western civilization. The question arises, then, of what historians mean by the concept *Western civilization*. What defines it in particular, as compared to other civilizations?

CHAPTER FOCUS What changes did Western civilization bring to human life?

The Concept of Western Civilization

It is difficult to give a precise definition of *Western civilization* because the concept involves three hotly debated topics: the concept of civilization in general, the vagueness of the idea of the West geographically, and—most controversial of all—the nature and the value of the West's ideas and ways of life. The history of Western civilization, in any case, begins with the history of Sumer in Mesopotamia and of Egypt in Africa and extends to the present day. The early history of the West focuses on the peoples who lived in and around the Mediterranean Sea in southwestern Asia, northern Africa, and southern Europe.

Defining Western Civilization

To define *Western civilization*, it is necessary first to define **civilization** in general (see "Terms of History," page 5). Historians traditionally define it as a way of life based in cities governed as political states under a central authority, with a complex organization of labor, trade, religion, and other central aspects of human life. The definition of *city* is also imprecise, but the word certainly refers to a densely settled urban area with large buildings and a population governed by a system of political authority. Other characteristics of civilization are also identified as a diverse economy generating surplus resources, strong social hierarchies, a sense of local identity, some knowledge of writing, and a military force for defense and, perhaps, conquest of the land and property of others.

We generally use *civilization* and related terms such as *civilized behavior* as if everyone agreed that the development of civilization brought progress, giving people opportunities for greater prosperity and creating more complex but nevertheless advantageous interactions. Some historians, however, deny that civilization represents a better way of life than the way human beings lived before civilization. They argue that people were healthier, more

---

civilization: A way of life based in cities with dense populations organized as political states, large buildings constructed for communal activities, the production of food, diverse economies, a sense of local identity, and some knowledge of writing.

4000–1000 B.C.E. Bronze Age in southwestern Asia, Egypt, and Europe

3050 B.C.E. Narmer (Menes) unites Upper and Lower Egypt into one kingdom

4000 B.C.E. — 3500 B.C.E. — 3000 B.C.E.

4000–3000 B.C.E. Mesopotamians invent writing and establish first cities

2687–2190 B.C.E. Old Kingdom in Egypt

TERMS OF HISTORY

Civilization

Our word *civilization* comes from the ancient Roman word *civilis*, which meant "suitable for a private citizen" and "behaving like an ordinary, down-to-earth person." Historians connect civilization especially with urbanization and the ways of life that characterize city existence. Also, the word *civilization* often expresses the judgment that being civilized means achieving a superior way of life. Consider, for example, these definitions from *The Random House Webster's College Dictionary* (1997), p. 240:

> *civilization*: **1.** an advanced state of human society, in which a high level of culture, science, and government has been reached. **2.** those people or nations that have reached such a state. **3.** any type of culture, society, etc. of a specific place, time, or group: *Greek civilization*. **4.** the act or process of civilizing or being civilized. **5.** cultural and intellectual refinement. **6.** cities or populated areas in general, as opposed to unpopulated or wilderness areas. **7.** modern comforts and conveniences, as made possible by science and technology.

All these definitions imply that *civilization* means an "advanced" or "refined" way of life compared to a "savage" or "rude" way. Ancient peoples often drew this sort of comparison between themselves and those whom they saw as crude. Much later, this notion of superiority became prominent in European thought after voyagers to the Americas reported on what they saw as the barbarian life of the peoples they called Indians. Because these Europeans saw Native American life as lacking discipline, government, and above all Christianity, it seemed to them to be "uncivilized." Today, this sense of comparative superiority in the word *civilization* has become so accepted that it can even be used in nonhuman contexts, such as in the following startling comparison: "some communities of ants are more advanced in civilization than others."[1]

Sometimes *civilization* is used without much definitional content at all, as in the Random House dictionary's third definition. Can the word have any deep meaning if it can be used to mean "any type of culture, society, etc. of a specific place, time, or group"? This broad definition reveals that studying civilization and deciding what it does—and should—mean still presents difficult challenges to students of history today. Should it not be their task to make *civilization* a word with intellectual content and a reality with meaning for improving human life, as those who first used the word thought that it was?

[1]Sir John Lubbock, *On the Origin and Metamorphoses of Insects*, 2nd ed. (London, 1874), 13.

equal in power, and more peaceful before they created cities, political states, and complex economies. Such comparisons are hard to make because there is so little evidence about early human life (see the Prologue). If there truly was less war before the emergence of civilization, the reason might simply be that many fewer people existed in early times and they were spread much farther apart—but it also probably matters that early peoples lacked the surpluses to finance long or distant wars. In any case, human beings all over the world chose to develop civilization, and no peoples have yet decided to reject it in favor of a simpler life.

Ancient peoples developed the idea that different civilizations are defined by their geography and their particular ideas and practices (their culture). The Greeks invented the geographic notion of the West. Building on ideas they probably learned from

2350 B.C.E. Sargon, king of Akkad, establishes the world's first empire

2300–2200 B.C.E. Enheduanna, princess of Akkad, composes poetry

2200 B.C.E. Minoans build their first palaces

2112–2004 B.C.E. Ur III dynasty rules in Sumer

2061–1665 B.C.E. Middle Kingdom in Egypt

2000 B.C.E.

1792–1750 B.C.E. Hammurabi rules Babylon and issues his law code

1750 B.C.E. Hittites establish their kingdom in Anatolia

1569–1081 B.C.E. New Kingdom in Egypt

1500 B.C.E.

1400 B.C.E. The Mycenaeans build their first palaces in Greece and take over Minoan Crete

1274 B.C.E. Battle of Kadesh in Syria between the Egyptians and the Hittites

1200–1000 B.C.E. Period of violence ends many kingdoms

1000 B.C.E.

their Near Eastern neighbors, they created the term *Europe* to indicate the West (where the sun sets), as distinct from the East (where the sun rises). The Greeks, like modern historians, were not sure exactly where to draw the boundaries of the West because its geographical meaning was then, as it remains now, vague. The boundaries shift depending on what period is being described, and the word *Western* in *Western civilization* sometimes refers to peoples and places beyond Europe, and sometimes not. For example, the region that is today Turkey was certainly part of Western civilization at the time of the Roman Empire; yet now in the twenty-first century, Europeans and Turks alike are debating what changes in Turkish life and politics it would take—and what the financial and cultural costs would be—for Turkey to be judged Western enough to join the European Union.

Because it is difficult to identify precisely what set of ideas and customs makes up the culture of a particular civilization, the most controversial questions about any given civilization are "What are its particular ideas and practices?," "Are those ideas and practices different from those of other civilizations?," and "If so, are they inferior or superior to those of other civilizations?" For example, Mesopotamian religion and Egyptian religion were both forms of **polytheism** (belief in many gods). The Mesopotamians in the region called Sumer, who built the world's first cities, believed that the deities were unpredictable and often harsh to humans, and that people had to ward off divine anger by serving the gods obediently, building them temples, worshipping them, and bringing them gifts. The Egyptians also believed that they had to respect the gods to find happiness, but they thought that their gods lovingly provided them with life's delights and that, if their king fulfilled his duties, the divinity Maat would bless them with justice. As we will see in Chapters 2 and 3, the Israelites made **monotheism** (belief in one god) a distinctive feature in Western civilization.

The Greeks inherited from their neighbors in the Near East the idea that regional differences meant that one people's culture was better than another's. Merikare's father, for instance, sternly warned him, "[Beware of the] miserable Asiatic [Near Easterner], wretched because of where he's from, a place with no water, no wood. . . . He doesn't live in one place, hunger propels his legs. . . . He doesn't announce the day of battle, he's like a thief darting around a crowd." The Greeks also later contributed to Western civilization new and unique ideas about alternative types of central political authority not involving kings and about the importance of reason for human thought.

In every known civilization, people have insisted on establishing social hierarchies. The invention of increasingly sophisticated metallurgy (the technology of working metals), for example, led to the creation of ever better tools and weapons, but it also turned out to be another factor prompting more visible differences in social status: people constructed status for themselves in part by acquiring metal objects, from jewelry to finely decorated weapons. Some contemporary scientists claim that this development was inevitable because human beings are by nature "status-protecting organisms."

It would be misleading, however, to define Western civilization by a simple list of characteristics: we have to find the nature and value of Western civilization by studying its history. As we shall see, Western civilization evolved to a large extent through cultural interaction provoked by trade and war. Contact with unfamiliar ways and technologies spurred people to learn from one another and to adapt for themselves the inventions and beliefs of others. Western civilization therefore developed in a mixing of different cultures. In the long run, the story of Western civilization expanded to include not only cultural and political interaction among the West's diverse peoples themselves but also between them and the peoples of the rest of the globe. It is clearly a mistake to understand the word *Western* to mean "fenced off in the West from the rest of the world."

The Societies of Early Western Civilization

Under the definition of *civilization* outlined here, civilization in the West locates its deepest foundations in two societies: (1) Mesopotamia, where the people of Sumer had developed separate cities and political states by 4000–3000 B.C.E., and (2) Egypt, in northeastern Africa, whose civilization emerged beginning around 3050 B.C.E., when a strong ruler made the country into a unified political state stretching along the Nile River. Both societies waged frequent wars to protect their civilization, to demonstrate their superiority over outsiders, and to seize resources through conquest.

The story of Western civilization next spreads beyond Mesopotamia and Egypt. By around 2000–1900 B.C.E., civilization had also appeared in

polytheism: The belief in and worship of multiple gods.

monotheism: The belief in and worship of only one god, as in Judaism, Christianity, and Islam.

Anatolia, Crete and other islands in the eastern Mediterranean Sea, and Greece. All these peoples learned from the older civilizations of Mesopotamia and Egypt, shared the sense that nothing in life was more important than religion, and waged war for defense and conquest. Comparably complex societies also emerged in India, China, and the Americas in different eras starting around 2500 B.C.E.; however, these societies pursued independent paths of development. Their direct connections to the West began only much later.

Since studying the history of Western civilization seems the best way to understand its definition, it is important to trace the interactions of its diverse peoples and regions in commerce, war, and ideas. We will follow that story here beginning with the Mesopotamians, the Egyptians, the Minoans on Crete and the Aegean islands, and the Mycenaeans in Greece. The insecurity of what we traditionally call civilization will become apparent when we come to the mysterious era of widespread violence that lasted from about 1200 to 1000 B.C.E. and threatened to destroy civilization in the West.

REVIEW QUESTION What are the challenges in defining the term *Western civilization*?

Mesopotamia, Home of the First Civilization, 4000–1000 B.C.E.

The Neolithic Revolution (see the Prologue, pages P-6–P-9) created the economic basis of civilization by providing enough surplus agricultural resources to allow many people to work full-time at occupations other than farming and by encouraging permanent settlements that could grow into cities. These changes in the physical conditions of life in turn generated changes in society. The first place where farming villages gradually became cities was Mesopotamia, in southwestern Asia (the ancient Near East). There, climate change had promoted agriculture and domestication of animals in the region called the Fertile Crescent. Sumer, the name for southern Mesopotamia, developed the first cities. By 4000–3000 B.C.E., the Sumerians had built large urban communities, each controlling its surrounding territory as a separate political state. Archaeological and textual evidence has revealed the interlocking physical and social conditions of the first civilization: cities, successful agriculture on arid plains made possible by complex irrigation, religion as the guide to life, a social hierarchy with kings at the top and slaves at the bottom, the invention of writing to keep track of economic transactions and record people's stories and beliefs, and war to demonstrate cultural superiority and gain land and riches from others.

The riches for which people now fought had a new component: metal. Items made of metal had become central to wealth and power after craft workers invented the technology of metallurgy about 4000 B.C.E. Historians label the period from about 4000 to 1000 B.C.E. the Bronze Age because at this time bronze, an alloy of copper and tin, was the most important metal for weapons and tools; iron was not yet in common use. The ownership of metal objects strengthened visible status divisions in society between men and women and rich and poor. Long-distance commerce increased to satisfy people's desire for resources and goods not available in their homelands and stimulated the invention of the alphabet to supplement earlier forms of writing. Rulers created systems of law to regulate the complex economic and social activities of their society, instruct their subjects to be obedient to their rulers, and show the gods that they were fulfilling the divine command to maintain order by dispensing justice.

The Emergence of Cities, 4000–2350 B.C.E.

The first cities, and therefore the first civilization, emerged in Sumer when its inhabitants figured out how to raise crops on the fertile but dry plains between and around the Euphrates and Tigris Rivers (Map 1.1). This flat region was spacious enough for the growth of cities, but it was not ideal for agriculture: little rain fell, temperatures soared to 120 degrees Fahrenheit, and devastating floods occurred, caused by heavy precipitation that fell in unpredictable patterns in the faraway northern mountains where the Euphrates and Tigris originated. First Sumerians and then other Mesopotamians turned this marginal environment into rich farmland by diverting water from the Tigris and Euphrates to irrigate the plains. The complex system of canals, which provided irrigation and also helped limit flooding, required constant maintenance. The need to organize workers to maintain the many canals promoted the growth of centralized authority in Mesopotamian city-states, which led to the

Anatolia: The large peninsula that is today the nation of Turkey.

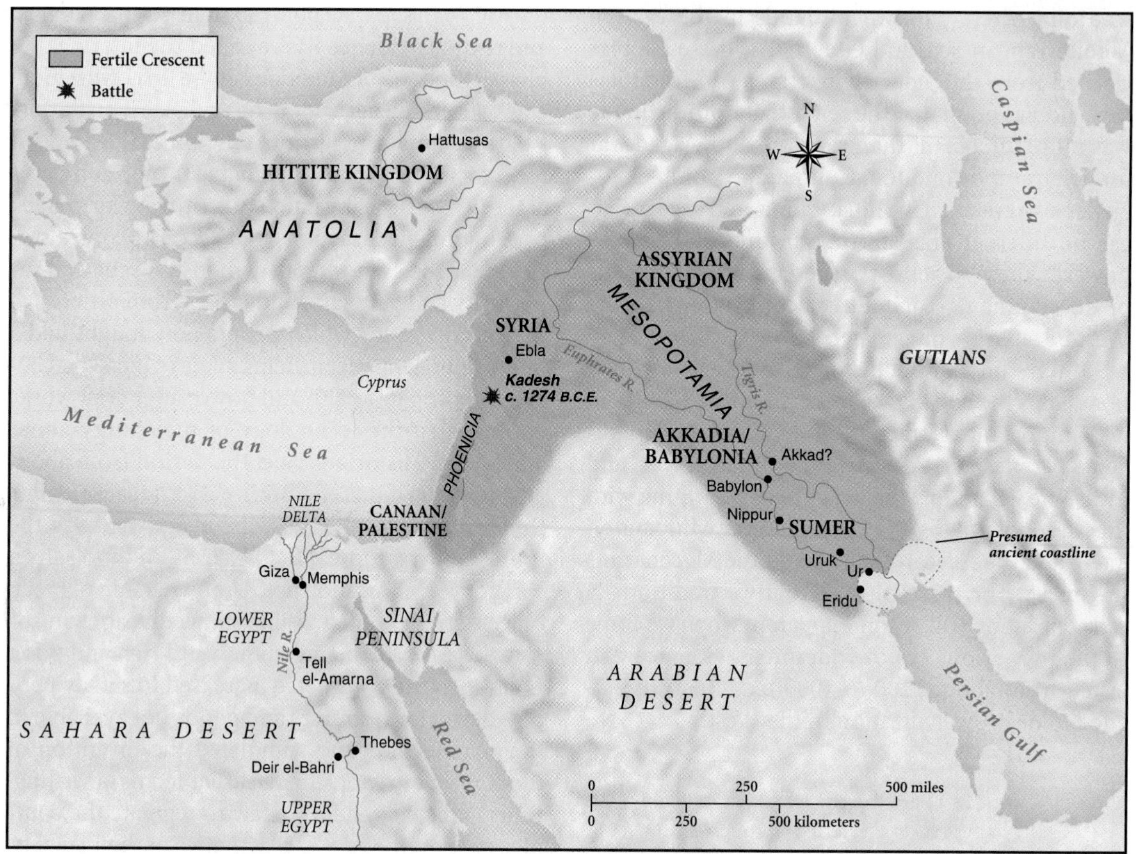

MAP 1.1 The Ancient Near East, 4000–3000 B.C.E.
The diverse region we call the ancient Near East included many different landscapes, climates, peoples, and languages. Kings ruled its independent city-states, the centers of the world's first civilizations, beginning around 4000–3000 B.C.E. Trade by land and sea for natural resources, especially metals, and wars of conquest kept the peoples of the region in constant contact and conflict with one another. | **How did geography facilitate—or hinder—the development of civilization in the Near East?**

emergence of kings as rulers. In this way, civilization created monarchy as a political system.

Food surpluses produced by Mesopotamian farmers stimulated population growth, increased the number of craft producers, and led to the emergence of cities. Each city controlled agricultural land outside its fortification walls and built large temples inside them. Historians call this arrangement—an urban center exercising political and economic control over the countryside around it—a **city-state**. Mesopotamia became a land of independent city-states, each with its own central political authority.

The Cities of Sumer | The origins of the Sumerians remain a mystery, and the background of the language they spoke remains obscure. What is known, however, is that by around 3000 B.C.E. the Sumerians had established twelve independent city-states—including Uruk, Eridu, and Ur—which remained fiercely separate communities warring over land and natural resources. By around 2500 B.C.E., each of the Sumerian cities had expanded to twenty thousand residents or more.

These first city-states had similar layouts. Irrigated fields filled their outlying territories, with villages housing agricultural workers closer to the urban center. A fortress wall surrounded the city itself. Outside the city's gates, bustling centers of trade developed, either at a harbor on the river or in a marketplace along the overland routes leading to the city. Inside the city, the most prominent buildings were the **ziggurats** (see the illustration on page 9), temples of a stair-step design that soared up to ten stories high.

---

city-state: An urban center exercising political and economic control over the surrounding countryside.

ziggurats (ZIH guh rats): Mesopotamian temples of massive size built on a stair-step design.

The Ziggurat at Ur in Sumer

Sumerian royalty built this massive temple (called a ziggurat) in the twenty-first century B.C.E. To construct its three huge terraces (placed one above another and connected with stairways), workers glued bricks together with tar around a central core. The walls had to be more than seven feet thick to hold the weight of the building, whose original height is uncertain. The first terrace reached forty-five feet above the ground. Still, the Great Pyramid in Egypt dwarfed even this large monument. *(© Michael S. Yamashita/Corbis.)*

Cities were crowded, though some space was left open for parks. Urban dwellers lived in mud-brick houses constructed around an open court. Most houses had only one or two rooms, but the wealthy constructed two-story dwellings that had a dozen or more rooms. Rich and poor alike could become ill from the water supply, which was often contaminated by sewage because no system of waste disposal existed. Pigs and dogs scavenged in the streets and areas where garbage was dumped before it could be cleared away.

Still, agriculture and trade made Sumerian city-states prosperous. They bartered grain, vegetable oil, woolens, and leather with one another and with foreign regions, from which they acquired natural resources not found in Sumer, such as metals, timber, and precious stones. Sailing for weeks, Sumerian traders traveled as far east as India, where the Indus civilization's large cities emerged about five hundred years after Sumer's. Technological innovation further strengthened the early Mesopotamian economy, especially beginning around 3000 B.C.E., when Sumerians invented the wheel in a form sturdy enough to be used on carts for transport.

Religious officials predominated in the early Sumerian economy because they controlled large farms and gangs of laborers, whose work for the gods supported the ziggurats and their related activities. Priests and priestesses supervised a large amount of property and economic activity. By around 2600 B.C.E., however, kings dominated the economy because their leadership in Mesopotamia's frequent wars won them control of their territories' resources; some private households also amassed significant wealth by working large fields.

Kings in Sumer Kings and their royal families were the highest-ranking people in the Sumerian social hierarchy. A king formed a council of older men as his advisers and praised the gods as his rulers, who made his power secure. This claim to divinely justified power gave priests and priestesses political influence. Although a Sumerian queen was respected as the wife of the king and the mother of the royal children, the king held supreme power in the patriarchal city-states of Mesopotamia. Still, women had more legal rights under Sumerian law than they would in later Mesopotamian societies; only Egypt would give women greater legal standing than Sumer did.

The king's supreme responsibility was to ensure justice, which meant pleasing the gods, developing law, keeping order among the people, and fighting wars against other city-states both for defense and for conquest. In return, the king extracted surpluses from the working population as taxes to support his

Gold Helmet from the Sumerian Royal Tomb at Ur
This helmet sculpted from gold was among the costly treasures placed in a grave in the royal cemetery at Ur in Sumer about 2600–2400 B.C.E. It was meant for ceremonial use rather than protection in war. The Sumerians buried such expensive goods with their kings and queens so that their royalty could maintain after death the position at the top of the social hierarchy that they had possessed while alive. *(The Granger Collection, New York/All rights reserved.)*

family, court, palace, army, and officials. If the surpluses came in regularly, the king mostly left the people alone to live their daily lives; from time to time, he released the poor from their debts as part of his divine mission to fight injustice.

To demonstrate their status atop the social hierarchy, Sumerian kings and their families lived in luxurious palaces that rivaled the size of the great temples. The palace served as the city-state's administrative center and the storehouse for the ruler's enormous wealth. Members of the royal family dedicated a significant portion of the community's economic surplus to displaying their superior status. Archaeological excavation of the immense royal cemetery in Ur, for example, has revealed the dazzling extent of the rulers' riches—spectacular possessions included crowns, weapons, tableware, and cosmetics sets crafted in gold, silver, and precious stones. The graves in Ur also yielded more gruesome evidence of the exalted status of the king and queen: the bodies of servants sacrificed to serve their royal masters after death. The spectacle of wealth and power that characterized Sumerian kingship reveals the enormous gap between the upper and lower ranks of Sumerian society.

Slaves in Sumer Just as it created monarchy, civilization also created slavery. Scholars dispute precisely how and why people began enslaving other people, but a rigid system of ranking people by status was slavery's foundation. Slaves were those confined to the bottom of this hierarchy. No single description of Mesopotamian slavery covers all its diverse forms or its social and legal consequences. Both the gods (through their temple officials) and private individuals could own slaves. People lost their freedom by being captured in war, by being born to slaves, by voluntarily selling themselves or their children to escape starvation, or by being sold by their creditors to satisfy debts. Foreigners enslaved as captives in war or in raids were considered inferior to citizens who fell into slavery to pay off debts. Children whose parents dedicated them as servants to the gods counted as slaves, but they could rise to prominent positions in the temple administrations.

In general, slaves worked without pay and lacked nearly all rights; they existed as property rather than people. Slave owners could demand sex from, beat, or even kill their slaves with impunity. Although slaves frequently married among themselves, had families, and sometimes formed relationships with free persons, masters could buy and sell slaves at will. Sumerians, like later Mesopotamians, apparently accepted slavery as a fact, and there is no evidence of any sentiment for abolishing it.

Slaves worked as household servants, craft producers, and farm laborers, but historians dispute their economic significance compared with that of free workers. Most labor for the city-state seems to have been performed by free persons who paid their taxes through work rather than with money (which consisted of measured amounts of food or precious metal; coins were not invented until around 700 B.C.E. in Anatolia). Under certain conditions slaves could gain their freedom: masters' wills could liberate them, or they could purchase their freedom with earnings they were sometimes allowed to save.

The Invention of Writing Writing was also a creation of civilization. Beginning around 3500 B.C.E., the Sumerians invented writing to do accounting because expanding populations and commerce had increased the complexity of economic transactions. Before writing, people drew small pictures on clay tablets to represent objects. At first, these pictographs symbolized concrete objects only, such as a cow. Over several centuries of development, nonpictorial symbols and marks were added to the pictographs to stand for the sounds of spoken language. The final version of Sumerian writing was not an alphabet, in which a symbol (a letter) represents one or more designated sounds, but rather a mixed system of phonetic symbols and pictographs that represented entire syllables or entire words.

Archaeologists call the Sumerians' fully developed script **cuneiform** (from *cuneus*, Latin for "wedge") because the writers used wedge-shaped marks pressed into clay tablets to record spoken language (Figure 1.1). Other Mesopotamian peoples subsequently adopted cuneiform to write their own languages. For a long time, only a few professionally trained men and women, known as scribes, mastered the new technology of writing. Schools sprang up to teach aspiring scribes, who could then find jobs as accountants. Kings, priests, and wealthy landowners employed scribes above all to record who had paid their taxes and who still owed.

Writing soon created a new way to hand down stories and beliefs previously preserved only in memory and speech. The scribal schools extended their curriculum to cover nature lore, mathematics, and foreign languages. Written literature provided a powerful new tool for passing on a culture's traditions to later generations. Enheduanna, an Akkadian woman of the twenty-third century B.C.E., is considered the world's first known author of written poetry. She was a priestess, prophetess, and princess, the daughter of King Sargon of the city of Akkad. Her poetry, written in Sumerian, praised the awesome power of the life-giving and life-taking goddess of love and war, Inanna (also known as Ishtar): "I great gods scattered from you like fluttering bats, unable to face your intimidating gaze . . . knowing and wise queen of all the lands, who makes all creatures and people multiply." Later princesses—who wrote love songs, lullabies, songs of mourning, and prayers—continued the Mesopotamian tradition of royal women as authors and composers.

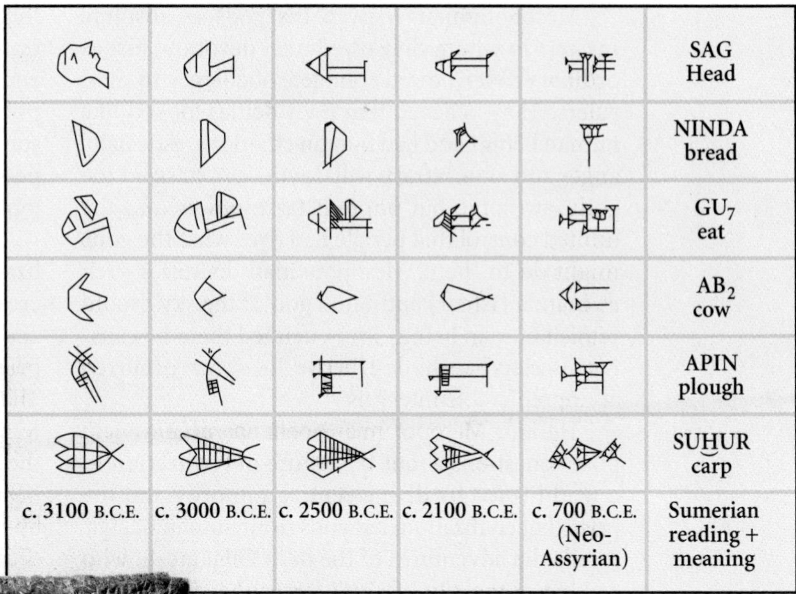

FIGURE 1.1 Cuneiform Writing
The earliest known form of writing developed in different locations in Mesopotamia in 4000–3000 B.C.E. when people began linking meaning and sound to signs such as those shown in the chart. Some scribes who mastered the system used sticks or reeds to press dense rows of small wedge-shaped marks into damp clay tablets; others used chisels to engrave them on stone. Cuneiform was used for at least fifteen Near Eastern languages and continued to be written for three thousand years. Written about 1900 B.C.E., the cuneiform text records a merchant's complaint that a shipment of copper contained less metal than he had expected. His letter, impressed on a clay tablet several inches long, was enclosed in an outer clay shell, which was then marked with the sender's private seal. This envelope protected the inner text from tampering or breakage. *(© The Trustees of The British Museum/Art Resource, NY.)*

cuneiform (kyoo NEE uh form): The earliest form of writing, invented in Mesopotamia and done with wedge-shaped characters.

Mesopotamian Myths and Religion

Writing developed into a crucial technology for supporting civilization because it provided a new way to record the traditions that helped hold communities together, especially myths (legendary stories about the gods and the origins of civilization that people saw as teaching important truths about the conditions of life) and religion (people's individual beliefs and group practices in worshipping the gods). Mesopotamians believed that the gods had created the universe as a hierarchy requiring that social inferiors obey their superiors. They also believed that the gods controlled all areas affecting human existence, from war to fertility to the weather. The more power over people's well-being that a divinity was believed to have, the more important the god. Each city-state honored a particular major deity as its special protector.

Mesopotamians viewed the gods as absolute masters to whom they owed total devotion, just as ordinary people owed complete obedience to their rulers. They believed that their deities looked like human beings and had human emotions, especially anger and an arbitrary will. Myths emphasized the gods' awesome but unpredictable power and the limited control that people had over what the gods might do to them. Mesopotamian divinities such as Inanna (Ishtar) and Enlil, god of the sky, would punish human beings who offended them by causing disasters like the destructive floods that occurred at unpredictable intervals.

The long Mesopotamian poem *Epic of Gilgamesh* poses questions about the nature of civilization in a world ruled by divine central authority and the price that civilization demands from human beings. It tells the adventures of the hero Gilgamesh, who as king of the city of Uruk forces the city's young men to construct a temple and a fortification wall, and its young women to sleep with him. When the distressed inhabitants beg Anu, lord of the gods, to grant them a rival to Gilgamesh, Anu calls on Aruru, the mother of the gods, to create a wild man, Enkidu, "hairy all over . . . dressed as cattle are." A week of sex with a prostitute tames this brute, preparing him for civilization: "Enkidu was weaker; he ran slower than before. But he had gained judgment, was wiser." After wrestling to a draw, Enkidu and Gilgamesh become friends and set out to conquer Humbaba (or Huwawa), the ugly, giant monster of the Pine Forest. Gilgamesh later insults the goddess Ishtar, who sends the Bull of Heaven to challenge him and Enkidu. The two comrades prevail, but when Enkidu makes matters worse by hurling the dead bull's haunch at Ishtar, the gods condemn him to death. In despair over human failure and weakness, Gilgamesh tries to find the secret of immortality, only to have his quest ended by a thieving snake. He realizes that immortality for human beings comes only from the fame of their achievements, above all building a great city such as Uruk, which spreads to "three square miles and its open ground." Only memory and gods live forever, Gilgamesh discovers.

A later version of the *Epic of Gilgamesh* includes a description of a huge flood that covers the earth, recalling the devastating deluges that often killed people and damaged the economy of Mesopotamia. Before sending the flood, the gods warn one man, Utnapishtim, of the coming disaster, telling him to build a boat. He loads his vessel with his relatives, his possessions, artisans, and domesticated and wild animals—"everything there was." After a week of drowning rains, he and his passengers land to repopulate the earth. This story shows that ancient Mesopotamians realized their civilization might be flawed—after all, it angered the gods enough to want to destroy it. The themes of Mesopotamian mythology, which lived on in poetry and song, powerfully influenced the mythology of distant peoples, especially the Greeks. The flood story also looks forward to the biblical account of Noah's ark.

Religion lay at the heart of Mesopotamian civilization because people believed that the divinely created hierarchy of the universe determined the conditions of their lives. As a result, the priest or priestess of a city's chief deity enjoyed high status. The most important duty of Mesopotamian priests was divination, the ritual process for discovering the gods' will and predicting the future. In performing divination, priests searched for divine messages by tracking the patterns of the stars, interpreting dreams, and cutting open animals to examine their organs for shapes signaling trouble ahead. These inspections helped people decide how to behave to persuade their unpredictable gods to give them a better future. Ordinary people joined priests in donating gifts to the gods and celebrating festivals to please their many deities. During the New Year holiday, for example, the reenactment of the mythical marriage of the goddess Inanna and the god Dumuzi was believed to ensure successful reproduction by the city's humans, animals, and plants for the coming year.

Metals and Empire Making: The Akkadians and the Ur III Dynasty, c. 2350–c. 2000 B.C.E.

The growth of agriculture and trade strengthened city-states in Mesopotamia. Their prosperity led them into competition and conflict, as rulers led armies on brutal campaigns to conquer their neighbors and win glory and wealth. Although agricultural production remained the greatest source of wealth, the desire to acquire metals pushed the kings of the city-state of Akkad to wage war to create the world's first **empire** (a political state in which one or more formerly independent territories or peoples are ruled by a single sovereign power).

Early metallurgy presents a clear example of a regular theme in history since the Neolithic Revolution: technological change leading to changes in social customs and values. In the case of metal, craftsmen invented ways to smelt ore and to make

---

empire: A political state in which one or more formerly independent territories or peoples are ruled by a single sovereign power.

metal alloys at high temperatures. Pure copper, which people had been using for some time, easily lost its shape and edge. The invention of bronze, a copper-tin alloy hard enough to hold a razor edge, enabled smiths to produce durable and deadly swords, daggers, and spearheads. The new technology of metallurgy led kings and the social elite of the Akkadian Empire to want new and more expensive luxury goods in metal; improved tools for agriculture and construction; and, above all, bronze weapons for war.

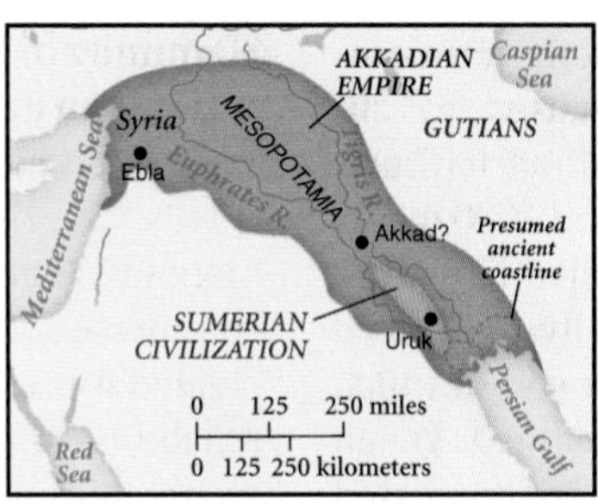

The Akkadian Empire, 2350–2200 B.C.E.

The desire to accumulate wealth and to possess status symbols stimulated demand for lavishly adorned weapons and exquisitely crafted jewelry. Rich men, especially, paid skilled metalworkers to make bronze swords and daggers decorated with expensive inlays, as on costly guns today. Such weapons increased visible social differences between men and women because they marked the status of the masculine roles of hunter and warrior.

Ambitious rulers chose to acquire metals by conquest rather than by trade, and they started wars to capture territory containing ore mines. The first empire began around 2350 B.C.E., when Sargon, king of Akkad, launched invasions far to the north and south of his homeland in mid-Mesopotamia. Through violent wars he conquered Sumer and the regions all the way westward to the Mediterranean Sea. Since Akkadians expressed their ideas about their own history in poetry and believed that the gods determined their fate, it was fitting that a poet of around 2000 B.C.E. credited Sargon's success to the favor of the god Enlil: "To Sargon the king of Akkad, from below to above, Enlil had given him lordship and kingship."

Sargon's grandson Naram-Sin continued the family tradition of conquering distant places to gain valuable resources, especially metals, and to prove the king's worthiness to rule. By around 2250 B.C.E., he had severely damaged Ebla, a large city whose site has been discovered in modern Syria, more than five hundred miles from his home base in Mesopotamia. Archaeologists have unearthed many cuneiform tablets at Ebla, some of them in more than one language. These discoveries suggest that the city thrived as an early center for learning and for trade.

The process of building an empire by force had the unintended consequence of spreading Mesopotamian literature and art throughout the Near East. The Akkadians spoke a language unrelated to Sumerian, but in conquering Sumer they took on most of the characteristics of that region's religion, literature, and culture. The other peoples whom the Akkadians conquered were then exposed to Sumerian beliefs and traditions, which they in turn adapted to suit their own purposes. In this way, war promoted cultural interaction.

Violence ended the Akkadian Empire. The traditional explanation for the empire's fall has been that the Gutians, a neighboring hill people, overthrew the Akkadian dynasty around 2200 B.C.E. by attacking from, in the words of a poet, "their land that rejects outside control, with the intelligence of human beings but with the form and stumbling words of a dog." Research has revealed, however, that civil war is a more likely explanation for the Akkadian Empire's fall. A newly resurgent Sumerian dynasty called Ur III (2112–2004 B.C.E.) then seized power in Sumer and presided over a flourishing of Sumerian literature. The Ur III rulers created a centralized economy, published the earliest preserved law code, and justified their rule by proclaiming their king to be divine. The best-preserved ziggurat was built in their era. Royal hymns, a new literary form, glorified the king; one example reads: "Your commands, like the word of a god, cannot be reversed; your words, like rain pouring down from heaven, are without number."

Mesopotamia remained politically unstable, and the development of civilization based on the centralized authority of kings did little to change that fact. The Ur III kings could not protect their dynasty from monarchy's fatal weakness—its tendency to inspire powerful and ambitious internal rivals to conspire to overthrow the ruling dynasty and take power themselves. When civil war weakened the regime, Amorite marauders from nearby saw their opportunity to conduct damaging raids. The Ur III dynasty collapsed after only a century of rule.

The Achievements of the Assyrians, the Babylonians, and the Canaanites, 2000–1000 B.C.E.

New kingdoms emerged in Assyria and Babylonia in the second millennium B.C.E. following the fall of the Akkadian Empire and the Sumerian Ur III dynasty. Assyrian innovations in long-distance commerce, Babylonian achievements in law, and the Canaanite invention of the alphabet were important contributions to the development of Western civilization. Such accomplishments are especially remarkable because they occurred while Mesopotamia

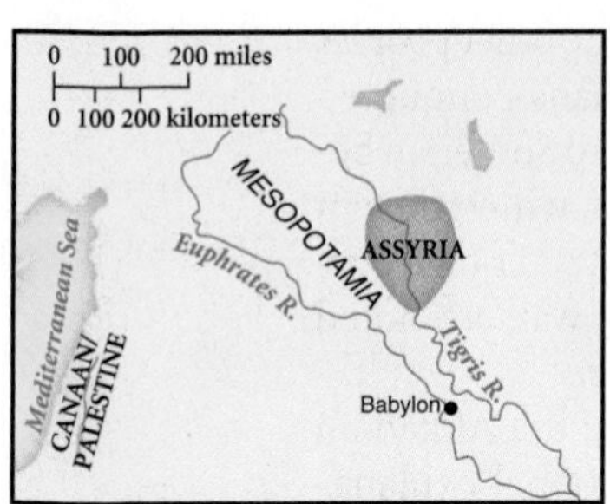

The Kingdom of Assyria, 1900 B.C.E.

was experiencing long-term economic troubles caused by climate change and agricultural pollution. By around 2000 B.C.E., the region's intensive irrigation had unintentionally increased the salt level of the soil so much that crop yields declined. When an extended period of decreased rainfall, especially in southern Mesopotamia, made the situation worse, the resulting economic stress generated political instability that lasted for centuries. In Canaan (ancient Palestine), on the eastern Mediterranean coast, strong trade by sea with many diverse regions and the export of timber from inland supported the growth of prosperous and independent city-states.

The Assyrians and Long-Distance Commerce

The Assyrians inhabited northern Mesopotamia, just east of Anatolia. They took advantage of their geography to build an independent kingdom whose rulers permitted long-distance trade conducted by private entrepreneurs. The city-states of Anatolia were rich sources of wood, copper, silver, and gold for many Mesopotamian states. By acting as intermediaries in this trade between Anatolia and Mesopotamia, the Assyrians became the leading merchants of the Near East. They exported woolen textiles to Anatolia in exchange for its raw materials, which they in turn sold to the rest of Mesopotamia.

The economies of Mesopotamian city-states had previously been dominated by centralized state monopolies in which the king's officials controlled international trade and redistributed goods according to their ideas of who needed what. This kind of **redistributive economy** managed by the state never disappeared in Mesopotamia, but by 1900 B.C.E. the Assyrian kings were allowing individuals to transact large commercial deals on their own initiative. This system allowed private entrepreneurs to maximize profits as a reward for taking risks in business. Private Assyrian investors, for example, provided funds to traders to purchase an export cargo of cloth. The traders then formed donkey caravans to travel hundreds of miles to Anatolia, where, if they survived the dangerous journey, they could make huge profits to be split with their investors. Royal regulators settled any complaints of trader fraud or losses in transit.

Hammurabi of Babylon and Written Law

To maintain social order, Mesopotamians established written laws that were made known to the people, an important development in Western civilization. The growth of private commerce and property ownership in Mesopotamia created a pressing need to guarantee fairness and reliability in contracts and other business agreements. Mesopotamians believed that the king had a sacred duty to make divine justice known to his subjects by rendering judgments in all sorts of cases, from commercial disputes to crime. Once written down, the record of the king's decisions amounted to what historians today call a law code. **Hammurabi** (r. c. 1792–c. 1750 B.C.E.), king of Babylon, a great city on the Euphrates River in what is today Iraq, became the most famous lawgiver in Mesopotamia (see Document, "Hammurabi's Laws for Physicians," page 15). In making his laws, he drew on earlier Mesopotamian legal traditions, such as the laws of the Sumerian Ur III dynasty.

In his code, Hammurabi proclaimed that his goals as ruler were to support "the principles of truth and equity" and to protect the less powerful members of society from exploitation. He gave a new emphasis to relieving the burdens of the poor as a necessary part of royal justice. The code legally divided society into three categories: free persons, commoners, and slaves. We do not know exactly how the first two categories differed, but they reflected a social hierarchy in which some people were assigned a higher value than others. An attacker who caused a pregnant woman of the free class to miscarry, for example, paid twice the fine levied for the same offense against a commoner. In the case of physical injury between social equals, the code specified "an eye for an eye" (an expression still used today). But a member of the free class who killed a commoner was not executed, only fined.

Many of Hammurabi's laws concerned the king's interests as a property owner who leased tracts of land to tenants in return for rent or services. The laws imposed severe penalties for offenses against property, including mutilation or a gruesome death for crimes ranging from theft to wrongful sales and careless construction. Women had only limited legal rights in this patriarchal society, but they could make business contracts and appear in court. A wife could divorce her husband for cruelty; a husband could divorce his wife for any reason. The law protected the wife's interests, however, by requiring a husband to restore his wife's property to her in the case of divorce.

---

redistributive economy: A system in which state officials control the production and distribution of goods.

Hammurabi (ha muh RAH bee): King of Babylonia in the eighteenth century B.C.E., famous for his law code.

DOCUMENT

Hammurabi's Laws for Physicians

In Hammurabi's collection of 282 laws, the following decisions set the fees for successful operations and the punishment for physicians' errors. The prescription of mutilation of a surgeon as the punishment for mutilation of a patient from the highest social class (law number 218) squares with the legal principle of equivalent punishment ("an eye for an eye") that occurs throughout Hammurabi's law code—a principle applied differently to patients of lower social classes.

215. If a physician performed a major operation on a freeman with a bronze scalpel and has saved the freeman's life, or he opened up the eye-socket of a freeman with a bronze scalpel and has saved the freeman's eye, he shall receive ten shekels[1] of silver.

216. If it was a commoner, he shall receive five shekels of silver.

217. If it was a freeman's slave, the owner of the slave shall give two shekels of silver to the physician.

218. If a physician performed a major operation on a freeman with a bronze scalpel and has caused the freeman's death, or he opened up the eye-socket of a freeman and has destroyed the freeman's eye, they shall cut off his hand.

219. If a physician performed a major operation on a commoner's slave with a bronze scalpel and has caused his death, he shall make good slave for slave.

220. If he opened up [the slave's] eye-socket with a bronze scalpel and has destroyed his eye, he shall pay half his value in silver.

Source: Adapted from James B. Pritchard, *Ancient Near Eastern Texts Relating to the Old Testament*, 3rd ed. with supplement (Princeton, NJ: Princeton University Press, 1969), 175.

[1]A shekel is a measurement of weight (about three-tenths of an ounce), not a coin. A hired laborer earned about one shekel per week. The average price of a slave was about twenty shekels.

Question to Consider

■ **What does the nature of these punishments reveal about the different social worth of the physician and his patients?**

Hammurabi's law code was based on an ideal of justice. For example, under the eye-for-an-eye principle, the penalty was meant to match the crime as literally as possible. In this same spirit, the code protected people from bad-faith prosecutions by imposing the death penalty on anyone who made a serious accusation but did not prove his case. It also relied on what might be called nature-decided justice by allowing an accused person to leap into a river to receive a judgment: if the accused person sank, he was guilty; if he floated, he was innocent.

In everyday practice, however, Hammurabi's laws apparently were not always followed to the letter. Babylonian documents show that legal penalties were often less severe than the code specified. The people themselves assembled in courts to determine most cases by their own judgments. Why, then, did Hammurabi have his laws written down? He announces his reasons at the beginning and end of his code: to show Shamash, the Babylonian sun god and god of justice, that he had fulfilled the moral responsibility imposed on him as a divinely installed monarch—to ensure justice and the moral and material welfare of his people: "So that the powerful may not oppress the powerless, to provide justice for the orphan and the widow . . . let the victim of injustice see the law which applies to him, let his heart be put at ease." The king's responsibility for his society's welfare corresponded to the strictly hierarchical and religious vision of society accepted by all Mesopotamian peoples.

Mesopotamian City Life and Learning Hammurabi's code offers glimpses into the daily life of Bronze Age Mesopotamian city dwellers. It suggests that crimes of burglary and assault were common in cities, for example, and it reveals that marriages were arranged by the bride's father and the groom, and sealed with a legal contract. The detailed laws on surgery make clear that doctors practiced in the cities. Because people believed that angry gods or evil spirits caused serious diseases, Mesopotamian medicine included magic: a doctor might prescribe an incantation along with potions and diet recommendations. Magicians or exorcists offered medical treatment that depended primarily on spells and on interpreting signs, such as the patient's dreams or hallucinations.

Archaeological evidence adds to the information on urban life found in Hammurabi's code. That cities had many taverns and wine shops, often run by women proprietors, indicates that Babylonians enjoyed having alcoholic drinks in a friendly setting. Contaminated drinking water caused many illnesses because sewage disposal was rudimentary. Citizens could find relief from the odors and crowding of the streets in the city's open spaces. The world's oldest known map, an inscribed clay tablet showing the outlines of the Babylonian city of Nippur about 1500 B.C.E., indicates a substantial area set aside as a city park.

Having large numbers of people living and interacting in cities helped stimulate intellectual developments. Mesopotamian achievements in mathematics and astronomy had a tremendous effect that endures to this day. Creating maps, for example, required sophisticated techniques of measurement and knowledge of spatial relationships. Mathematicians invented algebra, including the derivation of roots of numbers, to solve complex problems. They invented place-value notation, which makes a numeral's position in a number indicate ones, tens, hundreds, and so on. The system of reckoning based on sixty, still used in the division of hours and minutes and in the degrees of a circle, also comes from Mesopotamia. Mesopotamian expertise in recording the paths of the stars and planets probably arose from the desire to make predictions about the future, in accordance with the astrological belief that the movement of celestial bodies directly affects human life. The charts and tables compiled by Mesopotamian stargazers laid the foundation for later advances in astronomy.

Canaanites, Commerce, and the Alphabet The people of Canaan expanded their population by absorbing merchants from many lands. Some scholars believe that the political structure of the Canaanite communities even provided inspiration for the city-states of Greece. The interaction of traders and travelers from many different cultures in Canaanite cities encouraged innovation in the recording of business transactions. This multilingual business environment produced an overwhelmingly important writing technology about 1600 B.C.E.: the alphabet. In this new system of writing, a simplified picture—a letter—stood for only one sound in the language, a dramatic change from complicated scripts such as cuneiform. The alphabet developed in Canaanite cities later became the basis for the Greek and Roman alphabets and, from there, of modern Western alphabets. The Canaanite alphabet therefore ranks as one of the most important contributions to the history of Western civilization.

REVIEW QUESTION How did life change for people in Mesopotamia when they began to live in cities?

Egypt, the First Unified Country, 3050–1000 B.C.E.

Alongside Mesopotamian civilization, the other earliest example of Western civilization arose in Egypt, in northeastern Africa. The Egyptians built a wealthy, profoundly religious, and strongly centralized society ruled by kings. Unlike the Mesopotamian city-states, Egypt became a unified country, the world's first large-scale territorial state, whose prosperity and stability depended on the king's success in maintaining strong central authority and defeating enemies. Egypt was located close enough to Mesopotamia to learn from peoples there but was geographically protected enough to develop its own distinct culture, which Egyptians believed was superior to any other. Like the Mesopotamians, the Egyptians believed that a just society respected the gods, was structured in a hierarchy, and had a supreme ruler who made law for the rest of the people. The Egyptian rulers' belief in the soul's immortality and the possibility of a happy afterlife motivated them to construct the most imposing tombs in history, the pyramids. Egyptian architecture, art, and religious ideas influenced later Mediterranean peoples, especially the Greeks.

From the Unification of Egypt to the Old Kingdom, 3050–2190 B.C.E.

When climate change dried up the grasslands of the Sahara region of Africa about 5000–4000 B.C.E., people slowly migrated from there to the northeast corner of the continent, settling along the Nile River. They had formed a large political state by about 3050 B.C.E., when King Narmer (also called Menes)[1] united the previously separate territories of Upper (southern) Egypt and Lower (northern) Egypt. (*Upper* and *Lower* refer to the direction of the Nile River, which begins south of Egypt and flows northward to the Mediterranean.) The Egyptian ruler therefore referred to himself as King of the Two Lands. By around 2687 B.C.E., the monarchs had created a strong centralized state in these large territories. Historians refer to this first great unified Egyptian state as the Old Kingdom. It lasted until around 2190 B.C.E. (Map 1.2). Unlike their Mesopotamian counterparts, who ruled independent city-

[1]Representing ancient Egyptian names and dates presents serious problems. Since the Egyptians did not include vowel sounds in their writing, we are not sure how to spell their names. The spelling of names here is taken from *The Oxford Encyclopedia of Ancient Egypt*, edited by Donald B. Redford (2001), with alternate names given in cases where they might be more familiar. Dates are approximate and uncertain, and scholars bitterly disagree about them. (For an explanation of the problems, see Redford, "Chronology and Periodization," *The Oxford Encyclopedia*, vol. 1, 264–68.) The dates appearing in this book are compiled with as much consistency as possible from articles in *The Oxford Encyclopedia* and in the "Egyptian King List" given at the back of each of its volumes.

states in a divided land, Egyptian kings built only a few large cities in their united country. The first capital of the united country, Memphis (south of modern Cairo), grew into a metropolis packed with mammoth structures in and near its urban center. The most spectacular — and most mysterious — of the Old Kingdom architectural marvels is the so-called Great Sphinx. The oldest monumental sculpture in the world, this statue carved from stones has a human head on the body of a lion lying on its four paws. It is nearly 250 feet long and almost 70 feet high. A temple was built in front of it, perhaps to worship the sun as a god. The precise date and the purpose of this huge monument remain hotly contested issues. A thousand years later, Egyptians apparently regarded the Sphinx as a divinity, but no records exist to explain its original meaning. Most scholars believe that this enormous statue was erected in the Old Kingdom (although they disagree about exactly when to date it within that period). A few, however, citing weathering and erosion patterns on the stone of the statue, have argued that it is much older, indeed as old as 5000 B.C.E. If clear evidence supporting this date is ever discovered, then the history of early Egypt will have to be completely rewritten. This is just one of the many controversies about ancient Egypt that archaeological science may someday settle.

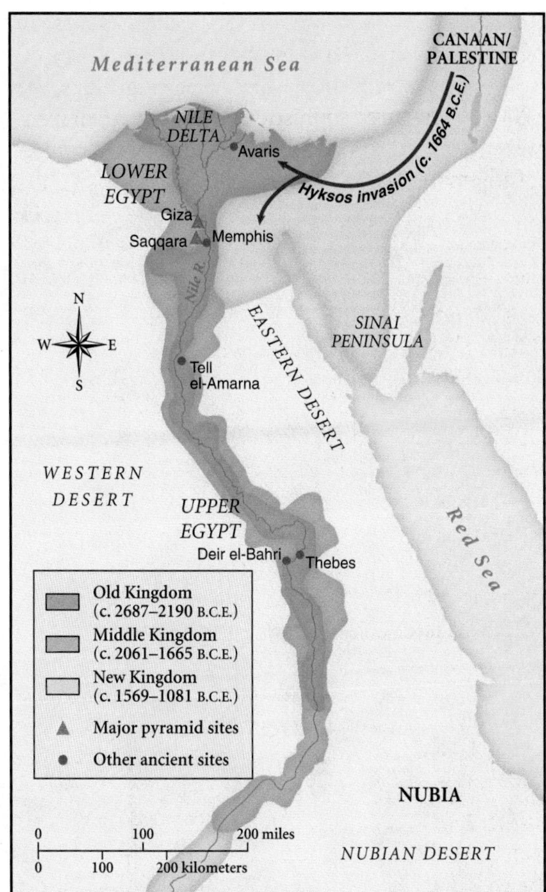

MAP 1.2 Ancient Egypt
Large deserts enclosed the Nile River on the west and the east. The Nile provided Egyptians with water to irrigate their fields and a highway for traveling north to the Mediterranean Sea and south to Nubia. The only easy land route into and out of Egypt lay through the northern Sinai peninsula into the coastal area of the eastern Mediterranean; Egyptian kings always fought to control this region to secure the safety of their land.

The Old Kingdom's costly architectural marvels indicate the prosperity and power that Narmer's unified state gradually acquired. That state's central territory consisted of a narrow strip of fertile land on either side of the Nile River. This ribbon of green fields zigzagged along the river's banks for seven hundred miles southward from the Mediterranean Sea. The great desert flanking the fields on the west and the east protected Egypt from invasion, except through the northern Nile delta and from Nubia in the south. The deserts also were sources of wealth because they contained large deposits of metal ores. Egypt's geography additionally contributed to its prosperity by supporting seaborne commerce in the Mediterranean sea to the north and the Indian Ocean to the east, as well as overland trade with peoples in central Africa to the south.

The most important sector of Egypt's economy was agriculture. Under normal weather conditions, the Nile River overflowed its channel for several weeks each year, when melting snow from the mountains of central Africa swelled its waters. This annual flood, which usually happened at a predictable time in the year, enriched the soil with nutrients from the river's silt and diluted harmful mineral salts, thereby making farming much more productive and supporting strong population growth. In sharp contrast to the unpredictable floods that harmed Mesopotamian peoples, the regular flooding of the Nile benefited Egyptians. Trouble came in Egypt only if the usual flood did not take place, as occasionally happened when not enough winter precipitation fell in the African mountains.

The plants and animals raised by Egypt's farmers on the flood-nourished lands fed a population that grew faster than in Mesopotamia. Egypt had expanded to perhaps several million people (the exact size is uncertain) by the time of the New Kingdom. Date palms, vegetables, grass for pasturing animals, and grain grew in abundance. From their ample supplies of grain, the Egyptians made bread and beer, the country's most popular beverage for people of all ages. Thicker and more nutritious than the modern version, ancient Egyptian beer was such an important food that it was sometimes used to pay workmen's wages. Egyptians, like other ancient societies, often flavored and sweetened their beer with fruits, usually dates.

The Great Sphinx of Egypt
This enormous stone sculpture of a sphinx, a mythical female creature with a human head and torso and lion's body, was built near the Great Pyramid in Egypt. Since no inscriptions tell us which king or kings ordered it built, or when or why, scholars still debate its place in ancient Egyptian history and thought. It remains the largest stone monument in the world. *(The Art Archive/Gianni Dagli Orti.)*

Egypt's diverse population included people whose skin color ranged from light to dark. Although many ancient Egyptians would be regarded as black by modern racial classification, ancient peoples did not observe such distinctions. The modern controversy over whether Egyptians were people of color is therefore not an issue that ancient Egyptians would have considered. If asked, they would probably have identified themselves by geography, language, religion, or traditions rather than skin color. Like many other ancient groups, the Egyptians called themselves simply The People. Later peoples, especially the Greeks, recognized the ethnic and cultural differences between themselves and the Egyptians, but they deeply admired Egyptian civilization for its long history and strongly religious character. The Greeks above all recognized that they had received many ideas about the gods from the traditions of the Egyptians, which they respected for their great age.

Although early Egyptians absorbed knowledge from both the Mesopotamians and their African neighbors to the south, the Nubians, they developed their own written scripts rather than using cuneiform. To write formal and official texts they used an ornate pictographic script known as **hieroglyphic** (Figure 1.2, page 19). They also developed other scripts for everyday purposes.

But some scholars believe that of all the outside influences, Nubian society was the one that most deeply influenced early Egypt. A Nubian social elite lived in dwellings much grander than the small

hieroglyphic: The ancient Egyptian pictographic writing system for official texts.

Hieroglyph	*Meaning*	*Sound value*
	vulture	glottal stop
	flowering reed	consonantal I
	forearm and hand	ayin
	quail chick	W
	foot	B
	stool	P
	horned viper	F
	owl	M
	water	N
	mouth	R
	reed shelter	H
	twisted flax	slightly guttural
	placenta (?)	H as in "loch"
	animal's belly	slightly softer than h
	door bolt	S
	folded cloth	S
	pool	SH
	hill	Q
	basket with handle	K
	jar stand	G
	loaf	T

FIGURE 1.2 Egyptian Hieroglyphs
Ancient Egyptians used pictures such as these to develop their own system of writing around 3000 B.C.E. Egyptian hieroglyphs include around seven hundred pictures in three categories: ideograms (signs indicating things or ideas), phonograms (signs indicating sounds), and determinatives (signs clarifying the meaning of the other signs). Because Egyptians employed this formal script mainly for religious inscriptions on buildings and sacred objects, Greeks referred to it as *ta hieroglyphica* ("the sacred carved letters"), from which comes the modern word *hieroglyphic*, used to designate this system of writing. Eventually, Egyptians also developed the handwritten cursive script called demotic (Greek for "of the people"), a much simpler and quicker form of writing. The hieroglyphic writing system continued until about 400 C.E., when it was replaced by the Coptic alphabet. Compare hieroglyphs with cuneiform shapes (see page 11). *(Victor R. Boswell Jr./National Geographic Stock.)*

huts housing most of the population. Egyptians interacted with Nubians while trading for raw materials such as gold, ivory, and animal skins, and scholars argue that Nubia's hierarchical political and social organization influenced the development of Egypt's politically centralized Old Kingdom. Eventually, however, Egypt's greater power led it to dominate its southern neighbor.

Religion and the Authority of the King

Although the Egyptians carved a new path for civilization by creating a large unified country under a central authority, keeping the country unified and politically stable turned out to be difficult. When the kings were strong, as during the Old Kingdom, the country was peaceful and rich, with flourishing international trade, especially by sea along the eastern Mediterranean coast. However, when regional governors became rebellious and the king was weak, political instability resulted.

The king derived power and success from the fulfillment of his religious obligations. Like the Mesopotamians, Egyptians centered their lives on religion. They worshipped a great variety of gods, who were often shown in paintings and sculptures as creatures with both human and animal features, such as the head of a jackal or a bird atop a human body. This style of representing deities did not mean that people worshipped animals, but rather that they believed the gods each had a particular animal through which they revealed themselves to human beings. At the most basic level, Egyptian gods were associated with powerful natural objects, emotions, qualities, and technologies — examples are Re, the sun god; Isis, the goddess of love and fertility; and Thoth, the god of wisdom and the inventor of writing. People worshipped the gods with rituals, prayers, and festivals that expressed their respect and devotion to these divine powers.

Modern historians' generalizations about religions should never be taken as adequate descriptions of an ancient people's beliefs, but it seems worth asking the question: Did Egyptians in general consider their gods as more kindly and helpful to human beings than did Mesopotamians, whose deities seem more harsh and even sometimes cruel? If this is indeed a significant difference between the religions of Egypt and Mesopotamia, one might ask whether it could reflect the difference in the two regions' natural environments: as noted above, the annual flooding of the Nile benefited the Egyptians, while the random flooding of the Euphrates and Tigris Rivers brought disaster to Mesopotamian peoples. Given that both Egyptians and Mesopotamians believed that the gods were responsible for the weather and the good or the bad that it brought to human beings, it seems possible that these cultures' respective environments played a role in their understanding of their deities.

In any case, the Egyptians regarded their king as a helpful divinity in human form, identified with the hawk-headed god Horus. In the Egyptian view, the king's rule was divine because he helped generate *maat* ("what is right"), the supernatural force that brought order and harmony to human beings if they maintained a stable hierarchy. The goddess **Maat** embodied this force, which was the source of justice in a world that would, the Egyptians believed, fall into violent disorder if the king did not rule properly. To fulfill his religious obligation to rule according to maat and therefore maintain the goodwill of the gods toward the people, the king had the duties of making law, keeping the forces of nature in balance for the benefit of his people, and waging war on Egypt's enemies.

To express the king's legitimacy as ruler, official art represented him carrying out his religious and military duties. The requirement for the king to show piety (proper religious belief and behavior) demanded strict regulation of his daily activities: he had specific times to take a bath, go for a walk, and make love to his wife. Most important, he had to ensure the country's fertility and prosperity. Above all, the king was supposed to guarantee a proper flooding of the Nile by performing his duties justly and in accordance with traditional order. Any failure of the flood to happen, which would devastate the country's economy and leave many people hungry, seriously weakened the king's authority and encouraged rebellions by rivals for power.

Pyramids and the Afterlife

Successful Old Kingdom rulers used expensive building programs to demonstrate their piety and exhibit their status atop the social hierarchy. In the desert outside Memphis, the Old Kingdom rulers erected stunning monuments displaying their status and their religious belief: their huge tombs. These tombs — the pyramids (see the illustration on page 21) — formed the centerpieces of elaborate groups of temples and halls for religious ceremonies and royal funerals. Although the pyramids were not the first monuments built from enormous worked stones (that title goes to a set of temples, admittedly much smaller in scale, on the Mediterranean island of Malta), they rank as the grandest, much larger even than the Great Sphinx.

Old Kingdom rulers spent vast resources on these huge complexes to proclaim their divine status and protect their mummified bodies for existence in the afterlife. King Khufu (r. 2609–2584 B.C.E.; also known as Cheops) commissioned the hugest monument of all — the Great Pyramid at Giza. At about 480 feet high, it stands taller than a forty-story skyscraper. Covering more than thirteen acres and 760 feet long on each side, it required more than two million blocks of limestone, some of which weighed fifteen tons apiece. Its exterior blocks were quarried along the Nile and then floated to the site on barges. Free workers (not slaves) dragged the blocks up ramps into position using rollers and sleds.

The Old Kingdom rulers' expensive preparations for death reflected their strong belief in an

---

Maat (MAH aht): The Egyptian goddess embodying truth, justice, and cosmic order. (The word *maat* means "what is right.")

eternal afterlife. A hieroglyphic text addressed to the god Atum expresses the hope that the ruler will have a safe existence after death: "O Atum, put your arms around King Neferkare Pepy II [r. c. 2300–2206 B.C.E.], around this construction work, around this pyramid. . . . May you guard lest anything happen to him evilly throughout the course of eternity." The royal family equipped their tombs with loads of comforts to use when they joined the world of the dead. Gilded furniture, sparkling jewelry, exquisite objects of all kinds — the dead kings had all this and more placed alongside their coffins, in which rested their mummies. Archaeologists have even uncovered two full-sized cedar ships buried next to the Great Pyramid, meant to carry King Khufu on his journey into eternity.

Hierarchy and Order in Egyptian Society The Old Kingdom ranked Egyptians in a tightly structured hierarchy to preserve their kings' authority and therefore support what they regarded as the proper order of a just society. Egyptians believed that their ordered society was superior to any other, and they despised foreigners, such as the Near Easterners criticized by Merikare's father.

The king and queen headed the hierarchy. Brothers and sisters in the royal family could marry each other, perhaps because such matches were believed necessary to preserve the purity of the royal line and to imitate the marriages of the gods. The priests, royal administrators, provincial governors, and commanders of the army ranked next in the hierarchy. Then came the free common people, most of whom worked in agriculture. Free workers had heavy obligations to the state. For example, in a system called corvée labor, the kings commanded commoners to work on the pyramids during slack times in farming. The state fed, housed, and clothed the workers while they performed this seasonal work, but their labor was a way of paying taxes. Rates of taxation reached 20 percent on the produce of free farmers. Slaves captured in foreign wars served the royal family and the priests in the Old Kingdom, but privately owned slaves working in free persons' homes or on their farms did not become numerous until after the Old Kingdom. The king hired mercenaries, many from Nubia, to form the majority of the army.

Hierarchy seemed less important when it came to gender. Egypt preserved more of the gender equality of the early Stone Age than did its neighbors, for reasons not easy to discover. Egyptian religion gave great respect to female divinities, but so did Mesopotamian religion. Perhaps the Egyptian myth of the goddess Isis, who restored life to her husband Osiris after he had been torn into pieces, expressed a special belief in the ability of women to restore order to life in times of great loss. Whatever

The Pyramids at Giza in Egypt
The kings of the Egyptian Old Kingdom constructed massive stone pyramids for their tombs, the centerpieces of large complexes of temples and courtyards stretching down to the banks of the Nile or along a canal leading to the river. The inner burial chambers lay at the end of long, narrow tunnels snaking through the pyramids' interiors. The biggest pyramid shown here is the so-called Great Pyramid of King Khufu (Cheops), erected at Giza (in the desert outside what is today Cairo) in the twenty-sixth century B.C.E. and soaring almost 480 feet high, several times taller than the famous Parthenon temple in fifth-century B.C.E. Athens (see page 85). *(Travel Pix Ltd./SuperStock.)*

the explanation, women in ancient Egypt generally enjoyed the same legal rights as free men. They could own land and slaves, inherit property, pursue lawsuits, transact business, and initiate divorces. Old Kingdom portrait statues show the equal status of wife and husband: each figure is the same size and sits on the same kind of chair. Men dominated public life, while women devoted themselves mainly to private life, managing their households and property. When their husbands went to war or were killed in battle, however, women often took on men's work. Women could serve as priestesses, farm managers, or healers to maintain stability and order in times of crisis.

The formal style of Egypt's art illustrates how much the civilization valued order and predictability. Almost all Egyptian sculpture and painting comes from tombs or temples, testimony to its people's deep desire to maintain proper relations with the gods by honoring them with appropriate art. Old Kingdom artists excelled in stonework, from carved ornamental jars to massive portrait statues of the kings. These statues represent the subject either standing stiffly with the left leg advanced or sitting on a chair or throne, stable and poised. The concern for decorum (suitable behavior) also appears in the Old Kingdom literature the Egyptians called instructions, known today as **wisdom literature**. These texts gave instructions for appropriate behavior by officials. In the *Instruction of Ptahhotep*, for example, the royal minister Ptahhotep instructs his son, who will succeed him in office, to seek advice from ignorant people as well as the wise and not to be arrogant or overconfident just because he is well educated. This kind of literature had a strong influence on later civilizations, especially the ancient Israelites.

The Middle and New Kingdoms in Egypt, 2061–1081 B.C.E.

The Old Kingdom began to disintegrate in the late third millennium B.C.E. The reasons remain mysterious. One suggestion is that climate changes caused the annual Nile flood to shrink and the ensuing agricultural failure discredited the regime—people believed the kings had betrayed Maat. Economic hard times probably fueled rivalry for royal rule between ambitious families, and civil war between a northern and a southern dynasty then ripped apart the Kingdom of the Two Lands. This destruction of the Old Kingdom's unity allowed regional governors to increase their power. Some governors, who had previously supported the kings while times were good, now seized independence for their regions. It was the troubles of this period that made Merikare's father's advice so pressing: famine and civil unrest during the so-called First Intermediate Period (2190–2061 B.C.E.) prevented the reestablishment of political unity.

The Middle Kingdom The kings of what historians label the Middle Kingdom (2061–1665 B.C.E.) gradually restored the strong central authority their Old Kingdom predecessors had lost. They waged war to extend the southern boundaries of Egypt, while to the north they expanded diplomatic and trade contacts in the eastern Mediterranean region and with the island of Crete.

Middle Kingdom literature reveals that the reclaimed national unity contributed to a deeply felt pride in the homeland. The Egyptian narrator of *The Story of Sinuhe*, for example, reports that he lived luxuriously during a forced stay in Syria but still longed to return: "Whichever god you are who ordered my exile, have mercy and bring me home! Please allow me to see the land where my heart dwells! Nothing is more important than that my body be buried in the country where I was born!" For this lost soul, love for Egypt outranked personal riches and comfort in a foreign land.

From Hyksos Rule to the New Kingdom The Middle Kingdom lost its unity during the Second Intermediate Period (1664–1570 B.C.E.), when the kings proved too weak to control aggressive foreigners who had migrated into Egypt and gradually set up independent communities. By 1664 B.C.E., diverse bands of a Semitic people originally from the eastern Mediterranean coast took advantage of the troubled times to become Egypt's rulers. The Egyptians called these foreigners Hyksos ("rulers of the foreign countries"). Recent archaeological discoveries have emphasized the role of Hyksos settlers in transplanting elements of foreign culture to Egypt: their capital, Avaris, boasted wall paintings done in the Minoan style current on the island of Crete. Some historians think the Hyksos also introduced such innovations as bronze-making technology, new musical instruments, humpbacked cattle, and olive trees; they certainly promoted frequent contact between Egypt and other Near Eastern states. Hyksos rulers also strengthened Egypt's capacity to make war by expanding the use of chariots on the battlefield and more powerful bows in the army.

After a long struggle with the Hyksos, the leaders of Thebes, in southern Egypt, reunited the kingdom. The series of royal dynasties they founded is called the New Kingdom (1569–1081 B.C.E.). Recent

---

wisdom literature: Texts giving instructions for proper behavior by officials.

archaeological discoveries reveal that Thebes may have drawn some of the strength that allowed it to reunite Egypt from its connections with prosperous settlements that emerged far out in the western desert, such as at Kharga Oasis. Oases featured abundant water from underground aquifers in the middle of an otherwise dry and scorching environment. An oasis settlement could flourish because it provided an essential stopping point for the caravans of merchants who endured dangerously harsh desert conditions to profit from commerce. Thebes seems to have benefited from access to trade provided by good relations with the peoples settled in the western desert. This expansion of contact is a clear sign that Egyptian society did not remain unchanged over time, shutting itself off behind its natural boundaries along the Nile. Similarly, contacts with peoples to the east across the Red Sea and along the Indian Ocean increased in the New Kingdom.

Hatshepsut as Pharaoh Offering Maat
This granite statue, eight and a half feet tall, portrayed Hatshepsut, queen of Egypt in the early fifteenth century B.C.E., as pharaoh wearing a beard and male clothing. She is performing her royal duty of offering *maat* (the divine principle of order and justice) to the gods. Egyptian religion taught that the gods "lived on maat" and that the land's rulers were responsible for providing it. Hatshepsut had this statue, and many others, placed in a huge temple she built outside Thebes, in Upper Egypt. Compare her posture to that of the statue of a woman grinding grain on page P-9. Why do you think Hatshepsut is shown as calm and relaxed, despite having her toes severely flexed? *(Egypt, eighteenth dynasty, ca. 1473–1458 B.C.E. Granite, H. 261.5 cm. [102 15/16 in.]; w. 80 cm. [31½ in.]; d. 137 cm. [53 15/16 in.]. Rogers Fund, 1929 [29.3.1]. The Metropolitan Museum of Art, New York, NY, U.S.A. Image copyright © The Metropolitan Museum of Art/Art Resource, NY.)*

The kings of the New Kingdom, known as pharaohs, rebuilt central authority by restricting the power of regional governors and promoting a renewed sense of national identity. To prevent invasions, the pharaohs followed up the Hyksos innovations in military technology by creating a standing army, another significant change in Egyptian society. These kings still employed many mercenaries, but they formed an Egyptian military elite to command national defense. Recognizing that knowledge of the rest of the world was necessary for safety, the pharaohs engaged in regular diplomacy with neighboring monarchs to increase their international contacts. In fact, the pharaohs regularly exchanged letters on matters of state with their "brother kings," as they called them, in Mesopotamia, Anatolia, and the eastern Mediterranean region.

Warrior Pharaohs The New Kingdom pharaohs sent their reorganized military into foreign wars to gain territory and show their superiority. They waged many campaigns abroad and presented themselves in official propaganda and art as the incarnations of warrior gods. They invaded lands to the south to win access to gold and other precious materials, and they fought up and down the eastern Mediterranean coast to control that crucial land route into Egypt. Their imperialism has today earned them the title *warrior pharaohs.*

Massive riches supported the power of the warrior pharaohs. Egyptian traders exchanged local fine goods, such as ivory, for foreign luxury goods, such as wine and olive oil transported in painted pottery from Greece. Egyptian rulers displayed their wealth most conspicuously in the enormous sums spent to build stone temples. Queen Hatshepsut (r. 1502–1482 B.C.E.), for example, built her massive mortuary temple at Deir el-Bahri, near Thebes, including a temple dedicated to the god Amun (or Amen), to express her claim to divine birth and the right to rule. After her husband (who was also her half brother) died, Hatshepsut proclaimed herself "female king" as co-ruler with her young stepson. In this way, she got around the restrictions of Egyptian political tradition, which did not recognize the right of a queen to reign in her own right. Hatshepsut also often had herself represented in official art as a king, with a royal beard and male clothing. Hatshepsut succeeded in her unusual rule because she demonstrated that a woman could ensure safety and prosperity by maintaining the goodwill of the gods toward the country and its people.

Religious Tradition and Upheaval Egyptians believed that their gods oversaw all aspects of life and death. Many large temples honored the traditional gods, and by the time of the New Kingdom, the gods' cults (that is, the traditions and rituals used in worship) enriched the religious life of the entire population. The principal festivals of the gods featured large public celebrations. A calendar based on the moon governed the dates of religious ceremonies. (The Egyptians also developed a calendar for administrative and fiscal purposes that had 365 days, divided into 12 months of 30 days each, with the extra 5 days added before the start of the next year. Our modern calendar comes from this source.)

The early New Kingdom pharaohs from Thebes promoted their state god Amun-Re (a combination of Thebes's patron god and the sun god) so energetically that he became far more important than the other gods. This Theban cult took in and subordinated the other gods, without denying their existence or the continued importance of their priests. The pharaoh Akhenaten (r. 1372–1355 B.C.E.) went a step further, however: he proclaimed that official religion would concentrate on worshipping Aten, who represented the sun. Akhenaten made the king and the queen the only people with direct access to the cult of Aten; ordinary people had no part in it. Some scholars identify Akhenaten's religious reform as a step toward monotheism, with Aten meant to be the state's sole god. Whatever may have been Akhenaten's attitude toward the question of whether the universe was ruled by one god or many, his main goal was to use religion to strengthen his personal rule as king.

To showcase the royal family and the concentration of power that he sought, Akhenaten built a new capital for his favorite god at Tell el-Amarna (see Map 1.2). He tried to force his revised religion on the priests of the old cults, but they resisted. Historians have blamed Akhenaten's religious zeal for leading him to neglect practical affairs and thus weaken his kingdom's defense, but recent research on international correspondence found at Tell el-Amarna has shown that the pharaoh tried to use diplomacy to turn foreign enemies against one another so that they would not become strong enough to threaten Egypt. His policy failed, however, when the Hittites from Anatolia defeated the Mitanni, Egypt's allies in eastern Syria. Akhenaten's religious reform also died with him. During the reign of his successor, Tutankhamun (r. 1355–1346 B.C.E.)—famous today through the discovery in 1922 of his rich, unlooted tomb—the cult of Amun-Re reclaimed its leading role. The crisis created by Akhenaten's attempted reform emphasizes the overwhelming importance of religious conservatism in Egyptian life and the control of religion by the ruling power.

Life and Belief in the New Kingdom

Most Egyptians' daily lives under the New Kingdom still revolved around their labor and the annual flood of the Nile. During the months when the river stayed between its banks, they worked their fields, rising early in the morning to avoid the searing heat. When the flooding halted agricultural work, the king required them to work on his building projects. They lived in workers' quarters erected next to the construction sites. Although slaves became more common as household workers in the New Kingdom, free workers, performing labor instead of paying taxes in money, did most of the work on this period's mammoth royal construction projects. Written texts reveal that workers lightened their burden by singing songs, telling adventure stories, and drinking a lot of beer. They accomplished a great deal with their labors: the majority of the ancient temples remaining in Egypt today were built during the New Kingdom.

Ordinary people worshipped many different gods, especially deities they hoped would protect them in their daily lives. They venerated Bes, for instance, a dwarf with the features of a lion, as a protector of the household. They carved his image on amulets, beds, headrests, and mirror handles. By the time of the New Kingdom, ordinary people believed that they, too, could have a blessed afterlife and therefore put great effort into preparing for it. Those who could afford it arranged to have their tombs outfitted with all the goods needed for the journey to their new existence. Most important, they paid burial experts to turn their corpses into mummies so that they could have a complete body in the afterlife. Making a mummy required removing the brain (through the nose with a long-handled spoon), cutting out the internal organs to store separately in stone jars, drying the body with mineral salts to the consistency of old leather, and wrapping the shrunken flesh in linen soaked with ointments.

Every mummy had to travel to the afterlife with a copy of the *Book of the Dead*, which included magical spells for avoiding dangers along the way as well as instructions on how to prepare for the judgment-day trial before the gods. To prove that they deserved a good fate after death, the dead had to convincingly recite claims such as the following: "I have not committed crimes against people; I have not mistreated cattle; I have not robbed the poor; I have not caused pain; I have not caused tears" (see Document, "Declaring Innocence on Judgment Day in Ancient Egypt," page 25). Only if the gods believed the dead person was he or she allowed to live a blessed afterlife.

DOCUMENT

Declaring Innocence on Judgment Day in Ancient Egypt

The Egyptian collection of spells and instructions for the dead—known today as the Book of the Dead—*instructed the dead person how to make a declaration of innocence to the gods judging the person's fate on the day of judgment. The declaration listed evils that the person denied having committed; presumably the divine judges could tell whether the deceased was speaking truthfully. This selection of denials, each directed to a specific deity, reveals what Egyptians regarded as just and proper behavior.*

Wide-of-Stride who comes from On: I have not done evil.
Flame-grasper who comes from Kheraha: I have not robbed.
Long-nosed who comes from Khmun: I have not coveted.
Shadow-eater who comes from the cave: I have not stolen.
Savage-faced who comes from Rostau: I have not killed people.
Lion-Twins who come from heaven: I have not trimmed the measure.
Flint-eyed who comes from Kehm: I have not cheated.
Fiery-one who comes backward: I have not stolen a god's property.
Bone-smasher who comes from Hnes: I have not told lies.
Flame-thrower who comes from Memphis: I have not seized food.
Cave-dweller who comes from the west: I have not sulked.
White-toothed who comes from Lakeland: I have not trespassed.
Blood-eater who comes from slaughterplace: I have not slain sacred cattle.
Entrail-eater who comes from the tribunal: I have not extorted.
Lord of Maat who comes from Maaty: I have not extorted.
Wanderer who comes from Bubastis: I have not spied.
Pale-one who comes from On: I have not prattled.
Villain who comes from Anjdty: I have contended only for my goods.
Fiend who comes from slaughterhouse: I have not committed adultery.
Examiner who comes from Min's temple: I have not defiled myself.
Chief of the nobles who comes from Imu: I have not caused fear.
Wrecker who comes from Huy: I have not trespassed.
Disturber who comes from the sanctuary: I have not been violent.
Child who comes from On: I have not been deaf to Maat.
Foreteller who comes from Wensi: I have not quarreled.
Bastet who comes from the shrine: I have not winked.
Backward-face who comes from the pit: I have not copulated with a boy.
Flame-footed who comes from the dusk: I have not been false.
Dark-one who comes from darkness: I have not reviled.

Source: Translation from Miriam Lichtheim, *Ancient Egyptian Literature* (Berkeley: University of California Press, 1978), vol. 2, 126–27.

Question to Consider

- **What do the crimes enumerated here reveal about the values embraced by Egyptian society?**

Magic played a large role in the lives of Egyptians. Professional magicians sold them spells and charms, both written and oral, they could use to promote their eternal salvation, protect themselves from demons, smooth the rocky course of love, exact revenge on enemies, and find relief from disease and injury. Egyptian doctors knew many medicinal herbs (knowledge they passed on to later civilizations) and could perform major surgeries, including opening the skull. Still, no doctor could cure severe infections; as in the past, sick people continued to rely on the help of supernatural forces through prayers and spells.

REVIEW QUESTION **How did religion guide the lives of both rulers and ordinary people in ancient Egypt?**

The Hittites, the Minoans, and the Mycenaeans, 2200–1000 B.C.E.

The first examples of Western civilization to emerge in the central Mediterranean region were located in Anatolia, dominated by the warlike Hittite kingdom (see Map 1.1); on the large island of Crete and nearby islands, home to the Minoans; and on the Greek mainland, where the Mycenaeans grew rich from raiding and trade (Map 1.3). As early as 6000 B.C.E., people from southwestern Asia, especially Anatolia, began migrating westward and southward to inhabit islands in the Mediterranean Sea. From this migration, the rich civilization of the Minoans gradually emerged on the island of Crete and other islands in

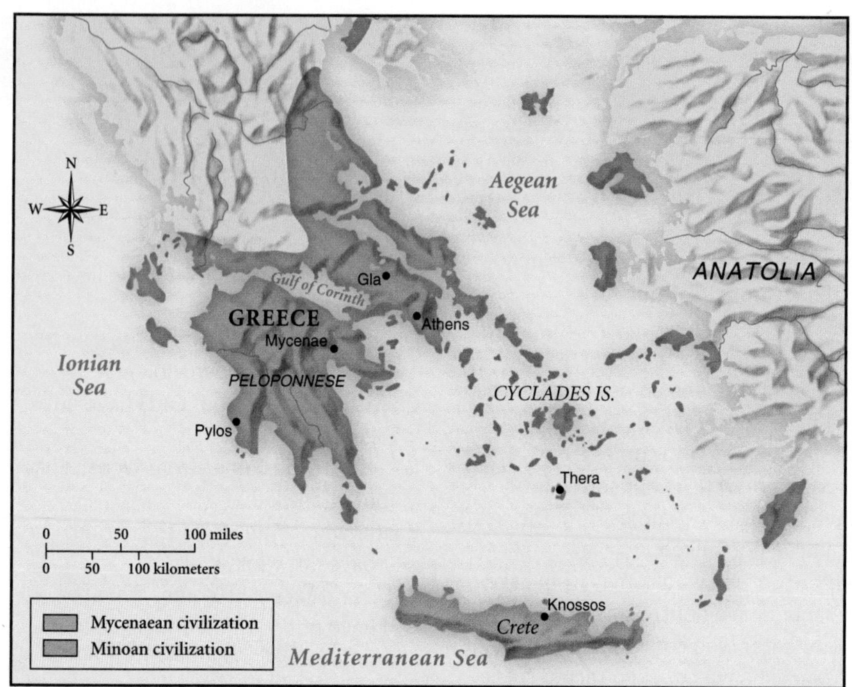

MAP 1.3 Greece and the Aegean Sea, 1500 B.C.E.

A varied landscape of mountains, islands, and seas defined the geography of Greece. The distances between settlements were mostly short, but rough terrain and seasonally stormy sailing made travel a chore. The distance from the mainland to the largest island in this region, Crete, where Minoan civilization arose, was sufficiently long to keep Cretans isolated from the wars of most of later Greek history.

the Aegean Sea by around 2200 B.C.E. In mainland Greece, civilization eventually arose among peoples who had moved into the area thousands of years before, again most likely from southwestern Asia.

The Hittites, the Minoans, and the Mycenaeans had advanced military technologies, elaborate architecture, striking art, a marked taste for luxury, and extensive trade contacts with Egypt and the Near East. The Hittites, like the Egyptians, created a unified state under a single central authority. The Minoans and the Mycenaeans, like the Mesopotamians, established separate city-states. All three peoples inhabited a dangerous world in which repeated raids and violent disruptions lasting from around 1200 to 1000 B.C.E. ultimately destroyed their prosperous cultures. Nevertheless, their accomplishments paved the way for the later civilization of Greece, which would greatly influence the history of Western civilization.

The Hittites, 1750–1200 B.C.E.

By around 1750 B.C.E. the Hittites had made themselves the most powerful people of central Anatolia. They had migrated from the Caucasus area, between the Black and Caspian Seas, and overcome indigenous Anatolian peoples to set up their centralized kingdom. It flourished because they inhabited a fertile upland plateau in the peninsula's center, excelled in war and diplomacy, and controlled trade in their region and southward. The Hittites' southward-knifing military campaigns eventually threatened Egypt's possessions on the eastern Mediterranean coast, bringing them into conflict with the warrior pharaohs of the New Kingdom.

Since the Hittites spoke an Indo-European language, they belonged to the linguistic family that over time populated most of Europe. The original Indo-European speakers, who were pastoralists and raiders, had migrated as separate groups into Anatolia and Europe, including Greece, most likely from western Asia. Recent archaeological discoveries in that general region have revealed graves of women buried with weapons. These burials suggest that women in these groups originally occupied positions of leadership in war and peace alongside men; the prominence of Hittite queens in documents, royal letters, and foreign treaties perhaps sprang from that tradition.

As in other early civilizations, rule in the Hittite kingdom depended on religion for its justification and structuring of authority. Hittite religion combined worship of Indo-European gods with worship of deities inherited from the original Anatolian population. The king served as high priest of the storm god, and Hittite belief demanded that he maintain a strict purity in his life as a demonstration of his justice and guardianship of social order. His drinking water, for example, always had to be strained. So strong was this insistence on purity that the king's water carrier was executed if so much as one hair was found in the water. Like Egyptian kings, Hittite rulers felt responsible for maintaining the gods' goodwill toward their subjects. King Mursili II (r. 1321–1295 B.C.E.), for example, issued a set of prayers begging the gods to end a plague: "What is this, o gods, that you have done? Our land is dying. . . . We have lost our wits, and we can do nothing right. O gods, whatever sin you behold, either let a prophet come forth to identify it . . . or let us see it in a dream!"

The kings conducted many religious ceremonies in their capital, Hattusas, which grew into one of the most impressive cities of its era. Ringed by massive defensive walls and stone towers, it featured huge palaces aligned along straight, gravel-paved streets. Sculptures of animals, warriors, and, especially, the royal rulers decorated public spaces. Hit-

Chariots in the Ancient Near East
Chariots appear frequently in hunting and war scenes in Assyrian, Egyptian, Hittite, and Persian art. The scenes often show a rider, usually a king or noble, shooting a bow at an animal or an enemy, with a charioteer to guide the charging horse. Textual evidence confirms that chariots were important weaponry in the ancient Near East, but scenes such as this one were primarily intended to impress viewers with the skill and majesty of the hunter or warrior rather than to give an exact picture of the battlefield or hunting ground. *(© C. M. Dixon/HIP/The Image Works.)*

tite kings maintained their rule by forging personal alliances—cemented by marriages and oaths of loyalty—with the noble families of the kingdom.

These rulers aggressively employed their troops to expand their power. In periods when ties between kings and nobles remained strong and the kingdom therefore preserved its unity, they launched extremely ambitious military campaigns. In 1595 B.C.E., for example, the royal army raided as far southeast as Babylon in Mesopotamia, destroying that kingdom. Scholars no longer accept the once popular idea that the Hittites owed their success in war to a special knowledge of making weapons from iron, although their craftsmen did smelt iron, from which they made ceremonial implements. (Weapons made from iron did not become common in the Mediterranean world until well after 1200 B.C.E.—at the end of the Hittite kingdom.) The Hittite army excelled in the use of chariots, and perhaps this skill gave it an edge.

The economic strength of the Hittite kingdom came from control over long-distance trade routes for essential raw materials, especially metals. The Hittites worked mightily to dominate the lucrative trade moving between the Mediterranean coast and inland northern Syria. The Egyptian New Kingdom pharaohs fiercely resisted Hittite expansion and power in this region. The Anatolian kingdom proved too strong, however, and in the bloody battle of Kadesh, around 1274 B.C.E., the Hittites fought the Egyptians to a standstill in Syria, leading to a political stalemate in that region. Fear of neighboring Assyria eventually led the Hittite king to negotiate with his Egyptian rival, and the two war-weary kingdoms became allies sixteen years after the battle of Kadesh by agreeing to a treaty that is a landmark in the history of international diplomacy. Remarkably, both Egyptian and Hittite copies of the treaty survive. In it, the two monarchs pledged to be "at peace and brothers forever." The alliance lasted, and thirteen years later the Hittite king gave his daughter in marriage to his Egyptian "brother."

The Minoans, 2200–1400 B.C.E.

Study of early Greek civilization traditionally begins with the people today known as Minoans, who inhabited Crete and other islands in the Aegean Sea by the late third millennium. The word *Minoan* was applied after the archaeologist Arthur Evans (1851–1941) searched the island for traces of King Minos, famous in Greek myth for building the first great navy and keeping the half-human/half-bull Minotaur in a labyrinth at his palace. Scholars today are not sure whether to count the Minoans as the earliest Greeks because they are uncertain whether the Minoan language, whose decipherment remains controversial, was related to Greek or belongs to another linguistic tradition.

Minoans apparently had no written literature, only official records. They wrote these records in a script today called Linear A. If further research confirms a recent suggestion that Minoan was a member of the Indo-European family of languages (the ancestor of many languages, including Greek, Latin, and, much later, English), then Minoans can be seen as the earliest Greeks. Regardless of how the Minoans' language is classified, their interactions with the mainland deeply influenced later Greek civilization.

By around 2200 B.C.E., Minoans on Crete and nearby islands had created what scholars call a **palace society**, in recognition of its sprawling multichambered buildings that apparently housed not only the rulers, their families, and their servants but also the political, economic, and religious administrative offices of the state. Minoan rulers combined the functions of ruler and priest, dominating both politics and religion. The palaces seem to have been largely independent, with no single Minoan community imposing unity on the others. The general population clustered around each palace in houses adjacent to one another; some of these settlements reached the size and density of small cities. The Cretan site Knossos, which Evans thought had been Minos's headquarters, is the most famous such palace complex. Other, smaller settlements dotted outlying areas of the island, especially on the coast. The Minoans' numerous ports supported extensive international trade, above all with the Egyptians and the Hittites.

The most surprising feature of Minoan communities is that they did not build elaborate defensive walls. Palaces, towns, and even isolated country houses apparently saw no need to fortify themselves. The remains of the newer palaces — such as the one at Knossos, with its hundreds of rooms in five stories, indoor plumbing, and colorful scenes painted on the walls — have led some historians to the controversial conclusion that Minoans avoided war among themselves, despite their having no single central authority over their independent settlements. Others object to this vision of peaceful Minoans as overly romantic, arguing that the most powerful Minoans on Crete dominated some neighboring islands. Recent discoveries of tombs on Crete have revealed weapons caches, and a find of bones cut by knives has even raised the possibility of human sacrifice. The prominence of women in palace frescoes and the numerous figurines of large-breasted goddesses found on Minoan sites have also prompted speculation that women dominated Minoan society, but no texts so far discovered have verified this. Minoan art certainly depicts women prominently and respectfully, but the same is true of contemporary civilizations that we know were controlled by men. More archaeological research is needed to resolve the controversies concerning gender roles in Minoan civilization.

Scholars agree, however, that the development of **Mediterranean polyculture** — the cultivation of olives, grapes, and grains in a single, interrelated agricultural system — greatly increased the health and wealth of Minoan society. This innovation made the most efficient use of a farmer's labor by combining crops that required intense work at different seasons. This system of farming, which still characterizes Mediterranean agriculture, had two major consequences. First, the combination of crops provided a healthy way of eating (the Mediterranean diet, as doctors call it today), which in turn stimulated population growth. Second, agriculture became both more diversified and more specialized, increasing production of the valuable products olive oil and wine.

Just as they had in Mesopotamia and Egypt, agricultural surpluses on Crete and nearby islands spurred the growth of specialized, often related crafts. To store and transport surplus food, Minoan artisans manufactured huge storage jars (the size of a modern refrigerator), in the process creating another specialized industry. Craft workers, producing sophisticated goods using time-consuming techniques, no longer had time to grow their own food or make the things, such as clothes and lamps, they needed for everyday life. Instead, they exchanged the products they made for food and other goods. In this way, Minoan society experienced increasing economic interdependence.

---

palace society: Minoan and Mycenaean social and political organization centered on multichambered buildings housing the rulers and the administration of the state.

Mediterranean polyculture: The cultivation of olives, grapes, and grains in a single, interrelated agricultural system.

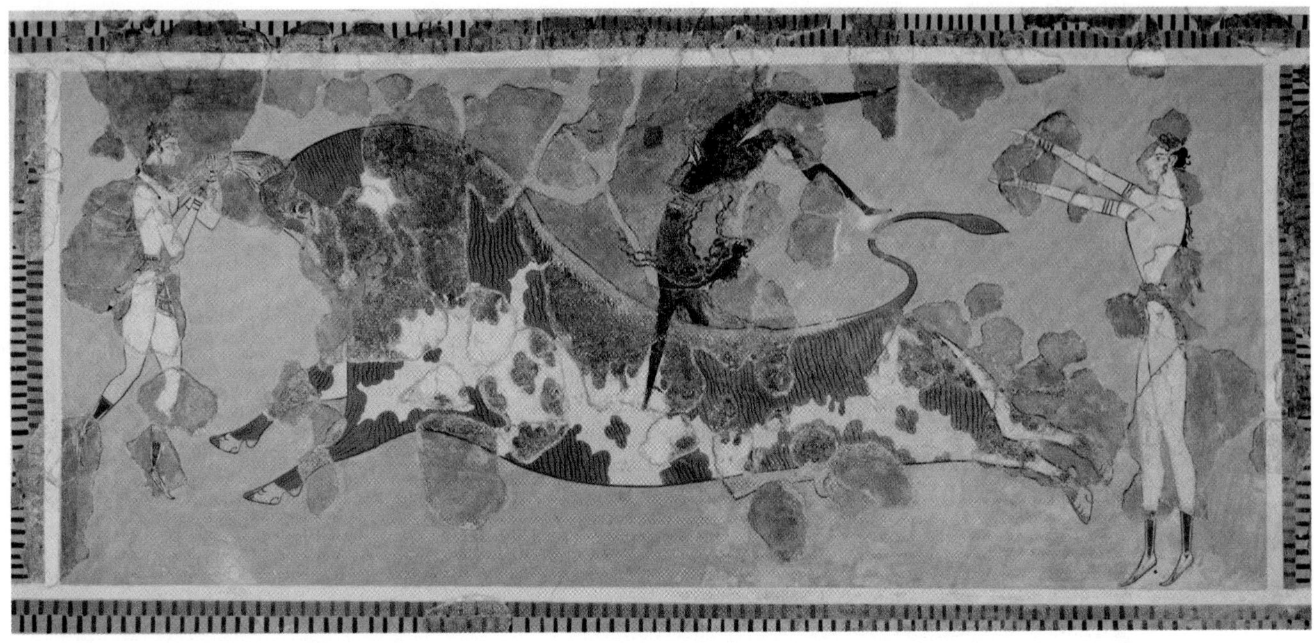

Wall Painting from Knossos, Crete

Minoan artists painted with vivid colors on plaster to enliven the walls of buildings. Unfortunately, time and earthquakes have severely damaged most Minoan wall paintings, and the versions we see today are largely reconstructions painted around surviving fragments of the originals. This painting from the palace at Knossos depicted an acrobatic performance in which a youth leaped in an aerial somersault over the back of a charging bull. Some scholars speculate this dangerous activity was a religious ritual instead of just a circus act. If it was a part of Minoan religion, what do you think this performance could symbolize? *(Archeological Museum of Heraklion, Crete, Greece/Bernard Cox/The Bridgeman Art Library International.)*

The vast storage areas in Minoan palaces suggest that the rulers, like some Mesopotamian kings before them, controlled this interdependence through a redistributive economic system. The Knossos palace, for example, held hundreds of gigantic jars capable of storing 240,000 gallons of olive oil and wine. Bowls, cups, and dippers crammed storerooms nearby. Palace officials would have decided how much each farmer or craft producer had to contribute to the palace storehouse and how much of those contributions would then be redistributed to each person in the community for basic subsistence or as an extra reward. In this way, people gave the products of their labor to the central authority, which redistributed them according to its own priorities.

The Mycenaeans, 1800–1000 B.C.E.

Ancestors of the Greeks had moved into the mainland region of Greece by perhaps 8000 B.C.E., yet the first civilization definitely identified as Greek because of its Indo-European language arose only in the early second millennium B.C.E., about the same time as the Hittite kingdom. These first Greeks are called Mycenaeans, a name derived from the hilltop site of Mycenae, famous for its multichambered palace, rich graves, and massive fortification walls. Located in the Peloponnese (the large peninsula forming southern Greece; see Map 1.3), Mycenae dominated its local area, but neither it nor any other settlement ever ruled all of Bronze Age Greece. Instead, the independent communities of Mycenaean civilization vied with one another in a fierce competition for natural resources and territory.

The nineteenth-century German millionaire Heinrich Schliemann was the first to discover treasure-filled graves at Mycenae. The burial objects revealed a warrior culture organized in independent settlements and ruled by aggressive kings. Constructed as stone-lined shafts, the graves contained entombed dead, who had taken hordes of valuables with them: golden jewelry, including heavy necklaces loaded with pendants, gold and silver vessels, bronze weapons decorated with scenes of wild animals inlaid in precious metals, and delicately painted pottery.

In his excitement at finding treasure, Schliemann proudly announced that he had found the grave of Agamemnon, the legendary king who commanded the Greek army against Troy, a city in northwestern Anatolia, in the Trojan War. Homer, Greece's first and most famous poet, immortalized this war in his epic poem *The Iliad*. Archaeologists now know the shaft graves date to around 1700–1600 B.C.E., long before the Trojan War could have taken place. Schliemann, who paid for his own excavation at Troy to prove to skeptics that the city had really existed, infuriated scholars with his self-promotion. But his passion to confirm that Greek myth preserved a kernel of historical truth motivated him to excavate at Mycenae. His discoveries provided the most spectacular evidence for mainland Greece's earliest civilization.

Mycenaean Interaction with Minoan Crete

Since the hilly terrain of Greece had little fertile land but many useful ports, settlements tended to spring up near the coast. Mycenaean rulers enriched themselves by dominating local farmers, conducting naval raids, and participating in seaborne trade. Palace records inscribed on clay tablets reveal that the Mycenaeans operated under a redistributive economy. On the tablets scribes made detailed lists of goods received and goods paid out, recording everything from chariots to livestock, landholdings, personnel, and perfumes, even broken equipment taken out of service. Like the Minoans, Mycenaeans apparently did not use writing to record the oral literature that scholars believe they created.

The existence of *tholos* tombs—massive underground burial chambers built in beehive shapes with closely fitted stones—shows that some Mycenaeans had become very rich by about 1500 B.C.E. The architectural details of the tholos tombs and the style of the burial goods placed in them testify to the far-flung expeditions for trade and war that Mycenaean rulers conducted throughout the eastern Mediterranean. Above all, however, their many decorative patterns clearly inspired by Minoan art indicate a close connection with Minoan civilization.

Underwater archaeology has revealed the influence of international commerce during this period in (unintentionally) promoting cultural interaction. Divers have discovered, for example, that a late-fourteenth-century B.C.E. shipwreck off Uluburun in Turkey carried a mixed cargo and varied personal possessions from many locations in the eastern Mediterranean, including Canaan, Cyprus, Greece, Egypt, and Babylon. The variety confirms that merchants and consumers involved in this sort of trade were exposed directly to the goods produced by others and indirectly to their ideas.

The sea brought the Mycenaean and Minoan civilizations into close contact, but they remained different in significant ways. The Mycenaeans spoke Greek and made burnt offerings to the gods; the Minoans did neither. The Minoans extended their religious worship outside their centers, establishing sacred places in caves, on mountaintops, and in country villas, while the mainlanders concentrated the worship of their gods inside their walled communities. When the Mycenaeans started building palaces in the fourteenth century B.C.E., they (unlike the palace society Minoans) designed them around *megarons*—rooms with prominent ceremonial hearths and thrones for the rulers. Some Mycenaean palaces had more than one megaron, which could soar two stories high with columns to support a roof above the second-floor balconies.

Documents found in the palace at Knossos reveal that by around 1400 B.C.E. the Mycenaeans had acquired dominance over Crete, possibly in a war over commerce in the Mediterranean. The documents were tablets written in **Linear B**, a pictographic script based on Minoan Linear A, an earlier writing system used for the Minoan language (which scholars still cannot fully decipher). The twentieth-century architect Michael Ventris proved that Linear B was used to write not Minoan, but in fact Greek. Because the Linear B tablets date from before the final destruction of Knossos in about 1370 B.C.E., they show that the palace administration had been keeping its records in a foreign language for some time and therefore that Mycenaeans were controlling Crete well before the end of Minoan civilization. By the middle of the fourteenth century B.C.E., then, the Mycenaeans had displaced the Minoans as the Aegean region's preeminent civilization.

War in Mycenaean Society

By the time Mycenaeans took over Crete, war at home and abroad was the principal concern of well-off Mycenaean men, a tradition that they passed on to later Greek civilization. Contents of Bronze Age tombs in Greece reveal that no wealthy man went to his grave without his war equipment. Armor and weapons were so central to a Mycenaean man's identity that he could not do without them, even in death. Warriors rode into battle on revolutionary transport—lightweight two-wheeled chariots pulled by horses. These expensive vehicles, perhaps introduced by Indo-Europeans migrating from Central Asia, first appeared in various Mediterranean and Near Eastern societies not long after 2000 B.C.E.; the first picture of such a chariot

---

Linear B: The Mycenaeans' pictographic script for writing Greek.

Decorated Dagger from Mycenae

The hilltop fortress and palace at Mycenae was the capital of Bronze Age Greece's most famous kingdom. The picture of a lion hunt inlaid in gold and silver on this sixteenth-century B.C.E. dagger expressed how wealthy Mycenaean men saw their roles in society: as courageous hunters and warriors overcoming the hostile forces of nature. The nine-inch blade was found in a circle of graves inside Mycenae's walls, where the highest-ranking people were buried with their treasures as evidence of their status. *(Nimatallah/Art Resource, NY.)*

in the Aegean region occurs on a Mycenaean grave marker from about 1500 B.C.E. Wealthy people evidently desired this new and costly equipment not only for war but also as proof of their social status.

The Mycenaeans seem to have spent more on war than on religion. In any case, they did not construct any giant religious buildings like Mesopotamia's ziggurats or Egypt's pyramids. Their most important deities were male gods concerned with war. The names of gods found in the Linear B tablets reveal that Mycenaeans passed down many divinities to the Greeks of later times, such as Dionysus, the god of wine.

The Violent End to Early Western Civilization, 1200–1000 B.C.E.

A state of political equilibrium, in which kings corresponded with one another and traders traveled all over the area, characterized the Mediterranean and Near Eastern world around 1300 B.C.E. Within a century, however, violence had destroyed or weakened almost every major political state in the region, including Egypt, some kingdoms of Mesopotamia, and the Hittite and Mycenaean kingdoms. Neither the civilizations united under a single central authority nor the ones with independent states survived. This period of international violence from about 1200 to 1000 B.C.E. remains one of the most fascinating and disturbing puzzles in the history of Western civilization.

The best clue to what happened comes from Egyptian and Hittite records. They document many foreign attacks in this period, especially from the sea. According to an inscription, in about 1190 B.C.E. a warrior pharaoh defeated a powerful coalition of seaborne invaders from the north, who had fought their way to the edge of Egypt. These **Sea Peoples**, as historians call them, were made up of many different groups operating separately. No single, unified group of Sea Peoples originated the tidal wave of violence starting around 1200 B.C.E. Rather, many different bands devastated the region. A chain reaction of attacks and flights in a recurring and expanding cycle put even more bands on the move. Some were mercenary soldiers who had deserted the rulers who had employed them; some were raiders by profession. Many may have been Greeks. The famous story of the Trojan War probably recalls this period of repeated violent attacks from abroad: it portrays an army from Greece crossing the Aegean Sea to attack and plunder Troy and the surrounding region in coastal Anatolia. The attacks also reached far inland. As a result, the Babylonian kingdom collapsed, the Assyrians were confined to their homeland, and much of western Asia and Syria was devastated.

It remains mysterious how so many attackers could be so successful over such a long time, but the consequences for the eastern Mediterranean region are clear. The once mighty Hittite kingdom fell around 1200 B.C.E., when raiders cut off its trade routes for raw materials. Invaders razed its capital city, Hattusas, which never revived. Egypt's New Kingdom turned back the Sea Peoples after a tremendous military effort, but the raiders destroyed

Sea Peoples: The diverse groups of raiders who devastated the eastern Mediterranean region in the period of violence 1200–1000 B.C.E.

the Egyptian long-distance trade network. By the end of the New Kingdom, around 1081 B.C.E., Egypt had shrunk to its original territorial core along the Nile's banks. These problems ruined the Egyptian state's credit. For example, when an eleventh-century B.C.E. Theban temple official traveled to Phoenicia to buy cedar for a ceremonial boat, the city's ruler demanded cash in advance. Although the Egyptian monarchy hung on, power struggles between pharaohs and priests, made worse by frequent attacks from abroad, prevented the reestablishment of centralized authority. No Egyptian dynasty ever again became an aggressive international power.

In Greece, homegrown conflict apparently led to the tipping point for Mycenaean civilization at the time when the Sea Peoples became a threat. The Mycenaeans reached the zenith of their power around 1400–1250 B.C.E. The enormous domed tomb at Mycenae, called the Treasury of Atreus, testifies to the riches of this period. The tomb's elaborately decorated front and soaring roof reveal the pride and wealth of the Mycenaean warrior princes. The last phase of the extensive palace at Pylos on the west coast of the Peloponnese also dates from this time. It boasted vivid wall paintings, storerooms bursting with food, and a royal bathroom with a built-in tub and intricate plumbing. But these prosperous Mycenaeans did not escape the widespread violence that began around 1200 B.C.E. Linear B tablets record the disposition of troops to the coast to guard the palace at Pylos from raids from the sea. The palace inhabitants of eastern Greece constructed defensive walls so massive that the later

MAPPING THE WEST

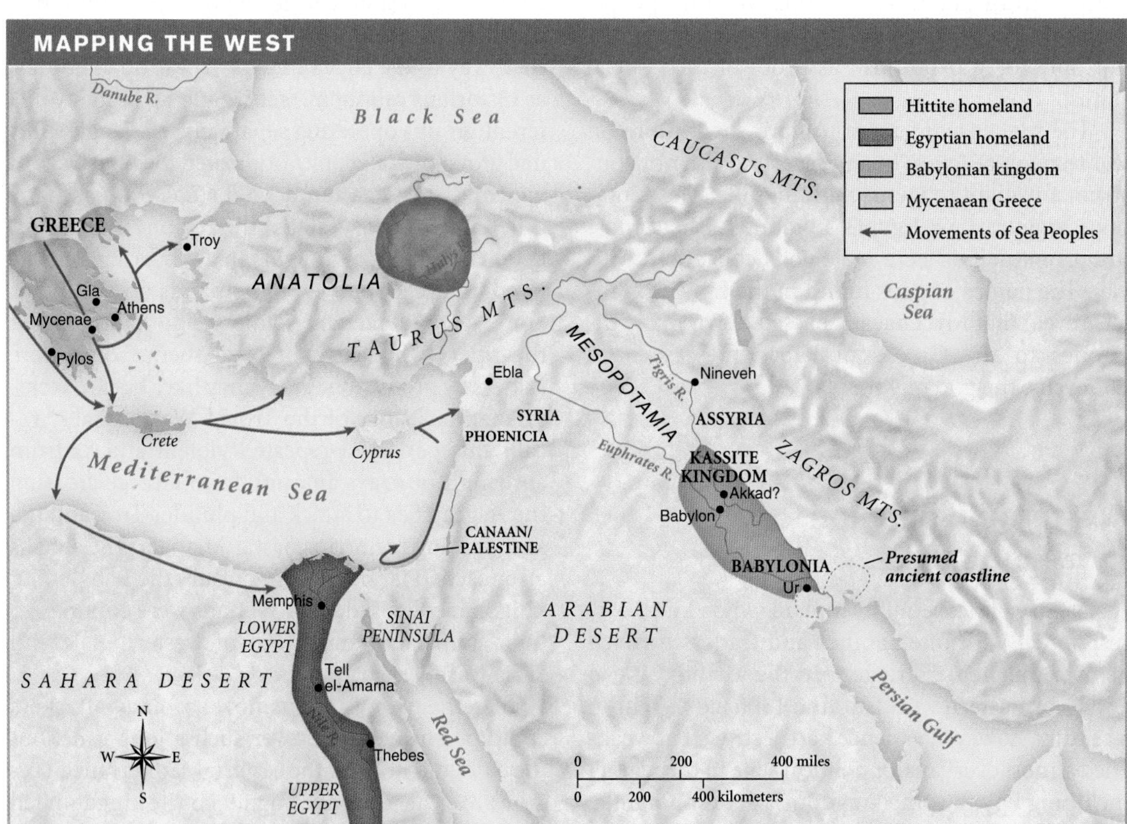

The Violent End to Early Western Civilization, 1200–1000 B.C.E.

Bands of wandering warriors and raiders set the eastern Mediterranean aflame at the end of the Bronze Age. This violence displaced many people and ended the power of the Egyptian, Hittite, and Mycenaean kingdoms. Even some of the Near Eastern states well inland from the eastern Mediterranean coast felt the effects of this period of unrest, whose causes remain mysterious. The Mediterranean Sea was a two-edged sword for the early civilizations that grew up around and near it: as a highway for transporting goods and ideas, it was a benefit; as an easy access corridor for attackers, it was a danger. The raids of the Sea Peoples that smashed the prosperity of the eastern Mediterranean region around 1200–1000 B.C.E. also set in motion the forces that led to the next step in our story, the reestablishment of civilization in Greece. Internal conflict among Mycenaean rulers turned the regional unrest of those centuries into a local catastrophe; fighting each other for dominance, they so weakened their monarchies that their societies could not recover from the effects of battles and earthquakes.

Greeks thought giants had built them. These fortifications would have protected coastal palaces against seafaring attackers, who could have been either outsiders or Greeks. The wall around the inland palace at Gla in central Greece, however, which foreign raiders could not easily reach, confirms that Mycenaean communities also had to defend themselves against other Mycenaean communities.

The internal conflict probably did more damage to Mycenaean civilization than the raids of the Sea Peoples. Major earthquakes also struck at this time, spreading further destruction among the Mycenaeans. Archaeology offers no evidence for the ancient tradition that Dorian Greeks invading from the north caused this damage. Rather, near-constant civil war by jealous local Mycenaean rulers overburdened the complicated administrative balancing system necessary for the palaces' redistributive economies and hindered recovery from earthquake damage. The violence killed many Mycenaeans, and the disappearance of the palace-based redistributive economy put many others on the road to starvation. The destruction of central authority left most Greeks with no organized way to defend or feed themselves and forced them to wander abroad in search of new places to settle and learn to farm. Like people from the earliest times, they had to move to build a better life.

REVIEW QUESTION How did war determine the fate of early Western civilization in Anatolia, Crete, and Greece?

Conclusion

The best way to create a meaningful definition of Western civilization is to study its history, which begins in Mesopotamia and Egypt; early societies there influenced the later civilization of Greece. Cities first arose in Mesopotamia around 4000 to 3000 B.C.E. Hierarchy had characterized society to some degree from the very beginning, but it, along with patriarchy, grew more prominent once civilization and political states with centralized authority became widespread.

Trade and war were constants, both aiming in different ways at profit and glory. Indirectly, they often generated cultural interaction by putting civilizations into close contact to learn from one another. Technological innovation was also a prominent characteristic of this long period. The invention of metallurgy, monumental architecture, mathematics, and alphabetic writing greatly affected people's lives. Religion was at the center of society; people believed that the gods demanded everyone, from king to worker, to display just and righteous conduct.

FOR FURTHER EXPLORATION

- **For additional primary-source material from this period**, see *Sources of the Making of the West*, Fourth Edition.
- **For Web sites, images, and documents related to topics in this chapter**, visit *Make History* at bedfordstmartins.com/hunt.

Chapter 1 Review

Online Study Guide bedfordstmartins.com/hunt

Key Terms and People

In the grid below, identify the term or person and explain its historical significance. (To do this exercise online, go to bedfordstmartins.com/hunt.)

Term	Who or What & When	Why It Matters
civilization (p. 4)		
polytheism (p. 6)		
monotheism (p. 6)		
Anatolia (p. 7)		
city-state (p. 8)		
ziggurats (p. 8)		
cuneiform (p. 11)		
empire (p. 12)		
redistributive economy (p. 14)		
Hammurabi (p. 14)		
hieroglyphic (p. 18)		
Maat (p. 20)		
wisdom literature (p. 22)		
palace society (p. 28)		
Mediterranean polyculture (p. 28)		
Linear B (p. 30)		
Sea Peoples (p. 31)		

Review Questions

1. What are the challenges in defining the term *Western civilization*?
2. How did life change for people in Mesopotamia when they began to live in cities?
3. How did religion guide the lives of both rulers and ordinary people in ancient Egypt?
4. How did war determine the fate of early Western civilization in Anatolia, Crete, and Greece?

Making Connections

1. Compare and contrast the environmental factors affecting the emergence of the world's first civilizations in Mesopotamia and Egypt.
2. What were the advantages and disadvantages of living in a unified country under a single central authority compared to living in a region with separate city-states?
3. Which were more important in influencing the development of early Western civilization: the intentional or the unintentional consequences of change?

Important Events

Date	Event	Date	Event
4000–1000 B.C.E.	Bronze Age in southwestern Asia, Egypt, and Europe	2061–1665 B.C.E.	Middle Kingdom in Egypt
4000–3000 B.C.E.	Mesopotamians invent writing and establish first cities	1792–1750 B.C.E.	Hammurabi rules Babylon and issues his law code
3050 B.C.E.	Narmer (Menes) unites Upper and Lower Egypt into one kingdom	1750 B.C.E.	Hittites establish their kingdom in Anatolia
2687–2190 B.C.E.	Old Kingdom in Egypt	1569–1081 B.C.E.	New Kingdom in Egypt
2350 B.C.E.	Sargon, king of Akkad, establishes the world's first empire	1400 B.C.E.	The Mycenaeans build their first palaces in Greece and take over Minoan Crete
2300–2200 B.C.E.	Enheduanna, princess of Akkad, composes poetry	1274 B.C.E.	Battle of Kadesh in Syria between the Egyptians and the Hittites
2200 B.C.E.	Minoans build their first palaces	1200–1000 B.C.E.	Period of violence ends many kingdoms
2112–2004 B.C.E.	Ur III dynasty rules in Sumer		

- Consider three events: **Mesopotamians invent writing and establish first cities (4000–3000 B.C.E.), Sargon establishes the world's first empire in Akkadia (2350 B.C.E.)**, and **Enheduanna composes poetry (2300–2200 B.C.E.)**. How might the invention of writing have promoted the growth of stronger city-states and the first empire? How might the creation of the Akkadian empire have fostered the development of literature?

SUGGESTED REFERENCES

The combination of archaeological and linguistic research informs scholarship on the history of the ancient Near East, Egypt, and Greece. New discoveries and new ideas both help historians achieve a clearer understanding of these earliest societies of Western civilization.

Baines, John. *Religion and Society in Ancient Egypt*. 2003.

Bertman, Stephen. *Handbook to Life in Ancient Mesopotamia*. 2003.

Bryce, Trevor. *Life and Society in the Hittite World*. 2004.

——, and Adam Hook. *Hittite Warrior*. 2007.

*Chavalas, Mark W., ed. *The Ancient Near East. Historical Sources in Translation*. 2006.

Cline, Eric H. *Oxford Handbook of the Bronze Age Aegean*. 2010.

Crouch, Carly L. *War and Ethics in the Ancient Near East*. 2009.

*Dalley, Stephanie, trans. *Myths from Mesopotamia: Creation, the Flood, Gilgamesh, and Others*. 1991.

Ikram, Salima. *Ancient Egypt: An Introduction*. 2010.

Mieroop, Marc Van De. *King Hammurabi of Babylon: A Biography*. 2005.

——. *A History of the Ancient Near East ca. 3000–323 B.C.* 2nd ed. 2007.

Partridge, Robert B. *Fighting Pharaohs: Weapons and Warfare in Ancient Egypt*. 2002.

Podany, Amanda H. *Brotherhood of Kings: How International Relations Shaped the Ancient Near East*. 2010.

Sanders, N. K. *The Sea Peoples: Warriors of the Ancient Mediterranean, 1250–1150 B.C.* Rev. ed. 1985.

Shelmerdine, Cynthia. *The Cambridge Companion to the Aegean Bronze Age*. 2008.

*Simpson, William Kelly, ed. *The Literature of Ancient Egypt. An Anthology of Stories, Instructions, and Poetry*. 3rd ed. 2003.

Szapakowska, Kasia. *Daily Life in Ancient Egypt: Recreating Lahun*. 2008.

Thebes in ancient Egypt: http://www.thebanmappingproject.com/

Tyldesley, Joyce. *Hatchepsut: The Female Pharaoh*. 1998.

*Primary source.

CHAPTER 2

Near East Empires and the Reemergence of Civilization in Greece

1000–500 B.C.E.

The Greek poet Homer in the eighth century B.C.E. told emotion-filled stories recalling the period of violence in 1200–1000 B.C.E. that had wrecked Greek civilization. In his epic poem *The Iliad*, he narrated bloody tales of the Trojan War that were rich with legends born from combined Greek and Near Eastern traditions, such as the story of the Greek hero Bellerophon. Driven from his home by a false charge of sexual assault, Bellerophon had to serve as "enforcer" for a foreign king, combating the king's most dangerous enemies. He had to fight—and kill—fierce tribesmen, Amazons, and even the king's own warriors, but his most famous contest pitted him against a monster. As Homer tells it, Bellerophon was ordered "to defeat the Chimera, an inhuman freak created by the gods, horrible with its lion's head, goat's body, and dragon's tail, breathing fire all the time." Riding on the winged horse Pegasus, Bellerophon triumphed by swooping down on the Chimera in an aerial attack. For such amazing heroics, the king gave Bellerophon his daughter in marriage and half his kingdom.

Black-Figure Vase from Corinth
This vase was made in Corinth about 600 B.C.E., painted in the so-called black-figure style in which artists carved details into the dark-baked clay. In the late sixth century B.C.E., this style gave way to red-figure, in which artists painted details in black on a reddish background instead of engraving them; the result was finer detail (compare this vase painting with that on page 5). The animals and mythical creatures on the vase shown here follow Near Eastern models, which inspired Archaic Age Greek artists to put people and animals into their designs again after their absence during the Dark Age. Why do you think the artist depicted the animal at the lower right with two bodies but only one head? (*© The Trustees of the British Museum/Art Resource, NY.*)

Homer's story provides evidence for the intercultural contact between the Near East and Greece that supported the reemergence of civilization in Greece after 1000 B.C.E. Both the Chimera and the horse-headed, hawk-bodied, lion-footed beast painted on the vase from Corinth shown in the chapter-opening illustration were creatures from Near Eastern myth taken over by Greeks. Greece's geography—countless ports on its long coastline and many islands—promoted contacts by sea through trade, travel, and war with its richer and stronger Near Eastern neighbors. In the centuries from

1000 to 500 B.C.E., these contacts—combined with the Greeks' value of competitive individual excellence, their sense of a communal identity, and their belief that people in general (and not just rulers) were responsible for maintaining justice and the goodwill of the gods toward the community—helped Greeks reestablish their prosperity and reinvent their civilization with a radically new concept of central authority: city-states governed not by kings but by groups of citizens.

Despite the violence and consequent economic failure that had destroyed so many Bronze Age communities in the eastern Mediterranean region by around 1000 B.C.E., people's desire for trade and cross-cultural contact endured and increased as conditions improved over the following centuries. The Near East, retaining monarchy as its traditional form of social and political organization, recovered more quickly than Greece. Near Eastern kings in this period extracted surpluses from subject populations to fund their palaces and their armies. They also continually sought new conquests to win glory, exploit the labor of conquered peoples, seize raw materials, and conduct long-distance trade.

Attacks of the Sea Peoples, internal wars, and earthquakes had destroyed the political and social organization of Minoan and Mycenaean Greece in 1200–1000 B.C.E. During Greece's initial recovery from poverty and depopulation around 1000 to 750 B.C.E., there emerged new political and social institutions and traditions rejecting the rule of kings. In this period, Greeks sailed the Mediterranean Sea to maintain trade and cross-cultural contact with the older civilizations of the Near East. Their mythology, as in Homer, and their art, as on the Corinthian vase, reveal that Greeks imported ideas and technology from that part of the wider world as they remade their lives during this difficult era.

By the eighth century B.C.E., Greeks had begun to create their own kind of city-state, the polis, as a new form of political and social organization. The polis was a radical innovation because it made citizenship—not subjection to kings—the basis for society and politics, and included the poor as citizens. It gave legal—though not political—rights to women, but no rights to slaves. With the exception of occasional tyrannies, Greek city-states governed themselves by having male citizens share political power. The extent of the power sharing varied, with small groups of upper-class men dominating in some places. In other places, however, the polis shared power among all free men, even the poor, eventually creating the world's first democracy. The Greeks' invention of democratic politics, limited though it might have been by modern standards, stands as a landmark in the history of Western civilization.

Religion and philosophy also changed greatly in this period. Leaders and thinkers in the Near East and Greece gradually created new ways of belief and thought that slowly filtered down to the mass of people and deeply influenced the development of Western civilization. In religion, the Persians developed beliefs that saw human life as a struggle between good and evil, and the Israelites evolved their monotheism. In philosophy, the Greeks began to use reason and logic to replace mythological explanations of nature.

CHAPTER FOCUS How did the forms of political and social organization that Greece developed after 1000 B.C.E. differ from those of the Near East?

From Dark Age to Empire in the Near East, 1000–500 B.C.E.

The widespread violence in 1200–1000 B.C.E. had weakened or obliterated many communities and populations in the eastern Mediterranean. Although

1000–750 B.C.E. Greece experiences its Dark Age

900 B.C.E. Neo-Assyrian Empire emerges

800 B.C.E. Greeks learn to write with an alphabet

776 B.C.E. Olympic Games founded in Greece

750 B.C.E. Greeks begin to create the polis

1000 B.C.E. — 900 B.C.E. — 800 B.C.E.

recent archaeological research shows that people in this era were still actively pursuing trade and intercultural contacts, historians have traditionally used the term *Dark Age* to refer to the times immediately following the period of violence, both because economic conditions were so gloomy for so many people and because our knowledge of what happened is so limited. The Dark Age in the Near East lasted less than a century, while in Greece it lasted over two hundred years.

By 900 B.C.E., a powerful centralized Assyrian kingdom had once again gained power in Mesopotamia. From this base, the Assyrians carved out a new empire even larger than the preceding one. The riches and power of this Neo-Assyrian Empire inspired first the Babylonians and then the Persians to build their own empires when Assyrian power collapsed. The traditional striving for empire remained constant in the Near East. In comparison, the Israelites had little military power, but they established a new path for civilization during this period by changing their religion. They developed monotheism and produced the Hebrew Bible (as it is known today), called the Old Testament by Christians.

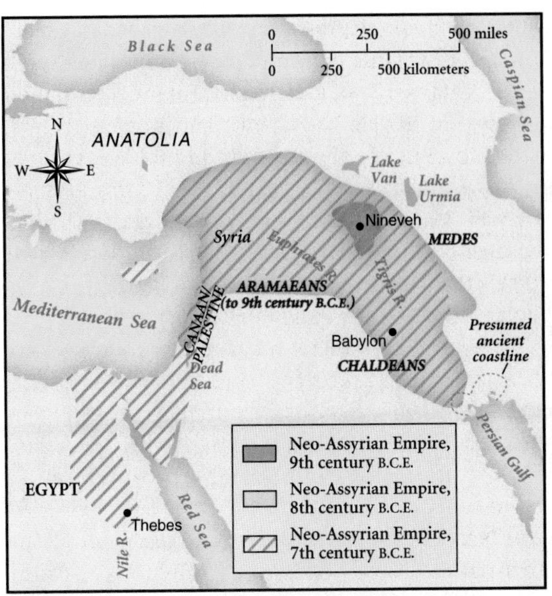

MAP 2.1 Expansion of the Neo-Assyrian Empire, c. 900–650 B.C.E.
Like their Akkadian, Assyrian, and Babylonian predecessors, the Neo-Assyrian kings dominated a vast region of the Near East to secure a supply of metals, access to trade routes on land and sea, and imperial glory. In this way, they built the largest empire the world had yet seen. Also like their predecessors, they treated disobedient subjects harshly and intolerantly to try to prevent their diverse territories from rebelling.

The New Empire of Assyria, 900–600 B.C.E.

When the Hittite kingdom fell around 1000 B.C.E., the Assyrians gained power by seizing supplies of metal—much prized by rulers—and controlling trade routes in the eastern Mediterranean (Map 2.1). By 900 B.C.E., Assyrian armies had punched westward all the way to the coast. The Neo-Assyrian kings conquered Babylon, in southern Mesopotamia, in the eighth century B.C.E., and they added Egypt to their empire in the seventh century. These kings proclaimed their pride at having restored and expanded the imperial power that Assyria had possessed in the past.

Neo-Assyrian Militarism and Imperial Brutality A warrior culture provided the foundation for the military strength that established the Neo-Assyrian Empire. A tactical innovation made Assyrian armies unstoppable: foot soldiers, not cavalry, were the Assyrians' main strike force. These infantrymen excelled in using military technology such as siege towers and battering rams, while swift chariots carried archers. Wars against foreign lands brought in revenues supplementing the domestic economy, which centered on agriculture, animal husbandry, and long-distance trade.

700 B.C.E. Spartans conquer Messenia and enslave its inhabitants as helots

657 B.C.E. Cypselus becomes tyrant in Corinth

597 and 586 B.C.E. Israelites exiled to Babylon

546–510 B.C.E. Peisistratus's family rules Athens as tyrants

508–500 B.C.E. Cleisthenes' reforms extend democracy in Athens

700 B.C.E. — 600 B.C.E. — 500 B.C.E.

700–500 B.C.E. Ionian philosophers invent rationalism

630 B.C.E. The lyric poet Sappho is born

594 B.C.E. Solon's reforms promote early democracy in Athens

539 B.C.E. Persian king Cyrus captures Babylon and permits Israelites to return to Canaan

Assyrian Warfare
The Assyrians relied on technology and bravery to attack walled cities. This sculpture shows a covered and wheeled battering ram and warriors climbing up a siege ladder to defeat their enemies. The crucified victims above and the bodies below reveal the brutal fate awaiting anyone who resisted the Assyrian army. The king and his entourage are shown as much larger than others to express their supreme status in society and to emphasize their rule. *(Ancient Art & Architecture Collection, Ltd.)*

Neo-Assyrian kings kept order by treating conquered peoples brutally. Those allowed to stay in their homelands had to pay annual tributes to the Assyrians: these payments included raw materials and luxury goods such as incense, wine, dyed linens, glasswork, and ivory. Worse was the fate of the large number of defeated people whom the kings routinely deported to Assyria for work on huge building projects — temples and palaces — in main cities. One unexpected consequence of this harsh policy was the undermining of the kings' native language: so many Aramaeans, for example, were deported from Canaan to Assyria that Aramaic had largely replaced Assyrian as the land's everyday language by the eighth century B.C.E.

Neo-Assyrian Life and Religion

When not making war, Neo-Assyrian men displayed their status and masculinity by hunting wild animals; the more dangerous the prey, the better. The king hunted lions to demonstrate his vigor and power and thus his capacity to rule. Royal lion hunts provided a favorite subject for sculptors, who carved long relief sculptures that narrated a connected story. Practical technology apparently also mattered to the kings. One, for example, boasted that he invented new irrigation equipment and a novel method of metal casting. The Neo-Assyrian kings also proclaimed that they were following the historical example of their ancestors in building an empire, and they prided themselves as authorities on that past. As one boasted, "I have read complicated texts, whose versions in Sumerian are obscure and in Akkadian hard to understand. I do research on the cuneiform texts on stone from before the Flood." Women of the social elite probably had a chance to become literate, but they were excluded from the male dominions of war and hunting.

Public religion, which included deities adopted from Babylonia, reflected the prominence of war in Assyrian culture: the cult of Ishtar, the goddess of love and war, glorified warfare, as it had in Babylonia. The Neo-Assyrian rulers' desire to demonstrate their respect for the gods motivated them to build huge and costly temples. These shrines' staffs of priests and slaves grew so numerous that the revenues from temple lands were insufficient to support them; the kings had to supply extra funds from the spoils of conquest.

The Neo-Assyrian kings' demand for revenue and generally harsh rule made their own people, especially the social elite, resent their regimes. Rebellions therefore became common throughout the history of the kingdom; a seventh-century B.C.E. revolt fatally weakened it. The Medes, an Iranian people, and the Chaldeans, a Semitic people who had driven the Assyrians from Babylonia, combined forces to invade the kingdom. Recent research has disproved the long-standing assumption that the attackers completely destroyed the Assyrian capital at Nineveh in 612 B.C.E., but their invasion nevertheless ended the Neo-Assyrian Empire.

The Neo-Babylonian Empire, 600–539 B.C.E.

As leaders of the allies who overthrew the Neo-Assyrian Empire, the Chaldeans seized the lion's share of territory. Originating among semi-nomadic herders along the Persian Gulf, by 600 B.C.E. the Chaldeans had established the Neo-Babylonian Empire, the most powerful in Babylonian history, though the shortest-lived: it fell to the Near East's next great empire, that of the Persians, in 539 B.C.E. The Neo-Babylonians spent great sums to increase the architectural splendor of Babylon, rebuilding the great temple of Marduk, the chief god, and constructing an elaborate city gate dedicated to the goddess Ishtar. Blue-glazed bricks and lions molded in yellow, red, and white decorated the gate's walls, which soared thirty-six feet high.

The Neo-Babylonians adopted ancestral Babylonian culture and preserved much Mesopotamian literature, such as the *Epic of Gilgamesh*. They also created many new works of prose and poetry, which the educated minority would often read aloud publicly for the enjoyment of the illiterate. Particularly popular were fables, proverbs, essays, and prophecies teaching morality and proper behavior. This so-called wisdom literature, a tradition going back at least to the Egyptian Old Kingdom, was a Near Eastern tradition that also was prominent in the religious writings of the Israelites.

The Neo-Babylonians passed their knowledge to others outside their region. Their advances in astronomy became so influential that the Greeks later used the word *Chaldean* to mean "astronomer." The primary motivation for observing the stars was the belief that the gods communicated their will to humans through natural phenomena, such as celestial movements and eclipses, abnormal births, patterns of smoke curling upward from a fire, and the trails of ants. The interpretation of these phenomena as messages from the gods exemplified the mixture of science and religion characteristic of ancient Near Eastern thought.

The Persian Empire, 557–500 B.C.E.

Cyrus (r. 557–530 B.C.E.) founded the Persian Empire in what is today Iran through his skills as a general and a diplomat who saw respect for others' religious practices as good imperial policy. He continued the region's tradition of kings waging war

Cyrus: Founder of the Persian Empire.

The Great King of Persia

Like their Assyrian predecessors, the Persian kings decorated their palaces with large relief sculptures emphasizing royal dignity and success. This one from Persepolis shows officials and petitioners giving the king proper respect when entering his presence. To symbolize their elevated status, the king and his son, who stands behind the throne, are shown larger than everyone else, as also in other Near Eastern royal art. Do you think the way the sculptors portrayed the figures from the side is more or less artistic than the technique used by the Egyptian painters in the image from the *Book of the Dead* on page 2. Why? *(Courtesy of the Oriental Institute of the University of Chicago.)*

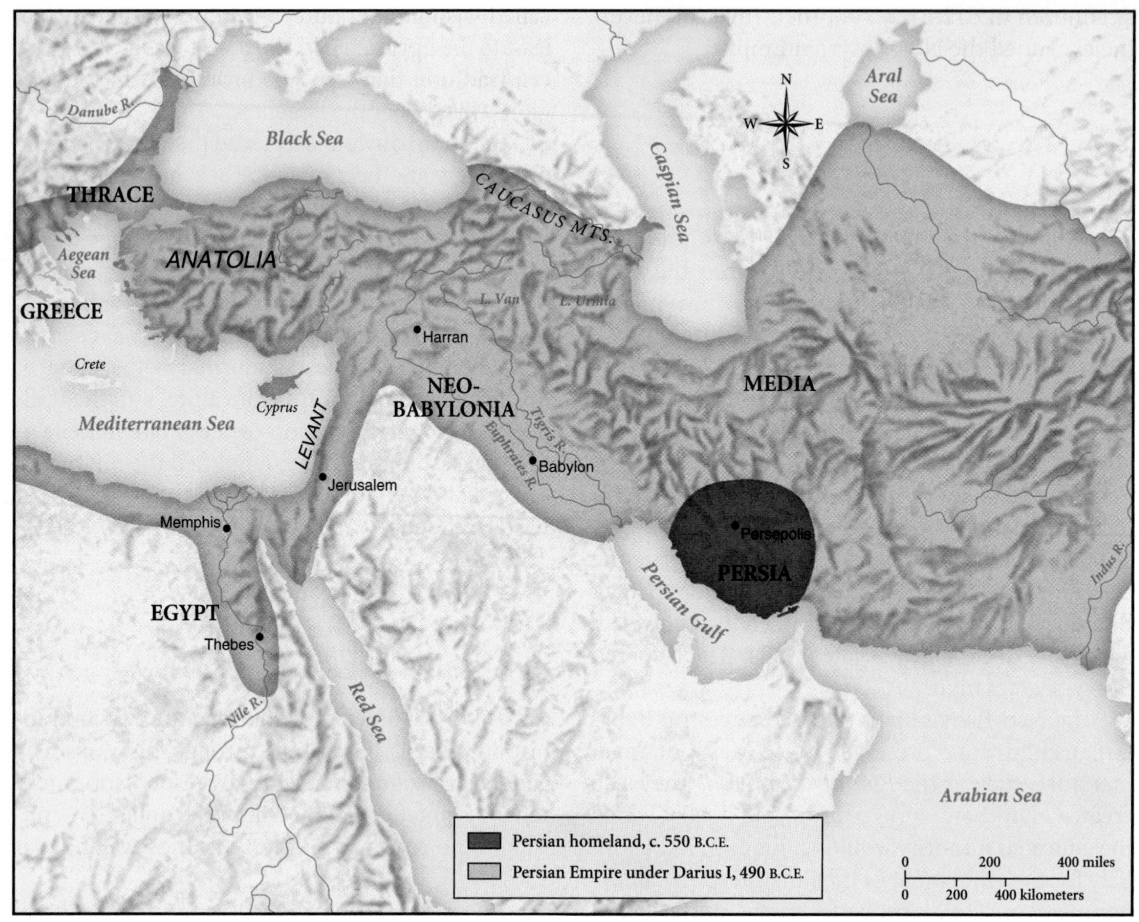

MAP 2.2 Expansion of the Persian Empire, c. 550–490 B.C.E.
Cyrus (r. 557–530 B.C.E.) founded the Persian Empire, which his successors expanded to be even larger than the Neo-Assyrian Empire that it replaced. The Persian kings made war outward from their inland center to gain coastal possessions for access to seaborne trade and naval bases. By late in the reign of Darius I (r. 522–486 B.C.E.), the Persian Empire had expanded eastward as far as the western edge of India, while to the west it reached Thrace, the eastern edge of Europe. Unlike their imperial predecessors, the Persian kings won their subjects' loyalty with tolerance of local customs and religion, although they treated rebels harshly.

to gain territory when he conquered Babylon in 539 B.C.E. Cyrus won local support there by presenting himself as the restorer of traditional religion. An ancient inscription has him proclaim: "I returned the statues of the gods [of Babylon] to their places. . . . Obeying the order of Marduk, the great lord, I put the gods of Sumer and Akkad in their homes."

Cyrus's successors expanded Persian rule via the same principles of military strength and cultural tolerance as foundations for maintaining order in an empire. At its height, the Persian Empire extended from Anatolia (today Turkey), the eastern Mediterranean coast, and Egypt on the west to present-day Pakistan on the east (Map 2.2). Since Persian kings believed that they had a divine right to rule everyone in the world, they never stopped trying to expand their empire.

Persian Royal Magnificence and Decentralized Rule

The Persian monarchy's revenues produced enormous wealth, and everything about the king emphasized his magnificence. His robes of purple outshone everyone else's; only he could step on the red carpets spread for him to walk on; his servants held their hands before their mouths in his presence so that he would not have to breathe the same air as they. As in other Near Eastern royal art, the Persian king was shown as larger than any other person in the sculpture adorning his immense palace at Persepolis. To display his concern for his loyal subjects as well as the gigantic scale of his resources, the king provided meals for fifteen thousand nobles and other guests every day—although he himself ate hidden from their view. Those who committed serious offenses against his laws or his

DOCUMENT

Excerpt from a Gatha

This excerpt from a Gatha *(one of the seventeen hymns believed to have been composed by Zarathustra) comes from the* Avesta, *the sacred scripture of Zoroastrianism. The dates of composition of the various parts of the Avesta are uncertain, but this text reflects Zoroastrians' belief in the divine power of their supreme god and creator of the world, Ahura Mazda, and in his loving and protective care for his worshippers.*

I announce and [will] complete [my worship] to Ahura Mazda, the creator, the radiant and glorious, the greatest and the best, the most beautiful, the most firm, the wisest, and the one of all whose body is the most perfect, who attains His ends the most infallibly, because of His Righteous Order, to Him who puts our minds in right order, who sends His joy-creating grace far and wide; who made us, and has fashioned us, and who has nourished and protected us, who is the most bounteous Spirit!

I announce and I (will) complete (my worship) to the Good Mind, and to Righteousness the Best, and to the Sovereignty which is to be desired, and to Piety the Bountiful, and to the two, the Universal Well-Being and Immortality. . . .

And I announce and complete my worship to all the stars . . . to the Moon . . . to the resplendent Sun . . . to Ahura Mazda . . . to the guardian spirits of the saints. . . .

And I announce and complete my worship to you, the Fire, O Ahura Mazda's son, together with all the fires, and to the good waters, even to all the waters made by Mazda, and to all the plants which Mazda made.

O all you lords, the greatest one, holy lords of the ritual order, if I have offended you by thought, or word or deed, whether with my will, or without intending error, I praise you [now the more] for this.

Source: *The Zend Avesta*, translated by James Darmesteter and L. H. Mills. Copyright © 1880, Oxford University Press.

Question to Consider

- **How does this song demonstrate the worshipper's understanding of his relationship to the supreme god?**

dignity the king punished brutally, mutilating their bodies and executing their families. Contemporary Greeks, in awe of the Persian monarch's power and his luxurious lifestyle, called him the Great King.

So long as his subjects — numbering in the millions and of many different ethnicities — remained peaceful, the king left them alone to live and worship as they pleased. The empire's smoothly functioning administrative structure sprang from Assyrian precedents: satraps (regional governors) ruled enormous territories with little interference from the kings. In this decentralized system, the governors' duties included keeping order, enrolling troops when needed, and sending revenues to the royal treasury.

Darius I (r. 522–486 B.C.E.) extended Persian power eastward to the western edge of India and westward to Thrace, northeast of Greece. This expansion created the Near East's greatest empire. Organizing this vast territory into provinces, Darius assigned each region taxes payable in the way best suited to its local economy — precious metals, grain, horses, slaves. He also required each region to send soldiers to the royal army. A network of roads and a courier system for royal mail provided communication among the far-flung provincial centers. The Greek historian Herodotus reported that neither snow, rain, heat, nor darkness slowed the couriers from completing their routes as swiftly as possible, a claim transformed centuries later into the U.S. Postal Service motto.

Persian Religion

Ruling as absolute autocrats, the Persian kings believed themselves superior to everyone. They claimed to be not gods but rather the agents of Ahura Mazda, the supreme god of Persia. As Darius I said in his autobiography, carved into a mountainside in three languages, "Ahura Mazda gave me kingship. . . . By the will of Ahura Mazda the provinces respected my laws."

Persian religion made Ahura Mazda the center of its devotion and took its doctrines from the teachings of the legendary prophet Zarathustra. (The religion is called Zoroastrianism today from Zoroaster, the Greek name for this holy man.) Zarathustra proclaimed Ahura Mazda to be "the father of Truth" and "creator of Good Thought," who demanded purity from his worshippers and promised help to those who lived with truthfulness and justice (see Document, "Excerpt from a Gatha," above). The most important doctrine of Zoroastrianism was **moral dualism**. This belief saw the world as the arena

moral dualism: The belief that the world is the arena for an ongoing battle for control between divine forces of good and evil.

for an ongoing battle between the two opposing divine forces of good and evil. Ahura Mazda, as the embodiment of good and light, constantly struggled against the evil darkness represented by the Satan-like figure Ahriman. Human beings had to choose between the way of the truth and the way of the lie, between purity and impurity. As in the judgment of the dead in ancient Egyptian religion, so too in Persian religion only those judged righteous after death made it across "the bridge of separation" to heaven and avoided falling from its narrow span into hell. Persian religion's emphasis on ethical behavior and on a supreme god had a lasting influence on others, especially the Israelites.

The Israelites, Origins to 539 B.C.E.

The Israelites' development of a monotheistic religion makes them a principal building block in the foundations of Western civilization, even though they never rivaled the political and military power of the great empires in the Near East. Their religion, known as Judaism, developed over a long time. It reflected influences from the Israelites' polytheistic neighbors in Canaan (ancient Palestine), but its ideas on the nature of a monotheistic divinity became a turning point in the history of religions.

Israelite Origins and the Bible

The influence of the Israelites on Western civilization came from the impact of the book that became their sacred scripture, the Hebrew Bible. This book deeply affected not only Judaism but also Christianity and, later, Islam. Unfortunately, no source provides definitive information on the historical background of the Israelites or their religion. The Bible tells stories to explain God's moral plan for the universe, not to give a full account of Israelite origins, and archaeology has not yielded a clear picture.

According to the Bible's account, the patriarch Abraham and his followers migrated from the Mesopotamian city of Ur to Canaan, perhaps around 1900 B.C.E. Once there, the Israelites continued to live as semi-nomads, tending flocks of animals on the region's scraggly grasslands and living in temporary tent settlements. They occasionally planted barley or wheat for a season or two and then moved on to new pastures. Traditionally believed to have been divided into twelve tribes, they never settled down or formed a political state in this period. The Canaanites remained the political and military power in the region.

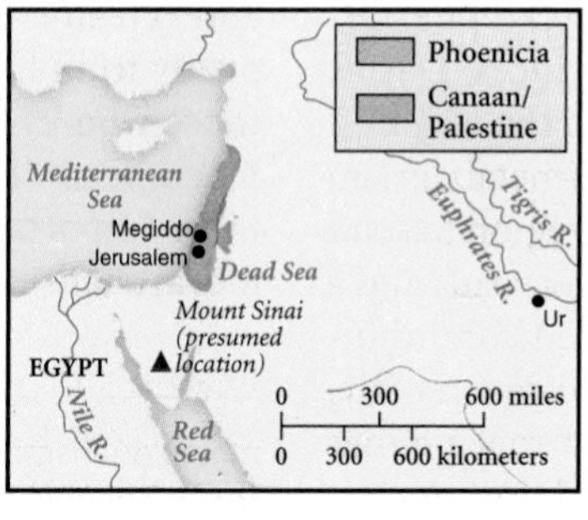

Phoenicia and Canaan/Palestine

Abraham's son Isaac moved his pastoral people to various locations to try to avoid disputes with local Canaanites over grazing rights. Isaac's son Jacob, the story continues, moved to Egypt late in life when his son Joseph brought Jacob and other relatives there to escape famine in Canaan. Joseph had previously used his intelligence and charisma to rise to an important position in the Egyptian administration. The biblical story of the movement of a band of Israelites to Egypt represents a crucial event in their early history, possibly reflecting a time when drought forced some Israelites to migrate gradually into the Nile delta of Egypt. They probably drifted in during the seventeenth or sixteenth century B.C.E. as part of the movement of peoples into Egypt at the time of Hyksos rule. By the thirteenth century B.C.E., the pharaohs had forced the Israelite men into slave-labor gangs for farming and for construction work on large building projects.

Although historians have found no secure evidence for the story, according to the biblical Book of Exodus, the Israelite deity, Yahweh, instructed Moses to lead the Israelites out of bondage in Egypt against the will of the king, perhaps around the mid-thirteenth century B.C.E. Yahweh sent ten plagues to compel the pharaoh to free the Israelites, but the king still tried to recapture them during their flight. Yahweh therefore miraculously parted the sea to allow them to escape eastward; the water swirled back together and drowned the pharaoh's army as it tried to follow.

Covenant, Monotheism, and Israelite Law

Next in the biblical narrative after the story of the exodus from Egypt comes the crucial event in the history of the Israelites: the formalizing of a contractual agreement (called a covenant in religious terminology) between them and their deity, who revealed himself to Moses on Mount Sinai in the desert northeast of Egypt. This contract between the Israelites and Yahweh specified that, in return for their worshipping him exclusively as their only god and living by his laws, Yahweh would make them his chosen people and lead them into a promised land of safety and prosperity. The form of the covenant with Yahweh followed the ancient Near Eastern tradition of treaties between a superior and subordinates, but its content differed from that of other ancient

Near Eastern religions because it made Yahweh the exclusive deity of his people.

This binding agreement demanded human obedience to divine law and promised punishment for unrighteousness. Yahweh described himself to Moses as "compassionate and gracious, patient, ever constant and true . . . forgiving wickedness, rebellion, and sin," yet he also declared that he was "one who punishes sons and grandsons to the third and fourth generation for their fathers' iniquity" (Exod. 34:6–7).

Because the earliest parts of the Hebrew Bible were probably composed about 950 B.C.E., more than three hundred years after the date implied in the Bible for the Israelites' exodus from Egypt, this narrative of the Israelite covenant and laws deals with a distant time for whose history there is no indisputable documentation. It is clear, however, that the early Israelites, like their neighbors in Canaan, originally worshipped a variety of gods, including spirits believed to reside in natural objects such as trees and stones. Yahweh may have originally been the deity of the tribe of Midian, to which Moses's father-in-law belonged. In the time of Moses, some Israelites, ignoring their leaders' instructions, continued to worship other local gods, such as Baal of Canaan.

The Hebrew Bible sets forth the religious and moral code the Israelites had to follow. The **Torah** (the first five books of the Hebrew Bible, called the Pentateuch by Christians) recorded numerous laws for righteous living. Most famous are the Ten Commandments, which required Israelites to worship Yahweh exclusively; make no idols; keep from misusing Yahweh's name; honor their parents; refrain from work on the seventh day of the week (the Sabbath); and abstain from murder, adultery, theft, lying, and covetousness. Many of the Israelites' laws shared the traditional form and content of earlier Mesopotamian laws, such as those of Hammurabi in Mesopotamia: if someone did a certain thing to another person, then a specified punishment was imposed on the perpetrator. For example, both Hammurabi's laws and Israelite law covered the case of an ox that had gored a person; the owner was penalized only if he had been warned about his beast's tendency to gore and had done nothing to restrain it. Also like Hammurabi's laws, Israelite law expressed an interest in the welfare of the poor as well as the rich. In addition, it secured protection for the lower classes and people without power, such as strangers, widows, and orphans. The correspondence between the Pentateuch and Hammurabi's laws, which date from centuries before the imputed date of the exodus, is of course an indication that Israelite legal traditions were not created in isolation from long-standing ideas about justice in Near Eastern societies.

Torah: The first five books of the Hebrew Bible, also referred to as the Pentateuch. It contains early Jewish law.

Goddess Figurines from Judah
Many small statues of this type, called Astarte figurines after a goddess of Canaan, have been found in private houses in Judah dating from about 800 to 600 B.C.E. Israelites evidently kept them as magical tokens to promote fertility and prosperity. The prophets fiercely condemned the worship of such figures as part of the development of Israelite monotheism and the abandoning of polytheism. Compare the shape of these figurines to the body shape of the Venus figurine on page P-5. What do you think these shapes represented? *(Collection of the Israel Antiquities Authority and Collection of The Israel Museum, Jerusalem. Photo © The Israel Museum, Jerusalem.)*

Israelite law and thus Israelite justice differed significantly from their Mesopotamian precedent, however, in applying the same rules and punishments to everyone, without regard to social rank. Israelite law also eliminated eye-for-an-eye punishment—a Mesopotamian tradition ordering, for example, that a rapist's wife be raped, or that the son of a builder be killed if his father's negligent work caused the death of someone else's son. Crimes against property did not carry the death penalty, as they frequently did in other Near Eastern societies. Israelite women and children had reduced legal rights compared to men: for example, wives had less freedom to divorce their husbands than husbands had to divorce their wives, much as in the laws of Hammurabi. Israelite laws also protected slaves against flagrant mistreatment by their masters. Slaves who lost an eye or a tooth from a beating were to be freed. Like free people, slaves enjoyed the right to rest on the Sabbath.

According to the Bible, the Israelites who fled from Egypt with Moses made their way back to Canaan, joining their relatives who had remained there and somehow carving out separate territories for themselves. The twelve Israelite tribes remained

Solomon's Walls at Megiddo
Rulers in the Near East often fought to control the city of Megiddo because it controlled an important pass along a main north-south route near the eastern Mediterranean coast. The Israelite king Solomon built strong fortification walls for it in the tenth century B.C.E., as recalled in the Hebrew Bible (1 Kings 9:15). A tunnel reaching hundreds of feet through rock to a spring hidden in a cave supplied water during a siege. Despite these defenses, the city later fell to the Egyptians and the Assyrians. *(Erich Lessing/Art Resource, NY.)*

politically distinct under the direction of separate leaders, called judges, until the eleventh century, when according to tradition their first monarchy emerged. Their monotheism gradually developed over the succeeding centuries.

The Consolidation of Israelite Monotheism Again, controversy rages among historians about the accuracy of the biblical account, according to which the Israelites achieved their first national organization with the creation of a monarchy in the late eleventh century B.C.E. Saul became their first king, and his successors David (r. 1010–970 B.C.E.) and Solomon (r. c. 961–922 B.C.E.) brought the Israelite kingdom to the height of its prosperity. The kingdom's wealth, based on international commerce conducted through its cities, was displayed above all in the great temple richly decorated with gold leaf that Solomon built in Jerusalem to be the house of Yahweh. Whatever one thinks about the truth of the details of these stories, the temple in Jerusalem and the sacrifices that took place there did become the center of the Israelites' religion.

The Israelites' initial unity and prosperity were short-lived. After Solomon's death, the monarchy split into two kingdoms: Israel in the north and Judah in the south. The Assyrians destroyed Israel in 722 B.C.E. and deported its population to Assyria. In 597 B.C.E., the Babylonians conquered Judah and captured its capital, Jerusalem. In 586 B.C.E., they destroyed the temple to Yahweh and banished the Israelite leaders, along with much of the population, to Babylon.

During their period of exile in Mesopotamia, the Israelites came into close contact with Zoroastrianism. Scholars strongly dispute the extent of influence that the religious ideas of this religion had on the beliefs of the exiled Israelites. Some argue that in reality the ideas of the Israelites influenced Zoroastrian religion. It is clear, however, that the religions of these two groups eventually (the timing is uncertain) came to share crucial concepts, such as the existence of God and Satan, angels and demons, God's day of judgment, and the arrival of a messiah. Even if we cannot make out the exact details of the effect on the Israelites of their exile in Babylon, it seems likely that this forced experience of living in a foreign culture would have altered their worldview.

When the Persian king Cyrus overthrew the Babylonians in 539 B.C.E., he permitted the Israelites to return to their part of Canaan. The Bible proclaimed Cyrus a messiah of the Israelites chosen by Yahweh as his "shepherd . . . to accomplish all his purpose" in restoring his people to their previous home (Isa. 44:28–45:1). This region was called Yehud, from the name of the southern Israelite kingdom, Judah. From this geographical term came the word *Jew*, a designation for the Israelites after their Babylonian exile. Cyrus allowed them to rebuild their main temple in Jerusalem and to practice their religion. After returning from exile, the Jews were forever a people subject to the political domination of various Near Eastern powers, except for a period of independence during the second and first centuries B.C.E.

Jewish prophets, both men and women, preached that their defeats were divine punishment for neglecting the Sinai covenant and mistreating their poor. Some prophets also predicted the coming end of the present world following a great crisis, a judgment by Yahweh, and salvation leading to a new and better world. This apocalypticism ("uncovering," or revelation), reminiscent of Babylonian prophetic wisdom literature, would later provide the worldview of Christianity. Yahweh would save the Israelite nation, the prophets thundered, only if Jews strictly observed divine law.

Jewish leaders therefore developed complex religious laws to maintain ritual and ethical purity in all aspects of life. Marrying non-Jews was forbidden, as was working on the Sabbath. Fathers had legal power over the household, subject to intervention by the male elders of the community; women gained honor as mothers. Only men could initiate divorce proceedings. Ethics applied not only to obvious crimes but also to financial dealings; cheating in business transactions was condemned. Jews had to pay taxes and offerings to support and honor the sanctuary of Yahweh, and they had to forgive debts every seventh year.

The Jews' hardships had taught them that their religious traditions and laws gave them the strength to survive even when separated from their homeland. Gradually, they created their monotheism by accepting their leaders' preaching that Yahweh was the only god and that they had to adhere to his divine will by obeying his laws. Jews retained their identity by following this religion, regardless of their personal fate or their geographical location. A remarkable outcome of these religious developments was that Jews who did not return to their homeland, instead choosing to remain in Babylon or Persia or Egypt, could maintain their Jewish identity by following Jewish law while living among foreigners. In this way, the **Diaspora** ("dispersion of population") came to characterize the history of the Jewish people.

Israelite monotheism made the preservation and understanding of a sacred text, the Bible, the center of religious life. The chief priests compiled an authoritative scripture by adding to the Torah the books of the prophets, such as Isaiah, and other writings, including Psalms and wisdom literature. Making scripture the focus of religion proved the most crucial development for the history not only of Judaism but also of Christianity and Islam, because these later religions made their own sacred texts—the Bible and the Qur'an, respectively—the centers of their belief and practice.

Although the ancient Israelites never formed a militarily powerful nation, their monotheistic religion created a new path for Western civilization. Through the continuing vitality of Judaism and its impact on the doctrines of Christianity and Islam, the early Jews passed on ideas—chiefly monotheism and the notion of a covenant bestowing a divinely ordained destiny on a people if they obey divine will—whose effects have endured to this day. These religious concepts constitute one of the most significant legacies to Western civilization from the Near East in the period 1000–500 B.C.E.

Diaspora (die ASS por a): The dispersal of the Jewish population from their homeland.

REVIEW QUESTION In what ways was religion important in the Near East from c. 1000 B.C.E. to c. 500 B.C.E.?

The Reemergence of Greek Civilization, 1000–750 B.C.E.

During the period of violence in 1200–1000 B.C.E., the Greeks lost the distinguishing marks of civilization: they no longer had unified states, prosperous large settlements, or writing. Thus, during their Dark Age (c. 1000–750 B.C.E.), they had to remake their civilization. Trade, cultural interaction, and technological innovation led to recovery: contact with the Near East promoted intellectual, artistic, and economic revival, while the introduction of metallurgy for making iron made farming more efficient. As conditions improved, a social elite distinguished by wealth and the competitive pursuit of individual excellence described in Homeric poetry replaced the hierarchy of Mycenaean times. In the eighth century B.C.E., the creation of the Olympic Games and the emphasis on justice in the poetry of Hesiod promoted the communal values that fueled the reemergence of Greek civilization. It also laid the foundation for a radically new form of political organization in which central authority was based on citizenship rather than on subjection to kings.

The Greek Dark Age

The fall of Mycenaean civilization brought to Greece the depressed economic conditions that so many people in other regions experienced during the worst years of their Dark Ages. One of the most startling indications of the severity of life in the Dark Age in Greece is that Greeks apparently lost their knowledge of writing when Mycenaean civilization fell. The Linear B script they had used to write Greek was difficult to master and probably known only by a few scribes, who used writing exclusively to track the flow of goods in and out of the palaces. When the Mycenaean states collapsed, the Greeks no longer needed scribes or writing.

The Greek Dark Age, 1000–750 B.C.E.

1000 B.C.E.	Almost all important Mycenaean sites except Athens destroyed by now
1000–900 B.C.E.	Greatest depopulation and economic loss
900–800 B.C.E.	Early revival of population and agriculture; beginning use of iron tools and weapons
800 B.C.E.	Greek trading contacts initiated with Al Mina in Syria
776 B.C.E.	First Olympic Games held
775 B.C.E.	Euboeans found trading post on island in the Bay of Naples
750 B.C.E.	Homeric poetry recorded in writing after Greeks learn to write again; Hesiod composes his poetry

MAP 2.3 Dark Age Greece, 1000–750 B.C.E.
During their Dark Age, Greeks lived in many fewer and smaller settlements than in the Bronze Age. It took centuries for the region as a whole to revive. Recent archaeological research, however, indicates that Greece was not as impoverished or as depopulated after the fall of the Mycenaean kingdoms as sometimes assumed. The many small ports along Greece's jagged coastline and the short distances between its islands allowed seafaring trade and communication to continue. By island-hopping, boats could make it safely across the Aegean Sea and beyond, keeping the routes open to the Near East.

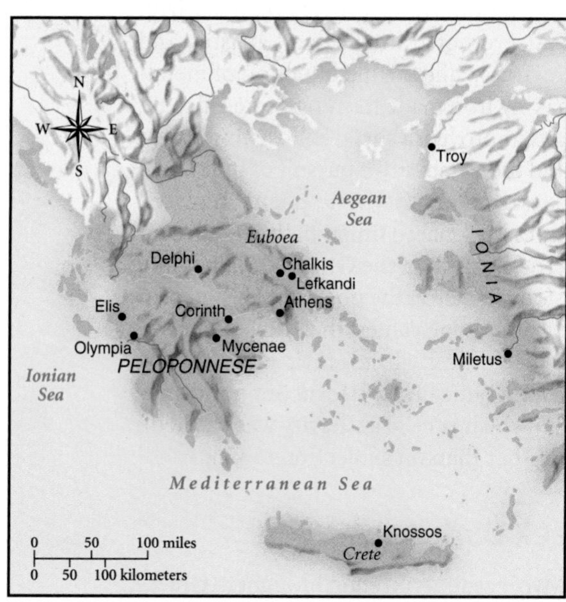

Only oral transmission kept Greek cultural traditions alive.

Archaeology reveals that the Mycenaean collapse meant that Greeks in the early Dark Age, although spread across roughly the same geographical area as before, cultivated much less land and had many fewer settlements (Map 2.3). No longer did powerful rulers sheltered in stone fortresses control redistributive economies. The number of ships carrying Greek adventurers, raiders, and traders dwindled. Large political states ceased to exist; people scratched out an existence as herders, shepherds, and subsistence farmers bunched in tiny settlements—as few as twenty people in many cases. The smaller population could not produce as much food as before, causing its numbers to drop still further as hunger and starvation killed many people. These two processes reinforced each other in a vicious circle, multiplying their negative effects.

With the decline of agriculture in their Dark Age, more Greeks than ever before made their living by herding animals. These herders necessarily no longer lived in permanent settlements: they needed to move their herds to new pastures once the animals had overgrazed their current location. Lucky ones might find a new spot where they could grow a crop of grain if they stayed long enough. In this transient lifestyle, people built only simple huts and kept few possessions. Unlike their Bronze Age ancestors, Greeks in the Dark Age had no monumental architecture, and they even lost an old tradition in their everyday art: they stopped including people and animals in their principal art form—paintings on ceramics—putting only nonfigural designs on their pots.

Trade, Innovation, and Recovery in Greece

Geography allowed the Greeks to continue seaborne trade with the civilizations of the eastern Mediterranean even during their Dark Age. Trade promoted cultural interaction, and the Greeks learned to write again about 800 B.C.E. They adopted the alphabet from the Phoenicians, seafaring traders from Canaan. Greeks changed and added letters to achieve independent representation of vowel sounds so that they could express their language and record their literature, beginning with Homer's and Hesiod's poetry in the eighth century B.C.E. Near Eastern art inspired Greeks to resume the production of ceramics with figural designs (as on the Corinthian vase on page 36). Seaborne commerce encouraged better-off Greeks to produce agricultural surpluses and goods they could trade for luxuries such as gold jewelry and gems from Egypt and Syria.

Most important, trade brought the new technology of iron metallurgy. The violence of 1200–1000 B.C.E. had interrupted the traditional trading routes for tin. Without tin, metalworkers could not forge bronze weapons and tools. To make up for this loss, smiths in the eastern Mediterranean devised technology to smelt iron ore. Greeks then learned this skill through their eastern trade contacts and mined their own iron ore, which was common in Greece. Iron eventually replaced bronze in many uses, above all for agricultural tools, swords, and spear points. The Greeks still used bronze for shields and armor, however, because it was easier to shape into thin, curved pieces.

The iron tools' lower cost allowed more people to acquire them. Because iron is harder than bronze, implements kept their sharp edges longer. Better and more plentiful farming implements of iron helped increase food production, which sustained population growth. In this way, technology imported from the Near East improved people's chances for survival and thus helped Greece recover from the Dark Age's depopulation.

The Greek Social Elite and the Homeric Ideal

With the Mycenaean rulers gone, leadership became an open competition in Dark Age Greece. Individuals who proved themselves excellent in action, words, charisma, and religious knowledge joined the social elite, enjoying higher prestige and authority in society. Competition as a social value defined Greek life. Excellence—***aretê*** in Greek—was earned by competing. Men competed with others for aretê as warriors and persuasive public speakers. Women won their highest aretê by being seen to manage a household of children, slaves, and storerooms that was more successful than those of struggling families. Members of the elite accumulated wealth by controlling agricultural land, which people of lower status worked for them as tenants or slaves.

The poems of **Homer**, Greece's first and most famous author, reflect the social elite's ideals, especially the competition for aretê. The Greeks believed that Homer was a blind poet from Ionia (today Turkey's western coast) who composed the epic poems *The Iliad* and *The Odyssey*. Most modern scholars believe that Homer was the last in a long line of poets who, influenced by Near Eastern mythology, had been singing these stories for centuries, orally transmitting cultural values from one generation to the next. *The Iliad* tells the story of the Greek army in the Trojan War. Camped before the walls of Troy for ten years, the heroes of the army compete for glory and riches by raiding the countryside, dueling Troy's best fighters, and quarreling with one another over prestige and booty. The greatest Greek warrior is Achilles, who proves his aretê by choosing to die in battle rather than accept the gods' offer to return home safely but without glory. *The Odyssey* recounts not only the hero Odysseus's ten-year adventure sailing home after the fall of Troy but also the struggle of his wife, Penelope, to protect their household from the schemes of rivals. Penelope proves her aretê by outwitting jealous neighbors to preserve her family's prosperity for her husband's return.

---

aretê **(ah reh TAY):** The Greek value of competitive individual excellence.

Homer: Greece's first and most famous author, who composed *The Iliad* and *The Odyssey*.

A Rich Woman's Model Granary from the Dark Age
This clay model of storage containers for grain was found in a woman's tomb in Athens from about 850 B.C.E. It apparently symbolizes the surpluses that the woman and her family were able to accumulate and indicates that she was wealthy by the standards of her time. The geometric designs painted on the pottery are characteristic of Greek art in this period, when human and animal figures were not used. By the Archaic Age, figures returned to Greek art, the result of Near Eastern influence. Contrast the lively animals painted some two hundred years later on the Corinthian vase illustrated at the opening of this chapter (page 36). *(American School of Classical Studies at Athens: Agora Excavations.)*

Homer reveals that the white-hot emotions inflamed by the competition for excellence could provoke a disturbing level of inhumanity. Achilles, in preparing to duel Hector, the prince of Troy, brutally rejects the Trojan's proposal that the winner return the loser's corpse to his family and friends: "Do wolves and lambs agree to cooperate? No, they hate each other to the roots of their being." The victor, Achilles, mutilates Hector's body. When Hecuba, the queen of Troy, sees this outrage, she bitterly shouts, "I wish I could sink my teeth into his liver in his guts to eat it raw." The endings of Homer's poems suggest that the gods could sometimes help people achieve reconciliation after violent conflict, but the amount of human suffering in his stories makes it clear that the pursuit of excellence can come at a high price.

As in Homer, the real world of the Greek Dark Age had a small but wealthy social elite. On the island of Euboea, for example, archaeologists have discovered the tenth-century B.C.E. grave of a couple who took such enormous riches with them to the next world that the woman's body was covered in gold ornaments. They had done well in the competition for prestige and wealth; most people of the time were, by comparison, desperately poor. Those who scratched out a hard living could only dream of

Athletic Competition
Greek vase painters often showed male athletes in action or training, perhaps in part because athletes were customers who would buy pottery with such scenes. As in this painting of an Athenian foot race from around 530 B.C.E., the athletes were usually shown nude, which is how they competed, revealing their superb physical condition and strong musculature. Being in excellent shape was a man's ideal for several reasons: it was regarded as beautiful, it enabled him to compete for individual glory in athletic contests, and it allowed him to fulfill his community responsibility by fighting as a well-conditioned soldier in the city-state's citizen militia. Why do you think the figure at the far left does not have a full beard? (See the caption on page 69 for a hint.) *([Euphiletos Painter [sixth century B.C.E.], Panathenaic prize amphora, ca. 530 B.C.E. Reverse. Terracotta, H. 24½ in. [62.2 cm.]. Archaic Greek, Attic. Rogers Fund, 1914. [14.130.12]. The Metropolitan Museum of Art, New York, U.S.A. Image copyright © The Metropolitan Museum of Art/Art Resource, NY.)*

the luxurious life and rich goods they heard about in Homer's poems.

The Values of the Olympic Games

Greece had recovered enough population and prosperity by the eighth century B.C.E. to begin creating new forms of social and political organization. The most vivid evidence is the founding of the Olympic Games, traditionally dated to 776 B.C.E. This international religious festival showcased the competitive value of aretê.

Every four years, the games took place in a huge sanctuary dedicated to Zeus, the king of the gods, at Olympia, in the northwestern Peloponnese. Male athletes from elite families vied in sports, imitating the aretê needed for war: running, wrestling, jumping, and throwing. Horse and chariot racing were added to the program later, but the main event remained a two-hundred-yard sprint, the *stadion* (hence our word *stadium*). The athletes competed as individuals, not on national teams as in the modern Olympic Games. Winners received not money but rather a garland made from wild olive leaves to symbolize the prestige of victory.

The Olympics illustrate Greek notions of proper behavior for each gender: crowds of men flocked to the games, but women were prohibited on pain of death. Women had their own separate Olympic festival on a different date in honor of Hera, queen of the gods. Only unmarried women could compete. These separate games existed because most Greeks believed it was not proper for men and women to observe nonslave strangers of the opposite gender wearing no or little clothing. In later times, professional athletes dominated the Olympics, earning their living from appearance fees and prizes at games held throughout the Greek world. The most famous winner was Milo, from Croton in Italy. Six-time Olympic wrestling champion, he stunned audiences with demonstrations of strength such as holding his breath until his veins expanded to snap a cord tied around his head.

Although the Olympics existed to glorify individual competitive excellence by identifying winners and losers, the games' organization reveals an important trend under way in Greek society: they were open to any socially elite Greek male good enough to compete and to any male spectator who could journey there. These rules represented beginning steps toward a concept of collective Greek identity. Remarkably for a land so often torn by internal wars, once every four years an international truce of several weeks was declared so that competitors and fans from all Greek communities could safely travel to and from Olympia. The Olympic Games, then, helped channel the competition for individual excellence into a new context of social cooperation and community values, essential preconditions for the creation of Greece's new political form, the city-state ruled by citizens.

Homer, Hesiod, and Divine Justice in Greek Myth

The Greeks' belief in divine justice inspired them to develop the cooperative values that remade their civilization. This idea came not from scripture—Greeks had none—but from poetry that told myths about the gods and goddesses and their relationships to humans. Myths could seem fantastically unrealistic, but at the same time they taught lessons about the nature of life in a world that Greeks saw as under the control of gods whose purposes were difficult to understand. Different myths often provided different lessons, teaching that human beings could not expect to have a clear understanding of the gods and had to make choices on their own about how to live.

Homer's poems reveal that the gods had plans for human existence. Zeus's will, for example, motivated the Trojan War's tragic events. This myth did not specify, however, that Zeus's purpose was just. Bellerophon, for example, the wronged hero whose brave efforts won him a princess bride and a kingdom, ended up losing everything. He became, in Homer's words, "hated by the gods and wandering the land alone, eating his heart out, a refugee fleeing from the haunts of men." The poem gives no explanation for this tragedy and therefore no reason to believe that a concern for justice motivated the gods in this case.

Hesiod's poetry, by contrast, reveals how other myths describing divine support for justice contributed to the feeling of community that motivated the creation of Greece's new social and political organization. Hesiod's vivid stories, which originated in Near Eastern creation myths, show that existence, even for deities, always involved struggle, sorrow, and violence. These stories also reveal, however, that the divine order of the universe could sometimes include a concern for justice.

Hesiod's epic poem *Theogony* (whose title means "genealogy of the gods") recounted the birth of the race of gods—including Sky and numerous others—from the intercourse of primeval Chaos and Earth. Hesiod explained that when Sky began to imprison his siblings, Earth persuaded her fiercest son, Kronos, to overthrow him violently because "Sky first schemed to do shameful things." When Kronos later began to swallow his own children to avoid sharing power with them, his wife, Rhea (who was also his sister), had their son Zeus violently force his father from power.

In *Works and Days*, his poem on conditions in his own time, Hesiod identified Zeus as the source of justice in human affairs, a force that punished evildoers: "Zeus commanded that fishes and wild beasts and birds should eat each other, for they have no justice; but to human beings he has given justice, which is far the best." People, however, were responsible for administering justice, and in the eighth century B.C.E. this meant the male social elite. They controlled their family members and household servants. Hesiod insisted that a leader should demonstrate aretê by employing persuasion instead of force: "When his people in their assembly get on the wrong track, he gently sets matters right, persuading them with soft words."

Hesiod complained that many elite leaders in his time failed to exercise their power in this way, instead creating conflict between themselves and the peasants—free proprietors of small farms owning a slave or two, oxen to work their fields, and a limited amount of goods acquired by trading the surplus of their crops. Hesiod warned "bribe-devouring chiefs," who used "crooked judgments" to settle disputes among their followers and neighbors, to fear divine justice. The outrage that peasants felt at not receiving equal treatment helped push the gradual movement toward a new form of social and political organization in Greece.

REVIEW QUESTION What factors proved most important in the Greek recovery from the troubles of the Dark Age?

The Creation of the Greek City-State, 750–500 B.C.E.

The Greek Dark Age led to what historians call the Archaic Age (c. 750–500 B.C.E.). This new era saw the creation of the Greek city-state—the **polis**—an independent community of citizens inhabiting

---

polis: The Greek city-state, an independent community of citizens not ruled by a king.

a city and the countryside around it. Greece's geography, dominated by mountains and islands, promoted the creation of hundreds of independent city-states in its heartland in and around the Aegean Sea. From these original locations, Greeks dispersed widely around the Mediterranean to settle hundreds more trading communities that often grew into new city-states. Individuals' drive for profit from trade, especially in raw materials, and for free farmland probably started this process of founding new settlements.

Though it took varying forms, the Greek polis differed from the Mesopotamian city-state primarily in being a community of citizens making laws and administering justice among themselves versus being a collection of inhabitants subject to a king. Another difference was that poor citizens of Greek city-states enjoyed a rough legal and political equality with the rich. Not different, however, were the subordination of women and the subjugation of slaves. Also, though this new direction in social and political organization gave the poor a share of power in the community, it was never able to eliminate tension between the interests of the social elite and those of ordinary people.

The Physical Environment of the Greek City-State

Culturally, Greeks identified with one another because they spoke the same language and worshipped the same gods. Still, the ancient Greeks never became a nation in the political sense because their many city-states never unified. Their homeland lay in and around the Aegean Sea, a section of the Mediterranean between modern Greece and Turkey dotted with large and small islands (Map 2.4).

The mountainous geography of Greece tended to isolate its communities and contributed to the city-states' often hostile relations. A single island could be home to multiple city-states; Lesbos, for example, had five. Because few city-states had enough farmland to support many people, most of them had populations of only several hundred to several thousand. Some that had revenues from international trade, like Athens or Corinth, grew to be much larger.

Only the sea offered practical long-distance transportation in Greece. Greek rivers were little more than creeks, while land travel was slow and expensive because rudimentary dirt paths and dry riverbeds provided the only roads. The most plentiful resource was timber from the mountains for building houses and ships. Deposits of metal ore were scattered throughout Greek territory, as were clays suitable for pottery and sculpture. Various quarries of fine stone such as marble provided material for special buildings and works of art. The uneven distribution of these resources meant that some areas were considerably wealthier than others.

None of the mountains wrinkling the Greek landscape rose higher than ten thousand feet, but their steep slopes limited agriculture. Only 20 to 30 percent of the total land area could be farmed. The scarcity of level terrain in most areas made it impossible to raise large herds of cattle and horses. Pigs, sheep, and goats were the common livestock, and the domestic chicken had been introduced from the Near East by the seventh century B.C.E. The Mediterranean climate (intermittent heavy rain during a few months and hot, dry summers) limited a farmer's options, as did the fragility of the environment. Grazing livestock, for example, could be so hard on plant life that winter downpours would wash away the shallow topsoil. Because the amount of annual precipitation varied greatly, farming was a precarious business of boom and bust. People preferred wheat, but since that grain was expensive to cultivate, the cereal staple of the Greek diet became barley. Wine grapes and olives were the other most important crops.

Trade and "Colonization," 800–580 B.C.E.

A desire for greater prosperity led Greeks to engage in long-distance trade by sea throughout the Mediterranean region. Greece's jagged coastline made sea travel practical: almost every community lay within forty miles of the Mediterranean Sea. But sailors faced dangers from pirates and, especially, storms. Seasonal winds and fierce gales almost ruled out sea travel during winter. Sailors tried to hug the coast, hopping from island to island and putting in to shore at night, but sometimes the drive for profit required long, nonstop voyages over open waters. As Hesiod commented, merchants took to the sea "because an income means life to poor mortals, but it is a terrible fate to die among the waves."

The search for metals and other scarce resources took traders far from home, and also brought them into frequent contact with other cultures. *The Odyssey* describes the basic strategy of this commodity trading, when the goddess Athena appears disguised as a metal trader: "I am here . . . with my ship and crew on our way across the wine-dark sea to foreign lands in search of copper; I am carrying iron now." By 800 B.C.E., the Mediterranean swarmed with entrepreneurs of many nationalities. The Phoenicians established settlements as far west as Spain's Atlantic coast to gain access to inland mines there. Their

North African settlement at Carthage (modern Tunis) would become one of the Mediterranean's most powerful cities in later times, dominating commerce west of Italy.

Greeks energetically joined this seaborne competition for profit as the scale of trade soared near the end of the Dark Age: archaeologists have found only two tenth-century B.C.E. Greek pots that were carried abroad, but eighth-century pottery has turned up at more than eighty foreign sites. By 750 B.C.E. (or earlier—the evidence is hard to date), Greeks had begun to settle far from their homeland, sometimes living in others' settlements, especially those of the Phoenicians in the western Mediterranean, and sometimes establishing trading posts of their own, as on an island in the Bay of Naples. Everywhere they traded with the local populations, such as the Etruscans in central Italy, who imported large amounts of Greek goods, as the vases found in their tombs reveal. Greeks staying abroad for the long term would also cultivate vacant land, gradually building permanent communities. Traders were not the only Greeks to leave home. As the population expanded following the Dark Age, a shortage of farmland in Greece drove some poor farmers abroad to find fields they could work. Apparently only males left home on trading and land-hunting expeditions, so they had to find wives wherever they settled, either through peaceful negotiation or by kidnapping.

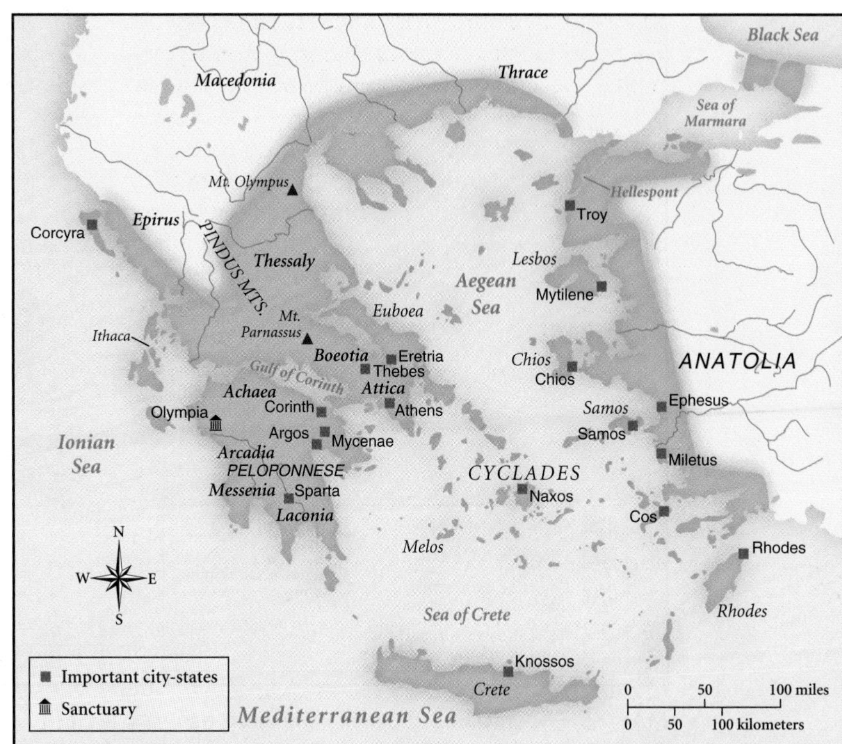

MAP 2.4 Archaic Greece, 750–500 B.C.E.
The Greek heartland lay in and around the Aegean Sea, in what is today the nation of Greece and the western edge of the nation of Turkey (ancient Anatolia). The "mainland," where Athens, Corinth, and Sparta are located, is the southernmost tip of the mountainous Balkan peninsula. The many islands of the Aegean area were home mainly to small city-states, with the exception of the large islands just off the western Anatolian coast, which were home to populous ones.

By about 580 B.C.E., Greek settlements had spread westward to Spain, present-day southern France, southern Italy, and Sicily; southward to North Africa; and eastward to the Black Sea coast (Map 2.5). The settlements in southern Italy and Sicily, such as Naples and Syracuse, eventually became so large and powerful that this region was called Magna Graecia ("Great Greece"). Its communities became rivals of Carthage for commercial dominance in the western Mediterranean.

Fewer Greeks settled in the eastern Mediterranean, perhaps because the monarchies there restricted immigration. Still, a Greek trading station had sprung up in Syria by 800 B.C.E., and in the seventh century B.C.E. the Egyptians permitted Greek merchants to settle in a coastal town. These close contacts with eastern Mediterranean peoples paid cultural as well as economic dividends. In addition to inspiring Greeks to reintroduce figures into their painting, Near Eastern art gave them models for statues: they began sculpting images that stood stiffly and stared straight ahead, imitating Egyptian statuary. (See "Seeing History," page 55.) When the improving economy of the later Archaic Age allowed Greeks again to afford monumental architecture in stone, their rectangular temples on platforms with columns reflected Egyptian architectural designs.

Historians have traditionally called the Greeks' settlement process in this era colonization, but recent research questions this term's accuracy because the word *colonization* implies the process by which modern European governments officially installed dependent settlements and regimes abroad. The evidence for these Greek settlements suggests rather that private entrepreneurship created most of them. Official state involvement was minimal, at least in the beginning. Most commonly, a Greek city-state in the homeland would establish ties with a settlement originally set up by its citizens privately and then claim it as its colony only after the community had grown into an economic success. Few instances are clearly recorded in which a Greek city-state sent out a group to establish a formally organized colony abroad.

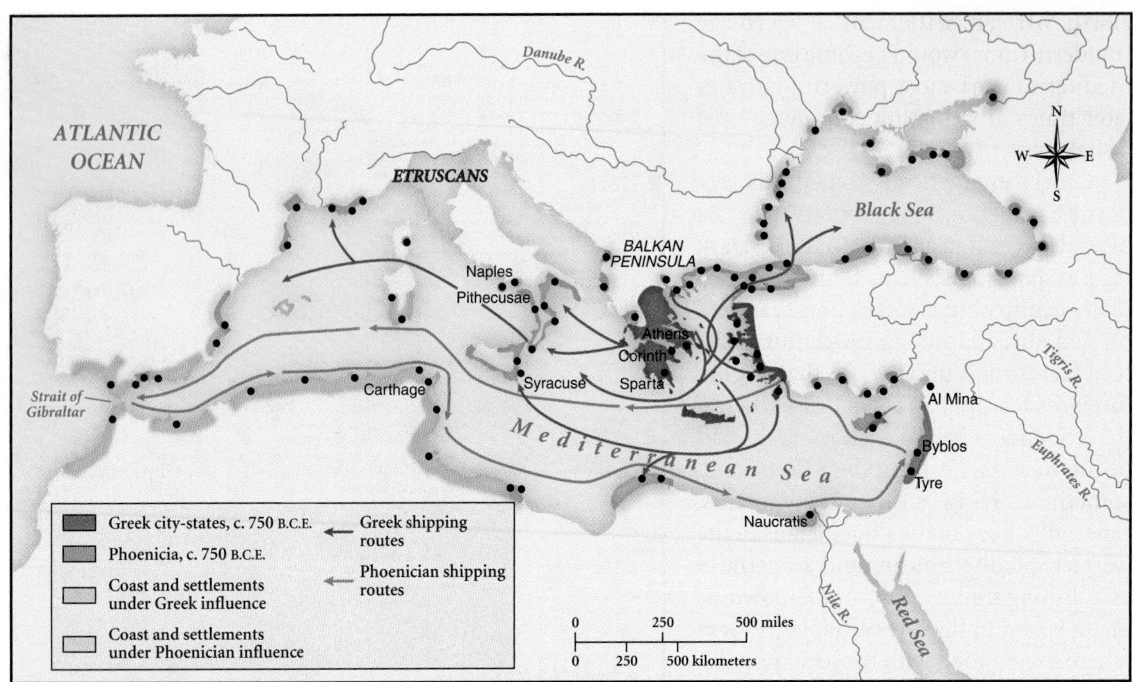

MAP 2.5 Phoenician and Greek Expansion, 750–500 B.C.E.
The Phoenicians were early explorers and settlers of the western Mediterranean. By 800 B.C.E. they had already founded the city of Carthage, which would become the main commercial power in the region. During the Archaic Age, groups of adventurous Greeks followed the Phoenicians' lead and settled all around the Mediterranean, hoping to improve their economic prospects by trade and farming. Sometimes they moved into previously established Phoenician settlements; sometimes they founded their own. Some Greek city-states established formal ties with new settlements or sent out their own expeditions to try to establish loyal colonies. | **Where did Phoenicians predominantly settle, and where did Greeks?**

Citizenship and Freedom in the Greek City-State

The creation of the polis filled the political vacuum left by Mycenaean civilization's fall. The Greek city-state was unique because it was based on the concept of citizenship for all its free inhabitants, rejected monarchy as its central authority, and made justice the responsibility of the citizens. Moreover, except in tyrannies (in which one man seized control of the city-state), at least some degree of shared governing was normal. This principle was manifest as early as the seventh century B.C.E., when the polis of Dreros on Crete inscribed on stone a law setting a term limit on its head judicial office, thereby ensuring that no single individual could dominate this crucial position.

Power sharing reached its widest form in democratic Greek city-states. Some historians argue that knowledge of the older cities on Cyprus and in Phoenicia influenced the Greeks in creating their new political systems. Since monarchs dominated their subjects in those eastern states, however, this theory cannot explain the origin of citizenship in all Greek city-states and the sharing of power in most. The most famous ancient analyst of Greek politics and society, the philosopher Aristotle (384–322 B.C.E.), insisted that the forces of nature had created the city-state: "Humans are beings who by nature live in a city-state." Anyone who existed outside such a community, Aristotle remarked, must be either a simple fool or superhuman. The polis's innovation in making shared power the basis of government did not immediately change the course of history—monarchy later became once again the most common form of government in ancient Western civilization—but it was important as proof that power sharing was a workable system of political organization.

Religion in the Greek City-State

Like all earlier ancient communities, Greek city-states were officially religious communities. As well as worshipping many deities, each city-state honored a particular god or goddess as its special protector, such as Athena at Athens. Different communities could choose the same deity: Sparta, Athens's chief rival in later times, also chose Athena as its defender. Greeks envisioned the twelve most important gods banqueting atop Mount Olympus, the

SEEING HISTORY

The Shift in Sculptural Style from Egypt to Greece

As Greek civilization revived during the Archaic Age (750–500 B.C.E.), artists took inspiration from the older civilizations of Egypt and the Near East, with sculpture in particular emerging as an important mode of cultural expression. Greek sculptors carved freestanding *kouros* ("young male") statues whose poses recalled the Egyptian style that remained unchanged for two thousand years: an erect posture, a striding leg, and a calm facial expression staring straight ahead. And yet important differences, both religious and stylistic, exist between Egyptian statuary and the Greek sculpture influenced by it.

Kaemheset (shown on the left) held a high government position during the Old Kingdom as Egypt's chief architect and supervisor of sculptors. Croesus (on the right) was a warrior from Athens who died in battle; the inscription on the base of his statue proclaimed: "Stand and mourn at this monument of Croesus, now dead; raging Ares [the Greek war god] destroyed him as he battled in the front ranks." Both statues were painted in bright colors (traces of red survive on Croesus's statue); Kaemheset's lively decoration remains because it stood inside his closed tomb, while Croesus's stood outside. Croesus's statue differs from Kaemheset's in that it portrays him nude, even though warriors went into battle wearing armor. What do you think could have been the reasons for placing statues inside or outside tombs and for portraying their subjects clothed or nude?

Look more closely at the details of the figures — musculature, hair, hands, facial expression, stride. What stylistic similarities do you see? Art historians have argued that, despite the similarities, the *kouros* statues of Greece's Archaic period already show signs of the increasing naturalism and idealization of the human body that would characterize the later Greek classical style (see the illustration on page 93). What evidence do you see of that in the differences between the two sculptures?

Question to Consider

- **What cultural factors do you think could account for Egyptian statues keeping the same style over time, while the style of Greek statues changed?**

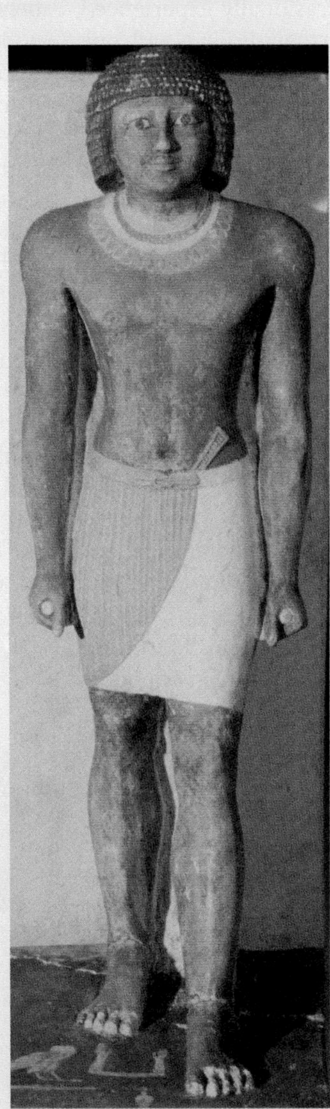

Limestone Statue of Kaemheset, Old Kingdom Egypt, c. 2400 B.C.E. *(Borromeo/Art Resource, NY.)*

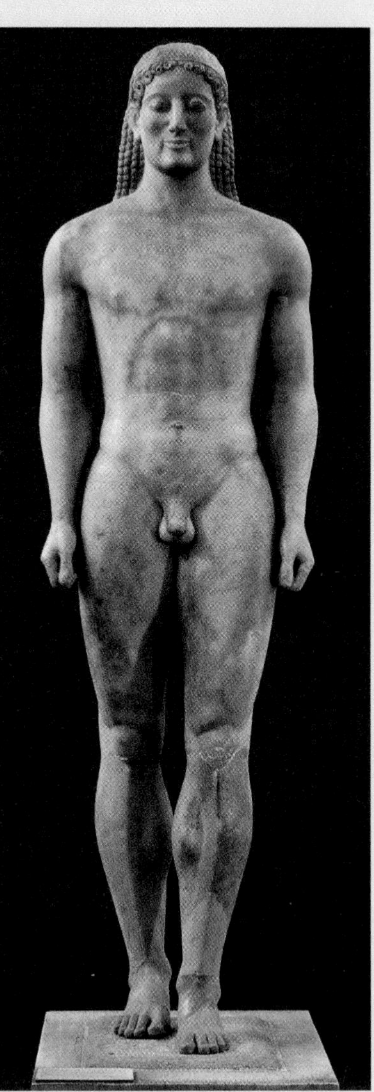

Marble Statue of Croesus, Archaic Age Greece, c. 530–520 B.C.E. *(The Art Archive/National Archeological Museum, Athens/Gianni Dagli Orti.)*

highest peak in mainland Greece. Zeus headed this pantheon; the others were Hera, his wife; Aphrodite, goddess of love; Apollo, sun god; Ares, war god; Artemis, moon goddess; Athena, goddess of wisdom and war; Demeter, earth goddess; Dionysus, god of pleasure, wine, and disorder; Hephaestus, fire god; Hermes, messenger god; and Poseidon, sea god. Like Homer's warriors, the Olympian gods were competitive, both with one another and with human beings, and they punished any disrespect. "I am well aware that the gods are competitively jealous and disruptive towards humans," remarked the sixth-century Athenian statesman Solon. The Greeks believed that their gods occasionally experienced temporary pain or sadness in their dealings with one another but were immune to permanent suffering because they were immortal.

Greek religion's core belief was that humans, both as individuals and as communities, must honor the gods to thank them for blessings received and to receive more blessings in return. Furthermore, the Greeks believed that the gods sent both good and bad into the world. The relationship between gods and humans generated sorrow as well as joy, punishment in the here and now, and only a limited hope for favored treatment in this life and in the underworld after death for the gods' favorites. Ordinary Greeks did not expect the gods to take them to a paradise at some future time when evil forces would be eliminated forever.

The idea of reciprocity between gods and humans underlay the Greek understanding of the nature of the gods. Deities did not love humans. Rather, they protected people who paid them honor and did not offend them. Gods could punish offenders by sending disasters such as floods, famines, earthquakes, epidemic diseases, and defeats in battle.

City-states honored gods by sacrificing animals such as cattle, sheep, goats, and pigs; decorating their sanctuaries with works of art; and celebrating festivals with songs, dances, prayers, and processions. A seventh-century B.C.E. bronze statuette, which a man named Mantiklos gave to a sanctuary of Apollo, makes clear why individuals offered such gifts. On its legs the donor inscribed his understanding of the transaction, using one of the god's titles: "Mantiklos gave this from his share to the Far Darter of the Silver Bow; now you, Apollo, do something for me in return."

People's greatest religious difficulty came in anticipating what might offend a deity. Mythology hinted at the gods' expectations of proper human behavior. For example, the Greeks told stories of the gods demanding hospitality for strangers or proper burial for family members. Other acts such as performing a sacrifice improperly, violating the sanctity of a temple area, or breaking an oath or sworn agreement also counted as disrespect for the gods. People believed that the deities were generally not concerned with most other crimes, which humans had to police themselves. Homicide, however, was such a serious offense that the gods were thought to punish it by casting a miasma (ritual contamination) on the murderer and on all those around him or her. Unless the members of the affected group purified themselves by punishing the murderer, they could all expect to suffer divine punishment, such as bad harvests or disease. In this way, the divine penalty for failing to punish the crime was extended to the entire community.

Oracles, dreams, divination, and the interpretations of prophets provided clues about what hu-

A Greek Woman at an Altar

This red-figure vase painting (contrast the black-figure vase on page 36) from the center of a large drinking cup shows a woman in rich clothing pouring a libation to the gods onto a flaming altar. In her other arm, she carries a religious object that has not been securely identified. This scene illustrates the most important and frequent role of women in Greek public life: participating in religious ceremonies, both at home and in community festivals. Greek women (and men) commonly wore sandals; why do you think they are usually depicted without shoes in vase paintings? *(Attributed to Makron [painter] and Hieron [potter], [Greek, from Athens], Kylix [Drinking Vessel], detail, Tondo:* Woman Sacrificing at an Altar, *ca. 490–480 B.C.E., wheel-thrown, slip-decorated earthenware, red-figure technique, h. 4 7/16 in. [11.3 cm.]; diam. at lip 11 5/16 in. [28.7 cm.]; diam. with handles 14¼ in. [36.2 cm.]. Toledo Museum of Art [Toledo, Ohio], Purchased with funds from the Libbey Endowment, Gift of Edward Drummond Libbey [1972.55].)*

DOCUMENT

Zaleucus's Law Code for a Greek City-State in Seventh-Century B.C.E. Italy

Zaleucus from the Greek city-state of Locri, in southern Italy, became the most famous early Greek lawmaker for his creation of a new law code for his community around 650 B.C.E. He founded his law code on belief in the gods as benefactors of human life. Some of his laws imposed harsh penalties for crimes, literally incorporating the eye-for-an-eye principle of equivalent punishment known from much earlier Mesopotamian law codes. Other laws took a different approach, as shown below. The Locrians respected Zaleucus's lawgiving so highly that three hundred years later they still required anyone who wished to change a law to make the proposal with a noose around his neck. If his proposal failed, he was strangled on the spot.

As you read, consider this: Do you think that fear of public shame or humiliation is a strong enough deterrent for certain crimes? If so, is it acceptable to use such a fear to change people's behavior?

Zaleucus's family came from Locri in Italy, and he was from the upper class. He was a student of the philosopher Pythagoras. Gaining a high reputation in his homeland, he was chosen as lawmaker. Creating a new law code from the foundation up, he began, first of all, with the gods of the heavens.

Immediately in the introduction to the entire code he said that the inhabitants of the city first of all must accept and believe that gods exist, and that, using their minds to inspect the heavens and their beautiful arrangement and order, they should judge that these things had been arranged not by chance or by human beings. Also, the inhabitants must worship the gods as being responsible for everything fine and good in life. They must keep their souls pure from every kind of wrongdoing, believing that the gods rejoice not at the sacrifices or expensive gifts of bad people, but at the just and fine ways of life of good men.

After urging the citizens in this introduction to pious worshipping and justice, he added the command that they should not regard a fellow citizen as an enemy with whom they could never be reconciled. Serious conflict should be conducted in such a way that they could come to a settlement and friendship. Anyone who behaves contrary to this should be considered by the citizens to be savage and wild in his soul. He instructed the officials not to be self-willed or arrogant, and not to give legal judgments based on hatred or friendship.

Among his various laws he came up with many on his own very wisely and extraordinarily. For, although everywhere else women who behaved badly were made to pay fines in money, Zaleucus corrected their out-of-control behavior with an ingenious penalty. He wrote the following: a freeborn woman may not be accompanied by more than one female slave, unless she is drunk; she may not leave the city during the night, unless she is committing adultery; she may not wear gold jewelry or clothing with a woven purple border, unless she is a hired "companion." A man may not wear a ring gleaming with gold or a cloak in the luxurious style of the city-state of Miletus unless he is partying with a "companion" or committing adultery.

In this way, with his (on the surface) shameful removal of penalties, he easily turned people away from harmful luxury and out-of-control habits. For no one wanted to be the object of ridicule among the citizens by seeming to approve of shameful out-of-control behavior.

He made other fine laws, such as those on contracts and other sources of disputes in life.

Source: Diodorus Siculus, *Library of History*, Book 12, chapter 20. Translation by Thomas R. Martin.

Question to Consider

■ **What presumptions about appropriate behavior for women and men are embedded in these laws? Why do you think this is so?**

mans might have done to anger the gods. The most important oracle was at Delphi, in central Greece, where a priestess in a trance provided Apollo's answers—in the form of riddles that had to be interpreted—to questions posed by city-states as well as individuals, who paid a fee for the information. Competition to consult the Delphic oracle concerning the will of the gods could be fierce because the priestess gave answers only on a limited number of days each year.

City-states and individuals alike paid respect to each god and goddess through a **cult**, a set of official, publicly funded religious activities for each deity overseen by priests and priestesses. To fulfill their religious obligations, people prayed, sang hymns of praise, offered sacrifices, and presented gifts at the deity's sanctuary. In these holy places a person could honor and thank the deities for blessings and beg them for relief when misfortune struck the community or the individual. People could also offer sacrifices at home with the household gathered around; sometimes the family's slaves were allowed to participate.

---

cult: In ancient Greece, a set of official, publicly funded religious activities for a deity overseen by priests and priestesses.

Priests and priestesses chosen from the citizen body performed the sacrifices of public cults; they did not use their positions to influence political or social matters. Their special knowledge consisted in knowing how to perform traditional religious rites. They were not guardians of correct religious thinking because Greek polytheism had no scripture or uniform set of beliefs and practices. It required its worshippers only to support the community's local rituals and to avoid religious pollution.

Citizenship for Rich and Poor In the Greek city-state, the concept of citizenship meant free people agreeing to form a political community that was a partnership of privileges and duties in common affairs under the rule of law (see Document, "Zaleucus's Law Code for a Greek City-State in Seventh-Century B.C.E. Italy," page 57). Citizenship was a remarkable political concept because, even in Greek city-states organized as tyrannies or oligarchies (rule by a small group), it meant a basic level of political equality among citizens. Most important, it carried the expectation (if not always the fulfillment) of equal treatment under the law for male citizens regardless of their social status or wealth. The degree of power sharing varied. In oligarchic city-states, where the social elite had a stranglehold on politics, small groups or even a single family could dominate the process of legislating. Women had the protection of the law, but they were barred from participation in politics on the grounds that female judgment was inferior to male. Regulations governing sexual behavior and control of property were stricter for women than for men.

In the most egalitarian version of the polis, all free adult male citizens shared in governing by attending and voting in a political assembly, where the laws and policies of the community were decided. In this direct democracy, all free men had the right to make proposals to be voted on in the assembly and to serve on juries. Even in democratic city-states, however, citizens did not enjoy perfect political equality. The right to hold office, for example, could be restricted to citizens possessing a certain amount of property. Equality prevailed most strongly in the justice system, in which all male citizens were treated the same, regardless of wealth or status.

Because monarchy and legal inequality had characterized the history of the ancient Near East and Greece in earlier times, making equality of male citizens the principle for the reorganization of Greek society and politics in the Archaic Age was a radical innovation. The polis—with its emphasis on equal protection of the laws for rich and poor alike—remained the preeminent form of political and social organization in Greece until the beginning of Roman control six centuries later.

How the poor originally gained the privileges of citizenship remains a mystery. The population increase in the late Dark Age and the Archaic Age was greatest among the poor. These families raised more children to help farm more land, which had been vacant after the depopulation brought on by the worst of the Dark Age. (See "Taking Measure," page 59.) There was no precedent in Western civilization for extending even limited political and legal equality to the poor, but the Greek city-states did so even as the number of poor people grew.

Historians have customarily believed that a hoplite revolution was the reason for expanded political rights, but recent research has undermined this interpretation. A **hoplite** was an infantryman who wore metal body armor and attacked with a thrusting spear. Hoplites made up the main strike force of the militia that defended each city-state; there were no permanent Greek armies at this period. Hoplites marched into combat arrayed in a rectangular formation called a phalanx. Staying in line and working together were the secrets to successful phalanx tactics. Greeks had fought in phalanxes for a long time, but only the elite could afford hoplite equipment. In the eighth century B.C.E.,

Grave Monument of a Greek Warrior

This inscribed flat pillar stood above the grave of a Greek warrior from Athens who died in the late sixth century B.C.E. An inscription preserves his name for future generations to remember: Aristion. The sculpture shows him with the muscular build that Greek hoplites (heavily armed infantry) worked to develop so that they could fight effectively while wearing metal armor. He holds the thrusting spear that was a hoplite's main battle weapon. *(AISA/Everett Collection.)*

hoplite: A heavily armed Greek infantryman. Hoplites constituted the main strike force of a city-state's militia.

TAKING MEASURE

Greek Family Size and Agricultural Labor in the Archaic Age

Using archaeological surveys and estimates of population size, modern demographers have calculated the changing relationship in the Archaic Age between the number of people in a farming family and the amount of land that the family could cultivate successfully. The graph shows how valuable healthy teenage children were to the family's prosperity. For example, when the family had two children old enough to work in the fields, it could farm over 50 percent more land, increasing its productivity significantly and thus making the family better off.

Source: Adapted from Thomas W. Gallant, *Risk and Survival in Ancient Greece: Reconstructing the Rural Domestic Economy* [1991], Fig. 4.10.

Question to Consider

■ **Given the information in this chart, what do you think childhood and adolescence looked like in this era?**

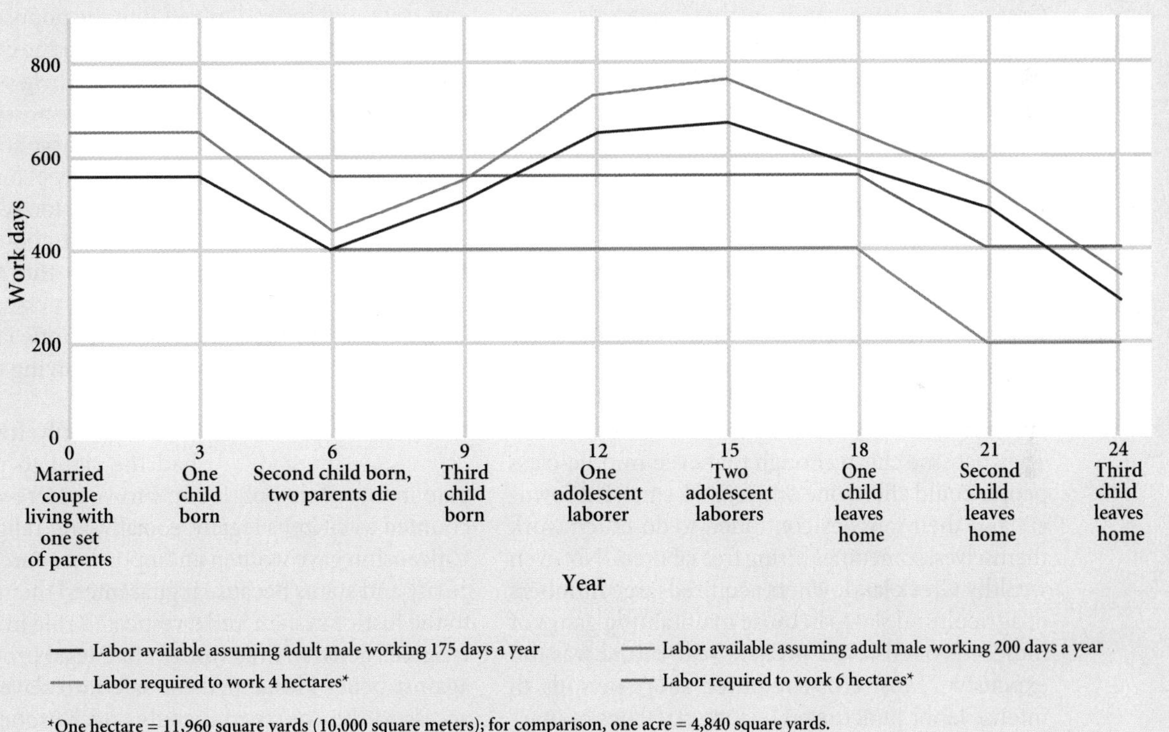

however, a growing number of men had become prosperous enough to buy metal weapons, especially because the use of iron had made such weapons more readily available.

According to the hoplite revolution theory, these new hoplites—feeling that they should enjoy political rights in exchange for buying their own equipment and training hard—forced the social elite to share political power by threatening to refuse to fight, which would cripple military defense. This interpretation correctly assumes that the hoplites had the power to demand and receive a voice in politics but ignores that hoplites were not poor. Furthermore, archaeology shows that not many men were wealthy enough to afford hoplite armor until the middle of the seventh century B.C.E., well after the earliest city-states had emerged. How then did poor men, too, win political rights?

The most likely explanation is that the poor earned respect by fighting to defend the community, just as hoplites did. Fighting as so-called light troops (that is, lightly armed), poor men could disrupt an enemy's heavy infantry by slinging barrages of rocks or shooting arrows. It is also possible that tyrants—sole rulers who seized power for their families in some city-states (see "Tyranny in the

City-State of Corinth," page 65)—boosted the status of poor men. Tyrants may have granted greater political rights to poor men as a means of gathering popular support. No matter how the poor became citizens who possessed a rough equality of political freedom and legal rights with the rich, this unprecedented change was Greek society's most remarkable innovation in the Archaic Age.

The Expansion of Greek Slavery

The growth of freedom and equality for citizens in Greece produced a corresponding expansion of slavery, as free citizens protected their status by drawing harsh lines between themselves and slaves. Many slaves were war captives. Pirates or raiders also seized people from non-Greek regions to the north and east to sell into slavery in Greece. The fierce bands in these areas also captured members from one another and sold them to slave dealers. Rich families prized educated Greek-speaking slaves, who could tutor their children (no public schools existed in this period).

City-states as well as individuals owned slaves. Publicly owned slaves enjoyed limited independence, living on their own and performing specialized tasks. In Athens, for example, special slaves were trained to detect counterfeit coinage. Temple slaves belonged to the deity of the sanctuary, for whom they worked as servants.

Slaves made up about one-third of the total population in some city-states by the fifth century B.C.E. They became cheap enough that even middle-class people could afford one or two. Still, small landowners and their families continued to do much work themselves, sometimes hiring free laborers. Not even wealthy Greek landowners acquired large numbers of agricultural slaves because maintaining gangs of hundreds of enslaved workers year-round was too expensive. Most crops required short periods of intense labor punctuated by long stretches of inactivity, and owners did not want to feed slaves who had no work.

Slaves did all kinds of jobs. Household slaves, often women, cleaned, cooked, fetched water from public fountains, helped the wife with the weaving, watched the children, accompanied the husband as he did the marketing, and performed other domestic chores. Neither female nor male slaves could refuse if their masters demanded sexual favors. Owners often labored alongside their slaves in small manufacturing businesses and on farms, although rich landowners might appoint a slave supervisor to oversee work in the fields. Slaves toiling in the narrow, landslide-prone tunnels of Greece's silver and gold mines had the worst lot: many died doing this dangerous, dark, backbreaking work.

Since slaves existed as property, not people, owners could legally beat or even kill them. But injuring or executing slaves would have made no economic sense—the master would have been crippling or destroying his own property. Under the best conditions, household workers could live free of violent punishment. They sometimes were allowed to join their owners' families on excursions and attend religious rituals. However, without families of their own, without property, and without legal or political rights, slaves remained alienated from regular society. In the words of an ancient commentator, slaves lived lives of "work, punishment, and food." Sometimes owners freed their slaves, and some promised freedom at a future date to encourage their slaves to work hard. Those slaves who gained their freedom did not become citizens in Greek city-states but instead mixed into the population of noncitizens officially allowed to live in the community. Freed slaves were still expected to help out their former masters when called on.

Greek slaves rarely rebelled on a large scale, except in Sparta, because they were usually of too many different origins and nationalities and too scattered to organize. No Greeks called for the abolition of slavery. The expansion of slavery in the Archaic Age reduced more and more unfree persons to a state of absolute dependence. As Aristotle later described their condition, slaves were "living tools."

Greek Women's Lives

Although only free men had the right to participate in city-state politics and to vote, free women counted as citizens legally, socially, and religiously. Citizenship gave women an important source of security and status because it guaranteed them access to the justice system and a respected role in official religious activity. Free women had legal protection against being kidnapped for sale into slavery and access to the courts in disputes over property, although they usually had to have a man speak for them. The traditional paternalism of Greek society required that all women have male guardians who acted as "fathers" to regulate their lives and safeguard their interests (as defined by men). Before a woman's marriage, her father served as her legal guardian; after marriage, her husband took over that duty.

The expansion of slavery made households bigger and added new responsibilities for women. While their husbands farmed, participated in politics, and met with their male friends, well-off wives managed the household: raising the children, supervising the preservation and preparation of food, keeping the family's financial accounts, weaving fabric for clothing, directing the work of the slaves, and tending them when they were ill. Poor women worked outside the home, laboring in the fields or selling produce and small goods such as ribbons and trinkets in the market that occupied the center of every settlement. Women's labor ensured the family's economic self-sufficiency and allowed male citizens the time to participate in public life.

Women's religious functions gave them prestige and freedom of movement. Women left the home to attend funerals, state festivals, and public rituals. They had access, for example, to the initiation rights of the popular cult of Demeter at Eleusis, near Athens. Women had control over cults reserved exclusively for them and also performed important duties in other official cults. In fifth-century B.C.E. Athens, for example, women officiated as priestesses for more than forty different deities, with benefits including salaries paid by the state.

Marriage Marriages were arranged, and everyone was expected to marry. A woman's guardian — her father or, if he was dead, her uncle or her brother — would often engage her to another man's son while she was still a child, perhaps as young as five. The engagement was a public event conducted in the presence of witnesses. The guardian on this occasion repeated the phrase that expressed the primary aim of the marriage: "I give you this woman for the plowing [procreation] of legitimate children." The wedding took place when the girl was in her early teens and the groom ten to fifteen years older. Hesiod advised a man to marry a virgin in the fifth year after her first menstruation, when the man was "not much younger than thirty and not much older."

A legal wedding consisted of the bride moving to her husband's dwelling; the procession to his house served as the ceremony. The bride's father bestowed on her a dowry (a certain amount of family property a daughter received at marriage); if she was wealthy, this could include land yielding an income as well as personal possessions that formed part of her new household's assets and could be inherited by her children. Her husband was legally obliged to preserve the dowry, use it to support his wife and their children, and return it in case of a divorce.

Except in certain cases in Sparta, monogamy was the rule in ancient Greece, as was a nuclear family (husband, wife, and children living together without other relatives in the same house). Citizen men, married or not, were free to have sexual relations with slaves, foreign concubines, female prostitutes, or willing pre-adult citizen males. Citizen women, single or married, had no such freedom. Sex between a wife and anyone other than her husband carried harsh penalties for both parties.

Greek citizen men placed Greek citizen women under their guardianship both to regulate marriage and procreation and to maintain family property. According to Greek mythology, women were a necessary evil. Zeus supposedly ordered the creation of the first woman, Pandora, as a punishment for men in retaliation against Prometheus, who had stolen fire from Zeus and given it to humans. To see what

A Bride's Preparation

This special piece of pottery was designed to fit over a woman's thigh to protect it while she sat down to spin wool. As a woman's tool, it appropriately carried a picture from a woman's life: a bride being helped to prepare for her wedding by her family, friends, and servants. The inscriptions indicate that this fifth-century B.C.E. piece shows the mythological bride Alcestis, famous for sacrificing herself to save her husband and then being rescued from Death by the hero Herakles. *(Deutsches Archeologisches Institut-Athens, Neg. Nr. DAI-ATHEN-NM 5126. Photo: E. M. Czako.)*

was in a container that had come as a gift from the gods, Pandora lifted its lid and accidentally released into a previously trouble-free world the evils that had been locked inside. When she finally slammed the lid back down, only hope still remained in the container. Hesiod described women as "big trouble" but thought any man who refused to marry to escape the "troublesome deeds of women" would come to "destructive old age" alone, with no heirs. In other words, a man needed a wife so that he could father children who would later care for him and preserve the family property after his death. This paternalistic attitude allowed Greek men to control human reproduction and consequently the distribution of property.

REVIEW QUESTION How did the physical, social, and intellectual conditions of life in the Archaic Age promote the emergence of the Greek city-state?

New Directions for the Greek City-State, 750–500 B.C.E.

Greek city-states developed three forms of social and political organization based on citizenship: oligarchy, tyranny, and democracy. Sparta provided Greece's most famous example of an oligarchy, in which a small number of men dominated policymaking in an assembly of male citizens. For a time Corinth had the best-known tyranny, in which one man seized control of the city-state, ruling it for the advantage of his family and loyal supporters, while acknowledging the citizenship of all (thereby distinguishing a tyrant from a king, who ruled over subjects). Athens developed Greece's best-known democracy by allowing all male citizens to participate in governing. Although assemblies of men had influenced some ancient Near Eastern kings (see "Contrasting Views," page 63), Greek democracies gave their male citizens an unprecedented degree of equality and political power.

The Archaic Age polis is justly famous as the incubator for democratic politics; it also provided the environment in which Greeks created new forms of artistic expression and new ways of thought. In this period they developed innovative ways of using reason to understand the physical world, their relations to it, and their relationships with one another. This intellectual innovation laid the foundation for the gradual emergence of scientific thought and logic in Western civilization.

Oligarchy in the City-State of Sparta, 700–500 B.C.E.

Uniquely among the Greek city-states, Sparta organized its society with laws directed at a single purpose: military readiness. This oligarchic city-state developed the mightiest infantry force in Greece during the Archaic Age. Its citizens were famous for their militaristic self-discipline. Sparta's urban center nestled in an easily defended valley on the Peloponnesian peninsula twenty-five miles from the Mediterranean coast. This separation from the sea kept the Spartans from becoming skilled sailors; their strength lay on land.

The Spartan oligarchy included three components of rule. First came the two hereditary, prestigious military leaders called kings, who served as the state's religious heads and the generals of its army. Despite their title, they were not monarchs but just one part of the ruling oligarchy. The second part was a council of twenty-eight men over sixty years old (the elders), and the third part consisted of five annually elected officials called *ephors* ("overseers"), who made policy and enforced the laws.

In principle, legislation had to be approved by an assembly of all Sparta's free adult males, who were called the Alike to stress their common status and purpose. The assembly had only limited power to amend the proposals put before it, however, and the council would withdraw a proposal when the assembly's reaction proved negative. "If the people speak crookedly," according to Spartan tradition, "the elders and the leaders of the people shall be withdrawers." The council would then resubmit the proposal after gaining support for its passage.

Spartan society demanded strict obedience to all laws. When the ephors took office, for example, they issued an official proclamation to Sparta's males: "Shave your mustache and obey the laws." The laws' importance was emphasized by the official story that the god Apollo had given them to Sparta. Unlike other Greeks, the Spartans never wrote down their laws. Instead, they preserved their system with a unique, highly structured way of life. All Spartan citizens were expected to put service to

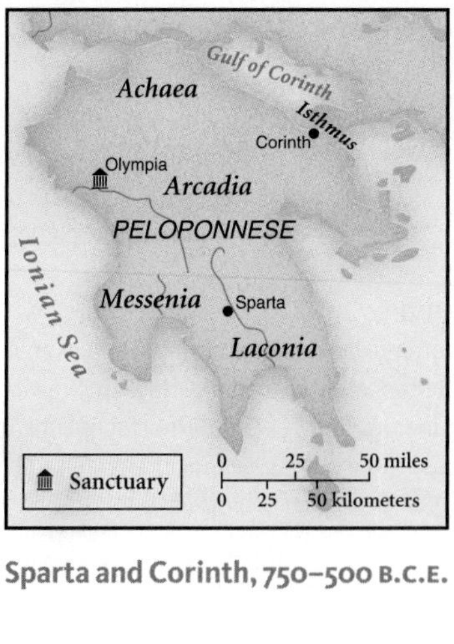

Sparta and Corinth, 750–500 B.C.E.

CONTRASTING VIEWS

Persians Debate Democracy, Oligarchy, and Monarchy

According to the Greek historian Herodotus, after a group of seven eminent Persians overthrew a false king in 522 B.C.E., they debated what would be the best type of government to establish in Persia. Otanes argued for democracy (or, as he calls it, "putting things in the middle"), Megabyzus for oligarchy, and Darius for monarchy. Four of the seven voted in favor of monarchy, and Darius became the new, legitimate king. Herodotus also says that some Greeks refused to believe that the debate ever took place, perhaps because there was no evidence that any system other than monarchy had ever been possible in Persia. In any case, these speeches present the earliest recorded contrasting views on systems of government, with special attention to the characteristics of monarchy.

Otanes recommended to the Persians to put things in the middle by saying this: "It doesn't seem right to me that one of us should be the monarch. There is nothing sweet or good about it. You know to what lengths violent arrogance [hubris] carried our former king Camybses, and you experienced that violent arrogance under the recent false king. How could monarchy be a suitable thing, when it allows the ruler to do whatever he wishes without any official accountability? Even the best of men would change his usual ideas if he had such a position of rule. Violent arrogance comes to him from the good things that he possesses, and jealousy has been part of human nature from the start. In having these two characteristics he has total bad character. Sated with his violent arrogance and jealousy, he does many outrageous things. A ruler with tyrannical power ought to be free of envy, for he possesses every good thing. But the opposite is true of his relations with the citizens. He is jealous if the best ones stay alive, delighted if the worst ones do; he's the best at listening to accusations. He is most difficult of men to deal with: if you only praise him in moderation, he gets angry because he is not being energetically flattered, but if someone flatters him energetically, he gets angry because the person is a flatterer. And now I am going to say the worst things of all: he overturns traditional customs, he rapes women, and he kills people without a trial. When the people are the ruler, the government has the best name: equality before the law. It does nothing of the things that a monarch does. It fills offices by lottery, its rule is subject to official accountability, and it has the community make all decisions. My judgment is that we should get rid of the monarchy and increase the power of the masses. For in the many is everything."

Otanes offered this judgment, but Megabyzus said they should entrust the government to an oligarchy, saying this: "What Otanes said about not having tyranny, I agree with, but as for giving power to the masses, he has missed the best judgment. There is nothing less intelligent or more violently arrogant than a useless crowd. It is certainly intolerable for men to flee the violent arrogance of the tyrant, only to fall victim to the violent arrogance of the people, who have no restraints upon them. If a tyrant does something, he does it from knowledge, but there is no knowledge in the people. How could someone have knowledge when he hasn't been taught anything fine and doesn't know it innately? He rushes into things without thought, like a river in its winter flood. Let those who intend evil to the Persians push for democracy, but let us choose a group of the best men and endow them with power. For we will be part of this group, and it is likely that the best plans will come from the best men."

Megabyzus offered this judgment, and Darius was the third to reveal his judgment, saying: "Megabyzus seems to me to speak correctly in what he says about the masses, but not correctly about oligarchy. For if we consider for argument's sake that all three systems are the best they can be—the best democracy, the best oligarchy, the best monarchy—then monarchy is far superior. For clearly nothing is better than the one best man. Relying on judgment that is the best he would direct the masses faultlessly, and he would be especially good at making plans against hostile men without them being divulged. In an oligarchy, where many men want to use their excellence for common interests, intense private hatreds tend to arise. For each one wants to be the head man and to win with his judgments, and they create great hatreds among themselves. From this come violent factions, and from factions comes murder, and from murder the system turns to monarchy. And in this one sees by how much monarchy is the best. Again, when the people rule, it is impossible that there not be evildoing. Moreover, when there is evildoing for the common interests, hatred doesn't arise among the evildoers; instead, strong friendships arise. For the evildoers act together to corrupt the common interests. This sort of thing happens until one man becomes the head of the people and stops these evildoers. With these actions he amazes the people, and being the object of amazement he clearly becomes a monarch. So, in this way, too, it is clear that monarchy is the strongest. To say it all together in one word: from where did our [i.e., Persian] freedom come, and who gave it to us? From the people, or an oligarchy, or a monarch? It is my judgment that, having obtained our freedom through one man, we should maintain our freedom in the same way, and we should also not do away with our sound traditional customs; for this is not better."

Source: Herodotus, *The Histories*, Book 3, chapters 80–82. Translation by Thomas R. Martin.

Question to Consider

- **Which arguments do you think are the most persuasive, and why?**

their city-state before personal concerns because their state's survival was continually threatened by its own economic foundation: the great mass of Greek slaves, called helots, who did almost all the work for citizens.

The Helots A **helot** was a slave owned by the Spartan city-state. They were Greeks captured in neighboring parts of Greece that the Spartans defeated in war. Most helots lived in Messenia, to the west, which Sparta had conquered by around 700 B.C.E. The helots outnumbered Sparta's free citizens. Harshly treated by their Spartan masters, helots constantly looked for chances to revolt.

Helots had some family life because they were expected to produce children to maintain their population, and they could own some personal possessions and practice their religion. They labored as farmers and household slaves so that Spartan citizens would not have to do such nonmilitary work. Spartan men wore their hair very long to show they were warriors rather than laborers, for whom long hair was inconvenient.

Helots lived under the constant threat of officially approved violence by Spartan citizens. Every year the ephors formally declared war between Sparta and the helots, allowing any Spartan to kill a helot without legal penalty or fear of offending the gods by committing murder. By beating the helots frequently, forcing them to get drunk in public as an object lesson to young Spartans, and humiliating them by making them wear dog-skin caps, the Spartans emphasized their slaves' "otherness." In this way Spartans created a justification for their harsh abuse of fellow Greeks. Contrasting the freedom of Spartan citizens from ordinary work with the ceaseless labor of the helots, a later Athenian observed, "Sparta is the home of the freest of the Greeks, and of the most enslaved."

Spartan Communal Life With helots to work the fields, male citizens could devote themselves full-time to preparation for war, training to protect their state both from hostile neighbors and its own slaves. Boys lived at home until their seventh year, when they were sent to live in barracks with other males until they were thirty. They spent most of their time exercising, hunting, practicing with weapons, and learning Spartan values by listening to tales of bravery and heroism at shared meals, where adult males in groups of about fifteen usually ate instead of at home. Discipline was strict, and the boys were purposely underfed so that they would learn stealth tactics by stealing food. If they were caught, punishment and disgrace followed immediately. One famous Spartan tale shows how seriously boys were supposed to fear such failure: having stolen a fox and hidden it under his clothing, a Spartan youth died because he let the panicked animal rip out his insides rather than letting himself be detected in the theft. A Spartan male who could not survive the tough training was publicly disgraced and denied the status of being an Alike.

Spending so much time in shared quarters schooled Sparta's young men in their society's values. The community took the place of a Spartan boy's family when he was growing up and remained his main social environment even after he reached adulthood. There he learned to call all older men Father to emphasize that his primary loyalty was to the group instead of his biological family. This way of life trained him for the one honorable occupation for Spartan men: obedient soldier. A seventh-century B.C.E. poet expressed the Spartan male ideal: "Know that it is good for the city-state and the whole people when a man takes his place in the front row of warriors and stands his ground without flinching."

An adolescent boy's life often involved what in today's terminology would be called a homosexual relationship, although the ancient concepts of heterosexuality and homosexuality did not match modern notions. An older male would choose a teenager as a special favorite, in many cases engaging him in sexual relations. Their bond of affection was meant to make each ready to die for the other, at whose side he would march into battle. Numerous Greek city-states included this form of homosexuality among their customs, although some made it illegal. The physical relationship could be controversial; the Athenian author Xenophon (c. 430–355 B.C.E.) wrote a work on the Spartan way of life denying that sex with boys existed there because he thought it a stain on the Spartans' reputation for virtue. However, other sources testify that such relationships did exist in Sparta and elsewhere. (The first modern histories of Greece suppressed discussion of this topic because their writers saw it as a form of child abuse.)

In such relationships the elder partner (the "lover") was supposed to help educate the young man (the "beloved") in politics and community values, and not just exploit him for physical pleasure. The relationship would not be lasting or exclusive: beloveds would grow up to get married, as lovers were, and would eventually become the older mem-

---

helot: A slave owned by the Spartan city-state; such slaves came from parts of Greece conquered by the Spartans.

ber of a new pair. Sex between adult males was considered disgraceful, as was sex between females of all ages (at least according to men).

Spartan women were known throughout the Greek world for their personal freedom. Since their husbands were so rarely at home, women controlled the households, which included servants, daughters, and sons who had not yet left for their communal training. Consequently, Spartan women exercised even more power at home than did women elsewhere in Greece. They could own property, including land. Wives were expected to stay physically fit so that they could bear healthy children to keep up the population. They were also expected to drum Spartan values into their children. One mother became legendary for handing her son his shield on the eve of battle and sternly telling him, "Come back with it or [lying dead] on it."

Demography determined Sparta's long-term fate. The population of Sparta was never large. Adult males—who made up the army—numbered between eight and ten thousand in the Archaic period. Over time, the problem of producing enough children to keep the Spartan army from shrinking became desperate, probably because losses in war far outnumbered births. Men became legally required to marry, with bachelors punished by fines and public ridicule. A woman could legitimately have children by a man other than her husband, if all three agreed.

Because the Spartans' survival depended on the exploitation of enslaved Greeks, they believed changes in their way of life must be avoided because any change might make them vulnerable to internal revolts. Some Greeks criticized the Spartan way of life as repressive and monotonous, but the Spartans' discipline and respect for their laws gained them widespread admiration.

Tyranny in the City-State of Corinth, 657–585 B.C.E.

In some city-states, competition among the social elite for political leadership became so bitter that a single family would suppress all its rivals and establish itself in rule for a time. The family's leader thus became a tyrant, a dictator who gained political dominance by force and was backed by his relatives and other supporters. Tyrants usually rallied support by promising privileges to poor citizens in city-states where they lacked full citizenship or felt disfranchised in political life. Successful tyrants kept their elite rivals out of power by cultivating the goodwill of the masses with economic policies favoring their interests, such as public employment schemes. Since few tyrants successfully passed their popularity on to their heirs, tyrannies tended to be short-lived.

Tyrants usually preserved their city-states' existing laws and political institutions. If a city-state had an assembly, for example, the tyrant would allow it to continue to meet, expecting it to follow his direction. Although today the word *tyrant* indicates a brutal or unwanted leader, tyrants in Archaic Greece did not always fit that description. Ordinary Greeks evaluated tyrants according to their behavior, opposing the ruthless and violent ones but welcoming the fair and generous ones.

Bronze Sculpture of a Spartan Youth

This sculpted handle of a bronze water jar from sixth-century B.C.E. Sparta shows a young male holding two lions by the tail on his shoulders. That spectacular pose portrayed the fearlessness and control over fierce nature that Sparta expected of its citizens. His hair is long in the self-conscious style of Spartan warriors, who prided themselves on not having the short hair that was common for laborers. *(Greek, Archaic, about 540 B.C.E. Place of manufacture: Greece, Laconia, Sparta. Bronze. H: 12.8 cm. [5 1/16 in.]. Museum of Fine Arts, Boston; Museum purchase with funds donated by contributions, 85.515. Photograph © 2011 Museum of Fine Arts, Boston.)*

The Temple of Apollo at Corinth
Built at Corinth in southern Greece to honor the god Apollo in the sixth century B.C.E., this temple exemplifies what is called the Doric architectural style. This called for fluted columns resting directly on the foundation and topped by flattened disks. Just as the worship of Apollo was meant to ensure divine protection for Corinth, the towering stone hill in the background served as its emergency fortress on an acropolis (central highpoint of a Greek city-state). *(The Art Archive/Gianni Dagli Orti.)*

The most famous early tyranny arose at Corinth in 657 B.C.E., when the family of Cypselus rebelled against the city's harsh oligarchic leadership. This takeover attracted wide attention in the Greek world because Corinth was such an important city-state. Its location on the isthmus controlling land access to the Peloponnese and a huge amount of seaborne trade made it the most prosperous city-state of the Archaic Age (see Map 2.4). Cypselus "became one of the most admired of Corinth's citizens because he was courageous, prudent, and helpful to the people, unlike the oligarchs in power, who were insolent and violent," according to a later historian. Cypselus's son succeeded him at his death in 625 B.C.E. and aggressively continued Corinth's economic expansion by founding colonies to increase trade. He also pursued commercial contacts with Egypt. Unlike his father, the son lost popular support by ruling harshly. He held on to power until his death in 585 B.C.E., but the hostility he had provoked soon led to the overthrow of his own heir. The social elite, to prevent tyranny, then installed an oligarchic government based on a board of officials and a council.

Democracy in the City-State of Athens, 632–500 B.C.E.

Only democracy, which the Greeks invented, instituted genuine political power sharing in the polis. Athens, located at the southeastern corner of central Greece, became the most famous of the democratic city-states because its government gave political rights to the greatest number of people; financed magnificent temples and public buildings; and, in the fifth century B.C.E., became militarily strong enough to force numerous other city-states to follow Athenian leadership in a maritime empire. Athenian democracy did not reach its full development until the mid-fifth century B.C.E., but its first steps in the Archaic Age allowed all male citizens to participate meaningfully in making laws and administering justice. Democracy has remained so important in Western civilization that understanding why and how Athenian democracy worked remains a vital responsibility for historians.

Athens's early development of a large middle class was a crucial factor in opening this new path for Western civilization. The Athenian population apparently expanded at a phenomenal rate when economic conditions improved rapidly from about 800 to 700 B.C.E. The ready availability of good farmland in Athenian territory and opportunities for seaborne trade along the long coastline allowed many families to achieve modest prosperity. These hardworking entrepreneurs evidently felt that their self-won economic success entitled them to a say in government. The democratic unity forged by the Athenian masses was evident as early as 632 B.C.E., when the people rallied "from the fields in a body," according to Herodotus, to block the attempt by an elite Athenian to install a tyranny.

By the seventh century B.C.E., all freeborn adult male citizens of Athens had the right to vote on public matters in the assembly, whose meetings regularly attracted several thousand participants. They also elected high officials called archons, who ran the judicial system by rendering verdicts in disputes and criminal accusations. Members of the elite dominated these offices; because archons received no pay, poor men could not afford to serve.

An extended economic crisis beginning in the late seventh century B.C.E. almost destroyed Athens's infant democracy. The first attempt to solve the crisis was the emergency appointment around 621 B.C.E. of a man named Draco to revise the laws. Athens's leaders hoped that reforming and clarifying the laws would bring social harmony through justice. Unfortunately, Draco's changes, which made death the penalty for even minor crimes, proved too harsh to work. Later Greeks said Draco (whose harshness inspired the word *draconian*) had written his laws in blood, not ink. By 600 B.C.E., economic conditions had become so terrible that poor farmers had to borrow constantly from richer neighbors and deeply mortgage their land. As the crisis grew worse, impoverished citizens were sold into slavery to pay off debts. Civil war seemed next.

Solon's Democratic Reforms

Desperate, Athenians appointed another emergency official in 594 B.C.E., a war hero named **Solon**. To head off violence, Solon gave both rich and poor something of what they wanted, a compromise called the "shaking off of obligations." He canceled private debts, which helped the poor but displeased the rich; he decided not to redistribute land, which pleased the wealthy but disappointed the poor. He banned selling citizens into slavery to settle debts and liberated citizens who had become slaves in this way. His elimination of debt slavery was a significant recognition of what today would be called citizen rights. Solon celebrated his success in poetry: "To Athens, their home established by the gods, I brought back many who had been sold into slavery, some justly, some not."

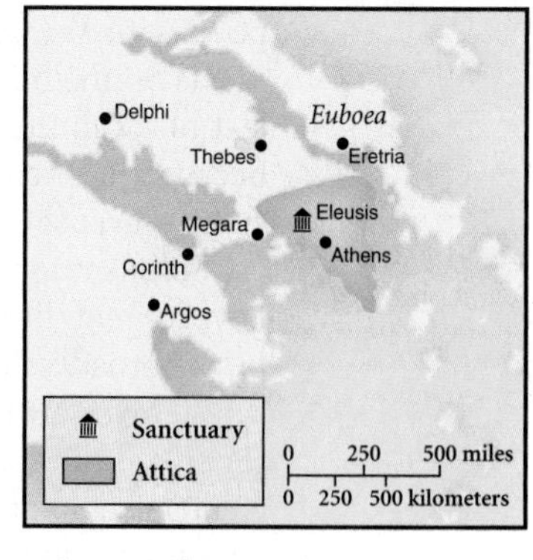

Athens and Central Greece, 750–500 B.C.E.

Solon was able to balance political power between rich and poor by reordering Athens's traditional ranking of citizens into four groups. Most important, he made the top-ranking division depend solely on wealth, not birth. This change eliminated inherited aristocracy at Athens. The groupings did not affect a man's treatment at law, only his eligibility for government office. The higher a man's ranking, the higher the post to which he could be elected, but higher also was the contribution he was expected to make to the community with his service and his money. Men at the poorest level, called laborers, were not eligible for any office. Solon did, however, confirm the laborers' right to vote in the legislative assembly. His classification scheme was consistent with democratic principles because it allowed for upward social mobility: a man who increased his wealth could move up the scale of eligibility for office.

Because the process of making decisions by persuasion can be glacially slow in large groups, the creation of a smaller council to prepare the agenda for the assembly was a crucial development in making Athenian democracy efficient. Solon may have been the one who created the council of four hundred men that decided what the assembly needed to discuss (though some evidence suggests it was instituted after his rule). The council members were chosen annually from the adult male citizenry by lottery — the most democratic method possible — which prevented the social elite from capturing too many seats.

Even more than his changes to the government, Solon's two reforms in the judicial system promoted democratic principles of equality. First, he directed that any male citizen could start a prosecution on behalf of any crime victim. Second, he gave people the right to appeal an archon's judgment to the assembly. With these two measures, Solon empowered ordinary citizens in the administration of justice. Characteristically, he balanced these democratic reforms by granting broader

---

Solon: Athenian political reformer whose changes promoted early democracy.

powers to the Areopagus Council ("council that meets on the hill of the god of war Ares"). This select body, limited to ex-archons, held great power because its members judged the most important cases — accusations against archons themselves.

Solon's reforms broke the traditional pattern of government limited to the elite. They extended power broadly through the citizen body and created a system of law that applied more equally than before to all the community's free men. A critic once challenged Solon, "Do you actually believe your fellow citizens' injustice and greed can be kept in check this way? Written laws are more like spiders' webs than anything else: they tie up the weak and the small fry who get stuck in them, but the rich and the powerful tear them to shreds." Solon replied that communal values ensure the rule of law: "People abide by their agreements when neither side has anything to gain by breaking them. I am writing laws for the Athenians in such a way that they will clearly see it is to everyone's advantage to obey the laws rather than to break them."

Some elite Athenians wanted oligarchy and therefore bitterly disagreed with Solon. The unrest they caused opened the door to tyranny at Athens. Peisistratus, helped by his upper-class friends and the poor whose interests he championed, made himself tyrant in 546 B.C.E. Like the Corinthian tyrants, he promoted the economic, cultural, and architectural development of Athens and bought the masses' support. He helped poorer men, for example, by hiring them to build roads, a huge temple to Zeus, and fountains to increase the supply of drinking water. He boosted Athens's economy and its image by minting new coins stamped with Athena's owl (a symbol of the goddess of wisdom; see the illustration on page 112) and organizing a great annual festival honoring the god Dionysus that attracted people from near and far to see its musical and dramatic performances.

Peisistratus's family could not maintain public goodwill after his death. Hippias, his eldest son, ruled harshly and was denounced as unjust by a rival elite family. These rivals convinced the Spartans, the self-proclaimed champions of Greek freedom, to "liberate" Athens from tyranny by expelling Hippias and his family in 510 B.C.E.

Cleisthenes, "Father of Athenian Democracy"

Peisistratus's support of ordinary people evidently had the unintended consequence of making them think that they deserved political equality. Tyranny at Athens thus opened the way to the most important step in developing Athenian democracy, the reforms of Cleisthenes. A member of the social elite, Cleisthenes found himself losing against rivals for election to office in 508 B.C.E. He turned his electoral campaign around by offering more political participation to the masses; he called his program "equality through law." Ordinary people so strongly favored his plan that they spontaneously rallied to repel a Spartan army that Cleisthenes' bitterest rival had convinced Sparta's leaders to send to block his reforms.

By about 500 B.C.E., Cleisthenes had engineered direct participation in Athens's democracy by as many adult male citizens as possible. First he created constituent units for the city-state's new political organization by grouping country villages and urban neighborhoods into units called **demes**. The demes chose council members annually by lottery in proportion to the size of their populations. To allow for greater participation, Solon's Council of Four Hundred was expanded to five hundred members. Finally, Cleisthenes required candidates for public office to be spread widely throughout the demes.

Cleisthenes helped his reforms succeed by grounding them in existing social conditions favorable to democracy. The creation of demes, for example, suggests that democratic notions stemmed from traditions of small-community life, in which each man was entitled to his say in running local affairs and had to persuade — not force — others to agree. Athenians remembered Cleisthenes as the father of their democracy. It took another fifty years of political struggle, however, before Athenian democracy reached its full development with the democratization of its judicial system.

New Ways of Thought and Expression in Greece, 630–500 B.C.E.

The idea that persuasion, rather than force or status, should drive political decisions matched the spirit of intellectual change rippling through Greece in the late Archaic Age. In city-states all over the Greek world, artists, poets, and philosophers pursued new ways of thought and new forms of expression. Through their contacts with the Near East, the Greeks encountered traditions to learn from and, in some cases, to alter for their own purposes.

---

demes (DEEMZ): The villages and city neighborhoods that formed the constituent political units of Athenian democracy in the late Archaic Age.

Vase Painting of a Music Lesson
This sixth-century B.C.E. red-figure vase shows a young man (seated on the left, without a beard) holding a lyre and watching an older, bearded man play the same instrument, while an adolescent boy and an older man listen. They all wear wreaths to show they are in a festive mood. The youth is evidently a pupil learning to play. Instruction in performing music and singing lyric poetry was considered an essential part of an upper-class Greek male's education. The teacher's lyre has a sounding board made from a turtle shell, as was customary for this instrument. *(Foto Marburg/Art Resource, NY.)*

Archaic Art and Literature

Early in the Archaic period Greek artists took inspiration from the Near East, but by the sixth century B.C.E. they had introduced innovations of their own. In ceramics, painters experimented with different clays and colors to depict vivid scenes from mythology and daily life. They became expert at rendering three-dimensional figures in an increasingly realistic style. Sculptors gave their statues balanced poses and calm, smiling faces.

Building on the Near Eastern tradition of poetry expressing personal emotions, Greeks created a new poetic form. This poetry, which sprang from popular song, was performed to the accompaniment of a lyre (a kind of harp) and thus called lyric poetry. Greek lyric poems were short, rhythmic, and diverse in subject. Lyric poets wrote songs both for choruses and for individual performers. Choral poems honored gods on public occasions, celebrated famous events in a city-state's history, praised victors in athletic contests, and enlivened weddings.

Solo lyric poems generated controversy because they valued individual expression and opinion over conventional views. Solon wrote poems justifying his reforms. Other poets criticized traditional values, such as strength in war. **Sappho**, a lyric poet from Lesbos born about 630 B.C.E. and famous for her poems on love, wrote, "Some would say the most beautiful thing on our dark earth is an army of cavalry, others of infantry, others of ships, but I say it's whatever a person loves." In this poem Sappho was expressing her longing for a woman she loved, who was now far away. Archilochus of Paros, who probably lived in the early seventh century B.C.E., became famous for poems mocking militarism, lamenting friends lost at sea, and regretting love affairs gone wrong. He became infamous for his lines about throwing away his shield in battle so that he could run away to save his life: "Oh, the hell with it; I can get another one just as good." When he taunted a family in verse after the father had ended Archilochus's affair with one of his daughters, the power of his ridicule reportedly caused the father and his two daughters to commit suicide.

Ionia and the Aegean, 750–500 B.C.E.

Greek Philosophy and Science

The study of philosophy ("love of wisdom") began in the seventh and sixth centuries B.C.E. when Greek thinkers created prose writing to express their innovative ideas, in particular their radically new explanations of the human world and its relation to the gods. Most of these philosophers lived in Ionia, on Anatolia's western coast, where they came in contact with Near Eastern knowledge in astronomy, mathematics, and myth. Because there were no formal schools in the Archaic Age, philosophers communicated their ideas by teaching privately and giving public lectures. Some also

---

Sappho (SAF oh): The most famous woman lyric poet of ancient Greece, a native of Lesbos.

composed poetry to explain their theories. People who studied with these philosophers or heard their presentations helped spread the new ideas.

Working from Babylonian discoveries about the regular movements of the stars and planets, Ionian philosophers such as Thales (c. 625–545 B.C.E.) and Anaximander (c. 610–540 B.C.E.), both of Miletus, reached the revolutionary conclusion that unchanging laws of nature (rather than gods' whims) governed the universe. Pythagoras, who emigrated from the island of Samos to the Greek city-state Croton in southern Italy about 530 B.C.E., taught that numerical relationships explained the world. He began the Greek study of high-level mathematics and the numerical aspects of musical harmony.

Ionian philosophers insisted that natural phenomena were neither random nor arbitrary. They applied the word *cosmos*—meaning "an orderly arrangement that is beautiful"—to the universe. The cosmos included not only the motions of heavenly bodies but also the weather, the growth of plants and animals, and human health. Because the universe was ordered, it was knowable; because it was knowable, thought and research could explain it. Philosophers therefore looked for the first or universal cause of all things, a quest that scientists still pursue. These first philosophers believed they needed to give reasons for their conclusions and to persuade others by arguments based on evidence. That is, they believed in logic. This new way of thought, called **rationalism**, became the foundation for the study of science and philosophy. This rule-based view of the causes of events and physical phenomena contrasted sharply with the traditional mythological view. Naturally, many people had difficulty accepting such a startling change in their understanding of the world, and the older tradition of explaining events as the work of deities lived on alongside the new approach.

These early Greek philosophers deeply influenced later times by being the first to clearly separate scientific thinking from myth and religion. Their idea that people must give reasons to justify their beliefs, rather than simply make assertions that others must accept without evidence, was their most

rationalism: The philosophic idea that people must justify their claims by logic and reason, not myth.

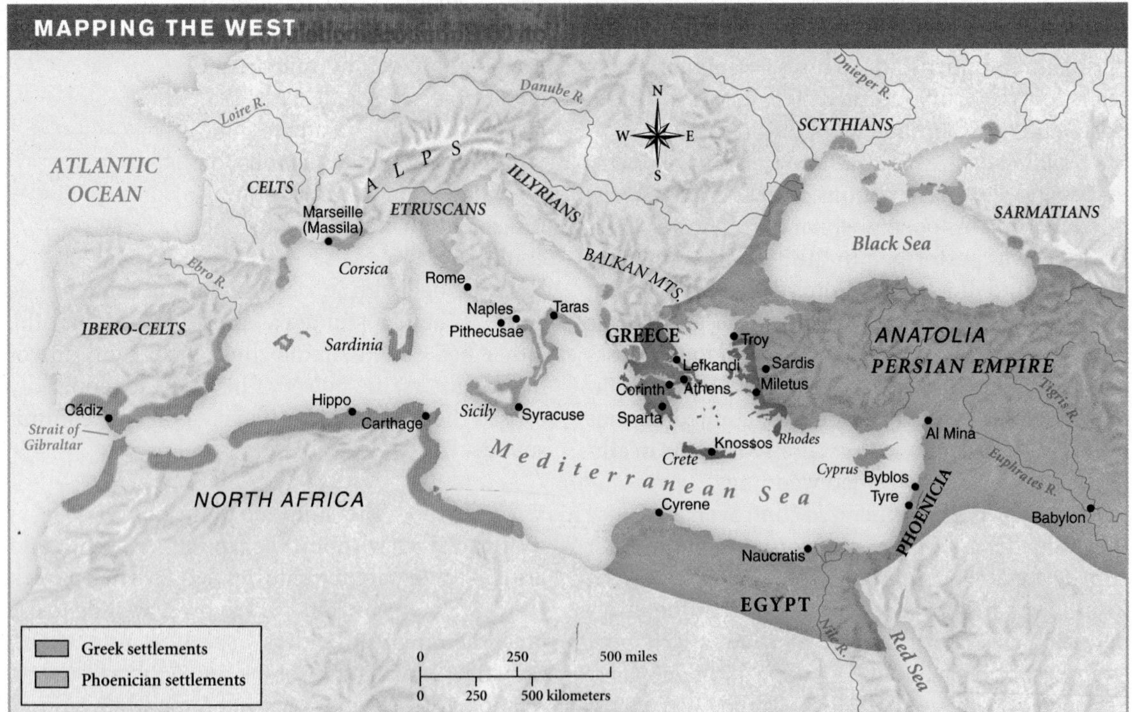

Mediterranean Civilizations, c. 500 B.C.E.

At the end of the sixth century B.C.E., the Persian Empire was by far the most powerful civilization touching the Mediterranean. Its riches and its unity gave it resources that no Phoenician or Greek city could match. The Phoenicians dominated economically in the western Mediterranean, while the Greek city-states in Sicily and southern Italy rivaled the power of those in the heartland. In Italy, the Etruscans were the most powerful civilization; the Romans were still a small community struggling to replace monarchy with a republic.

important achievement. This insistence on rationalism, coupled with the belief that the world could be understood as something other than the plaything of the gods, gave people hope that they could improve their lives through their own efforts. As Xenophanes of Colophon (c. 570–c. 478 B.C.E.) concluded, "The gods have not revealed all things from the beginning to mortals, but, by seeking, human beings find out, in time, what is better." This saying expressed the value Archaic Age philosophers gave to intellectual freedom, corresponding to the value that citizens gave to political freedom in the city-state. Even though these early concepts of freedom were not as complete as some modern thinkers believe that they should have been, they nevertheless represent a significant development in the history of Western civilization.

REVIEW QUESTION What were the main differences among the various forms of government in the Greek city-states?

Conclusion

Over different spans of time and with different results, both the Near East and Greece recovered from their Dark Ages brought on by the violence of the period 1200–1000 B.C.E. The Near East quickly revived its traditional pattern of social and political organization: empire with a strong central authority (monarchy). The Neo-Assyrians, the Neo-Babylonians, and the Persians succeeded one another as imperial powers. The moral dualism of Persian religion, Zoroastrianism, influenced later religions. The Israelites' development of monotheism based on scripture changed the course of religious history in Western civilization.

Greece's recovery from its Dark Age produced a new form of political and social organization: the polis, a city-state based on citizenship and shared governance. The rapidly growing population of the Archaic Age developed the sense of communal identity, personal freedom, and divine justice instituted by citizens that underlay the city-state. The degree of power sharing and the form of the political system varied in the Greek city-states. Some, like Sparta, were oligarchies; in others, like Corinth, rule was by tyranny. Over time, Athens developed the most extensive democracy, in which political power extended to all male citizens.

Just as revolutionary as the invention of democracy were the new methods of artistic expression and new ways of thought that Greeks developed. Building on Near Eastern traditions, Greek poets created lyric poetry to express personal emotion. Greek philosophers argued that laws of nature controlled the universe and that humans could discover these laws through reason and research, thereby establishing rationalism as the conceptual basis for science and philosophy.

The political and intellectual innovations of the Greek Archaic Age, which so profoundly affected later Western civilization, were almost lost to history. By about 500 B.C.E., Persia's awesome empire threatened the Greek world and its new values.

FOR FURTHER EXPLORATION

- **For additional primary-source material from this period**, see *Sources of the Making of the West*, Fourth Edition.
- **For Web sites, images, and documents related to topics in this chapter**, visit *Make History* at bedfordstmartins.com/hunt.

Chapter 2 Review

Online Study Guide bedfordstmartins.com/hunt

Key Terms and People

In the grid below, identify the term or person and explain its historical significance. (To do this exercise online, go to bedfordstmartins.com/hunt.)

Term	Who or What & When	Why It Matters
Cyrus (p. 41)		
moral dualism (p. 43)		
Torah (p. 45)		
Diaspora (p. 47)		
aretê (p. 49)		
Homer (p. 49)		
polis (p. 51)		
cult (p. 57)		
hoplite (p. 58)		
helot (p. 64)		
Solon (p. 67)		
demes (p. 68)		
Sappho (p. 69)		
rationalism (p. 70)		

Review Questions

1. In what ways was religion important in the Near East from c. 1000 B.C.E. to c. 500 B.C.E.?
2. What factors proved most important in the Greek recovery from the troubles of the Dark Age?
3. How did the physical, social, and intellectual conditions of life in the Archaic Age promote the emergence of the Greek city-state?
4. What were the main differences among the various forms of government in the Greek city-states?

Making Connections

1. What characteristics made the Greek city-state differ in political and social organization from the Near Eastern city-state?

How were the ideas of the Ionian philosophers different from mythic traditions?

...t extent were the most important changes in Western civilization in this period ...l or unintentional?

Important Events

Date	Event	Date	Event
1000–750 B.C.E.	Greece experiences its Dark Age	657 B.C.E.	Cypselus becomes tyrant in Corinth
900 B.C.E.	Neo-Assyrian Empire emerges	630 B.C.E.	The lyric poet Sappho is born
800 B.C.E.	Greeks learn to write with an alphabet	597 and 586 B.C.E.	Israelites exiled to Babylon
776 B.C.E.	Olympic Games founded in Greece	594 B.C.E.	Solon's reforms promote early democracy in Athens
750 B.C.E.	Greeks begin to create the polis	546–510 B.C.E.	Peisistratus's family rules Athens as tyrants
700 B.C.E.	Spartans conquer Messenia and enslave its inhabitants as helots	539 B.C.E.	Persian king Cyrus captures Babylon and permits Israelites to return to Canaan
700–500 B.C.E.	Ionian philosophers invent rationalism	508–500 B.C.E.	Cleisthenes' reforms extend democracy in Athens

- Consider three events: **Ionian philosophers develop rationalism (700–500 B.C.E.), The lyric poet Sappho is born (630 B.C.E.)**, and **Solon's reforms promote early democracy in Athens (594 B.C.E.).** How did the development of the Greek city-state (polis) encourage new modes of thinking and expression in science, philosophy, and literature?

SUGGESTED REFERENCES

Scholars today emphasize the importance of contact and inter-cultural influence among different peoples around the Mediterranean in helping us understand the history of the region as it recovered from the economic troubles and depopulation of the Dark Age.

Ancient Olympic Games: http://www.perseus.tufts.edu/Olympics/

Balot, Ryan K. *Greek Political Thought*. 2005.

*Barnes, Jonathan. *Early Greek Philosophy*. Rev. ed. 2002.

*Boyce, Mary, trans. *Textual Sources for the Study of Zoroastrianism*. 1990.

Bright, John. *A History of Israel*. 4th ed. 2000.

Brosius, Maria. *The Persians*. New ed. 2006.

Bryce, Trevor. *Life and Society in the Hittite World*. 2004.

*Dalley, Stephanie, trans. *Myths from Mesopotamia: Creation, the Flood, Gilgamesh, and Others*. Rev. ed. 2009.

Finkelstein, Israel, and Amihai Mazar. *The Quest for the Historical Israel: Debating Archaeology and the History of Early Israel*. Brian B. Schmidt, ed. 2007.

Hales, Shelley, and Tamar Hodos, eds. *Material Culture and Social Identities in the Ancient World*. 2009.

Hall, Jonathan M. *A History of the Archaic Greek World: ca. 1200–479 B.C.E.* 2006.

Hurwitt, Jeffrey M. *The Art and Culture of Early Greece, 1100–480 B.C.* 1985.

Kugel, James. *The God of Old: Inside the Lost World of the Bible*. 2003.

Lewis, John. *Solon the Thinker: Political Thought in Archaic Athens*. 2008.

*Malandra, William W. *An Introduction to Ancient Iranian Religion: Readings from the Avesta and the Achaemenid Inscriptions*. 1983.

Osborne, Robin. *Greece in the Making, 1200–479 B.C.* 2nd ed. 2009.

Shapiro, H. A. *The Cambridge Companion to Archaic Greece*. 2007.

*Primary source

The Greek Golden Age

CHAPTER

3

C. 500–C. 400 B.C.E.

A failure in international negotiations led to the greatest foreign danger ever to threaten Greece. In 507 B.C.E., Athens feared an attack from Sparta, its more powerful rival. The Athenian assembly therefore sent ambassadors to the Persian king, Darius I (r. 522–486 B.C.E.), to plead for a defensive alliance. The Athenian diplomats arranged for a meeting with the king's governor in Ionia (the western coast of modern Turkey), who controlled the Greeks living in that region. After the Athenians made their plea, the governor asked, "But who in the world are these people and where do they live that they are begging for an alliance with the Persians?" The mutual misunderstandings that resulted from this confused exchange helped start a prolonged conflict between mainland Greece and Persia in the early fifth century B.C.E.

This incident reveals external and internal reasons why war dominated Greece's history throughout that century, first with Greeks fighting Persians and then with Greeks fighting Greeks. The Persian king was eager to make more Greek city-states his subjects (those in Ionia had been his subjects for forty years) because their trade and growing wealth made them desirable prizes and because Persian kings believed it was their duty to expand their empire whenever possible. Unity seemed the Greeks' best defense, but the mainland city-states were so intensely competitive and suspicious of one another that they had never yet been able to come together to combat the Persians, not even to try to liberate the Greek city-states in Ionia from Persian control. Athens and Sparta so mistrusted each other that the Athenians appealed to foreigners for help against fellow Greeks.

Conflicting interests and mutual misunderstandings between Persia and Greece ignited a great conflict at the

Greek against Persian in Hand-to-Hand Combat (detail)
This red-figure painting appears on the interior of a Greek wine cup. Painted about 480 B.C.E. (during the Persian Wars), it shows a Greek hoplite (armored infantryman) striking a Persian warrior in hand-to-hand combat with swords. The Greek has lost his principal weapon, a spear, and the Persian can no longer shoot his, the bow and arrow. The Greek artist designed the painting to express multiple messages: the Persian's colorful outfit with sleeves and pants stresses the "otherness" of the enemy in Greek eyes, and their serene expressions at such a desperate moment dignify the horror of killing. Greek warriors often had heroic symbols painted on their shields, such as the winged horse Pegasus, an allusion to the brave exploits of Bellerophon. *(© National Museums of Scotland/The Bridgeman Art Library International.)*

start of the fifth century B.C.E.: the so-called Persian Wars (499–479 B.C.E.), in which Persia invaded Greece. The Persian invasions threatened the independence of the Greek mainland and Aegean islands. So dangerous was the threat that thirty-one Greek states (out of hundreds) temporarily laid aside their traditional competition to form an alliance to defeat the Persians. In victory, however, they lost their unity and fell to fighting one another. In the midst of nearly constant warfare spanning the century, Greeks (especially in Athens) created what later ages judged to be their most famous innovations in architecture, art, and theater. These cultural achievements have led historians to call this period from around 500 to around 400 B.C.E. the Golden Age. This Golden Age is the first part of the period called the Classical Age of Greece, which lasted from around 500 B.C.E. to the death of Alexander the Great in 323 B.C.E.

Most of the cultural achievements of the Golden Age took place in Athens, and only limited details about other important city-states, such as Corinth and Syracuse, emerge from the surviving literary and archaeological sources from this period. Many famous plays, histories, inscriptions, buildings, and sculptures survive from fifth-century B.C.E. Athens. For these reasons, studying the Greek Golden Age primarily means studying the Athenian Golden Age.

The confidence the Greeks gained from defeating the Persian invaders, combined with their traditional competitiveness, produced brilliant innovations in art, architecture, literature, education, and philosophy in the Golden Age. The new ideas in education and philosophy were hotly controversial at the time but have had a lasting influence on Western civilization. The controversy arose because many people saw the changes as attacks on ancient traditions, especially religion; they feared the gods would punish their communities for abandoning ancestral beliefs.

Political change also characterized the Athenian Golden Age. First, Athenian citizens made their city-state government more democratic than ever. Second, Athens also grew internationally powerful by using its navy to establish rule over other Greeks in a system dubbed "empire" by modern scholars. This naval power also promoted seaborne trade, and revenues from rule and trade brought Athens enormous prosperity. Athens's citizens voted to use the funds to finance new public buildings, art, and competitive theater festivals, and to pay for poorer men to serve as officials and jurors in an expanded democratic government.

The Golden Age ended when Sparta defeated Athens in the Peloponnesian War (431–404 B.C.E.) and the Athenians then fought a brief but bloody civil war (404–403 B.C.E.). The fifth century B.C.E., so famous for its cultural innovation, thus both began and ended with fierce wars, with Greeks standing together in the first one and tearing each other apart in the concluding one. Losing the Peloponnesian War bankrupted and divided Athens, turning its Golden Age to lead.

CHAPTER FOCUS Did war bring more benefit or more harm—politically, socially, and intellectually—to Golden Age Athens?

Wars between Persia and Greece, 499–479 B.C.E.

The Persian Wars had their roots in Athens's request for help from Persia in 507 B.C.E. The Athenian ambassadors agreed to the standard Persian requirement for an alliance: presenting tokens of earth and water to acknowledge submission to the Persian king. The Athenian assembly erupted in outrage at their diplomats' submitting to Persian authority but failed to inform King Darius that it rejected his terms; he continued to believe that Athens had agreed to obey him in return for his support. This misunderstanding planted the seed for two Persian attacks on Greece, one small and one huge. Since

500–323 B.C.E.
Classical Age of Greece

480–479 B.C.E.
Xerxes' invasion of Greece

451 B.C.E.
Pericles restricts Athenian citizenship to children whose parents are both citizens

500 B.C.E. — 475 B.C.E. — 450 B.C.E.

499–479 B.C.E.
Wars between Persia and Greece

490 B.C.E.
Battle of Marathon

480 B.C.E.
Battle of Salamis

461 B.C.E.
Ephialtes reforms Athenian court system

Early 450s B.C.E.
Pericles introduces pay for officeholders in Athenian democracy

the Persian Empire far outstripped the Greek city-states in soldiers and money, the conflict pitted the equivalent of a huge bear against a pack of undersized dogs.

From the Ionian Revolt to the Battle of Marathon, 499–490 B.C.E.

The lead-up from the Ionian Revolt to the Persian Wars is an example of a smaller conflict sparking a greater one—a common occurrence in the history of war. In 499 B.C.E., the Greek city-states in Ionia revolted against their Persian-installed tyrants, who were ruling harshly and unjustly, and ignored the demand of Darius I that the Ionians send more soldiers for his army. The Spartans refused to help the Ionian rebels, but the Athenians sent troops because they regarded the Ionians as close kin. A Persian counterattack sent the Athenians fleeing home and crushed the revolt by 494 B.C.E. (Map 3.1, page 79). Darius exploded in anger when he learned that the Athenians had attacked in Ionia. After all, he thought they were faithful allies. So bitter to him was this perceived betrayal that, according to the historian Herodotus, Darius ordered a slave to repeat three times at every meal, "Lord, remember the Athenians."

In 490 B.C.E., Darius sent a small fleet to punish Athens and install a puppet tyrant. He expected Athens to surrender without a fight. The Athenians refused to back down, however, confronting the invaders near the village of Marathon. The Athenian soldiers were stunned by the Persians' strange garb—colorful pants instead of the short tunics and bare legs that Greeks regarded as proper dress (see the chapter-opening photo)—but the Greek commanders in a tactical innovation had the hoplites (armored infantry) charge the enemy at a dead run instead of their usual slow advance. Running cut the time that the Athenians were exposed to the enemy's archers. The Greek soldiers, each wearing heavy metal armor, clanked across the Marathon plain through a hail of Persian arrows. In the hand-to-hand combat, the Greek hoplites used their heavier weapons to overwhelm the Persian infantry.

The Athenian infantry then hurried the twenty-six miles from Marathon to Athens to guard the city against the Persian navy. (Today's marathon races commemorate the legend of a runner speeding ahead to announce the victory and then dropping dead.) When the Persians sailed home, the Athenians rejoiced in disbelief. Thereafter, a family's greatest honor was to have a "Marathon fighter" among its ancestors.

Their unexpected success at Marathon evidently strengthened the Athenians' sense of community. When a fabulously rich strike was made in Athens's publicly owned silver mines in 483 B.C.E., a far-sighted leader named **Themistocles** convinced the assembly to spend the money on doubling the size of the navy to defend against possible foreign attack instead of distributing the money to the citizens to spend on themselves.

The Great Persian Invasion, 480–479 B.C.E.

Themistocles' foresight proved valuable when Darius's son Xerxes I (r. 486–465 B.C.E.) assembled an immense force to invade Greece to avenge his father's defeat and add the mainland city-states to the many lands paying him taxes. The Persians spared no expense, even digging a great canal through a peninsula in northern Greece to give their fleet safe passage. So huge was Xerxes' army, the Greeks claimed, that when the invasion began in 480 B.C.E. it took seven days and seven nights for the entire force to cross the Hellespont, the strip of sea between Anatolia and Greece, which Xerxes had bridged.

Themistocles (thuh MIST uh kleez): Athens's leader during the great Persian invasion of Greece.

450 B.C.E. Protagoras and other Sophists begin to teach in Athens

446–445 B.C.E. (winter) Peace treaty between Athens and Sparta; intended to last thirty years

441 B.C.E. Sophocles presents the tragedy *Antigone*

431–404 B.C.E. Peloponnesian War

425 B.C.E.

420s B.C.E. Herodotus finishes *Histories*

415–413 B.C.E. Enormous Athenian military expedition against Sicily

411 B.C.E. Aristophanes presents the comedy *Lysistrata*

404–403 B.C.E. Rule of the Thirty Tyrants at Athens

403 B.C.E. Restoration of democracy in Athens

400 B.C.E.

A Cylindrical Signet of Persia's King Darius
Like other kings in the ancient Mediterranean region, the Persian king hunted lions to show his courage and his ability to overcome nature's threats. Here on this cylindrical signet, used to impress the royal seal into wet clay to verify documents, King Darius (r. 522–486 B.C.E.) shoots arrows from a chariot driven for him by a charioteer. He is depicted wearing his crown so that his status as ruler would be obvious. The symbol of Ahura Mazda, the chief god of Persian religion, hovers in the sky to indicate that the king enjoys divine favor. *(The British Museum/akg-images.)*

Xerxes thought the Greek city-states would immediately surrender. Some did, but thirty-one made a decision new in Greek history: to unite as allies to defend their city-states' political freedom.

Their coalition became known as the Hellenic League, but it hardly represented the entire Greek world. The allies desperately wanted the major Greek city-states in Italy and Sicily to join the league because these western states were rich naval powers, but they refused. Syracuse, for example, the most powerful Greek state at the time, controlled a regional empire built on agriculture in Sicily's plains and seaborne commerce through its harbors on the Mediterranean's western trading routes. The tyrant ruling Syracuse rejected the league's appeal for help because he was fighting his own war against Carthage, a Phoenician city in North Africa, over control of the trade routes.

The Hellenic League chose Sparta to lead because of its reputation for military excellence. The Athenians swallowed their competitive desire for honor and agreed to follow. The Spartans demonstrated their courage in 480 B.C.E. when three hundred of their infantry (and a few hundred other troops) blocked Xerxes' army for several days at the narrow pass called Thermopylae ("gate of hot springs") in central Greece. When told the Persian archers were so numerous that their arrows darkened the sun, one Spartan reportedly remarked, "That's good news; we'll get to fight in the shade." They did—to the death. Their tomb's memorial proclaimed, "Go tell the Spartans that we lie buried here obedient to their orders."

When the Persians marched south, the Athenians, knowing they could not defend the city, evacuated their residents to the Peloponnese rather than surrender. The Persians then burned Athens. The panicked allies decided to retreat to the Peloponnese, but in the summer of 480 B.C.E. Themistocles and his Athenian political rival Aristides cooperated to win a tough argument with the other city-states' generals, convincing them to stay and fight a naval battle. Themistocles then tricked the Persian king into sending his ships into battle against the Greek fleet in the channel between the island of Salamis and the west coast of Athens: the narrowness of the channel prevented Xerxes from sending all his fleet (twice or more the size of the Greeks') into battle at the same time. The heavier Greek warships won the battle by ramming the flimsier Persian craft in the tight space. The battle of Salamis turned the tide of the war, and Xerxes retreated to Persia. The following summer (479 B.C.E.), the Spartans led the Greek infantry to dual victories over the remaining Persian land forces on the Greek mainland and, now on the offensive against the enemy,

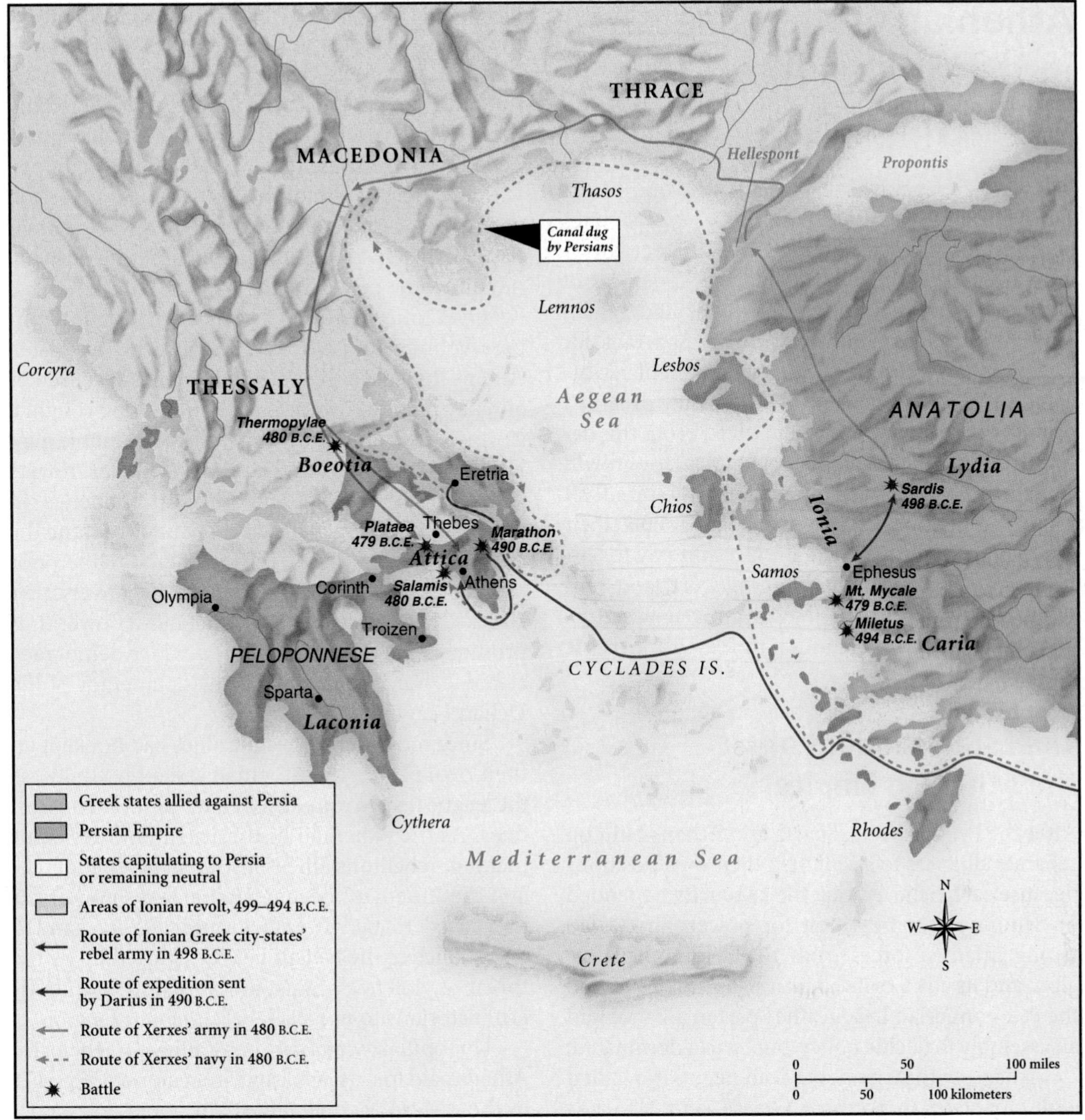

MAP 3.1 The Persian Wars, 499–479 B.C.E.
Following the example of King Cyrus (r. 557–530 B.C.E.), the founder of the Persian Empire, King Cambyses (r. 530–522 B.C.E.) and King Darius I (r. 522–486 B.C.E.) expanded the empire eastward and westward. Darius invaded Thrace more than fifteen years before the conflict against the Greeks that we call the Persian Wars. The Persians' unexpected defeat in Greece put an end to their attempt to extend their power into Europe.

on the Anatolian coast. Superior generalship and the Greek competitive spirit of aretê ("excellence") underlay these successes. When the victorious allies met to award a prize to the war's best Greek commander, Themistocles won the competition — every general voted for himself first and Themistocles second!

The Greeks won their battles against the Persians because their generals, especially Themistocles, had better strategic foresight, their soldiers had stronger body armor, their warships were more effective in close combat, and their tactics minimized the Persian advantage in numbers of troops and ships. Above all, the Greeks won the war because enough of them took the innovative step of uniting to fight together to keep their independence. Because the Greek forces included not only the social elites but also thousands of poorer men who rowed the warships, the victory over the Persians showed that rich and poor Greeks alike treasured the ideal of political freedom for their city-states that had emerged during the Archaic Age.

REVIEW QUESTION How did the Greeks overcome the dangers of the Persian invasions?

Athenian Confidence in the Golden Age, 478–431 B.C.E.

The struggle against the Persians was one of the rare occasions when at least some Greek city-states cooperated. Victory fractured this alliance, however, because the allies resented the harshness of Spartan command and the Athenians had gained the confidence to compete with the Spartans for leadership of Greece. No longer were Athenians satisfied to be followers of Sparta; now they dreamed of a much grander role for themselves. From this desire arose the so-called Athenian Empire. The growth of Athens's power over other Greeks inspired yet more confidence in its citizens, who broadened their democracy and spent vast amounts on pay for officials and jurors, public buildings, art, and religious festivals in which they competed with one another for public recognition in presenting music and drama.

The Establishment of the Athenian Empire

After the Persian Wars, Sparta and Athens built up separate alliances to strengthen their own positions because each believed that their security depended on winning a competition for power. Sparta led strong infantry forces from the Peloponnese region, and its ally Corinth had a sizable navy. Called the Peloponnesian League, the Spartan alliance had an assembly to decide policy, but Sparta dominated.

Athens, with Aristides as lead negotiator, allied with city-states in northern Greece, on the islands of the Aegean Sea, and along the Ionian coast — the places most in need of protection from Persian retaliation. This alliance, whose treasury was originally located on the Aegean island of Delos, was built on naval power and today is called the **Delian League**. The Delian League started out as a democratic alliance for collective security, but Athens came to control it through the allies' willingness to allow the Athenians to command and to set the financing arrangements for the league's fleet. At its height, the league included some three hundred city-states. Each paid dues according to its size; Athens as the league's leader controlled how the dues were used. Larger city-states paid their dues by sending **triremes** — warships propelled by 170 rowers on three levels and equipped with a battering ram at the bow (see Figure 3.1 on page 81) — complete with trained crews and their pay. Smaller states could share in building one ship or contribute cash instead.

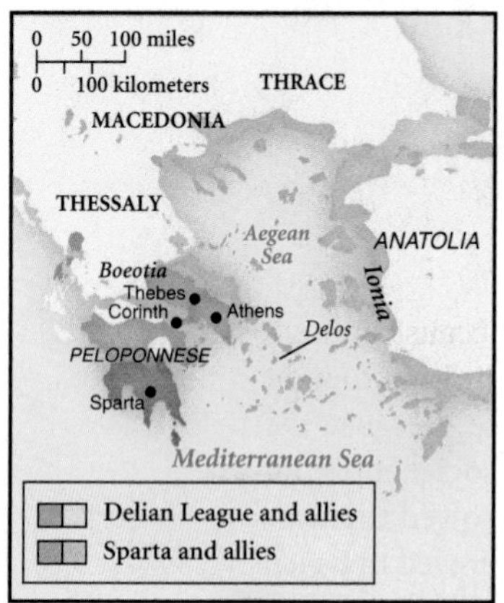

The Delian and Peloponnesian Leagues

Over time, more and more Delian League members voluntarily paid cash because it was easier. Athens then used this money to construct triremes and pay men to row them; oarsmen who brought a slave to row alongside them earned double pay. Drawn primarily from the poorest citizens, rowers gained both income and political influence in Athenian democracy because the navy became the city-state's main force. These benefits made poor citizens eager to expand Athens's power over other Greeks. The increase in Athenian naval power thus promoted the development of a wider democracy at home, but it undermined the democracy of the Delian League.

Since most Delian League allies had not kept up their own navies, the Athenian assembly could use the league fleet to force disobedient allies to pay cash dues. As the Athenian historian Thucydides commented, rebellious allies "lost their independence, and the Athenians became no longer as popular as they used to be." It was Athens's heavy-handed dominance of the Delian League, backed up by the threat of violence against allies, that has led modern historians to use the label *Athenian Empire.*

Unpopularity among many allies was the price Athens paid for making itself the major naval power in the eastern Mediterranean: by about 460 B.C.E., the Delian League's fleet had expelled remaining Persian garrisons from northern Greece and driven the enemy fleet from the Aegean Sea. This sweep eliminated the Persian threat for the next fifty years and proved the effectiveness of Athenian leadership.

Military success made Athens prosperous by bringing in spoils and cash dues from the Delian League, making seaborne trade safe, and benefiting rich and poor alike — the poor men who rowed the league's navy earned good pay, while elite commanders enhanced their chances for election to high office by spending their spoils on public festivals and buildings. The Athenian assembly debated how Athens should treat its league allies, but the majority consistently rejected complaints on the grounds that

---

Delian (DEE lee un) League: The naval alliance led by Athens in the Golden Age that became the basis for the Athenian Empire.

triremes (TRY reems): Greek wooden warships rowed by 170 oarsmen sitting on three levels and equipped with a battering ram at the bow.

the league was fulfilling its original duty by protecting everyone from Persian attack. In this way, there were direct links in Golden Age Athens among democracy for its own citizens, pay, and imperialism.

Radical Democracy and Pericles' Leadership, 461–431 B.C.E.

As the Delian League grew, the Athenian fleet's oarsmen realized that they provided the cornerstone for Athens's new power and prosperity. In the late 460s B.C.E., they decided that the time had come to increase their political power by making the court system of Athens just as democratic as the legislative assembly, in which all free adult male citizens could already participate. They wanted laws and political institutions that would finally make Cleisthenes' promise of equality through law a reality for everyone so that they would no longer be liable to unfair verdicts at the hands of the elite in criminal cases and civil suits. Members of the elite led this push for judicial reform, hoping to win popular support for election to high office by speaking out for the interests of the masses. A member of one of Athens's most distinguished families, **Pericles** (c. 495–429 B.C.E.), became Golden Age Athens's dominant politician by spearheading reforms to democratize its judicial system and provide pay for many public offices.

Creating Radical Democracy

The changes to Athenian democracy in the 460s and 450s B.C.E. have led historians to label the system *radical* ("from the roots") because it gave direct political power in the assembly and participation in the court system to all adult male citizens, not just elites. The government consisted of the assembly open to all these men, the Council of Five Hundred chosen annually by lottery, the Council of the Areopagus of ex-archons serving for life, an executive board of ten annually elected "generals," nine archons (now chosen by lottery every year), hundreds of other annual minor officials (most chosen by lottery), and the court system.

Athens's **radical democracy** balanced two competing goals: (1) participation by as many ordinary male citizens as possible in direct (not representative) democracy and (2) selective leadership by elite citizens. To achieve the first goal, Athenian voters established (1) random selection by lottery for most public offices, term limits, shared power, and salaries for most officials and members of the Council of Five Hundred (which prepared the assembly's agenda and supervised public matters); (2) open investigation and punishment of corruption; (3) equal protection under the law for citizens regardless of wealth; and (4) payment for and random selection of jurors. To achieve the second, the highest-level officials were elected, rather than chosen by lottery. The top officials (the board of ten generals, who oversaw military and financial affairs) ran for election every year, could be reelected an unlimited number of times, and received no pay so that they would not

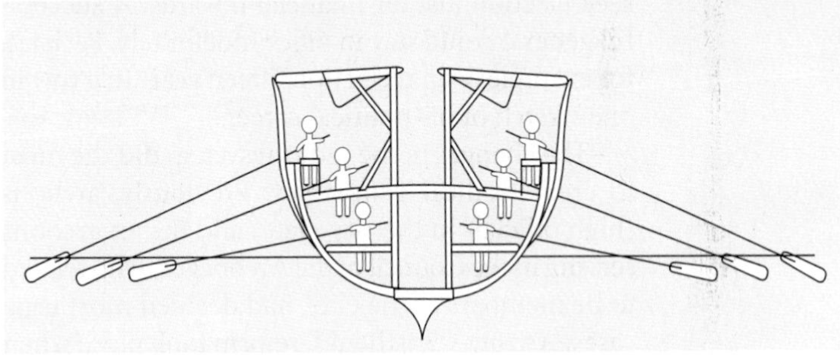

FIGURE 3.1 Triremes, the Foremost Classical Greek Warships
Innovations in military technology and training propelled a naval arms race in the fifth century B.C.E. when Greek shipbuilders designed larger and faster ramming ships powered by 170 rowers seated in three rows, each above the other. (See the line illustration of the rowers from behind.) Called triremes, these ships were expensive to build and required extensive crew training. Only wealthy and populous city-states such as Athens could afford to build and man large fleets of triremes. The relief sculpture found on the Athenian acropolis and dating from about 400 B.C.E. gives a glimpse of what a trireme looked like from the side when being rowed into battle. (Sails were used for power only when the ship was not in combat.) *(The Art Archive/Acropolis Museum, Athens/Gianni Dagli Orti.)*

Pericles (PEHR uh kleez): Athens's political leader during the Golden Age.

radical democracy: The Athenian system of democracy established in the 460s and 450s B.C.E. that extended direct political power and participation in the court system to all adult male citizens.

Potsherd Ballots for Ostracism
These two shards (*ostraka*) were broken from the same pot (as the breakage line shows) and inscribed for use as ballots in an ostracism at Athens. The lower fragment carries the name of Themistocles, the leader who engineered the Greek fleet's success against the Persian navy off the island of Salamis in 480 B.C.E. The upper one has the name of Cimon, the Delian League's most famous general. Political competition led to Themistocles' ostracism sometime in the late 470s B.C.E. and Cimon's in 461 B.C.E. Therefore, if these two ballots were intended for the same ostracism, it must have been that of Themistocles, or an earlier one when he was still in Athens. *(American School of Classical Studies at Athens: Agora Excavations.)*

seek election just for financial rewards. A successful general could stay in office indefinitely. Pericles, for example, won reelection fifteen years in a row in one stretch of his political career.

The changes in the judicial system did the most to create radical democracy. Previously, archons (high officials in the city-state) and the ex-archons serving in the Council of the Areopagus, who tended to be members of the elite, had decided most legal cases. As with Cleisthenes, reform took place when an elite man proposed it to support ordinary men's political rights and simultaneously win their votes against his rivals: in 461 B.C.E. Ephialtes won popular support by getting the assembly to establish a new system that took away jurisdiction from the archons and gave it to courts manned by citizen jurors. To make it more democratic and prevent bribery, jurors were selected by lottery from male citizens over thirty years old. They received pay to serve on juries numbering from several hundred to several thousand members. No judges or lawyers existed, and jurors voted by secret ballot after hearing speeches from the persons involved. As in the assembly, a majority vote decided matters; no appeals of verdicts were allowed.

Ostracism and Majority Rule

Athenian radical democracy included notions of privacy and legal protection for individuals, but the majority could overrule those protections on matters of public policy. A striking example was **ostracism** (from *ostrakon*, a piece of broken pottery used as a ballot). Once a year, all male citizens could cast a ballot on which they scratched the name of one man they thought should be exiled for ten years. If at least six thousand ballots were cast, the man whose name appeared on the greatest number was expelled from Athens. He suffered no other penalty; his family and property remained undisturbed.

Usually a man was ostracized because he had become so popular that a majority feared he would overthrow the democracy to rule as a tyrant. Sometimes a leader was ostracized when his political competitors ganged up to vote against him. This happened to Themistocles, who in a great irony ended up living in Persia as a favorite of King Xerxes, who valued his former enemy's intelligence. There was no guarantee of voters' motives in an ostracism, as a story about Aristides illustrates. He was nicknamed "the Just" because he had proved himself so fair-minded in setting the original level of dues for Delian League members. On the day of an ostracism, an illiterate citizen handed him a pottery fragment and asked him to scratch a name on it:

> "Certainly," said Aristides. "Which name shall I write?" "Aristides," replied the man. "All right," said Aristides as he inscribed his own name, "but why do you want to ostracize Aristides? What has he done to you?" "Oh, nothing. I don't even know him," sputtered the man. "I just can't stand hearing everybody refer to him as 'the Just.'"

True or not, this tale demonstrates that most Athenians believed the right way to support democracy was to trust a majority vote, regardless of its possible injustice to a particular individual.

Not all citizens approved of the equality of radical democracy. Some socially elite citizens bitterly criticized what they saw as its disregard for social merit in giving political power to the poor. Opponents of democracy blamed it for promoting the interests of those whom they called the "wicked" (i.e., the poor) over the interests of "useful" citizens (i.e., themselves, the rich). These critics became particularly vocal when Athens's democracy suffered periods of crisis, as at certain points in the great war with Sparta that was to erupt at the end of the Golden Age. They insisted that oligarchy—the rule of the few—was morally superior to radical democracy because they believed that the poor lacked the education and moral values needed for leadership and would use their majority rule to

---

ostracism (AHS truh sizm): An annual procedure in Athenian radical democracy by which a man could be voted out of the city-state for ten years; its purpose was to prevent tyranny.

strip the rich of their wealth by passing laws to make them pay for expensive public programs.

Pericles' Leadership Still, Pericles used his political vision and spellbinding public-speaking skills to convince the assembly to pass reforms that would strengthen the equality prized by poor citizens. These efforts contributed to his popularity and helped him become the most influential leader of his era. Pericles began his career by supporting Ephialtes' reform of the court system. Then, in the early 450s B.C.E., he boosted mass participation in democracy by introducing pay for service in the public offices filled by lottery. This reform used public funds to pay men for serving in numerous government posts, on the Council of Five Hundred, and on juries. Previously, because these offices had been unpaid, only wealthy men could afford to fill them. Now poor citizens could serve.

Pericles' citizenship reforms not only boosted the status of native-born Athenians from all classes but also recast who constituted a citizen. In 451 B.C.E., Pericles sponsored a law restricting citizenship to those whose mother and father were both Athenian by birth. Previously, wealthy men had often married foreign women from elite families. This change both increased the status of Athenian women, rich or poor, as potential mothers of citizens and made Athenian citizenship more valuable by reducing the number of people eligible for its legal and financial benefits. In another effort to enforce exclusiveness, officials reviewed everyone's identity and, some sources report, revoked the citizenship of thousands.

Pericles also convinced the assembly to launch naval campaigns (and thus provide poor Athenians an income as rowers) when war with Sparta broke out in the 450s B.C.E. over Athenian actions against Peloponnesian League states. He supported sending the fleet against Persian garrisons in Cyprus, Egypt, and the eastern Mediterranean to expand the Delian League's power and win war spoils. The voters in the assembly were so eager to compete for international power against both Persians and other Greeks that they authorized up to three major expeditions at a time. This large-scale militarism slowed in the late 450s B.C.E. after a large naval force sent to aid an Egyptian rebellion against Persian rule, in an effort to weaken Persian power in the eastern Mediterranean, suffered a horrendous defeat in which the Persian forces killed tens of thousands of oarsmen. In the winter of 446–445 B.C.E., Pericles arranged a peace treaty with Sparta with the goal of stabilizing the balance of power in Greece for thirty years and thus preserving Athenian control of the Delian League.

The Urban Landscape in Athens

Golden Age Athens prospered from Delian League dues, war plunder, and taxes on booming international seaborne trade. Its harbor in Piraeus promoted cross-Mediterranean commerce, its navy made its empire's numerous ports safe for merchants and travelers, and its courts resolved legal disputes. Its artisans produced goods traded far and wide; the Etruscans in central Italy, for example, imported countless painted vases for wine drinking at Greek-style dinner parties. The economic activity and international traffic of the mid-fifth century B.C.E. boosted Athens to its greatest prosperity ever.

Athenians spent their new riches not just on pay for citizens to participate in democratic government but also on their city's public buildings, art, and religious festivals. In private life, rich urban dwellers splurged on luxury goods influenced by Persian designs, but most houses retained their traditional modest size and plainness. Farmhouses could cluster in villages or stand isolated, while houses and apartments in the city wedged tightly against one another along narrow, winding streets. Recent archaeological study of the city of Olynthus in northeastern Greece shows that urban one-family homes were built on varying patterns, but one favorite plan grouped bedrooms, storerooms, and dining rooms around open-air courtyards. Poor city residents rented small apartments. Wall paintings or decorative artworks were rare, furnishings sparse. Toilets consisted of pots and a pit outside the front door. The city paid collectors to dump the dung outside its fortification walls.

Generals who wanted to display their excellence and also win the people's favor spent their war spoils on running tracks, shade trees, and public buildings. A popular building project was a stoa, a narrow structure open along one side that offered shelter from the weather. The super-rich commander Cimon, for example, paid for the Painted Stoa to be built on the edge of Athens's **agora**, the central market square. There, crowds of shoppers could admire the stoa's bright paintings depicting Cimon's family's military achievements, especially his father's leadership in the battle of Marathon. This sort of contribution was voluntary, but the laws required wealthy citizens to pay for festivals and equipping warships. This financial obligation on the rich was essential because Athens, like most other Greek city-states, had no regular property or income taxes.

---

agora (AH gore uh): The central market square of a Greek city-state, a popular gathering place for conversation.

MAP 3.2 Fifth-Century B.C.E. Athens
The urban center of Athens, with the agora and acropolis at its heart, measured about one square mile; it was surrounded by a stone wall with a circuit of some four miles. Gates guarded by towers and various smaller entries allowed traffic in and out of the city. Much of the Athenian population lived in the many demes (villages) of the surrounding countryside. Most of the city's water supply came from wells and springs inside the walls, but, unusual for a Greek city, Athens also had water piped in from outside. The Long Walls provided a protected corridor connecting the city to its harbor at Piraeus, where the Athenian navy was anchored and grain was imported to feed the people.

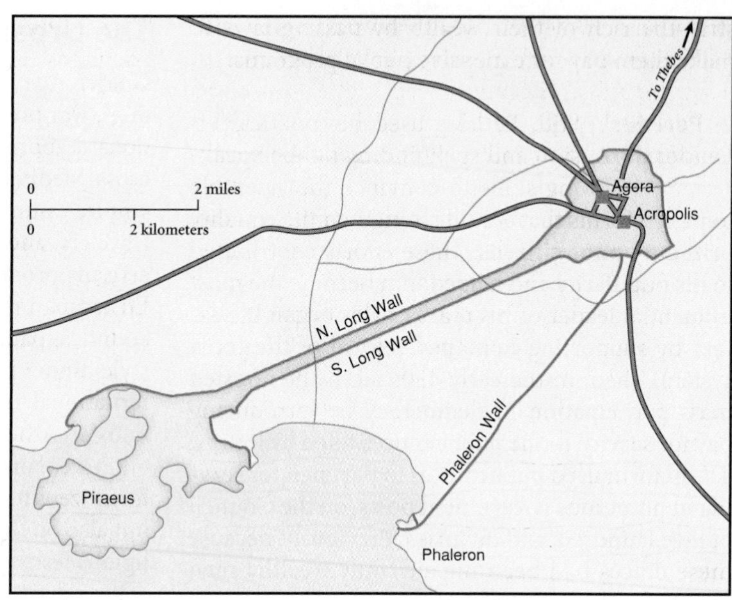

The Parthenon | On Athens's acropolis (the rocky hill at the city's center, Map 3.2), Pericles had the two most famous buildings of Golden Age Athens erected during the 440s and 430s B.C.E.: a mammoth gateway and an enormous marble temple of Athena called the **Parthenon**. Comparing a day's wage then and now, we can estimate that these buildings together cost more than the equivalent of a billion dollars, a phenomenal sum for a Greek city-state. Pericles' political rivals slammed him for spending too much public money on the project and diverting Delian League funds to beautify Athens.

The Parthenon ("virgin goddess's house") has become the foremost symbol of Athens's Golden Age. The Parthenon honored Athena, the city's patron deity, as the divine champion of Athenian military power and demonstrated her visible presence in the city. Inside the temple, a gold-and-ivory statue nearly forty feet high depicted the goddess in armor, holding in her outstretched hand a six-foot statue of Nike, the goddess of victory.

Like all Greek temples, the Parthenon was meant as a house for its divinity, not as a gathering place for worshippers. Its design followed standard temple architecture: a rectangular box on a raised platform lined with columns, a plan the Greeks probably derived from the stone temples of Egypt. The Parthenon's soaring columns fenced in a porch surrounding the interior chamber on all sides. They were carved in the simple style called Doric, in contrast to the more elaborate Ionic and Corinthian styles often imitated in columns on modern buildings (Figure 3.2).

The Parthenon's massive size and innovative style proclaimed the self-confidence of Golden Age Athens and its competitive drive to build a monument more spectacular than any other in Greece. Constructed from twenty thousand tons of Attic marble, the temple stretched some 230 feet long and 100 feet wide, with eight columns across the ends instead of the six normally found in Doric style and seventeen instead of thirteen along the sides. The temple's complex architecture demonstrated the

Parthenon (PAR thuh non): The massive temple to Athena as a warrior goddess built atop the Athenian acropolis in the Golden Age of Greece.

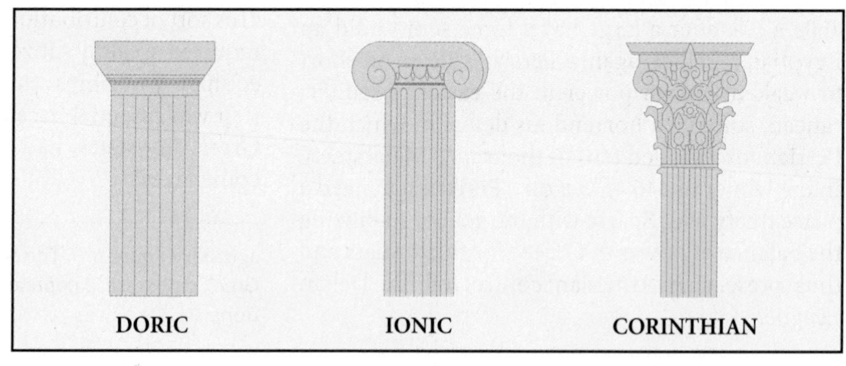

FIGURE 3.2 Styles of Greek Capitals
The Greeks decorated the capitals, or tops, of columns in these three styles to fit the different architectural "canons" (their word for precise mathematical systems of proportions) that they devised for designing buildings. These styles were much imitated in later times, as on many U.S. state capitols and the U.S. Supreme Court Building in Washington, D.C.

Athenian ambition to use human skill to improve nature: because perfectly rectilinear architecture appears curved to the human eye, subtle curves and inclines were built into the Parthenon to produce an illusion of completely straight lines and emphasize its massiveness.

The Parthenon's many sculptures communicated confident messages: the gods ensure triumph over the forces of chaos, and Athenians enjoy the gods' goodwill more than any other city-state's citizens do. The sculptures in each pediment (the triangular space atop the columns at either end of the temple) portrayed Athena as the city-state's benefactor. The metopes (panels sculpted in relief above the outer columns around all four sides) portrayed victories over hostile centaurs (creatures with the body of a horse but torso and head of a man) and other enemies of civilization. Most strikingly of all, a frieze (a continuous band of figures carved in relief) ran around the top of the walls inside the porch and was painted in bright colors to make it more visible. The Parthenon's frieze was special because usually only Ionic-style buildings had one. Although it had no inscription to state its subject, the frieze most likely portrayed Athenian men, women, and children on parade in the presence of the gods, the procession shown in motion like the pictures in a graphic novel or cartoon today.

The Parthenon frieze made a bold statement about how Athenians perceived their relationship to the gods — no other Greeks had ever adorned a temple with representations of themselves. Its sculpture staked a claim of unique closeness between the city-state and the gods, reflecting the Athenians' confidence after helping turn back the Persians, achieving leadership of a powerful naval alliance, and accumulating great wealth. Their success, the Athenians believed, proved that the gods were on their side, and their fabulous buildings displayed their gratitude.

Sculpture's New Message Like the unique Parthenon frieze, the innovations that Golden Age artists made in representing the human body shattered tradition. By the time of the Persian Wars, Greek sculptors had begun replacing the stiffly balanced style of Archaic Age statues with statues in motion in new poses. This style of movement in stone expressed an energetic balancing of competing forces, echoing a theme evident in radical democracy's principles.

Sculptors also began carving anatomically realistic but perfect-looking bodies, suggesting that humans could be confident in their potential for beauty and perfection. Female statues, for example, now displayed the shape of the curves underneath clothing,

The Acropolis of Athens
Most Greek city-states, including Athens, sprang up around a prominent rocky hill, called an acropolis ("height of the city"; compare the picture of Corinth on page 66). The summit of the acropolis usually housed sanctuaries for the city's protective deities and could serve as a fortress for the population during an enemy attack. Athens's acropolis boasted several elaborately decorated marble temples honoring the goddess Athena; the largest one was the Parthenon, seen here from its west (back) side. Recent research suggests that the ruins of a temple burned by the Persians when they captured Athens in 480 B.C.E. remained in place right next to the Parthenon. The Athenians left its charred remains to remind themselves of the sacrifices they had made in defending their freedom. (The walls in the lower foreground are from a theater built in Roman times.) *(akg-images.)*

Scene from the Parthenon Frieze
The Parthenon, the Athenian temple honoring Athena as a warrior goddess and patron of the Delian League, dominated the summit of the city's acropolis. A frieze (band of sculpture in relief), of which this is a small section, ran around the top of the temple's outside wall. Here, riders line up in the Pan-Athenaic festival's procession to the Parthenon; the artist layered the horses' legs to show depth. The original blazed with bright colors and details fashioned from metal, such as the horses' bridles. The elaborate folds of the riders' garments display the rich style characteristic of clothed figures in Classical Age sculpture. How would you compare the style of this relief to that of the Persian relief on page 41? *(The Art Archive/ Acropolis Museum, Athens/Gianni Dagli Orti.)*

while male ones showed bodybuilders' muscles. The faces showed a more relaxed and self-confident look in place of the rigid smiles of archaic statues.

As with relief sculptures on temples, freestanding Golden Age statues were erected to be seen by the public, whether they were paid for with private or government funds. Privately commissioned statues of gods were placed in sanctuaries as symbols of devotion. Wealthy families paid for statues of their deceased relatives, especially if they had died young in war, to be placed above their graves as memorials of their excellence and signs of the family's social status.

REVIEW QUESTION What factors produced political change in fifth-century B.C.E. Athens?

Tradition and Innovation in Athens's Golden Age

Golden Age Athens's prosperity and international contacts created unprecedented innovations in architecture, art, drama, education, and philosophy, but central aspects of the city-state's social and religious customs remained traditional, as they did elsewhere throughout Greece. This contrast between cultural change and social continuity generated tension between the desire to innovate and the pressure to preserve traditional ways, especially concerning the conduct of women and the practice of religion. In keeping with tradition, Athenian women, along with other Greek women, were expected to limit their public role to participation in religious ceremonies. In private life they were to manage their households and, if they were poor, work to help support their families. The startling new ideas of competitive philosophers and teachers called Sophists and the Athenian philosopher Socrates' views on personal morality and responsibility caused many people to fear that the gods would become angry at the community. The most famous response to the clash between innovation and tradition was the development of publicly funded drama festivals, whose contests for tragic and comic plays examined problems in city-state life, especially the social and personal hardships caused by war.

Religious Tradition in a Period of Change

Greeks maintained religious tradition publicly by participating in the city-state's sacrifices and festivals, and privately by seeking a personal relationship with the gods in the rituals of hero cults and mystery cults. Each cult had its own rituals, including everything from large-animal sacrifices to bloodless offerings of fruits, vegetables, and small cakes. The speechwriter Lysias (c. 445–380 B.C.E.), a Syracusan residing in Athens, explained the reason for publicly funded sacrifices:

> Our ancestors handed down to us the most powerful and prosperous community in Greece by

> performing the prescribed sacrifices. It is therefore proper for us to offer the same sacrifices as they, if only for the sake of the success which has resulted from those rites.

The public slaughter of a large animal provided an occasion for the community to reaffirm its ties to the divine world and for the worshippers to benefit by feasting on the roasted meat of the sacrificed beast. For poor people, the free food provided at religious festivals might be the only meat they ever tasted.

Golden Age Athens used its riches to pay for more religious festivals than any other city-state; nearly half the days of the year included one. The biggest festivals featured parades as well as contests with valuable prizes in music, dancing, poetry, and athletics. Laborers' contracts specified how many days off they received to attend such ceremonies. Some festivals were for women only, such as the three-day festival for married women in honor of Demeter, goddess of agriculture and fertility.

Privately, people took a keen interest in affirming their personal relations with the divine. Families marked significant events such as birth, marriage, and death with prayers, rituals, and sacrifices. They honored their ancestors with offerings made at their tombs, consulted seers about the meanings of dreams and omens, and paid magicians for spells to improve their love lives or curses to harm their enemies. Particularly important were hero cults and mystery cults. Hero cults included rituals performed at the tomb of an extraordinarily famous man or woman. Heroes' remains were thought to retain special power to reveal the future by inspiring oracles, healing sickness, and providing protection in battle. The strongman Herakles (or Hercules, as the Romans spelled his name) had cults all over the Greek world because his superhuman reputation gave him international appeal. **Mystery cults** involved a set of prayers, hymns, ritual purification, sacrifices, and other forms of worship that initiated members into secret knowledge about the divine and human worlds. Initiates believed that they gained divine protection from the cult's god or gods.

The Athenian mystery cult of Demeter and her daughter Persephone attracted worshippers from all parts of the world because it offered hope for protection on earth and in the afterlife. The cult's central rite was the Mysteries, a series of initiation ceremonies into secret knowledge. So important were the Mysteries that the Greek states observed an international truce—as with the Olympic Games—to allow travel even from distant corners of the world to attend them. The Mysteries were open to any free Greek-speaking individuals—women and men, adults and children—if they were clear of ritual pollution (for example, if they had not committed sacrilege, been convicted of murder, or had recent contact with a corpse or blood from a birth). Some slaves who worked in the sanctuary were also eligible to participate. The main stage of initiation took almost two weeks, culminating in the revelation of Demeter's central secret after a day of fasting. So seriously did Greeks take the initiation that no one ever revealed the secret during the cult's thousand-year history. Being initiated promised a better fate on earth and after death. A sixth-century B.C.E. poem read, "Richly blessed is the mortal who has seen these rites; but whoever is not an initiate and has no share in them, that one never has an equal portion after death, down in the gloomy darkness."

Mystery cults reveal that ancient Greeks thought their gods required action from their worshippers to receive blessings. Preserving religious tradition mattered deeply to most people because they saw it as a safeguard against the precariousness of life.

Women, Slaves, and Metics

Women, slaves, and **metics** (foreigners granted permanent residence status in return for paying taxes and serving in the military) made up the majority of Athens's population, but they lacked political rights. Women who were citizens enjoyed legal privileges and social status denied slaves and foreigners, and they earned respect through their roles in the family and in religion. Upper-class women managed their households, visited female friends, and participated in religious cults at home and in public. Poor women worked as small-scale merchants, crafts producers, and agricultural laborers. Slaves and metics also contributed much to Athens's prosperity, but they always remained outsiders in the city-state.

Property, Inheritance, and Marriage Bearing children in marriage earned women status because it was literally the source of family—the heart of Greek society. To defend this fundamental social institution, men were expected to respect and support their wives. Childbirth was dangerous under the medical conditions of the time. In *Medea*, a play of 431 B.C.E. by Euripides, the heroine shouts in anger at her husband, who has selfishly betrayed her: "People say that

mystery cults: Religious worship that provided initiation into secret knowledge and divine protection, including hope for a better afterlife.

metic: A foreigner granted permanent residence status in Athens in return for paying taxes and serving in the military.

CONTRASTING VIEWS

The Nature of Women and Marriage

Greeks believed that women had different natures from men and that both genders were capable of excellence, but in their own ways (Documents 1 and 2). Marriage was supposed to bring these natures together in a partnership of complementary strengths and obligations to each other (Document 3). Marriage contracts (Document 4), similar to modern prenuptial agreements, became common to define the partnership's terms. In reading these passages, consider whether you think they would have been different if they had been written by women instead of men.

1. Pericles Addresses the Athenians in the First Year of the Peloponnesian War (431–430 B.C.E.)

According to Thucydides, Pericles concluded his Funeral Oration, a solemn public occasion commemorating the valor of soldiers killed in battle and the excellences expected of citizens, with these terse remarks to the women in the audience. His comments reveal not only the assumption that women had a different nature from men but also the assumption that women best served social harmony by not becoming subjects of gossip. He kept these comments to a bare minimum in his long speech.

If it is also appropriate now for me to say something about what excellence means for women, I will signal all my thinking with this short piece of advice to those of you present who are now widows of the war dead: your reputation will be great if you don't fall short of your innate nature and men talk about you the least whether in praise of your excellence or blaming your faults.

Source: Thucydides, *History of the Peloponnesian War*, Book 2.45. Translation by Thomas R. Martin.

2. Melanippe Explains Why Men's Criticism of Women Is Baseless (late fifth century B.C.E.)

The Athenian playwright Euripides often portrayed female characters denouncing men for misunderstanding and criticizing women. The heroine of his tragedy Melanippe the Captive *is a mother who overcomes hardship and treachery to save her family. Preserved only on damaged papyrus scraps, Melanippe's speech unfortunately breaks off before finishing.*

Men's blame and criticism of women are empty, like the twanging sound a bow string makes without an arrow. Women are superior to men, and I'll demonstrate it. They make contracts with no need of witnesses [to swear they are honest]. They manage their households and keep safe the valuable possessions, shipped from abroad, that they have inside their homes. Without a woman, no household is elegant or happy. And then in the matter of people's relationship with the gods—this I judge to be most important of all—there we have the greatest role. For women prophesy the will of Apollo in his oracles [at Delphi], and at the hallowed oracle of Dodona by the sacred oak tree a woman reveals the will of Zeus to all Greeks who seek it. And then there are the sacred rites of initiation performed for the Fates and the Goddesses Without Names: these can't be done with holiness by men, but women make them flourish in every way. In this way women's role in religion is right and proper.

Therefore, should anyone put down women? Won't those men stop their empty fault-finding, the ones who strongly believe that all women should be blamed if a single one is found to be bad? I will make a distinction with the following argument: nothing is worse than a bad woman, but nothing is more surpassingly superior than a worthy one.

Source: Euripides, *Melanippe the Captive*, fragment 660 Mette. Translation by Thomas R. Martin.

3. Socrates Discusses Gender Roles in Marriage (late fifth century B.C.E.)

In this passage written by his follower and famous soldier Xenophon, Socrates discusses family life because it reveals the qualities of women as well as men. His analysis is part of his quest to discover the nature of human excellence. Socrates' upper-class friend Ischomachus has, as was common, married a young woman (whose name is not given), and the philosopher is quizzing him about their marriage. The new husband explains that it was a partnership based on the complementary natures of male and female.

Ischomachus: I said to her: . . . I for my sake and your parents for your sake [arranged our marriage] by considering who would be the best partner for forming a household and having children. I chose you, and your parents chose me as the best they could find. If God should give us children, we will then plan how to raise them in the best possible way. For our partnership provides us this good: the best

we women lead a safe life at home, while men have to go to war. What fools they are! I would much rather fight in battle three times than give birth to a child even once."

Athenian wives were expected to be partners with their husbands in owning and managing the household's property to help the family thrive. (See "Contrasting Views," above.) Rich women acquired property, including land—the most valued possession in Greek society because it could be farmed or rented out for income—through inheritance and dowry. A husband often had to put up valuable land of his own as collateral to guarantee repayment to his wife of the amount of her dowry if he

mutual support and the best maintenance in our old age. We have this sharing now in our household, because I've contributed all that I own to the common resources of the household, and so have you. We're not going to count up who brought more property, because the one who turns out to be the better partner in a marriage has made the greater contribution.

Ischomachus's wife: But how will I be able to partner you? What ability do I have? Everything rests on you. My mother told me my job was to behave with thoughtful moderation.

Ischomachus: Well, my father told me the same thing. Thoughtful moderation for a man, as for a woman, means behaving in such a way that their possessions will be in the best possible condition and will increase as much as possible by good and just means. . . . So, you must do what the gods made you naturally capable of and what our law requires. . . . With great forethought the gods have yoked together male and female so that they can form the most beneficial partnership. This yoking together keeps living creatures from disappearing by producing children, and it provides offspring to look after parents in their old age, at least for people. [He then explains that human survival requires outdoor work—to raise crops and livestock—and indoor work—to preserve food, raise infants, and manufacture clothing.] . . . And since the work both outside and inside required effort and care, God, it seems to me, from the start fashioned women's nature for indoor work and men's for outdoor. Therefore he made men's bodies and spirits more able to endure cold and heat and travel and marches, giving them the outside jobs, while assigning indoor tasks to women, it seems, because their bodies are less hardy. . . .

But since both men and women have to manage things, [God] gave them equal shares in memory and attentiveness; you can't tell which gender has more of these qualities. And God gave both an equal ability to practice self-control, with the power to benefit the most from this quality going to whoever is better at it—whether man or woman. Precisely because they have different natures, they have greater need of each other and their yoking together is the most beneficial, with the one being capable where the other one is lacking. And as God has made them partners for their children, the law makes them partners for the household.

Source: Xenophon, *Oeconomicus* 7.10–30. Translation by Thomas R. Martin.

4. Greek Marriage Contract from Egypt (311–310 B.C.E.)

Greeks living abroad customarily drew up written contracts to define the duties of each partner in a marriage because they wanted their traditional expectations to remain legally binding regardless of the local laws. The earliest surviving such contract comes from Elephantine, the site of a Greek military garrison far up the Nile.

Marriage contract of Heraclides and Demetria. Heraclides [of Temnos] takes as his lawful wife Demetria of Cos from her father Leptines of Cos and her mother Philotis. He is a free person; she is a free person. She brings a dowry of clothing and jewelry worth 1,000 drachmas. Heraclides must provide Demetria with everything appropriate for a freeborn wife. We will live together in whatever location Leptines and Heraclides together decide is best.

If Demetria is apprehended doing anything bad that shames her husband, she will forfeit all her dowry. Heraclides will have to prove any allegations against her in the presence of three men, whom they both must approve. It will be illegal for Heraclides to bring home another wife to Demetria's harm, or to father children by another woman, or to do anything bad to Demetria for any reason. If he is caught doing any of these things and Demetria proves it in the presence of three men whom they both approve, Heraclides must return her dowry in full and pay her 1,000 drachmas additional. Demetria and those who help her in getting this payment will have legal standing to act against Heraclides and all his property on land and sea. . . . Each shall have the right to keep a personal copy of this contract. [A list of witnesses follows.]

Source: O. Rubensohn, ed., *Elephantine Papyri* (Berlin: 1907), no. 1. Translation by Thomas R. Martin.

Questions to Consider

1. **What evidence and arguments for differing natures for men and women do these documents offer?**
2. **Do you think Athenian women would have found these arguments convincing? Why or why not?**

squandered it through bad investments or reckless spending.

Like fathers, mothers were expected to hand down property to their children to keep it in the family through male heirs, since only sons could maintain their father's family line; married daughters became members of their husband's family. The goal of keeping property in the possession of male heirs shows up most clearly in Athenian law about heiresses (daughters whose fathers died without any sons, which happened in about one of every five families): the closest male relative of the heiress's father—her official guardian after her father's death—was required to marry her. The goal was to produce a son to inherit the father's property. This rule applied regardless of whether either party was already married (unless the heiress had sons); the heiress and the male relative were both supposed to divorce their present spouses and marry each other. In real life, however, people often used legal technicalities to get around this requirement so that they could remain with their chosen partners.

Requiring property to be passed down in this way therefore met two traditional goals of male-dominated Greek society: continuing the father's bloodline and preventing property from piling up in the hands of unmarried women (and therefore out of the control of men). At Sparta, the famous scholar Aristotle (384–322 B.C.E.) reported, the inheritance laws were different (and, in his opinion, flawed); he claimed that women came to own 40 percent of Spartan territory.

Women's Daily Lives Tradition restricted women's freedom of movement in public; men claimed that this restriction protected women by limiting opportunities for seducers and rapists. Men wanted to ensure that their children were truly theirs, that family property went only to genuine heirs, and that the city had only legitimate citizens. Well-off women in the city were expected to avoid contact with male strangers and mainly to spend their time at home or with women friends in their houses. Recent research has discredited the idea that Greek homes had a defined "women's quarter" to which women were confined. Rather, women were granted privacy in certain rooms. If the house included an interior courtyard, women could walk there in the open air and talk with other members of the household, male and female. In the safety of her home, a well-to-do woman would spin wool for clothing, converse with visiting friends, direct her children, supervise the slaves, and present her opinions on various matters, including politics, to the men of the house as they came and went. Poor women had little time for such activities because they—like their husbands, sons, and brothers—had to leave the house, usually a crowded rental apartment, to set up small stalls to sell bread, vegetables, simple clothing, or trinkets they had made.

An elite woman careful of her reputation left home only for appropriate reasons, such as religious festivals, funerals, childbirths at the houses of relatives and friends, and trips to workshops to buy shoes or other domestic articles. Often her husband escorted her, but sometimes she took only a slave, setting her own itinerary.

Most upper-class women probably viewed their limited contact with men outside the household as a badge of superior social status. For example, a pale complexion, from staying inside so much, was much admired as a sign of an enviable life of leisure and wealth. Many women, unaware of the health risk, used powdered white lead as makeup to give themselves a fashionable lack of color in their skin.

Staying close to home and safeguarding one's reputation could afford some advantages. Women who bore legitimate children gained increased respect and freedom, as an Athenian man explained in his speech (written by Lysias) defending himself for having killed his wife's lover:

> After my marriage, I at first didn't interfere with my wife very much, but neither did I allow her too much independence. I kept an eye on her. . . . But after she had a baby, I started to trust her more and put her in charge of all my things, believing we now had the closest of relationships.

Vase Painting of a Woman Buying Shoes (detail) Greek vases frequently displayed scenes from daily life instead of mythological stories. Here, a woman is being fitted for a pair of custom-made shoes by a craftsman and his apprentice. Her husband has accompanied her, as was often the case for shopping, and he appears to be participating in the discussion of the purchase. This vase was painted in so-called black-figure technique, in which the figures are dark and have their details incised on a background of red clay. *(The Plousios Painter, Two-handled jar [amphora], Greek, Late Archaic Period, about 500–490 B.C.E. Place of manufacture: Greece, Attica, Athens. Ceramic, Black Figure. H: 36.1 cm. [14 3/16 in.]; diameter: 25.9 cm. [10 3/16 in.]. Museum of Fine Arts, Boston, Henry Lillie Pierce Fund, 01.8035. Photograph © 2011 Museum of Fine Arts, Boston.)*

Vase Painting of a Symposium
Upper-class Greek men often spent their evenings at a symposium, a drinking party that always included much conversation and usually featured music and entertainers. Wives were not included. The discussions could range widely, from literature to politics to philosophy. The man on the right is about to fling the dregs of his wine, playing a messy game called *kottabos*. The nudity of the female musician indicates she is a hired prostitute. *(Detail, Foundry Painter—Red-figured cup with symposium scene. Reproduced by permission of the Syndics of the Fitzwilliam Museum, Cambridge.)*

Bearing male children brought a woman special honor because sons meant security. Sons could appear in court to support their parents in lawsuits and protect them in the streets of Athens, which for most of its history had no regular police force. By law, sons were required to support elderly parents. So intense was the pressure to produce sons that stories circulated of women who smuggled in male babies born to slaves and passed them off as their own.

Extraordinary Women A few women in Athens escaped traditional restrictions by working as what Greeks called a **hetaira** ("companion"). Hetairas, usually foreigners, were unmarried, physically attractive, witty in speech, and skilled in music and poetry. Men might hire them to entertain at a symposium (a drinking party to which wives were not invited) with their playful conversation. Their much-admired skill at clever teasing and verbal insults allowed companions a freedom of speech denied to "proper" women. Hetairas nevertheless lacked the social status and respectability that wives and mothers possessed.

Sometimes hetairas also sold sex for a high price, and they could control their own sexuality by choosing their clients. Athenian men (but not women) could buy sex as they pleased without legal hindrance. "Certainly you don't think men father children out of sexual desire?" wrote the upper-class author Xenophon. "The streets and the brothels are swarming with ways to take care of that." Men (but, again, not women) could also have sex freely with female or male slaves, who could not refuse their masters.

Less successful hetairas lived precarious lives of exploitation and even violence at the hands of their male customers, but the most skilled of them attracted admirers from the highest levels of society and earned enough to live in luxury on their own. The most famous hetaira in Athens was Aspasia from Miletus, who became Pericles' lover and bore him a son. She dazzled men with her brilliant talk and wide knowledge. Pericles fell so deeply in love with her that he wanted to marry her, despite his own law of 451 B.C.E. restricting citizenship, which said that their children would not be citizens without a special law passed by the assembly.

Great riches could also free a woman from tradition, allowing her to speak to men openly and bluntly. The most outspoken Athenian woman of wealth was Elpinike, Cimon's sister. When controversy erupted over a speech in which Pericles supported Athens's attack on a rebellious Delian League ally, Elpinike publicly criticized him by sarcastically remarking in front of a group of women who were praising him, "This really is wonderful, Pericles. . . . You have caused the loss of many good citizens, not in battle against Phoenicians or Persians . . . but in suppressing an allied city of fellow Greeks."

Other sources, especially comic drama and fourth-century B.C.E. oratory, imply that not-so-rich women, too, had strong opinions about politics. They customarily expressed their views to their husbands and male relatives at home in private.

hetaira (heh TYE ruh): A witty and attractive woman who charged fees to entertain at a symposium.

Slaves and Metics Traditional social and legal restrictions in Golden Age Athens meant slaves and metics counted as outsiders, despite all the work they did in and for the city-state. Individuals and the city-state alike owned slaves, who could be purchased from traders or bred in the household. Unwanted newborns abandoned by their parents (an accepted practice called infant exposure) were often picked up by others and raised as slaves. Athens's commercial growth in this period increased the demand for slaves, who in Pericles' time made up around 100,000 of the city-state's total of perhaps 250,000 inhabitants (the numbers are extremely uncertain estimates from ancient reports of the army's numbers and probable household sizes). Slaves worked in homes, on farms, and in crafts shops; rowed alongside their owners in the navy; and, if they were really unlucky, toiled in Athens's dangerous silver mines. Unlike those at Sparta, Athens's slaves almost never rebelled, probably because they originated from too many different places to be able to unite. Many mining slaves did run away to the Spartan base established in Athenian territory during the Peloponnesian War; the Spartans probably resold them.

Golden Age Athens's wealth and cultural activities attracted many metics, who streamed to the city from all around the Mediterranean, hoping to make money as importers, crafts producers, entertainers, and laborers. By the start of the Peloponnesian War in 431 B.C.E., metics constituted perhaps 50,000 to 75,000 of the estimated 150,000 free men, women, and children in the city-state. Metics paid for the privilege of living and working in Athens through a special foreigners' tax and military service. Athenians valued metics' contributions to the city's prosperity, but their insistence on exclusive citizenship meant they were unwilling to share its legal and financial benefits with immigrants.

Innovative Ideas in Education, Philosophy, History, and Medicine

Building on the intellectual foundation of rationalism that emerged in the Archaic Age, thinkers in the Greek Golden Age developed innovative ideas in education, philosophy, history, and medicine. These innovations delighted some fifth-century Greeks, but they deeply upset others, who feared that these drastic changes from older ways of life and thought would undermine the traditions that held society together, especially religion, thereby provoking punishment from the angry gods. These controversial changes opened the way to the development of scientific study as an enduring characteristic of Western civilization.

Education and philosophy provided the hottest battles between tradition and innovation. Earlier, education had stressed the preservation of old ways. Parents controlled what children learned at home and from hired tutors (there were still no public schools). Controversy erupted when men known as Sophists appeared in the mid-fifth century B.C.E. and offered, for pay, classes to teenage and young-adult males that taught nontraditional philosophy and religious doctrines, as well as novel techniques for public speaking. Some philosophers' ideas about the nature of the cosmos challenged traditional religious views. The philosopher Socrates, who did not work as a Sophist, expressed such strict views on personal morality and responsibility that he provoked an equally fierce controversy. In history writing and medicine, innovators created models of interpretation and scientific method that stimulated argument over how to understand human experience and the body.

Disagreement over whether these changes in intellectual life were dangerous for Athenian society added to the political tension that had arisen at Athens by the 430s B.C.E. concerning Athens's harsh treatment of its own allies and its economic sanctions against Sparta's allies. This interaction occurred because the political, intellectual, and religious dimensions of life in ancient Athens were closely intertwined. Athenians would connect philosophic ideas about the nature of justice with their decisions about the city-state's domestic and foreign policy, while also being concerned about the attitude of the gods toward the community. (See Document, "Athenian Regulations for a Rebellious Ally," page 93.)

Education The only formal education available came from private teachers, to whom well-to-do families sent their sons to learn to read, write, play a musical instrument or sing, and develop athletic skills suitable for war. Physical training was considered a vital part of men's education because it both made their bodies beautiful and prepared them for service in the militia (to which they could be summoned anytime between ages eighteen and sixty). Therefore, men exercised nude every day in gymnasia, public open-air facilities paid for by wealthy families. Men frequently discussed politics and exchanged news at a gymnasium. The daughters of wealthy families usually received instruction at home from educated slaves, who were expensive because they were rare. The young girls learned reading, writing, and arithmetic so that they would be ready to help their future husbands by managing the household.

DOCUMENT

Athenian Regulations for a Rebellious Ally

The city-state of Chalcis on the island of Euboea rebelled from the Athenian-dominated Delian League in 446 B.C.E. After defeating the rebels, the Athenians forced the Chalcidians to swear compliance with new regulations, which were inscribed on stone in both cities. The text reveals that the terms were not the same for the two sides.

The Athenian Council and the jurors shall swear an oath in this form: "I will not expel Chalcidians from Chalcis nor will I reduce the city to ruins nor deprive any individual of his citizen rights nor punish him with exile nor imprison him nor kill him nor take property from anyone who has not had a trial without approval from the People [i.e., the assembly] of the Athenians, nor will I have a vote taken against the community or any single individual without their being called to trial, and when their representatives arrive, I will introduce them to the Council and People within ten days when I am in charge of the procedure, so far as I am able. These things I will guarantee the Chalcidians if they obey the People of the Athenians."

The Chalcidians shall swear an oath in this form: "I will not rebel from the People of the Athenians either by cunning or by any way at all either by word or by deed, and I will not obey anyone who rebels, and if anyone does rebel, I will denounce him to the Athenians, and I will pay the dues to the Athenians which I persuade the Athenians [to levy on me], and as an ally I will be the best and most just that I am able, and I will give support to and defend the People of the Athenians, if anyone wrongs the People of the Athenians, and I will obey the People of the Athenians."

Source: *Inscriptiones Graecae*, 3rd ed. (1981), no. 40. Translation by Thomas R. Martin.

Question to Consider

- **Would you regard the terms of the oaths each side was required to swear as harsh, given the circumstances?**

Poor girls and boys received no formal education; they learned a trade and perhaps a little reading, writing, and calculating by assisting their parents in their daily work or by serving as apprentices to skilled crafts workers. Scholars disagree about how many people could read well, but most likely they were a minority. Those with weak reading skills, however, could always find someone to read aloud any written text. In fact, oral communication was at the center of Greek life, whether in political speeches or in songs, plays, and stories from literature and history.

After their early education, young men from prosperous families would learn how to participate in public life, and especially Athenian democracy,

The Masculine Ideal

This sculpture of a male warrior/athlete, found in a shipwreck off the coast of Riace in southern Italy, was cast in bronze in the mid-fifth century B.C.E. Greeks preferred bronze over marble for top-rank statues, but few have survived because they were usually melted down and their metal reused (e.g., to make guns in later ages). The figure's relaxed pose displays the asymmetry—the head looking to one side, the arms in different positions, the torso tilted—that made Greek statues from the Classical Age appear less stiff than Archaic Age ones. The cap on his head was what warriors wore to cushion their helmet. The body displays the ideal build that Greek men strove to achieve through daily workouts. For male statues, nudity indicated a heroic ideal. *(Eric Lessing/Art Resource, NY.)*

not by taking formal lessons but by observing their fathers, uncles, and other older men as they debated in the Council of Five Hundred and the assembly, served in public office, and spoke in court. Often an older man would choose an adolescent boy as his special favorite to educate. The teenager would learn about public life by spending time with the older man. During the day the boy would listen to his mentor talking politics in the agora, help him perform his duties in public office, and work out with him in a gymnasium. They would spend their evenings at a symposium, whose agenda could range from serious political and philosophical discussion to riotous partying.

This older mentor/younger favorite relationship could lead to sexual relations between the youth and the older male, the latter of whom was usually married. Sex between mentors and favorites was considered acceptable in elite circles in many city-states, including Athens, Sparta, and Thebes. Other city-states banned this behavior because they believed, as the Athenian author Xenophon suggests, that it sprang from an adult man's shameful inability to control his lustful desires.

Sophists and Philosophers as a Threat to Tradition

By the time of radical democracy in Athens, young men eager to develop the essential political skill of public speaking could obtain higher education in a new way: by paying an expensive professional teacher to train them. These teachers, called **Sophists** ("men of wisdom"), sparked controversy because they strongly challenged traditional beliefs by teaching new skills of persuasion in speaking and new ways of thinking based on rational arguments. The term *sophist* later acquired a negative connotation (preserved in the English word *sophistry*) because clever Sophists could use complex reasoning to make deceptive arguments.

Starting about 450 B.C.E., Athens's booming economy and lively intellectual environment attracted Sophists from around the Greek world. These individual entrepreneurs competed with one another to attract pupils who could pay the hefty prices they charged for their innovative courses. As in every part of Greek intellectual life, the competition for prominence was intense. Sophists strove for excellence by offering specialized training in rhetoric—the skill of speaking persuasively. Every ambitious man wanted rhetorical training because it promised power in Athens's assembly, councils, and courts. The Sophists alarmed many tradition-minded Athenians, who feared their teachings would undermine established social and political traditions. Speakers trained by silver-tongued Sophists, they believed, might be able to mislead the assembly while promoting their private interests.

Prominent older leaders, Pericles among them, often joined the Sophists for discussions. The most notorious Sophist was Protagoras, a contemporary of Pericles from Abdera, in northern Greece. Protagoras moved to Athens around 450 B.C.E., when he was around forty, and spent most of his career there. His views on the nature of truth and morality outraged many Athenians: he argued that rationally there could be no absolute standard of truth because every issue had two irreconcilable sides. For example, if one person feeling a breeze thinks it warm whereas another person thinks it cool, neither judgment can be absolutely correct because the wind simply is warm to one and cool to the other. Protagoras summed up this subjectivism—the belief that there is no absolute reality behind and independent of appearances—in his work *Truth*: "The human being is the measure of all things, of the things that are that they are, and of the things that are not that they are not."

The subjectivism of Protagoras and other Sophists contained two main ideas: (1) human institutions and values are only matters of convention, custom, or *nomos* ("law") and not creations of *physis* ("nature"), and (2) since truth is subjective, speakers should be able to argue either side of a question with equal persuasiveness and rationality. The first view implied that traditional human institutions were arbitrary and changing rather than natural and permanent, while the second seemed to many people to make questions of right and wrong irrelevant. (See Document, "Sophists Argue Both Sides of a Case," page 95.)

The Sophists' critics therefore accused them of teaching moral relativism and threatening the shared public values of the democratic city-state. Aristophanes, author of comic plays, satirized Sophists for harming Athens by instructing students in persuasive techniques "to make the weaker argument the stronger." Protagoras, for one, energetically responded that his doctrines were not hostile to democracy, arguing that every person had a natural capability for excellence and that human society depended on the rule of law based on a sense of justice. Members of a community, he explained, must be persuaded to obey the laws, not because laws were based on absolute truth, which did not exist,

---

Sophists (SAH fists): Competitive intellectuals and teachers in ancient Greece who offered expensive courses in persuasive public speaking and new ways of philosophic and religious thinking beginning around 450 B.C.E.

DOCUMENT

Sophists Argue Both Sides of a Case

The Sophist Protagoras taught his students to argue both sides of any case, but he insisted he did not teach this skill for immoral purposes. Some teachers following in his footsteps were less ethical. This excerpt comes from an anonymous handbook of the late fifth century B.C.E. entitled Double Arguments, *which provided examples of how Sophists could make arguments in the fashion of Protagoras.*

Greek philosophers put forward double arguments concerning the good and the bad. Some say that the good is one thing and the bad another, but others say that they are the same, and that a thing might be good for some persons but bad for others, or at one time good and at another time bad for the same person. I myself agree with those who hold the latter opinion, which I shall examine using as an example human life and its concern for food, drink, and sexual pleasures: these things are bad for a man if he is sick but good if he is healthy and needs them. And, further, overindulgence in these things is bad for the one who overindulges but good for those who make a profit by selling these things. And again, sickness is bad for the sick but good for the doctors. And death is bad for those who die but good for the undertakers and makers of grave monuments. . . . Shipwrecks are bad for the ship owners but good for the ship builders. When tools are blunted and worn away it is bad for others but good for the blacksmith. And if a pot gets smashed, this is bad for everyone else but good for the potter. When shoes wear out and fall apart it is bad for others but good for the shoemaker. . . . In the *stadion* race for runners, victory is good for the winner but bad for the losers.

Source: *Dissoi Logoi* 1.1–6. Translation adapted from Rosamund Kent Sprague, ed., *The Older Sophists* (Columbia: University of South Carolina Press, 1972), 279–80.

Question to Consider

- **Do you think it is impossible ever to reach a firm conclusion about whether something is good or bad? Why or why not?**

but because rationally it was advantageous for everyone to be law-abiding. A thief, for example, who might claim that stealing was a part of nature, would have to be persuaded by reason that a man-made law forbidding theft was to his advantage because it protected his own property and the community in which he, like all humans, had to live in order to survive.

Even more disturbing to Athenians than the Sophists' ideas about truth were their ideas about religion. Protagoras angered people with his agnosticism (the belief that supernatural phenomena are unknowable): "Whether the gods exist I cannot discover, nor what their form is like, for there are many impediments to knowledge, [such as] the obscurity of the subject and the brevity of human life." His implication that even religious belief must be based on knowledge acquired through evidence was in keeping with the development of Greek rationalism and scientific thought, but it upset those who thought he was saying that conventional religion had no meaning. They worried that his words would provoke divine anger against the community that gave him a home.

Other fifth-century B.C.E. philosophers and thinkers, although not working as Sophists, also proposed new scientific theories about the nature of the cosmos and the origin of religion that offended believers in traditional religion. A philosopher friend of Pericles, for example, argued that the sun was a lump of flaming rock, not a god. Another philosopher invented an atomic theory of matter to explain how change was constant in the universe. Everything, he argued, consisted of tiny, invisible particles in eternal motion. Their random collisions caused them to combine and recombine in an infinite variety of forms, with no divine purpose guiding their collisions and combinations. These ideas seemed to invalidate traditional religion, which explained events as governed by the gods' will. Even worse was the idea advanced by the wealthy aristocrat Critias, who wrote a play in which religion was denounced as a clever but false system invented by powerful men to fool ordinary people into obeying moral standards through fear of divine punishment.

The Sophists' techniques of persuasion and ways of thought based on rational arguments helped their students forcefully advance their political opinions and defend themselves in court. But because only wealthy men could afford their classes, the Sophists threatened Athenian democracy by giving yet another advantage to the rich in the assembly's debates or speeches in court. In addition, moral relativism and the physical explanation of the universe struck many Athenians as dangerous: they feared that such teachings, by offending the gods, would destroy the divine goodwill they believed Athens enjoyed. These ideas so infuriated some Athenians that in the 430s B.C.E. they sponsored a law allowing citizens to bring charges of impiety against "those who fail to respect divine things or teach theories about the cosmos." Not even Pericles could prevent his philosopher friend from being convicted on this charge and expelled from Athens.

Socrates on Ethics Socrates (469–399 B.C.E.), the most famous philosopher of the Golden Age, became well known in his home state of Athens during this troubled time of the 430s, when people were anxious not just about the Sophists but also about the growing threat of war with Sparta. Socrates devoted his life to questioning people about their beliefs, but he insisted he was not a Sophist because he offered no courses and took no pay. Above all, he fought against the view that justice should be equated with power over others. By insisting that true justice was better than injustice under any and all circumstances, he gave a new direction to Greek philosophy: an emphasis on ethics (the study of ideal human values and moral duties). Although other thinkers before him (especially poets and authors of plays) had dealt with similar issues, Socrates was the first philosopher to make ethics his central concern.

Statuette of the Philosopher Socrates
The controversial Socrates, the most famous philosopher of Athens in the fifth century B.C.E., joked that he had a homely face and a bulging stomach. This small statue is an artist's impression of what Socrates looked like; we cannot be sure of the truth. Socrates was renowned for his irony, and he may have purposely exaggerated his physical unattractiveness to show his disdain for ordinary standards of beauty and his own emphasis on the quality of one's soul as the true measure of one's worth. Compare his body to that of the athletes shown in the vase painting on page 50 or of the statue of the warrior/athlete on page 93. *(Erich Lessing/Art Resource, NY.)*

Socrates lived an eccentric life that attracted constant attention. Sporting a stomach, in his words, "a bit too big to be convenient," he wore the same cheap cloak summer and winter and always went barefoot no matter how cold the weather. His physical stamina—including both his tirelessness as a soldier in Athens's infantry and his ability to outdrink anyone at a symposium—was legendary. Unlike the high-priced Sophists, he lived in poverty and disdained material possessions, though somehow he managed to support a wife and several children. He probably inherited some money and also accepted gifts from wealthy admirers.

Socrates spent his time in conversations all over Athens: participating in symposia, strolling in the agora, or watching young men exercise in a gymnasium. In this behavior he resembled his fellow Athenians, who placed great value on the importance and pleasure of speaking with one another at length. He wrote nothing. Our knowledge of his ideas comes from others' writings, especially those of his famous follower Plato (c. 428–348 B.C.E.). Plato portrays Socrates as a relentless questioner of his fellow citizens, foreign friends, and leading Sophists. Socrates' questions had the goal of making his conversational partners examine the basic assumptions of their way of life. Giving few answers, Socrates never directly instructed anyone. Instead, he led people to draw conclusions in response to his probing questions and refutations of their cherished assumptions. Today this procedure is called the **Socratic method**.

Socrates frequently upset and even outraged people because his method made them feel ignorant and baffled. His questions forced them to admit that they did not in fact know what they had assumed they knew very well. Even more painful to them was Socrates' fiercely argued view that the way they lived their lives—pursuing success in politics or business or art—was merely an excuse for avoiding the hard work of understanding and de-

---

Socratic method: The Athenian philosopher Socrates' method of teaching through conversation, in which he asked probing questions to make his listeners examine their most cherished assumptions.

veloping genuine aretê ("excellence"). Socrates insisted that he was ignorant of the best definition of excellence and what was best for human beings, but that his wisdom consisted of knowing that he did not know. He vowed he was trying to improve, not undermine, people's ethical beliefs, even though, as a friend put it, a conversation with Socrates made a man feel numb—as if a jellyfish had stung him.

Socrates especially wanted to use reasoning to discover universal, objective standards that justified individual ethics. He attacked the Sophists for their relativistic claim that conventional standards of right and wrong were merely "the chains that handcuff nature." This view, he protested, equated human happiness with power and "getting more."

Socrates insisted that the only way to achieve true happiness was to behave in accordance with a universal, transcendent standard of just behavior that people could understand rationally. Essentially, he argued that just behavior and excellence were identical to knowledge, and that true knowledge of justice would inevitably lead people to choose good over evil. They would therefore have truly happy lives, regardless of how rich or poor they were. Since Socrates believed that ethical knowledge was all a person needed for the good life, he argued that no one knowingly behaved unjustly and that behaving justly was always in the individual's interest. It was simply ignorant to believe that the best life was the life of unlimited power to pursue whatever one desired. The most desirable human life was concerned with excellence and guided by reason, not by dreams of personal gain.

Though very different from the Sophists' doctrines, Socrates' ideas proved just as disturbing because they rejected the Athenians' traditional way of life. His ridicule of commonly accepted ideas about the importance of wealth and public success angered many people. Unhappiest of all were the fathers whose sons, after listening to Socrates' questions reduce someone to utter bewilderment, came home to try the same technique on their parents, employing rational arguments to criticize as old-fashioned and worthless the values their family held dear. Men who experienced this reversal of the traditional educational hierarchy—the father was supposed to educate the son—felt that Socrates was undermining the stability of society by making young men question Athenian traditions. Socrates evidently did not teach women, but Plato portrays him as ready to learn from exceptional women, such as Pericles' companion Aspasia.

The worry that Socrates' ideas presented a danger to conventional society inspired Aristophanes to write his comedy *The Clouds* (423 B.C.E.). This play portrays Socrates as a cynical Sophist who, for a fee, offers instruction in Protagoras's technique of making the weaker argument the stronger. When the curriculum of Socrates' school, The Thinkery, transforms a youth into a public speaker who argues that a son has the right to beat his parents, his father burns the place down. None of these plot details seems to have been real; what was genuine was the fear that Socrates' radical views on individual morality endangered the city-state's traditional practices. This anxiety only grew worse as the Peloponnesian War dragged on with ever more casualties, and many citizens began to feel that their best hope for victory lay in strengthening tradition, not weakening it.

History Writing | Just as the Sophists and Socrates antagonized many people with their new ideas, the inventors of history writing drew attention because they took a critical attitude in their descriptions of the past. Herodotus of Halicarnassus (c. 485–425 B.C.E.) and Thucydides of Athens (c. 455–399 B.C.E.) became Greece's most famous historians and established Western civilization's tradition of history writing. The fifth-century B.C.E.'s unprecedented events—a coalition Greek victory over the world's greatest power and then the longest war ever between Greeks—apparently inspired them to create history as a subject based on strenuous research. They explained that they wrote histories because they wanted people to remember the past and to understand why wars had taken place.

In the 420s B.C.E., Herodotus finished a long, groundbreaking work called *Histories* ("inquiries" in Greek) to explain the Persian Wars as a clash between the cultures of the East and West. A typically competitive Greek intellectual, Herodotus—who by Roman times had become known as the Father of History—made the justifiable claim that he surpassed all those who had previously recorded the past by taking an in-depth and investigative approach to evidence, examining the culture of non-Greeks as well as Greeks, and expressing explicit and implicit judgments about people's actions. Because Herodotus recognized the necessity (and the delight) of studying other cultures with respect, he pushed his inquiries deep into the past, looking for longstanding cultural differences to help explain the Persian-Greek conflict. He showed that Greeks and non-Greeks were equally capable of good and evil. Unlike poets and playwrights, he focused on human psychology and interactions, not the gods, as the driving forces in history.

Thucydides redirected historical inquiry—and competed with Herodotus—by writing contemporary history and inventing the kind of analysis of power that today informs political science. His *History of the Peloponnesian War*, published after the end of the war, made power politics, not divine intervention, history's primary force. Deeply affected by the war's brutality, he used his experiences as a politician and failed military commander (he was exiled for losing a key outpost) to make his narrative vivid and frank in describing human moral failings. His insistence that historians should energetically seek out the most reliable sources and evaluate their testimony with objectivity set a high standard for later writers. Like Herodotus, he challenged tradition by revealing that Greek history was not just a story of glorious achievements but also had its share of shameful actions (such as the Athenian punishment of the Melians in the Peloponnesian War—see page 103).

Hippocrates and the Birth of Scientific Medicine

Hippocrates of Cos, a fifth-century B.C.E. contemporary of Thucydides, challenged tradition by grounding medical diagnosis and treatment in clinical observation. His fame continues today in the oath bearing his name that doctors swear at the beginning of their professional careers. Previously, medicine had depended on magic and ritual. Illness was believed to be caused by evil spirits, and various cults in Greek religion offered healing to patients through divine intervention. Competing to refute these earlier doctors' theories, Hippocrates insisted that only physical factors caused disease. He may have been the author of the view, dominant in later medicine, that four humors (fluids) made up the human body: blood, phlegm, black bile, and yellow bile. Health depended on keeping the proper balance among them; being healthy was to be in "good humor." This system for understanding the body corresponded to the division of the inanimate world into four parts: the elements earth, air, fire, and water.

Hippocrates taught that the physician's most important duty was to base his knowledge on careful observation of patients and their response to different treatments. Clinical experience, not abstract theory or religious belief, was the proper foundation for establishing effective cures. By putting his innovative ideas and practices to the test in competition with those of traditional medicine, Hippocrates established the truth of his principle, which later became a cornerstone of scientific medicine.

The Development of Greek Tragedy

Along with history and philosophy, Greek ideas about the problematic relationship between gods and humans inspired Golden Age Athens's most prominent cultural innovation: tragic drama. Plays called tragedies were presented over three days at the major annual festival of the god Dionysus in a contest for playwrights, in keeping with the competitive spirit characteristic of Greek life. Tragedies presented shocking stories involving fierce conflict and characters representing powerful forces, usually from myth but occasionally from recent history, that could be related to controversial issues in contemporary Athens. Therefore, these plays stimulated their large audiences to ponder the danger that ignorance, arrogance, and violence presented to the city-state's democratic society. Following the tradition of Homer and Hesiod, Golden Age playwrights explored top-

Divine Healing

This relief sculpture shows the god Asclepius healing Archinus (his name is inscribed at the bottom). Patients sought Asclepius's help by going to sleep and dreaming in his sanctuary, as shown at right. The god in the form of a snake is licking the patient's shoulder to heal it. At left, the god's power is symbolized by showing him as a heroic-sized figure, who is directly treating the injured shoulder. The Athenians brought Asclepius's cult from abroad to their city in 420 B.C.E. during the Peloponnesian War to try to alleviate epidemic disease and war injuries. The famous doctor and medical theorist Hippocrates challenged tradition by rejecting this kind of divine healing. *(The Art Archive/National Archeological Museum, Athens/Gianni Dagli Orti.)*

ics ranging from the roots of good and evil to the nature of individual freedom and responsibility in the family and the political community. As with other ancient texts, most of the Greek tragedies have not survived: only thirty-three still exist of the hundreds that were produced at Athens.

Athenian tragedy was a competitive public art form subsidized by tax revenues and mandatory contributions by the rich. The competition took place every year, with an official choosing three authors from a pool of applicants. Each of these finalists presented four plays during the festival: three tragedies in a row (a trilogy), followed by a semicomic play featuring satyrs (mythical half-man, half-animal beings) to end the day on a lighter note. Tragedies were written in verses of solemn language, and many were based on stories about the violent possibilities when gods and humans interacted. The plots often ended with a resolution to the trouble—but only after enormous suffering.

The performances of tragedies in Athens, as in many other cities in Greece, took place during the daytime in an outdoor theater. The theater at Athens was sacred to the god Dionysus and built into the southern slope of the acropolis; it held about fourteen thousand spectators overlooking an open, circular area in front of a slightly raised stage. A tragedy had eighteen cast members, all of whom were men: three actors to play the speaking roles (both male and female characters) and fifteen chorus members. Although the chorus leader sometimes engaged in dialogue with the actors, the chorus primarily performed songs and dances in the circular area in front of the stage, called the orchestra.

A successful tragedy offered a vivid spectacle. The chorus wore elaborate costumes and performed intricate dance routines. The actors, who wore masks, used broad gestures and booming voices to reach the upper tier of seats. A powerful voice was crucial to a tragic actor because words represented the heart of the plays, in which dialogue and long speeches predominated over physical action. Special effects were part of the spectacle. For example, a crane allowed actors playing the roles of gods to fly suddenly onto the stage. The actors playing lead roles, called the protagonists ("first competitors"), competed against one another for the designation of best actor. So important was a first-rate protagonist to a play's success that actors were assigned by lottery to the competing playwrights to give all three an equal chance to have a winning cast. Great protagonists became enormously popular, although they were not usually members of the social elite.

Playwrights were from the elite because only men of some wealth could afford the amount of time and learning this work demanded. They served as author, director, producer, musical composer, choreographer, and sometimes even actor. As citizens, playwrights also fulfilled the normal military and political obligations of Athenian men. The best-known Athenian tragedians—Aeschylus (525–456 B.C.E.), Sophocles (c. 496–406 B.C.E.), and Euripides (c. 485–406 B.C.E.)—all served in the army, and Sophocles was elected to Athens's highest public office. Authors of plays competed from a love of honor, not money. The prizes, determined by a board of judges, awarded high prestige but little cash. The competition was regarded as so important that any judge who took a bribe to award a prize was put to death.

Tragedy's plots explored the difficulties of telling right from wrong when humans came into conflict in the city-state and the gods became involved. Even though most tragedies were based on stories that referred to a legendary time before city-states existed, such as the period of the Trojan War, the moral issues pertained to the society and obligations of citizens in a city-state. For example, Aeschylus's trilogy *Oresteia* (458 B.C.E) uses the story of how the gods stop the murderous violence in the family of Orestes, son of Agamemnon, the Greek leader against Troy, to explain the divine origins of democratic Athens's court system. The plays suggest that human beings learn only by suffering but that the gods provide justice in the long run.

Sophocles' *Antigone* (441 B.C.E.) presents the story of the cursed family of Oedipus of Thebes as a drama of harsh conflict between a courageous woman, Antigone, and the city-state's stern male leader, her uncle Creon. After her brother dies in a failed rebellion, Antigone insists on her family's moral obligation to bury its dead in obedience to divine command, while Creon takes harsh action to preserve order and protect community values by prohibiting the burial of his nephew the traitor. In a horrifying story of raging anger and suicide that features one of the most famous heroines of Western literature, Sophocles exposes the right and wrong on each side of the conflict. His play offers no easy resolution of the competing interests of divinely sanctioned moral tradition and the state's political rules.

Ancient sources tell us that the audiences reacted strongly to the messages of the tragedies presented in the drama competition of the Dionysian festival. For one thing, they could see that the central characters of the plays were figures who fell into disaster even though they held positions of power and prestige. The characters' reversals of fortune came about not because they were absolute villains but because, as humans, they were susceptible to a lethal mixture of error, ignorance, and **hubris** (vio-

---

hubris (HYOO bris): The Greek term for violent arrogance.

lent arrogance that, according to the Greeks, drove the competitive spirit to excess). The Athenian Empire was at its height when audiences at Athens attended the tragedies written by competing playwrights. Thoughtful spectators could reflect on the possibility that Athens's current power and prestige, managed as they were by humans, might fall victim to the same kind of mistakes and conflicts that brought down the heroes and heroines of tragedy. Thus, tragedies not only entertained through their spectacle but also educated through their stories and words. In particular, they reminded male citizens — who governed the city-state in its assembly, council, and courts — that success created complex moral problems that self-righteous arrogance never solved.

The Development of Greek Comedy

Golden Age Athens developed comedy as its second distinctive form of public theater. Like tragedies, comedies were written in verse, performed in Dionysus festivals, and subsidized with public funds and contributions from the rich. Unlike tragedies, comedies commented directly on public policy and criticized current politicians and intellectuals. They did this with plots and casts presenting outrageous fantasies of contemporary life. For example, comic choruses, which had twenty-four dancing singers, could be colorfully costumed as talking birds or dancing clouds, or an actor could fly on a giant dung beetle to visit the gods.

Comic playwrights competed to win the award for the festival's best comedy by creating beautiful poetry, raising laughs with constant jokes and puns, and mocking self-important citizens and political leaders. Much of the humor concerned sex and bodily functions, delivered in a stream of imaginative profanity. Well-known men of the day were targets for insults as cowards or weaklings. Women characters portrayed as figures of fun and ridicule seem to have been fictional, to protect the dignity of actual female citizens.

Athenian comedies often made fun of political leaders. As the leading politician of radical democracy, Pericles came in for fierce criticism in comedy. Comic playwrights ridiculed his policies, his love life, even the shape of his skull ("Old Turnip Head" was a favorite insult). Aristophanes (c. 455–385 B.C.E.), Athens's most famous comic playwright, so fiercely satirized Cleon, the city's most prominent leader early in the Peloponnesian War, that Cleon sued him. A citizen jury ruled in Aristophanes' favor, upholding the Athenian tradition of free speech.

In several of Aristophanes' comedies, the main characters are powerful women who force the men of Athens to change their policy to preserve family life and the city-state. These plays even criticize the assembly's policy during wartime. Most famous is *Lysistrata* (411 B.C.E.), named after the female lead character of the play. In this fantasy, the women of Athens and Sparta unite to force their husbands to end the Peloponnesian War. To make the men agree to a peace treaty, they first seize the acropolis,

Greek Vase Painting of the Murder of King Agamemnon
This Greek vase from the fifth century B.C.E. shows Queen Clytemnestra (left) and her lover Aegisthus murdering her husband, King Agamemnon, after he returns home from leading the Greek army in its ten-year war against Troy. The painting shows Agamemnon as defenseless because he was ensnared in a gauzy robe that his wife gave him after he took a bath. The other side of the vase shows Agamemnon's son murdering Clytemnestra, his mother, in revenge. Greek mythology had many stories of murderous vengeance that emphasized how difficult it was to regulate human passions with social norms and laws. *(Greek, Early Classical Period, about 460 B.C.E. Place of manufacture: Greece, Attica, Athens. Ceramic, Red Figure. H: 51 cm. [20 1/16 in.]; diameter: 51 cm. [20 1/6 in.]. Museum of Fine Arts, Boston; William Francis Warden Fund, 63.1246. Photograph © 2011 Museum of Fine Arts, Boston.)*

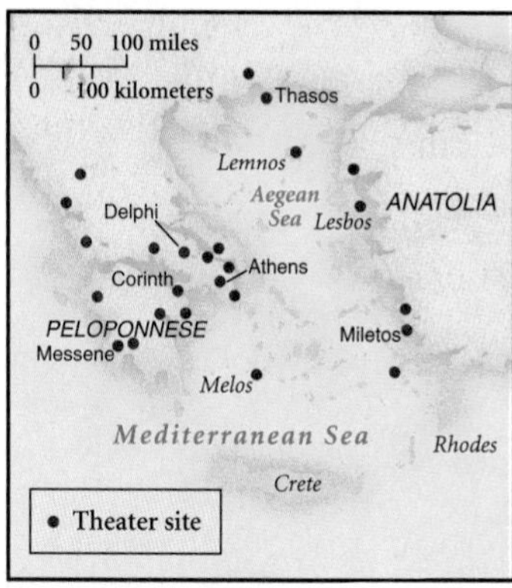

Theaters of Classical Greece

Statuettes of Comic Actors

Although these little statues are dressed in the kinds of masks and costumes that came into vogue later than the style of comedy that Aristophanes and his contemporaries wrote in the fifth century B.C.E. (for which no such pieces exist), they give a vivid sense of the exaggerated buffoonery that characterized the acting in Greek comedy. In Aristophanes' day, the grotesque unreality of comic costumes would have been even more striking because the male actors wore large leather phalluses (penises) attached below their waists that could be props for all sorts of ribald jokes. The use of masks in certain kinds of theater performances continued into Roman times. *(bpk, Berlin / Antikensammlung, Staaliche Musen, Berlin, Germany / photo by Johannes Laurentius / Art Resource, NY.)*

where Athens's financial reserves are kept, to prevent the men from squandering them further on the war. They then use sarcasm and pitchers of cold water to beat back an attack on their position by the old men who have remained in Athens while the younger men are out on campaign. Above all, the women steel themselves to refuse to sleep with their husbands when they return from battle. The effects of their sex strike on the men, portrayed in a series of explicit episodes, finally drive the warriors to make peace.

Lysistrata presents women acting bravely and aggressively against men who seem bent on destroying traditional family life—they are staying away from home for long stretches while on military campaigns and are ruining the city-state by prolonging a pointless war. Lysistrata insists that women have the intelligence and judgment to make political decisions: "I am a woman, and, yes, I have brains. And I'm not badly off for judgment. Nor has my education been bad, coming as it has from my listening often to the conversations of my father and the elders among the men." Her old-fashioned training and good sense allow her to see what needs to be done to protect the community. Like the heroines of tragedy, Lysistrata is a conservative, even a reactionary. She wants to put things back the way they were before the war ruined family life. To do that, however, she has to act like an impatient revolutionary. That irony sums up the challenge that fifth-century B.C.E. Athens faced in trying to resolve the tension between the dynamic innovation of its Golden Age and the importance of tradition in Greek life.

The remarkable freedom of speech of Athenian comedy allowed frank, even brutal, commentary on current issues and personalities. It cannot be an accident that this energetic, critical drama emerged in Athens at the same time as radical democracy, in the mid-fifth century B.C.E. The feeling that all citizens should have a stake in determining their government's policies evidently fueled a passion for using biting humor to keep the community's leaders from becoming arrogant and aloof.

REVIEW QUESTION How did new ways of thinking in the Golden Age change traditional ways of life?

The End of Athens's Golden Age, 431–403 B.C.E.

A war between Athens and Sparta that lasted a generation (431–404 B.C.E.) ended the Golden Age. Today it is called the Peloponnesian War because it matched Sparta's Peloponnese-based alliance against Athens and the Delian League. The war started, according to Thucydides, because the growth of Athenian power alarmed the Spartans, who feared that their interests and allies would fall to the Athenians' restless drive. Pericles, the most powerful politician in Athens at the time, persuaded its assembly to take a hard line when the Spartans demanded that Athens ease restrictions on city-states allied with Sparta. Corinth and Megara, crucial Spartan allies, complained bitterly to Sparta about Athens.

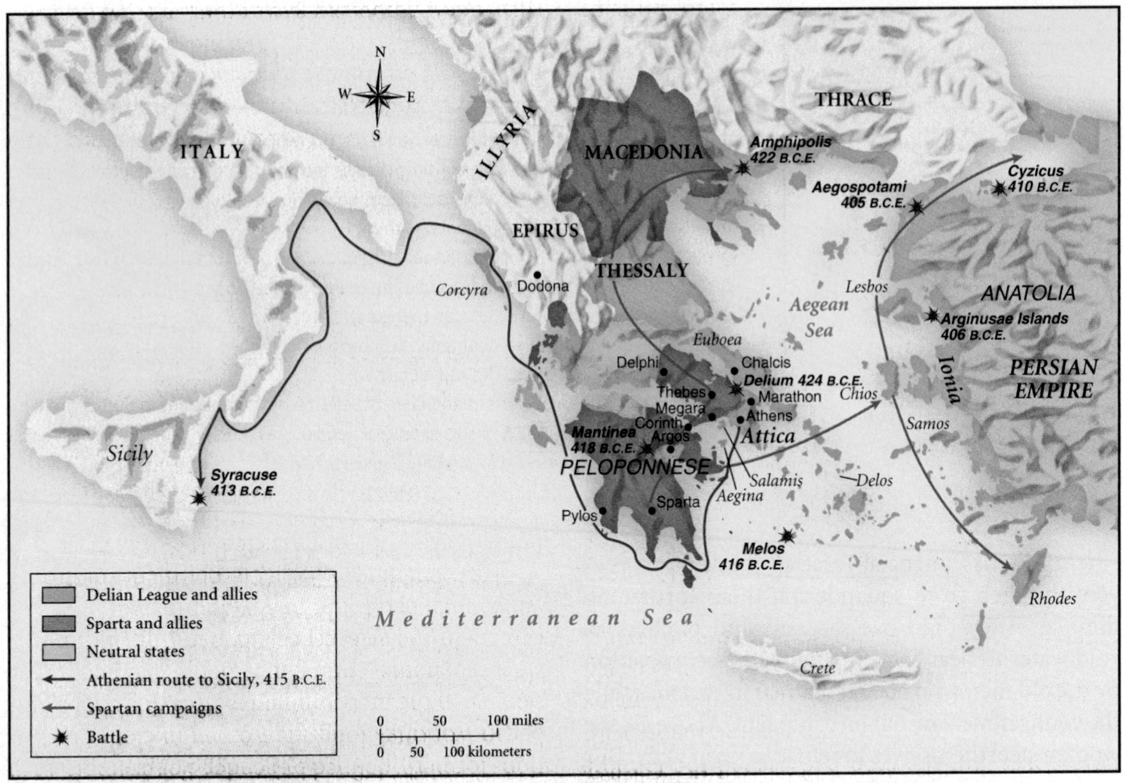

MAP 3.3 The Peloponnesian War, 431–404 B.C.E.
For the first ten years, the Peloponnesian War's battles took place largely in mainland Greece. Sparta, whose armies usually avoided distant campaigns, shocked Athens when its general Brasidas led successful attacks against Athenian forces in northeast Greece. Athens stunned the entire Greek world in the war's next phase by launching a huge naval expedition against Spartan allies in far-off Sicily. The last ten years of the war saw the action move to the east, on and along the western coast of Anatolia and its islands, on the boundary of the Persian Empire. Feeling threatened, the Persian king helped the Spartans build a navy there to defeat the famous Athenian fleet. | **Look at the route of Athens's expedition to Sicily; why do you think the Athenians took this longer voyage, rather than a more direct route?**

Finally, Corinth told Sparta to attack Athens, or else Corinth and its navy would change sides to the Athenian alliance. Sparta's leaders therefore gave Athens an ultimatum—stop mistreating our allies. Pericles convinced the Athenian assembly to reject the ultimatum on the grounds that Sparta had refused to settle the dispute through the third-party arbitration process called for by the 446–445 B.C.E. treaty. Pericles' critics claimed he was insisting on war against Sparta to revive his fading popularity. His supporters replied that he was defending Athenian honor and protecting foreign trade, a key to the economy. By 431 B.C.E. these disputes had shattered the peace treaty between Athens and Sparta negotiated by Pericles fifteen years before.

The Peloponnesian War, 431–404 B.C.E.

Lasting longer than any previous war in Greek history, the Peloponnesian War (Map 3.3) took place above all because Spartan leaders believed they had to fight now to keep the Athenians from using their superior long-distance offensive power—the Delian League's naval forces—to destroy Sparta's control of the Peloponnesian League. (See "Taking Measure," page 103) Sparta made the first strike of the war, but the conflict dragged on so long because the Athenian assembly failed to negotiate peace with Sparta when it had the chance and because the Spartans were willing to deal with Persia for money to build a fleet to win the war.

Dramatic evidence for the angry feelings that fueled the war comes from Thucydides' version of Pericles' stern oration to the Athenian assembly about not yielding to Spartan pressure:

> If we do go to war, have no thought that you went to war over a trivial affair. For you this trifling matter is the assurance and the proof of your determination. If you yield to their demands, they will immediately confront you with some larger demand, since they will think that you only gave way on the first point out of fear. But if you stand firm, you will show them that they

have to deal with you as equals. . . . When our equals, without agreeing to arbitration of the matter under dispute, make claims on us as neighbors and state those claims as commands, it would be no better than slavery to give in to them, no matter how large or how small the claim may be.

When Sparta invaded Athenian territory, Pericles advised a two-pronged strategy to win what he saw would be a long war: (1) use the navy to raid the lands of Sparta and its allies, and (2) avoid large infantry battles with the superior land forces of the Spartans, even when the enemy hoplites plundered the Athenian countryside outside the city. Athens's citizens could retreat to safety behind the city's impregnable walls, massive barriers of stone that encircled the city and the harbor, with the fortification known as the Long Walls protecting the land corridor between the urban center and the port (see Map 3.2). He insisted that Athenians should sacrifice their vast and valuable country property to save their population. In the end, he predicted, Athens, with its superior resources, would win a war of attrition, especially because the Spartans, lacking a base in Athenian territory, could not support long invasions.

Pericles' strategy and leadership might have made Athens the winner in the long run, but chance intervened to deprive Athens of his guidance: an epidemic struck Athens in 430 B.C.E. and killed Pericles the next year. This plague ravaged Athens's population for four years, killing thousands as it spread like wildfire among the people packed in behind the walls to avoid Spartan attacks. Despite their losses and the fears of many that the gods had sent the disease to punish them, the Athenians fought on. Over time, however, they abandoned the disciplined strategy that Pericles' prudent plan had required. The generals elected after his death, especially Cleon, pursued a much more aggressive strategy. At first this succeeded, especially when a group of Spartan hoplites surrendered after being blockaded by Cleon's forces at Pylos in 425 B.C.E. Their giving up shocked the Greek world and led Sparta to ask for a truce, but the Athenian assembly wanted more. When the daring Spartan general Brasidas captured Athens's possessions in northern Greece in 424 and 423 B.C.E., however, he turned the tide of war in the other direction by crippling the Athenian supply of timber and precious metals from this crucial region. When Brasidas and Cleon were both killed in 422 B.C.E., Sparta and Athens made peace in 421 B.C.E. out of mutual exhaustion.

Athens's most innovative and confident new general, Alcibiades, soon persuaded the assembly to reject the peace and to attack Spartan allies in 418 B.C.E. In 416–415 B.C.E., the Athenians and their allies overpowered the tiny and strategically meaningless Aegean island of Melos because it refused to abandon its allegiance to Sparta. Thucydides dramatically represents Athenian messengers telling the Melians they had to be conquered to show that Athens permitted no defiance to its dominance. Following their victory the Athenians executed the

TAKING MEASURE

Military Forces of Athens and Sparta at the Beginning of the Peloponnesian War (431 B.C.E.)

This chart compares the military forces of the Athenian side and the Spartan side when the Peloponnesian War broke out in 431 B.C.E. The numbers come from ancient sources, above all the Athenian general and historian Thucydides, who fought in the war. The bar graph starkly reveals the different characteristics of the competing forces: Athens relied on its navy of triremes and its archers (the fifth-century B.C.E. equivalent of artillery and snipers), while Sparta was superior in the forces needed for pitched land battles—hoplites (heavily armed infantry) and cavalry (shock troops used to disrupt opposing phalanxes). These differences dictated the differing strategies and tactics of the two sides: Athens in guerrilla fashion launching surprise raids from the sea, and Sparta trying to force decisive confrontations on the battlefield.

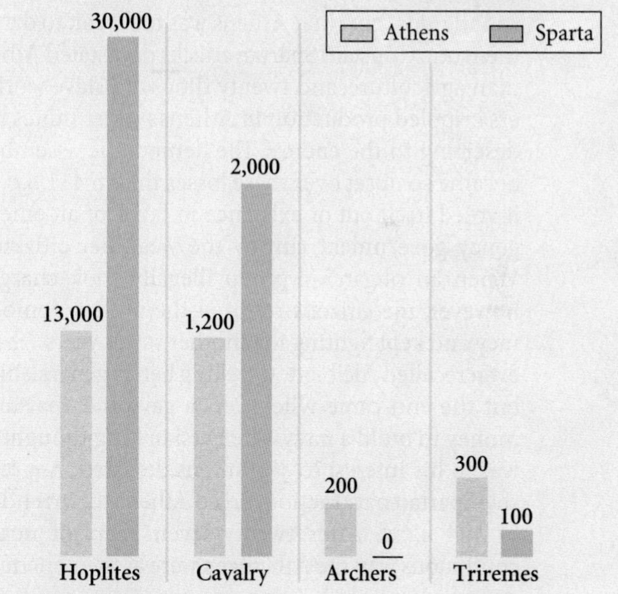

Question to Consider

■ **Given these figures, who at the start of the war would you have predicted would be the winner?**

Source: From Pamela Bradley, *Ancient Greece: Using Evidence* (Melbourne: Edward Arnold, 1990), 229.

Melian men, sold the women and children into slavery, and colonized the island.

The turning point in the war came soon thereafter when, in 415 B.C.E., Alcibiades persuaded the Athenian assembly to launch the greatest and most expensive campaign in Greek history. The expedition of 415 B.C.E. was directed against Sparta's allies in Sicily, far to the west. Alcibiades had dazzled his fellow citizens with the dream of conquering that rich island and especially its greatest city, Syracuse. Alcibiades' political rivals had him removed from his command, however, and the other generals blundered into catastrophic defeat in Sicily in 413 B.C.E. (see Map 3.3). The victorious Syracusans destroyed the allied invasion fleet and packed the survivors like human sardines into quarries under the blazing sun, with no toilets and only half a pint of drinking water and a handful of grain a day.

On the advice of Alcibiades, who had deserted to their side in anger at having lost his command, the Spartans in 413 B.C.E. seized a permanent base of operations in the Athenian countryside for year-round raids, now that Athens was too weak to drive them out. Constant Spartan attacks devastated Athenian agriculture, and twenty thousand slave workers crippled production in Athens's silver mines by deserting to the enemy. The democratic assembly became so upset over these losses that in 411 B.C.E. it voted itself out of existence in favor of an emergency government run by the wealthier citizens. When an oligarchic group illegally took charge, however, the citizens restored the radical democracy and kept fighting for another seven years. They even recalled Alcibiades, seeking better generalship, but the end came when Persia gave the Spartans money to build a navy. The Persian king thought it was in his interest to see Athens defeated. Aggressive Spartan naval action forced Athens to surrender in 404 B.C.E. After twenty-seven years of near-continuous war, the Athenians were at their enemy's mercy.

Athens Defeated: Tyranny and Civil War, 404–403 B.C.E.

Following Athens's surrender, the Spartans installed a regime of antidemocratic Athenians known as the Thirty Tyrants who were willing to collaborate with the victors. The collaborators were members of the social elite, and some, including their notoriously violent leader Critias, notorious for his criticism of religion, had been well-known pupils of the Sophists. Brutally suppressing democratic opposition, these oligarchs embarked on an eight-month period of murder and plunder in 404–403 B.C.E. The speechwriter Lysias, for example, reported that Spartan henchmen murdered his brother in order to steal the family's valuables, even ripping the gold rings from the ears of his brother's wife. Outraged at the violence and greed of the Thirty Tyrants, citizens who wanted to restore democracy banded together outside the city to fight to regain control of Athens. Fortunately for them, a feud between Sparta's two most important leaders paralyzed the Spartans, and they failed to send help to the Athenian collaborators. The democratic rebels defeated the forces of the Thirty Tyrants in a series of bloody street battles in Athens.

Democracy was thereby restored, but the city-state still seethed with anger and unrest. To settle the internal strife that threatened to tear Athens apart, the newly restored democratic assembly voted the first known amnesty in Western history, a truce agreement forbidding any official charges or recriminations stemming from the crimes of 404–403 B.C.E. Agreeing not to pursue grievances in court was the price of peace. As would soon become clear, however, some Athenians harbored grudges that no amnesty could dispel. In addition, Athens's financial and military strength had been shattered. At the end of the Golden Age, Athenians worried about how to remake their lives and restore the reputation that their city-state's innovative accomplishments had produced.

REVIEW QUESTION What factors determined the course of the Peloponnesian War?

Conclusion

When at the beginning of the fifth century B.C.E. some Greek city-states temporarily united to resist the Persian Empire, they surprised themselves by defeating the Persian invaders, who threatened their political independence. When the Persians retreated, however, so too did Greek unity. Following the Greek victory, Athens competed with Sparta for power. The Athenian Golden Age that followed the Persian Wars was based on empire and trade, and the city's riches funded the widening of democracy and brilliant cultural accomplishments.

As the money poured in, Athens built glorious and expensive temples, legislated pay for service in many government offices to strengthen democracy, and assembled the Mediterranean's most powerful navy. The poor men who rowed the ships demanded greater democracy; such demands led to political and legal reforms that guaranteed fairer treatment

MAPPING THE WEST

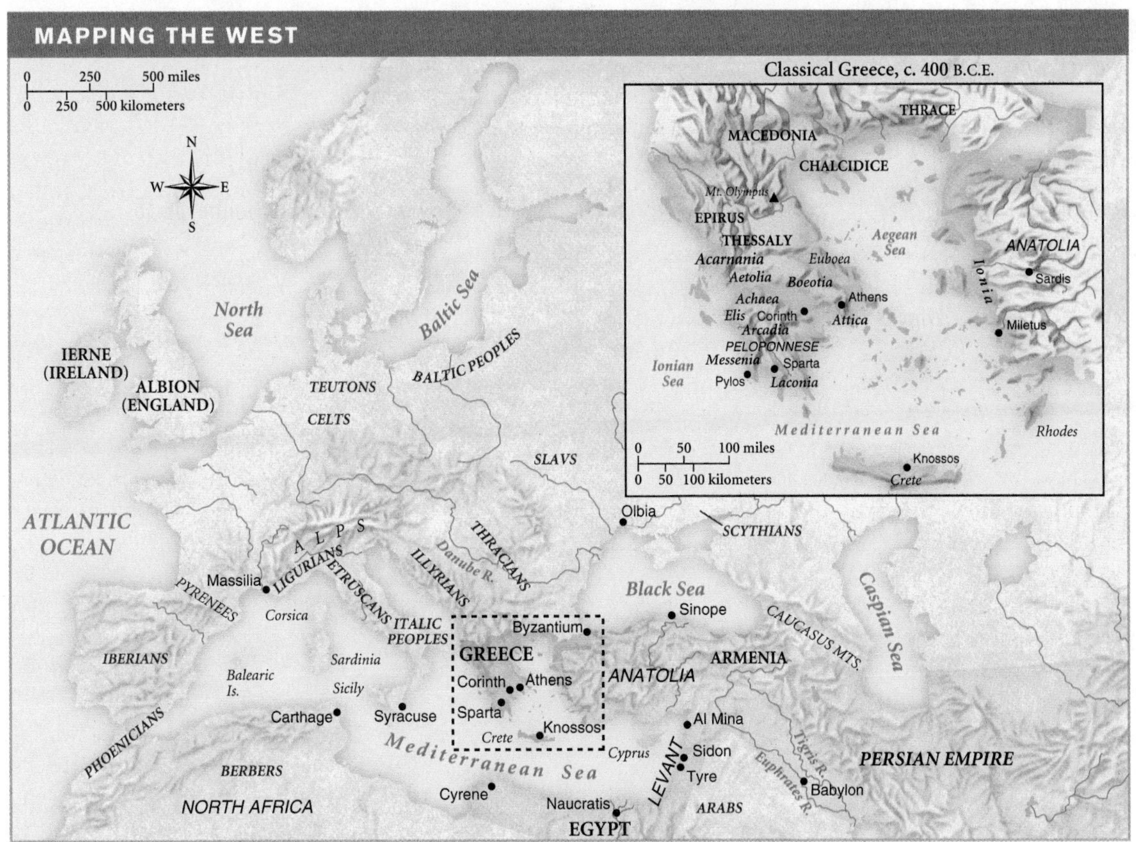

Greece, Europe, and the Mediterranean, 400 B.C.E.

No single power controlled the Mediterranean region at the end of the fifth century B.C.E. In the west, the Phoenician city of Carthage and the Greek cities on Sicily and in southern Italy were rivals for the riches to be won by trade. In the east, the Spartans, confident after their recent victory over Athens in the Peloponnesian War, tried to become an international power outside the mainland for the first time in their history by sending campaigns into Anatolia. This aggressive action aroused stiff opposition from the Persians because it was a threat to their westernmost imperial provinces. There was to be no peace and quiet in the Mediterranean even after the twenty-seven years of the Peloponnesian War.

for all. Pericles became the most famous politician of the Golden Age by leading the drive for radical democracy.

Religious practice and women's lives reflected the strong grip of tradition on everyday life, but dramatic innovations in education and philosophy created social tension. The Sophists' relativistic views disturbed tradition-minded people, as did Socrates' definition of virtue, which questioned ordinary people's love of wealth and success. Art and architecture broke out of old forms, promoting an impression of balanced motion rather than stability, while medicine gained a more scientific basis. Tragedy and comedy developed at Athens as public art forms commenting on contemporary social and political issues.

Wars framed the Golden Age. The Persian Wars sent Athens soaring to imperial power and prosperity, but the Athenians' high-handed treatment of allies and enemies combined with Spartan fears about Athenian power to bring on the disastrous Peloponnesian War. Nearly three decades of battle brought the stars of the Greek Golden Age crashing to earth: by 400 B.C.E. the Athenians found themselves in the same situation as in 500 B.C.E., fearful of Spartan power and worried whether the world's first democracy could survive. As it turned out, the next great threat to Greek stability and independence would once again come from a neighboring monarchy, this time not from Persia (to the east) but from Macedonia (to the north).

FOR FURTHER EXPLORATION

- **For additional primary-source material from this period**, see *Sources of the Making of the West*, Fourth Edition.
- **For Web sites, images, and documents related to topics in this chapter**, visit *Make History* at bedfordstmartins.com/hunt.

Chapter 3 Review

Online Study Guide bedfordstmartins.com/hunt

Key Terms and People

In the grid below, identify the term or person and explain its historical significance. (To do this exercise online, go to bedfordstmartins.com/hunt.)

Term	Who or What & When	Why It Matters
Themistocles (p. 77)		
Delian League (p. 80)		
triremes (p. 80)		
Pericles (p. 81)		
radical democracy (p. 81)		
ostracism (p. 82)		
agora (p. 83)		
Parthenon (p. 84)		
mystery cults (p. 87)		
metic (p. 87)		
hetaira (p. 91)		
Sophists (p. 94)		
Socratic method (p. 96)		
hubris (p. 99)		

Review Questions

1. How did the Greeks overcome the dangers of the Persian invasions?
2. What factors produced political change in fifth-century B.C.E. Athens?
3. How did new ways of thinking in the Golden Age change traditional ways of life?
4. What factors determined the course of the Peloponnesian War?

Making Connections

1. What were the most significant differences between Archaic Age Greece and Golden Age Greece?
2. For what sorts of things did Greeks of the Golden Age spend public funds? Why did they believe these things were worth the expense?
3. What price, in all senses, did Athens and the rest of Greece pay for the Golden Age? Was it worth it?

Important Events

Date	Event	Date	Event
500–323 B.C.E.	Classical Age of Greece	446–445 B.C.E. (WINTER)	Peace treaty between Athens and Sparta; intended to last thirty years
499–479 B.C.E.	Wars between Persia and Greece	441 B.C.E.	Sophocles presents the tragedy *Antigone*
490 B.C.E.	Battle of Marathon	431–404 B.C.E.	Peloponnesian War
480–479 B.C.E.	Xerxes' invasion of Greece	420S B.C.E.	Herodotus finishes *Histories*
480 B.C.E.	Battle of Salamis	415–413 B.C.E.	Enormous Athenian military expedition against Sicily
461 B.C.E.	Ephialtes reforms Athenian court system	411 B.C.E.	Aristophanes presents the comedy *Lysistrata*
EARLY 450S B.C.E.	Pericles introduces pay for officeholders in Athenian democracy	404–403 B.C.E.	Rule of the Thirty Tyrants at Athens
451 B.C.E.	Pericles restricts Athenian citizenship to children whose parents are both citizens	403 B.C.E.	Restoration of democracy in Athens
450 B.C.E.	Protagoras and other Sophists begin to teach in Athens		

- Consider three events: **Ephialtes reforms Athenian court system (461 B.C.E.)**, **Protagoras and other Sophists begin to teach in Athens (450 B.C.E.)**, and **Aristophanes presents the comedy *Lysistrata* (411 B.C.E.)**. How did the principles of radical democracy during the Athenian Golden Age help to make possible these different events?

SUGGESTED REFERENCES

The Greek city-states, especially Athens, reached the height of their political, economic, and military power in the fifth century B.C.E. following the defeat of the Persian invasion of mainland Greece; scholars continue to investigate how the frequent wars of this period influenced not only the democracy of Athens but also the famous dramatists and philosophers of this so-called Golden Age.

Blundell, Sue. *Women in Ancient Greece*. 1995.

Briant, Pierre. *From Cyrus to Alexander: History of the Persian Empire*. Translated by Peter Daniels. 2006.

Brunschwig, Jacques, and G. E. R. Lloyd, eds. *Greek Thought: A Guide to Classical Knowledge*. 2000.

Camp, John M. *The Archaeology of Athens*. 2004.

*Dillon, John, and Tania Gergel. *The Greek Sophists*. 2003.

*Grene, David, and Richmond Lattimore, eds. *The Complete Greek Tragedies*. 1992.

Hanson, Victor Davis. *A War Like No Other: How the Athenians and Spartans Fought the Peloponnesian War*. 2005.

Herman, Gabriel. *Morality and Behavior in Democratic Athens*. 2006.

*Herodotus. *The Histories*. Trans. Aubrey de Sélincourt. Revised by John Marincola. Rev. ed. 2003.

Mitchell-Boyask, Robin. *Plague and the Athenian Imagination: Drama, History, and the Cult of Asclepius*. 2008.

Papazarkadas, Nikolaus, et al., eds. *Interpreting the Athenian Empire*. 2009.

Parker, Robert. *Athenian Religion: A History*. 1996.

Parthenon: http://www.perseus.tufts.edu/cgi-bin/vor?x=16&y=13&lookup=parthenon

Patterson, Cynthia B. *The Family in Greek History*. 1998.

*Strassler, Robert B., ed. *The Landmark Thucydides. A Comprehensive Guide to the Peloponnesian War*. 1996.

Strauss, Barry. *The Battle of Salamis: The Naval Encounter That Saved Greece—and Western Civilization*. 2005.

Thorley, John. *Athenian Democracy*. 2004.

Wees, Hans van, ed. *War and Violence in Ancient Greece*. 2000.

Winkler, John J., and Froma I. Zeitlin, eds. *Nothing to Do with Dionysus? Athenian Drama in Its Social Context*. 1992.

*Primary source.

CHAPTER

From the Classical to the Hellenistic World

4

400–30 B.C.E.

About 255 B.C.E., an Egyptian camel trader far from home paid a scribe to write his Greek employer, Zeno, back in Egypt, to protest how Zeno's assistant, Krotos, was cheating him:

> You know that when you left me in Syria with Krotos I followed all your instructions concerning the camels and behaved blamelessly towards you. But Krotos has ignored your orders to pay me my salary; I've received nothing despite asking him for my money over and over. He just tells me to go away. I waited a long time for you to come, but when I no longer had life's necessities and couldn't get help anywhere, I had to run away . . . to keep from starving to death. . . . I am desperate summer and winter. . . . They have treated me like dirt because I am not a Greek. I therefore beg you, please, command them to pay me so that I won't go hungry just because I don't know how to speak Greek.

The trader's need for help from a foreigner holding power in his homeland reflects the changes in the eastern Mediterranean world during the Hellenistic Age (323–30 B.C.E.). The movement of Greeks into the Near East and their contacts with local peoples increased the cultural interaction of the Greek and the Near Eastern worlds to the highest level ever, forging a multicultural synthesis that set a new course for Western civilization in politics, art, philosophy, science, and religion. The first stage of this movement came after the Peloponnesian War, when thousands of Greeks became mercenary soldiers serving Near Eastern rulers. Alexander the Great (356–323 B.C.E.) then changed the course of history by conquering the Persian Empire, leading an army of Greeks and Macedonians to the border of India, taking Near Easterners into his army and imperial administration, and planting colonies of Greeks as far

The Rosetta Stone

Dug out of the wall of a fort in 1799 by a soldier in Napoleon's army near Rosetta, in the Nile River delta, this Hellenistic inscription in two different languages and three different forms of writing unlocked the lost secrets of how to read Egyptian hieroglyphs. The bands of text repeat the same message (priests praising King Ptolemy V in 196 B.C.E.) in hieroglyphs, demotic (a cursive form of Egyptian invented around 600 B.C.E.), and Greek. Bilingual texts were necessary to reach the mixed population of Hellenistic Egypt. Scholars deciphered the hieroglyphs by comparing them to the Greek version. They started with the hieroglyphs surrounded by an oval, which they guessed were royal names. *(Art Resource, NY.)*

east as Afghanistan. His amazing expedition—with its almost superhuman exploits—shocked the world and acted like a cultural whirlwind to give new creative energy to Western civilization by combining Near Eastern and Greek traditions as never before.

Politics changed in the Greek world when Alexander's successors revived monarchy by taking over territories to rule as their personal kingdoms. These new kingdoms, which became the dominant powers of the Hellenistic Age, restricted the freedom of Greece's city-states. The city-states retained local rule but lost their independence to compete with one another in foreign policy. The Hellenistic kings now controlled international affairs. They imported Greeks to fill royal offices, man their armies, and run businesses. This demographic change created tension with the kings' non-Greek subjects. Immigrant Greeks, such as Zeno in Egypt, formed a social elite that lorded it over the kingdoms' local populations. Egyptians, Syrians, or Mesopotamians who wanted to rise in society had to win the support of these Greeks and learn their language. Otherwise, they were likely to find themselves as powerless as the hungry camel merchant.

Over time, the Near East's local cultures interacted with the Greek overlords' culture to spawn a multicultural synthesis. Locals married Greeks, shared their artistic and religious traditions with the newcomers, passed along their agricultural and scientific knowledge, and learned Greek to win administrative jobs. Although Hellenistic royal society always remained hierarchical, with Greeks at the top, and never eliminated tension between rulers and ruled, its kings and queens did finance innovations in art, philosophy, religion, and science that combined Near Eastern and Greek traditions. The Hellenistic kingdoms fell in the second and first centuries B.C.E. when the Romans overthrew them one by one.

All this happened during an era of constant warfare. Cultural interaction, a characteristic of Western civilization from the beginning, reached a new level of intensity as an unintended consequence of Alexander's military campaigns. The new contacts between diverse peoples and the emergence of new ideas strongly influenced Roman civilization and therefore later Western civilization. In particular, Hellenistic artistic, scientific, philosophical, and religious innovations persisted even after the glory of Greece's Golden Age had faded, especially since Hellenistic religion provided the background for Christianity.

CHAPTER FOCUS What were the major political and cultural changes in the Hellenistic Age?

Classical Greece after the Peloponnesian War, 400–350 B.C.E.

The Greek city-states gradually regained their economic and political stability after the Peloponnesian War (431–404 B.C.E.), but daily life remained hard, especially for working people. The war's aftermath dramatically affected Greek philosophy. At Athens, citizens who blamed Socrates for inspiring the worst of the Thirty Tyrants brought him to trial; the jury condemned him to death. His execution helped persuade the philosophers Plato and Aristotle to detest democracy and develop new ways of thinking about right versus wrong and how human beings should live.

Although the city-states recovered after the war, their continuing competition for power in the fourth century B.C.E. drained their resources. After failing to control defeated Athens, the Spartans tried to expand their power into central Greece and Anatolia

399 B.C.E. Execution of Socrates

386 B.C.E. In King's Peace, Sparta surrenders control of Anatolian Greek city-states to Persia; Plato founds Academy

362 B.C.E. Battle of Mantinea leaves power vacuum in Greece

338 B.C.E. Battle of Chaeronea allows Macedonian Philip II to become the leading power in Greece

335 B.C.E. Aristotle founds Lyceum

334–323 B.C.E. Alexander the Great leads Greeks and Macedonians to conquer Persian Empire

307 B.C.E. Epicurus founds his philosophical group in Athens

306–304 B.C.E. Successors of Alexander declare themselves kings

c. 300 B.C.E. Euclid teaches geometry at Alexandria

300–260 B.C.E. Theocritus writes poetry at Ptolemaic court

400 B.C.E. — 350 B.C.E. — 300 B.C.E. — 250 B.C.E.

by collaborating with the Persians. This policy stirred up violent resistance from Thebes and from Athens, which had rebuilt its naval empire. By the 350s B.C.E., the strife among the Greek city-states so weakened all of them that they were unable to prevent the Macedonian kingdom (Alexander the Great's homeland) from gaining control of Greece.

Athens's Recovery after the Peloponnesian War

Athens provides the most evidence for Greek life after the Peloponnesian War. The devastation of Athens's rural economy by Spartan raids and the overcrowding in the wartime city produced friction between refugees from the countryside and city dwellers. Life became difficult for middle-class women whose husbands and brothers had died during the conflict. Traditionally, they had woven cloth at home for their families and supervised the household slaves, but the men had earned the family's income by farming or working at a trade. Now, with no man to provide for them and their children, many war widows had to work outside the home. The only jobs open to them — such as wet-nursing, weaving, or laboring in vineyards—were low-paying.

Resourceful Athenians found ways to profit from women's skills. The family of one of Socrates' friends, for example, fell into poverty when several widowed sisters, nieces, and female cousins moved in. The friend complained to Socrates that he was too poor to support his new family of fourteen plus their slaves. Socrates replied that the women knew how to make men's and women's cloaks, shirts, capes, and smocks, "the work considered the best and most fitting for women." He suggested they begin to sell the clothes outside the home. This plan succeeded financially, but the women complained that Socrates' friend was the household's only member who ate without working. Socrates advised the man to reply that the women should think of him as sheep did a guard dog — he earned his share of the food by keeping the wolves away.

Athens's postwar economy recovered because small-business owners and households engaged in trade and produced manufactured goods. Greek businesses, usually family-run, were small; the largest known was a shield-making company with 120 slave workers. Some changes occurred in occupations formerly defined by gender. For example, men began working alongside women in cloth production when the first commercial weaving shops outside the home sprang up. Some women made careers in the arts, especially painting and music, which men had traditionally dominated.

The rebuilding by 393 B.C.E. of Athens's destroyed Long Walls, which protected the transportation

Vase Painting of Women Fetching Water (detail)
This vase painting shows women filling water jugs at a public fountain to take back to their homes. Both freeborn and slave women fetched water for their households; few Greek homes had running water. Cities built attractive fountain houses such as the one depicted here, which dispensed fresh water from springs or piped it in through small aqueducts (compare the large Roman aqueduct on page 152.) Women often gathered at fountains for conversation with people from outside their household. *(The Priam Painter, Water jar [hydria], Athens, Attica, Greece. Place of manufacture: Athens, Attica, Greece. H. 53 cm. [20⅞ in.]; diameter: 37 cm. [14 9/16 in.]. Ceramic, Black Figure, Museum of Fine Arts, Boston, William Francis Warden Fund, 61.195. Photograph © 2011 Museum of Fine Arts, Boston.)*

30 B.C.E. Cleopatra VII dies and Rome takes over Ptolemaic Empire

200 B.C.E. | 150 B.C.E. | 100 B.C.E. | 50 B.C.E.

195 B.C.E. Seleucid queen Laodice endows dowries for girls

167 B.C.E. Maccabee revolt after Antiochus IV turns temple in Jerusalem into a Greek sanctuary

Silver Coins of Athens
The city-state of ancient Athens owned rich silver mines that financed its silver coinage, famous around the Greek world for purity and reliability. This coin from the fifth century B.C.E. was a tetradrachm ("four drachmas"), which was the amount that a worker or rower in the Athenian navy earned in four days. The images show Athena, the city-state's main goddess, and an owl with an olive branch, also symbols of Athena. The style of the images was kept old-fashioned and mostly unchanging so as not to harm the trust that people in foreign lands had in accepting Athenian coins in trade and commerce as a form of international currency. *(© C. M. Dixon/Ancient Art & Architecture Collection. Ltd.)*

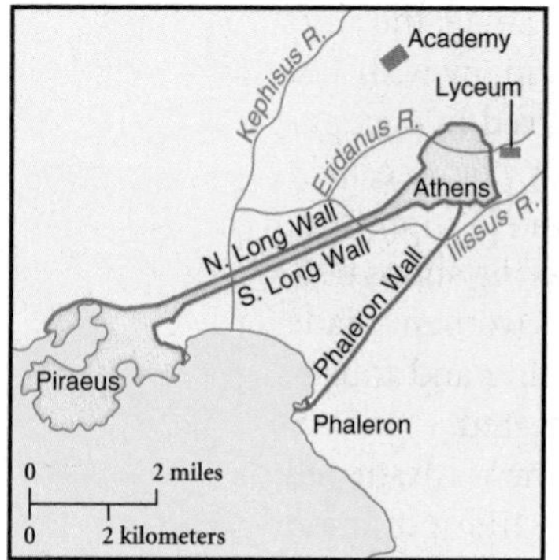

Athens's Long Walls as Rebuilt after the Peloponnesian War

corridor from the city to the port, gave evidence of a recovering economy. Exports of grain, wine, and pottery resumed, as did exports of silver from Athens's mines. The refortified harbor also allowed Athens to begin to rebuild its navy, which increased employment opportunities for poor men.

Even in an improving economy, daily life remained difficult for working people. Most workers earned barely enough to feed and clothe their families. They ate two meals a day, a light one at midmorning and a heavier evening meal. Bread baked from barley provided their main food; only rich people could afford wheat bread. A family bought bread from small bakery stands, often run by women, or made it at home, with the wife directing the slaves in grinding the grain, shaping the dough, and baking it in a clay oven heated by charcoal. People topped their bread with greens, beans, onions, garlic, olives, fruit, and cheese. The few households rich enough to afford meat boiled or grilled it over a fire. Everyone of all ages drank wine, diluted with water, with every meal.

The Execution of Socrates, 399 B.C.E.

Socrates, Athens's most famous philosopher in the Golden Age, fell victim to the bitterness many Athenians felt about the rule of the Thirty Tyrants following the Peloponnesian War. Since the amnesty proclaimed by the restored democratic assembly prohibited prosecutions for crimes committed under the tyrants' reign of terror, angry citizens had to bring other charges against those they hated. Some prominent Athenians hated Socrates because his follower Critias had been one of the Thirty Tyrants' most violent leaders.

These prominent citizens charged Socrates with impiety, a serious crime, claiming that he had angered the gods with his ideas and therefore threatened the city with divine punishment. In 399 B.C.E., they argued their case to a jury of 501 male citizens. They presented religious and moral arguments: Socrates, they claimed, rejected the city-state's gods, introduced new divinities, and lured young men away from Athenian moral traditions. Speaking in his own defense, Socrates refused to beg for sympathy, as was customary in trials. Instead, he repeated his dedication to goading his fellow citizens into examining their preconceptions about how to live justly. He vowed to remain their stinging gadfly no matter what.

When the jurors narrowly voted to convict the philosopher, Athenian law required them to decide between the penalty proposed by the prosecutors and that proposed by the defendant. The prosecutors proposed death. Everyone expected Socrates to offer exile as an alternative and the jury to accept it. The philosopher, however, said that he deserved a reward rather than punishment, until his friends made him propose a fine as his penalty. The jury chose death, requiring him to drink a poison concocted from powdered hemlock. Socrates accepted his sentence calmly, saying that "no evil can befall a good man either in life or in death." Ancient sources report that many Athenians soon came to regret Socrates' punishment as a tragic mistake and a severe blow to their reputation.

The Philosophy of Plato

Socrates' death made his follower and Greece's most famous philosopher, **Plato** (429–348 B.C.E.), hate democracy. From a well-to-do family and related to the infamous Critias, whom he wrote about favorably, Plato started out as a political consultant promoting the rule of philosopher-tyrants as the best form of government. He traveled to Sicily to advise Dionysius, tyrant of Syracuse, but when he failed to turn Dionysius into an ideal ruler, Plato gave up hope that political action could stop violence and greed. Instead, he turned to talking and writing about philosophy as the guide to life and established a philosophical school, the Academy, in Athens around 386 B.C.E. The Academy was an informal as-

---

Plato: A follower of Socrates who became Greece's most famous philosopher.

sociation of people who studied philosophy, mathematics, and theoretical astronomy under the leader's guidance. It attracted intellectuals to Athens for the next nine hundred years, and Plato's ideas about the nature of reality, ethics, and politics have remained central to philosophy and political science to this day.

Mosaic Depicting Plato's Academy
This Roman-era mosaic shows philosophers talking at Plato's school in Athens, the Academy. Founded about 386 B.C.E., the Academy became one of Greece's longest-lasting institutions, attracting scholars and students for more than nine hundred years. The columns and the tree in the mosaic express the harmonious blend of the natural and built environment of the Academy, which was meant to promote discussion. What message do the philosophers' bare chests convey? *(Erich Lessing/Art Resource, NY.)*

Plato's Ethical Thought

Plato's intellectual interests covered astronomy, mathematics, political philosophy, **metaphysics** (ideas about the ultimate nature of reality beyond the reach of the human senses), and ethics. His radical views on reality underlay his ethics. He presented his ideas in dialogues, which usually featured Socrates conversing with a variety of people. Plato wrote to provoke readers into thoughtful reflection, not to prescribe a set of beliefs. Nevertheless, he always maintained one essential idea based on his view of reality: ultimate moral qualities are universal, unchanging, and absolute, not relative. He thus rejected the relativism that the Sophists had taught.

Plato's dialogues explore his theory that justice, goodness, beauty, and equality exist on their own in a higher realm beyond the daily world. He used the word *Forms* (or *Ideas*) to describe the abstract, invariable, and ultimate realities of such ethical qualities. According to Plato, the Forms are the only genuine reality. All things that humans perceive with their senses on earth are only dim and imperfect copies of these metaphysical, ultimate realities. Forms are not defined by human experience of them—any earthly examples can always display the opposite quality. For example, returning a borrowed item might seem like justice. But what if the borrowed item is a weapon and the lender wants it back to commit murder? Returning the borrowed item would then support injustice. Therefore, every ethical quality is relative in the world that humans experience. But, Plato insists, they are absolute in the ultimate reality. Human experiences are like shadows of the absolutes cast on the wall of a cave. The difficult notion of Forms made metaphysics an important issue in philosophy.

Plato's ideas about the soul also deeply influenced later thought. He believed that humans possess immortal souls distinct from their bodies; this idea established the concept of **dualism**, a separation between soul (or mind) and body. Plato further explained that the human soul possesses preexisting knowledge put there by a god. The world has order because a rational deity created it. The god wanted to reproduce the Forms' perfect order in the material world, but the world turned out imperfect because matter is imperfect. Humans' present, impure existence is only a temporary stage in cosmic existence because, while the body does not last, the soul is immortal.

Building on earlier Greek rationalism, Plato argued that people must seek perfect order and purity in their souls by using rational thought to control irrational and therefore harmful desires. People who yield to irrational desires fail to consider the future of their body and soul. The desire to drink too much alcohol, for example, is irrational because the binge drinker fails to consider the painful hangover that will follow.

Plato's Republic

Plato presented his most famous ideas on politics in his dialogue *The Republic*. This work, whose Greek title means "system of government," discusses the nature of

---

metaphysics: Philosophical ideas about the ultimate nature of reality beyond the reach of human senses.

dualism: The philosophical idea that the human soul (or mind) and body are separate.

justice and the reasons people should never commit injustice. Democracy, Plato wrote, cannot create justice because people on their own cannot rise above narrow self-interest to knowledge of the ultimate reality of universal truth. Justice can come only under the rule of an enlightened oligarchy or monarchy. Therefore, a just society requires a strict hierarchy.

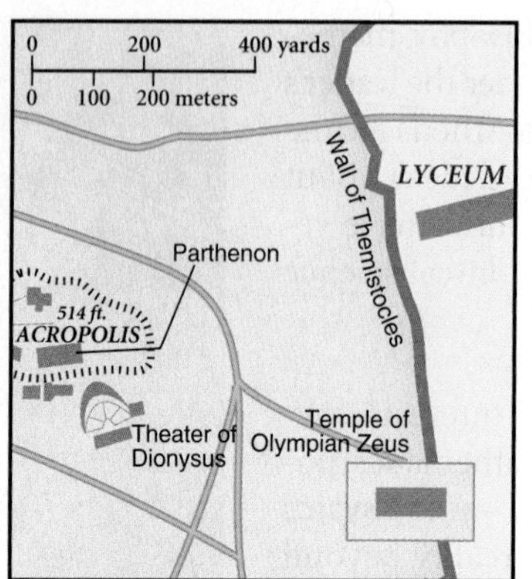

Aristotle's Lyceum, established 335 B.C.E.

Plato's *Republic* describes an ideal society with a hierarchy of three classes distinguished by their ability to grasp the truth of Forms. The highest class is the rulers, or "guardians," who must be educated in mathematics, astronomy, and metaphysics. Next come the "auxiliaries," who defend the community. "Producers" make up the bottom class; they grow food and make objects for everyone.

Women can be guardians because they possess the same virtues and abilities as men, except that the average woman has less physical strength than the average man. To minimize distraction, guardians are to have neither private property nor nuclear families. Male and female guardians are to live in houses shared in common, eat in the same dining halls, and exercise in the same gymnasia. They are to have sex with various partners so that the best women can mate with the best men to produce the best children. The children are to be raised together by special caretakers, not their parents. Guardians who achieve the highest level of knowledge can rule as philosopher-kings. Plato did not think humans could actually create the ideal society described in *The Republic*, but he did believe that imagining it was an important way to help people learn to live justly. For Plato, philosophy was an essential guide to human life.

Aristotle, Scientist and Philosopher

Aristotle (384–322 B.C.E.) was another Greek thinker who believed in the importance of philosophy as a guide to life. At age seventeen, he joined Plato's Academy. From 342 to 335 B.C.E., he earned a living by tutoring the teenage Alexander the Great in Macedonia. Returning to Athens in 335 B.C.E., Aristotle founded his own school, the **Lyceum**, and taught his own life-guiding philosophy, based on logic, scientific knowledge, and practical experience. Like Plato, he thought Athenian democracy was a bad system because it did not restrict decision making to the most educated and moderate citizens. His vast writings made him one of the world's most influential thinkers.

Aristotle's reputation rests on his scientific investigation of the natural world, development of rigorous systems of logical argument, and practical ethics. He regarded science and philosophy as the disciplined search for knowledge in every aspect of everyday life. That search brought the good life and genuine happiness. Aristotle lectured with dazzling intelligence on biology, medicine, anatomy, psychology, meteorology, physics, chemistry, mathematics, music, metaphysics, rhetoric, literary criticism, political science, and ethics. He also invented a system of logic for precise argumentation. By creating ways to identify valid arguments, Aristotle established grounds for determining whether an argument was logically valid or merely persuasive.

Aristotle required explanations to be based on strict rationality and common sense rather than metaphysics. He rejected Plato's theory of Forms because, he said, the separate, ultimate existence Plato postulated for Forms was not subject to demonstrable proof. Aristotle believed that the best way to understand anything was to observe it in its natural setting. He coupled detailed investigation with careful reasoning in biology, botany, and zoology. He was the first investigator to try to collect and classify all available information on animal species, recording facts and advancing knowledge about more than five hundred different kinds of animals, including insects. His recognition that whales and dolphins are mammals, for example, was overlooked by later writers on animals and not rediscovered for another two thousand years.

Not all of Aristotle's observations were accurate, and some of his views justified inequalities characteristic of his time. He regarded slavery as natural, arguing that some people were slaves by nature because their souls lacked the rational part

Aristotle: Greek philosopher famous for his scientific investigations, development of logical argument, and practical ethics.

Lyceum: The school for research and teaching in a wide range of subjects founded by Aristotle in Athens in 335 B.C.E.

DOCUMENT

Aristotle on the Nature of the Greek Polis

Aristotle's book Politics *discussed the origins of political states and the different ways to organize them. Reflecting on his research into many fields in science, Aristotle connected his theories on the structures of politics to his ideas that emerged from his investigations of the fundamental principles of the natural world. In this excerpt, Aristotle explains that the polis (city-state) was a creation of nature.*

Since we see that every city-state is a type of partnership and that every partnership is established for the sake of some good, for everything that everyone does is motivated by what seems to them to be a good, it is clear that, with all partnerships aiming at some good, the most authoritative partnership, which includes all other partnerships, does this the most of all and aims at the most authoritative of all goods. This is what is called the city-state, that is, the political partnership. . . .

If one looks at things as they grow from the beginning, one will make the best observations, on this topic and all others. Necessity first brings together those who cannot exist without each other, that is, on the one hand, the female and the male for the purpose of reproduction, and this is not a matter of choice, but just as with the other animals and with plants, it is a matter of nature to desire to leave behind another of the same kind. On the other hand, [necessity brings together] the ruler and the one who is naturally ruled for the sake of security, for the one who is able to foresee things with his mind is by nature a ruler and by nature a master, while the one who is able to do things with his body is the one who is ruled and is by nature a slave. For this reason the same thing benefits master and slave. . . .

From these two partnerships comes first the household, and Hesiod spoke correctly, saying, "First of all, [get yourself] a house and a wife and an ox for plowing,"[1] because the ox is a household slave for a poor man. Therefore, the partnership that is established first by nature for everyday purposes is the household. . . .

[1]A quotation from *Works and Days*, line 405.

The partnership that first arises from multiple households for the sake of more than everyday needs is the village. The village seems by nature to be a colony from the household. . . .

The final partnership of multiple villages is the city-state, which possesses the limit of self-sufficiency, so to speak. It comes into being for the sake of living, but it exists for the sake of living well. Every city-state therefore exists by nature, if it is true that the first partnerships do. . . . It is clear that the city-state belongs to the things existing by nature, and that humans are beings who by nature live in a city-state, and that the one who has no city-state by nature and not by chance is either a fool or a superhuman.

Source: Aristotle, *Politics*, Book 1.1–2, 1252a1–1253a19. Translation by Thomas R. Martin.

Question to Consider

- **On what specific ideas does Aristotle base his explanation of the origins and character of the city-state as a form of political and social organization? Does he make a convincing argument? Why or why not?**

that should rule in a human. He also concluded, on the basis of faulty biological observations, that nature made women inferior to men. He wrongly believed, for example, that in procreation the male's semen actively gave the fetus its design, whereas the female passively provided its matter. Mistaken biological information led Aristotle to evaluate females as incomplete males, a conclusion with disastrous results for later thought. At the same time, he believed that human communities could be successful and happy only if women and men both contributed. (See Document, "Aristotle on the Nature of the Greek Polis," above.)

In ethics, Aristotle emphasized the need to develop practical habits of just behavior to achieve happiness. People should achieve self-control by training their minds to win out over instincts and passions. Self-control meant finding "the mean," or balance, between denying and indulging physical pleasures. Aristotle claimed that the mind must rule in finding the balance leading to true happiness because the intellect is the finest human quality and the mind is the true self—indeed, the godlike part of a person.

Aristotle influenced ethics by insisting that standards of right and wrong have merit only if they are grounded in character and aligned with the good in human nature. They cannot work if they consist of abstract reasons for just behavior. That is, an ethical system must be relevant to real human situations. He argued that the life of the mind and experience of the real world are inseparable in defining a worthwhile and happy existence.

Greek Political Disunity

In the same period that Plato and Aristotle were developing their philosophies as guides to life, the Greek city-states were in a constant state of war. Sparta, Thebes, and Athens competed to dominate

Greece. None succeeded. Their endless fighting weakened their morale and their finances, leaving Greek independence vulnerable to external threat.

The Spartans provoked the competition by trying to conquer other city-states in central Greece and in Anatolia in the 390s B.C.E. Thebes, Athens, Corinth, and Argos then formed an anti-Spartan coalition. The Spartans checkmated the alliance by negotiating with the Persian king. Betraying their traditional claim to defend Greek freedom, the Spartans acknowledged the Persian ruler's right to control the Greek city-states of Anatolia—in return for permission to wage war in Greece without Persian interference. This agreement of 386 B.C.E., called the King's Peace, sold out the Greeks of Anatolia, returning them to submission to the Persian Empire, just as before the Persian Wars.

The Athenians rebuilt their military to compete with Sparta. The Long Walls restored Athens's invulnerability to invasion, and a new kind of light infantry—the *peltast*, armed with a small leather shield, a sword, and several javelins—fighting alongside hoplites gave Athenian ground forces greater tactical mobility and flexibility. Most important, Athens rebuilt its navy so that by 377 B.C.E. it had again become the leader of a naval alliance of Greek city-states. Members of this alliance insisted that their rights be specified in writing to prevent a repeat of Athenian domination as in the Delian League of the fifth century B.C.E.

The Thebans became Greece's main power in the 370s B.C.E. through brilliant generalship. They crushed the Spartan invasion of Theban territory in 371 B.C.E. and then invaded the Spartan homeland in the Peloponnese. They greatly weakened Sparta by freeing many helots. Since Thebes was only forty miles from Athens, the Thebans' success alarmed the Athenians, who allied with their hated enemies, the Spartans. The armies of Athens and Sparta confronted the Thebans in the battle of Mantinea in the Peloponnese in 362 B.C.E. Thebes won the battle but lost the war when its best general was killed and no capable replacement could be found.

The battle of Mantinea left the Greek city-states disunified and weak. As a commentator said, "Everyone had supposed that this battle's winners would become Greece's rulers and its losers their subjects; but there was only more confusion and disturbance in Greece after Mantinea than before." This judgment was confirmed when the Athenian naval alliance fell apart in a war between Athens and its allies over the negotiations some allies were conducting with Persia and Macedonia.

By the 350s B.C.E., no Greek city-state had the power to rule anything except its own territory. The city-states' competition for supremacy finally died out in a stalemate of exhaustion. By failing to cooperate, the Greeks opened the way for the rise of a new power—the kingdom of Macedonia—that would end their independence in international politics. The Macedonian kings did not literally enslave the Greeks, as the Spartans did the helots, or usually even change their local governments. They did, however, abolish the city-states' freedom to control their foreign policy.

REVIEW QUESTION **How did daily life, philosophy, and the political situation change in Greece during the period 400–350 B.C.E.?**

The Rise of Macedonia, 359–323 B.C.E.

The kingdom of Macedonia's rise to superpower status counts as one of the greatest surprises in ancient military and political history. In little more than a generation, the Macedonian kingdom, located just north of central Greece, took advantage of the Greek city-states' disunity to rocket from being a minor state to ruling the Greek and Near Eastern worlds. Two aggressive and charismatic Macedonian kings produced this transformation: Philip II (r. 359–336 B.C.E.) and his son **Alexander the Great** (r. 336–323 B.C.E.). Their conquests ended the Greek Classical Age and set in motion the Hellenistic Age's cultural changes.

The Roots of Macedonian Power

The Macedonians' power sprang from the characteristics of their monarchy and their people's ethnic pride. Macedonian kings had to listen to their people, who had freedom of speech. The king governed by maintaining the support of the elite, who ranked as his social equals and controlled many followers. Men spent their time training for war, hunting, and drinking heavily. The king had to excel in these activities to show that he deserved to lead the state. Queens and royal mothers received respect because they came from powerful families or the ruling houses of neighboring regions. In the king's absence these royal women exercised power at court.

Alexander the Great: The fourth-century B.C.E. Macedonian king whose conquest of the Persian Empire led to the greatly increased cultural interactions of Greece and the Near East in the Hellenistic Age.

Macedonian kings thought of themselves as ethnically Greek; they spoke Greek as well as they did their native Macedonian. Macedonians as a whole, however, looked down on the Greeks as too soft to survive life in their northern land. The Greeks returned this contempt. The famed Athenian orator Demosthenes (384–322 B.C.E.) mocked Philip II as "not only not a Greek nor related to the Greeks, but not even a barbarian from a land worth mentioning; no, he's a pestilence from Macedonia, a region where you can't even buy a slave worth his salt."

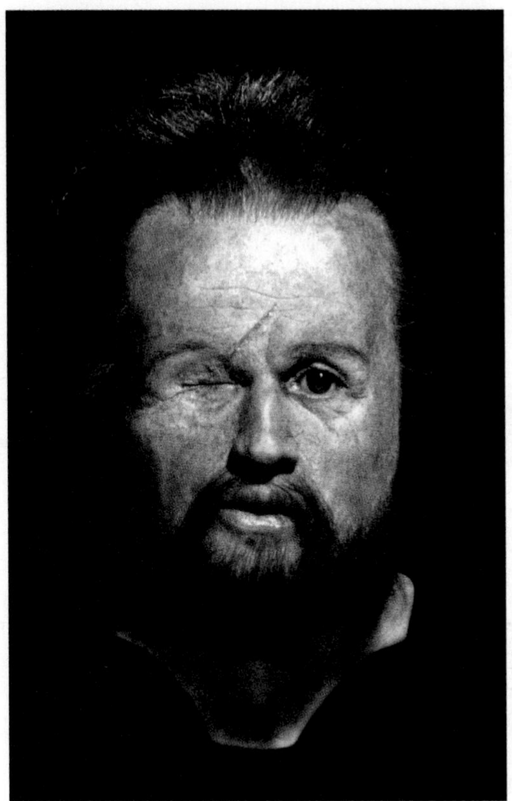

Reconstruction of the Head of King Philip II of Macedonia

Forensic archaeologists have reconstructed this head in wax to show what they think Philip II, King of Macedonia in the mid-fourth century B.C.E. and father of Alexander the Great, looked like. Philip's right eye was destroyed by an arrow, which left him disfigured but did not keep him out of battle as he went on to win the military and political leadership of mainland Greece. *(Reconstruction by Richard Neave/Photograph courtesy of the University of Manchester.)*

The Rule of Philip II, 359–336 B.C.E.

King Philip II forged Macedonia into an international power against heavy odds. Before his reign, the kingdom remained weak because of frequent strife between royals and the elite, and attacks from hostile neighbors. Princes married young, soon after the age of twenty, and possibly more than one wife, to try to produce male heirs to provide strong rule protecting the kingdom.

A military disaster in 359 B.C.E. brought Philip to the throne at a desperate moment. The Illyrians, neighbors to the west, had slaughtered the previous king and four thousand troops. Philip restored the Macedonian army's confidence by teaching his troops an unstoppable new tactic with their thrusting spears, which reached a length of sixteen feet and took two hands to wield: arranging them in the traditional phalanx formation, he created deep blocks of soldiers whose front lines bristled with outstretched spears like a lethal porcupine. Then he trained them to move around in battle in different directions without losing their formation. By moving as a unit, a mobile phalanx armed with such long spears could splinter the enemy's infantry. Deploying cavalry as a strike force to soften up the enemy while also protecting the infantry's flanks, Philip used his reorganized army to rout the Illyrians in the field, while at home he eliminated his local rivals for kingship.

Philip next moved southward into Greece, employing diplomacy, bribery, and military action to bulldoze the city-states into following him. A Greek contemporary labeled Philip "insatiable and extravagant; he did everything in a hurry . . . he never spared the time to reckon up his income and expenses." By the late 340s B.C.E., Philip had persuaded or forced most of northern and central Greece into alliance with him. Seeking glory for Greece and fearing the instability his strengthened army would create in his kingdom if the soldiers had nothing to do, he decided to lead a united Macedonian and Greek army to conquer the Persian Empire.

Philip justified attacking Persia as revenge for its invasion of Greece 150 years earlier. Some Greeks remained unconvinced. At Athens, Demosthenes bitterly criticized Greeks for not resisting Philip. They stood by, he thundered, "as if Philip was a hailstorm, praying that he would not come their way, but not trying to do anything to head him off." Moved by Demosthenes' words, Athens and Thebes rallied a coalition of southern Greek city-states to combat Philip, but in 338 B.C.E. the Macedonian king and his Greek allies crushed the coalition's forces at the battle of Chaeronea in Boeotia (Map 4.1). The defeated city-states retained their internal freedom, but Philip forced them to join his alliance. The battle of Chaeronea marked a turning point in Greek history: never again would the city-states of Greece be independent agents in foreign policy. City-states re-

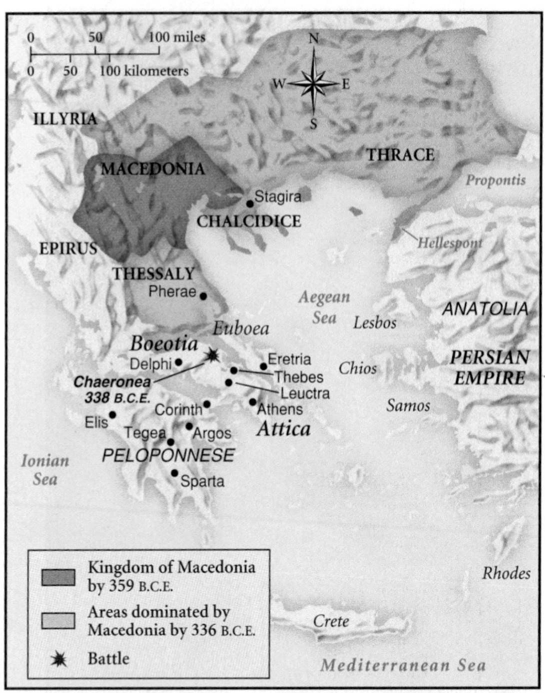

MAP 4.1 Expansion of Macedonia under Philip II, 359–336 B.C.E.
King Philip II expanded Macedonian power southward; mountainous terrain and warlike people blocked the way northward. The Macedonian royal house saw itself as ethnically Greek, and Philip made himself the leader of Greece by defeating a Greek coalition led by Athens at the battle of Chaeronea in 338 B.C.E. Sparta, far from Macedonia in the southern Peloponnese, did not join the coalition. Philip ignored it; Sparta's declining number of citizens made it too weak to matter.

mained Greece's central social and economic units, but they were always looking over their shoulders, worrying about the powerful kings who wanted to control them.

The Rule of Alexander the Great, 336–323 B.C.E.

If Philip had not been murdered by a Macedonian acquaintance in 336 B.C.E., we might be calling him Philip the Great. Instead, his assassination brought his son Alexander III to power. Rumors swirled that the son and his mother, Olympias, had arranged Philip's murder to seize the throne for the twenty-year-old Alexander, but our best guess is that the murderer acted out of personal anger at the king. Alexander secured his rule by killing his internal rivals and defeating Macedonia's enemies to the west and north in several lightning-fast strikes. Finally, Alexander forced the southern Greeks, who had defected from the alliance at the news of Philip's death, to rejoin. To demonstrate the price of disloyalty, in 335 B.C.E. Alexander destroyed Thebes for having rebelled.

Conquering the Persian Empire In 334 B.C.E., Alexander launched the most astonishing military campaign in ancient history by leading a Macedonian and Greek army against the Persian Empire to fulfill Philip's dream of avenging Greece. Alexander's conquest of all the lands from Turkey to Egypt to Uzbekistan while still in his twenties led later peoples to call him Alexander the Great. In his own time, he became a legend by motivating his men to victory after victory in hostile regions far from Macedonia.

Alexander inspired his troops by exhibiting reckless disregard for his own safety in battle. He often led the charge against the enemy's front line, riding his warhorse Bucephalas ("oxhead"). Everyone saw him speeding ahead in his plumed helmet, polished armor, and vividly colored cloak. He was so intent on conquest that he rejected advice to delay the war until he had fathered an heir. He gave away nearly all of his land to strengthen ties with his army officers. "What," one adviser asked, "do you have left for yourself?" "My hopes," Alexander replied. Alexander's hopes centered on making himself a warrior as famous as Achilles; under his pillow he always kept a copy of Homer's *Iliad*—and a dagger.

Alexander displayed his heroic ambitions as his army advanced. In Anatolia, he visited Gordion, where an oracle had promised the lordship of Asia to whoever could untie a massive knot of rope tying the yoke of an ancient chariot. Alexander, so the story goes, cut the Gordian knot with his sword. When Alexander later captured the Persian king's wives and daughters, he treated the women with respect. His honorable behavior toward the Persian royal women enhanced his claim to be the legitimate king of all Asia.

Building on Near Eastern traditions of siege technology and Philip's innovations, Alexander developed better military technology. When Tyre, a heavily fortified city on an island off the eastern Mediterranean coast, refused to surrender to him in 332 B.C.E., he built a massive stone pier as a platform for artillery towers, armored battering rams, and catapults flinging boulders to breach Tyre's walls. The successful use of this siege technology against Tyre showed that walls alone could no longer protect city-states. The knowledge that Alexander's army could overcome their fortifications made enemies much readier to negotiate a deal.

In his conquest of Egypt and the Persian heartland, Alexander revealed his strategy for ruling a vast empire: keeping an area's traditional administrative system in place while sprinkling cities of Greeks and Macedonians in conquered territory. In Egypt, he established his first new city, naming it Alexandria after himself. In Persia, he proclaimed himself the king of Asia and left the existing governing units intact, retaining selected Persian administrators. For local populations, Alexander's becoming their king changed their lives not a bit. They continued to send the same taxes to a remote master.

To India and Back Alexander led his army past the Persian heartland farther east into territory hardly known to the Greeks (Map 4.2). He aimed to outdo the heroes of legend by marching to the end of the world. Shrinking his army to reduce the need for supplies, he marched northeast into what is today Afghanistan and Uzbekistan. On the Jaxartes River, he founded a city called Alexandria the Furthest to show that he had penetrated deeper into this region than even Cyrus, the founder of the Persian Empire. Unable to subdue the local guerrilla forces, Alexander settled for an alliance sealed by his marriage to the Bactrian princess Roxane.

Alexander then headed east into India. Seventy days of marching through monsoon rains extinguished his soldiers' fire for conquest. In the spring of 326 B.C.E., they mutinied on the banks of the Hyphasis River and forced Alexander to turn back. The return journey through southeastern Iran's deserts cost many casualties from hunger and thirst; the survivors finally reached safety in the Persian heartland in 324 B.C.E. Alexander immediately began planning an invasion of the Arabian peninsula and, after that, of North Africa.

Alexander ruled more harshly after his return and began treating the Greeks as subjects instead of allies. He ordered the city-states to restore citizenship to the many exiles created by war, whose status as stateless persons was causing unrest. Even more striking was Alexander's announcement that he wished to receive the honors due a god. Most Greek city-states obeyed by sending religious delegations to him. A Spartan expressed the only prudent position on Alexander's deification: "If Alexander wishes to be a god, then we'll agree that he be called a god."

Personal motives best explain Alexander's announcement. He had come to believe he was truly the son of Zeus; after all, Greek myths said Zeus had mated with many human females who produced children. Since Alexander's superhuman accomplishments demonstrated that he had achieved godlike power, he must be a god himself. Alexander's divinity was, in ancient terms, a natural consequence of his power.

Alexander's premature death from a fever and heavy drinking in 323 B.C.E. aborted his plan to conquer Arabia and North Africa. His death followed months of depression provoked by the death of his best friend, Hephaistion. Some modern historians conclude that Alexander and Hephaistion were lovers, but no surviving ancient source reports this. Unfortunately for the stability of Alexander's immense conquests, by the time of his death he had not fathered an heir who could take over his rule. Roxane gave birth to their son only after Alexander's death. The story goes that, when at Alexander's deathbed his commanders asked him to whom he left his kingdom, he replied, "To the most powerful."

Alexander the Great
This marble portrait of Alexander (a copy of a bronze original) has him wearing a lion's head as a helmet to recall the hero Herakles (Hercules), whose myth said he killed the fiercest beast in Greece and wore its head as proof. Alexander gazes into the distance; he commanded that his portraits show him with this visionary expression. Why do you think he wanted the world to see him with these attributes? *(The Art Archive/National Archeological Museum, Athens/Dagli Orti Collection.)*

Alexander's Impact Scholars disagree on almost everything about Alexander, from whether his claim to divinity was meant to justify his increasingly authoritarian attitude toward the Greek city-states, to what he meant to achieve through conquest, to the nature of his character. Was he a bloodthirsty monster obsessed with war, or a romantic visionary intent on creating a multiethnic world open to all cultures? The ancient sources suggest that Alexander had interlinked goals reflecting his restless and ruthless nature: both to conquer and administer the known world and to explore and colonize new territory beyond.

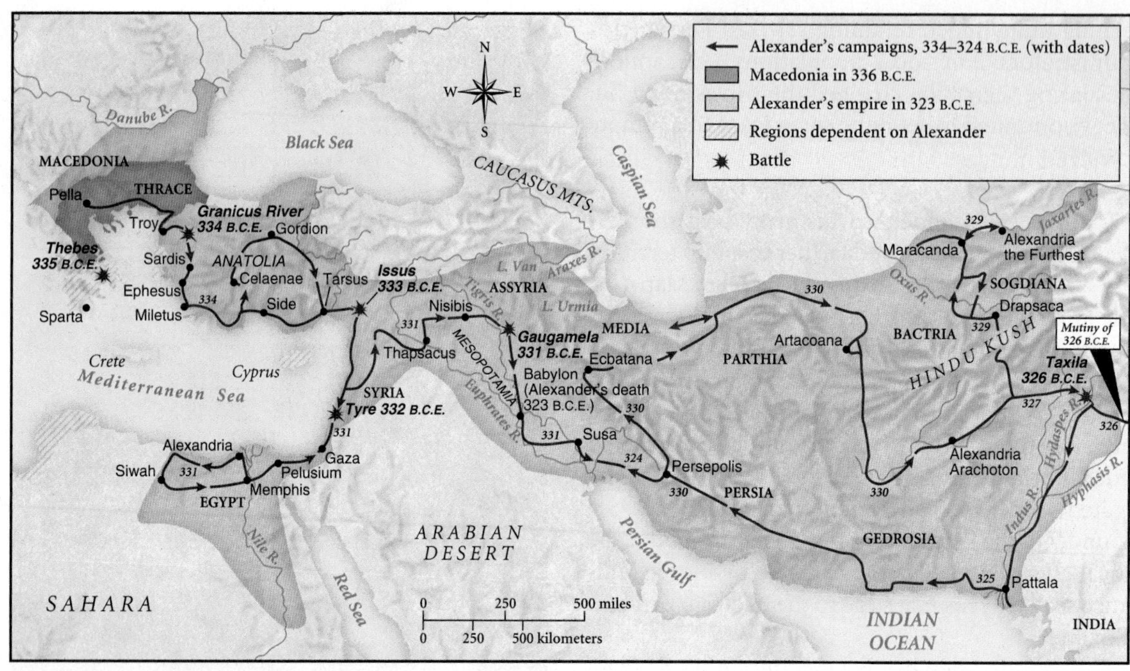

MAP 4.2 Conquests of Alexander the Great, 336–323 B.C.E.
From the time Alexander led his army against Persia in 334 B.C.E. until his death in 323 B.C.E., he was continually fighting military campaigns. His charismatic and fearless generalship, combined with effective intelligence gathering about his targets, generated an unbroken string of victories and made him a legend. His founding of garrison cities and preservation of local governments kept his conquests largely stable during his lifetime.

The ancient world agreed that Alexander was a marvel. An Athenian orator expressed the bewilderment many people felt over the events of Alexander's lifetime: "What strange and unexpected event has not occurred in our time? The life we have lived is no ordinary human one, but we were born to be an object of wonder to posterity." Alexander's fame increased after his death. Stories of reality-defying exploits attributed to him became popular folktales throughout the ancient world, even in distant regions such as southern Africa, where Alexander never set foot.

Alexander's conquests had consequences in many areas. His explorations benefited scientific fields from geography to botany because he took along knowledgeable writers to collect and catalog new knowledge. He had vast quantities of scientific observations dispatched to his old tutor Aristotle. Alexander's new cities promoted trade between Greece and the Near East. Most of all, his career brought these cultures into closer contact than ever before. This contact represented his career's most enduring impact.

REVIEW QUESTION What were the accomplishments of Alexander the Great, and what were their effects both for the ancient world and for later Western civilization?

The Hellenistic Kingdoms, 323–30 B.C.E.

Alexander's empire fragmented after his death, and new kingdoms arose. The period that extends from Alexander's death in 323 B.C.E. to the death of Cleopatra VII, the last Macedonian queen of Egypt, in 30 B.C.E. is known as the Hellenistic Age, a name given it by modern scholars. The word **Hellenistic** ("Greek-like") conveys the most significant characteristic of this period: the emergence in the eastern Mediterranean world of a mixture of Near Eastern and Greek traditions that generated innovations in politics, literature, art, philosophy, and religion. War stirred up this cultural mixing, and tension persisted between conquerors and subjects. The process promoted regional diversity: Greek ideas and practices had their greatest impact on the urban populations of Egypt and southwestern Asia, while the many people who farmed in the countryside had much less contact with Greek ways of life.

Hellenistic: An adjective meaning "Greek-like" that is today used as a chronological term for the period 323–30 B.C.E.

New kingdoms formed the Hellenistic period's dominant political structures. They reintroduced monarchy into Greek culture, there having been no kings in Greece since the fall of Mycenaean civilization nearly a thousand years earlier. Commanders from Alexander's army created the kingdoms after his death by seizing portions of his empire and proclaiming themselves kings in these new states. This process of state formation took more than fifty years of war. The self-proclaimed kings — called Alexander's successors — had to transform their families into dynasties and accumulate enough power to force the Greek city-states to give control of foreign policy to these new overlords. This process of transformation reinforced the hierarchical nature of Hellenistic society. Eventually, wars with the Romans brought all the Hellenistic kingdoms to an end.

Creating New Kingdoms

Alexander's early death left his succession an open question. His only legitimate son was born a few months later. Alexander's mother, Olympias, tried to protect her grandson, but Alexander's former commanders executed Olympias in 316 B.C.E. and later murdered the boy, Alexander IV, and his mother, Roxane. Having wiped out the royal family, the successors divided Alexander's conquests among themselves. Antigonus (c. 382–301 B.C.E.) took over Anatolia, the Near East, Macedonia, and Greece; Seleucus (c. 358–281 B.C.E.) seized Babylonia and the East as far as India; and Ptolemy (c. 367–282 B.C.E.) grabbed Egypt. These successors had to create their own form of monarchy based on military power and personal prestige because they did not inherit their positions legitimately: they were self-proclaimed rulers with no connection to Alexander's royal line. Several years after the elimination of Alexander's line, however, they announced that they were now kings.

In the beginning, the new kings' biggest enemies were one another. They fought constantly in the decades after Alexander's death, trying to annex more territory to their individual kingdoms. By the middle of the third century B.C.E., the three Hellenistic kingdoms had established their home territories (Map 4.3). The Antigonids had been reduced to a kingdom in Macedonia, but they also compelled the mainland Greek city-states to follow royal foreign policy. The Seleucids ruled in Syria and Mesopotamia, but they had to cede their easternmost territory to the Indian king Chandragupta (r. 323–299 B.C.E.). They also lost most of Persia to the Parthians, a northern Iranian people. The Ptolemies ruled the rich land of Egypt.

These territorial arrangements were never completely stable because the Hellenistic monarchs never stopped competing. Conflicts repeatedly arose over border areas. The Ptolemies and the Seleucids, for example, fought to control the eastern Mediterranean coast, just as the Egyptians and Hittites had

Greek-Style Buddha

The style of this statue of the founder of Buddhism, who expounded his doctrines in India, shows the mingling of eastern and western art. The Buddha's appearance, gaze, and posture stem from Indian artistic traditions, while the flowing folds of his garment recall Greek traditions. Compare the garment that Socrates is wearing on page 96. This combination of styles is called Gandhara, after the region in northwestern India where it began. What do you think are the possible motives for combining different artistic traditions? *(Borromeo/Art Resource, NY.)*

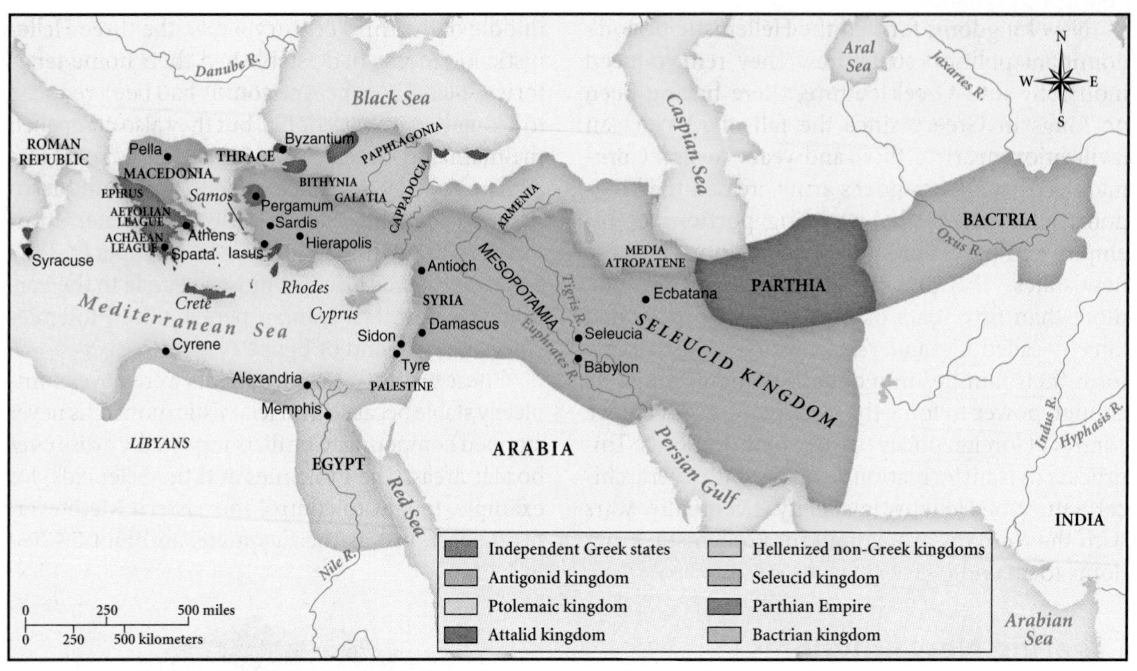

MAP 4.3 Hellenistic Kingdoms, 240 B.C.E.
Monarchy became the dominant political system in the areas of Alexander's conquests. By about eighty years after his death, the three major kingdoms established by his successors had settled their boundaries, after the Seleucids gave up their easternmost territories to an Indian king and the Attalids carved out their kingdom in western Anatolia.

done centuries earlier. The wars between the major kingdoms left openings for smaller, regional kingdoms to establish themselves. The most famous of these was the kingdom of the Attalids in western Anatolia, with the wealthy city of Pergamum as its capital. In Bactria in Central Asia, the Greeks—originally colonists settled by Alexander—broke off from the Seleucid kingdom in the mid-third century B.C.E. to found their own regional kingdom, which flourished for a time from the trade in luxury goods between India and China and the Mediterranean world.

Royal Silver Coin of Bactria
Bactria in central Asia (today part of Afghanistan, Pakistan, and Tajikistan) had been a province of the Persian Empire and then of the empire of Alexander the Great. After the fragmentation of Alexander's empire in the century after his death, Greeks established what scholars call Indo-Greek kingdoms there. This coin of King Demetrius I shows him wearing an elephant headdress, a symbol of his ambitions to conquer India. The other side shows the Greek mythological hero Heracles, who was said to have been the first Greek to visit this part of the world. *(The Granger Collection, New York—All rights reserved.)*

The Structure of Hellenistic Kingdoms

The Hellenistic kingdoms imposed foreign rule by Macedonian kings and queens on indigenous populations. The kings incorporated local traditions into their rule to build legitimacy. The Seleucids combined Macedonian with Near Eastern traditions, while the Ptolemies mixed Macedonian with Egyptian ones. The Ptolemaic royal family, for example, observed the Egyptian royal tradition of brother-sister marriage. Royal power was the ultimate source of control over the kingdoms' subjects, in keeping with the Near Eastern monarchical tradition that Hellenistic kings adopted. This tradition persisted above all in defining justice. Seleucus justified his rule on what he claimed as a universal truth of monarchy: "It is not the customs of the Persians and other people that I impose upon you, but the law which is common to everyone, that what is decreed by the king is always just." Hellenistic kings had to do more to survive than simply assert a right to rule, however. The survival of their dynasties depended on their ability to create strong armies, effective administrations, and close ties to urban elites. A letter from a Greek city summed up the situation while praising the Seleucid king Antiochus I (c. 324–261 B.C.E.): "His rule depends above all on his own excellence [aretê], and on the goodwill of his friends, and on his forces."

Royal Military Forces and Administration

Hellenistic royal armies and navies provided internal and external security. Professional soldiers manned these forces. To develop their military might, the Seleucid and Ptolemaic kings encouraged immigration by Greeks and Macedonians, who received land grants in return for military service. When this source of manpower gave out, the kings had to employ more local men as troops. Military competition put tremendous financial pressure on the kings to pay growing numbers of mercenaries and to purchase expensive new military technology. To compete effectively, a Hellenistic king had to provide giant artillery, such as catapults capable of flinging a 170-pound projectile up to two hundred yards. His navy cost a fortune because warships were now huge, requiring crews of several hundred men. War elephants, whose bellowing charges frightened opposing infantry, became popular after Alexander's encounters with them in India, and they were extremely costly to maintain.

Hellenistic kings needed effective administrations to collect revenues. Initially, they recruited mostly Greek and Macedonian immigrants to fill high-level posts. Following Alexander's example, however, the Seleucids and the Ptolemies also employed non-Greeks for middle- and lower-level positions, where officials had to be able to deal with the subject populations and speak their languages. Local men who wanted a government job bettered their chances if they could read and write Greek in addition to their native language. Bilingualism qualified them to fill positions communicating the orders of the highest-ranking officials, all Greeks and Macedonians, to local farmers, builders, and crafts producers. Non-Greeks who had successful government careers were rarely admitted to royal society because Greeks and Macedonians saw themselves as too superior to mix with locals. Greeks and non-Greeks therefore tended to live in separate communities.

Hellenistic royal administrations resembled those of the earlier Assyrian, Babylonian, and Persian Empires. Administrators' principal responsibilities were to maintain order and to direct the kingdoms' tax systems. Officials mediated disputes whenever possible, but they could call on soldiers to serve as police. The Ptolemaic administration used methods of central planning and control inherited from earlier Egyptian history. Its officials continued to administer royal monopolies, such as that on vegetable oil, to maximize the king's revenue. They decided how much land farmers could sow in oil-bearing plants, supervised production and distribution of the oil, and set prices for every stage of the oil business. The king, through his officials, also often entered into partnerships with private investors to produce more revenue.

Cities and Urban Elites

Cities were the Hellenistic kingdoms' economic and social hubs. Many Greeks and Macedonians lived in new cities founded by Alexander and the Hellenistic kings in Egypt and the Near East, and they also immigrated to existing cities there. Hellenistic kings promoted this urban immigration by adorning their new cities with the features of classical Greek city-states, such as gymnasia and theaters. Although these cities often retained the city-state's political institutions, such as councils and assemblies for citizen men, the need to follow royal policy limited their freedom; they made no independent decisions on foreign policy. In addition, the cities taxed their populations to send money demanded by the king.

Monarchy's reemergence in the Greek world also created a new relationship between rulers and the social elites, because the crucial element in the Hellenistic kingdom's political and social structure was the system of mutual rewards by which the kings and their leading urban subjects became partners in government and public finance. Wealthy people in the cities had the crucial responsibility of collecting taxes from the surrounding countryside as well as from their city and sending the money on to the royal treasury; the royal military and the administration were too small to perform these duties themselves. The kings honored and flattered the cities' Greek and Macedonian social elites because they needed their cooperation to ensure a steady flow of tax revenues. When writing to a city's council, the king would express himself in the form of polite requests, but the recipients knew he was giving commands.

This system thus continued the Greek tradition of requiring the wealthy elite to contribute to the common good. Cooperative cities received gifts from the king to pay for expensive public works like theaters and temples or for reconstruction after natural disasters such as earthquakes. Wealthy men and women in turn helped keep the general population peaceful by subsidizing teachers and doctors, financing public works, and providing donations and loans to ensure a reliable supply of grain to feed the city's residents.

The system of mutual rewards also required the kings to establish relationships with well-to-do non-Greeks living in the old cities of Anatolia and the Near East to keep their vast kingdoms peaceful and profitable. In addition, non-Greeks and non-Macedonians from eastern regions began moving westward to the new Hellenistic Greek cities in increasing numbers. Jews in particular moved from their ancestral homeland to Anatolia, Greece, and Egypt. The Jewish community eventually became an influential minority in Egyptian Alexandria, the most important Hellenistic city. In Egypt, as the Rosetta stone shows, the king also had to build good relationships with the priests who controlled the temples of the traditional Egyptian gods because the temples owned large tracts of rich land worked by tenant farmers.

The Layers of Hellenistic Society

Hellenistic monarchy reinforced social hierarchy. At the top were the royal family and the king's friends. The Greek and Macedonian elites of the major cities ranked next. Then came indigenous urban elites, leaders of large minority urban populations, and local lords in rural regions. Merchants, artisans, and laborers made up the free population's bottom layer. Slaves remained where they had always been, without any social status.

Emotion in Hellenistic Sculpture
Hellenistic sculptors introduced a new style into Greek art by depicting people's emotions. This statue of an elderly woman, for example, shows an expression of pain, disheveled clothing, and a body stooped from age and from carrying a basket of chickens and vegetables. The statue probably portrays a poor woman trying to survive by hawking food in the street. It is probably a later copy of a Hellenistic original. What sort of emotional response do you think this new style was meant to produce in the audience for such art? *(Statue of an old woman. Roman. Early Imperial, Julio-Claudian, 14–68 C.E. Marble, Pentelic, h. 49⅝ in. [125.98 cm.], Rogers Fund, 1909 [09.39]. The Metropolitan Museum of Art, New York, NY, U.S.A. Image copyright © The Metropolitan Museum of Art/Art Resource, NY.)*

The kingdoms' growth increased the demand for slave labor throughout the eastern Mediterranean; the island of Delos established a market where up to ten thousand slaves a day were bought and sold. The fortunate ones were purchased as servants for the royal court or elite households and lived physically comfortable lives, so long as they pleased their owners. The luckless ones labored, and often died, in the mines. Enslaved children could be taken far from home to work. For example, a sales contract from 259 B.C.E. records that Zeno, to whom the camel trader wrote, bought a girl about seven years old named Gemstone to work in an Egyptian textile factory. Originally from an eastern Mediterranean town, she had previously labored as the slave of a Greek mercenary soldier employed by a Jewish cavalry commander in the Transjordan region.

The Poor Like slaves, poor people—who made up the majority of the population—lived their lives as workers, most of them as laborers in agriculture, the foundation of the Hellenistic kingdoms' economies. There were some large cities, above all Alexandria in Egypt, but the majority of the population had their homes in country villages. Many of the poor were employed on the royal family's huge estates, but free peasants still worked their own small fields in addition to laboring for wealthy landowners. Rural people rose with the sun and began working before the heat became unbearable, raising the same kinds of crops and animals as their ancestors had, using the same simple hand tools. Perhaps as many as 80 percent of all adult men and women had to work the land to produce enough food to sustain the population. Poverty often meant hunger, even in fertile lands such as Egypt. In cities, poor women and men could work as small merchants, peddlers, and artisans, producing and selling goods such as tools, pottery, clothing, and furniture. Men could sign on as deckhands on the merchant ships that sailed the Mediterranean Sea and Indian Ocean.

Many country people in the Seleucid and Ptolemaic kingdoms existed in a state of dependency between free and slave. The peoples, as they were called, were tenants who farmed the estates belonging to the king. Although they could not be sold like slaves, they were not allowed to move away or abandon their tenancies. They owed a large quota of produce to the king, and this compulsory rent gave these tenant farmers little chance to escape poverty.

Women's Lives Hellenistic women's social and political status depended on their rank in the kingdom's hierarchy. Hellenistic queens commanded enormous riches and honors. The kingdoms based their legitimacy on the female as well as the male side. Hellenistic queens exercised power as the representatives of distinguished families; the mothers of a line of royal descendants; and patrons of artists, thinkers, and even cities. Later Ptolemaic queens essentially co-ruled with their husbands. Queens ruled on their own when no male heir existed. For example, Arsinoe II (c. 316–270 B.C.E.), the daughter of Ptolemy I, first married the Macedonian successor Lysimachus, who gave her four towns as her personal domain. After his death she married her brother Ptolemy II of Egypt and exerted at least as much influence on policy as he did. The excellences publicly praised in a queen reflected traditional Greek values for women. A city decree from about 165 B.C.E. honored Queen Apollonis of Pergamum by praising her piety toward the gods, reverence toward her parents, distinguished conduct toward her husband, and harmonious relations with her "beautiful children born in wedlock."

Some queens paid special attention to the condition of women. About 195 B.C.E., for example, the Seleucid queen Laodice gave a ten-year endowment to a city to provide dowries for needy girls. That Laodice funded dowries shows that she recognized the importance to women of controlling property, the surest guarantee of respect in their households.

Most women remained under the control of men. "Who can judge better than a father what is to his daughter's interest?" remained the dominant belief of fathers. Once a woman married, the words *husband* and *wife* replaced *father* and *daughter*. Most of the time, elite women continued to be separated from men outside their families, while poor women still worked in public. Greeks continued to abandon infants they did not want to raise—girls more often than boys—but other populations, such as the Egyptians and the Jews, did not practice infant exposure. Exposure differed from infanticide in that the parents expected someone to find the child and rear it, usually as a slave. A third-century B.C.E. comic poet overstated the case by saying, "A son, one always raises even if one is poor; a daughter, one exposes, even if one is rich." Daughters of wealthy parents were not usually abandoned, but scholars have estimated that up to 10 percent of other infant girls were.

Depending on their social class, women could sometimes achieve greater control over their lives in the Hellenistic period than before. A woman of exceptional wealth could enter public life by making donations or loans to her city and in return be rewarded with an official post in local government. In Egypt, women of all classes acquired greater say in married life as the marriage contract (see Chapter 3, "Contrasting Views," page 88) evolved from an agreement between the bride's parents and the groom to one in which the bride made her own arrangements with the groom.

The Wealthy Rich people showed increasing concern for the welfare of the less fortunate during the Hellenistic period. They were following the lead of the royal families, who emphasized philanthropy to build a reputation for generosity that would support their legitimacy in ruling. Sometimes wealthy citizens funded a foundation to distribute free grain to eliminate food shortages, and they also funded schools for children in various Hellenistic cities, the first public schools in the Greek world. In some places, girls as well as boys could attend school. Many cities also began sponsoring doctors to improve medical care: patients still had to pay, but at least they could count on finding a doctor.

The donors funding these services were repaid by the respect and honor they earned from their fellow citizens. Philanthropy even touched international relations. When an earthquake devastated Rhodes, many cities joined kings and queens in sending donations to help the residents recover. In return, they showered honors on their benefactors by appointing them to prestigious municipal offices and erecting inscriptions expressing the city's gratitude. In this system, the masses' welfare depended more and more on the generosity of the rich. Lacking democracy, the poor had no political power to demand support.

The End of the Hellenistic Kingdoms

All the Hellenistic kingdoms eventually lost their great riches and power, mostly through internal disunity in their ruling families. In their weakened condition, Hellenistic states could not prevent takeovers by the Romans, who over time intervened more and more forcefully in conflicts among kingdoms and Greek city-states in the eastern Mediterranean. Roman foreign policy was meant to protect their growing interests in this part of the world and ward off any danger to their own territory.

These interventions caused wars. Rome first established dominance over the Antigonid kingdom by the middle of the second century B.C.E. Next, the Seleucid kingdom fell to the Romans in 64 B.C.E. The Ptolemaic kingdom in Egypt survived a bit longer; by the 50s B.C.E., its royal family had split into warring factions, and the resulting weakness forced the rivals for the throne to seek Roman support. The end came when the famous queen Cleopatra, the last Macedonian to rule Egypt, chose the losing side in the civil war between Mark Antony and the future emperor Augustus in the late first century B.C.E. An invading Roman army ended Ptolemaic rule in 30 B.C.E. Rome thus became the heir to all the Hellenistic kingdoms (see Mapping the West, page 135).

REVIEW QUESTION How did the political and social organization of the new Hellenistic kingdoms compare with that of the earlier Greek city-states?

Seated Boxer
This Hellenistic-era sculpture in bronze shows an obviously tired boxer after a bout. He is still wearing the hard-edged leather gloves that made Greek and Roman boxing so brutal and dangerous. His pose, showing him looking up at the sky in weariness, or perhaps listening to his trainer or a fan, is characteristic of the tendency of Hellenistic artists to portray people in realistic rather than idealized ways. *(Museo Nazionale Romano delle Terme/akg-images/Jürgen Raible.)*

Hellenistic Culture

Hellenistic culture reflected three principal influences: the overwhelming impact of royal wealth, increased emphasis on private life and emotion, and greater interaction of diverse peoples. The kings drove developments in literature, art, science, and philosophy by deciding which scholars and artists to put on the royal payroll. The obligation of authors and artists to the kings meant that they could not criticize public policy; their works therefore concentrated on everyday life and individual emotion.

Cultural interaction between Near Eastern and Greek traditions occurred most prominently in language and religion. These developments deeply influenced the Romans as they took over the Hellenistic world. The Roman poet Horace (65–8 B.C.E.) described the effect of Hellenistic culture on his own by saying that "captive Greece captured its fierce victor."

The Arts under Royal Support

Hellenistic kings became the supporters of scholarship and the arts on a vast scale, competing with one another to lure the best scholars and artists to their capitals with lavish salaries. They funded intellectuals and artists because they wanted to boost their reputations by having these famous people produce books, poems, sculptures, and other prestigious creations at their courts.

The Ptolemies turned Alexandria into the Mediterranean's leading arts and sciences center, establishing the world's first scholarly research institute and a massive library. The librarians were instructed to collect all the books in the world. The library grew to hold half a million scrolls, an enormous number for the time. Linked to it was the building in which the hired research scholars dined together and produced encyclopedias of knowledge such as *The Wonders of the World* and *On the Rivers of Europe*. We still use the name of the research institute's building, the Museum ("place of the Muses," the Greek goddesses of learning and the arts), to designate institutions preserving knowledge. The Alexandrian scholars produced prodigiously. Their champion was the scholar Didymus (c. 80–10 B.C.E.), nicknamed "Brass Bowels" for writing nearly four thousand books commenting on literature. Sadly, not a single one has survived; the library was later destroyed by fire in wartime.

Literature at Court The writers and artists paid by Hellenistic kings had to please their paymasters with their works. The poet Theocritus (c. 300–260 B.C.E.) spelled out the deal

DOCUMENT

Epigrams by Women Poets

Anyte, Nossis, and Erinna were three of the most famous women poets of the Hellenistic period. They composed short poems about death, love, and sex, often centered on women. They also invented the tradition of writing poems about speaking animals. None of them was hired by a Hellenistic king to be a resident poet at court, so they had to create their poetic masterpieces on their own. We lack documentary evidence to tell us why women authors worked in this genre of creative literature, as opposed to writing longer works of epic or history; they may have preferred shorter poems for aesthetic and literary reasons, but it may also be because they lacked the financial backing to complete bigger projects.

Anyte on Mourning a Young Woman

The virgin Antibia I mourn for; many
young men came to her father's house
seeking to marry her,
drawn by the fame of her beauty and
wisdom. But everyone's
hopes deadly Fate tossed away.

Anyte on a Dolphin Speaking after Death

No longer taking joy in surging seas
will I stretch out my neck as I leap from
the depths,
no longer around the lovely bows of the
ship
will I jump, delighting in the figurehead,
my likeness.
No, the purple surge of the sea cast me
onto the land;
here I lie on this narrow strip of beach.

Nossis on the Joy of Sex

Nothing is sweeter than sexual passion;
every other blessing is second;
I spit out from my mouth even honey.
This is what Nossis says: anyone that
Aphrodite has not kissed
doesn't know what kind of flowers her
roses are.

Nossis on a Woman's Present to Aphrodite

The picture of herself Callo dedicated in
the temple of blond Aphrodite,
having her portrait made to look exactly
like herself.
How gracefully it stands; see how great
is the grace that blooms on it.
Best wishes to her! For she has no
blame in her life.

Erinna on the Death of the Bride Baukis

I am the grave marker of the bride
Baukis. As you pass by
this most wept-for pillar, say this to
Hades in the underworld:
"You are jealous of Baukis, Hades!" The
lovely letters that you see
announce the brutal fate Chance
brought to Baukis,
how with the pine-torches from the
wedding that they were using to
worship Hymenaeus [the god of
marriage]
the groom's father set afire her funeral
pyre.
And you, Hymenaeus, the tuneful song
of the wedding
converted to the sad cries of lamentation.

Source: *Palatine Anthology*, 7.490, 7.215, 5.170, 9.605, 7.712. Translations by Thomas R. Martin.

Question to Consider

- **What do these women's poems reveal about women's lives and concerns in the Hellenistic age?**

underlying royal support in a poem flattering King Ptolemy II: "The spokesmen of the Muses [that is, poets] celebrate Ptolemy in return for his benefactions." Poets such as Theocritus avoided political topics and stressed the social gap between the intellectual elite—to which the kings belonged—and the uneducated masses. They filled their new poetry with erudite references to make it difficult to understand and therefore exclusive. Only people with a deep literary education could appreciate the mythological allusions that studded these authors' elaborate poems.

Theocritus was the first Greek poet to express the divide between town and countryside, a poetic stance corresponding to a growing Hellenistic reality. His *Idylls* emphasized the discontinuity between urban life and the country bumpkins' bucolic existence, reflecting the Ptolemaic social division between the food consumers in the town and the food producers in the countryside. Theocritus presented a city dweller's idealized dream that country life was peaceful and stress-free, a fiction that deeply influenced later literature.

No Hellenistic women poets seem to have enjoyed royal financial support; rather, they created their art independently. They excelled in writing **epigrams**, a style of short poem originally used on tombstones to remember the dead. Highly literary poems by women from diverse regions of the Hellenistic world still survive (see Document, "Epigrams by Women Poets," above). Many epigrams were about women, from courtesans to respectable matrons, and the writer's personal feelings. No other

epigrams: Short poems written by women in the Hellenistic Age; many were about other women and the writer's personal feelings.

Hellenistic literature better conveys the depth of human emotion than the epigrams of women poets.

Hellenistic comedies also emphasized stories about emotions and stayed away from politics. Comic playwrights presented plays concerning the troubles of fictional lovers. These comedies of manners, as they are called, became enormously popular because, like modern situation comedies, they offered humorous views of daily life. Papyrus discoveries have restored comedies of Menander (c. 342–289 B.C.E.), the most famous Hellenistic comic poet, noted for his skill in depicting human personality (see "New Sources, New Perspectives," page 129). Hellenistic tragedy could take a multicultural approach: Ezechiel, a Jew living in Alexandria, wrote *Exodus*, a tragedy in Greek about Moses leading the Hebrews out of captivity in Egypt.

Emotion in Sculpture Hellenistic sculptors and painters also featured emotions in their works. Classical artists had given their subjects' faces an idealized serenity, but now sculptures depicted personal feelings. A sculpture from Pergamum, for example, commemorating the Attalid victory over invading Gauls (one of the Celtic peoples from what is now France), showed a defeated Celtic warrior stabbing himself after having killed his wife to prevent her enslavement by the victors.

The artists created their works mainly on order from royalty, and from the urban elites who wanted to show they had the same artistic taste as their royal superiors. The increasing diversity of subjects that emerged in Hellenistic art presumably represented a trend approved by kings, queens, and the elites. Sculpture best reveals this new preference for depicting people never before appearing in art: heartbreaking victims of war, drunkards, battered athletes, wrinkled old people. The female nude became common. A statue of Aphrodite by Praxiteles, which portrayed the goddess completely nude for the first time, became renowned as a religious object and tourist attraction in the city of Cnidos, which had commissioned it. The king of Bithynia offered to pay off the citizens' entire public debt if he could have the work of art. They refused.

Philosophy for a New Age

New philosophies arose in the Hellenistic period, all asking the same question: What is the best way to live? They recommended different paths to the same answer: individuals must achieve inner personal tranquillity to achieve freedom from the blows of outside forces, especially chance. It is easy to see why these philosophies had appeal: outside forces—the Hellenistic kings—had robbed the Greek city-states of their independence in foreign policy, and their citizens' fates ultimately rested in the hands of unpredictable monarchs. More than ever, human life seemed out of individuals' control. It therefore was appealing to look to philosophy for personal, private solutions to the unsettling new conditions of Hellenistic life.

Hellenistic philosophers concentrated on **materialism**, the doctrine that only things made of matter truly exist. Materialism denied Plato's metaphysical concept of the soul and indeed of all nonmaterial phenomena, following up Aristotle's doctrine that only things identified through logic or observation exist. Hellenistic philosophy was divided into three areas: (1) logic, the process for discovering truth; (2) physics, the fundamental truth about the nature of existence; and (3) ethics, how humans should achieve happiness and well-being through logic and physics. Materialism greatly influenced Roman thinkers and the many important Western philosophers who later read those thinkers' works.

---

materialism: A philosophical doctrine of the Hellenistic Age that denied metaphysics and claimed instead that only things consisting of matter truly exist.

Dying Barbarians

Hellenistic artists excelled in portraying emotional scenes, such as this murder-suicide of a Celtic warrior who is slaying himself after killing his wife, to prevent their capture by the enemy. (Celtic women followed their men to the battlefield.) The original was in bronze, forming part of a large sculptural group that Attalus I (r. 241–197 B.C.E.) erected at Pergamum to commemorate his victory over these barbarian raiders. Why did Attalus celebrate his victory by erecting a monument portraying the defeated enemy as brave, noble, and sympathetic? *(Erich Lessing/Art Resource, NY.)*

NEW SOURCES, NEW PERSPECTIVES

Papyrus Discoveries and Menander's Comedies

Fourth-century B.C.E. Greek playwrights invented a kind of comedy, called New Comedy, that is today's most popular entertainment—the situation comedy (sitcom). They wrote comedies that concentrated on the conflicts between personality types in everyday situations. The rocky course of love and marriage drove most plots. Avoiding political satire, comedians created type characters such as bubble-headed lovers, cranky fathers, rascally servants, and boastful soldiers, as revealed by their titles: *The Country Boob*, *Pot-Belly*, *The Stolen Girl*, *The Bad-Tempered Man*, and so on. Confusions of identity leading to hilarious misunderstandings were frequent, as were jokes about marriage, such as this one:

First Man: "He's married, you know."

Second Man: "What's that you say? Actually married? How can that be? I just left him alive and walking around!"

These comic plays inspired many imitations, especially Roman comedies, which inspired William Shakespeare (1564–1616) in England and Molière (1622–1673) in France. Their comedies, in turn, led to today's sitcoms.

The most famous author of this kind of comedy was Menander (343–291 B.C.E.) of Athens. Despite antiquity's "two thumbs up," none of Menander's comedies survived into modern times. Works of Greek and Roman literature had to be copied over and over by hand for centuries if they were to survive. For unknown reasons, people at some point stopped recopying New Comedy. So scholars knew Menander had been a star, but they had never read any of his plays—until archaeologists began finding ancient paper in Egypt.

The Egyptians made paper from the papyrus plant, and their super-dry climate preserved the paper that people used to wrap mummies or simply threw away after writing on it. The French emperor Napoleon's conquest of Egypt in 1798–1801 inspired a European craze for collecting papyrus. By unwrapping mummies and excavating ancient trash dumps, scholars have discovered thousands of texts of all kinds.

Incredibly, some of Menander's comedies turned up in these discoveries, beginning with *The Bad-Tempered Man*. Further detective work has yielded more, and today we can read most of *The Girl from Samos* and parts of other plays. In this way, Menander's characters, stories, and jokes have come back from the dead.

Recovering plays from papyrus is difficult. The handwriting is often difficult to make out, there are no gaps between words, punctuation is minimal, changes in speakers are indicated by colons or dashes rather than by names, and there are no stage directions. Sometimes the papyrus has been chewed by mice and insects, burned, or torn. One part of a play can turn up in the wrapping of one mummy and another part in a different one. However, the collaboration of archaeologists, historians, and literary scholars has brought back to life the ancestors of what remains our most crowd-pleasing form of comedy.

Questions to Consider

1. **What makes situation comedy so appealing?**
2. **Why would Greeks living in the fourth century B.C.E. prefer situation comedy to political satire or darker forms of humor?**

Further Reading

Bagnall, Roger. *Reading Papyri, Writing Ancient History*. 1995.

Menander: Plays and Fragments. Translated with an introduction by Norma Miller. 1987.

Parkinson, Richard, and Stephen Quirke. *Papyrus*. 1995.

Pompeian Wall Painting of Menander

A wealthy Roman had this painting of Menander put on a wall in his house at Pompeii. The owner appears to have loved Greek plays—he had the room's other walls decorated with images of the tragedian Euripides and possibly the Muses of Tragedy and Comedy. The faded lettering on the scroll identified the playwright: "Menander: he was the first to write New Comedy." The ivy wreath on his head symbolizes the poet's victory in the contests of comedies presented at the festivals of the god Dionysus, the patron of drama. *(Scala/Art Resource, NY.)*

Epicureanism One of the two most significant new Hellenistic philosophies was **Epicureanism**, named for its founder, Epicurus (341–271 B.C.E.), who settled his followers around 307 B.C.E. in an Athenian house surrounded by greenery—hence, his school came to be known as the Garden. Epicurus broke tradition by admitting both women and slaves to study philosophy in his group.

Epicureanism (eh puh KYUR ee uh nizm): The philosophy founded by Epicurus of Athens to help people achieve a life of true pleasure, by which he meant "absence of disturbance."

Praxiteles' Statue of Aphrodite

The fourth-century B.C.E. Athenian sculptor Praxiteles excelled at carving stone to resemble flesh and producing perfect surfaces, which he had a painter make lively with color. His masterpiece was the Aphrodite made for the city-state of Cnidos in southwestern Anatolia; the original is lost, but many Hellenistic-era copies like this one were made. Praxiteles was the first to show the goddess of love nude, and rumor said his lover was the model. Given that there was a long tradition of nude male statues, why do you think it took until the Hellenistic period for Greek sculptors to produce female nudes? *(Nimatallah/Art Resource, NY.)*

Epicurus's key idea was that people should be free of worry about death. Because all matter consists of tiny, invisible, irreducible pieces called atoms ("indivisible things") in random movement, he said, death is nothing more than the painless separating of the body's atoms. Moreover, all human knowledge must be empirical, that is, derived from experience and perception. Phenomena that most people perceive as the work of the gods, such as thunder, do not result from divine intervention in the world. The gods live far away in perfect tranquillity, ignoring human affairs. People therefore have nothing to fear from the gods, in life or in death.

Epicurus believed people should pursue pleasure, but by true pleasure he meant an "absence of disturbance." Thus, people should live free from the turmoil, passions, and desires of ordinary existence. A sober life spent with friends and separated from the cares of the common world provided Epicurean pleasure. Epicureanism therefore represented a serious challenge to the Greek tradition of political participation by citizens.

Stoicism The other important new Hellenistic philosophy, **Stoicism**, prohibited an isolationist life. Its name derives from the Painted Stoa in Athens, where Stoic philosophers discussed their doctrines. Stoics believed that fate controls people's lives but that individuals should still make the pursuit of excellence (that is, virtue) their goal. Stoic excellence meant putting oneself in harmony with the divine, rational force of universal nature by cultivating good sense, justice, courage, and temperance. These doctrines applied to women as well as men. In fact, some Stoics advocated equal citizenship for women, unisex clothing, and abolition of marriage and families.

The Stoic belief in fate raised the question of whether humans have free will. Stoic philosophers concluded that purposeful human actions do have significance even if fate rules. Nature, itself good, does not prevent evil from occurring, because excellence would otherwise have no meaning. What matters in life is striving for good. A person should therefore take action against evil by, for example, participating in politics. To be a Stoic also meant to shun desire and anger while calmly enduring pain and sorrow, an attitude that yields the modern meaning of the word *stoic*. Through endurance and self-control, adherents of Stoic philosophy gained inner tranquillity. They did not fear death because they believed that people live the same life over and over again. This repetition occurred because the world is periodically destroyed by fire and then re-formed.

Competing Philosophies Several other Hellenistic philosophies competed with Epicureanism and Stoicism. Some of these philosophies built on the work of earlier giants such as Pythagoras and Plato. Others struck out in new directions. Skeptics, for example, aimed at the same state of personal calm as did Epicureans, but from a completely different basis. They believed that secure knowledge about anything was impossible because the human senses perceive contradictory information about the world. All people can do, they insisted, is depend on perceptions and appearances while suspending judgment about their ultimate reality. These ideas had been influenced by the Indian ascetics (who practiced self-denial as part of their spiritual discipline) encountered on Alexander the Great's expedition.

For their part, Cynics rejected every convention of ordinary life, especially wealth and material comfort. The name *Cynic*, which means "like a dog,"

Stoicism: The Hellenistic philosophy whose followers believed in fate but also in pursuing excellence (virtue) by cultivating good sense, justice, courage, and temperance.

came from the notion that dogs had no shame. Cynics believed that humans should aim for complete self-sufficiency and that whatever was natural was good and could be done without shame before anyone. Therefore, public bowel movements and sexual intercourse were fine. Women and men alike should be free to follow their sexual inclinations. Above all, Cynics rejected life's comforts. The most famous early Cynic, Diogenes (d. 323 B.C.E.), wore borrowed clothing and slept in a storage jar. Also notorious was Hipparchia, a female Cynic of the late fourth century B.C.E. who once defeated a philosophical opponent named Theodorus the Atheist with the following remarks: "That which would not be considered wrong if done by Theodorus would also not be considered wrong if done by Hipparchia. Now if Theodorus punches himself, he does no wrong. Therefore, if Hipparchia punches Theodorus, she does no wrong."

Gemstone Showing Diogenes in His Jar
This engraved gem from the Roman period shows the famous philosopher Diogenes (c. 412–c. 324 B.C.E.) living in a storage jar and talking with a man holding a scroll. Diogenes was born at Sinope on the Black Sea but was exiled in a dispute over monetary fraud. He then lived at Athens and Corinth, becoming infamous as the founder of Cynic ("doglike") philosophy. To defy social convention, he lived as shamelessly as a dog, hence the name given to his philosophical views and the dog usually shown beside him in art. What kind of person do you think would have wanted this gemstone as a piece of jewelry? *(Inv. No. I 977, Diogenes in his pithos, in dispute with a seated man. Roman Republican ringstone, 100 B.C.E.–30 B.C.E. Thorvaldsens Museum.)*

Philosophy in the Hellenistic Age reached a wider audience than ever before. Although the working poor were too busy to attend philosophers' lectures, well-off members of society studied philosophy in growing numbers. Kings competed to attract famous philosophers to their courts, and Greek settlers took their interest in philosophy with them to even the most remote Hellenistic cities. Archaeologists excavating a city in Afghanistan—thousands of miles from Greece—uncovered a Greek philosophical text and inscriptions of moral advice recording Apollo's oracle at Delphi as their source. Sadly, this site, called Ai-Khanoum, was devastated in the twentieth century during the Soviet war in Afghanistan.

Scientific Innovation

Scientific investigation was separated from philosophy in the Hellenistic period. Science so benefited from this divorce that historians have called this era ancient science's golden age. Scientific innovation flourished because Alexander's expedition had encouraged curiosity and increased knowledge about the world's extent and diversity, royal families supported scientists financially, and the concentration of scientists in Alexandria promoted the exchange of ideas.

Advances in Geometry and Mathematics

The greatest advances in scientific knowledge came in geometry and mathematics. Euclid, who taught at Alexandria around 300 B.C.E., made revolutionary discoveries in analyzing two- and three-dimensional space. The utility of Euclidean geometry still endures. Archimedes of Syracuse (287–212 B.C.E.) calculated the approximate value of pi and invented a way to manipulate very large numbers. He also invented hydrostatics (the science of the equilibrium of fluid systems) and mechanical devices, such as a screw for lifting water to a higher elevation and cranes to disable enemy warships. Archimedes' shout of delight when he solved a problem while soaking in his bathtub has been immortalized in the modern expression "Eureka!" meaning "I have found it!"

Advances in Hellenistic mathematics energized other fields that required complex computation. Early in the third century B.C.E. Aristarchus was the first to propose the correct model of the solar system: the earth revolving around the sun. Later astronomers rejected Aristarchus's heliocentric model in favor of the traditional geocentric one (with the earth at the center) because conclusions drawn from his calculations of the earth's orbit failed to correspond to the observed positions of celestial objects. Aristarchus had assumed a circular orbit instead of an elliptical one, an assumption not corrected until much later. Eratosthenes (c. 275–194 B.C.E.) pioneered mathematical geography. He calculated the circumference of the earth with astonishing accuracy by simultaneously measuring the length of the shadows of widely separated but identically tall structures. Together, these researchers gave Western scientific

Tower of the Winds
This forty-foot octagonal tower, built in Athens about 150 B.C.E., used scientific knowledge developed in Hellenistic Alexandria to tell time and predict the weather. Eight sundials (now missing) carved on the walls displayed the time of day all year; a huge interior water clock showed hours, days, and phases of the moon. A vane on top showed wind direction. The carved figures represented the winds, which the Greeks saw as gods. Each figure's clothing predicted the typical weather from that direction, with the cold northern winds wearing boots and heavy cloaks, while the southern ones have bare feet and gauzy clothes. What were the goals, do you imagine, in erecting such a large clock in a public place? *(The Art Archive/Gianni Dagli Orti.)*

thought an important start toward its fundamental procedure of reconciling theory with observed data through measurement and experimentation.

Discoveries in Science and Medicine Hellenistic science and medicine made gains through royal support, especially in Alexandria, although rigorous experimentation was impossible because no technology existed to measure very small amounts of time or matter. The science of the age was as quantitative as it could be given these limitations. Ctesibius invented pneumatics by creating machines operated by air pressure. He also built a working water pump, an organ powered by water, and the first accurate water clock. Hero continued this development of mechanical ingenuity by building a rotating sphere powered by steam. As in most of Hellenistic science, these inventions did not lead to usable applications in daily life. The scientists and their royal patrons were more interested in new theoretical discoveries than in practical results, and the technology did not exist to produce the pipes, fittings, and screws needed to build metal machines.

Hellenistic science produced impressive military technology, such as more powerful catapults and huge siege towers on wheels. The most famous large-scale application of technology for nonmilitary purposes was the construction of the Pharos, a lighthouse three hundred feet tall, for the harbor at Alexandria. Using polished metal mirrors to reflect the light from a large bonfire, the Pharos shone many miles out over the sea. Awestruck sailors called it one of the wonders of the world.

Medicine also benefited from the Hellenistic quest for new knowledge as medical researchers worked on understanding human health. Increased contact between Greeks and people of the Near East made Mesopotamian and Egyptian medical knowledge better known in the West and promoted research on what made people ill. Hellenistic medical researchers discovered the value of measuring the pulse in diagnosing illness and studied anatomy by dissecting human corpses. It was rumored that they also dissected condemned criminals still alive; they had access to these subjects because the king authorized the research. Some of the terms then invented are still used, such as *diastolic* and *systolic* for blood pressure. Other Hellenistic advances in anatomy included the discovery of the nerves and nervous system.

Cultural and Religious Transformations

Along with scientific innovations, cultural transformations also shaped Hellenistic society. Wealthy non-Greeks increasingly adopted a Greek lifestyle to conform to the Hellenistic world's social hierarchy. Greek became the common language for international commerce and cultural exchange. The widespread use of the simplified form of the Greek language called **Koine** ("shared" or "common") reflected the emergence of an international culture based on Greek models; this was the reason the Egyptian camel trader stranded in Syria (recall the

---

Koine (koy NAY): The "common" or "shared" form of the Greek language that became the international language in the Hellenistic period.

story at the beginning of this chapter) had to communicate in Greek with a high-level official in Egypt. The most striking evidence of this cultural development comes from Afghanistan. There, King Ashoka (r. c. 268–232 B.C.E.), who ruled most of the Indian subcontinent, used Greek as one of the languages in his public inscriptions. These texts announced his plan to teach his subjects Buddhist self-control, such as abstinence from eating meat. Local languages did not disappear in the Hellenistic kingdoms, however. In one region of Anatolia, for example, people spoke twenty-two different languages. This sort of diversity was common in the Hellenistic world.

Changes in Greek and Egyptian Religion

Diversity and interaction in religion also grew. Traditional Greek cults remained popular, but new cults, especially those deifying kings, reflected changing political and social conditions. Preexisting cults that previously had only local significance gained adherents all over the Hellenistic world. In many cases, Greek cults and local cults from the eastern Mediterranean influenced each other. Their beliefs meshed well because these cults shared many assumptions about how to remedy the troubles of human life. In other instances, local cults and Greek cults existed side by side and even overlapped. Some Egyptian villagers, for example, continued worshipping their traditional crocodile god and mummifying their dead according to the old ways but also paid honor to Greek deities. Since they were polytheists (believers in multiple gods), people could worship in both old and new cults.

New cults incorporated a prominent theme of Hellenistic thought: concern for the relationship between the individual and what seemed the arbitrary power of divinities such as Tychê ("chance" or "luck"). Since advances in astronomy had furthered earlier Mesopotamian science on the mathematical precision of the movement of the universe's celestial bodies, religion now had to address the disconnect between heavenly uniformity and the shapeless chaos of earthly life. One increasingly popular approach to bridging that gap was to rely on astrology for advice based on the movement of the stars and planets, thought of as divinities. Another very common choice was to worship Tychê in the hope of securing good luck in life.

The most revolutionary approach in seeking protection from Tychê's unpredictable tricks was to pray for salvation from deified kings, who expressed their divine power in what are now called **ruler cults**.

ruler cults: Cults that involved worship of a Hellenistic ruler as a savior god.

Various populations established these cults in recognition of great benefactions. The Athenians, for example, deified the Macedonian Antigonus and his son Demetrius as savior gods in 307 B.C.E., when they liberated the city and bestowed magnificent gifts on it. Like most ruler cults, this one expressed the populations' spontaneous gratitude and a desire to flatter the rulers in the hope of obtaining additional favors, and the rulers' wish to have their power made clear. Many cities in the Ptolemaic and Seleucid kingdoms set up ruler cults for their kings and queens. An inscription put up by Egyptian priests in 238 B.C.E. concretely described the qualities appropriate for a divine king and queen:

> King Ptolemy III and Queen Berenice, his sister and wife, the Benefactor Gods, . . . have provided good government . . . and [after a drought] sacrificed a large amount of their revenues for the salvation of the population, and by importing grain . . . they saved the inhabitants of Egypt.

As these words make clear, the Hellenistic monarchs' tremendous power and wealth gave them the status of gods to the ordinary people who depended on their generosity and protection. The idea that a human being could be a god, present on earth to save people from evils, was now firmly established and would prove influential later in Roman imperial religion and Christianity.

Healing divinities offered another form of protection to anxious individuals. Scientific Greek medicine had rejected the notion of supernatural causes and cures for disease ever since Hippocrates in the fifth century B.C.E. Nevertheless, the cult of the god Asclepius, who offered cures for illness and injury at his many shrines, grew popular during the Hellenistic period. Suppliants seeking Asclepius's help would sleep in special locations at his shrines to await dreams in which he prescribed healing treatments. These prescriptions emphasized diet and exercise, but numerous inscriptions commissioned by grateful patients also testified to miraculous cures and surgery performed while the sufferer slept. The following example is typical:

> Ambrosia of Athens was blind in one eye. . . . She . . . ridiculed some of the cures [described in inscriptions in the sanctuary] as being incredible and impossible. . . . But when she went to sleep, she saw a vision; she thought the god was standing next to her. . . . He split open the diseased eye and poured in a medicine. When day came she left cured.

People's faith in divine healing gave them hope that they could overcome the constant danger of illness, which appeared to strike at random; there was no knowledge of germs as causing infections.

Underground Labyrinth for Healing
This underground stone labyrinth formed part of the enormous healing sanctuary of the god Asclepius at Epidaurus in Greece. Patients flocked to the site from all over the Mediterranean world. They descended into the labyrinth, which was covered and dark, as part of their treatment, which centered on reaching a trance state to receive dreams that would provide instructions on their healing and, sometimes, miraculous surgery. Do you think such treatment could be effective? *(The Art Archive/Dagli Orti.)*

Mystery cults promised secret knowledge to initiates as a key to worldly and physical salvation. The cults of the Greek god Dionysus and, in particular, the Egyptian goddess Isis attracted many people to their initiations in this period. Isis was beloved because her powers protected her worshippers in all aspects of their lives. King Ptolemy I boosted her popularity by establishing a headquarters for her cult in Alexandria. The cult of Isis, who became the most popular female divinity in the Mediterranean, involved extensive ceremonies, rituals, and festivals incorporating features of Egyptian religion mixed with Greek elements. Disciples of Isis hoped to achieve personal purification, as well as the aid of the goddess in overcoming the demonic power of Tychê. That an Egyptian deity like Isis could achieve such popularity among Greeks (and, later, Romans) is the best evidence of the cultural interaction of the Hellenistic world.

Hellenistic Judaism Cultural interaction between Greeks and Jews produced important changes in Judaism during the Hellenistic period. King Ptolemy II made the Hebrew Bible accessible to a wide audience by having his Alexandrian scholars produce a Greek translation — the Septuagint. Many Jews, especially those in the large Jewish communities that had grown up in Hellenistic cities outside their homeland, began to speak Greek and adopt Greek culture. These Greek-style Jews mixed Jewish and Greek customs, while retaining Judaism's rituals and rules and not worshipping Greek gods.

Internal conflict among Jews erupted in second-century B.C.E. Palestine over how much Greek tradition was acceptable for traditional Jews. The Seleucid king Antiochus IV (r. 175–164 B.C.E.) intervened to support Greek-style Jews in Jerusalem, who had taken over the high priesthood that ruled the Jewish community. In 167 B.C.E., Antiochus converted the great Jewish temple in Jerusalem into a Greek temple and outlawed the practice of Jewish religious rites, such as observing the Sabbath and circumcision. This action provoked a revolt led by Judah the Maccabee, which won Jewish independence from Seleucid control after twenty-five years of war. The most famous episode in this revolt was the retaking of the Jerusalem temple and its rededication to the worship of the Jewish god, Yahweh, commemorated by the Hanukkah holiday. That Greek culture attracted some Jews in the first place provides a striking example of the transformations that affected many — though far from all — people of the Hellenistic world. By the time of the Roman Empire, one of those transformations would be Christianity, whose theology had roots in the cultural interaction of Hellenistic Jews and Greeks and their ideas on apocalypticism (religious ideas revealing the future) and divine human beings.

REVIEW QUESTION How did the political changes of the Hellenistic period affect art, science, and religion?

MAPPING THE WEST

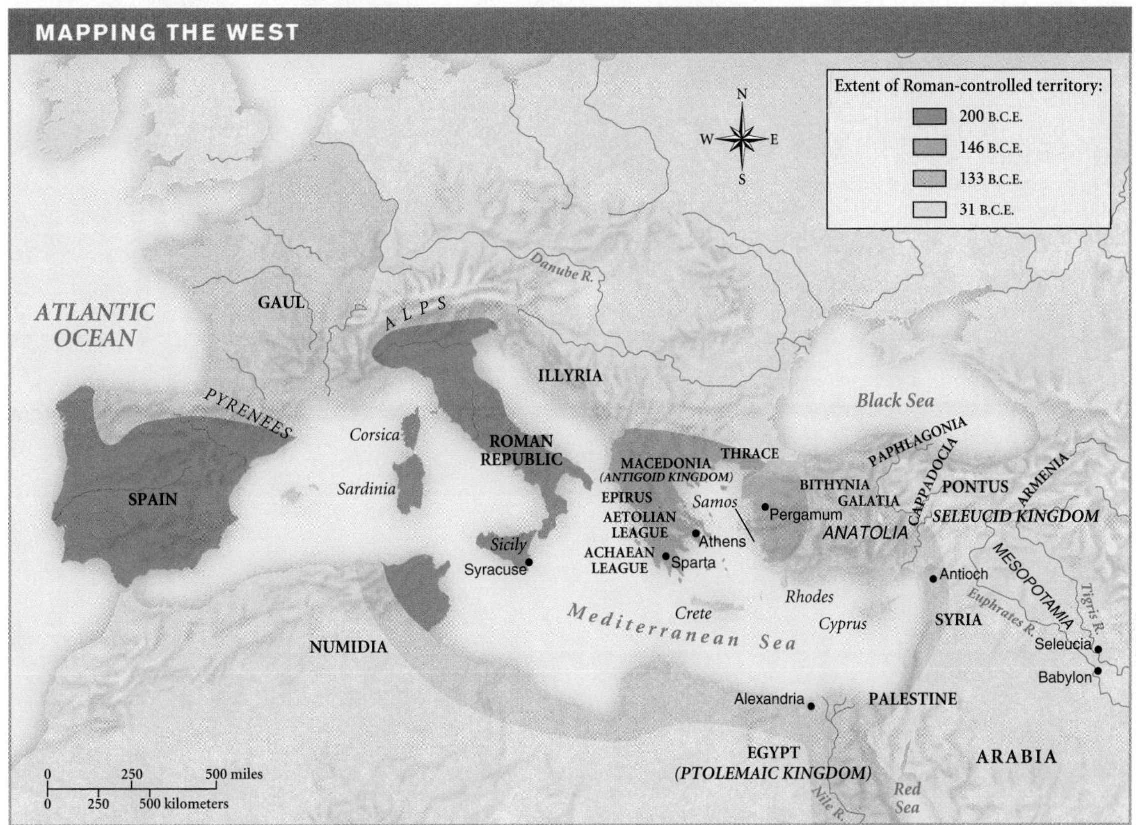

Roman Takeover of the Hellenistic World, to 30 B.C.E.

By the death of Cleopatra VII of Egypt in 30 B.C.E., the Romans had taken over the Hellenistic kingdoms of the eastern Mediterranean. This territory became the eastern half of the Roman Empire. Compare the political divisions on this map with those on the map at the end of Chapter 3 to see the differences from the Classical Age.

Conclusion

The aftermath of the Peloponnesian War led ordinary people as well as philosophers like Plato and Aristotle to question the basis of morality. The disunity of Greek international politics allowed Macedonia's aggressive leaders Philip II (r. 359–336 B.C.E.) and Alexander the Great (r. 336–323 B.C.E.) to make themselves the masters of the competing city-states. Inspired by Greek heroic ideals, Alexander the Great conquered the Persian Empire and set in motion the Hellenistic period's enormous political, social, and cultural changes.

When Alexander's commanders transformed themselves into Hellenistic kings after his death, they reintroduced monarchy into the Greek world, adding an administrative layer of Greek and Macedonian officials to the conquered lands' existing governments. Local elites cooperated with the new Hellenistic monarchs in governing and financing their hierarchical society, which was divided along ethnic lines, with the Greek and Macedonian elite ranking above local elites. To enhance their own reputations, Hellenistic kings and queens funded writers, artists, scholars, philosophers, and scientists, thereby energizing intellectual life. The traditional city-states continued to exist in Hellenistic Greece, but their freedom extended only to local governance; the Hellenistic kings controlled foreign policy.

Increased contacts between diverse peoples promoted greater cultural interaction in the Hellenistic world. What changed most of all was the Romans' culture once they took over the Hellenistic kingdoms' territory and came into close contact with their diverse peoples' traditions. Rome's rise to power took centuries, however, because Rome originated as a tiny, insignificant place that no one except Romans ever expected to amount to anything in the wider world.

FOR FURTHER EXPLORATION

- **For additional primary-source material from this period**, see *Sources of the Making of the West*, Fourth Edition.
- **For Web sites, images, and documents related to topics in this chapter**, visit *Make History* at bedfordstmartins.com/hunt.

Chapter 4 Review

Online Study Guide bedfordstmartins.com/hunt

Key Terms and People

In the grid below, identify the term or person and explain its historical significance. (To do this exercise online, go to bedfordstmartins.com/hunt.)

Term	Who or What & When	Why It Matters
Plato (p. 112)		
metaphysics (p. 113)		
dualism (p. 113)		
Aristotle (p. 114)		
Lyceum (p. 114)		
Alexander the Great (p. 116)		
Hellenistic (p. 120)		
epigrams (p. 127)		
materialism (p. 128)		
Epicureanism (p. 129)		
Stoicism (p. 130)		
Koine (p. 132)		
ruler cults (p. 133)		

Review Questions

1. How did daily life, philosophy, and the political situation change in Greece during the period 400–350 B.C.E.?
2. What were the accomplishments of Alexander the Great, and what were their effects both for the ancient world and for later Western civilization?
3. How did the political and social organization of the new Hellenistic kingdoms compare with that of the earlier Greek city-states?
4. How did the political changes of the Hellenistic period affect art, science, and religion?

Making Connections

1. What made ancient people see Alexander as "great"? Would he be regarded as "great" in today's world?
2. What are the advantages and disadvantages of governmental support of the arts and sciences? Compare such support in the Hellenistic kingdoms to that in the United States today (e.g., through the National Endowment for the Humanities, National Endowment for the Arts, and the National Science Foundation).
3. Is inner personal tranquillity powerful enough to make a difficult or painful life bearable?

Important Events

Date	Event	Date	Event
399 B.C.E.	Execution of Socrates	306–304 B.C.E.	Successors of Alexander declare themselves kings
386 B.C.E.	In King's Peace, Sparta surrenders control of Anatolian Greek city-states to Persia; Plato founds Academy	300–260 B.C.E.	Theocritus writes poetry at Ptolemaic court
362 B.C.E.	Battle of Mantinea leaves power vacuum in Greece	c. 300 B.C.E.	Euclid teaches geometry at Alexandria
338 B.C.E.	Battle of Chaeronea allows Macedonian Philip II to become the leading power in Greece	195 B.C.E.	Seleucid queen Laodice endows dowries for girls
335 B.C.E.	Aristotle founds Lyceum	167 B.C.E.	Maccabee revolt after Antiochus IV turns temple in Jerusalem into a Greek sanctuary
334–323 B.C.E.	Alexander the Great leads Greeks and Macedonians to conquer Persian Empire	30 B.C.E.	Cleopatra VII dies and Rome takes over Ptolemaic Empire
307 B.C.E.	Epicurus founds his philosophical group in Athens		

- Consider three events: **Alexander the Great leads Greeks and Macedonians to conquer Persian Empire (334–323 B.C.E.)**, **Epicurus founds his philosophical group in Athens (307 B.C.E.)**, and **Euclid teaches geometry at Alexandria (c. 300 B.C.E.)**. How might Alexander's expeditions have influenced developments in politics, philosophy, and science?

SUGGESTED REFERENCES

After the Peloponnesian War, the structure of international relations changed radically in the Greek world as the city-states became secondary in political power, first to the kingdom of Macedonia and then to the kingdoms of the Hellenistic period. Long-lasting cultural changes accompanied this political transformation.

*Aristotle. *Complete Works*. Ed. Jonathan Barnes. 1985.

Briant, Pierre. *Alexander the Great and His Empire: A Short Introduction*. Trans. Amélie Kuhrt. 2010.

Chaniotis, Angelos. *War in the Hellenistic World*. 2005.

Collins, John Joseph. *Between Athens and Jerusalem: Jewish Identity in the Hellenistic Diaspora*. 1999.

Dahmen, Karsten. *The Legend of Alexander the Great on Greek and Roman Coins*. 2006.

Empereur, Jean-Yves. *Alexandria: Jewel of Egypt*. 2002.

Evans, J. A. S. *Daily Life in the Hellenistic Age: From Alexander to Cleopatra*. 2008.

Hornblower, Simon. *The Greek World 479–323 B.C.* 4th ed. 2011.

Mikalson, Jon D. *Religion in Hellenistic Athens*. 1998.

*Plato. *The Collected Dialogues*. Ed. Edith Hamilton and Huntington Cairns. 1963.

*Plutarch. *The Age of Alexander*. Trans. Ian Scott-Kilvert. 1973.

Pollitt, J. J. *Art in the Hellenistic Age*. 1986.

Ptolemaic Egypt: http://www.houseofptolemy.org/

Rogers, Guy MacLean. *Alexander: The Ambiguity of Greatness*. 2004.

Sharples, R. W. *Stoics, Epicureans, and Sceptics: An Introduction to Hellenistic Philosophy*. 1996.

Shipley, Graham. *The Greek World after Alexander 323–30 B.C.* 1999.

Snyder, Jane M. *The Woman and the Lyre: Women Writers in Classical Greece and Rome*. 1989.

*Primary source.

CHAPTER 5

The Rise of Rome and Its Republic

753–44 B.C.E.

The Romans treasured legends about their state's transformation from a tiny village to a world power. They especially loved stories about their first king, Romulus, famous as a hot-tempered but shrewd leader. According to the tale later called "The Rape of the Sabine Women," Romulus's Rome needed more women to bear children to increase its population and build a strong army. The king therefore begged Rome's neighbors for permission for Romans to marry their women. Everyone turned him down, mocking Rome's poverty and weakness. Enraged, Romulus hatched a plan to use force where diplomacy had failed. Inviting the neighboring Sabines to a religious festival, he had his men kidnap the unmarried women. The Roman kidnappers immediately married the Sabine women, promising to cherish them as beloved wives and new citizens. When the Sabine men attacked Rome to rescue their kin, the women rushed into the midst of the bloody battle, begging their brothers, fathers, and new husbands either to stop slaughtering one another or to kill them to end the war. The men made peace on the spot and agreed to merge their populations under Roman rule.

This legend emphasizes that Rome, unlike the city-states of Greece, expanded by absorbing outsiders into its citizen body, sometimes violently, sometimes peacefully. Rome's growth became the ancient world's greatest expansion of population and territory, as a people originally housed in a few huts gradually created a state that fought countless wars and relocated an unprecedented number of citizens to gain control of most of Europe, North Africa, Egypt, and the eastern Mediterranean lands. The social, cultural, political, legal, and economic traditions that Romans developed in ruling this vast area created closer interconnections between many diverse peoples than ever before or since. Unlike the Greeks and Macedonians, the

The Wolf Suckling Romulus and Remus

This bronze statue relates to the myth that a she-wolf nursed the twin brothers Romulus and Remus, the offspring of the war god Mars and the future founders of Rome. Romans treasured this story because it meant that Mars loved their city so dearly that he sent a wild animal to nurse its founders after a cruel tyrant had forced their mother to abandon the infants. The myth also taught Romans that their state had been born in violence: Romulus killed Remus in an argument over who would lead their new settlement. The wolf is an Etruscan sculpture from the fifth century B.C.E.; the babies were added in the Renaissance. *(Scala/Art Resource, NY.)*

Romans maintained the unity of their state for centuries. Its long existence allowed many Roman values and traditions to become essential components of Western civilization.

Roman values and traditions originated with ancient Italy's many peoples, but Greek literature, art, and philosophy influenced Rome's culture most of all. This cross-cultural contact that so deeply influenced Rome was a kind of competition in innovation between equals, not "inferior" Romans imitating "superior" Greek culture. Like other ancient peoples, Romans often learned from their neighbors, but they adapted foreign traditions to their own purposes and forged their own cultural identity.

The kidnapping legend belongs to Rome's earliest history, when kings ruled (753–509 B.C.E.). Rome's most important history comes afterward, divided into two major periods of about five hundred years each—the republic and the empire. Under the republic (founded 509 B.C.E.), male voters elected their officials and passed laws (although an oligarchy of the social elite controlled politics). Under the empire, monarchs once again ruled. Rome's greatest expansion came during the republic. Romans' belief in a divine destiny fueled this tremendous growth. They believed that the gods wanted them to rule the world by military might and law and improve it through social and moral values. Their faith in a divine destiny is illustrated by the legend of the Sabine women, in which the earliest Romans used a religious festival as a cover for kidnapping. Their conviction that values should drive politics showed in their determination to persuade the Sabine women that loyalty and love would outweigh the crime of kidnapping that turned them into Romans.

Roman values emphasized family loyalty, selfless political and military service to the community, individual honor and public status, the importance of the law, and shared decision making. Unfortunately, these values conflicted with one another in the long run. By the first century B.C.E., power-hungry leaders such as Sulla and Julius Caesar had plunged Rome into civil war. By putting their personal ambition before the good of the state, they destroyed the republic.

CHAPTER FOCUS How did traditional Roman values affect both the rise and the downfall of the Roman republic?

Roman Social and Religious Traditions

Roman social and religious traditions shaped the history of the Roman republic. Rome's citizens believed that eternal moral values connected them to one another and required them to honor the gods in return for divine support. Hierarchy affected all of life: people at all social levels were obligated to patrons or clients; in families, fathers dominated; in religion, people at all levels of society owed sacrifices, rituals, and prayers to the gods who protected the family and the state.

Roman Moral Values

Roman values defined relationships with other people and with the gods. Romans guided their lives by the ***mos maiorum*** ("the way of the elders"), or values handed down from their ancestors. The Romans

---

mos maiorum: Literally, "the way of the elders"; the set of Roman values handed down from the ancestors.

753 B.C.E. Traditional date of Rome's founding as monarchy

509 B.C.E. Roman republic established

396 B.C.E. Defeat of Etruscan city of Veii; first great expansion of Roman territory

700 B.C.E. — 600 B.C.E. — 500 B.C.E. — 400 B.C.E.

509–287 B.C.E. Struggle of the orders

451–449 B.C.E. Creation of Twelve Tables, Rome's first written law code

387 B.C.E. Gauls sack Rome

preserved these values because, for them, *old* equaled "tested by time," while *new* meant "dangerous." Roman morality emphasized virtue, faithfulness, and respect. Being seen to behave morally was crucial to Romans because it earned them the respect of others.

Virtus ("manly virtue") was a primarily masculine quality comprising strength, loyalty, and courage, especially in war. It also included wisdom and moral purity, qualities that the social elite were expected to display in their public and private lives. In this broader sense, women, too, could possess virtus. In the second century B.C.E., the Roman poet Lucilius defined it this way:

> *Virtus* is to know the human relevance of each thing,
> To know what is humanly right and useful and honorable,
> And what things are good and what are bad, useless, shameful, and dishonorable. . . .
> *Virtus* is to pay what in reality is owed to honorable status,
> To be an enemy and a foe to bad people and bad values,
> But a defender of good people and good values. . . .
> And, in addition, *virtus* is putting the country's interests first,
> Then our parents', with our own interests third and last.

Fides (FEE dehs, "faithfulness") meant keeping one's obligations no matter the cost. Failing to meet an obligation offended the community and the gods. Faithful women remained virgins before marriage and monogamous afterward. Men demonstrated faithfulness by keeping their word, paying their debts, and treating everyone with justice—which did not mean treating everyone equally, but rather treating each person appropriately, according to whether he or she was a social superior, an equal, or an inferior.

Religion was part of faithfulness. Showing respect and devotion to the gods and to one's family was the supreme form of this value. Romans respected the superior authority of the gods and of the elders and ancestors of their families. Performing religious rituals properly was crucial: Romans believed they had to worship the gods faithfully to maintain the divine favor that protected their community.

Roman values required that each person maintain self-control and limit displays of emotion, to show other people that they respected themselves and their status in society. So strict was this value that not even wives and husbands could kiss in public without seeming emotionally out of control. It also meant that a person should never give up no matter how hard the situation. Persevering and doing one's duty were instilled from a young age.

The reward for living these values was respect from others. Women earned respect by bearing legitimate children and educating them morally; their reward was a good reputation among their families and friends. Respected men relied on their reputations to help them win election to government posts. A man of the highest reputation commanded so much respect that others would obey him regardless of whether he held an office with formal power over them. A man with this much prestige was said to possess authority.

The concept of authority based on respect reflected the Roman belief that some people were by nature superior to others and that society had to be hierarchical to be just. Thus, they determined status both by family history and by wealth. Romans believed that aristocrats, or people born into the best families, automatically deserved high respect. In return, aristocrats were supposed to live strictly by the highest values and serve the community.

264–241 B.C.E. Rome and Carthage fight First Punic War

220 B.C.E. Rome controls Italy south of Po River

218–201 B.C.E. Rome and Carthage fight Second Punic War

168–149 B.C.E. Cato writes *The Origins*, first history of Rome in Latin

149–146 B.C.E. Rome and Carthage fight Third Punic War

146 B.C.E. Carthage and Corinth destroyed

133 B.C.E. Tiberius Gracchus elected tribune; assassinated in same year

91–87 B.C.E. Social War between Rome and its Italian allies

60 B.C.E. First Triumvirate of Caesar, Pompey, and Crassus

49–45 B.C.E. Civil war, with Caesar the victor

45–44 B.C.E. Cicero writes his philosophical works on *humanitas*

44 B.C.E. Caesar appointed dictator with no term limit; assassinated in same year

300 B.C.E. — 200 B.C.E. — 100 B.C.E. — 0

In Roman legends about the early days, a person could be poor and still remain a proud aristocrat. Over time, however, money became overwhelmingly important to the Roman elite, for spending on showy luxuries, large-scale entertaining, and extremely costly gifts to the community. In this way, wealth became necessary to maintain high social status. By the later centuries of the Roman republic, ambitious men often trampled on other values to acquire riches and high status.

The Patron-Client System

The **patron-client system** underlay status in Roman society. It was an interlocking network of personal relationships that obligated people to one another. A patron was a man of superior status who could provide benefits, as they were called, to lower-status people; these were his clients, who in return owed him duties and paid him special attention. In this hierarchical system, a patron was often himself the client of a higher-status man.

patron-client system: The interlocking network of mutual obligations between Roman patrons (social superiors) and clients (social inferiors).

Sculpted Tomb of a Family of Ex-Slaves
The inscription on this tomb monument from, probably, the first century B.C.E. reveals that the couple started life as slaves but became free and thus Roman citizens. Their son (his head has been knocked off) is shown in the background holding a pet pigeon. This family had done well enough financially to afford a sculpted tomb, and the tablets the man is holding and the woman's hairstyle are meant to show that their family was literate and stylish. Compare the man's realistically lined face with the woman's softer, more idealized one. *(German Archeological Institute/Madeline Grimoldi.)*

Benefits and duties centered on mutual exchanges of financial and political help. Patrons would help their clients get started in making a living by giving them a gift or a loan and putting them in touch with others who could help them. In politics, a patron would jump-start a client's career by promoting his candidacy for elective office and providing money for campaigning and doing favors for influential supporters. A patron's most important obligation was to support a client and his family if they got into legal trouble.

Clients had to aid their patrons' campaigns for public office by swinging votes their way. They also had to lend money when patrons had huge expenses to provide public works and to fund their daughters' dowries. A patron expected his clients to gather at his house at dawn to accompany him to the forum, the city's public center, because it was a mark of great status to have numerous clients thronging around. A Roman leader needed a large house to hold this throng and to entertain his social equals. A crowded house indicated social success.

Patrons' and clients' mutual obligations endured for generations. Ex-slaves, who became the clients for life of the masters who freed them, often passed this relationship on to their children. Romans with contacts abroad could acquire clients among foreigners; Roman generals sometimes had entire foreign communities obligated to them. The patron-client system demonstrated the Roman idea that social stability and well-being were achieved by faithfully maintaining established ties.

The Roman Family

The family was Roman society's bedrock because it taught values and determined the ownership of property. Men and women shared the duty of teaching their children values, though by law the father possessed the ***patria potestas*** ("father's power") over his children — no matter how old — and his slaves. This power made him the sole owner of all his dependents' property. As long as he was alive, no son or daughter could officially own anything, accumulate money, or possess any independent legal standing. Unofficially, however, adult children did control personal property and money, and favored slaves could build up savings. Fathers also held legal power of life and death over these members of their households, but they rarely exercised this power except, like the

patria potestas **(PAH tree uh po TEHS tahs):** Literally, "father's power"; the legal power a Roman father possessed over the children and slaves in his family, including owning all their property and having the right to punish them, even with death.

Sculpture of a Woman Running a Store
This sculpture portrays a woman selling food from a small shop while customers make purchases or chat. Since Roman women could own property, it is possible that the woman is the store owner. The man standing behind her could be her husband or a servant. Much like malls of today, markets in Roman towns were packed with small stores. *(Art Resource, NY.)*

Greeks, through exposure of newborns, an accepted practice to limit family size and dispose of physically imperfect infants.

Patria potestas did not allow a husband to control his wife because "free" marriages — in which the wife formally remained under her father's power as long as the father lived — became common. But in the ancient world, few fathers lived long enough to oversee the lives of their married daughters or sons; four out of five parents died before their children reached age thirty. A Roman woman without a living father was relatively independent. Legally she needed a male guardian to conduct her business, but guardianship was largely an empty formality by the first century B.C.E. Upper-class women could even demonstrate publicly to express their opinions. In 195 B.C.E., for example, a group of women blocked Rome's streets for days, until the men abolished a wartime law meant to reduce tensions between rich and poor by limiting the amount of gold jewelry and fine clothing women could wear and where they could ride in carriages. A later legal expert commented on women's freedom of action: "The common belief, that because of their instability of judgment women are often deceived and that it is only fair to have them controlled by the authority of guardians, seems more false than true. For women of full age manage their affairs themselves."

A Roman woman had to grow up fast to assume her duties as teacher of values to her children and manager of her household's resources. Tullia (c. 79–45 B.C.E.), daughter of Rome's most famous politician and orator, Cicero, was engaged at twelve, married at sixteen, and widowed by twenty-two. Like every other wealthy married Roman woman, she managed the household slaves, monitored the nurturing of the young children by wet nurses, kept account books to track the property she personally owned, and accompanied her husband to dinner parties — something a Greek wife never did.

A mother's responsibility for shaping her children's values constituted the foundation of female virtue. Women like Cornelia, a famous aristocrat of the second century B.C.E., won enormous respect for loyalty to family. When her husband died, Cornelia refused an offer of marriage from King Ptolemy VIII of Egypt so that she could continue to oversee the family estate and educate her surviving daughter and two sons. (Her other nine children had died.) The boys, Tiberius and Gaius Gracchus, grew up to be among the most influential political leaders in the late republic. The number of children Cornelia bore reveals the fertility and stamina required of a Roman wife to ensure the survival of her husband's family line. Cornelia also became famous for her stylishly worded letters, which were still being read a century later.

Roman women had no official political role, but wealthy women like Cornelia could influence politics indirectly through expressing their opinions to their male relatives and friends in conversations at their homes and at dinner parties. Marcus Porcius Cato (234–149 B.C.E.), a famous politician and author, described this clout: "All mankind rule their wives, we [Roman men] rule all mankind, and our wives rule us."

Women could acquire property through inheritance and entrepreneurship. Archaeological discoveries reveal that by the end of the republic some women owned large businesses. Because both women and men could control property, prenuptial agreements determining the property rights of husband and wife were common. Divorce was legally simple, with fathers usually keeping the children, a reflection of the father's power over the members of his household. Most poor women, like poor men, had to toil for a living as field laborers or hawkers selling trinkets in cities. Women and men both worked in manufacturing, which mostly happened in the home. The men worked the raw materials — cutting, fitting, and polishing wood, leather, and metal — while the women sold the finished goods. The poorest women earned money through prostitution, which was legal but considered disgraceful.

Education for Public Life

Roman education aimed to make men and women effective speakers and exponents of traditional values. Most children received their education at home; there were no public schools, and only the rich could afford private teachers. Wealthy parents bought literate slaves (pedagogues) to educate their children; by the late republic, they often chose Greek slaves so that their children could learn to speak Greek and read Greek literature. Lessons emphasized memorization, and teachers used physical punishment to keep pupils attentive. In upper-class families, both daughters and sons learned to read. The girls were also taught literature and perhaps some music, and how to make educated conversation at dinner parties. The principal aim of women's education was to prepare them to teach traditional social and moral values to their children.

Sons received physical training and learned to fight with weapons, but rhetorical training dominated an upper-class Roman boy's education because a successful political career depended on the ability to speak persuasively in public. A boy would learn winning techniques by listening to speeches in political meetings and arguments in court cases. As the orator Cicero said, young men must learn to "excel in public speaking. It is the tool for controlling men at Rome."

Public and Private Religion

Romans followed Greek models in religion. Their chief deity, Jupiter, corresponded to the Greek god Zeus and was seen as a powerful, stern father. Juno (Greek Hera), queen of the gods, and Minerva (Greek Athena), goddess of wisdom, joined Jupiter to form the state religion's central triad. These three deities shared Rome's most revered temple.

Protecting Rome's safety and prosperity was the gods' major function. They were supposed to help Rome defeat enemies in war, but divine support for agriculture was also essential. Official prayers requested the gods' aid in growing abundant crops, healing disease, and promoting reproduction for animals and people. In times of crisis, Romans sought foreign gods for help, such as when the government imported the cult of the healing god Asclepius from

Household Shrine from Pompeii

This shrine stood inside the entrance to a house at Pompeii owned by successful businessmen, who spent heavily to decorate their home with 188 colorful wall paintings. This type of shrine housed statuettes of the deities protecting the household, shown here also in a painting, flanking a figure representing the spirit of the family's father. What do you think it signifies that the deities are dancing? The snake below, which is about to drink from a bowl probably holding milk, also symbolizes a protective force. The scene sums up the role Romans expected their gods to play: protecting people against harm and bad luck. *(Scala/Art Resource, NY.)*

Greece in 293 B.C.E., hoping he would save Rome from an epidemic.

The republic supported many other cults, including that of Vesta, goddess of the hearth and therefore protector of the family. Her shrine housed Rome's official eternal flame, which guaranteed the state's permanent existence. The Vestal Virgins, six unmarried women sworn to chastity and Rome's only female priests, tended Vesta's shrine. Their chastity was considered crucial to preserving Rome. They earned high status and freedom from their fathers' control by performing their most important duty: keeping the flame from going out. If the flame went out, the Romans assumed that one of the Vestal Virgins had had sex and buried her alive.

Religion was important in Roman family life. Each household maintained small indoor shrines housing statuettes of the spirits of the household and those of the ancestors, who were believed to protect the family's health and morality. Upper-class families kept death masks of ancestors hanging in the main room and wore them at funerals to commemorate the family's heritage and the current generation's responsibility to live up to the ancestors' values.

Because Romans believed that divine spirits participated in crucial events such as birth, marriage, and death, they performed many rituals seeking protection. Rituals also accompanied everyday activities, such as breast-feeding babies or fertilizing crops. Many public religious gatherings promoted the community's health and stability. For example, during the February 15 Lupercalia festival (whose name recalled the wolf, *luper* in Latin, that legend said had reared Romulus and his twin, Remus), near-naked young men streaked around the Palatine hill, lashing any woman they met with strips of goatskin. Women who had not yet borne children would run out to be struck, believing this would help them become fertile.

Like the Greeks, the Romans did not regard the gods as guardians of human morality. Cicero's description of Jupiter's titles explained public religion's closer ties to security and prosperity than to personal behavior: "We call Jupiter the Best and Greatest not because he makes us just or sober or wise but, rather, healthy, unharmed, rich, and prosperous." Roman officials preceded important actions with the ritual called taking the auspices, in which they sought Jupiter's approval by observing natural signs such as birds' flight direction or eating habits, or the appearance of thunder and lightning. Action proceeded only if the auspices were favorable.

Romans linked values and religion by regarding values as divine forces. *Pietas* ("piety"), for example, meant devotion and duty to family, friends, the state, and the gods; a temple at Rome held a statue personifying pietas as a female divinity. The personification of abstract moral qualities provided a focus for cult rituals.

The duty of Roman religious officials was to maintain peace with the gods. Socially prominent men served as priests, conducting sacrifices, festivals, and prayers. They were not professionals devoting their lives to religious activity; they were citizens performing public service. The chief priest, the *pontifex maximus* ("greatest bridge-builder"), served as the head of state religion and the ultimate authority on religious matters affecting government. The political powers of this priesthood motivated Rome's most ambitious men to seek it.

Disrespect for religious tradition brought punishment. Admirals, for example, took the auspices by feeding sacred chickens on their warships: if the birds ate energetically, Jupiter favored the Romans and an attack could begin. In 249 B.C.E., the commander Publius Claudius Pulcher grew frustrated when his chickens, probably seasick, refused to eat. Determined to attack, he finally hurled the birds overboard in a rage, sputtering, "Well then, let them drink!" When he promptly suffered a huge defeat, he was fined heavily.

REVIEW QUESTION What common themes underlay Roman values? How did Romans' behavior reflect those values?

From Monarchy to Republic

Romans' values and their belief in a divine destiny fueled their astounding growth from a tiny settlement into the Mediterranean's greatest power. The surviving evidence for the first five hundred years of Roman history down to the wars against Carthage is very limited, and therefore much remains uncertain about the development of Roman society, politics, and military power. The Romans spilled much blood as they gradually expanded their territory through war. From the eighth to the sixth century B.C.E., they were ruled by kings, but the later kings' violence provoked members of the social elite to overthrow the monarchy and create the republic, which lasted from the fifth through the first century B.C.E. The republic—from the Latin ***res publica*** ("the people's matter" or "the public business")—

res publica (REHS POOB lih kuh): Literally, "the people's matter" or "the public business"; the Romans' name for their republic and the source of our word *republic*.

distributed power by electing officials and making laws in open meetings of male citizens. This model of republican government, rather than Athens's direct democracy, influenced the founders of the United States in organizing their new nation as a federal republic. Rome gained land and population by winning aggressive wars and by absorbing other peoples. Its economic and cultural growth depended on contact with many other peoples around the Mediterranean.

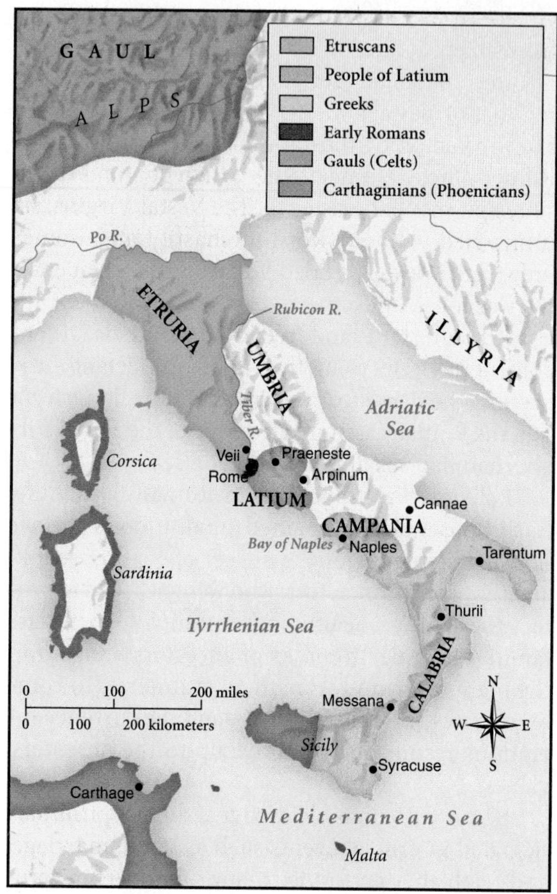

MAP 5.1 Ancient Italy, 500 B.C.E.
When the Romans removed the monarchy to found a republic in 509 B.C.E., they inhabited a relatively small territory in central Italy. Many different peoples lived in Italy at this time, with the most prosperous occupying fertile agricultural land and sheltered harbors on the peninsula's west side. The early republic's most urbanized neighbors were the Etruscans to the north and the Greeks in the city-states to the south, including on the island of Sicily. Immediately adjacent to Rome were the people of Latium, called Latins. | **How did geography aid Roman expansion?**

Roman Society under the Kings, 753–509 B.C.E.

Legend taught that Rome's original government had seven kings, ruling from 753 to 509 B.C.E. The kings created Rome's most famous and enduring government body: the Senate, a group of distinguished men chosen as the king's personal council. This council played the same role—advising government leaders—for a thousand years, as Rome changed from a monarchy to a republic and back to a monarchy (the empire). It was always a Roman tradition that one should never make decisions by oneself but only after consulting advisers and friends.

The kings began Rome's expansion by taking in outsiders whom they conquered, as reflected in the story of Romulus's assimilating the Sabines. This inclusionary policy of making others into citizens, which contrasted sharply with the exclusionary laws of the Greeks, proved crucial for Rome's growth and promoted ethnic diversity. Even more remarkably, Romans, unlike Greeks, granted citizenship to freed slaves. Though freedmen and freedwomen owed special obligations to their former owners and could not hold elective office or serve in the army, they enjoyed all other citizens' rights, such as legal marriage. Their children possessed citizenship without any limits. By the late republic, many Roman citizens were descendants of freed slaves.

Expansion and Cross-Cultural Contact By approximately 550 B.C.E., Rome had grown to between thirty and forty thousand people and, through war and diplomacy, had won control of three hundred square miles of surrounding territory. Rome's geography propelled its further expansion. The Romans originated in central Italy, a long peninsula with a mountain range down its middle like a spine and fertile plains on either side. In addition to possessing rich farmland, Rome controlled a river crossing on a major north–south route. Most important, Rome was ideally situated for international trade: the Italian peninsula stuck so far out into the Mediterranean that east–west seaborne traffic naturally encountered it (Map 5.1), and the city had a good port nearby.

The Romans' predecessors in Italy were peoples whose languages belonged to what linguists call the Indo-European family of related languages, which are found from Europe to India. Our only material evidence for these ancestors of the Romans comes from archaeological excavation of ninth- and eighth-century B.C.E. tombs. The Italian pre-Romans lived by herding animals, farming, and hunting. They became skilled metalworkers, especially in iron.

The earliest Romans' closest neighbors in central Italy were poor villagers, too, and spoke the same Indo-European language, Latin. Greeks lived to the south in Italy and Sicily, however, and contact with them had the greatest effect on Roman cultural development. Greek culture reached its most famous flowering in its fifth-century B.C.E. Golden Age, at the time when the Roman republic was taking shape and centuries before Rome had its own literature, theater, or monumental architecture. Romans developed a love-hate relationship with Greece, admiring its literature and art but looking down on its lack of military unity. They adopted many elements from Greek culture — from deities for their national cults to models for their poetry, prose, and architectural styles.

The Etruscans The Etruscans, a people to the north, also influenced Roman culture. Brightly colored wall paintings in tombs, portraying funeral banquets and games, reveal the splendor of Etruscan society. In addition to producing their own art, jewelry, and sculpture, the Etruscans also imported luxurious objects from Greece and the Near East. Most of the intact Greek vases known today were found in Etruscan tombs, and Etruscan culture was deeply influenced by that of Greece.

The relationship between the Etruscan and Roman cultures remains a controversial topic. Scholars long believed that the Etruscans completely reshaped Roman culture during a period of supposed political domination in the sixth century B.C.E. New research, however, shows the Romans' independence in developing their own cultural traditions: they borrowed from the Etruscans, as from the Greeks, whatever appealed to them and adapted these borrowings to their own circumstances.

Romans adopted ceremonial features of Etruscan culture, such as musical instruments, religious rituals, and lictors (attendants who walked in front of the highest officials carrying the fasces, a bundle of rods around an axe, symbolizing the officials' right to command and punish). The Romans also borrowed from the Etruscans the ritual of divination — determining the will of the gods by examining organs of slaughtered animals. The custom of wives joining husbands at dinner parties may also have come from the Etruscans.

Other features of Roman culture formerly seen as deriving from Etruscan influence were probably part of the ancient Mediterranean's shared practices. The organization of the Roman army — a citizen militia of heavily armed infantry troops fighting in formation — reflected the practice of many other peoples. The alphabet, which the Romans first learned from the Etruscans, was actually Greek; the Greeks had gotten it through their contact with the earlier alphabets of eastern Mediterranean peoples. Foreign trade and urban planning are other features of Etruscan life that Romans are said to have assimilated, but it is too simplistic to assume these cultural developments resulted from a superior culture instructing a less developed one. Rather, at this time in Mediterranean history, similar cultural developments were under way in many places.

Etruscan Painting of a Musician
This Etruscan painting, characteristically done with bright colors (now faded), shows a man playing the double pipe, a reed wind instrument with holes in both tubes that the player fingered simultaneously. This instrument originated in Greece, as did the designs above and below the central figure. The Etruscans adopted many cultural traditions from the Greeks, some of which they then passed on to the Romans. *(Italic, Etruscan, Late Archaic period or early Classical period, about 470 B.C.E. Terracotta, overall dimensions: 112.5 x 52 cm. [44 5/16 x 20½ in.]. Museum of Fine Arts, Boston, William Francis Warden Fund, 62.363. Photograph © 2011 Museum of Fine Arts, Boston.)*

DOCUMENT

The Rape and Suicide of Lucretia

This story explaining why the Roman elite expelled the monarchy in 509 B.C.E., thus opening the way to the republic, centers on female virtue and courage, as do other stories about significant political changes in early Roman history. The values attributed to Lucretia obviously reflect men's wishes for women's behavior, but it would be a mistake to assume that women could not hold the same views. The historian Livy wrote this document in the late first century B.C.E., at another crucial point in Roman history—the violent transition from republic to empire—when Romans were deeply concerned with the values of the past as a guide to the present.

Sextus Tarquinius, the son of Rome's king (Tarquin the Proud, r. 534–510 B.C.E.), came to Lucretia's home. She greeted him warmly and asked him to stay [as Roman hospitality demanded for such a high-status visitor]. Crazy with lust, he waited until he was sure the household was sleeping. Drawing his sword, he snuck into Lucretia's bedroom and placed the blade against her left breast, whispering, "Quiet, Lucretia; I am Sextus Tarquinius, and I am holding a sword. If you cry out, I'll kill you!" Rudely awakened, the desperate woman realized that no one could help her and that she was close to death. Sextus Tarquinius said he loved her, begging and threatening her in turn, trying everything to wear her down. When she wouldn't give in, even in the face of threats of murder, he added another intimidation. "After I've murdered you, I am going to put the naked corpse of a slave next to your body, and everybody will say that you were killed during a disgraceful adultery." This final threat defeated her, and after raping her he left, having stolen her honor.

Lucretia, overwhelmed by sadness and shame, sent messengers to her husband, Tarquinius Conlatinus, who was away, and her father at Rome, telling them, "Come immediately, with a good friend, because something horrible has happened." Her father arrived with a friend, and her husband came with Lucius Junius Brutus. . . . They found Lucretia in her room, overcome with grief. When she saw them, she started weeping. "How are you?" her husband asked. "Very bad," she replied. "How can anything be fine for a woman who has lost her honor? Traces of another man are in our bed, my husband. My body is defiled, though my heart is still pure; my death will be the proof. But give me your right hand and promise that you will not let the guilty escape. It was Sextus Tarquinius who returned our hospitality with hostility last night. With his sword in his hand, he came to have his fun, to my despair, but it will also be his sorrow—if you are real men." They pledged that they would catch him, and they tried to ease her sadness, saying that the soul did wrong, not the body, and where there were no bad intentions there could be no blame. "It is your responsibility to ensure that he gets what he deserves," she said; "I am blameless, but I will not free myself from punishment. No dishonorable woman shall hold up Lucretia as an example." Then she grabbed a dagger hidden underneath her robe and stabbed herself in the heart. She fell dead, as her husband and father cried out.

Brutus, leaving them to their tears, pulled the blade from Lucretia's wound and held it up drenched in blood, shouting, "By this blood, which was completely pure before the crime of the king's son, I swear before you, O gods, to drive out the king himself, his criminal wife, and all their children, by sword, fire, and everything in my power, and never to allow a king to rule Rome ever again, whether from that family or any other."

Source: Livy, *From the Foundation of the City*, 1.57–59. Translation by Thomas R. Martin.

Question to Consider

- **What notions of honor for men and for women are reflected in Livy's tale?**

The Early Roman Republic, 509–287 B.C.E.

The Roman social elite's hatred of monarchy motivated the creation of the republic. The upper class believed that power would inevitably corrupt a sole ruler. This belief was enshrined in the most famous legend about the fall of the Roman monarchy: the rape of the virtuous Roman woman Lucretia by the king's son and her subsequent suicide (see Document, "The Rape and Suicide of Lucretia," above). Declaring themselves Rome's liberators from tyranny, in 509 B.C.E. Lucretia's relatives and friends from the social elite drove out the king and founded the republic. Thereafter, the Romans prided themselves on having created a political system freer than that of many of their neighbors.

The Struggle of the Orders The Romans struggled for nearly 250 years to shape a stable government for the republic. Roman social hierarchy split the population into two **orders**: the **patricians** (a small group of the most aristocratic families) and the **plebeians** (the rest of the citizens). Bitter striving for power pitted the orders

---

orders: The two groups of people in the Roman republic—**patricians** (aristocratic families) and **plebeians** (all other citizens).

against each other; historians call this turmoil the struggle of the orders. The conflict finally ended in 287 B.C.E. when plebeians won the right to make laws in their own assembly.

Social and economic disputes underlay the struggle of the orders. Patricians constituted a tiny percentage of the population—numbering only about 130 families—but their inherited status entitled them to control public religion. Soon after the republic's founding, they used this power to monopolize political office. In this early period, many patricians were much wealthier than most plebeians. Some plebeians, however, were also rich, and they resented the patricians' dominance, especially their ban on intermarriage with plebeians. Patricians inflamed tensions by wearing special red shoes to set themselves apart; later they changed to black shoes adorned with a small metal crescent.

The struggle began when rich plebeians insisted on the right to marry patricians as social equals, while poor plebeians demanded farmland and relief from crushing debts. To pressure the patricians, the plebeians periodically refused military service. This tactic worked because Rome's army depended on plebeian manpower; the patricians were too few to defend Rome by themselves.

In response, between 451 and 449 B.C.E., the patricians agreed to the earliest Roman law code, guaranteeing greater equality and social mobility. This code, known as the **Twelve Tables**, formalized early Rome's legal customs in simply worded laws such as "If plaintiff calls defendant to court, he shall go," or "If a wind causes a neighbor's tree to be bent and lean over your farm, action may be taken to have that tree removed." The Twelve Tables prevented the patrician public officials who judged most legal cases from giving judgments only according to their own wishes. They became so important a symbol of the commitment to justice for all citizens that children were required to memorize them. The Roman belief in fair laws as the best protection against social unrest helped keep the republic united until the late second century B.C.E.

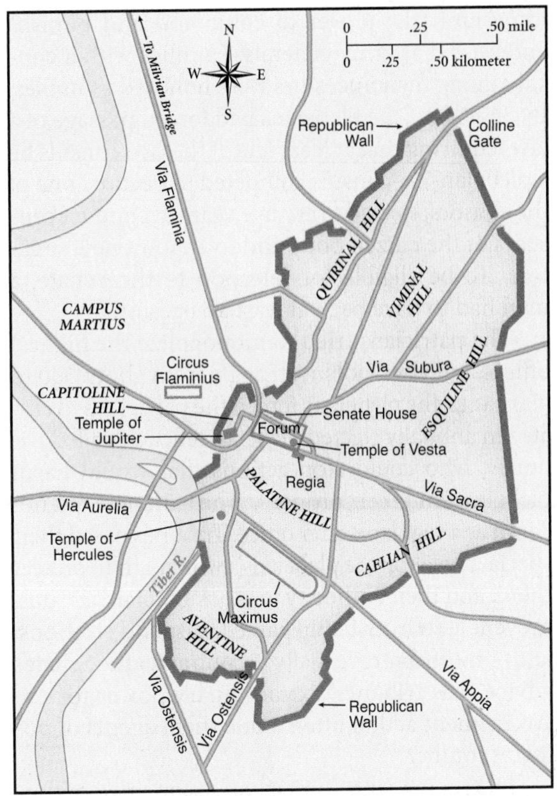

MAP 5.2 The City of Rome during the Republic
Roman tradition said that a king built Rome's first defensive wall in the sixth century B.C.E., but archaeology shows that the first wall encircling the city's center and seven hills on the east bank of the Tiber River belongs to the fourth century B.C.E.; this wall covered a circuit of about seven miles. By the second century B.C.E., the wall had been extended to soar fifty-two feet high and had been fitted with catapults to protect the large gates. Like the open agora surrounded by buildings at the heart of a Greek city, the forum remained Rome's political and social heart. | **How might modern cities benefit from having a large public space at their center?**

The Consuls, the Ladder of Offices, and the Senate

Elected officials ran Roman republican government; voting took place in and near the forum in the center of the city (Map 5.2). All officials joined committees, numbering from two to more than a dozen members, in accordance with the Roman value that rule should be shared. The highest officials, two elected each year, were called consuls. Their most important duty was commanding the army.

To be elected consul, a man had to win elections all the way up a **ladder of offices** (*cursus honorum*). Before politics, however, came ten years of military service from about ages twenty to thirty. The ladder's first step was getting elected quaestor, a financial administrator. The second step was getting elected as an aedile (supervisors of Rome's streets, sewers, aqueducts, temples, and markets). Few men reached the next step, election as praetor. Praetors performed judicial and military duties. The most successful praetors competed to be one of the two consuls elected each year. Praetors and consuls held

Twelve Tables: The first written Roman law code, enacted between 451 and 449 B.C.E.

ladder of offices: The series of Roman elective government offices from quaestor to aedile to praetor to consul.

imperium (the power to command and punish) and served as army generals. Families with a consul among their ancestors were honored as nobles. By 367 B.C.E., the plebeians had forced passage of a law requiring that at least one of the two consuls be a plebeian. Ex-consuls competed to become one of the censors, elected every five years to conduct censuses of the citizen body and to appoint new senators. To be eligible for selection to the Senate, a man had to have been at least a quaestor.

The patricians tried to monopolize the highest offices, but after violent struggle from about 500 to 450 B.C.E., the plebeians forced the patricians to create ten annually elected plebeian officials, called tribunes, who could stop actions that would harm plebeians and their property. The tribunate did not count as a regular ladder office. Tribunes based their special power on the plebeians' sworn oath to protect them, and their authority to block officials' actions, prevent laws from being passed, suspend elections, and—most controversially—contradict the Senate's advice. The tribunes' extraordinary power to veto government action often made them agents of political conflict.

In keeping with Roman values, men were supposed to compete for public office to win respect and glory, not money. Only well-off men could run for election because officials earned no salaries. In fact, they were expected to spend a great deal of their own money to win popular support by paying for expensive public shows featuring gladiators and wild animals, such as lions imported from Africa. Financing such exhibitions could put a candidate deeply in debt. Once elected, a magistrate had to pour his private funds into building and maintaining roads, aqueducts, and temples.

Early republican officials' only reward was the respect they earned for public service. As Romans conquered more and more overseas territory, however, the desire for money to finance electoral campaigns overcame many men's adherence to traditional Roman values of faithfulness and honesty. By the second century B.C.E., military officers enriched themselves not only legally by seizing booty from foreign enemies but also illegally by extorting bribes as administrators of newly conquered territories. Over time, acquiring money became more important than serving the public.

The Senate retained the role it had played under the monarchy: directing government policy by giving advice to its highest officials. Strictly speaking, the Senate did not make law, but the senators' high social standing gave their opinions the moral force of law. If a consul rejected or ignored the Senate's advice, a political crisis resulted. The Senate thus guided the republic in every area: decisions on war, domestic and foreign policy, state finance, official religion, and all types of legislation. To make their status visible, the senators wore black high-top shoes and robes with a broad purple stripe.

The Assemblies Male citizens meeting in three different assemblies decided legislation, government policy, election outcomes, and judgment in certain trials. The Centuriate Assembly, which elected praetors and consuls, was dominated by patricians and richer plebeians. The Plebeian Assembly, which excluded patricians, elected the tribunes. In 287 B.C.E., its resolutions, called **plebiscites**, became legally binding on all Romans. The Tribal Assembly mixed patricians with plebeians and became the republic's most important assembly for making policy, passing laws, and, until separate courts were later created, holding trials.

Assemblies met outdoors and were only for voting, not debates. Discussions of a sort took place before assembly meetings when orators gave speeches about the issues. Everyone, including women and noncitizens, could listen to these pre-vote speeches. The crowd expressed its agreement or disagreement with the speeches by applauding or hissing. This process mixed a small measure of democracy with the republic's oligarchic government. A significant restriction on democracy in the assemblies, however, was that voting took place by group, not by individuals. Each assembly was divided into groups with different numbers of men determined by status and wealth; each group had one vote.

The Judicial System The Roman republic's judicial system developed overlapping institutions. Early on, the praetors decided many legal cases; especially serious trials could be transferred to the assemblies. A separate jury system arose in the second century B.C.E., and senators repeatedly clashed with other upper-class Romans over whether these juries should consist exclusively of senators.

As in Greece, Rome had no state-paid prosecutors or defenders. Accusers and accused had to speak for themselves in court or have friends speak for them. Priests dominated in legal knowledge until the third century B.C.E., when senators with legal expertise began to offer legal advice. Called jurists, these senators operated as private citizens, not as officials. Developed over centuries and gradually incorporating laws from other peoples, Roman law,

---

plebiscites (PLEH buh sites): Resolutions passed by the Plebeian Assembly; such resolutions gained the force of law in 287 B.C.E.

especially on civil matters, became the basis for European legal codes still in use today.

The republic's complex system of political and judicial institutions evolved in response to conflicts over power. Laws could emerge from different assemblies, and legal cases could be decided by various institutions. Rome had no single highest court, such as the U.S. Supreme Court, to give final verdicts. The republic's stability therefore depended on maintaining the mos maiorum. Because they defined this tradition, the most socially prominent and richest Romans dominated politics and the courts.

REVIEW QUESTION How and why did the Roman republic develop its complicated political and judicial systems?

Roman Imperialism and Its Consequences

Expansion through war made military service central to Romans' lives; it also caused a huge number of citizens to migrate to communities that the government established as anchors in newly conquered areas. From the fifth to the third century B.C.E., the Romans fought war after war in Italy until Rome became the most powerful state on the peninsula. In the third and second centuries B.C.E., Romans warred far from home in every direction, above all against Carthage to the south. Their success in these campaigns made Rome the premier power in the Mediterranean by the first century B.C.E.

Fear of attacks and the desire for wealth propelled Roman imperialism. The senators' worries about national security made them advise preemptive attacks against potential enemies, while everyone longed to capture plunder and new farmland. Poor soldiers hoped to pull their families out of poverty; the elite, who commanded the armies, wanted to strengthen their campaigns for office by acquiring glory and greater wealth.

The wars in Italy and abroad transformed Roman life. Astonishingly, Rome had no literature until around 240 B.C.E.; the contact with others that conquest brought stimulated the first Roman written works of history and poetry. War's harshness also influenced Roman art, especially portraiture. On the social side, endless military service away from home created stresses on small farmers and undermined the stability of Roman society; so too did the relocation of numerous citizens and the importation of countless war captives to work as slaves on rich people's estates. Rome's great conquests thus turned out to be a two-edged sword: they brought expansion and wealth, but their unexpected social and political consequences disrupted traditional values and the community's stability.

Expansion in Italy, 500–220 B.C.E.

After defeating their Latin neighbors in the 490s B.C.E., the Romans spent the next hundred years warring with the nearby Etruscan town of Veii. Their 396 B.C.E. victory doubled the Romans' territory. By the fourth century B.C.E., the Roman infantry legion of five thousand men had surpassed the Greek and Macedonian phalanx as an effective fighting force because its soldiers were trained to throw javelins from behind their long shields and then rush in to finish off the enemy with swords. A devastating sack of Rome in 387 B.C.E. by marauding Gauls (Celts) from beyond the Alps proved only a temporary setback, though it made Romans forever fearful of foreign invasion. By around 220 B.C.E., Rome controlled all of Italy south of the Po River, at the northern end of the peninsula.

Rome and Central Italy, Fifth Century B.C.E.

The Romans combined brutality with diplomacy to control conquered people and territory. Sometimes they enslaved the defeated or forced them to surrender large parcels of land. Other times they struck generous peace terms with former enemies but required them to render military aid against other foes, for which they received a share of the booty, chiefly slaves and land. In this way, the Romans co-opted opponents by making them partners in the spoils of conquest.

To increase homeland security, the Romans planted numerous colonies of relocated citizens and constructed roads up and down the peninsula to allow troops to march faster. By connecting Italy's diverse peoples, these roads promoted a unified culture dominated by Rome.

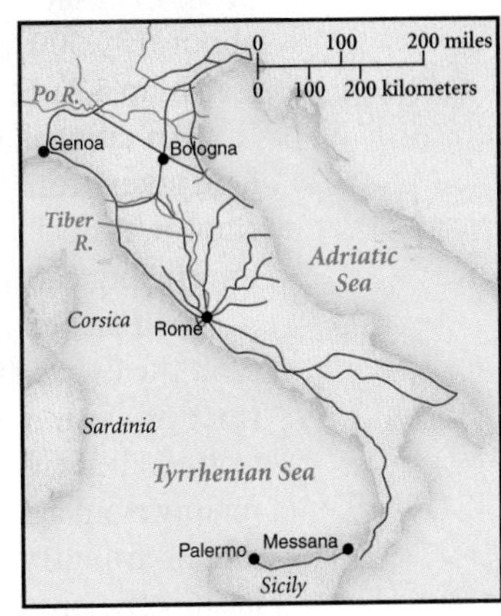

Roman Roads, 110 B.C.E.

Aqueduct at Nîmes in France
The Romans excelled at building complex delivery systems of tunnels, channels, bridges, and fountains to transport fresh water from far away. Compare the Greek city fountain shown in the vase painting on page 111. One of the best-preserved sections of a major aqueduct is the so-called Pont-du-Gard near Nîmes (ancient Nemausus) in France, erected in the late first century B.C.E. to serve the flourishing town there. Built of stones fitted together without clamps or mortar, the span soars 160 feet high and 875 feet long, carrying water along its topmost level from thirty-five miles away in a channel constructed to fall only one foot in height for every three thousand feet in length so that the flow would remain steady but gentle. What sort of social and political organization would be necessary to construct such a system? *(Hubertus Kanus/Photo Researchers, Inc.)*

Latin became the common language, although local tongues lived on, especially Greek in the south.

The wealth that the Roman army captured in the first two centuries of expansion attracted hordes of people to the capital because it financed new aqueducts to provide fresh, running water—a treasure in the ancient world—and a massive building program that employed the poor. By 300 B.C.E., about 150,000 people lived within Rome's walls (see Map 5.2). Outside the city, around 750,000 free Roman citizens inhabited various parts of Italy on land taken from local peoples. Much conquered territory was declared public land, open to any Roman for grazing cattle.

Rich plebeians and patricians cooperated to exploit the expanding Roman territories; the old distinction between the orders had become largely a technicality. This merged elite derived its wealth mainly from agricultural land and plunder acquired during military service. Since Rome had no regular income or inheritance taxes, families could pass down their wealth from generation to generation.

Wars with Carthage and in the East, 264–121 B.C.E.

Rome's leaders, remembering the Gauls' attack on the city in 387 B.C.E., feared foreign invasions and also saw imperialism as the route to riches. The republic therefore fought its three most famous wars against the wealthy city of Carthage in North Africa, which Phoenicians had founded around 800 B.C.E. In the third century B.C.E., Carthage, governed like Rome as a republic, controlled a powerful empire rich from farming in Africa and seaborne trade in the Mediterranean. Geography meant that an expansionist Rome would sooner or later come into conflict with Carthage. To Romans, Carthage seemed both a dangerous rival and a fine prize because it had grown so prosperous from agriculture and international commerce. Horror at the Carthaginians' alleged tradition of incinerating infants to placate their gods in times of trouble also fed Romans' hostility against people they saw as barbarians.

TAKING MEASURE

Census Records during the First and Second Punic Wars

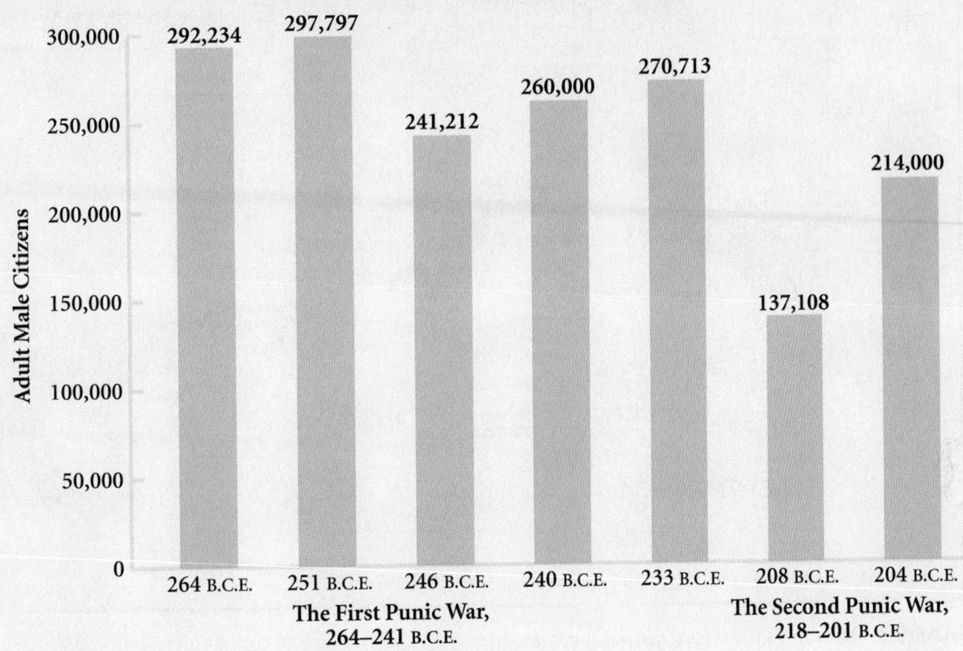

Writing hundreds of years apart, Livy (59 B.C.E.–17 C.E.) and Jerome (c. 347–420 C.E.) provide these numbers from Rome's censuses, which counted only adult male citizens (the men eligible for Rome's regular army), conducted during and between the first two wars against Carthage. Since the census did not include the Italian allies fighting on Rome's side, the census numbers understate the wars' total casualties; scholars estimate that they took the lives of nearly a third of Italy's adult male population, which would have meant perhaps a quarter of a million soldiers killed.

Source: Tenney Frank, *An Economic Survey of Ancient Rome*, vol. 1 (New York: Farrar, Straus and Giroux, 1959), 56.

Question to Consider

■ **What effects do you think the population changes shown in this graph might have had on Roman society?**

First Wars Abroad Rome's three wars with Carthage are called the Punic Wars (from the Latin word for "Phoenician"). The first one (264–241 B.C.E.) erupted over Sicily, where Carthage wanted to preserve its trading settlements and Rome wanted to prevent Carthaginian troops from being close to their territory. This long conflict revealed why the Romans won wars: the large Italian population provided deep manpower reserves, and the Roman government was prepared to sacrifice as many troops, spend as much money, and fight as long as it took to defeat the enemy. Previously unskilled at naval warfare, the Romans expended vast sums to build warships to combat Carthage's experienced navy; they lost more than five hundred ships and 250,000 men while learning how to win at sea. (See "Taking Measure," above.)

The Romans' victory in the First Punic War made them masters of Sicily, where they set up their first province (a foreign territory ruled and taxed by Roman officials). This innovation proved so profitable that they soon seized the islands of Sardinia and Corsica from the Carthaginians to create another province. These first successful foreign conquests increased the Romans' appetite for expansion outside Italy (Map 5.3). Fearing a renewal

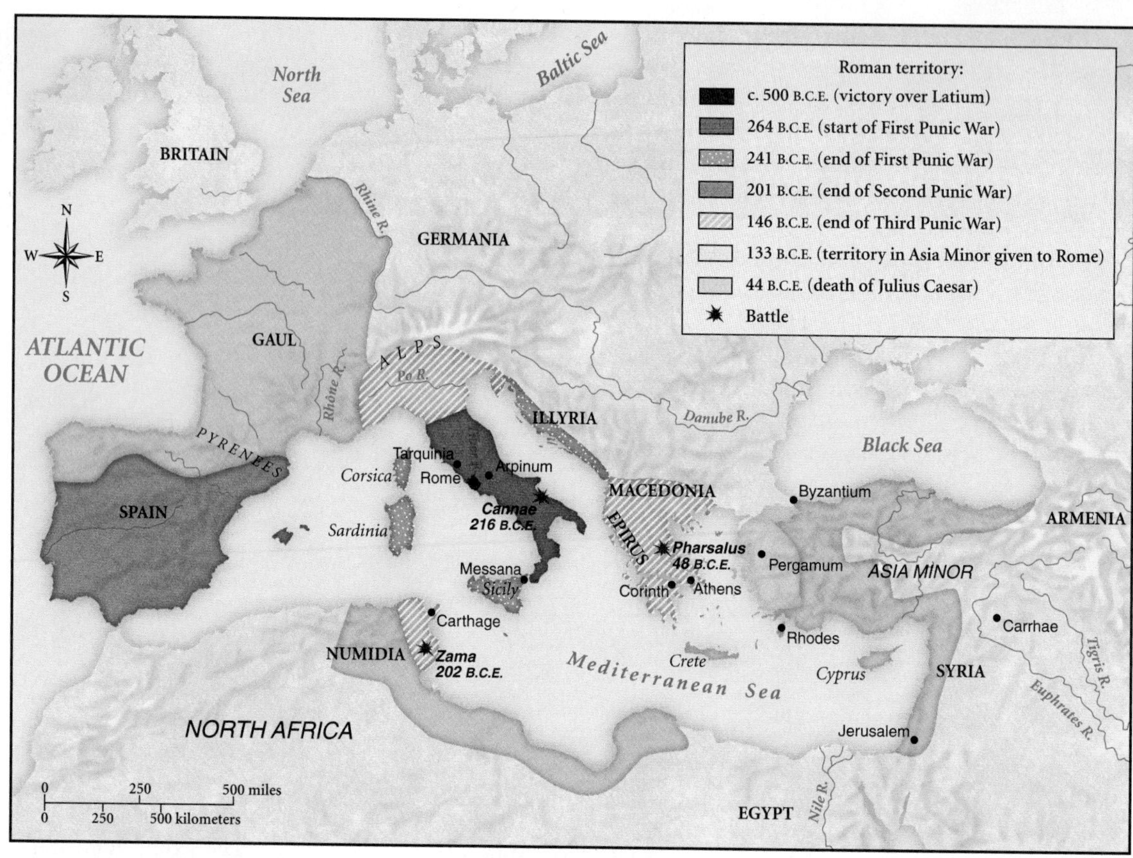

MAP 5.3 Roman Expansion, 500–44 B.C.E.
During its first two centuries, the Roman republic used war and diplomacy to extend its power north and south in the Italian peninsula. In the third and second centuries B.C.E., conflict with Carthage in the south and west and the Hellenistic kingdoms in the east extended Roman power outside Italy and led to the creation of provinces from Spain to Greece. The first century B.C.E. saw the conquest of Syria by Pompey and of Gaul by Julius Caesar (d. 44 B.C.E.).

of Carthage's power, the Romans cemented alliances with local peoples in Spain, where the Carthaginians were expanding from their southern trading posts.

A Roman ultimatum forbidding further expansion convinced the Carthaginians that another war was inevitable, so they decided to strike back. In the Second Punic War (218–201 B.C.E.), the daring Carthaginian general Hannibal terrified the Romans by marching troops and war elephants over the Alps into Italy. Slaughtering more than thirty thousand at Cannae in 216 B.C.E. in the bloodiest Roman loss ever, Hannibal tried to convince Rome's Italian allies to desert, but most refused to rebel. Hannibal's alliance in 215 B.C.E. with the king of Macedonia forced the Romans to fight on a second front in Greece. Still, they refused to crack despite Hannibal's ravaging of Italy from 218 to 203 B.C.E. Then the Romans turned the tables: invading the Carthaginians' African homeland, the Roman army prevailed at the battle of Zama in 202 B.C.E. The Senate imposed a punishing settlement on the enemy in 201 B.C.E., forcing Carthage to scuttle its navy, pay huge war indemnities, and hand over its lucrative holdings in Spain, which Rome made into provinces prosperous from their mines.

Dominance in the Mediterranean

The Third Punic War (149–146 B.C.E.) began when the Carthaginians, who had revived financially, retaliated against the aggression of the king of Numidia, a Roman ally. After winning the war, the Romans heeded the crusty senator Cato's repeated opinion, "Carthage must be destroyed!" They obliterated the city and converted its territory into a province. This disaster did not destroy Carthaginian culture, however, and under the Roman Empire this part of North Africa flourished economically and intellectually, creating a synthesis of Roman and Carthaginian traditions.

The Punic War victories extended Roman power beyond Spain and North Africa to Macedonia, Greece, and western Asia Minor. Hannibal's alliance with the king of Macedonia had brought Roman troops east of Italy for the first time. After defeating the Macedonian king for revenge and to prevent any threat of his invading Italy, the Roman commander proclaimed the "freedom of the Greeks" in 196 B.C.E. to show respect for Greece's glorious past. The Greek cities and federal leagues understood the proclamation to mean that they, as "friends" of Rome, could behave as they liked. They misunderstood. The Romans expected them to behave as clients and follow their new patrons' advice.

The Romans repeatedly intervened to make the kingdom of Macedonia and the Greeks observe their obligations as clients. The Senate in 146 B.C.E. ordered Corinth destroyed for asserting its independence and converted Macedonia and Greece into a province. In 133 B.C.E., the Attalid king increased Roman power with a stupendous gift: in his will he bequeathed his Asia Minor kingdom to Rome. In 121 B.C.E., the Romans made the lower part of Gaul across the Alps (modern southern France) into a province. By the late first century B.C.E., then, Rome governed and profited from two-thirds of the Mediterranean region; only the easternmost Mediterranean lay outside its control (see Map 5.3).

Comparison of Ancient Greek and Roman Developments, c. 750 B.C.E.–146 B.C.E.

	Greece	Rome
753 B.C.E.		Traditional date for the founding of Rome
750 B.C.E.	Polis begins to develop	
750–700 B.C.E.	First Greek poetry (Homer and Hesiod)	
509 B.C.E.		Overthrow of monarchy and establishment of the republic
508–500 B.C.E.	Cleisthenes' reforms to strengthen Athenian democracy	
500–450 B.C.E.		Struggle to establish office of tribune to protect the people
461 B.C.E.	Ephialtes' reforms to democratize Athens's courts	
451–449 B.C.E.		Rome's first law code established (Twelve Tables)
420s B.C.E.	The first Greek history (Herodotus)	
240–210 B.C.E.		First poetry in Latin (translation of Homer's *Odyssey*)
200 B.C.E.		First Roman history in Greek
168–149 B.C.E.		First Roman history in Latin (Cato)
146 B.C.E.	Rome makes Greece a province	

Greek Influence on Roman Literature and the Arts

Roman imperialism generated extensive cross-cultural contact with Greece. Although Romans looked down on Greeks for their military weakness, Roman authors and artists found inspiration in Greek literature and art. About 200 B.C.E., the first Roman historian used Greek to write his narrative of Rome's foundation and the wars with Carthage. The earliest Latin poetry was a translation of Homer's *Odyssey* by a Greek ex-slave, composed sometime after the First Punic War.

Roman literature combined the foreign and the familiar. Many famous early Latin authors were not native Romans but came from different regions of Italy, Sicily, and even North Africa. All found inspiration in Greek literature. Roman comedies, for example, took their plots and stock characters from Hellenistic comedy such as that of Menander, which featured jokes about family life and stereotyped personalities, such as the braggart warrior and the obsessed lover. (See the sculpture on page 156.)

Some Romans distrusted the effect of Greek culture on their own. In the mid-second century B.C.E., Cato, although he studied Greek himself, thundered against the influence of the "weakling" Greeks on the "sturdy" Romans. His history of Rome, *The Origins*, and his instructions on running a large farm, *On Agriculture*, established Latin prose. Cato predicted that if the Romans ever adopted Greek values, they would lose their power. In truth, despite its debt to Greek literature, early Latin literature reflected traditional Roman values. For example, the pathbreaking Latin epic *Annals*, a poetic version of Roman history by the poet Ennius, shows the influence of Greek epic but praises ancestral Roman traditions, as in this famous line: "On the ways and the men of old rests the Roman state."

Later Roman writers also took inspiration from Greek literature in both content and style. The first-century B.C.E. poet Lucretius wrote *On the Nature of Things* to persuade people not to fear death, a terror that only inflamed "the running sores of life." His ideas reflected Greek philosophy's "atomic theory," which said that matter was composed of tiny, invisible particles. Dying, the poem taught, simply meant the dissolving of the union of atoms, which had come together temporarily to make up a person's body. There could be no eternal punishment or pain after death, indeed no existence at all, because a person's soul, itself made up of atoms, perished along with the body.

Hellenistic Greek authors inspired Catullus in the first century B.C.E. to write witty poems ridiculing prominent politicians for their sexual behavior (see Document 2 in "Contrasting Views," page 162)

Actors in a Comedy

This sculpture from the first century C.E. shows actors portraying characters in one of the several kinds of comedy popular during the Roman republic. In this variety, which derived from Hellenistic comedy, the actors wore exaggerated masks designating stock personality types and acted broad, slapstick comedy. The plots ranged from burlesques of famous myths to stereotypes of family problems. Here, on the right, a son returns home after a night of binge drinking, leaning on his slave and accompanied by a hired female musician. On the left, his enraged father is being restrained by a friend from beating his drunken son with a cane. *(Scala/Art Resource, NY.)*

and lamenting his own disastrous love life. His most famous love poems revealed his obsession with a married woman named Lesbia, whom he begged to think only of immediate pleasures:

> Let us live, my Lesbia, and love; the gossip of stern old men is not worth a cent. Suns can set and rise again; we, when once our brief light has set, must sleep one never-ending night. Give me a thousand kisses, then a hundred, then a thousand more.

The orator and politician **Cicero** (106–43 B.C.E.) wrote speeches, letters, and treatises on political science, philosophy, ethics, and theology. He adapted Greek philosophy to Roman life and stressed the need to appreciate each person's uniqueness. His doctrine of ***humanitas*** ("humaneness, the quality of humanity") expressed an ideal for human life based on generous and honest treatment of others and a commitment to morality based on natural law (the rights that belong to all people because they are human beings, independent of the differing laws and customs of different societies). The spirit of humanitas that Cicero passed on to later Western civilization was one of the ancient world's most attractive ideals.

Greece also influenced Rome's art and architecture, from the style of sculpture and painting to the design of public buildings. Romans adapted Greek models to their own purposes, as portrait sculpture reveals. Hellenistic sculptors had pioneered a realistic style showing the ravages of age and infirmity on the human body. They portrayed only stereotypes, however, such as the "old man" or the "drunken woman," not specific people. Their portrait sculpture presented actual individuals in the best possible light, much like an airbrushed photograph today.

Roman artists applied Greek realism to male portraiture, as contemporary Etruscan sculptors also did. They sculpted men without hiding their unflattering features: long noses, receding chins, deep wrinkles, bald heads, careworn looks. Portraits of women, by contrast, were more idealized, probably representing the traditional vision of the bliss of family life (see the image of the sculpted family tomb on page 142). Because the men depicted in the portraits (or their families) paid for the busts, they must have wanted their faces sculpted realistically—showing the damage of age and effort—to emphasize how hard they had worked to serve the republic.

Stresses on Society from Imperialism

The wars of the third and second centuries B.C.E. proved disastrous for small farmers, confronting the republic with grave social and economic difficulties. The long deployments of troops abroad disrupted Rome's agricultural system, the economy's foundation. Before this time, Roman warfare had followed a pattern of short campaigns timed not to interfere with farmers' work. Now, however, a farmer absent during a protracted war had two unhappy choices: rely on a hired hand or slave to manage his crops and animals, or have his wife perform farmwork in addition to her usual domestic tasks.

The story of the consul Regulus, who won a great victory in Africa in 256 B.C.E., revealed the problems prolonged absence caused. When the man who managed Regulus's farm died while the consul was away fighting, a worker stole all the farm's tools and livestock. Regulus begged the Senate to send a replacement fighter so that he could return to save his wife and children from starving. The senators instead sent help to preserve Regulus's family and

---

Cicero (SIH suh roh): Rome's most famous orator and author of the doctrine of *humanitas*.

humanitas: The Roman orator Cicero's ideal of "humaneness," meaning generous and honest treatment of others based on natural law.

property because they wanted to keep him on the battle lines.

The Poor Ordinary soldiers could expect no special aid, and economic troubles hit their families particularly hard when, in the second century B.C.E., for reasons that remain unclear, there was not enough farmland to support the population. Scholars have usually concluded that the rich had deprived the poor of land, but recent research suggests that the problem stemmed from an unexplained increase in the number of births of young people. Not all regions of Italy suffered as severely as others, and some impoverished farmers and their families managed to survive by working as agricultural laborers for others. Still, the number of poor people with no way to make a living created a social crisis by the late second century B.C.E. Many homeless people relocated to Rome, where the men begged for work as day laborers and women sought piecework making cloth but often had to become prostitutes to survive.

This flood of desperate people increased the poverty-level population of Rome, and the landless poor became an explosive swing element in Roman politics. They backed any politician who promised to address their need for food, and the government had to feed them to avert riots. Like Athens in the fifth century B.C.E., Rome by the late second century B.C.E. needed to import grain to feed its swollen urban population. The poor's demand for low-priced (and eventually free) food distributed at state expense became one of the most divisive issues in late republican politics.

The Rich While the landless poor struggled, imperialism brought Rome's elite ample political and financial rewards. The need for commanders to lead military campaigns abroad created opportunities for successful generals to enrich their families. The elite enhanced their reputations by using their gains to finance public works that benefited the general population. Building new temples, for example, was thought to increase everyone's security because the Romans believed it pleased their gods to have many shrines. In 146 B.C.E., a victorious general paid for Rome's first marble temple, finally bringing this Greek style to the capital city.

Bedroom in a Rich Roman House

This bedroom from about 40 B.C.E. was in the house of a rich Roman family near Naples; it was buried—and preserved—by the eruption of the volcano Vesuvius in 79 C.E. The bright paintings showed a dazzling variety of outdoor scenes and architecture. The stone floor helped create a sensation of coolness in the summer. *(Cubiculum [bedroom] from the Villa of P. Fannius Synistor at Boscoreale, ca. 50–40 B.C.E. Fresco, Room: 8 ft. ½ in. x 10 ft .11½ in. x 19 ft. 7⅛ in. [265.4 x 334 x 583.9 cm.] Rogers Fund, 1903 [03.14.13a-g]. Location: the Metropolitan Museum of Art, New York, NY, U.S.A. Image copyright © The Metropolitan Museum of Art/Art Resource, NY.)*

The economic distress of small farmers benefited rich landowners because they could buy bankrupt farms to create large estates. They further increased their holdings by illegally occupying public land carved out of the territory seized from defeated enemies. The rich worked their huge farms, called *latifundia*, with free laborers as well as slaves, a ready supply of which were available from the huge numbers taken captive in the same wars that displaced so many farmers. Thus, the victories won by free but poor Roman citizens created a slave workforce with which they could not compete. The growing size of the slave crews working on latifundia was a mixed blessing for their wealthy owners. Although the owners did not have to pay these laborers, the presence of so many slave workers in one place led to periodic revolts that required military intervention.

The elite profited from Rome's expansion by filling the governing offices in the new provinces. Some governors ruled honestly, but others used their power to squeeze the provincials. Since provincial officials ruled by martial law, no one in the provinces could curb a greedy governor's appetite for graft, extortion, and landgrabbing. Often such offenders faced no punishment because their colleagues in the Senate excused their crimes.

The new opportunities for rich living strained the traditional values of moderation and frugality. Previously, a man could become legendary for his life's simplicity: Manius Curius (d. 270 B.C.E.), for example, boiled turnips for his meals in a humble hut despite his glorious military victories. Now, in the second century B.C.E., the elite acquired showy luxuries, such as large country villas for entertaining friends and clients. Money had become more valuable to them than the ancestral values of the republic.

REVIEW QUESTION What advantages and disadvantages did Rome's victories over foreign peoples create for both rich and poor Romans?

Civil War and the Destruction of the Republic

Beginning in the late second century B.C.E., members of the Roman upper class set in motion a series of events that for the next century turned politics into a violent competition. This conflict exploded into civil wars in the first century that destroyed the republic. Senators introduced violence to politics by murdering the tribunes Tiberius and Gaius Gracchus when the brothers pushed for reforms to help the poor by giving them land. When a would-be member of the elite, Gaius Marius, opened military service to the poor to boost his personal status, his creation of "client armies" undermined faithfulness to the general good of the community. The people's unwillingness to share citizenship with Italian allies sparked a damaging war in Italy. Finally, the out-of-control competition for leadership and power by the "great men" Sulla, Pompey, and Julius Caesar peaked in destructive civil wars.

The Gracchus Brothers and Violence in Politics, 133–121 B.C.E.

Tiberius and Gaius Gracchus based their political careers on pressing the rich to make concessions to strengthen the state. They came from the cream of Roman society: their grandfather had defeated Hannibal, and their mother was the Cornelia whom the king of Egypt had courted. Their policies supporting the poor angered many of their fellow members of the social elite. Tiberius explained the tragic circumstances that motivated them politically:

> The wild beasts that roam over Italy have their dens. . . . But the men who fight and die for Italy enjoy nothing but the air and light. They wander about homeless with their wives and children. . . . They fight and die to protect the wealth and luxury of others. They are called masters of the world, and have not a lump of earth they call their own.

When Tiberius won election as a tribune in 133 B.C.E., his opponents blocked his attempts at reform. He then took the radical step of disregarding the Senate's advice by having the Plebeian Assembly pass reform laws to redistribute public land to landless Romans. He again broke with tradition by ignoring the Senate in financing his farming reforms: he convinced the people pass a law to use the Attalid king's gift of his kingdom to equip new farms on the redistributed land.

Tiberius next announced he would run for reelection as tribune for the following year, violating the prohibition against consecutive terms. His opponents had had enough: Tiberius's cousin, an ex-consul, led a band of senators and their clients in a sudden attack on him, shouting, "Save the republic." Pulling up their togas over their left arms so they would not trip in a fight, they clubbed the tribune to death, along with many of his supporters and clients.

Gaius, whom the people elected tribune for 123 B.C.E. and, contrary to tradition, again for the next year, also pushed measures that outraged his fellow elite: more farming reforms, subsidized prices for grain, public works projects to employ the poor, and colonies abroad with farms for the landless. His most revolutionary measures proposed Roman citizenship for many Italians and new courts to try senators accused of corruption as provincial governors. The new juries would be manned not by senators but by ***equites*** ("equestrians" or "knights"). These were elite landowners who, in the earliest republic, had been men rich enough to provide horses for cavalry service but were now wealthy businessmen, whose careers in commerce instead of government made their interests different from the senators'. Because they did not serve in the Senate, the equites could convict senators for crimes without having to face peer pressure. Gaius's proposal marked the equites' emergence as a political force in Roman politics, angering the Senate.

When in 121 B.C.E. the senators blocked Gaius's plans, he assembled an armed group to threaten them. They responded by advising the consuls "to take all measures necessary to defend the republic," meaning the use of force to kill anyone identified, rightly or wrongly, as a threat to public order. When his enemies came to murder him, Gaius robbed them of their prize and proved his courage by committing suicide in dramatic fashion: he had one of his slaves cut his throat. The senators then killed hundreds of his supporters and their servants.

The violence from this conflict introduced factions (strongly aggressive interest groups) into Roman politics. From that point on, members of the elite identified themselves as either supporters of the people, the ***populares*** faction, or supporters of "the best," the ***optimates*** faction. Some chose a faction from genuine allegiance to its policies; others supported whichever side better promoted their own political advancement. The elite's splintering into bitterly hostile factions remained a source of murderous political violence until the end of the republic.

equites **(EHK wih tehs):** Literally, "equestrians" or "knights"; wealthy Roman businessmen who chose not to pursue a government career.

populares **(poh poo LAH rehs):** The Roman political faction supporting the common people; established during the late republic.

optimates **(op tee MAH tehs):** The Roman political faction supporting the "best," or highest, social class; established during the late republic.

Marius and the Origin of Client Armies, 107–100 B.C.E.

The republic needed innovative commanders to combat slave revolts and foreign invasions in the late second and early first centuries B.C.E. A new kind of leader arose to meet this need: the "new man," an upper-class man without a consul among his ancestors, who relied on sheer ability and often political violence to force his way to fame, fortune, and—his ultimate goal—the consulship.

Gaius Marius (c. 157–86 B.C.E.), who came from the equites class, set the pattern for this new kind of leader. Ordinarily, a man of Marius's status had no chance to crack the ranks of Rome's ruling oligarchy. Gaining fame for his brilliant military record as a junior officer and relying on voters' anger at the current war leadership, Marius won election as a consul for 107 B.C.E. In Roman terms this election made him a "new man"—that is, the first man in his family's history to become consul. Marius's continuing success as a commander, first in North Africa and next against German tribes who attacked southern France and then Italy, led the people to elect him consul six times, breaking all tradition.

For his victories, the Senate voted Marius a triumph, Rome's ultimate military honor. In the ceremony, huge crowds cheered him as he rode in a chariot through the streets of Rome. His soldiers shouted obscene jokes about him, to ward off the evil eye at this moment of supreme glory. For a former small-town member of the equites class like Marius, this honor was a supreme social coup. Yet, despite Marius's triumph, the optimates never accepted him as one of them. His support came from the common people, whom he had won over with his revolutionary reform of entrance requirements for the army. Previously, only men with property could usually enroll as soldiers. Marius opened the ranks to **proletarians**, men who had no property and could not afford weapons on their own. For them, serving in the army meant an opportunity to better their lot by acquiring booty and a grant of land. (See Document, "Polybius on Roman Military Discipline," page 160.)

Marius's reform changed Roman history by creating armies more loyal to their commander than to the republic. Proletarian troops felt immense goodwill toward a commander who led them to victory and then divided the spoils with them generously. The crowds of poor Roman soldiers thus began to behave like an army of clients following

proletarians: In the Roman republic, the mass of people so poor they owned no property.

DOCUMENT

Polybius on Roman Military Discipline

Polybius, a Greek commander who spent years on campaign with Roman armies in the second century B.C.E., describes the ideal centurion (an experienced soldier appointed to discipline the troops). He also notes the importance of harsh punishments and the fear of disgrace and shame for maintaining military discipline.

The Romans want centurions not so much to be bold and eager to take risks but rather to be capable of leadership and steady and solid in character. Nor do they want them to start attacks and start battles. They want men who will hold their position and stay in place even when they are losing the battle and will die to hold their ground. . . . Soldiers [convicted of neglecting sentry duty] who manage to live [after being beaten or stoned as punishment] don't thereby secure their safety. How could they? For they are not permitted to return to their homeland, and none of their relatives would dare to accept such a man into their households. For this reason men who have once fallen into this misfortune are completely ruined. . . . Even when clearly at risk of being wiped out by enormously superior enemy forces, troops in tactical reserve units are not willing to desert their places in the battle line, for fear of the punishment that would be inflicted by their own side. Some men who have lost a shield or sword or another part of their arms in battle heedlessly throw themselves against the enemy, hoping either to recover what they lost, or to escape the inevitable disgrace and the insults of their relatives by suffering [injury or death].

Source: Polybius, *Histories*, Book 6.24, 37. Translation by Thomas R. Martin.

Question to Consider

■ **What purpose does punishment serve in the maintenance of a fighting army, according to Polybius?**

their commander as patron. In keeping with the patron-client system, they supported his personal ambitions. Marius was the first to promote his own career in this way. He lost his political importance after 100 B.C.E. when, no longer consul, he tried but failed to win the backing of the optimates. Commanders after Marius used client armies to advance their political careers more ruthlessly than he had, thereby accelerating the republic's destruction.

Sulla and Civil War, 91–78 B.C.E.

One such commander, Lucius Cornelius Sulla (c. 138–78 B.C.E.), took advantage of uprisings by non-Romans in Italy and Asia Minor in the early first century B.C.E. to use his client army to seize Rome's highest offices and force the Senate to support his policies. His career revealed the dirty secret of politics in the late republic: traditional values no longer restrained commanders who—above peace and the good of the community—prized their own advancement and the enriching of their troops.

The Social War The uprisings in Italy occurred because many of Rome's Italian allies lacked Roman citizenship and therefore had no vote in decisions concerning their own interests. They became increasingly unhappy as wealth from conquests piled up in the late republic. Their upper classes wanted a greater share of the prosperity that war had brought to the citizen elite. The Roman people rejected the allies' demand for citizenship, from fear that sharing such status would lessen their own privileges.

The Italians' discontent erupted in 91–87 B.C.E. in the Social War (so named because the Latin word for "ally" is *socius*). Forming a confederacy to fight Rome, the allies demonstrated their commitment by the number of their casualties—300,000 dead. Although Rome's army prevailed, the rebels won the political war: the Romans granted citizenship and the vote to all freeborn people in Italy south of the Po River. The Social War's bloodshed therefore reestablished Rome's tradition of strengthening the state by granting citizenship to outsiders. The war's other significant outcome was that Sulla's successful generalship won him election as consul for 88 B.C.E.

Plunder Abroad and Violence at Home Sulla gained supreme power by taking advantage of events in Asia Minor in 88 B.C.E., when Mithridates VI (120–63 B.C.E.), king of Pontus on the Black Sea's southern coast, rebelled against Roman control. The peoples of Asia Minor hated Rome's tax collectors, who tried to make provincials pay much more than was required. Denouncing the Romans as "the common enemies of all mankind," Mithridates persuaded the locals to kill all the Italians there—tens of thousands of them—in a single day.

The Senate advised a military expedition to punish this treachery. Victory would mean capturing unimaginable booty from Asia Minor's wealthy cities. Born to a patrician family that had lost much of its status and all of its money, Sulla craved the command. When the Senate gave it to him, his jealous rival Marius, now an old man, immediately plotted to have it transferred to himself by plebiscite. Outraged, Sulla did the unthinkable: he marched his client army against Rome itself. All his officers except one deserted him in horror at this shameful attack, but his common soldiers followed him to a man. Neither they nor their commander shrank from starting a civil war. After capturing Rome, Sulla killed or exiled his opponents. He let his men rampage through the city and then led them off to Asia Minor, ignoring a summons to stand trial and sacking Athens on the way. In Sulla's absence, Marius embarked on his own reign of terror in Rome to try to regain his former power. In 83 B.C.E., Sulla returned victorious, having allowed his soldiers to plunder Asia Minor. Civil war erupted for two years until Sulla crushed his enemies at home.

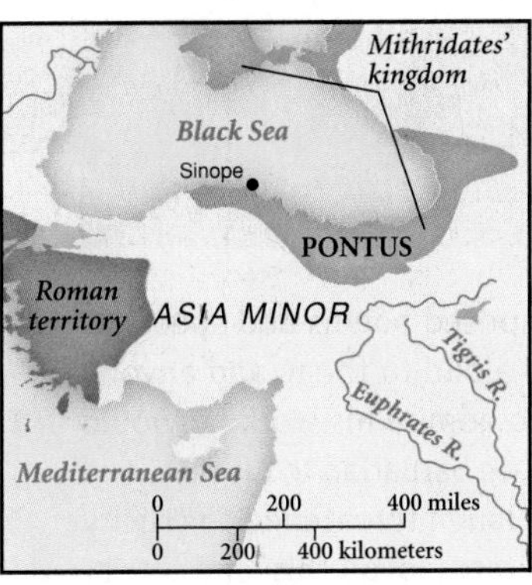

The Kingdom of Mithridates VI, 88 B.C.E.

Sulla then exterminated everyone who had opposed him. To speed the process, he devised a procedure called proscription—posting a list of people accused of being traitors so that anyone could hunt them down and execute them. Because proscribed men's property was confiscated, the victors fraudulently added to the list anyone whose wealth they coveted. The terrorized Senate appointed Sulla dictator—an emergency office supposed to be held only temporarily—and gave him permanent immunity from prosecution. As dictator, Sulla reorganized the government to favor the optimates—his social class—by making senators the only ones allowed to judge cases against their colleagues and forbidding tribunes from sponsoring legislation or holding any other office after their term.

The Effects of Sulla's Career

Sulla died before he could remake the republic's government, but his murderous career revealed the strengths and weaknesses of Roman values. First, the purpose of war had changed from defending the community to accumulating plunder for common soldiers as well as commanders. Second, the patron-client system led proletarian soldiers to feel stronger ties of obligation to their generals than to the republic.

Finally, the traditional competition for status worked both for and against political stability. When that value motivated men to seek office to promote the community's welfare—the traditional ideal of a public career—it exerted a powerful force for social unity and prosperity. But pushed to its extreme, as in the case of Sulla, the contest for individual prestige and wealth pulled the republic apart.

Julius Caesar and the Collapse of the Republic, 83–44 B.C.E.

Powerful generals after Sulla took him as their model: while declaring their loyalty to the community, they ruthlessly pursued their own advancement. Two Roman aristocrats' competition for power and money led to the civil war that brought the final destruction of the republic and opened the way for the return of monarchy. Those competitors were Gnaeus Pompey and Julius Caesar. (See "Contrasting Views," page 162.)

Pompey's Tradition-Shattering Career

Pompey (106–48 B.C.E.) was a better general than a politician. In his early twenties he won victories supporting Sulla. In 71 B.C.E., Pompey won the mop-up battles defeating a massive slave rebellion led by a fugitive gladiator named Spartacus, stealing the glory from the real victor, Marcus Licinius Crassus. (Spartacus had terrorized southern Italy for two years and defeated consuls with his army of 100,000 escaped slaves.) Pompey shattered tradition by demanding and receiving a consulship for 70 B.C.E., even though he was nowhere near the legal age of forty-two and had not been elected to any lower post on the ladder of offices. Three years later, he received a command with unlimited powers to exterminate the pirates then infesting the Mediterranean, a task he accomplished in a matter of months. This success made him wildly popular with many groups: the urban poor, who depended on a steady flow of imported grain; merchants, who depended on safe sea lanes; and coastal communities, which were vulnerable to pirates' raids. In 66 B.C.E., he defeated Mithridates, who was still stirring up trouble in Asia Minor. By annexing Syria as a province in 64 B.C.E., Pompey ended the Seleucid kingdom and extended Rome's power to the Mediterranean's eastern coast.

People compared Pompey to Alexander the Great and added *Magnus* ("the Great") to his name.

CONTRASTING VIEWS

What Was Julius Caesar Like?

Julius Caesar provoked strong reactions among people: some loved him, some hated him, some ridiculed him (Document 2), and some changed their minds (Document 3)—but only fools failed to recognize his extraordinary energy and will (Document 1). These excerpts, including one in his own words (Document 4), offer sample assessments of what different sources said this most famous Roman was like. The biographer Suetonius described both Caesar's strengths and faults (Document 5).

1. Caesar and the Pirates

About a century and a half after Caesar's death, the Greek scholar Plutarch wrote a biography to reveal the famous leader's character. He tells this story of Caesar as an eighteen-year-old (well before he became famous) refusing the dictator Sulla's politically motivated order to divorce his wife. When the teenage Caesar fled Rome to escape being murdered by Sulla's henchmen, he was captured by pirates while trying to get to safety in Asia Minor.

[To escape Sulla], Caesar sailed to King Nicomedes in Bithynia (in Asia Minor). On his voyage home, pirates from Cilicia captured him and held him on an island. When they demanded twenty talents [a huge sum] for his ransom, he laughed at them for not knowing who he was, and spontaneously promised to give them fifty talents instead. Next, after he had dispatched friends to various cities to gather the money, he had only one friend and two attendants left while a captive of the most murderous men in the world. Nevertheless, he felt so superior to them that whenever he wanted to sleep, he would order them to be quiet.

For thirty-eight days, as if the pirates were not his kidnappers but rather his bodyguards, he participated in their games and exercises with a carefree spirit. He also composed poems and speeches that he read aloud to them, and anyone who failed to admire his work he would call an illiterate barbarian to his face, and often with a laugh threatened to crucify them. The pirates loved this, and attributed his free speech to simplemindedness and youthful spirit.

After Caesar had paid the ransom and was released, he immediately manned ships and put to sea against the pirates. He caught them still anchored, and captured most of them. He took their loot as his booty and threw the men into prison, telling the Roman provincial governor that it was his job to punish them. But since the governor had his eyes on the pirates' rich loot and kept saying that he would consider their case when he had time, Caesar took the pirates out of prison and crucified them all, just as he had often warned them on the island that he was going to do, when they thought he was joking.

Source: Plutarch, *Life of Julius Caesar*, 1–2 (excerpted). Translation by Thomas R. Martin.

2. A Poet Mocks Caesar about Sex

*In about 58 B.C.E., the twenty-something Catullus ridiculed Caesar (in his early forties) and his follower Mamurra in several acid-tongued poems. The biographer Suetonius (*Life of Julius Caesar *73) reports that Caesar said the ridicule inflicted a permanent blot on his name, but that when Catullus apologized, Caesar invited the poet to dinner that very same day.*

They're a pretty good match, those fags,
Mamurra and that queer, Caesar.
And no wonder. They've both got the
  same stains,
One of them a City guy and the other
  from Formiae,
And they won't wash out.
One's just as sick as the other, those
  twins,
Two little brainiacs on the same little
  couch,
This one's just as greedy an adulterer as
  the other,
They're allies competing even for little
  girlies;
So, they're a pretty good match,
  those fags.

Source: Catullus, Poem 57. Translation by Thomas R. Martin.

3. Cicero Writes to a Friend about Caesar

Cicero, Rome's most famous orator, wrote many private letters that have survived. In this one, written to his friend Atticus a few days after Caesar began the civil war by crossing the Rubicon River in January 49 B.C.E., Cicero worriedly expresses his opinion of Caesar at the time.

What's going on? I'm in the dark. . . . That awful fool Caesar, who has never had even the slightest thought of "the good and the fair"! He claims he's doing all this for the sake of honor? But how can you have honor if you have no ethics? Is it ethical to lead an army without official confirmation of your command, to capture cities of Roman citizens to force your way more easily to our mother city, to plot abolition of debts and the recall of exiles, a thousand outrages, "all to obtain the greatest of divinities, sole rule"?

In this letter, written on March 1 of the same year, Cicero offers a different opinion.

Just look at the kind of man who has taken over the republic: clear thinking, sharp, on the ball. By god, if he doesn't murder anyone and doesn't take away people's property, the very people who lived in fear of him will worship him the most.

Source: Cicero, *Letters to Atticus*, 7.11, 8.13. Translation by Thomas R. Martin.

4. Caesar Explains Why He Fought the Civil War

In his memoirs, Caesar provided his own account of the civil war that made him Rome's most powerful man. Here he reports what he said to the Senate on April 1, 49 B.C.E., after Pompey left the capital and Caesar took it without a struggle. In his own writings Caesar refers to himself in the third person (i.e., the he *in this excerpt is Caesar).*

A meeting of the Senate convened, and he spoke about the wrongs his enemies had done him. He explained that he had only wanted a usual office [i.e., consul] . . . and was content with what any citizen could obtain. . . . He emphasized his moderation in asking on his own initiative that both his army and Pompey's be disbanded [to prevent war], a concession that would have cost him both status and office. He talked about how bitter his enemies had been . . . and how they had not laid down their command and armies, even at the cost of anarchy. He stressed how unfair they had been to try to deprive him of his legions, and how savage and arrogant in putting restrictions on the tribunes [who favored him]. He spoke about the offers he had made, the meeting that he had suggested but they had rejected. Given all this, he encouraged, he asked the Senators to take responsibility for the state and govern it together with him. But, he added, if they ran away out of fear, he would not run away from the job and would govern the state by himself. His opinion was that the Senate should send delegates to Pompey to arrange a settlement; he was not cowed by Pompey's recent remark in the Senate that to receive a delegation implied authority but sending it implied fear. That sort of thought revealed a weak and superficial spirit. He, by contrast, wished to win the competition to be just and fair in the same way in which he had striven to excel in his achievements.

Source: Julius Caesar, *The Civil War*, 1.32. Translation by Thomas R. Martin.

5. A Biographer Describes Caesar's Character

These excerpts about Caesar's character and behavior come from Suetonius's biography, written about 150 years after Caesar's assassination.

Caesar was somewhat overly concerned with how he looked, and he always had a careful haircut and shave, and even had excess hair removed. . . . His baldness embarrassed him because his enemies made fun of it. He therefore used to comb his little remaining hair forward, and more than any other honor bestowed by the Senate and people he treasured and used the right to wear a wreath of laurel leaves on his head all the time. . . .

The only sexual impropriety in his reputation was his relationship with the king of Bythinia, but that accusation was serious and lasted; everybody insulted him about it. . . . He seduced lots of women . . . and had love affairs with queens. . . . He drank only very little.

Both as a military commander and as a public official at Rome he used every trick to accumulate money. . . . As a public speaker and a general he either equaled or outstripped the fame of the most outstanding men of the past. . . . He wrote memoirs . . . which Cicero says "deserve the highest praise—they're simple and elegant at the same time."

On military campaigns he showed incredible endurance. . . . It's hard to say whether as a commander he relied more on caution or boldness because he never led his army into a spot where it could be ambushed without first making a careful scouting of the territory. . . . He never let concern for religious scruples deter him from action or slow him down. . . . Whenever his troops started to retreat, he often rallied them himself, using his body to block their way . . . even grabbing them by the throat and making them turn around to face the enemy. . . . He judged his soldiers not by their character or luck but only by how skilled they were, and he treated them all with the same strictness and the same indulgence. . . . He would sometimes overlook their mistakes and didn't punish them strictly according to the rules, but he always kept careful watch for soldiers deserting or mutinying, and these he punished with great harshness. . . . So, he made his men very devoted to him and also very brave.

Even as a young man he treated his clients faithfully. . . . He was always kind to his friends. . . . He never became so much of an enemy to anyone that he couldn't make them a friend when the chance came. . . . Even in seeking revenge he was naturally very merciful . . . and he certainly showed wonderful self-restraint and mercy while fighting the civil war and after he won. . . .

In the end, however, his other words and deeds outbalance all this, and there is the opinion that he abused his rule and that it was justice that he was murdered.

Source: Suetonius, *Life of Julius Caesar*, 45–76. Translation by Thomas R. Martin.

Questions to Consider

1. **How and why do a leader's personal characteristics matter for political success?**
2. **What methods can historians use to evaluate a leader when the evidence is inconsistent or conflicting?**

Bust of Pompey
Gnaeus Pompey (106–48 B.C.E.) became Julius Caesar's main political opponent, until Caesar defeated him in the civil war that destroyed the Roman republic. Pompey was a brilliant general, even when young. At twenty-three he raised a client army to fight on Sulla's side. So frightening was Pompey's power that Sulla could not refuse the youth's astonishing demand for a triumph—the ultimate military honor. Awarding the supreme honor to such a young man, who had held not a single public office, shattered the republic's traditions. But as Pompey told Sulla, "People worship the rising, not the setting, sun." *(Ny Carlsberg Glyptotek, Copenhagen, Denmark/The Bridgeman Art Library International.)*

His actions show the degree to which Roman foreign policy had become the personal business of "great men." He ignored the tradition of commanders consulting the Senate about conquering and administering foreign territories, behaving like an independent king rather than a Roman official. He summed up his attitude by replying to some foreigners who criticized his actions as unjust: "Stop quoting the laws to us," he told them. "We carry swords."

Pompey's enemies at Rome worked to undermine his popularity by seeking the people's support, proclaiming their concern for the problems of citizens in financial trouble. By the 60s B.C.E., Rome's urban population had soared to more than half a million. Hundreds of thousands of the poor lived crowded together in slum apartments, surviving on subsidized food distributions. Jobs were scarce. Danger haunted the streets because the city had no police force. Even many formerly wealthy property owners were in trouble: Sulla's confiscations had caused land values to plummet and produced a credit crunch by flooding the real estate market with properties for sale. Overextended investors were trying to borrow their way back to financial security, without success.

The First Triumvirate The senators, who saw the glory that Pompey won from his great military successes as posing a threat to their traditional status as the most important leaders at Rome, were especially eager to cut his power. They therefore blocked his reorganization of the former Seleucid kingdom and his distribution of land to his army veterans. Pompey therefore negotiated with his fiercest political rivals, Crassus and Caesar (100–44 B.C.E.). In 60 B.C.E., they formed an unofficial arrangement that historians call the **First Triumvirate** ("group of three"). Pompey then forced through laws confirming his earlier plans, thus reinforcing his status as a great patron. Caesar got the consulship for 59 B.C.E. and a special command in Gaul, where he could seize booty to build his own client army. Crassus received financial breaks for the Roman tax collectors in Asia Minor, who supported him politically and financially.

This coalition of political rivals revealed how private relationships had largely replaced communal values in politics. To cement their political bond, Caesar arranged to have his daughter, Julia, marry Pompey in 59 B.C.E., even though she had been engaged to another man. Pompey soothed Julia's jilted fiancé by offering the hand of his own daughter, who had been engaged to yet somebody else. Through these marital machinations, the two powerful antagonists now had a common interest: the fate of Julia, Caesar's only daughter and Pompey's new wife. (Pompey had earlier divorced his second wife after Caesar allegedly seduced her.) Pompey and Julia apparently fell deeply in love in their arranged marriage. As long as Julia lived, Pompey's affection for her kept him from breaking his alliance with her father.

Civil War During the 50s B.C.E., Caesar won his soldiers' loyalty with victories and plunder in Gaul, which he added to the Roman provinces, and he awed his troops with his boldness by crossing the channel to campaign in Britain. His political enemies in Rome dreaded him even more as his military successes mounted, and the bond allying him to Pompey shattered in 54 B.C.E. when Julia died in childbirth. The two leaders' rivalry then exploded into violence: gangs of their supporters battled each other in the streets of Rome. The violence became so bad in 53 B.C.E. that it was impossible to hold elections. The First Triumvirate soon dissolved, and in 52 B.C.E. Caesar's enemies convinced the Senate to make Pompey consul by himself, breaking the Republic's long tradition of two consuls sharing power at the head of the state.

First Triumvirate: The coalition formed in 60 B.C.E. by Pompey, Crassus, and Caesar. (The word *triumvirate* means "group of three.")

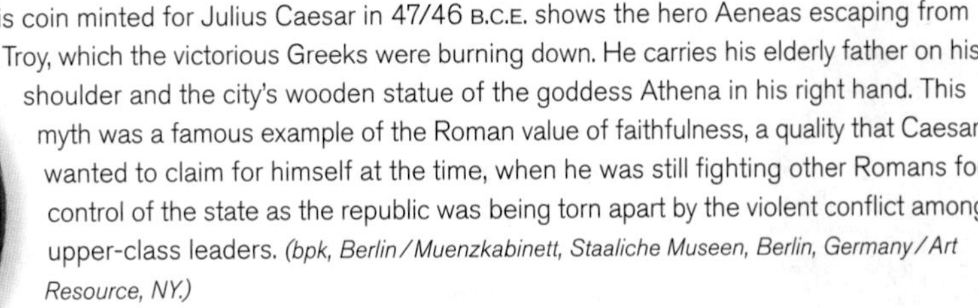

Escape from Troy on a Coin of Julius Caesar

This coin minted for Julius Caesar in 47/46 B.C.E. shows the hero Aeneas escaping from Troy, which the victorious Greeks were burning down. He carries his elderly father on his shoulder and the city's wooden statue of the goddess Athena in his right hand. This myth was a famous example of the Roman value of faithfulness, a quality that Caesar wanted to claim for himself at the time, when he was still fighting other Romans for control of the state as the republic was being torn apart by the violent conflict among upper-class leaders. *(bpk, Berlin/Muenzkabinett, Staaliche Museen, Berlin, Germany/Art Resource, NY.)*

Civil war exploded when the Senate ordered Caesar to surrender his command. Like Sulla, Caesar led his army against Rome. As he crossed the Rubicon River, the official northern boundary of Italy, in early 49 B.C.E., he uttered the famous words signaling that there was now no turning back: "Let's roll the dice." His troops followed him without hesitation, and the people in the countryside cheered him on. He had many backers in Rome, too: not only the masses counting on his legendary generosity for handouts but also impoverished members of the elite hoping to regain their fortunes through proscriptions of the rich.

The support for Caesar convinced Pompey and most senators, including the famous politician and orator Cicero, to flee to Greece. Caesar entered Rome peacefully, left to defeat the enemies he had in Spain, and then sailed to Greece. There he nearly lost the war when his supplies ran out, but his soldiers stayed loyal even when they were reduced to eating bread made from roots. When Pompey saw what Caesar's men were willing to live on, he cried, "I am fighting wild beasts." Caesar's nail-hard troops defeated the army of Pompey and the Senate at the battle of Pharsalus in central Greece in 48 B.C.E. Pompey fled to Egypt, where the ministers of the teenaged pharaoh Ptolemy XIII (63–47 B.C.E.) treacherously murdered him.

Caesar next invaded Egypt, winning a difficult campaign that ended when he restored Cleopatra VII (69–30 B.C.E.) to the throne of Egypt. As ruthless as she was intelligent, Cleopatra charmed Caesar into sharing her bed and supporting her rule. Their love affair shocked the general's friends and enemies alike: they thought Rome should seize power from foreigners, not share it with them.

Caesar's Dictatorship and Murder

By 45 B.C.E., Caesar had won the civil war. He now had to decide how to rule a shattered republic. He apparently believed that only a sole ruler could end the chaotic violence of the factions, but the republic's oldest tradition prohibited

Relief Carving of Cleopatra and Her Son Caesarion

This relief carving appears on the wall of a temple at Dendera in Egypt. It depicts Cleopatra VII, queen of Egypt, and her son by Julius Caesar, Caesarion ("Little Caesar"). They are shown wearing the traditional ceremonial clothing and crowns of Egyptian pharaohs, a sign of the claim of the Ptolemaic ruling family to be the legitimate rulers of Egypt despite their Macedonian ethnic origins. Both died in 30 B.C.E. when Octavian, the adopted son of Julius Caesar and soon to become Augustus and the ruler of Rome, conquered Egypt and made it a Roman province. *(© Ancient Art and Architecture Collection, Ltd.)*

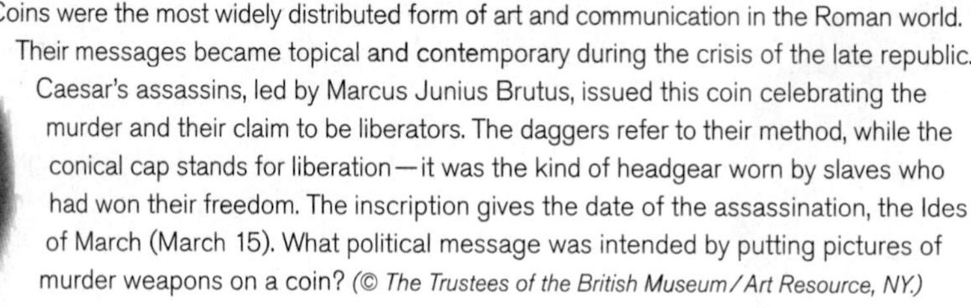

Ides of March Coin Celebrating Caesar's Murder
Coins were the most widely distributed form of art and communication in the Roman world. Their messages became topical and contemporary during the crisis of the late republic. Caesar's assassins, led by Marcus Junius Brutus, issued this coin celebrating the murder and their claim to be liberators. The daggers refer to their method, while the conical cap stands for liberation—it was the kind of headgear worn by slaves who had won their freedom. The inscription gives the date of the assassination, the Ides of March (March 15). What political message was intended by putting pictures of murder weapons on a coin? *(© The Trustees of the British Museum/Art Resource, NY.)*

monarchy. Still, Caesar decided to rule as a king, but without the title, taking instead the traditional Roman title of *dictator*, used for a temporary emergency ruler. In 44 B.C.E., he announced he would continue as dictator without a term limit. "I am not a king," he insisted. The distinction, however, was meaningless. As ongoing dictator, he controlled the government. Elections for offices continued, but Caesar manipulated the results by recommending candidates to the assemblies, which his supporters dominated.

Caesar's policies as dictator were meant to improve the financial situation and reward his supporters. As sole ruler, he offered them a moderate cancellation of debts; a cap on the number of people eligible for subsidized grain; a large program of public works, including public libraries; colonies for his veterans in Italy and abroad; plans to rebuild Corinth and Carthage as commercial centers; and citizenship for more non-Romans.

Unlike Sulla, Caesar did not proscribe his enemies. Instead, he treated them mildly, thereby obligating them to become his grateful clients. For example, he allowed Cicero to return to Rome without punishment. Caesar's decision not to seek revenge earned him unheard-of honors, such as a special golden seat in the Senate house and the renaming of the seventh month of the year after him (July). He also regularized the Roman calendar by having each year include 365 days, a calculation based on an ancient Egyptian calendar that forms the basis for our modern one.

Caesar's dictatorship satisfied the people but outraged the optimates. (See "Contrasting Views," page 162.) They resented being dominated by one of their own, a "traitor" who had deserted to the people's faction. Some senators, led by Caesar's former close friend Marcus Junius Brutus (85–42 B.C.E.) and inspired by the memory of the ancestor of Brutus who led the overthrow of Rome's first monarchy five hundred years before, conspired to murder him. They stabbed Caesar repeatedly in a shower of blood in the Senate house on March 15 (the Ides of March in the Roman calendar), 44 B.C.E. When Brutus struck him, Caesar gasped his last words—in Greek: "You, too, son?" He collapsed dead at the foot of a statue of Pompey.

The liberators, as they called themselves, had no new plans for government. They apparently expected the traditional republic to revive automatically after Caesar's murder, ignoring the political violence of the past century and the deadly imbalance in Roman values, with "great men" placing their competitive private interests above the community's well-being. The liberators were stunned when the people rioted at Caesar's funeral to vent their anger against the upper class that had robbed them of their generous patron. Instead of then forming a united front, the elite resumed their personal vendettas. The traditional values of the republic failed to save it.

REVIEW QUESTION What factors generated the conflicts that caused the Roman republic's destruction?

Conclusion

The two most remarkable features of the Roman republic's history were its phenomenal expansion and its violent disintegration. Rome expanded to control vast territories because it incorporated outsiders, its small farmers produced agricultural surpluses to support a growing population and army, and its leaders respected the traditional values stressing the common good. The Romans' willingness to endure great loss of life and property—the proof of their faithfulness—made their army unstoppable in prolonged conflicts: Rome might lose battles, but never wars. Because wars of conquest brought profits to leaders and the common people alike, peace seemed a wasted opportunity.

MAPPING THE WEST

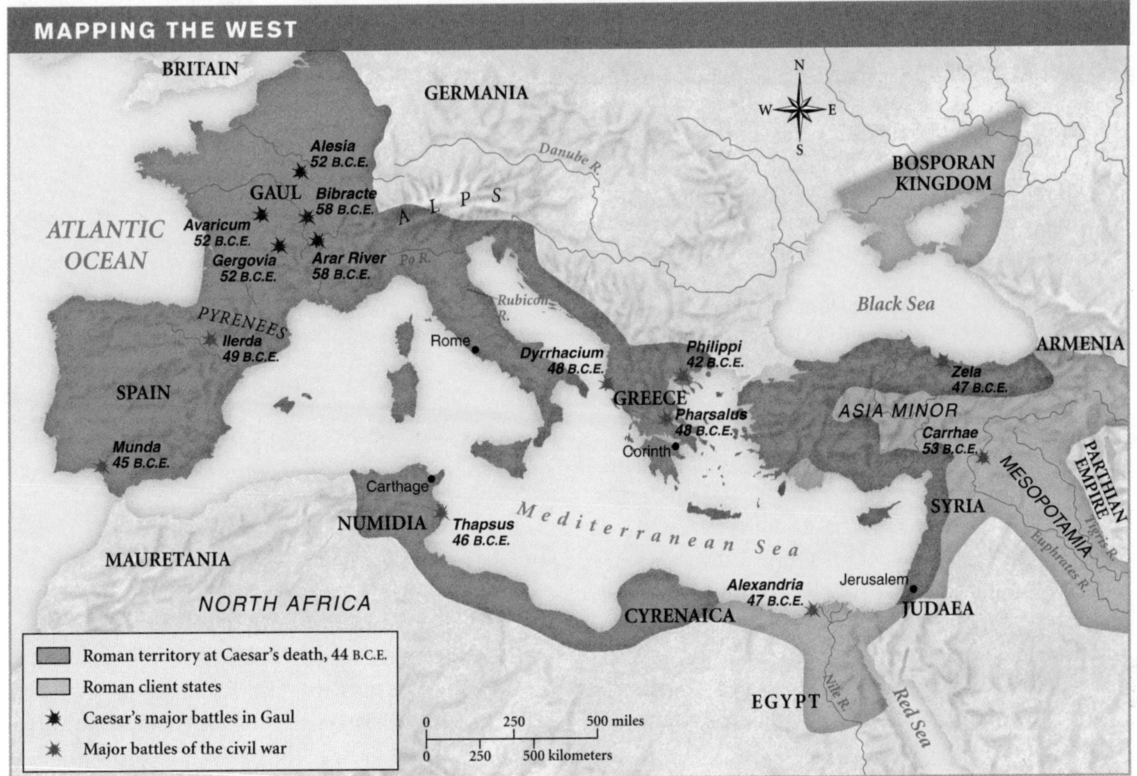

The Roman World at the End of the Republic, 44 B.C.E.
By the time of Julius Caesar's assassination in 44 B.C.E., the territory that would be the Roman Empire was almost complete. Caesar's young relative Octavian (the future Augustus) would conquer and add Egypt in 30 B.C.E. Geography, distance, and formidable enemies were the primary factors inhibiting further expansion—which Romans never stopped wanting, even when lack of money and political discord rendered it purely theoretical. The deserts of Africa and the once again powerful Persian kingdom in the Near East worked against expansion southward or eastward, while trackless forests and fierce resistance from local inhabitants made expansion into central Europe and the British Isles impossible to maintain.

But the republic's victories against Carthage and in Macedonia and Greece had unexpected consequences. Long military service ruined many farming families, and poor people flocked to Rome to live on subsidized food, becoming an unstable political force. Members of the upper class increased their competition with one another for the career opportunities presented by constant war. These rivalries became dangerous to the state when successful generals began acting as patrons to client armies of poor troops. In this dog-eat-dog atmosphere, violence and murder became the preferred means for settling political disputes. Communal values were drowned in the blood of civil war. No reasonable Roman could have been optimistic about the chances for an enduring peace following Caesar's assassination in 44 B.C.E. It would have seemed an impossible dream to imagine that Caesar's grandnephew and adopted son, Octavian—a teenage student at the time of the murder—would eventually bring peace by creating a new political system disguised as the restoration of the old republic.

FOR FURTHER EXPLORATION

- **For additional primary-source material from this period**, see *Sources of the Making of the West*, Fourth Edition.
- **For Web sites, images, and documents related to topics in this chapter**, visit *Make History* at bedfordstmartins.com/hunt.

Chapter 5 Review

Online Study Guide bedfordstmartins.com/hunt

Key Terms and People

In the grid below, identify the term or person and explain its historical significance. (To do this exercise online, go to bedfordstmartins.com/hunt.)

Term	Who or What & When	Why It Matters
mos maiorum (p. 140)		
patron-client system (p. 142)		
patria potestas (p. 142)		
res publica (p. 145)		
orders: patricians and plebeians (p. 148)		
Twelve Tables (p. 149)		
ladder of offices (p. 149)		
plebiscites (p. 150)		
Cicero (p. 156)		
humanitas (p. 156)		
equites (p. 159)		
populares (p. 159)		
optimates (p. 159)		
proletarians (p. 159)		
First Triumvirate (p. 164)		

Review Questions

1. What common themes underlay Roman values? How did Romans' behavior reflect those values?
2. How and why did the Roman republic develop its complicated political and judicial systems?
3. What advantages and disadvantages did Rome's victories over foreign peoples create for both rich and poor Romans?
4. What factors generated the conflicts that caused the Roman republic's destruction?

Making Connections

1. How do the political and social values of the Roman republic compare to those of the Greek city-state in the Classical Age?
2. What were the positive and the negative consequences of war for the Roman republic?
3. How can people decide what is the best balance between individual advancement and communal stability?

Important Events

Date	Event	Date	Event
753 B.C.E.	Traditional date of Rome's founding as monarchy	168–149 B.C.E.	Cato writes *The Origins*, first history of Rome in Latin
509 B.C.E.	Roman republic established	149–146 B.C.E.	Rome and Carthage fight Third Punic War
509–287 B.C.E.	Struggle of the orders	146 B.C.E.	Carthage and Corinth destroyed
451–449 B.C.E.	Creation of Twelve Tables, Rome's first written law code	133 B.C.E.	Tiberius Gracchus elected tribune; assassinated in same year
396 B.C.E.	Defeat of Etruscan city of Veii; first great expansion of Roman territory	91–87 B.C.E.	Social War between Rome and its Italian allies
387 B.C.E.	Gauls sack Rome	60 B.C.E.	First Triumvirate of Caesar, Pompey, and Crassus
264–241 B.C.E.	Rome and Carthage fight First Punic War	49–45 B.C.E.	Civil war, with Caesar the victor
220 B.C.E.	Rome controls Italy south of Po River	45–44 B.C.E.	Cicero writes his philosophical works on *humanitas*
218–201 B.C.E.	Rome and Carthage fight Second Punic War	44 B.C.E.	Caesar appointed dictator with no term limit; assassinated in same year

- Consider two events: **Cato writes *The Origins* (168–149 B.C.E.)** and **Carthage and Corinth are destroyed (146 B.C.E.)**. What attitudes prompted Cato's writings, and how were similar ideas reflected in the destruction of Carthage and Corinth?

SUGGESTED REFERENCES

Scholars continue to debate the causes and the effects of the rise and fall of the Roman republic, focusing in particular on the intended and unintended political, social, and cultural consequences of the many wars that the Romans fought in this period.

Beard, Mary, et al. *Religions of Rome*. 2 vols. 1998.

Billows, Richard. *Julius Caesar: The Colossus of Rome*. 2008.

Bradley, Keith. *Slavery and Society at Rome*. 1994.

*Caesar. *The Civil War*. Trans. John Carter. 1997.

*Cicero. *On the Good Life*. Trans. Michael Grant. 1971.

Cornell, Tim. *The Beginnings of Rome: Italy and Rome from the Bronze Age to the Punic Wars* (c. 1000–264 B.C.). 1995.

Daily life (and more): http://www.vroma.org/~bmcmanus/romanpages.html

Earl, Donald. *The Moral and Political Tradition of Rome*. 1967.

Flower, Harriet. *Roman Republics*. 2009

Gardner, Jane. *Women in Roman Law and Society*. 1986.

Goldworthy, Adrian. *The Punic Wars*. 2000.

Haynes, Sybill. *Etruscan Civilization: A Cultural History*. 2005.

Hoyos, Dexter. *The Carthaginians*. 2010.

Keaveney, Arthur. *Sulla: The Last Republican*. 2nd ed. 2005.

Lancel, Serge. *Carthage: A History*. Trans. Antonia Nevill. 1995.

*Plutarch. *The Fall of the Roman Republic*. Trans. Rex Warner. Rev. ed. 2006.

Ramage, Nancy H., and Andrew Ramage. *Roman Art*. 2008.

Roller, Duane W. *Cleopatra: A Biography*. 2010.

*Primary source.

CHAPTER 6

The Creation of the Roman Empire

44 B.C.E.–284 C.E.

In 203 C.E., Vibia Perpetua, wealthy and twenty-two years old, sat in a Carthage jail, nursing her infant while awaiting execution. She had received the death sentence for refusing to sacrifice to the gods for the Roman emperor's health and safety. One morning the jailer dragged her off to the city's main square, where a crowd had gathered. Perpetua described in her prison journal what happened when the local governor tried to persuade her to save her life:

> My father came carrying my son, shouting "Perform the sacrifice; take pity on your baby!" Then the governor said, "Think of your old father; show pity for your little child! Offer the sacrifice for the imperial family's well being." "I refuse," I answered. "Are you a Christian?" asked the governor. "Yes." When my father would not stop trying to change my mind, the governor ordered him thrown to the earth and whipped with a rod. I felt sorry for my father; it seemed they were beating me. I pitied his pathetic old age.

The brutality of Perpetua's punishment failed to break her: gored by a wild cow and stabbed by a gladiator, she died professing her faith.

Perpetua went to her death because she believed that Christianity required her not only to disregard the traditional Roman value of faithfulness to her family obligations but also to refuse the state's demand to show loyalty. Her decision to put her personal religious commitment ahead of her civic duty was a different version of the civil wars fought by the Roman republic's commanders because they valued their individual success above service to the common good.

Mosaic of Chariot Racing
Racing four-horse chariots was the most popular—and most expensive—sport in the Roman Empire. This mosaic, a picture made from thousands of tiny colored tiles put together like a giant jigsaw puzzle, shows a driver holding a branch signifying that he has just won a big race. Two attendants or race officials are in the background. Hundreds of thousands of spectators attended the largest races at the Circus Maximus in Rome, but many cities across the empire had tracks. Romans loved the races' action and potential violence, as chariots swerved at top speed around and around the tight turns of the track and sometimes collided in bloody accidents. *(National Museum of Archeology, Madrid, Spain/ullstein bild/AISA.)*

Following Julius Caesar's assassination in 44 B.C.E., his grandnephew and adopted son, Octavian (the future Augustus), eventually brought peace by transforming Roman government and creating what is today called the

Roman Empire. Ever after, Rome's rulers feared disloyalty above all because it threatened to reignite the civil wars that had destroyed the Roman Republic. The refusal of Christians such as Perpetua to perform traditional sacrifice was considered treason—the ultimate disloyalty—because Romans believed the gods would punish the entire community for sheltering people who refused to worship them.

This period of political transformation opened with a bloodbath: seventeen years of civil war followed Caesar's funeral. Finally, in 27 B.C.E., Augustus created a disguised monarchy to end the violence, ingeniously masking his creation as a restoration of the old Roman republic. Romans continued to call their new system by this old name throughout the long history of what in modern times is usually referred to as the Roman Empire. Augustus's system retained traditional institutions for sharing power—the Senate, the consuls, the courts—but in reality he and his successors governed like kings ruling an empire. More than a thousand years would pass before government under a true republic reappeared in Western civilization.

The challenge for Romans under the new system was to maintain political stability and prosperity. Augustus's political system brought peace for two hundred years, except for a struggle between generals for rule in 69 C.E. This **Pax Romana** ("Roman Peace") allowed agriculture and trade to flourish in the provinces, but war still determined Rome's long-term future because of its financial consequences. Under the republic, foreign wars had won huge amounts of land and money for Romans, but now the distances were too great, the adjoining lands too rough, and the foreign enemies too strong for continued conquest. The army became no longer an offensive weapon for expansion bringing in new taxes but instead a defense force protecting the frontier regions that had to be paid for out of current revenues. This change during the Pax Romana slowly created a financial crisis that weakened the principate and destabilized the government. The emergence of Christianity created a new religion that would over centuries transform the Roman world, but this change also created tension because the growing presence of Christians made other Romans worry about punishment from the gods. In the third century C.E., a crisis developed when generals competing to rule reignited prolonged civil war. By the 280s C.E., Roman government was once more on the brink of disintegration.

Pax Romana: Literally "Roman Peace"; the two centuries of relative peace and prosperity in the Roman Empire under the early principate begun by Augustus.

CHAPTER FOCUS How did Augustus's "restored republic" successfully keep the peace for more than two centuries, and why did it fail in the third century?

From Republic to Empire, 44 B.C.E.—14 C.E.

Inventing tradition takes time. Augustus created his new political system gradually; in keeping with one of his favorite sayings, Augustus "made haste slowly." He succeeded because he reinvented government, guaranteed the army's support, did not hesitate to use violence to win power, and built political legitimacy by communicating an image of himself as a dedicated leader and patron. His announced respect for tradition and his reign's length established his disguised monarchy as Rome's political system and saved the state from anarchy. Succeeding where Caesar had failed, he did it by making the new look old.

30 B.C.E. Octavian (the future Augustus) conquers Ptolemaic Egypt

30 C.E. Jesus crucified in Jerusalem

64 C.E. Great fire in Rome; Nero blames Christians

69 C.E. Civil war after death of Nero

50 B.C.E. — 0 — 50 C.E.

27 B.C.E. Augustus inaugurates the principate

70 C.E. Titus captures Jerusalem and destroys the Jewish temple

70–90 C.E. New Testament Gospels are written

80s C.E. Domitian leads campaigns against multiethnic invaders on northern frontiers

Civil War, 44–27 B.C.E.

Members of the social elite competing for power after Caesar's assassination in 44 B.C.E. started a civil war that lasted until 30 B.C.E. The main competitors were Caesar's friend Mark Antony and Caesar's eighteen-year-old grandnephew and adopted son, Octavian (the future Augustus). Octavian won over Caesar's soldiers by promising them money from their murdered general's wealth, which he had inherited. Marching these troops to Rome, the teenager forced the Senate to make him consul in 43 B.C.E., disregarding the rule that a man had to climb the ladder of offices before becoming consul.

Octavian and Antony put aside their differences—for a time—and with a general named Lepidus joined forces against Caesar's assassins and anyone else they thought dangerous. In late 43 B.C.E., the trio formed the so-called Second Triumvirate and forced the Senate to recognize them as an official panel for restoring the government. They then conducted a murderous proscription of their enemies, including some of their own relatives, and confiscated their property.

Octavian and Antony next forced Lepidus into retirement and began fighting each other. Antony controlled the eastern provinces by allying with the ruler of Egypt, Queen Cleopatra VII (69–30 B.C.E.), who had earlier allied with Caesar. Dazzled by her intelligence and personal magnetism, Antony, who was married to Octavian's sister, fell in love with Cleopatra. Octavian rallied support by claiming that Antony planned to make this foreign queen Rome's ruler. He made the residents of Italy and the western provinces swear allegiance to him. His victory in the naval battle of Actium in northwest Greece in 31 B.C.E. won the war. Cleopatra and Antony fled to Egypt, where they committed suicide in 30 B.C.E. The general first stabbed himself, bleeding to death in his lover's embrace. The queen then allowed a poisonous snake to bite her. Octavian's revenues from the capture of Egypt made him Rome's richest citizen.

The Creation of the Principate, 27 B.C.E.–14 C.E.

After distributing land to army veterans and creating colonies in the provinces, in 27 B.C.E. Octavian, in his own words, "gave back the state from [his] own power to the control of the Roman Senate and the people" and announced they should decide how to preserve it. Recognizing Octavian's overwhelming power, the senators asked him to safeguard the state, granted him special civil and military powers, and bestowed on him the honorary title **Augustus**, meaning "divinely favored." From this point Augustus became his name.

Inventing the Principate In reality, Augustus changed Rome's political system, but he kept up the appearance and the name of government under a republic. Citizens elected consuls, the Senate gave advice, and the assemblies met. Augustus occasionally served as consul, but mostly he let others hold that office. While making himself sole ruler, he concealed his monarchy by referring to himself not as a *rex* ("king") but only with the honorary title *princeps*, meaning "first man" (among social equals), a term from the republic indicating general agreement about who was the leading individual of the time or who was the most distinguished Roman senator. Princeps is thus the position we call emperor, and the Roman government in the early empire after 27 B.C.E. is best described as a ***principate***. Each new princeps was supposed to be chosen only with the Senate's approval, but in practice each ruler chose his own

---

Augustus: The honorary name meaning "divinely favored" that the Roman Senate bestowed on Octavian; it became shorthand for "Roman imperial ruler."

***principate*:** Roman political system invented by Augustus as a disguised monarchy with the *princeps* ("first man") as emperor.

161–180 C.E. Marcus Aurelius battles multiethnic bands attacking northern frontiers

230s–280s C.E. Third-century financial and political crisis

100 C.E. | 150 C.E. | 200 C.E. | 250 C.E.

212 C.E. Caracalla extends Roman citizenship to almost all free inhabitants of the provinces

249–251 C.E. Decius persecutes Christians

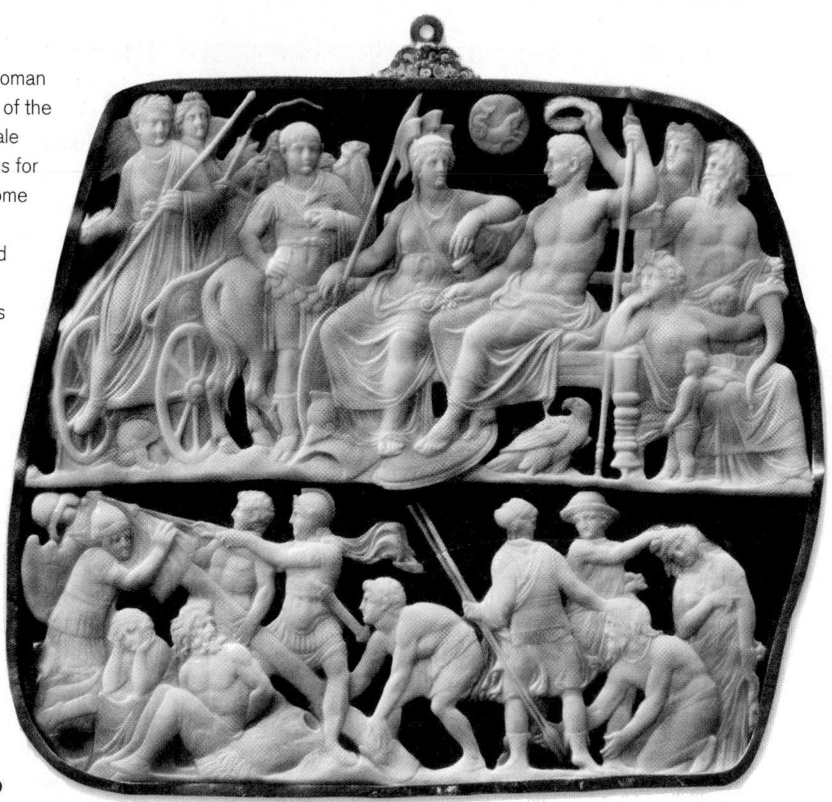

Cameo Celebrating Augustus
This cameo, about eight by nine inches, was carved early in the Roman Empire from a stone with layers of blue and white. Interpretations of the scenes vary, but the upper scene probably shows a standing female figure representing the Inhabited World who is crowning Augustus for rescuing Roman citizens. The seated female figure represents Rome and resembles Augustus's wife, Livia, his partner in rule. The man stepping out of a chariot is Tiberius, Augustus's choice to succeed him as princeps. Why do you think Tiberius carries a scepter like that held by Augustus? The lower scene shows defeated enemies subjected to Roman power. How do you think the lower scene relates to the upper scene? *(Erich Lessing/Art Resource, NY.)*

successor, like kings with a royal family. To preserve the tradition that no official should hold more than one post at a time, Augustus as princeps had the Senate grant him the powers, though not the office, of a tribune. That is, he possessed the legal power to act and to veto as if he were a tribune protecting the rights of the people, but he left all the positions of tribune open for other men to occupy. In 23 B.C.E., the Senate agreed that Augustus should also have a consul's power to command (*imperium*)—with the crucial addition that his power would be superior to that of the actual consuls.

Holding the power of a tribune and the "superior power" of a consul meant that Augustus could rule the state without filling any formal executive political office. He did not take the office of dictator that Sulla and Julius Caesar had used to rule. Augustus proclaimed that people obeyed him not because of his powers but because they so respected his *auctoritas* ("moral authority"). The truth was that Augustus and the rulers of the Roman Empire who followed him were able to exercise supreme power because they controlled the army and the treasury. Augustus knew, however, that symbols affect people's perception of reality, so he dressed and acted modestly, like a regular citizen in a republic, not an arrogant king. Livia, his wife, played a prominent role under his regime as his political adviser and partner in upholding old-fashioned values.

Augustus's choice of *princeps* as his public, though unofficial, title was a brilliant symbolic move because it used tradition to give legitimacy to a political revolution. He invented the principate to disguise a monarchy as a corrected and restored republic. Roman emperors after Augustus continued this same arrangement and proclaimed the same propaganda: they continued to refer to the state as the Roman republic, the senators and the consuls continued to exist, and the princeps continued to pretend to respect their positions. In truth, Augustus revolutionized the underlying power structure of Rome's government: no one previously could have exercised the powers of both tribune and "superior" consul simultaneously while also controlling the state's money and troops.

Augustus made the military the foundation of his power by turning the republic's citizen militia into a professional, full-time army and navy. He established regular lengths of service and substantial retirement benefits, changes that made the emperor the troops' patron and solidified their loyalty to him. To raise money for the added costs, Augustus imposed Rome's first inheritance tax on citizens, angering the rich. His other major military innovation was to station several thousand soldiers in Rome for the first time ever. These soldiers—the **praetorian guard**—would later play a crucial role in imperial politics by selecting the next emperor when the current one died. Augustus meant them to provide security for him and prevent rebellion in the capital by serving as a visible reminder that the superiority of the princeps was backed by the threat of armed force.

---

praetorian guard: The group of soldiers stationed in Rome under the emperor's control; first formed by Augustus.

Communicating the Emperor's Image In keeping with his policy of using both force and symbols, Augustus constantly communicated his image as patron and public benefactor (see Document, "Augustus, *Res Gestae* [My Accomplishments]," page 176). He used media as small as coins and as large as buildings. As the only mass-produced medium for official messages, Roman coins functioned like modern political advertising. They proclaimed slogans such as "Father of His Country" to remind Romans of Augustus's moral authority, or "Roads have been built" to emphasize his generosity in paying for highway construction.

Augustus used his personal fortune to erect spectacular public buildings in Rome. The huge Forum of Augustus, dedicated in 2 B.C.E., best illustrates his skill at sending messages through architecture (Figure 6.1). This public gathering space centered on a temple to Mars, the Roman god of war; Julius Caesar's sword was preserved there as a national treasure. Two-story colonnades extended from the temple like wings, sheltering statues of famous Roman heroes to serve as inspirations to future leaders. Augustus's forum provided space for religious rituals and the coming-of-age ceremonies of upper-class boys, but it also stressed his justifications for his rule: peace and security restored through military power, the foundation of a new age, devotion to the gods who protected Rome, respect for tradition, and generosity in spending money for public purposes.

Augustus's Motives Augustus never revealed his motives for establishing the principate, but his challenge was the one every Roman leader faced—balancing his own ambition with Rome's need for peace and its traditional commitment to its citizens' freedom of action. Augustus's solution was to employ traditional values to justify changes, as with his reinvention of the meaning of the word *princeps*. Above all, he transferred the traditional paternalism of social relations—the patron-client system—to politics by making the princeps everyone's most important patron, with the moral authority to guide their lives. This process reached its peak in 2 B.C.E. when the Senate joined the Roman people in formally proclaiming Augustus "Father of His Country" (a title that Cicero and Julius Caesar had also received). The title emphasized that the principate gave Romans a sole ruler who governed them like a father: stern but caring, expecting obedience and loyalty from his children, and obligated to take care of them in return. The goal of this arrangement was a combination of stability and order, not political freedom.

Augustus ruled until his death at age seventy-five in 14 C.E. The length of his reign—forty-one years—gave his transformation of Roman government time to become accepted. As the historian Tacitus (c. 56–120 C.E.) remarked, by the time Augustus died, "almost no one was still alive who had seen the republic." Through his longevity, command over the army, good relations with the capital's urban masses, and manipulation of political symbols and language to mask his power, Augustus restored political stability and created imperial Rome.

Daily Life in the Rome of Augustus

Archaeological and literary sources reveal a composite picture of life in Rome at the time of Augustus. Although some of the sources refer to times after Augustus and to cities other than Rome, they help us understand the Augustan period because economic and social conditions remained essentially unchanged in Roman cities during the early Roman Empire.

Augustan Rome's population of nearly one million was vast for the ancient world. No European city would have this many people again until London in the 1700s. Many people had no regular jobs and too little to eat. The streets were packed: "One man jabs me with his elbow, another whacks me with a pole; my legs are smeared with mud, and big feet step on me from all sides" was how one poet de-

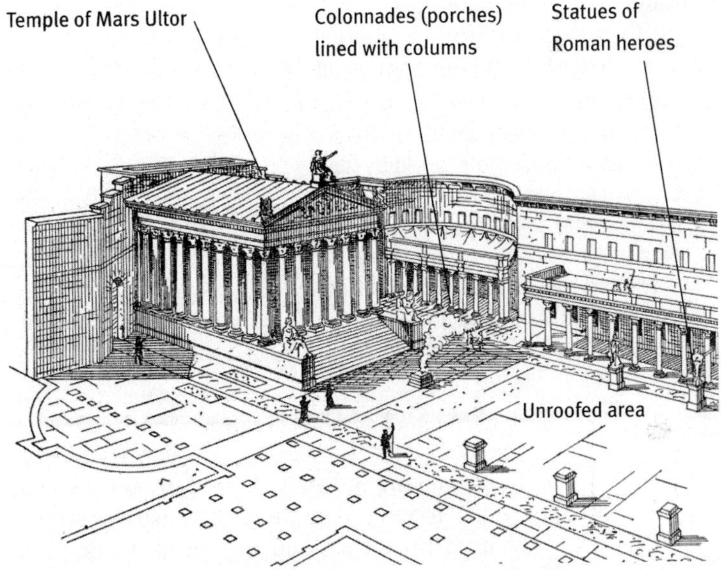

FIGURE 6.1 Cutaway Reconstruction of the Forum of Augustus
Augustus built this large forum (120 × 90 yards) to commemorate his victory over the assassins of Julius Caesar. The centerpiece was a marble temple to Mars Ultor ("Mars the Avenger"), and inside the temple were statues of Mars, Venus (the divine ancestor of Julius Caesar), and Julius Caesar (as a god), as well as works of art and Caesar's sword. The two spaces flanking the temple featured statues of Aeneas and Romulus, Rome's founders. The high stone wall behind the temple protected it from fire, a constant threat in the crowded neighborhood just behind.

DOCUMENT

Augustus, *Res Gestae* (My Accomplishments)

Augustus, the first Roman emperor, had an autobiographical report of his accomplishments displayed around the empire. These excerpts reveal his justifications for his rule, especially the peace and financial benefits that he had brought to Roman citizens, thereby making him their patron and morally obligating them to be loyal clients. Many of the sections not included here list his numerous and expensive personal payments for public works.

1. At the age of nineteen, on my own initiative and at my own expense, I raised an army, which I used to liberate the republic, which had been oppressed by the tyranny of a faction. For this reason the Senate passed honorary votes for me and made me a member [in 43 B.C.E.], at the same time granting me the rank of a consul in its voting, and it gave me the power of military command [imperium]. It ordered me as propraetor to see to it, along with the consuls, that no harm came to the state. Moreover, in the same year, when both consuls had died in the war, the people elected me consul and a triumvir with the duty of establishing the republic. . . .

3. I waged many wars, civil and foreign, throughout the whole world by land and by sea, and as victor I spared all citizens who asked for pardons. Foreign peoples who could safely be pardoned I preferred to spare rather than destroy. Approximately 500,000 Roman citizens swore military oaths to me. A little more than 300,000 of these, when their terms of service were ended, I settled in colonies or sent back to their own municipalities; I allotted lands or granted money to all of them as rewards for military service. . . .

5. I refused to accept the dictatorship offered to me [in 22 B.C.E.] by the people and by the Senate, both in my absence and my presence. During a severe scarcity of grain I accepted the supervision of the grain supply, which I so administered that within a few days I freed the whole people from imminent panic and danger by my expenditures and effort. The consulship, too, which was offered to me at that time as an annual office for life, I refused to accept.

6. [In 19, 18, and 11 B.C.E.], although the Roman Senate and people in unison agreed that I should be elected sole guardian of the laws and morals with supreme power, I refused to accept any office offered to me that was contrary to our ancestors' traditions [*mos maiorum*]. The measures that the Senate desired me to take at that time I carried out under the tribunician power. While holding this power I five times voluntarily requested and was given a colleague by the Senate.

7. . . . I have been ranking senator [*princeps senatus*] for forty years, up to the day on which I wrote this document. . . .

34. In my sixth and seventh consulships [28 and 27 B.C.E.], after I had put an end to the civil wars, having gained possession of everything through the consent of everyone, I returned the state from my own power [*potestas*] to the control of the Roman Senate and the people. As reward for this meritorious service, I received the title of Augustus by vote of the Senate, and the doorposts of my house were publicly decked with laurels, the civic crown was affixed over my doorway, and a golden shield was set up in the Julian Senate house, which, as the inscription on this shield testifies, the Roman Senate and people gave me in recognition of my valor, clemency, justice, and devotion. After that time I excelled all in authority [*auctoritas*], but I possessed no more power [*potestas*] than the others who were my colleagues in each magistracy.

35. When I held my thirteenth consulship [2 B.C.E.], the Senate, the equestrian order, and the entire Roman people gave me the title of "father of the country" [*pater patriae*]. . . . At the time I wrote this document I was in my seventy-sixth year.

Source: Herbert W. Benario, ed., *Caesaris Augusti Res Gestae et Fragmenta*, 2nd ed. (1990). Translation by Thomas R. Martin.

Question to Consider

- **Why do you think Augustus ends this justification of his rule with a list of his personal and moral qualities as officially recognized by the Roman Senate and people?**

scribed walking in Rome in the early second century C.E. To ease congestion in the narrow streets, the city banned carts and wagons in the daytime. This regulation made nights noisy with the creaking of axles and the shouting of drivers caught in traffic jams.

The Conditions of City Life Most urban residents lived in small apartments in multistoried buildings called islands. Outnumbering private houses by more than twenty to one, the islands' first floors housed shops, bars, and restaurants. Graffiti of all kinds—political endorsements, the posting of rewards, personal insults, and advertising—covered the exterior walls. The higher the floor, the cheaper the rent. Well-off tenants occupied the lower stories, while the poorest people lived in single rooms rented by the day on the top floors. Aqueducts delivered a plentiful supply of fresh water to public fountains, but apartment dwellers had to lug heavy jugs up the stairs. The wealthy few had piped-in water at ground level. Most tenants lacked bathrooms and had to use the public latrines or pots for toilets at home. Some buildings had cesspits, but most people had to carry buckets of excrement down to the streets to be emptied by sewage collectors. Lazy tenants flung these containers' foul-smelling contents out the window. Sanitation was an enormous problem in a city that generated sixty tons of human waste every day.

To keep clean, residents used public baths. Because admission fees were low, almost everyone could afford to bathe daily. Baths existed all over the city; like modern health clubs, they served as centers for exercising and socializing (see Document, "The Scene at a Roman Bath," page 178). Bathers progressed through a series of increasingly warm, humid areas until they reached a sauna-like room. They swam naked in their choice of hot or cold pools. Women had access to the public baths, but men and women bathed apart. Since bathing was thought to be helpful for sick people, the public baths unintentionally contributed to the spread of communicable diseases.

Augustus's care for citizens' everyday lives helped them accept his political changes. He did all he could to improve Rome's public safety and health. Since fire presented a constant danger, Augustus gave Rome the first public fire department in Western history. He also established the first permanent police force, despite his fondness for watching the frequent brawls in Rome's crowded streets. There were challenges in urban life, however, that not even his power and money could overcome. He greatly enlarged the city's main sewer, but its contents still emptied untreated into the Tiber River. The technology for sanitary disposal of waste did not exist. People often left human and animal corpses in the streets, to be gnawed by vultures and dogs. The poor were not the only people affected by such conditions: a stray mutt once brought a human hand to the table where Vespasian, who would be emperor from 69 to 79 C.E., was eating lunch. Flies everywhere and a lack of refrigeration contributed to frequent gastrointestinal ailments: the most popular jewelry of the time was supposed to ward off stomach trouble. Although the wealthy could not avoid such problems, they made their lives more pleasant with luxuries such as snow rushed from the mountains to ice their drinks and slaves to clean their houses, which were built around courtyards and gardens.

City residents faced hazards beyond infectious disease. Apartment dwellers often hurled debris out their windows, where it rained down on pedestrians. "If you are walking to a dinner party in Rome," a poet warned, "you would be foolish not to make out your will first. For every open window is a source of potential disaster." Roman architects built public structures from concrete, brick, and stone

A Roman Street
Like Pompeii, the town of Herculaneum on the Bay of Naples was frozen in time by the volcanic eruption of Mount Vesuvius in 79 C.E. Mud from the eruption buried the town and preserved its buildings. Herculaneum's straight roads paved with flat stones and sidewalks were typical for a Roman town. Balconies jutted from the houses, offering a shady viewing point for life in the streets. Roman houses often enclosed a garden courtyard instead of having yards in front or back. Why do you think urban homes had this arrangement? *(Scala/Art Resource, NY.)*

that lasted centuries, but crooked contractors cut costs by cheating on materials for private buildings; therefore, apartment buildings sometimes collapsed. Augustus imposed a height limit of seventy feet on new apartment buildings to limit the danger.

As the people's patron, Augustus used his own money to import grain to feed the urban poor. State distribution of grain had long been a tradition in the capital, but Augustus extended his welfare plan to reach 250,000 recipients. Counting the recipients' families, more than 700,000 people depended on the princeps to survive. Poor Romans cooked this grain into bread or soup — if they were lucky, they might add beans, leeks, or cheese — and they washed down their meals with cheap wine. The rich ate more costly food, such as roast pork or crayfish, flavored with sweet-and-sour sauce concocted from honey and vinegar.

Wealthy Romans increasingly spent money on luxuries and political careers instead of raising

DOCUMENT

The Scene at a Roman Bath

Life in the streets of Roman cities could be loud and crowded. People sought relaxation in public baths—which could, however, be just as hectic. In this letter, the Roman philosopher Seneca (4 B.C.E.–65 C.E.) wrote to a friend describing his experience living in a rented apartment located above one of the large and busy bathing and exercise establishments that existed in every sizable community in the Roman Empire.

I am staying in an apartment directly above a public bath. Imagine all the kinds of voices that I hear, enough to make me hate having ears! When the really strong guys are working out with heavy lead weights, when they are working hard or at least pretending to work hard, I hear their grunts. Whenever they let out the breath they've been holding in, I hear them hissing and panting loudly. When I happen to notice some sluggish type getting a cheap rubdown, I hear the slap of the hand pounding his shoulders, changing its sound according to whether it's a blow with an open or a closed fist. If a serious ball-player comes along and starts keeping score out loud, then I'm done for. Add to this the bruiser who likes to pick fights, the pickpocket who's been caught, and the man who loves to hear the sound of his own voice in the bath. And there are those people who jump into the swimming pool with a tremendous splash and lots of noise. Besides all the ones who have awful voices, imagine the "armpit hair plucker-outer" with his high, shrill voice—so he'll be noticed—always chattering and never shutting up, except when he is plucking armpits and making his customer yell instead of yelling himself. And there are also all the different cries from the sausage seller, and the fellow selling pastries, and all the food vendors screaming out what they have to sell, all of them with their own special tones.

Source: Seneca, *Moral Epistles*, 56.1–2. Translation by Thomas R. Martin.

Question to Consider

- **What do the sounds described by the Roman philosopher reveal about the kinds of people frequenting the bath and the nature of the community itself?**

families. Fearing that the falling birthrate would destroy the social elite on whom Rome relied for public service, Augustus granted legal privileges to the parents of three or more children. To strengthen marriages, he made adultery a crime and supported this reform so strongly that he exiled his own daughter—his only child—and a granddaughter for sex scandals. His legislation had little effect, however, and the prestigious old families dwindled over the coming centuries. Recent research suggests that up to three-quarters of senatorial families either lost their official status by spending all their money or died out every generation by failing to have children. Equites and provincials who won the emperor's favor filled the open places in the social hierarchy and the Senate.

Roman Slavery In a remarkable departure from the practice of other ancient states, Rome gave citizenship to freed slaves. All slaves—and there were many in Roman society—had the hope of someday becoming a free Roman citizen, regardless of whether they had originally become enslaved by being captured in wars against Romans, had been carried off from their home region by slave traders in raids in non-Roman territory and then sold to Roman owners, or had been born to slave women and therefore started life as the property of the mother's owner. Slaves' descendants, if they became wealthy, could become members of the social elite. This policy gave slaves reason to cooperate with their masters, as an owner might reward a slave's dutiful work with emancipation. Scholars lack the evidence to calculate precisely what percentage of Roman slaves were freed in their lifetimes, but it is clear that the tradition of giving citizenship to former slaves did eventually lead to most Romans having slave ancestors in their family history.

The harshness of slaves' lives varied widely. Slaves in agriculture and manufacturing lived a grueling existence. Most such workers were men, although women might assist the foremen who managed gangs of rural laborers. A second-century C.E. novelist described the grim situation of slaves in a flour mill: "Through the holes in their ragged clothes you could see all over their bodies the scars from whippings. Some wore only loincloths. Letters had been branded on their foreheads [to show they were slaves and should be captured and returned to their owners, if they escaped] and irons manacled their ankles." Worse than the mills were the mines, where the foremen whipped the miners to keep them working in such a dangerous environment.

Household slaves lived better. Most Romans owned slaves as home servants; modestly well-off families had one or two, while rich houses and the imperial palace owned large numbers. Domestic slaves were often women, working as nurses, maids, kitchen helpers, and clothes makers. Some male slaves ran businesses for their masters, and they were often allowed to keep part of the profits as an incentive; they saved to purchase their freedom someday. Women had less opportunity to earn money, though masters sometimes granted tips for sexual favors to female and male slaves. Many female prostitutes were slaves working for their owner in a brothel. Slaves with savings would sometimes buy other slaves, especially to have a mate; they were barred from legal marriage, because they and their children remained their master's property, but they could live as a shadow family. Fortunate slaves could buy themselves from their masters or be freed in their masters' wills. Some masters' tomb inscriptions record their affection for a slave, but even household slaves could experience painful treatment from cruel masters. Slaves had no right to bring legal charges against their owners. If slaves attacked their owners, the punishment was death.

Violence in Public Entertainment

While potential violence defined slaves' lives, actual violence featured in much Roman public entertainment, revealing that many Romans felt comfortable watching the suffering of other people and of animals. The emperors regularly provided shows featuring hunters killing fierce beasts, wild African animals mangling condemned criminals, mock naval battles in flooded arenas, blood-drenched gladiatorial combats, and wreck-filled chariot races. Spectators packed arenas for these shows, seated according to their social rank and gender following an Augustan law. The emperor and senators sat close to the action, while women and the poor were seated in the upper seats, to display the hierarchy that Romans believed necessary to social stability.

War captives, criminals, and slaves could be forced to fight as gladiators, but free people also voluntarily became gladiators, hoping to become sports celebrities and win rich prizes if they survived. Most gladiators were men, though women could also fight other women if they wished. The first female gladiators were the daughters of gladiators in the time of the Roman republic, trained by their fathers to compete in the arena. Women continued to fight each other in bloody spectacles until the emperor Septimius Severus (r. 193–211 C.E.) banned their appearance.

Gladiatorial shows had originated as part of rich funerals, but Augustus made them popular entertainment. Gladiators were often wounded or killed because the fights were so dangerous, but their contests rarely required a fight to the death, unless they were captives or criminals. Professional fighters could have extended careers and win riches and celebrity. To make the fights unpredictable, pairs of gladiators often competed with different weapons. One favorite bout pitted a lightly armored "net man," who used a net and a trident, against a more heavily armored "fish man," so named from the design of his helmet crest. Betting was popular, the crowds rowdy. As a Christian commentator complained: "Look at the mob coming to the show—already they're out of their minds! Aggressive, thoughtless,

Gladiator after a Kill
This first-century C.E. mosaic covered a villa floor in North Africa. It shows a gladiator staring at the opponent he has just killed. What feelings do you think his expression conveys? Gladiatorial combats originated as part of wealthy people's funeral ceremonies, symbolizing the human struggle to avoid death. Training an expert gladiator took many years and great expense. Like boxers today, gladiators fought only a couple of times a year. Because it cost so much to replace a dead gladiator, most fights were not to the death intentionally; however, kills often happened in the fury of combat. *(Photo courtesy Helmut Ziegert/University of Hamburg.)*

already in an uproar about their bets! They all share the same suspense, the same madness, the same voice."

Public entertainment served as two-way communication between ruler and ruled. Emperors provided gladiatorial combats, chariot races, and theater productions for the masses, and ordinary citizens staged protests at these festivals to express their wishes to the emperors, who were expected to attend. Poor Romans, for example, rioted to protest shortfalls in the free grain supply.

Changes in Education, Literature, and Art in Augustus's Rome

Elite culture changed in the Augustan period to serve the same goal as public entertainment: legitimizing the transformed political system. Oratory—the highest attainment of Roman education—lost its freedom. Under the republic, the ability to make frank speeches criticizing political opponents had been such a powerful weapon that it could catapult a "new man" like Cicero to a leadership role. Now, the emperor's supremacy ruled out honest political debate. Ambitious men required rhetorical skills only to praise the emperor. Criticism of the established political system in both oratory and the arts was too risky.

Education Education in oratory remained a privilege of the wealthy. Since Rome had no free public schools, the poor received no formal education. Most people had time for learning only practical skills. A character in a Roman satirical novel expresses this utilitarian attitude: "I didn't study geometry and literary criticism and worthless junk like that. I just learned how to read the letters on signs and how to work out percentages, and I learned weights, measures, and the values of the different kinds of coins."

Servants took care of rich boys and girls, who attended private elementary schools from ages seven to eleven to learn reading, writing, and basic arithmetic. Some children went on to the next three years of school, in which they studied literature, history, and grammar. Only a few boys then proceeded to the study of rhetoric. Advanced studies concerned literature, history, ethical philosophy, law, and dialectic (reasoned argument). Mathematics and science were rarely studied as separate subjects, but engineers and architects became proficient at calculation despite the difficulty of using Roman numerals for complex math.

Ideals in Literature and Sculpture So much famous literature comes from the Augustan period that scholars call it the Golden Age of Latin literature. The emperor, himself an author, served as a patron for writers and artists. His favorites were Horace (65–8 B.C.E.) and Virgil (70–19 B.C.E.). Horace entranced audiences with the rhythms and irony of his poems on public and private subjects. His poem celebrating Augustus's victory at Actium became famous for its opening line: "Now we have to drink!"

Virgil became the most admired Roman poet for his long poem *The Aeneid*, which both praised Augustus's new system and—very indirectly—alluded to problems in it. Inspired by Homer's epics,

Literacy and Social Status
This two-foot-high wall painting of a woman and her husband was found in a comfortable house in Pompeii, buried by twelve feet of ash from Mount Vesuvius's volcanic eruption in 79 C.E. The couple may have owned the bakery that adjoined the house. Both are holding items showing that they were literate and therefore deserving of social status. She has the notepad of the time, a hinged wooden tablet filled with wax for writing on with the stylus (thin stick) that she touches to her lips. He holds a scroll of papyrus or animal skin, the standard form for books at the time. Her hairstyle was one popular in the mid-first century C.E. *(Erich Lessing/Art Resource, NY.)*

The Aeneid told the story of the Trojan Aeneas, the legendary founder of Rome. Virgil balanced his praise for Roman civilization with recognition of the price in freedom to be paid for peace. *The Aeneid* thus revealed the complex mix of gain and loss created by Augustus's transformation of Roman politics.

Authors with a more independent streak had to be careful. The historian Livy (54 B.C.E.–17 C.E.) composed a history of Rome in which he recorded Augustus's ruthlessness in the civil war after Caesar's murder. The emperor scolded but did not punish Livy because his work proclaimed that stability and prosperity depended on traditional values of loyalty and self-sacrifice. The poet Ovid (43 B.C.E.–17 C.E.), however, wrote *Art of Love* and *Love Affairs* to mock the emperor's moral legislation with witty advice for conducting sexual affairs and picking up other men's wives. His work *Metamorphoses* undermined the idea of hierarchy as natural by telling bizarre stories of supernatural shape-changes, with people becoming animals and confusion between the human and the divine. In 8 B.C.E., after Ovid became embroiled in the scandal involving Augustus's granddaughter, the emperor exiled him.

Changes in public sculpture also reflected the emperor's influence. When Augustus was growing up, portraits were starkly realistic. The sculpture that Augustus ordered displayed an idealized style based on classical Greek models. In works such as the Prima Porta statue, Augustus had himself portrayed as serene and dignified, not careworn and sick, as he often was. As with architecture, Augustus used sculpture to project a calm and competent image of himself as the "Restorer of the Roman Republic" and founder of a new age for Rome.

Marble Statue of Augustus from Prima Porta
At six feet eight inches high, this statue of Augustus stood a foot taller than he did. Found at his wife Livia's country villa at Prima Porta ("First Gate"), the portrait was probably done about 20 B.C.E., when Augustus was in his forties; however, it shows him as younger, using the idealizing techniques of classical Greek art. Compare his smooth face to the realistic portraiture in Chapter 5. The statue's symbols communicate Augustus's image: his bare feet hint he is a near-divine hero, the Cupid refers to the Julian family's descent from the goddess Venus, and the breastplate's design shows a Parthian surrendering to a Roman soldier under the gaze of personified cosmic forces admiring the peace Augustus's regime has created. *(Scala/Art Resource, NY.)*

REVIEW QUESTION How did the peace gained through Augustus's "restoration of the Roman republic" affect Romans' lives in all social classes?

Politics and Society in the Early Roman Empire

Augustus made political changes to promote not only his personal glory but also stability and prosperity—above all by preventing civil war—but his new system lacked a way to block struggles for power when the princeps died. Since Augustus claimed not to have created a monarchy, no successor could automatically inherit his power without the Senate's approval. Augustus therefore decided to identify an heir whom he wished the senators to recognize as princeps after his death. This strategy succeeded and kept rule in his family, called the **Julio-Claudians**, until the death in 68 C.E. of Augustus's last descendant, the infamous Nero. It established the tradition that family dynasties ruled the "restored republic" of imperial Rome.

Under the principate, the emperor's main goals were preventing unrest, building loyalty, and financing the administration while governing the diverse provinces. Augustus set the pattern for effective imperial rule: take special care of the army, communicate the emperor's image as a just ruler and generous patron, and promote Roman law and culture as universal standards. The citizens, in

---

Julio-Claudians: The ruling family of the early principate from Augustus through Nero, descended from the aristocratic families of the Julians and the Claudians.

return for their loyalty, expected the emperors to be generous patrons—but the difficulties of long-range communication imposed practical limits on imperial support of or intervention in the lives of the residents of the provinces.

The Perpetuation of the Principate after Augustus, 14–180 C.E.

Augustus's claim that the republic continued meant that he needed the Senate's cooperation to give legitimacy to his successor and perpetuate his disguised monarchy. He had no son, so he adopted Livia's son by a previous marriage, Tiberius (42 B.C.E.–37 C.E.). Since Tiberius had a brilliant career as a general, the army supported Augustus's choice. Augustus had Tiberius granted the power of a tribune and the power of a consul equal to his own so that he would be recognized as emperor after Augustus's death. The senators did just that when Augustus died in 14 C.E., allowing the Julio-Claudian dynasty to begin.

The First Dynasty: The Julio-Claudians, 14–68 C.E. Tiberius (r. 14–37 C.E.) was able to stay in power for twenty-three years because he had the most important qualification for succeeding as emperor: the army's loyalty. He built the praetorian guard a fortified camp in Rome so that its soldiers could better protect the emperor. This change had the unintended consequence of guaranteeing the guards a role in determining all future successions—no emperor could come to power without their support. Tiberius described his position by saying, "I am the master of the slaves, the commander of the soldiers, and the princeps of the rest."

Tiberius's long reign provided the extended transition period that the principate needed to endure, establishing the compromise on power between the elite and the emperor essential for political stability. The traditional offices of consul, senator, and provincial governor continued, with elite Romans filling them and enjoying their prestige, but the emperors decided who received the offices and controlled law and government policy. In this way, the social elite performed valuable service, especially by keeping the peace and overseeing the collection of taxes while governing provinces that the emperor assigned them. (The emperor used his own assistants to govern the provinces that housed strong military forces.) Everyone saved face by pretending that the republic's political offices retained their original power.

Tiberius paid a bitter price to rule. To strengthen their family tie, Augustus forced Tiberius to divorce his beloved wife, Vipsania, to marry Augustus's daughter, Julia—and the marriage proved disastrously unhappy. When Tiberius's sadness led him to spend his reign's last decade in seclusion far from Rome, his neglect of the government permitted abuses in the capital and kept him from training a decent successor for the Senate to approve.

Tiberius designated Gaius, better known as Caligula (r. 37–41 C.E.), to be the next emperor because the young man was Augustus's great-grandson and Tiberius's uncritical supporter, not because he had leadership qualities. The third Julio-Claudian emperor might have been successful because he knew about soldiering: *Caligula* means "baby boots," the nickname the soldiers gave him as a child because he wore little leather shoes like theirs when he was growing up in the military garrisons his father commanded. Unfortunately, Caligula's enormous appetites outweighed his feeble virtues. Cruel and violent, he bankrupted the treasury to satisfy his desires. His biographer labeled him a monster for his murders and sexual crimes, which some said included incest with his sisters. He outraged the elite by fighting in mock gladiatorial combats and appearing in public in women's clothing or costumes imitating gods. He once said, "I'm allowed to do anything." The praetorian commanders murdered him in 41 C.E. to avenge personal insults.

The senators then debated the idea of truly restoring the republic by refusing to approve a new emperor. They backed down, however, when Claudius (r. 41–54 C.E.), Augustus's grandnephew and Caligula's uncle, bribed the praetorian guard to back him. The soldiers' insistence on there being an emperor so that they would have a patron to pay them indicated that the old republic was never coming back.

Claudius was an active emperor, commanding a successful invasion of Britain in 43 C.E. that made much of the island into a Roman province. He opened the way for provincial elites to expand their participation in government by enrolling men from Gaul in the Senate. In return for keeping their regions peaceful and ensuring tax payments, they would receive offices at Rome and the emperor's support. Claudius also transformed imperial bureaucracy by employing freed slaves as powerful administrators; since they owed their positions to the emperor, they could be expected to be loyal.

Power corrupted Claudius's teenage successor, Nero (r. 54–68 C.E.). Emperor at sixteen, he loved music and acting, not governing. The public entertainments he sponsored and the cash he distributed kept him popular with Rome's poor. His generals put down the revolt in Britain led by the woman commander Boudica in 60 C.E. and fought the Jewish rebels who tried to throw off Roman rule in Judaea in 66 C.E., but he himself had no military career. A giant fire in 64 C.E. (the event behind the legend that Nero fiddled while Rome burned) aroused suspicions that he ordered the city burned to make space for a new palace. Nero scandalized the senatorial class by appearing onstage to sing, and he emptied the treasury by building a palace called the Golden House. To raise money, he faked treason charges against senators and equites to seize their property. When his generals toppled his regime, Nero had a servant help him cut his own throat as he dug his grave, wailing, "I'm dying reduced to the status of a laborer!"

The Flavian Dynasty and the Imperial Cult, 69–96 C.E. Nero's death sparked a year of civil war in 69 C.E. during which four generals competed for power. Vespasian (r. 69–79 C.E.) won. His victory showed that the elite and the army wanted the principate to continue. To give legitimacy to his new dynasty (called Flavian, from his family name), Vespasian had the Senate grant him the same powers as previous emperors, pointedly leaving Caligula and Nero off the list. He encouraged the spread of the imperial cult (worship of the emperor as a living god and sacrifices for his household's welfare) in the provinces but not in Italy, where this innovation would have disturbed traditional Romans. The imperial cult communicated the same image of the emperor to the provinces as Rome's architecture and sculpture did: he was superhuman, provided benefactions, and deserved loyalty. Vespasian reportedly did not believe in his own divinity, to judge from his joking remark on his deathbed: "Oh me! I think I'm becoming a god."

Vespasian's sons, Titus (r. 79–81 C.E.) and Domitian (r. 81–96 C.E.), conducted hardheaded fiscal policy and high-profile military campaigns. Titus had become famous by finally suppressing the Jewish revolt and capturing Jerusalem in 70 C.E. He sent relief to Pompeii and Herculaneum when, in 79 C.E., Mount Vesuvius's volcanic eruption buried these towns. He built a state-of-the-art site for public entertainment by finishing Rome's **Colosseum**, outfitting the amphitheater seating fifty thousand spectators with awnings to shade the crowd. The Colosseum was deliberately constructed on the site of the former fishpond in Nero's Golden House to demonstrate the Flavian dynasty's commitment to the well-being of the people.

When Titus died suddenly after only two years as emperor, his brother Domitian stepped in. Domitian balanced the budget and campaigned against Germanic tribes threatening the empire's northern frontiers, a sign of the greater troubles to come for the empire from this region. Domitian's arrogance turned the senators against him; once he sent them a letter announcing, "Our lord god, myself, orders you to do this." Alarmed by an elite general's rebellion, Domitian executed numerous upper-class citizens as conspirators. Fearful that they, too, would become victims, his wife and members of his court murdered him in 96 C.E.

The Five "Good Emperors," 96–180 C.E. As Domitian's murder showed, the principate had not solved monarchy's inevitable weakness: rivalry among the elite for rule. The danger of civil war persisted, whether generated by ambitious generals or the emperor's jealous heirs. No one could predict whether a good ruler or a bad one would emerge. As Tacitus commented, emperors were like the weather: "We just have to wait for bad ones to pass and hope for good ones to appear."

Fortunately for Rome, fair weather dawned with the next five emperors: Nerva (r. 96–98 C.E.), Trajan (r. 98–117 C.E.), Hadrian (r. 117–138 C.E.), Antoninus Pius (r. 138–161 C.E.), and Marcus Aurelius (r. 161–180 C.E.). Historians call this period the Roman political Golden Age because it had peaceful successions for nearly a century. Nevertheless, it saw ample war and strife: Trajan fought to expand Roman control across the Danube River into Dacia (today Romania) and eastward into Mesopotamia (Map 6.1); Hadrian executed several senators as alleged conspirators, punished a Jewish revolt by turning Jerusalem into a military colony, and withdrew Roman forces from Mesopotamia; and Marcus Aurelius, who wanted to be a philosopher instead of an emperor, nevertheless faithfully did his duty by spending difficult years fighting off invaders from the Danube region as the dangers to imperial territory along the northern frontiers kept increasing.

Still, the five "good emperors" did preside over a political and economic Golden Age. They succeeded one another without murder or conspiracy—the first four, having no surviving sons, used adoption to find the best possible successor. The economy provided enough money to finance building projects such as the fortification wall Hadrian built across Britain. Most important, they kept the army

---

Colosseum: Rome's fifty-thousand-seat amphitheater built by the Flavian dynasty for gladiatorial combats and other spectacles.

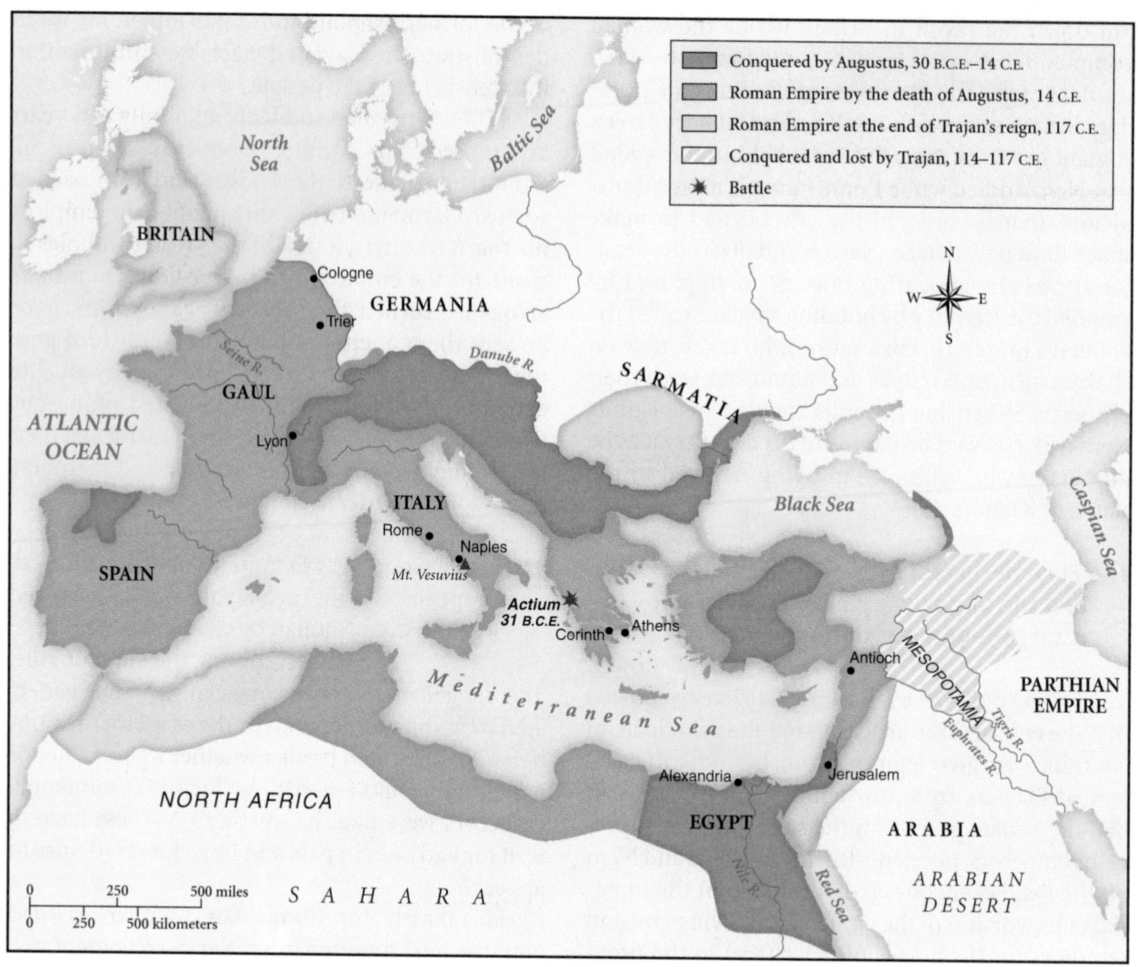

MAP 6.1 The Expansion of the Roman Empire, 30 B.C.E.–117 C.E.
When Octavian (the future Augustus) captured Egypt in 30 B.C.E. after the suicides of Mark Antony and Cleopatra, he greatly boosted Rome's economic strength. The land produced enormous amounts of grain and metals, and Roman power now almost encircled the Mediterranean Sea. When Emperor Trajan took over the southern part of Mesopotamia in 114–117 C.E., imperial conquest reached its height; Rome's control had never extended so far east. Egypt remained part of the empire until the Arab conquest in 642 C.E., but Mesopotamia was immediately abandoned by Hadrian, Trajan's successor, probably because it seemed too distant to defend. | **How did territorial expansion both strengthen and weaken the Roman Empire?**

obedient. Their reigns marked Rome's longest stretch without a civil war since the second century B.C.E.

Life in the Roman Golden Age, 96–180 C.E.

Peace and prosperity in Rome's Golden Age depended on defense by a loyal military, service by provincial elites in local administration and tax collection, common laws enforced throughout the empire, and a healthy population reproducing itself. The empire's vast size and the relatively small numbers of soldiers and imperial officials in the provinces meant that emperors had only limited control over these factors.

The Army in the Early Roman Empire In theory, Rome's military goal remained perpetual expansion because conquest brought land, money, and glory. Virgil expressed this idea in *The Aeneid* by describing Jupiter, the king of the gods, as promising Rome "imperial rule without limit." In reality, the emperors lacked the resources to expand the empire permanently much beyond what Augustus had controlled and had to concentrate on defending imperial territory.

Most provinces were peaceful and had no need for garrisons. Even Gaul, which had originally fiercely resisted Roman control, was, according to one witness, "kept in order by 1,200 troops—hardly more soldiers than it has towns." Most legions (units of five thousand troops) were stationed on frontiers to prevent invasions from barbarians to the north and Persians to the east. The long period of peace supported the Golden Age's prosperity and promoted long-distance trade to import luxury goods, such as spices and silk, from as far away as India and China. Roman merchants in search of profits took advantage of the patterns of the winds to sail from Egypt to India and back every year.

The army, which included both Romans and noncitizens from the provinces, reflected the population's diversity. Serving under Roman officers, the non-Romans could learn to speak Latin and to live by Roman customs. Upon discharge, they received Roman citizenship. Thus the army helped spread a common way of life.

Paying for Government and Defense

Paying for imperial government became an insoluble problem. In the past, foreign wars had brought in huge amounts of revenue from booty and prisoners of war sold into slavery. Conquered territory also provided regular income from taxes. Now the army was no longer making big conquests, but the soldiers had to be paid well to maintain discipline. As the army's patrons, emperors at their accession and other special occasions supplemented soldiers' regular pay with substantial bonuses. These rewards made a soldier's career desirable but cost the emperors dearly.

A tax on agriculture in the provinces (Italy was exempt) now provided the principal source of revenue for the imperial government and the army. The administration itself required relatively little money because it was small compared with the size of the territory being governed: no more than several hundred top officials governed a population of about fifty million. Most locally collected taxes stayed in the provinces to pay expenses there, especially legionnaires' pay. Senatorial and equestrian governors with small staffs ran the provinces, which eventually numbered about forty. In Rome, the emperor employed a large staff of freedmen and slaves, while equestrian officials called prefects managed the city.

The government's finances depended on tax collection carried out by provincial elites. Serving as **decurions** (members of municipal Senates), these wealthy men were required personally to guarantee that their area's financial responsibilities were met. If there was a shortfall in tax collection or local finances, the decurions had to make up the difference from their own pockets. Wise emperors kept taxes moderate. As Tiberius put it when refusing a request for tax increases from provincial governors, "I want you to shear my sheep, not skin them alive." The financial liability in holding civic office made that honor expensive, but the accompanying prestige made the elite willing to take the risk. Rewards for decurions included priesthoods in the imperial cult, an honor open to both men and women, although few women had the wealth to pay for the expected public sacrifices and other priestly responsibilities of the post.

The system worked because it observed tradition: the local elites were their communities' patrons and the emperor's clients. As long as there were enough rich, public-spirited provincials participating, the principate functioned by fostering the old ideal of community service by the upper class in return for respect and social status.

The Impact of Roman Culture on the Provinces

The provinces contained diverse peoples who spoke different languages, observed different customs, dressed in different styles, and worshipped different divinities (Map 6.2). In the countryside, Roman conquest only lightly affected local customs. In new towns that sprang up around Roman forts or settlements of army veterans, Roman influence predominated. Modern cities such as Trier and Cologne in Germany started as such towns. Roman culture had the greatest effect on western Europe, permanently rooting Latin (and the languages that would emerge from it) as well as Roman law and customs there. Over time, social and cultural differences lessened between the provinces and Italy. Eventually, emperors came from citizen-families in the provinces; Trajan, from Spain, was the first of those emperors.

Romanization, as historians call the spread of Roman law and culture in the provinces, raised the standard of living for many by providing roads and bridges, increasing trade, and establishing peaceful conditions for agriculture. The army's need for supplies created business for farmers and merchants. The prosperity that provincials enjoyed under Roman rule made Romanization acceptable. In addition, Romanization was not a one-way street. In western regions as diverse as Gaul, Britain, and North Africa, interaction between the local people and Romans produced mixed cultural traditions, especially in religion and art. Therefore, the process led to a gradual merging of Roman and local culture, not a mere imposition of the conquerors' way of life. (See the illustration on page 187.)

---

decurions (dih KYUR ee uhns): Municipal Senate members in the Roman Empire responsible for collecting local taxes.

Romanization: The spread of Roman law and culture in the provinces of the Roman Empire.

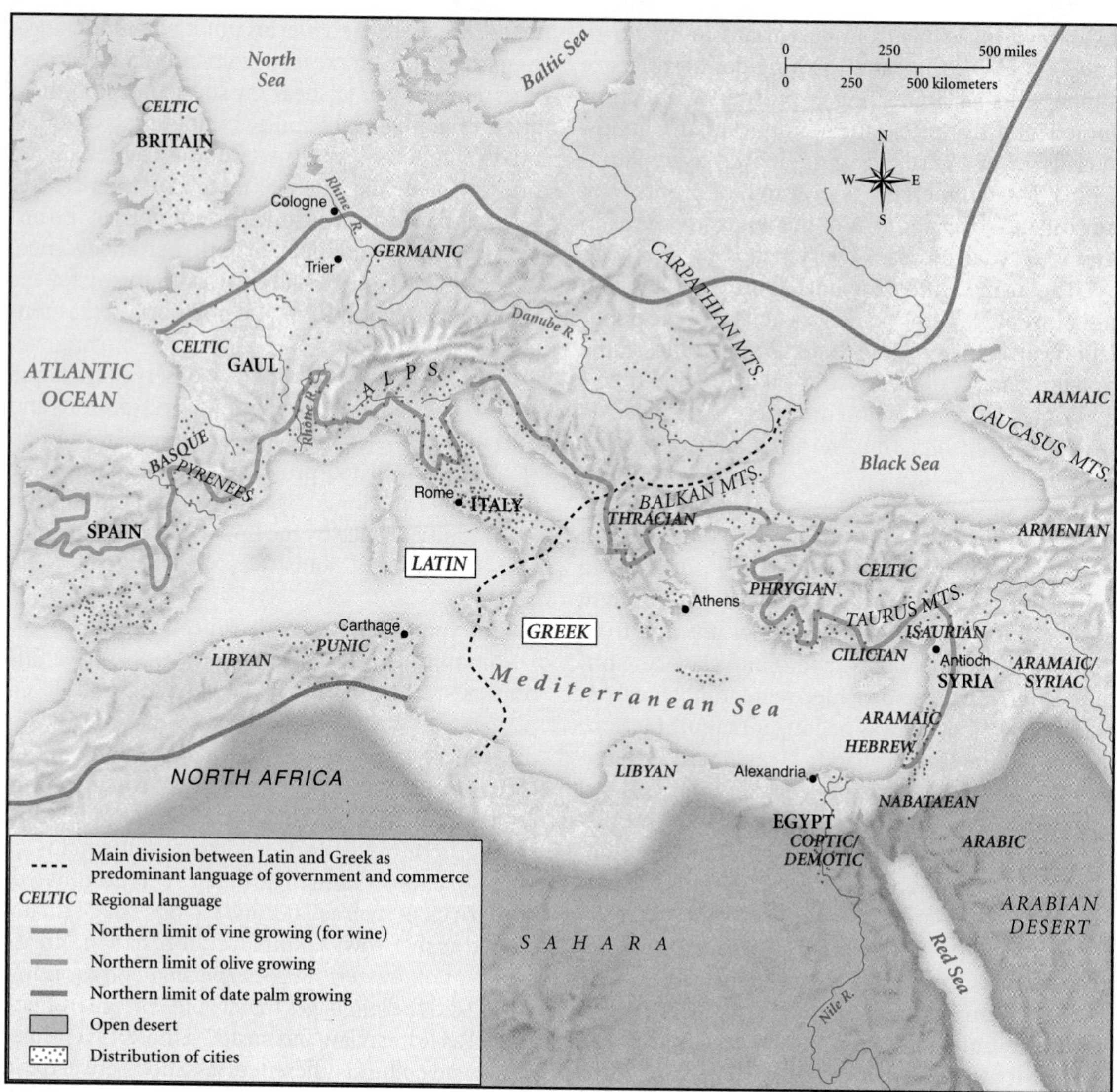

MAP 6.2 Natural Features and Languages of the Roman World
The environment of the Roman world included a large variety of topography, climate, and languages. The inhabitants of the Roman Empire, estimated to have numbered as many as fifty million, spoke dozens of different tongues, many of which survived well into the late empire. The two predominant languages were Latin in the western part of the empire and Greek in the eastern. Latin remained the language of law even in the eastern empire. Vineyards and olive groves were important agricultural resources because wine was regarded as an essential beverage, and olive oil was the principal source of fat for most people as well as being used to make soap, perfume, and other products for daily life. Dates and figs were popular sweets in the Roman world, which had no refined sugar.

Romanization affected the eastern provinces less, and they largely retained their Greek and Near Eastern characteristics. Huge Hellenistic cities such as Alexandria (in Egypt) and Antioch (in Syria) rivaled Rome in size and splendor. The eastern provincial elites readily accepted Roman governance because Hellenistic royal traditions had prepared them to see the emperor as their patron and themselves as his clients.

New Trends in Literature

The continuing vitality of Greek language and culture contributed to new trends in Roman literature. Lucian (c. 117–180 C.E.) composed satirical dialogues in Greek mocking stuffy and superstitious people. The essayist and philosopher Plutarch (c. 50–120 C.E.) also used Greek to write paired biographies of Greek and Roman men. His exciting stories made him favorite reading for centuries; William Shakespeare based several plays on Plutarch's biographies.

As for literature in Latin, modern scholars call the late first century and early to mid-second century C.E. its Silver Age, second only to the Augustan Golden Age. Tacitus (c. 56–120 C.E.) wrote historical works that exposed the Julio-Claudian emperors'

Roman Theater at Sabratha in North Africa
This theater, with its three-story scene building at the back of the stage, was built in the late third century C.E. at the coastal city of Sabratha in Libya. Phoenicians had founded Sabratha as a trading station some eight hundred years earlier; it was still flourishing under the Roman Empire. The size of this very expensive building shows the importance that Romans attached to public entertainment for large numbers of people. *(Frans Lemmens / The Image Bank / Getty Images.)*

ruthlessness. Juvenal (c. 65–130 C.E.) wrote poems ridiculing pretentious Romans while complaining about living broke in the capital. Apuleius (c. 125–170 C.E.) excited readers with his *Golden Ass*, a sexually explicit novel about a man turned into a donkey who regains his body and his soul through the kindness of the Egyptian goddess Isis.

Law and Order through Equity Romans prided themselves on their ability to order their society through law. As Virgil said, their divine mission was "to establish law and order within a framework of peace." Roman law influenced most modern European legal systems. Its foundation was the principle of equity, which meant doing what was "good and fair" even if that required ignoring the letter of the law. This principle taught that the intent in a contract outweighed its words, and that accusers should prove the accused guilty because it was unfair to make defendants prove their innocence. The emperor Trajan ruled that no one should be convicted on the grounds of suspicion alone because it was better for a guilty person to go unpunished than for an innocent person to be condemned. (See "Contrasting Views," page 188.)

The importance of hierarchy led Romans to create formal distinctions in society based on wealth. The elites constituted a tiny portion of the population. Only about one in every fifty thousand had enough money to qualify for the senatorial order, the highest-ranking class, while about one in a thousand belonged to the equestrian order, the second-ranking class. Different purple stripes on clothing identified these orders. The third-highest order consisted of decurions, the local Senate members in provincial towns.

Under the republic, Roman law had made a legal distinction between patricians and plebeians. This division became even stricter under the early Roman Empire. "Better people" included senators, equites, decurions, and retired army veterans. Everybody else — except slaves, who counted as property, not people — made up the vastly larger group of "humbler people." The law imposed harsher penalties on them than on "better people" for the same crime. "Humbler people" convicted of serious crimes were regularly executed by being crucified or torn apart by wild animals before a crowd of spectators. "Better people" rarely received the death penalty, and those who did were allowed a quicker and more dignified execution by the sword. "Humbler people" could also be tortured in criminal investigations, even if they were citizens. Romans regarded these differences as fair on the grounds that an elite per-

CONTRASTING VIEWS

Christians in the Empire: Conspirators or Faithful Subjects?

Romans worried that new religions would disrupt the "peace with the gods" that guaranteed their national safety and prosperity. Groups whose religious beliefs seemed likely to anger the traditional deities could therefore be accused of treason, but Christians insisted that they were loyal subjects who prayed for the safety of the emperors (Document 1). The early emperors tried to form a policy on religion that was fair both to Christian subjects and to those citizens who feared them (Document 2).

1. Tertullian's Defense of His Fellow Christians, 197 C.E.

A theologian from North Africa, Tertullian insisted that Christians supported the empire. He explained that even though Christians refused to pray to the emperor, they prayed for him and thus for the community's health and safety.

So that is why Christians are public enemies—because they will not give the emperors vain, false, and reckless honors; because, being men of a true religion, they celebrate the emperors' festivals more in heart than in a festival mood. . . .

On the contrary, the name faction may properly be given to those who join to hate the good and honest, who shout for the blood of the innocent, who use as a pretext to defend their hatred the absurdity that they take the Christians to be the cause of every disaster to the state, of every misfortune of the people. If the Tiber reaches the walls, if the Nile does not rise to water the fields, if the sky does not move [i.e., if there is no rain] or the earth does, if there is famine, if there is plague, the cry at once arises: "The Christians to the lions!"

For we do pray to the eternal God, the true God, the living God, for the safety of the emperors. . . . Looking up to heaven, the Christians—with hands outspread because innocent, with head bare because we do not blush, yes!, and without a prompter because we pray from the heart—are ever praying for all the emperors. We pray for a fortunate life for them, a secure rule, a safe house, brave armies, a faithful Senate, a virtuous people, a peaceful world. . . .

Should not our sect [i.e., Christianity] have been listed among the legal associations, when it commits no such actions as are commonly feared from unlawful associations? For unless I am mistaken, the reason for prohibiting associations clearly lay in care for public order—to save the state from being torn into factions, a thing very likely to disturb election assemblies, public gatherings, local Senates, meetings, even the public games, with the clashing and rivalry of partisans. . . . We, however, whom all the passion for glory and rank leave cold, have no need to combine; nothing is more foreign to us than the state. One state we recognize for all—the universe.

Source: Tertullian, *Apology*, 30.1, 30.4; 35.1; 38.1–3; 40.1–2. Translation (modified) by T. R. Glover, 1931.

2. Pliny on Early Imperial Policy toward Christians, 112 C.E.

As governor of the province of Bithynia, Pliny had to decide the fate of Christians accused of crimes by their neighbors. Knowing of no precedent to guide him, he tried to be fair and wrote to the emperor Trajan to ask if he had acted correctly. The emperor's reply set out official policy concerning Christians in the early empire.

[Pliny to the emperor Trajan]

It is my habit, my lord, to refer to you all matters concerning which I am in doubt. For who can better give guidance to my hesitation or inform my ignorance? I have never participated in trials of Christians. I therefore do not know what offenses it is the practice to punish or investigate, and to what extent. . . .

In the case of those who were denounced to me as Christians, I have observed the following procedure: I interrogated these as to whether they were

son's higher status required of him or her a higher level of responsibility for the common good. As one provincial governor expressed it, "Nothing is less equitable than mere equality itself."

Marriage and Reproduction Although competition for social status drove many aspects of Roman life, nothing mattered more to the empire's strength than steady population levels. The upper-class government official Pliny, for example, sent the following report to the grandfather of his third wife, Calpurnia: "You will be very sad to learn that your granddaughter has suffered a miscarriage. She is a young girl and did not realize she was pregnant. As a result she was more active than she should have been and paid a high price."

Concerns about marriage and reproduction thus filled Roman society; remaining single and childless represented social failure for both women and men. The propertied classes usually arranged marriages between spouses who hardly knew each other, although husband and wife could grow to love each other in a partnership devoted to family. As in earlier times, girls often married in their early teens, to have as many years as possible to bear children. Because so many babies died young, families had to produce numerous offspring to keep from disappearing. The tombstone of Veturia, a soldier's wife,

Christians; those who confessed I interrogated a second and a third time, threatening them with punishment; those who persisted I ordered executed. For I had no doubt that, whatever the nature of their religion, stubbornness and inflexible obstinacy surely deserve to be punished. There were others possessed of the same madness; but because they were Roman citizens, I signed an order for them to be transferred to Rome.

Soon accusations spread, as usually happens, because of the proceedings going on, and several incidents occurred. An anonymous document was published containing the names of many persons. Those who denied that they were or had been Christians, when they called on the gods in words dictated by me, offered prayer with incense and wine to your image, which I had ordered to be brought for this purpose together with statues of the gods, and moreover cursed Christ—none of which those who are really Christians, it is said, can be forced to do—these I thought should be set free. Others named by the informer declared that they were Christians, but then denied it, asserting that they had been but had ceased to be, some three years before, others many years, some as much as twenty-five years. They all worshipped your image and the statues of the gods, and cursed Christ.

They asserted, however, that the sum and substance of their fault or error had been that they were accustomed to meet on a fixed day before dawn and sing responsively a hymn to Christ as to a god, and to bind themselves by oath, not to some crime, but not to commit fraud, theft, or adultery, not to break their word, nor to refuse to return a trust when called upon to do so. When this was over, it was their custom to depart and to assemble again to eat together—but ordinary and innocent food. Even this, they affirmed, they had stopped doing after my edict by which, in accordance with your instructions, I had forbidden political associations. Accordingly, I judged it all the more necessary to find out what the truth was by torturing two female slaves who were called attendants. But I discovered nothing else except depraved, excessive superstition.

I therefore postponed the investigation and hastened to consult you. For the matter seemed to me to require consulting you, especially because of the numbers involved. For the infection of this superstition has spread not only to the cities but also to the villages and farms. But it seems possible to check and cure it. It is certainly quite clear that the temples, which had been almost deserted, have begun to be frequented, that the established religious rites, long neglected, are being resumed, and that from everywhere sacrificial animals are coming, for which until now very few purchasers could be found. Hence it is easy to imagine what a multitude of people can be reformed if an opportunity for repentance is given.

[Emperor Trajan to Pliny]

You followed proper procedure, my dear Pliny, in handling the cases of those who had been denounced to you as Christians. For it is not possible to lay down any general rule to serve as a kind of fixed standard. They are not to be searched for; if they are denounced and proved guilty, they are to be punished, with this reservation, that whoever denies that he is a Christian and really proves it—that is, by worshipping our gods—even though he was under suspicion in the past, shall obtain pardon through repentance. But anonymously posted accusations ought to have no place in any prosecution. For this is both a dangerous kind of precedent and out of keeping with [the spirit of] our age.

Source: Pliny, *Letters*, Book 10, nos. 96 and 97. Translation (modified) by Betty Radice, 1969.

Questions to Consider

1. **Do you think that Pliny's procedure in dealing with the accused Christians respected the Roman legal principle of equity? Explain.**
2. **How should a society treat a minority of its members whose presence severely disturbs the majority?**

tells a typical story: "Here I lie, having lived for twenty-seven years. I was married to the same man for sixteen years and bore six children, five of whom died before I did."

While the emphasis on childbearing brought status to mothers, the social pressure to bear numerous children also created many health hazards for women. The biology of reproduction was not well understood. Gynecologists erroneously recommended the days just after menstruation as the best time to become pregnant, when the woman's body was "not congested." Doctors possessed metal instruments for surgery and physical examinations, but many were freedmen (former slaves) from the provinces, usually with only informal training. There was no official licensing of medical personnel, and most people considered being a doctor a job with low status and therefore fit for ex-slaves. Complications in childbirth could easily lead to the mother's death because doctors could not stop internal bleeding or cure infections. When Romans did want to control family size, they practiced contraception (by obstructing the vagina or by administering drugs to the female partner) or they abandoned unwanted infants.

The emperors tried to support reproduction. They gave money to feed needy children in the hope they would grow up to have families. Following the

Midwife's Sign
Childbirth carried the danger of death from infection or internal hemorrhage. This terra-cotta sign from Ostia, the ancient port city of Rome, probably hung outside a midwife's room to announce her expertise in helping women give birth. It shows a pregnant woman clutching the sides of her chair, with an assistant supporting her from behind and the midwife crouched in front to help deliver the baby. Why do you think the woman is seated for delivery instead of lying down? Such signs were especially effective for people who were illiterate; a person did not have to read to understand the services that the specialist inside could provide. *(Scala/Art Resource, NY.)*

emperors' lead, wealthy people often adopted children in their communities. One North African man supported three hundred boys and three hundred girls each year until they grew up.

REVIEW QUESTION In the early Roman Empire, what was life like in the cities and in the country for the elite and for ordinary people?

The Emergence of Christianity in the Early Roman Empire

Christianity began as what scholars call "the Jesus movement," a Jewish splinter group in Judaea (today Israel and the Palestinian Territories). There, as elsewhere under Roman rule, Jews were allowed to worship in their ancestral religion. The emergence of the new religion was gradual: three centuries after the death of Jesus, Christians were still a minority in the Roman Empire. Moreover, Christians' beliefs created official suspicion and hostility. Christianity grew because of the attraction of Jesus's charismatic career, its message of salvation, its early members' sense of mission, and the strong bonds of community it inspired. Ultimately, Christianity's emergence proved the most significant development in Roman history.

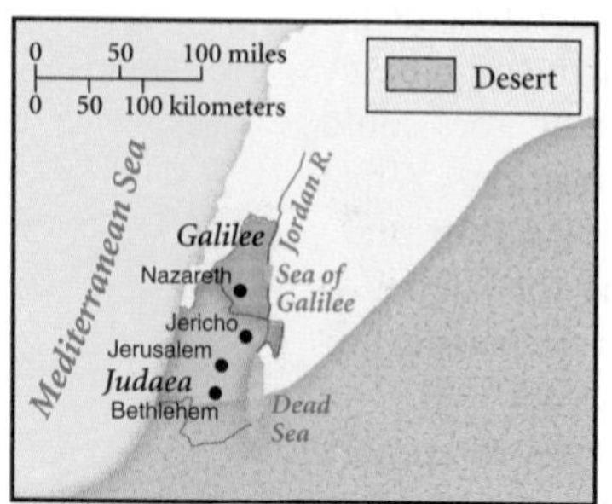

Palestine in the Time of Jesus, 30 C.E.

Jesus and His Teachings

Jesus (c. 4 B.C.E.–30 C.E.) grew up in a troubled region. Harsh Roman rule in Judaea had angered the Jews, and Rome's provincial governors worried about rebellion. Jesus's execution reflected the Roman policy of eliminating any threat to social order. In the two decades after his crucifixion, his followers, particularly Paul of Tarsus, developed and spread his teachings beyond his region's Jewish community to the wider Roman world.

Jewish Apocalypticism and Christianity Christianity offered an answer to a difficult question about divine justice raised by the Jews' long history of oppression under the kingdoms of the ancient and Hellenistic Near East: If God was just, as Hebrew monotheism taught, how could he allow the wicked to prosper and the righteous to suffer? Nearly two hundred years before Jesus's birth, persecution by the Seleucid king Antiochus IV (r. 175–164 B.C.E.) had provoked the Jews into revolt, a struggle that generated the concept of apocalypticism (see Chapter 2, page 46). According to this doctrine, evil powers controlled the world, but God would end their rule by sending the Messiah ("anointed one," *Mashiach* in Hebrew, **Christ** in Greek) to conquer them. A final judgment would soon follow, punishing the wicked and rewarding the righteous for eternity. Apocalypticism especially influenced the Jews living in Judaea under Roman rule and later inspired Christians and Muslims.

During Jesus's life, Jews disagreed among themselves about what form Judaism should take in such troubled times. Some favored getting along with the Romans, while others preached rejection of the non-Jewish world and its spiritual corruption. The local ruler, installed by the Romans, was Herod the Great (r. 37–4 B.C.E.). He was a Jew, but his Greek

---

Christ: Greek for "anointed one," in Hebrew *Mashiach* or in English *Messiah*; in apocalyptic thought, God's agent sent to conquer the forces of evil.

style of life ignored Jewish law and made him unpopular, despite his magnificent rebuilding of the great Jewish temple in Jerusalem. When a decade of unrest followed Herod's death, Augustus installed a Roman administration to suppress disorder. Life in Judaea was tense during Jesus's early life.

The Life and Ministry of Jesus

Jesus began his career as a teacher and healer during the reign of Emperor Tiberius. The books that would later become the New Testament Gospels, composed around 70 to 90 C.E., offer the earliest accounts of his life. Jesus wrote nothing down, and others' accounts of his words and deeds are often inconsistent. He taught not through direct instruction but through stories and parables that challenged his followers to reflect on what he meant.

Jesus's public ministry began with his baptism by John the Baptist, who preached a message of repentance before the approaching final judgment. The Jewish ruler Herod Antipas, a son of Herod the Great, executed John because he feared that John's apocalyptic preaching might cause riots. After John's death, Jesus continued his mission by traveling around Judaea's countryside teaching that God's kingdom was coming and that those who heard him needed to prepare spiritually for it. Some saw Jesus as the Messiah, but his apocalypticism did not call for immediate revolt against the Romans. Instead, he taught that God's true kingdom was to be found not on earth but in heaven. He stressed that this kingdom was open to believers regardless of their social status or apparent sinfulness. His emphasis on God's love for humanity and people's responsibility to love one another reflected Jewish religious teachings, such as the scriptural interpretations and moral teachings of the scholar Hillel, who lived in the time of Jesus.

Realizing that he had to reach more than country people to make an impact, Jesus took his message to the Jewish population of Jerusalem, the region's main city. His miraculous healings and exorcisms, combined with his powerful preaching, created a sensation. So popular was he that his followers created the Jesus movement; it was not yet Christianity but rather a Jewish sect, of which there were several, such as the Saduccees and Pharisees, competing for authority at the time. Jesus attracted the attention of Jewish leaders, who assumed that he wanted to replace them. Fearing Jesus might lead a Jewish revolt, the Roman governor Pontius Pilate ordered his crucifixion in Jerusalem in 30 C.E.

The Mission of Paul of Tarsus

Jesus's followers reported that they had seen him in person after his death, proclaiming that God had raised him from the dead. They convinced a few other Jews that he would soon return to judge the world and begin God's kingdom. At this time, his closest disciples, the twelve Apostles (Greek for "messengers"), still considered themselves faithful Jews and continued to follow the commandments of Jewish law. Their leader was Peter, who won acclaim as the greatest miracle worker of the Apostles, an ambassador to Jews interested in the Jesus movement, and the most important messenger proclaiming Jesus's teachings in the imperial capital. The later Christian church called him the first bishop of Rome.

A turning point came with the conversion of Paul of Tarsus (c. 10–65 C.E.), a pious Jew and a Roman citizen who had violently opposed Jews who accepted Jesus as the Messiah. A spiritual vision on the road to Damascus in Syria, which Paul interpreted as a divine revelation, inspired him to become a follower of Jesus as the Messiah, or Christ—a Christian, as members of the movement came to be known. Paul taught that accepting Jesus as divine and his crucifixion as the ultimate sacrifice for the sins of humanity was the only way of becoming righteous in the eyes of God. In this way alone could one expect to attain salvation in the world to come. Paul's new mission opened the way for Christianity to become a new religion separate from Judaism.

Seeking converts outside Judaea, Paul traveled to preach to Jews and Gentiles (non-Jews) who had adopted some Jewish practices in Asia Minor (today Turkey), Syria, and Greece. Although he stressed the necessity of ethical behavior as defined by Jewish tradition, especially the rejection of sexual immorality and polytheism, Paul also taught that converts did not have to live strictly according to Jewish law. To make conversion easier, he did not require male converts to undergo the Jewish initiation rite of circumcision. He also told his congregations that they did not have to observe Jewish dietary restrictions or festivals. These teachings generated tensions with Jewish authorities in Jerusalem as well as with followers of Jesus living there, who still believed that Christians had to follow Jewish law. Roman authorities arrested Paul as a troublemaker, and he was executed in about 65 C.E.

Hatred of Roman rule provoked Jews to revolt in 66 C.E. After crushing the rebels in 70 C.E., the Roman emperor Titus destroyed the Jerusalem temple and sold most of the city's population into slavery. In the aftermath of this catastrophe, in which Jews lost their religious center, Christianity began to separate more and more clearly from Judaism.

Paul's importance in early Christianity shows in the number of letters—thirteen—attributed to him among the twenty-seven Christian writings that were eventually put together as the New Testament. Christians came to regard the New Testament as having equal authority with the Jewish Bible, which they then called the Old Testament. Since teachers like Paul preached mainly in the cities to reach large crowds, congregations of Christians sprang up in urban areas. In early Christianity, women in some locations could be leaders—such as Lydia, a businesswoman who founded the congregation in Philippi in Greece—but many men, including Paul, opposed women's leadership.

Growth of a New Religion

Christianity faced serious obstacles as a new religion. Imperial officials, suspecting Christians such as Vibia Perpetua (mentioned in the opening of this chapter) of being traitors, could prosecute them for refusing to perform traditional sacrifices. Christian leaders had to build an organization from scratch to administer their growing congregations. Finally, Christians had to decide whether women could continue as leaders in their congregations.

The Rise of Persecution and Martyrdom

The Roman emperors found Christians baffling and troublesome. Unlike Jews, Christians professed a new faith rather than their ancestors' traditional religion. Roman law therefore granted them no special treatment. Most Romans feared that Christians' denial of the old gods and the imperial cult would bring down divine punishment upon the empire. Secret rituals in which Christians symbolically ate the body and drank the blood of Jesus during communal dinners, called Love Feasts, led to accusations of cannibalism and sexual promiscuity.

For these reasons, Romans were quick to blame Christians for disasters. Nero declared that Rome's great fire in 64 C.E. was caused by Christian arsonists, whom he had covered in wild animal skins to be torn to pieces by dogs or fastened to crosses and set on fire to light the streets at night. Nero's cruelty, however, earned Christians sympathy from Rome's population.

Persecutions like Nero's were infrequent. There was no law against Christianity, but officials could punish Christians, as they could anyone, to protect public order. Pliny's actions as a provincial governor in Asia Minor illustrated the situation. (See "Contrasting Views," page 188.) In about 112 C.E., Pliny asked a group of people accused of following this new religion if they were really Christians. When some said yes, he asked them to reconsider. He freed those who denied Christianity, so long as they sacrificed to the gods, swore loyalty to the imperial cult, and cursed Christ. He executed those who refused these actions. Christians argued that Romans had nothing to fear from their faith. Far from spreading immorality and subversion, they insisted, Christianity taught morality and respect for authority. It was not a foreign superstition but the true philosophy, combining the best features of Judaism and Greek rational thought.

The occasional persecutions in the early empire did not stop Christianity. Christians like Perpetua regarded public executions as an opportunity to be-

Catacomb Painting of Christ as the Good Shepherd

Catacombs (tunnels with underground rooms), cut deep into soft rock outside major cities in the Roman Empire, served as meeting places and burial chambers for Jews and Christians. Rome had 340 miles of catacombs. This painting from the catacomb at Rome named after Priscilla, who was probably a Christian from the first century C.E., shows Jesus as the Good Shepherd (John 10: 10–11). He is carrying an animal back to the flock, symbolizing his role as savior; he is dressed in the traditional fashion for a Roman man on a special occasion. Catacomb paintings such as this one were the earliest form of Christian art. *(Catacomb of Priscilla, Rome, Italy/photograph by Erich Lessing/Art Resource, NY.)*

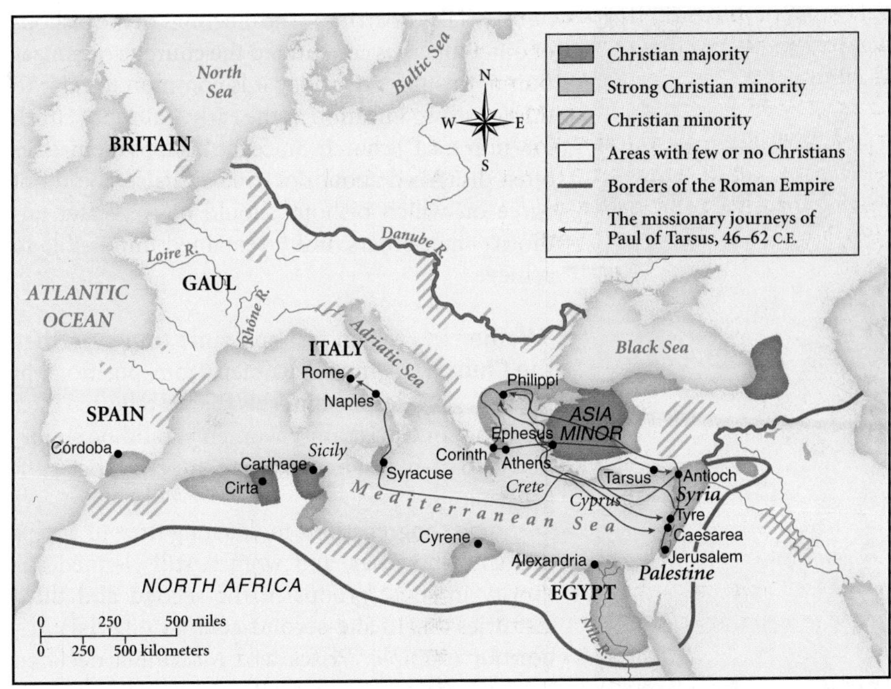

MAP 6.3 Christian Populations in the Late Third Century C.E.
Christians were still a minority in the Roman world three hundred years after Jesus's crucifixion. However, certain areas of the empire—especially Asia Minor, where Paul had preached—had a concentration of Christians. Most Christians lived in cities and towns, where the missionaries had gone to find crowds to hear their message. *Paganus*, a Latin word for "country person" or "rural villager," came to mean a believer in traditional polytheistic cults—hence the word *pagan* that modern historians sometimes use to indicate traditional polytheism. Paganism lived on in rural areas for centuries.

come a **martyr** (Greek for "witness"), someone who dies for his or her religious faith. Martyrs' belief that their deaths would send them directly to paradise allowed them to face torture. Some Christians actively sought to become martyrs. Tertullian (c. 160–240 C.E.) proclaimed that "martyrs' blood is the seed of the Church." Ignatius (c. 35–107 C.E.), bishop of Antioch, begged Rome's congregation, which was becoming the most prominent Christian group, not to ask the emperor to show him mercy after his arrest: "Let me be food for the wild animals [in the arena] through which I can reach God," he pleaded. "I am God's wheat, to be ground up by the teeth of beasts so that I may be found pure bread of Christ." Stories reporting the martyrs' courage inspired the faithful to accept hostility from non-Christians and helped shape the new religion as one that gave its believers the spiritual power to endure suffering.

Bishops and Christian Hierarchy

First-century C.E. Christians expected Jesus to return to pass judgment on the world during their lifetimes. When that did not happen, they began transforming their religion from an apocalyptic Jewish sect expecting the immediate end of the world into one that could survive indefinitely. This transformation was painful because early Christians fiercely disagreed about what they should believe, how they should live, and who had the authority to decide these questions. Some insisted Christians should withdraw from the everyday world to escape its evil, abandoning their families and shunning sex and reproduction. Others believed they could follow Christ's teachings while living ordinary lives. Many Christians worried they could not serve as soldiers without betraying their faith because the army participated in the imperial cult. This dilemma raised the further issue of whether Christians could remain loyal subjects of the emperor. Disagreement over these doctrinal questions raged in the many congregations that arose in the early empire around the Mediterranean, from Gaul to Africa to the Near East (Map 6.3).

The need to deal with such tensions and to administer the congregations led Christians to create an official hierarchy, headed by bishops meant to provide the connection of spiritual communion between congregations and Christ that promised salvation to believers. Bishops possessed authority both to define Christian doctrine and to administer the practical affairs of a growing religion. The emergence of bishops became the most important institutional development in early Christianity. Bishops received their positions according to the principle later called **apostolic succession**, which states that the Apostles appointed the first bishops as their successors, granting these new officials the author-

martyr: Greek for "witness," the term for someone who dies for his or her religious beliefs.

apostolic (ah puh STAH lihk) **succession:** The principle by which Christian bishops traced their authority back to the apostles of Jesus.

Woman Holding a Religious Musical Instrument
This sculpture dating from the early Roman Empire shows a woman standing next to her husband and holding a musical instrument called a *sistrum*. This percussion instrument consisted of a frame with rods piercing it that made a rattling sound when shaken. It was used especially in rituals in the worship of Isis, the Egyptian goddess whose cult as a mother figure/savior became widespread around the Mediterranean in Roman imperial times. *(© akg-images/Pietro Baguzzi/The Image Works.)*

ity Jesus had originally given to the Apostles. Those designated by the Apostles in turn appointed their own successors. Bishops had authority to ordain ministers with the holy power to administer the sacraments, above all baptism and communion, which believers regarded as necessary for achieving eternal life. Bishops also controlled their congregations' memberships and finances. The money financing the early church came from members' donations.

The bishops tried to suppress the disagreements that arose in the new religion. They used their authority to define **orthodoxy** (true doctrine) and **heresy** (false doctrine). The meetings of the bishops of different cities constituted the church's organization in this period. Today it is common to refer to this loose organization as the early Catholic (Greek for "universal") church. Since the bishops themselves often disagreed about doctrine and also could not agree on which bishops should have greater authority than others, unity remained impossible to achieve.

Women in the Church When bishops came to power, they demoted women from positions of leadership. This change reflected their view that in Christianity women should be subordinate to men, just as in Roman imperial society in general.

Some congregations took a long time to accept this shift, however, and women still claimed authority in some groups in the second and third centuries C.E. In late-second-century C.E. Asia Minor, for example, Prisca and Maximilla declared themselves prophetesses with the power to baptize believers in anticipation of the coming end of the world. They spread the apocalyptic message that the heavenly Jerusalem would soon descend in their region.

Excluded from leadership posts, many women chose a life without sex to demonstrate their devotion to Christ. Their commitment to celibacy gave these women the power to control their own bodies. Other Christians regarded women who reached this special closeness to God as holy and socially superior. By rejecting the traditional roles of wife and mother in favor of spiritual excellence, celibate Christian women achieved independence and status otherwise denied them.

Competing Religious Beliefs

Three centuries after Jesus's death, traditional polytheism was still the religion of the overwhelming majority of the Roman Empire's population. Polytheists, who worshipped a variety of gods in different ways in diverse kinds of sanctuaries, often reflecting regional religious rituals and traditions, never created a unified religion. Nevertheless, the stability and prosperity of the early empire gave traditional believers confidence that the old gods and the imperial cult protected them. Even those who preferred religious philosophy, such as Stoicism's idea of divine providence, respected the old cults because they embodied Roman tradition. By the third century C.E., the growth of Christianity, along with the persistence of Judaism and polytheistic cults, meant that people could choose from a number of competing beliefs. Especially appealing were beliefs that offered people hope that they could change their

---

orthodoxy: True doctrine; specifically, the beliefs defined for Christians by councils of bishops.

heresy: False doctrine; specifically, the beliefs banned for Christians by councils of bishops.

Mithras Slaying the Bull
Hundreds of shrines to the mysterious god Mithras have been found in the Roman Empire. Scholars debate the symbolic meaning of the bull slaying that is prominent in art connected to Mithras's cult, as in this wall painting of about 200 C.E. from the shrine at Marino, south of Rome. Here, a snake and a dog lick the sacrificial animal's blood, while a scorpion pinches its testicles as it dies in agony. The ancient sources do not clarify the scene's meaning. What do you think could be the explanation for this type of sacrifice? *(Scala/Art Resource, NY.)*

present lives for the better and also look forward to an afterlife.

Polytheistic religion had as its goal winning the goodwill of all the divinities who could affect human life. Its deities ranged from the state cults' major gods, such as Jupiter and Minerva, to spirits thought to inhabit groves and springs. International cults such as the Mysteries of Demeter and Persephone outside Athens remained popular; the emperor Hadrian traveled there to be initiated.

Isis and Mithras The cults of Isis and Mithras demonstrate how polytheism could provide a religious experience arousing strong emotions and demanding a moral way of life. The Egyptian goddess Isis had already attracted Romans by the time of Augustus, who tried to suppress her cult because it was Cleopatra's religion. But the fame of Isis as a kind, compassionate goddess who cared for her followers made her cult too popular to crush: the Egyptians said it was her tears for starving humans that caused the Nile to flood every year and bring them good harvests. Her image was that of a loving mother, and in art she was often depicted nursing her son. Her cult's central doctrine concerned the death and resurrection of her husband, Osiris. Isis also promised her believers a life after death.

Isis required her followers to behave righteously. Many inscriptions expressed her high moral standards by listing her own civilizing accomplishments: "I broke down the rule of tyrants; I put an end to murders; I caused what is right to be mightier than gold and silver." The hero of Apuleius's novel *The Golden Ass* shouts out his intense joy after his rescue and spiritual rebirth through Isis: "O holy and eternal guardian of the human race, who always cherishes mortals and blesses them, you care for the troubles of miserable humans with a sweet mother's love. Neither day nor night, nor any moment of time, ever passes by without your blessings." Other cults also required worshippers to lead upright lives. Inscriptions from Asia Minor, for example, record people's confessions to sins such as sexual transgressions for which their local god had imposed severe penance.

Archaeology reveals that the cult of Mithras had many shrines under the Roman Empire, but no texts survive to explain its mysterious rituals and symbols, which Romans believed had originated in Persia. Mithras's legend said that he killed a bull in a cave, apparently as a sacrifice for the benefit of his worshippers. As pictures show (see the illustration on page 195), this was no ordinary sacrifice because the animal was allowed to struggle as it was killed. Initiates in Mithras's cult proceeded through rankings named, from bottom to top, Raven, Male Bride, Soldier, Lion, Persian, Sun-runner, and Father—the latter a title of great honor.

Philosophy as the Science of Living In addition to following their religious beliefs, many upper-class Romans guided their lives by Greek philosophy. The most popular choice was Stoicism, which presented philosophy as the "science of living" and required self-discipline and duty from men and women alike. (See Chapter 4, page 130, and see Document, "A Roman Stoic Philosopher on the Capabilities of Women," page 197.) Philosophic individuals put together their own set of beliefs, such as those on duty expressed by the emperor Marcus Aurelius in his memoirs, entitled *To Myself* (or *Meditations*).

Christian and polytheist intellectuals debated Christianity's relationship to Greek philosophy. Origen (c. 185–255 C.E.) argued that Christianity was superior to Greek philosophical doctrines as a guide to correct living. At about the same time, Plotinus (c. 205–270 C.E.) developed the philosophy that had the greatest influence on religion. His spiritual philosophy was influenced by Persian religious ideas and, above all, Plato's philosophy, for which reason this new philosophy is called **Neoplatonism**. Plotinus's ideas deeply influenced many Christian thinkers as well as polytheists. He wrote that ultimate reality is a trinity of The One, Mind, and Soul. By turning away from the life of the body and relying on reason, individual souls could achieve a mystic union with The One, who in Christian thought would be God. To succeed in this spiritual quest required strenuous self-discipline in personal morality and spiritual purity as well as in philosophical contemplation.

REVIEW QUESTION **Which aspects of social, cultural, and political life in the early Roman Empire supported the growth of Christianity, and which opposed it?**

Neoplatonism: Plotinus's spiritual philosophy, based mainly on Plato's ideas, which was very influential for Christian intellectuals.

From Stability to Crisis in the Third Century C.E.

In the third century C.E., military expenses provoked a financial crisis that fed a political crisis lasting from the 230s to the 280s C.E. Invasions on the northern and eastern frontiers had forced the Roman emperors to expand the army for defense, but no new revenues came in to meet the additional costs. The emperors' desperate schemes to finance defense costs damaged the economy and infuriated the population. This anger at the regime encouraged generals to repeat the behavior that had destroyed the republic: commanding client armies to seize power. They created a civil war that lasted fifty years. Earthquakes and regional epidemics added to people's misery. By 284 C.E., this combination of troubles had destroyed the Pax Romana of the early empire.

Threats to the Northern and Eastern Frontiers of the Early Roman Empire

Emperors since Domitian in the first century had combated invaders. The most aggressive attackers were the multiethnic bands from northern Europe that crossed the Danube and Rhine Rivers to raid Roman territory. One theory is that these attacks were the result of a ripple effect of pressure on the northerners caused by wars in central Asia that disrupted trade and normal economic conditions like falling dominoes from east to west. Whatever motivated their incursions into the Roman Empire, these originally poorly organized northerners developed military discipline through their frequent fighting against the Roman army. They mounted especially damaging invasions during the reign of Marcus Aurelius (r. 161–180 C.E.). A major threat also appeared at the eastern edge of the empire, when a new Persian dynasty, the Sasanids, defeated the Parthian Empire and fought to recreate the ancient Persian Empire. By the early third century C.E., Persia's renewed military power forced the emperors to deploy a large part of the army to protect the rich eastern provinces, which took troops away from defense of the northern frontiers.

Recognizing the northern warriors' bravery, the emperors had begun hiring them as auxiliary soldiers for the Roman army in the late first century C.E. and settling them on the frontiers as buffers against other invaders. By the early third century, the army had expanded to enroll perhaps as many as 450,000 troops (the size of the navy remains unknown). Training constantly, soldiers had to be able to carry

DOCUMENT

A Roman Stoic Philosopher on the Capabilities of Women

Musonius Rufus was a Roman philosopher in the first century C.E. who lectured (in Greek) on Stoicism as "the science of living." Leading citizens in Rome became his students. He put his teaching to work by trying to serve as a mediator between the warring forces in the civil war that followed the emperor Nero's death. His ideas were regarded as subversive enough to be threatening to those in power: two different emperors expelled him from Rome, hoping to eliminate his influence. These excerpts reveal his views on the natural capacities of women, education in philosophy, and marriage. His arguments in favor of opportunities and greater equality for women expressed philosophical ideas first explored by earlier Greek philosophers; they did not reflect actual changes in Roman society under the empire.

The gods have given women the same ability to use their minds as men. . . . Women have the same senses as men: vision, hearing, smell, and everything else. . . . Women as well as men have an eagerness and a natural tendency towards excellence (virtue). . . . Therefore, why is it proper for men to investigate and examine to live rightly, that is, to study philosophy and live by its guidance, but not for women? Is it appropriate for men to be good, but not women?

To begin with, a woman must manage her household and pick out what is helpful for her home and take charge of the household slaves. I claim that philosophy is especially helpful for these actions, since each of them is a part of life, and philosophy is nothing other than the science of living. . . . Next, a woman must be chaste, and capable of keeping herself free from illegal love affairs, and pure in other self-indulgent pleasures. She must not delight in quarreling, not be extravagant, or overly concerned with her appearance. . . . She must control her anger, and not be overcome by grief, and stronger than every kind of emotion.

[A woman who is guided by philosophy knows to] love her children more than her own life. What woman could be more just than someone who behaves like that? Therefore, it follows that an educated woman will have more courage than an uneducated woman . . . because neither fear of death nor any concern about suffering would lead her to do anything shameful, and she would not be afraid of anyone just because he was from an important family or powerful or rich. . . .

It is easy to recognize that there are not different types of excellences for men and women. First, men and women both need to have common sense. . . . Second, both need to live just lives. An unjust man can not be a good citizen, and a woman can not run her household well, if she does not run it justly. . . . Third, a wife ought to be chaste, and so should a husband, for the laws punish both sides in cases of adultery. . . .

You might argue that only men need courage, but that is false. The best sort of woman must have the courage of a man and purge herself of cowardice, so that she will not give in to suffering or fear. If she can't do that, then how can she be chaste, if someone by threatening her or torturing her can force her to act disgracefully? . . . That women are able to use weapons, we know from the Amazons, who fought many peoples in battle. . . .

Well then, suppose someone asks, "Do you think that men should learn to work wool like women and that women should work out in the gymnasium like men?" No, that is not what I recommend. I say that, since in the case of human beings the males are naturally stronger . . . , appropriate work ought to be assigned to men and women, with the physically heavier tasks given to the stronger, and the lighter ones to the less strong. . . . Nevertheless, some men might fittingly undertake some of the lighter work and work regarded as more suitable for women, when the conditions of their body or necessity or time require it. For all human work is a common responsibility for men and women, and nothing is necessarily prescribed for one gender or the other. . . .

It is reasonable, then, for me to think that women should be educated like men concerning excellence, and they must be taught, beginning in their childhood, that this is good and that is bad, and that they are the same for both genders, and that this is beneficial and that harmful, and that an individual must do this, and not do that. Such lessons develop reasoning in both girls and boys, and there is no distinction between them. . . .

[In marriage], husband and wife join together to live their lives in common and to have children. . . . They should consider all their property to be shared, and nothing to belong only to themselves, not even their bodies. . . . There must be complete companionship and concern for each other by both husband and wife, in health and in sickness and at all times, because they entered upon the marriage for this reason, as well as to have children. When such caring for one another is perfect, and the married couple provide it for each another, and each works to outdo the other, then this is marriage as it ought to be. . . . But when one partner looks to their own interests alone and neglects the other's concerns . . . or is unwilling to pull together with their partner or to cooperate, then inevitably the marriage is destroyed, and although the two live together, their common interests do poorly, and finally they get a divorce, or they live on in an existence that is worse than loneliness.

Source: Musonius Rufus 3, 4, 13A, Lutz edition. Translation by Thomas R. Martin.

Question to Consider

- **What arguments does the Stoic philosopher make about the benefits of women studying philosophy?**

forty-pound packs twenty miles in five hours, swimming rivers on the way. Since the early second century C.E., the emperors had built many stone camps for permanent garrisons, but on the march an army constructed a fortified camp every night; soldiers transported all the makings of a wooden walled city everywhere they went. As one ancient commentator noted, "Infantrymen were little different from loaded pack mules." At one temporary fort in a frontier area, archaeologists found a supply of a million iron nails—ten tons' worth. The same encampment required seventeen miles of timber for its barracks' walls. To outfit a single legion with tents required fifty-four thousand calves' hides.

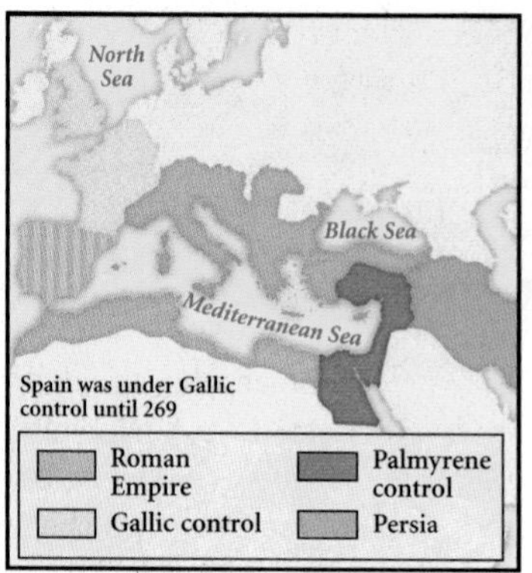

The Fragmented Roman Empire of the Third Century

The increased demand for pay and supplies strained imperial finances because successful conquests had become rare. The army had become a source of negative instead of positive cash flow to the treasury, and the economy had not expanded to make up the difference. To make matters worse, inflation had driven up prices. A principal cause of inflation may have been, ironically, the principate's long period of peace, which increased demand for goods and services to a level that outstripped the supply.

War Scene on Trajan's Column

The emperor Trajan erected a hundred-foot-tall column carved with some twenty-five hundred figures to show his conquest of Dacia (territory north of the Danube River). Our knowledge of Roman military equipment largely comes from the pictures on the column. The scenes spiral up the column in a continuing story, showing Trajan leading his troops and making sacrifices to the gods, with his soldiers preparing to march, crossing the river, building camps, and (as here) fighting hand-to-hand battles with the Dacians, who fought with no armor except shields. *(© Vittoriano Rastelli/Corbis.)*

In desperation, some emperors attempted to curb inflation by debasing imperial coinage to cut government costs. **Debasement of coinage** meant putting less silver in each coin without changing its face value. In this way, the emperors created more cash from the same amount of precious metal. (See "Taking Measure" on page 199.) But merchants soon raised prices to make up for the debased coinage's reduced value; this in turn produced more inflation. By the early third century, the furious spiral of rising prices had spun into a financial tornado. Still, the soldiers demanded that their patrons, the emperors, pay them well. This pressure drove imperial finances into collapse by the 250s C.E.

Uncontrolled Spending, Natural Disasters, and Political Crisis, 193–284 C.E.

The emperors Septimius Severus (r. 193–211 C.E.) and his son Caracalla (r. 211–217 C.E.) made financial crisis unavoidable when they drained the treasury to satisfy the army and their own dreams of glory. A soldier's soldier who came from North Africa, Severus became emperor when his predecessor's incompetence caused a government crisis and civil war. To restore imperial prestige and acquire money through foreign conquest, Severus pursued successful campaigns beyond the frontiers of the provinces in Mesopotamia and Scotland.

Since inflation had reduced their wages to almost nothing, soldiers expected the emperors, as their patrons, to provide gifts of extra money. Severus spent large sums on gifts and raised their regular pay by a third. The army's expanded size made this raise more expensive than the treasury could handle. This out-of-control spending did not bother Severus in the least. His deathbed advice to his sons Caracalla and Geta in 211 C.E. was to "stay on good terms with each other, be generous to the soldiers, and pay no attention to anyone else."

Caracalla and Civil War

Severus's sons followed his advice only on the last two points. Caracalla, after murdering his brother, ended the Roman Golden Age of peace

---

debasement of coinage: Putting less silver in a coin without changing its face value; a failed financial strategy during the third-century C.E. crisis in Rome.

and prosperity with his uncontrolled spending and cruelty. He increased the soldiers' pay by another 40 to 50 percent and spent gigantic sums on building projects, including the largest public baths Rome had ever seen, covering blocks and blocks of the city. These huge expenses put unbearable pressure on the local provincial officials responsible for collecting taxes and on the citizens, whom the officials in turn squeezed for ever larger payments.

In 212 C.E., Caracalla took his most famous step to try to fix the budget: he granted Roman citizenship to almost every man and woman in imperial territory except slaves. Since only citizens paid inheritance taxes and fees for freeing slaves, an increase in citizens meant an increase in revenues, most of which was earmarked for the army. But too much was never enough for Caracalla, whose cruelty to anyone who displeased him made contemporaries whisper that he was insane. His attempted conquests of new territory failed to bring in enough funds, and he wrecked imperial finances. Once when his mother reprimanded him for his excesses he replied, as he drew his sword, "Never mind, we won't run out of money as long as I have this."

The financial crisis generated political instability that led to a half century of civil war. This period of violent struggle broke the back of the principate. For fifty years, a parade of emperors and pretenders fought to rule. More than two dozen men, often several at once, held or claimed power in that time. Their only qualification was their ability to command a frontier army and to reward the troops for loyalty to their general instead of to the state.

The civil war devastated the population and the economy. Violence and hyperinflation made life miserable in many regions. Agriculture withered as farmers could not keep up normal production when armies searching for food ravaged their crops. City council members faced constantly escalating demands for tax revenues from the swiftly changing emperors. The endless financial pressure destroyed members' will to serve their communities.

Historians dispute how severely natural disaster worsened the empire's financial and political crisis, but earthquakes and epidemics did strike some of the provinces in the mid-third century. In some regions, the population declined significantly as food supplies became less dependable, civil war killed soldiers and civilians alike, and infection raged. The loss of population meant fewer soldiers for the army, whose strength as a defense and police force had been gutted by political and financial chaos. This weakness made frontier areas more vulnerable to raids and allowed roving bands of robbers to range unchecked inside the borders.

TAKING MEASURE

The Value of Roman Imperial Coinage, 27 B.C.E.–300 C.E.

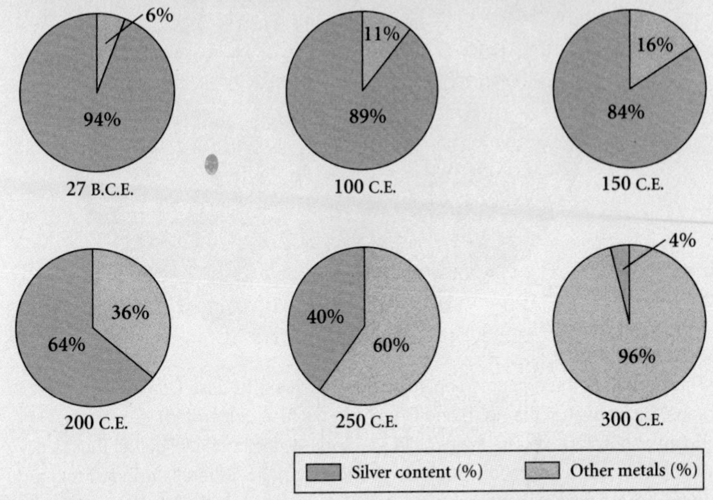

Ancient silver coinage got its value from its metallic content; the less silver in a coin, the less the coin was worth. When government and military expenses rose but revenues fell because no conquests were being made, emperors debased the coinage by reducing the amount of silver and increasing the amount of other, cheaper metals in each coin. These pie charts reveal that devaluation of the coinage was gradual until the third century C.E., when military expenses skyrocketed. By 300 C.E., coins contained only a trace amount of silver. Debasement fueled inflation because merchants and producers had to raise their prices for goods and services when they were paid with currency that was increasingly less valuable.

Source: Adapted from Kevin Greene, *The Archeology of the Roman Economy* (London: B. T. Batsford, Ltd., 1986), 60.

Question to Consider

- **How might the increasing devaluation have affected the lives of citizens at all levels in the Roman Empire?**

Foreign enemies to the north and east took advantage of the third-century crisis to attack. Roman fortunes hit bottom when Shapur I, king of the Sasanid Empire of Persia, invaded the province of Syria and captured the emperor Valerian (r. 253–260 C.E.). By this time, imperial territory was in constant danger of being captured. Zenobia, the warrior queen of Palmyra in Syria, for example, seized Egypt and Asia Minor. Emperor Aurelian (r. 270–275 C.E.) won back these provinces only with great difficulty. He also had to encircle Rome with a larger wall to ward off attacks from northern raiders, who were smashing their way into Italy.

Emperor Severus and His Family

This portrait of the emperor Septimius Severus; his wife, Julia Domna; and their sons, Caracalla (on the right) and Geta (with his face obliterated) was painted in Egypt about 200 C.E. The males hold scepters, symbolic of rule, but all four family members wear bejeweled golden crowns fit for royalty. Severus arranged to marry Julia without ever meeting her because her horoscope predicted she would become a queen, and she served as her husband's valued adviser. They hoped their sons would share rule, but when Severus died in 211 C.E., Caracalla murdered Geta so that he could rule alone. Why do you think the portrait's owner rubbed out Geta's face? *(bpk, Berlin/Antikensammlung, Staaliche Museen, Berlin, Germany/photo by Johannes Laurentius/Art Resource, NY.)*

Persecution of Christians Polytheists explained the third-century crisis in the traditional way: the state gods were angry about something. But what? The obvious answer was the presence of Christians, who denied the existence of the Roman gods and refused to worship them. Emperor Decius (r. 249–251 C.E.) therefore launched a systematic persecution to eliminate Christians and restore the goodwill of the gods. He proclaimed himself Restorer of the Cults while declaring, "I would rather see a rival to my throne than another bishop of Rome." He ordered all the empire's inhabitants to prove their loyalty to the state's well-being by sacrificing to its gods. Christians who refused were killed. This persecution did not stop the civil war, economic failure, and natural disasters that threatened Rome's empire, and Emperor Gallienus (r. 253–268 C.E.) ordered Christians to be left alone and their property restored. The crisis in government continued, however, and by the 280s C.E. the principate had reached a political dead end.

REVIEW QUESTION What were the causes and the effects of the Roman crisis in the third century C.E.?

Conclusion

Augustus created the principate and the Pax Romana by constructing a disguised monarchy as princeps while insisting that he was restoring the Roman republic. He succeeded because he ensured the loyalty of the army and the people by becoming their patron. He bought off the upper class by letting them keep their traditional offices and status. Provincials found this arrangement acceptable because it resembled the kind of top-down government that they had grown used to before Roman conquest. The imperial cult provided a focus for building and displaying loyalty to the emperor.

So long as the emperors had enough money to keep their millions of clients satisfied, stability prevailed. They provided food to the poor, built baths and arenas for public entertainment, paid their troops well, and helped out members of the elite when they needed it. The emperors of the first and second centuries expanded the military to protect their distant territories stretching from Britain to North Africa to Syria. By the second century, peace and prosperity had created an imperial Golden Age. Long-term financial difficulties set in, however, because the army, now concentrating on defense, no longer brought money in through frequent conquests. Severe inflation made the situation desperate. Since the provincial elites could no longer meet the demand for increased taxes without draining their fortunes, they lost their public-spiritedness and avoided their communal responsibilities. Loyalty to the state became too expensive.

The emergence of Christianity added to the instability because Roman officials doubted the loyalty of the Christians. The new religion evolved from Jewish apocalypticism to a hierarchical organization. Its

Sasanid Silver Plate with Royal Hunting Scene

This silver plate, plated with gold, shows the ruler of the Sasanid Empire hunting with a bow and arrow while riding a camel. The Sasanids ruled the territory of the ancient Persian Empire, centered in Iran, for four hundred years beginning in the third century C.E. The Roman emperors treated the Sasanid emperors as their equals, respecting their wealth and fearing their military power. *(© Ancient Art and Architecture Collection, Ltd.)*

MAPPING THE WEST

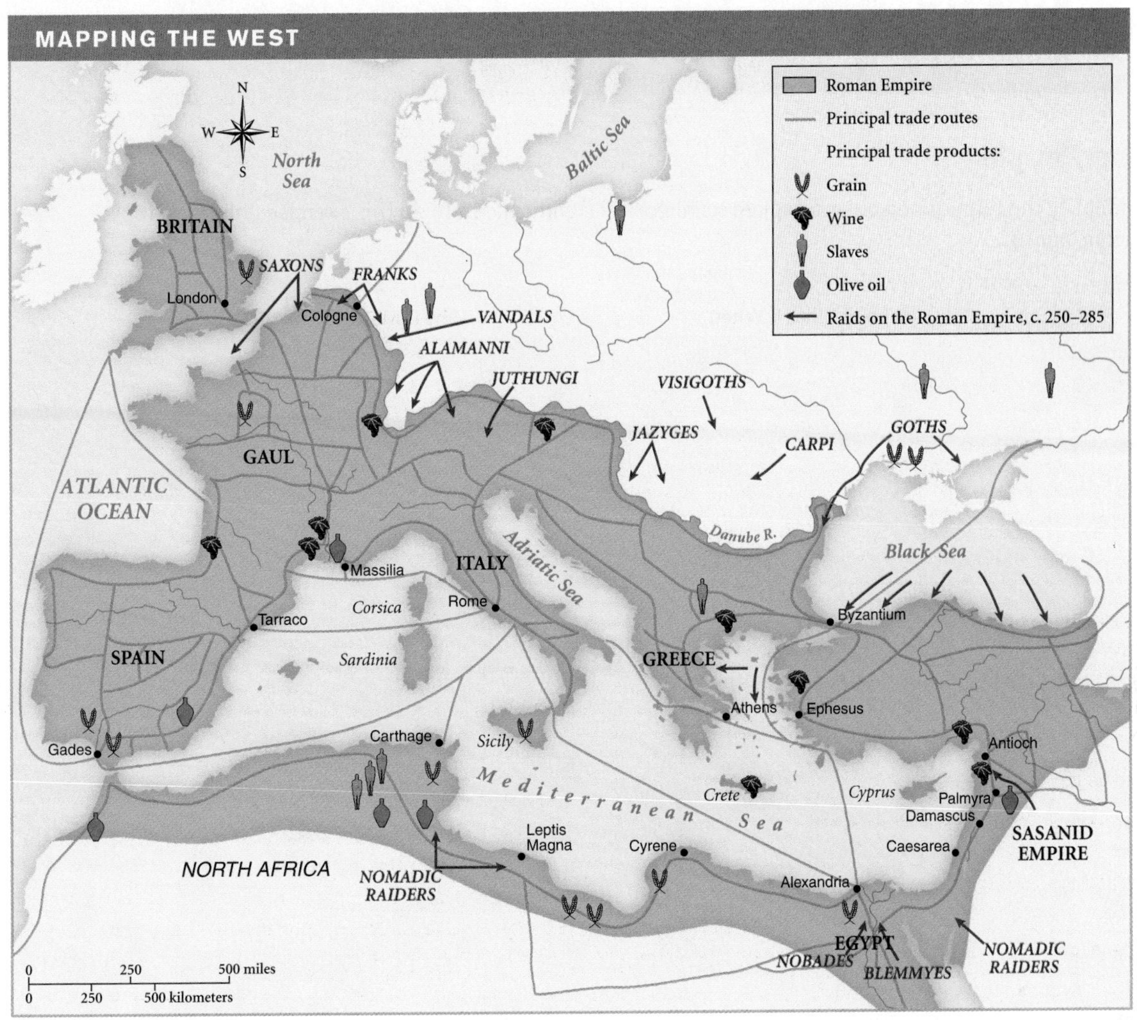

The Roman Empire in Crisis, 284 C.E.

By the 280s C.E., fifty years of civil war had torn the principate apart. Imperial territory retained the outlines inherited from the time of Augustus (compare Map 6.1 on page 184), except for the loss of Dacia to the Goths a few years before. Attacks from the north and east had repeatedly penetrated the frontiers, however. Long-distance trade had always been important to the empire's prosperity, but the decades of violence had made transport riskier and therefore more expensive, contributing to the crisis. | **What do you think would have been the greatest challenges in ruling such a vast empire in an age without swift communications or fast travel?**

believers argued with one another and with the authorities. Martyrs such as Vibia Perpetua worried the government with the depth of their beliefs; citizens placing loyalty to a single divinity ahead of loyalty to the state was a new and inexplicable phenomenon for Roman officialdom.

When financial ruin, natural disasters, and civil war combined to create a political crisis for the principate in the mid-third century C.E., the emperors lacked the money and the popular support to solve their problems. Not even persecutions of Christians could convince the gods to restore Rome's good fortunes. Threatened with the loss of peace, prosperity, and territory, the empire needed a political transformation to survive. That process began under the emperor Diocletian (r. 284–305 C.E.). Under his successor, Constantine (r. 306–337 C.E.), the Roman Empire also began the slow process of becoming officially Christian.

FOR FURTHER EXPLORATION

- **For additional primary-source material from this period**, see *Sources of the Making of the West*, Fourth Edition.
- **For Web sites, images, and documents related to topics in this chapter**, visit *Make History* at bedfordstmartins.com/hunt.

Chapter 6 Review

Online Study Guide bedfordstmartins.com/hunt

Key Terms and People

In the grid below, identify the term or person and explain its historical significance. (To do this exercise online, go to bedfordstmartins.com/hunt.)

Term	Who or What & When	Why It Matters
Pax Romana (Roman Peace) (p. 172)		
Augustus (p. 173)		
principate (p. 173)		
praetorian guard (p. 174)		
Julio-Claudians (p. 181)		
Colosseum (p. 183)		
decurions (p. 185)		
Romanization (p. 185)		
Christ (p. 190)		
martyr (p. 193)		
apostolic succession (p. 193)		
orthodoxy (p. 194)		
heresy (p. 194)		
Neoplatonism (p. 196)		
debasement of coinage (p. 198)		

Review Questions

1. How did the peace gained through Augustus's "restoration of the Roman republic" affect Romans' lives in all social classes?
2. In the early Roman Empire, what was life like in the cities and in the country for the elite and for ordinary people?
3. Which aspects of social, cultural, and political life in the early Roman Empire supported the growth of Christianity, and which opposed it?
4. What were the causes and the effects of the Roman crisis in the third century C.E.?

Making Connections

1. What were the similarities and differences between the crisis in the first century B.C.E. that undermined the Roman republic and the crisis in the third century C.E. that undermined the principate?
2. If you had been a first-century Roman emperor under the principate, what would you have done about the Christians and why? What if you had been a third-century emperor?
3. Do you think that the factors that caused the crisis in the Roman Empire could cause a similar crisis in the Western world of today?

Important Events

Date	Event	Date	Event
30 B.C.E.	Octavian (the future Augustus) conquers Ptolemaic Egypt	70–90 C.E.	New Testament Gospels are written
27 B.C.E.	Augustus inaugurates the principate	80s C.E.	Domitian leads campaigns against multiethnic invaders on northern frontiers
30 C.E.	Jesus crucified in Jerusalem	161–180 C.E.	Marcus Aurelius battles multiethnic bands attacking northern frontiers
64 C.E.	Great fire in Rome; Nero blames Christians	212 C.E.	Caracalla extends Roman citizenship to almost all free inhabitants of the provinces
69 C.E.	Civil war after death of Nero	230s–280s C.E.	Third-century financial and political crisis
70 C.E.	Titus captures Jerusalem and destroys the Jewish temple	249–251 C.E.	Decius persecutes Christians

- Consider three events: **Great fire in Rome; Nero blames Christians (64 C.E.), New Testament Gospels are written (70–90 C.E.)**, and **Decius persecutes Christians (249–251 C.E.)**. How were these persecutions similar to and different from one another, and what attitudes did they illustrate? How might polytheist and Christian ideas have contributed to these events?

SUGGESTED REFERENCES

Scholars continue to debate the nature and the significance of the many social, cultural, and (especially) religious changes that occurred under the early Roman Empire. Perhaps the most difficult question to answer is to what extent life became better or worse for most people—and indeed how to define *better* and *worse* in this context—once the empire stopped expanding into new territories.

Ando, Clifford. *The Matter of the Gods: Religion and the Roman Empire*. 2008.

Crossan, Dominic, and Jonathan Reed. *In Search of Paul: How Jesus's Apostle Opposed Rome's Empire with God's Kingdom*. 2005.

Denzey, Nicola. *The Bone Gatherers: The Lost Worlds of Early Christian Women*. 2007.

*Futrell, Allison. *The Roman Games: Historical Sources in Translation*. 2006.

Galinsky, Karl, ed. *The Cambridge Companion to the Age of Augustus*. 2005.

Goldsworthy, Adrian. *The Complete Roman Army*. 2003.

Green, Bernard. *Christianity in Ancient Rome: The First Three Centuries*. 2010.

Harris, W. V. *Rome's Imperial Economy*. 2010.

*Kraemer, Ross Shephard. *Her Share of the Blessings: Women's Religion among Pagans, Jews, and Christians in the Greco-Roman World*. 1992.

MacMullen, Ramsay. *Christianizing the Roman Empire (A.D. 100–400)*. 1984.

Mattingly, David J. *Imperialism, Power, and Identity: Experiencing the Roman Empire*. 2010.

Matz, David. *Life of the Ancient Romans: Daily Life through History*. 2008.

Roman emperors: http://www.roman-emperors.org/startup.htm

Roth, Roman, and Johannes Keller, eds. "Roman by Integration: Dimensions of Group Identity in Material Culture and Text." Special issue, *Journal of Roman Archaeology* (suppl. no. 66). 2007.

*Suetonius. *Lives of the Caesars*. Trans. Catharine Edwards. 2009.

Syme, Ronald. *The Roman Revolution*. 1939; repr. 2002.

*Tacitus. *The Complete Works*. Trans. Alfred John Church and William Jackson Brodribb. 1964.

*Primary source.

CHAPTER 7

The Transformation of the Roman Empire

284–600 C.E.

In 376, bands of Visigoths, desperate to escape the deadly attacks of the Huns, begged the Roman emperor Valens (r. 364–378) to let them cross the Danube River from their northern homelands into Roman territory.[1] Like emperors before him, Valens admitted them into the empire because he wanted to use their warriors in place of Romans, who could buy their way out of military service by paying for barbarian—that is, northern foreign—mercenaries to substitute for them. Roman officers charged with helping the barbarians instead greedily extorted bribes. They even forced the starving refugees to sell some of their own people into slavery to buy dogs to eat.

Furious, the barbarians massacred Valens's army at the battle of Adrianople in Thrace in 378. Valens trampled on the bleeding corpses of his men as he tried to escape. He did not make it, and his body was never found. Some said he was burned to death while hiding in a farmhouse, fulfilling the wish of citizens who often expressed their unhappiness with his reign by rioting in the streets and yelling, "We want to set Valens on fire alive!" Theodosius I (r. 379–395), Valens's successor, then had to allow the barbarians to settle permanently inside the borders in a kingdom under their own laws and give them annual "gifts" of money, in return for their fighting alongside Romans as federates (allies) protecting the empire.

The battle of Adrianople, Rome's bloodiest defeat since Hannibal invaded Italy six hundred years earlier,

Vandal General Stilicho and His Family

This ivory diptych ("folding tablet") from around 400 C.E. shows Stilicho, the top general in the Roman army in Europe and close adviser to the western Roman emperor, with his wife, Serena, and their son Eucherius. Stilicho's life reveals the mixing of cultures in the later Roman Empire: his father was from the Vandal tribe in Germany and his mother was Roman; he himself rose to prominence in Roman imperial government and society. Serena was the adoptive daughter of the emperor, and Stilicho and Serena's daughter Maria married the emperor's son. Stilicho is shown dressed in the richly decorated clothing appropriate for a member of the Roman elite, and he wears a metal clasp to fasten his robe, a symbol of his father's ethnicity. The images on his shield of the two emperors then ruling the divided Roman Empire proclaim his loyalty even as they point to the political and geographic fragmentation of the time. *(Basilica di San Giovanni Battista, Monza, Italy/The Bridgeman Art Library International.)*

[1]From this point on, dates are C.E. unless otherwise indicated.

illustrates the conflicted relationship that the emperors had with the peoples north and east of the Danube and Rhine Rivers in Europe: for centuries, Rome's rulers, recognizing the barbarians' bravery, had hired them as soldiers and let them bring their families into the empire, while at the same time looking down on them for their non-Roman ways and often allowing imperial officials to exploit them so cruelly that they rebelled. The unintended consequences of this relationship helped change the course of history by pushing the Roman Empire toward division into two halves with different destinies.

Competition between ambitious generals and would-be emperors had driven the empire's third-century political crisis. The emperor Diocletian (r. 284–305) finally restored temporary political stability. Tough enough to impose peace, he was also flexible enough to reorganize the administration by appointing a co-emperor and two assistant emperors. Regaining social stability proved more difficult because of suspicion between Christians and followers of traditional polytheistic cults concerning who was responsible for the divine anger that, they all believed, had sent the crisis. Diocletian convinced his co-rulers to persecute the Christians, whom he blamed. His successor Constantine (r. 306–337) ended the persecution by converting to Christianity and supporting his new faith with imperial funds and a policy of religious freedom. Even with official support, however, it took nearly a hundred years more for Christianity to become the state religion, and the church from early on was rocked by fierce disagreements over doctrine. The social and cultural transformations produced by the Christianization of the Roman Empire settled in even more slowly because many Romans clung to their traditional beliefs; Christian emperors had to employ non-Christians if they wanted to get the best possible administrators and generals.

Diocletian's reform of government only postponed the division of imperial territory: less than twenty years after the battle of Adrianople, Theodosius I split the empire in two, with one of his sons ruling the west and the other the east. The two emperors were supposed to cooperate, but in the long run this system of divided rule could not cope with the different pressures affecting the two regions.

In the western Roman empire, military and political events provoked social and cultural change when barbarian newcomers began living side by side with Romans. Both sides changed, with the barbarians creating kingdoms and laws based on Roman traditions yet adopting Christianity, while wealthy Romans increasingly fled from cities to seek safety in country estates when the western central government became ineffective. These changes in turn transformed the political landscape of western Europe in ways that

Coin Portrait of Emperor Constantine
Constantine had these special, extra-large coins minted to depict him for the first time as an overtly Christian emperor. The jewels on his helmet and crown, the fancy bridle on the horse, and the scepter indicate his status as emperor, while his armor and shield signify his military accomplishments. He proclaims his Christian rule with his scepter's new design—a cross with a globe—and the round badge sticking up from his helmet that carries the monogram signifying "Christ" that he had his soldiers paint on their shields to win God's favor in battle. *(The Art Archive.)*

293 Diocletian creates the tetrarchy

301 Diocletian issues edict on maximum prices and wages

303 Diocletian launches Great Persecution of Christians

312 Constantine wins battle of the Milvian Bridge and converts to Christianity

313 Religious freedom proclaimed in the Edict of Milan

323 Pachomius in Upper Egypt establishes the first monasteries

324 Constantine wins civil war and refounds Byzantium as Constantinople, the "new Rome"

325 Council of Nicaea defends Christian orthodoxy against Arianism

361–363 Julian the Apostate tries to reinstate polytheism as official state religion

378 Barbarian massacre of Roman army in battle of Adrianople

391 Theodosius I makes Christianity the official state religion

395 Theodosius I divides empire into western and eastern halves

410 Visigoths sack Rome

300 C.E. — 350 C.E. — 400 C.E.

foreshadowed Europe's later political states. In the east, the empire, economically vibrant and politically united, lived on for a thousand years beyond its disintegration and transformation in the west and helped pass on the memory of classical traditions to later Western civilization by preserving much ancient Greek and Roman literature. Despite financial pressures and the gradual loss of territory, the eastern half endured as the continuation of the Roman Empire until Turkish invaders conquered it in 1453.

CHAPTER FOCUS What were the most important sources of unity and of division in the Roman Empire from the reign of Diocletian to the reign of Justinian, and why?

From Principate to Dominate in the Late Roman Empire, 284–395

Diocletian and Constantine pulled Roman government from its extended crisis by increasing the emperors' authority, reorganizing the empire's defense, restricting workers' freedom, and changing the tax system to try to raise the money for all these changes. The two emperors also believed that they had to win back divine favor to ensure their people's safety. However, the effort to regain the gods' goodwill was complicated by worry about the growing number of Christians in the empire.

Diocletian and Constantine believed that they had to resolve the empire's problems by becoming more autocratic. Since for Romans strength had to be visible to be effective, they transformed their appearance as rulers to make their power seem awesome beyond compare, taking ideas from the self-presentation of the kings of the powerful contemporary Persian Empire. They hoped that their assertion of supremacy would help keep the empire united. In the long run and for multiple reasons, however, it proved impossible to preserve the empire on the scale once ruled by Augustus.

The Political Transformation and Division of the Roman Empire

The man to make the first attempt to restore and secure the empire was Diocletian. No one could have predicted his rise to power: he began life as an uneducated peasant in the Balkans, far from the center of power in Rome. In the third-century crisis, however, military talent counted for more than connections. Diocletian's leadership, courage, and intelligence propelled him through the ranks until the army made him emperor in 284. He ended a half a century of civil war by imposing the most autocratic system of rule in Roman history.

Inventing the Dominate The foremost symbol of Diocletian's new system was the title that he used after becoming emperor: *dominus*, meaning "lord" or "master"—what slaves called their owners. Historians refer to Roman rule from Diocletian onward as the ***dominate***. Like the emperors before them, the emperors of the dominate continued to refer to their government

dominate: The openly authoritarian style of Roman rule from Diocletian (r. 284–305) onward; the word was derived from *dominus* ("master" or "lord") and contrasted with *principate*.

426 Augustine publishes *The City of God*

451 Council of Chalcedon attempts to forge agreement on Christian orthodoxy

450 C.E.

475 Visigoths publish law code

476 German commander Odoacer deposes the final western emperor, the boy Romulus Augustulus ("fall of Rome")

493–526 Ostrogothic kingdom in Italy

500 C.E.

507 Clovis establishes Frankish kingdom in Gaul

527–565 Reign of eastern Roman emperor Justinian

529–534 Justinian publishes law code and handbooks

540 Benedict devises his rule for monasteries

550 C.E.

as the Roman republic (see, for example, the first line in the document "Diocletian's Edict on Maximum Prices and Wages," page 211), but they ruled autocratically. This new system eliminated the principate's ideal of the princeps ("first man") as the social equal of the senators, with whom he shared political power—the emperors of the dominate recognized no equals. The offices of senator, the consul, and so on from the ancient republic continued to exist but only as posts of honor. These officials had the responsibility to pay for public services, especially chariot races and festivals, but no power to govern. Imperial administrators were increasingly chosen from lower ranks of society according to their competence and their loyalty to the emperor.

The grandiose style of the dominate recalled the monarchies of the Near East rather than the modest manner of Augustus's principate. In particular, the dominate's emperors took ideas for emphasizing their superiority from the Sasanids in Persia, whose empire (224–651) they recognized as equal to their own in power and whose king and queen they addressed as "our brother" and "our sister." The Roman Empire's masters now broadcasted their majesty by surrounding themselves with courtiers and ceremony, presiding from a raised platform, and sparkling in jeweled crowns, robes, and shoes. Constantine took from Persia the tradition that emperors set themselves apart by wearing a diadem, a purple gem-studded headband, as a visible boast of supremacy that recalled the decorated ribbon Alexander the Great put on his head after conquering the Persian king. In another echo of Persian monarchy, a series of veils separated the palace's waiting rooms from the interior room where the emperor listened to people's pleas for help or justice, further emphasizing the difference between the emperor and ordinary people. Officials marked their rank in the rigidly hierarchical administration by wearing special shoes and belts and claiming grandiose titles such as "most perfect."

The dominate's emperors also asserted their supreme power through laws and punishments. Their word alone made law. Indeed, they came to be above the law because they were not bound by anyone else's decisions, not even those of their predecessors. To impose order, they raised punishments to often brutal levels. Violent criminals were executed in traditional fashion: tied in a leather sack with poisonous snakes and drowned in a river. New punishments included Constantine's order that the "greedy hands" of officials who took bribes "shall be cut off by the sword." The guardians of a young girl who allowed a lover to seduce her were executed by having molten lead poured into their mouths. Penalties

The Empire's Four Rulers

This sculpture shows the four rulers of the tetrarchy, the system of shared rule that the emperor Diocletian created in the 290s C.E. to try to administer and defend the Roman Empire more effectively. The sculptor divided the rulers into two pairs, each showing an emperor and a co-emperor (the junior member of the pair). Their gestures symbolize the closeness that the pairs were supposed to display in the tetrarchy, while their nearly identical faces imply that individuality was secondary to cooperation in the new system of governing. Their hands on swords emphasize that they were ready to use force to defend Roman territory and tradition. Originally erected in Constantinople, the capital of the eastern empire, the sculpture was probably looted when crusaders sacked that city in 1204. It was then carried back to Venice, where it was built into the wall of St. Mark's cathedral. *(Basilica di San Marco, Venice, Italy / The Bridgeman Art Library International.)*

grew ever harsher for the majority of the population, legally designated as "humbler people" to indicate they could be punished more severely than the "better people" for comparable offenses. In this way, the dominate strengthened the divisions between ordinary people and the rich.

Subdividing Imperial Rule Diocletian realized that he needed to reform imperial rule to prevent civil war and defend against invaders from the north and the east. The principle underlying his reforms—subdivide the government's power to strengthen it—was daring because it increased the chance of more civil war between ambitious leaders. By 293, he had put the first part of his plan into practice. He divided imperial territory into four loosely defined administrative districts, two in the west and two in the east. He then appointed three "partners" (a co-emperor, Maximian, and two assistant emperors, Constantius and Galerius, who were the designated successors) to join him in this new subdivision of power, called a **tetrarchy** ("rule by four"). Each ruler controlled one of the four districts. Diocletian served as supreme ruler and was supposed to receive the loyalty of the others. This system was Diocletian's attempt to put imperial government into closer contact with the empire's frontier regions, where the dangers of invasion and rebellious troops loomed.

Diocletian also subdivided the territory of the provinces themselves, thereby doubling their number to almost a hundred. He then grouped these smaller administrative units into twelve regions (dioceses) under separate governors, who reported to the four emperors' assistants, the praetorian prefects (Map 7.1). Finally, he tried to prevent provincial

tetrarchy: The "rule by four," consisting of two co-emperors and two assistant emperors/designated successors, initiated by Diocletian to subdivide the ruling of the Roman Empire into four regions.

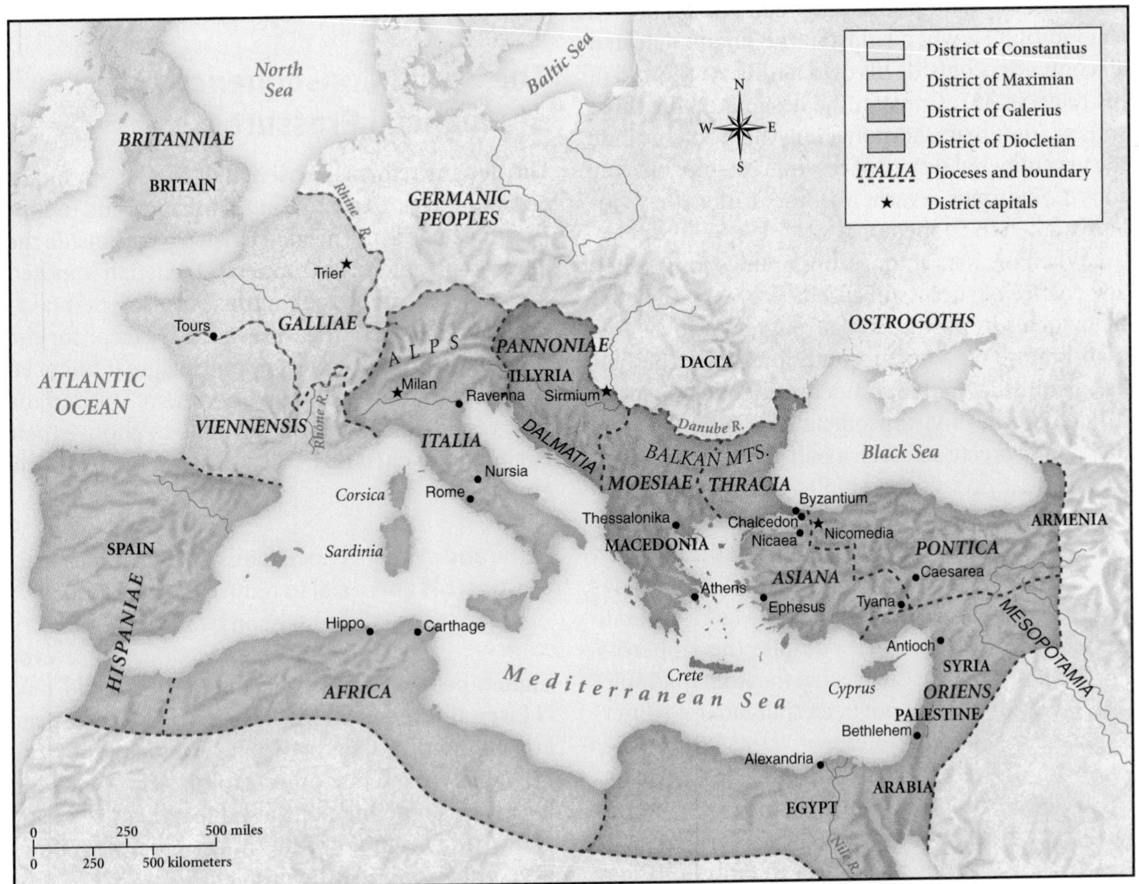

MAP 7.1 Diocletian's Reorganization of 293
Trying to prevent civil war, Emperor Diocletian reorganized Rome's imperial territory into a tetrarchy, to be ruled by himself, his co-emperor Maximian, and assistant emperors Constantius and Galerius, each the head of a large district. He subdivided the preexisting provinces into smaller units and grouped them into twelve dioceses, each overseen by a regional administrator. The four districts as shown here reflect the arrangement recorded by the imperial official Sextus Aurelius Victor in about 360. | **What were the advantages and disadvantages of subdividing the empire?**

administrators from rebelling by separating their civil and military authority—granting them control only of legal and financial affairs while entrusting defense to separate commanders, a process that Constantine completed.

Diocletian's successors dropped the tetrarchy, but his reforms mattered because appointing co-emperors continued to be tried in later times as a way to prevent political instability. His reforms also ended Rome's thousand years as the empire's most important city. Diocletian—who lived in Nicomedia, in Asia Minor—did not even visit Rome until 303, nearly twenty years after becoming emperor. Italy became just another section of the empire, on an equal footing with the other provinces and subject to the same taxation system, except for the district of Rome itself—the last trace of the city's traditional preeminence.

The Creation of the Eastern and Western Empires

Diocletian failed to bring long-lasting political stability to the Roman Empire. He resigned in 305 for unknown reasons, after which rivals for power fought off and on in civil wars until 324, when Constantine finally defeated all contenders outside his own family. At the end of his reign in 337, Constantine designated his three sons as joint heirs, admonishing them to continue the new imperial system of co-emperorship. Like the sons of Septimius Severus a century earlier, they violently failed to cooperate.

When the wars among Constantine's sons ruined any chance of successful co-emperorship, they put their forces in positions that roughly split the Roman Empire on a north–south line along the Balkan peninsula. In 395, Emperor Theodosius made this territorial division official. He intended this division to create an eastern half and a western half of the empire that would be co-ruled and cooperate politically and militarily, but in the long run the empire's halves would be governed largely as de facto separate territories despite the emperors' insistence that the Roman Empire had not been split into two different states.

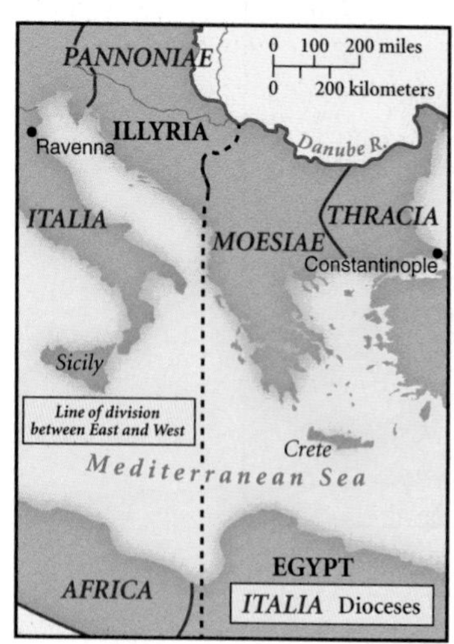

The Empire's East/West Division, 395

Each half had its own capital city. Constantinople ("Constantine's City")—formerly the ancient city of Byzantium (today Istanbul, Turkey)—was the eastern capital. Constantine—who had renamed it after himself in 324, boasting that it was a "new Rome"—had made it his capital because of its strategic military and commercial location: it lay at the mouth of the Black Sea on an easily fortified peninsula astride principal routes for trade and troop movements. To recall the glory of Rome and thus claim for himself the political legitimacy of the old capital, Constantine constructed a forum, an imperial palace, a hippodrome for chariot races, and monumental statues of the traditional gods in his refounded city. Constantinople grew to be the most important city in the Roman Empire.

Geography determined the site of the western capital as well. Honorius, Theodosius's son and successor in the west, wanted his palace in a city that he believed was easy to defend. In 404, he chose the port of Ravenna, an important commercial center on Italy's northeastern coast that housed a main naval base. Great marshes and walls protected it from attack by land, while access to the sea kept it from being starved out in a siege. Though the emperors enhanced it with churches covered in multicolored mosaics, Ravenna never rivaled Constantinople in size or splendor.

The Social Consequences of Financial Pressures

Diocletian's reforms carried high costs, both financial and social. To try to control inflation and to support the huge army needed to keep peace inside the empire and defend its frontiers, Diocletian imposed not only price and wage controls but also a new taxation system. These measures failed, except for the unintended consequence of putting great financial pressures on both rich and poor. Also, Diocletian's new restrictions on people's rights to choose their occupations curtailed freedoms for many in the empire.

Price and Wage Controls and Tax Increases

Diocletian realized it was crucial to reduce the hyperinflation brought on by the third-century civil wars. As prices rose ever higher, people hoarded whatever they could buy. "Hurry and spend all my money you have; buy me any kinds of goods at whatever prices they are available," wrote one official to his servant, trying to salvage something of the value of his savings by converting his money into things. Hoarding, however, only worsened the problem.

In 301, the inflation was so severe that Diocletian imposed harsh price and wage controls in the worst-hit areas (see Document, "Diocletian's Edict on Maximum Prices and Wages," page 211). This mandate, which blamed high prices not on government

DOCUMENT

Diocletian's Edict on Maximum Prices and Wages

In an effort to control high inflation caused by soaring government spending, Diocletian and his co-emperors issued an edict in 301 C.E. setting maximum prices and wages for the first time in Roman history. Their orders proved impossible to enforce across the vast empire. The chances for success were small in any case, as setting fixed prices tends to lead people to reduce production of goods and hoard those that are available. The high-sounding language was typical of imperial bureaucracy under the dominate.

Recalling the wars that we have successfully waged, it is to the fortune of our republic, next to the immortal gods, that we owe the peaceful state of our world, located in the lap of the deepest tranquillity, and the benefits of peace, which we worked for with great effort. Our honorable public and Rome's respectability and majesty long for this fortune to be faithfully established and suitably adorned. Therefore, we, who with the kind support of the gods in the past overcame the blazing raids of the barbarian peoples by slaughtering those nations, must fortify the tranquillity that we established for eternity with the necessary defenses of justice. . . .

It is agreed that we [the co-emperors], who are the parents of the human race, are to bring decisive justice to the situation, so that what humanity has long hoped for but not been able to provide will be conferred by the solutions of our foresight for the common improvement of everyone. . . .

Who then could be unaware that audacity lies in wait to attack the public interest wherever the common well-being of everyone demands that our armies be directed, not only in villages or towns but on every march, jacking up prices for goods for sale not four or eight times, but to such a height that the system of human speech cannot find names for this pricing and this deed. And so the result is that the sale of a single item deprives the soldier of his bonus and his pay, and that all the taxes paid by the entire world to support the armies fall victim to this detestable profit seeking. . . .

It is our decision that, if anyone makes an effort through daring to go against this edict, he shall be subject to capital punishment. . . .

Listed below are the prices for the sale of individual items; no one may exceed them. *[These examples are selections from the edict's long list of maximum allowed prices and wages. A sextarius was about half a liter. The Roman pound was about three-quarters of a U.S. pound. The silver coin was the denarius. A soldier at this date earned eighteen hundred silver coins per year.]*

Prices for food

Sextarius of first-quality old wine, 24 silver coins
Sextarius of country wine, 8 silver coins
Sextarius of beer from Gaul, 4 silver coins
Sextarius of beer from Egypt, 2 silver coins
Pound of pork, 12 silver coins
Pound of goat or sheep, 8 silver coins
Fattened pheasant, 250 silver coins
Pair of chickens, 60 silver coins
Pound of second-quality fish, 16 silver coins

Wages for workers

Daily pay for a farm laborer, with food, 25 silver coins
Daily pay for a finish carpenter, with food, 50 silver coins
Baker, with food, 50 silver coins
Mule doctor, for trimming and preparing hoofs, 6 silver coins per animal
Scribe, for first-quality writing, 25 silver coins per 100 lines
Scribe, for second-quality writing, 20 silver coins per 100 lines
Elementary teacher, 50 silver coins per student per month
Greek, Latin, or geometry teacher, 200 silver coins per student per month
Public speaking teacher, 250 silver coins per student per month
Legal expert or speaker in court, 1,000 silver coins per case

Source: *Diocletiani edictum de pretiis rerum venalium.* Translation by Thomas R. Martin.

Question to Consider

- **What do the maximum prices set reveal about what society most valued in the late Roman Empire?**

spending but on profiteers' "unlimited and frenzied avarice," forbade hoarding of goods and set ceilings on what could legally be charged or paid for about one thousand goods and services. Merchants refused to cooperate, however, and government officials were unable to enforce the mandate, despite the threat of death or exile as the penalty for violations. Diocletian's price and wage controls therefore only increased the financial pressures on the population.

The civil wars that followed Diocletian's resignation stoked the government's insatiable appetite for revenue. The emperors increased taxes mostly to support the army, which required enormous amounts of grain, meat, salt, wine, vegetable oil, horses, camels, and mules. The major sources of revenue were a tax on land, assessed according to its productivity, and a head tax on individuals. To supplement taxes paid in coin, the emperors began collecting some payments in goods and services.

The empire was too large to enforce the tax system uniformly. In some areas both men and women ages twelve to sixty-five paid the full tax, but in others women paid only half the tax assessment or none at all. The reasons for such differences are not

TAKING MEASURE

Peasants' Use of Farm Produce in the Roman Empire

This graph offers a speculative model (precise statistics have not survived) of how peasants during the Roman Empire perhaps used what they produced as farmers and herders to maintain their families, pay rent and taxes, and buy things they did not produce themselves. Individual families would have had widely varying experiences and there were definitely strong regional differences in the vast empire, but it is nevertheless likely that most families had to use most of their production just to maintain a subsistence level—a description of poverty by modern standards.

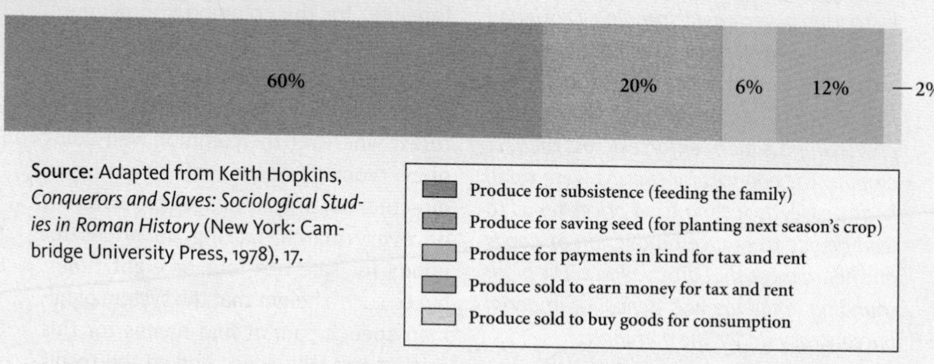

Source: Adapted from Keith Hopkins, *Conquerors and Slaves: Sociological Studies in Roman History* (New York: Cambridge University Press, 1978), 17.

Question to Consider

■ What does the distribution of farmers' produce reveal about priorities, as well as the nature of their life and existence?

recorded, so we cannot tell whether women were being granted a privilege (perhaps to recognize their role as caregivers for children) or being regarded as less valuable than men and therefore liable to a lower rate. Workers in cities probably owed taxes only on their property, perhaps to encourage crafts production; they periodically paid "in kind," that is, by laboring without pay on public works projects such as cleaning municipal drains or repairing buildings. People in commerce, from shopkeepers to prostitutes, still paid taxes in money, while members of the senatorial class were exempt from ordinary taxes but had to pay special levies.

Social Consequences The new tax system could work only if agricultural production remained stable and the government kept track of the people liable for the head tax (see "Taking Measure," above). Diocletian therefore restricted the movement of tenant farmers, called ***coloni*** ("cultivators"), whose work provided the empire's economic base. Coloni had traditionally been free to move from farm to farm as long as their debts were paid. Now male coloni, as well as their wives in areas where women were assessed for taxes, were increasingly tied to a particular plot of land. Their children were also bound to the family plot, making farming a hereditary obligation.

The government also regulated other occupations deemed essential. Bakers, who were required to produce free bread for Rome's many poor, a tradition begun under the republic to prevent food riots, could not leave their jobs, and anyone who acquired a baker's property had to assume that occupation. From Constantine's reign on, the military was another hereditary lifetime career: the sons of military veterans were obliged to serve in the army. As usual, however, conditions were not the same everywhere in the empire. Free workers earning wages apparently remained important in the economy of Egypt in the late Roman Empire, and archaeological evidence suggests that some regions may actually have become more prosperous. As always, no single or simple description can cover the varieties in the conditions of life in such a vast extent of territories and over long periods of time.

The emperors also decreed oppressive regulations for the **curials**, the social elite in the cities and towns. During this period, many men in the curial class were obliged to serve as decurions (un-

coloni **(kuh LOH ny):** Literally, "cultivators"; tenant farmers in the Roman Empire who became bound by law to the land they worked and whose children were legally required to continue to farm the same land.

curials (KYUR ee uhls): The social elite in Roman empires' cities and towns, most of whom were obliged to serve as decurions on municipal Senates and collect taxes for the imperial government, paying any shortfalls themselves.

salaried members of their city Senate) and to spend their own funds to support the community. Their financial responsibilities ranged from maintaining the water supply to feeding troops, but their most expensive duty was paying for shortfalls in tax collection. The emperors' demands for more and more revenue made this duty a crushing obligation, compounding the damage that the third-century crisis had inflicted on local elites. Scholars debate how effective imperial regulations were in forcing curials to take on burdensome public service and how deep dissatisfaction with the central government became, but it is clear that the emperors tried hard to squeeze more out of the curials.

For centuries, the empire's welfare had depended on a steady supply of property owners filling local offices in return for honor and the emperor's favor. Now this tradition broke down as some wealthy people avoided public service to escape financial ruin. So distorted had the situation become that service on a municipal council could be imposed as punishment for a crime. Eventually, to prevent curials from escaping their obligations, imperial policy decreed that they could not move away from the town where they had been born. Members of the elite sought exemptions from public service by petitioning the emperor, bribing imperial officials, or taking up an occupation that freed them from curial obligations (the military, imperial administration, or church governance). The most desperate simply fled, abandoning home and property to avoid fulfilling their traditional duties.

The restrictions on personal freedom caused by the pressures for higher taxes contributed to the erosion of communal values that had long motivated wealthy Romans. The drive to increase revenues also produced social discontent among poorer citizens: the tax rate on land eventually reached one-third of the land's gross yield, impoverishing small farmers. Financial troubles, especially severe in the west, kept the empire overall from ever regaining the prosperity of its Golden Age.

From the Great Persecution to Religious Freedom

Diocletian concluded that the gods' anger had caused the empire's third-century crisis. To win back divine goodwill, he called on citizens to follow the ancient gods who had guided Rome to power and virtue in the past: "Through the providence of the immortal gods, eminent, wise, and upright men have in their wisdom established good and true principles. It is wrong to oppose these principles or to abandon the ancient religion for some new one." Christianity was the new faith he meant.

Diocletian's Great Persecution and the Conversion of Constantine

To eliminate what he saw as a threat to national security, Diocletian in 303 launched the so-called **Great Persecution** to please the gods by suppressing Christianity. He expelled Christians from official posts, seized their property, tore down churches, and executed anyone who refused to participate in official religious rituals. His three partners in the tetrarchy applied the policy unevenly. In the western empire, official violence against Christians stopped after about a year; in the east, it continued for a decade. The public executions of Christians were so gruesome that they aroused the sympathy of some polytheists. The Great Persecution, like the edict on prices and wages, ultimately failed: it undermined social stability without destroying Christianity.

Constantine changed the world's religious history forever by converting to the new faith. He had learned to have a favorable view of Christians from his father, one of the empire's co-rulers, and believed that the Christian God brought him victory in a crucial battle that secured his political power. During the civil war that Constantine fought after Diocletian stepped down, before the battle of the Milvian Bridge in Rome in 312, Constantine reportedly experienced a dream promising him God's support and saw Jesus's cross in the sky surrounded by the words "In this sign you will be the victor." Constantine ordered his soldiers to paint "the sign of the cross of Christ" on their shields and won a great victory that ended the civil war. He attributed his success to the Christian God's miraculous power and goodwill, and declared himself a Christian.

Edict of Milan of 313

Following his conversion to the new faith, Constantine did not make polytheism illegal and did not make Christianity the official state religion. Instead, he forced his co-rulers to allow religious freedom, a policy that, following his father's lead, he had put into practice in the west as early as 306. The best evidence for this change survives in the so-called **Edict of Milan** of 313 (see Document, "The Edict of Milan on Religious Freedom," page 214). It proclaimed that Constantine and his polytheist co-emperor Licinius decreed free choice of religion for everyone under

---

Great Persecution: The violent program initiated by Diocletian in 303 to make Christians convert to traditional religion or risk confiscation of their property and even death.

Edict of Milan: The proclamation of Roman co-emperors Constantine and Licinius decreeing free choice of religion in the empire.

DOCUMENT

The Edict of Milan on Religious Freedom

In 313 C.E., Constantine, recently converted to Christianity, and his co-emperor, Licinius, a follower of traditional Roman religion, met to discuss official policy on religion. They agreed to abolish restrictions on Christianity and proclaim religious freedom in the eastern parts of the empire; Constantine had done this as early as 306 in the west. The document contains the letter of instructions later sent to governors in the eastern provinces; it is the best surviving evidence for the new policies. The long sentences (which are shortened here) and lofty language reflect the official imperial style.

When I, Constantine Augustus, and I, Licinius Augustus, had a successful meeting at Milan and discussed everything pertaining to the public benefit and security, among other things that we regarded as going to be of use to many people, we believed that first place should go to those matters having to do with reverence for divinity, so that we might give the Christians and everyone the free power of worshipping in the religion that they wish. In this way, whatever divinity exists in the heavenly seat may be appeased and be kind to us and to all those who are established under our power. And thus, believing that we should initiate this policy on a wholesome and most upright basis, we thought that to no one whatsoever should the opportunity be denied, whether he dedicates his mind to the worship of the Christians or to that religion, which he felt best suited him. Our purpose is so that the highest divinity, whose religion we follow with free minds, may provide his customary favor and kindness in all things. Wherefore it has pleased us for your Devotedness [the provincial governor] to know that all the restrictions on the Christian name set forth in letters given to your office previously are completely removed and that whatever seemed utterly sinister and foreign to our clemency should be repealed, and that now any person of those also wishing to observe the religion of the Christians may strive to do so freely and plainly without any worry or interference. We believed that these things should be made completely clear to your Solicitude so that you would know that we have given a free and absolute permission to these Christians to practice their religion. When you see that we have granted this to them, your Devotedness will know that we have likewise conceded an open and free power to others to practice their religion for the sake of the tranquillity of our age, so that each person may have free permission to worship in the manner he has chosen. We did this so that we shall not seem to have detracted from any observance or religion.

[The emperors next order people who bought or received Christians' property confiscated in the Great Persecution to return it at no cost and then to apply to an imperial representative for reimbursement through the emperors' "clemency."]

On all these matters you will be obligated to provide your most effectual aid to the body of Christians mentioned above, so that our orders may be carried out more quickly, whereby public tranquillity may be served also by our clemency. In this way it will happen, as was explained above, that divine favor toward us, which we have experienced in so many things, will endure for all time to give prosperity to our successes in company with the public happiness. Moreover, so that the content of this ordinance and of our kindness may come to everyone's attention, it should be put up everywhere above an announcement of your own and brought to the knowledge of everyone, so that this ordinance of our kindness shall not be concealed.

Source: Lactantius, *On the Deaths of the Persecutors*, 48, and Eusebius, *Ecclesiastical History*, 10.5.2–14. Translation by Thomas R. Martin.

Question to Consider

- **What reasons do Constantine and Licinius give for instituting this new policy of religious freedom?**

their rule and referred to protection of the empire by "the highest divinity"—an imprecise term meant to satisfy both polytheists and Christians.

Constantine tried to avoid angering traditional polytheists, who still greatly outnumbered Christians, but he also promoted his newly chosen religion. These conflicting goals called for a careful balancing act that continued the principle of subdividing power to try to maintain order and stability. In this case, he subdivided official support and respect for religion. For example, he returned all property confiscated from Christians during the Great Persecution, but he had the treasury compensate those who had bought it. When in 321 he made the Lord's Day of each week a holy occasion on which no official business or manufacturing work could be performed, he called it Sunday to blend Christian and traditional notions in honoring two divinities, God and the sun. He decorated his new capital of Constantinople with statues of traditional gods. Above all, he respected tradition by continuing to hold the office of *pontifex maximus* ("chief priest"), which emperors had filled ever since Augustus.

REVIEW QUESTION What were Diocletian's policies to end the third-century crisis, and how successful were they?

The Official Christianization of the Empire, 312–c. 540

Constantine's conversion in 312 set the empire on the path to official Christianization. The process was gradual: not until the end of the fourth century was Christianity proclaimed the state religion, and even after that many people for a long time continued to worship the traditional gods in private. Eventually, however, Christianity became the religion of the overwhelming majority by attracting converts among women and men of all classes, assuring believers of personal salvation, offering the social advantages and security of belonging to the emperors' religion, nourishing a strong sense of shared identity and community, developing a hierarchy to govern the church, and creating communities of devoted monks (male and female). The transformation from polytheist empire into Christian state was the Roman Empire's most important influence on Western civilization.

Polytheism and Christianity in Competition

Since almost everyone in the Roman Empire believed that religion was fundamental to the safety and prosperity of the community and the individual, polytheism and Christianity were in a serious competition for people's faith. (See "Seeing History," page 216.) Polytheists and Christians shared some similar beliefs. Both, for example, regarded spirits and demons as powerful and ever-present forces in life. Over time, the two competing faiths influenced each other to a limited degree. Some polytheists focused their beliefs on a supreme god who seemed almost monotheistic; some Christians took ideas from Neoplatonist philosophy. Some people perhaps merged the two faiths: a silver spoon used in the worship of the polytheist forest spirit Faunus, for example, has been found engraved with the outline of a fish, the common symbol whose Greek spelling (*ichthys*) was taken as an acronym for the Greek words "Jesus Christ the Son of God, the Savior." Some scholars think this image indicates a combination of pagan and Christian beliefs in the same cult.

The Persistence of Polytheism Unbridgeable differences remained, however, between the beliefs of traditional polytheists and Christians. People disagreed over whether there was one God or many, and what degree of interest the divinity (or divinities) paid to the human world. Most polytheists participated in frequent festivals and sacrifices to many different gods. Why, they wondered, were these joyous occasions not enough to satisfy everyone's need for contact with divinity?

Polytheists also could not accept a divine savior who promised eternal salvation for believers but had apparently lacked the will or the power to overthrow Roman rule and prevent his own execution as a rebel. The traditional gods, by contrast, had given their worshippers a world empire. Moreover, polytheists could say, cults such as that of the goddess Isis and philosophies such as Stoicism insisted that only the pure of heart and mind could be admitted to their fellowship. Christians, by contrast, embraced sinners. Why, wondered perplexed polytheists, would anyone want to associate with such people? In short, as the Greek philosopher Porphyry argued, Christians had no right to claim they possessed the sole version of religious truth, for no one had ever discovered a doctrine that provided "the sole path to the liberation of the soul."

The slow pace of Christianization revealed how strong polytheism remained in this period, especially at the highest social levels. In fact, the emperor known as **Julian the Apostate** (r. 361–363) rebelled against his family's Christianity—the word *apostate* means "renegade from the faith"—by trying to reverse official support of the new religion in favor of his own less

Julian the Apostate: The Roman emperor (r. 361–363), who rejected Christianity and tried to restore traditional religion as the state religion. *Apostate* means "renegade from the faith."

Relief Sculpture of Saturn from North Africa
This pillar depicts the solar divinity known to Romans as Saturn and to Carthaginians as Ba'al Hammon, from the cult of the Phoenician founders of Carthage. This syncretism (identifying deities as the same even though they carried different names in different places) was typical of ancient polytheism and allowed Roman and non-Roman cults to merge. The inscription dates the pillar to 323. Other objects testify to the prevalence of polytheistic cults in the Roman Empire until the end of the fourth century. What in this sculpture indicates that it depicts a god? (*© Martha Cooper/Peter Arnold, Inc./photolibrary.*)

SEEING HISTORY

Changing Religious Beliefs: Pagan and Christian Sarcophagi

Christianity became Rome's state religion in 391 when the emperor Theodosius I banned polytheist sacrifices, but the Christianization of the empire had begun long before. Over time, Christians found ways to testify publicly to their beliefs, often making creative use of methods previously employed to honor Rome's traditional gods. We can see this process in action by comparing scenes from two sarcophagi (stone coffins), one from the first century and one from the mid-fourth century. These decorated coffins were meant to be seen, not hidden in the ground, to make a statement about their owner's beliefs.

The left-hand image, from a pagan Roman sarcophagus, shows a religious procession by members of the cult of the god Dionysus. The worship of Dionysus as god of wine and theater was so complex

Scene of a Procession in Honor of the God Dionysus. Marble Sarcophagus, Roman, First Century C.E. *(Erich Lessing/Art Resource, NY.)*

traditional and more philosophical interpretation of polytheism. Like Christians, he believed in a supreme deity, but he based his religious beliefs on Greek philosophy when he said, "This divine and completely beautiful universe, from heaven's highest arch to earth's lowest limit, is tied together by the continuous providence of god, has existed ungenerated eternally, and is imperishable forever."

Making Christianity Official

Julian was killed in a military expedition against Persia, and the succeeding emperors were Christians. They provided financial support for their religion while denying it to traditional cults. They dropped the title *pontifex maximus* and ceased government-funded sacrifices. Symmachus (c. 340–402), a polytheist senator who also served as prefect (mayor) of Rome, objected to this suppression of religious diversity. In a last public plea for religious freedom, he echoed Porphyry: "We all have our own way of life and our own way of worship. . . . So vast a mystery cannot be approached by only one path."

Christianity officially replaced polytheism as the state religion in 391 when **Theodosius I** enforced a

Theodosius I: The Roman emperor (r. 379–395) who made Christianity the state religion by ending public sacrifices in the traditional cults and closing their temples. In 395 he also divided the empire into western and eastern halves to be ruled by his sons.

as even to seem contradictory, ranging from violent passion to peaceful rest; it showed both the good that could come from pleasure and the evil that resulted from going too far. Lively processions in his honor, some led by women, were popular. Dionysus is shown here in one of his many different forms: a chubby, lusty, old drunkard, whom the Romans called Bacchus. He reclines on a cart with a jar of wine, pulled by a horse and some kind of half man, half beast, perhaps a centaur. His entourage also includes female musicians, who dance along playing horns and beating tambourines. What other details can you make out? Do they offer hints about the values of the cult of Dionysus?

Compare this scene with the one shown on the right, a detail from the most spectacular surviving example of an early Christian sarcophagus. This coffin, from 359, held the remains of Junius Bassus, a prominent Roman official. Carved from marble in a classical style, the scenes are all taken from the Bible and center on the story of Christ. The absence of references to polytheistic mythology, which had been standard on earlier Christian sarcophagi, illustrates Christians' growing confidence in their own religious traditions, which they display in the same way that pagans had previously done. What accounts for the position of Adam's and Eve's hands? What do the scenes suggest about the roles of women in pagan and Christian religion?

Question to Consider

- **What similarities and differences do you see in these two images, and what do they suggest about the religious traditions by which they are inspired?**

Adam and Eve on the Sarcophagus of Junius Bassus, 359 C.E. *(Erich Lessing/Art Resource, NY.)*

ban on polytheist sacrifices, even if private individuals paid for the animals. He also announced that all polytheist temples had to close. Nevertheless, some famous shrines, such as the Parthenon in Athens, remained open for a long time. Pagan temples were gradually converted to churches during the fifth and sixth centuries. Non-Christian schools were not forced to close — the Academy, founded by Plato in Athens in the early fourth century B.C.E., endured for 140 years after Theodosius's reign — but Christians received advantages in official careers.

Jews posed a special problem for the Christian emperors. They seemed entitled to special treatment because Jesus had been a Jew. Previous emperors had allowed Jews to practice their religion, but the Christian emperors now burdened them with legal restrictions. Imperial decrees banned Jews from holding government posts but still required them to assume the financial burdens of curials without the status. By the late sixth century, the law barred Jews from marrying Christians, making wills, receiving inheritances, or testifying in court.

These restrictions began the long process that made Jews into second-class citizens in later European history, but they did not destroy Judaism. Magnificent synagogues had appeared in Palestine, where some Jews still lived, though most had been dispersed throughout the cities of the empire and the lands to the east. Jewish scholarship flourished in this period, culminating in the vast fifth-century C.E.

texts known as the Palestinian and the Babylonian Talmuds (learned opinions on the Mishnah, a collection of Jewish law) and the Midrash (commentaries on parts of Hebrew Scripture). These extremely detailed records of centuries of argument over everything from philosophical ideas to the rules for daily life eventually became authoritative for many Jews in medieval and modern Europe.

Christianity's Growing Appeal By the end of the fourth century, Christianity had been finding converts outside the Jewish community for three hundred years. Now that the faith had an official status, it attracted even more new believers, especially in the military. Since their emperors were now Christian, soldiers could convert and still serve in the army; previously, Christians had sometimes created disciplinary problems by renouncing their military oath. At his court-martial in 298 for refusing to continue his duties, one senior infantryman had said, "A Christian serving the Lord Christ should not serve the affairs of this world." Once the emperors had become Christians, however, soldiers saw military duty as serving Christ's regime.

Christianity's social values contributed to its appeal by offering believers a strong sense of shared identity and community in this world. Since the time of Paul, when Christians traveled, they could find a warm welcome in the local congregation (Map 7.2). The faith had also won converts from early on by promoting the tradition of charitable works characteristic of Judaism and some polytheist cults, which emphasized caring for poor people, widows, and orphans. By the mid-third century, for example, Rome's Christian congregation was supporting fifteen hundred widows and poor people. Fellowship and philanthropy to support believers in need contributed to the faith's growth.

Women were deeply involved in the new faith. **Augustine** (354–430), bishop of Hippo, in North Africa, and perhaps the most influential theologian in Western civilization, recognized women's contribution to the strengthening of Christianity in a letter he wrote to the unbaptized husband of a baptized woman: "O you men, who fear all the burdens imposed by baptism! Your women easily best you. Chaste and devoted to the faith, it is their presence in large numbers that causes the church to grow." Women could win a high reputation by giving their property to their congregation or by renouncing marriage to dedicate themselves to Christ. Consecrated virgins who chose not to marry and widows who chose not to remarry thus joined large donors as especially respected women. These women's choices challenged the traditional social order, in which women were supposed to devote themselves to raising families. Even these sanctified women, however, were largely excluded from leadership positions as the church's hierarchy came more closely to resemble the male-dominated world of imperial rule. There were still some women leaders in the church even in the fourth century, but they were a small minority.

Jesus as Sun God
This heavily damaged mosaic, perhaps from the mid-third century, depicts Jesus like the Greek god of the sun, Apollo, riding in a chariot pulled by horses with rays of light shining forth around his head. This symbolism—God is light—reached back to ancient Egypt. Christian artists used it to portray Jesus because he had said, "I am the light of the world" (John 8:12). The mosaic artist arranged the sunbeams to suggest the shape of the Christian cross. The cloak flaring from Jesus's shoulder suggests the spread of his motion across the heavens. *(Scala / Art Resource, NY.)*

Augustine: Bishop in North Africa whose writings defining religious orthodoxy made him the most influential theologian in Western civilization.

Hierarchy in the Church The need to organize believers to support the Christianization of the Roman Empire led to the creation of a hierarchy based on the authority of male bishops in charge of groups of congregations in different regions. That hierarchy replaced early Christianity's relatively loose communal organization, in which many women held leadership posts. Over time, the bishops replaced the curials as the emperors' partners in local rule, in return earning the right to control the distribution of imperial subsidies to the people. Regional councils of bishops appointed new bishops and addressed doctrinal disputes. There were regional differences concerning whether some bishops should outrank other bishops in the area, but bishops in the largest cities eventually became the most powerful leaders in the church. The main bishop of Carthage, for example, oversaw at least a hundred local bishops in the surrounding area. The bishop of Rome eventually emerged as the church's supreme leader in the western empire, claiming for himself a title previously applied to many bishops: pope (from *pappas*, a child's word for "father" in Greek), the designation still used for the head of the Roman Catholic church. Christians in the eastern empire never conceded this title to the bishop of Rome, however.

The bishops of Rome claimed they had leadership over other bishops on the basis of the New Testament, where Jesus addresses Peter, his head apostle: "You are Peter, and upon this rock I will build my church. . . . I will entrust to you the keys of the kingdom of heaven. Whatever you bind on earth shall be bound in heaven. Whatever you loose on earth shall be loosed in heaven" (Matt. 16:18–19). Noting that Peter's name in Greek means "rock" and that Peter had founded the Roman church, bishops in Rome eventually argued that they had the right to command the church as Peter's successors.

Portrait of Augustine

This fresco (painting on plaster) from the Lateran Basilica in Rome is the oldest surviving portrait of Augustine. It shows him reading a book in the form of a codex (that is, as books are made today, with bound pages instead of one long scroll of paper). This was an appropriate pose since Augustine was one of the most widely read scholars of the Roman Empire, as well as perhaps its most productive author, writing countless works on Christian thought and doctrine. *(The Granger Collection, NY— All rights reserved.)*

The Struggle for Clarification in Christian Belief

Jesus himself left no written teachings, and early Christians frequently argued over what their savior had meant them to believe. The church's expanding hierarchy struggled to establish clarity concerning what Christians should believe to ensure its members' spiritual purity. Bishops as well as rank-and-file believers often disagreed about theology, however, and doctrinal disputes repeatedly threatened the unity of the church.

Controversy centered on what was orthodoxy and what was heresy. (See Chapter 6, page 194.) After Christianity became official, the emperor was ultimately responsible for enforcing orthodox creed (a summary of correct beliefs) and could use force to compel agreement when disputes led to violence.

Arguing about God: Arianism Theological questions about the nature of the Christian Trinity—Father, Son, and Holy Spirit, three seemingly separate deities nevertheless conceived by orthodox believers to be a unified, co-eternal, and identical divinity—proved the hardest to clarify. The doctrine called **Arianism** generated fierce controversy for centuries. Named after its founder, Arius (c. 260–336), a priest from Alexandria, it maintained

---

Arianism: The Christian doctrine named after Arius, who argued that Jesus was "begotten" by God and did not have an identical nature with God the Father.

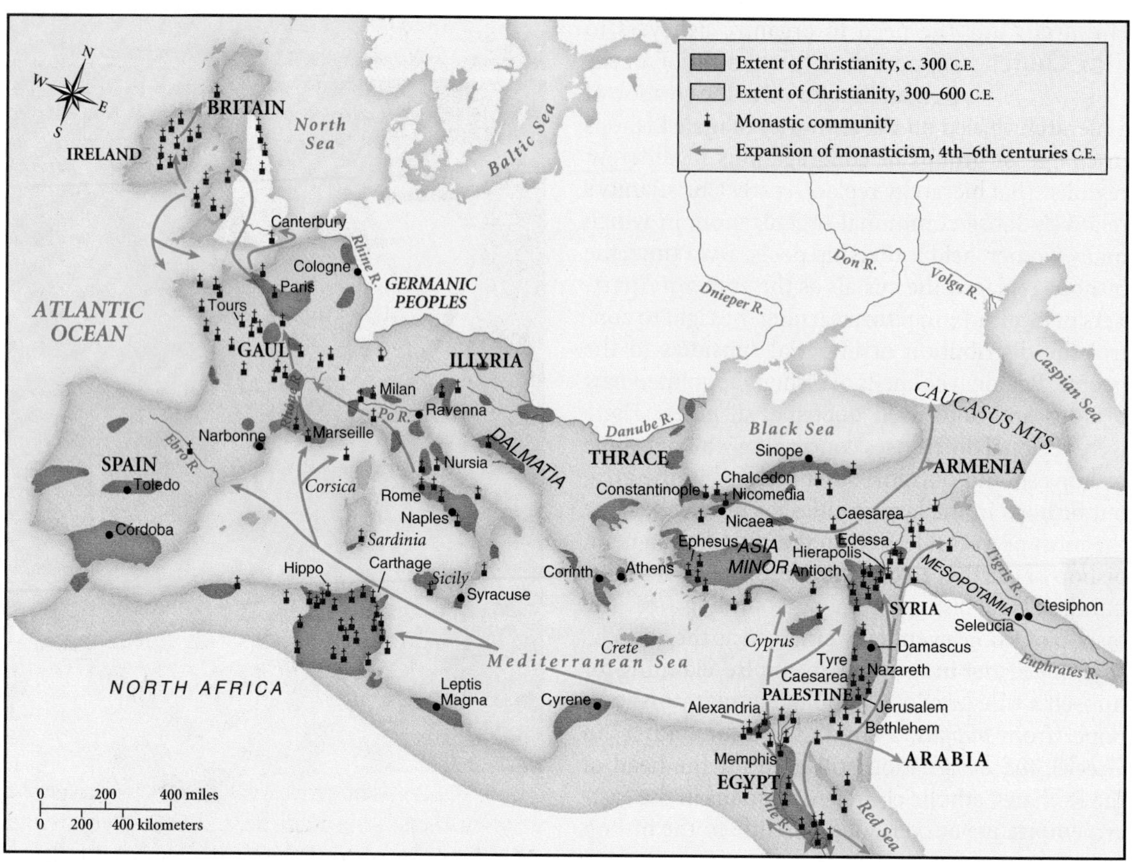

MAP 7. 2 The Spread of Christianity, 300–600

Christians were a minority in the Roman Empire in 300, although congregations existed in many cities and towns, especially in the eastern provinces. The emperor Constantine's conversion to Christianity in the early fourth century gave a boost to the new religion. It gained further strength during that century as the Christian emperors supported it financially and eliminated subsidies for the polytheist cults that had previously made up the religion of the state. By 600, Christians were numerous in all parts of the empire. *(From Henry Chadwick and G. R. Evans,* Atlas of the Christian Church *[Oxford: Andromeda Oxford Ltd., 1987], 28. Reproduced by permission of Andromeda Oxford Limited.)*

that God the Father begot (created) his son Jesus from nothing and gave him his special status. Thus, Jesus was not identical with God the Father and was, in fact, dependent on him. This view of Jesus as secondary did not fit with others' ideas about the nature of the Holy Trinity. Arianism found widespread support—the emperor Valens and his barbarian opponents were Arian Christians. Many people found this doctrine appealing because it eliminated the difficulty of understanding how a son could be the equal of his father and because its subordination of son to father corresponded to the norms of family life. Arius used popular songs to make his views known, and people everywhere became engaged in the controversy. "When you ask for your change from a shopkeeper," one observer remarked in describing Constantinople, "he harangues you about the Begotten and the Unbegotten. If you inquire how much bread costs, the reply is that 'the Father is superior and the Son inferior.'"

Disputes such as this led Constantine to try to restore ecclesiastical peace and lead the bishops in clarifying religious truth. In 325, he convened 220 bishops at the Council of Nicaea to discuss Arianism. The majority of bishops voted to come down hard on the heresy: they banished Arius to Illyria, a rough Balkan region, and declared in the **Nicene Creed** that the Father and the Son were *homoousion* ("of one substance") and co-eternal. So difficult were the issues, however, that Constantine later changed his mind twice, first recalling Arius from exile and then reproaching him again not long after. The doctrine lived on: Constantine's third son, Constantius II

Nicene Creed: The doctrine agreed on by the council of bishops convened by Constantine at Nicaea in 325 to defend orthodoxy against Arianism. It declared that God the Father and Jesus were *homoousion* ("of one substance").

Mosaic of a Family from Edessa

This mosaic, found in a cave tomb from c. 218–238 C.E., depicts an elite family from Edessa in the late Roman Empire. Their names are given in Syriac, the dialect of Aramaic spoken in their region, and their colorful clothing reflects local Iranian traditions. The mosaic's border uses decorative patterns from Roman art, illustrating the combining of cultural traditions in the Roman Empire. Edessa was the capital of the small kingdom of Osrhoëne, annexed by Rome in 216. It became famous in Christian history because its king Abgar (r. 179–216) was the first monarch to convert to Christianity, well before Constantine. The eastern Roman emperors proclaimed themselves the heirs of King Abgar. *(Photo by J. B. Segal, one of the authors, from* Vanished Civilizations: Forgotten Peoples of the Ancient World, *ed. by Edward Bacon, 1967. London: Thames and Hudson.)*

(r. 337–361), favored Arianism, and his missionaries converted many of the non-Roman peoples who later poured into the empire.

Monophysitism, Nestorianism, and Donatism

Numerous other disputes about the nature of Christ divided believers. The orthodox position held that Jesus's divine and human natures commingled within his person but remained distinct. Monophysites (a Greek term for "single-nature believers") argued that the divine took precedence over the human in Jesus and that he therefore had essentially only a single nature. They split from the orthodox hierarchy in the sixth century to found independent churches in Egypt (the Coptic church), Ethiopia, Syria, and Armenia.

Nestorius, who became the bishop of Constantinople in 428, argued that Mary in giving birth to Jesus produced the human being who became the temple for the indwelling God. Nestorianism therefore offended Christians who accepted the designation of *theotokos* (Greek for "bearer of God") for Mary. The bishops of Alexandria and Rome had Nestorius deposed and his doctrines officially rejected at councils held in 430 and 431; they condemned his writings in 435. Refusing to accept these decisions, Nestorian bishops in the eastern empire formed a separate church centered in Persia, where for centuries Nestorian Christians flourished under the tolerance of non-Christian rulers. They later became important agents of cultural diffusion by establishing communities that still endure in Arabia, India, and China.

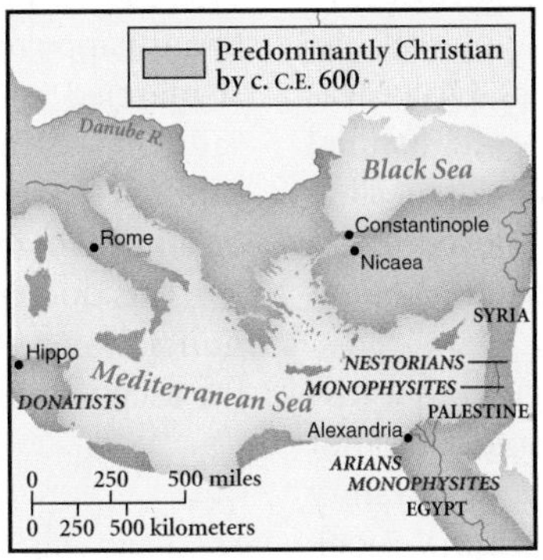

Original Areas of Christian Splinter Groups

Donatism best illustrates the level of ferocity that Christian disputes could generate. A conflict erupted in North Africa not over theology but over whether to readmit to their old congregations Christians who had cooperated with imperial authorities during the Great Persecution. The Donatists (followers of the North African priest Donatus) insisted that the church should not be polluted with such "traitors." So bitter was the clash that it even broke apart Christian families. One son threatened his mother, "I will join Donatus's followers, and I will drink your blood."

With emotions at a fever pitch, the church promoted orthodoxy as religious truth. A council organized in Chalcedon (a suburb of Constantinople) in 451 to settle the still-raging disagreement over Nestorius's views was the most important attempt to clarify orthodoxy. The conclusions of the Council of Chalcedon form the basis of what most Christians in the West still accept as doctrine. At the time, however, it failed to create unanimity, especially in the eastern empire, where Monophysites flourished.

Augustine on Order

The ideas of Augustine contributed largely to Christian orthodoxy in the western empire. By around 500, Augustine and other influential theologians such as Ambrose (c. 339–397) and Jerome (c. 345–420) earned the informal title *church fathers* because their views were cited as authoritative in disputes over orthodoxy. Augustine became the most famous of this group of patristic (from *pater,* Greek for "father") authors, and for the next thousand years his works would be the most influential texts in western Christianity except the Bible. He wrote so prolifically about religion and philosophy that a later scholar was moved to declare: "The man lies who says he has read all your works."

Augustine deeply affected later thinkers with his views on order in human life, expressed in *The City of God*, a "large and arduous work," as he called it, published in 426 after thirteen years of writing. In it, Augustine asserted that the basic dilemma for humans lay between the desire for earthly pleasures and the desire for spiritual purity. Emotion, especially love, was natural and commendable, but only when directed toward God. Humans were misguided to look for any value in life on earth. Only life in God's eternal city at the end of time had meaning.

Nevertheless, Augustine wrote, law and government are required on earth because humans are imperfect. God's original creation was perfect, but after Adam and Eve disobeyed God, humans lost their initial perfection and inherited a permanently flawed nature. According to this doctrine of original sin—a subject of theological debate since at least the second century—Adam and Eve's disobedience passed down to human beings a hereditary moral disease that made the human will a divisive force. This corruption necessitated governments that could suppress evil. The state therefore had a duty to compel people to remain loyal to the church, by force if necessary.

For Augustine, the purpose of secular authority was to maintain a social order based on a moral order. To help maintain order, Christians had a duty to obey the emperor and participate in political life. Soldiers, too, had to follow their orders. Order was so essential, Augustine argued, that it even justified what he admitted was the unjust institution of slavery. Although detesting slavery, he believed it was a lesser evil than the social disorder that he thought its abolition would create.

In *The City of God*, Augustine argued that history has a divine purpose, even if people could not see it. All that Christians could know with certainty was that history progressed toward an ultimate goal, but only God could know the meaning of each day's events:

> To be truthful, I myself fail to understand why God created mice and frogs, flies and worms. Nevertheless, I recognize that each of these creatures is beautiful in its own way. For when I contemplate the body and limbs of any living creature, where do I not find proportion, number, and order exhibiting the unity of concord? Where one discovers proportion, number, and order, one should look for the craftsman.

The repeated *I* in this passage indicates the intense personal engagement Augustine brought to matters of faith and doctrine. Many other Christians shared this intensity, a trait that energized their disagreements over orthodoxy and heresy.

Augustine and Sexual Desire

Next to the nature of Christ, the question of how to understand and regulate sexual desire presented Christians with the thorniest problem in the search for religious truth. Augustine became the most influential source of the idea that sex trapped human beings in evil and that they should therefore strive for **asceticism**, the practice of self-denial, especially through spiritual discipline. Augustine knew from personal experience how difficult it was to accept this doctrine. In his autobiographical work *Confessions*, written about 397, he described the deep conflict he felt between his sexual desires and his religious beliefs. Only after a long period of reflection and doubt, he wrote, did he find the inner strength to commit to chastity as part of his conversion to Christianity.

He advocated sexual abstinence as the highest course for Christians because he believed that Adam and Eve's disobedience had forever ruined the perfect harmony God created between the human will and human passions. According to Augustine, God punished his disobedient children by making sexual desire a disruptive force that human will would always struggle to control. He reaffirmed the value of marriage in God's plan, but he insisted that sexual intercourse even between loving spouses carried the unhappy reminder of humanity's fall from grace. A married couple should "descend with a certain sadness" to the task of procreation, the only acceptable reason for sex; sexual pleasure could never be a human good.

This doctrine ennobled virginity and sexual renunciation as the highest virtues; in the words of the ascetic biblical scholar Jerome, they counted as

---

asceticism (uh SEH tuh sih zuhm)**:** The practice of self-denial, especially through spiritual discipline; a doctrine for Christians emphasized by Augustine.

"daily martyrdom." By the end of the fourth century, Christians valued virginity as an ascetic virtue so highly that congregations began to call for virgin ministers and bishops.

The Emergence of Christian Monks

Christian asceticism reached its peak with the emergence of monks: men and women who withdrew from everyday society to live a life of extreme self-denial imitating Jesus's suffering, while praying for divine mercy on the world. In this movement, called monasticism, monks at first lived alone, but soon they formed communities for mutual support in the pursuit of holiness.

The Appeal of Monasticism Polytheists and Jews had strong ascetic traditions, but Christian monasticism was distinctive for the huge numbers of people drawn to it and the high status that they earned in the Christian population. Monks' fame came from their rejection of ordinary pleasures and comforts. They left their families and congregations, renounced sex, worshipped almost constantly, wore rough clothes, and ate so little they were always starving. To achieve inner peace detached from daily concerns, monks fought a constant spiritual battle against fantasies of earthly delights—plentiful, tasty food and the joys of sex.

The earliest monks emerged in Egypt in the second half of the third century. Antony (c. 251–356), the son of a well-to-do family, was among the first to renounce regular existence. After hearing a sermon stressing Jesus's command to a rich young man to sell his possessions and give the proceeds to the poor (Matt. 19:21), he left his property in about 285 and withdrew into the desert to devote the rest of his life to worshipping God through extreme self-denial.

Antony achieved fame for his ascetic life, illustrating a main appeal of monasticism: the chance to achieve excellence and recognition, a traditional ideal in the ancient Western world. This opportunity seemed especially valuable after the end of the Great Persecution. Becoming a monk—a living martyrdom—not only served as the substitute for dying a martyr's death but also emulated the sacrifice of Christ. Hermit monks went to great lengths to attract attention to their dedication. In Syria, "holy women" and "holy men" sought fame through feats of pious endurance; Symeon (390–459), for example, lived atop a tall pillar for thirty years, preaching to the people gathered at the foot of his perch. Egyptian Christians came to believe that their monks' supreme piety made them living heroes who ensured the annual flooding of the Nile, an event once associated with the pharaohs' religious power.

The influence of ascetics with reputations for exceptional holiness continued after their deaths. In a Christian tradition that had originated with martyrs, the relics of dead holy men and women—body parts or clothing—became treasured sources of protection and healing. Projecting the enduring power of saints (people venerated after their deaths for their holiness), relics gave believers faith in divine favor. Christian reverence for relics continued a more long-standing tradition: the fifth-century B.C.E. Athenians, for example, had believed that good fortune followed from the recovery of bones identified as the remains of Theseus, their legendary founder.

The Rise of Monastic Communities In about 323, an Egyptian Christian named Pachomius organized the first monastic community, establishing the tradition of single-sex settlements of male or female monks helping one another along the harsh path to holiness. This communal monasticism dominated Christian asceticism ever after. Communities of men and women were often built close together to share labor, with women making clothing, for example, while men farmed.

Some monasteries imposed military-style discipline, but there were large differences in the degree of control of the monks and the extent of contact allowed with the outside world (see the illustration on page 224). Some groups strove for complete self-sufficiency to avoid transactions with outsiders. The most isolationist groups lived in the eastern empire, but the followers of Martin of Tours (c. 316–397), an ex-soldier famed for his pious deeds, founded communities in the west as austere as any. Basil of Caesarea (c. 330–379), in Asia Minor, started an alternative tradition of monasteries in service to society. Basil (later dubbed "the Great") required monks to perform charitable deeds, especially ministering to the sick, a development that led to the foundation of the first hospitals, attached to monasteries.

A milder code of monastic conduct became the standard in the west beginning about 540. Called the Benedictine rule after its creator, Benedict of Nursia (c. 480–553), in central Italy, it mandated the monastery's daily routine of prayer, scriptural readings, and manual labor. This was the first time in Greek and Roman history that physical work was seen as noble, even godly. The rule divided the day into seven parts, each with a compulsory service of prayers and lessons, called the office. Unlike the harsh regulations of other monastic communities, Benedict's code did not isolate the monks from the outside world or deprive them of sleep, adequate food, or warm clothing. Although it gave the abbot (the head monk) full authority, it instructed him to listen to other members of the community before deciding important matters. He was not allowed to beat disobedient monks, as sometimes happened under other systems. Communities of women, such as those founded by Basil's sister Macrina and Benedict's sister Scholastica, generally followed the rules of the male monasteries, with an emphasis on the decorum thought necessary for women.

The thousands upon thousands of Christians who joined monasteries from the fourth century onward abandoned the outside world for social as well as theological reasons. Monastic piety held special appeal for women and the rich, as women could achieve greater status and respect for their holiness than ordinary life allowed them, while the rich could win fame on earth and hope for favor in heaven by endowing monasteries with large gifts of money. Jerome wrote, "[As monks,] we evaluate people's virtue not by their gender but by their character, and deem those to be worthy of the greatest glory who have renounced both status and riches." Some monks did not choose their life; monasteries took in children from parents who could not raise them or who, in a practice called oblation, gave them up to fulfill pious vows. Jerome once advised a mother who decided to send her young daughter to a monastery:

> Let her be brought up in a monastery, let her live among virgins, let her learn to avoid swearing, let her regard lying as an offense against God, let her be ignorant of the world, let her live the angelic life, while in the flesh let her be without the flesh, and let her suppose that all human beings are like herself.

When the girl reached adulthood as a virgin, he added, she should avoid the baths so that she would not be seen naked or give her body pleasure by dipping in the warm pools. Jerome emphasized tradi-

Monastery of St. Catherine at Mount Sinai

The sixth-century eastern Roman emperor Justinian built a wall to protect this monastery in the desert at the foot of Mount Sinai (on the peninsula between Egypt and Arabia). Justinian fortified the monastery to promote orthodoxy in a region dominated by Monophysite Christians. The monastery gained its name in the ninth century when the story was circulated that angels had recently brought the body of Catherine of Alexandria there. Catherine was said to have been martyred in the fourth century for refusing to marry the emperor because, in her words, she was the bride of Christ. *(Erich Lessing/Art Resource, NY.)*

tional values favoring males when he promised that God would reward the mother with the birth of sons in compensation for the dedication of her daughter.

Since monasteries were self-governing, they could find themselves in conflict with the church leadership. Bishops resented members of their congregations who withdrew into monasteries, especially because they then gave money and property to their new community instead of to their local churches. Moreover, monks represented a threat to bishops' authority because holy men and women earned their special status not by having it bestowed from the church hierarchy but through their own actions; strengthening the bishops' right to discipline monks who resisted their authority was one of the goals of the Council of Chalcedon. At bottom, however, bishops and monks shared a spiritual goal—salvation and service to God.

REVIEW QUESTION How did Christianity both unite and divide the Roman Empire?

Non-Roman Kingdoms in the Western Roman Empire, c. 370–550s

The residents of the western empire had special reason to pray for God's help because their territory came under great pressure from the many incursions of non-Roman peoples—barbarians, the Romans called them, meaning "brave but uncivilized"—that took place in the fourth and fifth centuries. The emperors had traditionally admitted some multiethnic groups from east of the Rhine River and north of the Danube River into the empire to fight in the Roman army, but eventually other barbarians fought their way in from the northeast. The barbarians had two strong motivations to move westward: to flee attacks by the Huns (nomads from central Asia) and to share in Roman prosperity. By the 370s, this human tide had swollen to a flood, provoking violence and a loss of order in the western empire.

Over the coming decades, the immigrants transformed themselves from loosely organized tribes into kingdoms with newly defined identities. By the 470s, one of their commanders ruled Italy—the political change that has been said to mark the so-called fall of the Roman Empire. However, the interactions of these non-Roman peoples with the empire's residents in western Europe and North Africa are better understood as causing a political, social, and cultural transformation—admittedly based on force more than cooperation—that made the immigrants the heirs of the western Roman Empire and led to the formation of medieval Europe.

Non-Roman Migrations into the Western Roman Empire

The non-Roman peoples who flooded into the empire had diverse origins; scholars in the past referred to them generically as Germanic peoples, but this label misrepresents the variety of languages and customs among these multiethnic groups. What we must remember is that the diverse barbarian peoples had no previously established sense of ethnic identity, and that many of them had had long-term contact with Romans through trade across the frontiers and service in the Roman army. By encouraging this contact, the emperors unwittingly set in motion forces that they could not in the end control. By late in the fourth century, attacks by the Huns had destabilized life for these bands across the Roman frontiers, and the families of warriors followed them into the empire seeking safety. Hordes of men, women, and children crossed into the empire as refugees. They came with no political or military unity and no clear plan. Loosely organized into tribes that often warred with one another, they shared only their terror of the Huns and their custom of conducting raids for a living in addition to farming small plots.

The inability to prevent immigrants from crossing the border or to integrate them into Roman society once they had crossed put great stress on the western central government. Persistent economic weakness rooted in the third-century crisis worsened this pressure. Tenant farmers and landlords fleeing crushing taxes had left as much as 20 percent of farmland unworked in the most seriously affected areas. The loss of revenue made the government unable to afford enough soldiers to control the frontiers. Over time, the immigrating non-Roman peoples forced the Roman government to grant them territory in the empire. Remarkably, they then began to develop separate ethnic identities and create new societies for themselves and the Romans living under their control.

Immigrant Traditions The traditions the newcomers brought with them from their barbarian homelands poorly prepared them for ruling others. There they had lived in small settlements whose economies depended on farming, herding, and ironworking; they had no experience with running kingdoms built on strong central authority (see "Contrasting Views," page 226).

CONTRASTING VIEWS

Debate: Did Romans or Huns Better Protect Life, Law, and Freedom?

In 448, a Roman named Priscus went as a diplomat to the court of Attila the Hun at a location north of the Danube River. His firsthand report of what he learned about life among the Huns during this visit includes this conversation with a stranger he met there. They exchanged contrasting views of whether life, law, and freedom were better protected among the Romans or the Huns (called Scythians here). According to descriptions of the Huns by other authors (such as the fourth-century historian and military man Ammianus Marcellinus), Romans recognized these barbarians as fearless and proud, and they respected them for their fierce dedication to their way of life. As a writer, Priscus could have been influenced by having read the bitter criticism of Roman society that Tacitus, the famous first-century C.E. Roman historian, put into the mouths of non-Romans in his works. But the details that Priscus gives about the stranger's personal appearance and life story perhaps increase the likelihood that he is reporting, in this document, a conversation held with a real person.

A man who I assumed was a barbarian from his Scythian-style clothes came up to me and said "Hello!" in Greek. I was surprised by a Scythian speaking Greek. For the subjects of the Huns, swept together from various lands, speak, in addition to their native barbarian languages, either Hunnic or Gothic, or—since many of them do business with the western Romans—Latin. None of them usually speak Greek, except captives from the Thracian or Illyrian coast; anyone who meets them easily recognizes, from their ripped clothing and the poor appearance of their heads, that they are individuals whose lives have taken a turn for the worse. This man, on the other hand, was well dressed in fancy Scythian clothes and a circular mullet-style haircut.

Returning his greeting, I asked him who he was and where he had come from into a barbarian land and chosen the Scythian lifestyle. When he asked me why I was eager to know, I told him that his speaking Greek had made me curious. Then he laughed and said that he was a Greek by birth and had gone as a merchant to trade in Viminacium, in the region of Moesia on the Danube River. He had lived there a long time and married a very rich wife. But barbarians captured the city, and his property was taken away. On account of his riches he was allotted as a captive to [the Hun] Onegesius in the division of the spoils, since it was customary that, after Attila, the chiefs of the Scythians, because they commanded many men, would keep the rich prisoners for themselves. He later fought bravely [in attacks by the Huns] against the Romans and the Acatiri tribe. Following the Scythian custom, he gave the spoils that he won to his master, and so got his freedom. He then married a barbarian wife and had children.

Since he had the privilege of eating at the table of Onegesius, he considered his new life among the Scythians better than his old life among the Romans. For he explained that once a war is over, the Scythians live at ease, each enjoying what he has got, with no, or only a little, bothering of others or being bothered themselves. The Romans, on the other hand, are very likely to be destroyed by war, as they have to pin their hopes of safety on other people: their tyrants do not permit everyone to use weapons. And Romans who do use them are harmed by the cowardly actions of their generals, who cannot stand up to the stresses of war. But the condition of Roman subjects in peacetime is far more burdensome than the evils of war, on account of the harshness of tax collection and the harm done by wrongdoers, since the laws do not apply to everyone. A member of the upper class who breaks the law does not face punishment. If a man is poor, however, and doesn't understand how to handle things, he suffers the penalty imposed by the law, if he doesn't leave this life before he gets to the trial, given how long lawsuits are dragged out and how much money has to be spent. The most painful thing of all is to have to pay in order to try to get justice. For no one will give his day in court to the man who has been treated unjustly unless he pays money to the judge and the judge's clerks.

As he was saying many other things like this, I calmly asked him to hear what I had to say. I insisted that the founders of the Roman Republic were wise and good

In their homelands the barbarians had lived in chiefdom societies, whose members could only be persuaded, not ordered, to follow the chief. Chiefs maintained their status by giving gifts to their followers and leading raids to capture cattle and slaves. They led clans—groups of households organized on kinship lines, following maternal as well as paternal descent. Members of a clan were supposed to keep peace among themselves, and violence against a fellow clan member was the worst possible offense. Clans in turn grouped themselves into tribes—fluctuating coalitions that anyone could join. Tribes differentiated themselves by their clothing, hairstyles, jewelry, weapons, religious cults, and oral stories.

Family life was patriarchal: men headed households and held authority over women, children, and slaves. Warfare preoccupied men, as their ritual

men. To prevent things from being done randomly, they arranged for some people to be guardians of the laws, while others were tasked with skill in weapons and to train for war, focused on nothing else but being ready for battle and having the spirit to go to war as if going to their usual exercises, having gotten rid of their fear ahead of time through their training. The founders arranged for others to do farming and care for the land, to feed both themselves and those who fought for them by contributing the tax that consists of the grain supply for the army. They arranged for others to pay attention to people who have been treated unjustly and to conduct rightful prosecutions for people who are too weak to advance their own case. Others they set up as judges to guard what the law wishes.

Since the founders were concerned for those involved in the judicial process, they also arranged for others whose job it is to make sure that a person who wins a judgment in court will in fact receive the damages that have been awarded, as well as that the person who was found guilty does not pay more than the legal judgment specified. If no one existed who would pay attention to such things, then the motivation for a second case at law would arise from the first one, because either the winner in the case would apply too much pressure, or the person who lost the case would continue to act unjustly.

There is indeed an amount of money that these officials are paid by those involved in court cases, just as the farmers pay a set amount to the soldiers. Isn't it proper to support those who help you and reward their good will, in the same way that feeding a horse helps a horseman . . . ? Whenever court costs have to be paid even though we've lost the case, shouldn't we blame our own unjust action instead of attributing the harm to someone else?

If it does happen that it takes too long to try a case, that's the result of a concern for justice, to prevent judges from judging cases carelessly and making mistaken judgments. For they believe that it is better to finish a case late than to wrong someone by hurrying and thereby committing an offense against God, the founder of justice. The laws do apply to everyone, so that even the Roman emperor obeys them. And it's not true, as was said in his accusation, that the rich use force against the poor without any risk, unless someone escapes prosecution because he never got caught. The poor can get away with things this way, too. Criminals under these circumstances get away because of the lack of evidence, something that happens among all peoples and not just the Romans.

You ought to thank chance for the freedom you enjoy, not the master who led you into war, where as a result of your inexperience you could have been killed by the enemy or punished by the one who possessed you if you ran away from the battlefield. The Romans usually treat even their household slaves better than this. They act like fathers or teachers to them, to restrain them from behaving stupidly and to get them to do what is considered right, and they teach them self-control when they make mistakes, just as with the children in their families. It is not legal for them to punish them with death, as the Scythians do.

There are many ways to freedom among the Romans. Not just the living but even those who have died gladly give it, arranging their estates however they wish. The law is that whatever each person wishes to happen to his possessions when he dies is valid.

In tears, he said that the laws were excellent and the Roman Republic [as the Romans still called the Empire] was good, but the officials were corrupting it by not living up to the same moral standards that the officials of the past did.

Source: Priscus, fr. 11.2 Müller *Fragmenta Historicorum Graecorum* (= *Exc. de Leg. Rom.* 3). Translation by Thomas R. Martin.

Questions to Consider

1. **Do you think that this is a fabricated account written by Priscus to demonstrate a point, a documentation of an actual exchange, or a combination of both? What evidence from the document supports your argument?**
2. **Do you think Priscus, in his reply, adequately answers the points raised by the stranger? Why or why not?**
3. **What do you think is the intended effect of Priscus's giving the stranger the last word in this exchange?**

sacrifices of weapons preserved in northern European bogs have shown. Women were valued for their ability to bear children, and rich men could have more than one wife and perhaps concubines as well. A division of labor made women responsible for growing crops, making pottery, and producing textiles, while men worked iron and herded cattle. Women enjoyed certain rights of inheritance and could control property, and married women received a dowry of one-third of their husband's property.

Assemblies of free male warriors made major decisions in the tribes. Their leaders' authority was restricted mostly to religious and military matters. Tribes could be unstable and prone to internal conflict—clans frequently feuded, with bloody consequences. Tribal law tried to determine what forms of violence were and were not acceptable in seeking revenge, but laws were oral, not written, and thus open to wide dispute.

Fleeing the Huns The migrations avalanched when the Huns invaded eastern Europe in the fourth century. The Huns arrived on the Russian steppes shortly before 370 as the vanguard of Turkish-speaking nomads moving west. Their warriors' appearance terrified their victims, who reported skulls elongated from having been bound between boards in infancy, faces grooved with decorative scars, and arms fearsome with elaborate tattoos. Huns excelled as raiders, launching cavalry attacks without warning. Skilled as horsemen, they could shoot their powerful bows accurately while riding full tilt and stay mounted for days, sleeping atop their horses and carrying snacks of raw meat between their thighs and the animal's back.

By later in the fourth century the Huns had moved as far west as the Hungarian plain north of the Danube, terrifying the peoples there and launching raids southward into the Balkans. The emperors in Constantinople began paying the Huns to spare their territory, so the most ambitious Hunnic leader, Attila (r. c. 440–453), pushed his domain westward toward the Alps. He led his forces as far west as central France and into northern Italy. At Attila's death in 453, the Huns lost their fragile unity and faded from history. By this time, however, the terror that they had inspired in the peoples living in eastern Europe had provoked the migrations that eventually transformed the western empire.

Visigoths: The First New Society The first non-Roman group that created a new identity and society for themselves inside the empire were the barbarians who defeated Valens at Adrianople (Map 7.3). Their history illustrates the pattern of the migrations: desperate barbarians in barely organized groups with no uniform

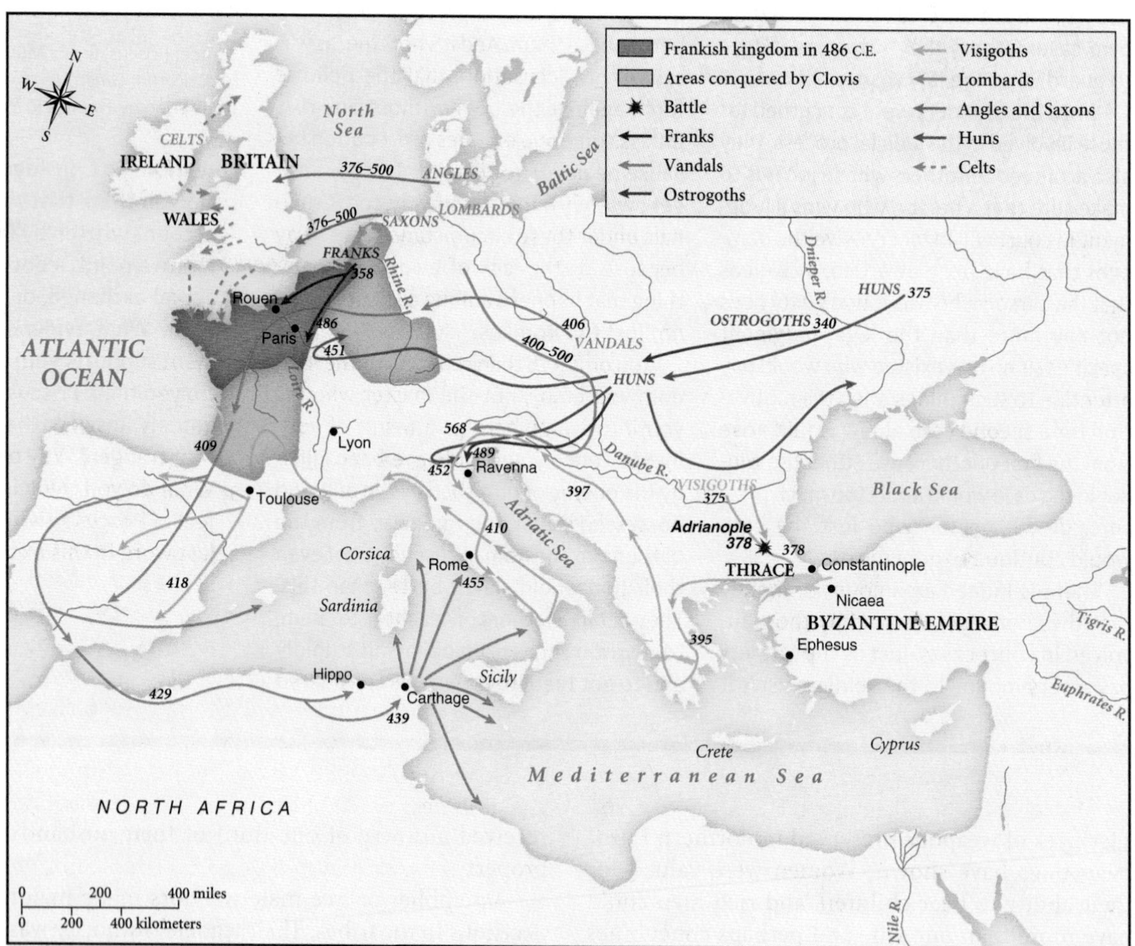

MAP 7.3 Migrations and Invasions of the Fourth and Fifth Centuries
The movements of non-Roman peoples into imperial territory transformed the Roman Empire. These migrations had begun as early as the reign of Domitian (r. 81–96), but in the fourth century they increased greatly when the Huns' attacks pushed numerous barbarian bands into the empire's northern provinces. Print maps offer only a static representation of dynamic processes such as movements of populations, but this map helps illustrate the variety of peoples involved, the wide extent of imperial territory that they affected, and their prominence in the western empire.

ethnic identity, seeking protection in the Roman Empire in return for military service but being mistreated, and then rebelling to form their own, new kingdom.

When the emperor Theodosius died in 395, the barbarians whom he had allowed to settle in the empire rebelled. United by Alaric into a tribe known as the **Visigoths**, they fought their way into the western empire. In 410, they stunned the world by sacking Rome itself. For the first time since the Gauls eight hundred years before, a foreign force occupied the ancient capital. They terrorized the population: when Alaric demanded all the citizens' goods, the Romans asked, "What will be left to us?" "Your lives," he replied.

Too weak to fend off the invaders, the western emperor Honorius in 418 reluctantly agreed to settle the newcomers in southwestern Gaul (present-day France), where they completed their unprecedented transition from tribe to kingdom, organizing a political state and creating their identity as Visigoths. In this process they followed the only model available: Roman tradition, especially having a code of law. They established mutually beneficial relations with local Roman elites, who used time-tested ways of flattering their new superiors to gain advantages. Sidonius Apollinaris (c. 430–479), for example, a well-connected noble from Lyon, once purposely lost a backgammon game to the Visigothic king as a way of winning a favor.

How the new non-Roman kingdoms raised revenues has become a much-debated question. Did the newcomers become landlords by forcing Roman property owners to redistribute a portion of their lands, slaves, and movable property as "ransom" to them? Or did Romans directly pay the expenses of the kingdom's soldiers, who lived mostly in urban garrisons? Whatever the new arrangements were, the Visigoths found them profitable enough to expand into Spain within a century of establishing themselves in southwestern Gaul.

The Vandals and the Spiral of Violence

The western government's concessions to the Visigoths led other groups to seize territory and create new kingdoms and identities. In 406, the Vandals, fleeing the Huns, crossed the Rhine into Roman territory. This huge group cut a swath through Gaul all the way to the Spanish coast. (The modern word *vandal*, meaning "destroyer of property," perpetuates their reputation for warlike ruthlessness.)

In 429, eighty thousand Vandals ferried to North Africa, where they soon broke their agreement to become federate allies and captured the region. They crippled the western empire by seizing North Africa's tax payments of grain and vegetable oil and disrupting the importation of food to Rome. They threatened the eastern empire with their strong navy and in 455 sailed to Rome, plundering the city. In Africa the Vandals caused tremendous hardship for local people by confiscating property rather than (like the Visigoths) allowing owners to make regular payments on the land. As Arian Christians, they persecuted North African Christians whose doctrines they considered heresy.

The Anglo-Saxons at the Empire's Western Edge

Small non-Roman groups took advantage of the disruption caused by bigger bands to break off distant pieces of the weakened western empire. The most significant group for later history was the Anglo-Saxons. Composed of Angles from what is now Denmark and Saxons from northwestern Germany, this mixed group invaded Britain in the 440s after the Roman army had been recalled from the province to defend Italy against the Visigoths. The Anglo-Saxons captured territory from the local Celtic peoples and the remaining Roman inhabitants. Gradually, their culture replaced the local traditions of the island's eastern regions. The Celts there lost most of their language, and Christianity gave way to Anglo-Saxon beliefs, surviving only in Wales and Ireland.

The Fall of Rome and the Ostrogoths

Another barbarian group, the Ostrogoths, carved out a kingdom in Italy in the fifth century. By the time the Ostrogothic king Theodoric (r. 493–526) came to power, there had not been a western Roman emperor for nearly twenty years, and there never would be again — the change that has traditionally, but simplistically, been called the fall of the Roman Empire. The story's details reveal the complexity of the political transformation of the western empire under the new kingdoms. The weakness of the western emperors' army had obliged them to hire foreign officers to lead the defense of Italy. By the middle of the fifth century, one non-Roman general after another decided who would serve as puppet emperor under his control. The employees were running the company.

The last such unfortunate puppet was only a child. His father, a former aide to Attila, tried to establish a royal house by proclaiming his young son as western emperor in 475. He gave the boy ruler the name Romulus Augustulus ("Romulus the Little

---

Visigoths: The name given to the barbarians whom Alaric united and led on a military campaign into the western Roman Empire to establish a new kingdom; they sacked Rome in 410.

Augustus") to match his young age and to recall both Rome's founder and its first emperor. In 476, following a dispute over pay, the boy emperor's non-Roman soldiers murdered his father and deposed him. Pitied as an innocent child, Little Augustus was given safe refuge and a generous pension. The rebels' leader, Odoacer, did not appoint another emperor. Instead, he had the Roman Senate petition Zeno, the eastern emperor, to recognize his leadership in return for his acknowledging Zeno as sole emperor over west and east. Odoacer thereafter oversaw Italy nominally as the eastern emperor's viceroy, but in fact he ruled as he liked.

Zeno later plotted to rid himself of an ambitious non-Roman general then resident in Constantinople—Theodoric—by sending him to fight Odoacer, whom the emperor had found too independent. Successfully eliminating Odoacer by 493, Theodoric then established his own Ostrogothic kingdom, ruling Italy from the capital at Ravenna.

Theodoric and his Ostrogothic nobles wanted to enjoy the luxurious life of the empire's elite, not destroy it, and to preserve the empire's prestige and status. They therefore left the Senate and consulships intact. An Arian Christian, Theodoric followed Constantine's example by announcing a policy of religious freedom. Like the other non-Romans, the Ostrogoths adopted and adapted Roman traditions that supported the stability of their own rule. For these reasons, some scholars consider it more accurate to speak of the western empire's "transformation" than of its "fall."

The Enduring Kingdom of the Franks Among the groups reshaping the western Roman Empire politically, socially, and culturally, the Franks were especially significant because they were the people who transformed Roman Gaul into Francia (from which comes the name *France*). Roman emperors had allowed some of the Franks to settle in a rough northern border region (now in the Netherlands) in the early fourth century; by the late fifth century they were a major presence in Gaul. In 507, their king Clovis (r. 485–511), with support from the eastern Roman emperor, overthrew the Visigothic king in Gaul. When the emperor named Clovis an honorary consul, Clovis celebrated this ancient honor by having himself crowned with a diadem in the style of the emperors since Constantine. He established western Europe's largest new kingdom in what is today mostly France, overshadowing the neighboring and rival kingdoms of the Burgundians and Alemanni in eastern Gaul. Probably persuaded by his wife, Clotilda, a Christian, to believe that God had helped him defeat the Alemanni, Clovis proclaimed himself an orthodox Christian and renounced Arianism, which he had reportedly embraced previously. To build stability, he carefully fostered good relations with the bishops as the regime's intermediaries with the population.

Clovis's dynasty, called Merovingian after the legendary Frankish ancestor Merovech, endured for another two hundred years, foreshadowing the kingdom that would emerge much later as the forerunner of modern France. The Merovingians survived so long because, better than any other kingdom, they successfully combined their own traditions of military bravery with Roman social and legal traditions. In addition, their location in far western Europe kept them out of the reach of the destructive invasions sent against Italy by the eastern emperor Justinian in the sixth century to reunite the Roman world.

Eagle Brooches from Gothic Spain
Wealthy Gothic women used brooches like these to fasten their clothes at the shoulder. The costly materials from which they were made displayed the wearer's status in society. The eagle design pointed both to the respect that those predator birds enjoyed in Gothic ideas about the natural world and to Roman power and majesty (the eagle had long been depicted on the standards carried in front of the Roman army's legions). In this way, the ornaments emphasized Gothic women's pride in their own heritage as well as their adaption to what was best (in their eyes) in Roman society. (Eagle Fibula, Anonymous, Visigothic, sixth century, gold over bronze with gemstones, glass and meerschaum. Object 54.421–422, photo © *The Walters Art Museum, Baltimore.*)

Social and Cultural Transformation in the Western Roman Empire

Western Europe's political transformation—the gradual replacement of imperial government by the new kingdoms—set in motion social and cultural transformations as well (Map 7.4). The newcomers and their Roman subjects created novel ways of life by combining old traditions, as the Visigoth

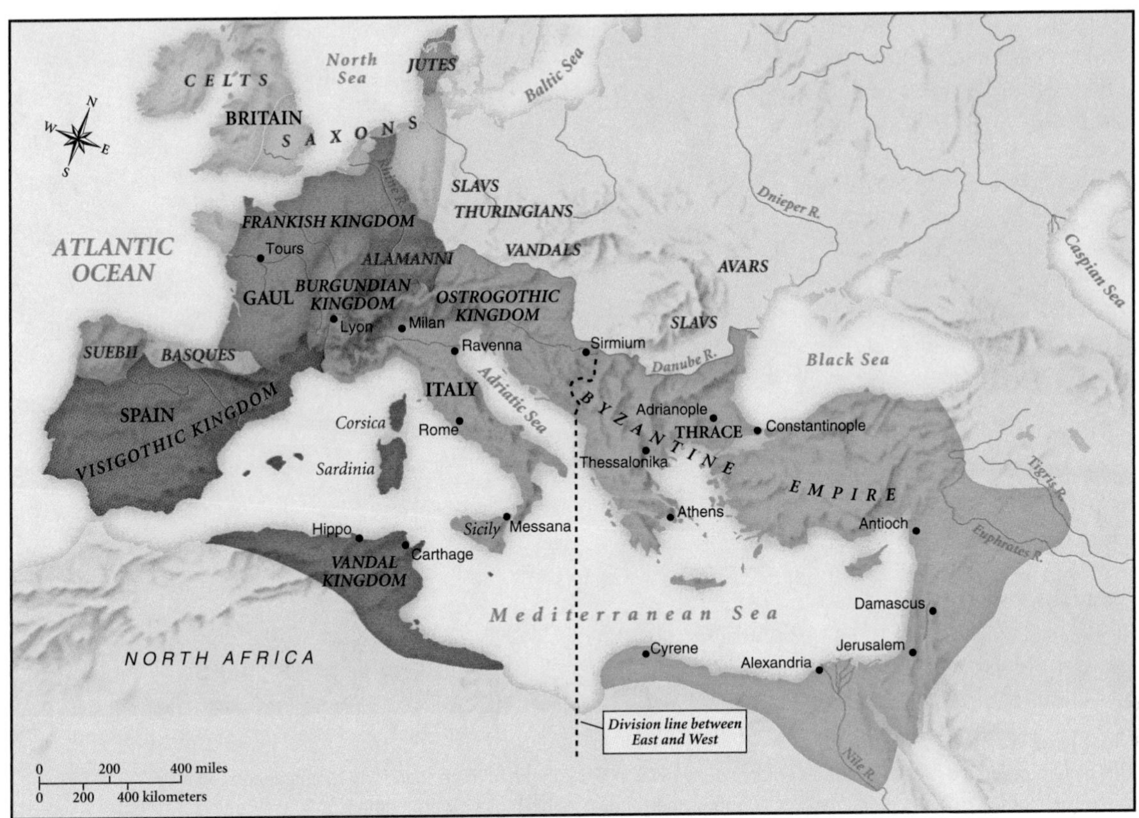

MAP 7.4 Peoples and Kingdoms of the Roman World, 526
The provinces of the Roman Empire had always been home to a population diverse in language and ethnicity. By the early sixth century, the territory of the western empire had become a mixture of diverse political units as well. Italy and most of the former western provinces were ruled by kingdoms organized by different non-Roman peoples, who had moved into former imperial territory over several centuries. The eastern empire remained under the political control of the emperor in Constantinople.

king Athaulf (r. 410–415) explained after marrying a Roman noblewoman:

> At the start I wanted to erase the Romans' name and turn their land into a Gothic empire, doing myself what Augustus had done. But I have learned that the Goths' freewheeling wildness will never accept the rule of law, and that state with no law is no state. Thus, I have more wisely chosen another path to glory: reviving the Roman name with Gothic vigor. I pray that future generations will remember me as the founder of a Roman restoration.

This process of social and cultural transformation promoted stability by producing new law codes but undermined long-term security by weakening the economic situation.

Visigothic and Frankish Law

Roman law was the most influential precedent for the new kings in their efforts to construct stable states. Their original tribal societies never had written laws, but their new states required legal codes to create a sense of justice and keep order. The Visigothic kings were the first to issue a written law code. Published in Latin in about 475, it made fines and compensation the primary method for resolving disputes. Clovis also emphasized written law for the Merovingian kingdom. His code, also published in Latin between about 507 and 511, promoted social order through clear penalties for specific crimes. In particular, he formalized a system of fines intended to defuse feuds and vendettas between individuals and clans. The most prominent component of this system was **wergild**, the payment a murderer had to make as compensation for his crime, to prevent feuds of revenge. The king received about one-third of the fine, with the rest paid to the victim's family.

Since laws indicate social values, the differing amounts of wergild in Clovis's code suggest the relative values of different categories of people in his kingdom. Murdering a woman of childbearing age,

---

wergild: Under Frankish law, the payment that a murderer had to make as compensation for the crime, to prevent feuds of revenge.

Mosaic of Women Exercising

This picture covered a floor in a fourth-century country villa in Sicily that had more than forty rooms decorated with thirty-five hundred square meters of mosaics. The women shown in this mosaic were perhaps dancers getting in shape for public appearances or athletes performing as part of a show. Members of the Roman elite built such enormous and expensive houses as the centerpieces of estates meant to insulate them from increasingly dismal conditions in cities and protect them from barbarian attack. In this case, the strategy apparently failed: the villa was likely seriously damaged by Vandal invaders. *(Erich Lessing/Art Resource, NY.)*

a boy under twelve, or a man in the king's retinue brought a massive fine of six hundred gold coins, enough to buy six hundred cattle. A woman past childbearing age (specified as sixty years), a young girl, or a freeborn man was valued at two hundred. Ordinary slaves rated thirty-five. Obviously these laws did not support true equality among people, but they did make clear that appropriate compensation had to be paid for the damage done by crimes, a requirement that was surely meant to help prevent an endless cycle of revenge in society. This feature of the so-called barbarian law codes had a long influence in later legal history.

A Transformed Economic Landscape

Law codes promoted social stability in the new kingdoms of the transformed western Roman Empire, but the migrations that had brought the new groups into Roman territory had the unintended consequence of harming the empire's already weakened economy. The Vandals' violent attacks severely damaged many towns in Gaul, hastening a decline in urban population. In the countryside, now beyond the control of any central government, wealthy Romans built sprawling villas on extensive estates, staffed by tenants bound to the land like slaves. These establishments aimed to operate as self-sufficient units by producing all they needed, defending themselves against barbarian raids, and keeping their distance from any authorities. The owners shunned municipal offices and tax collection, the public services that had supplied the lifeblood of Roman administration. Provincial government disappeared, and the new kingdoms never fully replaced its duties.

The situation only grew grimmer as the effects of these changes multiplied. In some areas now outside reach of the central government, the infrastructure of trade—roads and bridges—fell into disrepair with no public-spirited elite to maintain them. The elite holed up in their fortress-like households. They could afford to protect themselves: the annual income of the richest of them rivaled the revenue of an entire province in the old western empire.

In some cases, these fortunate few helped pass down Roman learning to later ages. Cassiodorus (c. 490–585), for one, founded a monastery on his ancestral estate in Italy in the 550s after a career in imperial administration. He gave the monks the task of copying manuscripts as old ones disintegrated. His own book, *Institutions*, summed up what he saw as the foundation of ancient Greek and Roman culture by listing the books an educated person should read; it included ancient classical literature as well as Christian texts. The most lasting effort to keep classical traditions alive, however, came in the eastern empire.

REVIEW QUESTION How did their migrations and invasions change the barbarians themselves and the Roman Empire?

The Roman Empire in the East, c. 500–565

The eastern Roman Empire (later called the Byzantine Empire—see Chapter 8) avoided the massive transformations that reshaped western Europe. Trade and agriculture kept the eastern empire from poverty, while its emperors used force, diplomacy, and bribery to prevent invasions from the north and repel attacks by the powerful Sasanid Empire in Persia, which was still making periodic strikes against the eastern empire.

The eastern emperors believed it was their duty to rule a united Roman Empire and prevent barbarians from degrading its culture. The most famous eastern Roman emperor, **Justinian** (r. 527–565), and his wife and partner in rule, **Theodora** (500–548), took this mission so seriously that for decades the eastern empire waged war against the barbarian kingdoms in the west, aiming to reunite the empire and restore the imperial glory of the Augustan period. Like Diocletian, Justinian increased imperial authority and tried to purify religion to provide what he saw as the strong leadership and divine favor necessary in troubled times. He and his successors in the eastern empire also contributed to the preservation of the memory of classical Greek and Roman culture by preserving a great deal of earlier literature, non-Christian and Christian.

Imperial Society in the Eastern Roman Empire

The sixth-century eastern empire enjoyed a vitality that had vanished in the west. Its social elite spent freely on luxuries such as silk, precious stones, and pepper and other spices imported from India and China. Markets in its large cities teemed with merchants from far and wide. Its churches' soaring domes testified to its confidence in the Christian God as its divine protector.

In keeping with Roman tradition, the eastern emperors sponsored religious festivals and entertainments on a massive scale to rally public support. Rich and poor alike crowded city squares, theaters, and hippodromes on these lively occasions. Chariot racing aroused the hottest passions. Constantinople's residents divided themselves into competitive factions called Blues and Greens after the racing colors of their favorite charioteers. Emperors sometimes backed one gang or the other to intimidate potential rivals.

Preserving "Romanness" The eastern emperors worked to maintain Roman tradition and identity, believing that "Romanness" was the best defense against what they saw as the barbarization of the western empire. They hired many foreign mercenaries, but they also tried to keep their subjects from adopting foreign ways. Styles of dress figured largely in this struggle. Ignoring the favored clothing of the chariot factions, eastern emperors ordered Constantinople's residents not to wear barbarian-style clothing (especially heavy boots and furs) instead of traditional Roman attire (sandals or light shoes and cloth robes).

The quest for cultural unity was hopeless because society in the eastern empire was thoroughly multilingual and multiethnic. The eastern empire's inhabitants regarded themselves as the heirs of ancient Roman culture: they referred to themselves as Romans, even though most of them spoke Greek as their native language and used Latin only for government and military communication. Many people retained their traditional languages, such as Phrygian and Cappadocian in western Asia Minor, Armenian farther east, and Syriac and other Aramaic dialects along the eastern Mediterranean coast. The streets of Constantinople reportedly rang with seventy-two languages.

Romanness definitely included Christianity, but the eastern empire's theological diversity rivaled its ethnic and linguistic complexity. Bitter controversies over doctrine divided eastern Christians; neither the emperors nor the bishops succeeded in imposing orthodoxy. Emperors used violence against heretics when persuasion failed. They had to resort to extreme measures, they believed, to save lost souls and preserve the empire's religious purity and divine goodwill. The persecution of Christian subjects by Christian emperors illustrates the disturbing consequences of the quest for a unitary identity.

Justinian and Theodora: Sixth-century emperor and empress of the eastern Roman Empire, famous for waging costly wars to reunite the empire.

Theodora and Her Court in Ravenna
This mosaic shows the empress Theodora and members of her court presenting a gift to the church at San Vitale in Ravenna. It faced the matching scene of her husband Justinian and his attendants (page 235). Theodora wears the jewels, pearls, and rich robes characteristic of eastern Roman monarchs. (Compare the style of the clothes in these two mosaics to those shown in the cameo from Augustus's time on page 174. What were the different styles of dress meant to convey about the leaders in each period?) Theodora extends in her hands a gem-encrusted wine cup as her present. Her gesture imitates the gift-giving of the Magi to the baby Jesus, the scene illustrated on the hem of her garment. The circle around her head, called a nimbus (Latin for "cloud"), indicates special holiness. *(Scala / Art Resource, NY.)*

Women in Society and at Court

Most women in eastern Roman society lived according to ancient Mediterranean tradition: they concentrated on their households and minimized contact with men outside that circle. Law barred them from performing many public functions, such as witnessing wills. Subject to the authority of their fathers and husbands, women veiled their heads (though not their faces) to show modesty. The strict views of Christian theologians on sexuality and reproduction made divorce more difficult and discouraged remarriage even for widows. Sexual offenses carried harsher legal penalties. Female prostitution remained legal and common, but emperors raised the penalties for those who forced girls or female slaves under their control into prostitution.

Women in the imperial family could achieve prominence unattainable for ordinary women. Empress Theodora demonstrated the influence high-ranking women could have in the eastern empire. Uninhibited by her humble origins (she was the daughter of a bear trainer and had been an actress with a scandalous reputation), she came to rival anyone in influence and wealth (see the illustration above). She had a hand in every aspect of Justinian's rule, advising him on personnel for his administration, pushing for her religious views in disputes over Christian doctrine, and rallying his courage at times of crisis. John Lydus, a contemporary government official and high-ranking administrator, judged her "superior in intelligence to any man."

Social Class and Government Services

Government in the eastern empire increased social divisions because it provided services according to people's wealth. Officials received fees for countless activities, from commercial permits to legal grievances. Some scholars argue that these arrangements actually promoted more effective action by government officials. People with money and status certainly found the situation useful: they relied on their social connections to get a hearing from the right official, and on their wealth to make payments to move matters along quickly. Whether seeking preferential treatment or just spurring administrators to do what they were supposed to do, the rich could make the system work. The poor, by contrast, had trouble affording the payments that government officials expected.

This fee-based system allowed the emperors to pay their civil servants tiny salaries and spend imperial funds for other purposes. John Lydus, for example, reported that he earned thirty times his annual salary in payments from people seeking services during his first year in office. To keep the sys-

Justinian and His Court in Ravenna
This mosaic scene dominated by the eastern Roman emperor Justinian stands opposite Theodora's mosaic (page 234) in San Vitale's Church in Ravenna. The emperor is shown presenting a gift to the church. Justinian and Theodora finished building the church, which the Ostrogothic king Theodoric had started, to commemorate their successful campaign to restore Italy to the Roman Empire and reassert control of the western capital, Ravenna. The inclusion of the portrait of Maximianus, bishop of Ravenna, standing on Justinian's left and identified by name, stresses the theme of cooperation between bishops and emperors in ruling the world. What do you think the inclusion of the soldiers at the left is meant to indicate? *(Scala / Art Resource, NY.)*

tem from destroying itself through extortion, the emperors published an official list of the maximum fees that their employees could charge.

The Reign of Emperor Justinian, 527–565

Justinian became the most famous eastern emperor by waging war to reunite the empire as it had been in the days of Augustus, making imperial rule more autocratic, constructing costly buildings in Constantinople, and instituting legal and religious reforms. Also the most intellectual emperor since Julian the Apostate two centuries earlier, Justinian had the same aims as all his predecessors: to preserve social order based on hierarchy and maintain divine goodwill (see the illustration above). Unfortunately, the cost of his plans forced him to raise taxes, generating civil strife.

Taxes and Social Unrest Justinian faced bitter resistance to his plans and their enormous cost. His unpopular taxes provoked a major riot in 532. Known as the Nika Riot, it arose when the Blue and Green factions, gathering to watch chariot races, unexpectedly united against the emperor, shouting "Nika! Nika!" ("Win! Win!") as their battle cry. After nine days of violence that left much of Constantinople in ashes, Justinian was ready to abandon his throne and flee in panic. But Theodora sternly rebuked him: "Once born, no one can escape dying, but for one who has held imperial power it would be unbearable to be a fugitive. May I never take off my imperial robes of purple, nor live to see the day when those who meet me will not greet me as their ruler." Her husband then sent in troops, who ended the rioting by slaughtering thirty thousand rioters trapped in the racetrack.

Justinian's most ambitious goal was to restore the empire to a unified territory, religion, and culture. Invading the former western provinces, his generals defeated the Vandals and Ostrogoths after campaigns that in some cases took decades to complete. At an enormous price in lives and money, Justinian's armies restored the old empire's geography, with its territory stretching from the Atlantic to the western edge of Mesopotamia.

Justinian's success in reuniting the western and eastern empires had unintended consequences: severe damage to the west's infrastructure and the east's finances. Italy endured the most physical destruction, while the eastern empire suffered because Justinian squeezed even more taxes out of his already overburdened population to finance his wars and pay the Persian kingdom not to attack while his home defenses were weakened. The tax burden crippled the economy, leading to constant banditry in the countryside. Crowds poured into the capital from rural areas, seeking relief from poverty and robbers.

Natural disaster compounded Justinian's problems. In the 540s, a horrific epidemic killed a third of his empire's inhabitants; a quarter of a million, half the capital's population, died in Constantinople alone. This was only the first of many pandemics that erased millions of people in the eastern empire over the next two centuries. Serious earthquakes, always a danger in this region, increased the death toll. The loss of so many people created a shortage of army recruits, requiring the emperor to hire expensive mercenaries, and left countless farms vacant, reducing tax revenues.

Strengthening Central Authority Justinian craved stability, which he sought by strengthening his authority in two ways: emphasizing his closeness to God and increasing the autocratic power of his rule. These traits became characteristic of eastern Roman emperors. Moreover, Justinian proclaimed the emperor the "living law," recalling the Hellenistic royal doctrine that the ruler's decisions defined law.

His building program in Constantinople communicated his overpowering supremacy and piety. Most spectacular of all was his reconstruction of Hagia Sophia (Church of the Holy Wisdom). Creating a new design for churches, Justinian's architects erected a huge building on a square plan capped by a dome 107 feet across and 160 feet high. Its interior walls glowed like the sun from the light reflecting off their four acres of gold mosaics. Imported marble of every color added to the sparkling effect. When he first entered his masterpiece, dedicated in 538, Justinian exclaimed, "I have defeated you, Solomon," claiming to have bested the glorious temple that the ancient king built for the Hebrews.

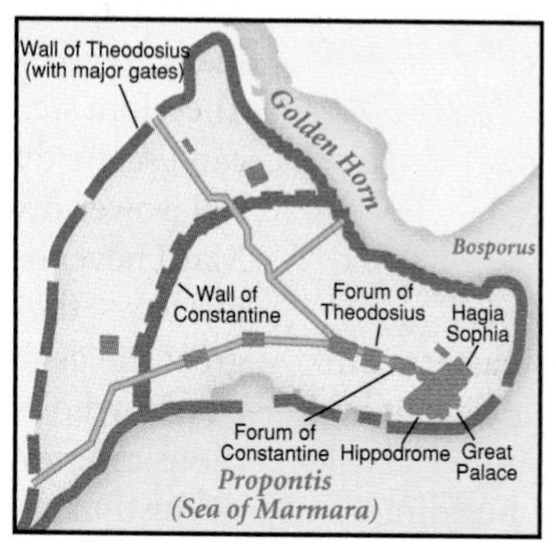

Constantinople during the Rule of Justinian

Justinian's autocratic rule reduced the autonomy of the empire's cities. Their councils ceased to govern; imperial officials took over instead. Provincial elites still had to ensure full payment of their area's taxes, but no longer could they decide local matters. Now the central government determined all aspects of decision making and social status. Men of property from the provinces who aspired to power and prestige could satisfy their ambitions only by joining the imperial administration in the capital.

Legal and Religious Reform To solidify his authority and bring uniformity to the confusing mass of decisions that earlier emperors had made, Justinian codified the laws of the empire. His *Codex* appeared in 529, with a revised version completed in 534. A team of scholars also condensed millions of words of regulations to produce the *Digest* in 533, intended to expedite legal cases and provide a syllabus for law schools. This collection, like the *Codex* written in Latin and therefore readable in the western empire, influenced legal scholars for centuries. Justinian's legal experts also compiled a textbook for students, the *Institutes*, which appeared in 533 and remained on law school reading lists until modern times.

To fulfill the emperor's sacred duty to secure the welfare of his people, Justinian acted to enforce their religious purity. Like the polytheist and Christian emperors before him, he believed his world could not flourish if its god became angered by the presence of religious offenders. As emperor, Justinian decided who the offenders were. Zealously enforcing laws against polytheists, he compelled them to be baptized or forfeit their lands and official positions. He also relentlessly purged heretical Christians who rejected his version of orthodoxy.

Justinian's laws made male homosexual relations illegal for the first time in Roman history. Earlier, same-sex unions between men had apparently been allowed, or at least officially ignored, until they were prohibited in 342 after Christianity became the emperors' religion. There had never before been any civil penalties imposed on men engaging in homosexual activity, perhaps because previous rulers considered it impractical to regulate men's sexuality, given that adult men lived their private lives free of direct oversight. All the previous emperors had, for example, simply taxed male prostitutes. The legal status of homosexual activity between women is uncertain, but women's restricted freedom made it easier for men to think that women's sexuality could and should be controlled. Homosexual activity between married women probably counted as adultery and thus as a crime. In reality, Justinian probably had limited success in changing people's sexual behaviors, but he saw his strengthened emphasis on greater purity of life as an important demonstration of his commitment to fulfilling his responsibilities as a Christian emperor with the duty of preserving God's favor toward his rule and his subjects.

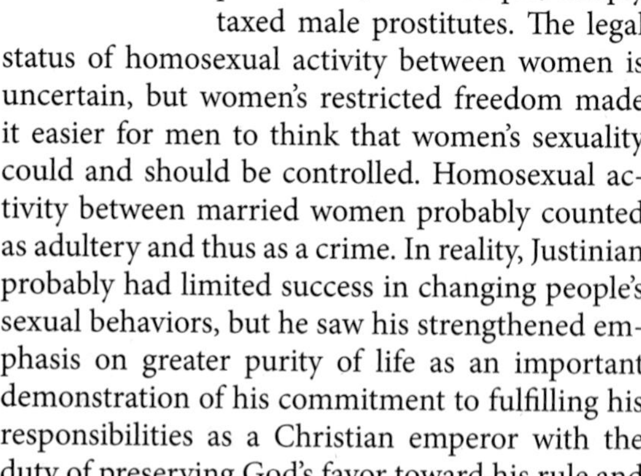

A brilliant theologian in his own right, Justinian tried to reconcile orthodox and Monophysite Christians by revising the creed of the Council of Chalcedon. But the church leaders in Rome and Constantinople had become too bitterly divided and too jealous of one another's prominence to agree on a unified church. The eastern and western churches were by now firmly launched on the diverging courses that would result in formal schism five hundred years later. Justinian's own ecumenical council in Constantinople ended in conflict in 553 when it jailed Rome's defiant Pope Vigilius while also managing to alienate Monophysite bishops. Probably no one could have done better, but Justinian's efforts to impose religious unity only drove Christians further apart and undermined his vision of a restored Roman world.

The Preservation of Classical Traditions in the Late Roman Empire

Since knowledge of a culture can disappear if its texts are not preserved, Christianization of the late Roman Empire endangered the memory of classical traditions. The greatest danger to the survival of the plays, histories, philosophical works, poems, speeches, and novels of classical Greece and Rome—which were polytheist and therefore potentially subversive of Christian belief—stemmed not so much from active censorship as simple neglect. As Christians became authors, which they did in great numbers, their works displaced ancient Greek and Roman texts as the most important literature of the age. Fortunately for later times, however, the eastern empire played a crucial role in passing on intellectual achievements from the past to later Western civilization.

Classical texts survived because Christian education and literature depended on non-Christian models, Latin and Greek. In the eastern empire, the region's original Greek culture remained the dominant influence, but Latin literature continued to be read because the administration was bilingual, with official documents and laws published in Latin along with Greek translations. Latin scholarship in the east received a boost when Justinian's Italian wars caused Latin-speaking scholars to flee for safety to Constantinople. There they helped conserve many works that might otherwise have disappeared. Scholars preserved classical literature because they regarded it as a crucial part of a high-level education. In other words, much of the classical literature available today survived because it formed part of an elite curriculum for Christians. At least some knowledge of some pre-Christian classics was required for a successful career in government service, the goal of every ambitious student. An imperial decree from 360 stated, "No person shall obtain a post of the first rank unless it shall be shown that he excels in long practice of liberal studies, and that he is so polished in literary matters that words flow from his pen faultlessly."

Another factor promoting the preservation of classical literature was that the principles of classical rhetoric provided the guidelines for the most effective presentation of Christian theology. When Ambrose, bishop of Milan from 374 to 397, composed the first systematic description of Christian ethics for young ministers, he consciously imitated the great classical orator Cicero. Theologians refuted heretical Christian doctrines by employing the dialogue form pioneered by Plato, and polytheist traditions of biography praising heroes inspired the hugely popular genre of saints' lives. Choricius, a Christian who held the official position of professor of rhetoric in Gaza, wrote works based on subjects from pre-Christian Greek mythology and history, such as the Trojan War or the Athenian general Miltiades. Similarly, Christian artists incorporated polytheist traditions in communicating their beliefs and emotions in paintings, mosaics, and carved reliefs. A favorite artistic motif of Christ with a sunburst surrounding his head, for example, took its inspiration from polytheist depictions of the radiant Sun as a god. (See the illustration on page 218.)

The growth of Christian literature generated a technological innovation used also to preserve classical literature. Polytheist scribes had written books on sheets of parchment (made from thin animal skin) or paper (made from papyrus). They then glued the sheets together and attached rods at both ends to form a scroll. Readers faced an awkward task in unrolling scrolls to read. For ease of use, Christians produced their literature in the form of the codex—a book with bound pages that not only stood up better to use but also held text more efficiently than scrolls. Eventually the codex became the standard form of book production.

Despite its continuing importance in education and rhetoric, classical Greek and Latin literature barely survived the war-torn world dominated by Christians. Knowledge of Greek in the west faded so drastically that by the sixth century almost no one there could read the original versions of Homer's *Iliad* and *Odyssey*, the traditional foundations of a classical literary education. Latin fared better, and scholars such as Augustine and Jerome knew Rome's ancient literature extremely well. But they also saw its classics as potentially too seductive for a pious Christian because the pleasure that came from

An Author or Scribe at Work

This illustration from a book produced in late Roman/early medieval times shows either an author writing a book or a scribe making a copy of a book by hand. This was the painstaking and slow process necessary to produce books in antiquity; mechanical printing had not yet been invented, and therefore mass production of books was not possible. As a result, books were expensive and precious objects, as indicated in the painting by their being carefully placed on their sides in the cabinet behind the writer to keep their weight from warping their spines and pages. *(The Granger Collection, NY—All rights reserved.)*

reading them could be a distraction from the worship of God. Jerome in fact once had a nightmare of being condemned on Judgment Day for having been more dedicated to Cicero than to Christ.

The closing around 530 of the Academy, founded in Athens by Plato more than nine hundred years earlier, demonstrated the dangers for classical learning in the later Roman Empire. This most famous of classical schools finally went out of business when many of its scholars emigrated to Persia to escape Justinian's tightened restrictions on polytheist teachers and its revenues dwindled because the Athenian elite, its traditional supporters, were increasingly Christianized. The Neoplatonist school at Alexandria, by contrast, continued. Its leader John Philoponus (c. 490–570) was a Christian. In addition to Christian theology, Philoponus wrote commentaries on the works of Aristotle. Some of his ideas anticipated those of Galileo a thousand years later. With his work, he achieved the kind of synthesis of old and new that was one of the fruitful possibilities in the cultural transformation of the late Roman world—he was a Christian subject of the eastern Roman Empire in sixth-century Egypt, heading a school founded long before by polytheists, studying the works of an ancient Greek philosopher as the inspiration for his forward-looking scholarship. The strong possibility that present generations could learn from the past would continue as Western civilization once again remade itself in medieval times.

REVIEW QUESTION What policies did Justinian undertake to try to restore and strengthen the Roman Empire?

Conclusion

The third-century civil wars brought the Roman Empire to a crisis that Diocletian's creation of the dominate and reorganization of government temporarily relieved, but Diocletian's reforms only delayed the division of the empire. In the late fourth century, migrations of non-Roman peoples fleeing the Huns brought intense pressures on the central government. Emperor Theodosius I divided the empire into western and eastern halves in 395 to try to improve its administration and defense. When Roman authorities bungled the task of integrating barbarian tribes into Roman society, the newcomers created kingdoms that eventually replaced imperial government in the west. Roman history increasingly divided into two regional streams, even though emperors as late as Justinian in the sixth century retained the dream of reuniting the empire and restoring its glory.

The large-scale immigration of barbarian tribes into the Roman Empire transformed not only the western empire's politics, society, and economy but also the tribes themselves, as they developed their own ethnic identities while organizing themselves into kingdoms inside Roman territory. The economic deterioration and political weakness that accompanied these often violent changes destroyed the public-spiritedness of the elite, which had been one of the foundations of imperial stability, as wealthy nobles retreated to self-sufficient country estates and shunned municipal office.

The eastern empire fared better economically than the western and avoided the worst violence of the migrations. Eastern emperors attempted to pre-

MAPPING THE WEST

Western Europe and the Eastern Roman Empire, c. 600

The eastern Roman emperor Justinian employed brilliant generals and expended huge sums of money to reconquer Italy, North Africa, and part of Spain to reunite the western and eastern halves of the former Roman Empire. His wars to regain Italy and North Africa eliminated the Ostrogothic and Vandal kingdoms, respectively, but at a huge cost in effort, time—the war in Italy took twenty years—and expense. The resources of the eastern empire were so depleted that his successors could not maintain the reunification. By the early seventh century, the Visigoths had taken back all of Spain. Africa, despite serious revolts by indigenous Berber tribes, remained under imperial control until the Arab conquest of the seventh century. Within five years of Justinian's death, however, the Lombards had set up a new kingdom controlling a large section of Italy. Never again would anyone in the ancient world attempt to reestablish a universal Roman Empire.

serve "Romanness" by maintaining Roman culture and political traditions. The financial drain of trying to reunite the empire by wars against the new kingdoms increased social discontent by driving tax rates to unbearable levels, while the concentration of authority in the capital weakened local communities.

Constantine's conversion to Christianity in 312 marked a turning point in Western history. Christianization of the empire occurred gradually, and it was not until 391 that it became the official state religion and public polytheist worship was completely banned. Christians disagreed among themselves over fundamental doctrines of faith, even to the point of deadly violence. Many Christians attempted to come closer to God by abandoning everyday society to live as monks. Monastic life redefined the meaning of holiness by creating communities of God's heroes who withdrew from this world to devote their service to glorifying the next. In the end, then, the imperial vision of unity faded in the face of the powerful effects of political and social transformation. Nevertheless, the memory of Roman power and culture remained potent and present, providing an influential inheritance to the peoples and states that would become Rome's heirs in the next stage of Western civilization.

FOR FURTHER EXPLORATION

- **For additional primary-source material from this period**, see *Sources of the Making of the West*, Fourth Edition.
- **For Web sites, images, and documents related to topics in this chapter**, visit *Make History* at bedfordstmartins.com/hunt.

Chapter 7 Review

Online Study Guide bedfordstmartins.com/hunt

Key Terms and People

In the grid below, identify the term or person and explain its historical significance. (To do this exercise online, go to bedfordstmartins.com/hunt.)

Term	Who or What & When	Why It Matters
dominate (p. 207)		
tetrarchy (p. 209)		
coloni (p. 212)		
curials (p. 212)		
Great Persecution (p. 213)		
Edict of Milan (p. 213)		
Julian the Apostate (p. 215)		
Theodosius I (p. 216)		
Augustine (p. 218)		
Arianism (p. 219)		
Nicene Creed (p. 220)		
asceticism (p. 222)		
Visigoths (p. 229)		
wergild (p. 231)		
Justinian and Theodora (p. 233)		

Review Questions

1. What were Diocletian's policies to end the third-century crisis, and how successful were they?
2. How did Christianity both unite and divide the Roman Empire?
3. How did their migrations and invasions change the barbarians themselves and the Roman Empire?
4. What policies did Justinian undertake to try to restore and strengthen the Roman Empire?

Making Connections

1. How did the principate and the dominate differ with regard to political appearance versus political reality?
2. What were the main similarities and differences between polytheism and Christianity as official state religions in the late Roman Empire?
3. What developments in the late Roman Empire would support the idea that it is possible for a state to be too large to be well governed and to remain united indefinitely?

Important Events

Date	Event	Date	Event
293	Diocletian creates the tetrarchy	395	Theodosius I divides empire into western and eastern halves
301	Diocletian issues edict on maximum prices and wages	410	Visigoths sack Rome
303	Diocletian launches Great Persecution of Christians	426	Augustine publishes *The City of God*
312	Constantine wins battle of the Milvian Bridge and converts to Christianity	451	Council of Chalcedon attempts to forge agreement on Christian orthodoxy
313	Religious freedom proclaimed in the Edict of Milan	475	Visigoths publish law code
323	Pachomius in Upper Egypt establishes the first monasteries	476	German commander Odoacer deposes the final western emperor, the boy Romulus Augustulus ("fall of Rome")
324	Constantine wins civil war and refounds Byzantium as Constantinople, the "new Rome"	493–526	Ostrogothic kingdom in Italy
325	Council of Nicaea defends Christian orthodoxy against Arianism	507	Clovis establishes Frankish kingdom in Gaul
361–363	Julian the Apostate tries to reinstate polytheism as official state religion	527–565	Reign of eastern Roman emperor Justinian
378	Barbarian massacre of Roman army in battle of Adrianople	529–534	Justinian publishes law code and handbooks
391	Theodosius I makes Christianity the official state religion	540	Benedict devises his rule for monasteries

- Consider three events: **Augustine publishes *The City of God* (426)**, **Council of Chalcedon attempts to forge agreement on Christian orthodoxy (451)**, and **Justinian publishes law code and handbooks (529–534)**. What connections can be drawn between these events in terms of the attitudes that informed them, their goals, and their effects on society?

SUGGESTED REFERENCES

Some scholars regard the political, social, and cultural changes in the late Roman Empire as evidence of a sad "decline and fall"; others judge them to have had mixed positive and negative consequences. The rise of Christianity to the status of an official religion also changed Roman life in complex ways that are still being investigated.

Brown, Peter. *The Body and Society: Men, Women, and Sexual Renunciation in Early Christianity*. 1988.

Cameron, Alan. *The Last Pagans of Rome*. 2010.

Daryaee, Touraj. *Sasanian Iran (224–651 C.E.): Portrait of a Late Antique Empire*. 2008.

*Drew, Katherine Fischer, ed. *The Laws of the Salian Franks*. 1991.

Elsner, Jas. *Imperial Rome and Christian Triumph: The Art of the Roman Empire, A.D. 100–450*. 1998.

*Grubbs, Judith Evans. *Women and Law in the Roman Empire: A Sourcebook on Marriage, Divorce, and Widowhood*. 2002.

Halsall, Guy. *Barbarian Migrations and the Roman West, 376–568*. 2008.

Heather, Peter. *Empires and Barbarians: The Fall of Rome and the Birth of Europe*. 2010.

Kelly, Christopher. *Ruling the Later Roman Empire*. 2006.

*Lee, A. D. *Pagans and Christians in Late Antiquity: A Sourcebook*. 2000.

Little, Lester K., ed. *Plague and the End of Antiquity: The Pandemic of 541–750*. 2006.

MacMullen, Ramsay. *Christianity and Paganism in the Fourth to Eighth Centuries*. 1997.

Odahl, Charles. *Constantine and the Christian Empire*. 2nd ed. 2010.

*Procopius. *The Secret History*. Trans. G. A. Williamson and Peter Sarris. 2007.

*Procopius. *The Wars*. Vols. I–V. Trans. H. B. Dewing. 1914–1928.

Rosen, William. *Justinian's Flea: The First Great Plague and the End of the Roman Empire*. 2008.

Southern, Pat, and Karen R. Dixon. *The Late Roman Army*. 1996.

Wickham, Chris. *Framing the Early Middle Ages: Europe and the Mediterranean*. 2007.

*Primary source.

CHAPTER

8

The Heirs of Rome: Islam, Byzantium, and Europe

600–750

In the eighth century, a Syrian monk named Joshua wrote about the first appearance of Islam in Roman territory. "The Arabs conquered the land of Palestine and the land as far as the great river Euphrates. The Romans fled," he marveled, and then continued:

> The first king was a man among them named Muhammad, whom they also called Prophet because he turned them away from cults of all kinds and taught them that there was only one God, creator of the universe. He also instituted laws for them because they were much entangled in the worship of demons.

Joshua was wrong about Muhammad leading the conquest of Palestine—Muhammad died in 632, six years before the fall of Palestine. But he was right to see the Arab movement as a momentous development, for in the course of a few decades the Arabs conquered much of the Persian and Roman Empires. Joshua was also right to emphasize Muhammad's teachings, for it was the fervor of Islam that brought the Arabs out of the Arabian peninsula and into the regions that hugged the Mediterranean in one direction and led to the Indus River in the other.

In the sixth century, as the western and eastern parts of the Roman Empire were going their separate ways, a third power—Arab and Muslim—was forming. These three powers have continued in various forms to the present: the western Roman Empire became western Europe; the eastern Roman Empire (occupying what is now Turkey, Greece, and some of the Balkans) became part of eastern Europe and helped create Russia; and the Arab world endures in North Africa and the Middle East (the ancient Near East).

As diverse as these cultures are today, they share many of the same roots: All were heirs of Rome. All adhered to monotheism. The western and eastern

The Dome of the Rock at Jerusalem (691)
Rivaling the great churches of Christendom, the mosque in Jerusalem called Dome of the Rock borrowed from late Roman and Byzantine forms even while asserting its Islamic identity. The columns and the capitals atop them, the round arches, the dome, and the mosaics are all from Byzantine models. In fact, the columns were taken from older buildings at Jerusalem. But the strips of Arabic writing on the dome itself—and in many other parts of the building—assert Islamic doctrine. *(Erich Lessing/Art Resource, NY.)*

halves of the Roman Empire had Christianity in common, although they differed at times in interpreting it. Adherents of Islam, the Arab world's religion, believed in the same God as the Jews and Christians. They understood Jesus, however, as God's prophet rather than his son.

The history of the seventh and eighth centuries is a story of the Roman Empire's persistence and transformation. Historians consider the changes in the eastern empire so important that they use a new term — Byzantine Empire — to describe it. They also speak of the end of antiquity and the beginning of the Middle Ages. (See "Terms of History," page 245.) Use of the term *Byzantine Empire* or *Byzantium*, which comes from the old Greek name for Constantinople, rightly implies that the center of power and culture in the eastern Roman Empire was now concentrated in this one city. Over the centuries, the Byzantine Empire shrank, expanded, and even nearly disappeared — but it hung on in one form or another until 1453.

During the period 600–750, all three heirs of the Roman Empire combined elements of their heritage with new values, interests, and conditions. The divergences among them resulted from disparities in geography and climate, material and human resources, skills, beliefs, and local traditions. But these differences should not obscure the fact that the Byzantine, Muslim, and western European cultures were related.

CHAPTER FOCUS What three cultures took the place of the Roman Empire, and to what extent did each of them both draw on and reject Roman traditions?

Islam: A New Religion and a New Empire

In the sixth century, a religion that called on all to believe in one God began in Arabia (today Saudi Arabia). Islam ("submission to God") emerged under **Muhammad** (c. 570–632), a merchant turned holy man from the city of Mecca. While many of the people living in Arabia were polytheists, Muhammad recognized one God, the same one worshipped by Jews and Christians. He understood himself to be God's last prophet and thus came to be called the Prophet — the person who received and in turn repeated God's final words to humans. Invited by the quarreling tribes of Medina to act as a mediator for them, Muhammad exercised the powers of both a religious and a secular leader. This dual role became the model for his successors, known as caliphs. Through a combination of persuasion and force, Muhammad and his co-religionists, the Muslims ("those who submit to Islam"), converted most of the Arabian peninsula. By the time Muhammad died in 632, conquest and conversion had begun to move northward into Byzantine and Persian territories. In the next generation, the Arabs conquered most of Persia and all of Egypt and were on their way across North Africa to Spain. Yet within the territories they conquered, daily life went on much as before.

Nomads and City Dwellers

In the seventh century, the vast deserts of the Arabian peninsula were populated by both sedentary and nomadic peoples. The sedentary peoples, who lived in one place, far outnumbered the nomads, who were often on the move. Some of the sedentary groups lived in oases, where they raised dates, a highly prized food. Some oases were prosperous enough to support merchants and artisans. The nomads were known as Bedouins; they lived in the desert, where they herded goats, camels, or sheep, surviving largely on the products of their animals: leather, milk, and meat. (The richer nomads herded camels and called themselves Arabs.) The Bedouins

---

Muhammad: The prophet of Islam (c. 570–632). He united a community of believers around his religious tenets, above all that there was one God whose words had been revealed to him by the angel Gabriel. Later, written down, these revelations became the Qur'an.

c. 486–751 Merovingian dynasty

572 Lombards conquer northern Italy

587 Conversion of Visigothic king Reccared

r. 590–604 Papacy of Pope Gregory the Great

603–623 War between Byzantium and Persia

622 Hijra to Medina; year 1 of the Islamic calendar

550 — 575 — 600 — 625

c. 570–632 Life of Muhammad, prophet of Islam

r. 573–c. 594 Bishop Gregory of Tours

c. 590 Arrival of Irish monk Columbanus in Gaul

624 Muhammad and Meccans fight battle of Badr

were warriors; valuing honor and bravery, Bedouin tribes raided one another to capture slaves or wives and to take belongings. Although they lacked written literature, their oral tradition of poetry expressed many things, including the bravado of a boast, the trials of a journey, and longing for a lost love, as in the following verse:

> To remember Salma! to recall
> times spent with her
> is folly, conjecture about the other side,
> a casting of stones.

The "follies of love" were part of a culture in which men practiced polygyny (having more than one wife at a time).

Islam began as a religion of the city dwellers, but it soon found support and military strength among the nomads. It had its start in Mecca, an important commercial center near the coast of the Red Sea. Mecca was also a religious center, the home of the Ka'ba, a shrine that contained the images of many gods. The Ka'ba was a sacred place within which war and violence were prohibited. The tribe that dominated Mecca, the Quraysh, controlled access to the shrine, taxing the pilgrims who flocked there and selling them food and drink. Visitors, assured of their safety, bartered on the sacred grounds, transforming the plunder from raids into trade.

The Prophet Muhammad and the Faith of Islam

Muhammad was born in Mecca. Orphaned at the age of six, he lived two years with his grandfather and then came under the care of his uncle, a leader of the Quraysh tribe. Eventually, Muhammad became a trader. At the age of twenty-five, he married Khadija, a rich widow who had once employed him. They had at least four daughters and lived (to all appearances) happily and comfortably. Yet Muhammad sometimes left home and spent a few days in a nearby cave in prayer and contemplation, practicing a type of piety similar to that of the early Christians.

In about 610, on one of these retreats, Muhammad heard a voice and had a vision that summoned him to worship the God of the Jews and Christians, Allah ("the God" in Arabic). He accepted the call as coming from God. Over the next years, he received messages that he understood to be divine revelations. Later, when these messages had been written down and compiled — a process completed in the seventh century, but after Muhammad's

TERMS OF HISTORY

Medieval

How did the word *medieval* come into being, and why is it a derogatory term today? No one who lived in the Middle Ages thought of himself or herself as "medieval." People did not say they lived in the "Middle Ages." The whole idea of the Middle Ages began in the sixteenth century. At that time, writers decided that their own age, known as the Renaissance (French for "rebirth"), and the ancient Greek and Roman civilizations were much alike. They dubbed the period in between—from about 600 to about 1400—with a Latin term: the *medium aevum*, or the "middle age." It was not a flattering term. Renaissance writers considered the *medium aevum* a single unfortunate, barbaric, and ignorant period.

Only with the Romantic movement of the nineteenth century and the advent of history as an academic discipline did writers begin to divide that middle age into several ages. Often they divided it into three periods: Early (c. 600–1100), High (c. 1100–1300), and Late (c. 1300–1400). Today there is no hard-and-fast rule about this terminology: Chapter 11 of this book, for example, covers the period 1150–1215 as the High Middle Ages.

The period before the High Middle Ages was sometimes called the Dark Ages, a term that immediately brings to mind doom and gloom. However, recent research disputes this view of the period, stressing instead its creativity, multiethnicity, and localism.

Newspaper reporters and others still sometimes use *medieval* as a negative term: for example, by calling a primitive prison system "medieval." Little do they know that when they do that, they are stuck in the sixteenth century.

661–750 Umayyad caliphate

664 Synod of Whitby; English king opts for Roman form of Christianity

680–754 Life of Boniface, who reformed the Frankish church

r. 717–741 Emperor Leo III the Isaurian

726–787 Period of iconoclasm at Byzantium

650 675 700 725

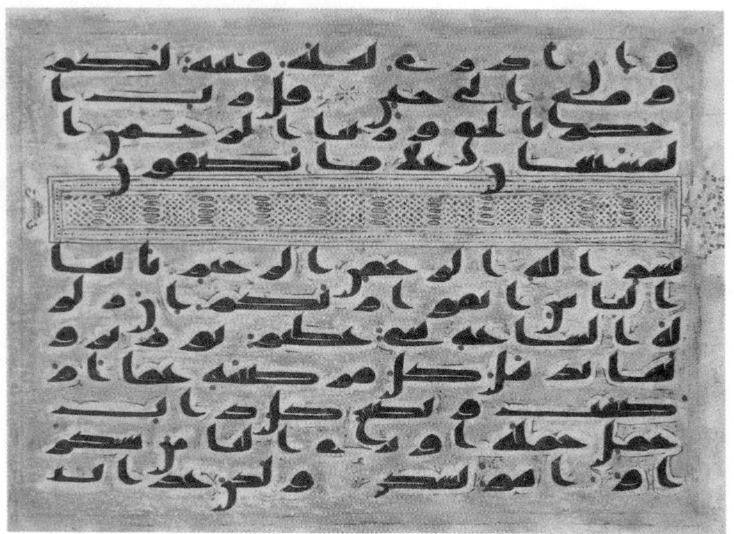

Qur'an
More than a holy book, the Qur'an represents for Muslims the very words of God that were dictated to Muhammad by the archangel Gabriel. In the Umayyad period, the Qur'an was written, as here, on pages wider than long. The first four lines on the top give the last verses of Sura 21. *(Freer Gallery of Art, Smithsonian Institution, Washington, DC, Purchase F1945.16.)*

death—they became the **Qur'an**, the holy book of Islam. *Qur'an* means "recitation"; each of the book's parts, or suras, is understood to be God's revelation as told to Muhammad by the archangel Gabriel—the very Gabriel of the Hebrew and Christian Bibles—and then recited by Muhammad to others. Written entirely in verse, the Qur'an changed the focus of traditional Bedouin poetry, which had emphasized the here and now. The Qur'an focuses on the divine, the "one of great power." In an early sura, Muhammad has a vision of this power:

> This is a revelation
> taught him by one of great power
> and strength that stretched out over
> while on the highest horizon—
> then drew near and came down
> two bows' lengths or nearer

Here the object of Muhammad's vision never quite reveals itself; nevertheless, it teaches him about its great power and strength, its astonishing ability to stretch to the horizon, and its willingness at the same time almost to touch him.

Beginning with the Fatihah ("opening"; see Document, "The Fatihah of the Qur'an," page 247), frequently also said as an independent prayer, the Qur'an continues with suras of gradually decreasing length. They cover the gamut of human experience and the life to come. For Muslims, the Qur'an contains the foundations of history, prophecy, and the legal and moral code by which men and women should live: "Do not set up another god with God. . . . Do not worship anyone but Him, and be good to your parents. . . . Give to your relatives what is their due, and to those who are needy, and the wayfarers." The Qur'an emphasizes the family—a man, his wife (or wives), and children—as the basic unit of Muslim society. For its adherents, Islam replaced the identity and protection of the tribe with a new identity as part of the *ummah*, the community of believers, who share both a belief in one God and a set of religious practices.

Stressing individual belief in God and adherence to the Qur'an, Islam had no priests or sacraments, though in time it came to have authoritative religious leaders who interpreted the Qur'an and related texts. The Ka'ba, with its many gods, had attracted tribes from the surrounding vicinity. Muhammad, with his one God, forged an even more universal religion.

Growth of Islam, c. 610–632

The first convert to Muhammad's faith was his wife, Khadija. A few friends and members of their immediate family joined them. Eventually, as Muhammad preached the new faith, others became adherents. Soon the new faith polarized Meccan society. Muhammad's insistence that the cults of all other gods be abandoned in favor of one brought him into conflict with leading members of the Quraysh tribe, whose control over the Ka'ba had given them prestige and wealth. Perceiving Muhammad as a threat, they insulted him and harassed his adherents.

Hijra: Muhammad's Journey from Mecca to Medina

Disillusioned with the people of Mecca, Muhammad looked elsewhere for a place and a population receptive to his message. In particular, he expected support from Jews, whose monotheism, in Muhammad's view, prepared them for his own faith. When a few of Muhammad's converts from Medina, an oasis about two hundred miles north of Mecca, promised to protect him if he would join them there, he eagerly accepted the invitation, in part because Medina had a significant Jewish population. Muhammad's journey to Medina—called the **Hijra**—proved to be a crucial event for the new faith. Although he was disappointed not to find much

---

Qur'an (Kur AN/Koo RAHN): The holy book of Islam, considered the word of Allah ("the God") as revealed to the Prophet Muhammad.

Hijra (HIJ ruh): The emigration of Muhammad from Mecca to Medina. Its date, 622, marks year 1 of the Islamic calendar.

support among the Jews at Medina, Muhammad did find others there ready to listen to his religious message and to accept him as the leader of their community. They expected him to act as a neutral and impartial judge in their interclan disputes. Muhammad's political position in the community set the pattern by which Islamic society would be governed afterward; rather than simply adding a church to political and cultural life, Muslims made their political and religious institutions inseparable. After Muhammad's death, the year of the Hijra, 622, was named the first year of the Islamic calendar; it marked the beginning of the new Islamic era.[1]

Although successful at Medina, Muhammad and his Muslim followers felt threatened by the Quraysh at Mecca, who actively opposed the public practice of Islam. For this reason, Muhammad led raids against them. At the battle of Badr in 624, the Muslims killed forty-nine of the Meccan enemy, took numerous prisoners, and confiscated rich booty. Thus, from the time of this conflict, the Bedouin tradition of plundering was grafted onto the Muslim duty of **jihad** ("striving in the way of God").

The battle of Badr was a great triumph for Muhammad, who was able to secure his position at Medina, gaining new adherents and silencing all doubters, including Jews. When the Jews of Medina did not convert to Islam as expected, Muhammad suspected them of supporting his enemies; he expelled two Jewish tribes from Medina and executed the male members of another. Although Muslims had originally prayed in the direction of Jerusalem, the center of Jewish worship, Muhammad now had them turn in the direction of Mecca.

DOCUMENT

The Fatihah of the Qur'an

The Fatihah is the prayer that begins the Qur'an. It emphasizes God's compassion for the believer, who needs to be guided "along the road straight"—God's highway. To convey the fluid nature of the phrases, which relate to one another in many ways and have no one meaning, the translation here uses no punctuation.

In the name of God
    the Compassionate the Caring
Praise be to God
    lord sustainer of the worlds
the Compassionate the Caring
master of the day of reckoning
To you we turn to worship
    and to you we turn in time of need
Guide us along the road straight
the road of those to whom you are giving
    not those with anger upon them
    not those who have lost the way

Source: *Approaching the Qur'an: The Early Revelations*, intro. and trans. Michael Sells (Ashland, OR: White Cloud Press, 1999), 42.

Question to Consider

- **According to this passage from the Fatihah, what are the attributes of God—and the corresponding attributes of those who believe in him?**

Defining the Faith

As Muhammad broke with the Jews, he instituted new practices to define Islam as a unique religion. Among these were the *zakat*, a tax on possessions to be used for alms; the fast of Ramadan, which took place during the ninth month of the Islamic year, the month in which the battle of Badr had been fought; the *hajj*, the pilgrimage to Mecca during the last month of the year, which each Muslim was to make at least once in his or her lifetime; and the *salat*, formal worship at least three times a day (later increased to five). The salat could include the *shahadah*, or profession of faith: "There is no divinity but God, and Muhammad is the messenger of God." Detailed regulations for these practices, sometimes called the **Five Pillars of Islam**, were worked out in the eighth and early ninth centuries.

Meanwhile, Muhammad sent troops to subdue Arabs north and south. In 630, he entered Mecca with ten thousand men and took over the city, assuring the Quraysh of leniency and offering alliances with its leaders. As the prestige of Islam grew, clans elsewhere converted. Through a combination of force, conversion, and negotiation, Muhammad was able to unite many, though by no means all, Arabic-speaking tribes under his leadership by the time of his death in 632.

Muhammad was responsible for social as well as religious change. The ummah included both men and women; Islam thus enhanced women's status. At

[1]Thus, 1 anno Hegirae (1 A.H.) on the Muslim calendar is equivalent to 622 C.E.

jihad: In the Qur'an, the word means "striving in the way of God." This can mean both striving to live righteously and striving to confront unbelievers, even through holy war.

Five Pillars of Islam: The five essential practices of Islam, namely, the *zakat* (alms); the fast of Ramadan; the *hajj* (pilgrimage to Mecca); the *salat* (formal worship); and the *shahadah* (profession of faith).

first, Muslim women joined men during the prayer periods that punctuated the day, but beginning in the eighth century, women began to pray apart from men. Men were allowed to have up to four wives at one time but were obliged to treat them equally; wives received dowries and had certain inheritance rights. Islam prohibited all infanticide, a practice that Arabs had long used largely against female infants. Like Judaism and Christianity, however, Islam retained the practices of a patriarchal society in which women's participation in community life was limited.

Even though the Islamic ummah was a new sort of community, it functioned in many ways as a tribe, or rather a "supertribe," obligated to fight common enemies, share plunder, and peacefully resolve any internal disputes. Muslims participated in group rituals, such as the salat and public recitation. The Qur'an was soon publicly sung by professional reciters, much as the old tribal poetry had been. Most significant for the eventual spread of Islam was that Bedouin converts to Islam turned their traditional warrior culture to its cause. Along the routes once taken by caravans to Syria, Muslim armies reaped profits at the point of a sword. But this differed from intertribal fighting; it was the jihad of people who were carrying out God's command against unbelievers as recorded in the Qur'an: "Strive, O Prophet, against the unbelievers and the hypocrites, and deal with them firmly. Their final abode is Hell: And what a wretched destination!"

The Caliphs, Muhammad's Successors, 632–750

In the new political community he founded in Arabia, Muhammad reorganized traditional Arab society by cutting across clan allegiances and welcoming converts from every tribe. He forged the Muslims into a formidable military force, and his successors, the caliphs, used this force to take the Byzantine and Persian worlds by storm.

War and Conquest After Muhammad's death, the Muslims moved to the north and west, quickly taking Byzantine territory in Syria and Egypt (Map 8.1). To the east, they invaded the Sasanid Empire, conquering the whole of Persia by 651. During the last half of the seventh century and the beginning of the eighth, Islamic warriors extended their sway westward to Spain and eastward to India.

How were such widespread conquests possible, especially in so short a time? First, the Islamic forces

MAP 8.1 Expansion of Islam to 750
In little more than a century, Islamic armies conquered a vast region that included numerous different people, cultures, climates, and living conditions. Yet under the Umayyads these disparate territories were administered by one ruler from the capital city at Damascus. The uniting force was the religion of Islam, which gathered all believers into one community, the *ummah*.

DOCUMENT

The Pact of Umar

Treaties such as the one excerpted here regulated the relations between Muslims and other monotheists in the regions conquered by the Muslims. The Muslims wished both to safeguard those who practiced other "religions of the book [the Bible]" and at the same time protect themselves and their religion from contamination by non-Muslims. The treaties also imposed a tax on non-Muslims. Historians used to think that this tax was simply a token, but recent studies argue that it was a considerable burden on many. The treaty given here is specifically for Christians, but those for Jews were similar. The numbering of the provisions here differs from the original.

1. If any of you [Christians] says of Muhammad or God's book or His religion something which is inappropriate for him to say, the protection of God, the commander of the faithful and all Muslims is removed from him; the conditions under which security was given will be annulled and the commander of the faithful will put that person's property and life outside the protection of the law, like the property and lives of enemies.
2. If one of you commits adultery with or marries a Muslim woman, or robs a Muslim on the highway, or turns a Muslim away from his religion . . . he has broken this agreement, and his life and property are outside the protection of the law. . . . We shall examine your every dealing between yourself and Muslims, and if you have had a part in anything that is unlawful for a Muslim, we shall undo it and punish you for it. . . . You will not give a Muslim any forbidden thing to eat or drink, and you will not allow him to marry in the presence of your witnesses, nor to partake in a marriage we consider illegal. [On the other hand] we shall not scrutinize nor inquire into a contract between you and any other unbeliever. . . .
3. You shall not display the cross nor parade your idolatry in any Muslim town, nor shall you build a church or place of assembly for your prayers, nor sound your bells. You will not use your idolatrous language about Jesus, son of Mary, or anyone else to any Muslim. . . .
4. For every free adult male of sound mind, there will be on his head a poll-tax of one dinar of full weight, payable at new year. He will not leave his land until he has paid the tax. . . .
5. These terms are binding on you and those who accept them; we have no treaty with those who reject them. We will protect you and your property which we deem lawful against anyone, Muslim or not, who tries to wrong you, just as we protect ourselves and our own property.

Source: "'Umar II and the 'protected people'" in *Classical Islam: A Sourcebook of Religious Literature*, ed. and trans. Norman Calder, Jawid Mojaddedi, and Andrew Rippin (London: Routledge, 2003), 90–92.

Question to Consider

■ **In what ways does this pact protect Christians, and in what ways does it coerce them?**

came up against weakened empires. The Byzantine and Sasanid states were exhausted from fighting each other, and the cities they fought over were depopulated and demoralized. Second, discontented Christians and Jews welcomed Muslims into both Byzantine and Persian territories. The Monophysite Christians in Syria and Egypt, for example, who had suffered persecution under the Byzantines, were glad to have new, Islamic overlords. The so-called Pact of Umar, which set out the terms by which Christians and Jews were to be integrated into the new Islamic empire, made clear that Christianity and Judaism could be practiced so long as Islam was accorded special honor (see Document, "The Pact of Umar," above).

There were also internal reasons for Islamic success. Arabs had long been used to intertribal warfare; now united as a supertribe, inspired by religious fervor, and fighting under the banner of jihad, they exercised their skills as warriors against unbelievers. Fully armed and mounted on horseback, using camel convoys to carry supplies and provide protection, they conquered with amazing ease. To secure their victories, they built garrison cities from which their soldiers requisitioned taxes and goods. Sometimes whole Arab tribes, including women and children, were resettled in conquered territory, as happened in parts of Syria. In other regions, such as Egypt, one small Muslim settlement sufficed to gather the spoils of conquest.

The Politics of Succession Muhammad died quietly at Medina in 632. The question of who should succeed him as leader of the new Islamic state was the origin of the tension between the two main Muslim factions—Shi'ite and Sunni—that continues today. The caliphs who followed Muhammad came not from the traditional tribal elite but rather from the inner circle of men who had participated in the Hijra and remained close to the Prophet. The first two caliphs ruled without serious opposition, but the third caliph,

Uthman (r. 644–656), a member of the Umayyad clan and son-in-law of Muhammad, aroused discontent among other members of the inner circle and soldiers unhappy with his distribution of high offices and revenues. Accusing Uthman of favoritism, they supported his rival, Ali, a member of the Hashim clan (to which Muhammad had belonged) and the husband of Muhammad's only surviving child, Fatimah. After a group of discontented soldiers murdered Uthman, civil war broke out between the Umayyads and Ali's faction. It ended when Ali was killed by one of his own former supporters, and the caliphate remained in Umayyad hands from 661 to 750.

Despite defeat, the Shi'at Ali ("Ali's faction"), did not fade away. Ali's memory lived on among **Shi'ite** Muslims, who saw in him a symbol of justice and righteousness. For them, Ali's death was the martyrdom of the only true successor to Muhammad. They remained faithful to his dynasty, shunning the mainstream caliphs of Sunni Muslims (whose name derived from the word *sunna*, the practices of Muhammad). The Shi'ites awaited the arrival of the true leader—the imam—who in their view could come only from the house of Ali.

Shi'ite: A Muslim of the "party of Ali" and his descendants. Shi'ites are thus opposed to the Sunni Muslims, who reject the authority of Ali.

Peace and Prosperity in Islamic Lands

Ironically, the definitive victories of the Muslim warriors in the seventh and early eighth centuries ushered in times of peace. While the conquerors stayed within their fortified cities or built magnificent hunting lodges in the deserts of Syria, the conquered went back to work, to study, to play, and—in the case of Christians and Jews, who were considered protected subjects—to live in accordance with the provisions of the Pact of Umar. Under the **Umayyad caliphate**, which lasted from 661 to 750, the Muslim world became a state. Its capital was at Damascus, in Syria.

Borrowing from institutions well known to the civilizations they had just conquered, the Muslims issued coins and hired Byzantine and Persian officials as civil servants (see "Seeing History," page 251). They made Arabic a tool of centralization, imposing it as the language of government on regions not previously united linguistically. At the same time, the Islamic world was startlingly multireligious and multiethnic, including Arabs, Syrians, Egyptians, Iraqis, and many other peoples.

Taking advantage of the vigorous economy in both the cities and the countryside, the Umayyads presided over a new literary and artistic flowering. At Damascus, local artists and craftspeople worked on the lavish decorations for a mosque that used Roman motifs. At Jerusalem, the mosque called the Dome of the Rock used Christian building models for its octagonal form and its interior arches,

Umayyad caliphate (oo MAH yuhd KAY luhf ayt): The caliphs (successors of Muhammad) who traced their ancestry to Umayyah, a member of Muhammad's tribe. The dynasty lasted from 661 to 750.

Mosaic from the Great Mosque at Damascus
Like the Dome of the Rock, the Umayyad mosque at Damascus in Syria, built at the beginning of the eighth century, drew on Byzantine forms. In this mosaic, which is one of many that decorate the interior of the mosque, the style is Byzantine. But the harmonious intertwining of trees, buildings, rocks, and water picks up on an Islamic theme: the new faith's conquest over both civilization and nature. *(© Umayyad Mosque, Damascus, Syria / Bildarchiv Steffens / The Bridgeman Art Library International.)*

SEEING HISTORY

Who Conquered Whom? A Persian and an Arabic Coin Compared

Do you see any differences between the two coins shown here? One is Persian; the other is Arabic and comes from a later period. Both were minted for use in Iran and Iraq, but at different times, when these lands were under different rule. The coin on the top is Persian and shows the image of a Sasanid King of Kings. In the margin are three crescents, each encompassing stars. It was minted under Chosroes II (r. 591–628), the ambitious conqueror of Jerusalem. The coin on the bottom was minted by an Umayyad provincial governor in 696/697, after Islamic armies had conquered Persia. True, one branch of Islam barred depicting the human form, but the early Ummayads were less condemning and saw nothing wrong with imitating traditional numismatic models. Although the image on the Arabic coin is still of a Sasanid ruler, the governor had his own name added in Arabic—it's in the right half of the central roundel, perpendicular to the nose. He also added in the margin of the coin an Arabic inscription that mentions Allah several times.

Consider these coins in conjunction with supplemental evidence. The Arabic word for this type of coin, *dirham*, comes from the Greek *drachma*, a monetary unit used under the Byzantines. In areas that had been under Byzantine rule, the early Umayyad rulers adopted Byzantine coin forms, reusing *their* images—just as here they used the face of a Sasanid ruler. In general, the Umayyad fiscal system, which preserved the Byzantine land taxes, was administered by Syrians, who had often served Byzantine rulers in the same capacity. What advantages did the Arabs derive from adopting these institutions? From this evidence, how might you argue that both Greek and Persian institutions captured the conquering Arabs?

Question to Consider

- **What do the images and history of these two coins suggest about how much the Islamic world borrowed from the Persian Empire that it conquered?**

Persian Silver Coin (minted 606). (*© The Trustees of the British Museum/Art Resource, NY.*)

Umayyad Silver Dirham (minted 696/697). (*© The Trustees of the British Museum/Art Resource, NY.*)

which rested on columns and piers (see the chapter-opening photo).

During the seventh and eighth centuries, Muslim scholars turned Arabic, previously an oral language primarily, into a written language as well. They determined the definitive form for the Qur'an and compiled pious narratives about Muhammad, called hadith literature. A literate class—consisting mainly of the old Persian and Syrian elites, now converted to Islam—created new forms of prose writing in Arabic, producing official documents and essays on every sort of topic. They also wrote poetry, exploring new worlds of thought and feeling. Supported by the caliphs, for whom written poetry served as an important source of propaganda and reinforcement for their power, the poets also reached a wider audience that delighted in their clever use of words, their satire, and their verses celebrating courage, piety, and sometimes erotic love:

> I spent the night as her bed-companion, each
> enamored of the other,
> And I made her laugh and cry, and stripped her
> of her clothes.
> I played with her and she vanquished me; I made
> her happy and I angered her.
> That was a night we spent, in my sleep, playing
> and joyful,
> But the caller to prayer woke me up.

Such poetry scandalized conservative Muslims, brought up on the ascetic tenets of the Qur'an. But this love poetry was a by-product of the new urban civilization of the Umayyad period, during which wealth, cultural mix, and the confidence born of conquest inspired diverse and experimental literary forms. By the time the Umayyad caliphate ended in 750, Islamic civilization was multiethnic, urban, and sophisticated—a true heir of Roman and Persian traditions.

REVIEW QUESTION How and why did the Muslims conquer so many lands in the period 632–750?

Byzantium Besieged

The Byzantines saw themselves as the direct heirs of Rome. In fact, as we have seen, Emperor Justinian (r. 527–565) had tried to re-create the old Roman Empire and, on the surface, had succeeded. His empire once again included Italy, North Africa, and the Balkans. Vestiges of the old Roman society persisted: an educated elite maintained its prestige, town governments continued to function, and old myths and legends were retold in poetry and depicted in works of art. Around 600, however, the eastern half of the Roman Empire began to undergo a transformation as striking as the one that had earlier remade the western half.

Almost constant war, beginning in the last third of the sixth century and continuing through the seventh century, shrank the eastern empire's territory drastically. Cultural and political change came as well. Cities decayed, and the countryside became the focus of governmental and military administration. In the wake of these shifts, the old elite largely disappeared and classical learning gave way to new forms of education, mainly religious in content. The traditional styles of urban life, dependent on public gathering places and community spirit, faded away. Historians have good reason to stop speaking of the eastern Roman Empire and call this something new—the Byzantine Empire.

At the same time, the transformations should not be exaggerated. A powerful emperor continued to rule at Constantinople. Roman laws and taxes remained in place. The cities, while shrunken, nevertheless survived, and Constantinople itself had a flourishing economic and cultural life even in Byzantium's darkest hours. The Byzantines continued to call themselves Romans. For them, the empire never ended: it just moved to Constantinople.

Wars on the Frontiers, c. 570–750

From about 570 to 750, the Byzantines waged war against invaders. One key challenge came from an old enemy, Persia. Another involved many new groups—Lombards, Slavs, Avars, Bulgars, and Muslims. In the wake of these onslaughts, Byzantium became smaller but tougher.

Invasions from Persia In the sixth century, before the Muslims came on the scene, the principal challenge to Byzantine power came from the Sasanid Empire of Persia (Map 8.2). From their capital city at Ctesiphon, where they built a grand palace complex, the Sasanid kings promoted an exalted view of themselves: they took the title *King of Kings* and gave the men at their court titles such as *priest of priests* and *scribe of scribes*. Dreams of military and imperial glory accompanied the display of splendor. Using the revenues from new taxes to strengthen the army, the Sasanids decided to invade major areas of the Roman Empire. Between 611 and 614, King Chosroes II (r. 591–628) took Syria and Jerusalem; he conquered Egypt in 620. The fall of Jerusalem particularly shocked the pious Byzantines, since Chosroes took as plunder the relic of the Holy Cross (on which Jesus was said to have died).

Responding to this affront, the Byzantine emperor **Heraclius** reorganized his army and inspired his troops to avenge the sack of Jerusalem. By 627, the Byzantines had regained all their lost territory. But the wars had changed much: Syrian, Egyptian, and Palestinian cities had grown used to being under Persian rule, and Christians who did not adhere to the orthodoxy at Byzantium preferred their Persian overlords. Even more important, the constant wars and plundering sapped the wealth of the region and the energy of its people.

Attack on All Fronts Preoccupied by war with the Sasanids, Byzantium was ill equipped to deal with other groups who were pushing into parts of the empire at about the same time. The **Lombards**, a Germanic people, entered northern Italy in 568 and by 572 were masters of the Po valley and some inland regions in Italy's south. In addition to Rome, the Byzantines retained only Bari, Calabria, Sicily, and a narrow swath of land through the middle called the Exarchate of Ravenna.

The Byzantine army could not contend anymore with the Slavs and other peoples just beyond the Danube River. The Slavs conducted lightning

---

Heraclius (her uh KLY uhs): The Byzantine emperor who reversed the fortunes of war with the Persians in the first quarter of the seventh century.

Lombards: The people who settled in Italy during the sixth century, following Justinian's reconquest. A king ruled the north of Italy, while dukes ruled the south. In between was the papacy, which felt threatened both by Lombard Arianism and by the Lombards' geographical proximity to Rome.

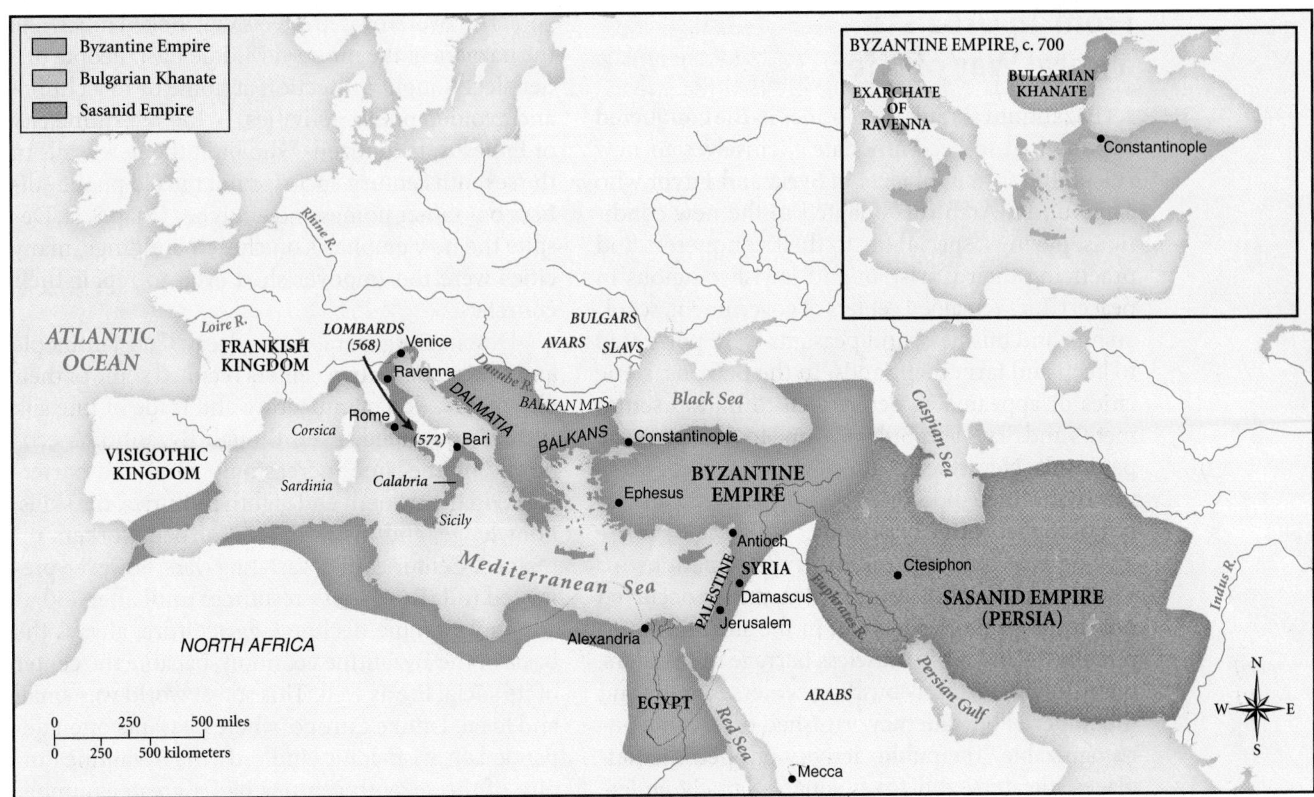

MAP 8.2 Byzantine and Sasanid Empires, c. 600

The emperor Justinian (r. 527–565) hoped to re-create the old Roman Empire, but just a century after his death Italy was largely conquered by the Lombards. Meanwhile, the Byzantine Empire had to contend with the Sasanid Empire to its east. In 600, these two major powers faced each other uneasily. Three years later, the Sasanid king attacked Byzantine territory. The resulting wars, which lasted until 627, exhausted both empires and left them open to invasion by the Arabs. By 700, the Byzantine Empire was quite small. | **Compare the inset map here with Map 8.1, on page 248. Where did the Muslims made significant conquests of Byzantine territory?**

raids on the Balkan countryside (part of Byzantium at the time); joined by the Avars, they attacked Byzantine cities as well. Meanwhile, the Bulgars entered what is now Bulgaria in the 670s, defeating the Byzantine army and in 681 forcing the emperor to recognize their new state.

Even as the Byzantine Empire was facing military attacks on all fronts, its power was being whittled away by more peaceful means. For example, as Slavs and Avars, who were not subject to Byzantine rulers, settled in the Balkans, they often intermingled with the native peoples there, absorbing local agricultural techniques and burial practices while imposing their language and establishing religious cults.

Consequences of Constant Warfare

Byzantium's loss of control over the Balkans meant the shrinking of its empire (see Map 8.2 inset). More important, the Balkan peninsula could no longer serve, as it had previously, as a major link between Byzantium and Europe. The loss of the Balkans exacerbated the growing separation between the eastern and western parts of the former Roman Empire. The political division between the Greek-speaking and Latin-speaking halves had begun in the fourth century; the events of the seventh century, however, made the split both physical and cultural. Avar and Slavic control of the Balkans effectively cut off trade and travel between Constantinople and the cities of the Dalmatian coast, while the Bulgarian khanate threw up a political barrier across the Danube. Perhaps as a result of this physical separation, historians in the East ceased to be interested in the western part of Europe, and Byzantine scholars no longer bothered to learn Latin. The two halves of the former Roman Empire communicated very little in the seventh century.

Byzantium's wars with the Sasanid Empire exhausted both Persian and Byzantine military strength. Both empires were now vulnerable to attack by the Muslim Arabs, whose military conquests created a new empire and introduced a new religion.

From an Urban to a Rural Way of Life

As Byzantium shrank, Byzantines in the conquered regions had to accommodate themselves to new rulers. Byzantine subjects in Syria and Egypt who came under Arab rule adapted to the new conditions, paying a special tax to their conquerors and practicing their Christian and Jewish religions in peace. Cities remained centers of government, scholarship, and business, and peasants were permitted to keep and farm their lands. In the Balkans, some cities disappeared as people fled to hilltop settlements and Slavs and Bulgars came to dominate the peninsula. Nevertheless, the newcomers recognized the Byzantine emperor's authority, and they soon began to flirt with Christianity.

Some of the most radical transformations for seventh- and eighth-century Byzantines occurred not in the territories lost but in the shrunken empire itself. Under the ceaseless barrage of invaders, many towns, formerly bustling centers of trade and the imperial bureaucracy, vanished or became unrecognizable. The public activity of open marketplaces, theaters, and town squares largely ended. City baths, once places where people gossiped, made deals, and talked politics and philosophy, disappeared in most Byzantine towns — with the significant exception of Constantinople. Warfare reduced some cities to rubble, and the limited resources available for rebuilding went to construct thick city walls and solid churches instead of spacious marketplaces and baths. Traders and craftspeople sold their goods on overcrowded streets that looked much like the bazaars of the modern Middle East. People under siege sought protection at home or in a church and avoided public activities. In the Byzantine city of Ephesus, the citizens who built the new walls in the seventh century enclosed not the old public edifices but rather homes and churches (Map 8.3). Despite the new emphasis on church buildings, many cities were too impoverished even to repair their churches.

Despite the general urban decay, Constantinople and a few other urban centers retained some of their old vitality. The manufacture and trade of fine silk textiles continued. Even though Byzantium's economic life became increasingly rural and barter-based in the seventh and eighth centuries, the skills, knowledge, and institutions of urban workers remained. Centuries of devastating wars, however, prevented full use of these resources until after 750.

As urban life declined, agriculture, always the basis of the Byzantine economy, became the center of its social life as well. This social world was small and local. Unlike Europe, where peasants often depended on aristocratic landlords, the Byzantine Empire of the seventh century had a greater number of free peasants who grew food, herded cattle, and tended vineyards on their own small plots of land. Farmers interacted mostly with members of their families or with monks at local monasteries; two or three neighbors were enough to ratify a land transfer. As Byzantine cities declined, the curials (town councilors), the elite who for centuries had mediated between the emperor and the people, disappeared. Now on those occasions when farmers came into contact with the state — to pay taxes, for example — they felt the impact of the emperor or his representatives directly. There were no local protectors any longer.

Emperors, drawing on the still-vigorous Roman legal tradition, promoted local, domestic life with new imperial legislation. The laws strengthened the nuclear family by narrowing the grounds for divorce and setting new punishments for marital infidelity. Husbands and wives who committed adultery were to be whipped and fined, and their noses slit. Abortion was prohibited, and new protections were set in place against incest. Mothers were given equal power with fathers over their offspring; if widowed, they became the legal guardians of their minor children and controlled the household property.

Silver Censer from Cyprus
This small dish, used for burning incense (and thus called a censer), was used during the Christian church service; it was carried and swung on three chains attached to the round rings on the lip of the censer. Each of the six sides shows a holy figure; pictured here is the Virgin Mary flanked by Saints John and James. By the seventh century, such precious objects were common in churches throughout the Byzantine Empire. *(© The Trustees of the British Museum/Art Resource, NY.)*

New Military and Cultural Forms

The shift from an urban-centered society to a rural one meant changes not only in daily life and the economy but also in the empire's military and cultural institutions. The Byzantine navy fought successfully at sea with its powerful weapon of "Greek fire," a mixture of crude oil and resin that was heated and shot via a tube over the water, engulfing enemy ships in flames. Determined to win wars on land as well, the imperial government tightened its control over the military by wresting power from other elite families and encouraging the formation of a middle class of farmer-soldiers. One seventh-century emperor, possibly Heraclius, divided the empire into military districts called ***themes*** and put all civil as well as military matters in each district into the hands of one general, a *strategos*. Landless men were lured to join the army with the promise of land and low taxes; they fought side by side with local farmers, who provided their own weapons and horses. The new organization effectively countered frontier attacks.

The disappearance of the old cultural elite meant a shift in the focus of education. Whereas the curial class had cultivated the study of the pagan classics, hiring tutors or sending their children (primarily their sons) to school to learn to read the works of Greek poets and philosophers, eighth-century parents showed far more interest in giving their children, both sons and daughters, a religious education. Even with the decay of urban centers, cities and villages often retained an elementary school. There teachers used the Book of Psalms (the Psalter) as their primer. Secular, classical learning remained decidedly out of favor throughout the seventh and eighth centuries; dogmatic writings, biographies of saints, and devotional works took center stage.

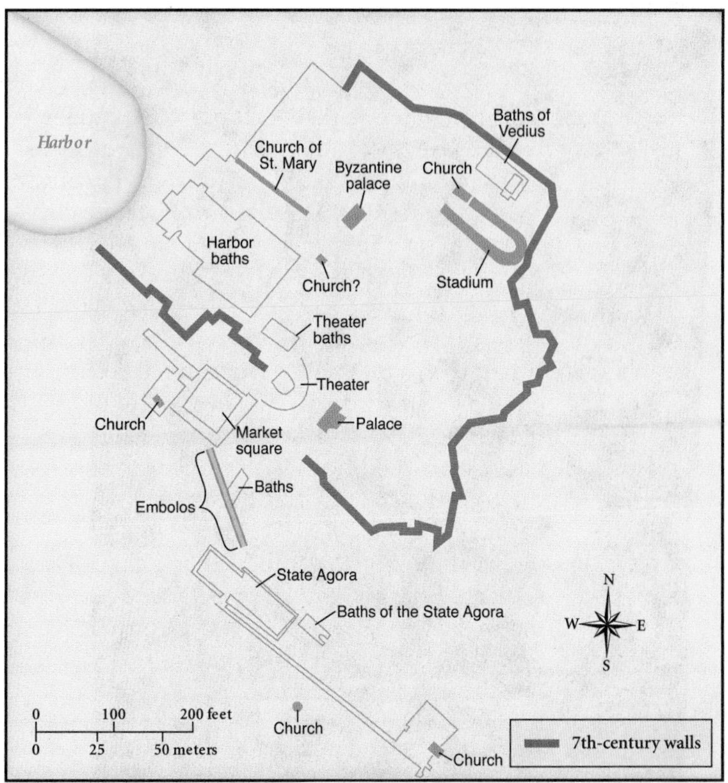

MAP 8.3 Plan of the City of Ephesus
Before the seventh century, Ephesus sprawled around its harbor. Nearest the harbor were baths and churches including, by 500, the bishop's Church of St. Mary. To the south was the Embolos—a long, marble-paved avenue adorned with fountains, statues, and arcades and bordered by well-appointed homes. Earthquakes, plague, and invasions changed much in the seventh century. Ephesians built a new wall to embrace the area around the harbor. The Embolos was neglected, and even within the narrow precinct protected by the new wall, baths were allowed to go to ruin, while people made their homes within the debris. After the Arabs invaded, the bishop moved out of the city altogether.

Religion, Politics, and Iconoclasm

The importance of religious learning and piety in the seventh century complemented both the autocratic imperial ideal and the powers of the bishops. While in theory imperial and church powers were separate, in practice they were interdependent. The emperor exercised considerable power over the church: he influenced the appointment of the chief religious official, the patriarch of Constantinople; he called church councils to determine dogma; and he regularly used bishops as local governors. Beginning with Heraclius, the emperors considered it one of their duties to baptize Jews forcibly, persecuting those who would not convert. In the view of the imperial court, this was part of the ruler's role in upholding orthodoxy.

Bishops and Monks Jostling for Power At the same time, although the curial lay elite had disappeared, bishops and their clergy formed a rich and powerful upper class, even in declining cities. They served as judges and tax collectors. They distributed food in times of famine or siege, provisioned troops, and set up military fortifications. As part of their charitable work, they cared for the sick and the needy. Byzantine bishops were part of a three-tiered system: they were appointed by metropolitans (bishops who headed an entire province), and the metropolitans were in turn appointed by the patriarchs (bishops with authority over whole regions).

Theoretically, monasteries were under the limited control of the local bishop, but in practice they were enormously powerful institutions that often defied the authority of bishops and even emperors. Because monks commanded immense prestige as

theme: A military district in Byzantium. The earliest themes were created in the seventh century and served mainly defensive purposes.

Icon of the Virgin and Child
Surrounded by two angels in the back and two soldier-saints at either side, the Virgin Mary and the Christ Child are depicted with still, otherworldly dignity. The sixth-century artist gave the angels transparent halos to emphasize their spiritual natures, while depicting the saints as earthly men, with hair and beards, and feet planted firmly on the ground. Icons like this were used for worship both in private homes and in Byzantine monasteries. *(Erich Lessing/Art Resource, NY.)*

the holiest of God's faithful, they could influence the many issues of doctrine that racked the Byzantine church.

Conflict over Icons The most important doctrinal issue of the Byzantine church in this period revolved around **icons**—images of holy people, such as Jesus; his mother, Mary; and the saints (see the illustration above). To Byzantine Christians, icons were far more than mere representations: they were believed to possess holy power that directly affected people's daily lives as well as their chances for salvation.

Many seventh-century Byzantines made icons the focus of their religious devotion. To them, the images were like the incarnation of Christ in that they turned spirit into material substance. That is, they believed that an icon manifested in physical form the holy person it depicted. Some Byzantines actually worshipped icons; others, particularly monks, considered icons a necessary part of Christian piety. Protected by his Muslim overlords, the Christian Syrian St. John of Damascus wrote a thundering defense of icons (see Document, "On Holy Images," page 257).

Other Byzantines abhorred icons. Most numerous of these were the soldiers on the frontiers. Unnerved by Arab triumphs, they attributed their misfortunes to disregard of the biblical command against graven (carved) images: "You shall not make for yourself a graven image, or any likeness of anything that is in heaven above, or that is in the earth beneath, or that is in the water under the earth" (Exod. 20:4). When they compared their defeats to Muslim successes, Byzantine soldiers could not help but notice that Islam prohibited all visual images of the divine. To these soldiers and others who shared their view, icons revived pagan idolatry and desecrated Christian divinity. As the movement toward **iconoclasm** ("icon breaking") grew, some churchmen became outspoken in their opposition to icons.

Byzantine emperors shared these religious objections, and they also had important political reasons for opposing icons. One reason was that the issue of icons became a test of their authority. Icons diluted loyalties, creating intermediaries between worshippers and God that undermined the emperor's exclusive place in the divine and temporal order. In addition, the emphasis on icons in monastic communities made the monks potential threats to imperial power; the emperors hoped to use this issue to weaken the monasteries. Above all, though, the emperors opposed icons because the army did, and they needed to retain the loyalty of their troops.

After Emperor Leo III the Isaurian (r. 717–741) defeated the Arabs besieging Constantinople at the beginning of his reign, he turned his attention to consolidating his political position. Officers of the

icons: Images of holy people such as Jesus, Mary, and the saints. Controversy arose in Byzantium over the meaning of such images. The iconoclasts considered them "idols," but those who adored icons maintained that they manifested the physical form of those who were holy.

iconoclasm: Literally, "icon breaking"; referring to the destruction of icons, or images of holy people. Byzantine emperors banned icons from 726 to 787; a modified ban was revived in 815 and lasted until 843.

DOCUMENT

On Holy Images

At Constantinople, no one could publicly oppose iconoclasm. But Christians in the Arab world had more freedom. John of Damascus (c. 675–749) was born in Syria after it came under Islamic rule. His father, though Christian, worked for the Arab governor there, and John soon did so as well. John wrote this ringing defense of icons shortly before he joined a monastery near Jerusalem. To be sure, the iconoclasts condemned his work, but he was vindicated in 787, when the ban was lifted (for a time).

I believe in one God, the source of all things, without beginning, uncreated, immortal, everlasting, incomprehensible, bodiless, invisible, uncircumscribed [i.e., in no one place], without form. I believe in one supersubstantial being [i.e., beyond all substance], one divine Godhead in three entities, the Father, the Son, and the Holy Ghost, and I adore Him alone with the worship [due God alone]. I adore one God, one Godhead but three Persons, God the Father, God the Son made flesh, and God the Holy Ghost, one God. I do not adore creation more than the Creator, but I adore the creature created as I am, adopting creation freely and spontaneously that He might elevate our nature and make us partakers of His divine nature. Together with my Lord and King I worship Him clothed in the flesh, not as if it were a garment or He constituted a fourth person of the Trinity—God forbid. That flesh is divine, and endures after its assumption. Human nature was not lost in the Godhead, but just as the Word made flesh remained the Word, so flesh became the Word remaining flesh, becoming, rather, one with the Word through union. Therefore I venture to draw an image of the invisible God, not as invisible, but as having become visible for our sakes through flesh and blood. I do not draw an image of the immortal Godhead. I paint the visible flesh of God, for if it is impossible to represent a spirit, how much more God who gives breath to the spirit.

Source: *St. John Damascene on Holy Images*, trans. Mary H. Allies (London: Thomas Baker, 1898), 1 (slightly modified).

Question to Consider

- **How does John's view of the nature of the Son (Jesus Christ) support his argument in favor of icons?**

imperial court tore down the great golden icon of Christ at the gateway of the palace and replaced it with a cross. In 726, Leo ordered all icons destroyed, a ban that remained in effect until 787. This is known as the period of iconoclasm in Byzantine history. A modified ban would be revived in 815 and last until 843.

Iconoclasm had an enormous impact on Byzantium. At home, where people had their own portable icons, the devout had to destroy their icons or worship them in secret. Iconoclasts (who were especially numerous at Constantinople itself) whitewashed the walls of churches, erasing all the images. They smashed portable icons. Artists largely ceased depicting the human form, and artistic production in general dwindled during this time. The power and prestige of the monasteries, which were associated with icons, diminished. As the tide of battle turned in favor of the Byzantines, imperial supporters and soldiers credited iconoclasm for their victories.

REVIEW QUESTION What stresses did the Byzantine Empire endure in the seventh and eighth centuries, and how was iconoclasm a response to those stresses?

Western Europe: A Medley of Kingdoms

In contrast to Byzantium—where an emperor still ruled as the successor to Augustus and Constantine, drawing on an unbroken chain of Roman legal and administrative traditions—western Europe saw a dispersal of political power in the seventh and eighth centuries. With the end of Roman imperial government in the western half of the empire, the region was divided into a number of kingdoms: various monarchs ruled in Spain, Italy, England, and Gaul. The primary foundations of power and stability in all of these kingdoms were kinship networks, church patronage, royal courts, and wealth derived from land and plunder. There were kings, to be sure, but in some places churchmen and rich magnates were even more powerful than royalty. Icons were not very important in the West, but in their place was the power of the saints as exercised through their relics—the bodies and body parts, even clothes and dust from the tombs of holy people. These represented and wielded the divine forces of God. Although the patterns of daily life and the procedures of government in western Europe remained recognizably Roman, they were also in the process of

TABLE 8.1 The Three Monotheistic Religions, c. 750*

Religion	Founder/ Prophet	Chief Religious Head(s)	Place of Worship	Important Elements of Worship	Key Religious Texts	Material Aids to Worship
Christianity						
Roman Catholic	Jesus	Bishops, increasingly pope at Rome	Church	Mass, prayer, fasting	Bible, especially the Psalms	Relics
Byzantine	Jesus	Patriarch of Constantinople	Church	Mass, prayer, fasting	Bible, especially the Psalms	Icons
Judaism	Abraham	Rabbis	Synagogue	Prayer, fasting	Hebrew Scriptures and rabbinic legal literature (Talmud)	Torah (first five books of the Bible)
Islam	Muhammad	Caliphs or, increasingly, religious scholars	Mosque	Prayer, fasting	Qur'an and commentaries on it	Qur'an

*None of these religions remained fixed in the form they had in 750.

change, borrowing from and adapting to local traditions and to the very powerful role of the Christian religion in every aspect of society.

Frankish Kingdoms with Roman Roots

The most important kingdoms in post-Roman Europe were Frankish. During the sixth century, the Franks had established themselves as dominant in Gaul, and by the seventh century the limits of their kingdoms roughly approximated the eastern borders of present-day France, Belgium, the Netherlands, and Luxembourg (Map 8.4). Moreover, the Frankish kings who constituted the **Merovingian dynasty** (c. 486–751) subjugated many of the peoples beyond the Rhine, foreshadowing the contours of the western half of modern Germany. Where there were cities, there were reminders of Rome. Elsewhere, the Roman heritage was less obvious.

Blending the Roman Past with the Frankish Present Imagine travelers going from Rome to Trier (near what is now Bonn, Germany) in the early eighth century, perhaps to visit its bishop and check up on his piety. No doubt they would have relied on river travel, even though some Roman roads were still in fair repair. Water routes were preferable because land travel was slow and because even large groups of travelers on the roads were vulnerable to attacks by robbers (see Taking Measure, page 260). Like the roads, other structures in the landscape would have seemed familiarly Roman. Traveling northward on the Rhône River, our voyagers would have passed Roman walled cities and farmlands neatly and squarely laid out by Roman land surveyors. The great stone palaces of villas would still have dotted the countryside. Once at Trier, the travelers would have felt at home seeing the city's great gate (now called the Porta Nigra; see the illustration on page 259), its monumental baths (some still standing today), and its cathedral, built on the site of a Roman palace. Being in Trier was almost like being in Rome.

Nevertheless, travelers would have had to have been unobservant not to notice that the cities that they passed through were not what they had once been in the heyday of the Roman Empire. True, cities still served as the centers of church administration. Bishops lived in them, and so did clergymen, servants, and others who helped the bishops. Cathedrals (the churches presided over by bishops) remained within city walls, and people were drawn to them for important rituals such as baptism. Nevertheless, many urban centers had lost their commercial and cultural vitality. Largely depopulated, they survived as skeletons of their former selves.

Whereas the chief feature of the Roman landscape had been cities, the Frankish landscape was characterized by dense forests, acres of marshes and bogs, patches of cleared farmland, and pasturage for

---

Merovingian (mehr oh VIN jian) dynasty: The royal dynasty that ruled Gaul from about 486 to 751.

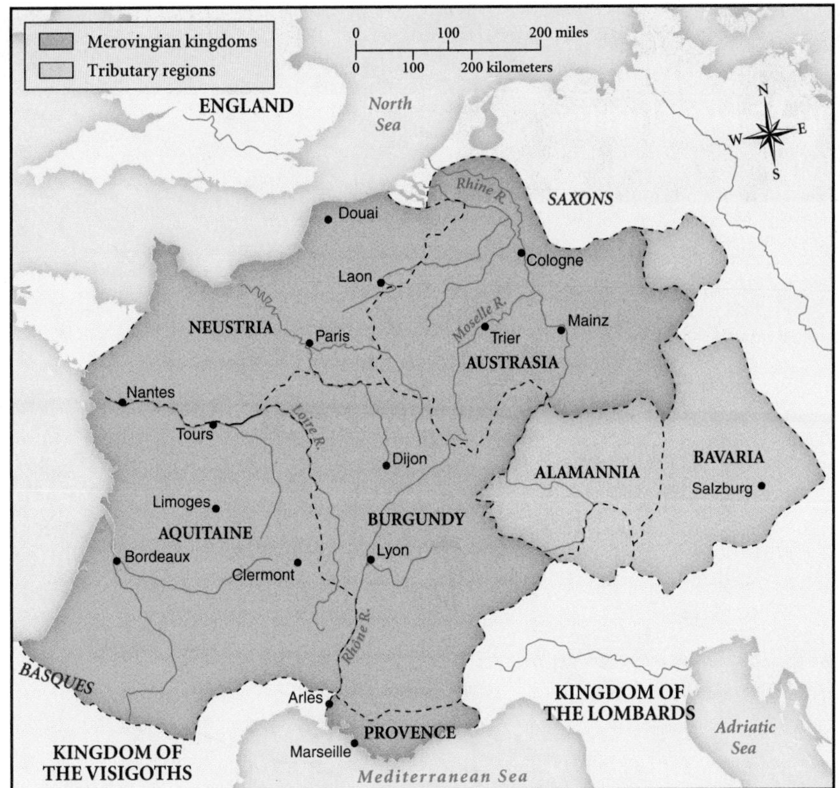

MAP 8.4 The Merovingian Kingdoms in the Seventh Century
By the seventh century, there were three powerful Merovingian kingdoms: Neustria, Austrasia, and Burgundy. The important cities of Aquitaine were assigned to these major kingdoms, while Aquitaine as a whole was assigned to a duke or other governor. Kings did not establish capital cities; they did not even stay in one place. Rather, they continually traveled throughout their kingdoms, making their power felt in person.

animals. These areas were not much influenced by Rome; they represented far more the farming and village settlement patterns of the Franks.

On the vast plains between Paris and Trier, most peasants were only semi-free. They were settled—in family groups—on small holdings called manses, which included a house, a garden, and cultivable land. The peasants paid dues and sometimes owed labor services to a lord (an aristocrat who owned the land). Some of the peasants were descendants of the *coloni* (tenant farmers) of the late Roman Empire; others were the sons and daughters of slaves, now provided with a small plot of land; and a few were people of free Frankish origin who for various reasons had come down in the world. At the lower end of the social scale, the status of Franks and Romans had become identical.

Romans (or, more precisely, Gallo-Romans) and Franks had also merged at the elite level. Although people south of the Loire River continued to be called Romans and people to the north Franks, their cultures—their languages, their settlement patterns, their newly military way of life—were strikingly similar (see "New Sources, New Perspectives," page 261).

The Porta Nigra at Trier
Although in Germania, Trier became one of Rome's capitals in the fourth century. The Porta Nigra was originally the northern gate of the city. During the course of the fifth century, the Porta Nigra came to be considered at best useless and at worst pagan, so bits and pieces of it were pillaged to be used in other building projects. However, this practice stopped when a hermit named Simeon moved into its eastern tower. After Simeon's death in 1035, the Porta Nigra was turned into a two-story church, which it remained until the early nineteenth century, when Napoleon, who conquered Trier, ordered the church to be dismantled and the site returned (more or less) to its original shape. *(The Art Archive/Gianni Dagli Orti.)*

TAKING MEASURE

Papal Letters Sent from Rome to Northern Europe, c. 600–c.700

Between 600 and 700, the pope at Rome sent many letters to kings, queens, aristocrats, and members of the clergy in northern Europe. But he didn't send the same number every month. This graph shows that papal communications were never sent in January and February, whereas their numbers peaked in June and July. The explanation? Very likely the popes had to wait for fine sailing weather to get their letters to their destination, since land routes were too uncertain.

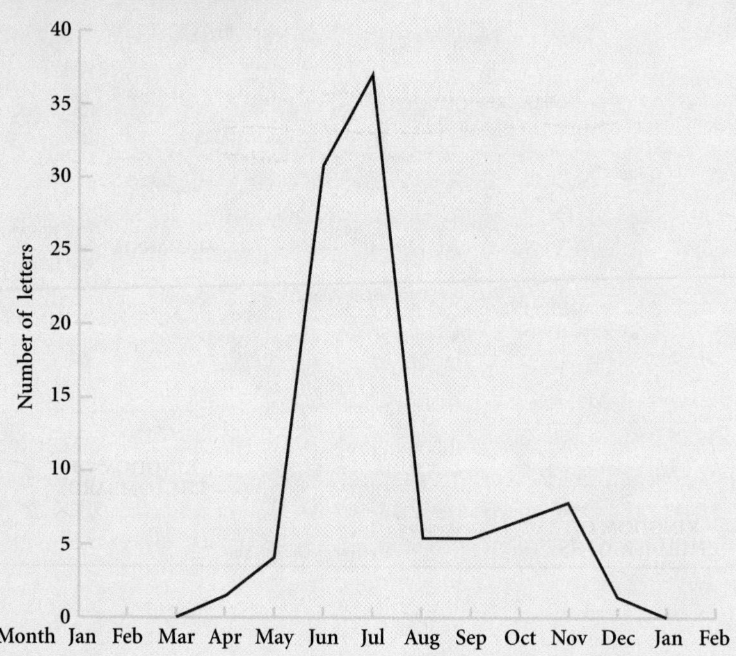

Source: Adapted from Michael McCormick, *Origins of the European Economy: Communications and Commerce, AD 300–900* (Cambridge: Cambridge University Press, 2001), chart 3.1, 80.

Question to Consider

- **How might the seasonal limitations on communication have affected the relationship between the pope and his church?**

The language that aristocrats spoke and (often) read depended on their location, not their ethnicity. Among the many dialects in the Frankish kingdoms, some were Germanic, especially to the east and north, but most were derived from Latin, yet no longer the Latin of Cicero. At the end of the sixth century, Bishop **Gregory of Tours** (r. 573–c. 594), wrote, "Though my speech is rude, . . . to my surprise, it has often been said by men of our day, that few understand the learned words of the rhetorician but many the rude language of the common people." This beginning to Gregory's *Histories*, a valuable source for the Merovingian period, testifies to Latin's transformation; Gregory expected that his "rude" Latin—the plain Latin of everyday speech—would be understood and welcomed by the general public.

The Frankish elites, like Frankish peasants, tended to live in the countryside rather than in cities. In fact, peasants and aristocrats tended to live together in villages. In many cases, these consisted of a large central building (probably for the aristocratic household to use), sometimes with stone foundations. It was surrounded by smaller buildings, some of which were no doubt houses for peasant families along with their livestock, which provided warmth in the winter. Such villages might boast populations a bit over a hundred.

The elites of the Merovingian period cultivated military—rather than civilian—skills. They went on hunts and wore military-style clothing: the men wore trousers, a heavy belt, and a long cloak; both men and women bedecked themselves with jewelry. As hardened warriors, or wanting to appear so, aristocrats no longer lived in grand villas, choosing instead modest wooden structures without baths or heating systems. That explains why the village great house and the smaller ones nearby looked very much alike.

Saints and Relics

Sometimes villages formed around old villas. In other instances they clustered around sacred sites. Tours—where Gregory was bishop—exemplified this new-style settlement. In Roman times, Tours was a thriving city; around 400, its population diminished (as happened elsewhere in Gaul) and it constructed walls

Gregory of Tours: Bishop of Tours (in Gaul) from 573 to 594, the chief source for the history and culture of the Merovingian kingdoms.

NEW SOURCES, NEW PERSPECTIVES

Anthropology, Archaeology, and Changing Notions of Ethnicity

At the end of the nineteenth century, scholars argued that ethnicity was the same as race and that both were biological. They measured skeletal features and argued that different human groups—blacks, whites, Jews, and Slavs, for example—were biologically distinct and that some were better than others according to "scientific" criteria. This same view was shared by historians, who spoke of the various groups who entered the Roman Empire—Franks, Visigoths, Saxons, Lombards—as if these people were biologically different from Romans and from one another. They thought, for example, that there was a real biological group called the Lombards who had migrated into the Roman Empire and set up the "Lombard kingdom" in Italy by conquering another real biological group called the Romans.

Some anthropologists challenged this view. In the early 1900s, for example, the anthropologist Franz Boas showed that American Indians were not biologically different from any other human group; their "ethnicity" was cultural. Boas meant that the characteristics that made Indians "Indian" were not physical but rather a combination of practices, beliefs, language, dress, and sense of identity. Soon archaeologists came to realize that no physical difference distinguished a Frankish skeleton from a Lombard or a Roman or a Slav skeleton. It was only the artifacts associated with skeletons in grave excavations—jewelry, weapons—that revealed to what ethnicity a person belonged.

If ethnicity were biological, it would be fixed. No one could be a Lombard unless he or she had been born into the group. But since ethnicity is cultural, "outsiders" can join, while "insiders" can be shed. Historians—especially those associated with the University of Vienna—have shown in detail how this was the case with the peoples that the Romans called barbarians. Walter Pohl, for example, has demonstrated how ethnic groups like the Lombards and Franks were made up of men and women from all sorts of backgrounds. Their sense of being Lombard or Frankish was a product of common myths that they accepted about themselves. The Lombards, for example, thought that their name came from a trick played by their women, who tied their long hair around their chins, humoring the war god Woden into calling them "Longbeards" and giving their men victory in battle. The Avars, for their part, were held together by their loyalty to their leader, the *khagan*. Avars who broke away from the khagan's political dominance were no longer considered part of the group—they were considered Bulgarians instead. In contrast, the less centrally organized Slavs recognized all sorts of people living in their territory as Slavs; their ethnicity was based on language and other cultural traditions, which could be learned even by newcomers.

Seeing ethnicity as cultural allows us to understand the origins of European states not as the result of the conquest of one well-defined group by another but rather as a historical process. France, Germany, and England were not created by fixed entities known for all time as, respectively, the Franks, the Germans, and the Angles. Rather, they were created and shaped by the will and imagination of men and women who intermingled, interacted, and adapted to one another over time.

The benefits of this view depend, to be sure, on whether the evidence bears it out. Recent critiques, by Andrew Gillett and others, point out that the primary sources for the discussion of Germanic identity are in Latin. These scholars suggest that France, Germany, and England were created not by ethnic groups but by Roman administrative structures and categories of thought that automatically associated peoples with geographical regions.

Pohl and others respond that there is no one foundation for ethnic identity. Rather, identities are the result of a series of acts: individuals identify themelves with a group that has an ethnic name for itself; groups identify themselves with an ethnic term; and outsiders identify groups with an ethnic epithet that sets them off from others. This view does not deny the contribution of Roman categories, but it views them as just one factor in a complex process of identification.

Questions to Consider

1. The society of the United States has been called a melting pot. In what ways might the same be said about European societies?
2. How do common myths nourish contemporary notions of ethnicity?
3. Does the language of a primary source matter in assessing its value for discussions of ethnicity?

Further Reading

Geary, Patrick J. *The Myth of Nations: The Medieval Origins of Europe*. 2002.

Gillett, Andrew. "Ethnogenesis: A Contested Model of Early Medieval Europe," *History Compass* 4/2 (2006): 241–60.

Pohl, Walter, and Gerda Heydemann, eds. *Strategies of Identification*. 2011.

around its now smaller acreage. By Gregory's day, however, it had gained a new center *outside* of the city walls. There a church had been built to house the remains of the most important and venerated person in the locale: St. Martin. This fourth-century soldier-turned-monk was long dead, but his relics remained at Tours, where he had served as bishop. The population of the surrounding countryside was pulled to his church as if to a magnet. Seen as a miracle worker, Martin acted as the representa-

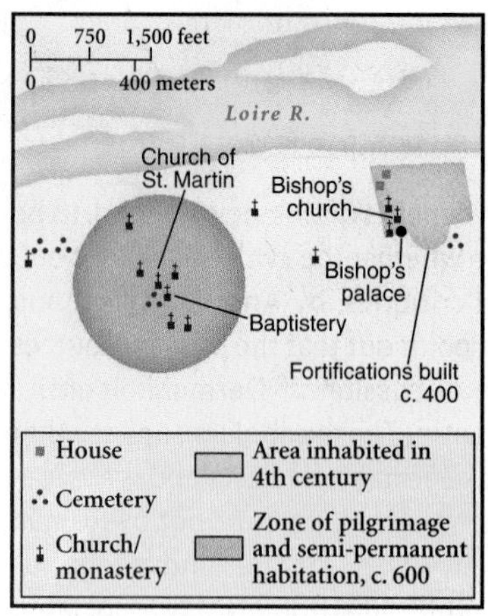

Tours, c. 600

(Nancy Gauthier and Henri Galinié, eds., Gregoire de Tours et l'espace gaulois [Tours: Actes du congrès internationale, 1997], 70.)

tive of God's power: a protector, healer, and avenger. In Gregory's view, Martin's relics (or rather God *through* Martin's relics) not only cured the lame and sick but even prevented armies from plundering local peasants. Martin was not the only human thought to have such great power; all saints were miracle workers.

The veneration of dead saints and their relics marked a major departure from practices of the classical age, in which the dead had been banished from the presence of the living. In the medieval world, the holy dead held the place of highest esteem. The church had no formal procedures for proclaiming saints in the early Middle Ages, but holiness was "recognized" by influential local people and the local bishop. When, for example, miracles were observed at the supposed tomb of the martyr Benignus in Dijon, the common people went there regularly to ask for help. But only after the martyr himself appeared to the local bishop in a vision, thus dispelling doubts about the tomb, was Benignus accorded saintly status. No one at Tours doubted that Martin had been a saint, however, and to tap into the power of his relics, the local bishop built a church directly over his tomb. For a man like Gregory of Tours and his flock, the church building was above all a home for the relics of the saints.

Reliquary

The cult of relics necessitated housing the precious parts of the saints in equally precious containers. This reliquary—made of cloisonné enamel (bits of enamel framed by metal), garnets, glass gems, and a cameo—is in the shape of a miniature sarcophagus. It was made in honor of St. Maurice, a venerated martyr, and was given to a monastery dedicated to Maurice, Saint-Maurice d'Agaune (today in Switzerland). Note the side hinges, which allowed the casket to be worn on a chain. No doubt the abbot of Saint-Maurice wore it when he traveled outside the monastery, to ensure him of the power and protection of the saint. *(Erich Lessing/Art Resource, NY.)*

Economic Activity in a Peasant Society

As a bishop, Gregory was aware of some sophisticated forms of economic activity that existed in early medieval Europe, such as long-distance trade, which depended on surpluses. Most people, however, lived on the edge of survival. Studies of Alpine peat bogs show that from the fifth to the mid-eighth century glaciers advanced and the mean temperature in Europe dropped. This climatic change spelled shortages in crops. Chronicles, histories, and biographies of saints also describe crop shortages, famines, and diseases as a normal part of life. For the year 591 alone, Gregory reported that

> a terrible epidemic killed off the people in Tours and in Nantes. . . . In the town of Limoges a number of people were consumed by fire from heaven for having profaned the Lord's day by transacting business. . . . There was a terrible drought which destroyed all the green pasture. As a result there were great losses of flocks and herds.

Subsistence and Gift Economies

An underlying reason for the calamities of the Merovingian period was the weakness of the agricultural economy. Even the meager population of the Merovingian world was too large for the land's productive capacities. Farmers could easily till the light, dry soil of the Mediterranean region with wooden implements. But the heavy, wet soils of northern Europe were difficult to turn and aerate. Technological limitations meant a limited food supply, and agricultural work was not equitably or efficiently allocated and managed. A leisure class of landowning warriors and churchmen lived off the work of peasant men, who tilled the fields, and peasant women, who wove cloth, gardened, brewed, and baked.

Occasionally surpluses developed, either from good harvests in peacetime or from plunder in warfare, and these changed hands, although rarely in an impersonal, commercial manner. Most economic transactions of the seventh and eighth centuries were part of a gift economy, a system of give-and-take: the rich took booty, demanded tribute, hoarded harvests, and minted coins—all to be redistributed to friends, followers, and dependents. Kings and other powerful men and women

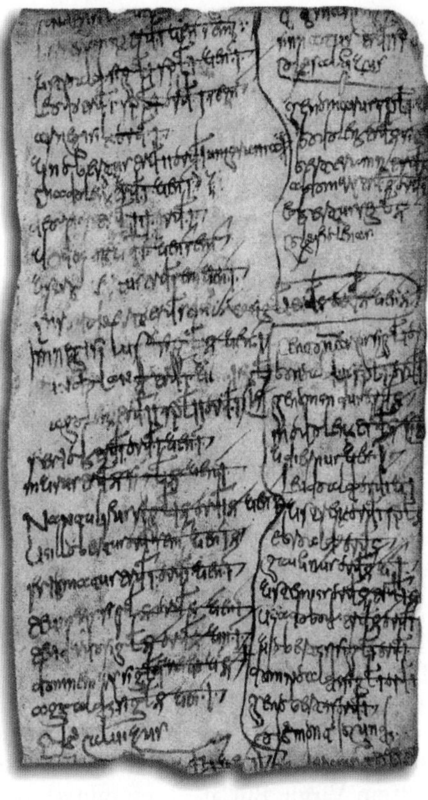

Early Medieval Accounting
In the seventh century, peasants in western Europe were lucky to produce more grain than they sowed. To make sure that it got its share of this meager production, the monastery of Saint-Martin at Tours kept a kind of ledger. This parchment sheet, dating from the second half of the seventh century, lists the amount of grain and wood that tenants owed to the monastery. It is one of the few such early accounts that have survived the ages. *(Bibliothèque nationale de France.)*

amassed gold, silver, ornaments, and jewelry in their treasuries and grain in their storehouses to mark their power, add to their prestige, and demonstrate their generosity. Those reaping benefits from the gifts of the rich included religious people and institutions: monks, nuns, bishops, monasteries, and churches. We still have a partial gift economy today; at holidays, for example, goods change hands for social purposes: to consecrate a holy event, to express love and friendship, to show off wealth and status. In the Merovingian world, the gift economy was the dynamic behind most of the exchanges of goods and money.

Trade and Traders However, some economic activity in this period was purely commercial and impersonal, especially long-distance trade. In these transactions, Europe supplied slaves and raw materials such as furs and honey. In return, it received luxuries and manufactured goods such as silks and papyrus. Byzantine, Islamic, and western European descendants of the Roman Empire kept in tenuous contact with one another by making voyages for trade, diplomatic ventures, and pilgrimages. Seventh- and eighth-century sources speak of Byzantines, Syrians, and Jews as the chief intermediaries of any long-distance trade that existed. Many of these intermediaries lived in the still-thriving port cities of the Mediterranean. Gregory of Tours associated Jews with commerce, complaining that they sold things "at a higher price than they were worth."

Although the population of the Merovingian world was overwhelmingly Christian, Jews were integrated into every aspect of secular life. They used Hebrew in worship, but otherwise they spoke the same languages as Christians and used Latin in their legal documents. Jews often gave their children the same names as Christians (and, in turn, Christians often took Old Testament names); they dressed as everyone else dressed; and they engaged in the same occupations. Many Jews planted and tended vineyards, in part because of the importance of wine in synagogue services and in part because they could easily sell the surplus. Some Jews were rich landowners, with slaves and dependent peasants working for them; others were independent peasants of modest means. Some Jews lived in towns with a small Jewish quarter that included both homes and synagogues, but most Jews, like their Christian neighbors, lived on the land. Only much later, in the eleventh century, would the status of Jews change, setting them markedly apart from Christians.

The Powerful in Merovingian Society

Monarchs and aristocrats held political power in Merovingian society. The Merovingian elite—who included monks and bishops as well as laypeople—obtained their power through hereditary wealth, status, and personal influence.

The Aristocrats Many aristocrats of the period were extremely wealthy. The will drawn up by a bishop and aristocrat named Bertram of Le Mans, for example, shows that he owned estates—some from his family, others given him as gifts—scattered over much of Gaul.

Along with administering their estates, many male aristocrats spent their time honing their proficiency as warriors. To be a great warrior in Merovingian society, just as in the otherwise very different world of the Bedouins, meant more than just fighting: it meant perfecting the virtues necessary for leading armed men. Merovingian warriors affirmed their skills and comradeship in the hunt; they proved their worth in the regular taking of booty; and they rewarded their followers afterward at generous banquets. At these feasts, as they gave abundantly to their dependents in keeping with the gift economy, the lords combined fellowship with the redistribution of wealth.

Merovingian aristocrats also spent time with their families. The focus of marriage was procreation. Important both to the survival of aristocratic families and to the transmission of their property and power, marriage was an expensive institution. It had two forms: in the most formal, the man gave a generous dowry of clothes, livestock, and land to his bride; after the marriage was consummated, he gave her a "morning gift" of furniture. Very wealthy men also might support one or more concubines, who enjoyed a less formal type of marriage, receiving a morning gift but no dowry. Churchmen in this period had many ideas about the value of marriages, but in practice they had little to do with the matter. Marriage was a family decision and a family matter; no one was married in a church.

Some sixth-century aristocrats still patterned their lives on those of the Romans, teaching their children classical Latin poetry and writing to one another in phrases borrowed from Virgil. But already in the seventh century their spoken language had come to diverge from literary Latin. Some still learned Latin, but they cultivated it mainly to read the Psalms. Just as in Byzantium, a religious culture that emphasized Christian piety over the classics was developing in Europe.

The arrival on the continent around 590 of the Irish monk St. Columbanus (c. 543–615) energized this heightened emphasis on religion. Columbanus's brand of monasticism — which stressed exile, devotion, and discipline — found much favor among the Merovingian elite. The monasteries St. Columbanus established in both Gaul and Italy attracted local recruits from the aristocracy, some of them grown men and women. Others were young children, given to the monastery by their parents in the ritual called oblation. This practice was not only accepted but also often considered essential for the spiritual well-being of both the children and their families. Irish monasticism introduced Merovingian aristocrats to a deepened religious devotion. Those aristocrats who did not join or patronize a monastery still often read (or listened to others read) books about penitence, and they chanted the Psalms.

Bishops ranked among the most powerful men in Merovingian society. Gregory of Tours, for example, considered himself the protector of "his citizens." When representatives of the king came to collect taxes in Tours, Gregory stopped them in their tracks, warning them that St. Martin would punish anyone who tried to tax his people. "That very day," Gregory reported, "the man who had produced the tax rolls caught a fever and died." Little wonder that Frankish kings let the old Roman land tax die out.

Like other aristocrats, many bishops chose to marry, even though church councils demanded celibacy. As the overseers of priests and guardians of morality, however, bishops were expected to refrain from sexual relations with their wives. Since bishops were ordinarily appointed late in life, long after they had raised a family, this restriction did not threaten the ideal of a procreative marriage.

Women of Power | Noble parents generally decided whom their daughters would marry, for such unions bound together not only husbands and wives but entire extended families as well. Brides received a dowry — often land, over which they had some control; if they were widowed without children, they were allowed to sell, give away, exchange, or rent out their dowry estates as they wished. Moreover, men could give property to their women kinfolk outright in written testaments. Because fathers often wanted to share their property with their daughters, an enterprising author created a formula for scribes to follow when drawing up wills in such cases. It began:

> For a long time an ungodly custom has been observed among us that forbids sisters to share with their brothers the paternal land. I reject this impious law: I make you, my beloved daughter, an equal and legitimate heir in all my patrimony [inheritance].

Praying Man

This incised brick, formed in the shape of a church, was a decorative element in an edifice (perhaps itself a church) built in the eighth century. The figure is a bearded man in prayer. Prior to the tenth or eleventh century, people did not pray with hands pressed together but rather with hands raised up on either side of the head. Here the artist gave the gesture special importance by exaggerating the man's arms and hands; his legs and feet hardly matter. *(Musée de l'Hôtel Goüin de la Société Archéologique de Touraine, France, nº d'inventaire HG 856.007.)*

Bequests, dowries, and other such gifts made many aristocratic women very rich. Childless widows frequently gave generous gifts to the church from their vast possessions. But a woman need not have been a widow to control enormous wealth. In 632, for example, the nun Burgundofara, who had never married, drew up a will giving her monastery the land, slaves, vineyards, pastures, and forests she had received from her two brothers and her father. She bequeathed other property that she owned to her brothers and sister.

York Helmet

This fine helmet—which belonged to a wealthy warrior named Oshere who lived near York, England, in the second half of the eighth century—was intended for both display and battle. The helmet, made of iron, and the back flap, made of flexible chain mail, gave excellent protection against sword blades. The cheek pieces were probably originally pulled close to the warrior's face by a leather tie. The nose piece is decorated with interlaced animals. Over the top, two bands of copper meet at the middle. They were inscribed "In the name of our Lord Jesus, the Holy Spirit, God, and with all, we pray. Amen. Oshere. Christ." What do the features of this helmet imply about the relationship between the Christian religion and the profession of warrior? *(York Museums Trust [Yorkshire Museum].)*

Though legally under the authority of her husband, a Merovingian woman often found ways to exercise some power and control over her life. Tetradia, wife of Count Eulalius, left her husband, taking all his gold and silver, because, as Gregory of Tours describes to us,

> he was in the habit of sleeping with the women-servants in his household. As a result he neglected his wife. . . . As a result of his excesses, he ran into serious debt, and to meet this he stole his wife's jewelry and money.

A court of law ordered Tetradia to repay Eulalius four times the amount she had taken from him, but she was allowed to keep and live on her own property.

Other women were able to exercise behind-the-scenes control through their sons. A woman named Artemia, for example, used the prophecy that her son Nicetius would become a bishop to prevent her husband from taking the bishopric himself. After Nicetius did become a bishop (thus fulfilling the prophecy), he remained at home with his mother well into his thirties, working alongside the servants and teaching the younger children to read the Psalms.

Some women exercised direct power. Rich widows with fortunes to bestow wielded enormous influence. Some Merovingian women were abbesses, rulers in their own right over female monasteries and sometimes over "double monasteries," with separate facilities for men and women. Monasteries under the control of abbesses could be substantial centers of population: the convent at Laon, for example, had three hundred nuns in the seventh century. Because women lived in populous convents or were monopolized by rich men able to support several wives or mistresses at one time, unattached aristocratic women were scarce.

The Power of Kings Atop the aristocracy were the Merovingian kings, rulers of the Frankish kingdoms. The Merovingian dynasty (c. 486–751) owed its longevity to good political sense: it had allied itself with local lay aristocrats and ecclesiastical (church) authorities. The kings relied on these men to bolster the power they derived from other sources, such as their leadership in war, their access to the lion's share of plunder, and their takeover of the public lands and legal framework of Roman administration. The kings' courts functioned as schools for the sons of the elite, tightening the bonds and loyalties between royal and aristocratic families. When kings sent officials—counts and dukes—to rule in their name in various regions of their kingdoms, these regional governors worked with and married into the aristocratic families who had long controlled local affairs.

Both kings and aristocrats had good reason to want a powerful royal authority. The king acted as arbitrator and intermediary for the competing interests of the aristocrats while taking advantage of local opportunities to appoint favorites and garner prestige by giving out land and privileges to supporters and religious institutions. Gregory of Tours's history of the sixth century is filled with stories of bitter battles between Merovingian kings, as royal brothers fought continuously. Yet what seemed to the bishop like royal weakness and violent chaos was in fact one way the kings contained local aristocratic tensions, organizing them on one side or another and preventing them from spinning out of royal control. By the beginning of the seventh century, three relatively stable Frankish kingdoms had emerged: Austrasia to the northeast; Neustria to the west, with its capital city at Paris; and Burgundy, incorporating the southeast (see Map 8.4). In an age that depended on local face-to-face contact, these divisions were so useful to aristocrats and Merovingian kings alike that even when royal power was united in the hands of one king, Clothar II (r. 613–623), he made his son the independent king of Austrasia.

As the power of the kings in the seventh century increased, however, so did the might of their chief court official, the mayor of the palace. As we shall see, one mayoral family allied with the Austrasian aristocracy would in the following century displace the Merovingian dynasty and establish a new royal line, the Carolingians.

Christianity and Classical Culture in the British Isles

The Merovingian kingdoms exemplify some of the ways in which Roman and non-Roman traditions combined; the British Isles show others. Ireland had never been part of the Roman Empire, but the Irish people were early converts to Christianity, as were people in Roman Britain and parts of Scotland. Invasions by various Celtic and Germanic groups—particularly the Anglo-Saxons, who gave their name to England, "the land of the Angles"—redrew the religious boundaries. Ireland, largely free of invaders, remained Christian; Scotland, also relatively untouched by invaders, had been slowly Christianized by the Irish from the west and in early years by the British from the south; England, which emerged from the invasions as a mosaic of about a dozen kingdoms ruled by separate Anglo-Saxon kings, became largely pagan until it was actively converted in the seventh century.

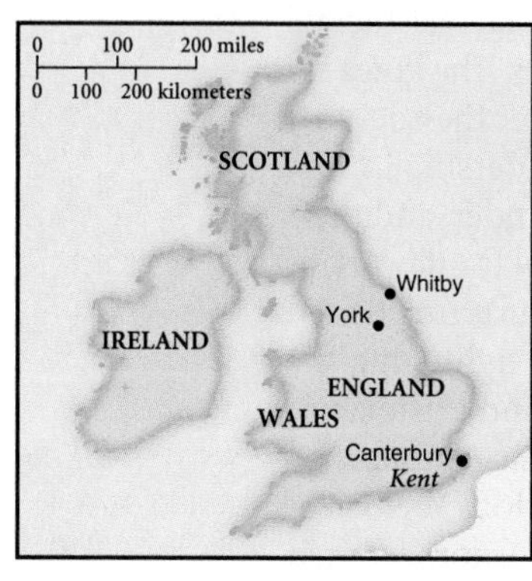

The British Isles

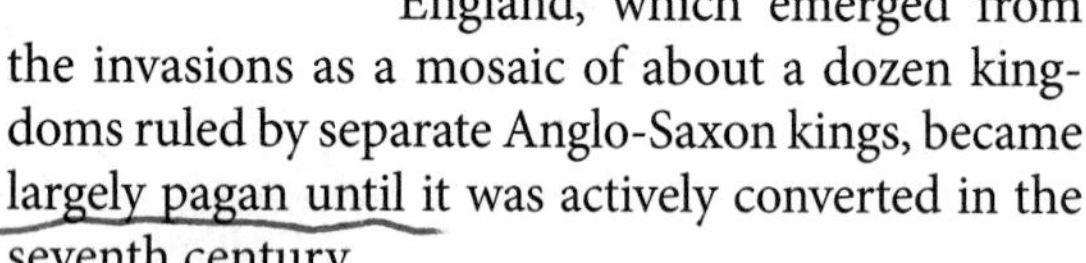

Competing Church Hierarchies in Anglo-Saxon England Christianity was introduced to Anglo-Saxon England from two directions. In the north of England, Irish monks brought their own brand of Christianity. Converted in the fifth century by St. Patrick and other missionaries, the Irish had evolved a church organization that corresponded to its rural clan organization. Abbots and abbesses, generally from powerful dynasties, headed monastic *familiae*, communities composed of blood relatives, servants, slaves, and of course monks or nuns. Bishops were often under the authority of abbots, since the monasteries rather than cities were the centers of population in Ireland. The Irish missionaries to England were monks, and they set up monasteries modeled on those at home.

In the south of England, Christianity came in 597 via missionaries sent by the pope known as **Gregory the Great** (r. 590–604). The missionaries, under the leadership of Augustine (not the same Augustine as the bishop of Hippo), intended to convert the king and people of Kent, the southernmost kingdom, and then work their way northward. But Augustine and his party brought with them Roman practices at odds with those of Irish Christianity, stressing ties to the pope and the organization of the church under bishops rather than abbots. Using the Roman model, they divided England into territorial units, called dioceses, headed by an archbishop and bishops. Augustine, for example, became archbishop of Canterbury. Because he was a monk, he set up a monastery right next to his cathedral; thus having a community of monks attached to the bishop's church became a characteristic of the English church. Later a second archbishopric was added at York.

A major bone of contention between the Roman and Irish churches involved the calculation of the date of Easter, celebrated by Christians as the day on which Christ rose from the dead. The Roman church insisted that Easter fall on the first Sunday following the first full moon after the vernal equinox. The Irish had a different method of determining when Easter should fall, and therefore they celebrated Easter on a different day. Because everyone agreed that believers could not be saved unless they observed Christ's resurrection properly and on the right date, the conflict was bitter. It was resolved by Oswy, king of Northumbria, who organized a meeting of churchmen, the **Synod of Whitby**, in 664. Convinced by the synod that Rome spoke with the voice of St. Peter, who was said in the New Testament to hold the keys of the kingdom of heaven, Oswy chose the Roman date. His decision paved the way for the triumph of the Roman brand of Christianity in England.

Literary Culture The authority of St. Peter was not the only reason for favoring Roman Christianity. For many English churchmen, Rome had great prestige because it was a treasure trove of knowledge, piety, and holy objects. Benedict

---

Gregory the Great: The pope (r. 590–604) who sent missionaries to Anglo-Saxon England, wrote influential books, tried to reform the church, and had contact with the major ruling families of Europe and Byzantium.

Synod of Whitby: The meeting of churchmen and King Oswy of Northumbria in 664 that led to the adoption of the Roman brand of Christianity in England.

Biscop (c. 630–690), the founder of two important English monasteries, made many difficult trips to Rome, bringing back relics, liturgical vestments, and even a cantor to teach his monks the proper melodies in a time before written musical notation. Above all, he went to Rome to get books. At his monasteries in the north of England, he built up a grand library. In Anglo-Saxon England, as in Scotland and Ireland, all of which lacked a strong classical tradition from Roman times, a book was considered a precious object, to be decorated as finely as a garnet-studded brooch. (See the illustration on the right.)

The Anglo-Saxons and Irish Celts had a thriving oral culture but extremely limited uses for writing. Books became valuable only when these societies converted to Christianity. Just as Islamic reliance on the Qur'an made possible a literary culture under the Umayyads, so Christian dependence on the Bible, liturgy, and the writings of the church fathers helped make England and Ireland centers of literature and learning in the seventh and eighth centuries. Archbishop Theodore (r. 669–690), who had studied at Athens and was one of the most learned men of his day, founded a school at Canterbury where students studied Latin and even some Greek in order to comment on biblical texts. Men like Benedict Biscop soon sponsored other centers of learning, using the texts from the classical past. Although women did not establish famous schools, many abbesses ruled over monasteries that stressed Christian learning. Here, as elsewhere in the British Isles, Latin writings, even pagan texts, were studied diligently, in part because Latin was so foreign a language that mastering it required systematic and formal study. One of Benedict Biscop's pupils was Bede ("the Venerable"; 673–735), an Anglo-Saxon monk and a historian of extraordinary breadth. Bede in turn taught a new generation of monks who became advisers to eighth-century rulers.

Much of the vigorous pagan Anglo-Saxon oral tradition was adapted to Christian culture. Bede encouraged and supported the use of the Anglo-Saxon language, urging priests, for example, to use it when they instructed their flocks. In contrast to other European regions, where Latin was the primary written language in the seventh and eighth centuries, England made use of the vernacular—the language normally spoken by the people. Written Anglo-Saxon (or Old English) was used in every aspect of English life, from government to entertainment.

The decision at the Synod of Whitby to favor Roman Christianity tied the English church to the church of Rome by doctrine, friendship, and conviction. The Anglo-Saxon monk and bishop Wynfrith even changed his name to the Latin Boniface to symbolize his loyalty to the Roman church. Preaching on the continent, Boniface (680–754) set up churches in Germany and Gaul that, like those in England, looked to Rome for leadership and guidance. Boniface was one of those travelers from Rome who went to Trier to check on the bishop's piety. He found it badly wanting! Boniface's efforts to reform the Frankish church gave the papacy new importance in Europe.

Page from the Lindisfarne Gospels

The lavishly illuminated manuscript known as the Lindisfarne Gospels, of which this is one page, was probably produced in the first third of the eighth century. For the monks at Lindisfarne (a tidal island off the northeast coast of England) and elsewhere in the British Isles, books were precious objects, to be decorated much like pieces of jewelry. (Compare the treatment of the figure here with the decoration of the eagle brooches on page 230, both of which rely on flat areas of color.) The page shown here depicts the Evangelist St. Mark, writing while also holding a book. Above his halo is his symbol, a winged lion; it is blowing a trumpet while its front paws rest on a book. What books might St. Mark and the lion be holding? *(© The British Library/HIP/The Image Works.)*

Unity in Spain, Division in Italy

In contrast to the British Isles, southern Gaul, Spain, and Italy had long been part of the Roman Empire and preserved many of its traditions. Nevertheless, as they were settled and fought over by new peoples, their histories diverged dramatically. When the Merovingian king Clovis (r. 485–511) defeated the Visigoths in 507, the Visigothic kingdom, which had sprawled across southern Gaul into Spain, was dismembered. By midcentury, the Franks had come into possession of most of its remnants in southern Gaul.

In Spain, the Visigothic king Leovigild (r. 569–586) established territorial control by military might. But no ruler could hope to maintain his position in Visigothic Spain without the support of the Hispano-Roman population, which included both the great landowners and leading bishops; and their backing was unattainable while the Visigoths remained Arian Christians (maintaining that Christ was not identical with God; see page 219). Leovigild's son Reccared (r. 586–601) took the necessary step in 587, converting to Roman Catholic Christianity. Two years later, at the Third Council of Toledo, most of the Arian bishops followed their king by announcing their conversion to Catholicism.

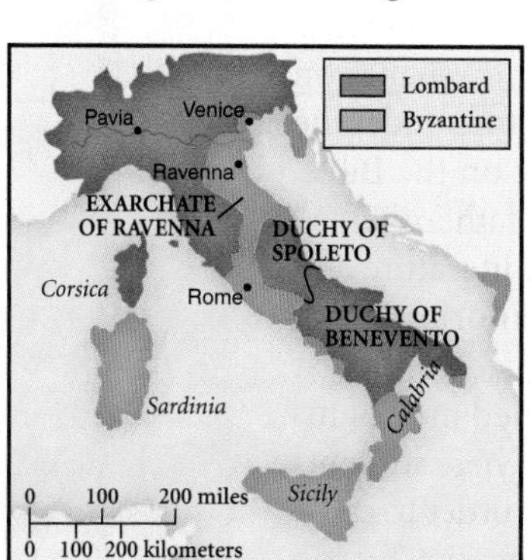

Lombard Italy, Early Eighth Century

Thereafter, the bishops and kings of Spain cooperated to a degree unprecedented in other regions. While the king gave the churchmen free rein to set up their own hierarchy (with the bishop of Toledo at the top) and to meet regularly at synods to regulate and reform the church, the bishops in turn supported their Visigothic king, who ruled as a minister of the Christian people. Rebellion against him was tantamount to rebellion against Christ. The Spanish bishops reinforced this idea by anointing the king, daubing him with holy oil in a ritual that paralleled the ordination of priests and demonstrated divine favor. Toledo, the city where the highest bishop presided, was also where the kings were "made" through anointment. While the bishops in this way made the king's cause their own, their lay counterparts, the great landowners, helped supply the king with troops, allowing him to maintain internal order and repel his external enemies.

Ironically, it was precisely the centralization and unification of the Visigothic kingdom that proved its undoing. When the Arabs arrived in 711, they needed only to kill the king, defeat his army, and capture Toledo to take the kingdom.

By contrast, in Italy the Lombard king constantly faced a hostile papacy in the center of the peninsula and virtually independent dukes in the south. Theoretically royal officers, the dukes of Benevento and Spoleto in fact ruled on their own behalf. Although many Lombards were Catholics, others, including important kings and dukes, were Arian. The "official" religion of Lombards in Italy varied with the ruler in power. Rather than signal a major political event, the conversion of the Lombards to Catholic Christianity occurred gradually, ending only around the mid-seventh century. Partly as a result of this slow development, the Lombard kings, unlike the Visigoths, Franks, or even the Anglo-Saxons, never enlisted the full support of any particular group of churchmen.

Although lacking united religious support, Lombard royal power still had strengths. Chief among these were the traditions of leadership associated with the royal dynasty, the kings' military ability and their control over large estates in northern Italy, and the Roman institutions that survived in Italy. The Italian peninsula had been devastated by the wars between the Ostrogoths and the Byzantine Empire, but the Lombard kings took advantage of the still-urban organization of Italian society and the economy, assigning dukes to city bases and setting up a royal capital at Pavia. Recalling emperors like Constantine and Justinian, the kings built churches, monasteries, and other places of worship in the royal capital; they maintained the city walls, issued laws, and minted coins. Revenues from tolls, sales taxes, port duties, and court fines filled their treasuries, although their inability to revive the Roman land tax was a major weakness. The greatest challenge for the Lombard kings came from sharing the peninsula with Rome. As soon as the kings began to make serious headway into southern Italy against the duchies of Spoleto and Benevento, the pope began to fear for his own position and called on the Franks for help.

Political Tensions and the Power of the Pope

In the year 600, the pope's position was ambiguous: he was both a ruler and a subordinate. On the one hand, believing he was the successor of St. Peter and head of the church, he wielded real secular power. Pope Gregory the Great in many ways laid the foundations for the papacy's spiritual and temporal ascendancy. During Gregory's reign, the papacy became the greatest landowner in Italy. Gregory organized the defenses of Rome and paid for its army; he heard court cases, made treaties, and

Mosaic from Sant'Agnese

The church of Sant'Agnese was founded by Constantine and rebuilt by Pope Honorius I (625–638). It has been much restored and reworked since then, but the apse mosaic is almost as it was when commissioned by Honorius. The mosaic shows St. Agnes flanked by two popes (one of them Honorius, holding a church) against a background of heavenly bands of gold. *(akg-images/Andrea Jemolo.)*

provided welfare services. The missionary expedition Gregory sent to England was only a small part of his involvement in the rest of Europe. He also maintained close ties with the churchmen in Spain who were working to convert the Visigoths from Arianism to Catholicism. He wrote letters to the Byzantine emperor and to European kings and queens. He admonished Brunhild, a Frankish queen well known to Gregory of Tours, to reform the church in Gaul:

> Evil priests cause ruin for the people . . . [so] see that you send us a letter of yours, and we shall send over a person with the assent of your authority, if you give the order, who together with other priests should inquire into these acts with great care, and correct them according to God's will.

A prolific author of spiritual works and biblical commentaries, Gregory digested and simplified the ideas of church fathers like St. Augustine of Hippo, making them accessible to a wider audience. His book *Pastoral Rule* was used as a guide for bishops throughout Europe.

Yet the pope was not independent. He was only one of many bishops in the Roman Empire, which was now ruled from Constantinople, and he was therefore subordinate to the emperor at Byzantium. For a long time the emperor's views on dogma, discipline, and church administration prevailed at Rome. This authority began to unravel in the seventh century. In 691, Emperor Justinian II convened a council that determined 102 rules for the church, and he sent them to Rome for papal endorsement. Most of the rules were unobjectionable, but Pope Sergius I (r. 687 or 689–701) was unwilling to agree to all of them because they permitted priests to marry (which the Roman church did not want to allow) and prohibited fasting on Saturdays in Lent (which the Roman church required). Outraged by Sergius's refusal, Justinian tried to arrest him, but Italian armies (theoretically under the emperor) came to the pope's aid, while Justinian's arresting officer cowered under the pope's bed. As this incident reveals, some local forces were already willing to rally to the side of the pope against the emperor. Constantinople's influence and authority over Rome was dwindling. Sheer distance, as well as diminishing imperial power in Italy, meant that the popes were, in effect, the leaders of the parts of Italy not controlled by the Lombards.

The gap between Byzantium and Rome widened in the early eighth century as Emperor Leo III tried to increase the taxes on papal property to pay for his war against the Arab invaders. The pope responded by leading a general tax revolt. Meanwhile, Leo's fierce policy of iconoclasm collided with the pope's tolerance of images. In Italy, as in other European regions, Christian piety focused more on relics than on icons. Nevertheless, the papacy would not allow sacred images and icons to be destroyed. The pope argued that holy images should be respected, though not worshipped. His support of images reflected popular opinion as well. A later commentator wrote that iconoclasm so infuriated the inhabitants of Ravenna and Venice that "if the pope had not prohibited the people, they would have attempted to set up a [different] emperor over themselves."

These difficulties with the emperor were matched by increasing friction between the pope and the Lombards. The Lombard kings had gradually managed to bring under their control the duchies of Spoleto and Benevento as well as part of the Exarchate of Ravenna. By the mid-eighth century, the popes feared that Rome would fall to the Lombards, and Pope Zachary (r. 741–752) looked northward for friends. He created an ally by giving his approval to the removal of the last Merovingian king and his replacement by the first Carolingian king, Pippin III (r. 751–768). In 753, Pope Stephen II (r. 752–757) called on Pippin to march to Italy with an army to fight the Lombards. Thus, events at Rome had a major impact on the history not only of Italy but of the Frankish kingdom as well.

REVIEW QUESTION What were the similarities and differences among the kingdoms that emerged in western Europe, and how did their histories combine and diverge?

MAPPING THE WEST

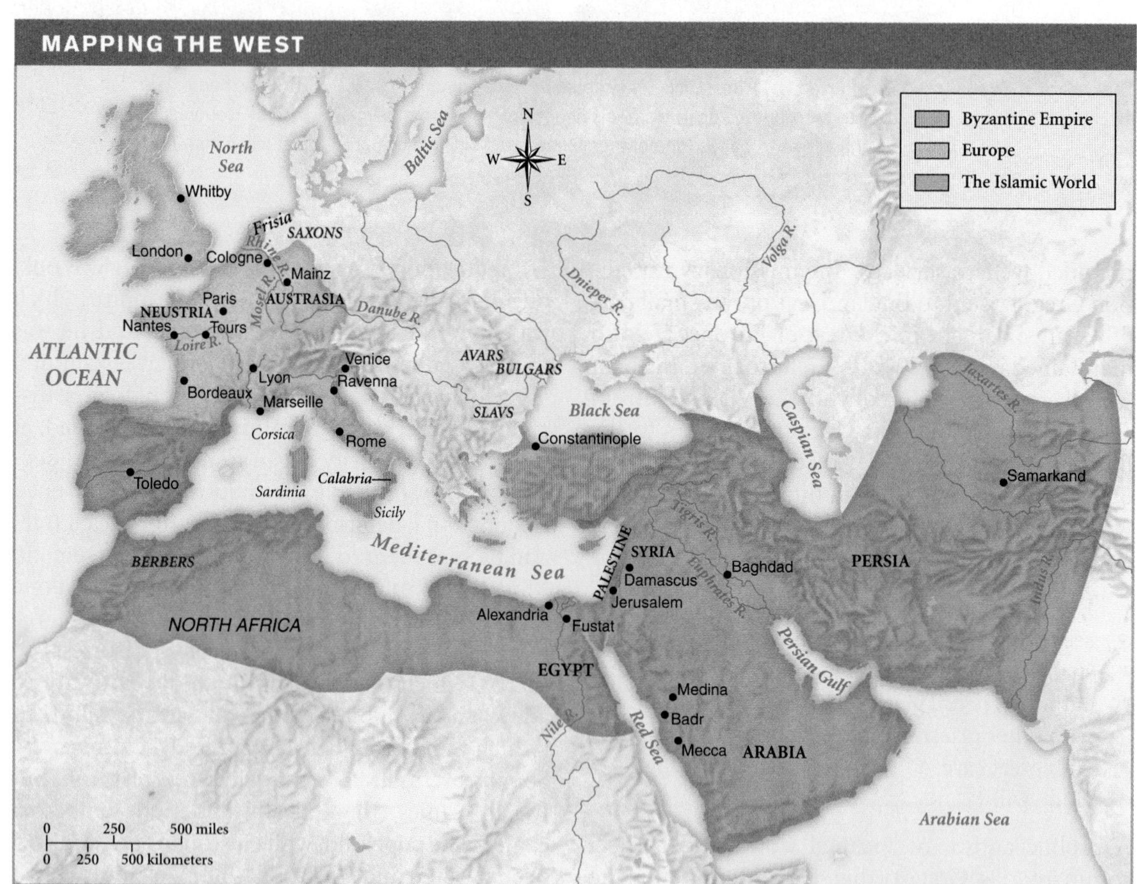

Rome's Heirs, c. 750

The major political fact of the period 600–750 was the emergence of Islam and the creation of an Islamic state that reached from Spain to the Indus River. The Byzantine Empire, once a great power, was dwarfed—and half swallowed up—by its Islamic neighbor. To the west were fledgling European kingdoms, mere trifles on the world stage. The next centuries, however, would prove their resourcefulness and durability.

Conclusion

The Islamic world, Byzantium, and western Europe were heirs of the Roman Empire, but they built on its legacies in different ways. Muslims were the newcomers to the Roman world, but their religion, Islam, was influenced by both Jewish and Christian monotheism, each with roots in Roman culture. Under the guidance of Muhammad the Prophet, Islam became both a coherent theology and a tightly structured way of life. Once the Muslim Arabs embarked on military conquests, they became the heirs of Rome in other ways: preserving Byzantine cities, hiring Syrian civil servants, and adopting Mediterranean artistic styles. Drawing on Roman and Persian traditions, the Umayyad dynasty created a powerful Islamic state, with a capital city in Syria and a culture that generally tolerated a wide variety of economic, religious, and social institutions so long as the conquered paid taxes to their Muslim overlords.

Byzantium directly inherited the central political institutions of Rome: its people called themselves Romans; its emperor was the Roman emperor; and its capital, Constantinople, was considered to be the new Rome. Byzantium also inherited the taxes, cities, laws, and religion—Christianity—of Rome. The changes of the seventh and eighth centuries—contraction of territory, urban decline, disappearance of the old elite, and a ban on icons—whittled away at this Roman character. By 750, Byzantium was less Roman than it was a new, resilient political and cultural entity, a Christian state on the borders of the new Muslim empire.

Western Europe also inherited—and transformed—Roman institutions. The Frankish kings built on Roman traditions that had earlier been modified by provincial and Germanic custom. In Anglo-Saxon England, once the far-flung northern outpost of the Roman Empire, parts of the Roman legacy—Latin learning and the Christian religion—had to be reimported in the seventh century. In Spain, the Visigothic kings converted from Arian to Roman Christianity and allied themselves with a Hispano-Roman elite that maintained elements of the organization and intellectual traditions of the late empire. In Italy and at Rome itself, the traditions of the classical past endured. The roads remained, the cities of Italy survived (although depopulated), and both the popes and the Lombard kings ruled according to the traditions of Roman government.

Muslim, Byzantine, and western European societies all suffered the ravages of war. In each one, the social hierarchy became simpler, with the loss of "middle" groups like the curials at Byzantium and the near suppression of tribal affiliations among Muslims. All tied politics to religion more tightly than ever before. In Byzantium, the emperor was a religious force, presiding over the destruction of icons. In the Islamic world, the caliph was the successor to Muhammad, a religious and political leader. In western Europe the kings allied with churchmen in order to rule. Despite their many differences, all these leaders had a common understanding of their place in a divine scheme: they were God's agents on earth, ruling over God's people. In the next century they would consolidate their power. Little did they know that, soon thereafter, local elites would be able to assert greater authority than ever before.

FOR FURTHER EXPLORATION

- **For additional primary-source material from this period**, see *Sources of the Making of the West*, Fourth Edition.
- **For Web sites, images, and documents related to topics in this chapter**, visit *Make History* at bedfordstmartins.com/hunt.

Chapter 8 Review

Online Study Guide bedfordstmartins.com/hunt

Key Terms and People

In the grid below, identify the term or person and explain its historical significance. (To do this exercise online, go to bedfordstmartins.com/hunt.)

Term	Who or What & When	Why It Matters
Muhammad (p. 244)		
Qur'an (p. 246)		
Hijra (p. 246)		
jihad (p. 247)		
Five Pillars of Islam (p. 247)		
Shi'ite (p. 250)		
Umayyad caliphate (p. 250)		
Heraclius (p. 252)		
Lombards (p. 252)		
theme (p. 255)		
icon (p. 256)		
iconoclasm (p. 256)		
Merovingian dynasty (p. 258)		
Gregory of Tours (p. 260)		
Gregory the Great (p. 266)		
Synod of Whitby (p. 266)		

Review Questions

1. How and why did the Muslims conquer so many lands in the period 632–750?
2. What stresses did the Byzantine Empire endure in the seventh and eighth centuries, and how was iconoclasm a response to those stresses?
3. What were the similarities and differences among the kingdoms that emerged in western Europe, and how did their histories combine and diverge?

Making Connections

1. What were the similarities and the differences in political organizations of the Islamic, Byzantine, and western European societies in the period 600–750?
2. Compare and contrast the roles of religion in the Islamic, Byzantine, and western European worlds in the period 600–750.
3. Compare the material resources of the Islamic, Byzantine, and western European governments in the period 600–750.

Important Events

Date	Event	Date	Event
c. 486–751	Merovingian dynasty	622	Hijra to Medina; year 1 of the Islamic calendar
c. 570–632	Life of Muhammad, prophet of Islam	624	Muhammad and Meccans fight battle of Badr
572	Lombards conquer northern Italy	661–750	Umayyad caliphate
r. 573–c. 594	Bishop Gregory of Tours	664	Synod of Whitby; English king opts for Roman form of Christianity
587	Conversion of Visigothic king Reccared	680–754	Life of Boniface, who reformed the Frankish church
c. 590	Arrival of Irish monk Columbanus in Gaul	r. 717–741	Emperor Leo III the Isaurian
r. 590–604	Papacy of Pope Gregory the Great	726–787	Period of iconoclasm at Byzantium
603–623	War between Byzantium and Persia		

- Consider three events: **Papacy of Pope Gregory the Great (r. 590–604); Hijra to Medina, year 1 of the Islamic calendar (622)**; and **Emperor Leo III the Isaurian (r. 717–741)**. How did these events reshape religious faith? What were the broader implications of those changes for social and political life?

SUGGESTED REFERENCES

Donner's book is insightful on the origins of Islam. Herrin gives a dazzling overview of Byzantine history. Smith's and Wickham's books are essential for understanding the early medieval West.

Ahmed, Leila. *Women and Gender in Islam: Historical Roots of a Modern Debate*. 1992.

*Bede. *A History of the English Church and People*. Trans. Leo Sherley-Price. 1991.

Berkey, Jonathan P. *The Formation of Islam: Religion and Society in the Near East, 600–1800*. 2003.

*Byzantine Sourcebook: http://www.fordham.edu/halsall/sbook1c.html

Cameron, Averil. *The Byzantines*. 2006.

Connor, Carolyn L. *Women of Byzantium*. 2004.

Donner, Fred McGraw. *Muhammad and the Believers: At the Origins of Islam*. 2010.

*Geanakoplos, Deno John, ed. and trans. *Byzantium: Church, Society, and Civilization Seen through Contemporary Eyes*. 1984.

Geary, Patrick. *Before France and Germany: The Creation and Transformation of the Merovingian World*. 1988.

*Gregory of Tours. *The History of the Franks*. Trans. Lewis Thorpe. 1976.

Haldon, J. F. *Byzantium in the Seventh Century: The Transformation of a Culture*. 1990.

Hen, Yitzhak. *Roman Barbarians: The Royal Court and Culture in the Early Medieval West*. 2007.

Herrin, Judith. *Byzantium: The Surprising Life of a Medieval Empire*. 2007.

Hodgson, Marshall G. S. *The Venture of Islam: Conscience and History in a World Civilization*. Vol. 1, *The Classical Age of Islam*. 1974.

*Islamic Sourcebook: http://www.fordham.edu/halsall/islam/islamsbook.html

Kennedy, Hugh. *The Prophet and the Age of the Caliphates: The Islamic Near East from the Sixth to the Eleventh Century*. 2nd ed. 2004.

Smith, Julia M. H. *Europe after Rome: A New Cultural History 500–1000*. 2005.

Whittow, Mark. *The Making of Byzantium, 600–1025*. 1996.

Wickham, Chris. *Framing the Early Middle Ages: Europe and the Mediterranean, 400–800*. 2005.

*Primary source.

CHAPTER

From Centralization to Fragmentation

9

750–1050

In 841, a fifteen-year-old boy named William went to serve at the court of Charles the Bald, king of the Franks. William's father, Bernard, was an extremely powerful noble. His mother, Dhuoda, was a well-educated, pious, and able woman; she administered the family's estates in the south of France while her husband was occupied with politics at court. In 841, however, politics had become a dangerous business. King Charles was fighting with his brothers over his portion of the Frankish Empire, and he doubted Bernard's loyalty. In fact, William was sent to Charles's court as a kind of hostage, to ensure Bernard's fidelity. Anxious about her son, Dhuoda wrote a handbook of advice for William, outlining what he ought to believe about God; about politics and society; about obligations to his family; and, above all, about his duties to his father, which she emphasized even over loyalty to the king:

> In the human understanding of things, royal and imperial appearance and power seem preeminent in the world, and the custom of men is to account those men's actions and their names ahead of all others. . . . But despite all this . . . I caution you to render first to him whose son you are special, faithful, steadfast loyalty as long as you shall live. . . . So I urge you again, most beloved son William, that first of all you love God. . . . Then love, fear, and cherish your father.

William heeded his mother's words, with tragic results: when Bernard ran afoul of Charles and was executed, William died in a failed attempt to avenge his father.

Dhuoda's handbook reveals the volatile political atmosphere of the mid-ninth century, and her advice to her son points to one of its causes: a crisis of loyalty. Loyalty to emperors, caliphs, and kings — all of whom were symbols of unity cutting across regional and family ties — competed with allegiances to local authorities; and

The Kiss of Judas
According to the Gospels, Judas, one of the original twelve Apostles, betrayed Jesus by giving him a kiss, in that way identifying him to the Roman and Hebrew authorities. In this depiction of the scene from the late tenth century, Judas is almost dancing with Jesus. Soldiers and the servants of the Hebrew high priest grab Jesus's arms from both sides. Meanwhile, St. Peter, the chief of the Apostles, has grabbed one of the priest's servants and is cutting off his ear. In the tenth century, people knew a great deal about loyalty and betrayal. Most of the institutions of government relied on oaths of fidelity, but these turned out to be fragile instruments for cohesion. *(Stadtbibliothek/Stadtarchiv, Trier.)*

those, in turn, vied with family loyalties. The period 600–750 had seen the startling rise of Islam, the whittling away of Byzantium, and the beginnings of stable political and economic development in an impoverished Europe. The period 750–1050 would see all three societies contend with internal issues of diversity even as they became increasingly conscious of their unity and uniqueness. At the beginning of this period, rulers built up and dominated strong, united political communities. By the end, these realms had fragmented into smaller, more local units. While men and women continued to feel some loyalty toward faraway emperors and caliphs, their most powerful allegiances often focused on local lords closer to home.

In Byzantium, military triumphs brought emperors enormous prestige. A renaissance (French for "rebirth")—that is, an important revival—of culture and art took place at Constantinople. Yet at the same time new elites began to dominate the Byzantine countryside. In the Islamic world, a dynastic revolution in 750 ousted the Umayyads from the caliphate and replaced them with a new family, the Abbasids. The Abbasid caliphs moved their capital from Damascus to Baghdad, in the area formerly called Persia. Even though the Abbasids' power began to ebb as regional Islamic rulers came to the fore, the Islamic world, too, saw a renaissance. In western Europe, Charlemagne—a Frankish king from a new dynasty, the Carolingians—forged a huge empire and presided over yet another cultural renaissance. Yet this newly unified kingdom was fragile, disintegrating within a generation of Charlemagne's death. In western Europe, even more than in the Byzantine and Islamic worlds, power fell into the hands of local lords.

Along the borders of these realms, new political entities began to develop, shaped by the religion and culture of their more dominant neighbors. The ancestor of Russia grew up in the shadow of Byzantium, as did Bulgaria and Serbia. Western Europe cast its influence over central European states. In the west, the borders of the Islamic world remained stable or were pushed back. (By contrast, Muslim expansion to the east changed the shape of central Asia.) By the year 1050, the contours of what were to become modern Europe and the Middle East were dimly visible.

CHAPTER FOCUS What forces led to the dissolution—or weakening—of centralized government in the period 750–1050, and what institutions took their place?

The Byzantine Emperor and Local Elites

Between 750 and 850, Byzantium staved off Muslim attacks in Asia Minor and began to rebuild. After 850, it went on the attack. Military victories brought new wealth and power to the imperial court, and the emperors supported a vast program of literary and artistic revival—the Macedonian renaissance—at Constantinople. But while the emperor dominated at the capital, a new landowning elite began to control the countryside. On its northern frontier, Byzantium helped create new Slavic realms.

Imperial Power

While the *themes*, with their territorial military organization, took care of attacks on Byzantine territory, *tagmata*—new mobile armies made up of the best troops—moved aggressively outward, beginning around 850. By 1025, the Byzantine Empire extended from the Danube in the north to the Euphrates in the south (Map 9.1). The Byzantines had not controlled so much territory since their wars with the Sasanid Persians four hundred years earlier.

750–c. 950 The Abbasid caliphate

751 Pippin III becomes king of the Franks, establishing Carolingian rule

768–814 Charlemagne rules as king of the Franks

786–809 Caliphate of Harun al-Rashid

800 Charlemagne crowned emperor at Rome

843 Treaty of Verdun

871–899 Reign of King Alfred of England

750 — 800 — 850

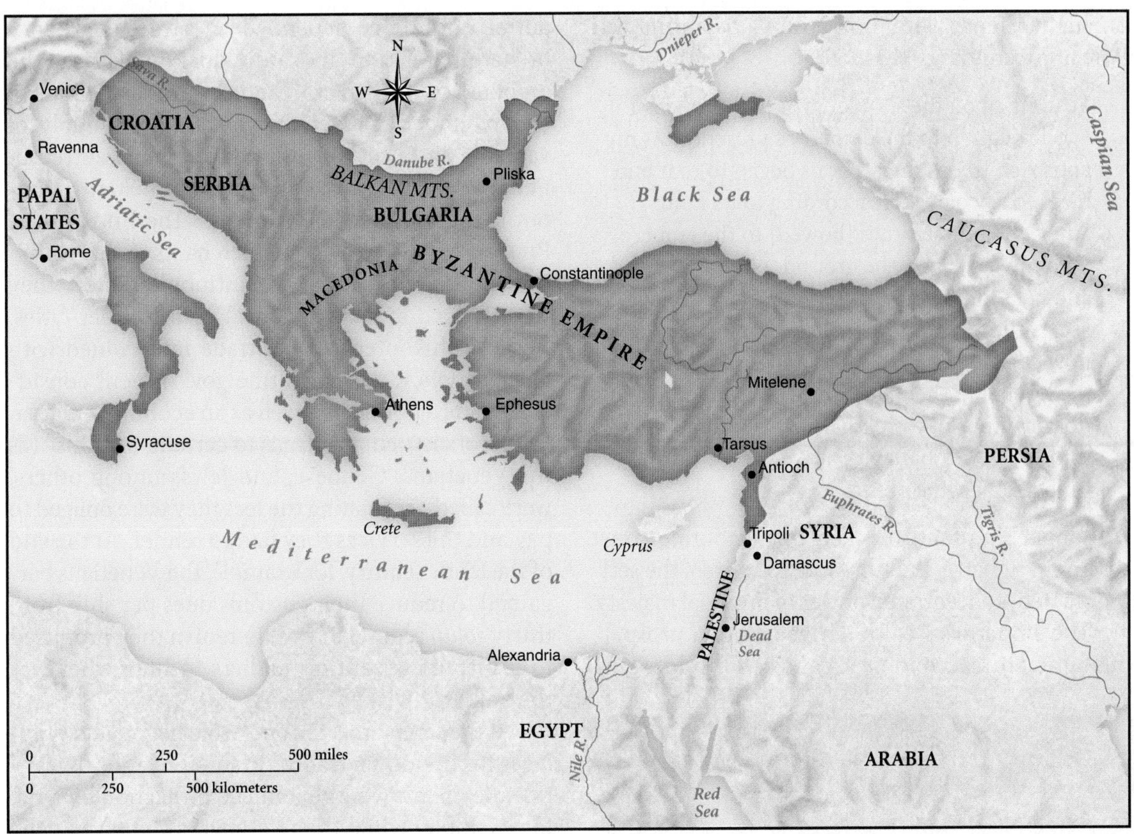

MAP 9.1 The Byzantine Empire, 1025
Under Emperor Basil II, the Byzantine Empire once again embraced the entire area of the Balkans, while its eastern arm extended around the Black Sea and its southern fringe reached nearly to Tripoli. The year 1025 marked the Byzantine Empire's greatest size after the rise of Islam.

Military victories gave new prestige and wealth to the army and to the imperial court. The emperors drew revenues from vast and growing imperial estates. They could demand services and money from the general population at will—requiring citizens to build bridges and roads, to offer lodging to the emperor and his attendants, and to pay taxes in cash. Emperors used their wealth to create a lavish court culture, surrounding themselves with servants, slaves, family members, and civil servants. Eunuchs (castrated men who could not pose a threat to the imperial line) were entrusted with some of the highest posts in government. From their powerful position, the emperors negotiated with other rulers, exchanging ambassadors and receiving and entertaining diplomats with elaborate ceremonies. One such diplomat, Liutprand, bishop of the northern Italian city of Cremona, reported

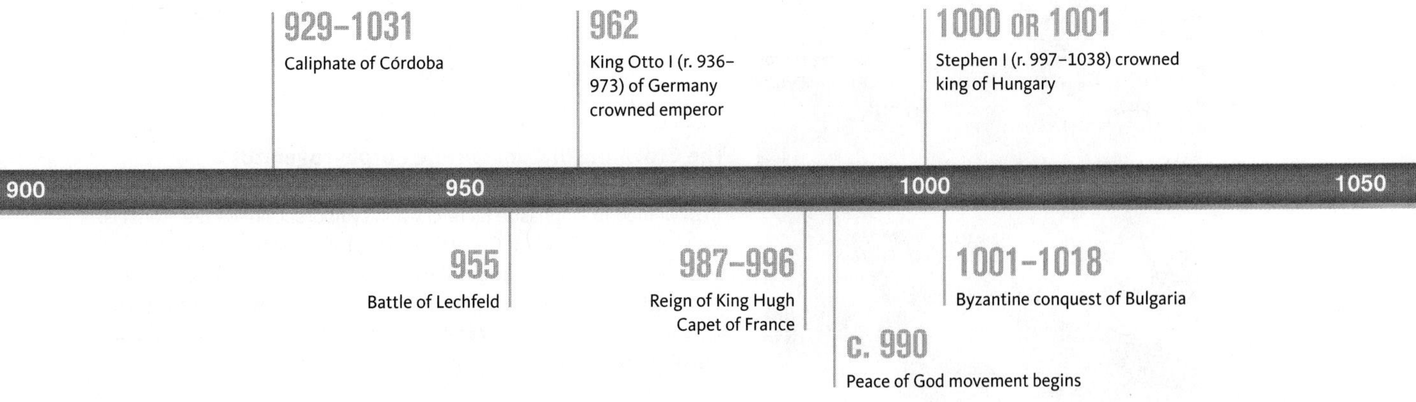

on his audience with Emperor Constantine VII Porphyrogenitos (r. 913–959):

> Leaning upon the shoulders of two eunuchs I was brought into the emperor's presence. At my approach [mechanical] lions began to roar and birds to cry out, each according to its kind. . . . After I had three times [bowed] to the emperor with my face upon the ground, I lifted my head, and behold! the man whom just before I had seen sitting on a moderately elevated seat had now changed his [clothing] and was sitting on the level of the ceiling. How it was done I could not imagine, unless perhaps he was lifted up by some such sort of device as we use for raising the timbers of a wine press.

Although Liutprand mocked this elaborate court ceremony, it had a real function: to express the serious, sacred, concentrated power of imperial majesty.

The emperor's wealth derived from a prosperous agricultural economy organized for trade. Byzantine commerce depended on a careful balance of state regulation and individual enterprise. The emperor controlled craft and commercial guilds to ensure imperial revenues and a stable supply of valuable and useful commodities, while entrepreneurs organized most of the markets held throughout the empire (see Document, "The Book of the Prefect," page 279). Foreign merchants traded within the empire, either at Constantinople (where they were lodged at state expense) or in border cities. Because this international trade intertwined with foreign policy, the Byzantine government considered trade a political as well as an economic matter. Emperors issued privileges to certain "nations" (as the Venetians, Genoese, and Jews, among others, were called), regulating the fees they were obliged to pay and the services they had to render. At the end of the tenth century, for example, the Venetians bargained to reduce their customs dues per ship from thirty *solidi* (coins) to two; in return they promised to transport Byzantine soldiers to Italy whenever the emperor wished.

At the same time, the emperors negotiated privileges for their own traders in foreign lands. Byzantine merchants were guaranteed protection in Syria, for example, while the two governments split the income on sales taxes. Thus, Byzantine trade flourished in the Middle East and, thanks to Venetian intermediaries, with western Europe. Equally significant was trade to the north; from the Kievan Rus the Byzantines imported furs, slaves, wax, and honey.

The Macedonian Renaissance, c. 870–c. 1025

Flush with victory and recalling Byzantium's past glory, the emperors revived classical intellectual pursuits. Basil I (r. 867–886) from Macedonia founded the imperial dynasty that presided over the so-called Macedonian renaissance. This renaissance was made possible by an intellectual elite who came from families that—even in the anxious years of the eighth century—had persisted in studying the classics in spite of the trend toward a simple religious education.

The Crowning of Constantine Porphyrogenitos
This ivory relief was carved at Constantinople in the mid-tenth century. The artist wanted to emphasize hierarchy and symbolism, not nature. Christ is shown crowning Emperor Constantine Porphyrogenitos (r. 913–959). What message do you suppose the artist wanted to telegraph by making Christ higher than the emperor and by having the emperor slightly incline his head and upper torso to receive the crown? *(Pushkin Museum, Moscow, Russia/The Bridgeman Art Library International.)*

DOCUMENT

The Book of the Prefect

Claiming to control all aspects of Byzantine life, emperors issued rules and regulations for every sort of profession. The Book of the Prefect, a decree issued in 911 or 912 by the emperor, shows the emperor's concern to implement God's harmonious intentions by making sure that no group infringed on the activities or duties of any other. Thus the book regulated numerous traders and craftspeople, including silk merchants, perfume dealers, candle makers, butchers, bakers, and—as illustrated here—notaries and jewelers. The prefect was the chief city official at Constantinople.

Preface

God, after having created all things that are and given order and harmony to the universe, with his own finger engraved the Law on the tables and published it openly so that men, being well directed thereby, should not shamelessly trample upon one another and the stronger should not do violence to the weaker but that all things should be apportioned with just measure. Therefore it has seemed good for Our Serenity [i.e., the emperor] also to lay down the following ordinances based on the statutes in order that the human race may be governed fittingly and no person may injure his fellow. .

I. The Notaries

1. Whoever wishes to be appointed a notary [a writer of legal or official documents] must be elected by a vote and decision both of the *primicerius* [the chief of the guild of notaries] and the notaries acting with him to ensure that he has a knowledge and understanding of the laws, that he excels in handwriting, that he is not garrulous [overly talkative] or insolent, and that he does not lead a corrupt life, but on the contrary is serious in his habits, guileless in his thoughts, eloquent, intelligent, a polished reader, and accurate in his diction, to guard against his being easily led to give a false meaning in places to what he writes or to insert deceptive clauses. And if at any time a notary is found to be doing something contrary to the law and the authorized written regulations, those who have acted as his witnesses shall be responsible.
2. The candidate must know by heart the forty titles of the *Manual of Law* [a short compilation of imperial laws] and must also know the sixty books of the Basilika [a much longer compilation]. He shall also have received a general education so that he may not make mistakes in formulating his documents and be guilty of errors in his reading. He shall also have abundant time to give proof of his ability both mental and physical. Let him prepare a handwritten document in a meeting of the guild, so that he may not later commit unforeseen errors; but if he should then be detected in any, let him be expelled, from the order. . . .

II. The Jewelers

1. We ordain that the jewelers may, if any one invites them, buy the things that pertain to them, such as gold, silver, pearls, or precious stones; but not bronze and woven linens or any other materials which others should purchase rather than they. However, they are not hereby prevented from buying anything they wish for private use.
2. They must not depreciate or increase the price of things for sale to the detriment of the vendors, but shall appraise them at their just value. If anyone acts deceitfully in this, he shall forfeit the appraised value of the things to the vendor. . . .
4. If a jeweler discovers a woman offering for sale objects of gold or silver, or pearls, or precious stones, he shall inform the Prefect of these things to prevent their being exported to foreign peoples.
5. If anyone adulterates uncoined metal and manufactures things for sale from it, he shall have his hand cut off.

Source: A. E. R. Boak, "Notes and Documents: The Book of the Prefect," *Journal of Economic and Business History* 1 (1929): 600–602, 604 (slightly modified).

Question to Consider

- **What sort of legal training did notaries have to have? How does modern legal training compare? What does this tell us about Byzantine life and society?**

Now, with the empire slowly regaining its military eminence and with icons permanently restored in 843, this scholarly elite thrived again. Byzantine artists produced new works, and emperors and other members of the new court society, liberated from the sober taboos of the iconoclastic period, sponsored lavish artistic productions. Emperor Constantine Porphyrogenitos wrote books of geography and history and financed the work of other scholars and artists. He even supervised the details of his craftspeople's products, insisting on exacting standards: "Who could enumerate how many artisans the Porphyrogenitos corrected? He corrected the stonemasons, the carpenters, the goldsmiths, the silversmiths, and the blacksmiths," wrote a historian supported by the same emperor's patronage.

The emperors were not alone in their support of the arts. Other members of the imperial court also sponsored writers, philosophers, and historians. Scholars wrote summaries of classical literature, encyclopedias of ancient knowledge, and commentaries on classical authors. Some copied manuscripts of religious and theological commentaries, such as homilies, liturgical texts, Bibles, and Psalters. The

A Depiction of David from the Macedonian Renaissance
This manuscript illumination, made at Constantinople in the mid-ninth century, combines Christian and classical elements in a harmonious composition. David, author of the Psalms, sits in the center. Like the classical Orpheus, he plays music that attracts and tames the beasts. In the right-hand corner, a figure labeled "Bethlehem" is modeled on a lounging river or mountain god. *(Bibliothèque nationale, Paris, France/The Bridgeman Art Library International.)*

merging of classical and Christian traditions is clearest in manuscript illuminations (painted illustrations or embellishments in hand-copied manuscripts). For example, to depict King David, the supposed poet of the Psalms, an artist illuminating a Psalter turned to a model of Orpheus, the enchanting musician of ancient Greek mythology. (See the illustration above.) Both in Byzantium and in the West, artists chose their subjects by considering the texts they were to illustrate and the ways in which previous artists had handled particular themes. As with the illustration of King David, they drew on traditional models to make their subjects identifiable. Like modern illustrators of Santa Claus who rely on a tradition dictating a plump man with a bushy white beard (Santa's "iconography"), medieval artists used particular visual cues to alert viewers to the identity of their subjects.

The *Dynatoi*: A New Landowning Elite

At Constantinople the emperor reigned supreme. But outside the capital, especially in the border regions of Anatolia, where leaders of the tagmata became famous as military heroes, extremely powerful military families began to compete with imperial power. The ***dynatoi*** ("powerful men"), as this new hereditary elite was called, got rich on booty and new lands taken in the aggressive wars of the tenth century. They took over or bought up whole villages, turning the peasants' labor to their benefit. For the most part they exercised their power locally, but they also sometimes occupied the imperial throne.

The Phocas family exemplifies the strengths as well as the weaknesses of the dynatoi. Probably originally from Armenia, they possessed military skills and exhibited loyalty to the emperor that together brought them high positions in both the army and at court in the last decades of the ninth century. In the tenth century, with new successes in the east, the Phocas family gained independent power. After some particularly brilliant victories, Nicephorus Phocas was declared emperor by his armies and ruled (as Nicephorus II Phocas) at Constantinople from 963 to 969. But opposing factions

---

dynatoi **(DY nuh toy):** The "powerful men" who dominated the countryside of the Byzantine Empire in the tenth and eleventh centuries, and to some degree challenged the authority of the emperor.

of the dynatoi brought him down. The mainstay of Phocas family power, as of that of all the dynatoi, was outside the capital, on the family's great estates.

As the dynatoi gained power, the social hierarchy of Byzantium began to resemble that of western Europe, where land owned by aristocratic lords was farmed by peasants bound by tax and service obligations to the fields they cultivated.

The Formation of Eastern Europe and Kievan Rus

What would become modern eastern Europe was shaped during the period 850–950. By 800, Slavic settlements dotted the area from the Danube River down to Greece and from the Black Sea to Croatia. The ruler of the Bulgarians, called a *khagan*, presided over the largest realm, northwest of Constantinople. Under the khagan Krum (r. c. 803–814) and his son, Bulgarian rule stretched west to the Tisza River in modern Hungary. At about the same time as Krum's triumphant expansion, however, the Byzantine Empire began its own campaigns to conquer, convert, and control these Slavic regions, today known as the Balkans.

Bulgaria and Serbia The Byzantine offensive to the north and west began under Emperor Nicephorus I (r. 802–811), who waged war against the Slavs of Greece in the Peloponnese, set up a new Christian diocese there, organized it as a new military theme, and forcibly resettled Christians in the area to counteract Slavic paganism. The Byzantines followed this pattern of conquest as they pushed northward. By 900, Byzantium ruled all of Greece.

Still under Nicephorus I, the Byzantines launched a massive attack against the Bulgarians, took the chief city of Pliska, plundered it, burned it to the ground, and then marched against Krum's encampment in the Balkan Mountains. Krum, however, attacked the imperial troops, killed Nicephorus, and brought home the emperor's skull in triumph. Cleaned out and lined with silver, the skull served as the victorious Krum's drinking goblet. In 816, the two sides agreed to a peace that lasted for thirty years. But hostility remained, and intermittent skirmishes between the Bulgarians and Byzantines gave way to longer wars throughout the tenth century.

Basil II: The Byzantine emperor (r. 976–1025) who presided over the end of the Bulgar threat (earning the name Bulgar-Slayer) and the conversion of Kievan Russia to Christianity.

Emperor **Basil II** (r. 976–1025) led the Byzantines in a slow, methodical conquest. Aptly called the Bulgar-Slayer, Basil brought the entire region under Byzantine control and forced its ruler to accept the Byzantine form of Christianity. Around the same time, the Serbs, encouraged by Byzantium to oppose the Bulgarians, began to form the political community that would become Serbia.

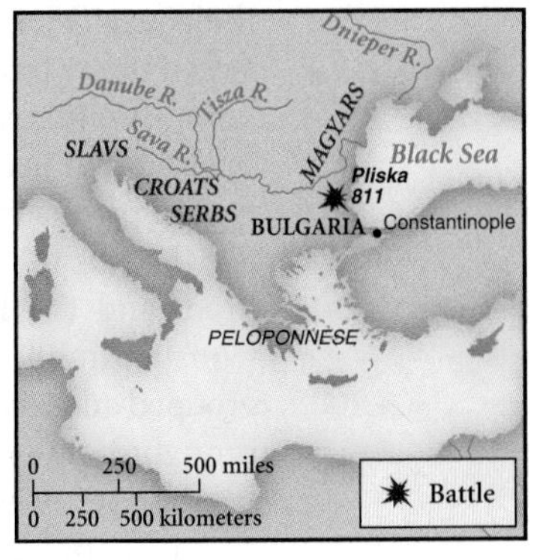

The Balkans, c. 850–950

Religion played an important role in the Byzantine conquest of the Balkans. In 863, the brothers Cyril and Methodius were sent as Christian missionaries from the Byzantines to the Slavs. Well educated in both classical and religious texts, they spoke one Slavic dialect fluently and devised an alphabet for Slavic (until then an oral language) based on Greek forms. It was the ancestor of the modern Cyrillic alphabet used in Bulgaria, Serbia, and Russia today.

Kievan Rus The region that would eventually become Russia lay outside the sphere of direct Byzantine rule in the ninth and tenth centuries. Like Serbia and Bulgaria, however, it came under increasingly strong Byzantine influence. In the ninth century, the Vikings — Scandinavian adventurers who ranged over vast stretches of ninth-century Europe seeking trade, booty, and land — penetrated the region below the Gulf of Finland, where they imposed their rule. By the end of the century they had moved southward, taking in the region around Kiev, a key commercial emporium. There the Rus, as they were called, adopted some of the ceremonial trappings of the nearby Khazar state, a formidable power at the mouth of the Volga River. From Kiev, which today is the capital of Ukraine, enterprising Rus sailed the Dnieper River and crossed the Black Sea in search of markets for their slaves and furs.

The relationship between Rus and Byzantium began with trade, continued with an interlude of war, and was soon sustained by a common religion. Already at the start of the tenth century the Rus had special trade privileges at Constantinople, where they were allowed to enter in groups of fifty, though only if unarmed. In 911, the Rus and the Byzantines drew up a detailed treaty that proclaimed

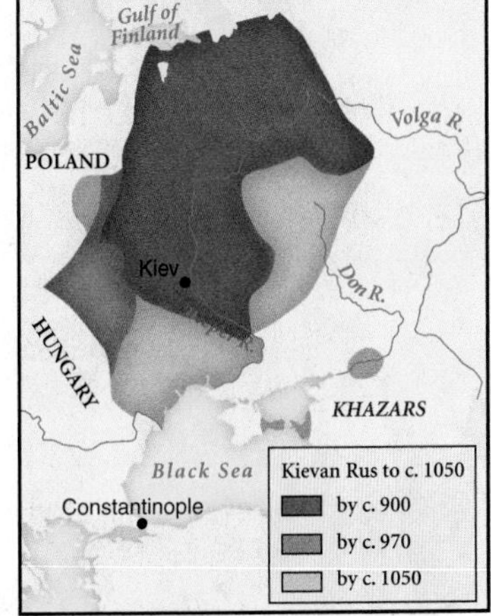

The Formation of Kievan Rus

their "amity" and "love." It regulated relations between the two peoples at Constantinople. "If a Rus kill a Byzantine, or a Byzantine a Rus, let him die where the murder has been committed," read one typical provision. But when the Byzantines tried to use the Rus to attack the Khazars, their plan backfired, and the Khazars forced the Rus to attack Constantinople in 941. Soon, however, the Rus regrouped and resumed trading with Byzantium. They brought home not only money but also Byzantine silks, some of which have survived in the burial chambers of well-to-do Rus women.

Few Rus were Christian (most were polytheists, others Muslims or Jews), but that changed at the end of the tenth century, when good relations between the Rus and the Byzantines were sealed by the conversion of the Rus ruler Vladimir (r. c. 978–1015). Emperor Basil II, in need of military help in 988, sent his sister Anna to marry Vladimir in exchange for an army of Rus. To seal the alliance, Vladimir was baptized and took his brother-in-law's name. The general population seems to have quickly adopted the new religion.

Vladimir's conversion represented a wider pattern: the Christianization of Europe. In the southeast, orthodox Byzantine Christianity was decisive, while in the west and northwest, Roman Catholicism tended to be most important. Slavic realms such as Moravia, Serbia, and Bulgaria adopted the Byzantine form of Christianity, while the rulers and peoples of Poland, Hungary, Denmark, and Norway were converted under the auspices of the Roman church. The conversion of the Rus was especially significant, because they were geographically as close to the Islamic world as to the Christian and could conceivably have become Muslims. By converting to Byzantine Christianity, the Rus made themselves heir to Byzantium and its church, customs, art, and political ideology. The adoption of Christianity linked Rus to the Christian world, but choosing the Byzantine form, rather than the Roman Catholic, later served to isolate the region from western Europe, as in the course of the centuries the Byzantine (Greek-speaking) and Roman (Latin-speaking) churches became estranged.

Wishing to counteract this isolation, Rus rulers at times sought to cement relations with central and western Europe, which were tied to Catholic Rome. Prince Iaroslav the Wise, who became sole ruler in 1034 or 1036, forged such links through his own marriage and those of his sons and daughters to rulers and princely families in France, Hungary, and Scandinavia. Iaroslav encouraged intellectual and artistic developments that would connect Russian culture to the classical past. At his own church of St. Sophia, in Kiev, which copied the one at Constantinople, Iaroslav created a major library.

When Iaroslav died in 1054, his kingdom was divided among his sons. Civil wars broke out between the brothers and eventually between cousins, shredding what unity Rus had known. Massive invasions by outsiders, particularly from the east, further weakened the Kievan rulers, who were eventually displaced by princes from the north. At the crossroads of East and West, Rus could meet and absorb a great variety of traditions; but its geographical position also opened it to unremitting military pressures.

Mosaic of Mary in the Cathedral of St. Sophia

Imitating Justinian's Hagia Sophia at Constantinople, the cathedral of St. Sophia in Kiev was built by Rus ruler Iaroslav the Wise (r. 1019–1054) around 1050. Here the Virgin Mary, who looms at the very center of the cathedral, is portrayed praying in the position of the praying man figure shown on page 264. Compare her to the icon of the Virgin and Child on page 256 to see how much the Russian artists borrowed from Byzantine styles. *(Cathedral of St. Sophia, Kiev, Russia/Vadim Gippenreiter/The Bridgeman Art Library International.)*

REVIEW QUESTION In what ways did the Byzantine emperor expand his power, and in what ways was that power checked?

The Rise and Fall of the Abbasid Caliphate

A new dynasty of caliphs—the Abbasids—first brought unity and then, in their decline, fragmentation to the Islamic world. Caliphs ruled in name only, as regional rulers took over the actual government in Islamic lands. Local traditions based on religious and political differences played an increasingly important role in people's lives. Yet, even in the eleventh century, the Islamic world had a clear sense of its own unity, based on language, commerce, and artistic and intellectual achievements that transcended regional boundaries.

The Abbasid Caliphate, 750–936

In 750, a civil war ousted the Umayyads and raised the **Abbasids** to the caliphate. The Abbasids found support in an uneasy coalition of Shi'ites (the faction of Islam loyal to Ali's memory) and non-Arabs who had been excluded from the Umayyad government and now demanded a place in political life. With the new regime, the center of Islamic rule shifted from Damascus, with its roots in the Roman tradition, to Baghdad, a new capital city built by the Abbasids right next to Ctesiphon, which had been the Sasanid capital. Here the Abbasid caliphs adhered even more firmly than the Umayyads to Persian courtly models. Their administration grew more and more centralized: the caliph's staff grew, and he controlled the appointment of regional governors.

From Baghdad, the Abbasid caliph Harun al-Rashid (r. 786–809) presided over a flourishing empire. His contemporary Frankish ruler, Charlemagne, was impressed with the elephant Harun sent him as a gift, along with monkeys, spices, and medicines. Such items were mainstays of everyday commerce in Harun's Iraq. A mid-ninth-century catalog of imports listed "tigers, panthers, elephants, panther skins, rubies, white sandal[wood], ebony, and coconuts" from India as well as "silk, chinaware, paper, ink, peacocks, racing horses, saddles, felts [and] cinnamon" from China.

The Abbasid dynasty began to decline after Harun's death. For eight years, his two sons waged war against each other, splintering the caliphate. During the war, the caliphs lost control over many regions, including Syria and Egypt. They needed to recruit an army that would be loyal to them alone. This they found in "outsiders," many of them Turks from east of the Caspian Sea (today Kazakhstan). Many of the Turks, later called Mamluks, were bought as slaves. One slave trader reported, "[The caliph sent me] to purchase Turks. Each year I would bring him a certain number such that . . . [he] accumulated some three thousand young men." Once purchased, the Turks were freed and paid a salary. They were crackerjack troops because they knew how to fire arrows while riding horseback. But to keep them employed, the Abbasids needed a good tax base, and this they did not have. Even in Iraq itself, serious uprisings just south of Baghdad kept huge swaths of territory outside the control of the caliphs. Other regions of the Islamic world easily went their own way. In the tenth century the caliphs became figureheads only, while independent regional rulers collected taxes and hired their own armies.

Thus, in the Islamic world, as in the Byzantine, new regional lords challenged the power of the central ruler. But the process was soon much more advanced in Islamic than in Byzantine territories. Map 9.1 (see page 277) correctly omits any indication of regional dynatoi because the key center of power in the Byzantine Empire continued to be Constantinople. Map 9.2, on the other hand, shows the fragmentation of the Abbasid caliphate, as local dynasties established themselves.

Regional Diversity in Islamic Lands

A faraway caliph could not command sufficient allegiance from local leaders once he demanded more in taxes than he gave back in favors. The forces of fragmentation were strong in the Islamic world, which was, after all, based on the conquest of many diverse regions, each with its own deeply rooted traditions and culture. The Islamic religion, with its Sunni/Shi'ite split, also became a source of polarization.[1] Western Europeans knew almost nothing about Muslims, calling all of them Saracens (from the Latin word for "Arabs") without distinction. But, like today, Muslims were of different ethnicities, practiced different customs, and identified with different regions. With the fragmentation of political and religious unity, each of the tenth- and early-eleventh-century Islamic states built on local traditions under local rulers.

Abbasids (A buh sihds): The dynasty of caliphs that, in 750, took over from the Umayyads in all of the Islamic realm except for Spain (al-Andalus). From their new capital at Baghdad, they presided over a wealthy realm until the late ninth century.

---

[1]The Shi'ites, originally followers of Ali, had by this time come to practice Islam differently from the Sunni. Each faction adhered to its own interpretation of the Prophet Muhammad's life and message.

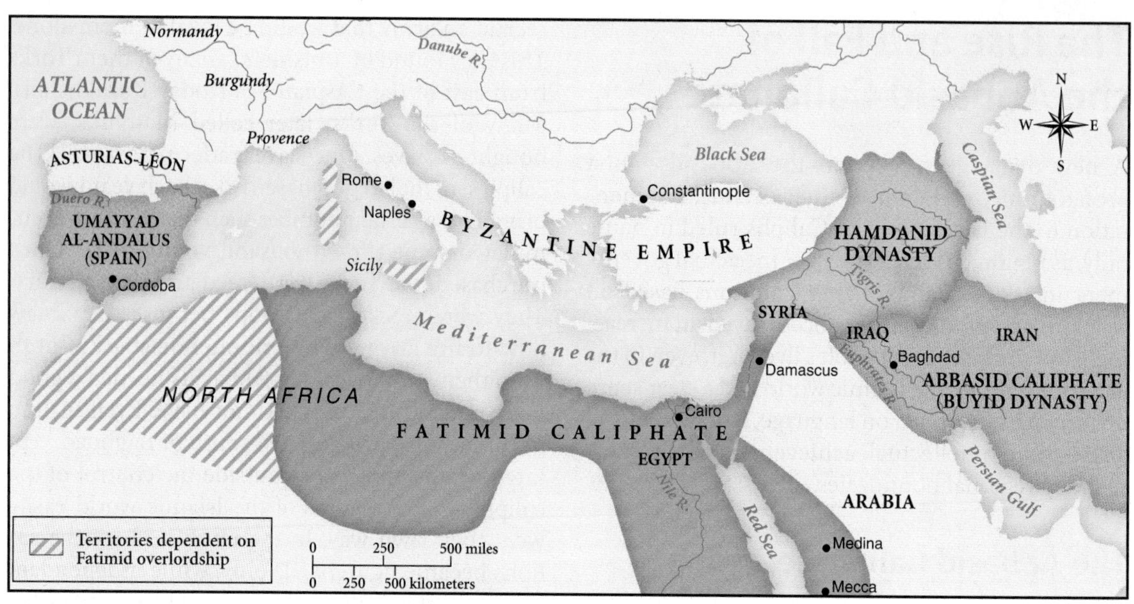

MAP 9.2 Islamic States, c. 1000
Comparing this map with Map 8.1 on page 248 will quickly demonstrate the fragmentation of the once united Islamic caliphate. In 750, one caliph ruled territory stretching from Spain to India. In 1000, there was more than one caliphate as well as several other ruling dynasties. The most important of those dynasties were the Fatimids, who began as organizers of a movement to overthrow the Abbasids. By 1000, the Fatimids had conquered Egypt and claimed hegemony over all of North Africa.

The Fatimid Dynasty In the tenth century, one group of Shi'ites, calling themselves the **Fatimids** (after Fatimah, daughter of Muhammad and wife of Ali), allied with the Berbers in North Africa and established themselves in 909 as rulers in the region now called Tunisia. The Fatimid Ubayd Allah claimed to be not only the true imam—the descendant of Ali—but also the *mahdi*, the "divinely guided" messiah, come to bring justice on earth. In 969, the Fatimids declared themselves rulers of Egypt. Their dynasty lasted for about two hundred years. Fatimid leaders also controlled North Africa, Arabia, and even Syria for a time. They established a lavish court culture that rivaled the one at Baghdad, and they supported industries such as lusterware (see the illustration on the right), that had once been a monopoly of the Abbasids.

Fatimids (FAT ih mihds): Members of the tenth-century Shi'ite dynasty who derived their name from Fatimah, the daughter of Muhammad and wife of Ali; they dominated in parts of North Africa, Egypt, and even Syria.

The Spanish Emirate Whereas the Shi'ites dominated Egypt, Sunni Muslims ruled al-Andalus, the Islamic central and southern heart of Spain. Unlike the other independent Islamic states, which were forged during the ninth and tenth centuries, the Spanish emirate of Córdoba (so called because its ruler took the secular title *emir*, "commander," and fixed his capital at Córdoba) was created near the start of the Abbasid

Fatimid Tableware
The elites under the Fatimid rulers cultivated a luxurious lifestyle that including dining on porcelain tableware, which was glazed and fired several times to produce the effect seen here. Trade contacts with China inspired the Islamic world to mimic Chinese pottery. *(Museum of Fine Arts, Cleveland/photo © Werner Forman/HIP/The Image Works.)*

caliphate. During the Abbasid revolution of 750, Abd al-Rahman—a member of the Umayyad family—fled to Morocco, gathered an army, invaded Spain, and after only one battle was declared emir in 756, becoming Abd al-Rahman I. He and his successors ruled a broad range of peoples, including many Jews and Christians. After the initial Islamic conquest of Spain, the Christians adopted so much of the new Arabic language and so many of the customs that they were called Mozarabs, that is, "like Arabs." The Arabs allowed them freedom of worship and let them live according to their own laws. Some Mozarabs were content with their status, others converted to Islam, and still others intermarried—most commonly, Christian women married Muslim men and raised their children as Muslims, since the religion of the father determined that of the children.

A Princely Pyxis
A pyxis is a small container, and this one, about six inches high and carved out of ivory, was made for the younger son of Abd al-Rahman III, the caliph of Córdoba. The prince is depicted in a decorative lozenge, sitting on a rug and holding a bottle and a flower. One servant sits beside him to cool him with a fan; another stands and plays the lute. Underneath the rug are lions, symbols of power. Outside the princely enclosure, falconers stand by, ready to accompany the prince to the hunt. The whole scene suggests order, skill, and elegance, all important features of the Islamic renaissance. *(Louvre, Paris, France/Peter Willi/The Bridgeman Art Library International.)*

Abd al-Rahman III (r. 912–961) was powerful enough to take the title of caliph, and the caliphate of Córdoba, which he created, lasted from 929 to 1031. Under Abd al-Rahman III's rule, members of all religious groups in al-Andalus enjoyed not only freedom of worship but also equal opportunity to rise in the civil service. The caliph also initiated diplomatic contacts with Byzantine and European rulers, ignoring the weak and tiny Christian kingdoms squeezed into northern Spain. Yet under later caliphs, al-Andalus experienced the same political fragmentation that was occurring everywhere else. The caliphate of Córdoba broke up in 1031, and rulers of small, independent regions, called *taifas*, took power.

Unity of Commerce and Language

Although the regions of the Islamic world were culturally and politically diverse, they maintained a measure of unity through trade networks and language. Their principal bond was Arabic, the language of the Qur'an. At once poetic and sacred, Arabic was also the language of commerce and government from Baghdad to Córdoba. Moreover, despite political differences, borders were open: an artisan could move from Córdoba to Cairo; a landowner in Morocco might very well own property in al-Andalus; a young man from North Africa would think nothing of going to Baghdad to find a wife; a young girl purchased as a slave in Mecca might become part of a prince's household in Baghdad. With few barriers to commerce (though every city and town had its own customs dues), traders regularly dealt in various, often exotic, goods.

The primary reason for these open borders was Islam itself, but the openness extended to non-Muslims as well. The commercial activities of the Tustari brothers, Jewish merchants from southern Iran, were typical in the Arabic-speaking world. By 1026, the Tustaris had established a flourishing business in Egypt. Although they did not have "branch offices," informal contacts with friends and family allowed them to import fine textiles from Iran to sell in Egypt and to export Egyptian fabrics to sell in Iran. Dealing in fabrics could yield fabulous wealth, for cloth was essential not only for clothing but also for home decoration: textiles covered walls; curtains separated rooms. The Tustari brothers held the highest rank in Jewish society and had contacts with Muslim rulers. The son of one of the brothers converted to Islam and became vizier (chief minister) to the Fatimids in Egypt.

The sophisticated Islamic society of the tenth and eleventh centuries supported commercial networks even more vast than those of the Tustari family. Muslim merchants brought tin from England; salt and gold from Timbuktu in west-central Africa; amber, gold, and copper from Rus; and slaves from every region. Equally widespread was the reach of the Islamic renaissance.

DOCUMENT

When She Approached

The tenth and eleventh centuries marked the golden age of Arabic poetry in al-Andalus. In the first of these centuries, the poets' patron was the caliph at Córdoba. In the eleventh century, as al-Andalus broke up into taifas *(see page 285), each taifa ruler supported his own artists. Ibn Darraj al-Quastali (958–1030) revealed his most intimate feelings when he wrote in this poem about leaving his wife and child behind to find employment at the court of a taifa ruler.*

When she approached to bid me farewell,
her sighs and moans breaking down my endurance,
reminding me of the times of love and joy,
while in the crib a little one gurgles,
unable to talk, but the sounds he makes
firmly lodge in the heart's whims. . . .
I disobeyed the promptings of my heart to stay with him,
led on by a habit of constant travel day and night,
and the wing of parting took off with me, while the fear
of parting flew high with many wings.

Source: Salma Khadra Jayyusi, "Andalusi Poetry: The Golden Period," in *The Legacy of Muslim Spain*, ed. Salma Khadra Jayyusi, 2 vols. (Leiden: Brill, 1994), 1:335.

Question to Consider

▪ **What image of family life does this poem project? What does it tell us about the different attractions of career and family in the Islamic world?**

The Islamic Renaissance, c. 790–c. 1050

Unlike the Macedonian renaissance, which was concentrated in Constantinople, the Islamic renaissance occurred throughout the Islamic world. The dissolution of the caliphate into separate political entities multiplied the centers of learning and intellectual productivity. The Islamic renaissance was particularly dazzling in capital cities such as Córdoba, where tenth-century rulers presided over a brilliant court culture, patronizing scholars, poets, and artists. The library at Córdoba contained the largest collection of books in Europe at that time (see Document, "When She Approached," above).

Elsewhere, already in the eighth century, the Abbasid caliphs endowed research libraries and set up centers for translation where scholars culled the writings of the ancients, including the classics of Persia, India, and Greece. Many scholars read, translated, and commented on the works of ancient philosophers. Some studied astronomy while others wrote on mathematical matters. Al-Khwarizmi (c. 780–c. 850) wrote a book on algebra (the word itself is from the Arab *al-jabr*) and another on the Indian method of calculation, using the numbers 1, 2, and 3. He introduced the zero, essential for differentiating 1 from 10, for example. When these numerals were introduced into western Europe in the twelfth century, they were known as Arabic, as they are still called today.

The newly independent Islamic rulers supported science as well as mathematics. Ibn Sina (980–1037), known in Christian Europe as Avicenna, wrote books on logic, the natural sciences, and physics. His *Canon of Medicine* systematized earlier treatises and reconciled them with his own experience as a physician. Active in the centers of power, he served as vizier to various rulers. In his autobiography, he spoke with pleasure and pride about his intellectual development:

> One day I asked permission [of the ruler] to go into [his doctors'] library, look at their books, and read the medical ones. He gave me permission, and I went into a palace of many rooms, each with trunks full of books, back-to-back. In one room there were books on Arabic and poetry, in another books on jurisprudence, and similarly in each room books on a single subject. . . . When I reached the age of eighteen, I had completed the study of all these sciences.

Long before there were universities in Europe, there were institutions of higher learning in the Islamic world. Rich Muslims, often members of the ruling elite, demonstrated their piety and charity by establishing schools. Each school, or madrasa, was located within or attached to a mosque. Sometimes visiting scholars held passionate public debates at these schools. More regularly, professors held classes throughout the day on the interpretation of the Qur'an and other literary or legal texts. Students, all male, attended the classes that suited their achievement level and interest. Most students paid a fee for learning, but there were also scholarship students. One tenth-century vizier was so solicitous of the welfare of the scholars he supported that each day he set out iced refreshments, candles, and paper for them in his own kitchen.

The use of paper, made from flax and hemp or rags and vegetable fiber, points to a major difference among the Islamic, Byzantine, and (as we shall see) Carolingian renaissances. Byzantine scholars worked to enhance the prestige of the ruling classes. Their work, written on expensive parchment (made from animal skins), kept manuscripts out of the hands of all but the very rich. This was true of scholarship in Europe as well. By contrast, Islamic scholars had goals that cut across all social classes: to be physicians to the rich, teachers to the young, and contributors to passionate religious debates. Their writings, on paper (less expensive than parchment), were widely available.

REVIEW QUESTION What forces contributed to the fragmentation of the Islamic world in the tenth and eleventh centuries, and what forces held it together?

The Carolingian Empire

Just as in the Byzantine and Islamic worlds, in Europe the period 750–1050 saw first the formation of a strong empire, ruled by one man, and then its fragmentation as local rulers took power into their own hands. A new dynasty, the Carolingians, came to rule in the Frankish kingdom at almost the very moment (c. 750) that the Abbasids gained the caliphate. Charlemagne, the most powerful Carolingian monarch, conquered new territory, took the title of emperor, and presided over a revival of Christian classical culture known as the Carolingian renaissance. He ruled at the local level through counts and other military men. Nevertheless, the unity of the Carolingian Empire—based largely on conquest, a measure of prosperity, and personal allegiance to Charlemagne—was shaky. Its weaknesses were exacerbated by attacks from Viking, Muslim, and Magyar invaders. Charlemagne's successors divided his empire among themselves and saw it divided further as local leaders took defense—and rule—into their own hands.

The Rise of the Carolingians

The Carolingians were among many aristocratic families on the rise during the Merovingian period, but they gained exceptional power by monopolizing the position of "palace mayor"—a sort of prime minister—under the Merovingian kings. Charles Martel ("Charles the Hammer"), mayor 714–741, gave the name **Carolingian** (from *Carolus*, Latin for "Charles") to the dynasty. Renowned for defeating an invading army of Muslims from al-Andalus near Poitiers in 732, he also contended vigorously against other aristocrats who were carving out independent lordships for themselves. Charles Martel and his family turned aristocratic factions against one another, rewarded supporters, crushed enemies, and dominated whole regions by supporting monasteries that served as focal points for both religious piety and land donations.

The Carolingians also allied themselves with the Roman papacy and its adherents. They supported Anglo-Saxon missionaries like Boniface (see page 267) who went to areas on the fringes of the Carolingian realm as the pope's ambassador. Reforming the Christianity that these regions had adopted, Boniface set up a hierarchical church organization and founded monasteries dedicated to the Benedictine rule. His newly appointed bishops were loyal to Rome and the Carolingians.

Pippin III (d. 768), Charles Martel's son, turned to the pope even more directly. When he deposed the Merovingian king in 751, taking over the kingship himself, Pippin petitioned Pope Zachary to legitimize the act; the pope agreed. The Carolingians returned the favor a few years later when the pope asked for their help against hostile Lombards. That papal request signaled a major shift. Before 754, the papacy had been part of the Byzantine Empire; after that, it turned to Europe for protection. Pippin launched a successful campaign against the Lombard king that ended in 756 with the so-called Donation of Pippin, a peace accord between the Lombards and the pope. The treaty gave back to the pope cities that had been taken by the Lombard king. The new arrangement recognized what the papacy had long before created: a territorial "republic of St. Peter" ruled by the pope, not by the Byzantine emperor. Henceforth, the fate of Italy would be tied largely to the policies of the pope and the Frankish kings to the north, not to the eastern emperors.

Partnership with the Roman church gave the Carolingian dynasty a Christian aura, expressed in symbolic form by anointment. Bishops rubbed holy oil on the foreheads and shoulders of Carolingian kings during the coronation ceremony, imitating the Old Testament kings who had been anointed by God.

Charlemagne and His Kingdom, 768–814

The most famous Carolingian king was Charles, called the Great (*le Magne* in Old French) by his contemporaries—thus, **Charlemagne** (r. 768–814). (See "Contrasting Views," pages 290–291.) Mod-

---

Carolingian: The Frankish dynasty that ruled a western European empire from 751 to the late 800s; its greatest vigor was in the time of Charlemagne (r. 768–814) and Louis the Pious (r. 814–840).

Charlemagne (SHAR luh mayn)**:** The Carolingian king (r. 768–814) whose conquests greatly expanded the Frankish kingdom. He was crowned emperor on December 25, 800.

Charlemagne's Chapel
Charlemagne was the first Frankish king to build a permanent capital city. He decided to do so in 789 and chose Aachen because of its natural warm springs. There he built a palace complex that, besides a grand living area for himself and his retinue, included a chapel (a small semiprivate church). Today the entire chapel is enclosed within Aachen's cathedral. *(© Aachen Cathedral, Aachen, Germany/Bildarchiv Steffens/The Bridgeman Art Library International.)*

ern historians are less dazzled than his contemporaries were, noting that Charlemagne was complex, contradictory, and sometimes brutal. He loved listening to St. Augustine's *City of God* as it was read aloud, and he supported major scholarly enterprises, yet he never learned to write. He was devout, building a beautiful chapel at his major residence at Aachen (see the illustration above), yet he flouted the advice of churchmen when they told him to convert pagans rather than force baptism on them. He admired the pope, yet he was furious when a pope placed the imperial crown on his head. He waged many successful wars, yet he thereby destroyed the buffer states surrounding the Frankish kingdoms, unleashing a new round of invasions even before his death.

Behind these contradictions, however, lay a unifying vision. Charlemagne dreamed of an empire that would unite the martial and learned traditions of the Roman and Germanic worlds with the legacy of Christianity. This vision lay at the core of his political activity, his building programs, and his support of scholarship and education.

Territorial Expansion During the early years of his reign, Charlemagne conquered lands in all directions (Map 9.3). He invaded Italy, seizing the crown of the Lombard kings and annexing northern Italy in 774. He then moved northward and began a long and difficult war against the Saxons, concluded only after more than thirty years of fighting, during which he forcibly annexed Saxon territory and converted the Saxon people to Christianity through mass baptisms at the point of the sword. To the southeast, Charlemagne fought the Avars. Charlemagne's courtier and biographer Einhard described this campaign as follows: "All the money and treasure that had been amassed over many years was seized, and no war in which the Franks have ever engaged within the memory of man brought them such riches and such booty." To the southwest, Charlemagne led an expedition to al-Andalus. Although suffering a defeat at Roncesvalles in 778 (immortalized later in the medieval epic *The Song of Roland*), he did set up a march, or military buffer region, between al-Andalus and his own realm.

By the 790s, Charlemagne's kingdom stretched eastward beyond the Elbe River (today in Germany), southeast to what is today Austria, and south to Spain and Italy. Such power in the West was unheard of since the time of the Roman Empire. Charlemagne began to imitate aspects of the imperial model: he sponsored building programs to symbolize his authority, standardized weights and measures, and acted as a patron of intellectual and artistic efforts. He built a capital city at Aachen, complete with a chapel that was patterned on Justinian's church of San Vitale (see pages 234–35) at Ravenna.

To discourage corruption, Charlemagne appointed special officials, called *missi dominici* ("those sent out by the lord king"), to oversee his regional governors — the counts — on the king's behalf. The missi — lay aristocrats or bishops — traveled in pairs throughout the kingdom. As one of Charlemagne's capitularies (summaries of royal decisions) put it, the missi "are to make diligent inquiry wherever people claim that someone has done them an injustice, so that the missi fully carry out the law and do justice for everyone everywhere, whether in the holy churches of God or among the poor, orphans, or widows."

MAP 9.3 Expansion of the Carolingian Empire under Charlemagne
The conquests of Charlemagne temporarily united almost all of western Europe under one ruler. Although this great empire broke apart (see the inset showing how the empire was divided by the Treaty of Verdun), the legacy of that unity remained, even serving as one of the inspirations behind today's European Union.

Imperial Coronation While Charlemagne was busy imitating Roman emperors through his conquests, his building programs, his legislation, and his efforts at church reform, the papacy was beginning to claim imperial power for itself. At some point, perhaps in the 760s, members of the papal chancery (writing office) created a document called the Donation of Constantine, which declared the pope the recipient of the fourth-century emperor Constantine's crown, cloak, and military rank along with "all provinces, palaces, and districts of the city of Rome and Italy and of the regions of the West." (The document was much later proved a forgery.) The tension between the imperial claims of the Carolingians and those of the pope was heightened by the existence of an emperor at Constantinople who also had rights in the West.

Pope Leo III (r. 795–816) upset the delicate balance among these three powers. In 799, accused of adultery and perjury by a faction of the Roman aristocracy, Leo narrowly escaped being blinded and having his tongue cut out. He fled northward to seek Charlemagne's protection. (See an anonymous poet's account of this event in Document 2 in "Contrasting Views," page 290.) Charlemagne had the pope escorted back to Rome under royal protection, and he soon arrived there himself to an imperial welcome orchestrated by Leo. On Christmas Day, 800, Leo put an imperial crown on Charlemagne's head, and the clergy and nobles who were present acclaimed the king Augustus, the title of the first Roman emperor. The pope hoped in this way to exalt the king of the Franks, to downgrade the Byzantine ruler, and to claim for himself the role of "emperor maker."

About twenty years later, when Einhard wrote about this coronation, he said that the imperial title at first displeased Charlemagne "so much that he

CONTRASTING VIEWS

Charlemagne: Roman Emperor, Father of Europe, or the Chief Bishop?

Charlemagne was crowned emperor, but was he really one of the successors of Augustus? Einhard (Document 1) thought so. An anonymous poet at Charlemagne's court claimed still more (Document 2): the king was the "father of Europe." Even while these secular views of Charlemagne were being expressed, other people—both in and outside the court—were stressing the king's religious functions and duties. Later on, these views became even more grandiose, as Notker the Stammerer's statement (Document 3) reveals.

1. Charles as Emperor

Probably at some point in the mid-820s, Einhard, who had spent time at the Carolingian court and knew Charlemagne well, wrote a biography of the emperor that took as its model the Lives of the Caesars *by Suetonius (c. 70–130). Although he did not emphasize Charlemagne's imperial title per se, Einhard stressed the classical moral values of his hero, including his "greatness of spirit" and steadfast determination. (See pages 140–41 for the traditional Roman virtues.)*

It is widely recognized that, in these ways [i.e., through conquests, diplomacy, and patronage of the arts], [Charlemagne] protected, increased the size of, and beautified his kingdom. Now I should begin at this point to speak of the character of his mind, his supreme steadfastness in good times and bad, and those other things that belong to his spiritual and domestic life.

After the death of his father [in 768], when he was sharing the kingdom with his brother [Carloman], he endured the pettiness and jealousy of his brother with such great patience, that it seemed remarkable to all that he could not be provoked to anger by him. Then [in 770], at the urging of his mother [Bertrada], he married a daughter of Desiderius, the king of the Lombards, but for some unknown reason he sent her away after a year and took Hildegard [758–783], a Swabian woman of distinct nobility. . . .

[Charlemagne] believed that his children, both his daughters and his sons, should be educated, first in the liberal arts, which he himself had studied. Then, he saw to it that when the boys had reached the right age they were trained to ride in the Frankish fashion, to fight, and to hunt. But he ordered his daughters to learn how to work with wool, how to spin and weave it, so that they might not grow dull from inactivity and [instead might] learn to value work and virtuous activity. . . .

Source: *Charlemagne's Courtier: The Complete Einhard*, ed. and trans. Paul Edward Dutton (Peterborough, Ont.: Broadview Press, 1998), 27–28.

2. The "Father of Europe"

Shortly after Pope Leo III fled northward to seek Charlemagne's help (799), an anonymous poet at the royal court composed an extremely flattering poem about the king. Here Charlemagne's virtues became larger than life.

The priests and the joyful people await
the pope's advent.
Now father Charles [i.e., Charlemagne]
sees his troops arrayed on the wide
field;
He knows that Pepin [his son] and the
highest pastor [the pope] are fast
approaching;
He orders his people to wait for them.
He divides his troops into a ring-like
shape,
In the center of which, he himself, that
blessed one, stands,
Awaiting the advent of the pope, but
higher up than his comrades
On the summit of the ring; he rises
above the assembled [Franks].

stated that, if he had known in advance of the pope's plan, he would not have entered the church that day." For more than a year after getting the imperial crown, Charlemagne used no title but *king*. However, it is unlikely that he was completely surprised by the imperial title; his advisers certainly had been thinking about it for him. He might have hesitated to adopt the title because he feared the reaction of the Byzantines, as Einhard went on to suggest, or he might have objected to the papal role in his crowning rather than to the crown itself. When Charlemagne finally did call himself emperor, after establishing a peace with the Byzantines, he used a long and revealing title: "Charles, the most serene Augustus, crowned by God, great and peaceful Emperor who governs the Roman Empire and who is, by the mercy of God, king of the Franks and the Lombards." According to this title, Charlemagne was not the Roman emperor crowned by the pope, but rather God's emperor who governed the Roman Empire along with his many other duties.

The Carolingian Renaissance, c. 790–c. 900

Charlemagne inaugurated—and his successors continued to support—a revival of learning designed to enhance the glory of the kings, educate their officials, reform the liturgy, and purify the faith. Like

Now Pope Leo approaches and crosses
the front line of the ring.
He marvels at the many peoples from
many lands whom he sees,
At their differences, their strange
tongues, dress, and weapons.
At once Charles hastens to pay his revere
nt respects,
Embraces the great pontiff, and
kisses him.
The two men join hands and walk
together, speaking as they go.
The entire army prostrates itself three
times before the pope,
And the suppliant throng three times
pays its respects.
The pope prays from his heart for the
people three times.
The king, the father of Europe, and Leo,
the world's highest pastor,
Walk together and exchange views,
Charles inquiring as to the pope's case
and his troubles.
He is shocked to learn of the wicked
deeds of the [Roman] people.
He is amazed by the pope's eyes which
had been blinded,
But to which sight had now returned,
And he marveled that a tongue muti-
lated with tongs now spoke.

Source: Paul Edward Dutton, ed., *Carolingian Civilization: A Reader*, 2nd ed. (Peterborough, Ont.: Broadview Press, 2004), 64–65.

3. The Chief Bishop

A monk at the Swiss monastery of St. Gall, Notker the Stammerer, wrote a biography of Charlemagne in 884 at the request of Charlemagne's great-grandson Charles the Fat. Here the emphasis is on Charlemagne's religious authority.

The Devil, who is skilful in laying ambushes and is in the habit of setting snares for us in the road which we are to follow, is not slow to trip us up one after another by means of some vice or other. The crime of fornication was imputed to a certain princely bishop—in such a case the name must be omitted. This matter came to the notice of his congregation, and then through tale-tellers it eventually reached the ears of the most pious Charles, the chief bishop of them all. . . . Charlemagne, that most rigorous searcher after justice, sent two of his court officials who were to turn aside that evening to a place near to the city in question and then come unexpectedly to the bishop at first light and ask him to celebrate Mass for them. If he should refuse, then they were to compel him in the name of the Emperor to celebrate the Holy Mysteries in person. The bishop did not know what to do, for that very night he had sinned before the eyes of the Heavenly Observer [God], and yet he did not dare to offend his visitors. Fearing men more than he feared God, he bathed his sweaty limbs in ice-cold springwater and then went forward to offer the awe-inspiring sacraments. Behold, either his conscience gripped his heart tight, or the water penetrated his veins, for he was seized with such frosty chill that no attention from his doctors was of use to him. He was brought to his death by a frightful attack of fever and compelled to submit his soul to the decree of the strict and eternal Judge.

Source: *Einhard and Notker the Stammerer: Two Lives of Charlemagne*, trans. Lewis Thorpe (Harmondsworth, England: Penguin, 1969), 121–22.

Questions to Consider

1. **How does the anonymous poet describe the relationship between Charlemagne and the pope?**
2. **According to Notker, how important is the Mass?**
3. **What did Einhard consider to be the chief imperial virtues?**

the renaissances of the Byzantine and Islamic worlds, the Carolingian renaissance resuscitated the learning of the past. Scholars studied Roman imperial writers such as Suetonius and Virgil, read and commented on the works of the church fathers, and worked to establish complete and accurate texts of everything they read and prized.

The English scholar Alcuin (c. 732–804), a member of the circle of scholars whom Charlemagne recruited to form a center of study, brought with him the traditions of Anglo-Saxon scholarship that had been developed by men such as Benedict Biscop and Bede. Invited to Aachen, Alcuin became Charlemagne's chief adviser, writing letters on the king's behalf, counseling him on royal policy, and tutoring the king's household, including the women and girls. He also prepared an improved edition of the Vulgate, the Latin Bible used by the clergy in all church services.

The Carolingian renaissance depended on an elite staff of scholars such as Alcuin, yet its educational program had broader appeal. In one of his capitularies, Charlemagne ordered that the cathedrals and monasteries of his kingdom teach reading and writing to all who were able to learn. Some churchmen expressed the hope that schools for children would be established even in small villages and hamlets. Although this dream was never realized, it shows that, at just about the same time as the Islamic world was organizing its madrasas, the Carolingians

David in the Carolingian Renaissance

In this sumptuous illustration from a Bible made for Charlemagne's grandson Charles the Bald, the central figure is David, the composer of the Psalms, who is playing the harp and dancing on a cloud. Above and below him are his musicians with their instruments. The influence of earlier models is clear in the two figures flanking David, who are dressed like soldiers in the late Roman Empire. Compare this depiction of David with the one painted during the Macedonian renaissance on page 289. *(Scala/White Images/Art Resource, NY.)*

were thinking about the importance of religious education for more than a small elite.

Art, like scholarship, served Carolingian political and religious goals. Carolingian artists turned to models from Byzantium (perhaps some refugees from Byzantine iconoclasm joined them) and Italy to illustrate Bibles (see the illustration above), Psalters, scientific treatises, and literary manuscripts.

The ambitious educational program endured, even after the Carolingian dynasty had faded to a memory. The work of locating, understanding, and transmitting models of the past continued in a number of monastic schools. In the twelfth century, scholars would build on the foundations laid by the Carolingian renaissance. The very print of this textbook depends on one achievement of the period: modern letter fonts are based on the clear and beautiful letter forms, called Caroline minuscule, invented in the ninth century to standardize manuscript handwriting — and make it more readable — across the whole empire.

Charlemagne's Successors, 814–911

When Charlemagne died (of a fever at age sixty-six), his son Louis the Pious (r. 814–840) took his role as leader of the Christian empire even more seriously than his father did. He brought the monastic reformer Benedict of Aniane to court and issued a capitulary in 817 imposing a uniform way of life, based on the Benedictine rule, on all the monasteries of the empire. Although some monasteries opposed this legislation, and in the years to come the king was unable to impose his will directly, this moment marked the effective adoption of the Benedictine rule as the monastic standard in Europe.

In a new development of the coronation ritual, Louis's first wife, Ermengard, was crowned empress by the pope in 816. In 817, their firstborn son, Lothar, was given the title emperor and made co-ruler with Louis. Their other sons, Pippin and Louis (later called Louis the German), were made subkings under imperial rule. Louis the Pious hoped in this way to ensure the unity of the empire while satisfying the claims of all his sons. Should any son die, only his firstborn could succeed him, a measure intended to prevent further splintering. But Louis's hopes were thwarted by events. Ermengard died, and Louis married Judith, reputed to be the most beautiful woman in the kingdom. In 823, she and Louis had a son, Charles (later known as Charles the Bald, to whose court Dhuoda's son William was sent). The sons of Ermengard, bitter over the birth of another royal heir, rebelled against their father and fought one another for more than a decade.

Finally, after Louis the Pious's death in 840, the **Treaty of Verdun** (843) divided the empire among his three remaining sons (Pippin had died in 838) — in an arrangement that would roughly define the future political contours of western Europe (see the inset in Map 9.3). The western third, bequeathed to Charles the Bald (r. 843–877), would eventually become France, and the eastern third, handed to Louis the German (r. 843–876), would become Ger-

---

Treaty of Verdun: The treaty that, in 843, split the Carolingian Empire into three parts; its borders roughly outline modern western European states.

many. The "Middle Kingdom," which was given to Lothar (r. 840–855) along with the imperial title, had a different fate: parts of it were absorbed by France and Germany, and the rest eventually formed what were to become the modern states of the Netherlands, Belgium, Luxembourg, Switzerland, and Italy.

By 843, Charlemagne's European-wide empire had dissolved. Forged by conquest, it had been supported by a small group of privileged aristocrats with lands and offices stretching across its entire expanse. Their loyalty—based on shared values, friendship, expectations of gain, and sometimes formal ties of vassalage and fealty (see page 298)—was crucial to the success of the Carolingians. The empire had also been supported by an ideal, shared by educated laymen and churchmen alike, of conquest and Christian belief working together to bring good order to the earthly state. But powerful forces operated against the Carolingian Empire. Once the empire's borders were fixed and conquests ceased, the aristocrats could not hope for new lands and offices. They put down roots in particular regions and began to gather their own followings. Powerful local traditions such as different languages also undermined imperial unity. Finally, as Dhuoda revealed in the handbook she wrote for her son, some people disagreed with the imperial ideal. By asking her son to put his father before the emperor, Dhuoda demonstrated her belief in the primacy of the family and the personal ties that bound it together. Her ideal represented a new sensibility that saw real value in the breaking apart of Charlemagne's empire into smaller, more intimate local units.

Land and Power

The Carolingian economy, based on trade and agriculture, contributed to both the rise and the dissolution of the Carolingian Empire. At the onset, the empire's wealth came from land and plunder. After the booty from war ceased to pour in, the Carolingians still had access to money and goods. To the north, in Viking trading stations such as Haithabu (today Hedeby, in northern Germany), archaeologists have found Carolingian glass and pots alongside Islamic coins and cloth, evidence that the Carolingian economy intermingled with that of the Abbasid caliphate. Silver from the Islamic world probably came north up the Volga River through Russia to the Baltic Sea. There the coins were melted down and the silver was traded to the Carolingians in return for wine, jugs, glasses, and other manufactured goods. The Carolingians turned the silver into coins of their own, to be used throughout the empire for small-scale local trade. The weakening of the Abbasid caliphate in the mid-ninth century, however, disrupted this far-flung trade network and contributed to the weakening of the Carolingians at about the same time.

Land provided the most important source of Carolingian wealth and power. Like the landholders of the late Roman Empire and the Merovingian period, Carolingian aristocrats held many estates, scattered throughout the Frankish kingdoms. In the Merovingian period these estates were rare, but in the Carolingian period they became more common and better organized for production. We also know much more about them than about their predecessors because their tenants and the dues and services they owed were carefully noted down in registers. Modern historians often call these estates manors.

A typical manor was Villeneuve Saint-Georges, which belonged to the monastery of Saint-Germain-des-Près (today in Paris) in the ninth century. Villeneuve consisted of arable fields, vineyards, meadows where animals could roam, and woodlands, all scattered about the countryside rather than connected in a compact unit. Peasant families tilled the fields, and each family had its own manse, which consisted of a house, a garden, and small sections of the arable land. Besides farming the land that belonged to them, the families—which ordinarily lived in households of no more than two generations: a mother, a father, and their minor children—also worked the demesne, the very large manse of the lord, in this case the abbey of Saint-Germain. Grown children would found their own families, and their parents' land would be subdivided to give them a share. In many ways, the peasant household of the Carolingian period was the precursor of the modern nuclear family.

Peasants at Villeneuve practiced the most progressive sort of plowing, known as the three-field system, in which they farmed two-thirds of the arable land at one time (see Figure 9.1). They planted one-third of their arable land in the fall with winter wheat and one-third in the spring with summer crops, leaving the remaining third fallow to restore its fertility. The crops sown and the fallow field then rotated so that land use was repeated only every three years. This method of organizing the land produced larger yields (because two-thirds of the land was cultivated each year) than the still-prevalent two-field system, in which only half of the arable land was cultivated one year while the other half lay fallow.

All the peasants at Villeneuve were dependents of the monastery and owed dues and services to Saint-Germain. Their status and obligations varied enormously. One family, for example, owed four silver coins, wine, wood, three hens, and fifteen eggs every year, and the men had to plow the fields of

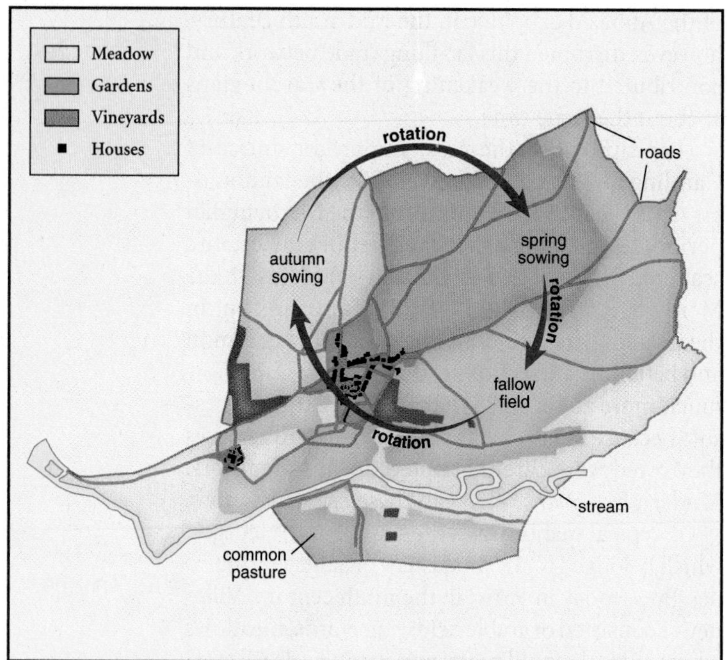

FIGURE 9.1 Diagram of a Manor and Its Three-Field System
This schematic diagram of a manor shows that peasants lived clustered together in a village that consisted of houses and gardens. One of the buildings was a church. Nearby were vineyards. A bit beyond were the fields, pastureland, and meadows, well connected by dirt roads. The field sown with spring crops (such as oats) this year would have been sown with winter wheat the next year, while the fallow field would get a spring crop. *(Based on Map IV in Marc Bloch,* French Rural History: An Essay on Its Basic Characteristics. *Berkeley: University of California Press, 1966.)*

the demesne. Another family owed the intensive labor of working the vineyards. One woman was required to weave cloth and feed the chickens. Peasant women spent much time at the lord's house in the *gynaeceum*—the workshop where women made and dyed cloth and sewed garments—or in the kitchens, as cooks. Peasant men spent most of their time in the fields.

Manors organized on the model of Villeneuve were profitable. Like other lords, the Carolingians benefited from their extensive manors. Nevertheless, farming was still too primitive to return great surpluses, and as the lands belonging to the king were divided up in the wake of the partitioning of the empire and new invasions, the Carolingians' dependence on manors scattered throughout their kingdom proved to be a source of weakness.

Viking, Muslim, and Magyar Invasions, c. 790–955

Beginning around the time of Charlemagne's imperial coronation and extending to the mid-tenth century, new groups—Vikings, Muslims, and Magyars—confronted the Carolingian Empire and many of the other kingdoms of Europe (Map 9.4). Some rulers fought off the invaders; others allied with the newcomers. By around the year 1000, the Vikings and Magyars had largely been integrated into European politics and society, while the Muslims were largely pushed out, except in Sicily and, of course, al-Andalus.

Vikings | About the same time as they made their eastward forays into the region below the Gulf of Finland, the Vikings moved westward as well. The Franks called them Northmen; the English called them Danes. They were, in fact, much less united than their victims thought. When they began their voyages at the end of the eighth century, they did so in independent bands. Both merchants and pirates, Vikings followed a chief, seeking profit, prestige, and land. Many traveled as families: husbands, wives, children, and slaves.

The Vikings perfected the art of navigation. They crossed the Atlantic in their longships, not only settling Iceland and Greenland but also (in about the year 1000) landing on the coast of North America. Other Viking bands navigated the rivers of Europe. The Vikings were pagans, and to them monasteries and churches—with their reliquaries, chalices, and crosses—were simply storehouses of booty.

Parts of the British Isles were especially hard hit. In England, for example, the Vikings raided regularly in the 830s and 840s; by midcentury, they were spending winters there. The Vikings did not just destroy. In 876, they settled in the northeast of England, plowing the land and preparing to live on it. The region where they settled and imposed their own laws was later called the Danelaw. (See England in the Age of King Alfred, page 303.)

In Wessex, the southernmost kingdom of England, King Alfred the Great (r. 871–899) bought time and peace by paying tribute and giving hostages. Such tribute, later called Danegeld, eventually became the basis of a relatively lucrative taxation system in England. In 878, Alfred led an army that, as his biographer put it, "gained the victory through God's will. He destroyed the Vikings with great slaughter and pursued those who fled, . . . hacking them down." Thereafter, the pressures of invasion eased as Alfred reorganized his army, set up strongholds, and deployed new warships.

On the continent, too, Viking invaders set up trading stations and settled where originally they had raided. Beginning about 850, their attacks became well-organized expeditions for regional control. At the end of the ninth century, one contingent settled in the region of France that soon took the name Normandy ("land of the Northmen"). In

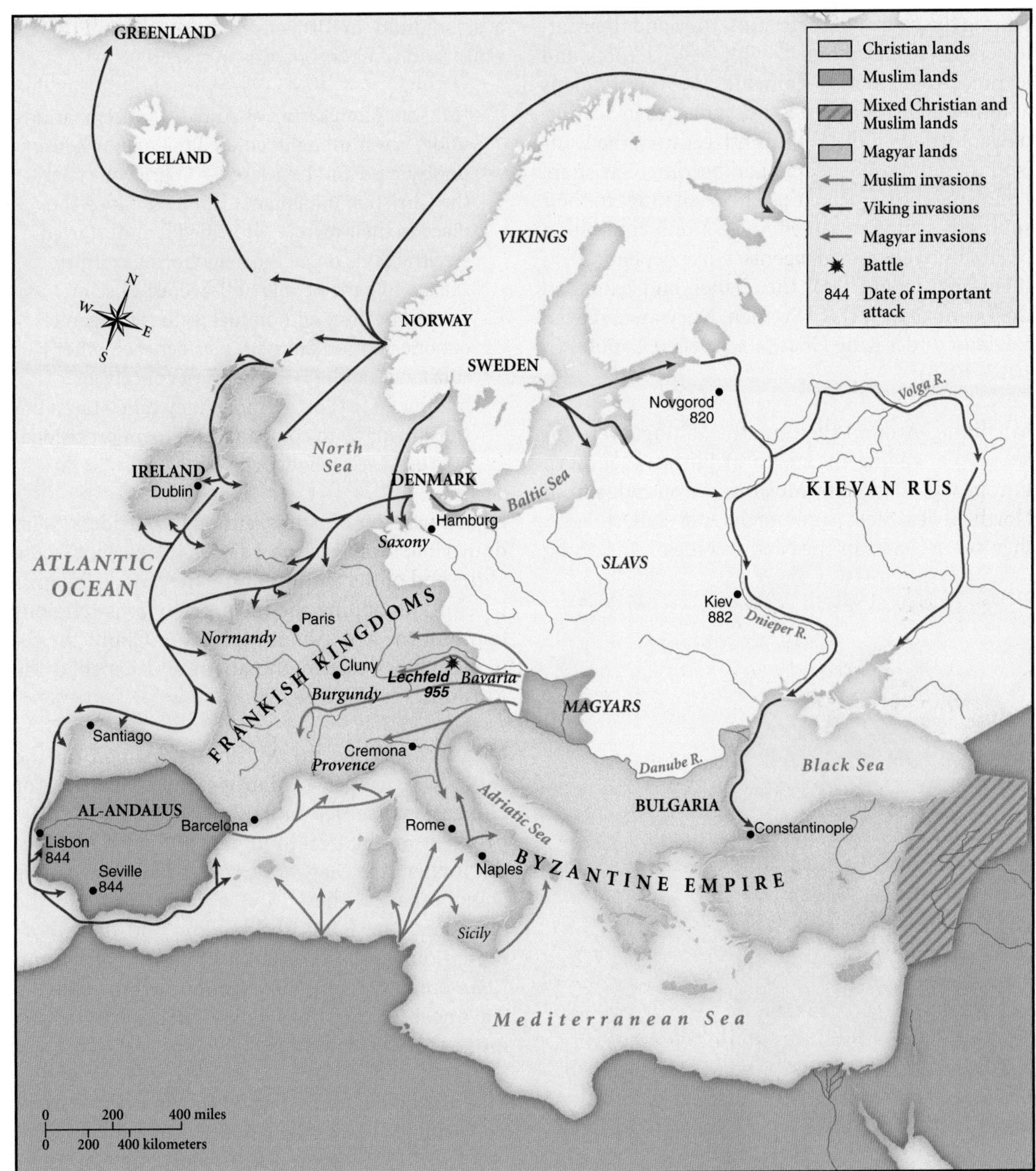

MAP 9.4 Muslim, Viking, and Magyar Invasions of the Ninth and Tenth Centuries

Bristling with arrows of different colors, this map suggests that western Europe was continually and thoroughly pillaged by invaders for almost two centuries. That impression, only partially true, must be offset by several factors. First, not all the invaders came at once. The Viking raids were nearly over when the Magyar attacks began. Second, the invaders were not entirely unwelcome. The Magyars were for a time enlisted as mercenaries by an Italian ruler, and some Muslims were allied to local lords in Provence. Third, the invasions, though widespread, were local in effect. Note, for example, that the Viking raids were largely limited to rivers or coastal areas. | **Why might the Vikings have raided primarily in these areas?**

911, the Frankish king Charles the Simple ceded the region to Rollo, the Viking leader there. In turn, Rollo converted to Christianity.

Normandy was not the only new Christian polity created in the north during the tenth and eleventh centuries. Scandinavia itself was transformed with the creation of the powerful kingdom of Denmark. There had been kings in Scandinavia before the tenth century, but they had been weak, their power challenged by nearby chieftains. The Vikings had been led by these chieftains, each competing for booty to win prestige, land, and power back home.

During the course of their raids, they and their followers came into contact with new cultures and learned from them. Meanwhile the Carolingians and the English supported missionaries in Scandinavia. By the middle of the tenth century, the Danish kings and their people had become Christian. Following the model of the Christian kings to their south, they built up an effective monarchy, with a royal mint and local agents who depended on them. By about 1000, the Danes had extended their control to parts of Sweden, Norway, and even England under King Cnut (also spelled Canute) (r. 1017–1035).

Muslims Around the time the Vikings were invading the north of Europe, southern Europe was attacked by Muslims. Adventurers from North Africa, Sicily, and northeastern al-Andalus, they set up bases in the Mediterranean, including a stronghold in Provence (in southern France). Liutprand of Cremona was outraged:

> [Muslim pirates from al-Andalus], disembarking under cover of night, entered the manor house unobserved and murdered — O grievous tale! — the Christian inhabitants. They then took the place as their own . . . [fortified it and] started stealthy raids on all the neighboring country. . . . Meanwhile the people of Provence close by, swayed by envy and mutual jealousy, began to cut one another's throats, plunder each other's substance, and do every sort of conceivable mischief. . . . [Furthermore, they called upon the Muslims] and in company with them proceeded to crush their neighbors.

In this way the Muslims, although outsiders, were drawn into local Provençal disputes. However, when, at the end of the tenth century, they made the mistake of kidnapping the most prestigious religious figure of the age, Abbot Maiolus of Cluny, the regional elites rescued the abbot and expelled the Muslims.

Magyars While the Muslims remained on the fringes of Europe, the Magyars (or Hungarians) settled in its very center. A nomadic people from the Ural Mountains (today northeastern Russia), the Magyars arrived around 899 in the Danube basin. They drove a wedge between the Slavs near the Frankish kingdom and those bordering on Byzantium. The Bulgarians, Serbs, and Rus were forced into the Byzantine orbit, while the Slavs nearer the Frankish kingdom came under the influence of Germany.

From their bases in present-day Hungary, the Magyars raided far to the west, attacking Germany, Italy, and even southern Gaul frequently between 899 and 955. Then in 955 the German king Otto I (r. 936–973) defeated a marauding party of Mag-

Viking Picture Stone
Picture stones — some elaborate, others with simple incisions — were made on the island of Gotland, today part of Sweden, from the fifth to the twelfth century. This one, dating from the eighth or ninth century, has four interrelated scenes. The bottom scene is a battle between people defending a farm and archers outside. The woman in the enclosure above is either Gudrun mourning her brother Gunnar, who was thrown into a snake pit, or Sigyn, the faithful wife of the god Loke, catching in a bowl the venom that a snake pours down on her chained husband. The ship in the next scene is the ship of death that takes heroes to Valhalla (heaven). At the very top is Valhalla, where the heroes hunt and feast for all eternity. *(The Granger Collection, NY—All rights reserved.)*

yars at the battle of Lechfeld. Otto's victory, his subsequent military reorganization of his eastern frontiers, and the cessation of Magyar raids around this time made Otto a great hero to his contemporaries. However, historians today think the containment of the Magyars had more to do with their internal transformation from nomads to farmers than with their military defeat. Soon they converted to the Roman form of Christianity. Hungary's position between East and West made it a frontier region, vulnerable to invasion and immigration, but also open to new experiments in assimilation and integration.

The Viking, Muslim, and Magyar invasions were the final onslaught western Europe experienced from outsiders. In some ways they were a continuation of the invasions that had rocked the Roman Empire in the fourth and fifth centuries. Loosely organized in war bands, the new groups entered western Europe looking for wealth but stayed on to become absorbed in the region's post-invasion society.

REVIEW QUESTION What were the strengths and weaknesses of Carolingian institutions of government, warfare, and defense?

After the Carolingians: The Emergence of Local Rule

The Carolingian Empire was too diverse to cohere. Although Latin was the language of official documents and most literary and ecclesiastical texts, few people spoke it; instead they used a wide variety of different languages and dialects. The king demanded loyalty from everyone, but most people knew only his representative, the local count. The king's power ultimately depended on the count's allegiance, but as the empire ceased to expand and came under attack by outsiders, the counts and other powerful men stopped looking to the king for new lands and offices and began to develop and exploit what they already had. Commanding allegiance from vassals, controlling the local peasantry, building castles, setting up markets, collecting revenues, and keeping the peace, they regarded themselves as independent regional rulers. In this way, a new warrior class of lords and vassals came to dominate post-Carolingian society.

Not all of Europe, however, came under the control of rural leaders. In northern and central Italy, where cities had never lost their importance, urban elites ruled over the surrounding countryside. Everywhere kings retained a certain amount of power; in some places, such as Germany and England, they were extremely effective. Central European monarchies formed under the influence of Germany.[2] Still, throughout this period, it was local allegiance—lord and vassal, castellan and peasant, bishop and layman—that mattered most to the societies of Europe.

Public Power and Private Relationships

Both kings and less powerful men commanded others through institutions designed to ensure personal loyalty. In the ninth century, the Carolingian kings had their *fideles* ("faithful men"), among whom were the counts. In addition to a share in the revenues of their administrative district—known as the county—counts received benefices, later also called **fiefs**, temporary grants of land given in return for service. These short-term arrangements often became permanent when a count's son inherited the job and the fiefs of his father. By the end of the ninth century, fiefs could often be passed on to heirs.

Vassals, Lords, and Ladies In the wake of the Viking, Magyar, and Muslim invasions, more and more warriors were drawn into networks of dependency, but not with the king: they became the faithful men—the vassals—of local lords. From the Latin *feodum* ("fief") comes the word *feudal*, and some historians call the social and economic system created by the relationship among vassals, lords, and fiefs **feudalism**. (See "Terms of History," page 298.)

Medieval people often said that their society consisted of three groups: those who prayed, those who fought, and those who worked. People of all these groups were involved in a hierarchy of depen-

---

[2]Names such as *Germany*, *France*, and *Italy* are used here for the sake of convenience. They refer to regions, not to the nation-states that would eventually become associated with those names.

fiefs: Grants of land, theoretically temporary, from lords to their noble dependents (*fideles* or, later, vassals) given in recognition of services, usually military, done or expected in the future; also called *benefices*.

feudalism: The whole complex of lords, vassals, and fiefs (from the Latin *feodum*) as an institution. The nature of that institution varied from place to place, and in some regions it did not exist at all.

TERMS OF HISTORY

Feudalism

Feudalism is a modern word, like *capitalism* and *communism*. No one in the Middle Ages used it, or any of its related terms, such as *feudal system* or *feudal society*. Many historians today think that it is a misleading word and should be discarded. The term poses two serious problems. First, historians have used it to mean different things. Second, it implies that one way of life dominated the Middle Ages, when in fact social, political, and economic arrangements varied widely.

Consider the many different meanings that *feudalism* has had. Historians influenced by Karl Marx's powerful communist theory used (and still use) the word *feudalism* to refer to an economic system in which nobles dominated subservient peasant cultivators. When they speak of feudalism, they are speaking of manors, lords, and serfs. Other historians, however, call that system *manorialism*. They reserve the word *feudalism* for a system consisting of vassals (who did no agricultural labor but only military service), lords, and fiefs. For example, in *Feudalism*, an influential book written in the mid-1940s, F. L. Ganshof considered the tenth to the thirteenth centuries to be the "classical age of feudalism" because during this period lords regularly granted fiefs to their vassals, who fought on their lord's behalf in return.

But, writing around the same time as Ganshof, Marc Bloch included in his definition of feudalism every aspect of the political and social life of the Middle Ages, including peasants, fiefs, knights, vassals, the fragmentation of royal authority, and even the survival of the state.

Today some historians argue that talking about feudalism distorts the realities of medieval life. The fief—whose Latin form, *feodum*, gave rise to the word *feudalism*—was by no means important everywhere. And even where it was important, it did not necessarily have anything to do with lords, vassals, or military obligations. For such historians, feudalism is a myth. Other historians, however, think that the term is extremely useful as long as its multiple forms are recognized. These historians are now starting to speak of "feudalisms"—in the plural.

dency and linked by personal bonds, but the upper classes—those who prayed (monks) and those who fought (knights)—were free. Their brand of dependency was prestigious, whether they were vassals, lords, or both. In fact, a typical warrior was lord of several vassals even while serving as the vassal of another lord. Monasteries normally had vassals to fight for them, and their abbots in turn were often vassals of a king or other powerful lord.

Vassalage served both as an alternative to public power and as a way to strengthen what little public power there was. Given the impoverished economic conditions of western Europe, its primitive methods of communication, and its lack of unifying traditions, kings relied on vassals personally loyal to them to muster troops, collect taxes, and administer justice. When in the ninth century the Carolingian Empire broke up politically and power fell into the hands of local lords, those lords, too, needed "faithful men" to protect them and carry out their orders. And vassals needed lords. At the low end of the social scale, poor vassals depended on their lords to feed, clothe, house, and arm them. They hoped that they would be rewarded for their service with a fief of their own, with which they could support themselves and a family. At the upper end of the social scale, landowning vassals looked to lords to give them still more land.

Many upper-class laywomen participated in the society of those who fought as wives and mothers of vassals and lords. A few women were themselves vassals, and some were lords (or, rather, ladies). Other women entered convents and joined the group of those who prayed. Through its abbess or a man standing in for her, a convent often had vassals as well. Many elite women engaged in property transactions, whether alone, with other family members, or as part of a group such as a convent. (See "Taking Measure," page 299.)

Becoming a vassal involved both ritual gestures and verbal promises. In a ceremony witnessed by others, the vassal-to-be knelt and, placing his hands between the hands of his lord, said, "I promise to be your man." This act, known as homage, was followed by the promise of fealty—fidelity, trust, and service—which the vassal swore with his hand on relics or a Bible. Then the vassal and the lord kissed. In an age when many people could not read, a public ceremony such as this represented a visual and verbal contract. Vassalage bound the lord and vassal to one another with reciprocal obligations, usually military. Knights, as the premier fighters of the day, were the most desirable vassals.

Lords and Peasants At the bottom of the social scale were those who worked—the peasants. In the Carolingian period, many peasants were free; they did not live on a manor or, if they did, they owed very little to its lord. (Manors like Villeneuve were the exceptions.) But as power fell into the hands of local rulers, fewer and fewer peasants remained free. Rather, they were made dependent on lords, not as vassals but as serfs. A serf's dependency was completely unlike that of a vassal. Serfdom was not voluntary but rather inherited. No serf did homage or fealty to his lord; no serf kissed his lord as an equal. Whereas vassals served their

TAKING MEASURE

Sellers, Buyers, and Donors, 800–1000

How did ladies get their wealth, and what did they do with it? Two counties in northeastern Spain, Osona and Manresa, are particularly rich in documentation for the period 880–1000. We have 2,121 charters (legal documents) attesting to sales, purchases, and donations of land from this period. As the graph shows, few women purchased property, which suggests that they gained their lands mainly through inheritance. As for what they did with it: by themselves they were more likely to sell property than men alone, and as part of a married couple, they were often involved in sales. They were less likely than men to make donations, many of which went to churches or monasteries.

Source: Lluís to Figueras, "Dot et douaire dans la société rurale de Catalogne," in *Dots et douaires dans le haut moyen âge*, ed. F. Bougard, L. Feller, and R. Le Jan (École française de Rome, 2002), 193, Table 1.

Question to Consider

- **How do you account for the differences between the ways in which women and men inherited and used their property?**

lords as warriors, serfs worked as laborers on their lord's land and paid taxes and dues to their lord. Peasants constituted the majority of the population, but unlike knights, who were celebrated in song, they were barely noticed by the upper classes—except as a source of revenue. While there were still free peasants who could lease land or till their own soil without paying dues to a lord, serfs—who could not be kicked off their land but who were also not free to leave it—became the norm.

New methods of cultivation and a slightly warmer climate helped transform the rural landscape, making it more productive and thus able to support a larger population. Along with a growing number of men and women to work the land, however, population increase meant more mouths to feed and the threat of food shortages. Landlords began reorganizing their estates to run more efficiently. In the tenth century, the three-field system became more prevalent; heavy plows that could turn wet, clayey northern soils came into wider use; and horses (more effective than oxen) were harnessed to pull the plows. The results were surplus food and a better standard of living for nearly everyone. (See the illustration on page 300.)

In search of greater profits, some lords lightened the dues and services of peasants to allow them to open up new lands by draining marshes and cutting down forests. Some landlords converted dues and labor services into money payments, a boon for both lords and peasants. Rather than getting hens and eggs they might not need, lords now received money to spend on what they wanted. Peasants benefited because their dues were fixed despite inflation. Thus, as the prices of their hens and eggs went up, they could sell them, reaping a profit in spite of the payments they owed their lords.

By the tenth century, many peasants had begun living in populous rural settlements, true villages. Surrounded by arable lands, meadows, woods, and wastelands, villages developed a sense of community. Boundaries—sometimes real fortifications,

Peasants at the Plow

When peasants used the three-field system, the month of January, which this illumination illustrates, was the month in which to start spring crops. The peasant at the plow guides it as the blade cuts into the soil. Behind him is another peasant, sowing seeds. Four oxen pull the plow, and a peasant ahead of the animals keeps them in line. *(akg-images/The British Library.)*

sometimes simple markers—told nonresidents to stay away or to find shelter in huts located outside the village limits.

The church often formed the focal point of village activity. There people met, received the sacraments, drew up contracts, and buried their dead. Religious feasts and festivals joined the rituals of farming to mark the seasons. The church dominated the village in another way: men and women owed it a tax called a tithe (one-tenth of their crops or income, paid in money or in kind), which was first instituted on a regular basis by the Carolingians.

Village peasants developed a sense of common purpose based on their interdependence, as they shared oxen or horses for the teams that pulled the plow or turned to village craftsmen to fix their wheels or shoe their horses. A sense of solidarity sometimes encouraged people to band together to ask for privileges as a group. Near Verona, in northern Italy, for example, twenty-five men living around the castle of Nogara joined together in 920 to ask their lord, the abbot of Nonantola, to allow them to lease plots of land, houses, and pasturage there in return for a small yearly rent and the promise to defend the castle. The abbot granted their request.

Village solidarity could be compromised, however, by conflicting loyalties and obligations. A peasant in one village might very well have one piece of land connected with a certain manor and another piece on a different estate; and he or she might owe several lords different kinds of dues. Even peasants of one village working for one lord might owe him varied services and taxes.

Obligations differed even more strikingly across the regions of Europe than within particular villages. The principal distinction was between free peasants—such as small landowners in Saxony and other parts of Germany, who had no lords—and serfs, who were especially common in France and England. In Italy, peasants ranged from small independent landowners to leaseholders (like the tenants at Nogara); most were both, owning a parcel in one place and leasing another nearby.

As the power of kings weakened, the system of peasant obligations became part of a larger system of local rule. When landlords consolidated their power over their manors, they collected not only dues and services but also fees for the use of their flour mills, bake houses, and breweries. Some built castles, fortified strongholds, collected taxes, heard court cases, levied fines, and mustered men for defense.

In France, for example, as the king's power waned, political control fell into the hands of counts and other princes. By 1000, castles had become the key to their power. In the south of France, power was so fragmented that each man who controlled a castle—a **castellan**—was a virtual ruler, although

---

castellan (KAS tuh luhn): The holder of a castle. In the tenth and eleventh centuries, castellans became important local lords. They mustered men for military service, collected taxes, and administered justice.

often with a very limited reach. In northwestern France, territorial princes, basing their rule on the control of many castles, dominated much broader regions. For example, Fulk Nera, count of Anjou (987–1040), built more than thirteen castles and captured others from rival counts. By the end of his life, he controlled a region extending from Blois to Nantes along the Loire valley.

Castellans extended their authority by subjecting everyone near their castle to them. Peasants, whether or not they worked on his estates, had to pay the castellan a variety of dues for his "protection" and judicial rights over them. Castellans also established links with wealthy landholders in the region, tempting or coercing them to become vassals. Lay castellans often supported local monasteries and controlled the appointment of local priests. But churchmen themselves sometimes held the position of territorial lord, as did, for example, the archbishop of Milan in the eleventh century.

The development of virtually independent local political units, dominated by a castle and controlled by a military elite, marks an important turning point in western Europe. Although this development did not occur everywhere simultaneously (and in some places it hardly occurred at all), the social, political, and cultural life of Europe was now dominated by landowners who were both military men and regional rulers.

Warriors and Warfare

Not all medieval warriors were alike. At the top of this elite group were the kings, counts, and dukes. Below them, but on the rise, were the castellans; and still further down the social scale were ordinary knights. Yet all shared in a common lifestyle.

Knights and their lords fought on horseback. High astride his steed, wearing a shirt of chain mail and a helmet of flat metal plates riveted together, the knight marked a military revolution. The war season started in May, when the grasses were high enough for horses to forage. Horseshoes allowed armies to move faster than ever before and to negotiate rough terrain previously unsuitable for battle. Stirrups, probably invented by nomadic Asiatic tribes, allowed the mounted warrior to hold his seat and thrust at the enemy with heavy lances. The light javelin of ancient Roman warfare was abandoned.

Lords and their vassals often lived together. In the lord's great hall they ate, listened to entertainment, and bedded down for the night. They went out hunting together, competed with one another in military games, and went off to the battlefield as a group. Some powerful vassals—counts, for example—lived on their own fiefs. They hardly ever saw their lord (probably the king), except when doing homage and fealty—once in their lifetime—or serving him in battles, for perhaps forty days a year (as was the custom in eleventh-century France). But they themselves were lords of knightly vassals who were not married and who lived and ate and hunted with them.

No matter how old they might be, unmarried knights who lived with their lords were called youths by their contemporaries. Such perpetual bachelors were something new, the result of a profound transformation in the organization of families and inheritance. Before about 1000, noble families had recognized all their children as heirs and had divided their estates accordingly. In the mid-ninth century, Count Everard and his wife, for example, willed their large estates, scattered from Belgium to Italy, to their four sons and three daughters (although they gave the boys far more than the girls, and the oldest boy far more than the others).

By 1000, however, adapting to diminished opportunities for land and office and wary of fragmenting the estates they had, French nobles changed both their conception of their family and the way property passed to the next generation. Recognizing the overriding claims of one son, often the eldest, they handed down their entire inheritance to him. (The system of inheritance in which the heir is the eldest son is called **primogeniture**.) The heir, in turn, traced his lineage only through the male line, backward through his father and forward through his own eldest son. Such **patrilineal** families left many younger sons without an inheritance and therefore without the prospect of marrying and founding a family; instead, the younger sons lived at the courts of the great as youths, or they joined the church as clerics or monks. The development of territorial rule and patrilineal families went hand in hand, as fathers passed down to one son not only manors but also titles, castles, and the authority of the ban.

Patrilineal inheritance tended to bypass daughters and so worked against aristocratic women, who lost the power that came with inherited wealth. In families without sons, however, widows and daughters did inherit property. And wives often acted as lords of estates when their husbands were at war. Moreover, all aristocratic women played an important role in this warrior society, whether in the

---

primogeniture: An inheritance practice that left all property to the oldest son.

patrilineal: Relating to or tracing descent through the paternal line (for example, through the father and grandfather).

monastery (where they prayed for the souls of their families) or through their marriages (where they produced children and helped forge alliances between their own natal families and the families of their husbands).

Efforts to Contain Violence

The rise of the castellans meant an increase in violence. Supported by their knights, castellans were keen to maintain their new authority over the peasants in their vicinity in the face of older regional powers, like counts and dukes. Threatened from below, those higher-ranking authorities looked to the bishops for help. The bishops, themselves resentful of local castellan claims and, moreover, generally members of the same elite families as counts and dukes, were glad to oblige. To do so, they enlisted the lower classes—peasants who were tired of wars that destroyed their crops or forced them to join regional infantries. The result was the **Peace of God**, which united bishops, counts, and peasants in an attempt to contain local violence. The movement began in the south of France around 990 and by 1050 had spread over a wide region. At impassioned meetings of bishops, lords, and crowds of enthusiastic men and women, the clergy set forth the provisions of this peace. "No man in the counties or bishoprics shall seize a horse, colt, ox, cow, ass, or the burdens which it carries. . . . No one shall seize a peasant, man or woman," ran the decree of one early council. Anyone who violated this peace was to be excommunicated: cut off from the community of the faithful, denied the services of the church and the hope of salvation.

The Peace of God proclaimed at local councils like this limited some violence but did not address the problem of conflict between armed men. A second set of agreements, the Truce of God, soon supplemented the peace. The truce prohibited fighting between warriors at certain times: on Sunday because it was the Lord's day, on Saturday because it was a reminder of Holy Saturday, on Friday because it symbolized Good Friday, and on Thursday because it stood for Holy Thursday. Enforcement of the truce fell to the local knights and nobles, who swore over saints' relics to uphold it and to fight anyone who broke it.

The Peace of God and the Truce of God were only two of the mechanisms that attempted to contain or defuse violent confrontations in the tenth and eleventh centuries. At times, lords and their vassals mediated wars and feuds at grand judicial assemblies. In other instances, monks or laymen tried to find solutions to disputes that would leave the honor of both parties intact. Rather than establishing guilt or innocence, winners or losers, these methods of adjudication often resulted in compromises on both sides.

Peace of God: A movement begun by bishops in the south of France around 990, first to limit the violence done to property and to the unarmed, and later, with the Truce of God, to limit fighting between warriors.

Political Communities in Italy, England, and France

The political systems that emerged following the breakup of the Carolingian Empire were as varied as the regions of Europe. In northern and central Italy, cities were the centers of power, still reflecting, if feebly, the political organization of ancient Rome. In England, strong kings came to the fore. In France, where the king was relatively weak, great lords dominated the countryside.

Urban Power in Northern and Central Italy Unlike their counterparts in France, where great landlords built their castles in the countryside, Italian elites tended to construct their family castles within the walls of cities such as Milan and Lucca. Also built within the city walls were churches—as many as fifty or sixty—the proud work of rich laymen and laywomen or of bishops. Although residing in the city, these elites normally controlled the land and people in the surrounding countryside.

Italian cities also served as marketplaces where peasants sold their surplus goods, artisans and merchants lived, and foreign traders offered their wares. These members of the lower classes were supported by the wealthy elite, who depended, here more than elsewhere, on cash to satisfy their desires. In the course of the ninth and tenth centuries, the peasants in the countryside became renters who paid in currency, helping meet their landlords' need for cash.

Family organization in Italy was quite different from that of the patrilineal families of France. To stave off the partitioning of its properties among heirs, the Italian family became a kind of economic corporation in which all male members shared the profits of the family's inheritance and all women were excluded. In the coming centuries, this successful model would also serve as the foundation of most early Italian businesses and banks.

Alfred and His Successors: Kings of All the English Whereas much of Italy was urban, most of England was rural. Having successfully repelled the Viking invaders, **Alfred the Great**, king of Wessex (r. 871–899), developed new mechanisms of royal government, instituting reforms that his successors continued. He fortified settlements throughout Wessex and divided the army into two parts, one with the duty of defending these fortifications, the other operating as a mobile unit. Alfred also started a navy. The money to pay for these military innovations came from assessments on peasants' holdings.

Along with its regional fortifications, Alfred sought to strengthen his kingdom's religious integrity. In the ninth century, people interpreted invasions as God's punishment for sin. Hence, Alfred began a program of religious reform by bringing scholars to his court. Above all, Alfred wanted to translate key religious works from Latin into Anglo-Saxon (or Old English). He was determined to "turn into the language that we can all understand certain books which are the most necessary for all men to know." Alfred and the scholars under his guidance translated works by church fathers such as Gregory the Great and St. Augustine. Even the Psalms, until now sung only in Hebrew, Greek, and Latin, were rendered into Anglo-Saxon. In most of ninth- and tenth-century Europe, Latin remained the language of scholarship, government, and writing, separate from the language people spoke. In England, however, the vernacular—the common spoken language—was also a literary language. With Alfred's reign giving it greater legitimacy, Anglo-Saxon came to be used alongside Latin for both literature and royal administration.

Alfred's reforms strengthened not only defense, education, and religion but also royal power. He consolidated his control over Wessex and fought the Danish kings, who by the mid-870s had taken Northumbria, northeastern Mercia, and East Anglia. Eventually, as he successfully fought the Danes who were pushing south and westward, he was recognized as king of all the English not under Danish rule. He issued a law code, the first by an English king since 695. Unlike earlier codes, which had been drawn up for each separate kingdom of England, Alfred drew his laws from and for all of the English kingdoms. In this way, Alfred became the first king of all the English.

Alfred's successors rolled back the Danish rule in England. "Then the Norsemen departed in their nailed ships, bloodstained survivors of spears," wrote one poet about a battle the Vikings lost in 937. But many Vikings remained. Converted to Christianity, their great men joined Anglo-Saxons in attending the English king at court. As peace returned, new administrative subdivisions for judicial and tax purposes were established throughout England: shires (the English equivalent of counties) and hundreds (smaller units). The powerful men of the kingdom swore fealty to the king, promising to be enemies of his enemies, friends of his friends. England was united and organized to support a strong ruler.

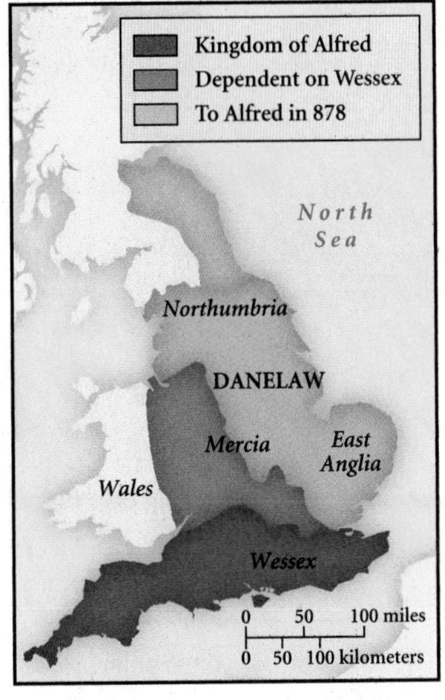

England in the Age of King Alfred, 871–899

Alfred's grandson Edgar (r. 957–975) commanded all the possibilities early medieval kingship offered. He was the sworn lord of all the great men of the kingdom. He controlled appointments to the English church and sponsored monastic reform. In 973, following the continental fashion, he was anointed king. The fortifications of the kingdom were in his hands, as was the army, and he took responsibility for keeping the peace by proclaiming certain crimes—arson and theft—to be under his special jurisdiction and by mobilizing the machinery of the shire and the hundred to find and punish thieves.

Despite its apparent centralization, England was not a unified state in the modern sense, and the king's control was often tenuous. Many royal officials were great landowners who (as on the continent) worked for the king because it was in their best interest. When it was not, they allied with different claimants to the throne. This political fragility may have helped the Danish king Cnut to conquer England. As king there from 1017 to 1035, Cnut reinforced the already strong connections between England and Scandinavia while keeping intact much of the administrative, ecclesiastical, and military apparatus already established in England by the Anglo-Saxons. By Cnut's time, Scandinavian traditions had largely merged with those of the rest of Europe and the Vikings were no longer an alien culture.

Capetian Kings of Franks: Weak but Prestigious French kings had a harder time than the English coping with invasions because their realm was much larger. They had no chance to build up their defenses slowly from one powerful base. During most of the tenth century, Carolin-

Alfred the Great: King of Wessex (r. 871–899) and the first king to rule over most of England. He organized a successful defense against Viking invaders, had key Latin works translated into the vernacular, and wrote a law code for the whole of England.

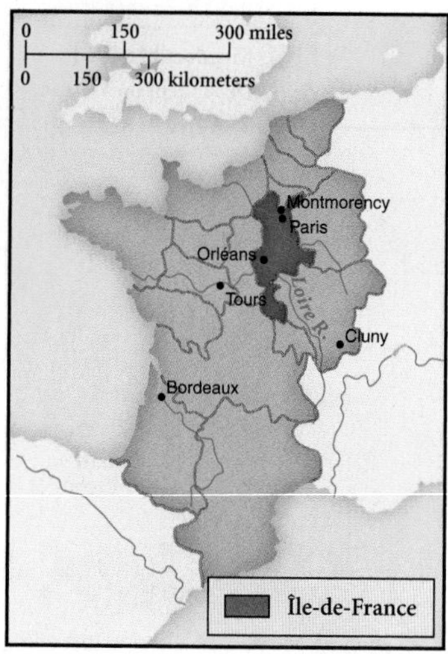

The Kingdom of the Franks under Hugh Capet, 987–996

gian kings alternated on the throne with kings from a family that would later be called the Capetian. As the Carolingian dynasty waned, the most powerful men of the kingdom—dukes, counts, and important bishops—came together to elect as king Hugh Capet (r. 987–996), a lord of great prestige yet relatively little power. His choice marked the end of Carolingian rule and the beginning of the **Capetian dynasty**, which would hand down the royal title from father to son until the fourteenth century.

In the eleventh century, territorial lordships limited the reach of the Capetian kings. The king's scattered but substantial estates lay in the north of France, in the region around Paris—the Île-de-France ("island of France"). His castles and his vassals were there. Independent castellans, however, controlled areas nearby. In the sense that he was a neighbor of castellans and not much more powerful militarily than they, the king of the Franks—who would only later take the territorial title of king of France—was just another local leader. Yet the Capetian kings had considerable prestige. They were anointed with holy oil, and they represented the idea of unity inherited from Charlemagne. Most of the counts, at least in the north of France, became their vassals. They did not promise to obey the king, but they did vow not to try to kill or depose him.

Emperors and Kings in Central and Eastern Europe

In contrast to the development of territorial lordships in France, Germany's fragmentation had hardly begun before it was reversed. The **Ottonian kings** of Germany consolidated their rule there; took the title *emperor*; and then, hand in hand with the papacy, fostered the emergence of new Christian monarchies. Aligned with the Roman church, these new kingdoms were the ancestors of today's Czech and Slovak Republics, Poland, and Hungary.

Ottonian Power in Germany

Five duchies (regions dominated by dukes) emerged in Germany in the late Carolingian period, each much larger than the counties and castellanies of France. When Louis the Child, the last Carolingian king in Germany, died in 911, the dukes elected one of themselves as king. Then, as the Magyar invasions increased, the dukes gave the royal title to the duke of Saxony, Henry I (r. 919–936), who proceeded to set up fortifications and reorganize his army, crowning his efforts with a major defeat of a Magyar army in 933.

Otto I (r. 936–973), the son of Henry I, was an even greater military hero. In 951, he marched into Italy and took the Lombard crown. His defeat of the Magyar forces in 955 at Lechfeld gave him prestige and helped solidify his dynasty. Against the Slavs, with whom the Germans shared a border, Otto created marches (border regions specifically set up for defense) from which he could make expeditions and stave off counterattacks. After the pope crowned him emperor in 962, Otto claimed the Middle Kingdom carved out by the Treaty of Verdun and cast himself as the agent of Roman imperial renewal. His kingdom was called "the Empire," as if it were the old Roman Empire revived. Some historians call it the "Holy Roman Empire" to distinguish it from the Roman Empire. But Otto and his successors never distinguished it from the Roman Empire; they considered it a continuation. In this book, it will be called the Empire.

Otto's victories brought tribute and plunder, ensuring him a following but also raising the German nobles' expectations for enrichment. He and his successors—including Otto II (r. 973–983) and Otto III (r. 983–1002), for which reason the dynasty is called the Ottonian—were not always able or willing to provide the gifts and inheritances their family members and followers expected. To maintain centralized rule, for example, the Ottonians did not divide their kingdom among their sons: like castellans in France, they created a patrilineal pattern of inheritance. But the consequence was that younger sons and other potential heirs felt cheated, and disgruntled royal kin led revolt after revolt against the Ottonian kings. The rebels found followers among the aristocracy, where the trend toward the patrilineal family prompted similar feuds and thwarted expectations.

Relations between the Ottonians and the German clergy were more harmonious. With a ribbon of new bishoprics along his eastern border, Otto I

Capetian (kuh PAY shuhn) dynasty: A long-lasting dynasty of French kings, taking their name from Hugh Capet (r. 987–996).

Ottonian (ah TOH nee uhn) kings: The tenth- and early-eleventh-century kings of Germany; beginning with Otto I (r. 936–973), they claimed the imperial crown and worked closely with their bishops to rule a vast territory.

Otto III Receiving Gifts

This triumphal image is in a book of Gospels made for Otto III (r. 983–1002). The crowned women on the left are personifications of the four parts of Otto's empire: Sclavinia (the Slavic lands), Germania (Germany), Gallia (Gaul), and Roma (Rome). Each offers a gift in tribute and homage to the emperor, who sits on a throne holding the symbols of his power (orb and scepter) and flanked by representatives of the church (on his right) and of the army (on his left). Why do you suppose the artist separated the image of the emperor from that of the women? What does the body language of the women indicate about the relations Otto wanted to portray between himself and the parts of his empire? Can you relate this manuscript, which was made in 997–1000, to Otto's conquest over the Slavs in 997? *(bpk, Berlin/Bayerische Staasbibliothek, Munich, Germany/Art Resource, NY.)*

appointed bishops, gave them extensive lands, and subjected the local peasantry to their overlordship. Like Charlemagne, Otto believed that the well-being of the church in his kingdom depended on him. The Ottonians placed the churches and many monasteries of Germany under their control. They gave bishops the powers of the ban, allowing them to collect revenues and call men to arms. Answering to the king and furnishing him with troops, the bishops became royal officials, while also carrying out their religious duties. German kings claimed the right to select bishops, even the pope at Rome, and to "invest" them (install them in their office) by participating in the ceremony that made them bishops. The higher clergy joined royal court society. Most came to the court to be schooled; in turn, they taught the kings, princes, and noblewomen there.

Like all the strong rulers of the day, whether in Europe or in the Byzantine and Islamic worlds, the Ottonians presided over a renaissance of learning. For example, the tutor of Otto III was Gerbert, the best-educated man of his time. Placed on the papal throne as Pope Sylvester II (r. 999–1003), Gerbert knew how to use the abacus and to calculate with Arabic numerals. He spent "large sums of money to pay copyists and to acquire copies of authors," as he put it. He studied the Latin classics as models of rhetoric and argument, and he reveled in logic and debate. Not only did churchmen and kings support Ottonian scholarship, but to an unprecedented extent noblewomen in Germany also acquired an education and participated in the intellectual revival. Aristocratic women spent much of their wealth on learning. Living at home with their kinfolk and servants or in convents that provided them with comfortable

The Ottonian Empire, 936–1002

private apartments, noblewomen wrote books and occasionally even Roman-style plays. They also supported other artists and scholars.

Despite their military and political strength, the kings of Germany faced resistance from dukes and other powerful princes, who hoped to become regional rulers themselves. The Salians, the dynasty that succeeded the Ottonians, tried to balance the power among the German dukes but could not meld them into a corps of vassals the way the Capetian kings tamed their counts. In Germany, vassalage was considered beneath the dignity of free men. Instead of relying on vassals, the Salian kings and their bishops used ministerials (specially designated men who were legally serfs) to collect taxes, administer justice, and fight on horseback. Ministerials retained their servile status even though they often rose to wealth and high position. Under the Salian kings, ministerials became the mainstay of the royal army and administration.

Supported by their prestige, their churchmen, and their ministerials, the German kings expanded their influence eastward, into the region from the Elbe River to Russia. Otto I was so serious about expansion that he created an extraordinary "elastic" archbishopric: it had no eastern boundary, so it could extend as far as future conquests and conversions to Christianity would allow.

The Emergence of Catholic Bohemia, Poland, and Hungary

Hand in hand with the popes, German kings insisted on the creation of new, Catholic polities along their eastern frontier. The Czechs, who lived in the region of Bohemia, converted under the rule of Václav (r. 920–929), who thereby gained recognition in Germany as the duke of Bohemia. He and his successors did not become kings, remaining politically within the German sphere. Václav's murder by his younger brother made him a martyr and the patron saint of Bohemia, a symbol around which later movements for independence rallied.

The Poles gained a greater measure of independence than the Czechs. In 966, Mieszko I (r. 963–992), the leader of the Slavic tribe known as the Polanians, accepted baptism to forestall the attack that the Germans were already mounting against pagan Slavic peoples along the Baltic coast and east of the Elbe River. Busily engaged in bringing the other Slavic tribes of Poland under his control, Mieszko adroitly shifted his alliances with various German princes to suit his needs. In 991, he placed his realm under the protection of the pope, establishing a tradition of Polish loyalty to the Roman church. Mieszko's son Boleslaw the Brave (r. 992–1025) greatly extended Poland's boundaries, at one time or another holding sway from the Bohemian border to Kiev. In 1000, he gained a royal crown with papal blessing.

Hungary's case was similar to that of Poland. As we have seen, the Magyars settled in the region known today as Hungary. Under Stephen I (r. 997–1038), they accepted Roman Christianity. According to legend, the crown placed on Stephen's head at his coronation (in late 1000 or early 1001) was sent to him by the pope. Stephen was canonized in 1083, and to this day the crown of St. Stephen remains the most hallowed symbol of Hungarian nationhood.

Symbols of rulership such as crowns, consecrated by Christian priests and accorded a prestige almost akin to saints' relics, were among the most vital sources of royal power in central Europe. The economic basis for the power of central European rulers was largely agricultural. As happened elsewhere, here too centralized rule gradually gave way to regional rulers.

REVIEW QUESTION After the dissolution of the Carolingian Empire, what political systems developed in western, northern, eastern, and central Europe, and how did these systems differ from one another?

Conclusion

In 800, the three heirs of the Roman Empire all appeared to be organized like their parent: centralized, monarchical, imperial. Byzantine emperors writing their learned books, Abbasid caliphs holding court in their new resplendent palace at Baghdad, and Carolingian emperors issuing their directives for reform all mimicked the Roman emperors. Yet leaders in the three realms confronted tensions and regional pressures that tended to put political power into the hands of local lords. Byzantium felt this fragmentation least, yet even there the emergence of a new elite, the *dynatoi*, weakened the emperor's control over the countryside. In the Islamic world, quarrels between Abbasid heirs, army disloyalty, economic weakness, and the ambitions of powerful local rulers decisively weakened the caliphate and opened the way to separate successor states. In Europe, powerful independent landowners strove with greater or lesser success (depending on the region) to establish themselves as effective rulers. By 1050, most of the states of modern Europe — western, central, and eastern — had begun to form.

In western Europe, local conditions determined political and economic organizations. Between 900

MAPPING THE WEST

Europe and the Mediterranean, c. 1050

The clear borders and distinct colors of the "states" on this map distort an essential truth: none of the areas shown had centralized governments that controlled whole territories, as in modern states. Instead, there were numerous regional rulers within each, and there were often competing claims of jurisdiction and conflicting allegiances. Consider Sicily: it was conquered by Muslims in the tenth century, but by 1060 it had been taken over by the Normans—adventurers from Normandy (in France). Its predominantly Greek-speaking population, however, was Greek Orthodox in religion, a legacy of its Byzantine past.

and 1000, for example, French society was transformed by the rise of castellans, the formation of patrilineal families, and the spread of ties of vassalage. These factors figured less prominently in Germany, where a central monarchy remained, buttressed by churchmen, ministerials, and conquests to the east.

After 1050, however, the German king would lose his supreme position as a storm of church reform whirled around him. The economy changed, becoming more commercial and urban, and the papacy asserted itself with new force in the life of Europe.

FOR FURTHER EXPLORATION

- **For additional primary-source material from this period**, see *Sources of the Making of the West*, Fourth Edition.
- **For Web sites, images, and documents related to topics in this chapter**, visit *Make History* at bedfordstmartins.com/hunt.

Chapter 9 Review

Online Study Guide bedfordstmartins.com/hunt

Key Terms and People

In the grid below, identify the term or person and explain its historical significance. (To do this exercise online, go to bedfordstmartins.com/hunt.)

Term	Who or What & When	Why It Matters
dynatoi (p. 280)		
Basil II (p. 281)		
Abbasids (p. 283)		
Fatimids (p. 284)		
Carolingian (p. 287)		
Charlemagne (p. 287)		
Treaty of Verdun (p. 292)		
fiefs (p. 297)		
feudalism (p. 297)		
castellan (p. 300)		
primogeniture (p. 301)		
patrilineal (p. 301)		
Peace of God (p. 302)		
Alfred the Great (p. 303)		
Capetian dynasty (p. 304)		
Ottonian kings (p. 304)		

Review Questions

1. In what ways did the Byzantine emperor expand his power, and in what ways was that power checked?
2. What forces contributed to the fragmentation of the Islamic world in the tenth and eleventh centuries, and what forces held it together?
3. What were the strengths and weaknesses of Carolingian institutions of government, warfare, and defense?
4. After the dissolution of the Carolingian Empire, what political systems developed in western, northern, eastern, and central Europe, and how did these systems differ from one another?

Making Connections

1. How were the Byzantine, Islamic, and European economies similar? How did they differ? How did these economies interact?
2. How did the powers and ambitions of castellans compare with those of the dynatoi of Byzantium and of Muslim provincial rulers?
3. Compare the effects of the barbarian invasions into the Roman Empire with the effects of the Viking, Muslim, and Magyar invasions into Carolingian Europe.

Important Events

Date	Event	Date	Event
750–c. 950	The Abbasid caliphate	929–1031	Caliphate of Córdoba
751	Pippin III becomes king of the Franks, establishing Carolingian rule	955	Battle of Lechfeld
768–814	Charlemagne rules as king of the Franks	962	King Otto I (r. 936–973) of Germany crowned emperor
786–809	Caliphate of Harun al-Rashid	987–996	Reign of King Hugh Capet of France
800	Charlemagne crowned emperor at Rome	c. 990	Peace of God movement begins
843	Treaty of Verdun	1000 or 1001	Stephen I (r. 997–1038) crowned king of Hungary
871–899	Reign of King Alfred of England	1001–1018	Byzantine conquest of Bulgaria

- Consider two events: **Peace of God movement begins (c. 990)** and **Stephen I (r. 997–1038) crowned King of Hungary (1000 or 1001)**. How do these events illustrate Christianity's ability to unify and mobilize people in this era?

SUGGESTED REFERENCES

A few books, like Brubaker and Smith's, try to bridge the divides between the Byzantine, Islamic, and western European worlds. Nevertheless, for the most part these regions are treated separately. For Byzantium, Whittow is essential. For insight into the Islamic world, see especially Cooperson. For the Carolingian world, De Jong provides a new approach. For the post-Carolingian West, see Head and Landes, who value fragmentation and the diversity of developments that it permitted.

Becher, Matthias. *Charlemagne.* 2003.

Berend, Nora. *At the Gate of Christendom: Jews, Muslims, and "Pagans" in Medieval Hungary, c. 1000–c. 1300.* 2001.

Brubaker, Leslie, and Julia M. H. Smith. *Gender in the Early Medieval World: East and West, 300–900.* 2004.

**Chronicle of Zuqnin, Parts III and IV, A.D. 488–775.* Trans. Amir Harrak. 1999.

Cooperson, Michael. *Al Ma'mun.* 2005.

De Jong, Mayke. *The Penitential State: Authority and Atonement in the Age of Louis the Pious, 814–840.* 2009.

Duby, Georges. *The Early Growth of the European Economy: Warriors and Peasants from the Seventh to the Twelfth Century.* Trans. H. B. Clark. 1974.

*Dutton, Paul Edward, ed. *Carolingian Civilization: A Reader.* 1993.

*———, ed. and trans. *Charlemagne's Courtier: The Complete Einhard.* 1998.

*Einhard and Notker the Stammerer. *Two Lives of Charlemagne.* Trans. Lewis Thorpe. 1969.

Fine, Jon V. A., Jr. *The Early Medieval Balkans: A Critical Survey from the Sixth to the Late Twelfth Century.* 1983.

Franklin, Simon, and Jonathan Shepard. *The Emergence of Rus, 750–1200.* 1996.

Garver, Valerie L. *Women and Aristocratic Culture in the Carolingian World.* 2009.

Head, Thomas, and Richard Landes, eds. *The Peace of God: Social Violence and Religious Response in France around the Year 1000.* 1992.

Jones, Anna Trumbore. *Noble Lord, Good Shepherd: Episcopal Power and Piety in Aquitaine, 877–1050.* 2009.

Kennedy, Hugh. *The Armies of the Caliphs: Military and Society in the Early Islamic State.* 2001.

Maguire, Henry, ed. *Byzantine Court Culture from 829 to 1204.* 1997.

*Psellus, Michael. *Fourteen Byzantine Rulers: The Chronographia.* Trans. E. R. A. Sewter. 1966.

Sweeney, Del, ed. *Agriculture in the Middle Ages: Technology, Practice, and Representation.* 1995.

Whittow, Mark. *The Making of Byzantium, 600–1025.* 1996.

*Primary source.

CHAPTER 10

Commercial Quickening and Religious Reform

1050–1150

In the middle of the twelfth century, a sculptor was hired to add some friezes depicting scenes from the Old and New Testaments to the facade of the grand new hilltop cathedral at Lincoln, England. He portrayed in striking fashion the deaths of the poor man Lazarus and the rich man Dives. Their fates could not have been more different. While Lazarus was carried to heaven by two angels, a contented-looking devil poked Dives and two other rich men straight into the mouth of hell—headfirst.

The sculptor's work reflected a widespread change in attitude toward money. In the Carolingian and post-Carolingian period (up to, say, 1050), wealth was considered, in general, a very good thing. Rich kings were praised for their generosity; expensively produced manuscripts, illuminated with gold leaf and precious colors, were highly prized; and splendid churches like Charlemagne's chapel at Aachen were widely admired. Such views changed over the course of the eleventh century.

The most striking feature of the period 1050–1150 was the rise of a money economy in western Europe. Agricultural production swelled, fueling the growth of trade and the expansion of cities. A new class of well-heeled merchants, bankers, and entrepreneurs emerged. These developments were met with a wide variety of responses. Some people fled the cities and their new wealth altogether, seeking isolation and poverty. Others, even the participants in the new economy, condemned it and emphasized its corrupting influence: Lincoln's new cathedral was built right next to a marketplace, and its twelfth-century bishops—who were themselves rich men—wanted to warn moneymaking parishioners about the perils of wealth. Most people embraced the new money economy, however—some eagerly, others cautiously.

Dives and Lazarus
At the time this sculpted depiction of Dives and Lazarus was made, the town of Lincoln was expanding both within and without its Roman walls. Within the walls were the precincts of the fishmongers, the grain sellers, and the poultry merchants. Outside the walls were the bakers, the soapmakers, and the salt sellers. The town was highly attuned to moneymaking—both its pleasures and its dangers. *(Conway Library, The Courtauld Institute of Art, London.)*

The development of a profit-based economy quickly transformed the landscape and lifestyles of western Europe. Many villages and fortifications became cities where traders, merchants, and artisans conducted business. In some places, town dwellers began to determine their own laws and administer their own justice. Although most people still lived in sparsely populated rural areas, their lives were touched in many ways by the new cash economy. Economic concerns helped drive changes within the church, where a movement for reform gathered steam and exploded in three directions: the Investiture Conflict, new monastic orders emphasizing poverty, and the crusades. Money even helped popes, kings, and princes redefine the nature of their power.

CHAPTER FOCUS How did the commercial revolution affect religion and politics?

The Commercial Revolution

As the population of Europe continued to expand in the eleventh century, cities, long-distance trade networks, local markets, and new business arrangements meshed to create a profit-based economy. With improvements in agriculture and more land in cultivation, the great estates of the eleventh century produced surpluses that helped feed—and therefore make possible—a new urban population.

Commerce was not new to the history of western Europe, but the **commercial revolution** of the Middle Ages spawned the institutions that would be the direct ancestors of modern businesses: corporations, banks, accounting systems, and, above all, urban centers that thrived on economic vitality. Whereas ancient cities had primarily religious, social, and political functions, medieval cities were centers of production and economic activity. Wealth meant power: it allowed city dwellers to become self-governing.

commercial revolution: A term for the western European development (starting around 1050) of a money economy centered in urban areas but affecting the countryside as well.

Fairs, Towns, and Cities

The commercial revolution took place in three venues: markets, fairs, and permanent centers. In some places, markets met weekly to sell local surplus goods. In others, fairs—which lasted anywhere from several days to a few months—took place once a year and drew traders from longer distances (Map 10.1). Some fairs specialized in particular goods: at Skania, in southern Sweden, the chief product was herring. At Saint-Denis, a monastery near Paris that had had a fair since at least the seventh century, the star attraction was wine. Most fairs offered a wide variety of products: at six different fairs in Champagne, merchants arrived from Flanders with woolen fabrics, from Lucca with silks, from Spain with leather goods, from Germany with furs. Bankers attended as well, exchanging coins from one currency into another—and charging for their services. (Sometimes, the currency was in peppercorns or other spices; see Document, "Peppercorns as Money," page 314.) Local inhabitants did not have to pay taxes or tolls, but traders from the outside—protected by guarantees of safe conduct—were charged stall fees as well as entry and exit fees. Local landlords reaped great profits, and as the fairs came under royal control, kings did so as well.

Permanent commercial centers—cities and towns—developed around castles and monasteries and within the walls of ancient Roman towns.

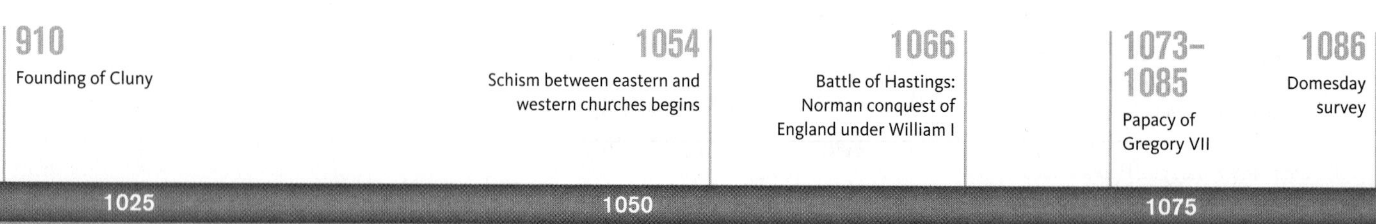

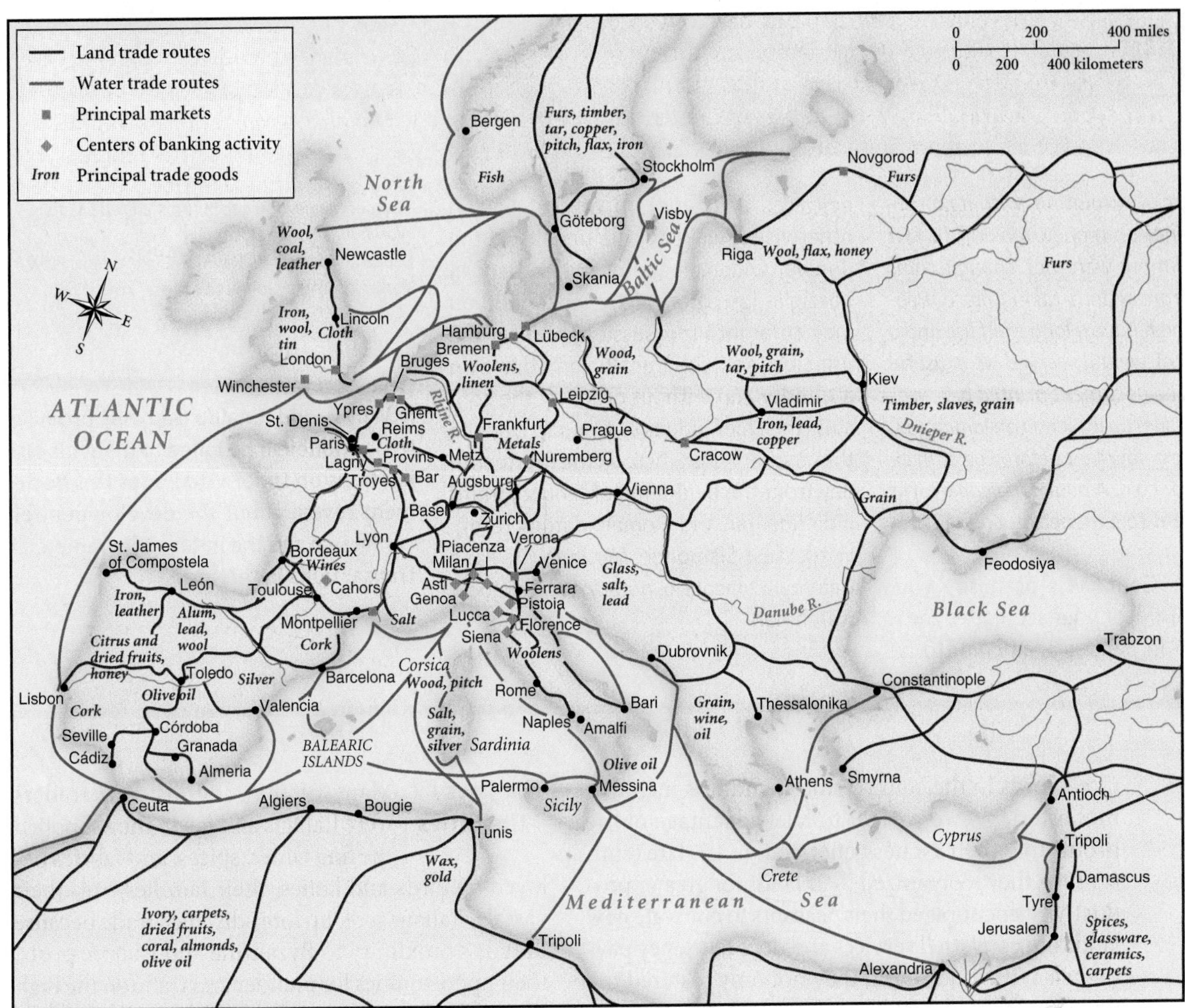

MAP 10.1 Medieval Trade Routes in the Eleventh and Twelfth Centuries
In the medieval world, bulk goods from the north (furs, fish, and wood) were traded for luxury goods from the south (ivory, spices, medicines, perfumes, and dyes). Already regions were beginning to specialize. England, for example, supplied raw wool, but Flanders (Ypres, Ghent) specialized in turning that wool into cloth and shipping it farther south, to the fairs of Champagne (whose capital was Troyes) or Germany. Italian cities channeled goods from the Muslim and Byzantine worlds northward and exported European goods southward and eastward.

1095
Council of Clermont;
Pope Urban II calls First Crusade

1108–1137
Reign of Louis VI

1122
Concordat of Worms ends Investiture Conflict

c. 1140
Gratian's *Decretum* published

1100 — 1125 — 1150

1097
Establishment of commune at Milan

1109
Establishment of the crusader states

1096–1099
First Crusade

1147–1149
Second Crusade

DOCUMENT

Peppercorns as Money

The commercial revolution, with its growing dependence on money, took off so fast that there simply were not enough coins for all the transactions taking place. Peppercorns, which have a long shelf life and a fairly uniform weight, served as a useful substitute. The document printed here was a contract drawn up in Genoa on January 14, 1156, to make a payment before Easter in either pepper or coin. A pound of peppercorns was equivalent to a monetary pound.

I, Rinaldo Gauxone, promise you, Lamberto Grillo, or your accredited messenger, £6½ in pepper or in coin [to be delivered any time] up to next Easter; otherwise [I will pay] the penalty of the double, under pledge of my orchard in Sozziglia [a region of Genoa]. And you may enter into [possession] of it for the principal and the penalty on your own authority and without order by the consuls [the chief judges of Genoa]. Done in the chapter house, 1156, on the fourteenth day from the beginning of January, third indiction [an old Roman dating term]. Witnesses: Sismondo Muscula, B. Papa Canticula Macobrio, notary, Baldo Rubeo, watchman.

Source: *Medieval Trade in the Mediterranean World: Illustrative Documents*, trans. Robert S. Lopez and Irving W. Raymond (1955; repr. New York: Columbia University Press, 2001), 145.

Question to Consider

- **Why would Rinaldo Gauxone promise to pay double if he failed to meet his obligations on time? What does this document reveal about the development of commerce and the nature of commercial transactions in this era?**

Great lords in the countryside—and this included monasteries—were eager to take advantage of the profits that their estates generated. In the late tenth century, they reorganized their lands for greater productivity, encouraged their peasants to cultivate new land, and converted services and dues to money payments. With ready cash, they not only fostered the development of local markets and yearly fairs, where they could sell their surpluses and buy luxury goods, but also encouraged traders and craftspeople to settle down near them. For example, at Bruges (today in Belgium), the local lord's castle became the magnet around which a city formed. As a medieval chronicler observed:

> To satisfy the needs of the people in the castle at Bruges, first merchants with luxury articles began to surge around the gate: then the winesellers came; finally the innkeepers arrived to feed and lodge the people who had business with the prince. . . . So many houses were built that soon a great city was created.

Other commercial centers clustered around monasteries and churches. Still other markets formed just outside the walls of older cities; these gradually merged into new and enlarged urban communities as town walls were built around them to protect their inhabitants. Sometimes informal country markets were housed in permanent structures. Along the Rhine and in other river valleys, cities sprang up to service the merchants who traversed the route between Italy and the north.

The Jews in the Cities Many of the long-distance traders were Italians and Jews. They supplied the fine wines, spices, and fabrics beloved by lords and ladies, their families, and their vassals. Italians took up long-distance trade because of Italy's proximity to Byzantine and Islamic ports, their opportunities for plunder and trade on the high seas, and their never entirely extinguished urban traditions. The Jews of Mediterranean regions—especially Italy and Spain—had been involved in commerce since Roman times. That trade had centered on the Mediterranean; now it extended to the north as well. For Jews living in the port cities of the old Roman Empire, little had changed. But for many Jews in northern Europe, the story was different. They had settled on the land alongside other peasants, and during the Carolingian period their properties bordered those of their Christian neighbors. As political power fragmented in the course of the tenth century—and the countryside was reorganized under the ban (controlling powers) of local lords—many Jews were driven off the land. They found refuge in the new towns and cities. Some became scholars, doctors, and judges within their communities; many became small-time pawnbrokers; and still others became moneylenders and financiers.

By the eleventh century, most Jews lived in cities but were not citizens. They were, in general, serfs of the king or, in the Rhineland, under the safeguard of the local bishop. This status was ambiguous: they were "protected" but also exploited, since their protectors constantly demanded steep taxes. Regular town trade groups, craft organizations, and town governments often rested on a conception of the common good sealed by an oath among Christians—and thus, by definition, excluded Jews. Nevertheless, Jews had their own institutions, centered on the synagogue, their place of worship (see the illustration on the right). Although they often lived in a "Jewish quarter," they were not forcibly segregated from other townspeople. In many cities they lived near Christians, purchased products from Christian craftspeople, and hired Christians as servants. In turn, Christians purchased luxury goods from Jewish long-distance traders and often borrowed money from Jewish lenders.

Synagogue Inscription from the City of Worms
This inscription is the oldest artifact we have from a synagogue in Europe. It says that Jacob ben David and his wife, Rahel, used their fortune to construct and furnish the synagogue, which was completed in 1034. They express the belief that this act of piety is as pleasing to God as having children. *(Jüdisches Museum im Raschihaus, Worms, Germany.)*

The "Unplanned" Town

The fact that Jews and Christians could live side by side had less to do with tolerance than with lack of planning. Most towns in medieval Europe grew haphazardly. Typically, towns had a center, where the church and town governments had their headquarters, and around this were the shops of tradespeople and craftspeople, generally grouped by specialty. Around the marketplace at Reims, for example, was a network of streets whose names (many of which still exist) revealed their commercial functions: Street of the Butchers, Street of the Wool Market, Street of the Wheat Market.

The look and feel of such developing cities varied enormously, but nearly all cities included a marketplace, a castle, and several churches. The streets—made of packed clay or gravel—were often narrow, dirty, dark, and winding. Most people had to adapt to increasingly crowded conditions. Archaeologists have discovered, for example, that at the end of the eleventh century in Winchester, England, city plots were still large enough to accommodate houses parallel to the street; but the swelling population soon necessitated destroying those houses and building instead long, narrow, hall-like tenements, constructed at right angles to the thoroughfare. These were built on a frame made from strips of wood filled with wattle and daub—twigs woven together and covered with clay. If they were like the stone houses built in the late twelfth century (a period about which we know a good deal), they had two stories: a shop or warehouse on the lower floor and living quarters above. Behind this main building was the kitchen and perhaps also enclosures for livestock. As this building style demonstrates, even city dwellers clung to rural pursuits, living largely off the food they raised themselves.

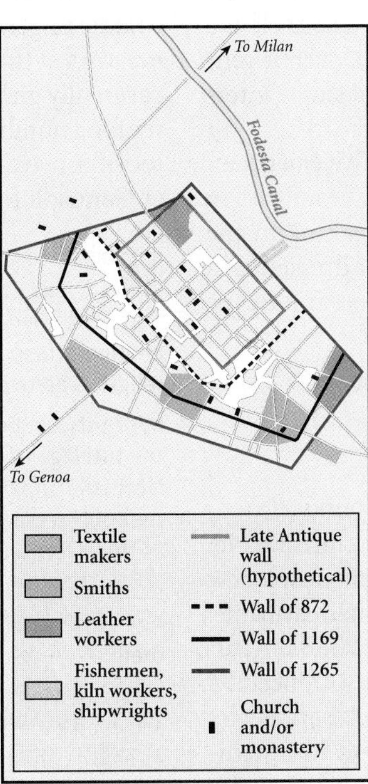

The Walls of Piacenza

The construction of houses and markets was part of a building boom that began in the tenth century and continued at an accelerated pace through the thirteenth. Towns put up specialized buildings for trade and city government—charitable houses for the sick and indigent, city halls, and warehouses. They also expanded their walls. Workers at Piacenza, for example, first pulled down the late antique wall and replaced it with a more extensive one in 872. Then, in 1169, Piacenzans took down the ninth-century wall and replaced it with one that was still more expansive. (See The Walls of Piacenza, left.)

Outside the cities, new bridges spanned the rivers. Before the eleventh century, Europeans had depended on boats and waterways for bulky long-distance transport; in the twelfth century, carts could haul items overland because new roads through the countryside linked the urban markets and because strengthened governments could protect overland travelers. Still, although commercial centers developed throughout western Europe, they grew fastest and most densely in

Baptismal Font at Liège, 1107–1118

This detail from a large bronze baptismal font cast at Liège (a city today in Belgium) illustrated the words of Luke 3:12–14: "Tax collectors also came to be baptized, and said to [Jesus], 'Teacher, what shall we do?' And he said to them, 'Collect no more than is appointed you.' Soldiers also asked him, 'And we, what shall we do?' And he said to them, 'Rob no one . . . and be content with your wages.'" In this representation, the tax collectors are dressed like twelfth-century city dwellers, while a soldier is dressed like a knight of the period. *(akg-images.)*

regions along key waterways: the Mediterranean coasts of Italy, France, and Spain; northern Italy along the Po River; the Rhône-Saône-Meuse river system; the Rhineland; the English Channel; the shores of the Baltic Sea. During the eleventh century, these waterways became part of a single interdependent economy.

What did townspeople look like? We can get an idea from a twelfth-century baptismal font cast in Liège (see above). It shows Jesus speaking to the soldiers and publicans: the soldier is dressed as a medieval knight, while the publicans wear the caps and clothes of well-to-do city dwellers.

Organizing Crafts and Commerce

In modern capitalism, there are few craftspeople: machines weave textiles, for example, and people sew pieces (a collar, perhaps) rather than whole garments. Piecework was just beginning in the Middle Ages, when most manufactured goods were produced by hand or with primitive machines and tools (see the illustration on page 317). Nevertheless, most medieval industries, though not mechanized, were highly organized. The fundamental unit of organization was the guild, a sort of club for craftspeople and tradespeople. Similarly, the ancestors of modern business corporations—which rely on capital pooled from various sources—originated in the Middle Ages.

Guilds | It was not by chance that city streets were named for various occupations: in a medieval city, crafts and trades were collective endeavors. Each was organized as a **guild**. Originally these were religious and charitable associations of people in the same line of trade. In Ferrara, Italy, for example, the shoemakers' guild started as a prayer confraternity, an association whose members gathered and prayed for one another. But soon guilds became professional corporations defined by statutes and rules. They charged dues, negotiated with lords and town governments, set the standards of their trade, and controlled their membership.

The manufacture of finished products often required the cooperation of several guilds. The production of wool cloth, for example, involved numerous guilds—shearers, weavers, fullers (who thickened the cloth), dyers—generally working under the supervision of the merchant guild that imported the raw wool. Some guilds were more prestigious than others: in Florence, for example, professional guilds of notaries and judges ranked above craft guilds. Within each guild of artisans, merchants, or professionals existed another kind of hierarchy. **Apprentices** were at the bottom, **journeymen** and **journeywomen** (that is, male or female day laborers—the word comes from the Middle English for "a day's work") in the middle, and **masters** at the top. Apprentices were boys (and occasionally girls) placed under the tutelage of a master for a number of years to learn a trade. At Paris, it took four years of apprenticeship to become a baker; at Genoa, it took ten to become a silversmith.

---

guild: A trade organization within a city or town that controlled product quality and cost and outlined members' responsibilities. Guilds were also social and religious associations.

apprentices: Boys (and occasionally girls) placed under the tutelage of a master craftsman in the Middle Ages. Normally unpaid, they were expected to be servants of their masters, with whom they lived, at the same time as they were learning their trade.

journeymen/journeywomen: Laborers in the Middle Ages whom guildmasters hired for a daily wage to help them produce their products.

masters: Men (and occasionally women) who, having achieved expertise in a craft, ran the guilds in the Middle Ages. They had to be rich enough to have their own shop and tools and to pay an entry fee into the guild. Often their positions were hereditary.

Learning a trade was not the same as becoming a master. A young person would spend many years as a day laborer hired by a master who needed extra help. Masters occupied the top of the guild hierarchy, dominating the offices and policies of the guild. They drew up the guild regulations and served as its chief overseers, inspectors, and treasurers. Because the number of masters was few and the turnover of official posts frequent, most masters eventually had a chance to serve as guild officers. Occasionally they were elected, but more often they were appointed by town governments or local rulers.

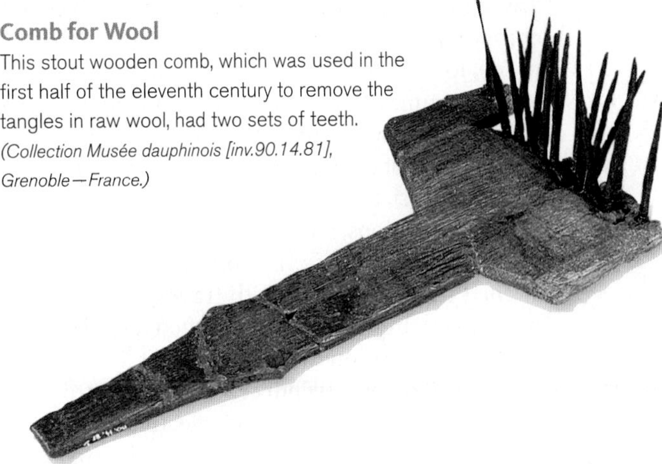

Comb for Wool
This stout wooden comb, which was used in the first half of the eleventh century to remove the tangles in raw wool, had two sets of teeth. *(Collection Musée dauphinois [inv.90.14.81], Grenoble—France.)*

Partnerships, Contracts, and the Rise of Industry In the course of the eleventh and twelfth centuries, people created new kinds of business arrangements through partnerships, contracts, and large-scale productive enterprises—the ancestors of modern **capitalism**. Although they took many forms, all of these business agreements had the common purpose of bringing people together to pool their resources and finance larger initiatives. Short-lived partnerships were set up for the term of one sea voyage; longer-term partnerships were created for land trade. In northern and central Italy, for example, long-term ventures took the form of a family corporation formed by extended families. Everyone who contributed to this corporation bore joint and unlimited liability for all losses and debts. This provision enhanced family solidarity, because each member was responsible for the debts of all the others, but it also risked bankrupting everyone in the family.

The commercial revolution also fostered the development of contracts for sales, exchanges, and loans. Loans were the most problematic. In the Middle Ages, as now, interest payments were the chief inducement for an investor to supply money. To circumvent the church's ban on usury (lending money at interest), a contract often disguised interest as a "penalty for late payment." The new willingness to finance business enterprises with loans signaled a changed attitude toward credit: risk was acceptable if it brought profit.

Contracts and partnerships made large-scale productive enterprises possible. In fact, light industry began in the eleventh century. One of the earliest products to benefit from new industrial technologies was cloth. Water mills powered machines such as presses to extract oil from fibers, and flails to clean and thicken cloth. Machines also exploited raw materials more efficiently: new deep-mining technology provided Europeans with hitherto untapped sources of metals. At the same time, forging techniques improved, and iron was for the first time since antiquity regularly used for agricultural tools and plows. Iron tools—which were more durable than wood—made farming more productive, which in turn fed the commercial revolution. People also fashioned metals into objects ranging from weapons and armor to ornaments and coins.

capitalism: The modern economic system characterized by an entrepreneurial class of property owners who employ others and produce (or provide services) for a market in order to make a profit.

Communes: Self-Government for the Towns

In the eleventh and twelfth centuries, townspeople—traders, artisans, ship captains, innkeepers, and money changers—did not fit into the old categories of medieval types as those who prayed, those who fought, or those who labored on the land. Just knowing they were different from those groups gave townspeople a sense of solidarity. But practical reasons also contributed to their feeling of common purpose: they lived in close quarters, and they shared a mutual interest in reliable coinage, laws to facilitate commerce, freedom from servile dues and duties, and independence to buy and sell as the market dictated. Already in the early twelfth century, the king of England granted to the citizens of Newcastle-upon-Tyne the privilege that any unfree peasant who lived there unclaimed by his lord for a year and a day would thereafter be a free person. This privilege became general. To townspeople, freedom meant having their own officials and law courts. They petitioned the political powers that ruled them—bishops, kings, counts, castellans—for the right to govern themselves. Often they had to fight for this freedom and, if successful, paid a hefty sum for it.

Town institutions of self-government were called **communes**; citizens swore allegiance to the commune, forming a legal corporate body.

Communes were especially common in northern and central Italy, France, and Flanders. Italian cities were centers of regional political power even before the commercial revolution. Castellans constructed their fortifications, and bishops ruled the countryside from such cities. The commercial revolution swelled the Italian cities with tradespeople, whose interest in self-government was often fueled by religious as well as economic concerns. At Milan in the second half of the eleventh century, popular discontent with the archbishop, who effectively ruled the city, led to numerous armed clashes. In 1097, the Milanese succeeded in transferring political power from the archbishop and his clergy to a government of leading men of the city, who called themselves consuls. The title recalled the government of the ancient Roman republic, affirming the consuls' status as representatives of the people. As the archbishop's power had done, the consuls' rule extended beyond the town walls into the *contado*, the outlying countryside.

Outside Italy, movements for city independence took place within the framework of larger kingdoms or principalities. Such movements were sometimes violent, as at Milan, but at other times they were peaceful. For example, William Clito, who claimed the county of Flanders (today in Belgium), willingly granted the citizens of St. Omer the privileges they asked for in 1127 in return for their support of his claims: he recognized them as legally free, gave them the right to mint coins, allowed them their own laws and courts, and lifted certain tolls and taxes. Whether violently or peacefully, the men and women of many towns and cities gained a measure of self-rule.

The Commercial Revolution in the Countryside

The countryside, too, was caught in the new networks of trade. Country people brought local products to markets and fairs. By 1150, rural life in many regions was organized for the marketplace. The commercialization of the countryside opened up opportunities for both peasants and lords, but it also burdened some with unwelcome obligations.

Great lords hired trained, literate agents to administer their estates, calculate their profits and losses, and make marketing decisions. Aristocrats needed money not only because they relished luxuries but also because their honor and authority continued to depend on their personal generosity, patronage, and displays of wealth. In the twelfth century, when some townsmen could boast fortunes that rivaled the riches of the landed aristocracy, the economic pressures on the nobles increased as their extravagance exceeded their income. Many went into debt.

The lord's need for money integrated peasants, too, into the developing commercial economy. The increase in population and the resultant greater demand for food required bringing more land under cultivation. By the middle of the twelfth century, the cultivation of new land had changed from a sporadic activity to a planned program. Great lords offered special privileges to peasants who would do the backbreaking work of plowing marginal land or draining marshes. For example, in Flanders, where land was regularly inundated by seawater, the great monasteries sponsored drainage projects. Canals linking the cities to the agricultural districts let boats ply the waters to virtually every nook and cranny of the region. With its dense population, Flanders provided not only a natural meeting ground for long-distance traders from England and France but also numerous markets for local traders.

Sometimes free peasants acted on their own to clear land and relieve the pressure of overpopulation, as when the small freeholders in England's Fenland region cooperated to build banks and dikes to reclaim the land that led out to the North Sea. Villages were founded on the drained land, and villagers shared responsibility for repairing and maintaining the dikes even as each peasant family farmed its new holding individually.

On old estates the rise in population strained to the breaking point the Carolingian period's manse organization, in which each household had been settled on the land that supported it. Now, in the twelfth century, twenty peasant families might live on what had been, in the tenth century, the manse of one family. With the manse supporting so many more people, labor services and dues had to be recalculated, and peasants and their lords often turned services and dues into money rents, payable once a year. Peasants sometimes formed commune-like collectives to buy their liberty for a high price, paid out over many years to their lord. Like town citizens, they gained a new sense of identity and solidarity as they bargained with a lord keen to increase his income at their expense.

---

commune: In a medieval town, a sworn association of citizens who formed a legal corporate body. The commune appointed or elected officials, made laws, kept the peace, and administered justice.

The commercial revolution and the resulting money economy brought both benefits and burdens to peasants. They gained from rising prices, which made their fixed rents less onerous. They had access to markets where they could sell their surplus and buy what they lacked. Increases in land under cultivation and the use of iron tools meant greater productivity. Peasants also gained increased personal freedom as they shook off direct control by lords. Nevertheless, these advantages were partially canceled out by their cash obligations. Peasants touched by the commercial revolution ate better than their forebears had eaten, but they also had to spend more money.

REVIEW QUESTION What new institutions resulted from the commercial revolution?

Church Reform

The commercial revolution affected the church no less than it affected other institutions of the time. Bishops ruled over many cities, and many bishops were appointed by kings or powerful local lords. This transaction involved gifts: churchmen gave gifts and money to secular leaders in return for their offices. Soon these transactions were being condemned by the same sorts of people who appreciated the fates of Dives and Lazarus. The impulse to free the church from "the world"—from rulers, wealth, sex, money, and power—was as old as the origins of monasticism; but, beginning in the tenth century and increasing to fever pitch in the eleventh, reformers demanded that the church as a whole remodel itself and become free of secular entanglements.

This freedom was, from the start, as much a matter of power as of religion. Most people had long believed that their ruler—whether king, duke, count, or castellan—reigned by the grace of God and had the right to control the churches in his territory. But by the second half of the eleventh century, more and more people saw a great deal wrong with secular power over the church. They looked to the papacy to lead the movement of church reform. The matter came to a head during the so-called Investiture Conflict, when Pope Gregory VII clashed with Emperor Henry IV (whose empire embraced both Germany and Italy). The Investiture Conflict ushered in a major civil war in Germany and a great upheaval in the distribution of power across western Europe. By the early 1100s, a reformed church—with the pope at its head—was penetrating into areas of life never before touched by churchmen. Church reform began as a way to free the church from the world, but in the end the church was thoroughly involved in the new world it had helped create.

Beginnings of Reform

The project of freeing the church from the world began in the tenth century with no particular plan and only a vague idea of what it might mean. Local reformers—both clerical and lay—took some early steps to make the clergy not only celibate but also independent of the laity. But church reform did not take final shape until the papacy embraced it and turned it into a blueprint for reorganizing the church under papal leadership. The movement to "liberate the church" in fact began in unlikely circles: with the very rulers who were controlling churches and monasteries, appointing churchmen, and using bishops as their administrators.

Cluniac Reform The Benedictine monastery of Cluny (today in France) may serve to represent the early phases of the reform. The duke and duchess of Aquitaine founded Cluny in 910 and endowed it with property. Then they did something new: instead of retaining control over the monastery, as other monastic founders did, they gave it and its worldly possessions to Saints Peter and Paul. In this way, they put control of the monastery into the hands of heaven's two most powerful saints. They designated the pope, as the successor of St. Peter, to be the monastery's worldly protector if anyone should bother or threaten it.

The whole notion of "freedom" at this point was vague. But Cluny's prestige was great because of its status as St. Peter's property and the elaborate round of prayers that the monks carried out there with scrupulous devotion. The Cluniac monks fulfilled the role of "those who pray" in a way that dazzled their contemporaries. Through their prayers, they seemed to guarantee the salvation of all Christians. Rulers, bishops, rich landowners, and even serfs (if they could) donated land to Cluny, joining their contributions to the land of St. Peter and the fate of their souls to Cluny's efficacious prayers. Powerful men and women called on the Cluniac monks to reform other monasteries along the Cluniac model.

The abbots of Cluny came to see themselves as reformers of the world as well. They advocated clerical celibacy, arguing against the prevailing norm in which parish priests and even some bishops were married. They thought that the laity could be reformed, become more virtuous, and cease its oppression of the poor. In the eleventh century, the Cluniacs began to link their program of internal monastic and external worldly reform to the papacy. When bishops and laypeople encroached on their lands, they appealed to the popes for help. At the same time, the papacy itself was becoming interested in reform.

Church Reform in the Empire Around the time the Cluniacs were joining their fate to that of the popes, a small group of clerics and monks in the Empire, the political entity created by the Ottonians, began calling for systematic reform within the church. They buttressed their arguments with new interpretations of canon law—the laws decreed over the centuries at church councils and by bishops and popes. They concentrated on two breaches of those laws: clerical marriage and **simony** (buying church offices).[1] Later they added the condemnation of **lay investiture**—the installation of clerics into their offices by lay rulers. In the investiture ritual, the emperor or his representative symbolically gave the church and the land that went with it to the priest or bishop or archbishop chosen for the job.

Many of the men who promoted the reform lived in the highly commercialized regions of the empire—Italy and the regions along the northern half of the Rhine River. Familiar with the impersonal practices of a profit economy, they regarded the gifts that churchmen usually gave in return for their offices as no more than crass purchases.

Emperor Henry III (r. 1039–1056) supported the reformers. Taking seriously his position as the anointed of God, Henry felt responsible for the well-being of the church in his empire. He denounced simony and refused to accept money or gifts when he appointed bishops to their posts. When in 1046 three men, each representing a different faction of the Roman aristocracy, claimed to be pope, Henry, as ruler of Rome, traveled to Italy to settle the matter. The Synod of Sutri (1046), over which he presided, deposed all three popes and elected another. In 1049, Henry appointed a bishop from the Rhineland to the papacy as Leo IX (r. 1049–1054). But this appointment did not work out as Henry had expected, for Leo set out to reform the church under his own, not the emperor's, control.

Leo IX and the Expansion of Papal Power During Leo's tenure, the pope's role expanded. Leo traveled to France and Germany, holding councils to condemn bishops guilty of simony. He sponsored the creation of a canon law textbook—*Collection in 74 Titles*—that emphasized the pope's power. To the papal court, Leo brought the most zealous reformers of his day, including Humbert of Silva Candida and Hildebrand (later Pope Gregory VII).

At first, clergy and secular rulers alike ignored Leo's claims to new power over the church hierarchy. Only a few bishops attended the Council of Reims, which Leo called in 1049; the king of France boycotted it entirely. Nevertheless, the pope turned the council into a forum for exercising his authority. Placing the relics of St. Remigius (the patron saint of Reims) on the altar of the church, he demanded that the attending bishops and abbots say whether or not they had purchased their offices. A few confessed, some did not respond, and others gave excuses. New and extraordinary was the fact that all present felt accountable to the pope and accepted his verdicts.

In 1054, his last year as pope, Leo sent Humbert of Silva Candida to Constantinople on a diplomatic mission to argue against the patriarch of Constantinople on behalf of the new, lofty claims of the pope. Furious at the contemptuous way he was treated by the patriarch, Humbert excommunicated him. In retaliation, the patriarch excommunicated Humbert and his party, threatening them with eternal damnation. Clashes between the two churches had occurred before and had been patched up, but this one, the schism between the eastern and western churches, (1054), proved insurmountable.[2] Thereafter, the Roman Catholic and the Greek Orthodox churches were largely separate.

Leo also had to confront a new power to his south. Under Count Roger I (c. 1040–1101), the Normans created a county that would eventually stretch from Capua to Sicily (see the map on page 322). Leo, threatened by this great power, tried to curtail it: in 1053 he sent a military force to Apulia, but it was soundly defeated. Leo's successors were obliged to change their policy. In 1058, the reigning pope "invested"—in effect, gave—Apulia, nearby

---

[1]The word *simony* comes from the name Simon Magus, the magician in the New Testament who wanted to buy the gifts of the Holy Spirit from St. Peter.

simony (SY muh nee): The sin of giving gifts or paying money to get a church office.

lay investiture: The installation of clerics into their offices by lay rulers.

[2]The mutual excommunications led to a permanent breach between the churches that largely remained in effect until 1965, when Pope Paul VI and Patriarch Athenagoras I made a joint declaration regretting "the offensive words" and sentences of excommunication on both sides, deploring "the effective rupture of ecclesiastical communion," and expressing the hope that the "differences between the Roman Catholic Church and the Orthodox Church" would be overcome in time.

Leo IX
This eleventh-century manuscript shows not so much a portrait of Pope Leo IX as an idealized image of his power and position. What might the halo signify? Why do you suppose Leo stands at least three heads taller than the other figure in the picture, Warinus, the abbot of St. Arnulf of Metz? What is Leo doing with his right hand? With his left hand he holds a little church (symbol of a real one) that is being presented to him by Warinus. What did the artist intend to convey about the relationship of this church to papal power? *(Burgerbibliothek Bern, Cod. 292, f. 73r.)*

Calabria, "and in the future, with the help of God and St. Peter," even Sicily to Roger's brother, even though none of this was the pope's to give. The papacy was particularly keen to see the Normans conquer Sicily. Once part of the Byzantine Empire, the island had been taken by Muslims in the tenth century; now the pope hoped to bring it under Catholic control. Thus, the pope's desires to convert Sicily nicely meshed with the territorial ambitions of Roger and his brother. The agreement of 1058 included a promise that all of the churches of southern Italy and Sicily would be placed under papal jurisdiction. No wonder that when the Investiture Conflict broke out, Roger and his army played an important role as a military arm of the papacy.

The popes were in fact becoming more and more involved in military enterprises. They participated in wars of expansion in Spain, for example. There, political fragmentation into small and weak *taifas* (see page 285) made al-Andalus fair game for the Christians to the north. Slowly the idea of the ***reconquista***, the Christian "reconquest" of Spain from the Muslims, took shape, fed by religious fervor as well as by greed for land and power. In 1063, just before a major battle, the pope issued an indulgence to all who would fight—a grant that, if it did not go so far as to forgive all sins, nevertheless lifted the knights' obligation to do penance. (For such penances, see Document: "Penances for the Invaders," page 338).

The Gregorian Reform and the Investiture Conflict, 1075–1122

Historians associate the papal reform movement above all with Gregory VII (r. 1073–1085) and therefore often call it the **Gregorian reform**. Beginning as a lowly Roman cleric named Hildebrand, with the job of administering the papal estates, he rose slowly through the hierarchy. A passionate advocate of papal primacy (the theory that the pope was the head of the church), Gregory was not afraid to clash head-on with **Henry IV** (r. 1056–1106), ruler of Germany and much of Italy, over leadership of the church. As his views crystallized, Gregory came to see an anointed ruler as just another layman who had no right to meddle in church affairs. At the time, this was an astonishing position, given the traditional religious and spiritual roles associated with kings and emperors.

Gregory was, and remains, an extraordinarily controversial figure. He certainly thought that as pope he was acting as the vicar, or representative, of St. Peter on earth. Describing himself, he declared, "I have labored with all my power that Holy Church, the bride of God, our Lady Mother, might come again to her own splendor and might remain free, pure, and Catholic." He thought that the reforms he advocated and the upheavals he precipitated were necessary to free the church from the evil rulers of

---

reconquista **(ray con KEE stuh):** The collective name for the wars waged by the Christian princes of Spain against the Muslim-ruled regions to their south. These wars were considered holy, akin to the crusades.

Gregorian reform: The papal movement for church reform associated with Gregory VII (r. 1073–1085); its ideals included ending three practices: the purchase of church offices, clerical marriage, and lay investiture.

Henry IV: King of Germany (r. 1056–1106), crowned emperor in 1084. From 1075 until his death, he was embroiled in the Investiture Conflict with Pope Gregory VII.

the world. But his great nemesis, Henry IV, had a very different view of Gregory. He considered him an ambitious and evil man who "seduced the world far and wide and stained the Church with the blood of her sons." Not surprisingly, modern historians are only a bit less divided in their assessment of Gregory. Few deny his sincerity and deep religious devotion, but many speak of his pride, ambition, and single-mindedness. He was not an easy man.

Henry IV was less complex. He was raised in the traditions of his father, Henry III, a pious church reformer who considered it part of his duty to appoint bishops and even popes to ensure the well-being of both church and state. Henry IV believed that he and his bishops—who were, at the same time, his most valuable supporters and administrators—were the rightful leaders of the church. He had no intention of allowing the pope to become head of the church; he didn't see that new religious ideals were sweeping away the old traditions. (See Contrasting Views, page 324.)

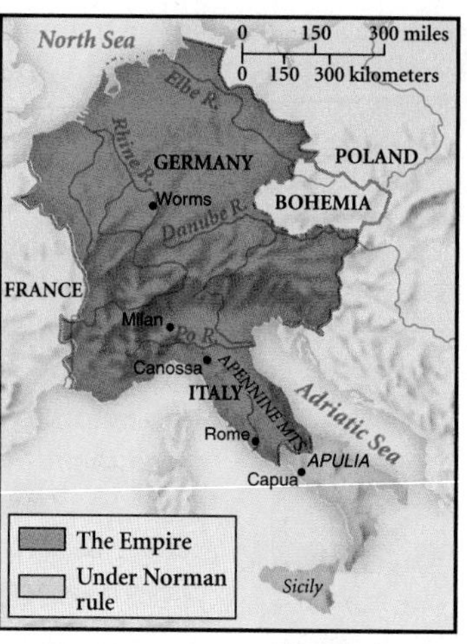

The World of the Investiture Conflict, c. 1070–1122

The Investiture Conflict

The great confrontation between Gregory and Henry that historians call the **Investiture Conflict**[3] began in 1075 over the appointment of the archbishop of Milan and a few other Italian prelates. When Henry insisted on appointing these clergymen, Gregory admonished the king. Henry responded by calling on Gregory to step down as pope. In turn, Gregory called a synod that both excommunicated and suspended Henry from office:

> I deprive King Henry [IV], son of the emperor Henry [III], who has rebelled against [God's] Church with unheard-of audacity, of the government over the whole kingdom of Germany and Italy, and I release all Christian men from the allegiance which they have sworn or may swear to him, and I forbid anyone to serve him as king.

It was this last part of the decree that made it politically explosive; it authorized everyone in Henry's kingdom to rebel against him. Henry's enemies, mostly German princes (as German aristocrats were called), now threatened to elect another king. They were motivated partly by religious sentiments, as many had established links with the papacy through their support of reformed monasteries, and partly by political opportunism, as they had chafed under the strong German king, who had tried to keep their power in check. Some bishops joined forces with Gregory's supporters. This was a great blow to royal power because Henry desperately needed the troops supplied by his churchmen.

Attacked from all sides, Henry traveled to intercept Gregory, who was journeying northward to visit the rebellious princes. In early 1077, king and pope met at a castle belonging to Matilda, countess of Tuscany, at Canossa, high in central Italy's snowy Apennine Mountains. Gregory remained inside the fortress there; Henry stood outside as a penitent, begging forgiveness. Henry's move was astute, for no priest could refuse absolution to a penitent; Gregory had to lift the excommunication and receive Henry back into the church. But Gregory now had the advantage of enjoying the king's humiliation before the majesty of the pope.

Although Henry was technically back in the church's fold, nothing of substance had been resolved. The princes elected an antiking (a king chosen illegally), and Henry and his supporters elected an antipope. From 1077 until 1122, papal and imperial armies and supporters waged intermittent war in both Germany and Italy.

Outcome of the Investiture Conflict

The Investiture Conflict was finally resolved long after Henry IV and Gregory VII had died. The **Concordat of Worms** of 1122 ended the fighting with a compromise. Henry V, the heir of Henry IV, gave up the right in the investiture ceremony to confer the ring and the pastoral

---

[3]This movement is also called the Investiture Controversy, Investiture Contest, or Investiture Struggle. The epithets all refer to the same thing: the disagreement and eventually war between the pope and the emperor over the right to invest churchmen in particular and power over the church hierarchy in general.

Investiture Conflict: The confrontation between Pope Gregory VII and Emperor Henry IV that began in 1075 over the appointment of prelates in some Italian cities and grew into a dispute over the nature of church leadership. It ended in 1122 with the Concordat of Worms.

Concordat of Worms: The agreement between pope and emperor in 1122 that ended the Investiture Conflict.

Matilda of Tuscany
How often is a woman the dominant figure in medieval art? In this illustration made around 1115, Matilda, countess of Tuscany, towers above the king (Henry IV) and upstages the abbot of Cluny (Hugh). Matilda was a key supporter of Pope Gregory VII. It was at her castle at Canossa that Henry IV did penance. The words underneath the picture emphasize Henry's abjection. They read: "The king begs the abbot and supplicates Matilda as well." *(Biblioteca Apostolica Vaticana, The Vatican, Italy/Flammarion/The Bridgeman Art Library International.)*

staff—symbols of spiritual power. But he retained, in Germany, the right to be present when bishops were elected. In effect, he would continue to have influence over those elections. In both Germany and Italy he also had the right to give the scepter to the churchman in a gesture meant to indicate the transfer of the temporal, or worldly, powers and possessions of the church—the lands by which it was supported.

Superficially, nothing much had changed; the Concordat of Worms ensured that secular rulers would continue to have a part in choosing and investing churchmen. In fact, however, few people would now claim that a king could act as head of the church. Just as the concordat broke the investiture ritual into two parts—one spiritual, with ring and staff, the other secular, with the scepter—so too it implied a new notion of kingship that separated it from priesthood. The Investiture Conflict did not produce the modern distinction between church and state—that would develop slowly—but it set the wheels in motion.

The most important changes brought about by the Investiture Conflict, however, were on the ground: the political landscape in both Italy and Germany was irrevocably transformed. In Germany, the princes consolidated their lands and their positions at the expense of royal power. In Italy, the emperor lost power to the cities. The northern and central Italian communes were formed in the crucible of the war between the pope and the emperor. In fierce communal struggles, city factions, often created by local grievances but claiming to fight on behalf of the papal or the imperial cause, created their own governing bodies. In the course of the twelfth century, these Italian cities became accustomed to self-government.

The Sweep of Reform

Church reform involved much more than the clash of popes, emperors, and their supporters. It penetrated into the daily lives of ordinary Christians, inspired new ways to think about church institutions such as the sacraments, brought about a new systemization of church law, changed the way the papacy operated, inspired new monastic orders dedicated to poverty, and led to the crusades.

New Emphasis on the Sacraments

According to the Catholic church, the **sacraments** were the regular means by which God's heavenly grace infused mundane existence; they included rites such as baptism, the Eucharist (communion), and marriage. But this did not mean that Christians were clear about how many sacraments there were, how they worked, or even what their significance was. Eleventh-century church reformers began the process—which would continue into the thirteenth century—of emphasizing the importance of the sacraments and the special nature of the priest, whose chief role was to administer them.

Marriage, for example, became a sacrament only after the Gregorian reform. Before the twelfth century, priests had little to do with weddings, which were family affairs. After the twelfth century, however, priests were expected to consecrate marriages. When the knight Arnulf of Ardres got married in 1194, for example, priests blessed and sprinkled him and his wife with holy water as the couple lay in their nuptial bed. Churchmen also began to assume jurisdiction over marital disputes, not simply in cases involving royalty (as they had always done) but also in those involving lesser aristocrats. Because the no-

---

sacraments: In the Catholic church, the institutionalized means by which God's heavenly grace is transmitted to Christians. Examples of sacraments include baptism, the Eucharist (communion), and marriage.

CONTRASTING VIEWS

Henry IV

Henry III was a church reformer in the old mold: he had ensured the well-being of the church by appointing excellent prelates. When he died in 1056, he left his six-year-old son, Henry IV, as his heir. Document 1 is a sympathetic account of the young king, whose minority gave many powerful groups in Germany a chance to exploit him. When he turned fifteen and was therefore no longer legally a minor, Henry freed himself from their grasp and began to restore royal power. This meant, in part, asserting his right to appoint bishops and archbishops, as he did in 1075 to the sees of Milan, Fermo, and Spoleto. In Document 2, Gregory VII scolds Henry for these appointments and demands that he heed the pope, or rather St. Peter, in whose place the pope stands. In Gregory's view, Henry was disobeying God. Henry's response to Gregory's scolding letter is in Document 3: there he portrays himself as the ordained of God and calls on Gregory to resign the papacy. Gregory reacted to this letter by excommunicating Henry, declaring him no longer king, and releasing all his subjects from their obedience to him. Suddenly Henry found himself nearly abandoned. To regain his position, he needed Gregory to lift the excommunication. In January 1077, Henry stood barefoot in the snow at Canossa, acting as a penitent. Document 4 describes that moment.

1. Anonymous Account of Henry's Minority

A biographer of Henry IV wrote this account shortly after the emperor's death in 1106. By then, the Investiture Conflict had raged for decades, and most people had taken sides. This biographer was on Henry's side.

But since immature age inspires too little fear, and while awe languishes, audacity increases, the boyish years of the king excited in many the spirit of crime. Therefore everyone strove to become equal to the one greater than him, or even greater, and the might of many increased through crime; nor was there any fear of the law, which had little authority under the young boy-king.

And so that they could do everything with more license, they first robbed of her child the mother [Empress Agnes, wife of Henry III] whose mature wisdom and grave habits they feared, pleading that it was dishonorable for the kingdom to be administered by a woman (although one may read of many queens who administered kingdoms with manly wisdom). But after the boy-king, once drawn away from the bosom of his mother, came into the hands of the princes to be raised, whatever they prescribed for him to do, he did like the boy he was. Whomever they wished, he exalted; whomever they wished, he set down; so that they may rightly be said not to have ministered to their king so much as to have given orders to him. When they dealt with the affairs of the kingdom, they took counsel not so much for the affairs of the kingdom as for their own; and in everything they did, it was their primary concern to put their own advantage above everything else. . . .

But when [at the age of fifteen] he passed into that measure of age and mind in which he could discern what was honorable, what shameful, what useful, and what was not, he reconsidered what he had done while led by the suggestion of the princes and condemned many things which he had done. And, having become his own judge, he changed those of his acts which were to be changed. He also prohibited wars, violence, and rapine; he strove to recall peace and justice, which had been expelled to restore neglected laws, and to check the license of crime.

Source: "The Life of the Emperor Henry IV" in *Imperial Lives and Letters of the Eleventh Century*, trans. Theodor E. Mommsen and Karl F. Morrison (New York: Columbia University Press, 2000), 106.

2. Gregory VII Admonishes Henry (1075)

Gregory had written letters to Henry before 1075, but this was the first one that scolded him. The issue was Henry's attempt to appoint prelates to three Italian sees (the seat, jurisdiction, or office of a bishop). Gregory complained that Henry's candidates were unknown and inappropriate. He did not yet object to royal investiture.

We marvel exceedingly that you have sent us so many devoted letters and displayed such humility by the spoken words of your legates . . . and yet in action showing yourself most bitterly hostile to the canons and apostolic decrees in those duties especially required by loyalty to the Church. Not to mention other cases, the way you have observed your promises in the Milan affair, made through your mother and through bishops, our colleagues, whom we sent to you, and what your intentions were in making them is evident to all. And now, heaping wounds upon wounds, you have handed over the sees of Fermo and Spoleto—if indeed a church may be given over by any human power—to persons entirely unknown to us, whereas it is not lawful to consecrate anyone except after probation and with due knowledge.

It would have been becoming to you, since you confess yourself to be a son of the Church, to give more respectful attention to the master of the Church, that is, to Peter, prince of the Apostles. To him, if you are of the Lord's flock, you have been committed for your pasture, since Christ said to him: "Peter, feed my sheep" (John 21:17), and again: "To thee are given the keys of Heaven, and whatsoever thou shalt bind on earth shall be bound in Heaven and whatsoever thou shalt loose on earth shall be loosed in Heaven" (Matt. 16:19). Now, while we, unworthy sinner that we are, stand in his place of power, still whatever you send to us, whether in writing or by word of mouth, he [Peter] himself receives, and while we read what is written or hear the voice of those who speak, he discerns with subtle insight from what spirit the message comes.

Source: *The Correspondence of Pope Gregory VII*, trans. Ephraim Emerton (New York: W. W. Norton, 1969), 87.

3. Henry's Response to Gregory's Admonition (early 1076)

A meeting called by Henry and attended by nobles and bishops in Germany produced two documents in response to Gregory's scolding letter: a harsh retort meant to be circulated in Germany as propaganda for Henry, and a gentler version to be sent to Gregory himself. Both called on Gregory to step down as pope. The harsh letter, part of which is printed here, makes clear Henry's exalted view of his own role in the church.

Henry, King not by usurpation, but by the pious ordination of God, to Hildebrand, now not Pope, but false monk:

You have deserved such a salutation as this because of the confusion you have wrought; for you left untouched no order of the Church which you could make a sharer of confusion instead of honor, of malediction instead of benediction.

For to discuss a few outstanding points among many: Not only have you dared to touch the rectors of the holy Church—the archbishops, the bishops, and the priests, anointed of the Lord as they are—but you have trodden them under foot like slaves who know not what their lord may do. . . .

And we, indeed, bore with all these abuses, since we were eager to preserve the honor of the Apostolic See. But you construed our humility as fear, and so you were emboldened to rise up even against the royal power itself, granted to us by God. You dared to threaten to take the kingship away from us—as though we had received the kingship from you, as though kingship and empire were in your hand and not in the hand of God.

Our Lord, Jesus Christ, has called us to kingship, but has not called you to the priesthood.

Source: *Imperial Lives and Letters of the Eleventh Century*, trans. Theodor E. Mommsen and Karl F. Morrison (New York: Columbia University Press, 2000), 150.

4. Lampert of Hersfeld Describes Henry at Canossa (c. 1077)

Lampert of Hersfeld was a German monk whose monastery, Hersfeld, supported Henry. However, in his Annales, *from which this excerpt is taken, Lampert emphasizes how weak the king had become as he awaited the pope's absolution at Canossa.*

Leaving Speyer a few days before Christmas with his wife and infant son, the journey [to Canossa] was begun. That noble man [Henry IV] left the realm accompanied by not a soul from Germany save one notable neither for his lineage nor his wealth. Since he needed resources for so long a journey, Henry sought aid from many men he had often benefited when his kingdom was intact. There were very few, however, who relieved his necessity to any extent, moved either by memory of past favors or by the present spectacle of human events. And thus the king descended suddenly from the height of glory and greatest wealth to such distress and calamity! . . .

Henry came [to the walls of Canossa], as he was ordered to, and since that castle had been enclosed by a triple wall, having been received within the space of the second wall, his band of retainers having been left outside, his regalia laid aside, displaying nothing pertaining to the kingship, showing no ceremony, with bare feet and fasting from morning until vespers, he waited for the decision of the Roman Pontiff. He did this a second day, and then a third. On the fourth day, finally having been admitted into the pope's presence, after many opinions were voiced on each side, he was finally absolved from the excommunication under these conditions: that on the day and at the place designated by the pope, he promptly call a general council of the German princes . . . [and there] it would be decided according to ecclesiastical law whether Henry should retain the realm.

Source: Maureen C. Miller, ed., *Power and the Holy in the Age of the Investiture Conflict: A Brief History with Documents* (Boston: Bedford/St. Martin's, 2005), 91–97.

Questions to Consider

1. **How important was Henry's minority in weakening royal authority?**
2. **Why did Gregory consider Henry impious when he appointed churchmen?**
3. **Why did Henry consider Gregory a false pope?**
4. **If the events at Canossa led to the king's absolution, why did Lampert and others consider it a sign of royal weakness?**

bility kept its inheritance intact by transferring it to a single male heir, the heir's marriage was crucial to the family strategy. The clergy's prohibition of marriage partners as distant as seventh cousins (since marriage between cousins was considered incest) had the potential to control dynastic alliances.

At the same time, churchmen began to stress the sanctity of marriage. Hugh of St. Victor, a twelfth-century scholar, dwelled on the sacramental meaning of marriage:

> Can you find anything else in marriage except conjugal society which makes it sacred and by which you can assert that it is holy? . . . Each shall be to the other as a same self in all sincere love, all careful solicitude, every kindness of affection, in constant compassion, unflagging consolation, and faithful devotedness.

In other words, Hugh saw marriage as a matter of Christian love.

The reformers also proclaimed the special importance of the sacrament of the Eucharist (holy communion), received by eating the wafer (the body of Christ) and drinking wine (the blood of Christ) during the Mass. Gregory VII called the Mass "the greatest thing in the Christian religion." No layman, regardless of how powerful, and no woman of any class or status at all could perform anything equal to it, for the Mass was the key to salvation.

Clerical Celibacy The new emphasis on the sacraments, which were now more thoroughly and carefully defined, along with the desire to set priests clearly apart from the laity (all who were not part of the clergy) led to vigorous enforcement of an old element of church discipline: the celibacy of priests. The demand for a celibate clergy had far-reaching significance for the history of the church. It distanced western clerics even further from their eastern Orthodox counterparts (who did not practice celibacy), exacerbating the east-west church schism of 1054. It also broke with traditional local practices, as clerical marriage was customary in some places. Gregorian reformers exhorted every cleric from the humble parish priest to the exalted bishop to refrain from marriage or to abandon his wife. Naturally, many churchmen resisted. The historian Orderic Vitalis (1075–c. 1142) reported that one zealous archbishop in Normandy

> fulfilled his duties as metropolitan [bishop] with courage and thoroughness, continually striving to separate immoral priests from their mistresses [and wives]: on one occasion when he forbade them to keep concubines he was stoned out of the synod.

Undaunted, the reformers persisted, and in 1123 the pope proclaimed all clerical marriages invalid. With its new power, the papacy was largely able to enforce the rule.

The Papal Monarchy Some of the new powers of the papacy rested on the consolidation and imposition of canon, or church, law. These laws had begun simply as rules determined at church councils. Later they were supplemented with papal declarations. Churchmen had made several attempts to gather together and organize these laws before the eleventh century. But the proliferation of rules during that century, along with the desire of Gregory's followers to clarify church law as they saw it, made a systematic collection of rules even more necessary. Around 1140, a teacher of canon law named Gratian achieved this goal with a landmark synthesis, the *Decretum*. Collecting nearly two thousand passages from the decrees of popes and councils as well as the writings of the church fathers, Gratian intended to demonstrate their essential agreement. In fact, his book's original title was *Harmony of Discordant Canons*. If he found any discord in his sources, Gratian usually imposed the harmony himself by arguing that the passages dealt with different situations. A bit later, another legal scholar revised and expanded the *Decretum*, adding ancient Roman law to the mix.

Even while Gratian was writing, the papal curia (government), centered in Rome, resembled a court of law with its own collection agency. In the course of the eleventh and twelfth centuries, the papacy developed a bureaucracy to hear cases, such as disputed elections of bishops. Churchmen not involved in litigation went to the papal curia for other purposes as well: to petition for privileges for their monasteries or to be consecrated by the pope. All these services were expensive, requiring lawyers, judges, hearing officers, notaries, and collectors. The lands owned by the papacy were not sufficient to support the growing cost of its administrative apparatus, and the petitioners and litigants themselves had to pay, a practice they resented. A satire written about 1100, in the style of the Gospels, made bitter fun of papal greed:

> There came to the court a certain wealthy clerk, fat and thick, and gross. . . . He first gave to the dispenser, second to the treasurer, third to the cardinals. But they thought among themselves that they should receive more. The Lord Pope, hearing that his cardinals had received many gifts, was sick, nigh unto death. But the rich man sent to him a couch of gold and silver and immediately he was made whole. Then the Lord Pope called his cardinals and ministers to him and said to them: "Brethren, look, lest anyone deceive you

with vain words. For I have given you an example: as I have grasped, so you grasp also."

The pope, with his law courts, bureaucracy, and financial apparatus, had become a monarch.

New Monastic Orders of Poverty

Like the popes, the monks of Cluny and other Benedictine monasteries were reformers. Unlike the popes, they spent nearly their entire day in large and magnificently outfitted churches singing a long and complex liturgy consisting of Masses, prayers, and psalms. These "black monks"—so called because they dyed their robes black—reached the height of their popularity in the eleventh century. Their monasteries often housed hundreds of monks, though convents for Benedictine nuns were usually less populated. Cluny was one of the largest monasteries, with some four hundred brothers in the mid-eleventh century.

In the twelfth century, the black monks' lifestyle came under attack by groups seeking a religious life of poverty. They considered the opulence of a huge and gorgeous monastery like Cluny to be a sign of greed rather than honor. (See the illustration below.) The Carthusian order founded by Bruno of Cologne in the 1080s was one such group. Each monk took a vow of silence and lived as a hermit in his own small hut. Monks occasionally joined others for prayer in a common prayer room, or oratory. When not engaged in prayer or meditation, the Carthusians copied manuscripts. They considered this task part of their religious vocation, a way to preach God's word with their hands rather than their mouths. The Carthusian order grew slowly. Each monastery was limited to only twelve monks, the number of the Apostles.

The Cistercians, by contrast, expanded rapidly. Their guiding spirit was **St. Bernard** (c. 1090–1153), who arrived at the Burgundian monastery of Cîteaux (in Latin, Cistercium, hence the name of the monks) in 1112 along with about thirty friends and relatives. Soon he became abbot of Clairvaux, one of a cluster of Cistercian monasteries in Burgundy. By the mid-twelfth century, more than three hundred monasteries spread throughout Europe were following what they took to be the customs of Cîteaux. Nuns too—as eager as monks to live the life of simplicity and poverty that they believed the Apostles had enjoyed and endured—adopted Cistercian cus-

St. Bernard: The most important Cistercian abbot (early twelfth century) and the chief preacher of the Second Crusade.

Cluny (twelfth century)
The church of the monastery of Cluny, built under the abbot Hugh (who appears with Matilda on page 323), was the largest and grandest in all of Christendom in the twelfth century. In its cavernous stone building, the sounds of the liturgy echoed throughout the day. Unfortunately, much of the church was torn down after the French Revolution in 1789. The depiction here is an image of the interior that relies on the best archaeological insights combined with computer-enhanced technologies. *(Major Ecclésia © on-situ/Arts et Metiers ParisTech/Centre des Monuments Nationaux—2010.)*

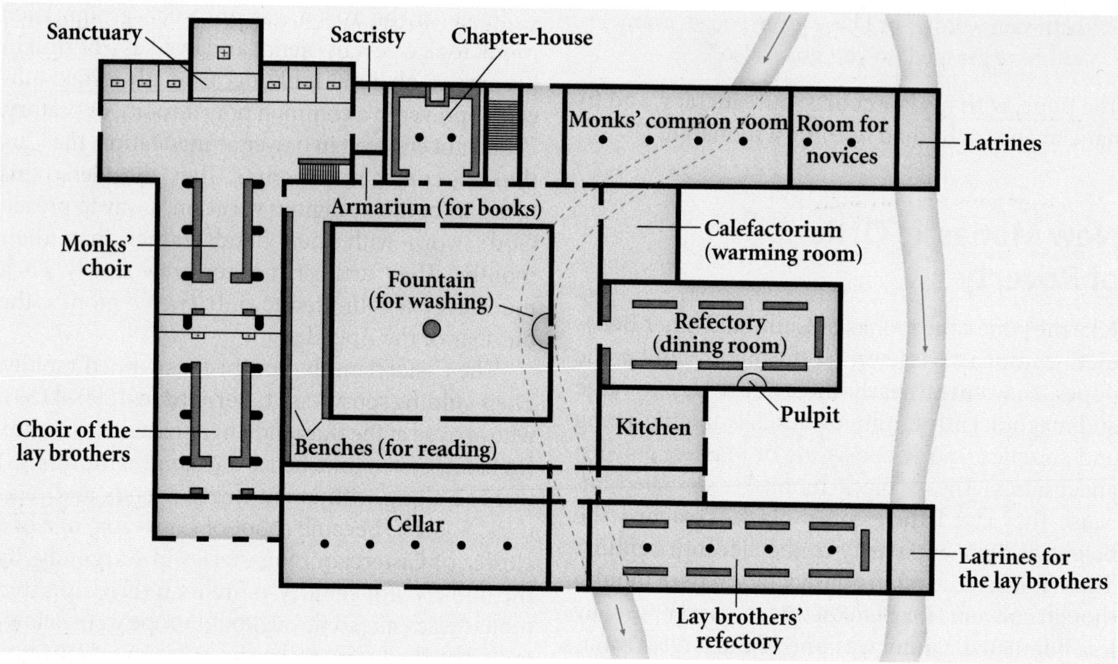

FIGURE 10.1 Floor Plan of a Cistercian Monastery
Cistercian monasteries seldom deviated much from this standard plan, which perfectly suited their dual nature—one half for the lay brothers, who worked in the fields, the other half for the monks, who performed the devotions. This plan shows the first floor. Above were the dormitories. The lay brothers slept above their cellar and refectory, the monks above their chapter house, common room, and room for novices. No one had a private bedroom, just as the rule of St. Benedict prescribed. *(Adapted from Wolfgang Braunfels,* Monasteries of Western Europe *[Princeton, NJ: Princeton University Press, 1972], 75.)*

Le Thoronet
Le Thoronet, a Cistercian monastery founded in 1136, boasted a small and plain church devoid of any wall paintings, ornaments, or sculpture. Nothing was to interfere with the contemplative inner lives of the monks worshipping there. *(Giraudon/The Bridgeman Art Library International.)*

toms. By the end of the twelfth century, the Cistercians were an order: all of their houses followed rules determined at the General Chapter, a meeting at which the abbots met to hammer out legislation.

Although they held up the rule of St. Benedict as the foundation of their monastic life, the Cistercians created a lifestyle all their own, largely governed by the goal of simplicity. Rejecting even the conceit of blackening their robes, they left them undyed (hence their nickname, the "white monks"). Cistercian monasteries were remarkably standardized. As shown in Figure 10.1, there were two halves to each monastery: the eastern half was for the monks, and the western half was for the lay brothers. The lay brothers did the hard manual labor necessary to keep the other monks—the "choir" monks—free to worship.

Cistercian churches reflected the order's emphasis on poverty. The churches were small, made of smoothly hewn, undecorated stone. Wall paintings and sculpture were prohibited. St. Bernard wrote a scathing attack on the sort of decorative sculpture shown in this chapter's opening illustration, the frieze depicting Dives and Lazarus:

> What is the point of ridiculous monstrosities in the cloister where there are brethren reading—I mean those extraordinary deformed beauties

> and beautiful deformities? What are those lascivious apes doing, those fierce lions, monstrous centaurs, half-men and spotted leopards? . . . It is more diverting to decipher marble than the text before you.

The Cistercians had no such visual diversions, but the simplicity of their buildings and of their clothing also had its beauty. Illuminated by the pure white light that came through clear glass windows, Cistercian churches like the one at Le Thoronet (see the illustration on page 328) were bright, cool, and serene.

True to this emphasis on purity, the communal liturgy of the Cistercians was shorn of the many additions found in the houses of the black monks. The white monks dedicated themselves to monastic administration as well as to private prayer and contemplation. Each house had large and highly organized farms and grazing lands called granges. Cistercian monks spent much of their time managing their estates and flocks, both of which were yielding handsome profits by the end of the twelfth century. Although they reacted against the wealth of the commercial revolution, the Cistercians became part of it, and managerial expertise was an integral part of their monastic life.

At the same time, the Cistercians emphasized a spirituality of intense personal emotion. St. Bernard said:

> Often enough when we approach the altar to pray our hearts are dry and lukewarm. But if we persevere, there comes an unexpected infusion of grace, our breast expands as it were, and our interior is filled with an overflowing love.

The Cistercians emphasized not only human emotion but also Christ's and Mary's humanity. While pilgrims continued to stream to the tombs and reliquaries of saints, the Cistercians dedicated all their churches to the Virgin Mary (for whom they had no relics) because for them she signified the model of a loving mother. Indeed, the Cistercians regularly used maternal imagery (as St. Bernard's description invoking the metaphor of a flowing breast illustrates) to describe the nurturing care that Jesus provided to humans. The Cistercian Jesus was approachable, human, protective, even mothering.

Many who were not members of the Cistercian order held similar views of God; their spirituality signaled wider changes. For example, around 1099, St. Anselm wrote a theological treatise entitled *Why God Became Man*, arguing that since man had sinned, only a sinless man could redeem him. St. Anselm's work represented a new theological emphasis on the redemptive power of human charity, including that of Jesus as a human being. As Anselm was writing, the crusaders were heading for the very place of Christ's crucifixion, making his humanity more real and powerful to people who walked in the holy "place of God's humiliation and our redemption," as one chronicler put it. Yet this new stress on the loving bonds that tied Christians together also led to the persecution of non-Christians, especially Jews and Muslims.

REVIEW QUESTION What were the causes and consequences of the Gregorian reform?

The Crusades

The crusades were the culmination of two separate historical movements: pilgrimages and holy wars. As pilgrimages to the Holy Land, the place where Jesus had lived and died, they drew on a long tradition of making pious voyages to sacred shrines to petition for help or cure. The relics of Jesus's crucifixion in Jerusalem, and even the region around it, attracted pilgrims long before the First Crusade was called in 1095.

As holy wars blessed by church leaders, the crusades had a prehistory. The Truce of God, begun in the late tenth century, depended on knights ready to go to battle to uphold it. The Normans' war against Sicily had the pope's approval. Already, as we have seen, the battle of 1063 in the reconquista of Spain was fought with a papal indulgence.

European crusaders established states in the Middle East that lasted for two hundred years. A tiny strip of crusader states along the eastern Mediterranean survived — perilously — until 1291. Although the crusades ultimately failed, in the sense that the crusaders did not succeed in permanently retaining the Holy Land for Christendom, they were a pivotal episode in Western civilization, marking the first stage of European overseas expansion.

Calling the Crusade

The events leading to the First Crusade began with the entry of the Seljuk Turks into Asia Minor (Map 10.2). As noted in Chapter 9, the Muslim world had splintered into numerous small states during the 900s. Weakened by disunity, those states were easy prey for the fierce Seljuk Turks — Sunni Muslims inspired by religious zeal to take over both Islamic and infidel (unbeliever) regions. By the 1050s, they had captured Baghdad, subjugated the Abbasid caliphate, and begun to threaten Byzantium.

The difficulties the Byzantine emperor Romanus IV had in pulling together an army to attack the Turks reveal how weak his position had become. Unable to muster Byzantine troops — which

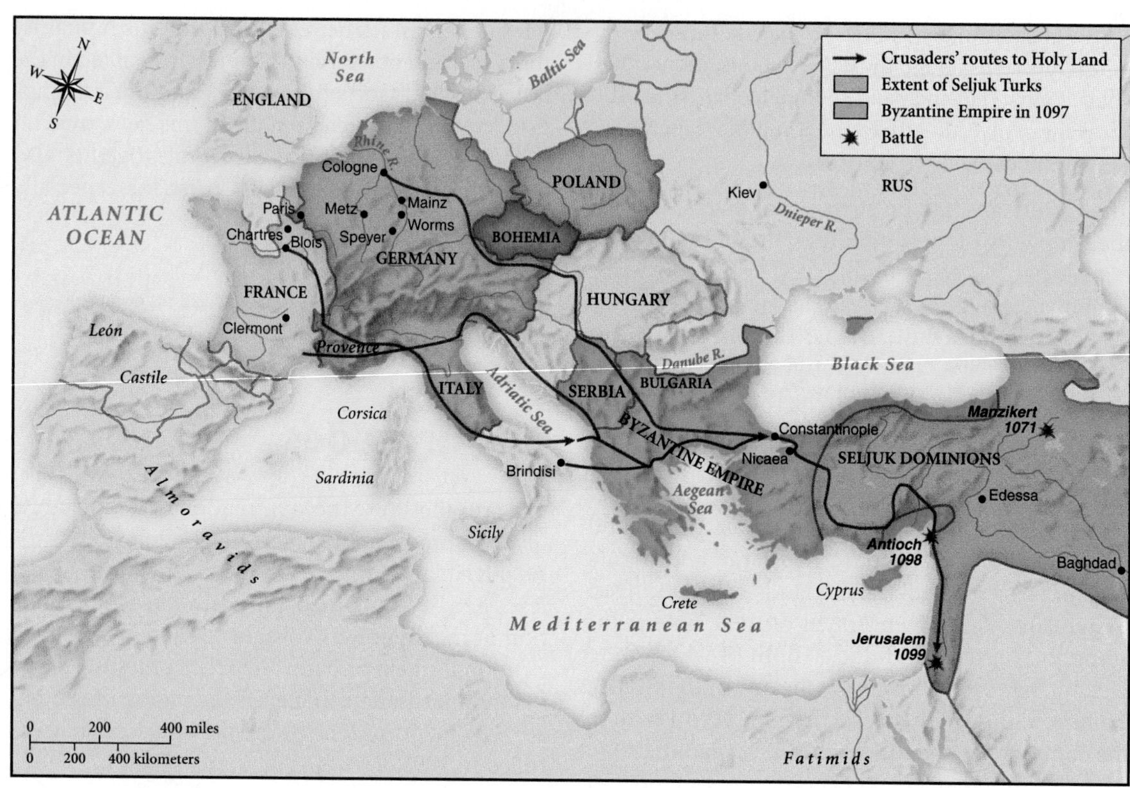

MAP 10.2 The First Crusade, 1096–1099

The First Crusade was a major military undertaking that required organization, movement over both land and sea, and enormous resources. Four main groups were responsible for the conquest of Jerusalem. One began at Cologne, in northern Germany; a second group started out from Blois, in France; the third originated just to the west of Provence; and the fourth launched ships from Brindisi, at the heel of Italy. All joined up at Constantinople, where their leaders negotiated with Alexius Comnenus for help and supplies in return for a pledge of vassalage to the emperor.

were either busy defending their own districts or were under the control of *dynatoi* (see page 280) wary of sending support to the emperor—Romanus had to rely on a mercenary army made up of Normans, Franks, Slavs, and even Turks. This motley force met the Seljuks at Manzikert in what is today eastern Turkey. The battle was a disaster for Romanus: the Seljuks routed the Byzantine army and captured the emperor. The battle of Manzikert (1071) marked the end of Byzantine domination in the region.

Gradually settling in Asia Minor, the Turks extended their control across the empire and beyond, all the way to Jerusalem, which had been under Muslim control since the seventh century and most recently had been under the rule of the Shi'ite Fatimids. In 1095, the Byzantine emperor **Alexius I (Alexius Comnenus)** (r. 1081–1118) appealed for help to Pope Urban II, hoping to get new mercenary troops for a fresh offensive.

Urban II (r. 1088–1099) chose to interpret the request in his own way. He made a long voyage through France, consecrating churches, cemeteries, and other holy places. In 1095 he attended a church council in Clermont; after the council had finished the usual business of proclaiming the Truce of God and condemning simony among the clergy, Urban moved outside the church and addressed an already excited throng:

> Oh, race of Franks, race from across the mountains, race beloved and chosen by God. . . . Let hatred depart from among you, let your quarrels end, let wars cease, and let all dissensions and controversies slumber. Enter upon the road to the Holy Sepulcher; wrest that land from the wicked race, and subject it to yourselves.

Alexius I (Alexius Comnenus): The Byzantine emperor (r. 1081–1118) whose leadership marked a new triumph of the *dynatoi*. His request to Pope Urban II for troops to fight the Turks turned into the First Crusade.

Urban II: The pope (r. 1088–1099) responsible for calling the First Crusade in 1095.

The crowd reportedly responded with one voice: "God wills it." Urban offered all who made the difficult trek to the Holy Land an indulgence—the forgiveness of sins. The pains of the trip would substitute for ordinary penance.

Historians remain divided over Urban's motives for his massive call to arms. Certainly he hoped to win Christian control of the Holy Land. He was also anxious to fulfill the goals of the Truce of God by turning the entire "race of Franks" into a peace militia dedicated to holy purposes, an army of God. Just as the Truce of God mobilized whole communities to fight against anyone who broke the truce, so the First Crusade mobilized armed groups sworn to free the Holy Land of its enemies. Finally, Urban's call placed the papacy in a new position of leadership, one that complemented in a military arena the position the popes had gained in the church hierarchy.

Inspired by local preachers, men and women, rich and poor, young and old, laypeople and clerics heeded Urban's call to go on the **First Crusade** (1096–1099). Between 60,000 and 100,000 people abandoned their homes and braved the rough journey to the Holy Land to fight for God. They also went to gain land; this was especially true of younger sons of aristocrats, who because of the tradition of primogeniture (whereby the oldest son alone was heir) could not expect an inheritance. Some knights went because they were obligated to follow their lord. Others hoped for plunder.

Although women were discouraged from going, some crusaders were accompanied by their wives. Other women went as servants; a few may have been fighters. Children and old people, not able to fight, made the cords for siege engines—giant machines used to hurl stones at enemy fortifications. As Christians undertook more crusades during the twelfth century, the transport and supply of these armies became a lucrative business for the commercial classes of maritime Italian cities such as Venice, strategically located on the route eastward.

Statuette of a Crusader
This statuette, perhaps made by the Normans in southern Italy, shows a crusader in his war gear—a coat of mail, a helmet, a lozenge-shaped shield strapped to his left shoulder, a sword, and a heavy lance held at the ready under his right arm. *(Réunion des Musées Nationaux/Art Resource, NY.)*

The First Crusade

The armies of the First Crusade were organized not as one military force but rather as separate militias, each commanded by a different individual. Fulcher of Chartres (c. 1059–c. 1127), an eyewitness, reported: "There grew armies of innumerable people coming together from everywhere. Thus a countless multitude speaking many languages and coming from many regions was to be seen." Fulcher was describing the armies led by nobles and authorized by the pope. There were also irregular armies with their own agendas; most were soon decimated. The main forces, despite numerous difficulties, managed to achieve their goal to take Jerusalem.

Attacking the Jews A number of armed groups, not heeding the pope's official departure date in August, took off in late spring. Historians have called these loosely affiliated groups the People's (or Peasants') Crusade. Some of the participants were peasants, others knights. Inspired by the fiery and charismatic orator Peter the Hermit and others like him, they took off for the Holy Land via the Rhineland. This unlikely route was no mistake: the crusaders took it to kill Jews. By 1095, three cities of the Rhineland—Speyer, Worms, and Mainz—had especially large and flourishing Jewish populations. (See the illustrations on pages 315 and 332.) They had long-established relationships with the local bishops, and in 1090 Emperor Henry IV had granted the Jews of Speyer and Worms a privilege of special protection.

It was against such Jewish communities that the People's Crusade—joined by local nobles, knights, and townspeople—vented its fury. As one commentator put it, the crusaders considered it ridiculous to attack Muslims when other infidels lived in their own backyards: "That's doing our work backward." The Rhineland Jews faced either forced conversion or death. Some of their persecutors relented when

---

First Crusade: The massive armed pilgrimage to Jerusalem that lasted from 1096 to 1099. It resulted in the massacre of Jews in the Rhineland (1095), the sack of Jerusalem (1099), and the setting up of the crusader states.

Window from a Mikvah
A mikvah is a ritual bathhouse. Within each one is a pool of water deep enough for a person to be totally immersed. The mikvah is used in purification rituals, most typically when Jewish women purify themselves in the pool after their menstrual period. This mikvah window at Speyer was carved by the same stonemasons who made the Speyer Cathedral windows, attesting to the close relations between Christians and Jews in that city before the attacks of the First Crusade. *(Historisches Museum der Pfalz, Speyer.)*

the Jews paid them money; others, however, attacked. Many Jews in Speyer found refuge in the bishop's castle, but at Worms and Mainz hundreds were massacred. Similar pogroms—systematic persecutions of the Jews—took place a half century later, when the preaching of the Second Crusade led to new attacks on the Jews.

Miserable as it was to die, Jews believed, it was glorious to be a martyr. The Rhineland Jews met their persecutors with uncustomary fervor, preferring to kill themselves and their children rather than be polluted by the enemy's sword. A new kind of Hebrew literature was created, celebrating the "beautiful death" of those who died in this way:

> Youths like saplings pleaded with their fathers:
> "Hurry! Hasten to do our Maker's Will!
> The One God is our portion and destiny
> Our days are over, our end has come."

Taking the Holy Land Some members of the People's Crusade died or dropped out; the rest continued through Hungary to Constantinople, where Alexius Comnenus promptly shipped them across the Bosporus—most to meet their death in Asia Minor. In the autumn, the main armies of the crusaders began to arrive, their leaders squabbling with Alexius as their expectations and his clashed. Eventually, they promised that whatever they conquered they would return to the Byzantine Empire. They didn't keep the promise.

Considering them too weak to bother with, the Turks spared the arriving crusaders, who made their way south to the Seljuk capital at Nicaea. At first, their armies were uncoordinated and their food supplies uncertain, but soon the crusaders organized themselves, setting up a "council of princes" that included their best leaders, while the Byzantines supplied food at a nearby port. The crusaders managed to defeat a Turkish army that attacked from nearby; then, surrounding Nicaea and besieging it with catapults and other war machines, they took the city on June 18, 1097, dutifully handing it over to Alexius.

Gradually, the crusaders left the Byzantine orbit. Most of them went toward Antioch, which stood in the way of their conquest of Jerusalem, but one led his followers to Edessa, where they took over the city and its outlying area, creating the first of the crusader states: the county of Edessa. Meanwhile, the main body of crusaders remained stymied for eight months before the thick and heavily fortified walls of Antioch. Then, in a surprise turnaround, they entered the town and found themselves besieged by Turks from the outside. Their mood grim, they rallied when a peasant named Peter Bartholomew reported that he had seen buried in the main church in Antioch the Holy Lance that had pierced Christ's body. (Antioch had a flourishing Christian population even under Muslim rule.) After a night of feverish digging, the crusaders found an object they believed to be the Holy Lance and prepared for a decisive confrontation with the Turks. "Then with God's right hand fighting with us," wrote Fulcher of Chartres, "we forced them to drive together to flee, and to leave their camps with everything in them."

From Antioch, it was only a short march to Jerusalem. But disputes among the leaders delayed that next step for over a year. One crusader claimed Antioch. Another eventually took charge—provisionally—of the expedition to Jerusalem. Quarrels among Muslim rulers eased his way, and an alliance with one of them allowed free passage through what would have been enemy territory. In early June 1099, a large force of crusaders amassed before the walls of Jerusalem and set to work building siege engines—some an astonishing three stories high. In mid-July they attacked, breached the walls, and entered the city. "Now that our men had possession of the walls and towers, wonderful sights were to be seen," wrote Raymond d'Aguiliers, a priest serving one of the crusade leaders. He continued:

> Some of our men (and this was the more merciful) cut off the heads of their enemies; others shot them with arrows, so that they fell from the towers; others tortured them longer by casting them into the flames. Piles of heads, hands, and

feet were to be seen in the streets of the city. . . . In the Temple and porch of Solomon, men rode in blood up to their knees and bridle reins. Indeed, it was a just and splendid judgment of God that this place should be filled with the blood of the unbelievers, since it had suffered so long from their blasphemies.

The Crusader States

The main objective of the First Crusade — to wrest the Holy Land from the Muslims and subject it to Christian rule — had now been accomplished. The leaders of the expedition did not give the conquered territories to Alexius but held onto them instead. By 1109 they had carved out several tiny states in the Holy Land.

Because the crusader states were created by conquest, they were treated as lordships. The rulers granted fiefs to their own vassals, and some of these men in turn gave portions of their holdings as fiefs to their own vassals. Many other vassals simply lived in the households of their lords. Since most Europeans went home after the First Crusade, the rulers who remained learned to coexist with the indigenous population, which included Muslims, Jews, and Greek Orthodox Christians (see "New Sources, New Perspectives," page 334). They encouraged a lively trade at their ports, visited by merchants from Italy, Byzantium, and Islamic cities.

The main concerns of these rulers, however, were military. They set up castles and recruited knights from Europe. So organized for war was this society that it produced a new and militant kind of monasticism: the Knights Templar. The Templars vowed themselves to poverty and chastity. But unlike monks, the Templars, whose name came from their living quarters in the area of the former Jewish Temple at Jerusalem, devoted themselves to warfare. Their first mission — to protect the pilgrimage routes from Palestine to Jerusalem — soon diversified. They manned the town garrisons of the crusader states, and they transported money from Europe to the Holy Land. In this way, the Order of the Templars became enormously wealthy (even though individual monks owned nothing), with branch "banks" in major cities across Europe.

The Disastrous Second Crusade

The presence of the Knights Templar did not prevent the Seljuks from taking the county of Edessa in 1144. This was the beginning of the slow but steady shrinking of the crusader states, and it sparked the Second Crusade (1147–1149). Called by Pope Eugenius III (r. 1145–1153), it attracted, for the first time, ruling monarchs to the cause: Louis VII of France and Emperor Conrad III in Germany. (The First Crusade had been led by counts and dukes.) St. Bernard, the charismatic and influential Cistercian abbot, was its tireless preacher. But Bernard and the pope were equally interested in other ventures. Eugenius supported Alfonso VI of Castile in his bid to continue the reconquista of Spain. He also encouraged German nobles to turn their interest in crusading not toward the Holy Land but rather northeastward — to conquer the pagans on the Baltic coast. St. Bernard inspired Flemings and Germans to attack the Portuguese city of Lisbon, aiding the king of Portugal in his own bid to expand into Muslim territory.

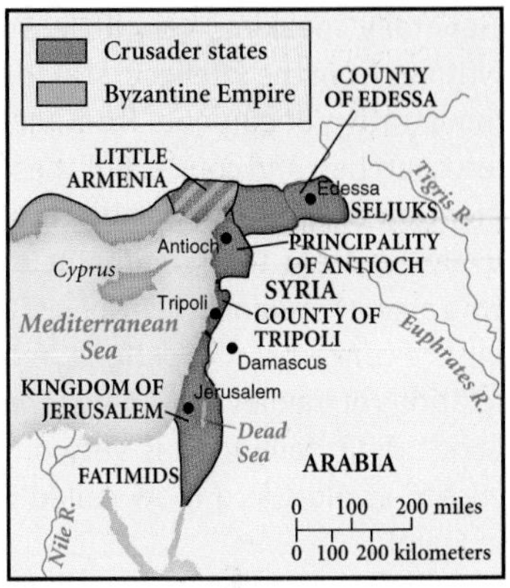

The Crusader States in 1109

Little organization or planning went into the Second Crusade. The emperor at Byzantium was hardly involved. Louis VII and Conrad had no coordinated strategy, and after Conrad had crossed the Bosporus to Asia Minor, it was too late for Louis to beg him to wait. As a chronicler of the crusade remarked, "Those whose common will had undertaken a common task should also use a common plan of action."

In fact, the Germans themselves had no clear plan, breaking into two groups that went their separate ways. All the armies — both French and German — were badly hurt by Turkish attacks. Furthermore, they largely acted at cross-purposes with the Christian rulers still in the Holy Land.

At last the leaders met at Acre and agreed to storm Damascus, which was under Muslim control and a thorn in the side of the Christian king of Jerusalem. On July 24, 1148, they were on the city's outskirts, but, encountering a stiff defense, they abandoned the attack after five days, suffering many losses as they retreated. The crusade was over.

The Second Crusade had one decisive outcome: it led Louis VII to divorce his wife, Eleanor, the heiress of Aquitaine. He was already primed to do this, since she had provided him with a daughter but no son. During the crusade, on which she accompanied her husband, he came to suspect her of infidelity, and after she gave birth to yet another daughter, their marriage was "dissolved" by the pope — that is, found to have been uncanonical in the first place. Eleanor promptly married Henry, count of Anjou and duke of Normandy. This marriage had far-reaching consequences, as we shall see, when Henry became King Henry II of England in 1154.

NEW SOURCES, NEW PERSPECTIVES

The Cairo Geniza

What do historians know about the daily life of ordinary people in the Middle Ages? Generally speaking, very little. We have writings from the intellectual elite and administrative documents from monasteries, churches, and courts. But these rarely mention ordinary folk, and if they do, it is always from the standpoint of those who are not ordinary themselves. Glimpsing the concerns, occupations, and family relations of medieval people as they went about their daily lives is very difficult—except at old Cairo (now called Fustat), in Egypt.

Cairo is exceptional because of a cache of unusual sources that were discovered in the *geniza* ("depository") of the Jewish synagogue near the city. Because their writings might include the name of God, members of the Jewish community left everything that they wrote, including their notes, letters, and even shopping lists, in the geniza to await ceremonial burial. Cairo was not the only place where this was the practice. But by chance at Cairo, the papers were left untouched in the depository and not buried. In 1890, when the synagogue was remodeled, workers tore down the walls of the geniza and discovered literally heaps of documents.

Many of these documents were purchased by American and English collectors and ended up in libraries in New York, Philadelphia, and Cambridge, England, where they remain. As is often the case in historical research, the questions that scholars ask are just as important as the sources themselves. At first, historians did not ask what the documents could tell them about everyday life. They wanted to know how to transcribe and read them; they wanted to study the evolution of their handwriting (a discipline called paleography). They also needed to organize the material. Dispersed among various libraries, the documents were a hodgepodge of lists, books, pages, and fragments. For example, the first page of a personal letter might be in one library, the second page in a completely different location. For decades, scholars were busy simply transcribing the documents with a view to printing and publishing their contents. Not until 1964 was a bibliography of these published materials made available.

Only then, when they knew where to find the sources and how to piece them together, did historians, most notably S. D. Goitein, begin to work through the papers for their historical interest. What Goitein learned through the remains of the geniza amplified historians' understanding of the everyday life of much of the Mediterranean world. He discovered a cosmopolitan community occupied with trade, schooling, marriages, divorces, poetry, litigation—all the common issues and activities of a middle-class society. For example, some documents showed that middle-class Jewish women disposed of their own property and that widows often reared and educated their children on their own.

More recently, Mark R. Cohen has looked at the underclass—the poor and needy—represented in the geniza documents. He has discovered workers down on their luck, starving children, and refugees in need of aid. At moments of crisis, these people wrote letters appealing for help. These were private messages, usually addressed to wealthier individuals or a small group: "I have been earning a livelihood, just managing to get by," wrote a man named Yahya sometime around 1100 to a hoped-for benefactor. He continued:

> I have responsibility for children and a family and an old mother advanced in years and blind. I incurred losses because of debts owed to Muslims in Alexandria. I remained in hiding. . . . Unable to go out, I began watching my children and old mother starve. . . . I heard that your excellency has a heart for his fellow Jews and is a generous person, who acts to receive reward from God and seeks to do good works, so I throw myself before God and you to help me.

In the last few years, the Friedberg Genizah Project (FGP) has begun digitizing, transcribing, and posting on the Web all of the geniza documents along with an exhaustive bibliography. A demo is readily available online at http://www.genizah.org/.

So think twice the next time you throw away a piece of paper. If a historian of the year 3000 were to read your notes, lists, or letters, what would he or she learn about your culture?

Questions to Consider

1. **What do the documents in the geniza tell us about Muslim as well as Jewish life in medieval Cairo?**
2. **What new questions might historians explore with the geniza documents?**
3. **How might digitization and Web access change the questions that historians ask?**

Further Reading

Cohen, Mark R. *The Voice of the Poor in the Middle Ages: An Anthology of Documents from the Cairo Geniza.* 2005.

Goitein, S. D. *A Mediterranean Society: The Jewish Communities of the Arab World as Portrayed in the Documents of the Cairo Geniza.* 6 vols. 1967–1983.

http://www.genizah.org/

Source: Quote is from Mark R. Cohen, *The Voice of the Poor in the Middle Ages: An Anthology of Documents from the Cairo Geniza* (Princeton: Princeton University Press, 2005), 22–23.

The Long-Term Impact of the Crusades

The success of the First Crusade was a mirage. The European toehold in the Middle East could not last. Numerous new crusades were called, and eight major ones were fought between the first in 1096 and the last at the end of the thirteenth century. But most Europeans were not willing to commit the vast resources and personnel that would have been necessary to maintain the crusader states, which fell to the Muslims permanently in 1291. In Europe, the crusades to the Holy Land became a sort of myth—an elusive goal that receded before more pressing ventures nearer to home. Yet they inspired far-flung expeditions like Columbus's in 1492. Although the crusades stimulated trade a bit, especially enhancing the prosperity of Italian cities like Venice, the commercial revolution would have happened without them. On the other hand, modern taxation systems may well have been stimulated by the machinery of revenue collection used to finance the crusades.

In the Middle East, the crusades worsened—but did not cause—Islamic disunity. Initially, the Muslims were perplexed by Europeans meddling in a region that had had only peripheral importance to them as a place of pilgrimage. Before the crusades, Muslims had a complex relationship with the Christians in their midst—taxing but not persecuting them, allowing their churches to stand and be used, permitting pilgrims into Jerusalem to visit the holy sites of Christ's life and death. In many ways, the split between Shi'ite and Sunni Muslims was more serious than the rift between Muslims and Christians. The crusades, and especially the conquest of Jerusalem, which was extraordinarily brutal, shocked and dismayed Muslims: "We have mingled blood with flowing tears," wrote one of their poets, "and there is no room left in us for pity."

REVIEW QUESTION How and why was the First Crusade a success, and how and why was it a failure?

The Revival of Monarchies

Even as the papacy was exercising its new authority by annulling marriages and calling crusades, kings and other rulers were, for the most part, enhancing and consolidating their own power. They created new ideologies and dusted off old theories to justify their hegemony (dominating influence), they

Alexius Comnenus Stands before Christ
In this twelfth-century manuscript illumination, the Byzantine emperor Alexius is shown in the presence of Christ. Note that both are almost exactly the same height, and the halos around their heads are the same size. What do you suppose is the significance of Christ sitting on a throne while the emperor is standing? Compare this image of the emperor with that on page 278. What statement is the twelfth-century artist making about the relationship between Christ and Alexius? *(© Biblioteca Apostolica Vaticana [Vatican Library] Vat. Lat.)*

hired officials to work for them, and they found vassals and churchmen to support them. Money gave them greater effectiveness, and the new commercial economy supplied them with increased revenues. The exception was the emperor in Germany, weakened by the Investiture Conflict.

Reconstructing the Empire at Byzantium

Ten years after the disastrous battle at Manzikert, Alexius Comnenus became the Byzantine emperor. He was an upstart — from a family of dynatoi — who saw the opportunity to seize the throne in a time of crisis. The people of Constantinople were suffering under a combination of high taxes and rising living costs. In addition, the empire was under attack on every side — from Normans in southern Italy, Seljuk Turks in Asia Minor, and new groups in the Balkans. (It is no wonder that an artist of his time hopefully pictured Alexius receiving Christ's blessing [see the illustration on page 335].) However, the emperor managed to avert the worst dangers. We have already seen how astutely he handled the crusaders who arrived on his doorstep.

To wage all the wars he had to fight, Alexius relied on mercenaries and allied dynatoi, armed and mounted like European knights and accompanied by their own troops. In return for their services, he gave these nobles lifetime possession of large imperial estates and their dependent peasants. Meanwhile, Alexius satisfied the urban elite by granting them new offices. He normally got on well with the patriarch and Byzantine clergy, for emperor and church depended on each other to suppress heresy and foster orthodoxy. The emperors of the Comnenian dynasty (1081–1185) thus gained in prestige and military might, but at the price of significant concessions to the nobility.

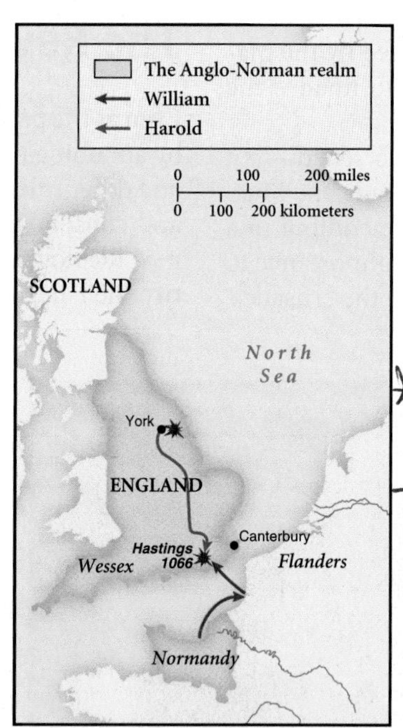

Norman Conquest of England, 1066

England under Norman Rule

In the twelfth century, the kings of England were the most powerful monarchs of Europe in large part because they ruled their whole kingdom by right of conquest. When the Anglo-Saxon king Edward the Confessor (r. 1042–1066) died childless in 1066, three main contenders vied for the English throne: Harold, earl of Wessex, an Englishman close to the king but not of royal blood; Harald Hardrada, the king of Norway, who had unsuccessfully attempted to conquer the Danes and now turned hopefully to England; and William, duke of Normandy, who claimed that Edward had promised him the throne fifteen years earlier. On his deathbed, Edward had named Harold of Wessex to succeed him, and a royal advisory committee that had the right to choose the king had confirmed the nomination.

The Norman Invasion, 1066 When he learned that Harold had been anointed and crowned, William (1027–1087) prepared for battle. Appealing to the pope, he received the banner of St. Peter and with this symbol of God's approval launched the invasion of England, filling his ships with warriors recruited from many parts of France.

Just before William's invasion force landed, Harold defeated Harald Hardrada at Stamford Bridge, near York, in the north of England. When he heard of William's arrival, Harold turned his forces south, marching them 250 miles and picking up new soldiers along the way to meet the Normans.

The two armies clashed at the **battle of Hastings** on October 14, 1066, in one of history's rare decisive battles. Both armies had about seven or eight thousand men, Harold's in defensive position on a slope, William's attacking from below. All the men were crammed into a very small space as they began the fight. Most of Harold's men were on foot, armed with battle-axes and stones tied to sticks, which could be thrown with great force. William's army consisted of perhaps three thousand mounted knights, a thousand archers, and the rest infantry.

At first William's knights broke rank, frightened by the deadly battle-axes thrown by the English; but then some of the English also broke rank as they pursued the knights. William removed his helmet so his men would know him, rallying them to surround and cut down the English who had

---

battle of Hastings: The battle of 1066 that replaced the Anglo-Saxon king with a Norman one and thus tied England to the rest of Europe as never before.

broken away. Gradually Harold's troops were worn down, particularly by William's archers, whose arrows flew a hundred yards, much farther than an Englishman could throw his battle-ax. (Some of the archers are depicted on the lower margin of the Bayeux "Tapestry," below.) By dusk, King Harold was dead and his army utterly defeated. No other army gathered to oppose the successful claimant. (See Document, "Penances for the Invaders," page 338.)

Some people in England gladly supported William, considering his victory a verdict from God and hoping to gain a place in the new order themselves. But William — known to posterity as William the Conqueror — wanted to replace, not assimilate, the Anglo-Saxons. During William's reign, families from the continent almost totally supplanted the English aristocracy. Although the English peasantry remained — now with new lords — they were severely shaken. A twelfth-century historian claimed to record William's deathbed confession:

> I have persecuted [England's] native inhabitants beyond all reason. Whether gentle or simple, I have cruelly oppressed them; many I unjustly disinherited; innumerable multitudes, especially in the county of York, perished through me by famine or the sword.

Modern historians estimate that one out of five people in England died as a result of the Norman conquest and its immediate aftermath.

Institutions of Norman Kingship

Although the Normans destroyed a generation of English men and women, they preserved and extended many Anglo-Saxon institutions. For example, the new kings used writs — terse written instructions — to communicate orders, and they retained the old administrative divisions and legal system of the shires. However, the Norman kings also drew from continental institutions. They set up a graded political hierarchy, culminating in the king, whose strength was reinforced by his castles and made visible to all. Because all of England was the king's by conquest, he could treat it as his booty; William kept about 20 percent of the land for himself and divided the rest, distributing it in large but scattered fiefs to a relatively small number of his barons and family members, lay and ecclesiastical, as well as to some lesser men, such as personal servants and soldiers. In turn, these men maintained their own vassals; they owed the king military service—and the service of a fixed number of their vassals—along with certain dues, such as reliefs (money paid upon inheriting a fief) and aids (payments made on important occasions).

Bayeux "Tapestry" (detail)

This famous "tapestry" is misnamed; it is really an embroidery, 230 feet long and 20 inches wide, created to tell the story of the Norman conquest of England from William's point of view. In this detail, the Norman archers are lined up along the lower margin, in a band below the armies. In the central band, the English warriors are on foot (the one at the farthest right holds a long battle-ax), while the Norman knights are on horseback. Who seems to be winning?

(Detail of the Bayeux Tapestry—eleventh century. By special permission of the City of Bayeux.)

DOCUMENT

Penances for the Invaders (1070)

Although William's conquest of England took place with papal blessing, nevertheless the church still insisted that the shedding of blood was a sin requiring penance. This explains why the indulgence (forgiveness of sins) offered by the pope to those who fought in Spain against the Muslims in 1063 or to those went on the First Crusade in 1096 was so important. Such an indulgence was not given to those who participated in the invasion of England. In this document the Norman bishops impose penances on those who participated in the invasion and conquest.

This is an institution of penance according to the decrees of the bishops of the Normans, confirmed by the authority of the pope through his legate Ermenfrid, bishop of [Sion, Switzerland]. It is to apply to those men whom William, duke of the Normans [commanded], and who gave him military service as their duty.

Anyone who knows that he killed a man in the great battle [of Hastings] must do penance for one year for each man that he killed.

Anyone who wounded a man, and does not know whether he killed him or not, must do penance for forty days for each man he thus struck (if he can remember the number), either continuously or at intervals.

Anyone who does not know the number of those he wounded or killed must, at the discretion of his bishop, do penance for one day in each week for the remainder of his life; or, if he can, let him redeem his sin by a perpetual alms [charity], either by building or by endowing a church.

The [churchmen] who fought, or who were armed for fighting, must do penance as if they had committed these sins in their own country, for they are forbidden by the canons [church law] to do battle.

Source: David C. Douglas and George W. Greenaway, eds., *English Historical Documents*, vol. 2: *1042–1189*, 2nd ed. (London: Routledge, 1981), 649.

Question to Consider

- **What impact would the imposition of penance have on the daily life of an ordinary warrior?**

Domesday Apart from the revenues and rights expected from the nobles, the king of England commanded the peasantry as well. Twenty years after his conquest, in 1086, William ordered a survey and census of England, popularly called Domesday because, like the reckoning Christians expected at doomsday, it provided facts that could not be appealed. It was the most extensive inventory of land, livestock, taxes, and population that had ever been compiled in Europe (see "Taking Measure," page 339). According to a contemporary observer, the king

> sent his men over all England into every shire and had them find out how many hundred hides [a measure of land] there were in the shire, or what land and cattle the king himself had in the country, or what dues he ought to receive every year from the shire. . . . So very narrowly did he have the survey to be made that there was not a single hide or yard of land, nor indeed . . . an ox or a cow or a pig left out.

The king's men conducted local surveys by consulting Anglo-Saxon tax lists and by taking testimony from local jurors, men sworn to answer a series of formal questions truthfully. From these inquests, scribes wrote voluminous reports filled with facts and statements from villagers, sheriffs, priests, and barons. These reports were then summarized in Domesday itself, a concise record of England's resources that supplied the king and his officials with information such as how much and what sort of land England had, who held it, and what revenues—including the lucrative Danegeld, which was now in effect a royal tax—could be expected from it.

England and the Continent The Norman conquest tied England to the languages, politics, institutions, and culture of the continent. Modern English is an amalgam of Anglo-Saxon and Norman French, the language the Normans spoke. English commerce was linked to the wool industry in Flanders. St. Anselm, the archbishop of Canterbury and author of *Why God Became Man*, was born in Italy and served as the abbot of a monastery in Normandy before crossing the Channel to England.

The barons of England retained their estates in Normandy and elsewhere, and the kings of England often spent more time on the continent than they did on the island. When William's son Henry I (r. 1100–1135) died without male heirs, civil war soon erupted: the throne of England was fought

TAKING MEASURE

English Livestock in 1086

Domesday provided important data for the English king in 1086, and those data remain important for historians today. Although relatively few Domesday records discuss livestock—apart from the oxen that pulled the plows—documents from East Anglia and the southwest are exceptions to this rule. They show that the great preponderance of animals raised was sheep. These were grazed on the marshes of both regions. Apart from milk and meat, sheep provided wool. It is no wonder that England soon became the great exporter of raw wool to textile manufacturers in Flanders.

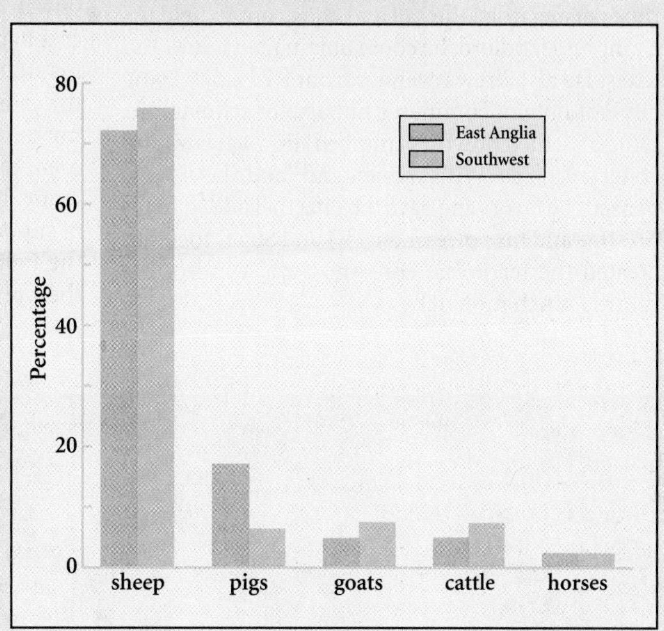

Source: Robert Bartlett, *England Under the Norman and Angevin Kings, 1075–1225* (Oxford: Clarendon Press, 2000), Fig. 7, 306).

Question to Consider

- **Why do you suppose the people of East Anglia concentrated on raising sheep instead of other types of livestock?**

over by two French counts, one married to Henry's daughter, the other to his sister. The story of England after 1066 was, in miniature, the story of Europe.

Praising the King of France

The twelfth-century kings of France were much less obviously powerful than their English and Byzantine counterparts. Yet they, too, took part in the monarchical revival. Louis VI, called Louis the Fat (r. 1108–1137), so heavy that he had to be hoisted onto his horse by a crane, was a tireless defender of royal power. We know a good deal about him and his reputation because a contemporary and close associate, Suger (1081–1152), abbot of Saint-Denis, wrote Louis's biography.

Although a churchman, Suger was a propagandist for his king. When Louis set about consolidating his rule in the Île-de-France, Suger portrayed him as a righteous hero. He thought that the king had rights over the French nobles because they were his vassals. He believed that the king had a religious role as the protector of the church and the poor. He saw Louis as another Charlemagne, a ruler for all society, not merely an overlord of the nobility. In Suger's view, Louis waged war to keep God's peace.

To be sure, the Gregorian reform had made its mark: Suger did not claim Louis was the head of the church. But he nevertheless emphasized the royal dignity and its importance to the papacy. When a pope arrived in France, Louis, not yet king, and his father, Philip I (r. 1052–1108), bowed low, but (Suger wrote), "the pope lifted them up and made them sit before him like devout sons of the apostles. In the manner of a wise man acting wisely, he conferred with them privately on the present condition of the church." In this passage Suger shows the pope in need of royal advice. Meanwhile, Suger stressed Louis's piety and active defense of the faith:

> Helped by his powerful band of armed men, or rather by the hand of God, he abruptly seized the castle [of Crécy] and captured its very strong tower as if it were simply the hut of a peasant. Having startled those criminals, he piously slaughtered the impious.

When Louis VI died in 1137, Suger's notion of the might and right of the king of France reflected reality in an extremely small area. Nevertheless, Louis laid the groundwork for the gradual extension of royal power in France. As the lord of vassals, the king could call on his men to aid him in times of war, though the most powerful among them sometimes disregarded the call and chose not to help. As a king and landlord, he could obtain many dues and taxes. He also drew revenues from Paris, a thriving city not only of commerce but also of scholarship. Officials called provosts enforced his royal laws and collected taxes. With money and land, Louis dispensed the favors and gave the gifts that added to his prestige and his power. Louis VI and Suger together created the territorial core and royal ideal of the future French monarchy.

Surviving as Emperor

As we have seen, Henry IV, king of Germany and emperor-to-be, began his reign as a child. Taken advantage of by powerful princes, he lost much of the power over the church and over Italy that his father had wielded. The Investiture Conflict thwarted his attempts to revive it: he could no longer control the church hierarchy in Germany and northern Italy, nor could he depend on bishops to work as government officials. The rebellion of the princes of Germany during the conflict was a symptom of his lack of support there, and the growing independence of the Italian cities ended his control over them and their revenues.

MAPPING THE WEST

Europe and the Mediterranean, c. 1150

A comparison with Mapping the West on page 307 reveals the major changes wrought during the century 1050–1150. England was politically tied to the continent with the Norman invasion of 1066. Soon the Seljuk Turks settled most of Anatolia, and the eastern wing of Byzantium was tightly wedged around Constantinople. At the end of the eleventh century, a narrow ribbon of crusader states was set up in the Holy Land. Meanwhile, Sicily and southern Italy came under Norman rule.

When Henry IV died and his son, Henry V (r. 1105–1125), came to the throne, the Investiture Conflict was still raging. Years of fruitless negotiations and numerous wars ended only in 1122 with the Concordat of Worms. This conceded considerable power within the church to the king, since he was understood to invest the bishops with their temporal goods—including the church buildings, estates, and taxes that belonged to them. But the concordat said nothing about the ruler's relations with the German princes or the Italian cities. When Henry V died childless in 1125, the position of the emperor was extremely uncertain.

When a German king died childless, the great bishops and princes would meet together to elect the next emperor. In 1125, numerous candidates were put forward; the winner, Lothar III (r. 1125–1137), was chosen largely because he was *not* the person designated by Henry V. Lothar had little time to reestablish royal control before he, too, died childless, leaving the princes to elect Conrad III. It was Conrad's nephew, Frederick Barbarossa, who would have a chance to find new sources of imperial power in a post-Gregorian age.

REVIEW QUESTION **Which ruler—Alexius Comnenus, William the Conqueror, or Louis VI—was the strongest, which the feeblest, and why?**

Conclusion

The commercial revolution and the building boom it spurred profoundly changed Europe. New trade, wealth, and business institutions became common in its thriving cities. Merchants and artisans became important people. Mutual and fraternal organizations like the guilds and communes expressed and reinforced the solidarity and economic interests of city dwellers. The countryside became reorganized for the market.

Sensitized by the commercial revolution to the corrupting effects of money and inspired by the model of Cluny, which seemed to "free the church from the world," reformers at the papal court began to demand a new and purified church. They were joined by ordinary laypeople, who feared that their immortal souls were jeopardized by priests who married or committed simony. Under Pope Gregory VII, the reform asserted a new vision of the church with the pope at the top. But too many people—especially rulers—depended on the old system, in which kings and bishops together kept the temporal and spiritual peace. Henry IV was particularly affected, and for him the Gregorian reform meant war: the Investiture Conflict. Although officially ended by a compromise, the conflict in fact greatly enhanced the power of the papacy and weakened that of the emperor.

The First Crusade was both cause and effect of the new power of the papacy. But the crusades were not just papal projects. They were fueled by enormous popular piety as well as the ambitions of European rulers. They resulted in a ribbon of crusader states along the Eastern Mediterranean that lasted until 1291.

Apart from the emperor, rulers in the period after the Investiture Conflict gained new prestige and, with the wealth of the commercial revolution, the ability to hire civil servants and impose their will as never before. The Norman ruler of England is a good example of the new-style king; William the Conqueror was interested not only in waging war but also in setting up the most efficient possible taxation system in times of peace. The successes of these rulers signaled a new era: the flowering of the Middle Ages.

FOR FURTHER EXPLORATION

- **For additional primary-source material from this period**, see *Sources of the Making of the West*, Fourth Edition.
- **For Web sites, images, and documents related to topics in this chapter**, visit *Make History* at bedfordstmartins.com/hunt.

Chapter 10 Review

Online Study Guide bedfordstmartins.com/hunt

Key Terms and People

In the grid below, identify the term or person and explain its historical significance. (To do this exercise online, go to bedfordstmartins.com/hunt.)

Term	Who or What & When	Why It Matters
commercial revolution (p. 312)		
guild (p. 316)		
apprentices (p. 316)		
journeymen/journeywomen (p. 316)		
masters (p. 316)		
capitalism (p. 317)		
commune (p. 318)		
simony (p. 320)		
lay investiture (p. 320)		
reconquista (p. 321)		
Gregorian reform (p. 321)		
Henry IV (p. 321)		
Investiture Conflict (p. 322)		
Concordat of Worms (p. 322)		
sacraments (p. 323)		
St. Bernard (p. 327)		
Alexius I (Alexius Comnenus) (p. 330)		
Urban II (p. 330)		
First Crusade (p. 331)		
battle of Hastings (p. 336)		

Review Questions

1. What new institutions resulted from the commercial revolution?
2. What were the causes and consequences of the Gregorian reform?
3. How and why was the First Crusade a success, and how and why was it a failure?
4. Which ruler—Alexius Comnenus, William the Conqueror, or Louis VI—was the strongest, which the feeblest, and why?

Making Connections

1. What were the similarities—and what were the differences—between the powers wielded by the Carolingian kings and those wielded by twelfth-century rulers?
2. In what ways was the movement for church reform a consequence of the commercial revolution?
3. How may the First Crusade be understood as a consequence of the Gregorian reform?

Important Events

Date	Event	Date	Event
910	Founding of Cluny	1095	Council of Clermont; Pope Urban II calls First Crusade
1049–1054	Papacy of Leo IX	1096–1099	First Crusade
1054	Schism between eastern and western churches begins	1097	Establishment of commune at Milan
1066	Battle of Hastings: Norman conquest of England under William I	1108–1137	Reign of Louis VI
1071	Battle between Byzantines and Seljuk Turks at Manzikert	1109	Establishment of the crusader states
1073–1085	Papacy of Gregory VII	1122	Concordat of Worms ends Investiture Conflict
1077	Henry IV does penance before Gregory VII at Canossa; war breaks out	c. 1140	Gratian's *Decretum* published
1086	Domesday survey	1147–1149	Second Crusade

- Consider three events: **Papacy of Gregory VII (1073–1085)**, **Concordat of Worms ends Investiture Conflict (1122)**, and **Gratian's *Decretum* published (c. 1140)**. How did these events serve to enhance the power of the papacy? How might the papacy have looked different had any of these events not occurred?

SUGGESTED REFERENCES

Lopez was the first to recognize the importance of the commercial revolution, and Little makes crucial connections between the new commerce and religious reform. Miller's running narrative and primary sources provide the best introduction to the Investiture Conflict and its aftermath. Asbridge offers a vivid account of the crusades, while Nicholson gives a quick overview along with primary sources. The new western monarchies are well covered by Hallam, Fuhrmann, Waley, and Huscroft.

Akbari, Suzanne Conklin. *Idols in the East: European Representations of Islam and the Orient, 1100–1450*. 2009.

Asbridge, Thomas. *The Crusades: The Authoritative History of the War for the Holy Land*. 2010.

*Bayeux Tapestry: http://www.bayeuxtapestry.org.uk/Index.htm

Clanchy, Michael. *From Memory to Written Record: England 1066–1307*. 3rd ed. 2006.

Epstein, Steven A. *An Economic and Social History of Later Medieval Europe, 1000–1500*. 2009.

Fuhrmann, Horst. *Germany in the High Middle Ages, c. 1050–1200*. 2002.

Hallam, Elizabeth M., and Judith Everard. *Capetian France, 987–1328*. 2nd ed. 2001.

Huscroft, Richard. *The Norman Conquest: A New Introduction*. 2009.

*Kerak (crusader) castle: http://www.vkrp.org/studies/historical/town-castle

Little, Lester K. *Religious Poverty and the Profit Economy in Medieval Europe*. 1978.

Lopez, Robert S. *The Commercial Revolution of the Middle Ages, 950–1350*. 1976.

*——, and Irving W. Raymond. *Medieval Trade in the Mediterranean World*. 1955.

Melve, Leidulf. *Inventing the Public Sphere: The Public Debate during the Investiture Contest (c. 1030–1122)*. 2 vols. 2007.

*Miller, Maureen C. *Power and the Holy in the Age of the Investiture Conflict*. 2005.

Moore, Robert I. *The First European Revolution, c. 970–1215*. 2000.

Morris, Colin. *The Papal Monarchy: The Western Church from 1050 to 1250*. 1989.

Nicholson, Helen. *The Crusades*. 2004.

*Peters, Edward, ed. *The First Crusade: The Chronicle of Fulcher of Chartres and Other Source Materials*. 1971.

Robinson, Ian S. *Henry IV of Germany*. 2000.

*Suger. *The Deeds of Louis the Fat*. Trans. Richard C. Cusimano and John Moorhead. 1992.

Tyerman, Christopher. *God's War: A New History of the Crusades*. 2006.

Waley, Daniel. *The Italian City-Republics*. 1969.

*Primary source.

CHAPTER 11

The Flowering of the Middle Ages

1150–1215

In 1194 a raging fire burned most of the town of Chartres, in France—including its cathedral. Worried citizens feared that their most prized relic, the sacred tunic worn by the Virgin Mary when Christ was born, had gone up in flames as well. Had the Virgin abandoned the town? Suddenly the bishop and his clerics emerged from the cathedral crypt, carrying the sacred tunic, which had remained unharmed. Not only had the Virgin *not* abandoned her city, but she had made clear that she wanted a new and more magnificent cathedral to house her relic. The town dedicated itself to the task; the bishop, his clerics, and the town guilds all gave generously to pay for stonecutters, carvers, glaziers, countless other workmen, and a master builder. Donations poured in from the counts and dukes of France and from the royal house. The new cathedral was finished in an incredible twenty-six years—in an age when such churches usually took a century or more to build. Its vault soared 116 feet high; its length stretched more than one hundred yards, longer than a modern football field. Its western portals, which had been spared the flames, retained the sculptural decoration—carved around 1150—of the old church: three doorways surrounded and surmounted by figures that demonstrated the close relationship between the truths of divine wisdom, the French royal house, and the seven liberal arts—grammar, rhetoric, logic, arithmetic, geometry, music, and astronomy. The rest of the church was built in a new style: Gothic.

The rebuilt cathedral at Chartres sums up in stone the key features that characterized the period 1150–1215 and would mark the rest of the Middle Ages. Its Gothic style—with its high vault, flying buttresses, and enormous stained-glass windows—became the quintessential style of medieval architecture. The celebration of the liberal arts on one of its doorways mirrors the new schools that flourished in the twelfth century and culminated in the universities of the thirteenth. The twenty-four statues of Old Testament figures flanking its western portals were meant to prefigure the kings of France; they

Chartres Cathedral
Rebuilt after a fire in 1194, the cathedral of Chartres reconciled old and new. The three doorways of its west end (shown here) were remnants of the former church. But they were crowned by a rose window, a form newly in vogue. *(The Art Archive/Neil Setchfield.)*

demonstrate the extraordinary importance of powerful princes in this period, when monarchies and principalities ceased to be the personal creation of each ruler and became—with varying success in different places—permanent institutions, with professional bureaucratic staffs. The outpouring of popular support that culminated in the building of the cathedral is evidence of a vibrant vernacular (non-Latin-speaking) culture, which expressed itself not only in stone but in literature as well. Finally, the emphasis at Chartres on the divine wisdom echoes the age's fervor about Christian truths, a zeal that led to the creation of new religious movements even as it stoked the fires of the crusade movement.

CHAPTER FOCUS What tied together the cultural and political achievements of the late twelfth century?

New Schools and Churches

Key to the flowering of the Middle Ages was a new emphasis on learning and a new form of church architecture—the Gothic style. In many ways, these developments laid the foundation for other trends of the period. The princely bureaucrats who kept governments running efficiently even when the ruler himself was absent were literate men trained in the schools; theological speculation and debate, a product of the schools as well, fed the new religious fervor—and dissent. The new architectural style gave special luster to its rich patrons, the increasingly powerful rulers of the time. At the same time, without the support of these rulers, neither the new institutions of learning nor the new style of architecture would have had a chance to flourish.

The New Learning and the Rise of the University

Schools had been connected to monasteries and cathedrals since the Carolingian period. They served to train new recruits to become either monks or priests. Some were better endowed with books and masters (or teachers) than others; a few developed a reputation for a certain kind of theological approach or specialized in a particular branch of learning, such as literature, medicine, or law. By the end of the eleventh century, the best schools were generally in the larger cities: Reims, Paris, and Montpellier in France and Bologna in Italy.

Eager students sampled nearly all of them. The young monk Gilbert of Liège was typical: "Instilled with an insatiable thirst for learning, whenever he heard of somebody excelling in the arts, he rushed immediately to that place and drank whatever delightful potion he could draw from the master there," wrote a contemporary observer. For Gilbert and other students, a good lecture had the excitement of theater. Teachers at cathedral schools found themselves forced to find larger halls to accommodate the crush of students. Other teachers simply declared themselves "masters" and set up shop by renting a room. If they could prove their mettle in the classroom, they had no trouble finding paying students (see the illustration on page 347).

Wandering scholars like Gilbert were probably all male, and because schools hitherto had been the training ground for clergymen, all students were considered clerics, whether or not they had been ordained. Wandering became a way of life as the consolidation of castellanies, counties, and kingdoms made violence against travelers less frequent. Markets, taverns, and lodgings sprang up in urban centers to serve the needs of transients.

Using Latin, Europe's common language, students could drift from, say, Italy and Spain to France

1139–1153 Civil War in England

1154–1189 Reign of King Henry II

1176 Battle of Legnano

1182–1226 Francis of Assisi

1125 — 1150 — 1175

1152–1190 Reign of Frederick Barbarossa

1180–1223 Reign of Philip II Augustus

and England, wherever a noted master had settled. Students joined crusaders, pilgrims, and merchants to make the roads of Europe crowded indeed. What the students sought, above all, was knowledge of the seven liberal arts. Grammar, rhetoric, and logic (or dialectic) belonged to the beginning arts, the so-called trivium. Logic, involving the technical analysis of texts as well as the application and manipulation of mental constructs, was a transitional subject leading to the second part of the liberal arts, the quadrivium. This comprised four areas of study that we might call theoretical math and science: arithmetic, geometry, music (theory), and astronomy.

Of all these arts, logic appealed the most to twelfth-century students. Medieval students and masters were convinced that logic could bring together, order, and clarify every issue, even questions about the nature of God. St. Anselm, a major theologian as well as an abbot and archbishop, saw logic as a way for faith to "seek understanding." Emptying his mind of all ideas except that of God, he attempted to use the tools of logic to prove God's existence.

After studying the trivium, students went on to schools of medicine, theology, or law. Paris was renowned for theology, Montpellier for medicine, and Bologna for law. All of these schools trained men for jobs. The law schools, for example, taught men who went on to serve popes, bishops, kings, princes, and communes. Scholars interested in the quadrivium, by contrast, tended to pursue those studies outside of the normal school curriculum, and few gained their living through such pursuits. With books expensive and hard to find, lectures were the chief method of communication. Students committed the lectures to memory.

The remarkable renewal of scholarship in the twelfth century had an unexpected benefit: we know a great deal about the men involved in it—and a few of the women—because they wrote so much,

A Teacher and His Students
This miniature, which illustrates the hierarchical relationship between students and teachers in the twelfth century, appears in a late-twelfth-century manuscript of a commentary written by Gilbert (d. 1154), bishop of Poitiers. Some considered Gilbert's ideas in this commentary to be heretical. Nevertheless, Gilbert escaped condemnation. The artist asserts Gilbert's orthodoxy by depicting Gilbert with a halo, in the full dress of a bishop, speaking from his throne. Below Gilbert are three of his disciples, also with halos. The artist's positive view of Gilbert is echoed by modern historians, who recognize Gilbert as a pioneer in his approach to scriptural commentary. *(Erich Lessing/Art Resource, NY.)*

1189–1192 The Third Crusade

1202–1204 The Fourth Crusade

1204 Philip takes Normandy, Anjou, Maine, Touraine, and Poitou from John

1204 Fall of Constantinople to crusaders

1209–1229 Albigensian Crusade

1212 Battle of Las Navas de Tolosa; triumph of the reconquista

1214 Battle of Bouvines

1215 Magna Carta

1200 — 1225

often about themselves. Three important figures may serve to typify the scholars of the period: Abelard and Heloise, who were early examples of the new learning; and Peter the Chanter, the product of a slightly later period.

Abelard and Heloise Born into a family of the lower nobility in Brittany and destined for a career as a warrior and lord, Peter Abelard (1079–1142) instead became one of the twelfth century's greatest thinkers. In his autobiographical account, *The Story of My Misfortunes*, Abelard described his shift from the life of the warrior to the life of the scholar:

> I was so carried away by my love of learning, that I renounced the glory of a soldier's life, made over my inheritance and rights of the eldest son to my brothers, and withdrew from the court of Mars [war] in order to kneel at the feet of Minerva [learning].

Arriving eventually at Paris, Abelard studied with one of the best-known teachers of his day, William of Champeaux. Soon he began to lecture and to gather students of his own. Around 1122–1123, he composed a textbook for his students, *Sic et Non* (*Yes and No*). It consisted of opposing positions on 156 subjects, among them "That God is one and the contrary," "That all are permitted to marry and the contrary," and "That it is permitted to kill men and the contrary." Arrayed on both sides of each question were passages from the Bible, the church fathers, the letters of popes, and other sources. The juxtaposition of authoritative sources was nothing new; what was new was calling attention to their contradictions. Abelard's students loved the challenge: they were eager to find the origins of the quotes, consider the context of each one carefully, and seek to reconcile the opposing sides by using the tools of logic.[1]

Abelard's fame as a teacher was such that a Parisian cleric named Fulbert gave Abelard room and board and engaged him as tutor for Heloise (c. 1100–c. 1163/1164), Fulbert's niece. Heloise is one of the few learned women of the period who left written traces. Brought up under Fulbert's guardianship, Heloise had been sent as a young girl to a convent school, where she received a thorough grounding in a literary education. Her uncle had hoped to continue her education at home by hiring Abelard. Abelard, however, became Heloise's lover as well as her tutor. "Our desires left no stage of love-making untried," wrote Abelard in his *Misfortunes*.

At first their love affair was secret. But Heloise became pregnant, and Abelard insisted they marry. They did so clandestinely to prevent damaging Abelard's career, for the new emphasis on clerical celibacy meant that Abelard's professional success and prestige would have been compromised if news of his marriage were made public. After they were married, Heloise and Abelard rarely saw one another; Abelard's sister took in their child, Astrolabe. Fulbert, suspecting that Abelard had abandoned his niece, plotted a cruel revenge against him: he paid a servant to castrate Abelard. Soon after, Abelard and Heloise entered separate monasteries.

For Heloise, separation from Abelard was a lasting blow. Although she became a successful abbess, carefully tending to the physical and spiritual needs of her nuns, she continued to call on Abelard for "renewal of strength." In a series of letters addressed to him, she poured out her feelings as "his handmaid, or rather his daughter, wife, or rather sister":

> You know, beloved, as the whole world knows, how much I have lost in you, how at one wretched stroke of fortune that supreme act of flagrant treachery robbed me of my very self in robbing me of you. . . . You alone have the power to make me sad, to bring me happiness or comfort.

For Abelard, however, the loss of Heloise and even his castration were not the worst disasters of his life. The heaviest blow came later, and it was directed at his intellect. He wrote a book that applied "human and logical reasons" (as he put it) to the Trinity; the book was condemned at the Council of Soissons in 1121, and he was forced to throw it, page by page, into the flames. Bitterly weeping at the injustice, Abelard lamented, "This open violence had come upon me only because of the purity of my intentions and love of our Faith, which had compelled me to write."

Peter the Chanter By the second half of the twelfth century, masters like Abelard had become far more common. Many of them were at Paris, though others taught at Montpellier, Bologna, and Oxford in England. Peter the Chanter (d. 1197) was one of the most influential and prolific. Like Abelard, he came from a family of

---

[1]Abelard's students did not yet have the sophisticated rules of logic that had been worked out by the ancient philosopher Aristotle (see page 114). Until the middle of the twelfth century, very little of Aristotle's work was available in Europe because it had not been translated from Greek into Latin. By the end of the century, however, that situation had been rectified by translators who traveled to cities such as Córdoba in Spain and Syracuse in Sicily, where they found Islamic scholars who had already translated Aristotle's Greek into Arabic and could help them translate from Arabic to Latin.

the lower nobility. He studied at the cathedral school at Reims and was given the honorary title of chanter of Notre Dame in Paris in 1183. The chant, as we shall see, consisted of the music and words of the church liturgy. But Peter had his underlings work with the choir singers; he himself was far more interested in lecturing, disputing, and preaching.

Peter's lectures followed the pattern established by other masters. The lecture began with the recitation of a passage from an important text. The master then explained the text, giving his comments. He then "disputed"—mentioning other explanations and refuting them, often drawing on the logic of Aristotle, which by Peter's time was fully available. Sometimes masters held public debates on their interpretations.

Peter chose to comment on biblical texts. There were many ways to interpret the Bible. Some commentators chose to talk about it as an allegory; others preferred to stress its literal meaning. Peter was interested in the morals it taught. While most theology masters commented on just the Psalms and the New Testament, Peter taught all the books of the Bible. He wrote two important treatises and was particularly interested in exploring social issues and the sacrament of penance.

Peter also took the fruits of his classroom experience to the people. His sermons have not survived, but he inspired a whole group of men to preach in and around Paris. One of his protégés, for example, was renowned for turning prostitutes, usurers, and immoral clerics from their sinful ways.

Universities | Around 1200, the pope wrote to the masters of theology, church law, and the liberal arts at Paris. He called them a *universitas*—the Latin word for a corporation or guild. The pope was right: universities were guilds. Like guilds, they evolved from earlier institutions (schools, in the case of universities; religious associations, in the case of craft guilds). Universities were schools that had become corporations and issued regulations for themselves. They had apprentices (students) and masters (schoolmasters). They issued rules to cover their trade (the acquisition and dissemination of knowledge). They had provisions for disciplining, testing, and housing students. They regulated the masters in similar detail. For example, masters at the University of Paris were required to wear long black gowns, follow a particular order in their lectures, and set the standards by which students could become masters themselves. The University of Bologna was unique in having two guilds, one of students and one of masters. At Bologna, the students participated in the appointment of masters and paid their salaries.

The University of Bologna was unusual because it was principally a school of law, where the students were often older men, well along in their careers and used to wielding power. The University of Paris, however, attracted younger students, drawn particularly by its renown in the liberal arts and theology. The universities of Salerno and Montpellier specialized in medicine. Oxford, once a sleepy town where students clustered around one or two masters, became a center of royal administration, and its university soon developed a reputation for teaching the liberal arts, theology, and—extraordinarily—science.

University curricula differed in content and duration. At the University of Paris in the early thirteenth century, for example, a student had to spend at least six years studying the liberal arts before he could begin to teach. If he wanted to continue his studies with theology, he had to attend lectures on the subject for at least another five years.

With few exceptions, masters and students were considered clerics. This had two important consequences: first, it meant that there were no university women, and second, it ensured that university men would be subject to church courts rather than to the secular jurisdiction of towns or lords. Many universities received generous privileges from popes and kings, who valued the services of scholars. Thus, for example, in 1200 the king of France promised that "neither our provost nor our judges shall lay hands on a student [at the University of Paris] for any offense whatever."

The combination of clerical status and special privileges made universities virtually self-governing corporations within the towns. This sometimes led to friction. For example, when a student at Oxford was suspected of killing his mistress and the townspeople tried to punish him, the masters protested by refusing to teach and leaving town. Incidents such as this explain why historians speak of the hostility between "town" and "gown." Yet, as in our own time, university towns depended on scholars to patronize local restaurants, shops, and hostels. Town and gown normally learned to negotiate with each other to their mutual advantage.

Architectural Style: From Romanesque to Gothic

While Peter the Chanter lectured at Notre Dame, the cathedral itself was going up around him—in Gothic style. At the time, this was a new architectural fashion, attempted only in the Île-de-France and nearby cities. It was associated with the luster of the Capetian kings of France. Elsewhere—in

Painted Vault
This fresco of Christ as ruler of the universe, his hand raised in a gesture of blessing, is one of many paintings in the Romanesque church of San Isidore de León, built in northwest Spain in the eleventh century. Surrounding Christ are the symbols of the four evangelists: the ox for Luke, the lion for Mark, the eagle for John, and the man for Matthew. *(The Art Archive / Real Collegiata San Isidoro León / Collection Dagli Orti.)*

France, Germany, Italy—the reigning style was Romanesque. But in the course of the thirteenth century Gothic style took Europe by storm, and by the fourteenth it was the quintessential cathedral style.

Romanesque Solidity

Romanesque is the term art historians use to describe the massive church buildings making up eleventh-century monasteries like Cluny. Heavy, serious, and solid, Romanesque churches were decorated with brightly colored wall paintings and sculpture. (See the illustration above.) The various parts of the church—the chapels in the *chevet*, or apse (the east end), for example—were handled as discrete units, with the forms of cubes, cones, and cylinders (Figure 11.1). Inventive sculptural reliefs, both inside and outside the church, enlivened these pristine geometrical forms. Emotional and sometimes frenzied, Romanesque sculpture depicted themes ranging from the beauty of Eve to the horrors of the Last Judgment. (See the frieze depicting Dives and Lazarus on page 310 for an example.)

Romanesque churches were above all houses for prayer, which was neither silent nor private. Prayer was sung in a musical style called plainchant, or Gregorian chant. Plainchant melodies were sung in unison and without instrumental accompaniment. Although rhythmically free, lacking a regular beat, chant's melodies ranged from extremely simple to highly ornate and embellished. By the twelfth century, a large repertoire of melodies had grown up, at first through oral composition and transmission and then, starting in the ninth century, in written notation. Echoing within the stone walls and the cavernous choirs, plainchant worked well in a Romanesque church.

Gilded reliquaries (where sacred relics were housed) and altars made of silver, precious gems, and pearls were considered the fitting accoutrements of worship in Romanesque churches. The prayer, decoration, and music complemented the gift economy of the period before the commercial revolution: wearing vestments of the finest materi-

---

Romanesque: An architectural style that flourished in Europe between about 1000 and 1150. It is characterized by solid, heavy forms and semicircular arches and vaults. Romanesque buildings were often decorated with fanciful sculpture and wall paintings.

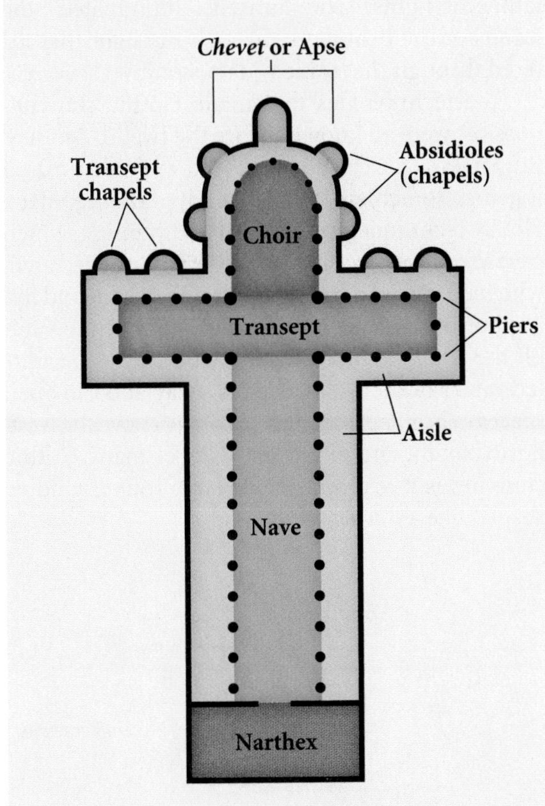

FIGURE 11.1 Floor Plan of a Romanesque Church
As churchgoers entered a Romanesque church, they passed through the narthex, an anteroom decorated with sculptures depicting scenes from the Bible. Walking through the portal of the narthex, they entered the church's nave, at the east end of which—just after the crossing of the transept and in front of the choir—was the altar. Walking down the nave, they passed tall, massive piers leading up to the vault (the ceiling) of the nave. Each of these piers was decorated with sculpture, and the walls were brightly painted. Romanesque churches were both lively and colorful (because of their decoration) and solemn and somber (because of their heavy stones and massive scale).

als, intoning the liturgy in the most splendid of churches, monks and priests offered up the gift of prayer to God, begging in return the gift of salvation of their souls and the souls of all the faithful.

Gothic Style | **Gothic architecture**, to the contrary, was a style of the cities, reflecting the self-confidence and wealth of merchants, guildspeople, bishops, and kings.[2] Usually a cathedral—the bishop's principal church—rather than a monastic church, the Gothic church was the religious, social, and commercial focal point of a city. The style, popular from the twelfth to fifteenth centuries, was characterized by pointed arches, ribbed vaults, and stained-glass windows. The arches began as architectural motifs but were soon adopted in every art form. Gothic churches appealed to the senses the way that Peter the Chanter's lectures and disputations appealed to human logic and reason: both were designed to lead people to knowledge that

Sant'Andrea
The church of Sant'Andrea at Vercelli suggests that Italian church architects and patrons adopted what they liked of French Gothic, particularly its pointed arches, while remaining uninterested in soaring heights and grand stained-glass windows. The real interest of the interior of Sant'Andrea is its inventive and lively use of contrasting light and dark stone. *(Scala/Art Resource, NY.)*

[2]*Gothic* is a modern term, originally meant to denigrate the style's "barbarity" but now used admiringly.

Gothic architecture: The style of architecture that started in the Île-de-France in the twelfth century and eventually became the quintessential cathedral style of the Middle Ages, characterized by pointed arches, ribbed vaults, and stained-glass windows.

touched the divine. The atmosphere of a Gothic church was a foretaste of heaven.

The style had its beginnings around 1135, with the project of Abbot Suger, the close associate of King Louis the Fat of France (see page 339), to remodel portions of the church of Saint-Denis. Suger's rebuilding was part of the fruitful melding of royal and ecclesiastical interests and ideals in the north of France. At the west end of his church, the place where the faithful entered, Suger decorated the portals with figures of Old Testament kings, queens, and patriarchs, signaling the links between the present king and his illustrious predecessors. At the eastern end, behind the altar, Suger used pointed arches and stained glass to let in light, which Suger believed would transport the worshipper from the "slime of earth" to the "purity of Heaven." Suger said that the father of lights, God himself, "illuminated" the minds of the beholders through the light that filtered through the stained-glass windows.

The technologies that made Gothic churches possible were all known before the twelfth century. But Suger's church showed how they could be used together to achieve a particularly dazzling effect. Gothic techniques included ribbed vaulting, which gave a sense of precision and order; the pointed arch, which produced a feeling of soaring height; and flying buttresses, which took the weight of the vault off the walls (Figure 11.2). The buttresses permitted much of the wall to be cut away and the open spaces to be filled with glass. Soaring above the west, north, south, and often east ends of many Gothic churches is a rose window: a large round window shaped like a flower.

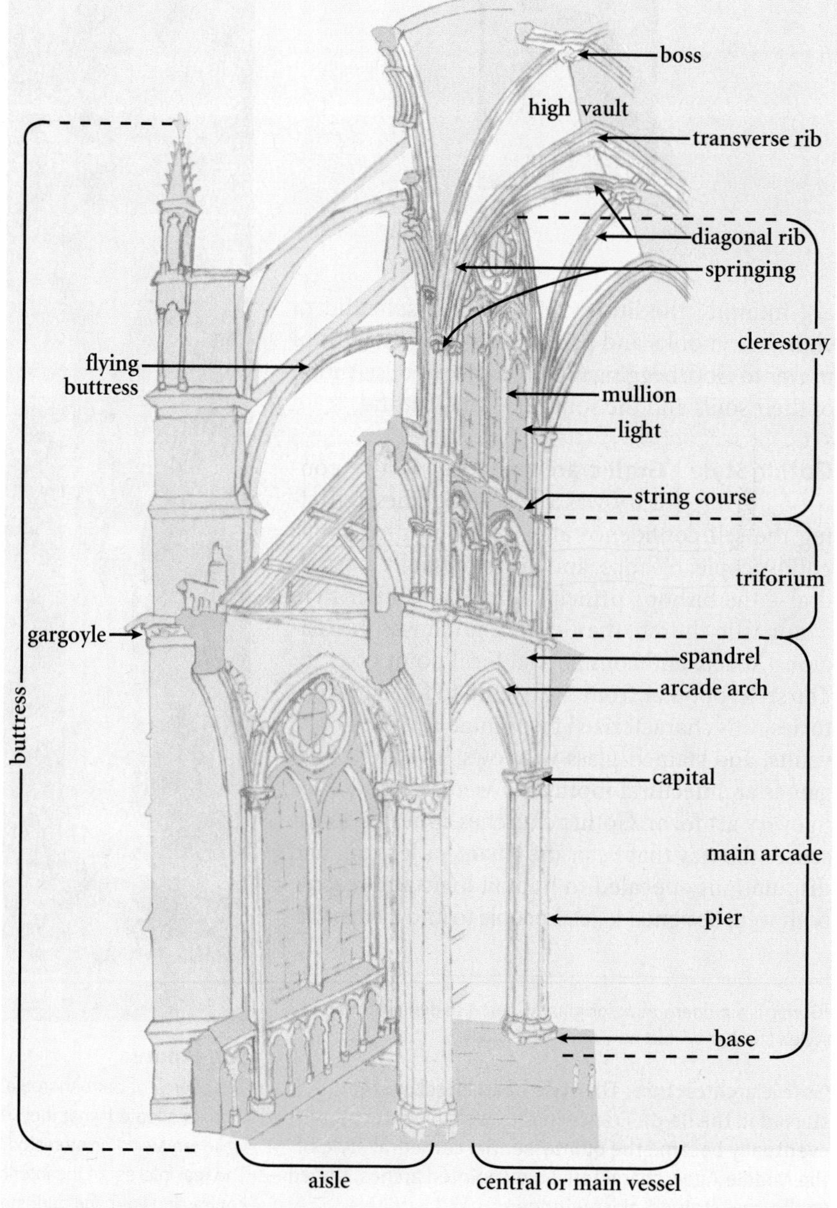

FIGURE 11.2 Elements of a Gothic Cathedral
Bristling on the outside with flying buttresses of stone, Gothic cathedrals were lofty and serene on the inside. The buttresses, which held the weight of the vault, allowed Gothic architects to pierce the walls with enormous windows. Thick piers anchored on sturdy bases became thin columns as they mounted over the triforium and clerestory, blossoming into ribs at the top. Whether plain or ornate, the ribs gave definition and drew attention to the high pointed vault. *(Figure adapted from Michael Camille,* Gothic Art: Glorious Visions *[New York: Abrams, 1996].)*

SEEING HISTORY

Romanesque versus Gothic: The View Down the Nave

When you enter a church, which, in the Middle Ages, you always did from the west end, you find yourself looking down its nave, toward the choir and the altar (the focal points of the church). That view changed over time, and the change tells us a lot about new architectural tastes in the Middle Ages. The church on the left, Saint-Savin, built near Poitiers, in France, in the early twelfth century, is a representative Romanesque church. The one on the right is Bourges, a Gothic church built (about a hundred miles to the east of Saint-Savin) around a century later. Comparing the views down the nave systematically will allow us to discover what makes the Romanesque and Gothic styles distinctive. You might first consider the vaults. Which one is more like a tunnel, and what contributes to that effect? Does one interior create more of a soaring effect? How? What elements of the architecture contribute to this impression? Which one has paintings? Which one lets in the most light? What architectural features make this possible? In which church are the capitals of the columns (the very tops) elaborately carved? In which one are the columns themselves highly articulated, with multiple pillars? From these considerations, name the features that make a Gothic church "Gothic."

Question to Consider

■ **What twelfth-century social and cultural trends are reflected in the shift from Romanesque to Gothic?**

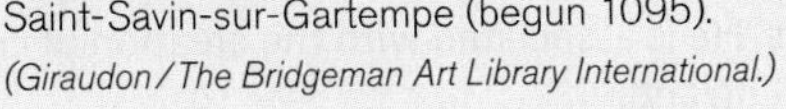

Saint-Savin-sur-Gartempe (begun 1095). *(Giraudon/The Bridgeman Art Library International.)*

Bourges (begun 1195). *(Scala/Art Resource, NY.)*

Unlike Romanesque churches, whose exteriors prepare visitors for what they will see within them, Gothic cathedrals surprise. The exterior of a Gothic church has an opaque, bristling, and forbidding look owing to the dark surface of its stained glass and its flying buttresses. The interior, however, is just the opposite. All is soaring lightness, harmony, and order. (See "Seeing History," page 353.)

By the mid-thirteenth century, Gothic architecture had spread from France to other European countries. The style varied by region, most dramatically in Italy. At Sant'Andrea in Vercelli, shown on page 351, for example, there are only two stories, and light filters in from small windows. Yet with its pointed arches and ribbed vaulting, Sant'Andrea is considered a Gothic church. At its east end is a rose window.

REVIEW QUESTION What was new about education and church architecture in the twelfth and early thirteenth centuries?

Governments as Institutions

Around the same time that architects, workers, patrons, theologians, and city dwellers were coming together to produce Gothic cathedrals, and masters and students were incorporating themselves as universities, rulership was becoming institutionalized. By the end of the twelfth century, western Europeans for the first time spoke of their rulers not as kings of a people (for example, the king of the Franks) but as kings of a territory (for example, the king of France). This new designation reflected an important change in medieval rulership. However strong earlier rulers had been, their political power had been personal (depending on ties of kinship, friendship, and vassalage) rather than territorial (touching all who lived within the borders of their state). Renewed interest in Roman law, a product of the schools, served as a foundation for strong, central rule. Money allowed kings to hire salaried professionals—talented, literate officials, many of whom had been schooled in the new universities cropping up across Europe—to carry out the new ideology. The process of state building had begun.

In England, the governmental system was institutionalized early, with royal officials administering both law and revenues. In other regions, such as France and Germany, bureaucratic administration did not develop so far. In eastern Europe, it hardly existed at all. At Byzantium, the bureaucracy that had long been in place frayed badly, leaving the state open to conquest by western crusaders.

England: Unity through Common Law

In the mid-twelfth century, the government of England was by far the most institutionalized in Europe. The king hardly needed to be present: royal government functioned smoothly without him, since officials handled all the administrative matters and record keeping. The very circumstances of the English king favored the growth of an administrative staff—the king's frequent travels to and from the continent meant that officials needed to work in his absence, and his enormous wealth meant that he could afford them. **Henry II** (r. 1154–1189) was the driving force in extending and strengthening the institutions of English government.

Accession of Henry II, 1154 Henry II became king in the wake of a terrible civil war. Henry I (r. 1100–1135), son of William the Conqueror, had no male heir. Before he died, he called on the great barons to swear that his daughter Matilda would rule after him. The effort failed; the Norman barons could not imagine a woman ruling over them. Many were glad to see Stephen of Blois (r. 1135–1154), Henry's nephew, take the throne. With Matilda's son, the future Henry II, only two years old when Stephen took the crown, the struggle for control of England during Stephen's reign became part of a larger territorial contest between the house of Anjou (Henry's family) and the house of Blois (Stephen's family) (Figure 11.3). Continual civil war (1139–1153) in England benefited the English barons and high churchmen, who gained new privileges and powers as the monarch's authority waned. Newly built private castles, already familiar on the continent, now appeared in England as symbols of the rising power of the English barons. Stephen's coalition of barons, high clergymen, and townsmen eventually fell apart, and he agreed to the accession of Henry of Anjou. Thus began what would be known as the Angevin (from Anjou) dynasty.[3]

[3]Henry's father, Geoffrey of Anjou, was nicknamed "Plantagenet" from the *genet*, a shrub he liked. Historians sometimes use the name to refer to the entire dynasty, so Henry II was the first Plantagenet as well as the first Angevin king of England.

Henry II: King of England (r. 1154–1189) who ended the period of civil war there and affirmed and expanded royal powers. He is associated with the creation of common law in England.

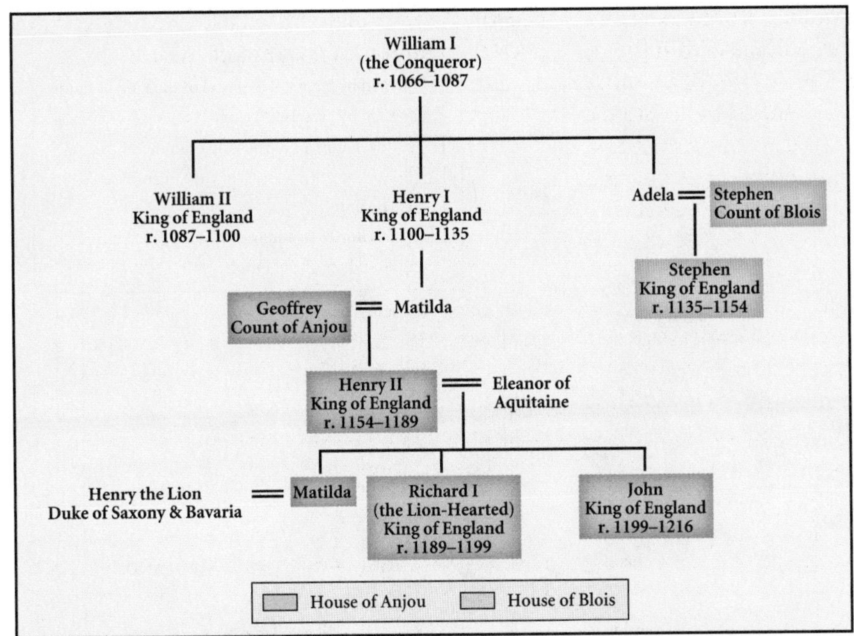

FIGURE 11.3 Genealogy of Henry II
King William I of England was succeeded by his sons, William II and Henry I. When Henry I died, the succession was disputed by two women and their husbands. One was William I's daughter, Adela, married to Stephen, count of Blois; the other was Henry's daughter, Matilda, wife of the count of Anjou. Although the English crown first went to the house of Blois, it reverted in 1154 to the house of Anjou, headed by Matilda's son, Henry. Henry II thus began the Angevin dynasty in England.

Henry's marriage to Eleanor of Aquitaine in 1152, after her marriage to Louis VII of France was annulled, brought the enormous inheritance of the duchy of Aquitaine to the English crown. Although he remained the vassal of the king of France for his continental lands, Henry in effect ruled a territory that stretched from England to southern France (Map 11.1).

Eleanor brought Henry not only an enormous inheritance but also the sons he needed to maintain his dynasty. He gave her much less. As queen of France, Eleanor had enjoyed an important position: she disputed with St. Bernard, the Cistercian abbot who was the most renowned churchman of the day, and when she accompanied Louis on the Second Crusade, she brought more troops than he did. Of independent mind, she determined to separate from Louis even before he considered leaving her. But with Henry, she lost much of her power, for he dominated her just as he came to dominate his barons. Turning to her offspring in 1173, Eleanor, disguised as a man, tried to join her eldest son, Henry the Younger, in a plot against his father. But the rebellion was put down, and she spent most of her years

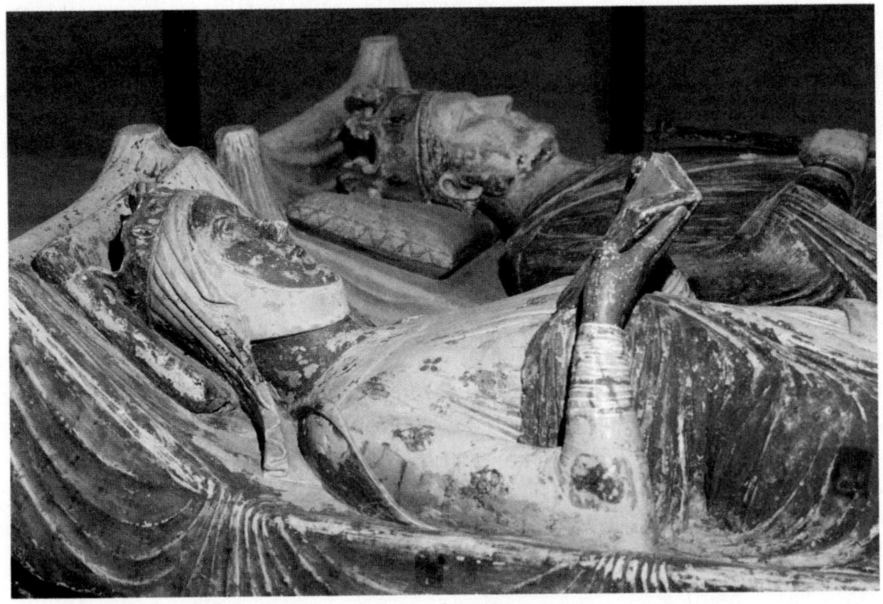

Eleanor and Henry
Nothing about their side-by-side tombs suggests the stormy relationship of Eleanor of Aquitaine and King Henry II of England. Their effigies, carved of limestone and walnut, suggest peace and piety. How does Eleanor's book help project this image? What do you suppose she is reading? The placement of the couple's tombs also attests to their religious fervor: they were buried in the powerful monastery of Fontevraud, a "double monastery" consisting (in separate quarters) of both monks and nuns. An abbess presided over all. *(Hervé Champollion / © Cephas Picture Library / Alamy.)*

MAP 11.1 Europe in the Age of Henry II and Frederick Barbarossa, 1150–1190
The second half of the twelfth century was dominated by two men, King Henry II and Emperor Frederick Barbarossa. Of the two, Frederick seemed to control more land, but this was deceptive. Although he was emperor, he had great difficulty ruling the territory that was theoretically part of his empire. Frederick's base was in central Germany, and even there he had to contend with powerful vassals. Henry II's territory was more compact but also more surely under his control.

thereafter, until her husband's death in 1189, confined under guard at Winchester Castle. (In death, however, she gained dignity, with her tomb next to Henry's. See the illustration on page 355.)

Royal Authority and Common Law When Henry II became king of England, he immediately set about to undo the damage to the monarchy caused by the civil war. He destroyed or confiscated the new castles and regained crown land. Then he proceeded to extend monarchical power, above all by imposing royal justice.

Henry's judicial reforms built on an already well-developed English system. The Anglo-Saxon kings had royal district courts: the king appointed sheriffs to police the shires, muster military levies, and haul criminals into court. The Norman kings retained these courts, which all the free men of the shire were summoned to attend. To these established institutions, Henry II added a system of judicial visitations called eyres (from the Latin *iter*, "journey"). Under this system, royal justices made regular trips to every locality in England. Henry declared that some crimes, such as murder, arson, and rape, were so heinous that they violated the "king's peace" no matter where they were committed. The king required local representatives of the knightly class to meet during each eyre and either give the sheriff the names of those suspected of committing crimes in the vicinity or arrest the suspects themselves and hand them over to the royal justices.

During the eyres, the justices also heard cases between individuals, today called civil cases. Free men and women (that is, people of the knightly class or above) could bring their disputes over such matters as inheritance, dowries, and property claims to the king's justices. Earlier courts had generally relied on duels between litigants to determine verdicts. Henry's new system offered a different option, an inquest under royal supervision.

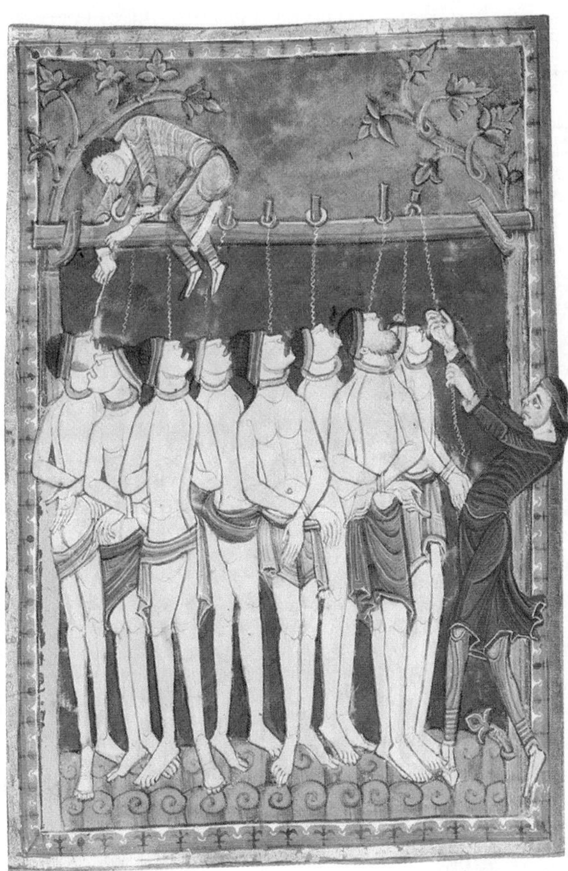

Hanging Thieves
The development of common law in England meant mobilizing royal agents to bring charges and arrest people throughout the land. In 1124, the royal justice Ralph Basset hanged forty-four thieves. It could not have been very shocking in that context to see, in this miniature from around 1130, eight thieves hanged for breaking into the shrine of St. Edmund. Under Henry II, all cases of murder, arson, and rape were considered crimes against the king himself. The result was not just the enhancement of the king's power but also new definitions of crime, more thorough policing, and more systematic punishments. Even so, hanging was probably no more frequent than it had been before. (The Thieves Are Hanged. *From* The Life, Passion, and Miracles of St. Edmund, King and Martyr, *in Latin. Bury St. Edmund's, c. 1130. MS. M.736, f. 19v. The Pierpont Morgan Library/Art Resource, NY.)*

The new system of **common law**—law that applied to all of England—was praised for its efficiency, speed, and conclusiveness in a twelfth-century legal treatise known as *Glanvill* (after its presumed author): "This legal institution emanates from perfect equity. For justice, which after many and long delays is scarcely ever demonstrated by the duel, is advantageously and speedily attained through this institution." *Glanvill* might have added that the king also speedily gained a large treasury. The exchequer, as the financial bureau of England was called, recorded all the fines paid for judgments and the sums collected for writs. The amounts, entered on parchment sewn together and stored as rolls, became the Receipt Rolls and Pipe Rolls, the first of many such records of the English monarchy and an indication that writing had become a mechanism for institutionalizing royal power in England.

The stiffest opposition to Henry's extension of royal courts came from the church, where a separate system of trial and punishment had long been available to the clergy and to others who enjoyed church protection. The punishments for crimes meted out by church courts were generally quite mild. Protective of their special status, churchmen refused to submit to the jurisdiction of Henry's courts. Henry insisted, and the ensuing contest between Henry II and his archbishop, Thomas Becket (1118–1170), became the greatest battle between the church and the state in the twelfth century. The conflict simmered for six years, with Becket refusing to allow "criminous clerics"—clergy suspected of committing a crime—to come before royal courts. Then Henry's henchmen murdered Thomas, right in his own cathedral. The desecration unintentionally turned Becket into a martyr. Although Henry's role in the murder remained ambiguous, he was forced by the general outcry to do public penance for the deed. In the end, both church and royal courts expanded to address the concerns of an increasingly litigious society. (See the illustration on page 358.)

Henry II was an English king with an imperial reach. He was lord over almost half of France, though much of this territory was in the hands of his vassals, and he was, at least theoretically, vassal to the French king (see Map 11.1). In England, he made the king's presence felt everywhere through his system of traveling royal courts. On the conti-

common law: Begun by Henry II (r. 1154–1189), the English royal law carried out by the king's justices in eyre (traveling justices). It applied to the entire kingdom and thus was "common" to all.

The Murder of Thomas Becket
Almost immediately after King Henry II's knights murdered Archbishop Thomas Becket in his church at Canterbury, Becket was viewed as a martyr. In this early depiction of the event, one of the murderers knocks off Becket's cap, while another hits the arm of Becket's supporter, who holds the bishop's cross-staff. *(British Library, London, UK/© British Library Board. All Rights Reserved./The Bridgeman Art Library International.)*

nent, he maintained his position through a combination of war and negotiation, but rebellions begun by his own sons with help from the king of France dogged him throughout his life.

Henry's Successors Under Henry II and his sons Richard I (r. 1189–1199) and John (r. 1199–1216), the English monarchy was omnipresent and rich. Its omnipresence derived largely from its eyre system of justice and its administrative apparatus. Its wealth came from court fees, income from numerous royal estates both in England and on the continent, taxes from cities, and customary feudal dues (reliefs and aids) collected from barons and knights. These dues were paid on such occasions as the knighting of the king's eldest son and the marriage of the king's eldest daughter. Enriched by the commercial economy of the late twelfth century, the English kings encouraged their knights and barons not to serve them personally in battle but instead to pay the king a tax called scutage in lieu of service. The monarchs preferred to hire mercenaries both as troops to fight external enemies and as police to enforce the king's will at home.

Richard I was known as the Lion-Hearted for his boldness. Historians have often criticized him for being an "absentee" king, yet it is hard to see what he might have done differently. He went on the Third Crusade the very year he was crowned; on his way home, he was captured and held for ransom by political enemies for a long time; and he died defending his possessions on the continent. Richard's real tragedy was that he died young.

Richard's successor, John, has also been widely faulted. Even in his own day, he was accused of asserting his will in a highhanded way. To understand John, it is necessary to appreciate how desperate he was to keep his continental possessions. In 1204, the king of France, **Philip II (Philip Augustus)** (r. 1180–1223), confiscated the northern French territories held by John. Between 1204 and 1214, John did ev-

---

Philip II (Philip Augustus): King of France (r. 1180–1223) who bested the English king John and won most of John's continental territories, thus immeasurably strengthening the power of the Capetian dynasty.

erything he could to add to the crown revenues so that he could pay for an army to win back the territories. He forced his vassals to pay ever-increasing scutages and extorted money in the form of new feudal dues. He compelled the widows of his vassals to either marry men of his choosing or pay him a hefty fee. Despite John's heavy investment in this war effort, his army was defeated in 1214 at the battle of Bouvines. The defeat caused discontented English barons to rebel openly against the king. At Runnymede in June 1215, John was forced to agree to the charter of baronial liberties that has come to be called **Magna Carta** ("Great Charter").

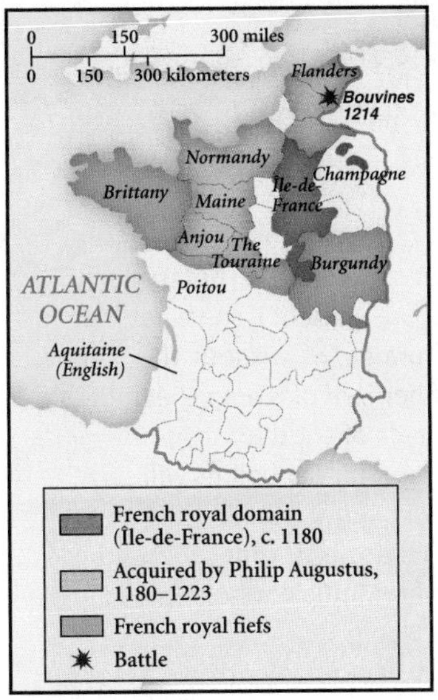

The Consolidation of France under Philip Augustus, 1180–1223

Magna Carta, 1215 | The English barons intended Magna Carta to be a conservative document defining the "customary" obligations and rights of the nobility and forbidding the king to break from these customs without consulting his barons. It also maintained that all free men in the land had certain rights that the king was obligated to uphold. (See "Contrasting Views," pages 360–61.) In this way, Magna Carta implied that the king was not above the law. The growing royal power was matched by the self-confidence of the English barons, certain of their rights and eager to articulate them. In time, as the definition of *free men* expanded to include all the king's subjects, Magna Carta came to be seen as a guarantee of the rights of Englishmen (and eventually Englishwomen) in general.

France: Consolidation and Conquest

Whereas the power of the English king led to a baronial movement to curb it, the weakness of the French monarchy ironically led to its expansion. In 1180, the French crown passed from the Capetian king Louis VII (first husband of Eleanor of Aquitaine) to his fourteen-year-old son, Philip Augustus. When the new king came to the throne, the royal domain, the Île-de-France, was sandwiched between territory controlled by the counts of Flanders, Champagne, and Anjou. By far the most powerful ruler on the continent was King Henry II of England. He was the count of Anjou and the duke of Normandy, and he held the duchy of Aquitaine through his wife and also controlled Poitou and Brittany (see Map 11.1, page 356).

Henry and the counts of Flanders and Champagne vied to control the youthful new king of France. Philip, however, quickly learned to play off the three rulers against one another, in particular by setting the sons of Henry II against their father. Contemporaries were astounded when Philip successfully gained territory: he wrested land from Flanders in the 1190s and Normandy, Anjou, Maine, the Touraine, and Poitou from King John of England in 1204. No wonder he was given the epithet *Augustus*, after the first Roman emperor.

After Philip's army confirmed its triumph over most of John's continental territories in 1214, the French monarch could boast that he was the richest and most powerful ruler in France. Most important, Philip had sufficient support and resources to keep a tight hold on Normandy.[4] He received homage and fealty from most of the Norman aristocracy, and his officers carried out their work there in accordance with Norman customs. For ordinary Normans, the shift from English duke to French king brought few changes.

Wherever he ruled, Philip instituted new administrative practices, run by officials who kept accounts and files. Before Philip's day, most French royal arrangements were committed to memory rather than to writing. If decrees were recorded at all, they were saved by the recipient, not by the government. The king did keep some documents, which he generally carried with him in his travels like personal possessions. But in 1194, in a battle with the king of England, Philip lost his meager cache of documents along with much treasure when he had to abandon his baggage train. After 1194, the king had all his decrees written down,

Magna Carta: Literally "Great Charter"; the charter of baronial liberties that King John was forced to agree to in 1215. It implied that royal power was subject to custom and law.

[4]Philip was particularly successful in imposing royal control in Normandy; later French kings gave most of the other territories to collateral members of the royal family.

CONTRASTING VIEWS

Magna Carta

Magna Carta ("Great Charter"), today considered a landmark of constitutional government, began as a demand by English barons and churchmen for specific rights and privileges. Reacting to King John's "abuses," they forced him in 1215 to affix his seal to a "charter of liberties" (Document 1). It set forth the customs that the king was expected to observe and, in its sixty-first clause, in effect allowed the king's subjects to declare war against him if he failed to carry out the charter's provisions. In 1225, Henry III, John's son, issued a definitive version of the charter. By then, it had become more important as a symbol of liberty than for its specific provisions. It was, for example, invoked by the barons in 1242 when they were summoned to one of the first Parliaments (Document 2).

1. Magna Carta, 1215

In these excerpts, the provisions that were dropped by Henry III in the definitive version of 1225 are starred. Explanatory notes are in brackets. The original charter had sixty-three clauses. In every clause John refers to himself by the royal "we."

1. First of all [we, i.e., John] have granted to God, and by this our present charter confirmed for us and our heirs for ever that the English church shall be free, and shall have its rights undiminished and its liberties unimpaired. . . .

8. No widow shall be forced to marry so long as she wishes to live without a husband, provided that she gives security [pledges] not to marry without our consent if she holds [her land] from us, or without the consent of her lord of whom she holds, if she holds of another.

9. Neither we nor our bailiffs will seize for any debt any land or rent, so long as the chattels [property] of the debtor are sufficient to repay the debt. . . .

*10. If anyone who has borrowed from the Jews any sum, great or small, dies before it is repaid, the debt shall not bear interest as long as the heir is under age, of whomsoever [lord] he holds [his land]; and if the debt falls into our hands [which might happen, as Jews were serfs of the crown], we will not take anything except the principal mentioned in the bond.

*12. No scutage or aid [money payments owed by a vassal to his lord] shall be imposed in our kingdom unless by common counsel of our kingdom, except for ransoming our person, for making our eldest son a knight, and for once marrying our eldest daughter; and for these only a reasonable aid shall be levied. . . .

30. No sheriff, or bailiff of ours, or anyone else shall take the horses or carts of any free man [for the most part, a member of the elite] for transport work save with the agreement of that freeman.

31. Neither we nor our bailiffs will take, for castles or other works of ours, timber which is not ours, except with the agreement of him whose timber it is. . . .

39. No free man shall be arrested or imprisoned or disseised [deprived of his land] or outlawed or exiled or in any way victimized, neither will we attack him or send anyone to attack him, except by the lawful judgment of his peers or by the law of the land. . . .

*61. Since . . . we have granted all these things aforesaid . . . we give and grant [the barons] the underwritten security, namely, that the barons shall choose any twenty-five barons of the kingdom they wish, who must with all their might observe, hold, and cause to be observed, the peace and liberties which we have granted and confirmed to them by this present charter of ours, so that if we, or our justiciar [the king's chief minister], or our bailiffs or any one of our servants offend in any way against anyone or transgress any of the articles of the peace or the security . . . , [the barons] shall come to us . . . and laying the transgression before us, shall petition us to have that transgression corrected without delay. And if we do not correct the transgression . . . within forty days . . . those twenty-five bar-

and he established permanent repositories in which to keep them.

Like the English king, Philip relied largely on members of the lesser nobility—knights and clerics, many of whom were masters educated in the city schools of France. They served as officers of his court, tax collectors, and overseers of the royal estates, making the king's power felt locally as never before.

Germany: The Revived Monarchy of Frederick Barbarossa

Theoretically, Henry V and his successors were kings of Germany and Italy, and at Rome they received the crown and title of emperor from the popes as well. But the Investiture Conflict (see page 322) had reduced their power and authority. Meanwhile, the German princes strengthened their position, enjoy-

ons together with the community of the whole land shall distrain and distress us in every way they can, namely, by seizing castles, lands, possessions, and in such other ways as they can, saving [not harming] our person.

Source: Harry Rothwell, ed., *English Historical Documents*, vol. 3 (London: Eyre & Spottiswoode, 1975), 317–23.

2. The Barons at Parliament Refuse to Give the King an Aid, 1242

Henry III convoked the barons to a meeting (parliament), expecting them to ratify his request for money to wage war for his French possessions. According to the writer of this document, Matthew Paris (a monk, artist, and chronicler of his time), the barons considered his request an excessive imposition. Magna Carta was a justification for their flat rejection of the king's request.

Since he had been their ruler they had many times, at his request, given him aid, namely, a thirteenth of their movable property, and afterwards a fifteenth and a sixteenth and a fortieth. . . . Scarcely, however, had four years or so elapsed from that time, when he again asked them for aid, and, at length, by dint of great entreaties, he obtained a thirtieth, which they granted him on the condition that neither that exaction nor the others before it should in the future be made a precedent of. And regarding that he gave them his charter. Furthermore, he then [at that earlier time] granted them that all the liberties contained in Magna Carta should thenceforward be fully observed throughout the whole of his kingdom. . . .

Furthermore, from the time of their giving the said thirtieth, itinerant justices have been continually going on eyre [moving from place to place] through all parts of England, alike for pleas of the forest [to enforce the king's monopoly on forests] and all other pleas, so that all the counties, hundreds, cities, boroughs, and nearly all the vills of England are heavily amerced [fined]; wherefore, from that eyre alone the king has, or ought to have, a very large sum of money, if it were paid, and properly collected. They therefore say with truth that all in the kingdom are so oppressed and impoverished by these amercements and by the other aids given before that they have little or no goods left. And because the king had never, after the granting of the thirtieth, abided by his charter of liberties [namely, Magna Carta], nay had since then oppressed them more than usual . . . they told the king flatly that for the present they would not give him an aid.

Source: Harry Rothwell, ed., *English Historical Documents*, vol. 3 (London: Eyre & Spottiswoode, 1975), 355–56.

John's Seal on Magna Carta

King John did not sign Magna Carta; he sealed it. From the thirteenth through the fifteenth century, kings, queens, and many other individuals and groups at all levels of society used seals to authenticate their charters—what we would call legal documents. The seal itself was made of wax or lead that was melted and pressed with a matrix of hard metal, such as gold or brass, that was carved in the negative, to produce a raised image. These seals reminded the public of the status as well as the name of the sealer. What image did John wish to project? *(The British Library/Ancient Art & Architecture Collection, Ltd.)*

Questions to Consider

1. **What do the clauses of Magna Carta that say what will henceforth *not* be done suggest about what the king *had been* doing?**
2. **How did the barons of 1242 use Magna Carta as a symbol of liberty?**
3. **Why didn't John sign Magna Carta?**

ing near independence as they built castles on their properties and established control over whole territories. When they elected a new king, the princes made sure that he would give them new lands and powers. The German kings were in a difficult position: they had to balance the many conflicting interests of their royal and imperial offices, their families, and the German princes, and they had to contend with the increasing influence of the papacy and the Italian communes, which made alliances with one another and with the German princes. All this prevented the consolidation of power under a strong German monarch during the first half of the twelfth century.

During the Investiture Conflict, the two sides (imperial and papal) were represented by two noble families. Leading the imperial party were the Staufer, or Hohenstaufen, clan; opposing them were the

Welfs. (Two later Italian factions, the Ghibellines and the Guelphs, corresponded, respectively, to the Hohenstaufens and the Welfs.) The enmity between these families was legendary, and warfare between the groups raged even after the Concordat of Worms in 1122. Decades of constant battles exhausted all parties, who began to long for peace. In an act of rare unanimity, they elected **Frederick I (Barbarossa)**. In Frederick (r. 1152–1190) they seemed to have a candidate who could end the strife: his mother was a Welf, his father a Staufer. Contemporary accounts of the king's career represented Frederick in the image of Christ as the cornerstone that joined two houses and reconciled enemies.

Frederick I (Barbarossa): King of Germany (r. 1152–1190) and emperor (crowned 1155) who tried to cement the power of the German king through conquest (for example, of northern Italy) and the bonds of vassalage.

New Foundations of Power

Frederick's appearance impressed his contemporaries—the name *Barbarossa* referred to his red-blond hair and beard. But beyond appearances, Frederick impressed those around him by what they called his firmness. He affirmed royal rights, even when he handed out duchies and allowed others to name bishops, because in return for these political powers Frederick required the princes to concede formally and publicly that they held their rights and territories from him as their lord. By making them his vassals, although with nearly royal rights within their principalities, Frederick defined the princes' relationship to the German king: they were powerful yet personally subordinate to him. In this way, Frederick hoped to save the monarchy and to coordinate royal and princely rule, thus ending Germany's chronic civil wars. Frederick used the lord–vassal relationship to give him a free hand to rule while placating the princes.

Frederick Barbarossa
In this image of Frederick, made during his lifetime, the emperor is dressed as a crusader, and the inscription tells him to fight the Muslims. The small figure on the right is the abbot of the Monastery of Schäftlarn, who gives Frederick a book that contains an account of the First Crusade. *(HIP/Art Resource, NY.)*

DOCUMENT

Frederick I's Reply to the Romans

Frederick I's conception of his rights and powers is well illustrated by the speech that he reportedly gave upon his entry into Rome in 1155 for his imperial coronation. The pope considered it his right to confer the crown on the king. But when Frederick came to Rome, envoys from the new city government that had been established there greeted him with an offer to give him the crown instead. Frederick reacted forcefully: the crown was not theirs to give; it was his by right. The gist of his reply to the Romans was recorded by his counselor and chronicler, Bishop Otto of Freising.

We have heard much heretofore concerning the wisdom and the valor of the Romans, yet more concerning their wisdom. Wherefore we cannot wonder enough at finding your words insipid with swollen pride rather than seasoned with the salt of wisdom. You set forth the ancient renown of your city. You extol to the very stars the ancient status of your sacred republic. Granted, granted! To use the words of your own writer, "There was, *there was once*, virtue in this republic." "Once," I say. And oh that we might truthfully and freely say "now"! Your Rome—nay, ours also—has experienced the vicissitudes of time. She could not be the only one to escape a fate ordained by the Author of all things for all that dwell beneath the orb of the moon. What shall I say? It is clear how first the strength of your nobility was transferred from this city of ours to the royal city of the East [Constantinople], and how for the course of many years the thirsty Greekling sucked the breasts of your delight. Then came the Frank, truly noble, in deed as in name, and forcibly possessed himself of whatever freedom was still left to you. Do you wish to know the ancient glory of your Rome? The worth of the senatorial dignity? The impregnable disposition of the camp? The virtue and the discipline of the equestrian order, its unmarred and unconquerable boldness when advancing to a conflict? Behold our state. All these things are to be found with us. All these have descended to us, together with the empire.

Source: Brian Tierney, *The Crisis of Church and State, 1050–1300: With Selected Documents* (Englewood Cliffs, NJ: Prentice Hall, 1964), 103–4.

Question to Consider

- **Why did Frederick think that Germany had inherited the Roman Empire along with all its power and glory?**

As the king of Germany, Frederick had the traditional right to claim the imperial crown. When, in 1155, he marched to Rome to be crowned emperor, the fledgling commune there protested that it alone had the right to give him the crown. Frederick interrupted them, asserting that the glory of Rome, together with its crown, came to him by right of conquest (see Document, "Frederick I's Reply to the Romans," above). He was equally insistent with the pope, who wrote to tell him that Rome belonged to St. Peter. Frederick replied that his imperial title gave him rights over the city. In part, Frederick was influenced by the revival of Roman law—the laws of Theodosius and Justinian—that was taking place in the schools of Italy. In part, too, he was convinced of the sacred—not just secular—origins of the imperial office. Frederick called his empire *sacer* ("sacred"), asserting that it was in its own way as precious, worthwhile, and God-given as the church.

Frederick buttressed this high view of his imperial right with worldly power. He married Beatrice of Burgundy, whose vast estates in Burgundy and Provence enabled him to establish a powerful political and territorial base centered in Swabia (today southwestern Germany).

Frederick and Italy Frederick Barbarossa then looked south to Italy. Its flourishing commercial cities could make him rich. Taxes on agricultural production there alone yielded thirty thousand silver talents annually, an incredible sum equal to the annual income of the richest ruler of the day, the king of England. Swabia and northern Italy together would give Frederick a compact and centrally located territory.

Some historians have faulted Frederick for "entangling" himself in Italy, but no emperor could leave Italy alone. The very title came from the Roman emperor, who had controlled the city of Rome and all of Italy. It would have seemed laughable to be "emperor" without holding at least some of this territory.

Nevertheless, Frederick's ambitions in Italy were problematic. Since the Investiture Conflict, the emperor had ruled Italy in name only. The communes of the northern cities guarded their liberties jealously, while the pope considered Italy his own sphere of influence. Frederick's territorial base just north of Italy threatened those interests (see Map 11.1, page 356). In 1157, soon after Frederick's imperial coronation, the pope's envoys arrived at a meeting called by the emperor with a letter detailing the dignities, honors, and other *beneficia* the papacy had showered on Frederick. The word *beneficia* angered Frederick and his supporters because it meant not only "benefits" but also "fiefs," casting Frederick as the pope's vassal. The incident opened old wounds from the Investiture Conflict and revealed the gulf between papal and imperial conceptions of worldly authority.

Despite the opposition of the cities and the pope, Frederick was determined to conquer northern Italy, which he managed to do by 1158. Adopting an Italian solution for governing the communes—appointing outsiders as magistrates—Frederick appointed his own men to these powerful positions. But that was where Frederick made his mistake. He chose German officials who lacked a sense of Italian communal traditions. The heavy hand of Frederick's magistrates created enormous resentment. For example, the magistrates at Milan immediately ordered an inventory of all taxes due the emperor and levied new and demeaning labor duties, even demanding that citizens carry the wood and stones of their plundered city to Pavia, twenty-five miles away, for use in constructing new houses there. By 1167, most of the cities of northern Italy had joined with the pope to form the Lombard League against Frederick. Defeated by the league at the battle of Legnano in 1176, Frederick made peace and withdrew most of his forces from Italy. The battle marked the triumph of the city over the crown in Italy, which would not have a centralized government until the nineteenth century; its political history would instead be that of its various regions and their dominant cities.

Frederick was the victim of traditions that were rapidly being outmoded. He based much of his rule in Germany on the bond of lord and vassal at the very moment when rulers elsewhere were relying less on such personal ties and more on salaried officials. He lived up to the meaning of *emperor*, with all its obligations to rule Rome and northern Italy, when other leaders were consolidating their terri-

Henry the Lion and Matilda

In this illustration from a deluxe manuscript of a liturgical book made for Henry the Lion, the duke and his wife are shown being crowned from heaven. Behind them are their royal and ducal forefathers. *(IAM/akg/World History Archive.)*

torial rule bit by bit. In addition, as "universal" emperor, he did not recognize the importance of local pride, language, customs, and traditions; he tried to rule Italian communes with his own men from Germany, and he failed.

Henry the Lion: Lord and Vassal

Frederick Barbarossa also had problems in Germany, where he had to contend with princes of near-royal status who acted as independent rulers of their principalities, though acknowledging Frederick as their feudal lord. One of the most powerful was Henry the Lion (c. 1130–1195). Married to Matilda, daughter of the English king Henry II and Eleanor of Aquitaine, Henry was duke of Saxony and Bavaria, which gave him important bases in both the north and the south of Germany. (See the illustration on page 364.) A self-confident and aggressive ruler, Henry dominated his territory by investing bishops (usurping the role of the emperor as outlined in the Concordat of Worms), collecting dues from his estates, and exercising judicial rights over his duchies. He also actively extended his rule, especially in Slavic regions, pushing northeast past the Elbe River to reestablish dioceses and to build the commercial city of Lübeck.

Henry was lord of many vassals and ministerials (people of unfree status but high prestige). He organized a staff of clerics and ministerials to collect taxes and tolls and to write up his legal acts. Here, as elsewhere, administration no longer depended entirely on the personal involvement of the ruler.

Yet like kings, princes could fall. Henry's growing power so threatened other princes and even Frederick that in 1179 Frederick called Henry to the king's court for violating the peace. When Henry chose not to appear, Frederick exercised his authority as Henry's lord and charged him with violating his duty as a vassal. Because Henry refused the summons to court and avoided serving his lord in Italy, Frederick condemned him, confiscated his holdings, and drove him out of Germany in 1180.

Late-twelfth-century kings and emperors often found themselves engaged in a balancing act of ruling yet placating their powerful vassals. The process was almost always risky. Successfully challenging one recalcitrant prince/vassal meant negotiating costly deals with the others, since their support was vital. Frederick wanted to retain Henry's duchy for himself, as Philip Augustus had managed to do with Normandy. But Frederick was not powerful enough to do so and was forced to divide and distribute it to the supporters he had relied on to enforce his decrees against Henry.

Eastern Europe and Byzantium, c. 1200

Eastern Europe and Byzantium: Fragmenting Realms

The importance of governmental and bureaucratic institutions such as those developed in England and France is made especially clear by comparing the experience of regions where they were not established. In eastern Europe, the characteristic pattern was for states to form under the leadership of one great ruler and then to fragment under his successor. For example, King Béla III of Hungary (r. 1172–1196) built up a state that looked superficially like a western European kingdom. He married a French princess, sent his officials to Paris to be educated, and built his palace in the French Romanesque style. The annual income from his estates, tolls, dues, and taxes equaled that of the richest western monarchs. But he did not set up enduring governmental institutions, and in the decades that followed Béla's death, wars between his sons splintered his monarchical holdings and aristocratic supporters divided the wealth.

Rus underwent a similar process. Although twelfth-century Kiev was politically fragmented, autocratic princes to the north constructed Vladimir (also known as Suzdalia), the nucleus of the later Muscovite state. Within the clearly defined borders of this principality, well-to-do towns prospered and monasteries and churches flourished; one chronicler wrote that "all lands trembled at the name [of its ruler]." Yet early in the thirteenth century this nascent state began to crumble as princely claimants fought one another for power, much as Béla's sons had done in Hungary. Soon Rus would be conquered by the Mongols (see page 402).

Although the Byzantine Empire was already a consolidated, bureaucratic state, after the mid-twelfth century it gradually began to show weaknesses. Traders from the west — the Venetians especially — dominated its commerce. The Byzantine emperors who ruled during the last half of the twelfth century downgraded the old civil servants, elevated imperial relatives to high offices, and favored the military elite, who nevertheless rarely came to the aid of the emperor. As Byzantine rule grew more personal and European rule became more bureaucratic, the two gradually became more alike.

The Byzantine Empire might well have continued like this for a long time. Instead, its heart was knocked out by the warriors of the Fourth Crusade (1202–1204). At the instigation of Venice, the crusaders made a detour to Constantinople on their way to the Holy Land, capturing the city in 1204. Although one of the crusade leaders was named "emperor" and ruled in Constantinople and its surrounding territory, the Byzantine Empire itself continued to exist, though disunited and weak. It retook Constantinople in 1261, but it never regained the power that it had had in the eleventh century.

REVIEW QUESTION What new sources and institutions of power became available to rulers in the second half of the twelfth century?

The Growth of a Vernacular High Culture

With their consolidation of territory, wealth, and power in the last half of the twelfth century, kings, barons, princes, and their wives and daughters supported new kinds of literature and music. For the first time on the continent, though long true in England, poems and songs were written in the vernacular, the spoken language, rather than in Latin. They celebrated the lives of the nobility and were meant to be read or sung aloud, sometimes with accompanying musical instruments. They provided a common experience for aristocrats at court. Whether in the cities of Italy or the more isolated courts of northern Europe, patrons and patronesses spent the profits from their estates and commerce on the arts. Their support helped develop and enrich the spoken language while it heightened their prestige as aristocrats.

The Troubadours: Poets of Love and Play

Already at the beginning of the twelfth century, Duke William IX of Aquitaine (1071–1126), the grandfather of Eleanor, had written lyric poems in Occitan, the vernacular of southern France. Perhaps influenced by Arabic and Hebrew love poetry from al-Andalus, his own poetry in turn provided a model for poetic forms that gained popularity through repeated performances. The final four-line stanza of one such poem demonstrates the composer's skill with words:

Per aquesta fri e tremble,	For this one I shiver and tremble,
quar de tan bon' amor l'am;	I love her with such a good love;
qu'anc no cug qu'en nasques semble	I do not think the like of her was ever born
en semblan de gran linh n'Adam.	in the long line of Lord Adam.

The rhyme scheme of this poem appears to be simple—*tremble* goes with *semble*, *l'am* with *n'Adam*—but the entire poem has five earlier verses, all six lines long and all containing the *-am*, *-am* rhyme in the fourth and sixth lines, while every other line within each verse rhymes as well.

Troubadours, lyric poets who wrote in Occitan, varied their rhymes and meters endlessly to dazzle their audiences with brilliant originality. Most of their rhymes and meters resemble Latin religious poetry of the same time, indicating that the vernacular and Latin religious cultures overlapped. Such similarity is also evident in the troubadours' choice of subjects. The most common topic, love, echoed the twelfth-century church's emphasis on the emotional relationship between God and humans.

The troubadours invented new meanings for old images. When William IX sang of his "good love" for a woman unlike any other born in the line of Adam, the words could be interpreted in two ways: they reminded listeners of the Virgin Mary, a woman unlike any other, but they also referred to William's lover, recalled in another part of the poem, where he had complained

If I do not get help soon
and my lady does not give me love,
by Saint Gregory's holy head I'll die
if she doesn't kiss me in a chamber or under
a tree.

His lady's character is ambiguous: she is like the Virgin Mary, but she is also his mistress.

Troubadours, both male and female, expressed prevalent views of love much as popular singers do

---

troubadours: Vernacular poets in southern France in the twelfth and early thirteenth centuries who sang of love, longing, and courtesy.

today. The Contessa de Dia (flourished c. 1160) wrote about her unrequited love for a man:

> So bitter do I feel toward him
> whom I love more than anything.
> With him my mercy and *cortesia* [fine manners]
> are in vain.

The key to troubadour verse is the idea of *cortesia.* The word refers to courtesy (the refinement of people living at court) and to the struggle to achieve an ideal of virtue.

Historians and literary critics used to use the term *courtly love* to emphasize one of the themes of courtly literature: overwhelming love for a beautiful married noblewoman who is far above the poet in status and utterly unattainable. But this theme was only one of many aspects of love that the troubadours sang about: some of the songs boasted of sexual conquests, others played with the notion of equality between lovers, and still others preached that love was the source of virtue. The real overall theme of this literature is not courtly love; it is the power of women. No wonder Eleanor of Aquitaine and other aristocratic women patronized the troubadours: they enjoyed the image that troubadour verse gave them of themselves. Until recently, historians thought that the image was a delusion and that twelfth-century aristocratic women were valuable mainly as heiresses to marry and as mothers of sons. But new research has revealed that there were many powerful female lords in southern France. They owned property, had vassals, led battles, decided disputes, and entered into and broke political alliances as their advantage dictated. Both men and women appreciated troubadour poetry, which recognized and praised women's power even as it eroticized it.

Troubadour poetry was not read; it was sung, typically by a *jongleur*, a medieval musician. No written troubadour music exists from before the thirteenth century, and even for poems written thereafter we have music for only a fraction. This music was written on four- and five-line staves, so scholars can at least determine relative pitches, and modern musicians can sing some troubadour songs with the hope of sounding reasonably like the original. This popular music is the earliest that can be recreated authentically (Figure 11.4).

From southern France, the troubadours' songs spread to Italy, northern France, England, and Germany. Similar poetry appeared in other vernacular languages: the *minnesingers* ("love singers") sang in German; the *trouvères* sang in the Old French of northern France. One trouvère was the English king Richard the Lion-Hearted. Taken prisoner on his re-

FIGURE 11.4 Troubadour Song: "I Never Died for Love"
This music is the first part of a song written by troubadour poet Peire Vidal sometime between 1175 and 1205. It has been adapted here for the treble clef. There is no time signature, but the music may easily be played by calculating one beat for each note, except for the two-note slurs, which fit into one beat together. *(From Samuel N. Rosenberg, Margaret Switten, and Gerard Le Vot, eds.,* Songs of the Troubadours and Trouvères. *Copyright © 1997 by Samuel N. Rosenberg, Margaret Switten, and Gerard Le Vot. Reprinted by permission of Taylor & Francis/Garland Publishing, http://www.taylorandfrancis.com.)*

turn from the Third Crusade, Richard wrote a poem expressing his longing not for a lady but for the good companions of war, the knightly "youths" he had joined in battle:

> They know well, the men of Anjou and Touraine,
> those bachelors, now so magnificent and safe,
> that I am arrested, far from them, in another's
> hands.
> They used to love me much, now they love me
> not at all.
> There's no lordly fighting now on the barren
> plains,
> because I am a prisoner.

Clearly some troubadour poetry was about war rather than love. (See Document: "Bertran de Born, 'I love the joyful time of Easter,'" page 368.)

The Birth of Epic and Romance Literature

War was not as common a topic in lyric poetry as love, but long narrative poems appeared frequently

DOCUMENT

Bertran de Born, "I love the joyful time of Easter"

The troubadours mainly sang of love. But they also sometimes wrote about war. Bertran de Born, whose poems date from the second half of the twelfth century, celebrated warfare. In "I love the joyful time of Easter," he satirized the many poems that proclaimed springtime to be the moment for lovers.

I love the joyful time of Easter,
that makes the leaves and flowers come forth,
and it pleases me to hear the mirth
of the birds, who make their song
resound through the woods,
and it pleases me to see upon the meadows
tents and pavilions planted,
and I feel a great joy
when I see ranged along the field
knights and horses armed for war.

And it pleases me when the skirmishers
make the people and their baggage run away,
and it pleases me when I see behind them coming
a great mass of armed men together,
and I have pleasure in my heart
when I see strong castles besieged,
the broken ramparts caving in,
and I see the host [army] on the water's edge,
closed in all around by ditches,
with palisades, strong stakes close together.

And I am as well pleased by a lord
when he is first in the attack,
armed, upon his horse, unafraid,
so he makes his men take heart
by his own brave lordliness.

Source: Frederick Goldin, ed. and trans., *Lyrics of the Troubadours and Trouvères: An Anthology and a History* (Garden City: Anchor Books, 1973), 243–45.

Question to Consider

- **In what ways was war like love for Bertran?**

in vernacular writing. Such poems, called **chansons de geste** ("songs of heroic deeds"), followed a long oral tradition and appeared at about the same time as love poems. Like the songs of the troubadours, these epic poems implied a code of behavior for aristocrats, in this case on the battlefield.

By the end of the twelfth century, warriors wanted a guide for conduct and a common identity. Nobles and knights had begun to merge into one class as they felt threatened from below by newly rich merchants and from above by newly powerful kings. Their ascendancy on the battlefield, where they unhorsed one another with lances and long swords and took prisoners rather than killing their opponents, was also beginning to wane in the face of mercenary infantrymen who wielded long hooks and knives that ripped easily through chain mail. A knightly ethos and sense of group solidarity emerged in the face of these social, political, and military changes. The protagonists of heroic poems yearned for battle:

> The armies are in sight of one another. . . . The cowards tremble as they march, but the brave hearts rejoice for the battle.

Examining the moral issues that made war both tragic and inevitable, poets played on the contradictory values of their society, such as the conflicting loyalties of friendship and vassalage or a vassal's right to a fief versus a son's right to his father's land.

These vernacular narrative poems, later called epics, focused on war. Other long poems, later called romances, explored the relationships between men and women. Romances reached their zenith of popularity during the late twelfth and early thirteenth centuries. The legend of King Arthur inspired many of them. For example, in a romance by the poet Chrétien de Troyes (c. 1150–1190) the heroic knight Lancelot, who is in love with King Arthur's wife, Queen Guinevere, comes across a comb bearing some strands of her radiant hair:

> Never will the eye of man see anything receive such honor as when [Lancelot] begins to adore these tresses. . . . Even for St. Martin and St. James he has no need.

Chrétien was evoking the familiar imagery of relics, such as bits of hair or the bones of saints, as items of devotion. Making Guinevere's hair an object of adoration not only conveyed the depth of Lancelot's feeling but also poked a bit of fun at him. Like the troubadours, the romantic poets enjoyed the interplay between religious and amorous feelings. Just as the ideal monk merges his will in God's

---

chansons de geste (shahn SOHN duh ZHEST): Epic poems of the twelfth century about knightly and heroic deeds.

will, Lancelot loses his will to Guinevere. When she sees him—the greatest knight in Christendom—fighting in a tournament, she tests him by asking him to do his "worst." The poor knight is obliged to lose all his battles until she changes her mind.

Lancelot was the perfect chivalric knight. The word **chivalry** derives from the French word *cheval* ("horse"); the fact that the knight was a horseman marked him as a warrior of the most prestigious sort. Perched high on his horse, his heavy lance couched in his right arm, the knight was an imposing and menacing figure. Chivalry made him gentle—except to his enemies on the battlefield. The chivalric hero was a knight constrained by a code of refinement, fair play, piety, and devotion to an ideal. Historians debate whether real knights lived up to the codes implicit in epics and romances, but there is no doubt that knights saw themselves mirrored there. They were the poets' audience; sometimes they were the poets' subject as well. For example, when the knight William the Marshal died, his son commissioned a poet to write his biography. In it, William was depicted as a model knight, courteous with the ladies and brave on the battlefield.

REVIEW QUESTION What do the works of the troubadours and vernacular poets reveal about the nature of entertainment—its themes, its audience, its performers—in the twelfth century?

Religious Fervor and Crusade

The new vernacular culture was merely one sign of the growing wealth, sophistication, and self-confidence of the late twelfth century. New forms of religious life were another. Unlike the reformed orders of the early half of the century, which had fled the cities, the new religious groups embraced (and were embraced by) urban populations. Rich and poor, male and female joined these movements. They criticized the existing church as too wealthy, impersonal, and spiritually superficial. Intensely interested in the life of Christ, men and women in the late twelfth century made his childhood, agony, death, and presence in the Eucharist—the bread and wine that became the body and blood of Christ in the Mass—the emotional focus of their own lives.

Religious fervor mixed with greed in new crusades that had little success in the Holy Land but were victorious on the borders of Europe and, as we have already seen, at Constantinople. These were the poisonous flowers of the Middle Ages.

New Religious Orders in the Cities

The quick rebuilding of the cathedral at Chartres reveals the religious fervor of late-twelfth-century city dwellers. New religious orders in the cities speak to that fervor as well. Appealing to people who did not want to leave urban society but who nevertheless wished to deepen their religious lives, the new orders—including the Franciscans and the Beguines—had enormous success. Some of these urban movements, however, so threatened established doctrine and church hierarchy that they were condemned as heresies.

Francis and the Franciscans St. Francis (c. 1182–1226) founded the most famous orthodox religious movement—the **Franciscans**. Francis was a child of city life and commerce. Expected to follow his well-to-do father in the cloth trade at Assisi in Italy, Francis began to experience doubts, dreams, and illnesses that spurred him to religious self-examination. Eventually, he renounced his family's wealth, dramatically marking the decision by casting off all his clothes and standing naked before his father, a crowd of spectators, and the bishop of Assisi. Francis then put on a simple robe and went about preaching penance to anyone who would listen.

Clinging to poverty as if, in his words, "she" were his "lady" (and thus borrowing the vocabulary of chivalry), he accepted no money, walked without shoes, and wore only one coarse tunic. Francis brought religious devotion out of the monastery and into the streets. Intending to follow the model of Christ, he received, as his biographers put it, a miraculous gift of grace: the stigmata, bleeding sores corresponding to the wounds Christ suffered on the cross.

By all accounts Francis was a spellbinding speaker, and he attracted many followers. Because they went about begging, those followers were called

---

chivalry: An ideal of knightly comportment that included military prowess, bravery, fair play, piety, and courtesy.

Franciscans: The religious order founded by St. Francis (c. 1182–1226) and dedicated to poverty and preaching, particularly in towns and cities.

mendicants, from the Latin verb *mendicare* ("to beg"). Recognized as a religious order by the pope, the Brothers of St. Francis (or friars, from the Latin term for "brothers") spent their time preaching, ministering to lepers, and doing manual labor. Eventually they dispersed, setting up fraternal groups throughout Italy and then in France, Spain, the Holy Land, Germany, and England. The friars sought town society, preaching to crowds and begging for their daily bread.

St. Francis converted both men and women. In 1212, an eighteen-year-old noblewoman, Clare, formed the nucleus of a community of pious women, which became the Order of the Sisters of St. Francis. At first, the women worked alongside the friars; but both Francis and the church hierarchy disapproved of their activities in the world, and soon Franciscan sisters were confined to cloisters under the rule of St. Benedict.

The Beguines | Clare was one of many women who sought a new kind of religious expression. Some women joined convents; others became recluses, living alone, like hermits; still others sought membership in new lay sisterhoods. In northern Europe at the end of the twelfth century, laywomen who lived together in informal pious communities were called Beguines. Without permanent vows or an established rule, the Beguines chose to be celibate (though they were free to leave and marry) and often made their living by weaving cloth or tending to the sick and old. Some of them may have prepared and illustrated their own reading materials. (See the illustration on the left.) Although their daily occupations were ordinary, the Beguines' spiritual lives were often emotional and ecstatic, infused with the combined imagery of love and religion so pervasive in both monasteries and courts. One renowned Beguine, Mary of Oignies (1177–1213), who like St. Francis was said to have received stigmata, felt herself to be a pious mother entrusted with the Christ child. As her biographer, Jacques de Vitry, wrote, "Sometimes it seemed to her that for three or more days she held [Christ] close to her so that He nestled between her breasts like a baby, and she hid Him there lest He be seen by others."

Heresies | In addition to the orthodox religious movements that took off at the end of the twelfth century, there was a veritable explosion of ideas and doctrines that contradicted those officially accepted by church authorities and were therefore labeled heresies. Heresies were not new in the twelfth century. But the eleventh-century Gregorian reform had created for the first time in the West a clear church hierarchy headed by a pope who could enforce a single doctrine and discipline. Clearly defined orthodoxy meant that people in western Europe now perceived heresy as a serious problem. When intense religious feeling led to the fervent espousal of new religious ideas, established authorities often felt threatened and took steps to preserve their power.

Beguine Psalter
Although emphasizing labor and caring for others, most Beguines were also literate. The Psalter (book of Psalms) illustrated here was probably made by Beguines. The painting focuses on Mary: in the bottom tier is the Annunciation, when she learns that she will give birth to the Savior. At the top she reigns as Queen of Heaven, with a crown on her head and the baby Jesus on her lap. *(© The British Library Board. All Rights Reserved. Liège Psalter, BL Add. Ms. 2114, fol. 8v.)*

Among the most visible heretics were dualists who saw the world as being torn between two great forces—one good, the other evil. Already important in Bulgaria and Asia Minor, dualism became a prominent ingredient in religious life in Italy and the Rhineland by the end of the twelfth century. Another center of dualism was Languedoc, an area of southern France; there the dualists were called Albigensians, a name derived from the town of Albi.

Calling themselves "Christ's poor"—though modern historians have given them the collective name Cathars (from a Greek word meaning "pure")—these men and women believed that the devil had created the material world. Therefore, they renounced the world, abjuring wealth, meat, and sex. Their repudiation of sex reflected some of the attitudes of eleventh-century church reformers (whose orthodoxy, however, was never in doubt), while their rejection of wealth echoed the same concerns that moved St. Francis to embrace poverty. In many ways, the dualists simply took these attitudes to an extreme; but unlike orthodox reformers, they also challenged the efficacy and legitimacy of the church hierarchy. Attracting both men and women, young and old, literate and unlettered, and giving women access to all but the highest positions in their church, the dualists saw themselves as followers of Christ's original message. But the church called them heretics.

The church also condemned other, nondualist groups as heretical, not on doctrinal grounds but because these groups allowed their lay members to preach, challenging the authority of the church hierarchy. In Lyon (in southeastern France) in the 1170s, for example, a rich merchant named Waldo decided to take literally the Gospel message "If you wish to be perfect, then go and sell everything you have, and give to the poor" (Matt. 19:21). The same message had inspired countless monks and would worry the church far less several decades later, when St. Francis established his new order. But when Waldo went into the street and gave away his belongings, announcing, "I am not really insane, as you think," he scandalized not only the bystanders but the church as well. Refusing to retire to a monastery, Waldo and his followers—men and women who called themselves the Poor of Lyon but were called Waldensians by their enemies—lived in poverty. They spent their time preaching, quoting the Gospel in the vernacular so that everyone would understand. But the papacy rebuffed Waldo's bid to preach freely, and his community—denounced, excommunicated, and expelled from Lyon—wandered to Languedoc, Italy, northern Spain, and the Mosel valley in Germany. Most were persecuted and eventually exterminated, but a few remnants survived and their descendants were absorbed into the sixteenth-century Protestant Reformation.

Disastrous Crusades to the Holy Land

Did religious fervor also inspire the new crusades of the later twelfth century? At least some Europeans thought so. The pope called the Third Crusade "an opportunity for repentance and doing good." A poet in Bavaria wrote, "If any man now will not have pity upon [Christ's] cross and his Sepulcher [in Jerusalem], then he will not be given heavenly bliss."

In the twelfth century, the Seljuk Empire fell apart. Following the crushing defeat of the crusaders in the Second Crusade, the Muslim hero Nur al-Din united Syria and presided over a renewal of Sunni Islam. His successor, Saladin (1138–1193), fought the Christian king of Jerusalem over Egypt, which Saladin ruled, together with Syria, by 1186. Caught in a pincer, Jerusalem fell to Saladin's armies in 1187. The Third Crusade, an unsuccessful bid to retake Jerusalem from Saladin, marked a military and political turning point for the crusader states. The European outpost survived, but it was reduced to very little. Christians could continue to enter Jerusalem as pilgrims, but Islamic hegemony over the Holy Land would remain a fact of life for centuries.

The Third Crusade, 1189–1192

Led by the greatest rulers of Europe—Emperor Frederick I (Barbarossa), Philip II of France, Leopold of Austria, and Richard I of England—the Third Crusade reflected political tensions among the European ruling class. Richard, in particular, seemed to cultivate enemies. The most serious of these was Leopold, whom he offended at the siege of Acre. But the apparent personal tensions indicated a broader hostility between the kings of England and France. In this, Leopold was Philip's ally. On his return home, Richard was captured by Leopold and held for a huge ransom. He had good reason to write his plaintive poem bemoaning his captivity and the lost "love" of former friends.

The Third Crusade accomplished little and exacerbated tensions with Byzantium. Frederick Barbarossa went overland on the crusade, passing through Hungary and Bulgaria and descending into the Byzantine Empire (Map 11.2). Before his untimely death by drowning, he spent most of his time harassing the Byzantines.

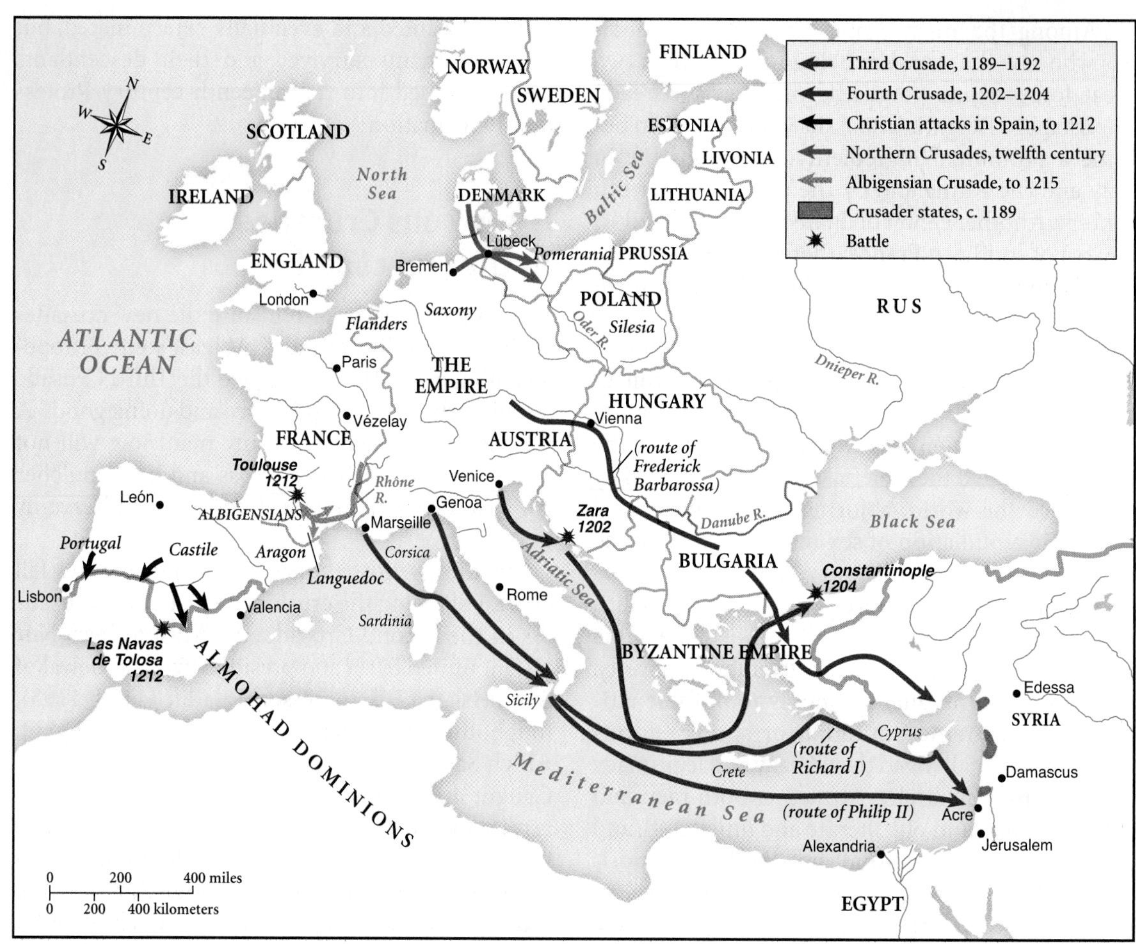

MAP 11.2 Crusades and Anti-Heretic Campaigns, 1150–1215
Europeans aggressively expanded their territory during the second half of the twelfth century. To the north, knights pushed into the Baltic Sea region. To the south, warriors pushed against the Muslims in al-Andalus and waged war against the Cathars in southern France. To the east, the new crusades were undertaken to shore up the tiny European outpost in the Holy Land. Although most of these aggressive activities had the establishment of Christianity as at least one motive, the conquest of Constantinople in 1204 had no such justification. It grew in part out of general European hostility toward Byzantium but mainly out of Venice's commercial ambitions.

The Fourth Crusade, 1202–1204 The hostilities that surfaced during the Third Crusade made it a dress rehearsal for the Fourth. Resentment had built up against the Byzantine Greeks ever since the First Crusade, when they had abandoned the crusaders after the battle of Nicaea (see page 332). During the **Fourth Crusade** prejudice and religious zeal combined to persuade many of the crusaders to change their plans and capture Constantinople rather than Jerusalem (see Map 11.2). (Some were disgusted by the new goal and went home.)

The Venetians instigated the change of plans. After the pope called the crusade, the Venetians fitted out a fine fleet of ships and galleys for the expedition. But when the crusaders arrived in Venice, there were far fewer fighters to pay for the transport than had been anticipated. To defray the costs of the ships and other expenses, the Venetians convinced the crusaders to do them some favors before taking off against the Muslims. First, they had the crusaders attack Zara, a Christian city in Dalmatia (today's Croatia) that was Venice's competitor in the Adriatic. Then they urged the army to attack Constantinople itself, where they hoped to gain commercial advantage over their rivals. Convinced of the superiority of their brand of Christianity over that of the Byzantines, the crusaders killed the inhabitants of Constantinople and ransacked the city for treasure and relics. "Never," wrote a contemporary, "was so great

---

Fourth Crusade: The crusade that lasted from 1202 to 1204; its original goal was to recapture Jerusalem, but the crusaders ended up conquering Constantinople instead.

DOCUMENT

The Children's Crusade (1212)

In some regions, intense lay piety led groups of unarmed young people, accompanied by priests and other adults, to attempt to free the Holy Sepulcher at Jerusalem. Chroniclers recorded their activities, some with dismay, others with amusement or admiration. The account below comes from the Ebersheim Chronicle, *written in Germany.*

Unheard-of events appeal to us from their outset, challenging us to preserve their memory. A certain little boy named Nicholas, who came from the region of Cologne, spurred on a great gathering of children through some unknown counsel, claiming that he could walk across the waves of the sea without wetting his feet and could provide sufficient provisions for those following him. The rumor of such a marvelous deed resounded through the cities and towns, and however many heard him, boys or girls, they abandoned their parents, marked themselves as crusaders, and prepared to cross the sea. And so throughout all Germany and France an infinite number of serving-boys, handmaids, and maidens followed their leader and came to Vienne, which is a city by the sea.[1] There they were taken on board some ships, carried off by pirates, and sold to the Saracens. Some who tried to return home wasted away with hunger; and many girls who were virgins when they left were pregnant when they returned. Thus, one can clearly see that this journey issued from the deception of the devil because it caused so much loss.

[1]Vienne isn't by the sea, but the child crusaders did get to various Mediterranean port cities.

Source: John Shinners, ed., *Medieval Popular Religion 1000–1500: A Reader*, 2nd ed. (Peterborough, Ontario: Broadview Press, 2007), 418–19.

Question to Consider

- **What factors help to explain the phenomenon of a mass crusade of young people?**

an enterprise undertaken by any people since the creation of the world." When one crusader discovered a cache of relics, a chronicler recalled, "he plunged both hands in and, girding up his loins, he filled the folds of his gown with the holy booty of the Church."

The pope decried the sack of Constantinople, but he also took advantage of it, ordering the crusaders to stay there for a year to consolidate their gains. Plans to go on to the Holy Land were never carried out. The crusade leaders chose one of themselves—Baldwin of Flanders—to be emperor, and he, the other princes, and the Venetians divided the conquered lands among themselves.

Popes continued to call crusades to the Holy Land until the mid-fifteenth century, but the Fourth Crusade marked the last major mobilization of men and leaders for such an enterprise. Working against these expeditions were the new values of the late twelfth century, which placed a premium on the interior pilgrimage of the soul and valued rulers who stayed home and cared for their people. (See Document, "The Children's Crusade [1212]," above.)

Victorious Crusades in Europe and on Its Frontiers

Armed expeditions against those perceived as infidels were launched not only to the Holy Land but also much nearer to home. In the second half of the twelfth century, the Spanish reconquista continued with increasing success and virulence, new wars of conquest were waged at the northern edge of Europe, and a crusade was launched against the Albigensians living in Europe itself.

The War in Spain In the second half of the twelfth century, Christian Spain achieved a political configuration that would last for centuries, dominated to the east by the kingdom of Aragon; in the middle by Castile, whose ruler styled himself emperor; and in the west by Portugal, whose ruler similarly transformed his title from *prince* to *king*. The three leaders competed for territory and power, but above all they sought an advantage against the Muslims to the south (Map 11.3).

Muslim disunity aided the Christian reconquest of Spain. The Muslims of al-Andalus were themselves beset from the south by new waves of Berber Muslims from North Africa. Claiming religious purity, these North African zealots declared their own holy war against the Andalusians. Threatened from both north and south, the Muslim leaders of Spain tried to negotiate with their Christian neighbors, sometimes even swearing vassalage to them.

But the crusading ideal held no room for such subtleties. The reconquista was set back by Berber victories, and competition between the Christian Spanish states prevented a coordinated effort. Nevertheless, piecemeal conquests—followed by the granting of law codes to regulate relations among

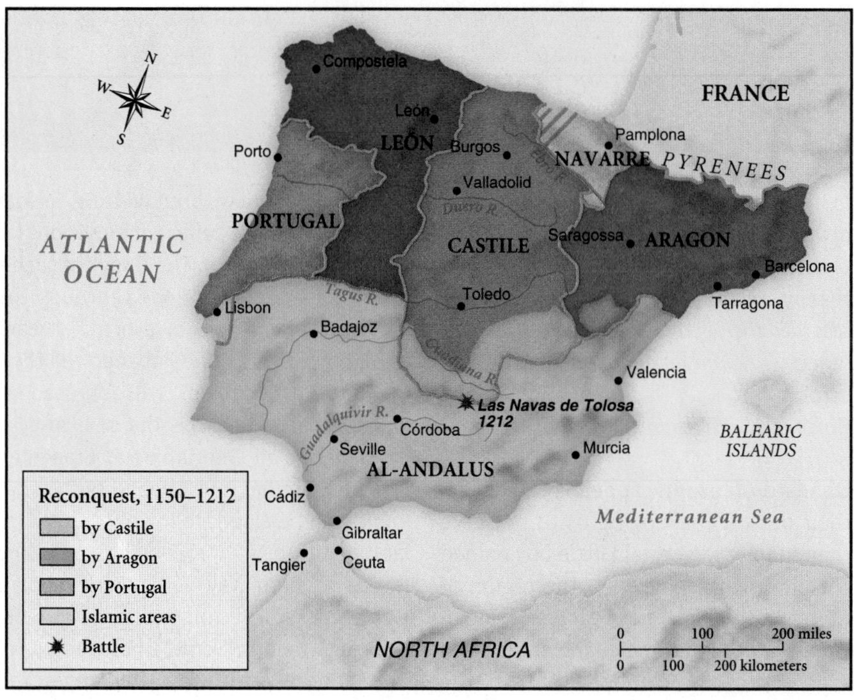

MAP 11.3 The Reconquista, 1150–1212
Slowly but surely the Christian kingdoms of Spain encroached on al-Andalus, taking Las Navas de Tolosa, deep in Islamic territory, in 1212. At the center of this activity was Castile. It had originally been a tributary of León, but in the twelfth century it became a power in its own right. (In 1230, León and Castile merged into one kingdom.) Meanwhile, the ruler of Portugal, who had also been dependent on León, began to claim the title of king, which was recognized officially in 1179, when he put Portugal under the protection of the papacy. Navarre was joined to Aragon until 1134, when it became, briefly, an independent kingdom. (In 1234, the count of Champagne came to the throne of Navarre, and thereafter its history was as much tied to France as to Spain.)

new Christian settlers as well as the Muslims, Mozarabs (Christians who had lived under the Muslims), and Jews who remained—gradually brought more territory under the control of the north. In 1212, a crusading army of Spaniards led by the kings of Aragon and Castile defeated the Muslims decisively at the battle of Las Navas de Tolosa. "On their side 100,000 armed men or more fell in the battle," the king of Castile wrote afterward, "but of the army of the Lord . . . incredible though it may be, unless it be a miracle, hardly 25 or 30 Christians of our whole army fell. O what happiness! O what thanksgiving!" The decisive turning point in the reconquista had been reached, though all of Spain came under Christian control only in 1492.

The Northern Crusades

Christians flexed their military muscle along Europe's northern frontiers as well. By the twelfth century, the peoples living along the Baltic coast—partly pagan, mostly Slavic- or Baltic-speaking—had learned to glean a living and a profit from inhospitable soil and climate. Through fishing and trading, they supplied the rest of Europe and Russia with slaves, furs, amber, wax, and dried fish. Like the earlier Vikings, they combined commercial competition with outright raiding, so that the Danes and the Germans of Saxony both benefited and suffered from their presence. As noted in Chapter 10 (page 333), during the Second Crusade a number of campaigns had been launched against the people on the Baltic coast. Thus began the Northern Crusades, which continued intermittently until the early fifteenth century.

The Danish king Valdemar I (r. 1157–1182) and the Saxon duke Henry the Lion led the first phase of the Northern Crusades. Their initial attacks on the Slavs were uncoordinated—in some instances, the Danes and Saxons even fought each other. But in key raids in the 1160s and 1170s, the two leaders worked together briefly to bring much of the region west of the Oder River under their control. They took some land outright—Henry the Lion apportioned conquered territory to his followers, for example—but more often the Slavic princes surrendered and had their territories reinstated once they became vassals of the Christian rulers. Meanwhile, churchmen arrived: the Cistercians came long before the first phase of fighting had ended, confidently building their monasteries to the very banks of the Oder River. Slavic peasants surely suffered from the conquerors' fire and pillage, but the Slavic ruling classes ultimately benefited from the northern crusades. Once converted to Christianity, they found it advantageous for both their eternal salvation and their worldly profit to join new crusades to areas still farther east.

Meanwhile German traders, craftspeople, and colonists poured in, populating new towns and cities along the Baltic coast and dominating the shipping that had once been controlled by non-Christians. The leaders of the crusades gave these townsmen some political independence but demanded a large share of the cities' wealth in return.

Although less well known than the crusades to the Holy Land, the Northern Crusades had far more lasting effects: they settled the Baltic region with German-speaking lords and peasants and forged a permanent relationship between northeastern Europe and its neighbors to the south and west. With the Baltic dotted with churches and monasteries and its peoples dipped into baptismal waters, the region would gradually adopt the institutions of western medieval society—cities, guilds, universities, castles, and manors. The Livs (whose region was eventually known as Livonia) were conquered by 1208, and their bishop sent knights northward to conquer the Estonians. A cooperative venture between the Polish and German aristocracy conquered the Prussians, and German peasants eventually settled Prussia. Only the Lithuanians managed to resist western conquest, settlement, and conversion.

The Albigensian Crusade

The first crusade to be launched within Europe itself was against the Cathars in southern France. It began with papal missions to preach to the people there, convert the heretics, and, if necessary use force. The Dominican Order had its start in this way. Its founder, St. Dominic (1170–1221), recognized that preachers of Christ's word who came to the region on horseback, followed by a crowd of servants and wearing fine clothes, had no moral leverage with their audience. Dominic and his followers, like their heretical adversaries, rejected material riches and instead went about on foot, preaching and begging. They resembled the Franciscans, both organizationally and spiritually, and were also called friars.

The missions did not have the success anticipated, however, and in 1208, the murder of a papal

Almourol Castle

In the early twelfth century, the papacy recognized the reconquista as equivalent to a crusade, and the rulers of Portugal, Castile, and Aragon persuaded the Templars and other military orders to help them hold on to regions that had formerly been Muslim. When the Portuguese ruler conquered the western end of the Tagus River valley in the mid-twelfth century, he entrusted some of the Muslim strongholds there to the Templars. They rebuilt one of them as Almourol castle, using it to defend Portugal's new frontier. *(© Patrick Frilet/Hemis/Corbis.)*

legate in southern France prompted the pope to demand that northern princes take up the sword, invade Languedoc, wrest the land from the heretics, and populate it with orthodox Christians. The Albigensian Crusade (1209–1229) marked the first time the pope offered warriors fighting an enemy within Christian Europe all the spiritual and temporal benefits of a crusade to the Holy Land. The crusaders' monetary debts were suspended, and they were promised that their sins would be forgiven after forty days' service. Like all other crusades, the Albigensian Crusade had political as well as religious dimensions. It pitted southern French princes, who often had heretical sympathies, against northern leaders eager to demonstrate their piety and win new possessions. After sixteen years of warfare, the Capetian kings of France took over leadership of the crusade. By 1229, all resistance was broken, and Languedoc was brought under the French crown.

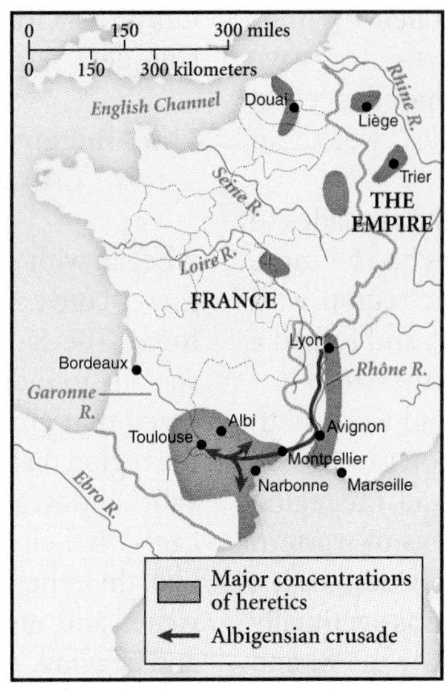

The Albigensian Crusade, 1209–1229

REVIEW QUESTION How did the idea of crusade change from the time of the original expedition to the Holy Land?

Conclusion

In the second half of the twelfth century, Christian Europe expanded from the Baltic Sea to the southern Iberian peninsula. European settlements in the Holy Land, by contrast, were nearly obliterated. When western Europeans sacked Constantinople in 1204, Europe and the Islamic world became the dominant political forces in the West.

Powerful territorial kings and princes established institutions of bureaucratic authority. They hired staffs to handle their accounts, record acts, collect taxes, issue writs, and preside over courts. A money economy provided the finances necessary to support the personnel now hired by medieval governments. Cathedral schools and universities became the training grounds for the new administrators. A new lay vernacular culture celebrated the achievements and power of the ruling class, while Gothic architecture reflected above all the pride and power of the cities.

New religious groups blossomed — Beguines, Franciscans, Dominicans, and heretics. However dissimilar the particulars, their beliefs and lifestyles all reflected the fact that people, especially city dwellers, yearned for a deeper spirituality.

Intense religiosity helped fuel the flames of crusades, which were now fought more often and against an increasing variety of foes, not only in the Holy Land but also in Spain, in southern France, and on Europe's northern frontiers. With heretics voicing criticisms and maintaining their beliefs, the church, led by the papacy, now defined orthodoxy and declared dissenters its enemies. The peoples on the Baltic coast became targets for new evangelical zeal; the Byzantines became the butt of envy, hostility, and finally enmity. European Christians still considered Muslims arrogant heathens, and the deflection of the Fourth Crusade did not stem the zeal of popes to call for new crusades to the Holy Land.

Confident and aggressive, the leaders of Christian Europe in the thirteenth century would attempt to impose their rule, legislate morality, and create a unified worldview impregnable to attack. But this drive for order would be countered by unexpected varieties of thought and action, by political and social tensions, and by intensely personal religious quests.

FOR FURTHER EXPLORATION

- **For additional primary-source material from this period**, see *Sources of the Making of the West*, Fourth Edition.
- **For Web sites, images, and documents related to topics in this chapter**, visit *Make History* at bedfordstmartins.com/hunt.

MAPPING THE WEST

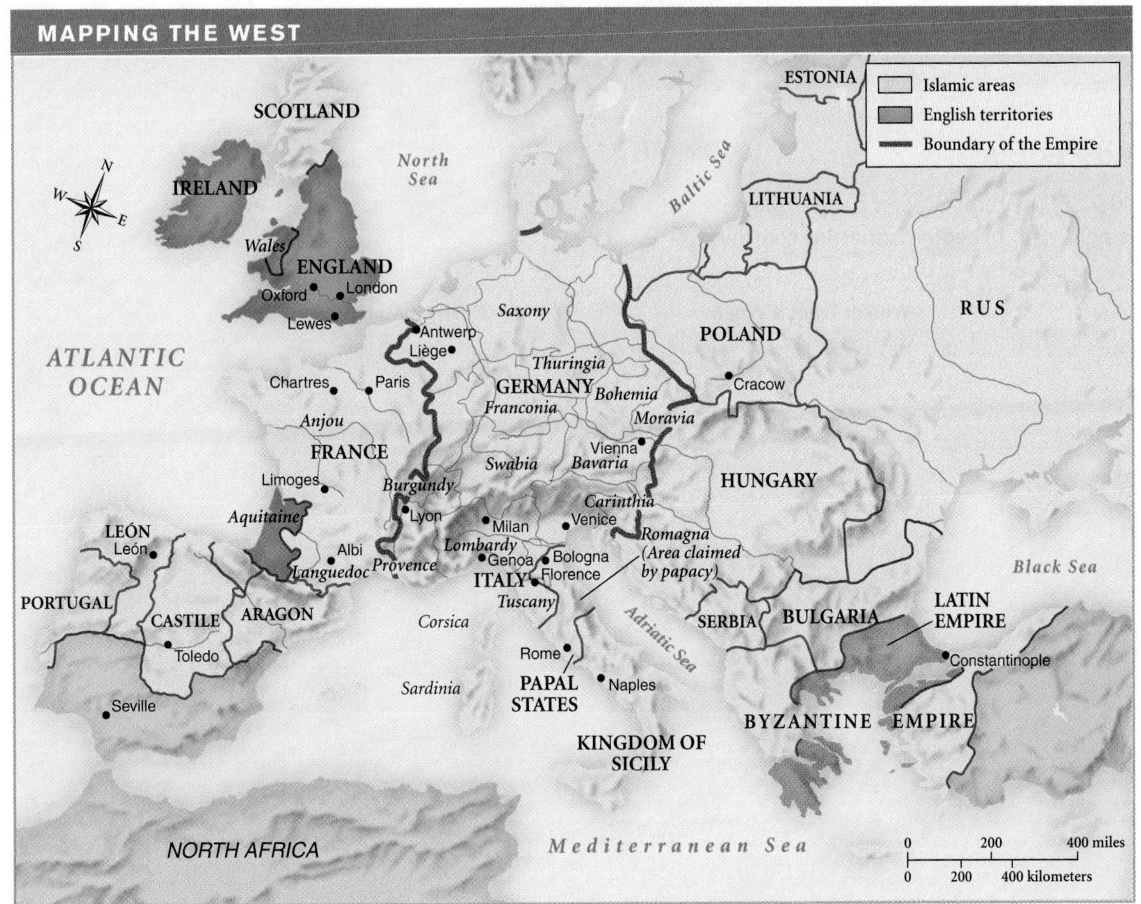

Europe and Byzantium, c. 1215

The major transformation in the map of the West between 1150 and 1215 was the conquest of Constantinople and the setting up of European rule there until 1261. The Byzantine Empire was now split into two parts. Bulgaria once again gained its independence. If Venice had hoped to control the Adriatic by conquering Constantinople, it must have been disappointed, for Hungary became its rival over the ports of the Dalmatian coast.

Chapter 11 Review

Online Study Guide bedfordstmartins.com/hunt

Key Terms and People

In the grid below, identify the term or person and explain its historical significance. (To do this exercise online, go to bedfordstmartins.com/hunt.)

Term	Who or What & When	Why It Matters
Romanesque (p. 350)		
Gothic architecture (p. 351)		
Henry II (p. 354)		
common law (p. 357)		
Philip II (Philip Augustus) (p. 358)		
Magna Carta (p. 359)		
Frederick I (Barbarossa) (p. 362)		
troubadours (p. 366)		
chansons de geste (p. 368)		
chivalry (p. 369)		
Franciscans (p. 369)		
Fourth Crusade (p. 372)		

Review Questions

1. What was new about education and architecture in the twelfth and early thirteenth centuries?
2. What new sources and institutions of power became available to rulers in the second half of the twelfth century?
3. What do the works of the troubadours and vernacular poets reveal about the nature of entertainment—its themes, its audience, its performers—in the twelfth century?
4. How did the idea of crusade change from the time of the original expedition to the Holy Land?

Making Connections

1. What were the chief differences that separated the ideals of the religious life in the period 1150–1215 from those of the period 1050–1150?
2. How was the gift economy associated with Romanesque architecture and the money economy with the Gothic style?
3. How do political developments—the growth of bureaucratic institutions, the development of strong monarchies, the growth of city governments—help explain the rise and popularity of vernacular literature and song in the twelfth and thirteenth centuries?

Important Events

Date	Event	Date	Event
1139–1153	Civil War in England	1202–1204	The Fourth Crusade
1152–1190	Reign of Frederick Barbarossa	1204	Fall of Constantinople to crusaders
1154–1189	Reign of King Henry II	1204	Philip takes Normandy, Anjou, Maine, Touraine, and Poitou from John
1176	Battle of Legnano	1209–1229	Albigensian Crusade
1180–1223	Reign of Philip II Augustus	1212	Battle of Las Navas de Tolosa; triumph of the reconquista
1182–1226	Francis of Assisi	1214	Battle of Bouvines
1189–1192	The Third Crusade	1215	Magna Carta

- Consider three events: **The Third Crusade (1189–1192)**, **The Fourth Crusade (1202–1204)**, and the **Albigensian Crusade (1209–1229)**. What were their various causes and results? How were they differently waged and led?

SUGGESTED REFERENCES

For the new schools, Abelard is a key primary source, while Clanchy provides perceptive background. Cultural and artistic developments are discussed in both Burl and Coldstream. Bartlett and Bradbury are essential for politics.

*Abelard's *The Story of My Misfortunes:* http://www.fordham.edu/halsall/source/abelard-sel.html

Aurell, Martin. *The Plantagenet Empire, 1154–1224*. Trans. David Crouch. 2007.

Bartlett, Robert. *England under the Norman and Angevin Kings, 1075–1225*. 2000.

Bouchard, Constance Brittain. *"Every Valley Shall Be Exalted": The Discourse of Opposites in Twelfth-Century Thought*. 2003.

Bradbury, Jim. *Philip Augustus: King of France*. 1998.

Burl, Aubrey. *Courts of Love, Castles of Hate: Troubadours and Trobairitz in Southern France, 1071–1321*. 2008.

Cheyette, Fredric L. *Ermengard of Narbonne and the World of the Troubadours*. 2001.

*Chrétien de Troyes. *Yvain: The Knight of the Lion*. Trans. Burton Raffel. 1987.

Christiansen, Eric. *The Northern Crusades*. 2nd ed. 1998.

Clanchy, Michael. *Abelard: A Medieval Life*. 1997.

Coldstream, Nicola. *Medieval Architecture*. 2002.

**Crusade of Frederick Barbarossa: The History of the Expedition of the Emperor Frederick and Related Texts*. Trans. G. A. Loud. 2010.

Gaunt, Simon, and Sarah Kay. *The Troubadours: An Introduction*. 1999.

*Goldin, Frederick. *Lyrics of the Troubadors and Trouvères: Original Texts, with Translations*. 1973.

Gothic architecture: http://www.bc.edu/bc_org/avp/cas/fnart/arch/gothic_arch.html

Hudson, John. *The Formation of the English Common Law: Law and Society in England from the Norman Conquest to Magna Carta*. 1996.

Moore, R. I. *The Formation of a Persecuting Society: Power and Deviance in Western Europe, 950–1250*. 2nd ed. 2007.

Pegg, Mark Gregory. *A Most Holy War: The Albigensian Crusade and the Battle for Christendom*. 2008.

Robson, Michael. *The Franciscans in the Middle Ages*. 2006.

Stephensen, David. *Heavenly Vaults: From Romanesque to Gothic in European Architecture*. 2009.

Troubadour poetry:
http://globegate.utm.edu/french/globegate_ mirror/occit.html

*Primary source.

CHAPTER 12

The Medieval Synthesis—and Its Cracks

1215–1340

In the second half of the thirteenth century, a wealthy patron asked a Parisian workshop specializing in manuscript illuminations to decorate Aristotle's *On the Length and Shortness of Life*. Most Parisian illuminators knew very well how to illustrate the Bible, liturgical books, and the writings of the church fathers. But Aristotle was a Greek who had lived before the time of Christ, and he was skeptical about the possibility of an afterlife. His treatise on life ended with death. The workshop's artists did not care about this fact. They illustrated Aristotle's work as if he had been a Christian and had believed in the immortal soul. As shown in the illustration opposite this page, the artists decorated one of the opening letters of the text with a depiction of the Christian Mass for the dead, a rite that is performed for the eternal salvation of Christians. In this way, the artists subtly but surely incorporated the pagan Aristotle into Christian belief and practice.

In the period 1215–1340, Europeans at all levels, from workshop artisans to kings and popes, thought that they could harmonize all ideas with Christianity, all aspects of this world with the next, and all of nature with revelation. Sometimes, as in the case of the illumination made for Aristotle's work, or in the writings of scholars seeking to bring together faith and reason, the synthesis seemed to work. But often it was forced, fragile, or elusive: not all people were willing to subordinate their beliefs to the tenets of Christianity; kings and popes debated without resolution the limits of their power; and theologians fought over the place of reason in matters of faith. Discord continually threatened expectations of unity and harmony.

Christianizing Aristotle
This illumination was created for a thirteenth-century Latin translation of Aristotle's *On the Length and Shortness of Life*. Although Aristotle did not believe in the eternity of the soul, the artists nevertheless placed a depiction of the Christian Mass for the dead in one of the book's initials, in this way revealing their conviction that the ancient teachings of Aristotle and Christian practice worked together. *(© Biblioteca Apostolica Vaticana [Vatican Library] Vat. Lat. 2071, f. 297.)*

New institutions of power and control were created to ensure the medieval synthesis. In 1215, the church set forth a comprehensive set of laws for both clergy and laity. Designed to create an orderly Christian society, these laws sought to regulate lay life and suppress heresy. They led to the establishment of courts of inquisition designed to find and punish heretics—those who dissented from church teachings and authority. Ironically, the Inquisition called attention to divergence even as it intended to enforce unity.

Around the same time, many Christian laypeople spontaneously sought new ways to express their religious zeal. This resulted in new devotional practices. It also led to the persecution of others—such as Jews and lepers—who were seen as contaminating the purity of a newly fervent Christian life.

On the whole, however, people did not so much seek to stamp out opposition as to reconcile opposites and find common ground in differences. Medieval thinkers, writers, musicians, and artists attempted to reconcile faith and reason and to find the commonalities in the sacred and secular realms. At the level of philosophy, this quest led to a new method of inquiry and study known as scholasticism. Yet even some scholastic thinkers pointed out cracks and disjunctions in the syntheses achieved.

To impose greater order and unity, kings and other rulers found new ways to extend their influence over their subjects. They used the tools of taxes, courts, and even representative institutions to control their realms. Yet the laws did not prevent dissent, and rulers often did not gain all the power they wanted. During this period the Empire weakened, the papacy was forced to move out of Rome, and the Mongols challenged Christian rulers. Soon natural disasters—crop failures and famine—added to the tension.

CHAPTER FOCUS **In what areas of life did thirteenth-century Europeans try to find harmony and impose order, and how successful were these attempts?**

The Church's Mission

The church had long sought to reform the secular world. In the eleventh century, during the Gregorian reform, such efforts focused on the king. In the thirteenth century, however, the church hoped to purify all of society. It tried to strengthen its institutions of law and justice to combat heresy and heretics, and it supported preachers who would bring the official views of the church to the streets. In this way, the church attempted to reorder the world in the image of heaven, with everyone following one rule of God in harmony. To some degree, the church succeeded in this endeavor; but it also came up against the limits of control, as dissident voices and forces clashed with its vision.

Innocent III and the Fourth Lateran Council

Innocent III (r. 1198–1216) was the most powerful, respected, and prestigious of medieval popes. As pope, he allowed St. Francis's group of impoverished followers to become a new church order, and he called the Fourth Crusade, which mobilized a large force drawn from every level of European society. The first pope to be trained at universities, Innocent studied theology at Paris and law at Bologna. From theology, he learned to tease new meaning out of canonical writings to magnify papal authority: he thought of himself as ruling in the place of Christ the King, with kings and emperors existing to help the pope. From law, Innocent gained his conception of the pope as lawmaker and of law as an instrument of moral reformation.

Innocent III: The pope (r. 1198–1216) who called the Fourth Lateran Council; he was the most powerful, respected, and prestigious of medieval popes.

1188 King Alfonso IX summons townsmen to the *cortes*

1215 Fourth Lateran Council

1232 Frederick II finalizes Statute in Favor of the Princes

1175 — 1200 — 1225 — 1250

1212–1250 Reign of Frederick II

1226–1270 Reign of Louis IX (St. Louis)

1240 Mongols capture Kiev

Innocent used the traditional method of declaring church law: a council. Presided over by Innocent, the **Fourth Lateran Council** (1215) attempted to regulate all aspects of Christian life. The comprehensive legislation it produced aimed at reforming both the clergy and the laity. Innocent and the bishops who met at the council hoped in this way to create a society united under God's law. They expected that Christians, lay and clerical alike, would work together harmoniously to achieve the common goal of salvation. They did not anticipate either the sheer variety of responses to their message or the persistence of those who defied it altogether.

The Laity and the Sacraments For laypeople, perhaps the most important canons (church laws) of the Fourth Lateran Council concerned the sacraments, the rites the church believed Jesus had instituted to confer sanctifying grace. Building on the reforms of the eleventh century, the council made the obligations that the sacraments imposed on the laity more precise and detailed. One canon required Christians to attend Mass and to confess their sins to a priest at least once a year. The increasing importance of the Eucharist as God's powerful instrument of salvation was reinforced by the council's definition:

> [Christ's] body and blood are truly contained in the sacrament of the altar under the forms of bread and wine, the bread and wine having been changed in substance [transubstantiated], by God's power, into his body and blood, so that in order to achieve this mystery of unity we receive from God what he received from us. Nobody can effect this sacrament except a priest who has been properly ordained according to the church's keys, which Jesus Christ himself gave to the apostles and their successors.

The council's emphasis on this moment of transformation, which it termed transubstantiation, gave the host—the bread taken at communion—new importance.

Other canons of the Fourth Lateran Council codified the traditions of marriage. The church declared that it had the duty to discover any impediments to a union (such as a close relationship by blood), and it claimed jurisdiction over marital disputes. The canons further insisted that children conceived within clandestine or forbidden marriages be declared illegitimate; they were not to inherit from their parents or become priests.

The impact of these provisions was perhaps less dramatic than church leaders hoped. Well-to-do London fathers still included their bastard children in their wills. On English manors, sons conceived out of wedlock regularly took over their parents' land. Men and women continued to marry in secret, and even churchmen had to admit that the consent of both parties made any marriage valid. Nevertheless, many men and women accepted the obligation to take communion and confess once a year, and priests proceeded to call out the banns (announcements of marriages) to discover any impediments to them.

Labeling the Jews Innocent III had wanted the Fourth Lateran Council to condemn Christian men who had sexual intercourse with Jewish women and then claimed ignorance as their excuse. But, building on the anti-Jewish feelings that had been mounting throughout the twelfth century, the council went even further, requiring all Jews to advertise their religion by some outward sign: "We decree that [Jews] of either sex in every Christian province at all times shall be distinguished

---

Fourth Lateran Council: The council that met in 1215 and covered the important topics of Christianity, among them the nature of the sacraments, the obligations of the laity, and policies toward heretics and Jews.

1265 English commons summoned to Parliament

1273 Thomas Aquinas publishes the *Summa Theologiae*

1275

1302 First Meeting of the French Estates General

1300

1309–1378 Avignon papacy

1313–1321 Dante writes *Divine Comedy*

1315–1322 Great Famine

1325

Jewish Couple

In this illustration from a Hebrew prayer book, a couple sits in a garden of lilies under a starry sky, illustrating the Bible's Song of Solomon 4:8: "come with me from Lebanon my bride." Hebrew commentators interpreted the bride as standing for Israel, while the speaker, the groom, was God. The groom wears a traditional Jewish hat, while the bride, Israel, wears a crown. There is an irony here: Christians portrayed the church as a crowned female. However, in this case the woman wears a blindfold, making her like the Christian depiction of the allegorical figure of the Jewish synagogue. Thus, this seemingly innocuous illustration gives the synagogue the status and dignity of the church. *(Staats- und Universitätsbibliothek Hamburg Carl von Ossietzky, Cod. Levy 37, fol. 169.)*

from other people by the character of their dress in public."

As with all church laws, these took effect only when local political powers enforced them. In many instances, rulers did so with zeal, not so much because they were eager to humiliate Jews but rather because they could make money selling exemptions to Jews who were willing to pay to avoid the requirements. Nonetheless, sooner or later Jews almost everywhere had to wear a badge as a sign of their second-class status. In southern France and in a few places in Spain, Jews were supposed to wear round badges. In England, Oxford required a rectangular badge, while Salisbury demanded that Jews wear special clothing. In Vienna and Germany, they were told to put on pointed hats. (See the illustration above.)

The Suppression of Heretics The Fourth Lateran Council's longest decree blasted heretics: "Those condemned as heretics shall be handed over to the secular authorities for punishment." If the secular authority did not carry out the punishment, the heretic was to be excommunicated. If he or she had vassals, they were to be released from their oaths of fealty. The lands of heretics were to be taken over by orthodox Christians.

Rulers heeded these declarations. Already some had taken up arms against heretics in the Albigensian Crusade (1209–1229). As a result of this crusade, southern France, which had been the home of most Albigensians, came under French royal control. The continuing presence of heretics there and elsewhere led church authorities inspired by the Fourth Lateran Council to set up a court of papal inquisitors. The Inquisition became permanent in 1233.

The Inquisition

The word *inquisition* simply means "investigation"; secular rulers had long used the method to summon people together, either to discover facts or to uncover and punish crimes. In its zeal to end heresy and save souls, the thirteenth-century church used the Inquisition to ferret out "heretical depravity." Calling suspects to testify, inquisitors, aided by secular authorities, rounded up virtually entire villages and interrogated everyone. (See "New Sources, New Perspectives," page 386.)

Typically, the inquisitors first called the people of a district to a "preaching," where they gave a sermon and promised clemency to those who promptly confessed their heresy. Then, at a general inquest, they questioned each man and woman who seemed to know something about heresy: "Have you ever seen any heretics? Have you heard them preach? Attended any of their ceremonies? Adored heretics?" The judges assigned relatively lenient penalties to those who were not aware that they held heretical beliefs and to heretics who quickly recanted. But unrepentant heretics were punished severely because the church believed that such people threatened the salvation of all.

In the thirteenth century, for the first time, long-term imprisonment became a tool to repress heresy, even if the heretic confessed. "It is our will," wrote one tribunal, "that [Raymond Maurin and Arnalda, his wife,] because they have rashly transgressed against God and holy church . . . be thrust into perpetual prison to do [appropriate] penance, and we command them to remain there in perpetuity." The inquisitors also used imprisonment to force people to recant, to give the names of other heretics, or to admit a plot. As the quest for religious control spawned wild fantasies of conspiracy, the inquisitors pinned their fears on real people.

Lay Piety

The church's zeal to reform the laity was matched by the desire of many laypeople to become more involved in their religion. They flocked to hear the preaching of friars and took what they heard to heart. Some women found new outlets for their piety by focusing on the Eucharist.

Preaching Friars and Receptive Townspeople The friars made themselves a permanent feature of the towns. At night they slept in their friaries, but they spent their days preaching. So, too, did other men, often trained in the universities and willing to take to the road to address throngs of townsfolk. When Berthold, a Franciscan who traveled the length and breadth of Germany giving sermons, came to a town, a high tower was set up for him outside the city walls. A pennant advertised his presence and let people know which way the wind would blow his voice. St. Anthony of Padua preached in Italian to huge audiences that had lined up hours in advance to be sure they would have a place to hear him.

Townspeople flocked to hear such preachers because they wanted to know how the Christian message applied to their daily lives. They were concerned, for example, about the ethics of moneymaking, sex in marriage, and family life. In turn, the preachers represented the front line of the church. They met the laity on their own turf, spoke in the vernacular that all could understand, and taught them to shape their behaviors to church teachings.

Laypeople further tied their lives to the mendicants, particularly the Franciscans, by becoming tertiaries. They adopted the practices of the friars—prayer and works of charity, for example—while continuing to live in the world, raising families and tending to the normal tasks of daily life, whatever their occupation. Even kings and queens became tertiaries.

The Piety of Women All across Europe, women in the thirteenth century sought outlets for their intense piety. As in previous centuries, powerful families founded new nunneries, especially within towns and cities. On the whole, these were set up for the daughters of the very wealthy. Ordinary women found different modes of religious expression. Some sought the lives of quiet activity and rapturous mysticism of the Beguines, others chose the lives of charity and service of women's mendicant orders, and still others decided on domestic lives of marriage and family punctuated by religious devotions. Elisabeth of Hungary, who married a German prince at the age of fourteen, raised three children. At the same time, she devoted her life to fasting, prayer, and service to the poor.

Many women were not as devout as Elisabeth. In the countryside, they cooked their porridge, brewed their ale, and raised their children. They attended church only on major feast days or for churching—the ritual of purification after a pregnancy. In the cities, working women scratched out a meager living. They sometimes made pilgrimages to relic shrines to seek help or cures. Religion was a part of these women's lives, but it did not dominate them.

For some urban women, however, religion was the focus of life, and the church's attempt to define and control the Eucharist had some unintended results. The new emphasis on the holiness of the transformed wine and bread induced some of these pious women to eat nothing but the Eucharist. One such woman, Angela of Foligno, reported that the consecrated bread swelled in her mouth, tasting sweeter than any other food. For these women, eating the Eucharist was truly eating God: they believed that Christ's crucifixion was the literal sacrifice of his body, to be eaten by sinful men and women as the way to redeem themselves and others. Renouncing all other foods became part of a life of service, because many of these devout women gave the poor the food they refused to eat.

Such women both accepted and challenged the pronouncements of the Fourth Lateran Council about the meaning of the Eucharist. They agreed that only priests could say Mass, but some of them bypassed their own priests, receiving the Eucharist (as they explained) directly from Christ in the form of a vision. Although men dominated the institutions that governed political, religious, and economic affairs, these women found ways to control their own lives and to some extent the lives of those around them, both those whom they served and those they lived with. Typically involved with meal preparation and feeding, like other women of the time, these holy women found a way to use their control over ordinary food to gain new kinds of social and religious power.

Jews and Lepers as Outcasts

While Christian women found new roles for themselves, non-Christians were pushed further into the category of "outsiders." To be sure, the First and Second Crusades gave outlet to anti-Jewish feeling. Nevertheless, they were abnormal episodes in the generally stable if tense relationship between Christians and Jews in Europe up to the middle of the

NEW SOURCES, NEW PERSPECTIVES

The Peasants of Montaillou

While historians can learn from material evidence how medieval peasants lived and worked, it is nearly impossible to find out what peasants thought. Almost all of our written sources come from the elite classes, who, if they noticed peasants at all, certainly did not care about their ideas. How, then, can historians hear and record the voices of peasants themselves? Until the 1960s, historians cared little about hearing those voices. They wanted to know about economic structures rather than peasant mentalities.

For that reason, historians did not notice an extremely important source of peasant voices, the Inquisition register made at the command of Bishop Fournier of Pamiers in the years 1318–1325. Fournier was a zealous anti-heretic, and when he became bishop of a diocese that harbored many Albigensians, he put the full weight of his office behind rounding them up. He concentrated on one particularly "heretic-infested" village, Montaillou, in the south of France near the Spanish border. Interrogating 114 people (including 48 women) over seven years, he committed their confessions and testimony to parchment with a view to punishing those who were heretics. Fournier was not interested in the peasants' voices; he simply wanted to know their religious beliefs and every other detail of their lives and thoughts. However, the long-term result of Fournier's zealous inquest—though he would not be happy to hear it—was to preserve the words of a whole village of peasants, shepherds, artisans, and shopkeepers. Fournier's register gathered dust in the Vatican archives for centuries, until it was transcribed and published in 1965. Only in 1975 was its great potential for peasant history made clear; in that year, Emmanuel Le Roy Ladurie published *Montaillou: The Promised Land of Error*, which for the first time brought a medieval peasant village to life.

Le Roy Ladurie's book reveals the myths, beliefs, rivalries, tensions, love affairs, tendernesses, and duplicities of a small peasant community in which all the people, even those who were relatively well off, worked with their hands; in which wealth was calculated by the size of a family's herd of livestock; and in which the church's demands for tithes seemed outrageously unfair.

The register shows a community torn apart by the opportunities the Inquisition gave to informers. The village priest, from a well-off family, was very clear about why he was denouncing his parishioners. He liked the Albigensians, he said (he was probably one himself), but he added: "I want to be revenged on the peasants of Montaillou, who have done me harm, and I will avenge myself in every possible way." However, the register also shows a community united by love: parents cared about their children, husbands and wives loved one another, and illicit lovers were caught up in passion. One affair took place between the village priest and a woman of somewhat higher rank. The priest courted the woman, Béatrice, for half a year, and after she gave in they met two or three nights a week. In the end, though, Béatrice decided to marry someone else and left the village.

Béatrice was not the only person of independent mind in Montaillou. Many people there were indeed heretics in the sense that their beliefs defied the teachings of the church. But they called themselves "good Christians." Other villagers remained in the Catholic fold. And still others in the region had their own ideas, as may be seen from Raimond de l'Aire's testimony, on the right.

---

twelfth century. Then things changed dramatically, as kings became more powerful, popular piety deepened, and church law singled Jews out for particular discrimination.

Jews were not alone in this new segregation. Lepers, too, had to wear a special costume, were forbidden to touch children, could not eat with the unafflicted, and were kept in leper houses.

Jews Exploited and Expelled As noted in Chapter 10, when Christian lords came to dominate the countryside, most Jews were forced off the manors and into the cities. Their opportunities narrowed with the growing monopoly of guilds, which prohibited Jewish members. Thus in many places Jews were barred from the crafts and trades. In effect, many were compelled to become usurers (moneylenders) because other fields were closed to them. Even with Christian moneylenders available (for some existed despite the Bible's prohibition against charging interest for loans), lords, especially kings, borrowed from Jews and encouraged others to do so because, along with their newly asserted powers, European rulers claimed the Jews as their serfs and Jewish property as their own. In England, where Jews had arrived with the Norman conquest in 1066, a special royal exchequer of the Jews was created in 1194 to collect unpaid debts due after the death of a Jewish creditor.

Even before 1194, the king of England had imposed new and arbitrary taxes on the Jewish community. Similarly in France, persecuting Jews and confiscating their property benefited both the treasury and the authoritative image of the king. In 1198, the French king declared that Jews must be mon-

Fournier's register became a "new" source because Le Roy Ladurie had new questions and sought a way to answer them, treating his evidence the way ethnographers treat reports by native peoples they have interviewed. Today, some historians question Le Roy Ladurie's approach, arguing that an Inquisition record cannot be handled in the same way that ethnographers consider information from their informants. For example, they point out that the words of the peasants were translated from Occitan, the language they spoke, to Latin for the official record. What readers hear are not the voices of the peasants but rather their ideas filtered through the vocabulary and summaries of the elite. Moreover, the peasants called before the tribunal were held in prison, feared for their lives, and were forced to talk about events that had taken place ten or more years earlier. In light of these circumstances, to what extent is their testimony a direct window onto their lives? Nevertheless, the register remains a precious source for learning at least something about what ordinary people thought and felt in a small village about seven hundred years ago.

Raimond de l'Aire's Testimony

One witness Fournier recorded was Raimond de l'Aire, who was not from Montaillou but rather from Tignac, a small town in Fournier's diocese. An older man had told [Raimond de l'Aire] that a mule has a soul as good as a man's, and, Fournier wrote,

> from this belief he [Raimond] had by himself deduced that his own soul and those of other men are nothing but blood, because when a person's blood is taken away, he dies. He also believed that a dead person's soul and body both die, and that after death nothing human remains. . . . From this he believed that the human soul after death [is] neither good nor evil, and that there is no hell or paradise in another world where human souls are rewarded or punished.

Source for Raimond de l'Aire: *Heresy and Authority in Medieval Europe: Documents in Translation*, ed. Edward Peters (Philadelphia: University of Pennsylvania Press, 1980), 253.

Further Reading

Boyle, Leonard. "Montaillou Revisited: *Mentalité* and Methodology." In J. A. Raftis, ed., *Pathways to Medieval Peasants*. 1981.

Le Roy Ladurie, Emmanuel. *Montaillou: The Promised Land of Error*. 1978. The original French version was published in 1975.

Resaldo, Renato. "From the Door of His Tent: The Fieldworker and the Inquisitor." In James Clifford and George E. Marcus, eds., *Writing Culture: The Poetics and Politics of Ethnography*. 1986.

Questions to Consider

1. **In what ways are modern court cases like Fournier's Inquisition register? In what ways are they unlike such a source? Could you use modern court cases to reconstruct the life of a community?**
2. **What are the advantages and the pitfalls of using a source such as the register for historical research?**
3. **Do you think that Raimond might have made up his testimony? Why or why not?**
4. **What does this testimony suggest about the impact of church doctrines in the French countryside?**

eylenders or money changers exclusively. Their activities were to be taxed and monitored by royal officials.

Limiting Jews to moneylending in an increasingly commercial economy clearly served the interests of kings. But lesser lords who needed cash also benefited: they borrowed money from Jews and then, as happened in York (England) in 1190, they orchestrated an attack to rid themselves of their debts and of the Jews to whom they owed money. Churchmen, too, used credit in a money economy but resented the fiscal obligations it imposed. With their drive to create centralized territorial states and their desire to make their authority known and felt, powerful rulers of Europe—churchmen and laymen alike—exploited and coerced the Jews while drawing on and encouraging a wellspring of elite and popular anti-Jewish feeling.

Attacks against Jews were inspired by more than resentment against Jewish money and the desire for power and control. They also, ironically, grew out of the codification of Christian religious doctrine and the anxiety of Christians about their own institutions. For example, in the twelfth century, the newly rigorous definition of the Eucharist represented by the word *transubstantiation* meant to many pious Christians that the body of Christ literally lay on the altar. Reflecting this unsettling view, sensational stories, originating in clerical circles but soon widely circulated, told of Jews who secretly sacrificed Christian children in a morbid revisiting of the crucifixion of Jesus.

In 1144, in one of the earliest instances of this charge, the body of a young boy named William was found in the woods near Norwich (England). His uncle, a priest, accused local Jews of killing the

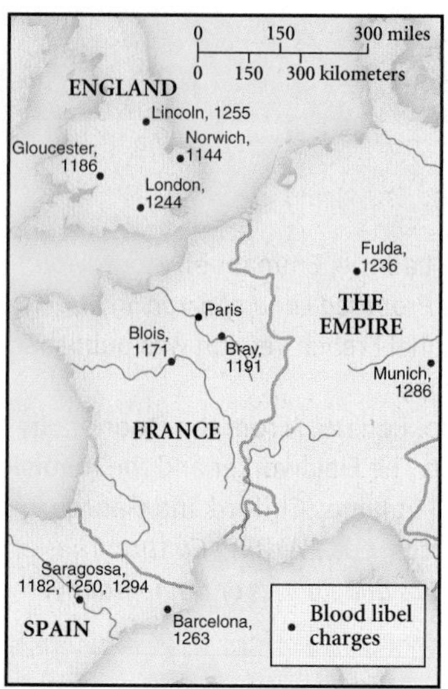

Blood Libel Charges in Europe, c. 1100–1300 *(Adapted from David Ditchburn, Simon MacLean, and Angus MacKay, eds.,* Atlas of Medieval Europe, *2nd ed. [London: Routledge, 2007].)*

child. A monk connected to the cathedral at Norwich, Thomas of Monmouth, took up the cause. He had visions that told him to exhume the body from the cemetery and bring it into the monastery. Miracles followed, and soon Thomas wrote *The Life and Martyrdom of St. William of Norwich.* According to his account, the Jews carefully prepared at Passover for the horrible ritual slaughter of the boy, whom they had chosen "to be mocked and sacrificed in scorn of the Lord's passion." This charge, which historians have called **blood libel**, was made frequently about other "martyrs" and led to massacres of Jews in cities in England, France, Spain, and Germany. (In truth, however, Jews had no rituals involving blood sacrifice at all.)

Some communities simply expelled Jews. At Bury-Saint-Edmunds, which was under the jurisdiction of the abbot of the monastery, a chronicler of the time described one such expulsion:

> And when they had been sent forth and conducted under armed escort to other towns [in England], the abbot ordered that all those who from that time forth should receive Jews or harbor them in the town of St. Edmund should be solemnly excommunicated in every church and at every altar.

Eventually, in 1291, the Jews were cast out from the entire kingdom of England. Most dispersed to France and Germany, but to a sad welcome. In 1306, for example, King Philip the Fair had them driven from France, though they were allowed to reenter, tentatively, in 1315.

Fearing the Contamination of Lepers People attacked by **leprosy**—a disease that causes skin lesions and attacks the peripheral nerves—were an unimportant minority in medieval society until the eleventh century. Then, beginning around 1075 and extending to the fourteenth century, lepers, though still a small minority, became the objects of both charity and disgust. Houses for lepers were set up both to provide for them and to segregate them from everyone else.

Leprosy delivered three blows: it was horribly disfiguring; it was associated with sin in the Bible; and it was contagious. In 1179, the Third Lateran Council took note of the fact that "lepers cannot dwell with the healthy or come to church with others" and asked that, where possible, special churches and cemeteries be set aside for them. No doubt this inspired a boom in the foundation of leper houses, which peaked between 1175 and 1250.

Before the leper went to such a house, he or she was formally expelled from the community of Christians via a ceremony of terrible solemnity. In northern France, for example, the leper had to stand in a cemetery, his or her face veiled. Mass was intoned, and the priest threw dirt on the leper as if he or she were being buried. "Be dead to the world, be reborn in God," the priest said, continuing:

> I forbid you to ever enter the church or monastery, fair, mill, marketplace, or company of persons. I forbid you to ever leave your house without your leper's costume [usually gloves and a long robe], in order that one recognize you and that you never go barefoot. I forbid you to wash your hands or any thing about you in the stream or in the fountain.

In 1321, the prohibition against drinking in the stream or fountain gained more sinister meaning as false rumors spread that Muslims had recruited both Jews and lepers to poison all the wells of Christendom.

REVIEW QUESTION **How did people respond to the teachings and laws of the church in the early thirteenth century?**

Reconciling This World and the Next

Just as the church wanted to regulate worldly life in accordance with God's plan for salvation, so contemporary thinkers, writers, musicians, and artists sought to harmonize the secular with the sacred realms. Scholars wrote treatises that reconciled faith with reason, poets and musicians sang of the links between heaven and human life on earth, and artists expressed the same ideas in stone and sculpture and on parchment. In the face of many contradictions, all of these groups were largely successful in communicating an orderly image of the world.

---

blood libel: The charge that Jews used the blood of Christian children in their Passover ritual; though false, it led to massacres of Jews in cities in England, France, Spain, and Germany in the thirteenth century.

leprosy: A bacterial disease that causes skin lesions and attacks the peripheral nerves. In the later Middle Ages, lepers were isolated from society.

The Achievement of Scholasticism

Scholasticism was the culmination of the method of logical inquiry and exposition pioneered by masters like Peter Abelard and Peter the Chanter (see Chapter 11). In the thirteenth century, the method was used to summarize and reconcile all knowledge. Many of the thirteenth-century scholastics (those who practiced scholasticism) were members of the Dominican and Franciscan orders and taught in the universities. On the whole, they were confident that knowledge obtained through the senses and reason was compatible with the knowledge derived from faith and revelation.

One of the scholastics' goals was to demonstrate this harmony. The scholastic summa, or summary of knowledge, was a systematic exposition of the answer to every possible question about human morality, the physical world, society, belief, action, and theology. Another goal of the scholastics was to preach the conclusions of these treatises. As one scholastic put it, "First the bow is bent in study, then the arrow is released in preaching": first you study the summa, and then you hit your mark—convert people—by preaching. Many of the preachers who came to the towns were students and disciples of scholastic university teachers.

The method of the summa borrowed much of the vocabulary and many of the rules of logic long ago outlined by Aristotle. Even though Aristotle was a pagan, scholastics considered his coherent and rational body of thought the most perfect that human reason alone could devise. Because they had the benefit of Christ's revelations, the scholastics believed they could take Aristotle's philosophy one necessary step further and reconcile human reason with Christian faith. Confident in their method and conclusions, scholastics embraced the world and its issues.

Some scholastics considered questions about the natural world. Albertus Magnus (c. 1200–1280) was a major theologian who also contributed to the fields of biology, botany, astronomy, and physics. His reconsideration of Aristotle's views on motion led the way to distinctions that helped scientists in the sixteenth and seventeenth centuries arrive at the modern notion of inertia.

St. Thomas Aquinas (1225–1274) was perhaps the most famous scholastic. A hefty man who was renowned for his composure in scholastic disputation, Thomas came from a noble Neapolitan family that had hoped to see him become a powerful bishop rather than a poor university professor. When he was about eighteen years old, he thwarted his family's wishes and joined the Dominicans. Soon he was studying at Cologne with Albertus Magnus. At thirty-two, he became a master at the University of Paris.

Like many other scholastics, Thomas considered Aristotle to be "the Philosopher," the authoritative voice of human reason, which he sought to reconcile with divine revelation in a universal and harmonious scheme. In 1273, he published his monumental *Summa Theologiae* (sometimes called the *Summa Theologica*), intended to cover all important topics, human and divine. He divided these topics into questions, exploring each one thoroughly and concluding with a decisive position and a refutation of opposing views. Yet even Thomas departed from Aristotle, who had explained the universe through human reason alone. In Thomas's view, God, nature, and reason were in harmony, so even though Aristotle's arguments could be used to explore both the human and the divine order, there were some exceptions. "Certain things that are true about God wholly surpass the capability of human reason, for instance that God is three and one," Thomas wrote. But he thought these exceptions were rare.

Many of Thomas's questions spoke to the keenest concerns of his day. He asked, for example, whether it was lawful to sell something for more than its worth. (See the illustration on page 390.) Thomas arranged his argument systematically, first quoting authorities that seemed to declare every sort of selling practice, even deceptive ones, to be lawful; this was the *sic* ("yes") position. Then he quoted an authority that opposed selling something for more than its worth; this was the *non*. Following that, he gave his own argument, prefaced by the words "I answer that." Unlike Abelard, who had not supplied answers, Thomas came to clear conclusions that harmonized both the yes and the no responses. In the case of selling something for more than it was worth, he pointed out that price and worth depended on the circumstances of the buyer and seller. He concluded that charging more than a seller had originally paid could be legitimate at times, as, for example, "when a man has great need of a certain thing, while another man will suffer if he is without it."

For townspeople engaged in commerce and worried about biblical admonitions against greed, Thomas's ideas about selling practices addressed burning questions. Hoping to go to heaven as well as to reap the profits of their business ventures, laypeople listened eagerly to preachers who delivered

---

scholasticism: The method of logical inquiry used by the scholastics, the scholars of the medieval universities; it applied Aristotelian logic to biblical and other authoritative texts in an attempt to summarize and reconcile all knowledge.

Friars and Usurers
Although clerics sometimes borrowed money, the friars had a different attitude. St. Francis, son of a merchant, refused to touch money altogether. In this illumination from about 1250, a Franciscan (in light-colored robes) and a Dominican (in black) reject offers from two usurers, whose profession they are thus shown to condemn. Other friars, including Thomas Aquinas, worked out justifications for some kinds of moneymaking professions, though not usury. *(bpk, Berlin/Bibliothèque Nationale, Paris, France/photo by Gerard Le Gall/Art Resource, NY.)*

their sermons in the vernacular but who based their ideas on the Latin summae (the plural of *summa*) of Thomas and other scholastics. Thomas's conclusions aided townspeople in justifying their worldly activities.

Scholastics like Thomas were enormous optimists. They believed that everything had a place in God's scheme of things, that the world was orderly, and that human beings could make rational sense of it. Their logical arguments filled the classrooms, spilled into the friars' convents, found their way into the shops of artisans, and even crept between the sheets of lovers. (See Document: "Thomas Aquinas Writes about Sex," page 391.) Scholastic philosophy helped give ordinary people a sense of purpose and a guide to behavior.

Yet even among scholastics, unity was elusive. In his own day, Thomas was accused of placing too much emphasis on reason and relying too fully on Aristotle. Later scholastics argued that reason could not find truth through its own faculties and energies. In the summae of John Duns Scotus (c. 1266–1308), for example, the world and God were less compatible. John, whose name Duns Scotus reveals his Scottish origin, was a Franciscan who taught at both Oxford and Paris. For John, human reason could know truth only through the "special illumination of the uncreated light," that is, by divine illumination. But unlike his predecessors, John believed that this illumination came not as a matter of course but only when God chose to intervene. John—and others—experienced God as sometimes willful rather than reasonable. Human reason could not soar to God; God's will alone determined whether or not a person could know him. In this way, John separated the divine and secular realms, and the medieval synthesis cracked.

New Syntheses in Writing and Music

Thirteenth-century writers and musicians, like scholastics, presented complicated ideas and feelings as harmonious and unified syntheses. Writers explored the relations between this world and the next, whereas musicians found ways to bridge sacred and secular forms of music.

Vernacular Literature Comes of Age

Vernacular literature may be said to have reached its full development with the work of Dante Alighieri (1265–1321), who harmonized the mysteries of faith with the poetry of love. Born in Florence in a time of political turmoil, Dante incorporated the major figures of history and his own day into his most famous poem, *Commedia*, written between 1313 and 1321. Later known as *Divina commedia* (*Divine Comedy*), Dante's poem describes the poet taking an imaginary journey from hell to purgatory and finally to paradise.

The poem is an allegory in which every person and object must be read at more than one level. At the most literal level, the poem is about Dante's travels. At a deeper level, it is about the soul's search for meaning and enlightenment and its ultimate discovery of God in the light of divine love. Just as Thomas Aquinas employed Aristotle's logic to reach important truths, so Dante used the pagan poet Virgil as his guide through hell and purgatory. And just as Thomas believed that faith went beyond reason to even higher truths, so Dante found a new guide representing earthly love to lead him through most of paradise. That guide was Beatrice, a Florentine girl with whom Dante had fallen in love as a boy and whom he never forgot. But only faith, in the form of the divine love of the Virgin Mary, could bring Dante to the culmination of his journey—a blinding and inexpressibly awesome vision of God:

> What I then saw is more than tongue can say.
> Our human speech is dark before the vision. The
> ravished memory swoons and falls away.

DOCUMENT

Thomas Aquinas Writes about Sex

Glad to broach every topic, human and divine, the scholastic Thomas Aquinas (1225–1274) took up the issue of sex in his Summa against the Gentiles. *He wrote this work around 1260 to provide arguments against the scientific views of—among others—elite Muslim scholars of ancient Greek learning, such as Averroes. The section on sex came when Thomas took up issues involved in living a moral life. As usual, he first offered arguments [here 1–3] for the position that he disagreed with: that sex outside of marriage ("fornication") was not a sin. Then he offered a long rebuttal [excerpted here as 4–6].*

The Reason Why Simple Fornication Is a Sin According to Divine Law, and That Matrimony Is Natural

[1] . . . We can see the futility of the argument of certain people who say that simple fornication is not a sin. For they say: Suppose there is a woman who is not married, or under the control of any man, either her father or another man. Now, if a man performs the sexual act with her, and she is willing, he does not injure her, because she favors the action and she has control over her own body. Nor does he injure any other person, because she is understood to be under no other person's control. So, this does not seem to be a sin.

[2] Now, to say that he injures God would not seem to be an adequate answer [against this argument]. For we do not offend God except by doing something contrary to our own good, as has been said. But this does not appear contrary to man's good. Hence, on this basis, no injury seems to be done to God.

[3] Likewise, it also would seem an inadequate answer to say that some injury is done to one's neighbor by this action, inasmuch as he may be scandalized. Indeed, it is possible for him to be scandalized by something which is not in itself a sin. In this event, the act would be accidentally sinful. But our problem is not whether simple fornication is accidentally a sin, but whether it is so essentially.

[4] Hence, we must look for a solution in our earlier considerations. We have said that God exercises care over every person on the basis of what is good for him. Now, it is good for each person to attain his end, whereas it is bad for him to swerve away from his proper end. Now, this should be considered applicable to the parts, just as it is to the whole being; for instance, each and every part of man, and every one of his acts, should attain the proper end. Now, though the male semen is superfluous in regard to the preservation of the individual, it is nevertheless necessary in regard to the propagation of the species. Other superfluous things, such as excrement, urine, sweat, and such things, are not at all necessary; hence, their emission contributes to man's good. Now, this is not what is sought in the case of semen, but, rather, to emit it for the purpose of generation, to which purpose the sexual act is directed. But man's generative process would be frustrated unless it were followed by proper nutrition, because the offspring would not survive if proper nutrition were withheld. Therefore, the emission of semen ought to be so ordered that it will result in both the production of the proper offspring and in the upbringing of this offspring.

[5] It is evident from this that every emission of semen, in such a way that generation cannot follow, is contrary to the good for man. And if this be done deliberately, it must be a sin. Now, I am speaking of a way from which, in itself, generation could not result: such would be any emission of semen apart from the natural union of male and female. For which reason, sins of this type are called contrary to nature. But, if by accident generation cannot result from the emission of semen, then this is not a reason for it being against nature, or a sin; as for instance, if the woman happens to be sterile.

[6] Likewise, it must also be contrary to the good for man if the semen be emitted under conditions such that generation could result but the proper upbringing would be prevented. We should take into consideration the fact that, among some animals where the female is able to take care of the upbringing of offspring, male and female do not remain together for any time after the act of generation. This is obviously the case with dogs. But in the case of animals of which the female is not able to provide for the upbringing of offspring, the male and female do stay together after the act of generation as long as is necessary for the upbringing and instruction of the offspring. Examples are found among certain species of birds whose young are not able to seek out food for themselves immediately after hatching. In fact, since a bird does not nourish its young with milk, made available by nature as it were, as occurs in the case of quadrupeds, but the bird must look elsewhere for food for its young, and since besides this it must protect them by sitting on them, the female is not able to do this by herself. So, as a result of divine providence, there is naturally implanted in the male of these animals a tendency to remain with the female in order to bring up the young. Now, it is abundantly evident that the female in the human species is not at all able to take care of the upbringing of offspring by herself, since the needs of human life demand many things which cannot be provided by one person alone. Therefore, it is appropriate to human nature that a man remain together with a woman after the generative act, and not leave her immediately to have such relations with another woman, as is the practice with fornicators.

Source: Thomas Aquinas, *Summa contra Gentiles*, book 3, Part II. Translated by Vernon J. Bourke at http://dhspriory.org/thomas/ContraGentiles3b.htm#122.

Question to Consider

- **Why might Thomas have based his arguments against fornication on what is good for man rather than on citations from the Bible?**

DOCUMENT

The Debate between Reason and the Lover

Jean de Meun (d. c. 1305) was the continuator of the Romance of the Rose, *a poem about a lover's quest for his beloved. Jean organized his part of the poem as a series of dialogues between the lover and various figures he encountered on his journeys. Meeting with the figure of Reason, the lover hears the following jaundiced definition of love.*

[Reason says:]
If I know anything of love, it is
Imaginary illness freely spread
Between two persons of opposing sex,
Originating from disordered sight,
Producing great desire to hug and kiss
And see enjoyment in a mutual lust.
[To which the Lover responds:]
Madam, you would betray me; should I scorn
All folk because the God of Love now frowns?
Shall I no more experience true love,
But live in hate? Truly, so help me God,
Then were I moral sinner worse than thief!

Source: Guillaume de Lorris and Jean de Meun, *The Romance of the Rose*, trans. Harry W. Robbins (New York: Dutton, 1962), 97, 102.

Question to Consider

■ **Whose point of view—Reason's or the lover's—do you think Jean de Meun agrees with, and why do you think so?**

Dante's poem electrified a wide audience. By elevating one dialect of Italian—the language that ordinary Florentines used in their everyday life—to a language of exquisite poetry, Dante was able to communicate an orderly and optimistic vision of the universe in an even more exciting and accessible way than the scholastics had. So influential was his work that it is no exaggeration to say that modern Italian is based on Dante's Florentine dialect.

Other writers of the period used different methods to express the harmony between heaven and earth. The anonymous author of the *Quest of the Holy Grail* (c. 1225), for example, wrote about the adventures of some of the knights of King Arthur's Round Table to convey the doctrine of transubstantiation and the wonder of the vision of God. In *The Romance of the Rose*, begun by one poet and finished by another, a lover seeks the rose, his true love. In the long dream that the poem describes, the narrator's search for the rose is thwarted by personifications of Love, Shame, Reason, Abstinence, and so on. They present him with arguments for and against love. In the end, sexual love is made part of the divine scheme—and the lover plucks the rose. (See Document, "The Debate between Reason and the Lover," at left.)

Polyphony and the Motet Just as some writers asserted the harmony of heavenly and earthly things, so musicians experimented at this time with combining sacred and secular music. This was quite new. The music before this time, plainchant (see Chapter 11), had a particular sequence of notes for a given text. It is true that sometimes a form of harmony was achieved when two voices sang exactly the same melody an interval apart. This was the first form of polyphony, the simultaneous sounding of two or more melodies. In the twelfth century, musicians experimented with freer melodies. One voice might go up the scale, for example, while the other went down, achieving even so a pleasing harmony. Or one voice might hold a pitch while the other danced around it.

Now, in the thirteenth century, some musicians put secular and sacred tunes together. This form of music, which probably originated in Paris, was called the motet (from the French *mot*, meaning "word"). The typical thirteenth-century motet had two or three melody lines, or "voices". The lowest, usually from a chant melody that was used in a church service, had only one or two words; sometimes, it was played on an instrument rather than sung. The remaining melodies had different texts, either Latin or French (or one of each), which were sung simultaneously. Latin texts were usually sacred, whereas French ones were secular, dealing with themes such as love and springtime. The motet thus wove the sacred (the chant melody in the lowest voice) and the secular (the French texts in the upper voices) into a sophisticated tapestry of words and music.

Like the scholastic summae, motets were written by and for a clerical elite. (See the illustration on page 393.) Yet they incorporated the music of ordinary people, such as the calls of street vendors and the boisterous songs of students. In turn, they touched the lives of everyone, for polyphony influenced every form of music, from the Mass to popular songs that entertained laypeople and churchmen alike.

Complementing the motet's complexity was the development of a new notation for rhythm. A primitive form of musical notation had been created in the ninth century; by the eleventh century, composers could indicate pitch but had no way to show the duration of the notes. Music theorists of the thirteenth century, however, developed increasingly

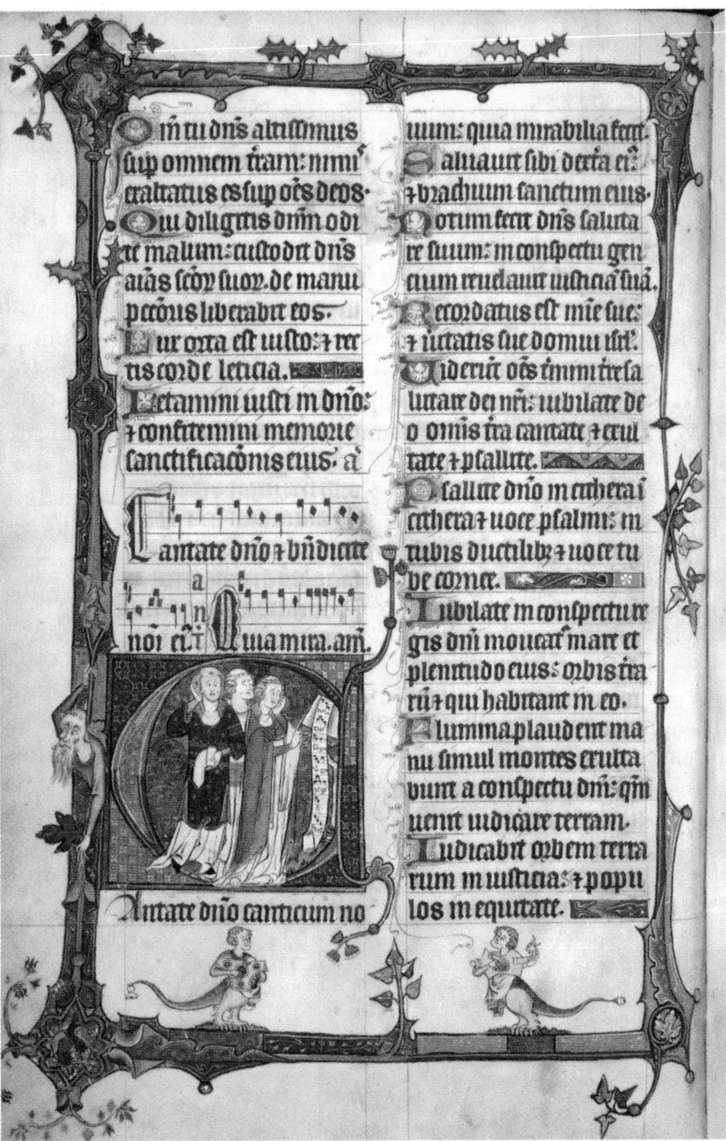

Singing a Motet
In this fourteenth-century English Psalter, the artist has illustrated the first letter of Psalm 96, which begins, "O sing to the Lord a new song," with a depiction of three clerics singing a motet. Its words and musical notation are written on a scroll draped over a lectern. *(© The British Library Board, All Rights Reserved. Arundel 83, fol. 63v.)*

precise methods to indicate rhythm. Franco of Cologne, for example, in his *Art of Measurable Song* (c. 1280), used different shapes to mark the number of beats each note should be held. His system became the basis of modern musical notation. Because each note could now be allotted a specific duration, written music could express new and complicated rhythms. The music of the thirteenth century reflected both the melding of the secular and the sacred and the possibilities of greater order and control.

Gothic Art

Gothic architecture—like philosophy, literature, and music—melded the sacred and the secular. By the end of the thirteenth century, the Gothic style, which had its beginnings at Saint-Denis and Chartres (see Chapter 11), had spread across most of Europe. Elements of Gothic style began to appear as well in other forms of art: stained glass, sculpture, painting, and the decorative motifs in manuscript illuminations.

Stained Glass Because pointed arches and flying buttresses allowed the walls of a Gothic church to be pierced with large windows, stained glass became a newly important art form. (See the illustrations on page 394.) To make this colored glass, workers added chemicals to sand, heated the mixture until it was liquid, and then blew and flattened it. Adding cobalt produced blue glass; copper oxide made red. Yellow, a rare color, was produced by painting clear glass with silver nitrate, then firing it in a kiln. Artists cut shapes from these colored glass sheets and held them in place with lead strips. They painted details right on the glass. As the sun shone through the finished windows, they glowed like jewels.

Last Judgment
Stained glass could illustrate complex theological truths. In this thirteenth-century depiction of the Last Judgment from Bourges Cathedral in France, two colorful devils force two naked sinners into the toothy mouth of hell. Licks of red flame greet them. While the devils enjoy their task (the green one is smiling), the sinners grimace and seem to cry out in pain. *(Saint-Etienne Cathedral, Bourges, France/The Bridgeman Art Library International.)*

The size of the windows allowed glaziers to depict complicated themes. The windows at Sainte-Chapelle, for example, tell the story of salvation in 1,134 scenes, starting with events of the Old Testament and ending with the Apocalypse. (All such windows must be read from bottom to top.) Themes ranged from heaven to hell. (See the illustration at left.)

Sculpture | Gothic cathedrals were decorated with sculpture. This was not new: Romanesque architecture had also featured sculpture (see the opening illustration for Chapter 10, page 310). But Gothic figures were separated from their background and sculpted in the round. The figures evoked motion—turning, moving, and interacting; at times, they even smiled. (See the illustration on page 395, bottom left.) Taken together, they were often meant to be "read" like a scholastic summa. The south portal of Chartres cathedral is a good example of the way in which Gothic sculpture could be used to sum up a body of truths. The sculptures in each massive doorway have related themes: the left doorway depicts the martyrs, the right the confessors, and the center the Last Judgment. Like Dante's *Divine Comedy*, these portals tell the story of the soul's pilgrimage from the suffering of this world to eternal life.

Sainte-Chapelle
Gothic architecture opened up the walls of the church to windows, as may be seen at Sainte-Chapelle, the private chapel of the French king Louis IX (St. Louis). Consecrated in 1248, it was built to house Christ's crown of thorns and other relics of the Passion. This photo shows the interior of the upper chapel looking east. *(Giraudon/The Bridgeman Art Library International.)*

Gothic sculpture began in France and was adopted, with many variations, elsewhere in Europe during the thirteenth century. The Italian sculptor Nicola Pisano (c. 1220–1278?), for example, crafted dignified figures inspired by classical forms. German sculptors created excited, emotional figures that sometimes gestured dramatically to one another.

Painting By the early fourteenth century, the naturalistic sculptures so prominent in architecture were reflected in painting as well. This new style is evident in the work of Giotto (1266–1337), a Florentine artist who changed the emphasis of painting, which had been predominantly symbolic, decorative, and intellectual. When Giotto filled the walls of a private chapel at Padua with paintings depicting scenes of Christ's life, he experimented with the illusion of depth. Giotto's figures, appearing weighty and voluminous, express a range of emotions as they move across interior and exterior spaces. (See the illustration below.) In bringing sculptural naturalism to a flat surface, Giotto stressed three-dimensionality, illusional space, and human emotion. By fusing earthly forms with religious meaning, Giotto found yet another way to fuse the natural and divine realms.

Gothic style also appeared in paintings as a decorative motif. Manuscript illuminations feature the shape of stained-glass windows and pointed vaults as common background themes. (See the illustration on page 396 for one example.) The colors of Gothic manuscripts echoed the rich hues of stained glass.

REVIEW QUESTION **How did artists, musicians, and scholastics try to link the physical world with the divine?**

The Annunciation
Figures decorating Gothic churches, such as this one at Reims (in northern France), were carved in the round. Here the angel Gabriel (on the left) turns and smiles joyfully at Mary, who looks down modestly as he announces that she will give birth to Jesus. *(Scala/Art Resource, NY.)*

Giotto's *Birth of the Virgin*
This depiction of the Virgin Mary's birth pays attention to the homey details of a thirteenth-century Florentine aristocratic household. Those details portray a sequence: the baby is bathed and swaddled by maidservants in the bottom tier, while above she is handed to her mother, St. Anne, who reaches out eagerly for the child. *(The Art Archive/Scrovegni Chapel, Padua/Dagli Orti.)*

Louis IX and Blanche of Castile
This miniature shows St. Louis, portrayed as a young boy, sitting opposite his mother, Blanche of Castile. Blanche served as regent twice in Louis's lifetime, once when he was too young to rule and a second time when he was away on crusade. The emphasis on the equality of queen and king may be evidence of Blanche's influence on and patronage of the artist. *(Detail from* Moralized Bible, *France, c. 1230. MS. M. 240, F.8. The Pierpont Morgan Library/Art Resource, NY.)*

The Politics of Control

The quest for order, control, and harmony also became part of the political agendas of princes, popes, and cities. These rulers and institutions imposed—or tried to impose—their authority ever more fully and systematically through taxes, courts, and sometimes representative institutions. Vestiges of these systems live on in modern European parliaments and in the U.S. Congress.

Louis IX of France is a good example of a ruler whose power increased during this period. In contrast, the emperor—who once claimed both Germany and Italy—gave up most of his power in Germany and lost it in Italy as well, while the papacy moved from Rome to Avignon, a real blow to its prestige. In Italy the rise of *signori* (lords) meant that the communes, which had long governed many cities, gave way to rule by one strong man.

A new political entity, the Mongols, directly confronted the rulers of Russia, Poland, and Hungary. Installing themselves in Russia, the Mongols became a new fixture in the West. In the end, they vitalized European trade, opening up routes to the East. But just as this was taking place, a challenge to the political and economic order came in the form of the calamities known collectively as the Great Famine, a period of devastating food shortages that lasted from 1315 to 1322.

The Weakening of the Empire

During the thirteenth century, both popes and emperors sought to dominate Italy. The clash of the German emperor and the papacy had its origins in Frederick Barbarossa's failure to control northern Italy, which was crucial to imperial policy. The model of Charlemagne required his imperial successors to exercise hegemony there. Moreover, Italy's prosperous cities beckoned as rich sources of income. When Barbarossa failed in the north, his son tried a new approach to gain Italy: he married Constance, the heiress of Sicily. From this base near the southern tip of Italy, he hoped to make good his imperial title. But he died suddenly, leaving his three-year-old son, Frederick II, to take up his plan. It was a perilous moment.

Italy at the End of the Thirteenth Century

While Frederick was a child, the imperial office became the plaything of the German princes and the papacy. Both wanted an emperor, but a virtually powerless one. Therefore, when Frederick's uncle attempted to become interim king until Frederick reached his majority, many princes and the papacy blocked the move. They supported Otto of Brunswick, the son of Henry the Lion and an implacable foe of Frederick's family. Otto promised the pope that he would not intervene in Italy, and Pope Innocent III crowned him emperor in return.

But Innocent had miscalculated. No emperor worthy of the name could leave Italy alone. Almost immediately after his coronation, Otto invaded Sicily, and Innocent excommunicated him in 1211. In 1212, Innocent gave the imperial crown to **Frederick II** (r. 1212–1250), now a young man ready to take up the reins of power.

Frederick was an amazing ruler: *stupor mundi* ("wonder of the world") his contemporaries called him. Heir to two cultures, Sicilian on his mother's side and German on his father's, he cut a worldly and sophisticated figure. In Sicily, he moved easily within a diverse culture of Jews, Muslims, and Christians. Here he could play the role of all-powerful ruler. In Germany, he was less at home. There Christian princes, often churchmen with ministerial retinues, were acutely aware of their crucial role in royal elections and jealously guarded their rights and privileges.

Both emperor and pope needed to dominate Italy to maintain their power and position. The papacy under Innocent III was expansionist, gathering money and troops to make good its claim to the Papal States, the band of territory stretching from Rome to Ferrara in the north and Fermo in the east. The pope expected dues and taxes, military service, and the profits of justice from this region. To ensure its survival, the pope refused to tolerate any imperial claims to Italy.

Frederick, in turn, could not imagine ruling as an emperor unless he controlled Italy. He attempted to do this throughout his life, as did his heirs. Frederick had a three-pronged strategy. First, he revamped the government of Sicily to give him more control and yield greater profits. His *Constitutions of Melfi* (1231), an eclectic body of laws, set up a system of salaried governors who worked according to uniform procedures. The *Constitutions* called for nearly all court cases to be heard by royal courts, regularized commercial privileges, and set up a system of taxation. Second, to ensure that he would not be hounded by opponents in Germany, Frederick granted them important concessions in his **Statute in Favor of the Princes**, finalized in 1232. These concessions allowed the German princes to turn their principalities into virtually independent states. Third, Frederick sought to enter Italy through Lombardy, as his grandfather had done.

Each of the four popes who ruled after the death of Innocent, in 1216, followed Frederick's every move and excommunicated the emperor a number of times. The most serious of these condemnations came in 1245, when the pope and other churchmen assembled at the Council of Lyon and excommunicated and deposed Frederick, absolving his vassals and subjects of their fealty to him and, indeed, forbidding anyone to support him. By 1248, papal legates were preaching a crusade against Frederick and all his followers. Frederick's death, in 1250, ensured their triumph.

The fact that Frederick's vision of the empire failed is of less long-term importance than the way it failed. His concessions to the German princes meant that Germany would not be united until the nineteenth century. The political entity now called Germany was simply a geographical expression, divided among many independent princes. Between 1254 and 1273, the princes kept the German throne empty. Splintered into factions, they elected two different foreigners, who spent their time fighting each other. In one of history's great ironies, it was during this low point of the German monarchy that the term *Holy Roman Empire* was coined to denote the empire that had begun with the crowning of Charlemagne in 800. In 1273, the princes at last united and elected a German, Rudolf (r. 1273–1291), whose family, the Habsburgs, was new to imperial power. Rudolf used the imperial title to help him consolidate control over his own principality, Swabia, but he did not try to fulfill the meaning of the imperial title elsewhere. For the first time, the word *emperor* was freed from its association with Italy and Rome. For the Habsburgs, the title *Holy Roman Emperor* was a prestigious but otherwise meaningless honorific.

The failure of Frederick II in Italy meant that the Italian cities would continue their independent course. To ensure that Frederick's heirs would not continue their rule in Sicily, the papacy called successively on other rulers to take over the island—first Henry III of England and then Charles of Anjou. Forces loyal to Frederick's family turned to the king of Aragon (Spain). The move left two enduring claimants to Sicily's crown—the kings of Aragon and the house of Anjou—and it spawned a long war that impoverished the region.

The popes won the war against Frederick, but at a cost. Even the king of France criticized the popes for doing "new and unheard-of things." By making its war against Frederick part of its crusade

---

Frederick II: The grandson of Barbarossa who became king of Sicily and Germany, as well as emperor (r. 1212–1250), who allowed the German princes a free hand as he battled the pope for control of Italy.

Statute in Favor of the Princes: A statute finalized by Frederick II in 1232 that gave the German princes sovereign power within their own principalities.

against heresy, the papacy came under attack for using religion as a political tool.

Louis IX and a New Ideal of Kingship

In hindsight, we can see that Frederick's fight for an empire that would stretch from Germany to Sicily was doomed. The successful rulers of medieval Europe were those content with smaller, more compact, more united polities. "National" states, like France and England, were in the future. (However, the existence of such states, too, may just be one phase of Western civilization.) In France, the new ideal of a stay-at-home monarch started in the thirteenth century with the reign of **Louis IX** (r. 1226–1270). Louis's two crusades to the Holy Land made clear to his subjects just how much they needed him in France, even though his place was ably filled the first time by his mother, Blanche of Castile. The two are pictured on page 396.

Louis was revered not because he was a military leader but because he was an administrator, a judge, and a "just father" of his people. On warm summer days, he would sit under a tree in the woods near his castle at Vincennes on the outskirts of Paris, hearing disputes and dispensing justice personally. Through his administrators, he vigorously imposed his laws and justice over much of France. At Paris he appointed a salaried chief magistrate, who could be supervised and fired if necessary. During Louis's reign, the influence of the parlement of Paris (the royal court of justice) increased significantly. Originally a changeable and movable body, part of the king's personal entourage when he dealt with litigation, the parlement was now permanently housed in Paris and staffed by professional judges who heard cases and recorded their decisions.

Unlike his grandfather Philip Augustus, Louis did not try to expand his territory. He inherited a large kingdom that included Poitou and Languedoc (Map 12.1), and he was content. Although at first Henry III, the king of England, attacked France continually to try to regain territory lost under Philip Augustus, Louis remained unprovoked. Rather than prolong the fighting, he conceded a bit and made peace. At the same time, Louis was a zealous crusader. He took seriously the need to defend the Holy Land when most of his contemporaries were weary of the idea.

Louis was respectful of the church and the pope; he accepted limits on his authority in relation to the church and never claimed power over spiritual matters. Nevertheless, he vigorously maintained the dignity of the king and his rights. He expected royal and ecclesiastical power to work in harmony, and he refused to let the church dictate how he should use his temporal authority. For example, French bishops wanted royal officers to support the church's sentences of excommunication. But Louis declared that he would authorize his officials to do so only if he was able to judge each case himself, to see if the excommunication had been justly pronounced or not. The bishops refused, and Louis held his ground. Royal and ecclesiastical power would work side by side, neither subservient to the other.

It would be easy to fault Louis for his policies toward Jews. His hatred of them was well known. He did not exactly advocate violence against them, but he sometimes subjected them to arrest, canceling the debts owed to them (but collecting part into the royal treasury) and confiscating their belongings. In 1253, he ordered them to live "by the labor of their hands" or leave France. He meant that they should no longer lend money, in effect taking away their one means of livelihood. Louis's contem-

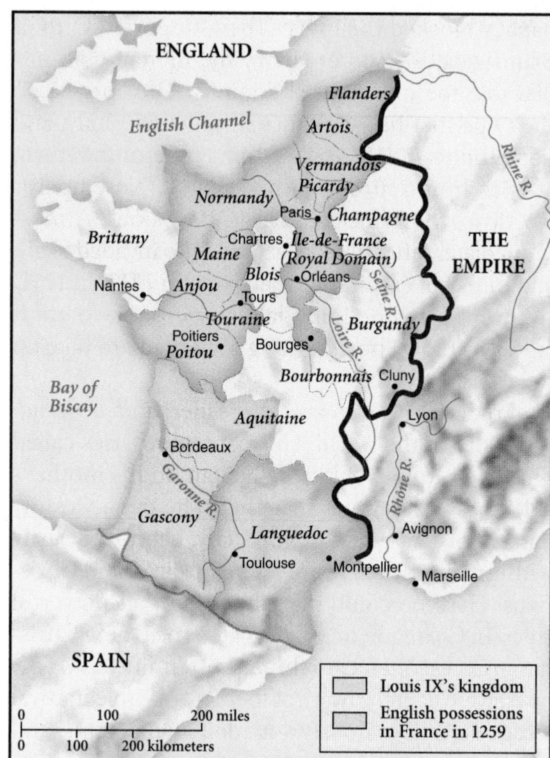

MAP 12.1 France under Louis IX, r. 1226–1270
Louis IX did not expand his kingdom as dramatically as his grandfather Philip Augustus had done. He was greatly admired, nevertheless, for he was seen by contemporaries as a model of Christian piety and justice. After his death, he was recognized as a saint and thus posthumously enhanced the prestige of the French monarchy.

Louis IX: A French king (r. 1226–1270) revered as a military leader and a judge; he was declared a saint after his death.

poraries did not criticize him for his Jewish policies. If anything, his hatred of Jews enhanced his reputation.

In fact, many of Louis's contemporaries considered him a saint, praising his care for the poor and sick, the pains and penances he inflicted on himself, and his regular participation in church services. In 1297, Pope Boniface VIII canonized him as St. Louis. The result was enormous prestige for the French monarchy. This prestige, joined with the renown of Paris as the center of scholarship and the repute of French courts as the hubs of chivalry, made France the cultural model of Europe.

The Birth of Representative Institutions

As thirteenth-century monarchs and princes expanded their powers, they devised a new political tool to enlist more broadly based support: all across Europe, from Spain to Poland, from England to Hungary, rulers summoned parliaments. These grew out of the ad hoc advisory sessions kings had held in the past with men from the two most powerful classes, or orders, of medieval society—the nobility and the clergy. In the thirteenth century, the advisory sessions turned into solemn, formal meetings of representatives of the orders to the kings' chief councils—the precursor of parliamentary sessions. Eventually these bodies became organs through which people not ordinarily present at court could articulate their wishes.

In practice, thirteenth-century kings did not so much command representatives of the orders to come to court as they simply summoned the most powerful members of their realm—whether clerics, nobles, or important townsmen—to support their policies. In thirteenth-century León (part of present-day Spain), for example, the king sometimes called only the clergy and nobles; sometimes he sent for representatives of the towns, especially when he wanted the help of town militias. As townsmen gradually began to participate regularly in advisory sessions, kings came to depend on them and their support. In turn, commoners became more fully integrated into the work of royal government.

Spanish Cortes | The ***cortes*** of Castile-León were among the earliest representative assemblies called to the king's court and the first to include townsmen. Enriched by plunder, fledgling villages soon burgeoned into major commercial centers. Like the cities of Italy, Spanish towns dominated the countryside. Hence, it was no wonder that King Alfonso IX (r. 1188–1230) summoned townsmen to the cortes in the first year of his reign, getting their representatives to agree to his plea for military and financial support and for help in consolidating his rule. Once convened at court, the townsmen joined bishops and noblemen in formally counseling the king and assenting to royal decisions. Beginning with Alfonso X (r. 1252–1284), Castilian monarchs regularly called on the cortes to participate in major political and military decisions and to assent to new taxes to finance them.

English Parliament | The English Parliament also developed as a new tool of royal government.[1] In this case, however, the king's control was complicated by the power of the barons, manifested, for example, in Magna Carta. In the twelfth century, King Henry II had consulted prelates and barons at Great Councils, using these parliaments as his tool to ratify and gain support for his policies. Although Magna Carta had nothing to do with such councils, the barons thought the document gave them an important and permanent role in royal government as the king's advisers and a solid guarantee of their customary rights and privileges. Henry III (r. 1216–1272) was crowned at the age of nine and was king in name only for the first sixteen years of his reign. Instead, England was governed by a council consisting of a few barons, university-trained administrators, and a papal legate. Although not quite "government by Parliament," this council set a precedent for baronial participation in government.

A parliament that included commoners came only in the midst of war and as a result of political weakness. Once in power, Henry III so alienated nobles and commoners alike by his wars, debts, choice of advisers, and demands for money that the barons threatened to rebel. At a meeting at Oxford in 1258, they forced Henry to dismiss his foreign advisers; rule with the advice of the Council of Fifteen, chosen jointly by the barons and the king; and limit the terms of his chief officers. However, this new government was itself riven by strife among the barons, and civil war erupted in 1264. At the battle

cortes (kawr TEHZ): The earliest European representative institution, called initially to consent to royal wishes; first convoked in 1188 by the king of Castile-León.

[1]Although *parlement* and *Parliament* are similar words, both deriving from the French word *parler* ("to speak"), the institutions they named were very different. The parlement of France was a law court, whereas the English Parliament, although beginning as a court to redress grievances, had by 1327 become above all a representative institution. The major French representative assembly, the Estates General, first convened at the beginning of the fourteenth century (see page 401).

of Lewes in the same year, the leader of the baronial opposition, Simon de Montfort (c. 1208–1265), routed the king's forces, captured the king, and became England's de facto ruler.

Because only a minority of the barons followed him, Simon sought new support by convening a parliament in 1265, to which he summoned not only the earls, barons, and churchmen who backed him but also representatives from the towns, the "commons"—and he appealed for their help. Thus, for the first time the commons were given a voice in English government. Even though Simon's brief rule ended that very year and Henry's son Edward I (r. 1272–1307) became a rallying point for royalists, the idea of representative government in England had emerged, born out of the interplay between royal initiatives and baronial revolts.

The Weakening of the Papacy

In contrast with England, representative institutions developed in France out of the conflict between Pope **Boniface VIII** (r. 1294–1303) and King Philip IV (r. 1285–1314), known as Philip the Fair. At the time, this confrontation seemed to be just one more episode in the ongoing struggle between medieval popes and secular rulers for power and authority. Throughout the thirteenth century the papacy confidently asserted its prerogatives. (See the illustration at right.) In fact, however, kings were gradually gaining ground. The conflict between Boniface and Philip signaled the turning point, when royal power trumped papal power.

Portrait of a Pope
Celebrating the power of the papacy, Pope Nicholas III (r. 1277–1280) sponsored a thorough redecoration of Rome's ancient basilica of St. Paul's Outside the Walls (the burial place of St. Paul). In the space above each of the columns running down the nave, he had his artists paint portraits of the popes, linking all to one another and ultimately to St. Peter (whose portrait was nearest the altar). In this image of Anacletus (c. 79–c. 91), the artist asserted the pope's gravity, solemnity, and otherworldliness. Anacletus wears a pallium, a white scarf symbolizing papal power, even though the pallium did not exist in the first century. *(Nimatallah/Art Resource, NY.)*

Taxing the Clergy For centuries, the clergy had maintained a special status within the medieval state. Since the twelfth century, popes had declared the clergy under their jurisdiction. Clerics were not taxed except in the case of religious wars; they were not tried except in clerical courts. At the end of the thirteenth century, royal challenges to these principles provoked angry papal responses. The clashes began over taxing the clergy. Philip the Fair and the English king Edward I both financed their wars (mainly against one another) by taxing the clergy along with everyone else. The new principle of national sovereignty that they were claiming led them to assert jurisdiction over all people, even churchmen, who lived within their borders. For the pope, however, the principle at stake was his role as head of the clergy. Thus, Pope Boniface VIII declared that only the pope could authorize taxes on clerics. Threatening to excommunicate kings who taxed prelates without papal permission, he called on clerics to disobey any such royal orders.

Edward and Philip reacted swiftly. Taking advantage of the role English courts played in protecting the peace, Edward declared that all clerics who refused to pay his taxes would be considered outlaws—literally "outside the law." Clergymen who were robbed, for example, would have no recourse against their attackers; if accused of crimes, they would have no defense in court. Relying on a different strategy, Philip forbade the exportation of precious metals, money, or jewels—effectively sealing the French borders. Immediately, the English clergy cried out for legal protection, while the papacy itself cried out for the revenues it had long enjoyed from French pilgrims, litigants, and travelers. Boniface was forced to back down, conceding

---

Boniface VIII: The pope (r. 1294–1303) whose clash with King Philip the Fair of France left the papacy considerably weakened.

in 1297 that kings had the right to tax their clergy in emergencies. But this concession did not end the confrontation.

The King's New Tools: Propaganda and Popular Opinion In 1301, Philip the Fair tested his jurisdiction in southern France by arresting Bernard Saisset, the bishop of Pamiers, on a charge of treason for slandering the king by comparing him to an owl, "the handsomest of birds which is worth absolutely nothing." Saisset's imprisonment violated the principle, maintained both by the pope and by French law, that a clergyman was not subject to lay justice. Boniface reacted angrily, and Philip seized the opportunity to deride and humiliate him, orchestrating a public relations campaign against Boniface. Philip convened representatives of the clergy, nobles, and townspeople to explain, justify, and propagandize his position. This new assembly, which met in 1302, was the ancestor of the French representative institution, the Estates General. The pope's reply, the bull[2] *Unam Sanctam* (1302), intensified the situation to fever pitch by declaring bluntly "that it is altogether necessary to salvation for every human creature to be subject to the Roman Pontiff." At meetings of the king's inner circle, Philip's agents declared Boniface a false pope, accusing him of sexual perversion, various crimes, and heresy.

Papal Defeat In 1303, French royal agents, acting on Philip's orders, invaded Boniface's palace at Anagni (southeast of Rome) to capture the pope, bring him to France, and try him. Fearing for the pope's life, however, the people of Anagni joined forces and drove the French agents out of town. Yet even after such public support for the pope, the king made his power felt. Boniface died very shortly thereafter, and the next two popes quickly pardoned Philip and his agents for their actions.

Just as Frederick II's failure revealed the weakness of the empire, so Boniface's humiliation demonstrated the limits of papal control. The two powers that claimed "universal" authority had very little weight in the face of new, limited, but tightly controlled national states such as France and England. After 1303, popes continued to denounce kings and emperors, but their words had less and less impact. In the face of newly powerful medieval states—undergirded by vast revenues, judicial apparatuses, representative institutions, and even the loyalty of churchmen—the papacy could make little headway. The delicate balance between church and state, reflecting a sense of universal order and harmony and a hallmark of the reign of St. Louis, broke down at the end of the thirteenth century.

The Avignon Papacy In 1309, forced from Rome by civil strife, the papacy settled at Avignon, a city then belonging to the Angevin rulers of Naples and very close to—and influenced by—France. Here the popes remained until 1378, and thus the period 1309–1378 is called the **Avignon papacy**. Europeans ashamed that the pope lived so far from Rome called it the Babylonian captivity. They were thinking of the Old Testament story of the Hebrews captured and brought into slavery in ancient Babylon.[3] The Avignon popes, many of them French, established a sober and efficient organization that took in regular revenues and gave the papacy more say than ever before in the appointment of churchmen. Slowly, they abandoned the idea of leading all of Christendom, tacitly recognizing the growing power of the secular states to regulate their internal affairs.

The Rise of the *Signori*

During the thirteenth century, new groups, generally made up of the non-noble classes—the ***popolo*** ("people"), who fought on foot—attempted to take over the reins of power from the nobility in many Italian communes. The popolo incorporated members of city associations such as craft and merchant guilds, parishes, and the commune itself. In fact, the popolo was a kind of alternative commune. Armed and militant, the popolo demanded a share in city government, particularly to gain a voice in matters of taxation. In 1223 at Piacenza, for example, the popolo's members and the nobles worked out a plan to share the election of their city's government. Such power sharing was a typical result of the popolo's struggle. In some cities, however, nobles dissolved the popolo, while in others the popolo virtually excluded the nobles from government. Such factions turned northern Italian cities into centers of civil discord.

---

[2]An official papal document is called a bull, from the *bulla*, or seal, that was used to authenticate it.

[3]See 2 Kings 24–25.

Avignon (AH vee NYAW) papacy: The period (1309–1378) during which the popes ruled from Avignon rather than from Rome.

***popolo*:** Literally, "people"; a communal faction, largely made up of merchants, that demanded (and often obtained) power in thirteenth-century Italian cities.

Weakened by this constant friction, the communes were tempting prey for great regional nobles who, allying with one or another urban group, often succeeded in establishing themselves as *signori* (singular *signore*, "lord") of the cities, keeping the peace at the price of repression. Thirteenth-century Piacenza was typical: first dominated by nobles, the popolo gained a voice by 1225; but then by midcentury both the nobles and the popolo were eclipsed by the power of a signore.

The Mongol Takeover

Europeans were not the only warring society in the thirteenth century: to the east, the Mongols (sometimes called Tatars or Tartars) created an aggressive army under the leadership of Chingiz (or Genghis) Khan (c. 1162–1227) and his sons. In part, economic necessity drove them out of Mongolia: changes in climate had reduced the grasslands that sustained their animals and their nomadic way of life. But they were also inspired by Chingiz's hope of conquering the world. By 1215, the Mongols held Beijing and most of northern China. Some years later, they moved through central Asia and skirted the Caspian Sea (Map 12.2).

The Golden Horde in Russia In the 1230s, the Mongols began concerted attacks in Russia, Poland, and Hungary, where native princes were weak. Only the death of the Great Khan, Chingiz's son Ogodei (1186–1241), and disputes over his succession prevented a concentrated assault on Germany. In the 1250s, the Mongols took Iran and Iraq.

The Mongols' sophisticated military tactics contributed to their overwhelming success. They devised two- and three-flank operations. The invasion of Hungary, for example, was two-pronged, with divisions arriving from Russia, Poland, and Germany. The Mongols—fighting mainly on horseback with heavy lances and powerful bows and arrows whose shots traveled far and penetrated deeply—crushed the Hungarian army of mixed infantry and cavalry.

In the West, the Mongol rule in Russia lasted the longest. Their most important victory there was the capture of Kiev in 1240. Making the mouth of the Volga River the center of their power in Russia, the

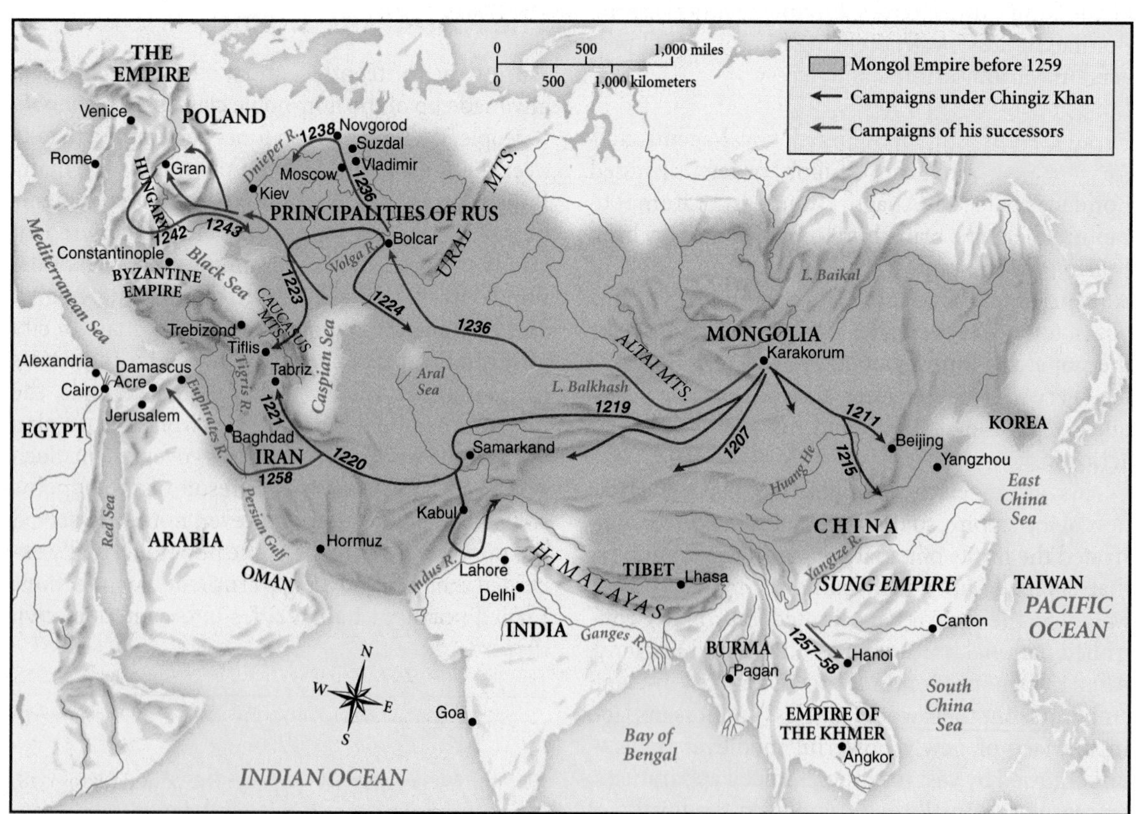

MAP 12.2 The Mongol Invasions to 1259

The Mongols tied East Asia to the west. Their conquest of China, which took place at about the same time as their invasions of Russia and Iran, created a Eurasian economy. | **Compare this map with the Mapping the West map on page 377. Why were the Mongol invasions a threat to the Muslim world?**

Mongols dominated all of Russia's principalities for about two hundred years. The Mongol Empire in Russia, later called the **Golden Horde** (*golden* probably from the color of their leader's tent; *horde* from a Turkish word meaning "camp"), adopted much of the local government apparatus and left many of the old institutions in place. They allowed Russian princes to continue ruling as long as they paid homage and tribute to the khan, and they tolerated the Russian church, exempting it from taxes. The Mongols' chief undertaking was a series of population censuses on the basis of which they recalculated taxes and recruited troops.

The Opening of China to Europeans The Mongol invasion changed the political configuration of Europe and Asia. Because the Mongols were willing to deal with Westerners, one effect of their conquests was to open China to European travelers for the first time. Missionaries, diplomats, and merchants went to China over land routes and via the Persian Gulf. Some of these voyagers hoped to enlist the aid of the Mongols against the Muslims; others expected to make new converts to Christianity; still others dreamed of lucrative trade routes.

The most famous of these travelers was Marco Polo (1254–1324), son of a merchant family from Venice. Marco's father and uncle had already made the round trip to China once when Marco joined them on a second expedition. He stayed in China for nearly two years. Others stayed even longer. In fact, evidence suggests that an entire community of Venetian traders lived in the city of Yangzhou in the mid-fourteenth century.

Merchants paved the way for missionaries. Friars (preachers to the cities of Europe) became missionaries to new continents as well. In 1289, the pope made the Franciscan John of Monte Corvino his envoy to China. Preaching in India along the way, John arrived in China four or five years after setting out, converting one local ruler, and building a church. A few years later, now at Beijing, he boasted that he had converted six thousand people, constructed two churches, and translated the New Testament and Psalms into the native language.

The long-term effect of the Mongols on the West was to open up new land routes to the East that helped bind together the two halves of the known world. Travel stories such as Marco Polo's account of his journeys stimulated others to seek out the fabulous riches — textiles, ginger, ceramics, copper — of China and other regions of the East. In a sense, the Mongols initiated the search for exotic goods and missionary opportunities that culminated in the European "discovery" of a new world, the Americas.

The Great Famine

While the Mongols stimulated the European economy, natural disasters coupled with political ineptitude brought on a terrible period of famine in northern Europe. The **Great Famine** (1315–1322) left many hungry, sick, and weak while it fueled social antagonisms.

Hunger and Its Effects An anonymous chronicler looking back on the events of 1315 wrote:

> The floods of rain have rotted almost all the seed, so that the prophecy of Isaiah might seem now to be fulfilled, . . . and in many places the hay lay so long under water that it could neither be mown nor gathered. Sheep generally died and other animals were killed in a sudden plague. . . . [In the next year, 1316,] the dearth of grain was much increased. Such a scarcity has not been seen in our time in England, nor heard of for a hundred years. For the measure of wheat sold in London and the neighboring places for forty pence [a very high price], and in other less thickly populated parts of the country thirty pence was a common price.

Thus did the writer chronicle the causes and effects of the famine: uncommonly heavy rains, a disease that killed farm animals important not only for their meat and fleeces but also for their labor; and, finally, the economic effects, as scarcity drove up the prices of ordinary foods. All of these led to hunger, disease, and death.

Had the rains gone back to normal, the European economy would no doubt have recovered. But the rains continued, and the crops kept failing. In many regions, the crisis lasted for a full seven years. Hardest hit were the peasants and the poor. In rural areas, wealthy lords, churches, monasteries, and well-to-do peasants profited from the newly high prices they could charge. (See Taking Measure, "Grain Prices during the Great Famine," page 404.) In the cities, some merchants and ecclesiastical institutions benefited as well. But on the whole, even

---

Golden Horde: The political institution set up by the Mongols in Russia, lasting from the thirteenth to the fifteenth century.

Great Famine: The shortage of food and accompanying social ills that besieged northern Europe between 1315 and 1322.

TAKING MEASURE

Grain Prices during the Great Famine

Famine was caused not just by a shortage of food but also by spikes in prices that made it impossible for the poor to buy enough to eat. The graph shown here represents the prices of grain produced on the English manor of Hinderclay between 1272 and 1324. It is clear that prices fluctuated greatly and that during the period of the Great Famine, 1315–1322, they rose dramatically, with the years 1316–1317 particularly striking. Note that the price of wheat was always higher than the prices of barley and rye, which were considered inferior grains. (That notion would change as beer, which is made with barley, gained favor.) The spikes in prices suggest that very little charitable distribution of grain was taking place on Hinderclay manor.

Source: Based on Phillipp R. Schofield, "The Social Economy of the Medieval Village in the Early Fourteenth Century," *Economic History Review* 61 (2008): 44, Figure 1.

Question to Consider

- **What explains the extraordinary price fluctuations shown on this graph?**

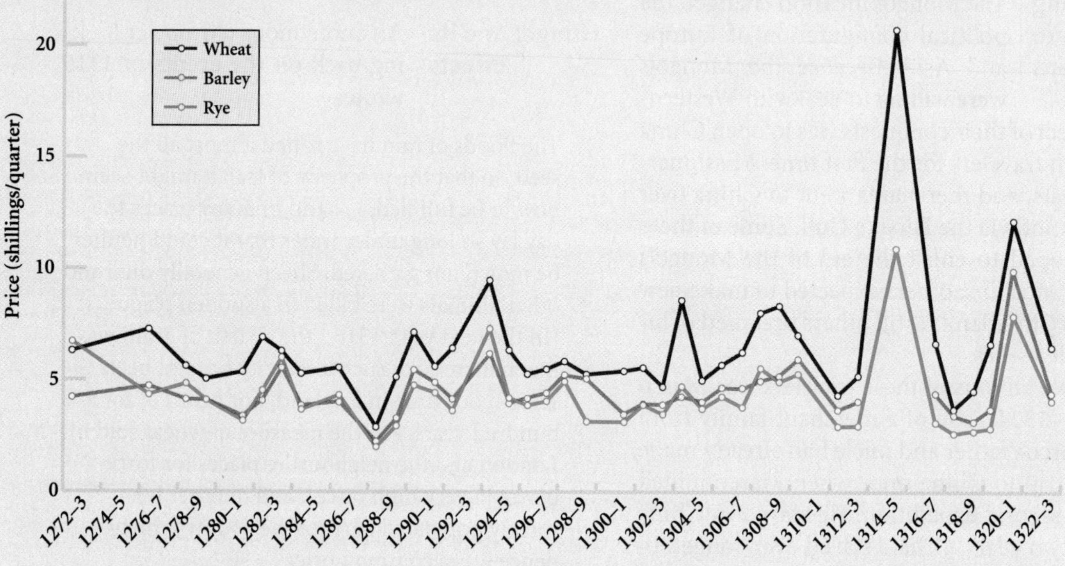

the well-to-do suffered, as both rural and urban areas lost fully 5 to 10 percent of their population. The impact was enormous, for loss of population meant erosion of manpower and falling productivity.

People did attempt to cope with and contain these disasters. The clergy offered up prayers and urged their congregations to do penance, for the famine was seen as God's punishment for the sins of humanity. In the countryside, charitable monasteries gave out food; conscientious kings tried to control high interest rates on loans; and hungry peasants migrated from west to east—to Poland, for example, where land was more plentiful. In the cities, where starving refugees from rural areas flocked for food, wealthy men and women sometimes opened their storehouses or distributed coins. Other rich townspeople founded hospitals for the poor. Town councils sold municipal bonds at high rates of interest, gaining some temporary solvency. These towns became the primary charitable institutions of the era, importing grain and selling it at or slightly below cost.

Social Causes and Consequences of the Great Famine

Contributing to the crop failure was population growth that challenged the productive capabilities of the age. The exponential leap in population from the tenth to the twelfth century slowed to zero around the year 1300, but all the land that could be cultivated had been settled by this time. No new technology had been developed to increase crop yields. The swollen population demanded a lot from the productive capacities of the land. Just a small shortfall could dislocate the whole system of distribution.

The policies of rulers added to the problems of too many people and too little food. The anonymous chronicler who considered "floods of rain" the cause of the famine also observed "that in Northumbria [the north of England] dogs and horses and other unclean things were eaten. For there, on account of the frequent raids of the Scots, work is more irksome, as the accursed Scots despoil the people daily of their food." Scottish troops were not the only ones who destroyed the crops. The king of England sent his soldiers to ravage Scotland in turn. The kings of Norway, Denmark, and Sweden regularly fought one another. The king of France was at war with rebellious Flemings to control Flanders. These wars not only ruined the crops but also diverted manpower and resources to arms and castles, at the same time disrupting normal markets and trade routes.

In order to wage wars, rulers imposed heavy taxes and, as the famine became worse, requisitioned grain to support their troops. Consequently, the effects of the famine grew worse, and in many regions people rose up in protest. In France, the merchants were enraged to see their grain taken off the open market, where they could hope to profit. The king tried to mollify them. In England, peasants resisted tax collectors. In a more violent reaction, poor French shepherds, outcasts, clerics, and artisans entered Paris to storm the prisons. They then marched southward—burning royal castles and attacking officials, Jews, and lepers. They were pursued by the king, who succeeded in putting down the movement. But the limits of the politics of control were made clear in this confrontation, which exacerbated the misery of the famine while doing nothing to contain it.

REVIEW QUESTION **How did the search for harmony result in cooperation—and confrontation—between secular rulers and other institutions, such as the church and the towns?**

A Famine in Florence

Starvation did not end with the last year of the Great Famine. This miniature from a manuscript detailing grain prices shows the effects—and the artist's interpretation—of a famine in 1329. The scene is the Orsanmichele, the Florentine grain market. The market was dominated by an image of the Virgin Mary, here depicted on the right-hand side. Extending beyond the margin on the far left, a mother with two children raises her hands and eyes to heaven in prayer. In the back, soldiers guard the market's entrance. The market itself bustles with rich buyers, who hand over their money and pack their bags with grain. Above flies an angel with broken trumpets, while a demon takes center stage and says, among other things, "I will make you ache with hunger and high prices." *(Biblioteca Laurenziana, Florence, Italy/Scala/Art Resource, NY.)*

Conclusion

The thirteenth century sought harmony and synthesis but discovered how elusive these goals could be. Theoretically, the papacy and empire were supposed to work together; instead they clashed in bitter warfare, leaving the government of Germany to the princes and northern Italy to its communes and *signori*. Theoretically, faith and reason were supposed to arrive at the same truths. They sometimes did so in the hands of scholastics, but not always. Theoretically, all Christians practiced the same rites and followed the teachings of the church. In practice, local enforcement determined which church laws took effect—and to what extent. Moreover, the search for order was never able to bring together all the diverse peoples, ideas, and interests of thirteenth-century society. Heretics and Jews were set apart.

Synthesis was more achievable in the arts. Heaven, earth, and hell were melded harmoniously together in stained glass and sculpture. Musicians wove disparate melodic and poetic lines into motets. Writers melded heroic and romantic themes with theological truths and mystical visions.

Political leaders also aimed at harmony. Via representative institutions, they harnessed the various

MAPPING THE WEST

Europe, c. 1340

The Empire, which in the thirteenth century came to be called the Holy Roman Empire, still dominated the map of Europe in 1340, but the emperor himself had less power than ever. Each principality—often each city—was ruled separately and independently. To the east, the Ottoman Turks were just beginning to make themselves felt. In the course of the next century, they would disrupt the Mongol hegemony and become a great power.

social orders to their quest for greater order and control. They asserted sovereignty over all the people who lived in their borders, asserting unity while increasing their revenues, expanding their territories, and enhancing their prestige. The kings of England and France and the governments of northern and central Italian cities largely succeeded in these goals, while the king of Germany failed miserably. Germany and Italy remained fragmented until the nineteenth century. Ironically, the Mongols, who began as invaders in the West, helped unify areas that were far apart by opening trade routes.

Events at the end of the thirteenth century thwarted the search for harmony. The mutual respect of church and state achieved under St. Louis in France disintegrated into irreconcilable claims to power under Pope Boniface VIII and Philip the Fair. The carefully constructed tapestry of St. Thomas's summae began to unravel in the teachings of John Duns Scotus. An economy stretched to the breaking point resulted in a terrible period of famine. Disorder and anxiety—but also extraordinary creativity—would mark the next era.

FOR FURTHER EXPLORATION

- **For additional primary-source material from this period**, see *Sources of the Making of the West*, Fourth Edition.
- **For Web sites, images, and documents related to topics in this chapter**, visit *Make History* at bedfordstmartins.com/hunt.

Chapter 12 Review

Online Study Guide bedfordstmartins.com/hunt

Key Terms and People

In the grid below, identify the term or person and explain its historical significance. (To do this exercise online, go to bedfordstmartins.com/hunt.)

Term	Who or What & When	Why It Matters
Innocent III (p. 382)		
Fourth Lateran Council (p. 383)		
blood libel (p. 388)		
leprosy (p. 388)		
scholasticism (p. 389)		
Frederick II (p. 397)		
Statute in Favor of the Princes (p. 397)		
Louis IX (p. 398)		
cortes (p. 399)		
Boniface VIII (p. 400)		
Avignon papacy (p. 401)		
popolo (p. 401)		
Golden Horde (p. 403)		
Great Famine (p. 403)		

Review Questions

1. How did people respond to the teachings and laws of the church in the early thirteenth century?
2. How did artists, musicians, and scholastics try to link the physical world with the divine?
3. How did the search for harmony result in cooperation—and confrontation—between secular rulers and other institutions, such as the church and the towns?

Making Connections

1. Why was Innocent III more successful than Boniface VIII in carrying out his objectives?
2. How did the growth of lay piety help bolster the prestige and power of kings like Louis IX?
3. Comparing the goals and methods of Abelard's scholarship with those of Thomas Aquinas, explain the continuities and the differences between the twelfth-century schools and the scholastic movement.

Important Events

Date	Event	Date	Event
1188	King Alfonso IX summons townsmen to the *cortes*	1265	English commons summoned to Parliament
1212–1250	Reign of Frederick II	1273	Thomas Aquinas publishes the *Summa Theologiae*
1215	Fourth Lateran Council	1302	First Meeting of the French Estates General
1226–1270	Reign of Louis IX (St. Louis)	1309–1378	Avignon papacy
1232	Frederick II finalizes Statute in Favor of the Princes	1313–1321	Dante writes *Divine Comedy*
1240	Mongols capture Kiev	1315–1322	Great Famine

- Consider three events: **Fourth Lateran Coucil (1215)**, **Dante writes *Divine Comedy* (1313–1321)**, and **Thomas Aquinas publishes the *Summa Theologiae* (1273)**. How did the papacy, vernacular literature, and scholastic philosophy represent different aspects of the medieval search for order?

SUGGESTED REFERENCES

For the church's mission, see Bynum, Sayers, and Kessler and Zacharias. The Inquisition and other forms of persecution are the subjects of the books by Given, Jordan (on the Jews), and Nirenberg. Colish's collected essays discuss the many forms of scholasticism. Abulafia, Jones, Le Goff, Maddicott, and O'Callaghan each helpfully cover the political developments of the period.

Abulafia, David. *Frederick II: A Medieval Emperor*. 1988.

Bynum, Caroline Walker. *Holy Feast and Holy Fast: The Religious Significance of Food to Medieval Women*. 1987.

Colish, Marcia L. *Studies in Scholasticism*. 2006.

*Fourth Lateran Council:
http://www.fordham.edu/halsall/source/ lat4-select.html

Gaposchkin, M. Cecilia. *The Making of Saint Louis: Kingship, Sanctity, and Crusade in the Later Middle Ages*. 2008.

Given, James Buchanan. *Inquisition and Medieval Society*. 2001.

Jackson, Peter. *The Mongols and the West*. 2005.

*Joinville, Jean de, and Geoffroy de Villehardouin. *Chronicles of the Crusades*. Trans. M. R. B. Shaw. 1963.

Jones, Philip. *The Italian City-State: From Commune to Signoria*. 1997.

Jordan, William Chester. *The French Monarchy and the Jews: From Philip Augustus to the Last Capetians*. 1989.

——. *The Great Famine: Northern Europe in the Early Fourteenth Century*. 1996.

Kessler, Herbert L., and Johanna Zacharias. *Rome 1300: On the Path of the Pilgrim*. 2000.

Le Goff, Jacques. *Saint Louis*. Trans. Gareth Evan Gollrad. 2009.

Maddicott, J. R. *Simon De Montfort*. 1994.

Nichols, Aidan. *Discovering Aquinas: An Introduction to His Life, Work and Influence*. 2003.

Nirenberg, David. *Communities of Violence: Persecution of Minorities in the Middle Ages*. 1996.

O'Callaghan, Joseph F. *The Cortes of Castille-León, 1188–1350*. 1989.

Panofsky, Erwin. *Gothic Architecture and Scholasticism*. 1951.

Richardson, H. G., and G. O. Sayles. *The English Parliament in the Middle Ages*. 1981.

Sayers, Jane. *Innocent III: Leader of Europe, 1198–1216*. 1994.

*Thomas Aquinas: http://www.newadvent.org/summa

Strayer, Joseph R. *The Reign of Philip the Fair*. 1980.

*Primary source.

CHAPTER

13

Crisis and Renaissance

1340–1492

In 1453, the Ottoman Turks turned their cannons on Constantinople and blasted the city's walls. The fall of Constantinople, which spelled the end of the Byzantine Empire, was an enormous shock to Europeans. Some, like the pope, called for a crusade against the Ottomans; others, like the writer Lauro Quirini, sneered, calling them "a barbaric, uncultivated race, without established customs, or laws, [who lived] a careless, vagrant, arbitrary life."

But the Turks didn't consider themselves uncultivated or arbitrary. In fact, they saw themselves as the true heirs of the Roman Empire, and they shared many of the values and tastes of the very Europeans who were so hostile to them. Sultan Mehmed II employed European architects to construct his new palace — the Topkapi Saray — in the city once known as Constantinople and now popularly called Istanbul. He commissioned the Venetian artist Gentile Bellini to paint his portrait, a genre invented in Burgundy to celebrate the status and individuality of important and wealthy patrons.

Mehmed's actions and interests sum up the dual features of the period of crisis and Renaissance that took place from the middle of the fourteenth century to the late fifteenth century. What was a crisis from one point of view — the fall of the Byzantine Empire — was at the same time stimulus for what historians call the Renaissance. Both to confront and to mask the crises of the day, people discovered new value in ancient, classical culture; they created a new vocabulary drawn from classical literature as well as astonishing new forms of art and music based on ancient precedents. The classical revival provided the stimulus for new styles of living, ruling, and thinking.

Along with the fall of the Byzantine Empire, other crises marked the period from 1340 to 1492. These were matched by equally significant gains. The plague, or Black Death, tore at the

Portrait of Mehmed II
The Ottoman ruler Mehmed II saw himself as a Renaissance patron of the arts, and he called upon the most famous artists and architects of the day to work for him. The painter of this portrait, Gentile Bellini, was from a well-known family of artists in Venice and served at Mehmed's court in 1479–1480. The revival of portraiture, so characteristic of Renaissance tastes, was as important to the Turkish sultans as to European rulers. *(Erich Lessing/Art Resource, NY.)*

fabric of communities and families; but the survivors and their children reaped the benefits of higher wages and better living standards. The Hundred Years' War, fought between France and England, involved many smaller states in its slaughter and brought untold misery to the French countryside; but it also helped create the glittering court of Burgundy, patron of new art and music. By the war's end, both the French and the English kings were more powerful than ever. Following their conquest of Constantinople, the Ottoman Turks penetrated far into the Balkans; but this was a calamity only from the European point of view. Well into the sixteenth century, the Ottomans were part of the culture that nourished the artistic achievements of the Renaissance. A crisis in the church overlapped with the crises of disease and war as a schism within the papacy—pitting pope against pope—divided Europe into separate camps; but a church council, whose members included Renaissance humanists, eventually resolved the papal schism reestablishing the old system: a single pope who presided over the church from Rome.

CHAPTER FOCUS How were the crises of 1340–1492 and the Renaissance related?

Crisis: Disease, War, and Schism

In the mid-fourteenth century, a series of crises shook the West. The Black Death swept through Europe and decimated the population, especially in the cities. Two major wars redrew the map of Europe between 1340 and 1492. The first was the Hundred Years' War, fought from 1337 to 1453 (thus actually lasting 116 years). This war turned a dynastic struggle over the kingdom of France into a military confrontation that transformed the nature of warfare itself. The second war began with the Ottoman domination of Byzantium in the 1360s and culminated in the Ottoman conquest of Constantinople in 1453—the same year the Hundred Years' War ended. Because Constantinople was the last buffer between Europe and the Islamic world, its fall marked a major shift in global power. The Ottomans now had a secure base from which to move into Europe. As the wars raged and attacks of the plague came and went, a crisis in the church also weighed on Europeans. Attempts to return the papacy from Avignon to Rome resulted in the Great Schism (1378–1417), when first two and then three rival popes asserted universal authority. In the wake of these crises, many ordinary folk sought solace in new forms of piety, some of them condemned by the church as heretical.

The Black Death, 1347–1352

The **Black Death**, so named by later historians, was a calamitous disease. It decimated the population wherever it struck and wreaked havoc on social and economic structures. Yet in the wake of this plague, those fortunate enough to survive benefited from an improved standard of living through greater access to jobs and resources. Unprofitable farms were abandoned, and a more diversified agriculture developed. Birthrates climbed, and new universities were established to educate the post-plague generations.

A "Pestilential Disease" A harbinger of the Black Death was noted in 1346, perhaps in the region between the Black and Caspian Seas. A year later, the Byzantine scholar Nicephorus Gregoras was already familiar with it.

Black Death: The term historians give to the disease that swept through Europe in 1347–1352.

1337–1453 Hundred Years' War

1347–1352 Black Death in Europe

1358 Jacquerie uprising in France

1378 Ciompi Revolt in Florence

1378–1417 Great Schism divides papacy

1381 Wat Tyler's Rebellion in England

1386 Union of Lithuania and Poland

1325 | 1350 | 1375 | 1400

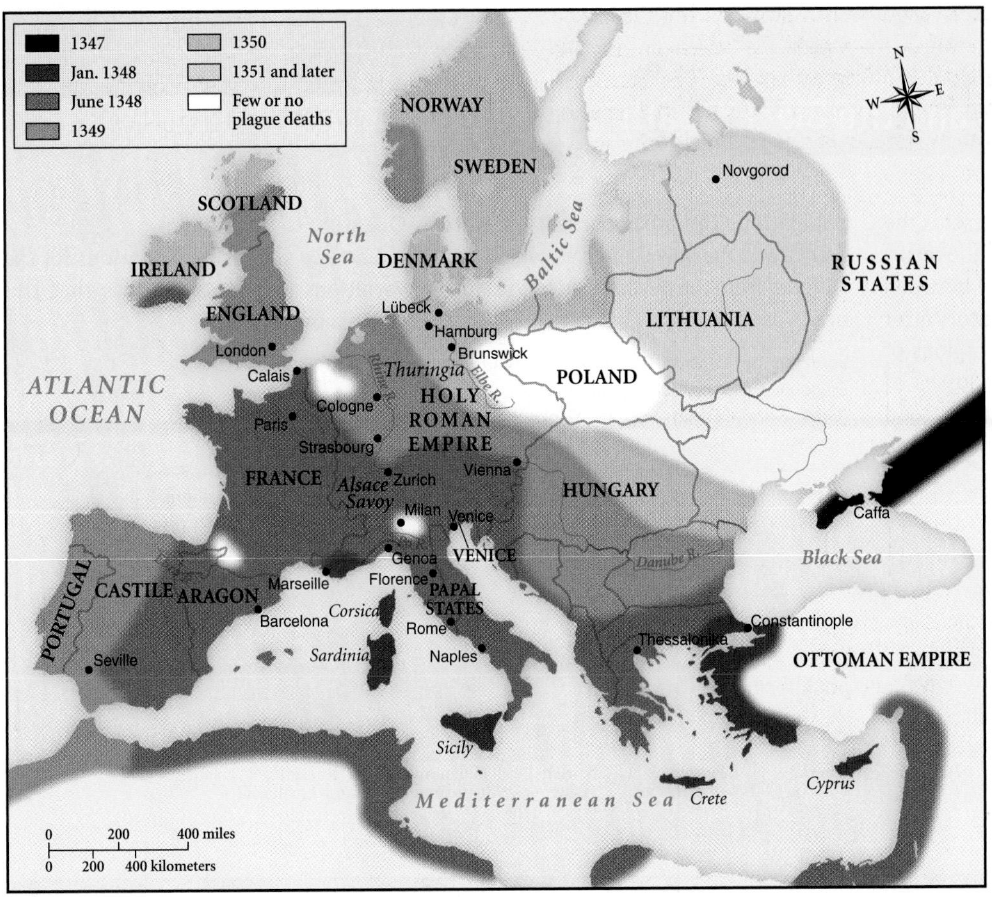

MAP 13.1 Advance of the Black Death, 1346–1352
Hitting the West in 1346, the Black Death quickly worked its way across the Mediterranean and then northward. Its path generally followed waterways and roads. With the exception of a few regions that were spared, it killed between one-third and one-half of the population of western Europe. However, in eastern Europe its impact was far less. The plague recurred—at first every ten to twelve years and then at longer intervals.

Calling it a "pestilential disease," he described its symptoms: "The prominent signs of this disease, signs indicating early death, were tumorous outgrowths at the roots of thighs and arms and simultaneously bleeding ulcerations." The Black Death was almost certainly caused by the bacterium *Yersinia pestis*, the same organism responsible for outbreaks of plague today. From its breeding ground, it traveled westward to the Middle East, the North African coast, and Europe (Map 13.1).

Probably carried by fleas traveling on the backs of rats, it hitched boat rides with spices, silks, and

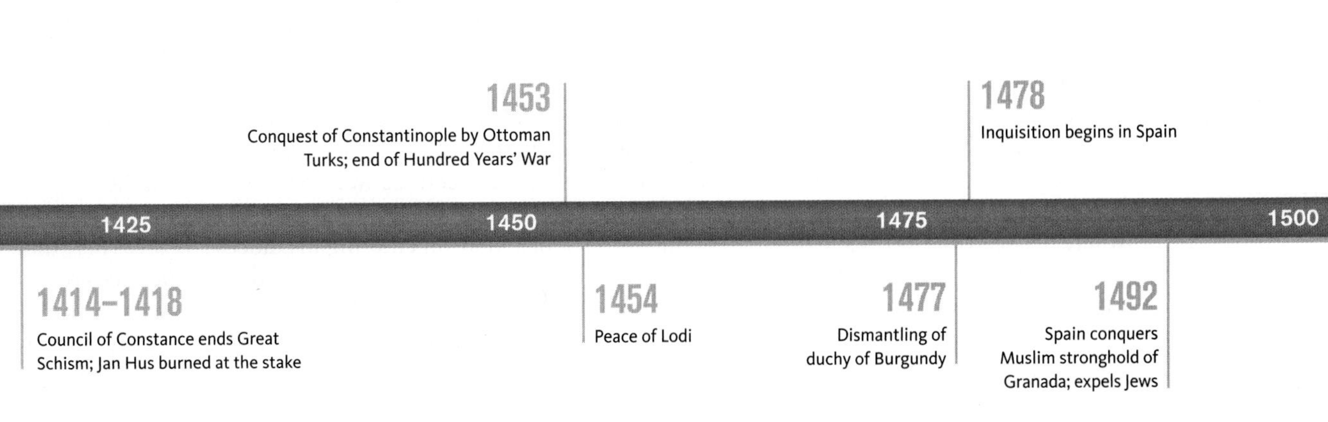

TAKING MEASURE

Population Losses and the Black Death

The bar chart dramatically represents the impact of the Black Death and the recurrent epidemics that hit Europe between 1340 and 1450. More than a century after the Black Death, none of the regions of Europe had made up for the losses of population. The population of 1450 stood at about 75–80 percent of the pre-plague population. The areas hardest hit were France and the Low Countries, which also suffered from the devastation of the Hundred Years' War.

Source: From Carlo M. Cipolla, ed., *Fontana Economic History of Europe: The Middle Ages* (Great Britain: Collins/Fontana Books, 1974), 36.

Question to Consider

- **Can you suggest explanations for the variations in population loss that this chart shows?**

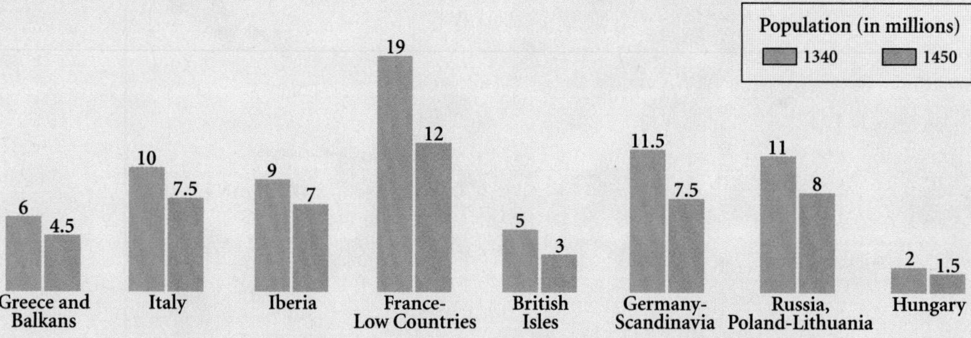

porcelain. In 1347, people in the Genoese colony in Caffa, on the north edge of the Black Sea, contracted the disease. Soon after that, it arrived in Constantinople and at the same time in Europe—in Sicily, Sardinia, Corsica, and Marseille. Within a few months it spread to Aragon, all of Italy, the Balkans, and most of France. It then crept northward to Germany, England, Scandinavia, and Russia. Meanwhile, it attacked the Islamic world as well—Baghdad, North Africa, and the bit of al-Andalus that remained. This was just the beginning. The disease recurred every ten to twelve years throughout the fourteenth century (though only the outbreak of 1347–1352 is called the Black Death), and it continued, though at longer intervals, until the eighteenth century.

The effects of the Black Death were spread across Europe yet oddly localized. At Florence, in Italy, nearly half of the population died, yet two hundred miles to the north, Milan suffered very little. Conservative estimates put the death toll in Europe anywhere between one-third and one-half of the entire population, but some historians put the mortality rate as high as 60 percent. (See "Taking Measure," above.)

What made the Black Death so devastating? The overall answer is simple: it confronted a population already weakened by disease or famine. The Great Famine that began in 1315 may have been over by 1322, but it was followed by local famines such as the one that hit Italy in 1339–1340. Epidemic diseases followed the famines: smallpox, influenza, and tuberculosis all took their toll.

Consequences of the Black Death Some responses came from local governments. The government of the Italian city of Pistoia, for example, decreed in 1348 that no citizen could go to nearby Pisa or Lucca, nor could people from those cities enter Pistoia; in effect, Pistoia set up a quarantine. Thinking that "bad air" brought the plague, the Pistoian leaders provided for better sanitation, declaring that "butchers and retailers of meat shall not stable horses or allow any mud or dung in the shop or other place where they sell meat." Elsewhere reactions were religious. The archbishop of York in England, for example, tried to prevent the plague from entering his diocese by ordering "that devout processions [be] held every Wednesday and Friday in our cathedral church . . . and in every parish church in our city and diocese."

Some people took more extreme measures. Lamenting their sins—which they believed had

Dance of Death
Figures meant to represent all the "types" in medieval society are depicted in this fresco, painted in 1474 on a wall of a cemetery church in Croatia. It should be read from right to left. Not pictured here, but first in line, is the pope, followed by a cardinal and a bishop. The portion shown here comes next: the king, who holds a scepter; the queen; and a landlord, carrying a small barrel. At the far left is a child. Even farther to the left (but not shown here) come a beggar, a knight, and a shopkeeper. All the figures are flanked by gleeful, dancing skeletons. The message is clear: everyone, even the most exalted, ends up in the grave. *(Alfredo Dagli Orti/Art Resource, NY.)*

brought on the plague—and attempting to placate God, men and women wandered from city to city with whips in their hands. Entering a church, they took off their shirts or blouses, lay down one by one on the church floor, and, according to the chronicler Henry of Hervordia (d. 1370),

> one of them would strike the first with a whip, saying, "May God grant you remission [forgiveness] of all your sins. Arise." And he would get up, and do the same to the second, and all the others in turn did the same. When they were all on their feet, and arranged two by two in procession, two of them in the middle of the column would begin singing a hymn in a high voice, with a sweet melody.

The church did not approve of this practice. Only members of the clergy were supposed to determine acts of penance, but the flagellants—as the people who whipped themselves were called (from the Latin *flagellum*, meaning "whip")—imposed penance on themselves. To Henry, the flagellants were "a race without a head," with neither sense nor a leader.

Yet Henry also thought that "a man would need a heart of stone to watch [the flagellants] without tears." They aroused enormous popular feeling wherever they went. This religious enthusiasm often culminated in violence against the Jews, as rumors circulated that the Jews were responsible for the Black Death. Christians revived old charges that Jews were plotting to "wipe out all the Christians with poison and had poisoned wells and springs everywhere," as one Franciscan friar put it. In Germany, especially, thousands of Jews were slaughtered. Many Jews fled to Poland, where the epidemic affected fewer people and where the authorities welcomed Jews as productive taxpayers. In western and central Europe, however, the persecutions impoverished the Jews.

Preoccupation with death led to the popularity of a theme called the Dance of Death as a subject of art, literature, and performance. It featured a procession of people of every age, sex, and rank mak-

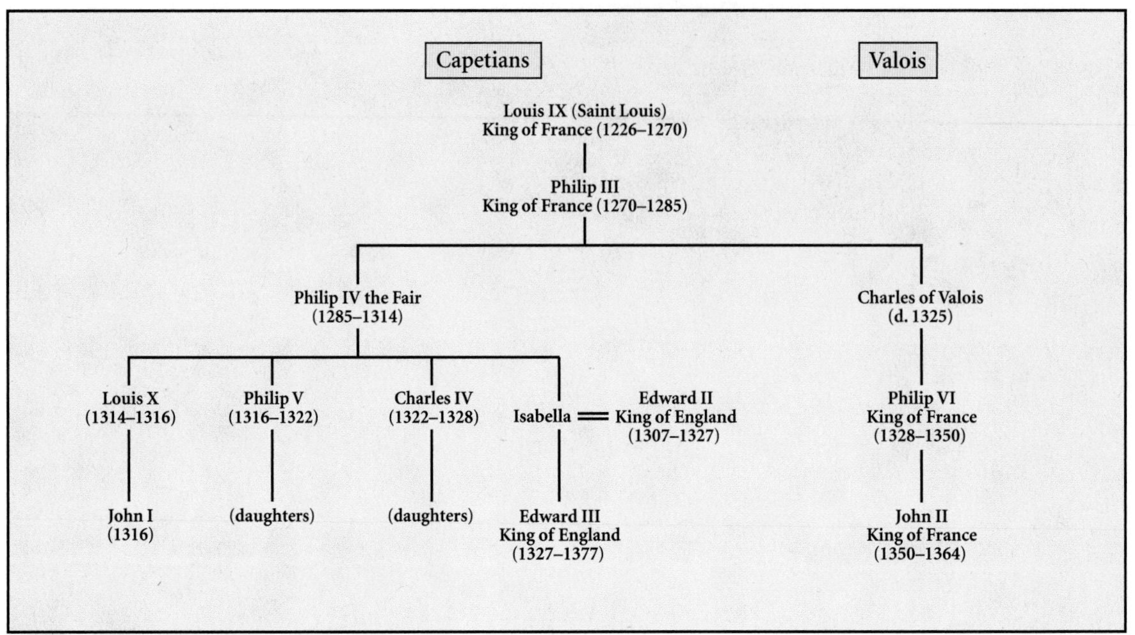

FIGURE 13.1 The Valois Succession
When Capetian King Charles IV died in 1328, his daughter was next in line for the French throne, but prejudice in France against female succession was so strong that the crown went to the Valois branch of the family. Meanwhile English King Edward III, as son of the French princess Isabella, claimed to be the rightful king of France.

ing their way to the grave. In works of art, skeletal figures of Death, whirling about, laughed as they abducted their prey. These were often life-size paintings that ran horizontally for many feet. They were meant to be "mirrors" in which viewers could see themselves. The Dance of Death was also sometimes performed—in a church or at a princely court. Preachers talked about the theme; poets wrote dialogues between Death and his victims. "Thus Death takes us all; that is certain," one poet concluded.

At the same time that it helped inspire this bleak view of the world, the Black Death brought new opportunities for those who survived its murderous path. With a smaller population to feed, less land was needed for farming. Marginal land that had been cultivated was returned to pasture, meadow, or forest. Landlords diversified their products. Wheat had been the favored crop before the plague, but barley—the key ingredient of beer—turned out to be more profitable afterward. Animal products continued to fetch a high price, and some landlords switched from raising crops to raising animals.

These changes in agriculture meant a better standard of living. The peasants and urban workers who survived the plague were able to negotiate better conditions or higher wages from their landlords or employers. With more money to spend, people could afford a better and more varied diet that included beer and meat.

A few years after each attack of the disease came a slight jump in the birthrate. It is unlikely that women became more fertile. Rather, the cause of the increased birthrate was more subtle: with good employment opportunities, couples married at younger ages and with greater frequency than they had previously. For example, before the Black Death, about seventeen couples per year married at Givry, a small town in Burgundy. But once the plague hit, an average of forty-seven couples there wed each year. "After the end of the epidemic," one chronicler wrote, "the men and women who stayed alive did everything to get married."

The Black Death also affected patterns of education. The post-plague generations needed schooling. The pestilential disease spared neither the students nor the professors of the old universities. As the disease ebbed, survivors built new local colleges and universities, partly to train a new generation for the priesthood and partly to satisfy local donors—many of them princes—who, riding on a sea of wealth left behind by the dead, wanted to be known as patrons of education. Thus, in 1348, in the midst of the Black Death, Holy Roman Emperor Charles IV chartered a university at Prague. The king of Poland founded Cracow University, and a Habsburg duke created a university at Vienna. Rather than traveling to Paris or Bologna, young men living east of the Rhine River now tended to study nearer home.

The Hundred Years' War, 1337–1453

Adding to people's miseries during the Black Death were the ravages of war. One of the most brutal was the **Hundred Years' War**, which pitted England against France. Since the Norman conquest of England in 1066, the king of England had held land on the continent. The French kings continually chipped away at it, however, and by the beginning of the fourteenth century England retained only the area around Bordeaux, called Guyenne. In 1337, after a series of challenges and skirmishes, King Philip VI of France (whose dynasty, the Valois, took over when the Capetians had no male heir) declared Guyenne to be his. In turn, King Edward III of England, son of Philip the Fair's daughter, declared himself king of France (Figure 13.1). The Hundred Years' War had begun.

The war had two major phases. In the first, the English gained ground, and a new political entity, the duchy of Burgundy, allied itself with England. This phase culminated in 1415, when the English achieved a great victory at the battle of Agincourt and took over northern France. In the second phase, however, fortunes reversed entirely: the French, after a major victory at the battle of Formigny, ousted the English (Map 13.2).

Joan of Arc How did the French achieve this turnaround? The answer lies partly in the inspiration of a sixteen-year-old peasant girl who presented herself at the court of the dauphin (the man who had been designated as king but had not yet been anointed and crowned) as the heaven-sent savior of France. Inspired by visions in which God told her to lead the war against the English, and calling herself "the Maid" (a virgin), **Joan of Arc** (1412–1431) arrived at court in 1429 wearing armor, riding a horse, and leading a small army. Full of charisma and confidence at a desperate hour, Joan was carefully questioned and examined (to be sure of her virginity) before her message was accepted. She convinced the French that she had been sent by God when she fought courageously (and was wounded) in the successful battle of Orléans. With Joan at his side, the dauphin traveled deep into enemy territory to be anointed and crowned as King Charles VII at the cathedral in Reims, following the tradition of French monarchs.

Portrait of Charles VII

The French artist who created this portrait of King Charles VII, Jean Fouquet (d. 1481), studied in Italy and knew about the new, naturalistic styles that were coming into vogue there (see the discussion of Renaissance art beginning on page 430). His portrait of Charles shows a broad-shouldered and serious man. The only hints of the monarch's royal status are his hat of blue and gold (reminiscent of the French crown) and the words that frame him above and below: "The Very Victorious King of France, Charles, Seventh of the Name." *(Louvre, Paris, France/Giraudon/The Bridgeman Art Library International.)*

The victory at Orléans and the anointing of Charles began the French about-face, but Joan herself suffered greatly. A promise to take Paris proved empty, and she was captured and turned over to the English. Tried as a witch, she was burned at the stake in 1431. (See "Contrasting Views," page 418.)

The Hundred Years' War as a World War The Hundred Years' War, although directly fought by England and France, drew people from other states of Europe into its vortex. Both the English and the French hired mercenaries from Germany, Switzerland, and the Netherlands; the best crossbowmen came from Genoa. Since the economies of England and Flanders (for Flanders, see Map 13.2) were interdependent, with England

---

Hundred Years' War: The long war between England and France, 1337–1453 (actually 116 years); it produced numerous social upheavals yet left both states more powerful than before.

Joan of Arc: A peasant girl (1412–1431) whose conviction that God had sent her to save France in fact helped France win the Hundred Years' War.

CONTRASTING VIEWS

Joan of Arc: Who Was "the Maid"?

The figure of Joan of Arc gives shape to the confused events and personalities of the Hundred Years' War. But who was this young woman? Joan herself emphasized her visions and divine calling (Document 1). The royal court was unsure whether to consider her a fraud (or, worse, the devil's tool) or a gift from heaven (Document 2). A neighbor of the young Joan recalled her as an ordinary young country girl (Document 3).

1. Joan the Visionary

Joan first referred to her visions at length after her capture by her enemies, who were eager to prove that she was inspired by the devil. The light and voices that she testified to echoed the experiences of many medieval visionaries. But we do not have Joan's exact words; her account was written up by her examiners, who composed it in Latin even though Joan spoke in French.

She confessed that when she was aged thirteen, she had a voice from God to help her to guide herself. And the first time she was greatly afraid. And this voice came around noon, in summer, in the garden of her father, and Joan had not fasted on the preceding day. She heard the voice on the right-hand side, towards the church, and she rarely heard it without a light. This light came from the same side that she heard the voice, but generally there was a great light there. And when Joan came to France [Lorraine, where Joan was raised, was not considered part of France], she often heard this voice. . . .

She said, in addition, that if she was in a wood, she clearly heard the voices coming to her. She also said that it seemed to her that it was a worthy voice and she believed that this voice had been sent from God, and that, after she had heard this voice three times, she knew that this was the voice of an angel. She said also that this voice had always protected her well and that she understood this voice clearly.

Asked about the instruction that this voice gave to her for the salvation of her soul, she said that it taught her to conduct herself well, to go to church often, and that it was necessary that she should travel to France. Joan added that her interrogator would not learn from her, on this occasion, in what form that voice had appeared to her. . . . She said moreover that the voice had told her that she, Joan, should go to find Robert de Baudricourt in the town of Vaucouleurs [a tiny holdout in eastern France that was not under English control], of which he was captain, and that he would provide her with men to travel with her. Joan then replied that she was a poor girl who did not know how to ride on horseback or to lead in war. [But she obeyed the voice, met with Robert de Baudricourt, and in the end got the escort that she needed to go to the court of the dauphin, the future Charles VII.]

Source: *Joan of Arc: La Pucelle*, trans. and annotated by Craig Taylor (Manchester: Manchester University Press, 2006), 141–42.

2. Messenger of God?

When Joan appeared at the court of the dauphin, her reputation as the messenger of God had preceded her. The French court received her with a mixture of wonder, curiosity, and skepticism. The dauphin's counselors debated about whether Joan should be taken seriously, and the dauphin referred the case to a panel of theologians to determine whether Joan's mission was of divine origin. The following account of Joan's first visit to the dauphin was given by Simon Charles, president of the royal Chamber of Accounts, at an investigation begun in 1455 to nullify Joan's sentence of 1429.

Questioned first on what he could depose and testify . . . [Simon Charles] said and declared upon oath that he only knew what follows: . . . that when Joan arrived at the town of Chinon, the council discussed whether the King should hear her or not. She was first asked why she had

exporting the wool that Flemish workers turned into cloth, it was inevitable that Flanders would be drawn into the conflict. In fact, once the war broke out, Flemish townsmen allied with England against their count, who supported the French king.

The duchy of Burgundy became involved in the war when the marriage of the heiress to Flanders and the duke of Burgundy in 1369 created a powerful new state. Calculating shrewdly which side—England or France—to support and cannily entering the fray when it suited them, the dukes of Burgundy created a glittering court, a center of art and culture. Had Burgundy maintained its alliance with England, the map of Europe would be entirely different today. But, sensing France's new strength, the duke of Burgundy broke off with England in 1435. The duchy continued to prosper until its expansionist policies led to the formation of a coalition against it. The last duke, Charles the Bold, died fighting in 1477. His daughter, his only heir, tried to save Burgundy by marrying the Holy Roman Emperor, but the move was to little avail. The duchy broke up, with France absorbing its western bits.

come and what she wanted. Although she did not wish to say anything except to the King, she was nevertheless forced on behalf of the King to reveal the purpose of her mission. She said that she had two commands from the King of Heaven, that is to say one to raise the siege of Orléans, and the other to conduct the King to Reims for his coronation and consecration. Having heard this, some among the King's councilors said that the King should not have any faith in this Joan, and the others said that, since she declared that she had been sent by God and that she had certain things to say to the King, the King should at least hear her. But the King decided that she should first be examined by the clerks and churchmen, which was done.

Source: *Joan of Arc: La Pucelle*, trans. and annotated by Craig Taylor (Manchester: Manchester University Press, 2006), 317–18.

3. Normal Girl?

At the same trial, various inhabitants in and near Domremy, Joan's village, recalled her as a normal young girl. The following account was given by Jean Morel, a laborer from a town near Joan's. He knew her as Jeannette.

He declared upon oath that the Jeannette in question was born at Domremy and was baptized at the parish church of Saint-Rémy in that place. Her father was named Jacques d'Arc, her mother Isabelle, both laborers living together at Domremy as long as they lived. They were good and faithful Catholics, good laborers, of good reputation, and of honest behavior. . . .

He declared upon oath that from her earliest childhood, Jeannette was well brought up in the faith as was appropriate, and instructed in good morals, as far as he knew, so that almost everyone in the village of Domremy loved her. Just like the other young girls she knew the *Credo*, the *Pater Noster*, and the *Ave Maria* [all three basic texts of Christian belief].

He declared that Jeannette was honest in her behavior, just as any similar girl is, because her parents were not very rich. In her childhood, and right up to her departure from her family home, she followed the plow and sometimes minded the animals in the fields; she did the work of a woman, spinning and making other things.

He declared upon oath that, as he saw, this Jeannette often went to church willingly to the extent that sometimes she was mocked by the other young people. . . .

He declared upon oath that on the subject of the tree called "of the Ladies," he once heard it said that women or supernatural persons—they were called fairies—came long ago to dance under that tree. But, so it is said, since a reading of the gospel of St. John, they did not come there any more. He also declared that in the present day . . . the young girls and lads of Domremy went under this tree to dance [on a particular Sunday in Lent], and sometimes also in the spring and summer on feast days; sometimes they ate at that place. On their return, they went to the spring of Thorns, strolling and singing, and they drank from the water of this spring, and all around they had fun gathering flowers. He also declared that Joan the Pucelle ["the Maid"] went there sometimes with the other girls and did as they did; he never heard it said that she went alone to the tree or to the spring, which is nearer to the village than the tree, for any other reason than to walk about and to play just like the other young girls.

Source: *Joan of Arc: La Pucelle*, trans. and annotated by Craig Taylor (Manchester: Manchester University Press, 2006), 267–68.

Questions to Consider

1. **Given the norms of the time, in what ways was Joan ordinary?**
2. **What do you suppose was the royal court's reaction to the testimony of Simon Charles? And to the testimony of Jean Morel?**

From Chivalry to Modern Warfare When he first started to write about the Hundred Years' War, the chronicler Jean Froissart (d. c. 1405) considered it a chivalric adventure—chivalry being the medieval code of refinement, fair play, and piety followed by knights. He expected it to display the gallantry and bravery of the medieval nobility. He said that he was writing his account

> in order that the honorable enterprises, noble adventure, and deeds of arms which took place during the wars waged by France and England should be fittingly related and preserved for posterity, so that brave men should be inspired thereby to follow such examples.

Froissart described knights like the Englishman Walter de Manny, who was so eager to show off his prowess that he privately gathered a group of followers and attacked a French town in order to fulfill a vow made "in the hearing of ladies and lords that, 'If war breaks out, . . . I'll be the first to arm myself and capture a castle or town in the kingdom of France.'"

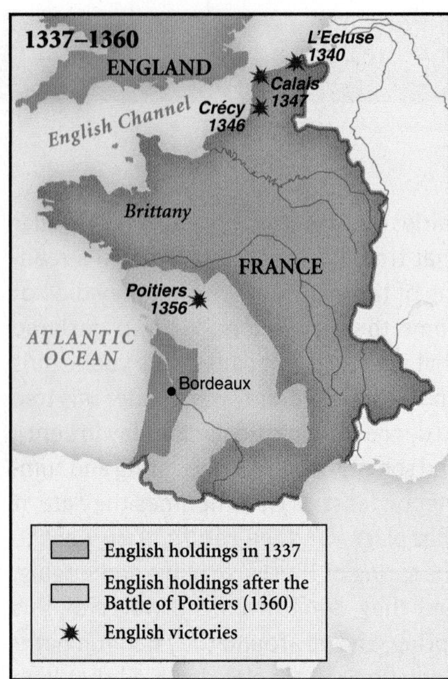

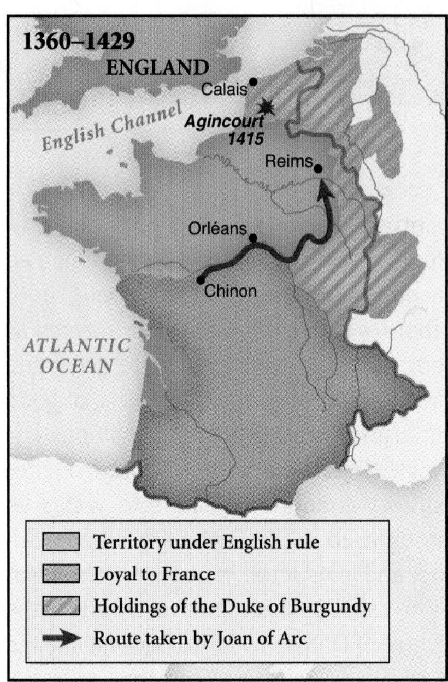

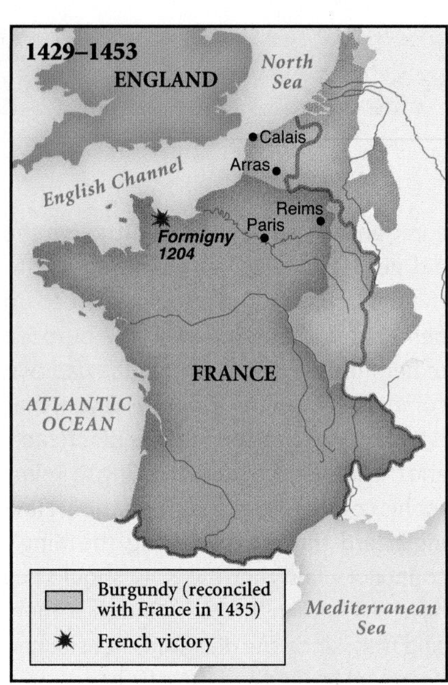

MAP 13.2 The Hundred Years' War, 1337–1453
During the Hundred Years' War, English kings—aided by the new state of Burgundy—contested the French monarchy for the domination of France. For many decades, the English seemed to be winning, but the French monarchy prevailed in the end.

But even Froissart could not help but notice that most of the men who went to battle were not wealthy knights on a lark like Walter de Manny. Nor were they ordinary foot soldiers, who had always made up a large portion of all medieval armies. The soldiers of the Hundred Years' War were primarily mercenaries: men who fought for pay and plunder, heedless of the king for whom they were supposed to be fighting. During lulls in the war, these so-called Free Companies lived off the French countryside, terrorizing the peasants and exacting "protection" money. Froissart wrote of "men-at-arms and irregulars from various countries, who subdued and plundered the whole region between the Seine and the Loire. . . . They roamed the country in troops of twenty, thirty, or forty, and they met no one capable of putting up a resistance to them."

The ideal chivalric knight fought on horseback with other armed horsemen. But in the Hundred Years' War, foot soldiers and archers were far more important than swordsmen. The French tended to use crossbows, whose heavy, deadly arrows were released by a mechanism that even a townsman could master. (See the illustration on page 421.) The English employed longbows, which could shoot five arrows for every one launched on the crossbow. Large groups of English archers could wreak havoc with a volley of arrows. Meanwhile, gunpowder was slowly being introduced and cannons forged. Handguns were beginning to be used, their effect about equal to that of crossbows.

By the end of the war, chivalry was only a dream—though one that continued to inspire soldiers even up to the First World War. Heavy artillery and foot soldiers, tightly massed together in formations of many thousands of men, were the face of the new military. Moreover, the army was becoming more professional and centralized. In the 1440s, the French king created a permanent army of mounted soldiers. He paid them a wage and subjected them to regular inspection. Private armies—such as the one Walter de Manny recruited for his own ambitions—were prohibited.

The War's Progeny: Uprisings in Flanders, the Jacquerie, and Wat Tyler's Rebellion

The outbreak of the Hundred Years' War led to revolts in Ghent and other great textile centers in Flanders. Dependent on England for the raw wool they processed, Flemish cities could not afford to have their count, Louis I, side with the French. The cities revolted and succeeded for a time in ousting the count, who fled to France in 1339. But discord among the cities and within each town allowed Louis I's successor, count Louis II, to return in 1348. Revolts continued to flare up thereafter, but Louis allowed a measure of self-government to the towns, maintained some distance from French influence, and managed on the whole to keep the peace.

In France, the Parisians chafed against the high taxes they were forced to pay to finance the war.

Crossbows at a Siege
This manuscript illumination from the fifteenth century shows city defenders using hand bows and arrows to fight against armed attackers. One of the besiegers uses a hand bow while another shoots a crossbow. Two of the attackers are in the process of spanning their crossbows, using a device to draw back the string. The heavy bolts (as crossbow arrows were called) were deadly, but crossbows were not ideal weapons because spanning took up precious time. *(© The British Library/HIP/The Image Works.)*

When the English captured the French king John at the battle of Poitiers in 1358, Étienne Marcel, provost of the Paris merchants, and other disillusioned members of the estates of France (the representatives of the clergy, nobility, and commons) met in Paris to discuss political reform, the incompetence of the French army, and taxes. Under Marcel's leadership, a crowd of Parisians killed some nobles and for a short while took control of the city. But troops soon blockaded Paris and cut off its food supply. Later that year, Marcel was assassinated and the Parisian revolt came to an end.

Also in that year, peasants weary of the Free Companies (who were ravaging the countryside) and disgusted by the military incompetence of the nobility rose up in protest. The French nobility called the peasant rebellion the **Jacquerie**, probably taken from a derisive name for male peasants: Jacques Bonhomme ("Jack Goodfellow"). Froissart was scandalized by the peasants' behavior:

> They banded together and went off . . . unarmed except for pikes and knives, to the house of a knight who lived near by. They broke in and killed the knight with his lady and his children, big and small, and set fire to the house. Next they went to another castle and did much worse.

If the peasants were in fact guilty of these atrocities, the nobles soon gave as good as they got. The Jacquerie was put down with exceptional brutality. Froissart described the moment with relish: "They [the nobles] began to kill those evil men [the peasants] and to cut them to pieces without mercy."

Similar revolts took place in England. The movement known as Wat Tyler's Rebellion, for example, started as an uprising in much of southern and central England when royal agents tried to collect poll taxes (a tax on each household) to finance the Hundred Years' War. Refusing to pay and refusing

---

Jacquerie (zhah kuh ree): The 1358 uprising of French peasants against the nobles amid the Hundred Years' War; it was brutally put down.

DOCUMENT

Wat Tyler's Rebellion (1381)

An anonymous chronicler wrote about Wat Tyler's Rebellion shortly after it took place in 1381. The author was hostile to the rebels yet understood their motives quite well. After converging on London from various parts of southern England, the rebels, led by men like Wat Tyler, demanded that the king end the unjust taxes collected by local officials. The fourteen-year-old King Richard II (r. 1377–1399) eventually met with them and seemed to give in to their demands, but another meeting the next day led to Tyler's death and the dispersal of the demonstrators. The excerpt here chronicles the very beginning of the movement, before the march on London.

Because in the year 1380 the subsidies [taxes] were over lightly granted at the Parliament of Northampton and because it seemed to divers lords and to the commons that the said subsidies were not honestly levied, but commonly exacted from the poor and not from the rich, to the great profit and advantage of the tax-collectors, and to the deception of the king and the commons, the Council of the King ordained certain commissions to make inquiry in every township how the tax had been levied. Among these commissions, one for Essex was sent to one Thomas Bampton [one of the tax collectors]. . . . He had summoned before him the townships of a neighboring hundred, and wished to have from them new contributions. . . .

Among these townships was Fobbing, whose people made answer that they would not pay a penny more, because they already had a receipt from himself for the said subsidy. On which the said Thomas threatened them angrily. . . . And for fear of his malice the folks of Fobbing took counsel with the folks of Corringham, and the folks of these two places . . . sent messages to the men of Stanford. . . . Then the people of these three townships came together to the number of a hundred or more, and with one assent went to the said Thomas Bampton, and roundly gave him answer that they would have no traffic with him, nor give him a penny. . . .

And afterwards the said commons assembled together . . . to the number of some 50,000, and they went to the manors and townships of those who would not rise with them, and cast their houses to the ground or set fire to them. At this time they caught three clerks of Thomas Bampton, and cut off their heads, and carried the heads about with them for several days stuck on poles as an example to others. For it was their purpose to slay all lawyers, and all jurors, and all the servants of the king whom they could find.

Source: Charles Oman, *The Great Revolt of 1381* (Oxford: Clarendon Press, 1906), 186–88.

Question to Consider

- **What did the author consider to be the main causes of the rebellion?**

to be arrested, the commons—peasants and small householders—rose up in rebellion in 1381. They massed in various groups, vowing "to slay all lawyers, and all jurors, and all the servants of the King whom they could find," as one chronicler put it. Marching to London to see the king, whom they professed to support, they began to make a more radical demand: an end to serfdom. Although the rebellion was put down and its leaders executed, the death knell of serfdom in England had been sounded, as peasants returned home to bargain with their lords for better terms. (See Document, "Wat Tyler's Rebellion," above.)

The Ottoman Conquest of Constantinople, 1453

The end of the Hundred Years' War coincided with an event that was even more decisive for all of Europe: the conquest of Constantinople by the Ottoman Turks. The Ottomans, who were converts to Islam, were one of several tribal confederations in central Asia. Starting as a small enclave between the Mongol Empire and Byzantium, and taking their name from a potent early leader, Osman I (r. 1280–1324), the Ottomans began to expand in the fourteenth century in a quest to wage holy war against infidels, or unbelievers.

During the next two centuries, the Ottomans took over the Balkans and Anatolia by both negotiations and arms (Map 13.3). Under Murad I (r. 1360–1389), they reduced the Byzantine Empire to the city of Constantinople and treated it as a vassal state. At the Maritsa River in 1364, Murad defeated a joint Hungarian-Serbian army, setting off a wave of crusading fervor in Europe that led (in the end) to only a few unsuccessful expeditions. In 1389, Murad's forces won the battle of Kosovo—still invoked in Serbia today as a great struggle between Christians and Muslims, even though a number of Serbian princes fought on the Ottoman side.

After a lull, when the Ottoman thrust was stopped, Sultan Mehmed I (r. 1410–1421) resumed the conquests; eventually, his grandson **Mehmed II** (r. 1451–1481) determined to take the city of Constantinople itself. Preparations began about a year in advance, when Mehmed II built an enormous fortress near the capital and fitted it out with a large number of soldiers and several brass cannons. In March 1453, he launched the attack. Perhaps eighty thousand men confronted some three thousand defenders (the entire population of Constantinople was no more than fifty thousand) and a fleet from Genoa. The city held out until the end of May, when Mehmed's forces attacked by both land and sea. The decisive moment came when the sultan's cannons breached the city's land walls. Mehmed's troops entered the city and plundered it thoroughly, killing the emperor and displaying his head in triumph.

The conquest of Constantinople marked the end of the Byzantine Empire. But that was not the way Mehmed saw the matter. He conquered Constantinople in part to be a successor to the Roman emperors — a Muslim successor, to be sure. He turned Hagia Sophia, the great church built by the emperor Justinian in 538, into a mosque, as he did with most of the other Byzantine churches. He retained the city's name, the City of Constantine — Qustantiniyya in Turkish — though it was popularly referred to as Istanbul, meaning, simply, "the city."

Like the French and English kings after the Hundred Years' War, the Ottoman sultans were centralizing monarchs who guaranteed law and order. The core of their army consisted of European Christian boys, who were requisitioned as tribute every five years. Trained in arms and converted to Islam, these young fighters made up the Janissaries — a highly disciplined military force also used to supervise local administrators throughout formerly Byzantine regions. Building a system of roads that crisscrossed their empire, the sultans made long-distance trade easy and profitable.

Once Constantinople was his, Mehmed embarked on an ambitious program of expansion and conquest. He brought all of Serbia under Ottoman control in 1458; he crossed the Aegean Sea and took over Athens and the Peloponnese by 1460; six years later, he gained Bosnia. By 1500, the Ottoman Empire was a new and powerful state bridging Europe and the Middle East.

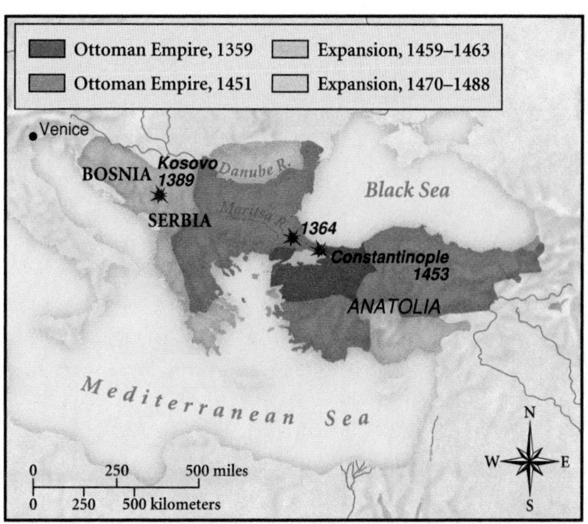

MAP 13.3 Ottoman Expansion in the Fourteenth and Fifteenth Centuries

The Balkans were the major theater of expansion for the Ottoman Empire. The Byzantine Empire was reduced to the city of Constantinople and surrounded by the Ottomans before its final fall in 1453.

The Great Schism, 1378–1417

Even as war and disease threatened their material and physical well-being, a crisis in the church, precipitated by a scandal in the papacy, tore at Europeans' spiritual life. The move of the papacy from Rome to Avignon in 1309 had caused an outcry, especially among Italians, distraught by the election of French popes and anxious to see the papacy return to Rome. Some critics, such as Marsilius of Padua, became disillusioned with the institution of the papacy itself. Marsilius, a physician and lawyer by training, argued in *The Defender of the Peace* (1324) that the source of all power lay with the people: "the law-making power or the first and real effective source of law is the people or the body of citizens or the prevailing part of the people according to its election or its will expressed in general convention by vote." Applied to the papacy, Marsilius's argument meant that Christians themselves formed the church and that the pope should be elected by a general council representing all Christians.

William of Ockham (c. 1285–1349), an English Franciscan who was one of the most eminent theologians of his age, was an even more thoroughgoing critic of the papacy. He believed that church power derived from the congregation of the faithful, both laity and clergy, not from the pope or a church council. Rejecting the confident synthesis of Christian doctrine and Aristotelian philosophy by Thomas Aquinas, Ockham believed that universal concepts had no reality in nature but instead existed only as mere representations, names in the mind — a philosophy that came to be called nominalism. Perceiving and analyzing such concepts as "man" or "papal infallibility" offered no assurance that the concepts expressed truth. Observation and human reason

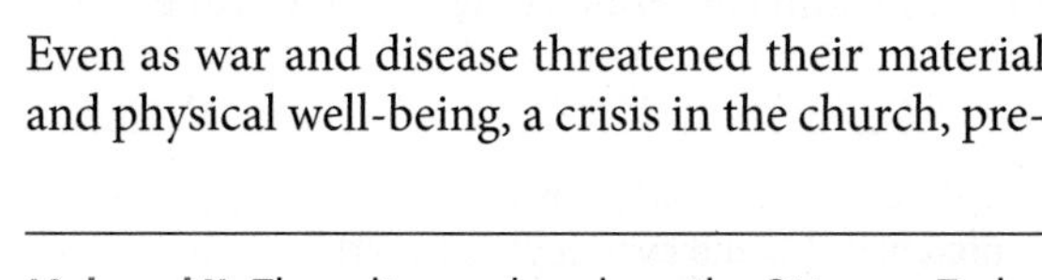
Mehmed II: The sultan under whom the Ottoman Turks conquered Constantinople in 1453.

Martin V at the Council of Constance

The events at the Council of Constance (1414–1418) were important both locally and across Europe. That is why a citizen of Constance, Ulrich von Richental, wrote a chronicle of the council. It was full of details about every event and richly illustrated. On this page, the bareheaded and newly elected Oddo di Colonna is led to the altar by two cardinals to gain the papal tiara as Martin V. *(akg-images/Interfoto/Bildarchiv Hansmann.)*

were limited tools with which to understand the universe and to know God. The principle that simple explanations were superior to complex ones became known as Ockham's razor (to suggest the idea of shaving away unnecessary hypotheses). Imprisoned by Pope John XXII for heresy in 1328, Ockham escaped within the year and found refuge with Emperor Louis of Bavaria.

Stung by his critics, Pope Gregory XI (r. 1370–1378) left Avignon to return to Rome in 1377. The scandal of the Avignon papacy seemed to be over. But Rome itself presented a problem. Glad to have the papacy back, the Romans were determined never to lose it again. When the cardinals — many of whom came from Spain, Italy, and France — met to elect Gregory's successor, the *popolo*, the communal faction who controlled the city, demanded that they choose a Roman: "A Roman! A Roman! A Roman or at least an Italian! Or else we'll kill them all." Expecting to gain an important place in papal government, the cardinals chose an Italian, who took the name Urban VI. But Urban had no intention of kowtowing to the cardinals: he exalted the power of the pope and began to reduce the cardinals' wealth and privileges. The cardinals from France decided that they had made a big mistake. Many left Rome for a meeting at Anagni, where they claimed that Urban's election had been irregular and called on him to resign. When he refused, they elected a Frenchman as pope; he took the name Clement VII and soon moved his papal court to Avignon, but not before he and Urban had excommunicated each other. The **Great Schism** (1378–1417), which split the loyalties of all of Europe, had begun.

The king of France supported Clement; the king of England favored Urban. Some European states — Burgundy, Scotland, and Castile, for example— lined up on the side of France. Others — the Holy Roman Empire, Poland, and Hungary — supported Urban. Portugal switched sides four times, depending on which alliance offered it the most advantages. Each pope declared that those who followed the other were to be deprived of the rights of church membership; in effect, everyone in Europe was excommunicated by one pope or the other.

The Conciliar Movement

Contrary to the ideas of Marsilius, church law said that only a pope could summon a general council of the church — a sort of parliament of high churchmen. But given the state of confusion in Christendom, many intellectuals argued that the crisis justified calling a general council to represent the body of the faithful, even against the wishes of an unwilling pope — or popes. They spearheaded the conciliar movement — a movement to have the cardinals or the emperor call a council.

In 1408, long after Urban and Clement had passed away and new popes had followed, the conciliar movement succeeded when cardinals from both sides met and declared their resolve "to pursue the union of the Church . . . by way of abdication of both papal contenders." With support from both England and France, the cardinals called for a

---

Great Schism: The papal dispute of 1378–1417 when the church had two and even (between 1409 and 1417) three popes. The Great Schism was ended by the Council of Constance.

council to be held at Pisa in 1409. Both popes refused to attend, and the council deposed them, electing a new pope.

But the "deposed" popes refused to budge, even though most of the European powers abandoned them. There were now three popes. The successor of the newest one, John XXIII, turned to the emperor to arrange for another council.

The Council of Constance (1414–1418) met to resolve the papal crisis as well as to institute church reforms. The delegates deposed John XXIII and accepted the resignation of the pope at Rome. After long negotiations with rulers still supporting the Avignon pope, all allegiance to him was withdrawn and he was deposed. The council then elected Martin V, who was recognized as pope by every important ruler of Europe. Finally, the Great Schism had come to an end.

Book of Hours
This illustration for June in a Book of Hours made for the duke of Berry was meant for the contemplation of a nobleman. In the background is a fairy-tale depiction of the duke's palace and the tower of a Gothic church, while in the foreground graceful women rake the hay and well-muscled men swing their scythes. *(Réunion des Musées Nationaux, Art Resource, NY.)*

New Forms of Piety

The Great Schism, no doubt abetted by the miseries of the plague and the distresses of war, caused enormous anxiety among ordinary Christians. Worried about the salvation of their souls now that the church was fractured by multiple popes, pious men and women eagerly sought new forms of religious solace. The church offered the plenary indulgence — full forgiveness of sins, which had been originally offered to crusaders who died while fighting for the cause — to those who made a pilgrimage to Rome and other designated holy places during declared Holy Years. People could wipe away their sins through confession and contrition, but they retained some guilt that they could remove only through good deeds or in purgatory. The idea of purgatory — the place where sins were fully purged — took precise form at this time, and with it **indulgences** became popular. These remissions of sin were offered for good works to reduce the time in purgatory. Thus, for example, the duchess of Brittany was granted a hundred days off of her purgatorial punishments when she allowed the Feast of Corpus Christi to be preached in her chapel. Lesser folk might obtain indulgences in more modest ways.

Both clergy and laity became more interested than ever in the education of young people as a way to deepen their faith and spiritual life. The Brethren of the Common Life — laypeople, mainly in the Low Countries (the region comprising today's Belgium, Luxembourg, and the Netherlands) who devoted themselves to pious works — set up a model school at Deventer. In Italy, humanists (see page 428) emphasized primary school education. Priests were expected to teach the faithful the basics of the Christian religion.

Home was equally a place for devotion. Portable images of Mary, the mother of God, and of the life and passion of Christ proliferated. They were meant

---

indulgence: A step beyond confession and penance, an indulgence (normally granted by popes or bishops) lifted the temporal punishment still necessary for a sin already forgiven. Normally, that punishment was said to take place in purgatory. But it could be remitted through good works (including prayers and contributing money to worthy causes).

to be contemplated by ordinary Christians at convenient moments throughout the day. People purchased or commissioned copies of Books of Hours, which contained prayers to be said on the appropriate day at the hours of the monastic office. Books of Hours included calendars, sometimes splendidly illustrated with depictions of the seasons and labors of the year. (See the illustration on page 425.) Other illustrations reminded their users of the life and suffering of Christ.

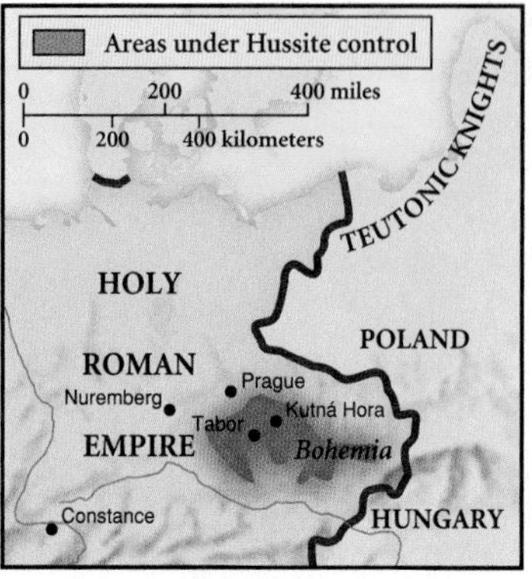

The Hussite Revolution, 1415–1436

On the streets of towns, priests marched in dignified processions, carrying the sanctified bread of the Mass—the very body of Christ—in tall and splendid monstrances that trumpeted the importance and dignity of the Eucharistic wafer. (See the illustration below.) Like images of the Lord's life and crucifixion, the monstrance emphasized Christ's body. Christ's blood was perhaps even more important. It was thought of as "wonderful blood," the blood that brought man's redemption. Thus, the image of a bleeding, crucified Christ was repeated over and over in depictions of the day. Viewers were meant to think about Christ's pain and feel it themselves, mentally participating in his death on the cross. Flagellants, as we have seen, literally drew their own blood.

New Heresies: The Lollards and the Hussites

Religious anxieties, intellectual dissent, and social unrest combined to create new heretical movements in England and Bohemia. In England were the Lollards, a term that was derogatory in the hands of their opponents and yet a proud title when used by the Lollards themselves. The Lollards were initially inspired by the Oxford scholar John Wycliffe (c. 1330–1384), who, like Marsilius of Padua and William of Ockham in an earlier generation, came to believe that the true church was the community of believers rather than the clerical hierarchy. Wycliffe criticized monasticism, excommunication, and the Mass. He emphasized Bible reading in the vernacular, arguing that true believers, not corrupt priests, formed the church.

The Lollard movement included scholars and members of the gentry (lesser noble) class as well as artisans and other humbler folk. Women were able and enthusiastic participants. Although suffering widespread hostility and persecution into the sixteenth century, the Lollards were extremely active, setting up schools for children (girls as well as boys), translating the Bible into English, preaching numerous sermons, and inspiring new recruits, clerical as well as lay.

On the other side of Europe were the Bohemian Hussites—named after one of their leaders,

Monstrance

Elaborate vessels such as the one held by angels in this woodcut became popular church furnishings in the fifteenth century. The monstrance, a term that comes from a Latin word meaning "to show," displayed the consecrated bread of the Eucharist to the laity in fitting splendor, as if it were a relic. *(© The Trustees of the British Museum/Art Resource, NY.)*

Jan Hus (1372?–1415), an admirer of Wycliffe. Their central demand—that the faithful receive not just the bread (the body) but also the wine (the blood) at Mass—brought together several passionately held desires and beliefs. The blood of Christ was particularly important to the devout, and the Hussite call to allow the laity to drink the wine from the chalice reflected this focus on the blood's redemptive power. Furthermore, the call for communion with *both* bread and wine signified a desire for equality. Bohemia was an exceptionally divided country, with an urban German-speaking elite, including merchants, artisans, bishops, and scholars, and a Czech-speaking nobility and peasantry that was beginning to seek better opportunities. (Hus himself was a Czech of peasant stock who became a professor at the University of Prague.) When priests celebrated Mass, they had the privilege of drinking the wine. The Hussites, who were largely Czech laity, wanted the same privilege and, with it, recognition of their dignity and worth.

The Bohemian nobility protected Hus after the church condemned him as a heretic, but the Holy Roman Emperor Sigismund lured him to the Council of Constance "to justify himself before all men." Though promised safe conduct, Hus was arrested when he arrived at the council. When he refused to recant his views, the church leaders burned him at the stake.

Hus's death caused an uproar, and his movement became a full-scale national revolt of Czechs against Germans. Sigismund called crusades against the Hussites, but all of his expeditions were soundly defeated. Radical groups of Hussites organized several new communities in southern Bohemia at Mount Tabor, named after the New Testament spot where the Transfiguration of Christ was thought to have taken place (Matt. 17:1–8). Here the radicals attempted to live according to the example of the first apostles. They recognized no lord, gave women some political rights, and created a simple liturgy that was carried out in the Czech language. Negotiations with Sigismund and his successor led to the Hussites' incorporation into the Bohemian political system by 1450. Though the Hussites were largely marginalized, they had won the right to receive communion in "both kinds" (wine and bread) and they had made Bohemia intensely aware of its Czech, rather than German, identity.

REVIEW QUESTION **What crises did Europeans confront in the fourteenth and fifteenth centuries, and how did they handle them?**

The Renaissance: New Forms of Thought and Expression

Some Europeans confronted the crises they faced by creating the culture of the Renaissance (French for "rebirth"). The period associated with the Renaissance, about 1350 to 1600, revived elements of the classical past—the Greek philosophers before Aristotle, Hellenistic artists, and Roman rhetoricians. (See "Terms of History," page 428.) Disillusioned with present institutions, many people looked back to the ancient world; in Greece and Rome they found models of thought, language, power, prestige, and the arts that they could apply to their own circumstances. Humanists modeled their writing on the Latin of Cicero, architects embraced ancient notions of public space, artists adopted classical forms, and musicians used classical texts. In reality, Renaissance writers and artists built much of their work on medieval precedents, but they rarely acknowledged this fact. They found great satisfaction in believing that they were resuscitating the glories of the ancient world—and that everything between them and the classical past was a contemptible "Middle Age."

Renaissance Humanism

Three of the delegates at the Council of Constance—Cincius Romanus, Poggius Bracciolinus, and Bartholomaeus Politianus—reveal the attitudes of the Renaissance. Although busy with church work, they decided to take time off for a "rescue mission." Cincius described the escapade to one of his Latin teachers back in Italy:

> In Germany there are many monasteries with libraries full of Latin books. This aroused the hope in me that some of the works of Cicero, Varro, Livy, and other great men of learning, which seem to have completely vanished, might come to light, if a careful search were instituted. A few days ago, [we] went by agreement to the town of St. Gall. As soon as we went into the library [of the monastery there], we found *Jason's Argonauticon*, written by C. Valerius Flaccus in verse that is both splendid and dignified and not far removed from poetic majesty. Then we found some discussion in prose of a number of Cicero's orations.

Cicero, Varro, Livy, and Valerius Flaccus were pagan Latin writers. Even though Cincius and his friends were working for Pope John XXIII, they loved the writings of the ancients, whose Latin was, in their

TERMS OF HISTORY

Renaissance

The word *renaissance* was first used in the sixteenth century to refer to a historical moment. At that time it meant the rebirth of classical poetry, prose, and art of that period alone. Only later did historians borrow the word to refer to earlier rebirths. One of the first persons to herald the fifteenth-century Renaissance was the Italian painter and architect Giorgio Vasari (1511–1574) in his *Lives of the Most Excellent Italian Architects, Painters, and Sculptors* (1550). Vasari argued that Greco-Roman art declined after the dissolution of the Roman Empire, to be followed by a long period of barbarity. Only in the past generations had Italian artists begun to restore the perfection of the arts, according to Vasari, a development he called *rinascita*, the Italian for "rebirth." It was the French equivalent—*renaissance*—that stuck.

Referring initially to a rebirth in the arts and literature, the word *renaissance* came to mean a new consciousness of modernity and individuality. Prizing the ancient world, Renaissance humanists were convinced that they lived in a new age that recalled that lost glory. They called the period between their age and the ancient one "the Middle Age." (That's why today we call it the Middle Ages.) They reveled in their human potential and their individuality.

The Renaissance was an important movement in Italy, France, Spain, the Low Countries, and central Europe. The word itself acquired widespread recognition with the 1860 publication of Jakob Burckhardt's *The Civilization of the Renaissance in Italy*. A historian at the University of Basel, Burckhardt considered the Renaissance a watershed in Western civilization. For him, the Renaissance ushered in a spirit of modernity, freeing the individual from the domination of society and creative impulses from the repression of the church; the Renaissance represented the beginning of secular society and the preeminence of individual creative geniuses.

Although very influential, Burckhardt's ideas have also been strongly challenged by many recent scholars. Some point out the various continuities between the Middle Ages and the Renaissance, others argue that the Renaissance was not a secular but a profoundly religious age, and still others see the Renaissance as only the beginning of a long period of transition from the Middle Ages to modernity. The consensus among scholars today is that the Renaissance represents a distinct cultural period lasting from the fourteenth to the sixteenth century, centered on the revival of classical learning. Historians disagree about its significance, but they generally understand it to represent some of the complex changes that characterized the passing from medieval society to modernity.

view, "splendid and dignified," unlike the Latin used in their own time, which they found debased and faulty. They saw themselves as the resuscitators of ancient language, literature, and culture. Cincius continued:

> When we carefully inspected the nearby tower of the church of St. Gall in which countless books were kept like captives and the library neglected and infested with dust, worms, soot, and all the things associated with the destruction of books, we all burst into tears. . . . Truly if this library could speak for itself, it would cry loudly: ". . . Snatch me from this prison. . . ." There were in that monastery an abbot and monks totally devoid of any knowledge of literature. What barbarous hostility to the Latin tongue! What damned dregs of humanity!

The monks were barbarians, in Cincius's view, while he and his companions were heroic raiders swooping in to liberate the captive books. **Humanism** was a literary and linguistic movement—an attempt to revive classical Latin (and later Greek) as well as the values and sensibilities that came with the language. It began among men and women living in the Italian city-states, where many saw parallels between their urban, independent lives and the experiences of the city-states of the ancient world. Humanism was a way to confront the crises—and praise the advances—of the fourteenth through sixteenth centuries. Humanists wrote poetry, history, moral philosophy, and grammar books, all patterned on classical models, especially the writings of Cicero.

That Cincius was employed by the pope yet considered the monks of St. Gall barbarians was no oddity. Most humanists combined sincere Christian piety with a new appreciation of the pagan past. Besides, they needed to work in order to live, and they took employment where they found it. Some humanists worked for the church, others were civil

humanism: A literary and linguistic movement cultivated in particular during the Renaissance (1350–1600) and founded on reviving classical Latin and Greek texts, styles, and values.

Petrarch
About seventy-five years after Petrarch's death, the artist Andrea del Castagno was commissioned to decorate the walls of a villa near Florence with a cycle of nine famous men and women. The three women he illustrated were drawn from the Bible or legend; one of them was Queen Esther. Three of the men were well-known Florentine military heroes. The three remaining men were poets whom Florence claimed as its own: Dante, Boccaccio, and (shown here) Petrarch. The monumentality, seriousness, and dignity of this portrait conveyed the importance of humanists, who in the eyes of contemporaries were equal to the most praiseworthy heroes and heroines. *(Galleria degli Uffizi, Florence, Italy/Giraudon/The Bridgeman Art Library International.)*

servants, and still others were notaries. A few were rich men who had a taste for literary subjects.

The first humanist, most historians agree, was **Francis Petrarch** (1304–1374). He was born in Arezzo, a town about fifty miles southeast of Florence. As a boy, he moved around a lot (his father was exiled from Florence), ending up in the region of Avignon, where he received his earliest schooling and fell in love with classical literature. After a brief flirtation with legal studies at the behest of his father, Petrarch gave up law and devoted himself to writing poetry, both in Italian and in Latin. When writing in Italian, he drew on the traditions of the troubadours, dedicating poems of longing to an unattainable and idealized woman named Laura; who she really was, we do not know. When writing in Latin, Petrarch was much influenced by classical poetry.

On the one hand, a boyhood in Avignon made Petrarch sensitive to the failings of the church: he was the writer who coined the phrase "Babylonian captivity" to liken the Avignon papacy to the Bible's account of the Hebrews' captivity in Babylonia. On the other hand, he took minor religious orders there, which gave him a modest living. Struggling between what he considered a life of dissipation (he fathered two children out of wedlock) and a religious vocation, he resolved the conflict at last in his book *On the Solitary Life*, in which he claimed that the solitude needed for reading the classics was akin to the solitude practiced by those who devoted themselves to God. For Petrarch, humanism was a vocation, a calling.

Less famous, but for that reason perhaps more representative of humanists in general, was Lauro Quirini (1420–1475?), the man who (as we saw at the start of this chapter) wrote disparagingly about

---

Francis Petrarch: An Italian poet (1304–1374) who revived the styles of classical authors; he is considered the first Renaissance humanist.

the Turks as barbarians. Educated at the University of Padua, Quirini eventually got a law degree there. He wrote numerous letters and essays, corresponding with other humanists on topics such as the nature of the state and the character of true nobility. He spent the last half of his life in Crete, where he traded various commodities—alum, cloth, wine, Greek books. Believing that the Ottomans had destroyed the libraries of Constantinople, he wrote to Pope Nicholas V: "The language and literature of the Greeks, invented, augmented, and perfected over so long a period with such labor and industry, will certainly perish." But the fact that he himself participated in the lively trade of Greek books proves his prediction wrong.

If Quirini represents the ordinary humanist, Giovanni Pico della Mirandola (1463–1494) was perhaps the most flamboyant. Born near Ferrara of a noble family, Pico received a humanist education at home before going on to Bologna to study law and to Padua to study philosophy. Soon he was picking up Hebrew, Aramaic, and Arabic. A convinced eclectic (one who selects the best from various doctrines), he thought that Jewish mystical writings supported Christian scriptures, and in 1486 he proposed that he publicly defend at Rome nine hundred theses drawn from diverse sources. The church found some of the theses heretical, however, and banned the whole affair. But Pico's *Oration on the Dignity of Man*, which he intended to deliver before his defense, summed up the humanist view: the creative individual, armed only with his (or her) "desires and judgment," could choose to become a boor or an angel. Humanity's potential was unlimited.

Christine de Pisan (c. 1365–c. 1430) exemplifies a humanist who chose to fashion herself into a writer and courtier. Born in Venice and educated in France, Christine was married and then soon widowed. Forced to support herself, her mother, and her three young children, she began to write poems inspired by classical models, depending on patrons to admire her work and pay her to write more. Many members of the upper nobility supported her, including Duke Philip the Bold of Burgundy, Queen Isabelle of Bavaria, and the English earl of Salisbury. But this cast of characters did not mean she sided with the English during the Hundred Years' War. On the contrary, she lamented the violence on all sides, and Joan of Arc's early victories inspired her to write a hymn to the Maid:

> We've never heard
> About a marvel quite so great,
> For all the heroes who have lived
> In history can't measure up
> In bravery against the Maid.

The Arts

The lure of the classical past was as strong in the visual and performing arts as in literature—and for many of the same reasons. Architects and artists admired ancient Athens and Rome, but they also

The Renaissance Facade at Santa Maria Novella

When Italians wished to transform their churches into the Renaissance style, they did not tear them down; they gave them a new facade. At Santa Maria Novella in Florence, the architect Leon Battista Alberti designed a facade that was inspired by classical models—hence the round-arched entranceway and columns. At the same time he paid tribute to the original Gothic church by including a round window. *(Scala/Art Resource, NY.)*

Pietro Perugino, *Christ Giving the Keys to St. Peter*
In this fresco on one of the side walls of the Sistine Chapel in the papal palace at Rome (now the Vatican), the artist Perugino depicted the transfer of power in Christ's church. Inspired by the architecture of the ancient world, Perugino set the action in a large piazza flanked by Roman triumphal arches. *(Vatican Museums and Galleries, Vatican City, Italy/The Bridgeman Art Library International.)*

modified these classical models, melding them with medieval artistic traditions. In music, Renaissance composers incorporated classical texts and allusions into songs that were based on the motet and other forms of polyphony. Working for patrons—whether churchmen, secular rulers, or republican governments—Renaissance artists and musicians used both past and present to express the patriotism, religious piety, and prestige of their benefactors.

From Agora to Piazza Medieval cities had grown without planning. Streets turned back on themselves. Churches sat cheek-by-jowl with private houses. Renaissance architects, however, reimagined the whole city as a place of order and harmony. The Florentine architect Leon Battista Alberti (1404–1472) proposed that each building in a city be proportioned to fit harmoniously with all the others and that city spaces allow for all necessary public activities—there should be market squares, play areas, grounds for military exercises. In Renaissance cities, the agora and the forum (the open, public spaces of the classical world) appeared

Lorenzo Ghiberti, *The Sacrifice of Isaac*
This bronze relief, which was entered into the competition to decorate the doors of the San Giovanni Baptistery in Florence, captures the dramatic moment (on the right-hand side) when the angel intervenes as Abraham prepares to kill Isaac, a story told in the Hebrew Scriptures. *(Museo Nazionale del Bargello/akg-images/Rabatti-Domingie.)*

once again, but in a new guise: the piazza—a plaza or open square. Architects carved out spaces around their new buildings, and they built porticoes—graceful covered walkways of columns and arches. The artist Pietro Perugino (1445–1523) depicted Christ giving the keys of the kingdom of heaven to the apostle Peter in an idealized city piazza, at the center of which was a perfectly proportioned church (see the illustration on the top of page 431).

The same principles applied to the architecture of the Renaissance court. At Urbino, Duke Federico, a great patron of humanists and artists, commissioned a new palace. The architect, probably Luciano Laurana, designed its spacious and airy courtyard as a public space, a sort of piazza within a palace. Later the courtier Baldassare Castiglione reminisced about this building: "[Duke Federico] built on the rugged site of Urbino a palace thought by many the most beautiful to be found anywhere in all Italy, and he furnished it so well with every suitable thing that it seemed not a palace but a city in the form of a palace." A city had both public and private spaces; similarly, public rooms at the ducal palace gave way to a modest space for the duke's private quarters, a bedroom, a bathroom, a chapel, and, most important, his study, filled with books.

The Gothic cathedral of the Middle Ages was a cluster of graceful spikes and soaring arches. Renaissance architects appreciated its vigor and energy, but they tamed it with regular geometrical forms inspired by classical buildings. Classical forms were applied to previously built structures as well as new ones. Florence's Santa Maria Novella, for example, had been a typical Gothic church when it was first built. But when Alberti, the man who believed in public spaces and harmonious buildings, was commissioned to replace its facade, he drew on Roman temple forms. (See the illustration on page 430.)

Sculpture and Painting

In 1400, the Florentines sponsored a competition for new bronze doors for their baptistery. The entry of Lorenzo Ghiberti (1378?–1455) depicted a scene from the Old Testament story in which God tested Abraham's faith by ordering him to sacrifice his son Isaac (see the illustration on page 431). Cast in one piece, a major technological feat at the time, it shows a young, nude Isaac modeled on the masculine ideal of ancient Greek sculpture. At the same time, Ghiberti drew on medieval models for his depiction of Abraham and for his

Jan van Eyck, *The Virgin of Chancellor Rolin*
Van Eyck portrays the Virgin and Chancellor Nicolas Rolin as if they were contemporaries sharing a nice chat. Only the angel, who is placing a crown on the Virgin's head, suggests that something out of the ordinary is happening. *(Erich Lessing/Art Resource, NY.)*

Sandro Botticelli, *The Birth of Venus*
Other artists had depicted Venus, but Botticelli was the first since antiquity to portray her in the nude. *(Galleria degli Uffizi, Florence, Italy/The Bridgeman Art Library International.)*

Leonardo da Vinci, *The Annunciation*
Working with a traditional Christian theme—the moment when the angel Gabriel announced to the Virgin Mary that she would give birth to Christ—Leonardo produced a work of great originality, drawing the viewer's eye from a vanishing point in the distance to the subject of the painting. The ability to subordinate the background to the foreground was the key contribution of Renaissance perspective. *(Scala/Ministero per i Beni e le Attività culturali/Art Resource, NY.)*

quatrefoil frame. In this way, he gracefully melded old and new elements — and won the contest.

In addition to using the forms of classical art, Renaissance artists also mined the ancient world for new subjects. Venus, the Roman goddess of love and beauty, had numerous stories attached to her name. At first glance, *The Birth of Venus* by Sandro Botticelli (c. 1445–1510) seems simply an illustration of the tale of Venus's rise from the sea (see page 433). A closer look, however, shows that Botticelli's work is complicated, drawing on the ideas of the humanist philosopher Marsilio Ficino (1433–1499) and the poetry of Angelo Poliziano (1454–1494). According to Ficino, Venus was *humanitas* — the essence of the humanities. For Poliziano, she was

> fair Venus, mother of the cupids.
> Zephyr bathes the meadow with dew
> spreading a thousand lovely fragrances:
> wherever he flies he clothes the countryside
> in roses, lilies, violets, and other flowers.

In Botticelli's painting, Zephyr (one of the winds) blows while Venus herself is about to be clothed in a fine robe embroidered with leaves and flowers.

The Sacrifice of Isaac and *The Birth of Venus* show some of the ways in which Renaissance artists used ancient models. Other artists perfected perspective — the illusion of three-dimensional space — to a degree that even classical antiquity had not anticipated. The development of the laws of perspective accompanied the introduction of long-range weaponry, such as cannons. In fact, some of perspective's practitioners — Leonardo da Vinci (1452–1519), for example — were military engineers as well as artists. In Leonardo's painting *The Annunciation*, sight lines meeting at a point on the horizon open wide precisely where the angel kneels and Mary responds in surprise (see the illustration at the bottom of page 433).

Ghiberti, Botticelli, and Leonardo were all Italian artists. While they were creating their works, a northern Renaissance was taking place as well. At the court of Burgundy during the Hundred Years' War, the dukes commissioned portraits of themselves — sometimes unflattering ones — just as Roman leaders had once commissioned their own busts. Soon it was the fashion for everyone who could afford it to have a portrait made, as naturalistically as possible. Around 1433, the chancellor Nicolas Rolin, for example, commissioned the Dutch artist Jan van Eyck to paint his portrait (see page 432). Though opposite the Virgin and the baby Jesus, Rolin, in a pious pose, is the key figure in the picture. The grand view of a city behind the figures was meant to underscore Rolin's prominence in the community. In fact Rolin *was* an important man: he worked for the duke of Burgundy and was also the founder of a hospital at Beaune and a religious order of nurses to serve it. Van Eyck's portrait emphasized not only Rolin's dignity and status but also his individuality. The artist took pains to show even the wrinkles of his neck and the furrows on his brow.

New Harmonies in Music

Using music to add glamour and glory to their courts and reputations, Renaissance rulers spent as much as 6 percent of their annual revenue to support musicians and composers. The Avignon papacy, in its own way one such court, was a major

Music in the Streets

Music in the Renaissance was as important in public places — even in the streets — as it was in the courts. In this satirical woodcut, one of many illustrating a book by Sebastian Brant called *The Ship of Fools* (1494), musicians dressed as fools serenade a nude lady. She is attempting to get rid of them by emptying her chamber pot on their heads. The picture makes fun of courtly gallantry even as it depicts the sort of thing that could really happen on a town street. *(© Lebrecht Music and Arts/The Image Works.)*

sponsor of sacred music. People appreciated music, whether secular or religious, for its ability to express their innermost feelings.

Every proper court had its own musicians. Some served as chaplains, writing music for the ruler's private chapel—the place where his court and household heard Mass. When Josquin Desprez (1440–1521) served as the duke of Ferrara's chaplain, he wrote a Mass that used the musical equivalents of the letters of the duke's name (the Italian version of *do re mi*) as its theme. Isabella d'Este (1474–1539), the daughter of the duke, employed her own musicians—singers, woodwind and string players, percussionists, and keyboard players—while her husband, the duke of Mantua, had his own band. Bartolomeo Tromboncino was Isabella's favorite musician. When her brother sent her poems to recopy, she had Tromboncino set them to music. This was one of the ways in which humanists and musicians worked together: the poems that interested Tromboncino were of the newest sort, patterned on classical forms. He and Isabella particularly favored Petrarch's poems.

The church, too, was a major sponsor of music. Every feast required music, and the papal schism inadvertently encouraged more musical production than usual, as rival popes tried to best one another in the realm of pageantry and sound. Churches needed choirs of singers, and many choirboys went on to become composers, while others sang well into adulthood: in the fourteenth century, the men who sang in the choir at Reims received a yearly stipend and an extra fee every time they sang the Mass and the liturgical offices of the day.

Isabella d'Este as Patron of the Arts

At the beginning of the sixteenth century, Isabella d'Este commissioned Lorenzo Costa to make five paintings to decorate her "little studio"—her special retreat—at the Mantuan ducal palace. In this painting, he depicted a "coronation," perhaps of Isabella herself. Cupid, held by his mother, Venus, places a laurel wreath on the lady's head. A battle rages far away, but the chief figures—personifications at one and the same time of music and poetry and the virtues—bask in peace and harmony. Pleased by the painting, Isabella made Costa the official painter of the court. *(Louvre, Paris, France/Giraudon/The Bridgeman Art Library International.)*

Vladislav Hall
The interior of this hall, built by Bohemian king Vladislav to house grand tournaments, is largely based on Gothic forms. Note, for example, the elaborate ribs of the vault. But the rectangular windows echo Renaissance architecture, the first such borrowing north of the Alps. *(© Franz-Marc Frei/Corbis.)*

When the composer Johannes Ockeghem—chaplain for three French kings—died in 1497, his fellow musicians vied in expressing their grief in song. Josquin Desprez was among them, and his composition illustrates how the addition of classical elements to very traditional musical forms enhanced music's emotive power. Josquin's work combines personal grief with religious liturgy and the feelings expressed in classical elegies. The piece uses five voices. Inspired by classical mythology, four of the voices sing in the vernacular French about the "nymphs of the wood" coming together to mourn. But the fifth voice intones the words of the liturgy: *Requiescat in pace* ("May he rest in peace"). At the very moment in the song that the four vernacular voices lament Ockeghem's burial in the dark ground, the liturgical voice sings of the heavenly light. The contrast makes the song more moving. By drawing on the classical past, Renaissance musicians found new ways in which to express emotion.

REVIEW QUESTION How and why did Renaissance humanists, artists, and musicians revive classical traditions?

Consolidating Power

The shape of Europe changed between 1340 and 1492. In Eastern Europe, the Ottoman Empire took the place (though not the role) of Byzantium. The capital of the Holy Roman Empire moved to Prague, bringing Bohemia to the fore. Meanwhile, the duke of Lithuania married the queen of Poland, uniting those two states. In western Europe, a few places organized and maintained themselves as republics; the Swiss, for example, consolidated their informal alliances in the Swiss Confederation. Italy, which at the beginning of the period was dotted with numerous small city-states, was by the end dominated by five major powers: Milan, the papacy, Naples, and the republics of Venice and Florence. Most western European states—England and France, for example—became centralized monarchies. The union of Aragon and Castile via the marriage of their respective rulers created Spain. Whether monarchies, principalities, or republics, states throughout Europe used their new powers to finance humanists, artists, and musicians—and to persecute heretics, Muslims, and Jews with new vigor.

New Political Formations in Eastern Europe

In the eastern half of the Holy Roman Empire, Bohemia gained new status as the seat of the Luxembourg imperial dynasty, whose last representative was Emperor Sigismund. This development led to a religious and political crisis when the Hussites clashed with Sigismund (see page 427). The chief beneficiaries of the violence were the nobles, both Catholic and Hussite, but they quarreled among themselves, especially about who should be king. No Joan of Arc appeared to declare the national will, and most of Europe considered Bohemia a heretic state. Countering this isolation from the rest of Europe, the Bohemian king Vladislav Jagiello (r. 1471–1516) borrowed some Renaissance architectural motifs for his palace.

Cracow in the Fifteenth Century
In the fifteenth century, Poland, united with Lithuania, was growing both in population and diversity. Relatively untouched by the plague, towns like Cracow were part of thriving trade networks, while Cracow itself boasted a university established along the lines of the one at Paris. No wonder that when Michael Wohlgemut's workshop was commissioned to make woodcuts for Hartmann Schedel's *World Chronicle* in 1493 (an early printed book), Cracow was depicted as not only densely packed but even spilling beyond its walls. *(Interfoto/Ancient Art & Architecture Collection, Ltd.)*

Farther north, it was the cities rather than the landed nobility that held power. Allied cities, known as *Hanse*, were common. The most successful alliance was the **Hanseatic League**, a loose federation of mainly north German cities formed to protect their mutual interests in defense and trade—and art. The Dance of Death, for example, painted at the Hanse town of Reval (see page 415), was made by the artist Bernt Notke, who hailed from Lübeck, another Hanse town. The Hanseatic League linked the Baltic coast with Russia, Norway, the British Isles, France, and even (via imperial cities like Augsburg and Nuremberg) the cities of Italy. When threatened by rival powers in Denmark and Norway in 1367–1370, the league waged war and usually won. But in the fifteenth century it confronted new rivals and began a long, slow decline.

Hanseatic League: A league of northern European cities formed in the fourteenth century to protect their mutual interests in trade and defense.

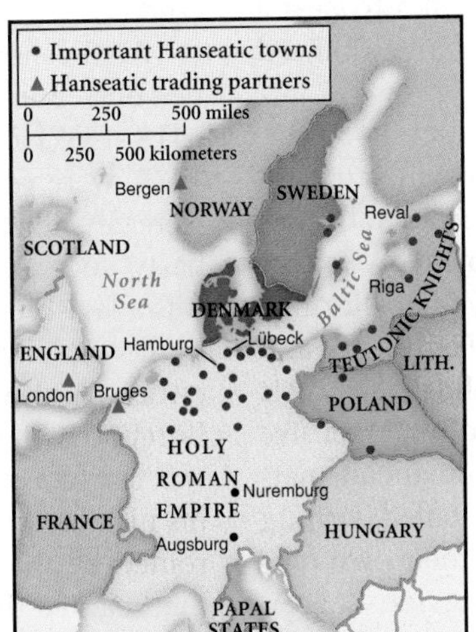

The Hanseatic League

To the east of the Hanseatic cities, two new monarchies took shape in northeastern Europe: Poland and Lithuania. Poland had begun to form in the tenth century. Powerful nobles soon dominated it, and Mongol invasions devastated the land. But recovery was under way by 1300. Unlike almost every other part of Europe, Poland expanded demographically and economically during the fourteenth century. Jews migrated there to escape persecutions in western Europe, and both Jewish and German settlers helped build thriving towns like Cracow. Monarchical consolidation began thereafter.

On Poland's eastern flank was Lithuania, the only major holdout from Christianity in eastern Europe. But as it expanded into southern Russia, its grand dukes flirted with both the Roman Catholic and Orthodox varieties. In 1386, Grand Duke Jogailo (c. 1351–1434), taking advantage of a hiatus in the Polish ruling dynasty, united both states when he married Queen Jadwiga of Poland, received a Catholic baptism, and was elected by the Polish nobility as King Wladyslaw II Jagiello. As part of the negotiations prior to these events, he promised to convert Lithuania, and after his coronation he sent churchmen there to begin the long, slow process. The union of Poland and Lithuania lasted, with some interruptions, until 1772. (See Mapping the West, page 445.)

Powerful States in Western Europe

Four powerful states dominated western Europe during the fifteenth century. The kingdom of Spain and the duchy of Burgundy were created by marriage; the newly powerful kingdoms of France and England were forged in the crucible of war. By the end of the century, however, Burgundy had disappeared, leaving three exceptionally powerful monarchies.

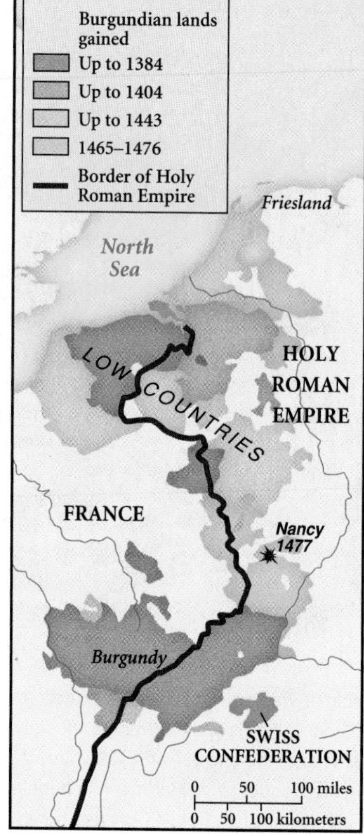

The Expansion of Burgundy, 1384–1476

Spain Decades of violence on the Iberian peninsula ended when Isabella of Castile and Ferdinand of Aragon married in 1469 and restored law and order in the decades that followed. Castile was the powerhouse, with Aragon its lesser neighbor and Navarre a pawn between the two. When the king and queen joined forces, they ruled together over their separate dominions, allowing each to retain its traditional laws and privileges. The union of Castile and Aragon was the first step toward a united Spain and a centralized monarchy there.

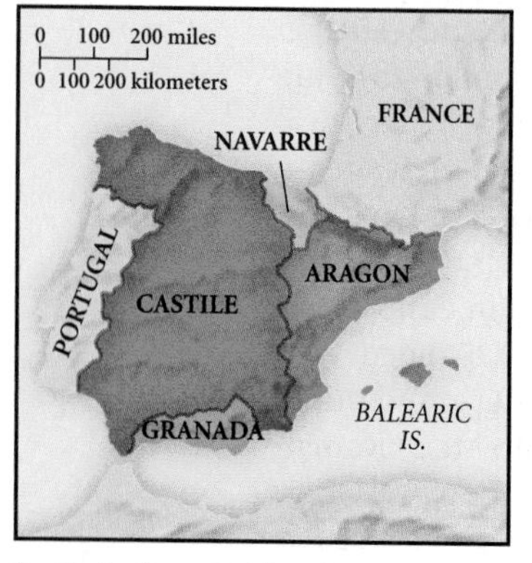

Spain before Unification, Late Fifteenth Century

Relying on a lucrative taxation system, pliant meetings of the *cortes* (the representative institution that voted on taxes), and an ideology that glorified the monarchy, Ferdinand and Isabella consolidated their power. They had an extensive bureaucracy for financial matters and a well-staffed writing office. They sent their own officials to rule over towns that had previously been self-governing, and they established regional courts of law.

Burgundy The duchy of Burgundy—created when the duke of Burgundy and heiress of Flanders married in 1369—was disunited linguistically and geographically. Its success and expansion in the fifteenth century resulted from military might and careful statecraft.

Part of the French royal house, the Burgundian dynasty expanded its power rapidly by acquiring land, primarily in the Netherlands. Between 1384 and 1476, the Burgundian state filled the territorial gap between France and Germany, extending from the Swiss border in the south to Friesland (Germany) in the north. Through purchases, inheritance, and conquests, the dukes ruled over French-, Dutch-, and German-speaking subjects, creating a state that resembled a patchwork of provinces and regions, each jealously guarding its laws and traditions. The Low Countries, with their flourishing cities, constituted the state's economic heartland, while the region of Burgundy itself, which gave the state its name, offered rich farmlands and vineyards. Unlike England, whose island geography made it a natural political unit; or France, whose borders were forged in the national experience of repelling English invaders; or Spain, whose national identity came from centuries of warfare against Islam, Burgundy was an artificial creation whose coherence depended entirely on the skillful exercise of statecraft.

At the heart of Burgundian politics was the personal cult of its dukes. Philip the Good (r. 1418–1467) and his son Charles the Bold (r. 1467–1477) were very different kinds of rulers, but both were devoted to enhancing the prestige of their dynasty and the security of their dominion. Philip was a lavish patron of the arts who commissioned numerous illuminated manuscripts, chronicles, tapestries, paintings, and music in his efforts to glorify Burgundy. Charles, by contrast, spent more time on war than at court. Renowned for his courage (hence his nickname), he died in 1477 when his army was routed by the Swiss at the town of Nancy, a loss that marked the end of Burgundian power.

The Burgundians' success depended in large part on their personal relationship with their sub-

Philip the Good's *History of Alexander the Great* Tapestries
In 1459 Duke Philip of Burgundy bought a series of tapestries that told the story of Alexander's adventures. These had been recounted in popular vernacular romances; now they were illustrated in silk, gold, and silver threads. In this detail, Alexander flies in the sky in a decorated cage held by winged mythical creatures known as griffons. Just to the right of that, he appears on the ground, surrounded by his courtiers. Next, he is inside a glass bell; you can just barely see him behind the white scrim made of sea creatures. *(Partial view, from* Episodes in the Life of Alexander: Flight of Alexander *and* Alexander Plumbs the Depths of the Oceans, *Galleria Doria Pamphilij. Rome/photo: akg-images/Pirozzi.)*

jects. Not only did the dukes travel constantly from one part of their dominion to another, but they also staged elaborate ceremonies to enhance their power and promote their legitimacy. Their entries into cities and their presence at weddings, births, and funerals became the centerpieces of a "theater state" in which the dynasty provided the only link among diverse territories. (See Document, "The Ducal Entry into Ghent," page 440.) New rituals became propaganda tools. Philip's revival of chivalry at court transformed the semi-independent nobility into courtiers closely tied to the prince. But, as mentioned earlier in this chapter (page 418), when Charles the Bold died in 1477, the duchy was parceled out to France and the Holy Roman Empire.

France Because of its quick recovery from the Hundred Years' War, France was powerful enough to take a large bite out of Burgundy. Under Louis XI (r. 1461–1483), the French monarchy both expanded its territory and consolidated its power. Soon after Burgundy fell to him, Louis inherited most of southern France after the Anjou dynasty died out. When the French king inherited claims to the duchy of Milan and the kingdom of Naples, he was ready to exploit other opportunities in Italy. By the end of the century, France had doubled its territory, assuming boundaries close to its modern ones, and was looking to expand even further.

To strengthen royal power at home, Louis promoted industry and commerce, imposed permanent salt and land taxes, maintained western Europe's first standing army (created by his predecessor), and dispensed with the meetings of the Estates General, which included the clergy, the nobility, and representatives from the major towns of France. The French kings had already increased their power with important concessions from the papacy. The Pragmatic Sanction of Bourges (1438) asserted the superiority of a general church council over the pope. Harking back to a long tradition of the high Middle Ages, the Pragmatic Sanction established what would come to be known as Gallicanism (after Gaul, the ancient Roman name for France), in which the French king would effectively control ecclesiastical revenues and the appointment of French bishops.

England In England the Hundred Years' War led to intermittent civil wars that came to be called the Wars of the Roses. Those wars ended

DOCUMENT

The Ducal Entry into Ghent (1458)

The dukes of Burgundy made numerous ceremonial entries into the cities of their duchy. Such events, elaborately planned and exactingly executed, enhanced the duke's prestige as well as the standing of those who participated in or contributed to the performance. Entries cemented (or repaired) ties with townspeople even as they cost the cities an enormous amount of money. In the case of Ghent, the entry of 1458 marked a reconciliation: several years before this time, the town had unsuccessfully rebelled against the duke. The description here is from the Chronicle of Flanders; *it presents the point of the view of the townspeople.*

The Joyous Entry of my most redoubted [awesome] lord and prince Philip [the Good] . . . which he made into his city of Ghent on the feast of St. George, Sunday, April 23, 1458, and which was organized by the aldermen and others of the same city of Ghent in the following manner. . . .

Outside the Walpoort [one of the gates of Ghent], on the outskirts of the city along both sides of the street to the end of the Waldamme [near the Walpoort] as far as the ramparts [city walls], the deacons and all the sworn members of the weavers [guild] were spread as far out as possible, each finely dressed in his long cloak of office down to the ground and as many as 500 in number, each bearing a lit torch in his hand. When they became aware of the approach of my redoubted lord, they fell to their knees and removed their hats in fine and graceful order. . . .

Between the crenellations of the gate there were many trumpeters and minstrels who played most agreeably from the arrival of my redoubted lord until he was led far into the city, and they were all richly dressed in the [coat of] arms [the heraldic devices] of my said lord and of the city as befitted the occasion. . . . All of the parish priests and other priests of the city, people in minor orders, and the beguines of both the beguinages were present within the city close by the gate each in their most precious copes, habits, and chasubles [names for various liturgical garments] of their churches in the manner of a fine procession. . . .

Inside the said Walpoort, opposite the house called *De Roze*, there was a stage covering the street next to the ca-

with the victory of Henry Tudor, who took the title of Henry VII (r. 1485–1509). Though long, the Wars of the Roses caused relatively little damage; the battles were generally short and, in the words of one chronicler, "neither the country, nor the people nor the houses, were wasted, destroyed or demolished, but the calamities and misfortunes of the war fell only upon the soldiers, and especially on the nobility."

As a result, the English economy continued to grow during the fifteenth century. The cloth industry expanded considerably, and the English used much of the raw wool that they had been exporting to the Low Countries to manufacture goods at home. London merchants, taking a vigorous role in trade, also assumed greater political prominence, not only in governing London but also as bankers to kings and members of Parliament. In the countryside the landed classes—the nobility, the gentry (the lesser nobility), and the yeomanry (free farmers)—benefited from rising farm and land-rent income as the population increased slowly but steadily. The Tudor monarchs took advantage of the general prosperity to bolster both their treasury and their power.

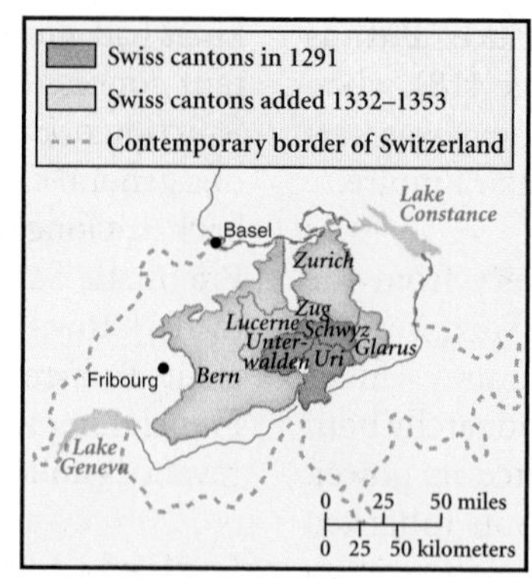

The Growth of the Swiss Confederation, to 1353

Power in the Republics

Within the fifteenth-century world of largely monarchical power were three important exceptions: Switzerland, Venice, and Florence. Republics, they prided themselves on traditions of self-rule. At the same time, however, they were in every case dominated by elites—or even by one family.

The Swiss Confederation The cities of the Alpine region of the Holy Roman Empire, like those of the Hanseatic League in the Baltic, had long had alliances with one another. In the fourteenth century, their union became more binding, and they joined with equally well-organized communities in rural and forested areas in

nal, and upon it stood the figure of the Prodigal Son who had ignobly squandered his portion, finely presented in the following manner. The father wore a long hooded gown and a small hat with a red brim, with three servants dressed in black behind him. The son was poorly dressed, his doublet in tatters, his stockings rent at the knee, and the father met him in this pitiful state and pardoned him as a result of the son acknowledging his misdeeds. Beneath the said stage were written the words, "Father, I have sinned against Heaven and against you. Luke [15:21]." . . .

Across the Holstraat there stood a stage which bore a great black lion with its jaws gaping as if it was roaring. In its paw the lion held a fine standard bearing the [coat of] arms of our most redoubted lord. Opposite this lion there was another, a beautiful white female meekly stretched out, and between them lay three white lion cubs which seemed to be half-dead. When the black lion roared, they awoke and were brought back to life. Everything was masterfully crafted and lifelike. On the edge of this stage was written "He will roar like a lion and the children will be afraid. Hosea [11:10]." . . .

In front of the gate of the residence of my redoubted lord . . . children sweetly sang a new song that had been composed for the Entry of my redoubted lord . . . :

Long live Burgundy! That's our cry.
We sing from the heart. I prithee,
On this, his joyous Entry,
Let us spare no expense.
Since he has come to his land,
All our sadness is gone. . . .

[After a speech by an important official of Ghent] the prince [Duke Philip] made a gracious reply and all returned to their homes or lodgings. It was fully nine in the evening, and my lord had spent more than four hours passing between the gate and his palace.

Source: Andrew Brown and Graeme Small, eds., *Court and Civic Society in the Burgundian Low Countries, c. 1420–1530* (Manchester: Manchester University Press, 2007), 176–86, slightly modified.

Question to Consider

- **Considering that Ghent and the duke had recently been at war against one another, what might be the symbolic meanings of the various staged dramas?**

the region. Their original purpose was to keep the peace, but soon they also pledged to aid one another against the Holy Roman Emperor. By the end of the fourteenth century, they had become an entity: the Swiss Confederation. While not united by a comprehensive constitution, they were nevertheless an effective political force.

Wealthy merchants and tradesmen dominated the cities of the Swiss Confederation, and in the fifteenth century they managed to supplant the landed nobility. At the same time, the power of the rural communes gave some ordinary folk political importance. No king, duke, or count ever became head of the confederation. In its fiercely independent stance against the Holy Roman Empire, it became a symbol of republican freedom. On the other hand, poor Swiss foot soldiers made their living by hiring themselves out as mercenaries, fueling the wars of kings in the rest of Europe.

The Republic of Venice By the fifteenth century, Venice, a city built on a lagoon, ruled an extensive empire. Its merchant ships plied the waters stretching from the Black Sea to the Mediterranean and out to the Atlantic Ocean. It had an excellent navy. Now, for the first time in its career, it turned to conquer land in northern Italy. In the early fifteenth century, Venice took over Brescia, Verona, Padua, Belluno, and many other cities, eventually coming up against the equally powerful city-state of Milan to its west. Between 1450 and 1454, two coalitions, one led by Milan, the other by Venice, fought for territorial control of the eastern half of northern Italy. Financial exhaustion and fear of an invasion by France or the Ottoman Turks led to the Peace of Lodi in 1454. Italy was a collection no longer of small cities, each with its own *contado* (surrounding countryside), but of large territorial city-states.

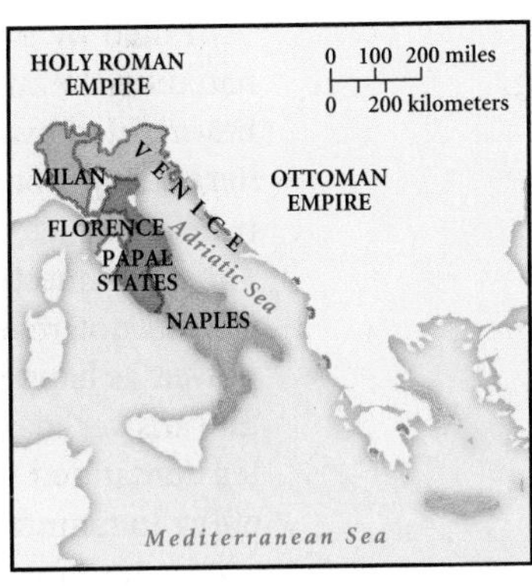

Italy at the Peace of Lodi, 1454

It is no accident that the Peace of Lodi was signed one year after the Ottoman conquest of Constantinople: Venice wanted to direct its might against the Turks. But the Venetians also knew that peace was good for business; they traded with the Ottomans, and the two powers influenced each other's art and culture: Gentile Bellini's portrait of Mehmed (see the chapter-opening illustration) is a good example of

Gentile Bellini, *Procession in Piazza San Marco*
After he returned to Venice from Istanbul, Bellini was commissioned by a prestigious confraternity—the Grand School of St. John—to paint a large canvas of the procession of the Holy Cross for the school's new Renaissance-style Great Hall. Bellini set the scene in the Piazza San Marco, Venice's central square. *(Erich Lessing/Art Resource, NY.)*

the importance of the Renaissance at the Ottoman court.

Ruled by the Great Council, which was dominated by the most important families, Venice was never ruled by a *signore* ("lord"). Far from being a hereditary monarch, the doge—the leading magistrate at Venice—was elected by the Great Council. The great question is why the lower classes at Venice did not rebel and demand their own political power, as happened in so many other Italian cities. The answer may be that Venice's foundation on water demanded so much central planning, so much effort to maintain buildings and services, and such a large amount of public funds to provide the population with necessities that it fostered a greater sense of common community than could be found elsewhere.

While Venice was not itself a center of humanism, its conquest of Padua in 1405 transformed its culture. After studying rhetoric at the University of Padua, young Venetian nobles returned home convinced of the values of a humanistic education for administering their empire. Lauro Quirini was one such man; his time at Padua was followed by a long period on Crete, which was under Venetian control.

Like humanism, Renaissance art also became part of the fabric of the city. Because of its trading links with Byzantium, Venice had long been influenced by Byzantine artistic styles. As it acquired a land-based empire in northern Italy, however, its artists adopted the Gothic styles prevalent elsewhere. In the fifteenth century, Renaissance art forms began to make inroads as well. Venice achieved its own unique style, characterized by strong colors, intense lighting, and sensuous use of paint—adapting the work of classical antiquity for its own purposes. Most Venetian artists worked on commission from churches, but lay confraternities—lay religious organizations devoted to charity—also sponsored paintings. (For one of these, see the illustration above.)

Florence | Florence, like Venice, was also a republic. But unlike Venice, its society and political life were turbulent, as social classes and political factions competed for power. The most important of these civil uprisings was the so-called Ciompi Revolt of 1378. Named after the wool workers (*ciompi*), laborers so lowly that they had not been allowed to form a guild, the revolt led to the creation of a guild for them, along with a new distribution of power in the city. But by 1382, the upper classes were once again monopolizing the government, and now with even less sympathy for the commoners.

By 1434, the **Medici** family had become the dominant power in this unruly city. The patriarch of this family, Cosimo de' Medici (1389–1464), founded his political power on the wealth of the Medici bank, which handled papal finances and had numerous branch offices in Italian and northern European cities. Backed by his money, Cosimo took over Florentine politics. He determined who could take public office, and he established new committees made up of men loyal to him to govern the city. He kept the old forms of the Florentine constitution intact, governing behind the scenes not by force but through a broad consensus among the ruling elite.

Cosimo's grandson Lorenzo "the Magnificent" (1449–1492), who assumed power in 1467, bolstered the regime's legitimacy with his patronage of the humanities and the arts. He himself was a poet and an avid collector of antiquities. He intended to build a grand library made of marble at his palace but died before it was complete. More successful was his sculpture garden, which he filled with ancient works and entrusted to the sculptor Bertoldo di Giovanni to tend. Serving on various Florentine committees in charge of building, renovating, and adorning the churches of the city, Lorenzo employed important artists and architects to work on his own palaces. He probably encouraged the young Michelangelo; he certainly patronized the poet Angelo Poliziano, whose verses inspired Botticelli's *Venus*. No wonder humanists and poets sang his praises.

But the Medici family also had enemies. In 1478, Lorenzo narrowly escaped an assassination attempt, and his successor was driven out of Florence in 1494. The Medici returned to power in 1512, only to be driven out again in 1527. In 1530, the republic fell for good as the Medici once again took power, this time declaring themselves dukes of Florence.

Medici (MEH dih chee): The ruling family of Florence during much of the fifteenth to the seventeenth centuries.

Venetian Art
When he was commissioned in the 1490s to depict the legend of Saint Ursula, Vittore Carpaccio chose Venice as the backdrop. Found in the very popular thirteenth-century *Golden Legend* by Jacobus de Voragine, the tale begins in England, where a pagan king is so inspired by hearing of the virtue of Ursula, daughter of the Christian king of Brittany, that he sends his ambassadors to ask for her hand for his son. In this detail, Carpaccio shows the English ambassadors arriving in a gondola. Note the glass-like colors and the evocation of atmosphere, both characteristic of Venetian style. *(Detail from the Ursula Cycle, 1490–96 (oil on canvas), Vittore Carpaccio, Galleria dell' Accademia, Venice, Italy/Cameraphoto Arte Venezia/The Bridgeman Art Library International.)*

Lorenzo's "Gardener"
Bertoldo di Giovanni presided over the antiquities collected by the Medici and exhibited in their sculpture garden. He was himself a fine artist, pioneering small bronze statuettes such as this one, which drew upon Homer's *Iliad* for its subject. It shows the hero Bellerophon capturing the winged horse Pegasus as part of his quest to defeat the Chimera, a ferocious monster. The underside of the base explains that Bertoldo was the designer, while Adriano Fiorentino cast it in bronze. Bertoldo found the model for his design in Roman art of the classical period, some of which was still where it had originally been placed. *(Kunsthistorisches Museum, Vienna, Austria/Erich Lessing/Art Resource, NY.)*

The Tools of Power

Whether monarchies, duchies, or republics, the newly consolidated states of the fifteenth century exercised their powers more thoroughly than ever before. Sometimes they reached into the intimate lives of their subjects or citizens; at other times they persecuted undesirables with new efficiency.

New Taxes, New Knowledge A good example of the ways in which governments peeked into the lives of their citizens—and picked their pockets—is the Florentine *catasto*. This was an inventory of households within the city and its outlying territory made for the purposes of taxation in 1427. The Domesday survey conducted in England in 1086 had been the most complete census of its day. But the catasto bested Domesday in thoroughness and inquisitiveness. It inquired about names, types of houses, and animals. It asked people to specify their trade, and their answers revealed the levels of Florentine society, ranging from agricultural laborers with no land of their own to soldiers, cooks, grave diggers, scribes, great merchants, doctors, wine dealers, innkeepers, and tanners. The list went on and on. The catasto inquired about private and public investments, real estate holdings, and taxable assets. Finally, it turned to the sex of the head of the family, his or her age and marital status, and the number of mouths to feed in the household. An identification number was assigned to each household.

The catasto showed that in 1427 Florence and its outlying regions had a population of more than 260,000. Although the city itself had only 38,000 inhabitants (about 15 percent of the total population), it held 67 percent of the wealth. Some 60 percent of the Florentine households in the city belonged to the "little people" (a literal translation from the Italian term; it referred to artisans and small merchants). The "fat people" (what we would call the upper middle class) made up 30 percent of the urban population and included wealthy merchants, leading artisans, notaries, doctors, and other professionals. At the very bottom of the hierarchy were slaves and servants, largely women from the surrounding countryside employed in domestic service. At the top, a tiny elite of wealthy patricians, bankers, and wool merchants controlled the state and owned more than one-quarter of its wealth. This was the group that produced the Medici family.

Most Florentine households consisted of at least six people, not all of whom were members of the family. Wealthier families had more children, while childless couples existed almost exclusively among the poor. The rich gave their infants to wet nurses to breast-feed, while the poor often left their children to public charity. Florence was rightly proud of its orphanage: it both provided for the city's poor children and was built in the newest and finest Renaissance style.

Driving Out Muslims, Heretics, and Jews European kings had long fought Muslims and expelled Jews from their kingdoms. But in the fifteenth century, their powers became concentrated and centralized. Newly rich from national taxes, buttressed by political theo-

Alfonso de Espina and the Jews

As a Franciscan friar and university rector, Alfonso de Espina was an influential man. His *The Fortress of Faith against the Jews, Muslims, and Other Enemies of the Christian Faith* devoted a whole chapter to "the cruelties of the Jews." It included a plan to ferret out heretical conversos, called for an Inquisition, and recommended the expulsion of the Jews from Spain. In this woodcut, made c. 1474 to illustrate the book, a well-armed Alfonso walks by a fortress. Ahead of him are devils. Behind are blindfolded Jews. What do you suppose the blindfolds were meant to signify? *(© Topham/The Image Works.)*

MAPPING THE WEST

Europe, c. 1492
By the end of the fifteenth century, the shape of early modern Europe was largely fixed as it would remain until the eighteenth century. The chief exception was the disappearance of an independent Hungarian kingdom after 1529.

ries that glorified their power, masters of the new expensive technologies of war (like cannons and mercenary armies), fifteenth-century kings in western Europe—England, France, Spain—commanded what we may call modern states. They used the full force of their new powers against their internal and external enemies.

Spain is a good example of this new trend. Once Ferdinand and Isabella established their rule over Castile and Aragon, they sought to impose religious uniformity and purity. They began systematically to persecute the *conversos* (converts); these were Jews who converted to Christianity in the aftermath of vicious attacks on Jews at Seville, Cordova, Toledo, and other Spanish towns in 1391. During the first half of the fifteenth century they and their descendants (still called conversos, even though their children were born and baptized in the Christian faith) took advantage of the opportunities open to educated Christians, in many instances rising to high positions in both the church and the state and marrying into so-called Old Christian families.

The conversos' success bred resentment, and their commitment to Christianity was questioned as well. Local massacres of conversos began. In Toledo in 1467, two conversos were caught and hanged "as traitors and captains of the heretical conversos." The terms *traitors* and *heretics* are telling. Conversos were no longer Jews, so their persecution was justified by branding them as heretics who undermined the monarchy. In 1478, Ferdinand and Isabella set up the Inquisition in Spain to do on behalf of the crown what the towns had started. Treating the conversos as heretics, the inquisitors imposed harsh sentences, expelling or burning most of them. That was not enough (in the view of the monarchs) to purify the land. In 1492, Ferdinand and Isabella decreed that all Jews in Spain must convert or leave the country. Some did indeed convert, but the experiences of the former conversos soured most on the prospect, and a large number of Jews—perhaps 150,000—left Spain, scattering around the Mediterranean.

Meanwhile, Ferdinand and Isabella determined to rid Spain of its last Muslim stronghold, Granada. Disunity within the ruling family at Granada allowed the conquest to proceed, and in January 1492—just a few months before they expelled the Jews—Ferdinand and Isabella made their triumphal entry into the Alhambra, the former residence of the Muslim king of Granada. While they initially promised freedom of religion to the Muslims who chose to remain, the royal couple also provided a fleet of boats to take away those who chose exile. In 1502, they demanded that all Muslims adopt Christianity or leave the kingdom.

REVIEW QUESTION How did the monarchs and republics of the fifteenth century use (and abuse) their powers?

Conclusion

The years from 1340 to 1492 marked a period of crisis in Europe. The Hundred Years' War broke out in 1337, and ten years later, in 1347, the Black Death hit, taking a heavy toll. In 1378, a crisis shook the church when first two and then three popes claimed universal authority. Revolts and riots plagued the cities and countryside. The Ottoman Turks took Constantinople in 1453, changing the very shape of Europe and the Middle East.

The revival of classical literature, art, architecture, and music helped men and women cope with these crises and gave them new tools for dealing with them. The Renaissance began mainly in the city-states of Italy, but it spread throughout much of Europe via the education and training of humanists, artists, sculptors, architects, and musicians. At the courts of great kings and dukes—even of the sultan—Renaissance music, art, and literature served as a way to celebrate the grandeur of rulers who controlled more of the apparatuses of government (armies, artillery, courts, and taxes) than ever before.

Consolidation was the principle underlying the new states of the Renaissance. Venice absorbed nearby northern Italian cities, and the Peace of Lodi confirmed its new status as a power on land as well as the sea. In eastern Europe, marriage joined together the states of Lithuania and Poland. A similar union took place in Spain when Isabella of Castile and Ferdinand of Aragon married. The Swiss Confederation became a permanent entity. The king of France came to rule over all of the area that we today call France. The consolidated modern states of the fifteenth century would soon look to the Atlantic Ocean and beyond for new lands to explore and conquer.

FOR FURTHER EXPLORATION

- **For additional primary-source material from this period**, see *Sources of the Making of the West*, Fourth Edition.
- **For Web sites, images, and documents related to topics in this chapter**, visit *Make History* at bedfordstmartins.com/hunt.

Chapter 13 Review

Online Study Guide bedfordstmartins.com/hunt

Key Terms and People

In the grid below, identify the term or person and explain its historical significance. (To do this exercise online, go to bedfordstmartins.com/hunt.)

Term	Who or What & When	Why It Matters
Black Death (p. 412)		
Hundred Years' War (p. 417)		
Joan of Arc (p. 417)		
Jacquerie (p. 421)		
Mehmed II (p. 423)		
Great Schism (p. 424)		
indulgences (p. 425)		
humanism (p. 428)		
Francis Petrarch (p. 429)		
Hanseatic League (p. 437)		
Medici (p. 443)		

Review Questions

1. What crises did Europeans confront in the fourteenth and fifteenth centuries, and how did they handle them?
2. How and why did Renaissance humanists, artists, and musicians revive classical traditions?
3. How did the monarchs and republics of the fifteenth century use (and abuse) their powers?

Making Connections

1. How did the rulers of the fourteenth century make use of the forms and styles of the Renaissance?
2. On what values did Renaissance humanists and artists agree?
3. What tied the crises of the period (disease, war, schism) to the Renaissance (the flowering of literature, art, architecture, and music)?

Important Events

Date	Event
1337–1453	Hundred Years' War
1347–1352	Black Death in Europe
1358	Jacquerie uprising in France
1378–1417	Great Schism divides papacy
1378	Ciompi Revolt in Florence
1381	Wat Tyler's Rebellion in England
1386	Union of Lithuania and Poland
1414–1418	Council of Constance ends Great Schism; Jan Hus burned at the stake
1453	Conquest of Constantinople by Ottoman Turks; end of Hundred Years' War
1454	Peace of Lodi
1477	Dismantling of duchy of Burgundy
1478	Inquisition begins in Spain
1492	Spain conquers Muslim stronghold of Granada; expels Jews

- Consider two events: **Hundred Years' War (1337–1453)** and the **Black Death in Europe (1347–1352)**. How did these events represent both major crises and new opportunities? How was the Renaissance both a crisis itself and a response to the crises of this period?

SUGGESTED REFERENCES

Aberth provides a good overview of the crises. Blumenfeld-Kosinski and Bynum each explore various aspects of late medieval piety. Nauert treats the many ramifications of Renaissance humanism, and Hale gives a useful overview of political developments.

Aberth, John. *From the Brink of the Apocalypse: Confronting Famine, War, Plague, and Death in the Later Middle Ages.* 2001.

*Beg, Tursun. *The History of Mehmed the Conqueror.* Trans. Halil Inalcik and Rhoads Murphey. 1978.

**The Black Death.* Ed. and trans. Rosemary Horrox. 1994.

Blumenfeld-Kosinski, Renate. *Poets, Saints, and Visionaries of the Great Schism, 1378–1417.* 2006.

Bynum, Caroline. *Wonderful Blood: Theology and Practice in Late Medieval Northern Germany and Beyond.* 2006.

Byrne, Joseph P. *The Black Death.* 2004.

Cohn, Samuel K., Jr. *Lust for Liberty: The Politics of Social Revolt in Medieval Europe, 1200–1425.* 2006.

Grendler, Paul F. *The Universities of the Italian Renaissance.* 2002.

Hale, J. R. *Renaissance Europe, 1480–1520.* 2nd ed. 2000.

Herlihy, David, and Christiane Klapisch-Zuber. *Tuscans and Their Families: A Study of the Florentine Catasto of 1427.* 1985.

Imber, Colin. *The Ottoman Empire, 1300–1650: The Structure of Power.* 2002.

**Joan of Arc: La Pucelle.* Trans. and ed. Craig Taylor. 2006.

Kent, F. W. *Lorenzo de' Medici and the Art of Magnificence.* 2004.

Kirkpatrick, Robin. *The European Renaissance: 1400–1600.* 2002.

Knecht, Robert. *Valois: Kings of France, 1328–1589.* 2004.

Lambert, Malcolm. *Medieval Heresy: Popular Movements from the Gregorian Reform to the Reformation.* 3rd ed. 2002.

Nauert, Charles G. *Humanism and the Culture of the Renaissance Europe.* 2nd ed. 2006.

**The Renaissance in Europe: An Anthology.* Ed. Peter Elmer, Nick Webb, and Roberta Wood. 2000.

Rollo-Koster, Joëlle, and Thomas M. Izbicki, eds. *A Companion to the Great Western Schism (1378–1417).* 2009.

**Selections from English Wycliffite Writings.* Ed. and trans. Anne Hudson. 1978.

*Primary source.

Appendix

Useful Facts and Figures

Prominent Roman Emperors

Julio-Claudians

27 B.C.E.–14 C.E.	Augustus
14–37	Tiberius
37–41	Gaius (Caligula)
41–54	Claudius
54–68	Nero

Flavian Dynasty

69–79	Vespasian
79–81	Titus
81–96	Domitian

Golden Age Emperors

96–98	Nerva
98–117	Trajan
117–138	Hadrian
138–161	Antoninus Pius
161–180	Marcus Aurelius

Severan Emperors

193–211	Septimius Severus
211–217	Antoninus (Caracalla)
217–218	Macrinus
222–235	Severus Alexander

Period of Instability

235–238	Maximinus Thrax
238–244	Gordian III
244–249	Philip the Arab
249–251	Decius
251–253	Trebonianus Gallus
253–260	Valerian
270–275	Aurelian
275–276	Tacitus
276–282	Probus
283–285	Carinus

Dominate

284–305	Diocletian
306	Constantius
306–337	Constantine I
337–340	Constantine II
337–350	Constans I
337–361	Constantius II
361–363	Julian
363–364	Jovian
364–375	Valentinian I
364–378	Valens
367–383	Gratian
375–392	Valentinian II
378–395	Theodosius I (the Great)

The Western Empire

395–423	Honorius
406–407	Marcus
407–411	Constantine III
409–411	Maximus
411–413	Jovinus
412–413	Sebastianus
423–425	Johannes
425–455	Valentinian III
455–456	Avitus
457–461	Majorian
461–465	Libius Severus
467–472	Anthemius
473–474	Glycerius
474–475	Julius Nepos
475–476	Romulus Augustulus

Prominent Byzantine Emperors

Dynasty of Theodosius

395–408	Arcadius
408–450	Theodosius II
450–457	Marcian

Dynasty of Leo

457–474	Leo I
474	Leo II
474–491	Zeno
475–476	Basiliscus
484–488	Leontius
491–518	Anastasius

Dynasty of Justinian

518–527	Justin
527–565	Justinian I
565–578	Justin II
578–582	Tiberius II
578–582	Tiberius II (I) Constantine
582–602	Maurice
602–610	Phocas

Dynasty of Heraclius

610–641	Heraclius
641	Heraclonas
641	Constantine III
641–668	Constans II
646–647	Gregory
649–653	Olympius
669	Mezezius
668–685	Constantine IV
685–695	Justinian II (banished)
695–698	Leontius
698–705	Tiberius III (II)
705–711	Justinian II (restored)
711–713	Bardanes
713–716	Anastasius II
716–717	Theodosius III

Isaurian Dynasty

717–741	Leo III
741–775	Constantine V Copronymus
775–780	Leo IV
780–797	Constantine VI
797–802	Irene
802–811	Nicephorus I
811	Strauracius
811–813	Michael I
813–820	Leo V

Phrygian Dynasty

820–829	Michael II
821–823	Thomas
829–842	Theophilus
842–867	Michael III

Macedonian Dynasty

867–886	Basil I
869–879	Constantine
887–912	Leo VI
912–913	Alexander
913–959	Constantine VII Porphrogenitos
920–944	Romanus I Lecapenus
921–931	Christopher
924–945	Stephen
959–963	Romanus II
963–969	Nicephorus II Phocas
976–1025	Basil II
1025–1028	Constantine VIII (IX) alone
1028–1034	Romanus III Argyrus
1034–1041	Michael IV the Paphlagonian
1041–1042	Michael V Calaphates
1042	Zoe and Theodora
1042–1055	Constantine IX Monomachus
1055–1056	Theodora alone
1056–1057	Michael VI Stratioticus

Prelude to the Comnenian Dynasty

1057–1059	Isaac I Comnenos
1059–1067	Constantine X (IX) Ducas
1068–1071	Romanus IV Diogenes
1071–1078	Michael VII Ducas
1078–1081	Nicephorus III Botaniates
1080–1081	Nicephorus Melissenus

Comnenian Dynasty

1081–1118	Alexius I
1118–1143	John II
1143–1180	Manuel I
1180–1183	Alexius II
1183–1185	Andronieus I
1183–1191	Isaac, Emperor of Cyprus

Dynasty of the Angeli

1185–1195	Isaac II
1195–1203	Alexius III
1203–1204	Isaac II (restored) with Alexius IV
1204	Alexius V Ducas Murtzuphlus

Lascarid Dynasty in Nicaea

1204–1222	Theodore I Lascaris
1222–1254	John III Ducas Vatatzes
1254–1258	Theodore II Lascaris
1258–1261	John IV Lascaris

Dynasty of the Paleologi

1259–1289	Michael VIII Paleologus
1282–1328	Andronicus II
1328–1341	Andronicus III
1341–1391	John V
1347–1354	John VI Cantancuzenus
1376–1379	Andronicus IV
1379–1391	John V (restored)
1390	John VII
1391–1425	Manuel II
1425–1448	John VIII
1449–1453	Constantine XI (XIII) Dragases

Prominent Popes

314–335	Sylvester
440–461	Leo I
590–604	Gregory I (the Great)
687–701	Sergius I
741–752	Zachary
858–867	Nicholas I
1049–1054	Leo IX
1059–1061	Nicholas II
1073–1085	Gregory VII
1088–1099	Urban II
1099–1118	Paschal II
1159–1181	Alexander III
1198–1216	Innocent III
1227–1241	Gregory IX
1243–1254	Innocent IV
1294–1303	Boniface VIII
1316–1334	John XXII
1447–1455	Nicholas V
1458–1464	Pius II
1492–1503	Alexander VI
1503–1513	Julius II
1513–1521	Leo X
1534–1549	Paul III
1555–1559	Paul IV
1585–1590	Sixtus V
1623–1644	Urban VIII
1831–1846	Gregory XVI
1846–1878	Pius IX
1878–1903	Leo XIII
1903–1914	Pius X
1914–1922	Benedict XV
1922–1939	Pius XI
1939–1958	Pius XII
1958–1963	John XXIII
1963–1978	Paul VI
1978	John Paul I
1978–2005	John Paul II
2005–	Benedict XVI

The Carolingian Dynasty

687–714	Pepin of Heristal, Mayor of the Palace
715–741	Charles Martel, Mayor of the Palace
741–751	Pepin III, Mayor of the Palace
751–768	Pepin III, King
768–814	Charlemagne, King
800–814	Charlemagne, Emperor
814–840	Louis the Pious

West Francia

840–877	Charles the Bald, King
875–877	Charles the Bald, Emperor
877–879	Louis II, King
879–882	Louis III, King
879–884	Carloman, King

Middle Kingdoms

840–855	Lothair, Emperor
855–875	Louis (Italy), Emperor
855–863	Charles (Provence), King
855–869	Lothair II (Lorraine), King

East Francia

840–876	Ludwig, King
876–880	Carloman, King
876–882	Ludwig, King
876–887	Charles the Fat, Emperor

German Kings Crowned Emperor

Saxon Dynasty

962–973	Otto I
973–983	Otto II
983–1002	Otto III
1002–1024	Henry II

Franconian Dynasty

1024–1039	Conrad II
1039–1056	Henry III
1056–1106	Henry IV
1106–1125	Henry V
1125–1137	Lothair II (Saxony)

Hohenstaufen Dynasty

1138–1152	Conrad III
1152–1190	Frederick I (Barbarossa)
1190–1197	Henry VI
1198–1208	Philip of Swabia
1198–1215	Otto IV (Welf)
1220–1250	Frederick II
1250–1254	Conrad IV

Interregnum, 1254–1273: Emperors from Various Dynasties

1273–1291	Rudolf I (Habsburg)
1292–1298	Adolf (Nassau)
1298–1308	Albert I (Habsburg)
1308–1313	Henry VII (Luxemburg)
1314–1347	Ludwig IV (Wittelsbach)
1347–1378	Charles IV (Luxemburg)
1378–1400	Wenceslas (Luxemburg)
1400–1410	Rupert (Wittelsbach)
1410–1437	Sigismund (Luxemburg)

Habsburg Dynasty

1438–1439	Albert II
1440–1493	Frederick III
1493–1519	Maximilian I
1519–1556	Charles V
1556–1564	Ferdinand I
1564–1576	Maximilian II
1576–1612	Rudolf II
1612–1619	Matthias
1619–1637	Ferdinand II
1637–1657	Ferdinand III
1658–1705	Leopold I
1705–1711	Joseph I
1711–1740	Charles VI
1742–1745	Charles VII (not a Habsburg)
1745–1765	Francis I
1765–1790	Joseph II
1790–1792	Leopold II
1792–1806	Francis II

Rulers of France

Capetian Dynasty

987–996	Hugh Capet
996–1031	Robert II
1031–1060	Henry I
1060–1108	Philip I
1108–1137	Louis VI
1137–1180	Louis VII
1180–1223	Philip II (Augustus)
1223–1226	Louis VIII
1226–1270	Louis IX (St. Louis)
1270–1285	Philip III
1285–1314	Philip IV
1314–1316	Louis X
1316–1322	Philip V
1322–1328	Charles IV

Valois Dynasty

1328–1350	Philip VI
1350–1364	John
1364–1380	Charles V
1380–1422	Charles VI
1422–1461	Charles VII
1461–1483	Louis XI
1483–1498	Charles VIII
1498–1515	Louis XII
1515–1547	Francis I
1547–1559	Henry II
1559–1560	Francis II
1560–1574	Charles IX
1574–1589	Henry III

Bourbon Dynasty

1589–1610	Henry IV
1610–1643	Louis XIII
1643–1715	Louis XIV
1715–1774	Louis XV
1774–1792	Louis XVI

After 1792

1792–1799	First Republic
1799–1804	Napoleon Bonaparte, First Consul
1804–1814	Napoleon I, Emperor
1814–1824	Louis XVIII (Bourbon Dynasty)
1824–1830	Charles X (Bourbon Dynasty)
1830–1848	Louis Philippe
1848–1852	Second Republic
1852–1870	Napoleon III, Emperor
1870–1940	Third Republic
1940–1944	Vichy government, Pétain regime
1944–1946	Provisional government
1946–1958	Fourth Republic
1958–	Fifth Republic

Monarchs of England and Great Britain

Anglo-Saxon Monarchs

829–839	Egbert
839–858	Ethelwulf
858–860	Ethelbald
860–866	Ethelbert
866–871	Ethelred I
871–899	Alfred the Great
899–924	Edward the Elder
924–939	Ethelstan
939–946	Edmund I
946–955	Edred
955–959	Edwy
959–975	Edgar
975–978	Edward the Martyr
978–1016	Ethelred the Unready
1016–1035	Canute (Danish nationality)
1035–1040	Harold I
1040–1042	Hardicanute
1042–1066	Edward the Confessor
1066	Harold II

Norman Monarchs

1066–1087	William I (the Conqueror)
1087–1100	William II
1100–1135	Henry I

House of Blois

1135–1154	Stephen

House of Plantagenet

1154–1189	Henry II
1189–1199	Richard I
1199–1216	John
1216–1272	Henry III
1272–1307	Edward I
1307–1327	Edward II
1327–1377	Edward III
1377–1399	Richard II

House of Lancaster

1399–1413	Henry IV
1413–1422	Henry V
1422–1461	Henry VI

House of York

1461–1483	Edward IV
1483	Edward V
1483–1485	Richard III

House of Tudor

1485–1509	Henry VII
1509–1547	Henry VIII
1547–1553	Edward VI
1553–1558	Mary
1558–1603	Elizabeth I

House of Stuart

1603–1625	James I
1625–1649	Charles I

Commonwealth and Protectorate (1649–1660)

1653–1658	Oliver Cromwell
1658–1659	Richard Cromwell

House of Stuart (Restored)

1660–1685	Charles II
1685–1688	James II
1689–1694	William III and Mary II
1694–1702	William III (alone)
1702–1714	Anne

House of Hanover

1714–1727	George I
1727–1760	George II
1760–1820	George III
1820–1830	George IV
1830–1837	William IV
1837–1901	Victoria

House of Saxe-Coburg-Gotha

1901–1910	Edward VII

House of Windsor

1910–1936	George V
1936	Edward VIII
1936–1952	George VI
1952–	Elizabeth II

Prime Ministers of Great Britain

Term	Prime Minister	Government
1721–1742	Sir Robert Walpole	Whig
1742–1743	Spencer Compton, Earl of Wilmington	Whig
1743–1754	Henry Pelham	Whig
1754–1756	Thomas Pelham-Holles, Duke of Newcastle	Whig
1756–1757	William Cavendish, Duke of Devonshire	Whig
1757–1761	William Pitt (the Elder), Earl of Chatham	Whig
1761–1762	Thomas Pelham-Holles, Duke of Newcastle	Whig
1762–1763	John Stuart, Earl of Bute	Tory
1763–1765	George Grenville	Whig
1765–1766	Charles Watson-Wentworth, Marquess of Rockingham	Whig
1766–1768	William Pitt, Earl of Chatham (the Elder)	Whig
1768–1770	Augustus Henry Fitzroy, Duke of Grafton	Whig
1770–1782	Frederick North (Lord North)	Tory
1782	Charles Watson-Wentworth, Marquess of Rockingham	Whig
1782–1783	William Petty FitzMaurice, Earl of Shelburn	Whig
1783	William Henry Cavendish Bentinck, Duke of Portland	Whig
1783–1801	William Pitt (the Younger)	Tory
1801–1804	Henry Addington	Tory
1804–1806	William Pitt (the Younger)	Tory
1806–1807	William Wyndham Grenville (Baron Grenville)	Whig
1807–1809	William Henry Cavendish Bentinck, Duke of Portland	Tory
1809–1812	Spencer Perceval	Tory
1812–1827	Robert Banks Jenkinson, Earl of Liverpool	Tory
1827	George Canning	Tory
1827–1828	Frederick John Robinson (Viscount Goderich)	Tory
1828–1830	Arthur Wellesley, Duke of Wellington	Tory
1830–1834	Charles Grey (Earl Grey)	Whig
1834	William Lamb, Viscount Melbourne	Whig
1834–1835	Sir Robert Peel	Tory
1835–1841	William Lamb, Viscount Melbourne	Whig
1841–1846	Sir Robert Peel	Tory
1846–1852	John Russell (Lord)	Whig
1852	Edward Geoffrey–Smith Stanley Derby, Earl of Derby	Whig
1852–1855	George Hamilton Gordon Aberdeen, Earl of Aberdeen	Peelite
1855–1858	Henry John Temple Palmerston, Viscount Palmerston	Tory
1858–1859	Edward Geoffrey–Smith Stanley Derby, Earl of Derby	Whig
1859–1865	Henry John Temple Palmerston, Viscount Palmerston	Tory
1865–1866	John Russell (Earl)	Liberal
1866–1868	Edward Geoffrey–Smith Stanley Derby, Earl of Derby	Tory
1868	Benjamin Disraeli, Earl of Beaconfield	Conservative
1868–1874	William Ewart Gladstone	Liberal
1874–1880	Benjamin Disraeli, Earl of Beaconfield	Conservative
1880–1885	William Ewart Gladstone	Liberal
1885–1886	Robert Arthur Talbot, Marquess of Salisbury	Conservative
1886	William Ewart Gladstone	Liberal
1886–1892	Robert Arthur Talbot, Marquess of Salisbury	Conservative
1892–1894	William Ewart Gladstone	Liberal
1894–1895	Archibald Philip–Primrose Rosebery, Earl of Rosebery	Liberal
1895–1902	Robert Arthur Talbot, Marquess of Salisbury	Conservative
1902–1905	Arthur James Balfour, Earl of Balfour	Conservative
1905–1908	Sir Henry Campbell-Bannerman	Liberal
1908–1915	Herbert Henry Asquith	Liberal
1915–1916	Herbert Henry Asquith	Coalition
1916–1922	David Lloyd George, Earl Lloyd-George of Dwyfor	Coalition
1922–1923	Andrew Bonar Law	Conservative
1923–1924	Stanley Baldwin, Earl Baldwin of Bewdley	Conservative
1924	James Ramsay MacDonald	Labour
1924–1929	Stanley Baldwin, Earl Baldwin of Bewdley	Conservative
1929–1931	James Ramsay MacDonald	Labour
1931–1935	James Ramsay MacDonald	Coalition
1935–1937	Stanley Baldwin, Earl Baldwin of Bewdley	Coalition
1937–1940	Neville Chamberlain	Coalition
1940–1945	Winston Churchill	Coalition
1945	Winston Churchill	Conservative
1945–1951	Clement Attlee, Earl Attlee	Labour
1951–1955	Sir Winston Churchill	Conservative
1955–1957	Sir Anthony Eden, Earl of Avon	Conservative
1957–1963	Harold Macmillan, Earl of Stockton	Conservative
1963–1964	Sir Alec Frederick Douglas-Home, Lord Home of the Hirsel	Conservative
1964–1970	Harold Wilson, Lord Wilson of Rievaulx	Labour
1970–1974	Edward Heath	Conservative
1974–1976	Harold Wilson, Lord Wilson of Rievaulx	Labour
1976–1979	James Callaghan, Lord Callaghan of Cardiff	Labour
1979–1990	Margaret Thatcher (Baroness)	Conservative
1990–1997	John Major	Conservative
1997–2007	Tony Blair	Labour
2007–2010	Gordon Brown	Labour
2010–	David Cameron	Conservative

Rulers of Prussia and Germany

1701–1713	*Frederick I
1713–1740	*Frederick William I
1740–1786	*Frederick II (the Great)
1786–1797	*Frederick William II
1797–1840	*Frederick William III
1840–1861	*Frederick William IV
1861–1888	*William I (German emperor after 1871)
1888	Frederick III
1888–1918	*William II
1918–1933	Weimar Republic
1933–1945	Third Reich (Nazi dictatorship under Adolf Hitler)
1945–1952	Allied occupation
1949–1990	Division of Federal Republic of Germany in west and German Democratic Republic in east
1990–	Federal Republic of Germany (reunited)

*King of Prussia.

Rulers of Austria and Austria-Hungary

1493–1519	*Maximilian I (Archduke)
1519–1556	*Charles V
1556–1564	*Ferdinand I
1564–1576	*Maximilian II
1576–1612	*Rudolf II
1612–1619	*Matthias
1619–1637	*Ferdinand II
1637–1657	*Ferdinand III
1658–1705	*Leopold I
1705–1711	*Joseph I
1711–1740	*Charles VI
1740–1780	Maria Theresa
1780–1790	*Joseph II
1790–1792	*Leopold II
1792–1835	*Francis II (emperor of Austria as Francis I after 1804)
1835–1848	Ferdinand I
1848–1916	Francis Joseph (after 1867 emperor of Austria and king of Hungary)
1916–1918	Charles I (emperor of Austria and king of Hungary)
1918–1938	Republic of Austria (dictatorship after 1934)
1945–1956	Republic restored, under Allied occupation
1956–	Free Republic

*Also bore title of Holy Roman Emperor.

Leaders of Post–World War II Germany

West Germany (Federal Republic of Germany), 1949–1990

Years	*Chancellor*	*Party*
1949–1963	Konrad Adenauer	Christian Democratic Union (CDU)
1963–1966	Ludwig Erhard	Christian Democratic Union (CDU)
1966–1969	Kurt Georg Kiesinger	Christian Democratic Union (CDU)
1969–1974	Willy Brandt	Social Democratic Party (SPD)
1974–1982	Helmut Schmidt	Social Democratic Party (SPD)
1982–1990	Helmut Kohl	Christian Democratic Union (CDU)

East Germany (German Democratic Republic), 1949–1990

Years	*Communist Party Leader*
1946–1971	Walter Ulbricht
1971–1989	Erich Honecker
1989–1990	Egon Krenz

Federal Republic of Germany (reunited), 1990–

Years	*Chancellor*	*Party*
1990–1998	Helmut Kohl	Christian Democratic Union (CDU)
1998–2005	Gerhard Schroeder	Social Democratic Party (SPD)
2005–	Angela Merkel	Christian Democratic Union (CDU)

Rulers of Russia, the USSR, and the Russian Federation

c. 980–1015	Vladimir
1019–1054	Yaroslav the Wise
1176–1212	Vsevolod III
1462–1505	Ivan III
1505–1553	Vasily III
1553–1584	Ivan IV
1584–1598	Theodore I
1598–1605	Boris Godunov
1605	Theodore II
1606–1610	Vasily IV
1613–1645	Michael
1645–1676	Alexius
1676–1682	Theodore III
1682–1689	Ivan V and Peter I
1689–1725	Peter I (the Great)
1725–1727	Catherine I
1727–1730	Peter II
1730–1740	Anna
1740–1741	Ivan VI
1741–1762	Elizabeth
1762	Peter III
1762–1796	Catherine II (the Great)
1796–1801	Paul
1801–1825	Alexander I
1825–1855	Nicholas I
1855–1881	Alexander II
1881–1894	Alexander III
1894–1917	Nicholas II

Union of Soviet Socialist Republics (USSR)*

1917–1924	Vladimir Ilyich Lenin
1924–1953	Joseph Stalin
1953–1964	Nikita Khrushchev
1964–1982	Leonid Brezhnev
1982–1984	Yuri Andropov
1984–1985	Konstantin Chernenko
1985–1991	Mikhail Gorbachev

Russian Federation

1991–1999	Boris Yeltsin
1999–2008	Vladimir Putin
2008–	Dmitry Medvedev

*USSR established in 1922.

Rulers of Spain

1479–1504	Ferdinand and Isabella
1504–1506	Ferdinand and Philip I
1506–1516	Ferdinand and Charles I
1516–1556	Charles I (Holy Roman Emperor Charles V)
1556–1598	Philip II
1598–1621	Philip III
1621–1665	Philip IV
1665–1700	Charles II
1700–1746	Philip V
1746–1759	Ferdinand VI
1759–1788	Charles III
1788–1808	Charles IV
1808	Ferdinand VII
1808–1813	Joseph Bonaparte
1814–1833	Ferdinand VII (restored)
1833–1868	Isabella II
1868–1870	Republic
1870–1873	Amadeo
1873–1874	Republic
1874–1885	Alfonso XII
1886–1931	Alfonso XIII
1931–1939	Republic
1939–1975	Fascist dictatorship under Francisco Franco
1975–	Juan Carlos I

Rulers of Italy

1861–1878	Victor Emmanuel II
1878–1900	Humbert I
1900–1946	Victor Emmanuel III
1922–1943	Fascist dictatorship under Benito Mussolini (maintained in northern Italy until 1945)
1946 (May 9–June 13)	Humbert II
1946–	Republic

Secretaries-General of the United Nations

Years	Secretary-General	Nationality
1946–1952	Trygve Lie	Norway
1953–1961	Dag Hammarskjöld	Sweden
1961–1971	U Thant	Myanmar
1972–1981	Kurt Waldheim	Austria
1982–1991	Javier Pérez de Cuéllar	Peru
1992–1996	Boutros Boutros-Ghali	Egypt
1997–2006	Kofi A. Annan	Ghana
2007–	Ban Kimoon	South Korea

United States Presidential Administrations

Term(s)	President	Political Party
1789–1797	George Washington	No party designation
1797–1801	John Adams	Federalist
1801–1809	Thomas Jefferson	Democratic-Republican
1809–1817	James Madison	Democratic-Republican
1817–1825	James Monroe	Democratic-Republican
1825–1829	John Quincy Adams	Democratic-Republican
1829–1837	Andrew Jackson	Democratic
1837–1841	Martin Van Buren	Democratic
1841	William H. Harrison	Whig
1841–1845	John Tyler	Whig
1845–1849	James K. Polk	Democratic
1849–1850	Zachary Taylor	Whig
1850–1853	Millard Filmore	Whig
1853–1857	Franklin Pierce	Democratic
1857–1861	James Buchanan	Democratic
1861–1865	Abraham Lincoln	Republican
1865–1869	Andrew Johnson	Republican
1869–1877	Ulysses S. Grant	Republican
1877–1881	Rutherford B. Hayes	Republican
1881	James A. Garfield	Republican
1881–1885	Chester A. Arthur	Republican
1885–1889	Grover Cleveland	Democratic
1889–1893	Benjamin Harrison	Republican
1893–1897	Grover Cleveland	Democratic
1897–1901	William McKinley	Republican
1901–1909	Theodore Roosevelt	Republican
1909–1913	William H. Taft	Republican
1913–1921	Woodrow Wilson	Democratic
1921–1923	Warren G. Harding	Republican
1923–1929	Calvin Coolidge	Republican
1929–1933	Herbert C. Hoover	Republican
1933–1945	Franklin D. Roosevelt	Democratic
1945–1953	Harry S. Truman	Democratic
1953–1961	Dwight D. Eisenhower	Republican
1961–1963	John F. Kennedy	Democratic
1963–1969	Lyndon B. Johnson	Democratic
1969–1974	Richard M. Nixon	Republican
1974–1977	Gerald R. Ford	Republican
1977–1981	Jimmy Carter	Democratic
1981–1989	Ronald W. Reagan	Republican
1989–1993	George H. W. Bush	Republican
1993–2001	William J. Clinton	Democratic
2001–2009	George W. Bush	Republican
2009–	Barack Obama	Democratic

Major Wars of the Modern Era

1546–1555	German Wars of Religion
1526–1571	Ottoman wars
1562–1598	French Wars of Religion
1566–1609, 1621–1648	Revolt of the Netherlands
1618–1648	Thirty Years' War
1642–1648	English Civil War
1652–1678	Anglo-Dutch Wars
1667–1697	Wars of Louis XIV
1683–1697	Ottoman wars
1689–1697	War of the League of Augsburg
1702–1714	War of Spanish Succession
1702–1721	Great Northern War
1714–1718	Ottoman wars
1740–1748	War of Austrian Succession
1756–1763	Seven Years' War
1775–1781	American Revolution
1796–1815	Napoleonic wars
1846–1848	Mexican-American War
1853–1856	Crimean War
1861–1865	United States Civil War
1870–1871	Franco-Prussian War
1894–1895	Sino-Japanese War
1898	Spanish-American War
1904–1905	Russo-Japanese War
1914–1918	World War I
1939–1945	World War II
1946–1975	Vietnam wars
1950–1953	Korean War
1990–1991	Persian Gulf War
1991–1997	Civil War in the former Yugoslavia
2001–	War in Afghanistan
2003–	Iraq War

Glossary of Key Terms and People

This glossary contains definitions of terms and people that are central to your understanding of the material covered in this textbook. Each term or person in the glossary is in boldface in the text when it is first defined, then listed again in the corresponding Chapter Review section to signal its importance. We have also included the page number on which the full discussion of the term or person appears so that you can easily locate the complete explanation to strengthen your historical vocabulary.

For words or names not defined here, two additional resources may be useful: the index, which will direct you to many more topics discussed in the text, and a good dictionary.

Abbasids (283): The dynasty of caliphs that, in 750, took over from the Umayyads in all of the Islamic realm except for Spain (al-Andalus). From their new capital at Baghdad, they presided over a wealthy realm until the late ninth century.

agora (83): The central market square of a Greek city-state, a popular gathering place for conversation.

Alexander the Great (116): The fourth-century B.C.E. Macedonian king whose conquest of the Persian Empire led to the greatly increased cultural interactions of Greece and the Near East in the Hellenistic Age.

Alexius I (Alexius Comnenus) (330): The Byzantine emperor (r. 1081–1118) whose leadership marked a new triumph of the *dynatoi*. His request to Pope Urban II for troops to fight the Turks turned into the First Crusade.

Alfred the Great (303): King of Wessex (r. 871–899) and the first king to rule over most of England. He organized a successful defense against Viking invaders, had key Latin works translated into the vernacular, and wrote a law code for the whole of England.

Anatolia (7): The large peninsula that is today the nation of Turkey.

apostolic succession (193): The principle by which Christian bishops traced their authority back to the apostles of Jesus.

apprentices (316): Boys (and occasionally girls) placed under the tutelage of a master craftsman in the Middle Ages. Normally unpaid, they were expected to be servants of their masters, with whom they lived, at the same time as they were learning their trade.

aretê (49): The Greek value of competitive individual excellence.

Arianism (219): The Christian doctrine named after Arius, who argued that Jesus was "begotten" by God and did not have an identical nature with God the Father.

Aristotle (114): Greek philosopher famous for his scientific investigations, development of logical argument, and practical ethics.

asceticism (222): The practice of self-denial, especially through spiritual discipline; a doctrine for Christians emphasized by Augustine.

Augustine (218): Bishop in North Africa whose writings defining religious orthodoxy made him the most influential theologian in Western civilization.

Augustus (173): The honorary name meaning "divinely favored" that the Roman Senate bestowed on Octavian; it became shorthand for "Roman imperial ruler."

Avignon papacy (401): The period (1309–1378) during which the popes ruled from Avignon rather than from Rome.

Basil II (281): The Byzantine emperor (r. 976–1025) who presided over the end of the Bulgar threat (earning the name Bulgar-Slayer) and the conversion of Kievan Russia to Christianity.

battle of Hastings (336): The battle of 1066 that replaced the Anglo-Saxon king with a Norman one and thus tied England to the rest of Europe as never before.

Black Death (412): The term historians give to the disease that swept through Europe in 1347–1352.

blood libel (388): The charge that Jews used the blood of Christian children in their Passover ritual; though false, it led to massacres of Jews in cities in England, France, Spain, and Germany in the thirteenth century.

Boniface VIII (400): The pope (r. 1294–1303) whose clash with King Philip the Fair of France left the papacy considerably weakened.

Capetian dynasty (304): A long-lasting dynasty of French kings, taking their name from Hugh Capet (r. 987–996).

capitalism (317): The modern economic system characterized by an entrepreneurial class of property owners who employ others and produce (or provide services) for a market in order to make a profit.

Carolingian (287): The Frankish dynasty that ruled a western European empire from 751 to the late 800s; its greatest vigor was in the time of Charlemagne (r. 768–814) and Louis the Pious (r. 814–840).

castellan (300): The holder of a castle. In the tenth and eleventh centuries, castellans became important local lords. They mustered men for military service, collected taxes, and administered justice.

chansons de geste (368): Epic poems of the twelfth century about knightly and heroic deeds.

Charlemagne (287): The Carolingian king (r. 768–814) whose conquests greatly expanded the Frankish kingdom. He was crowned emperor on December 25, 800.

chivalry (369): An ideal of knightly comportment that included military prowess, bravery, fair play, piety, and courtesy.

Christ (190): Greek for "anointed one," in Hebrew *Mashiach* or in English *Messiah*; in apocalyptic thought, God's agent sent to conquer the forces of evil.

Cicero (156): Rome's most famous orator and author of the doctrine of *humanitas*.

city-state (8): An urban center exercising political and economic control over the surrounding countryside.

civilization (4): A way of life based in cities with dense populations organized as political states, large buildings constructed for communal activities, the production of food, diverse economies, a sense of local identity, and some knowledge of writing.

coloni (212): Literally, "cultivators"; tenant farmers in the Roman Empire who became bound by law to the land they worked and whose children were legally required to continue to farm the same land.

Colosseum (183): Rome's fifty-thousand-seat amphitheater built by the Flavian dynasty for gladiatorial combats and other spectacles.

commercial revolution (312): A term for the western European development (starting around 1050) of a money economy centered in urban areas but affecting the countryside as well.

common law (357): Begun by Henry II (r. 1154–1189), the English royal law carried out by the king's justices in eyre (traveling justices). It applied to the entire kingdom and thus was "common" to all.

commune (318): In a medieval town, a sworn association of citizens who formed a legal corporate body. The commune appointed or elected officials, made laws, kept the peace, and administered justice.

Concordat of Worms (322): The agreement between pope and emperor in 1122 that ended the Investiture Conflict.

cortes (399): The earliest European representative institution, called initially to consent to royal wishes; first convoked in 1188 by the king of Castile-León.

cult (57): In ancient Greece, a set of official, publicly funded religious activities for a deity overseen by priests and priestesses.

cuneiform (11): The earliest form of writing, invented in Mesopotamia and done with wedge-shaped characters.

curials (212): The social elite in Roman empires' cities and towns, most of whom were obliged to serve as decurions on municipal Senates and collect taxes for the imperial government, paying any shortfalls themselves.

Cyrus (41): Founder of the Persian Empire.

debasement of coinage (198): Putting less silver in a coin without changing its face value; a failed financial strategy during the third-century C.E. crisis in Rome.

decurions (185): Municipal Senate members in the Roman Empire responsible for collecting local taxes.

Delian League (80): The naval alliance led by Athens in the Golden Age that became the basis for the Athenian Empire.

demes (68): The villages and city neighborhoods that formed the constituent political units of Athenian democracy in the late Archaic Age.

demography (P-9): The study of the size, growth, density, distribution, and vital statistics of the human population.

Diaspora (47): The dispersal of the Jewish population from their homeland.

dominate (207): The openly authoritarian style of Roman rule from Diocletian (r. 284–305) onward; the word was derived from *dominus* ("master" or "lord") and contrasted with *principate*.

dualism (113): The philosophical idea that the human soul (or mind) and body are separate.

dynatoi (280): The "powerful men" who dominated the countryside of the Byzantine Empire in the tenth and eleventh centuries, and to some degree challenged the authority of the emperor.

Edict of Milan (213): The proclamation of Roman co-emperors Constantine and Licinius decreeing free choice of religion in the empire.

empire (12): A political state in which one or more formerly independent territories or peoples are ruled by a single sovereign power.

Epicureanism (129): The philosophy founded by Epicurus of Athens to help people achieve a life of true pleasure, by which he meant "absence of disturbance."

epigrams (127): Short poems written by women in the Hellenistic Age; many were about other women and the writer's personal feelings.

equites (159): Literally, "equestrians" or "knights"; wealthy Roman businessmen who chose not to pursue a government career.

Fatimids (284): Members of the tenth-century Shi'ite dynasty who derived their name from Fatimah, the daughter of Muhammad and wife of Ali; they dominated in parts of North Africa, Egypt, and even Syria.

feudalism (297): The whole complex of lords, vassals, and fiefs (from the Latin *feodum*) as an institution. The nature of that institution varied from place to place, and in some regions it did not exist at all.

fiefs (297): Grants of land, theoretically temporary, from lords to their noble dependents (*fideles* or, later, vassals) given in recognition of services, usually military, done or expected in the future; also called *benefices*.

First Crusade (331): The massive armed pilgrimage to Jerusalem that lasted from 1096 to 1099. It resulted in the massacre of Jews in the Rhineland (1095), the sack of Jerusalem (1099), and the setting up of the crusader states.

First Triumvirate (164): The coalition formed in 60 B.C.E. by Pompey, Crassus, and Caesar. (The word *triumvirate* means "group of three.")

Five Pillars of Islam (247): The five essential practices of Islam, namely, the *zakat* (alms); the fast of Ramadan; the *hajj* (pilgrimage to Mecca); the *salat* (formal worship); and the *shahadah* (profession of faith).

Fourth Crusade (372): The crusade that lasted from 1202 to 1204; its original goal was to recapture Jerusalem, but the crusaders ended up conquering Constantinople instead.

Fourth Lateran Council (383): The council that met in 1215 and covered the important topics of Christianity, among them the nature of the sacraments, the obligations of the laity, and policies toward heretics and Jews.

Franciscans (369): The religious order founded by St. Francis (c. 1182–1226) and dedicated to poverty and preaching, particularly in towns and cities.

Frederick I (Barbarossa) (362): King of Germany (r. 1152–1190) and emperor (crowned 1155) who tried to cement the power of the German king through conquest (for example, of northern Italy) and the bonds of vassalage.

Frederick II (397): The grandson of Barbarossa who became king of Sicily and Germany, as well as emperor (r. 1212–1250), who allowed the German princes a free hand as he battled the pope for control of Italy.

Golden Horde (403): The political institution set up by the Mongols in Russia, lasting from the thirteenth to the fifteenth century.

Gothic architecture (351): The style of architecture that started in the Île-de-France in the twelfth century and eventually became the quintessential cathedral style of the Middle Ages, characterized by pointed arches, ribbed vaults, and stained-glass windows.

Great Famine (403): The shortage of food and accompanying social ills that besieged northern Europe between 1315 and 1322.

Great Persecution (213): The violent program initiated by Diocletian in 303 to make Christians convert to traditional religion or risk confiscation of their property and even death.

Great Schism (424): The papal dispute of 1378–1417 when the church had two and even (between 1409 and 1417) three popes. The Great Schism was ended by the Council of Constance.

Gregorian reform (321): The papal movement for church reform associated with Gregory VII (r. 1073–1085); its ideals included ending three practices: the purchase of church offices, clerical marriage, and lay investiture.

Gregory of Tours (260): Bishop of Tours (in Gaul) from 573 to 594, the chief source for the history and culture of the Merovingian kingdoms.

Gregory the Great (266): The pope (r. 590–604) who sent missionaries to Anglo-Saxon England, wrote influential books, tried to reform the church, and had contact with the major ruling families of Europe and Byzantium.

guild (316): A trade organization within a city or town that controlled product quality and cost and outlined members' responsibilities. Guilds were also social and religious associations.

Hammurabi (14): King of Babylonia in the eighteenth century B.C.E., famous for his law code.

Hanseatic League (437): A league of northern European cities formed in the fourteenth century to protect their mutual interests in trade and defense.

Hellenistic (120): An adjective meaning "Greek-like" that is today used as a chronological term for the period 323–30 B.C.E.

helot (64): A slave owned by the Spartan city-state; such slaves came from parts of Greece conquered by the Spartans.

Henry II (354): King of England (r. 1154–1189) who ended the period of civil war there and affirmed and expanded royal powers. He is associated with the creation of common law in England.

Henry IV (321): King of Germany (r. 1056–1106), crowned emperor in 1084. From 1075 until his death, he was embroiled in the Investiture Conflict with Pope Gregory VII.

Heraclius (252): The Byzantine emperor who reversed the fortunes of war with the Persians in the first quarter of the seventh century.

heresy (194): False doctrine; specifically, the beliefs banned for Christians by councils of bishops.

hetaira (91): A witty and attractive woman who charged fees to entertain at a symposium.

hierarchy (P-5): The system of ranking people in society according to their status and authority.

hieroglyphic (18): The ancient Egyptian pictographic writing system for official texts.

Hijra (246): The emigration of Muhammad from Mecca to Medina. Its date, 622, marks year 1 of the Islamic calendar.

Homer (49): Greece's first and most famous author, who composed *The Iliad* and *The Odyssey*.

Homo sapiens sapiens (P-3): The scientific name (in Latin) of the type of early human being identical to people today; it means "wise, wise human being."

hoplite (58): A heavily armed Greek infantryman. Hoplites constituted the main strike force of a city-state's militia.

hubris (99): The Greek term for violent arrogance.

humanism (428): A literary and linguistic movement cultivated in particular during the Renaissance (1350–1600) and founded on reviving classical Latin and Greek texts, styles, and values.

humanitas (156): The Roman orator Cicero's ideal of "humaneness," meaning generous and honest treatment of others based on natural law.

Hundred Years' War (417): The long war between England and France, 1337–1453 (actually 116 years); it produced numerous social upheavals yet left both states more powerful than before.

hunter-gatherers (P-3): Human beings who roam to hunt and gather food in the wild and do not live in permanent, settled communities.

iconoclasm (256): Literally, "icon breaking"; referring to the destruction of icons, or images of holy people. Byzantine emperors banned icons from 726 to 787; a modified ban was revived in 815 and lasted until 843.

icons (256): Images of holy people such as Jesus, Mary, and the saints. Controversy arose in Byzantium over the meaning of such images. The iconoclasts considered them "idols," but those who adored icons maintained that they manifested the physical form of those who were holy.

indulgence (425): A step beyond confession and penance, an indulgence (normally granted by popes or bishops) lifted the temporal punishment still necessary for a sin already forgiven. Normally, that punishment was said to take place in purgatory. But it could be remitted through good works (including prayers and contributing money to worthy causes).

Innocent III (382): The pope (r. 1198–1216) who called the Fourth Lateran Council; he was the most powerful, respected, and prestigious of medieval popes.

Investiture Conflict (322): The confrontation between Pope Gregory VII and Emperor Henry IV that began in 1075 over the appointment of prelates in some Italian cities and grew into a dispute over the nature of church leadership. It ended in 1122 with the Concordat of Worms.

Jacquerie (421): The 1358 uprising of French peasants against the nobles amid the Hundred Years' War; it was brutally put down.

jihad (247): In the Qur'an, the word means "striving in the way of God." This can mean both striving to live righteously and striving to confront unbelievers, even through holy war.

Joan of Arc (417): A peasant girl (1412–1431) whose conviction that God had sent her to save France in fact helped France win the Hundred Years' War.

journeymen/journeywomen (316): Laborers in the Middle Ages whom guildmasters hired for a daily wage to help them produce their products.

Julian the Apostate (215): The Roman emperor (r. 361–363), who rejected Christianity and tried to restore traditional religion as the state religion. *Apostate* means "renegade from the faith."

Julio-Claudians (181): The ruling family of the early principate from Augustus through Nero, descended from the aristocratic families of the Julians and the Claudians.

Justinian and Theodora (233): Sixth-century emperor and empress of the eastern Roman Empire, famous for waging costly wars to reunite the empire.

Koine (132): The "common" or "shared" form of the Greek language that became the international language in the Hellenistic period.

ladder of offices (149): The series of Roman elective government offices from quaestor to aedile to praetor to consul.

lay investiture (320): The installation of clerics into their offices by lay rulers.

leprosy (388): A bacterial disease that causes skin lesions and attacks peripheral nerves. In the Middle Ages, lepers were isolated from society.

Linear B (30): The Mycenaeans' pictographic script for writing Greek.

Lombards (252): The people who settled in Italy during the sixth century, following Justinian's reconquest. A king ruled the north of Italy, while dukes ruled the south. In between was the papacy, which felt threatened both by Lombard Arianism and by the Lombards' proximity to Rome.

Louis IX (398): A French king (r. 1226–1270) revered as a military leader and a judge; he was declared a saint after his death.

Lyceum (114): The school for research and teaching in a wide range of subjects founded by Aristotle in Athens in 335 B.C.E.

Maat (20): The Egyptian goddess embodying truth, justice, and cosmic order. (The word *maat* means "what is right.")

Magna Carta (359): Literally, "Great Charter"; the charter of baronial liberties that King John was forced to agree to in 1215. It implied that royal power was subject to custom and law.

martyr (193): Greek for "witness," the term for someone who dies for his or her religious beliefs.

masters (316): Men (and occasionally women) who, having achieved expertise in a craft, ran the guilds in the Middle Ages. They had to be rich enough to have their own shop and tools and to pay an entry fee into the guild. Often their positions were hereditary.

materialism (128): A philosophical doctrine of the Hellenistic Age that denied metaphysics and claimed instead that only things consisting of matter truly exist.

Medici (443): The ruling family of Florence during much of the fifteenth to the seventeenth centuries.

Mediterranean polyculture (28): The cultivation of olives, grapes, and grains in a single, interrelated agricultural system.

Mehmed II (423): The sultan under whom the Ottoman Turks conquered Constantinople in 1453.

Merovingian dynasty (258): The royal dynasty that ruled Gaul from about 486 to 751.

metaphysics (113): Philosophical ideas about the ultimate nature of reality beyond the reach of human senses.

metic (87): A foreigner granted permanent residence status in Athens in return for paying taxes and serving in the military.

monotheism (6): The belief in and worship of only one god, as in Judaism, Christianity, and Islam.

moral dualism (43): The belief that the world is the arena for an ongoing battle for control between divine forces of good and evil.

mos maiorum (140): Literally, "the way of the elders"; the set of Roman values handed down from the ancestors.

Muhammad (244): The prophet of Islam (c. 570–632). He united a community of believers around his religious tenets, above all that there was one God whose words had been revealed to him by the angel Gabriel. Later, written down, these revelations became the Qur'an.

mystery cults (87): Religious worship that provided initiation into secret knowledge and divine protection, including hope for a better afterlife.

Neolithic Age (P-2): The "New Stone" Age, dating from around 10,000 to 4000 B.C.E.

Neolithic Revolution (P-6): The invention of agriculture, the domestication of animals, and the consequent changes in human society that occurred about 10,000–8000 B.C.E. in the Near East.

Neoplatonism (196): Plotinus's spiritual philosophy, based mainly on Plato's ideas, which was very influential for Christian intellectuals.

Nicene Creed (220): The doctrine agreed on by the council of bishops convened by Constantine at Nicaea in 325 to defend orthodoxy against Arianism. It declared that God the Father and Jesus were *homoousion* ("of one substance").

optimates (159): The Roman political faction supporting the "best," or highest, social class; established during the late republic.

orders (148): The two groups of people in the Roman republic—**patricians** (aristocratic families) and **plebeians** (all other citizens).

orthodoxy (194): True doctrine; specifically, the beliefs defined for Christians by councils of bishops.

ostracism (82): An annual procedure in Athenian radical democracy by which a man could be voted out of the city-state for ten years; its purpose was to prevent tyranny.

Ottonian kings (304): The tenth- and early-eleventh-century kings of Germany; beginning with Otto I (r. 936–973), they claimed the imperial crown and worked closely with their bishops to rule a vast territory.

palace society (28): Minoan and Mycenaean social and political organization centered on multichambered buildings housing the rulers and the administration of the state.

Paleolithic Age (P-2): The "Old Stone" Age, dating from around 200,000 to 10,000 B.C.E.

Parthenon (84): The massive temple to Athena as a warrior goddess built atop the Athenian acropolis in the Golden Age of Greece.

patria potestas (142): Literally, "father's power"; the legal power a Roman father possessed over the children and slaves in his family, including owning all their property and having the right to punish them, even with death.

patriarchy (P-13): Dominance by men in society and politics.

patricians: *See* orders.

patrilineal (301): Relating to or tracing descent through the paternal line (for example, through the father and grandfather).

patron-client system (142): The interlocking network of mutual obligations between Roman patrons (social superiors) and clients (social inferiors).

Pax Romana (172): Literally, "Roman Peace"; the two centuries of relative peace and prosperity in the Roman Empire under the early principate begun by Augustus.

Peace of God (302): A movement begun by bishops in the south of France around 990, first to limit the violence done to property and to the unarmed, and later, with the Truce of God, to limit fighting between warriors.

Pericles (81): Athens's political leader during the Golden Age.

Petrarch, Francis (429): An Italian poet (1304–1374) who revived the styles of classical authors; he is considered the first Renaissance humanist.

Philip II (Philip Augustus) (358): King of France (r. 1180–1223) who bested the English king John and won most of John's continental territories, thus immeasurably strengthening the power of the Capetian dynasty.

Plato (112): A follower of Socrates who became Greece's most famous philosopher.

plebeians: *See* orders.

plebiscites (150): Resolutions passed by the Plebeian Assembly; such resolutions gained the force of law in 287 B.C.E.

polis (51): The Greek city-state, an independent community of citizens not ruled by a king.

political states (P-2): People living in a defined territory with boundaries and organized under a system of government with powerful officials, leaders, and judges.

polytheism (6): The belief in and worship of multiple gods.

popolo (401): Literally, "people"; a communal faction, largely made up of merchants, that demanded (and often obtained) power in thirteenth-century Italian cities.

populares (159): The Roman political faction supporting the common people; established during the late republic.

praetorian guard (174): The group of soldiers stationed in Rome under the emperor's control; first formed by Augustus.

primogeniture (301): An inheritance practice that left all property to the oldest son.

principate (173): Roman political system invented by Augustus as a disguised monarchy with the *princeps* ("first man") as emperor.

proletarians (159): In the Roman republic, the mass of people so poor they owned no property.

Qur'an (246): The holy book of Islam, considered the word of Allah ("the God") as revealed to the Prophet Muhammad.

radical democracy (81): The Athenian system of democracy established in the 460s and 450s B.C.E. that extended direct political power and participation in the court system to all adult male citizens.

rationalism (70): The philosophic idea that people must justify their claims by logic and reason, not myth.

reconquista (321): The collective name for the wars waged by the Christian princes of Spain against the Muslim-ruled regions to their south. These wars were considered holy, akin to the crusades.

redistributive economy (14): A system in which state officials control the production and distribution of goods.

res publica (145): Literally, "the people's matter" or "the public business"; the Romans' name for their republic and the source of our word *republic*.

Romanesque (350): An architectural style that flourished in Europe between about 1000 and 1150. It is characterized by solid, heavy forms and semicircular arches and vaults. Romanesque buildings were often decorated with fanciful sculpture and wall paintings.

Romanization (185): The spread of Roman law and culture in the provinces of the Roman Empire.

ruler cults (133): Cults that involved worship of a Hellenistic ruler as a savior god.

sacraments (323): In the Catholic church, the institutionalized means by which God's heavenly grace is transmitted to Christians. Examples of sacraments include baptism, the Eucharist (communion), and marriage.

Sappho (69): The most famous woman lyric poet of ancient Greece, a native of Lesbos.

scholasticism (389): The method of logical inquiry used by the scholastics, the scholars of the medieval universities; it applied Aristotelian logic to biblical and other authoritative texts in an attempt to summarize and reconcile all knowledge.

Sea Peoples (31): The diverse groups of raiders who devastated the eastern Mediterranean region in the period of violence 1200–1000 B.C.E.

Shi'ite (250): A Muslim of the "party of Ali" and his descendants. Shi'ites are thus opposed to the Sunni Muslims, who reject the authority of Ali.

simony (320): The sin of giving gifts or paying money to get a church office.

Socratic method (96): The Athenian philosopher Socrates' method of teaching through conversation, in which he asked probing questions to make his listeners examine their most cherished assumptions.

Solon (67): Athenian political reformer whose changes promoted early democracy.

Sophists (94): Competitive intellectuals and teachers in ancient Greece who offered expensive courses in persuasive public speaking and new ways of philosophic and religious thinking beginning around 450 B.C.E.

St. Bernard (327): The most important Cistercian abbot (early twelfth century) and the chief preacher of the Second Crusade.

Statute in Favor of the Princes (397): A statute finalized by Frederick II in 1232 that gave the German princes sovereign power within their own principalities.

Stoicism (130): The Hellenistic philosophy whose followers believed in fate but also in pursuing excellence (virtue) by cultivating good sense, justice, courage, and temperance.

Synod of Whitby (266): The meeting of churchmen and King Oswy of Northumbria in 664 that led to the adoption of the Roman brand of Christianity in England.

tetrarchy (209): The "rule by four," consisting of two co-emperors and two assistant emperors/designated successors, initiated by Diocletian to subdivide the ruling of the Roman Empire into four regions.

theme (255): A military district in Byzantium. The earliest themes were created in the seventh century and served mainly defensive purposes.

Themistocles (77): Athens's leader during the great Persian invasion of Greece.

Theodosius I (216): The Roman emperor (r. 379–395) who made Christianity the state religion by ending public sacrifices in the traditional cults and closing their temples. In 395 he also divided the empire into western and eastern halves to be ruled by his sons.

Torah (45): The first five books of the Hebrew Bible, also referred to as the Pentateuch. It contains early Jewish law.

Treaty of Verdun (292): The treaty that, in 843, split the Carolingian Empire into three parts; its borders roughly outline modern western European states.

triremes (80): Greek wooden warships rowed by 170 oarsmen sitting on three levels and equipped with a battering ram at the bow.

troubadours (366): Vernacular poets in southern France in the twelfth and early thirteenth centuries who sang of love, longing, and courtesy.

Twelve Tables (149): The first written Roman law code, enacted between 451 and 449 B.C.E.

Umayyad caliphate (250): The caliphs (successors of Muhammad) who traced their ancestry to Umayyah, a member of Muhammad's tribe. The dynasty lasted from 661 to 750.

Urban II (330): The pope (r. 1088–1099) responsible for calling the First Crusade in 1095.

Visigoths (229): The name given to the barbarians whom Alaric united and led on a military campaign into the western Roman Empire to establish a new kingdom; they sacked Rome in 410.

wergild (231): Under Frankish law, the payment that a murderer had to make as compensation for the crime, to prevent feuds of revenge.

wisdom literature (22): Texts giving instructions for proper behavior by officials.

ziggurats (8): Mesopotamian temples of massive size built on a stair-step design.

Additional Credits

Chapter 1, page 15: "Hammurabi's Laws for Physicians." From James Pritchard, *Ancient Near Eastern Texts Relating to the Old Testament*, Third Edition with Supplement. Copyright © 1950, 1955, 1969, renewed 1978 by Princeton University Press. Reprinted by permission of Princeton University Press. **Page 25:** "Declaring Innocence on Judgment Day in Ancient Egypt." From "The Declaration to the Forty-two Gods" in *The Book of the Dead*, reprinted in Miriam Lichtheim, trans., *Ancient Egyptian Literature: A Book of Readings*, vol. 2, *The New Kingdom*. Copyright © 1978 by the Regents of the University of California. Reprinted by permission of the University of California Press.

Chapter 3, page 95: "Sophists Argue Both Sides of a Case." Excerpt from *Dissoi Logio* 1.1–6. Translation adapted from *The Older Sophists*, edited by Rosamond Kent Sprague. Copyright © 1972 by Rosamond Kent Sprague. Reprinted by permission of the University of South Carolina Press.

Chapter 6, page 188: "Tertullian's Defense of His Fellow Christians, 197 C.E." Reprinted by permission of the publishers and the Trustees of the Loeb Classical Library from *Tertullian*, Loeb Classical Library Volume 250, translated by T. R. Glover, Cambridge, Mass.: Harvard University Press. Copyright © 1931 by the President and Fellows of Harvard College. The Loeb Classical Library ® is a registered trademark of the President and Fellows of Harvard College. **Page 188:** "Pliny on Early Imperial Policy toward Christians, c. 112 C.E." From *The Letters of the Younger Pliny*, translated with an introduction by Betty Radice (Penguin Classics, 1963; repr., 1969), Book 10, nos. 96 and 97. Copyright © Betty Radice, 1963, 1969. Reproduced by permission of Penguin Books Ltd.

Chapter 8, page 247: "The Fatihah of the Qur'an." From *Approaching the Qur'ān: The Early Revelations*, introduced and translated by Michael Sells. Copyright © 1999 by White Cloud Press. Reprinted by permission of White Cloud Press. **Page 249:** "The Pact of Umar." From "Umar II and the 'Protected People'" in *Classical Islam: A Sourcebook of Religious Literature*, edited and translated by Norman Calder, Jawid Mojaddedi, and Andrew Rippin. Copyright © 2003 Routledge. Reproduced by permission of Taylor & Francis Books UK.

Chapter 9, page 286: "When She Approached" by Ibn Darraj al-Quastali. From "Andalusi Poetry: The Golden Period" in *The Legacy of Muslim Spain*, edited by Salma Khadra Jayyusi, 2 volumes (Leiden: Brill, 1994), 1:335. Copyright © 1994 by Brill. Reprinted by permission of Koninklijke Brill NV. **Page 290:** "Charles as Emperor." From *Charlemagne's Courtier: The Complete Einhard*, edited and translated by Paul Edward Dutton. Copyright © 1998 by Paul Edward Dutton. Broadview Press (University of Toronto Press Higher Education Division). Reprinted with permission of the publisher. **Page 290:** "The 'Father of Europe.'" From *Carolingian Civilization: A Reader*, 2nd edition, edited by Paul Edward Dutton. Copyright © 2004 by Paul Edward Dutton. Broadview Press (University of Toronto Press Higher Education Division). Reprinted with permission of the publisher. **Page 291:** "The Chief Bishop." From *Two Lives of Charlemagne* by Einhard and Notker the Stammerer, translated with an introduction by Professor Lewis Thorpe (Penguin Classics, 1969). Copyright © Professor Lewis Thorpe, 1969. Reproduced by permission of Penguin Books Ltd.

Chapter 10, page 314: "Peppercorns as Money." From *Medieval Trade in the Mediterranean World: Illustrative Documents*, translated by Robert S. Lopez and Irving W. Raymond. Copyright © 1955, 1990, 2001 Columbia University Press. Reprinted with permission of the publisher. **Page 324:** "Anonymous Account of Henry's Minority." From *The Life of the Emperor Henry IV* in *Imperial Lives and Letters of the Eleventh Century*, translated by Theodor E. Mommsen and Karl F. Morrison. Copyright © 2000 Columbia University Press. Reprinted by permission of the publisher and Karl F. Morrison. **Page 324:** "Gregory VII Admonishes Henry." From *The Correspondence of Pope Gregory VII: Selected Letters from the Registrum*, translated by Ephraim Emerton. Copyright © 1932, 1960, 1990 Columbia University Press. Reprinted by permission of the publisher. **Page 325:** "Henry's Response to Gregory's Admonition." Excerpt from *The Letters of Henry IV* in *Imperial Lives and Letters of the Eleventh Century*, trans. Theodor E. Mommsen and Karl F. Morrison. Copyright © 2000 Columbia University Press. Reprinted by permission of the publisher and Karl F. Morrison. **Page 334:** "Excerpt from a letter by Yahya, c. 1100." From Mark R. Cohen, *The Voice of the Poor in the Middle Ages*. Copyright © 2005 Princeton University Press. Reprinted by permission of Princeton University Press. **Page 338:** "Penances for the Invaders." From *English Historical Documents*, vol. 2, *1042–1189*, edited by David C. Douglas and George W. Greenaway, 2nd ed. Copyright © 1996 Routledge. Reproduced by permission of Taylor & Francis Books UK.

Chapter 11, page 360: Magna Carta (excerpt). From *English Historical Documents*, vol. 3, *1189–1327*, edited by Harry Rothwell. Copyright © 1975 Routledge. Reproduced by permission of Taylor & Francis Books UK. **Page 361:** "The Barons at Parliament Refuse to Give the King an Aid, 1242." From *English Historical Documents*, vol. 3, *1189–1327*, edited by Harry Rothwell. Copyright © 1975 Routledge. Reproduced by permission of Taylor & Francis Books UK. **Page 363:** "Frederick I's Reply to the Romans." Reprinted with the permission of Simon & Schuster, Inc., from *The Crisis of Church and State, 1050–1300* by Brian Tierney. Copyright © 1964 by Prentice-Hall, Inc.; copyright renewed © 1992 by Brian Tierney. All rights reserved. **Page 367:** "Troubadour Song: I Never Died for Love" by Peire Vidal. From *Songs of the Troubadours and Trouvères/1*, edited by Samuel N. Rosenberg, Margaret Switten, and Gerard Le Vot (Routledge, 1998). Copyright © 1997 by Samuel N. Rosenberg, Margaret Switten, and Gerard Le Vot. Reprinted by permission of Taylor & Francis Group LLC Books. **Page 368:** "Bertran de Born, 'I love the joyful time of Easter.'" From *Lyrics of the Troubadours and Trouvères*, translated by Frederick Goldin. Copyright © 1973 by Frederick Goldin. Used by permission of Doubleday, a division of Random House, Inc. **Page 373:** "The Children's Crusade." From *Medieval Popular Religion, 1000–1500: A Reader*, edited and translated by John Shinners. Copyright © 1997 by John Shinners. Broadview Press (University of Toronto Press Higher Education Division). Reprinted with permission of the publisher.

Chapter 12, page 387: "Raymond de l'Aire's Testimony." Excerpted from "The Inquisitorial Register of Jacques Fournier" in *Heresy and Authority in Medieval Europe: Documents in Translation*, edited by Edward Peters. Copyright © 1980 University of Pennsylvania Press. Reprinted with permission of the University of Pennsylvania Press. **Page 391:** "Thomas Aquinas Writes about Sex." From "The Reason Why Simple Fornication Is a Sin According to Divine Law, and That Matrimony Is Natural" in Saint Thomas Aquinas, *Summa Contra Gentiles*, Book 3: *Providence*, Part II, translated by Vernon J. Bourke (Notre Dame, Ind.: University of Notre Dame Press, 1975). Copyright © 1975. Reprinted by permission of the University of Notre Dame Press. **Page 392:** "The Debate between Reason and the Lover." From *The Romance of the Rose* by Guillaume de Lorris and Jean de Meun, edited by Charles W. Dunn and translated by Harry W. Robbins. Copyright © 1962 by Florence L. Robbins. Used by permission of Dutton, a division of Penguin Group (USA) Inc. and Charlotte G. Larmee.

Chapter 13, page 418: "Joan the Visionary," "Messenger of God?" and "Normal Girl?" Excerpted from *Joan of Arc: La Pucelle*, translated and annotated by Craig Taylor. Copyright © 2006 by Manchester University Press. Reprinted by permission of Manchester University Press. **Page 440:** "The Ducal Entry into Ghent" (1458). From *Court and Civic Society in the Burgundian Low Countries, c. 1420–1530*, ed. Andrew Brown and Graeme Small. Copyright © 2007 by Manchester University Press. Reprinted by permission of Manchester University Press.

Index

A note about the index:
Names of individuals appear in bold face; biographical dates are included for major historical figures.
Letters in parentheses following pages refer to:
(i) illustrations, including photographs and artifacts
(f) figures, including charts, graphs, and tables
(m) maps
(b) boxed features (such as "Contrasting Views")

Elevation
Feet
Meters
Over 13,120
Over 4,001
6,561–13,120
2,001–4,000
1,641–6,560
501–2,000
661–1640
201–500
0–660
0–200
Below sea level
Below sea level
National capital
Major city
0
150
300 miles
0
150
300 kilometers
N
E
S
W
ATLANTIC OCEAN
North Sea
English Channel
Bay of Biscay
NORWAY
SWEDEN
Bergen
Oslo
Stockholm
Göteborg
Aarhus
DENMARK
Copenhagen
Baltic S
Kaliningr
Gdansk
NORTHERN IRELAND
SCOTLAND
Glasgow
Edinburgh
Belfast
Dublin
IRELAND
Cork
UNITED KINGDOM
Liverpool
WALES
Birmingham
ENGLAND
Thames R.
London
NETHERLANDS
Amsterdam
Rotterdam
Antwerp
Brussels
BELGIUM
LUXEMBOURG
Luxembourg
Elbe R.
Berlin
Vistula R.
POLAND
GERMANY
Rhine R.
Frankfurt
Oder R.
Prague
Cracc
CZECH REP.
Brno
Paris
Seine R.
Loire R.
FRANCE
LIECHTENSTEIN
Munich
Vienna
SLOVAK
Bratislava
Danube R.
Zürich
Vaduz
Bern
Innsbruck
AUSTRIA
SWITZERLAND
Graz
Budapest
HUNGAR
Lyon
ALPS
SLOVENIA
Ljubljana
Milan
Zagreb
CROATIA
Po R.
Belgrac
Rhone R.
San Marino
SAN MARINO
BOSNIA AND HERZEGOVINA
Sarajevo
Split
Adriatic Sea
Podgorica
MONTENEGRO
Tirana
ALBAN
ANDORRA
Andorra la Vella
PYRENEES
Ebro R.
Marseille
MONACO
APENNINES
Oporto
PORTUGAL
Madrid
Barcelona
Corsica
Lisbon
SPAIN
Rome
ITALY
Naples
Sardinia
Tyrrhenian Sea
BALEARIC IS.
Seville
Gibraltar (Br.)
Algiers
Palermo
Sicily
Ionian Sea
Tunis
Rabat
Valletta
MALTA
MOROCCO
TUNISIA
Mediterranean
ALGERIA
Tripoli
LIBYA

INLAND
Helsinki
St. Petersburg
Tallinn
ESTONIA
Pärnu
URAL MTS.
Moscow
Riga
ava
LATVIA
RUSSIAN FEDERATION
Ural R.
THUANIA
Kaunas
SIA
Vilnius
Volga R.
Minsk
KAZAKHSTAN
BELARUS
Gomel
arsaw
Brest
Kharkiv
Kiev
Dnieper R.
UKRAINE
CARPATHIAN MTS.
skolc
MOLDOVA
Chisinau
Tiraspol
Odessa
Cluj
Caspian Sea
imisoara
ROMANIA
CAUCASUS MTS.
Bucharest
Baku
GEORGIA
Tbilisi
Black Sea
Danube R.
ARMENIA
Yerevan
RBIA
BULGARIA
istina
Sofia
OVO
Plovdiv
AZERBAIJAN
Skopje
Istanbul
CEDONIA
Tehran
Salonica
Ankara
TURKEY
IRAN
Aegean Sea
Izmir
REECE
Tigris R.
Athens
SYRIA
Baghdad
Nicosia
Crete
IRAQ
Beirut
CYPRUS
Damascus
LEBANON
Euphrates R.
Sea
ISRAEL
Kuwait City
Tel Aviv
Amman
KUWAIT
Jerusalem
JORDAN
Alexandria
SAUDI ARABIA
Cairo
EGYPT
Nile R.

80°N
60°N
40°N
20°N
0°
Equator
20°S
40°S
60°S
80°S
160°W
140°W
120°W
100°W
80°W
60°W
40°W
20°W
Alaska (U.S.)
Greenland (Den.)
ICELAND
CANADA
UNITED STATES
Azores (Port.)
Madeira (Port.)
Canary Is. (Sp.)
Western Sahara (Mor.)
ATLANTIC OCEAN
Hawaii (U.S.)
MEXICO
BAHAMAS
CUBA
HAITI
DOMINICAN REPUBLIC
Puerto Rico (U.S.)
JAMAICA
BELIZE
ST. KITTS AND NEVIS
ANTIGUA AND BARBUDA
Guadeloupe (Fr.)
DOMINICA
Martinique (Fr.)
ST. VINCENT AND THE GRENADINES
ST. LUCIA
BARBADOS
GRENADA
TRINIDAD AND TOBAGO
GUATEMALA
HONDURAS
EL SALVADOR
NICARAGUA
COSTA RICA
PANAMA
VENEZUELA
GUYANA
SURINAME
French Guiana (Fr.)
COLOMBIA
CAPE VERDE
SENEGAL
GAMBIA
GUINEA-BISSAU
GUINEA
SIERRA LEONE
LIBERIA
CÔTE D'IVOIR
BURKINA FAS
GHA
PACIFIC OCEAN
Galápagos Is. (Ec.)
ECUADOR
PERU
BRAZIL
BOLIVIA
PARAGUAY
CHILE
URUGUAY
ARGENTINA
SAMOA
TONGA
Easter I. (Chile)
0
1,500
3,000 miles
0
1,500
3,000 kilometers
Falkland Is. (U.K.)
ATLANTIC OCEAN

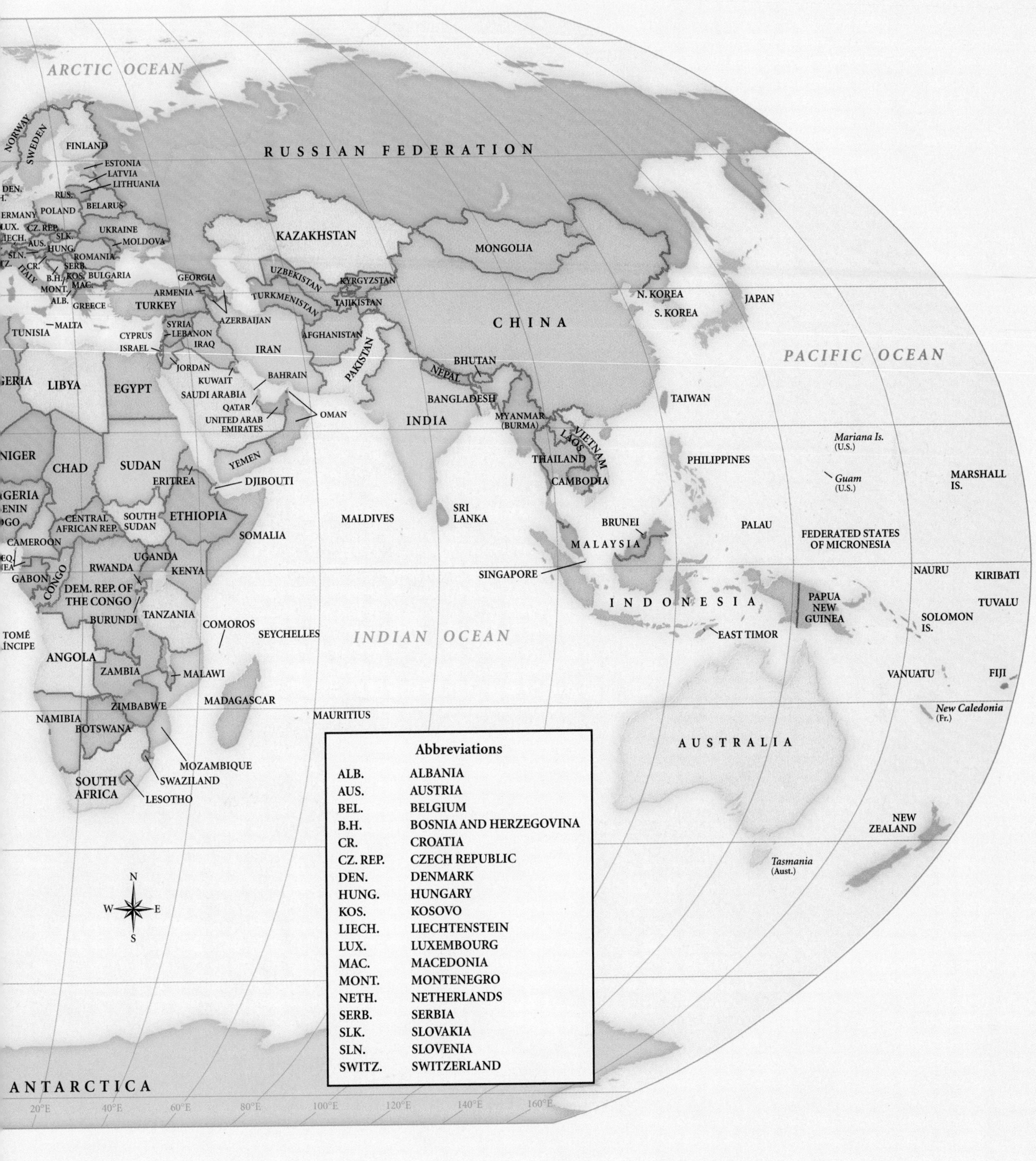
ARCTIC OCEAN
RUSSIAN FEDERATION
NORWAY
SWEDEN
FINLAND
ESTONIA
LATVIA
LITHUANIA
RUS.
BELARUS
POLAND
UKRAINE
MOLDOVA
CZ. REP.
SLK.
AUS.
HUNG.
ROMANIA
SLN.
CR.
ITALY
SERB.
KOS.
BULGARIA
B.H.
MONT.
MAC.
ALB.
GREECE
KAZAKHSTAN
MONGOLIA
UZBEKISTAN
KYRGYZSTAN
TURKMENISTAN
TAJIKISTAN
GEORGIA
ARMENIA
TURKEY
AZERBAIJAN
N. KOREA
S. KOREA
JAPAN
CHINA
PACIFIC OCEAN
TUNISIA
MALTA
CYPRUS
SYRIA
LEBANON
ISRAEL
IRAQ
IRAN
AFGHANISTAN
PAKISTAN
JORDAN
KUWAIT
BAHRAIN
NEPAL
BHUTAN
LIBYA
EGYPT
SAUDI ARABIA
QATAR
UNITED ARAB EMIRATES
OMAN
BANGLADESH
INDIA
MYANMAR (BURMA)
LAOS
VIETNAM
TAIWAN
NIGER
CHAD
SUDAN
YEMEN
THAILAND
PHILIPPINES
Mariana Is. (U.S.)
Guam (U.S.)
MARSHALL IS.
ERITREA
DJIBOUTI
CAMBODIA
CENTRAL AFRICAN REP.
SOUTH SUDAN
ETHIOPIA
MALDIVES
SRI LANKA
BRUNEI
PALAU
FEDERATED STATES OF MICRONESIA
CAMEROON
SOMALIA
MALAYSIA
UGANDA
RWANDA
GABON
CONGO
KENYA
DEM. REP. OF THE CONGO
SINGAPORE
NAURU
KIRIBATI
INDONESIA
PAPUA NEW GUINEA
TUVALU
BURUNDI
TANZANIA
COMOROS
SEYCHELLES
INDIAN OCEAN
EAST TIMOR
SOLOMON IS.
ANGOLA
ZAMBIA
MALAWI
VANUATU
FIJI
ZIMBABWE
MADAGASCAR
NAMIBIA
BOTSWANA
MAURITIUS
New Caledonia (Fr.)
AUSTRALIA
MOZAMBIQUE
SOUTH AFRICA
SWAZILAND
LESOTHO
NEW ZEALAND
Tasmania (Aust.)
N
W
E
S
Abbreviations
ALB. ALBANIA
AUS. AUSTRIA
BEL. BELGIUM
B.H. BOSNIA AND HERZEGOVINA
CR. CROATIA
CZ. REP. CZECH REPUBLIC
DEN. DENMARK
HUNG. HUNGARY
KOS. KOSOVO
LIECH. LIECHTENSTEIN
LUX. LUXEMBOURG
MAC. MACEDONIA
MONT. MONTENEGRO
NETH. NETHERLANDS
SERB. SERBIA
SLK. SLOVAKIA
SLN. SLOVENIA
SWITZ. SWITZERLAND
ANTARCTICA
20°E
40°E
60°E
80°E
100°E
120°E
140°E
160°E

About the authors

Lynn Hunt (Ph.D., Stanford University) is Eugen Weber Professor of Modern European History at the University of California, Los Angeles. She is the author or editor of several books, including most recently *Bernard Picart and the First Global Vision of Religion; The Book That Changed Europe: Picart and Bernard's Religious Ceremonies of the World; Measuring Time, Making History;* and *Inventing Human Rights.*

Thomas R. Martin (Ph.D., Harvard University) is Jeremiah O'Connor Professor in Classics at the College of the Holy Cross. He is the author of *Ancient Greece* and *Sovereignty and Coinage in Classical Greece* and is one of the originators of *Perseus: Interactive Sources and Studies on Ancient Greece* (www.perseus.tufts.edu). He is currently conducting research on the career of Pericles as a political leader in classical Athens as well as on the text of Josephus's *Jewish War.*

Barbara H. Rosenwein (Ph.D., University of Chicago) is professor of history at Loyola University Chicago. She is the author or editor of several books including *A Short History of the Middle Ages* and *Emotional Communities in the Early Middle Ages.* She is currently working on a general history of the emotions in the West.

Bonnie G. Smith (Ph.D., University of Rochester) is Board of Governors Professor of History at Rutgers University. She is the author or editor of several books including *The Oxford Encyclopedia of Women in World History; The Gender of History: Men, Women and Historical Practice;* and *Ladies of the Leisure Class.* Currently she is studying the globalization of European culture and society since the seventeenth century.

About the cover image

Mosaic of Lord Julius, 4th Century

This fourth-century mosaic pavement, which decorated a private home in the countryside near Carthage, depicts daily life on the estate of a wealthy lord. The lord and his wife are shown being assisted by servants and peasants as well as participating in a variety of seasonal activities. The seasons are represented by the elements of the landscape — such as wheat, olives, and flowers — and by the nature of the figures' activities, such as harvesting particular crops or hunting certain types of game. This mosaic thus provides insight into both rural social structures and the seasonal tasks typical of a rich country estate.